Sixth Edition

The Legal, Ethical, &
International Environment
of Business

Herbert M. Bohlman

Associate Professor
Arizona State University
Judge Pro Tempore, Maricopa County Superior Court

Mary Jane Dundas

Associate Professor
Arizona State University

THOMSON
SOUTH-WESTERN

WEST

Australia · Canada · Mexico · Singapore · Spain · United Kingdom · United States

THOMSON
SOUTH-WESTERN

WEST

The Legal, Ethical, and International Environment of Business, 6e
Herbert M. Bohlman and Mary Jane Dundas

VP/Editorial Director:
Jack W. Calhoun

VP/Editor-in-Chief:
George Werthman

Publisher:
Rob Dewey

Acquisitions Editor:
Steve Silverstein, Esq.

Sr. Developmental Editor:
Jan Lamar

Exec. Marketing Manager:
Lisa Lysne

Production Editor:
Amy McGuire

Technology Project Editor:
Christine Wittmer

Sr. Media Editor:
Amy Wilson

Manufacturing Coordinator:
Rhonda Utley

Production House:
Trejo Production

Printer:
Quebecor World
Taunton, MA

Design Project Manager:
Bethany Casey

Internal Designer:
Bethany Casey

Cover Designer:
Bethany Casey

Cover Images:
© PhotoDisc, Inc.

Dedication

M. J. D. dedicates this book to the memory
of her parents, R. J and Marie A. Dundas, and
her sisters, Jean and Marilyn, and their families.

H. M. B. dedicates this book to his wife, Mimi, and his
children, Bill, Patti, Mike, and Laura, and their families.

Brief Contents

Contents

CHAPTER 3

The Judicial System and Litigation 61

CHAPTER 4

Alternative Dispute Resolution Procedures 95

CHAPTER 5

The Constitution and the Regulation of Business 124

CHAPTER 6

Administrative Agencies and the Regulation of Business 159

Unit 2   Business and Private Law

CHAPTER 9

Contract Formation 253

CHAPTER 10

Contract Defenses and Remedies 280

CHAPTER 11

Sales Law and Product Liability 305

CHAPTER 13

International Business Law 378

CHAPTER 14

Rights of Consumers, Debtors, and Creditors 413

Unit 3   Business Formation

CHAPTER 19

Corporate Law and Franchising Law 575

Unit 4   Business and Government Regulation

CHAPTER 24
Environmental Law 730

Appendices

Preface

During the last four decades, the legal, ethical, and international landscape both in the United States and the around the world has changed tremendously. The law will be more dynamic as events and cultural changes mold the law in the future. No one contemplated legal and environmental issues surrounding space debris forty years ago. Ethics continues to be underrated by the business community as to the amount of impact ethics has on the economic and political worlds. International business expands as more countries join in the global expansion of trade. As trade grows, legal problems arise and must be resolved.

Businesses must influence and adapt to these ever-changing landscapes. *The Legal, Ethical, and International Environment of Business*, Sixth Edition, was written to present to the student the breadth of the legal, ethical, and international environment in which business operates as well as integrating the regulatory and technological conditions that impact businesses. The book can serve in part as a foundation that a student can use in his or her business or government career. Where appropriate, comments are made about the political and social aspects of the legal environment.

To accomplish these goals, we have presented materials that cover both private and public legal aspects of business. Unit I provides students with an introduction to law, ethics, and the World Wide Web. This unit includes chapters on ethics, the judicial system, and alternatives to the judicial system called dispute resolution procedures. The chapters on constitutional law, administrative agencies, and criminal law introduce students to the regulatory issues.

Unit II covers business and private law. Topics include torts; contracts; sales law; negotiable instruments; international business law; rights of consumers, debtors, and creditors; consumer protection; and property and intellectual property law.

Unit III examines the formation of business entities and agency and employment law.

Unit IV sets out the various aspects of government regulation, which includes securities, antitrust, labor, employment, equal opportunity, and environmental laws.

The sixth edition includes ethical, international, and technological sections in every chapter. Students are provided an opportunity to study the historical development of the U.S. legal system along with a general discussion of how constitutional issues affect businesses. The text integrates the American Assembly of Collegiate Schools of Business (AACSB) curriculum standards to cover ethical, global, political, social, legal regulatory, environmental, and technological issues.

New to the Sixth Edition

New to the sixth edition is the *Infotrac* feature, which is in every chapter. Students are guided in research using *Infotrac*, which is a database containing thousands of articles on various business and legal topics. Students are encouraged to read a number of articles in order to expand their knowledge base.

Each chapter has a court case decided in 2000 or later. These latest cases keep the students interested in the current law. Business-oriented issues, such as the downfall of many businesses over ethical and legal scandals are included in this edition.

With the 2001 terrorist attacks on the United States, the Congress passed the USA Patriot Act. This piece of legislation is sweeping in nature. Parts of the act are included in the appropriate chapters.

Product liability material is moved to the chapter covering torts. The new Third Restatement of Torts position on product liability is likewise presented in the section on product liability.

The materials on the Uniform Commercial Code, Article 2, Sales, are now covered in one chapter. Additional material is included in this chapter. This approach will guide students in distinguishing between Article 2 and the law on contracts. The two topics are different approaches to similar transactions. The rules are different depending on what is subject to sale and purchase.

The reference in each chapter to a fictitious business called *Artiste Login Products, Inc.*, is highlighted in every chapter. This fictitious business is used to emphasize the overall view of each chapter, as well as to distinguish points of law.

A large Web data-base accompanies this textbook at **http://bohlman.westbuslaw.com**. Each chapter has its own summary of Web addresses. The Web addresses on the inside back cover have been updated to make it easy for students to find commonly used Web addresses, such as **http://www.whitehouse.gov**. Because faculty and students have access to the Web, each chapter has two *Web Activities*. Additionally, the last problem in the *Questions and Case Problems* section includes an additional Web activity. All Web addresses, such as those in the *Using the World Wide Web* feature, the chapter, and the *Finding the Law on the Web* feature are included on Web site for the book. Instead of typing in the Web addresses, the student can open the Web site for the textbook and click on the Web address.

In addition to the Web addresses located on the Web site for the text,the text Web site also provided links to selected statutes and a special appendix on critical thinking. A list of the selected statutes is provided at the end of the text along with the following appendices: *Appendix A, Constitution of the United States of America, Appendix B, Web References for Selected Materials.*

Total Learning/ Teaching Package

This text constitutes what we believe to be a total learning/teaching package. It contains numerous pedagogical aids and high-interest additions.

Case Selection and Presentation

Each chapter has several cases to illustrate the application of the law to specific business problems. We have tried to create a balance between classic cases that are well recognized and recent cases that have changed the law significantly. Each case starts with the citation that includes the court, the date, the federal or state reporter (if available), the West reporter, and, when possible, a Web citation.

The *Background and Facts* section focuses on the setting in which the case arose and identifies the plaintiffs and defendants. Text from an actual court case is then presented in an abbreviated form. Although the case is in an abbreviated form, enough judicial material is included to allow the professor to facilitate a discussion with the students to explore the reasoning and impact of the case. Finally, the *Decision and Remedy* section clearly states who prevailed in the case and why. When appropriate, we include a *Comment* section that presents additional material not available from the case itself or that indicates future trends. Each case ends with a *Critical Thinking* problem that helps the students reach a deeper level of understanding of the law and public policy.

Chapter Features

Each chapter includes one or more of the following special sections. These segments are designed to be instructive as well as interesting.

Quotations
Each chapter opens with a brief quotation that is appropriate to the chapter material. The source of the quote is included.

Ethical Considerations
The emphasis on ethics in academic studies is reflected in the standards set by the AACSB. These standards require that ethics be integrated into the study of business, and this text likewise integrates ethics into each chapter. Chapter 2, *Ethics and Corporate Social Responsibility*, covers ethical theories and provides a basis for class discussion of the ethical problems set out at the beginning of each chapter. A model is provided in Chapter 2 and reprinted on the inside front cover to assist students in resolving ethical issues.

Fictitious Business
Contained in each chapter is a fictitious business called *Artiste Login Products, Inc.* This business is featured in the final portion of the Introduction to each chapter. When appropriate, this business example is also integrated in some of the chapters, such as in Chapter 3 where *Artiste Login Products, Inc.*, is involved in a lawsuit. In other chapters, the business is used in the Web Activities or the Internet problem at the end of the Questions and Case Problems section.

To add versatility to the use of *Artiste Login Products, Inc.* as a legal example throughout the text, the business has a Web presence, sells both unique, handmade items, and a variety of other common goods, such as dinnerware. The instructor can build problems, current issues, and critical thinking around this business.

CyberLaw

The feature entitled *CyberLaw* includes a discussion on a specific legal topic involving the Web. Interesting problems are discussed, such as the authentication of electronic signatures, along with twists on old problems, such as privacy in the electronic age.

Exhibits

Most chapters have at least one exhibit to illustrate important aspects of the law. Some exhibits are charts, such as the one setting out the federal court system; others focus on classifications or summaries; and others illustrate forms used in the legal or business world, such as a sample credit sale contract.

Legal Highlights

All chapters have a feature entitled *Legal Highlight*. This feature is used to present stories and to provide practical advice, such as how to check on a Social Security account or examples of how the law was applied in an unusual situation.

International Considerations

The economic future of the United States is dependent on international trade. People involved with international business need a working knowledge of how international trade functions and the legal problems that may arise. The AACSB also is concerned with integrating global issues into the academic studies of business. Each chapter has an *International Consideration* that discusses international aspects of the chapter's subject matter. Chapter 13, *International Business Law*, covers various aspects of doing business in the global environment.

Practical Tips

Toward the end of each chapter is material entitled *Practical Tips*. In each such discussion we have attempted to present a factual situation that a businessperson could confront in his or her career. These situations concern problems that are collateral to the rest of the material contained within the chapter. They provide students with practical advice on how to apply the law.

Using the World Wide Web

Each chapter has a variety of references to Web sites. This sixth edition integrates into the textual material references to Web sites relating to cases, statutes, regulations, and organizations. Professors and students can use these references to find more information on the issues discussed in the chapter. *Using the World Wide Web* begins with a short discussion, followed by two *Web Activities* that are posted on the text Web site. This summary makes finding Web sites easier. At the end of each chapter, there is a research problem involving the use of the Web.

Key Terms

Each chapter includes a list of *Key Terms*. The terms are first identified in the chapter by boldfaced type at which point a definition is provided. A key term used immediately prior to the definition is identified by the use of italics.

Questions and Case Problems

At the end of each chapter, there are ten *Questions and Case Problems*. The problems are a mix of hypothetical questions and actual case problems. The case problems are summaries of appellate court cases for which full citations are given. The last question involves a problem to be researched on the Web.

Complete answers to all of the *Ethical Considerations* and the *Questions and Case Problems* are found in a separate manual entitled *Answers to Ethical Considerations, Critical Thinking, Web Activities, Questions and Case Problems*.

Appendices

This book can serve as a reference for the *Constitution of the United States of America* and *Web References for Selected Materials*. Links for selected statutes are provided on the Web site for the text, which is **http:// bohlman.westbuslaw.com**. Also, an appendix on critical thinking is available on the text Web site.

Located at the end of the book:

A   Constitution of the United States of America
B   Web References for Selected Materials

Links available on the Web site are: the UCC, the Sherman Act, the Clayton Act, the Federal Trade Commission Act, the National Labor Relations Act, the Federal Civil Rights Acts, and the International Top-Level Domains (ITLDs). Also, appendices on Spanish Equivalents for Important Legal Terms, Critical Thinking, Selected World Wide Web Addresses, and International Top-Level Domains are available on the text Web site.

Supplements

Study Guide

Thomas Brierton of the University of the Pacific wrote the *Study Guide* (0-324-26986-2). Each chapter reinforces what the text has presented. The *Study Guide* consists of descriptions of general principles discussed in each chapter, chapter summaries in sentence outline form, and true-false, fill-in-the-blank, and multiple-choice questions to test students' comprehension.

Instructor's Manual

Michael Hogg of Tulane University wrote the *Instructor's Manual* (0-324-26987-0). Each chapter includes a chapter overview, lecture outline, case comments, ethical and international considerations comments, and instructional suggestions.

Test Bank

Dinah Payne of the University of New Orleans wrote the *Test Bank* (0-324-26988-9). Each chapter of the *Test Bank* includes approximately twenty-five true-false questions and seventy-five multiple-choice questions; many chapters have more items.

The *Test Bank* is available on *ExamView*™, which is computerized testing software program containing all of the questions in the printed test bank. This program is an easy-to-use test creation software package compatible with Microsoft Windows. Instructors can add or edit questions, instructions, and answers, and select questions by previewing them on the screen, selecting them randomly, or selecting them by number. Instructors can also create and administer quizzes online, whether over the Internet, a local-area network, or a wide-area network. Instructors should contact their West sales representative to inquire about acquiring *ExamView*™.

Answers to Ethical Considerations, Critical Thinking, Web Activities, Questions and Case Problems

Text authors H. M. Bohlman and Mary Jane Dundas prepared the *Answers to Ethical Considerations, Critical Thinking, Web Activities, Questions and Case Problems* (0-324-22122-3). The answer manual provides model answers to the *Ethical Considerations* that begin each chapter. This portion is followed by solutions to the *Questions and Case Problems* found in the end of each chapter.

Transparency Acetates

The supplements package contains a set of approximately thirty transparency acetates (0-324-26991-9).

PowerPoint Presentation Slides

Developed by Rhonda Carlson, more than 200 PowerPoint slides (0-324-23281-0) are available to supplement course content, adding structure and visual dimension to lectures.

Product Support Web Site

A rich Web site at **http://bohlman.westbuslaw. com** complements the text providing many extras including learning and teaching resources, case updates, a product tour, a *Talk to Us* section, a critical thinking appendix, a Spanish Equivalents for Important Legal Terms in English appendix, and links to various Web sites.

Video Library

The video library includes such videos as *Court TV*® and the *Drama of the Law* video series. For more information on the video library, go to **http://videos. westbuslaw.com**.

West's Digital Video Library

Featuring 55 segments on the most important topics in Business Law, West's Digital Video Library helps make the connection between the textbook and the business world. Three types of clips are represented. **Legal Conflicts in Business** features modern business scenarios, **Ask the Instructor** clips offer concept review, and **Drama of the Law** presents classic legal situations. Upon instructor request, an access card for the videos will be bundled with each new copy of this textbook. Students who buy used copies may purchase access to the digital video library at **http://digitalvideolibrary.westbuslaw.com**.

Info Trac

A four-month subscription for *Info Trac College Edition* is packaged with every new copy of the textbook. It is a fully searchable online university library containing complete articles and their images. Its database allows access to hundreds of scholarly and popular publications—all reliable sources, including magazines, journals, encyclopedias, and newsletters.

Acknowledgments

Many people are involved in the production of a textbook. The initial impetus for *The Legal, Ethical, and International Environment of Business*, Sixth Edition, came from Rob Dewey, our editor, who has been a strong supporter of this project. A heartfelt thanks to Jan Lamar, our developmental editor, who coordinated all the reviews, provided expert analysis, and made suggestions that make for a stronger textbook. A hearty thanks to Amy McGuire, our production editor, who kept the project moving in a timely manner.

We acknowledge the important contribution of Professor Arthur Gross Schaefer from Loyola Marymount University in Los Angeles. His credentials as an attorney, certified public accountant, and rabbi, along with his work in the development of ethical audits for profit and nonprofit organizations, make him a unique individual with a very broad background. His work as an ethicist with practicing attorneys and judges, moreover, has provided him with a critical outlook on dealing effectively with real-life situations. He has used these perspectives to create the ethics decision model, the ethics cases within each chapter, and model answers found in the *Answers to Ethical Considerations, Critical Thinking, Web Activities, Questions and Case Problems*. This material is an integral part of our book and greatly improved the book's overall presentation.

A number of reviewers were kind enough to give us their ideas and comments on various drafts of the manuscript. They are listed below for the six editions.

Reviewers for the Sixth Edition

Robert B. Bennett, Jr., Butler University
Thomas Brierton, University of the Pacific
George P. Generas, Jr., University of Hartford
John A. Miller, Pima Community College
Jeffrey Pittman, Arkansas State University
Bruce L. Rockwood, Bloomsburg University

Reviewers for the Fifth Edition

Thomas M. Apke, California State University, Fullerton
Thomas D. Brierton, University of the Pacific
Marc. A. Hall, Auburn University
Glen Jones, Henderson State University
Frank Julian, Murray State University
Peter B. Macky, Susquehanna University
S. Andrew Ostapski, Valdosta State University
Dinah Payne, University of New Orleans
Daniel R. Vaughen, University of Central Florida
William B. Woodward, Jr., University of Alabama, Huntsville
Raymond A. Zimmerman, The University of Texas at El Paso

Reviewers for the Fourth Edition

Patricia Billow, University of Akron
Frank Cavaliere, Lamar University
Howard Ellis, Millersville University
George Generas, University of Hartford
Cliff Koen, University of New Orleans
A. Robert Lamb, The University of the Incarnate Word
Alan Schlact, Kennesaw State University
Mark E. Smith, University of Louisville

Reviewers for the Third Edition

Gamewell D. Gantt III, Idaho State University
Arthur Gross Schaefer, Loyola Marymount University
A. Robert Lamb, Sr., Incarnate Word College
Michael Litka, University of Akron
Michael G. Walsh, Villanova University
Kay Wilburn, The University of Alabama at Birmingham
Raymond A. Zimmerman, The University of Texas at El Paso

Reviewers for the Second Edition

Thomas M. Apke, California State University, Fullerton

Thomas D. Brierton, University of the Pacific

Frank J. Cavallere, Lamar University

Michael Litka, University of Akron

Paul Lyons, Frostburg State University

Charles W. McGuire, DeVry Institute

Dinah Payne, University of New Orleans

Jeffrey R. Pittman, Arkansas State University

Martha Sartoris, North Hennepin Community College

Darryl L. Webb, University of Alabama

Kay Wilburn, The University of Alabama at Birmingham

Reviewers for the First Edition

David L. Baumer, North Carolina State University

Katherine Beebe, Salt Lake Community College

Thomas H. Brucker, University of Washington

Mark A. Buchanan, St. Cloud State University

Daylin J. Butler, Kansas State University

Lawrence S. Clark, Louisiana State University in Shreveport

Gamewell D. Gantt III, Idaho State University

John Geary, Appalachian State University

Amy Zoe Gershenfeld, University of Kentucky

Martin F. Grace, Georgia State University

Gerard Halpern, University of Arkansas

Marsha E. Hass, College of Charleston

James P. Hill, Central Michigan University

E. C. Hipp, Clemson University

David D. Jaeger, University of Cincinnati

Marianne M. Jennings, Arizona State University

Jack E. Karns, University of North Dakota

Nancy P. Klintworth, University of Central Florida

Paul Lansing, University of Iowa

Andrew Laviano, University of Rhode Island

F. Raymond Lewis, Northeastern Illinois University

Nancy R. Mansfield, Georgia State University

S. Scott Massin, Emory University

John E. McDonald, Jr., University of North Carolina at Charlotte

Sheel P. Pawar, Idaho State University

Jordan B. Ray, University of Florida

Nim Razook, University of Oklahoma

Daniel L. Reynolds, Middle Tennessee State University

Rene Sacasas, University of Miami Florida

Scott Sibray, California State University, Chino

Lou Ann Simpson, Drake University

S. Jay Sklar, Temple University

Lucy L. Spalding, Illinois State University

Larry Strate, University of Nevada at Las Vegas

Donald J. Swanz, St. Bonaventure University

Irvin Tankersley, Memphis State University

Bernard F. Thiemann, Bellarmine College

Daphney Thomas, James Mason University

Wayne R. Wells, St. Cloud State University

We thank our colleagues who encouraged us, supported us, and spent hours reviewing our rough drafts: Professors Luis Aranda, Eileen Aranda, Marianne Moody Jennings, Ethan Lock, Peter Reiss, and the late Claude Olney, all of Arizona State University; and Professor Marc Ruzicka, University of Tennessee, Knoxville. They were extremely helpful with our initial drafts and with giving us their creative ideas and thoughts. They also gave us the motivation to keep going on all five editions.

As careful as we have attempted to be, there are, no doubt, errors in this text for which we take full responsibility. We welcome comments from all users of the text, for it is by incorporating such comments that we can make this text even better in future editions.

Herbert M. Bohlman
Mary Jane Dundas

Unit 1

Introduction

Chapter 1

Basics of the Law

The educated citizen has an obligation to uphold the law. This is the obligation of every citizen in a free and peaceful society—but the educated citizen has a special responsibility by the virtue of his greater understanding. For, whether he has ever studied history or current events, ethics or civics, the rules of a profession or the tools of a trade, he knows that only a respect for the law makes it possible for free men to dwell together in peace and progress.

He knows that law is the adhesive force of the cement of society, creating order out of chaos and coherence in place of anarchy. He knows that for one man to defy a law or court order he does not like is to invite others to defy those which they do not like, leading to a breakdown of all justice and all order.

He knows, too, that every fellow man is entitled to be regarded with decency and treated with dignity. Any educated citizen who seeks to subvert the law, to suppress freedom, or to subject other human beings to acts that are less than human, degrades his inheritance, ignores his learning, and betrays his obligations.

Certain other societies may respect the rule of force—we respect the rule of law.

John Fitzgerald Kennedy, 1917–1963 Thirty-fifth president of the United States of America, 1961–1963 Speech at Vanderbilt University, Nashville, Tennessee, May 13, 1963, as quoted in the *New York Times*, May 19, 1963, p. 62.

Chapter Outline

Ethical Consideration

Ethical Attitudes

Enron, WorldCom, Tyco, Global Crossing, Adelphia Communications Company, Kmart, Xerox, Vivendi Universal, and Arthur Andersen—these are all names of companies that leapt to public prominence not because of their good works, but as a result of probable unethical and possibly criminal activity. Some were forced into bankruptcy, or were required to restate their earnings going back several years, or were compelled to restructure their businesses. Left behind were investors holding valueless stocks, former employees facing the bleak task of finding jobs during an employment slump, current and former employees bearing the burden of being left without savings or retirement funds, and suppliers and lenders left unpaid with little hope of recovering any payment.

A few top-level managers, before they were fired or retired, earned multimillions in salary, were granted multimillion dollar loans that were forgiven, and sold multi-thousands of shares of stock for multimillions prior to the collapse of their respective companies. In contrast, others, such as employees, investors, suppliers, and lenders, lost billions. Employees were especially hard hit when they lost their jobs, their homes, and their savings and retirement accounts. All of this bad news came during a prolonged economic slump.

This debacle highlighted once again the relationship among ethical principles, business conduct, and the legal system. **Ethics**, a section of philosophy, embody the principles used to differentiate right from wrong. These principles guide a person's conduct. Ethical principles establish standards that provide the foundation for our legal system. In turn, the legal system attempts to set minimum ethical standards. Ethical standards are not the same as legal standards; ethical standards encompass more. To behave in an ethical manner requires more than simply meeting minimum legal standards.

Companies recognize their business must be conducted with integrity and in an ethical manner to ensure long-term profits. Lost in all the outrage about how Enron, WorldCom, Tyco, and others acted were the thousands of businesses that operate in an ethical manner while remaining profitable. Magazines, such as *Fortune, Forbes,* and *Business Week* feature businesses that embrace ethical conduct. A motto used by W. P. Carey & Co. LLP, a real estate finance company headquartered in New York City, is "Doing good, while doing well." This motto reflects the attitude and practice of many businesses.

Introduction

Entrepreneurs abound in the United States and around the world. Whether they work for a company or, indeed, have their own businesses, every business-person needs to have a basic understanding of the law. The law permeates the business world no matter where the business is located, whether online or in a bricks-and-mortar building.

This chapter reviews the background of the legal system and provides information on the sources of American law, the classifications within the law, and schools of legal philosophy. The differences between the courts of law and the courts of equity are discussed. The different citation systems for cases, statutes, and administrative agencies are explained. The chapter ends with an explanation of and guidelines for briefing a case.

Artiste Login. Carlo and Carlotta are twins who are each famous international artists in their own right. Demand for their work has continued to grow each year, so they created an online business called Artiste Login Products, Inc., which is located on the World Wide Web (WWW or Web). Customers can order personalized pieces from a large variety of offerings. Each accepts work for commissioned pieces of art based on a customer's request. If they are unable to create the requested piece, Artiste Login turns to a number of creative artists under contract who work in different mediums.

From the time they created their business, Carlo and Carlotta have been aware that they have very little knowledge of the legal issues surrounding their business. They want to improve their knowledge of the law. Carlotta and Carlo can learn more either by taking a law course or by learning as they encounter business-related legal issues.

Definition of Law

Law is one of the most basic of all social institutions. A precise definition of the law, however, is illusive. Oliver Wendell Holmes, Jr., in a speech to the Suffolk Bar Association in 1885 observed "This abstract called the Law, wherein, as in a magic mirror, we see reflected not only our own lives, but the lives of all men that have been!"[1] In many ways, the law reflects its historical development.

Kermit Hall, a legal historian, expands on Holmes's explanation with this observation:

> *Law is, after all, a human institution; its history is a tale of human choices. Its abstract rules deal with the most central of human issues: the preservation of life, the protection of property the exercise of individual liberty, the fashioning of creative knowledge, and the allocating of scarce resources. All encounters in the law, therefore, have been personal, human encounters. Its history is that of individuals caught up in the efforts of the state to allocate blame, to deter criminal behavior, to punish wrongdoing, and encourage socially valuable activity.*[2]

Law in the United States is used in both a singular and a plural sense. Law, in the singular sense, means a law that must be obeyed and followed by society's members. Anyone who disobeys a law is subject to a sanction or legal consequences. If a person breaks a contract without a valid reason, she can be sued and the harmed party can recover money damages. If a person robs a bank, he can be prosecuted by the government and sentenced to prison.

Law, in the plural sense, is how society is governed. The governing institutions are legislative, executive, and judicial bodies. Laws are created, enforced, and interpreted by these government agencies. These three institutions keep society functioning and from turning violent.

The legislative body, Congress or state legislatures, has the constitutional duty to create laws. The Congress has two bodies, the House of Representatives and the Senate. When a bill is passed by the House and a similar bill is passed by the Senate, the two bills will not be exactly alike. To obtain a bill that will be exactly the same and will be agreeable to both sides, the two bodies appoint a joint conference committee.

The joint committee will work out the differences until the members agree on the language. The revised bill is returned to the House and to the Senate for final passage, then sent to the president for his signature or veto. If the president signs the bill, it becomes law and is placed in the appropriate statutes.

The key is that the Congress, an elective body, has the constitutional authority to create laws and embody them in statutes. No private person has the authority to create or modify laws. For example, Amy is for peace and does not want any of her taxes to support the Department of Defense. The portion of the budget spent on defense is 3 percent. Amy owes $1,000 in taxes, so she deducts 3 percent ($30), and files her income tax return with a check for $970. She can be successfully prosecuted for tax evasion. Amy has no right to create her own law.

The judicial branch at the federal level is appointed and at the state level may be elected or appointed. These judges have the authority to hear and decide cases. The key is that the judicial branch has the constitutional authority to sit in judgment on matters brought before it. No private person has the authority to sit in judgment of his or her own case.

The executive branch, the president at the federal level or governor at the state level, has two functions. First, the executive enforces the statutes passed by Congress. If Congress adopts a law requiring all passenger baggage to be screened prior to being loaded on an aircraft, it falls to the executive to enforce this statute. Enforcement authority flows from the president to the Department of Homeland Security then to the Transportation Security Agency, which conducts the actual baggage screening.

Second, the executive enforces judicial decisions. In a criminal case, a court sentences a person to prison. The executive takes custody and escorts the person to prison. In a civil case, the judge orders a $100,000 judgment. The defendant fails to pay the judgment. The plaintiff can return to court for assistance in collecting

---

[1] Oliver Wendell Holmes. Jr., *The Speeches of Oliver Wendell Holmes* (Boston: Little, Brown and Company, 1891), p. 17.
[2] Hermit L. Hall, *The Magic Mirror: Law in American History* (Oxford, UK: Oxford University Press, 1989), p. 4.

the judgment. The court can issue a command to the executive, the sheriff in this case, to assist in collecting the monies.

The key is that the executive branch enforces federal statutes and court orders. No private person has enforcement authority. For instance, the Border Patrol, under the Department of Homeland Security, enforces the laws concerning immigrants crossing illegally into the United States. A rancher cannot hire a helicopter and hunt down and shoot illegal immigrants. The rancher does not have any authority in this area. Moreover, no private person can enforce a court judgment. The plaintiff who was awarded the $100,000 judgment cannot go to the home or business of the defendant and take enough from those places to equal the amount of the judgment.

Society could not exist if people did as they pleased without regard for the rights of others. Only those institutions with constitutional or statutory authority can create, enforce, and interpret laws. Anyone reading newspapers, watching television news, or using the Web can observe how countries without a system of law fall into chaos and brutal civil wars. One example is Afghanistan in 2001. This country currently is rebuilding and starting a functioning government.

Sources of American Law

American law has evolved continuously since the first landings of English settlers near Jamestown, Virginia, in 1607, and at Plymouth Rock, Massachusetts, in 1620. The colonies naturally relied heavily on the English legal system.

During the new nation's early decades, however, Americans enriched their emerging legal system with French and German influences. These borrowed ideas and philosophies helped to shape our current legal system.

Constitutions

The constitution is the highest source of law. The two levels of constitutions are the U.S. Constitution and individual state constitutions. The U.S. Constitution has two functions: To establish the government and to protect people from overreaching government powers. State constitutions have the same two functions.

The U.S. Constitution is the supreme law of the land (Article VI, Section 2, U.S. Constitution).

The supreme law mandate is set out in the following provision:

> *This constitution, and the Laws of the United States which shall be made in Pursuance thereof; and all Treaties made, or which shall be made, under the Authority of the United States, shall be the supreme Law of the Land; and the Judges in every State shall be bound thereby, any Thing the Constitution or Laws of any State to the Contrary notwithstanding.*

Any law in conflict with the federal Constitution, regardless of its source, cannot be enforced. Similarly, a state constitution, although supreme within that state's borders, must conform to the U.S. Constitution.

Treaties

Treaties are agreements signed by the president with other sovereign states. The senate must ratify a treaty before it becomes law. Treaties can involve boundary disputes and economic issues or can end wars. For example, the Treaty of Paris formally ended the war in 1783 between England and the thirteen colonies that would eventually form the United States of America.

Statutes and Ordinances

A **statute** is a law passed by Congress or a state legislature, the legislative bodies, and generally is signed into law by the president or a governor. An **ordinance** is a law enacted by a city or county legislative body. Statutes and ordinances are referred to as **codes** or as the **codified law**.

Congress can only pass legislation that falls within the delegated powers granted to it under the U.S. Constitution (Amendment X, U.S. Constitution). State statutes and local ordinances must comply with the U.S. Constitution and the applicable state constitution. Cases before the courts often involve statutes. The courts must interpret the legislative intent of a law and apply that interpretation to the facts in the case.

Executive Powers in Creating Law

The president of the United States and governors of the states have the power to create law. The executive acts as a legislative leader, although not a part of the legislature, by influencing legislation. The president recommends legislation and sends proposed bills to Congress. The Congress may choose to ignore these bills, hence the phrase "dead on arrival." More commonly, a member of the Congress places a bill in the legislative system. Once a bill is before Congress, it is assigned to a committee to hold hearings, to conduct investigations, and then, based on the information gathered, to draft a bill. The bill must be passed by both houses of Congress. After the bill is passed, it is sent to the president so she can sign or veto the bill.

The president has the constitutional authority to issue *executive orders* and *military orders*. **Executive orders** are broad in nature. Such orders may be issued to give guidance on policy, to coordinate activities among agencies, or to create an **administrative agency**. A recent example is when President George W. Bush[3] initially created the Office of Homeland Security within the executive office. Eventually, Congress created the Department of Homeland Security and moved it from the executive office to a department as part of the president's cabinet. As commander-in-chief, the president issues **military orders** to guide military activities.

Governors of states have similar powers. Like the president, a governor recommends legislation, vetoes bill passed by the legislature, and oversees some of the state agencies. In some states, a governor has the power to issue executive orders.

Administrative Rules and Regulations

Administrative agencies usually are created by Congress, or at the state level by state legislatures, to implement and administer statutes. Although created by the legislative branch, these agencies function either under the executive branch of government or as independent agencies

Agencies regulate different aspects of society, such as education, public health, and taxation. To carry out their duties, these agencies adopt **administrative rules and regulations** that have the force of law.

Administrative law consists of regulations issued by governmental agencies regulating individuals and businesses. For example, assume the Occupational Safety and Health Administration has proposed a regulation requiring that restaurant noise be reduced. The restaurant industry has a chance to respond and can raise objections on the grounds that the proposed regulation would raise costs excessively in comparison with any benefits that may result.

Case Law

Written court decisions constitute the **common law**, also known as **case law**. The origins of common law lie in England's ancient, unwritten law. Disputes were settled according to local custom. In 1066, the Normans, led by William the Conqueror, conquered England. He and his successors began the long process of unifying the country.

One of the means used for unification was the king's court. This court established a common or uniform set of customs for the whole country. A person was given the right to appeal a local decision to the king. Over time, so many appeals were made that the king established a separate court system to hear these appeals.

The rules set out in the cases heard by the king's court formed the beginnings of common law. As the number of courts and cases increased, each year's important decisions were recorded in yearbooks. Judges, settling current disputes similar to ones previously decided, used the yearbooks as the basis for their decisions. If a case were unique, judges created new law by virtue of making a decision, but still based those decisions on the general principles adopted by earlier cases. The body of judge-made common law developed under this system is used today in both England and the United States.

In many legal areas, statutory law has replaced common law. For example, landlord–tenant law originally was created by common law. Today, much of the landlord–tenant law is statutory. In a particular case, the court looks first to the codified law on which to base its decision. If it finds none, the court looks to case law.

When a case before the court involves an issue for which no legislation exists, the court refers to the common law to make a decision. Provided that a common law decision does not conflict with a constitutional provision or with a statute, common law carries the same authority as statutory law. Even when statutes have been substituted for common law, courts often rely on common law to interpret the legislation based on the supposition that the drafters of the statute had intended to codify a previous common law rule.

---

[3]George W. Bush (1946 to present) was sworn in as the forty-third president for a term that runs from 2001 to 2005. The Department of Homeland Security was created in response to the attacks on the United States on September 11, 2001.

Most states have adopted common law by legislative decree. For example, the California Civil Code, Section 22.2, states that the "common law of England, so far as it is not repugnant to or inconsistent with the Constitution of the United States, or the Constitution or laws of this State, is the rule of decision in all the courts of this State."

Louisiana, formerly a French colony, is unique in that it adopted the *civil law system* that originated in continental Europe. The **civil law system** is based strictly on statutory provisions.

Stare Decisis

A cornerstone of the American judicial system is the practice of deciding new cases with reference to decisions made in prior similar cases. Known as the doctrine *of **stare decisis*** (let the decision stand), the judge uses **precedent**, that is, the decision of a previous similar case, to decide the outcome of the current case. The process of *stare decisis* acknowledges the experience and wisdom of the past and at the same time creates the common law.

LEGAL HIGHLIGHT

Common Law Writs

The common law originally developed through the issuance of writs. Historically, a *writ* was a command; thus, only the English king or his emissaries could issue writs. The king issued substantive writs.

Substantive writs created rights. In past centuries, if a person were injured in a horse-and-carriage accident caused by someone else, that person could bring an action to recover damages from the wrongdoer under a writ called "trespass on the case."

Substantive writs no longer exist because they evolved over the centuries into many of the modern legal rights. For example, the writ of trespass on the case evolved into the modern negligence laws. Today,

when a person is injured in an automobile accident caused by someone else, a lawsuit based on negligence can be filed. The person is not dependent on a writ issued by the king.

As centuries passed, the court system developed. Eventually, the king allowed the courts to issue substantive writs. Unlike the king, the courts, however, needed a way to enforce those writs. Over time, the courts began issuing procedural writs that were used to enforce rights created by the substantive writs.

Many procedural writs survived the centuries and are still issued today by the courts. The following are examples of modern procedural writs used today to enforce procedural rights.

Common Law Procedural Writs

Writ	Meaning	Purpose
Habeas corpus	You have the body.	*Habeas corpus* requires that the person held or detained be brought before the court. Used in criminal law and child custody cases.
Mandamus	We command.	*Mandamus* is used to require a specifically named public official to do her or his job. For example, *mandamus* may be sought to require the fire chief to activate a fire hydrant.
Quo warranto	By what authority?	*Quo warranto* may be sought to revoke a corporation's charter when the corporation is involved in illegal conduct.
Replevin	Redeliver.	*Replevin* directs the sheriff to seize personal property.
Certiorari	Review or inquiry.	*Certiorari* is a discretionary writ used by appellate courts to review a lower court's decision. If granted, the case will be reviewed. The writ of *certiorari* is used routinely by the U.S. Supreme Court.

Functions of *Stare Decisis*. *Stare decisis* has several functions: efficiency, uniformity, stability, and predictability. *Stare decisis* allows the courts to be more efficient. A judge reads the reasons that previous courts have developed to reach a particular legal decision. These previous court decisions can serve as a guide for the current decision-making process, because other judges have confronted similar issues, have reasoned through those problems, and have issued opinions. The judge can apply the reasoning used in previous cases to the current case.

Stare decisis results in a more just and uniform decision-making system. Decisions based on precedent can neutralize the personal prejudices of individual judges. Judges today are required to use precedent as the basis for their decisions. In spite of the use of precedent, however, some variations in law will occur because of the diverse applications of precedents in accordance with local law. Reasonable judges can differ in their interpretation and application of the law.

Finally, use of precedent makes the law more stable and predictable. If case decisions for a particular subject are well established, people tend to abide by and accept the law as it is applied by the courts. For example, today no one would expect a lawsuit to segregate schools on the basis of race to succeed. A law that is stable encourages people to use the judicial system and to accept the results.

Flexibility of *Stare Decisis*. *Stare decisis* provides stability, yet allows the law to be flexible. Kermit Hall described the history of U.S. law as "one of systematic change, of law and society reacting to and reinforcing one another."[4] When the precedent is no longer applicable, the courts can abandon it. For example, changes in technology, business practices, or social attitudes necessitate changes in the law

In most cases, the law follows events that change society. For example, the law changed in several ways after the attacks on America on September 11, 2001. Congress passed the USA Patriot Act of 2001 and reorganized the federal government. The reorganization created the Department of Homeland Security (DHS) and moved many agencies from other departments into DHS. As a result of the Patriot Act, federal courts have upheld some police procedures that would have been illegal prior the attacks of September 11, 2001. Society was changed by these attacks, the law was amended to reflect these changes, and the courts, if presented with a case that involves a particular law, will decide the constitutionality of the changed laws.

Although judges are reluctant to overrule a precedent, they have the power to do so. Without that power, legal thinking and reasoning would be frozen in time. A judge's decision to deviate from precedent depends on the subject of the case, the number and prestige of prior decisions, the degree of social change affecting the case, and the identity of the deciding court. The United States Supreme Court, as the highest authority in the land, is freer than a lower court to change the direction of the law. The cases of *Plessy v. Ferguson* and *Brown v. Board of Education,* which are discussed later, illustrate how the Court influences the direction of the law.

Case of First Impression. Occasionally, judges must make a decision on a case of first impression, that is, where no law exists on the topic, such as in evolving areas of electronic commerce (e-commerce) or the Internet. In these situations, a court uses one or more of the following guidelines in making its decision.

First, if the court can find a precedent that is relatively similar to the case under review, the court can draw an analogy from the prior cases to the current case to make its decision. For example, the court can make the following analogy. States have passed laws governing the license and use of gas-powered motor vehicles. In the future, courts will decide whether this law covers electric- or solar-powered vehicles, such as golf carts and scooters. A court could draw an analogy and apply the law to the electric-and solar-powered vehicles or the court could decide that the law does not apply.

Second, the court can consider social expectations to develop a policy. For example, the courts are currently debating the rights of ownership and privacy of electronic mail (e-mail). Does an e-mail user or recipient have the right to expect privacy? Does an e-mail message belong to the sender-creator, the employer, or the network provider? Is the employer or network provider legally responsible for the acts of others? By studying e-mail owners' policies and users' expectations, the courts can establish legal rules for this form of communication.

---

[4]Kermit L. Hall, *The Magic Mirror Law in American History* (Oxford, UK: Oxford University Press. 1989), p. 336.

Third, the court can balance interests of the parties in the lawsuit. In making its decision, the court might consider employer versus employee interests, government versus individual interests, and state versus federal government interests. By weighing these interests, the court attempts to make a just decision.

***Stare Decisis,* Two Cases.** Cases that overturn precedent often receive much publicity. For example, the famous case of *Brown v. Board of Education* (1954), in essence, overruled *Plessy v. Ferguson* (1896) and marked the beginning of the end of official racial segregation. The magnitude of the publicity that surrounds the reversal of major cases might lead the layperson to believe that case law is overturned frequently. Actually, most cases uphold the common law. The overturning of *Plessy v. Ferguson* by the later case of *Brown v. Board of Education* illustrates the Supreme Court's logic in reversing its position of sixty years earlier. A portion of the *Plessy v. Ferguson* case follows.

CASE 1.1

Supreme Court of the
United States, 1896
163 U.S. 537, 16 S. Ct.
1138, 41 L. Ed. 256
http://www.findlaw.com
http://supct.law.cornell.
edu/supct/

PLESSY v. FERGUSON

LANDMARK CASE

BACKGROUND AND FACTS Plessy, the petitioner, a resident of Louisiana, was of mixed blood, seven-eighths Caucasian and one-eighth African. He purchased a first-class ticket on the East Louisiana Railway to travel from New Orleans to Covington, Louisiana. He sat in a vacant seat in a coach where only white passengers were accommodated.

The conductor requested that Plessy take a seat in another coach for persons who were not white. The only reason Plessy was asked to move was that he was deemed under Louisiana law not to be a white person. On his refusal to move, he was forcibly ejected from the coach, arrested, and jailed. He was charged with violation of the 1890 Louisiana criminal statute providing for separate railroad coaches for whites and blacks.

Plessy brought a petition against the criminal court judge to prevent the judge from enforcing the statute. Plessy argued that the statute violated his federal constitutional rights.

Justice BROWN delivered the opinion of the Court.

. . . .

So far, then, as a conflict with the fourteenth amendment is concerned, the case reduces itself to the question whether the statute of Louisiana is a reasonable regulation, and with respect to this there must necessarily be a large discretion on the part of the legislature. In determining the question of reasonableness, it is at liberty to act with reference to the established usages, customs, and traditions of the people, and with a view to the promotion of their comfort, and the preservation of the public peace and good order. Gauged by this standard, we cannot say that a law which authorizes or even requires the separation of the two races in public conveyances is unreasonable, or more obnoxious to the fourteenth amendment than the acts of Congress requiring separate schools for colored children in the District of Columbia, the constitutionality of which does not seem to have been questioned, or the corresponding acts of state legislatures.

Justice HARLAN dissenting.

. . . .

The white race deems itself to be the dominant race in this country. And so it is, in prestige, in achievements, in education, in wealth, and in power. So, I doubt not, it will continue to be for all time, if it remains true to its great heritage, and holds fast to the principles of constitutional liberty. But in view of the constitution, in the eye of the law, there is in this country no superior, dominant, ruling class of citizens. There is no caste here. Our constitution is color-blind, and neither knows nor tolerates classes among citizens. In respect of civil rights, all citizens are equal before the law. The humblest is the peer of the most powerful. The law regards man as man, and takes no account of his surroundings or of his color when his civil rights as guaranteed by the supreme law of the land are involved. It is therefore to be regretted that this high tribunal, the final expositor of the fundamental law of the land, has reached the conclusion that it is competent for a state to regulate the enjoyment by citizens of their civil rights solely upon the basis of race.

In my opinion, the judgment this day rendered will, in time, prove to be quite as pernicious as the decision made by this tribunal in the *Dred Scott* Case.

DECISION AND REMEDY In 1896, the United States Supreme Court upheld the individual states' rights to require separate but equal facilities based solely on race. That decision legitimized an era of racial segregation in which the facilities were always separate, but never equal.

COMMENT The *Dred Scott* case, to which the Court referred, was decided in 1857. Dred Scott was a black slave whose owner took him to Illinois, a state that prohibited slavery. Later he and his owner returned to Missouri, a slave state. Scott brought a lawsuit in federal court in St. Louis, Missouri, to obtain his freedom based on previous decisions that residence in a free state conferred freedom. The United States Supreme Court found that Scott could not bring a lawsuit in federal court because blacks, whether free or slave, were not U.S. citizens. Shortly after the Court's decision, Dred Scott was sold to a new owner who granted him his freedom two months after the decision.

The ruling infuriated the North and brought the nation a little closer to the Civil War (1861–1865). It also influenced the introduction and passage of the Fourteenth Amendment to the U.S. Constitution in 1868. This amendment extended citizenship to former slaves and granted former male slaves full civil rights. As a side note, women, black or white, did not have full civil rights until the ratification in 1920 of the Nineteenth Amendment granting women the right to vote. People of the Chinese race (including those living in Hawaii, a territory of the United States) were not able to immigrate into the United States and those who were already in the United States were not eligible to apply for citizenship after Congress passed the Chinese Exclusion Act of 1882. The ban on both immigration and right to apply for citizenship was lifted in 1943 when Congress passed the Chinese Exclusion Repeal Act.

CRITICAL THINKING: REASONING Compare and contrast Justice Brown's opinion with Justice Harlan's opinion.

The next case, *Brown v. Board of Education,* illustrates the flexibility of the common law in adapting to changing social mores. During the fifty-eight years from *Plessy* in 1896 to *Brown* in 1954, two world wars had been fought, African Americans in large numbers had moved from the rural South to northern industrialized urban centers, and women had been granted the right to vote by the Nineteenth Amendment to the U.S. Constitution.

Fundamental structures and attitudes in our society had changed. Normally, the law lags behind such societal changes. When these changes are momentous, however, the law adapts to accommodate them as shown by the following case.

CASE 1.2

Supreme Court of the
United States, 1954
347 U.S. 483, 74 S. Ct.
686, 98 L. Ed. 873
http://www.findlaw.com
http://supct.law.cornell.
edu/supct/index.php

LANDMARK CASE

BROWN v. BOARD OF EDUCATION

BACKGROUND AND FACTS Five cases originating one each from Kansas, South Carolina, Virginia, Delaware, and the District of Columbia were joined because of the common legal issues involved. The lead case was from Kansas. The plaintiff, Linda Brown, was a five-year-old African-American child living in Topeka. Her father brought this action on her behalf in the U.S. District Court to prohibit enforcement of a Kansas statute that permitted cities with a population of more than 15,000 to maintain separate school facilities for African-American students.

The Topeka Board of Education had elected to establish segregated elementary schools. Linda was assigned to an elementary school based on her race and not to the school that was closest. During the lawsuit, the three-judge federal district court found that segregation in public education had a detrimental effect on African-American children. The court denied a remedy, however, on the grounds that the African-American and white schools substantially were equal with respect to buildings, transportation, curricula, and the educational qualifications of their teachers. Brown appealed.

Chief Justice WARREN delivered the opinion of the Court.

. . . .

. . . It is true that public school education at the time of the [Fourteenth] Amendment had advanced further in the North, but the effect of the Amendment on Northern States was generally ignored in the congressional debates. Even in the North, the conditions of public education did not approximate those existing today. The curriculum was usually rudimentary; ungraded schools were common in rural areas; the school term was but three months a year in many states; and compulsory school attendance was virtually unknown. As a consequence, it is not surprising that there should be so little in the history of the Fourteenth Amendment relating to its intended effect on public education.

. . . .

Here . . . . there are findings below that the Negro and white schools involved have been equalized, or are being equalized, with respect to buildings, curricula, qualifications and salaries of teachers, and other "tangible" factors. Our decision, therefore, cannot turn on merely a comparison of these tangible factors in the Negro and white schools involved in each of the cases. We must look instead to the effect of segregation itself on public education.

In approaching this problem, we cannot turn the clock back to 1868 when the Amendment was adopted, or even to 1896 when *Plessy v. Ferguson* was written. We must consider public education in the light of its full development and its present place in American life throughout the Nation. Only in this way can it be determined if segregation in public schools deprives these plaintiffs of the equal protection of the laws.

Today, education is perhaps the most important function of state and local governments. Compulsory school attendance laws and the great expenditures for education both demonstrate our recognition of the importance of education to our democratic society. It is required in the performance of our most basic public responsibilities, even service in the armed forces. It is the very foundation of good citizenship. Today it is a principal instrument in awakening the child to cultural values, in preparing him for later professional training, and in helping him to adjust normally to his environment. In these days, it is doubtful that any child may reasonably be expected to succeed in life if he is denied the opportunity of an education. Such an opportunity, where the state has undertaken to provide it, is a right which must be made available to all on equal terms.

We come then to the question presented: Does segregation of children in public schools solely on the basis of race, even though the physical facilities and other "tangible" factors may be equal, deprive the children of the minority group of equal educational opportunities? We believe that it does.

. . . .

We conclude that in the field of public education the doctrine of "separate but equal" has no place. Separate educational facilities are inherently unequal. Therefore, we hold that the plaintiffs and others similarly situated for whom the actions have been brought are, by reason of the segregation complained of, deprived of the equal protection of the laws guaranteed by the Fourteenth Amendment.

DECISION AND REMEDY The United States Supreme Court held that separate but equal public school facilities were inherently unconstitutional when the segregation was based on race. This decision laid the foundation for the desegregation of all public facilities. Ten years later the Civil Rights Act of 1964, which attempted to end all overt discrimination, was passed. As a result, *Plessy v. Ferguson* is no longer valid law.

COMMENT The *Brown* decision was pivotal for the nation. The Court understood the impact that its decision would have on the country; Thus, the justices came together in a 9-to-0 vote. The decision itself is only three and one-half pages long, double spaced. The Supreme Court rarely reads a decision in open court prior to releasing the material to the public. But to acknowledge the stature of the decision, Chief Justice Warren read the opinion out loud in open court, which was packed with the parties to the case, visitors, and the press.[a] One of the associate justices was Justice John Marshall Harlan,[b] the grandson of Justice John Marshall Harlan[c] who wrote the dissent in *Plessy v. Ferguson*.

The short opinion was reproduced in magazines and newspapers across the country. With no satellites to help speed transmission of this decision, the Voice of America, a radio broadcasting company, translated the *Brown* decision into thirty-four languages and, by the end of an hour, was broadcasting it around the world.

The *Brown* case did not include remedy, however. Instead, the Court set the case for a hearing. In 1955, in the case known as *Brown II,* the Court ordered the remedy to desegregate with "all deliberate speed." Unfortunately, desegregation did not mean automatic racial integration.

During the period between *Plessy* and *Brown,* neither Congress nor the state legislatures took steps toward overturning the concept of separate but equal because of political considerations. The courts provided the impetus for change by declaring segregation illegal.

Thurgood Marshall[d] (1908–1993) represented the plaintiffs from the five cases. During his years of litigation, he won twenty-nine of the thirty-two cases he argued before the Court. In 1967, he was appointed to the Supreme Court by President Lyndon Johnson[e] (1908–1973). Justice Marshall served on the Court from 1967 to 1991.

CRITICAL THINKING: POLITICAL CONSIDERATION Why was it necessary for the federal government to become involved in school desegregation at the state level?

---

[a] *University of Detroit Law Journal* 18 (1954), p. 64.

[b] John Marshall Harlan (1899–1971) served as associate justice on the U.S. Supreme Court from 1955 to 1971.

[c] John Marshall Harlan (1833–1911) served as associate justice on the U.S. Supreme Court from 1877 to 1911.

[d] Information about Thurgood Marshall is available at http://www.thurgoodmarshall.com.

[e] The Lyndon Baines Johnson Library is part of a system of presidential libraries administered by the National Archives and Records Administration. The library can be accessed at http://www.archives.gov (click on "Presidential Libraries") or at http://www.lbjlib.utexas.edu.

Brown v. Board of Education was first argued in 1952. The Court decided that it needed more information and reset the case for argument in 1953. Before the second hearing, Chief Justice Fred Vinson died and President Dwight Eisenhower[5] (1890–1969) appointed Earl Warren[6] (1891–1974) as chief justice of the United States (1953–1969). Recognizing the importance of the case, the newly appointed chief justice decided that he needed to hear the oral arguments. The case was then argued a second time before the Court. The Court issued its opinion two years after it was first argued.

At first glance, the cases of *Plessy v. Ferguson* and *Brown v. Board of Education* may seem out of place in a textbook concerned with the legal environment of business. Both cases, however, had important impacts on the business world.

Plessy v. Ferguson promoted an era of segregation. Businesses provided separate facilities for whites and non-whites, including separate entrances, restrooms, and drinking fountains. Tremendous costs were incurred in building and maintaining separate facilities. Citizens of this country were discriminated against in the job market, in housing, and in transportation based solely on their skin color. Segregation was imposed on other ethnic and religious groups, such as Native Americans, Asians, Hispanics, Irish, Jews, and Catholics. Victims of discrimination varied according to the region and the era.

Brown v. Board of Education began the nation's long journey toward desegregation and integration, a journey that continues today. Congress has passed a series of civil rights acts over the years. Businesses have spent and are still spending billions of dollars in attempts to comply with federal statutes and administrative regulations on equal opportunity and affirmative action, such as recruiting and training programs for minorities and women. Businesses are spending additional sums to defend against charges of violating an employee's constitutional and statutory rights. The financial losses resulting from wasted and unused talent are incalculable.

Classifications of Law

The law is divided into a number of classifications, according to its various functions and jurisdictions, with

[5]The Dwight D. Eisenhower Library is located at http://www.eisenhower.archives.gov and at http://www.archives.gov, click on "Presidential Libraries." He served as president from 1953 to 1961.
[6]A Web site for Earl Warren is found at http://provost.ucsd.edu/warren/welcome/facts/earl.html.

some overlap. These classifications are somewhat arbitrary, but a study of the various classifications provides a sense of the depth and breadth of our legal system.

Comparison of Substantive Law with Procedural Law

Substantive law defines, describes, regulates, and creates legal rights and obligations. Take the following example. Restaurants are subject to health standards because they sell food and drinks to the public. A restaurant may be fined or even closed if found to be in violation of the health standards. Another example of substantive law is the rule that a person who, through his own fault, injures another must pay damages. Substantive law sets out legal rights and liabilities.

Procedural law establishes the processes and methods of enforcing the legal rights created by substantive law. For example, procedural law regulates the procedures to initiate a lawsuit, to select the court in which the lawsuit should be filed, to select a jury, to enforce court decisions, and to determine which legal papers need to be filed.

Comparison of Public Law with Private Law

Public law addresses the relationship between the people and the government. An example is public contract law, such as a contract between a government agency and a private contractor to build a school.

Private law governs the legal relationships among individuals, such as a contract between a person and a private contractor to build a house. Whether a law is classified as public or private depends on the types of parties involved. Both public and private law are subdivisions of substantive law.

Comparison of Civil Law with Criminal Law

Civil law encompasses the legal rights and duties that exist among persons or between citizens and the government. Civil law is concerned with a person's legally recognized rights and duties in relationship with others. Contract law, corporate law, and partnership law, for example, are part of the civil law.

Criminal law involves a violation or wrong committed by a person. Although the criminal act may involve only one victim, it is also an offense against

LEGAL HIGHLIGHT

Law Terms Are Easy to Learn!

At first glance, new legal terms seem like a foreign language, but legal terms can be easy to decipher. Some legal terms have remained in the original Latin, while others have been translated into English over the centuries. Whenever a Latin term is used in this text, an explanation follows.

Numerous legal terms end in one of two suffixes: "-or" or "-ee." See the following chart.

Examples of "-or" and "-ee"

"-or"	"-ee"
Promisor	Promisee
Offeror	Offeree
Grantor	Grantee
Trustor	Trustee
Mortgagor	Mortgagee

A word ending in "-or" is making or creating the word that precedes the "-or." The promisor is the party making a promise; the offeror makes an offer; the grantor creates a grant, such as a conveyance of a title to real property; the trustor creates a trust; and the mortgagor creates a mortgage.

A word ending in "-ee" is receiving what precedes it. The promisee receives the promise, the offeree receives the offer, the grantee receives the grant, the trustee is the person who receives the assets for the trust, and the mortgagee receives the benefits of the mortgage. In a mortgage, the debtor, or mortgagor, is the one who creates the mortgage, thus the mortgagee is the creditor.

Legal terms appear formidable because they are not used in daily language. Keeping the "-or" and "-ee" rules in mind makes the terms intelligible.

---

society. Criminal acts are prohibited by the government to protect the public. All law not classified as criminal is civil.

Criminal law falls under public law jurisdiction, whereas civil law is sometimes public and sometimes private. A criminal act often violates a civil right as well. For example, drunk driving is a criminal act. If an accident occurs, the government can prosecute the accused for driving under the influence of alcohol. If the accused injures someone in the accident, the victim can sue in civil court for damages.

Courts of Law and Courts of Equity

Early in American legal history, the legal system followed the English model of courts and was divided into two systems, *courts of law* and *courts of equity.* A **court of law** grants a **judgment** (legal decision) for an **award** of monetary damages, while a **court of equity** grants a **remedy**, a legal means to enforce personal rights or to correct a wrong. In most states, courts of law and courts of equity have merged, but vestiges of the distinctions between the two remain.

Historically, the early English courts of law became so strict and complicated that justice was not served. In those days, the alleged facts were presumed to be true. Thus, the outcome of the case depended on using the correct procedure. If the lawyer used the wrong procedural writ, the person would lose the case. The only appeal was to the king. The effect still lingers in the consciousness of society. For example, the phrase "you must cross every *t* and dot every *i*" when dealing with legal matters has not been true for decades, but the phrase is still used.

By the thirteenth century, the courts of law were basically restricted to granting money damages and possession of property, such as a trial to determine the title to real estate, as a remedy. Depending on the degree of harm, a victim might not be compensated by these limited legal remedies. The only means of redress was to petition the king for justice for equitable relief. These petitions became so numerous that the king sent them to the lord **chancellor**, the king's principal minister, for resolution. By the fourteenth century, the petitions were sent directly to the chancellor.

By the middle of the fourteenth century, the chancery court became a separate court system. The chancellor had the ability to grant new and unique remedies that fit the facts of the particular case. Eventually, a body of rules and remedies was established for this new court. Chancery courts gradually became called *courts of equity*. The following section clarifies the distinctions that exist today between courts of law and courts of equity.

Distinctions

Several differences exist between courts of law and courts of equity. The major distinctions include the use of a jury, time limitations, and legal decisions.

First, a jury is allowed in a court of law, whereas in an equity court the judge makes the decision. Historically, juries were never used in courts of equity. Today, however, an advisory jury sometimes is allowed when equitable relief is sought, but its decision is not binding. For example, an injunction is decided by a judge, not a jury.

Second, the two courts differ in the time limitations for filing a lawsuit. In a court of law, the victim, after the harm has occurred, has a maximum time limitation to file a lawsuit or he forfeits the right to do so. The time limitations are set in the various **statutes of limitations** and are measured, usually, in years. For example, if a contract has been broken, the person who has been harmed may sue at any time during a four-year period. If the person sues one day after the four years have passed, the case will not be heard by a court. The statute of limitations is designed to prevent undue delay in bringing the suit to court so that the evidence on both sides is fresh and the witnesses still are available.

INFOTRAC RESEARCH ACTIVITY

Log on to InfoTrac. Search for "statute of limitations" or "limitations of actions." Compare two articles written for periodicals concerning the statute of limitations.

Courts of equity are bound by the **doctrine of laches**, which requires a person to sue within a reasonable time period. Individuals who fail to act promptly to protect their rights will lose the right to the equity court's assistance. (See Legal Highlight: Equitable Maxims.) For example, if a business seeks an injunction to prevent a labor union from carrying out its threat to strike within a week, management must file its request within a reasonable time period, usually within a few days. Depending on the nature of the cases heard, a reasonable time may range from a few days to several decades; thus, setting specific time limitations is impossible.

Third, a court of law's judgment awards money damages. A court of equity, on the other hand, issues a *decree* or *order*. A **decree** determines the parties' rights in the case before the court. For example, a divorce decree dissolves the marital bonds between a husband and wife. An **order**, which is usually part of a decree, also determines the parties' temporary or permanent rights, such as child support.

Courts of law award monetary damages, whereas courts of equity grant other types of relief. The following are some differences between *remedies at law* and *equitable remedies.*

Courts of Law: Remedies at Law. Today, most people sue in court for monetary damages, that is, they want money to replace their loss.

Artiste Login. A customer orders a bronze statue from Carlo. The customer and Carlo work out all of the details. Carlo molds and casts the bronze statue and has it delivered to the customer's home as agreed. The customer does not pay for the statue. Carlo could sue in a court of law for money damages, that is, the contract price on which both agreed. If Carlo prevails in court, the court will issue a judgment for money damages, also called a **remedy at law** or **legal remedy**.

Courts of Equity: Equitable Remedies. Equity courts are grounded in justice and fair dealing. These courts grant **equitable remedies** that provide solutions other than the money damage awards available in a court of law. Occasionally, people seeking equity may be granted money even though it was not the primary relief originally sought. In an equitable case, money is granted when the plaintiff asserts that the money is rightfully his. In a case at law, on the other hand, money is awarded to compensate for specific damages caused by the wrongdoer.

Equitable remedies try to correct a situation by granting the harmed party relief. Generally, the courts will not consider applying equitable principles and granting equitable relief unless no adequate legal redress is available. The most common equitable remedies are *specific performance, injunction, rescission, reformation,* and *accounting.* Detailed explanations of each follow.

Specify Performance. A plaintiff may ask a court to issue a decree of **specific performance**, which orders a defendant to perform the acts that she promised to do in a contract. The subject matter of the contract must be unique for a court to order specific performance.

For example, in most states, land and one-of-a-kind personal property, like a rare diamond, are considered to be unique. A court of law can only order payment of money for damages, but, in many cases, this payment is not a satisfactory remedy.

Artiste Login. Take the case of Carlo's contract to sell the bronze statue. Let's say that after Carlo created the statue, he failed to deliver it. If the customer has paid in full, she could sue for specific performance. The statue is a unique creation by Carlo and the customer wants the statue, not money damages. If Carlo fails to obey the court's order for specific performance, he could be held in contempt of court.

A court cannot order specific performance of personal services, however, because that would be considered involuntary servitude. Besides, such an order would be unenforceable in a practical sense.

Artiste Login. Carlo receives an order for a marble fountain. A dispute arises. If Carlo has not already created the marble fountain, a court could not issue a specific performance order that in effect would order

Carlo to construct the marble fountain, since it is a unique item. An equity court cannot order a person to perform this type of personal performance.

Injunction. A plaintiff might request an **injunction** to prevent a certain activity from happening or to stop an activity from continuing. For example, although a court cannot order a softball player to play, it could stop the softball player from playing for another team by issuing an injunction. The softball club would seek an injunction, in this case, an order to refrain him from doing a particular act, that is, playing for another team.

A **temporary restraining order (TRO)** is a temporary injunction that orders a person to refrain from an activity for the time period between the filing of the lawsuit and the conclusion of the trial. A TRO might be issued to preserve evidence or to protect the plaintiff's rights. Here, the softball club first would seek a TRO, which will be converted into a permanent injunction if the club prevails in court.

INFOTRAC RESEARCH ACTIVITY

Search for articles on "temporary restraining order." Compare an article describing why a court granted a temporary restraining order with an article discussing why a court did not grant the order.

Rescission. A person signs and performs a contract. Unfortunately, the basis of the contract was misrepresented by the other party. On discovery of the misrepresentation, the injured party wants to return to the position that he had before signing the contract. A court of equity can remedy the situation equitably by ordering a **rescission**. A rescission cancels the agreement and reinstates both parties to the **status quo**, that is, to their original positions.

For a rescission order to be issued by the court, the injured party must show that he relied on misrepresentations when signing the contract. If the equity court grants rescission, the plaintiff is entitled to have any property or money returned to him. All rights and duties created by the agreement are rescinded.

Artiste Login. Carlo signs a sales agreement not knowing that the supplier is misrepresenting the quality of the raw bronze metal he needs to make a statue. If Carlo discovers the fraud before money or goods have changed hands, Carlo can request the court to allow equitable relief to have the agreement rescinded, that is, to have the contract declared null and void. If, however, Carlo has paid the supplier before the fraud was discovered, Carlo can seek a rescission of the contract and request the court to order the supplier to repay his money.

Reformation. Occasionally, a written contract does not correctly reflect the original oral agreement. The court of equity may order a **reformation** or change of the written contract to reflect the true intent of the parties. Reformation actions result from either fraud or mistake in a contract situation.

Artiste Login. Carlotta goes to an insurance agent to purchase disability insurance for herself and her brother. Because they recently started an online business, they have very limited finances and can only afford maximum monthly payments of $50. They each need disability income coverage that will pay them each $400 a month to cover the loan payments on their respective motor vehicles. The insurance agent prepares the application for coverage of $400 a month.

After Carlotta leaves the office, the agent realizes that the $50 monthly premium will purchase coverage of

LEGAL HIGHLIGHT

Equitable Maxims

How do judges make a decision when one party asks for an equitable remedy and the opposing party disagrees? For example, Racing Farms contracts with Jed to purchase from him a race horse named Speedster. One week after the contract was signed, Jed raced Speedster one more time. Speedster won the race. Now Jed has seller's remorse and informs Racing Farms that he wants to keep Speedster because of the horse's potential for winning.

Racing Farms can sue for specific performance. Racing Farms requests the judge to order Jed to turn over the horse. Jed argues against the remedy. The judge is faced with making a decision as to whether to grant the request for specific performance.

From medieval times, judges have developed six principles, called *equitable maxims,* to guide their decision making. These equitable maxims are based on common sense and fairness.

1. *Whoever seeks equity must do equity.* Plaintiffs who seek an equitable remedy want to be treated fairly, but, to obtain justice, they, in turn, must have treated others fairly.

2. *Where there is equal equity, the law must prevail.* When both the plaintiff and the defendant have meritorious positions, the court must apply the law instead of searching for an equitable remedy.

3. *Equity regards substance rather than form.* The equity court is more interested in justice and fairness than in legal technicalities.

4. *One seeking the aid of an equity court must come to the court with clean hands.* The plaintiff must have acted honestly and fairly to seek aid from the court.

5. *Equity will not suffer a right to exist without a remedy.* When the plaintiff has a right to relief and no adequate remedy at law exists, the equity court is charged with identifying and awarding an equitable remedy.

6. *Equity aids the vigilant, not those who rest on their rights.* Individuals who find that they have been wronged must act within a reasonable time period to protect their rights. This maxim is the basis for the doctrine of laches, discussed earlier in this chapter.

The maxims do not have legal authority because they are not codified. They do have precedential value, however, because they have been relied on for centuries and are cited in numerous cases. These commonsense principles are often used by judges when deciding cases in equity. In this case, the judge will issue a specific performance order to Jed to turn over the horse to Racing Farms. Jed may have seller's remorse, but he does not have any legal reason not to turn over the horse.

only $200 a month. He erases the $400 and inserts $200. The insurance company does not realize that a change has been made and issues a policy for coverage of $200 per month. After six months, Carlotta becomes disabled and makes a claim for income of $400 a month. The insurance company informs Carlotta that the maximum amount is $200 a month. She files a lawsuit seeking reformation of the contract. Carlotta provides a copy of the original contract and shows the court the eraser marks, which are clear on the agent's copy. In this case, the court will reform the contract to the original amount of $400 based on the fraud committed by the agent.

Accounting. When parties that have a close relationship involving money or other property have a disagreement, one or both may request a court of equity for an **accounting**. For example, one business partner accuses the other of misappropriating some of the business assets. The accuser may file a lawsuit in a court of equity and request a full accounting of the missing assets. Normally, the court appoints a certified public accountant to conduct a full accounting. The court could order the wrongdoer to pay for the value of the missing assets to the innocent party.

Merged Court Systems. Anyone filing a lawsuit during the period between the fourteenth century and the middle of the twentieth century had to decide whether to file in a court of law or in a court of equity. Today, most states have merged the two court systems; thus, a person may request both legal and equitable remedies in the same lawsuit.

In states that have merged the two systems, trial court judges have the authority to grant both forms of relief. Judges decide questions of equity without a jury. As noted previously, a jury rarely is involved with equity cases. When a plaintiff requests only monetary damages, a judge alone or a jury may hear the case. The merging of the courts of law and equity has not diminished the importance of distinguishing between these two systems.

Schools of Legal Philosophy

Jurisprudence means the philosophy of law and describes the foundations and workings of our dynamic legal system. Jurisprudence explains the philosophical basis for the law, the reasons for the law, and the process by which the law can be changed.

A number of schools of legal philosophy exist. In the following sections, we review six current schools of thought, the *natural law school,* the *analytical school,* the *historical school,* the *legal realists school,* the *economic school,* and the *feminist school.* Each school explains some areas of the law, but each has its limitations. No unified philosophy of the law exists that can be applied to all areas of the law.

Natural Law School

The advocate of the **natural law school** believes that an ideal state of being exists that derives naturally from either human nature or a divine source. Natural law is discovered through reason and the knowledge of good and evil. Ethical values are the source of the law's authority.

Documents such as the Magna Carta, the Declaration of Independence, the U.S. Constitution (see Appendix A for the complete text), and the U.N. Declaration of Human Rights have the natural law as their philosophical basis. Natural law ideals are expressed in phrases such as this one from the Declaration of Independence: "We hold these truths to be self-evident, that all Men are created equal, that they are endowed by their Creator with certain unalienable Rights. . . ."

The civil rights movement of the late 1950s and early 1960s protested the existence of racial segregation. All levels of government had laws that specifically segregated the races, such as lunch counters where only whites could be seated or buses where only whites could sit in the front section. In a number of cities, African Americans were arrested for sitting at lunch counters or sitting in the fronts of buses. They were criminally charged.

The civil rights movement used the natural law philosophy as its foundation. The legal defense for the African Americans was based on the premise that segregation is inherently wrong. The defense asserted that a higher law provided meaning to the words found in the U.S. Constitution, such as equal protection in the Fourteenth Amendment, that sanctioned the defendants' acts of defiance. Although those defendants at that time were convicted of criminal acts, the Congress eventually made the segregation laws illegal.

Analytical School

A proponent of the **analytical school** examines the structure and subject matter of legal codes and cases, analyzing them logically to extract the underlying principles. By analyzing cases and rules, the analytical school develops general principles. These principles form the basis for legal reasoning. Logic shapes the analytical school's approach to the law.

The American Law Institute (ALI) has reviewed thousands of cases decided in the last 200 years to determine the law in specific areas. Based on this extensive review, the ALI has written **Restatements** for various sections of the law, including agency, contract, tort, and trust law.

The *Restatements* are volumes of sequentially organized compilations of cases on particular topics. The purpose of the *Restatements* is to set out the history, development, and logic of particular laws. Judges often use the *Restatements* to support their reasoning in case opinions. If a *Restatement* section is adopted by a state's supreme court, it becomes the law of that state.

Historical School

A student of the **historical school** concentrates on the legal system's origin and history to determine the principles of contemporary law. Legal principles that have withstood the passage of time are best suited for shaping present laws.

In 1540, the English Parliament passed the Statute of Wills. The statute permitted a person to sign a will; thus, the person was able to control to whom his real property was to be distributed after death. Prior to this statute, all real property belonged to the king and the king controlled how property was to be distributed after a person's death.

Centuries later, with the exception of Louisiana, all other states in the United States have adopted some version of this English law governing *probate*. **Probate** is the legal process of settling a person's estate by collecting property owned by the deceased (also called the *decedent*), paying his debts, and transferring ownership of the decedent's property to his heirs. These rules, based on historical precedent, have worked well for centuries, so they remain intact.

Legal Realists School

Advocates of the **school of legal realism** contend that the law is shaped by social forces and is an instrument of social control. The legal realists school of philosophy relies on the pragmatic and empirical sides of law, that is, life experience.

For example, in 1919, the Constitution's Eighteenth Amendment was adopted, prohibiting the manufacture and sale of alcohol. People in large numbers, however, continued to manufacture and sell intoxicating beverages, albeit illegally. Police and judges basically ignored the law, although occasionally police staged raids, generally for publicity purposes, during which they smashed moonshine equipment and arrested notorious criminals. Prohibition proved to be a dismal failure. In 1933, the Twenty-First Amendment repealed the Eighteenth Amendment, ending Prohibition.

Legal realists see law as a means to a social end; thus, they try to predict and influence lawmaking. In the legal realist school, the same set of facts does not always result in the same conclusion. For the legal realist, the legitimacy of law and of legal institutions is measured by the degree to which they meet the needs of society.

Economic School

A supporter of the **economic school** holds that people evaluate the law in accordance with economic principles. The theory assumes that everyone in the legal system is rational and will act to maximize personal welfare. For example, Jo has been injured in an automobile accident. She has a choice of filing a lawsuit or settling her claim. Chances are high that she will settle the claim because a settlement is faster and less costly than a trial. According to the economic school, efficiency is the key by which people analyze and evaluate the law.

The economic school of philosophy plays an important role in business decision making. For example, a manufacturer knows that one customer out of every 500,000 will be injured using its product. The manufacturer estimates the settlement cost for such an injury to be $300,000. The company considers this cost in pricing its product, reserving an appropriate amount for future claims.

Feminist School

A supporter of the **feminist school** believes that the female point of view is not represented, but only the male viewpoint, in the law. As a result, a bias in favor of males has resulted in women and children not being treated fairly by the law.

Historically, women were the victims of discrimination. Women were not allowed to vote until the passage in 1920 of the Nineteenth Amendment to the

Constitution. Many states in the past did not allow a married woman to enter into contracts, own real estate, or work in many types of jobs. In 1862, a North Carolina court held that a husband had a right to physically punish his wife to control her from an "unruly temper, or an unbridled tongue." Women were ruled by their husbands and they had few, if any, basic rights.

A century passed (1862–1962) and husbands still could beat their wives without much fear of the police interference. Although by 1962, a married woman could enter into contracts and own real property, she was required to take the residency of her husband in order to vote, could not have credit in her own name, could not control her salary since it belonged to her husband, and could not sell the real property without her husband's written approval.

To reverse this type of public policy, a body of law developed called *feminist jurisprudence*. Subscribers to the feminist school work to persuade legislators, judges, and other legal, social, and political forces to change attitudes so women will be treated equally under the law. Here is a sample legislative bill that illustrates the point. When the prescription male impotency pill Viagra first became available, the cost was quickly covered by health insurance. The prescription cost, however, for birth control pills taken by women since the 1960s was rarely covered by health insurance. The proposed legislation would require insurance companies that covered the prescription costs of Viagra to also cover the prescription costs of birth control pills.

After 1962, statutes were passed that prohibited spouses from beating one another. Married women could sell real property, could have residency apart from their husbands, establish credit in their own names, and control their salary.

Locating the Law

Trial courts hear factual issues and make decisions on the law in cases that are brought before them. The side that loses has the right to appeal that decision based on issues involving the law to a higher court, called an **appellate court**. The following material examines the publication of trial court and appellate court decisions.

Publishing Court Decisions

Court decisions are published in chronological order and typically reflect only the decisions of appellate courts. A few states, including California and New York, publish their trial court decisions. The published decisions of the federal district courts, the trial courts for the federal government, are available in law libraries and on computer databases.

Of the thousands of trial court decisions made each year, fewer than 1 percent finish the appeal process, and only a few of those decisions are available in law libraries and on computer databases. The appellate courts publish the decisions of cases containing the important legal issues.

The cases in this book have been taken from reported appellate court decisions. The following section addresses the system for locating reported cases.

Reporter System for Case Decisions

Many state governments publish their state appellate court decisions. State cases also appear in regional units of the *National Reporter System,* published privately by West Group[7] (West). (See Exhibit 1-1.) If the state government does not publish its own material, it may designate West as the official publisher of the state's legal materials. West is the unofficial publisher of all reported decisions by the federal trial and appellate courts.

United States Supreme Court decisions have one official citation and two unofficial citations. First, the official reports are printed by the U.S. Government Printing Office in the *United States Reports* (U.S.). The second and third citations refer to the two unofficial reporters, the *Supreme Court Reporter* (S. Ct.), published by West Group, and the *Lawyers' Edition* of the United States Supreme Court Reports (L. Ed.), published by Matthew Bender & Company, Inc.

Case Citations. Appellate court decisions normally have two citations: the official citation and the unofficial citation. The official citation is provided by the U.S. Government Printing Office and the unofficial citation is the one from the *National Reporter System*. The case is cited (referred to) by the case name, the volume number, name of the state report (if any), and page number; followed by the volume number, abbreviation of the *National Reporter,* and page number. The year in which the decision was filed appears at the end. (See Exhibit 1-2.)

[7]A West Group Web site for students is found at http://www.westbuslaw.com/learning_resources.html.

Exhibit 1–1   National Reporter System—Regional and Federal

Regional Reporters	Coverage Beginning	Coverage
Atlantic Reporter (A. or A.2d)	1885	Connecticut, Delaware, Maine, Maryland, New Hampshire, New Jersey, Pennsylvania, Rhode Island, Vermont, and District of Columbia.
North Eastern Reporter (N.E. or N.E.2d)	1885	Illinois, Indiana, Massachusetts, New York, and Ohio.
North Western Reporter (N.W. or N.W.2d)	1879	Iowa, Michigan, Minnesota, Nebraska, North Dakota, South Dakota, and Wisconsin.
Pacific Reporter (P. or P.2d)	1883	Alaska, Arizona, California, Colorado, Hawaii, Idaho, Kansas, Montana, Nevada, New Mexico, Oklahoma, Oregon, Utah, Washington, and Wyoming.
South Eastern Reporter (S.E. or S.E.2d)	1887	Georgia, North Carolina, South Carolina, Virginia, and West Virginia.
South Western Reporter (S.W. or S.W.2d)	1886	Arkansas, Kentucky, Missouri, Tennessee, and Texas.
Southern Reporter (So. or So.2d)	1887	Alabama, Florida, Louisiana, and Mississippi.

Federal Reporters		
Federal Reporter (F., F.2d or F.3d)	1880	U.S. Circuit Court from 1880 to 1912; Commerce Court of the United States from 1911 to 1913; U.S. district courts from 1880 to 1932; U.S. Court of Claims (now called U.S. Court of Federal Claims) from 1929 to 1932 and since 1960; U.S. Court of Appeals since 1891; U.S. Court of Customs and Patent Appeals since 1929; and U.S. Emergency Court of Appeals since 1943.
Federal Supplement (F.Supp.)	1932	U.S. Court of Claims from 1932 to 1960; U.S. district courts since 1932; and U.S. Customs Court since 1956.
Federal Rules Decisions (F.R.D.)	1939	U.S. district courts involving the Federal Rules of Civil Procedure since 1939 and Federal Rules of Criminal Procedure since 1946.
Supreme Court Reporter (S.Ct.)	1882	United States Supreme Court since the October term of 1882.
Bankruptcy Reporter (B.R.)	1980	Bankruptcy decisions of U.S. bankruptcy courts, U.S. district courts, U.S. Courts of Appeals, and United States Supreme Court.
Military Justice Reporter (M.J.)	1978	U.S. Court of Appeals for the Armed Forces and Army, Navy-Marine Corps, Air Force, and Coast Guard Courts of Criminal Appeals.

NATIONAL REPORTER SYSTEM MAP

Exhibit 1–2   **Case Citation Examples**

A. State Appellate Court Case

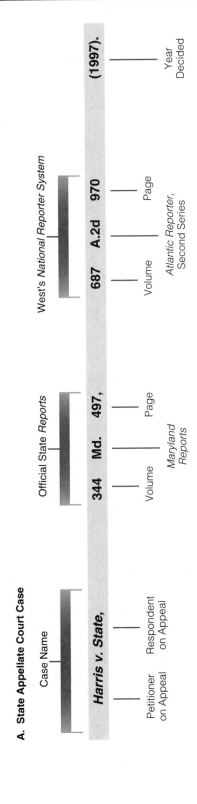

Note: There is no way to tell who was the original plaintiff or defendant at the trial level. The order of the names at the appellate level is based on who brings the petition for appeal; this is usually the party who lost at the lower level. A few states, however, follow the rule that the plaintiff's name always appears first on the citation.

B. United States Supreme Court Case

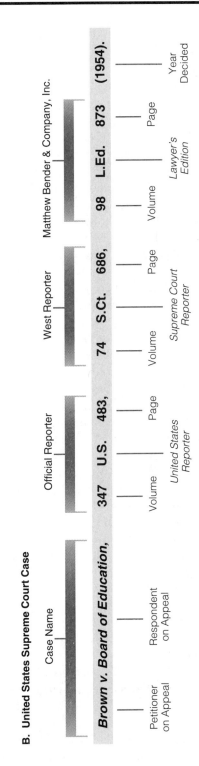

Note: Not all states have official reports, as Maryland does. Some states rely on West's *National Reporter System* as their official reports.

For example, consider the following citation to a case decided by the Maryland Court of Appeals: *Harris v. State,* 344 Md. 497, 687 A.2d 970 (1997). The names of the parties, Harris and the State, appear first. The opinion appears in volume 344 of the official *Maryland Reports,* published by the state of Maryland, beginning on page 497, as well as in volume 687 of the *Atlantic Reporter,* Second Series, published by West Group, beginning on page 970. The appellate court decision was filed in 1997. In the title of a case, such as *Harris v. State,* the *v* or *vs.* stands for *versus,* which means "against."

The appellate court often places the name of the party appealing the decision first. In this case, Harris appealed the trial court's decision. In some states, however, the appellate courts retain the order of names from the trial court. It is impossible from the case name to distinguish the **plaintiff**, the person filing the lawsuit and seeking relief from a harm allegedly caused by the **defendant**, the person being sued and accused of generating harm. The facts of each case must be read carefully to identify each party's role; Otherwise, the appellate court's discussion will be difficult to understand.

Uniform System of Citation. The American Bar Association (ABA) is recommending a new uniform system of citation. This system standardizes references made in published cases, whether in printed or electronic form.

Individual case references include the case name, the year of the decision, the court issuing the decision, and the decision's sequential number. Cases are numbered to correspond with the sequence in which the court decides them. To cite part of a case, a paragraph number, instead of a page number, follows the sequential number.

Here is a fictitious example. *Cotton v. Grady,* 2004 AZ 30, ¶58; 502 P.2d 1482, 1499. The name of the case is *Cotton v. Grady.* The first citation, 2004 AZ 30, ¶58 uses the uniform system of citation. The case was decided in 2004. The court name, AZ, stands for Arizona Supreme Court. The number 30 indicates that this case was the thirtieth sent to publication. Finally, the symbol ¶58 indicates the specific paragraph where the information sought is located.

The second citation, 502 P.2d 1482, is a standard citation and indicates that the case can be located in volume 502, on page 1482, in the Pacific second series of the *National Reporter System.* The number 1499 is the page where the material sought is located. The reader will have to read the whole page to find the information, unless the paragraphs are numbered.

Statute Publications

Statutes are passed by a legislative body as a bill that consists of various parts. A bill may specify actions that are deemed consumer protection, such as lifetime contracts for health spas, and a section specifying criminal sanctions for violating those consumer protections. These parts are individually assigned by topic to different areas of the statutory scheme.

The books containing statutes, whether state or federal, are commonly updated by the use of pocket parts that are inserted in the back binder of the book in a space created for this purpose. One pocket part is issued for each volume.

For publication purposes, statutes are organized by subject matter, such as the topics of consumer protection and the criminal law. Cases, on the other hand, are organized and published on a chronological basis.

Statutory Citations. As a result of the fact that statutes are organized differently from cases, statutory citations differ from those of cases. In a statutory citation, the first number is the title number, and the second number indicates the section within the title in which the statute can be located. (See Exhibit 1-3.)

Federal statutes can be found in the *United States Code* (U.S.C., published by the U.S. Government Printing Office). The expanded version is the *United State Code Annotated* (U.S.C.A.) published by West Group, which provides short summaries of all the cases decided under that statute.

For example, Thelma decides to research the federal law on bank robberies. She finds a specific statute on bank robberies, 18 U.S.C.A. §2113. The number 18 is the title number, not the volume number. Title 18, *Crimes and Criminal Procedure,* consists of a number of volumes and contains the federal criminal statutes. The symbol § stands for "section," which is followed by the number. In this example, the name of Section 2113 is *Bank Robbery and Incidental Crimes.*

Administrative Agency Regulations

An *administrative agency* is created by the legislative or, occasionally, the executive branch of the government. Each agency adopts regulations to facilitate the carrying

Exhibit 1-3   Statute Citation Examples

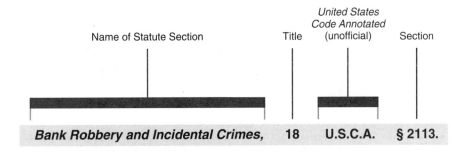

Note: Several other ways to cite statutes also are used, such as those found in *Statutes at Large, Public Law,* and in the official volumes of the *United States Code.*

out of its statutory duties. A regulation has the force of law unless a court overturns it. Federal agencies include the Federal Trade Commission, the Environmental Protection Agency, and the Internal Revenue Service. State and local agencies include the department of motor vehicles, public utility commissions, and pardon and parole boards.

The federal government publishes its administrative agencies' regulations in the *Code of Federal Regulations* (C.F.R.), a series of softbound books. Regulations issued by state governments are published either in softbound editions or in loose-leaf manuals. Both federal and state regulations change frequently, which explains why they are published in a hardcopy format that is inexpensive to produce and easy to change. (As discussed in the next section, regulations are also made available on the World Wide Web, which is a convenient way to disseminate information that changes frequently.)

Legal Research Using Computers

The two most widely used private, high-speed data delivery systems are WESTLAW by West Group and LEXIS-NEXIS by Reed Elsevier Properties, Inc. Both are computer-assisted legal research services that allow researchers to interact with the delivery system.

User interaction with the data-delivery system can be initiated anywhere in the world from a computer running a WESTLAW or LEXIS-NEXIS software access program. These systems can also be accessed by using a Web browser. Once the user is logged on the

system, a search request can be sent to the data bank. If the appropriate information is found, it appears on the user's computer screen. The user can print the information or download it to the hard drive or other storage device.

For a fee, WESTLAW, LEXIS-NEXIS, and similar computerized data-search systems can access virtually any case, statute, or regulation in the United States with minimum time and effort. Today, the latest case outcomes are available within days on the computer, far in advance of printed copies that are sent to law libraries and subscribers. This legal information is also available on CD-ROM and is updated frequently.

A congressional mandate requires all federal governmental agencies to make their information available on the World Wide Web. State, city, and county governments also post legal information on the Web. (See Exhibit 1-4.)

Problems arise with legal information available on the Web. First, only relatively recent information is available. A limited number of high-profile historic cases and statutes are available, but the amount is meager compared to the volumes of printed materials produced over several centuries. Second, the information on the Web is poorly organized, often difficult to locate, and unreliable for official research because of errors or lack of updating. Third, those who key in the information rarely include a date as to when the information was posted. The person accessing the legal documents, such as statutes or administrative regulations, has no reference point as to whether the material is current.

Exhibit 1–4   **Legal Research on the World Wide Web**

Background The Internet is a data–delivery system that consists of connected networks composed of several elements. The two popular ones are electronic mail (e-mail) and the World Wide Web (WWW). The WWW is popular because it supports text, graphics, video, and audio capabilities, all with interactive capabilities.

In the 1960s, the U.S. government began the development and construction of a system of computer networks, now called the Internet, but its use was restricted to authorized government, academic, and military users. After the end of the Cold War in 1989, the Internet was opened to the public. Since then, Internet use has grown exponentially. Millions of computers provide services linking the world's nations into a seamless web of computer connections that use telephone and cable lines, fiber optics, and satellite feeds.

Internet Service Providers The Internet is accessed using Internet service providers (ISPs), such as America Online (AOL), AT&T WorldNet Service, MindSpring, and Microsoft Internet Network. The ISP provides Internet access and related services, such as home pages and e-mail. Other common sources of Internet access and e-mail are places of employment, academic institutions, public libraries, and shopping malls.

Search Engines Search engines allow the user to locate information posted on the Internet. The popular Internet browsers, such as Netscape Navigator and Microsoft Internet Explorer, each have their own search engines. Other popular search engines are Ask Jeeves, Excite, Infoseek, Lycos, Savvysearch, Webcrawler, Google, and Yahoo.

Domain Name System Each computer that serves the WWW can be located through its Internet address. The address is based on the Domain Name System (DNS). Seven top-level domains exist in the United States. Country domains are identified by two-letter abbreviations. Each state in the United States is listed under the U.S. country domain of ".us". Appendix I lists the two-letter country domain and those for each of the fifty states. (See Appendix I at **http://bohlman.westbuslaw.com**.)

Current Domains The following table describes the top-level domains in the United States. A source for information about domains is the Internet Corporation for Assigned Names and Numbers at **http://www.icann.org/**.

Original Magnificent Seven Generic Top-Level Domains (gTLDs)

Abbreviation	Explanation
World Wide Web gTLDs	
.com	Commercial organizations. Businesses use this domain. If the growth pattern continues, this category may be subdivided.
.edu	Educational and academic organizations. In the past, this domain was used for all U.S. educational institutions. Now, the edu is restricted to four-year colleges and universities. Elementary and secondary schools and two-year colleges are registered in the country domain, such as ".us", and use either K–12 (kindergarten through twelfth grade) or community college names.
.int	Organizations established by international treaties or having international databases.
.net	Network providers, that is, NIC (network information center) and NOC (network operations center) computers.
.org	Organizations not included in other domains, such as research and not-for-profit organizations.
United States Only gTLDs	
.gov	Originally intended for all government agencies. Now reserved for the U.S. government. State and local agencies are registered in the U.S. domain, such as for Arizona at http://www.state.az.us.
.mil	Military organizations within the U.S. Department of Defense.

Exhibit 1–4 (continued)

New Domains Seven additional new gTLDs have been adopted. The new ones are shown in the next table. At the bottom are other new domains that are being considered.

New Additional Magnificent Seven gTLDs

Abbreviation	Explanation
.aero	For the aviation industry.
.biz	For businesses and is an alternative to .com.
.coop	For business cooperatives.
.info	For those providing general information services.
.museum	For museums.
.name	For individual or personal nomenclature; a personal *nom de plume* identifier.
.pro	For professionals.

New Possible gTLDs?

.health	For health information.
.news	For news media.
.travel	For travel information.

Reading Addresses In this textbook, bold face set off the actual address. An example of a WWW address follows: **http://www.law.cornell.edu**. Reading the example backwards, the computer is located at an educational site, Cornell University, which contains law-related topics. Although this address is easy to read and figure out, most addresses are not so easily readable because the letters and symbols used in the address do not have any readily apparent meaning. All addresses, however, are converted to numbers through a domain name server. If these numbers are known, they can be entered and they will take the searcher directly to the site.

Here is another example: **http://www.lawsoc.org.uk/**

The ".org" in the address might lead one to think that the site is for a not-for-profit organization in the United States. A closer look shows ".uk" follows ".org", indicating that this site is located in the United Kingdom. In fact, it is the site for the Law Society, an English not-for-profit organization. What is found at this site is English, not American, law.

Helpful Hints Occasionally, a top-domain address is typed in, but the site fails to respond. One reason

might be that the server is busy, similar to a telephone busy signal. If it remains busy after repeated tries, one solution is to enter a forward slash (/) following the top domain (i.e., .com, .edu, .gov), so it reads **http://thomas.loc.gov/**. That may do the trick. If the top-domain address has characters typed after a slash, try deleting everything to the right of the slash. For example, at one time **http://www.lawsoc.org.uk/lawsc02a.html** was a valid address, but today it no longer works. Often, by deleting the characters following the forward slash after the top domain, that is, by using **http://www.lawsoc.org.uk** instead, the address will work.

Sometimes in the address, a small symbol that is not very visible follows the first slash after the top domain. Three symbols, the tilde (~), the underscore (_), and the hyphen (-), are used often and can be difficult to see. The tilde often follows the top domain and first forward slash (/).

Millions of persons, businesses, and governments have their site names registered on the WWW. But sites, just like people, move or cease to exist. The Web addresses provided in this textbook as references are current as of the print date.

Analyzing Case Law

Reported court cases constitute the common law. The court's written opinion reflects the reasoning process used to reach a decision about a case. Often, an opinion describes the important facts in the case and the judge's application of the law to those facts, including references to precedents.

The cases in this book were edited to make them easier to read. Each case is separated into the following sections: *Background and Facts*; the court's opinion; *Decision and Remedy; Comment*, when it is appropriate; and *Critical Thinking* questions. In the section that is the **court's opinion**, the focus is on that part which illustrates a point; thus, much of the case is omitted. Three ellipses (. . .) mean that part of a sentence or paragraph has been deleted; four ellipses (. . . .) mean that one or more paragraphs were deleted. To ease the reading of the cases, references to other cases or statutes usually are omitted.

How to Brief a Case

To brief a case, read the case carefully. Follow this checklist when briefing a case.

1. *Case Name and Citation* State the case name, the level of court that decided the case, the decisions by prior courts, if given, and the year in which the case was decided.

2. *Facts* Summarize the facts. In this book, some of the facts appear in the Background and Facts section, while others appear in the case. This section can be fairly lengthy.

3. *Issue* Set out the issue of the case in the form of a question that can be answered yes or no. The issue is the question that the court answers to determine which party will prevail. The court often starts the issue with the words "whether or not" or "the issue is." This section is short.

4. *Holding* State the court's decision. This section is short.

5. *Reasoning* Summarize the court's reasoning that led to the holding. This section describes the court's application of the rule of law to the facts. The rule of law is a principle of general application that guides a judge in making a decision. This section is usually the longest part of a brief.

An appellate court has two alternatives when it reviews a case. If the court **affirms** a case, it is upholding (agreeing with) the lower court's decision. If the court **reverses** the case, it is disagreeing with the lower court's decision. An appellate court may choose to affirm part of a case and reverse the rest. Regardless of the appellate court's decision, the case is **remanded** (sent back) to the lower court to carry out the appellate court's instructions. The trial court is the one that normally carries out the decision of the appellate court.

CYBERLAW

The Internet

The World Wide Web (WWW) was created at CERN, the European Laboratory for Particle Physics, located outside Geneva, Switzerland. The WWW, which is part of the Internet (opened two years previously), was released for universal use in 1991 with a rudimentary **browser**, which is a program that provides a graphical user interface with the Web. A browser interfaces with **servers**, which are special software programs running on mainframe computers or personal computers (PCs). When connected to the Internet, the computers can serve information, including text, graphics, audio, and video, to the browser.

With the creation of the multimedia browsers and secured lines for making purchases, commercial use of the Internet grew exponentially. The amount of business conducted on the Web in 1993 was zero. By 2003, business-to-consumer e-commerce had reached $146 billion and business-to-business e-commerce grew to more than $1.3 trillion.

To purchase items online, a secure server is necessary. Once the purchaser is logged on to a secure server, the address should read "https" or "wwws." Additionally, somewhere on the screen, usually in the lower lefthand corner, a lock or other symbol should show that it is locked or secured. Once those two items are visible, the purchaser can purchase the item with relative assurance that the information provided will remain private.

During the past decade, this technology has created

new legal and social dilemmas. What is a digital signature? What is an electronic signature? Who owns e-mail? If the business owns the e-mail, does it have a right to monitor it, if it is business related or if it is personal? Concerns abound over the loss of privacy because of the information collected and stored in large databases without the knowledge of the consumer.

The Web allowed businesses another avenue to market and sell products and services. Called *e-commerce* (electronic commerce), brick-and-mortar businesses found another outlet to reach consumers, while new businesses pioneered an exclusive electronic presence on the Web. New questions arose. Can the state and federal government tax the income of these electronic businesses? What about applying sales taxes to the Web business transactions? If the e-merchant cannot send ordered items for a period of time, is the e-merchant obliged to notify the customer? How does the customer return the item if dissatisfied?

Other issues abound. Is the e-business able to sell shares of its company to investors over the Web? Can a Web site distribute copyrighted material without permission and without paying royalties? Which government has jurisdiction over crimes committed using the Web? How can a person or company defend against untruths posted on the Web? Can the Web be used to vote in elections? The questions previously posed cover only a few of the legal issues that must be considered by the legislatures and courts in the future.

No government or business owns the Internet. Yet, the Internet-related standards are global. The global Internet is powerful and is changing the dynamics of how business is conducted, how capital is raised, and how flexible companies must be to survive. The legal system is being challenged in the age of instantaneous and mass communications. Information on court cases, bills pending before a legislative body, and statutes was available only in a few places in the past, but now is obtainable using the Web.

International Consideration

Treaties, Conventions, and Agreements

The financial success of the United States depends on international trade. Every sovereign state (nation) has its own body of law, such as U.S. law, Egyptian law, German law, Japanese law, or Mexican law. **International law** does not exist as a unified set of codes. Instead, international law is reflected in trade, economic, legal, and other political relationships among nations. These relationships are established through treaties, *conventions*, and *agreements.*

Treaties are agreements made among nations. A nation that signs a treaty or a convention is referred to as a *signatory.* Treaties cover a wide scope of topics, ranging from regulation of migratory bird flight patterns to the destruction of nuclear weapons.

Treaties can create international organizations. A treaty signed by most nations created the United Nations in 1945. The 1957 Treaty of Rome created the European Economic Community (EEC).[8] Later amendments to the Treaty of Rome led to the European Union.

In the United States, the president signs treaties with his foreign counterparts. The U.S. Constitution requires treaties to be ratified by two-thirds of the Senate to become law.

A **convention** is a law adopted by an international organization that was created by a treaty, such as the United Nations' Convention on Climate Change. For a convention to be binding on a member nation, the treaty must grant the power for the organization to pass binding conventions. Each sovereign state has the power to adopt or disapprove conventions. If a nation adopts a convention, the treaty usually has provisions for a nation to later withdraw that permission. No nation has ever given up complete sovereignty to an international organization, nor can any international organization dictate a nation's adherence to the organization's code without that nation's permission.

An **agreement** is defined rather loosely as an agreement that can obligate a country, but that usually is less formal or less significant than a treaty or convention. Like treaties and conventions, agreements are made between or among heads of state. An example of an agreement is the North American Free Trade Agreement (NAFTA), which was approved by both the U.S. Senate and House of Representatives.

---

[8]The European Economic Community existed until 1992. The EEC evolved into the European Community (EC), which in turn evolved into the European Union (EU). The EU was created in 1991 by the Treaty on European Union (commonly known as the Maastricht Treaty), which amended the Treaty of Rome. Although legal differences exist between the EC and the EU, the terms are used interchangeably.

A businessperson needs a working knowledge of the laws of the United States, the laws of the countries in which her business is conducted, and the international laws that govern the relationship among the countries. Businesspeople need to obtain independent legal advice from a professional who knows not only the laws of the other countries, but also the laws contained within the treaties and lower level agreements.

PRACTICAL TIPS

A Manager's Role in Preventive Law

According to an adage, "A business is not successful until it has been sued." This statement is based on the experience of many successful businesses. When a business has assets and is a functioning operation, it needs to be concerned with the prospect of litigation.

As a manager of a new small business, your firm has not yet employed attorneys, known as in-house legal counsel. The best approach is to conduct your business affairs with the idea of staying out of the courtroom. Litigation is expensive and time consuming even when the business prevails in the lawsuit. The key, you believe, is to practice preventive law.

To achieve this goal, as the manager, you need to retain a law firm that operates with the same philosophy. One good preventive law strategy is to have understandable contracts with your employees, suppliers, and customers; to educate your employees; and to have a good system of documentation. The following checklist provides some guidance.

Checklist

✔ *Contracts in Plain English* Contracts with your employees, suppliers, and customers that are written in plain English will clarify your business obligations and support your working relations. For a contract to be effective, your employees, who will be working under the contract, must thoroughly review and understand it. As you plan the contents of the contract, consider including a clause that requires alternatives to litigation in resolving disputes, such as those discussed in Chapter 4.

✔ *Training for Employees* Employees who deal with legal issues should be well versed in the legal aspects of their jobs. For example, the personnel in the company's department of human resources should be educated in the pertinent statutes and cases pertaining to employment law. Other managers also should receive at least minimum training in personnel law, such as the laws involving sexual and racial harassment.

✔ *Effective Documentation* Documentation procedures and requirements should be well thought out. The length of time various documents are retained needs to be based on legal requirements or, if none exists, on common sense. Documents need to be stored so they can be swiftly retrieved. If a governmental agency or a lawyer inquires about a particular action or procedure, the business must have access to the appropriate documentation. For example, documents that chronicle the work performed in product design may prevent a lawsuit or, if a lawsuit is filed, aid in defending against allegations that the product failed to function properly. Often e-mail is used to exchange information. The company needs a records-retention policy that sets the length of time that documents, such as e-mails, will be retained.

Chapter Summary

As the English language evolved, the word *law* developed two definitions. First, law is a system that gives order to society by establishing rules of moral conduct that attempt to ensure justice. Second, law refers to specific principles represented by a rule or rules.

The court examines various sources of the law when making a decision. If applicable, the state or federal constitution, statutes, and regulations are examined. In addition, the courts review the case law, also known as the common law. Common law uses *stare decisis*. This doctrine of law makes the common law stable yet flexible with the passage of time.

The law also can be classified in several ways: substantive law or procedural law, public law or private law, and civil law or criminal law. The remedies that a court can apply can be divided into remedies at law and equitable remedies. Courts of law and courts of equity were compared.

The schools of legal philosophy are the natural law school, the analytical school, the historical school, the legal realists school, the economic school, and the feminist school. A number of methods can be used to locate the law. Law is covered by the Constitution, statutes, and cases. The mechanics of briefing a case were discussed.

Using the World Wide Web

Two useful WWW sites referenced frequently throughout the book are the FindLaw Web site and the legal site located at Cornell Law School.

The FindLaw Web site is extensive with more than 15,000 publications available. The user can access cases, statutes, current news, and some administrative regulations. The Cornell site also contains a wide-ranging amount of legal material. Statutes, cases, international material, and current news are available.

All federal government agencies and many officials, state governments, county and city governments, and other local governments, such as school boards, have Web sites. Using e-mail, citizens can easily transmit their ideas and views to their elected and appointed officials.

The federal government actively uses the WWW. To make information accessible to people, Congress has mandated that federal information be available on the Web.

Additionally, federal funding is available for academic institutions, schools, libraries, and state and local governments to enable them to place materials on the WWW.

For *Web Activities*, links to Web sites mentioned in the chapter, and additional Web sites that relate to the chapter topics, go to **http://bohlman.westbuslaw.com**, click on "Internet Applications," and select Chapter 1.

Web Activities

Go to **http://bohlman.westbuslaw.com**, click on "Internet Applications," and select Chapter 1.
1–1 Congressional Bills
1–2 Presidential Speeches

Key Terms

accounting	codified law	international law	remedy
administrative agency	common law	judgment	remedy at law
administrative law	convention	jurisprudence	rescission
administrative regulations	court of equity	law	*Restatements*
	court of law	legal remedy	reverse
administrative rules	court's opinion	military orders	school of legal realism
affirm	criminal law	natural law school	server
agreement	decree	order	specific performance
analytical school	defendant	ordinance	*stare decisis*
appellate court	doctrine of laches	plaintiff	status quo
award	economic school	precedent	statute
browser	equitable remedy	private law	statute of limitations
case law	ethics	probate	substantive law
chancellor	executive orders	procedural law	temporary restraining order (TRO)
civil law	feminist school	public law	
civil law system	historical school	reformation	treaty
code	injunction	remand	

Questions and Case Problems

1–1 Law Compare and contrast the definitions of the word *law*. Why are there two different definitions for one word?

1–2 Common Law Discuss the differences between common law and statutory law.

1–3 Philosophies of Law Identify and distinguish among the reasoning processes used to explain the law.

1–4 Philosophies of Law Describe the philosophical schools of law and classify each according to the appropriate reasoning process.

1–5 Citation Identify and describe the parts of the following citation: *Miranda v. Arizona,* 384 U.S. 436, 86 S. Ct. 1602,16 L. Ed. 2d 694 (1966).

1–6 *Stare Decisis* Define *stare decisis* and describe its functions and flexibility.

1–7 Classification Discuss the differences between private law and public law.

1–8 Law and Equity Discuss the differences between courts of law and courts of equity.

1–9 Law or Equity Fully discuss whether each of the following breach of contract situations warrants specific performance or money damages as a remedy.

a. Connie signs a contract to sell her house and lot to Juan. A few days later she finds another buyer who is willing to pay a higher price. Connie now refuses to sell to Juan. What remedies are available to Juan?

b. Broken Hearts, a country music group, contracts to appear for a week at a Branson, Missouri, hotel showroom. Two days before the scheduled engagement, the group informs the management that it refuses to appear. What remedies are available to the Branson Hotel?

c. Bill signs a contract to purchase a rare stamp from Al, who is breaking up his stamp collection. Before the stamp is turned over to Bill, Al decides to keep the stamp collection and refuses to deliver the stamp to Bill. What remedies are available to Bill?

1–10 Internet Go to **http://www.house.gov/** and find your representative to the House of Representatives. Go to **http://www.senate.gov/** and find your state's two senators. Find their e-mail addresses. What biographical information is posted at the site? What information is available that benefits the congressperson's constituency?

Chapter 2

Ethics and Corporate Social Responsibility

I would prefer to fail with honor than win by cheating.

> Sophocles, ca. 496–406 B.C.
> Sophocles was one of classical Athens' great writers of tragedy.

No man is justified in doing evil on the grounds of expedience.

> President Theodore Roosevelt,
> 1858–1919
> Twenty-sixth president of the United States of America, 1901–1909
> Nobel Peace Prize, 1906

Chapter Outline

Introduction

The basis on which a business analyzes its goals, particularly its goal to earn profits, influences its decisions and impacts its ethical standards. Emphasis on short-term profits sometimes creates the temptation to act unethically—although, certainly, a business's short-term success does not necessarily indicate that the business has been unethical. Still, when a business considers profits over the long term, rather than on a quarterly or annual basis, ethical considerations and social responsibility are reinforced.

The chapter begins with a discussion of several ethical theories. The relationship between ethics and the law is examined. The effect of business decisions on various groups is studied. Near the end of the chapter, an ethical decision-making model is provided and is applied to a sample problem. The chapter concludes with a discussion of ethics in the legal profession.

Artiste Login. Anyone who owns a business, such as the online business Artiste Login Products, Inc., owned by Carlo and Carlotta, is involved daily in making business decisions based on ethical standards. Ethical businesspeople recognize the responsibility owed to others and to themselves to maintain principles.

Theories of Ethical Conduct

Ethics are systematic statements of right and wrong behavior based on a philosophical system. The term ethics is from the Greek word *ethos*; the word moral comes from the Latin word *moralis*. Morals reflect values about right and wrong.

Ethics, in the simplest form, set a standard for determining right and wrong by making reflective choices and by directing the selected choice of action toward good. Constant clarification of those standards enables people to resolve ethical conflicts and to stimulate higher visions of what is good. For example, a common business practice in the mid-1800s was to drive competitors out of business by selling goods below cost, then raising the selling price exorbitantly once the competitors were eliminated. By the late 1800s and the early 1900s, this practice was not only regarded as unethical, but eventually was made illegal after Congress passed various laws.

Ethical decisions should neither depend on the mechanical aspects of an action (Is this action ethical?) nor on an action's legality (Is this action within the limitations of the law?). The ethical question is this: Should the action be taken based on social good?

Although ethics provide moral guidelines, individuals must apply these guidelines when making decisions. Business ethics is not a separate theory of ethics, but rather an application of ethics in the commercial arena. Although all people have ethical responsibilities, a higher set of standards is imposed on professionals who serve as social models, such as physicians, attorneys, and accountants.

The Western foundation of ethics is based on the writings of the ancient Greek philosophers. (See *Legal Highlight: The Ancient Greek Philosophers Are Still Relevant*.) Over the centuries, a number of different philosophical frameworks developed that established the standards of ethical conduct. The following subsections briefly describe only two of the major frameworks: ethical standards based on universal duties and ethical standards based on consequences.

Ethical Standards Based on Universal Duties

Deontology is the philosophical practice of defining and adhering to an absolute set of standards by which ethical behavior can be measured. Deontology attempts to define universal duties that serve as moral guides to decision making, such as those discussed by Immanuel Kant[1] and John Rawls.[2] When a moral dilemma arises, a person can apply these universal standards to determine whether a particular course of action is good.

A person who embraces deontology expects others to follow these universal duties without exception. For example, a person who believes that killing another is

---

[1]Kant (1724–1804), who was from Konigsberg, Prussia, based his philosophy in reason. He believed a universal set of ethical principles existed that could serve as action-guiding rules. Through the reasoning process, this absolute and finite set of rules could be determined. His rules were duty based. For example, he believed that truth-telling was a universal rule. If lying were to become the universal rule—if everyone lied—life would be impossible because no one could trust anyone. If truth-telling were the universal rule, everyone's moral duty would be to tell the truth. Kant's logic did not consider the consequences of the absolutism of universal rules.

[2]Rawls (1921–2002) was a professor of philosophy at Harvard University. He put forth the view that because society is not heterogeneous, people will hold opposing and sometimes irreconcilable views. As a result, democracy requires tolerance, which will lead to the principle of extensive individual liberty.

The Ancient Greek Philosophers Are Still Relevant

Western philosophy is based on and influenced by ancient Greek philosophers whose writings are still studied. The most powerful ideas came from Socrates, Plato, and Aristotle.

Socrates (ca. 470–399 B.C.) believed that wrong actions arose from ignorance. He believed that the way to discover universal rules was to use inductive reasoning. Through the questioning process, people would progress from general to more specific knowledge and eventually discover a universal rule that applies to all examples. The Socratic method of questioning is named after him. Graduate schools and law schools often use the Socratic method in class.

Plato (ca. 428–348 B.C.) was a student and friend of Socrates. Plato believed that all people desire happiness. Because people try to act in ways that produce happiness, actions contrary to this objective are mistakes caused by ignorance. According to Plato, if people know that moral virtue will lead to happiness, they will act virtuously.

Aristotle (ca. 384–322 B.C.) was Plato's student. Aristotle regarded ethics as the study of practical knowledge. He believed that people's goal was to attain happiness, which was achieved when they fulfilled a function. Thus, they had to discover what function

made them happy. Moral virtue fell between extremes. For example, generosity falls between stinginess and wastefulness, while courage falls between the extremes of cowardice and foolhardiness.

Various philosophical schools evolved in ancient Greece. One such school was called the Cynics. Founded by Antisthenes (ca. 445–365 B.C.), the Cynics claimed that people achieved happiness by leading a life of self-control and being free from material desires and pleasures. Antisthenes reasoned that individuals could not control these appetites for long.

The Epicureans were founded by Epicurus (ca. 341–270 B.C.). This school equated happiness with seeking moderate pleasure and avoiding pain. Pleasure was gained through prudence, moderation, courage, justice, and friendships.

The Stoics grew to be a very influential school. Stoicism was founded by Zeno (ca. 335–263 B.C.), who was from Citium, a city located on Cyprus. The Stoics thought it was foolish to try to shape circumstances to human desires. A divine intelligence guides and governs circumstances and directs all things ultimately toward goodness.

The ancient Greek philosophers remain influential. Their ideas stimulated other philosophers throughout the intervening centuries to build on and develop new ways of thinking about the meaning of justice, ethics, and goodness.

wrong must oppose capital punishment, war, and killing in self-defense. A person who follows the Ten Commandments without exception applies the concept of deontology.

In deontology, a person who fulfills an absolute moral duty embodies the concept of good, and the outcome of following that moral duty—whether good or bad—is inconsequential. When an ethical conflict arises, a person decides which action to take by determining if a particular action is morally right or wrong. The flaw with deontology is that importance is placed on the act of carrying out a duty and the concept of good does not include the results of the act. Deontology

does not help a person resolve conflicts that arise among the various universal standards. The following conflict illustrates this point.

The universal standard (moral duty) to keep promises is good. You make a promise to your friend that you will not tell anyone where she lives. Under deontology that promise is morally binding; therefore, you must keep the promise. Another universal standard, however, is to tell the truth. If a police officer asks you to tell him where your friend lives because her life is in danger, do you tell the police officer? Compliance with the universal duty of truth-telling would compromise the universal duty of promise-keeping.

Importance is placed on keeping the promise, not on the consequences. By keeping the promise, you say "no comment" to the police officer, thus, keeping your promise to your friend while adhering to the duty of truth-telling, but the consequence is that your friend is killed. If you break your promise, you are violating your moral duty, but the consequence of telling the police officer of your friend's whereabouts is that she will live.

Deontology does not provide guidance for prioritizing universal duties, for example, between promise-keeping and truth-telling. Following a universal rule usually is good, such as in keeping a promise. But sometimes consequences can be detrimental and harm can result from blindly obeying one moral duty while disregarding the other.

Another school of philosophers developed the concept of utilitarianism. This school looks at the consequences of ethical standards.

Ethical Standards Based on Consequences

Utilitarianism establishes ethical standards based on the consequences of an action. Philosophers, such as Jeremy Bentham[3] and John Stuart Mill,[4] believed that decisions should be made on the basis of their utility or usefulness.

Utilitarianism defines good as "the greatest happiness for the greatest number." It evaluates ideas, institutions, and actions on the basis of their utility or benefit. Any source of happiness has utility, because individuals care about increasing their pleasure and decreasing their pain. Rather than supporting selfishness in the quest for personal happiness, however, utilitarianism encourages people to seek their own happiness in the happiness of others.

---

[3]Bentham (1748–1832), a British philosopher, attempted to determine ethical judgments by observations and empirical study. He believed that an action's consequences in terms of its effect on others rather than an action's intended outcome is what mattered the most. He developed a method to measure happiness.
[4]Mill (1806–1873), a British philosopher, worked for the East India Company and eventually, like his father, became a director. He also served in the British Parliament. Mill believed that the quality of pleasure an action produced was a crucial factor in determining the actions that one should take. He also believed that some actions were more valuable than others.

Often "the greatest happiness for the greatest number" is misinterpreted to suggest that if the majority wants something, then the act produced is ethical. What the phrase really connotes is that the moral act is judged to be good or bad by the consequences produced in terms of social benefit or utility.

To illustrate this concept, in criminal cases the exclusionary rule prohibits the police from conducting a search without permission of the person or without a search warrant issued by the court. This rule is based on the Fourth Amendment of the U.S. Constitution. In a criminal trial, the judge will not allow any evidence found by the police during an unauthorized search to be introduced against the accused defendant. The reason for the exclusionary rule is to protect everyone from police abuse and to uphold the Fourth Amendment prohibition against unreasonable searches.

When polls are taken of the American people concerning the exclusionary rule, the majority disapproves of the rule. People reason that the rule prevents courts from convicting people accused of crimes because evidence that could potentially establish the accused person's guilt is not allowed to be introduced at the trial. Without that evidence, the jury is not able to consider this information when reaching a verdict. The majority, therefore, would ban the exclusionary rule.

In spite of the majority's motivation for a ban, the exclusionary rule benefits society. The number of people not tried for a crime they committed under the rule is small compared with the number of people who might suffer from police abuse if the rule were abolished. The ethical person using utilitarianism to determine right from wrong should not ask, "What is my greatest satisfaction or happiness?" but instead, "What is the greatest benefit (happiness, utility) for the greatest number?"

One flaw with utilitarian theory is that prediction of the success, failure, or utility of certain behaviors is impossible. In some situations, the temptation is to use the accumulation of wealth as a tangible measure of success and not how the wealth was accumulated.

Another weakness in utilitarian theory is that an individual's well-being can be sacrificed for social benefit. One individual might suffer more as a result of behavior that brings society greater happiness. For example, the payment of substandard wages to illegal migrant farm workers lowers the cost of food available to society.

Ethical Behavior and Legal Behavior

Managers can confuse legality and ethics, thinking that if an act is legal (or, at least, not forbidden), it is also ethical. Although legality and ethics often coincide, they are not one and the same. Agreement can be reached as to whether a particular type of conduct is or is not ethical. In almost all cases, what is illegal is generally considered to be unethical. The converse is generally considered to be true in society, that is, what is legal is considered to be ethical. Exceptions exist—conduct that is legal may be unethical, such as in the past when legal segregation based on race was legal.

The law has evolved as constitutions, statutes, cases, executive orders, and administrative regulations have changed to reflect changes over time. Development of the law is basically a reactive process. For example, laws forbidding computer crimes were not written before the first crime of that sort was committed. Only after computer crimes became more frequent were laws passed by legislative bodies in response to the public outcry by victims of computer crimes. During the period when there were no specific laws forbidding theft by computer, were those thefts ethical? Of course not.

Even when a law exists, it may not always be obeyed or even enforced. The law cannot cure ethical problems resulting from business behavior. For this reason, businesspeople must prioritize their inclusion of ethical guidelines and legal information in their decision-making process.

During recent years, television, the Internet, and the print media reported a series of revelations about executives being paid excessive compensation, boards of directors failing to govern and, hence, allowing corporate fraud to occur, independent auditing firms letting accounting fraud and accounting errors escape detection, and businesses filing for large-scale bankruptcies. With the enormous media coverage, people wondered if any companies were well run or had any corporate ethics. In fact, only a few companies grabbed the headlines, while the vast majority of the businesses quietly earned money without violations of ethics or the law.

What went wrong with these few companies? Why did some business leaders act in an unethical manner and possibly even criminally? To attempt to answer these questions, we need to review what happened.

Throughout the decade of the 1990s, the stock markets climbed higher in value as the result of the longest bull market ever seen. The good times finally came to a halt in February 2000 as the markets entered the longest bear market to date. In general, even well-run companies declined in value. Companies built on fraud, greed, poor management, or accounting errors, however, were unable to hide their problems from the market.

Companies such as Enron, WorldCom, Tyco, Global Crossing, Adelphia Communications Company, Kmart, Xerox, Vivendi Universal, HealthSouth, and Arthur Andersen found themselves garnering negative headlines. Most did not seek protection in bankruptcy court but restated earnings that had been based in part on flawed accounting practices. The common threads throughout all of these companies were top executives indulging their greed, auditors failing to perform their jobs, regulators missing irregularities and illegal transactions, and boards of directors neglecting to perform their duties.

The No More Enrons coalition, funded by consumer groups and labor unions, issued a report in late 2002. Losses in value within the 401(k) retirement accounts as a result of corporate executives' malfeasance were estimated to be approximately $175 billion. Public pension funds, including state, county, and city plans, lost a minimum of $6.4 billion. More than a million workers lost their jobs, health plans, and retirement funds, while company executives, in contrast, collected millions from their salaries, bonuses, and the sale of stock options in the year prior to the collapse. The federal government lost $13 billion in tax revenues from companies that underreported their profits to the Internal Revenue Service.[5]

The lack of ethics and violations of law led to these failures. Good business practice dictates that management ascertain which groups will be affected by their business, ethical, and legal decisions; determine a balance when a conflict of interest arises among the groups; and choose an action based on social good. The next section examines those groups.

[5]The Internal Revenue Service Web site is http://www.irs.gov.

Enron

A sculpture of the tilted *E*, its logo, graced the front of Enron's world headquarters in Houston, Texas, for more than a decade. After Enron went into bankruptcy, however, the sculptured *E*, which by that time was infamously called the "crooked *E*," was sold at auction for $45,000. What happened to this company which was among the most admired for its futurist vision and thinking out of the box qualities?

Enron was a company that held virtual assets and not hard assets, such as power stations, which were notoriously capital intensive with low returns and ongoing debt. Having virtual assets meant Enron was in the business of creating markets by trading energy. Enron's executives were hailed as financial geniuses. Its executives lobbied the Congress and state legislatures to deregulate the electrical industry. They argued that free markets should regulate the energy business and not sluggish government regulators even though the government guaranteed the returns, albeit low, on the capital invested. The company was acclaimed as one of the best to work for. Enron was the darling of the media and business schools. Graduating students armed with their master's in business administration (MBA) actively sought to work at this dynamic company.

The decline in the market starting in 2000, however, uncovered the house of cards on which Enron was built, eventually forcing the company into bankruptcy. What comprised this financially shaky company? Debt hidden in hundreds of off-the-books transactions. Enron used a number of types of financial structures to hide parts of its debts. To understand one favorite mechanism, one needs only to review the laws.

Special-purpose entities (SPEs) were authorized by Congress for, as the name indicates, a particular purpose. A company could create a SPE, but at this point, any debt of the SPE was carried on the books of the creating company. The debt, however, could be transferred from the creating company to the SPE if an independent third business purchased a minimum of a 3 percent interest (now raised to 10 percent) in the SPE. If the SPE had a value of $100 million, the third company needed to make a minimum purchase of $3 million in shares. At this point, the company could move the debt concerning this transaction to the books of the SPE and with the sale of the 3 percent interest, it was able to report the amount received, $3 million, as income.

This financial structure soon become a favorite of Enron, which created more than 900 SPEs. Enron called it "monetizing" or "syndicating" the assets. Over time, these structured finance transactions involved transfers from Enron to the SPEs involving between $15 and $20 billion of debt. The general description given earlier of the creation and operation of an SPE complies with the law. Enron, however, did not often follow this model, because many of its SPEs involved fraud. One SPE, called E-Barge, illustrates how debt was hidden as a result of fraud. The E-Barge transaction was far more complicated than the following description.

Enron had a contract to supply electricity to Lagos, a state within the country of Nigeria. For this contract, Enron purchased three electrical barges—barges carrying generators that were operated by various types of fuels and were capable of producing electricity—and anchored them in a waterway in Lagos. At that time, Nigeria owned and operated the National Electric Power Authority. Nigeria, sensing that its monopoly on electrical power was being challenged by the state of Lagos, became involved in a year-long dispute with Lagos as to whether Enron would be allowed to supply any electricity. Finally, Nigeria and Lagos ended their dispute and Enron was allowed to supply electricity. During that year, however, Enron was paying the loans on the barges while not collecting income.

In December 2000, Enron was faced with the end-of-the year reports and the need to meet Wall Street's earnings estimates of 31 cents a share. It was evident to the top executives at Enron that it was not going to meet the earnings estimates. Prior to December, Enron tried to sell the three barges, but found no takers. In an elaborate series of financial deals, Enron convinced Merrill Lynch, a stock brokerage firm, to create E-Barge.

Enron placed the electrical supply contracts and the barges in the SPE. Merrilll Lynch paid $7 million for an equity position in E-Barge. Enron transferred $21 million in debt to E-Barge; thus, Enron's books no longer carried the debt and reported the $7 million as income. This transaction was partially responsible for raising the earnings to 31 cents a share. As a result, the value of Enron's stock rose 27 percent. Without this and other SPE transactions, Enron would have earned only 24 cents a share. Everything looked legal to the casual observer. Let's see what really happened and which information was not disclosed.

The real structure of the transaction violated the SPE statutory requirements. Enron and Merrill Lynch had a good working relationship, with Merrill Lynch serving as underwriter, fund-raiser, investor, partner, lender, and analyst. Although Enron paid Merrill Lynch more than $38 million in stock and bond fees for advice, income from the fees paid by Enron made up less than 1 percent of Merrill Lynch's income. Enron, however, was a valued customer. When Enron called Merrill Lynch to purchase an equity share, costing $7 million, Merrill Lynch was interested, but reluctant.

Enron, in order to entice Merrill Lynch into the transaction, promised to make a $250,000 payment, to repay the $7 million at 15 percent interest, and to find a buyer for the stock within three months. In other words, Merrill Lynch did not have an equity—at risk—position in E-Barge. Merrill Lynch had a debt position since Enron was paying a fee of $250,000 to attract Merrill Lynch into the SPE and was guaranteeing repayment of the $7 million payment with interest, which is legally a loan. Merrill Lynch did not have any money at risk.

As a result of the "sale" to Merrill Lynch, Enron showed the $7 million as cash income and did not show that the amount was really a loan to be repaid. Enron was not legally required to reflect on its books any of the debt of the Nigerian electrical contract ($21 million). In effect, all of the debt and losses incurred with the Nigerian electrical contract were hidden from stock analysts, investors, and the government regulators.

By December 2001, Enron, the seventh largest company in the United States had filed for bankruptcy and the fraud was exposed. Its stock, which was trading at $90 in January 2001, was selling for pennies at the end of the year. In 2003, Merrill Lynch agreed to settle with the Securities and Exchange Commission (SEC) by paying $80 million. Documents showed that executives on both sides understood that the transactions were designed solely to allow Enron to claim increased earnings for the year. Merrill Lynch knew that the investment was really a short-term loan. Additionally, the SEC filed charges against four former Merrill Lynch executives who by that time were fired or had retired. Both civil and criminal charges are pending against Enron and its officers.

Stakeholders

When dealing with ethical issues, a business must consider at least five constituencies. These groups are called **stakeholders**, because they form a network with a stake in the decisions made by the business. A business making a decision must determine which stakeholders will be affected and the impact any decision will have on them.

Stakeholders include (1) the investors, including the owners; (2) the employees, who may be investors; (3) the supply chain, which includes customers and suppliers; (4) the government; and (5) the community or public at large. Emphasizing one of these groups when making decisions sometimes has the ultimate effect of benefiting or harming the others. Business managers must balance the interests of all stakeholders in order to make ethical decisions.

Top management is responsible for adopting and embracing ethical standards. These standards are useless, however, until top management implements those policies in day-to-day operations. All employee must understand what the standards are and how the standards are applied. Once the employees know and apply these ethical standards, their conduct will affect the other stakeholders.

A business can adopt a formal code of ethics. By adopting and implementing a code of ethics, businesses gain a reputation for integrity and honesty, thereby attracting investors, employees, suppliers, and customers. Businesses with ethical reputations are welcomed into communities.

Artiste Login. Carlo and Carlotta, as owners of Artiste Login, need to adopt a code of ethics, distribute it among the employees, and post the code on Artiste Login's Web site. Once the code is in place and has been used for a while, they should decide whether to hire an ethics review consultant to conduct an ethics audit. This audit can reveal which parts of the code are being followed and which are not. The consultant can then recommend a plan of action.

Owners

One of the prime objectives of our capitalist society is for a business, over the long run, to maximize its profits. Businesses need profits to survive and to increase their viability.[6]

The owners are the *shareholders* in a corporation or they may be called by other names in other business structures, but all hold an equitable interest in the business. An owner expects a monetary return from the

[6]Milton Friedman, "The Social Responsibility of Business Is to Increase Its Profits," *New York Times Magazine*, September 13, 1970.

business's activities. This return basically comes from the business's profits.

Owners expect that their interests will be fully protected by management. When owners believe management has acted improperly, they have the right to file a lawsuit to correct any such mismanagement. Management, however, is given wide latitude in setting aside the demands of owners, including management's right to refuse to declare dividends or other distributions.

Numerous reasons may exist for management's refusal to declare dividends or other distributions. If those reasons are to improve the welfare of the business's employees and lower the costs to customers, an ethical conflict arises between management's behavior toward employees and customers versus its behavior toward the owners.

The following case, decided in 1919, illustrates how disputes arise. A conflict arose between a business's behavior toward its shareholders versus its behavior toward employees and customers. Here is how the court resolved the conflict.

LANDMARK CASE

| CASE 2.1 | **DODGE v. FORD MOTOR CO.** |

Supreme Court of Michigan, 1919
204 Mich. 459, 170 N.W. 668

BACKGROUND AND FACTS Ford Motor Company was formed in 1903. Henry Ford, the president and majority shareholder, attempted to run the corporation as if it were a one-person operation. The business expanded rapidly and, in addition to regular quarterly dividends, often paid special dividends. Sales and profits were as follows:

· 1910—18,664 cars; $4,521,509 profit

· 1911—34,466 cars; $6,275,031 profit

· 1912—68,544 cars; $13,057,312 profit; $14,475,095 surplus

· 1913—168,304 cars; $25,046,767 profit; $28,124,173 surplus

· 1914—248,307 cars; $30,338,454 profit; $48,827,032 surplus

· 1915—264,351 cars; $24,641,423 profit; $59,135,770 surplus.

By 1919, accumulated earnings totaled $111,960,907. Originally, the Ford car sold for more than $900. From time to time, the price was reduced. In 1916, it sold for $440. For the year beginning August 1, 1916, the price was reduced, again, to $360. In the interests of setting aside money for future investment and expansion, Ford Motor Company paid no special dividends after October 1915. The plaintiffs were minority stockholders, who owned one-tenth of the shares of the corporation. They petitioned the court to compel the directors to declare a dividend.

Chief Justice OSTRANDER

. . . .

This declaration of the future policy, it is charged in the [complaint,] was published in the public press in the city of Detroit and throughout the United States in substantially the following language:

> *" 'My ambition,' declared Mr. Ford, 'is to employ still more men; to spread the benefits of this industrial system to the greatest possible number, to help them build up their lives and their homes. To do this, we are putting the greatest share of our profits back into the business.' "*

It is charged further that the said Henry Ford stated to plaintiffs personally, in substance, that as all the stockholders had received back in dividends more than they had invested they were not entitled to receive anything additional to the regular dividend of 5 percent a month, and that it was not his policy to have larger dividends declared in the future, and that the profits and earnings of the company would be put back into the business for the purpose of extending its operations and increasing the number of its employe[e]s, and that, inasmuch as the profits were to be represented by investment in plants and capital investment, the stockholders would have no right to complain. . . .

. . . .

> *"It is a well-recognized principle of law that the directors of a corporation, and they alone, have the power to declare a dividend of the earnings of the corporation, and to determine its amount. Courts of equity will not interfere in the management of the directors unless it is clearly made to appear that they are guilty of fraud or misappropriation of the corporate funds, or refuse to declare a dividend when the corporation has a surplus of net profits which it can, without detriment to its business, divide among its stockholders, and when a refusal to do so would amount to such an abuse of discretion as would constitute a fraud, or breach of that good faith which they are bound to exercise towards the stockholders."*

. . . .

There is committed to the discretion of directors, a discretion to be exercised in good faith, the infinite details of business, including the wages which shall be paid to employees, the number of hours they shall work, the conditions under which labor shall be carried on, and the price for which products shall be offered to the public.

. . . [I]t is not within the lawful powers of a board of directors to shape and conduct the affairs of a corporation for the merely incidental benefit of shareholders and for the primary purpose of benefitting others, and no one will contend that, if the avowed purpose of the defendant directors was to sacrifice the interests of shareholders, it would not be the duty of the courts to interfere.

. . . .

Defendants say, and it is true, that a considerable cash balance must be at all times carried by such a concern. But, as has been stated, there was a large daily, weekly, monthly, receipt of cash. The output was practically continuous and was continuously, and within a few days, turned into cash. Moreover, the contemplated expenditures were not to be immediately made. The large sum appropriated for the smelter plant was payable over a considerable period of time: So that, without going further, it would appear that, accepting and approving the plan of the directors, it was their duty to distribute on or near the 1st of August, 1916, a very large sum of money to stockholders.

In reaching this conclusion, we do not ignore, but recognize, the validity of the proposition that plaintiffs have from the beginning profited by, if they have not lately, officially, participated in, the general policy of expansion pursued by this corporation. We do not lose sight of the fact that it had been, upon an occasion, agreeable to the plaintiffs to increase the capital stock to $100,000,000 by a stock dividend of $98,000,000. These things go only to answer other contentions now made by plaintiffs, and do not and cannot operate to stop them to demand proper dividends upon the stock they own. It is obvious that an annual dividend of 60 percent upon $2,000,000 or $1,200,000 is the equivalent of a very small dividend upon $100,000,000, or more.

DECISION AND REMEDY The defendant, Ford Motor Company, was ordered by the court to declare a dividend.

COMMENT The two Dodge brothers received enough money from their share of the dividends and the sale of their stock to Henry Ford to establish their own automobile company, which produced Dodge automobiles. This company became part of the Chrysler Corporation in 1928 and in 1998 it became DaimlerChrysler.

Henry Ford was, at times, a farsighted business leader. He had a real concern for his employees. In 1914, when most of his competitors were requiring twelve-hour workdays, he instituted the eight-hour workday. When his competitors were paying $1 a day for unskilled labor and $2.50 for skilled workers, Henry Ford increased his minimum wage to $5 a day. This type of management resulted in more dedicated and efficient workers at Ford Motor Company.

As a result of the court decision, Ford purchased back all of the outstanding stock and took the company private. The corporation went public again in 1956 after his death.

CRITICAL THINKING: MANAGEMENT CONSIDERATION What was Mr. Ford's management philosophy? Although this case was decided in 1919, does the same problem still face businesses today?

Decisions made by management to increase employee wages and benefits, to lower prices, to improve product quality and safety for the consumer, or to contribute to community improvement projects lowers, at least for the short term, the owner's return on its investment. These actions are calculated to increase employee productivity, foster customer loyalty, and enhance community relationships, which in turn will lead to higher profitability and increased returns on the owner's investment.

Employees

Employees are essential to run a business. Some businesses have only one employee, while others have hundreds of thousands of employees. Employees are covered by federal and state employment laws. Not all aspects of employment law are covered by statutes. Areas covered by statutes include civil rights, benefits, wages, overtime, safety, and record requirement issues.

Employers have, at a minimum, an ethical duty to treat employees in a reasonable manner when no statute applies. To do otherwise, especially when legal duty exists, is costly because violations invite lawsuits. Employees who have been harmed increasingly are filing lawsuits against their employers.

Over the decades, employers have created a record-keeping system for their employees. Many records are mandated by the law, such as wages, while other records are not, such as how frequently an employee accessed the Internet from the work computer. The extent and detail of these records create a

LEGAL HIGHLIGHT

Dynamic Duo, Milton and Chainsaw Al

Milton is Milton Friedman, recipient of the 1976 Nobel Prize for economics and professor emeritus at the University of Chicago. He advocates profit maximization. He has written "[T]here is one and only one social responsibility of business—to use its resources and engage in activities designed to increase its profits so long as it stays within the rules of the game, which is to say, engages in open and free competition, without deception or fraud."[a] He has a disciple in Albert J. Dunlap.

"Chainsaw Al" and "Rambo in Pinstripes" were nicknames for Dunlap, awarded to him over the years in response to his aggressive business activities. Businesses brought in Dunlap to reverse pending financial disasters. One of his trademarks was to announce a mass firing. Those employees who still held their jobs no longer needed to worry about further cuts because Dunlap restructured a business only once.

Dunlap started his turnaround artistry with Lily-Tulip Company (1983–1986), a manufacturer of disposable cups. He cut the headquarters staff by 50 percent and the salaried staff by 20 percent. From Lily-Tulip he moved to Crown-Zellerbach (1986–1989), where he cut staff by 22 percent and reduced the number of distribution centers from twenty-two to four.

He spent nearly a year at Australian National Industries (1989), where he reduced the workforce by 47 percent and staff headquarters from 200 to 23. Leaving there, he went to Consolidated Press Holdings (1991–1993), where he sold off 300 of the 413 companies that made up the large conglomerate.

Next up was Scott Paper Co. (1994–1995), where Dunlap laid off 11,200 employees, nearly 31 percent of the workforce, including 71 percent of the headquar-

ters staff. He ended all research and development, plant improvements, and all of Scott's philanthropic programs. The palatial corporate headquarters was sold for $39 million and moved from Philadelphia, Pennsylvania, to Boca Raton, Florida. The move saved $6 million in maintenance and climate-control costs. Scott's $2.5-billion debt was nearly eliminated within two years. The value, measured by the outstanding shares, grew from $2.5 billion in 1993 to $9 billion by 1995. Scott was then sold to Kimberly-Clark and Dunlap personally made $100 million.

At Sunbeam-Oster (1996–1998), he laid off 6,000 of the 12,000 employees. He released layers of executives then sold the airplanes, automobiles, and condominiums, and cut or eliminated other benefits. The stock value increased from $12 to $39 within nine months. After Sunbeam acquired Coleman Co., Signature Brands USA, Inc., and First Alert, Inc., for $2.5 billion in 1997, Dunlap announced an additional 6,400 job cuts.

The common stock, however, plunged 65 percent in just three months when Dunlap could not meet the earnings forecasts. Eventually, he was terminated in June 1998 amid open cheers from Sunbeam-Oster employees. At the time of his dismissal, the board of directors issued a statement that it had lost confidence in his leadership based in part on his short-term accounting gimmicks. In 2002, after an investigation, the Securities and Exchange Commission settled with him for $500 million and permanently banned him from serving as director or officer of any public company based on findings of bogus accounting that occurred in the 1990s.

Putting the shareholders first, wherever he went, Dunlap's first act was to end all philanthropical contributions by the business. He believed that individuals may choose to donate their assets, but that a business should not give away assets. For Dunlap, only one stakeholder existed: the shareholder. Unfortunately, he forgot the last portion of Professor Friedman's philosophy, " without deception or fraud."

[a]Milton Friedman, *Capitalism and Freedom* (Chicago: University of Chicago Press, 1962), p. 133.

LEGAL HIGHLIGHT

Tyco

Tyco International, Ltd., is a large conglomerate with a diverse business involved with various products, such as electronics, plastic packaging, medical supplies, and alarm systems. Dennis Kozlowski started with Tyco in 1976 when it was a small industrial manufacturer. In 1992, Kozlowski became the chief executive officer (CEO).

During the following decade, Tyco paid $60 billion for 200 major corporate acquisitions and hundreds of smaller ones. Starting around 1998, Tyco acquired nearly 700 small businesses for $8 billion, but never informed Tyco's shareholders as required by law. Its largest purchase was Citigroup for $10 billion. Tyco is incorporated in Bermuda to avoid U.S. taxes, while its U.S. headquarters is located in Exeter, New Hampshire.

Kozlowski's downfall came when he tried to dodge paying $1 million in sales taxes that he personally would have owed to the state of New York if he were purchasing artwork. Allegedly using Tyco funds, he purchased $13 million in art, including paintings by Renoir and Monet, from a New York art dealer. Since Tyco apparently was making the purchase, it would owe the sales tax. Kozlowski attempted to exempt Tyco from the sale taxes by having the art dealer ship part of the artwork out of state to the company's office in Exeter. The office immediately reshipped the artwork, to Kozlowski's Fifth Avenue apartment in New York City. Other parts of the original purchase were shipped directly by the art dealer to the New York City apartment while empty boxes purporting to hold those specific pieces of art were shipped to the office in Exeter.

After the New York State banking department notified the Manhattan District Attorney's Office of a wire transfer of nearly $4 million from a Tyco account in Pittsburgh, Pennsylvania, to the New York bank account of an art dealer who in turned transferred the money to an account in the Bahamas, an investigation ensured.

Though Kozlowski was aware of the investigation, he did not notify the board of directors that an indict-

ment on criminal evasion of taxes was possible. Most companies have a reporting system requiring a disclosure to the board and shareholders when the CEO's ability to function may be impaired. After he was indicted for tax evasion, the board of directors fired him. His firing triggered more investigations, leading to the discovery of more problems.

Loans were made without the board of directors' knowledge or approval. Kozlowski was granted a loan of $40 million, then the loan was forgiven without any apparent disclosure to the board or shareholders. Tyco's general counsel received $35 million in undisclosed pay, which is in violation of the SEC rules that require reports to be filed disclosing the CEO's pay and the pay of the four other most highly compensated officers.

The investigation revealed Kozlowski's personal purchases, such as the $2,400 gilded wastebasket, $2,900 coat hangers, $6,000 shower curtain, $15,000 dog umbrella stand, and $2.1 million for a birthday party held in Sardinia for his wife. The problem is not the expensive items themselves, but whether Kozlowski paid for these items with his personal funds or with Tyco's funds. Questions also arose as to whether Kozlowski or Tyco paid for the New York City apartment.

In September 2002, Kozlowski and three others were indicted. He stood accused of operating a "criminal enterprise," stealing more than $170 million from the company, and obtaining $430 million from fraudulent securities sales. Records revealed that he and the chief financial officer had sold between them more than $500 million worth of shares back to Tyco, while publicly declaring they rarely sold their shares. The trial began in the fall of 2003.

Under new management, Tyco sold Citigroup, one of its major acquisitions, at half price. The value of Tyco's shares plummeted after Kozlowski was indicted and other alleged misconduct of its officers was disclosed. Tyco was left struggling, but was not forced into bankruptcy.

conflict between the employer's potential legal liability and the employee's right of privacy. The trust between employer and employee can easily become strained. The employer has an ethical conflict: generating detailed records, developed sometimes through surveillance, to protect the business from legal liability versus retaining the employee's privacy and trust.

Businesses must balance the interests of their employees with the other competing stakeholders. Should the employee's wages, working conditions, and benefits be increased? Should the amount of the investor's dividends be increased? Or should the amount spent on improving the quality and safety of a product for the customer be increased? These choices present various conflicts that management must resolve. The more employees receive, presumably the less owners will receive. Higher wages, however, may mean higher productivity, which, in turn, will reduce total costs and increase revenue, thus, benefiting the owners and customers.

The Supply Chain: Suppliers and Customers

The supply chain is defined as the management of all resources necessary to move a product from initial concept through its life cycle, that is, from the raw material stage to the product stage to the reuse, recycling, or final disposal stage. The supply chain encompasses both products and services. All businesses depend on both their suppliers and their customers.

Supplier and customer issues center around service, quality, safety, pricing, availability, fraudulent business practices, confidentiality, and advertising. These issues place pressure on middle managers, who are often the ones facing ethical dilemmas.

Middle managers must be concerned with the mandates and reactions of upper management, the requirements mandated by law, the needs of lower level employees, the expectations of external customers, and the demands of internal customers from the marketing, accounting, and operations departments. The profitability of the middle manager's department often is affected directly by customer satisfaction. Is it the

middle manager's ethical responsibility, then, to disclose quality problems to customers or the government, even if the situation is clearly under someone else's control and that person is content to ignore the problem? Is it upper management's ethical responsibility to ensure that ethical problems are discussed openly and guidance provided for all levels of managers?

In today's business world, supply chains are forged among large purchasers and their many suppliers. For example, Ford Motor Company has 300 primary suppliers that, in turn, have their own suppliers of products and services. Ford competes not as an individual company selling cars, but its whole supply chain is competing with other automobile manufacturers' supply chains. The supply chain that can supply its customer with the lowest price, the highest quality, and quickest availability will prevail over slower, more expensive supply chains.

Purchasers in a supply chain relationship with their suppliers have ethical concerns about privacy. As these supply chain relationships develop, a partnership is formed among the company and its suppliers. The supplier is required to divulge information that in the past was confidential in nature, such as its pricing strategy. As more proprietary information is shared by the supplier with its purchaser, what ethical duties are imposed on the customer to keep this information confidential and not to use this information as a weapon against the supplier in order to force it to sell at lower prices?

Companies owe a duty to their current and future customers to develop truthful advertisements. These advertisements must not deceive the reader by omitting important information. As a result of scandalous fraudulent advertisements in the past, this field is regulated by the Federal Trade Commission and is discussed in more detail in Chapter 14. All fifty states today have consumer protection laws and also regulate advertisements.

The following case represents a situation in which a business considered its short-term profits to be more important than its ethical responsibility for truthful advertising. In reviewing the case, consider whether these marketing practices best served this company's long-term interests.

CASE 2.2

Appellate Court of Illinois,
Fourth District, 2000
311 Ill. App. 3d 886, 726
N.E.2d 51
http://caselaw.findlaw.com

OLIVEIRA v. AMOCO OIL COMPANY

BACKGROUND AND FACTS Plaintiff, Oliveira, appealed the dismissal of his complaint against the defendant, Amoco Oil Company (Amoco). Oliveira was an Illinois consumer who alleged in his complaint that Amoco's advertisements for its premium gasolines were false and he and others purchased those premium brands because of the advertisements. He asserted that Amoco had violated the Illinois Consumer Fraud and Deceptive Business Practices Act (Act).

The complaint alleged Amoco began a multistate advertising campaign on November 6, 1991, which falsely represented:

(A) Amoco Ultimate gasoline is superior to all other brands of premium gasoline with respect to engine performance or environmental benefits because it is refined more than all other such brands;

(B) The clear color of Amoco Ultimate gasoline demonstrates the superior engine performance and environmental benefits Amoco Ultimate provides compared to other premium brands of gasolines that are not clear in color;

(C) A single tankful of Amoco Silver or Ultimate gasoline will make dirty or clogged fuel injectors clean;

(D) Amoco Silver or Ultimate gasoline provides superior fuel injector cleaning compared to other brands of gasoline; and

(E) Automobiles driven more than 15,000 miles with regular gasoline generally suffer from lost engine power or acceleration which will be restored by the higher octane of Amoco Silver gasoline.

The complaint alleges Amoco knew these statements were untrue. The result of its deceptive advertising campaign was to increase demand for its premium gasoline, thereby commanding an inflated and otherwise unsustainable price for the premium gasolines. All consumers paid this price whether or not they had relied on or seen the ads. Oliveira argued that all consumers who purchased defendant's premium gasolines during the advertising period were damaged by Amoco's misrepresentations.

The trial court granted Amoco's motion to dismiss. The court held that the marketing theory pleaded by Oliveira, that is, Amoco's misleading advertising, did not cause increased demand, which, in turn, did not create inflated prices for its gasoline. Therefore, no fraud was committed by Amoco. Oliveira appealed.

Justice KNECHT

. . . .

Section 2 of the Act delineates an unlawful practice as follows:

"Unfair methods of competition and unfair or deceptive acts or practices, including but not limited to the use or employment of any deception, fraud, false pretense, false promise, misrepresentation or the concealment, suppression or omission of any material fact, with intent that others rely upon the concealment, suppression or omission of such material fact, . . . in the conduct of any trade or commerce are hereby declared unlawful whether any person has in fact been misled, deceived or damaged thereby."

An action for damages under the Act may be brought pursuant to section 10a(a). "Any person who suffers actual damage as a result of a violation of this Act committed by any other person may bring an action against such person." The definition of "person" under the Act includes a corporation, company, or other business entity. Thus, defendant is included as a person who could commit a violation of the Act.

The Act has been construed liberally to give effect to the legislative goals behind its enactment. The Act's policy is to give broader protection than common law fraud by prohibiting any "deception, fraud, false pretense, false promise, misrepresentation or the concealment, suppression or omission of any material fact, with intent that others rely upon the concealment . . . in the conduct of any trade or commerce." The standard of proof for a violation of the Act is lenient as it does not require "any person has in fact been misled, deceived or damaged thereby."

. . . .

Defendant contends it provided affidavits to counter those supplied by plaintiff and which provide evidence the overall demand for its premium gasolines went down, as did prices during the relevant period; therefore, its advertising did not proximately cause any damages to plaintiff. . . . [T]he question is not whether demand for the premium gasolines went down but whether demand and prices were artificially high for the relevant time period due to misleading advertising. In other words, without the advertising, would the demand and prices of defendant's premium gasolines have been even lower during the relevant time period?

. . . .

DECISION AND REMEDY The court found Oliveira's complaint adequately stated a cause of action for consumer fraud under the Act. The complaint adequately pled a deceptive act or practice by defendant. Specifically, Oliveira alleged Amoco represented in its advertising that its premium gasolines had special features that would produce increased performance in automobiles and had environmental benefits, but that this information was false.

CRITICAL THINKING: LEGAL CONSIDERATION Do you think this type of advertising should be considered fraud or is it just trade puffing? *Trade puffing* refers to the use of words or phrases that do not promise anything or are not truly intended to be believed as in advertising for cosmetics.

With the global economy, suppliers must also consider their ethical responsibility to consumers in other countries. The Environmental Protection Agency prohibited the sale of insecticides containing DDT[7] in the United States because it might have long-term carcinogenic effects. Is it then ethical for the manufacturer to sell the product in countries where its sale is still legal? This example demonstrates an ethical conflict between short-term profits for shareholders and long-term concern for the well-being of its customers. When such a conflict arises, ethical businesses consider the long-term effects of their products on customers rather than only considering the short-range profit picture.

[7]DDT stands for d(ichloro)d(iphenyl)t(richloroethane), a human-made toxic compound found in insecticides.

Government

When businesses fail to act in an ethical manner, public pressure will mount until Congress adopts statutes governing the abusive business behavior. Once passed, a statute is assigned to administrative agencies to regulate and monitor. As a result, the government incurs increased costs to administer these statutes. Increased costs translate into increased taxes paid by individuals and businesses to the government. Businesses must comply with these new regulations or risk civil, and possibly criminal, charges.

The government's ability to tax and to adopt statutes influences business behavior. For example, when airline passengers had their flights delayed, baggage lost, and generally were treated poorly by airline personnel, Congress proposed a statute that would

LEGAL HIGHLIGHT

Kmart

Kmart, founded in 1900, grew over the decades and became a mainline retail store. Popular for decades with shoppers, it grew and prospered. By the 1980s and 1990s, Kmart was facing stiff competition from competitors, such as Wal-mart and Costco. The new competitors used an integrated computer network, took advantage of lower cost overseas suppliers, and located stores in newer neighborhoods.

By 2001, allegations of widespread wrongdoing abounded. Kmart filed for bankruptcy in January 2002. This once venerable business had fallen to a low point. The board of directors ordered a probe and discovered ten executives had engaged in misconduct serious enough that they would have been fired if they had not resigned during the previous year.

The executives devised plans to hide the precarious financial problems Kmart faced. Under the "Project Slow It Down" plan, the company did not pay its suppliers in a timely manner. Another plan involved the fraudulent reporting of millions on Kmart's books paid by vendors in return for stocking or promoting their goods. In fact, the vendor allowances were never arranged. While the company was bleeding financially, President Mark Schwartz and Chairman and Chief Executive Officer Chuck Conaway authorized the purchase of two company jets. The company probe revealed that the planes were used by executives for personal use. A number of executives drove luxury automobiles that were leased by Kmart.

Months before the bankruptcy, the board of directors authorized $28 million in loans to twenty-five of its top executives. The board was unaware of the seriousness of the company's financial situation until it read an analyst's report in January 2002. By then it was too late. In May 2002, Kmart restated its earnings for the first three quarters of 2001 to reflect additional losses of $554 million. As a result, more than 59,000 persons lost their jobs, 600 stores were closed, and criminal and civil lawsuits were filed. Whether Kmart is strong enough to restructure its business and emerge successfully from bankruptcy is a question that will be answered in the future.

---

provide passengers with rights. The airline industry reacted by voluntarily adopting rules governing their behavior in an effort to prevent Congress from passing any statutes. Congress, in response, delayed consideration of the airline passenger bill.

The U.S. government is one of the largest customers in the world. Unfortunately, the federal government discovered its suppliers were engaging in fraud and overcharging it. Congress reacted to this discovery by passing the **False Claims Act**[8] in 1986. The act authorizes the government to sue any party filing a fraudulent payment claim for products or services. The government receives information from a number of sources. One valuable source is the person known as a **whistleblower** who informs public officials or the news media of the company's unsafe, illegal, or unethical activities.

The information provided by a whistleblower is often the first notice that something is amiss. The government will conduct an investigation and if the information can be substantiated, the U.S. government will pursue a settlement or file a lawsuit. If the evidence used to build the case comes from a whistleblower, that person may be awarded from 15 to 25 percent of any damages awarded or fines assessed by the court in favor of the government. If the United States does not proceed with the litigation, but the informer continues with it and prevails, he is entitled to 25 to 30 percent of the awarded damages. Naturally, the law forbids a person who helped to plan and execute the fraud to collect under the federal False Claims Act.

[8]31 U.S.C.A. §§ 3729–3732. See also http://www.law.cornell.edu/uscode/31/ch37.html. The first formal False Claims Act was passed in 1863 as a result of suppliers engaging in fraudulent activities, such as selling faulty war supplies during the Civil War (1861–1865). The act was amended in 1943, which severely restricted the application of the original act. The 1986 amendments provided new life to the act by establishing the burden of proof as preponderance of the evidence, allowing the informant to seek damages, and protecting the informant from retaliation by the employer.

Many whistleblowers are employees who must decide whether to become a whistleblower. The employee who keeps quiet compromises her own ethical standards and the employer may required her to participate in the illegal actions. Choosing the alternative, however, may lead to undesirable results. Whistleblowers usually are fired for some unrelated offense. Frequently, the whistleblower will not find another job in that industry.

The federal government offers statutory protection for whistleblowers. These laws authorize whistleblowers to sue their employer if they are discharged or suffer discrimination as the result of informing the federal government of the employer's illegal activities.[9]

[9]Whistleblower information is provided by the Department of Labor's Whistleblower Collection found at http://www.oalj.dol.gov/libwhist.htm.

These statutes allow the court to award double the amount of back pay, attorneys' fees, and costs to an informer. If the employee is fired, the court can order that the employee be reinstated with the same seniority. To encourage employees to speak out, forty-five states have followed the lead of the federal government and have also enacted statutes that protect whistleblowers employed by the state government. Some state laws extend whistleblower protection to employees working in private industry.

In 1987, only 33 cases were filed under the act. By 2002, the number of cases had climbed to 320. Although the plaintiff prevailed in only 11 percent of the cases, those who do prevail receive large awards because of the amounts involved. For example, in two different Medicare fraud cases, the respective plaintiffs each received awards of $20 million and $9 million.

LEGAL HIGHLIGHT

Was She a Real Whistleblower?

Sherron Watkins was catapulted into the national scene in 2002. After working for the accounting firm of Arthur Andersen for more than a decade, Watkins joined the fast-paced, energetic Enron in 1993. Working in a number of departments, she moved in the summer of 2001 to a finance unit that researched which Enron assets to sell. The head of the unit was Andrew Fastow, the chief financial officer.

Not long after she had moved to the unit, she quickly understood what was happening. She saw that sham accounting companies were being misused to hide debt. After giving the matter a lot of thought, she decided to write a memorandum warning that Enron would "implode in a wave of accounting scandals."

She believed it would be useless to approach Fastow who was the creator and a participant in some of these shell companies. She decided to meet with Kenneth Lay, chairman of Enron. She informed Lay of her evaluations of the accounting house of cards and how Enron's future was imperiled. She also requested to be moved to another department. She believed that Lay would take the steps necessary to keep Enron as a dynamic company without any accounting tricks.

A number of events happened between the time she wrote her memorandum and the collapse of Enron. On September 11, 2001, the United States was attacked by terrorists. The stock market, which had been attempting to pull out of the two-year declining market, continued its decline. Unable to hide the amount of debt, in October 2001, Lay held a news conference, disclosed the sham companies, and announced a $1 billion charge against earnings. It was too late; Enron filed for bankruptcy in December 2001.

In 2002, Watkins testified before congressional panels while sitting next to Fastow. Transferred to a low-level job, shunned by others, removed from key projects, she paid a professional and an emotional price for revealing the weaknesses of Enron. Eventually, she left Enron to pursue her own interests.

Watkins was not a whistleblower in the true legal sense since she did not report her evaluations to the government, in this case, the Securities and Exchange Commission. She started with the person who had the power to make changes. In hindsight, she might have taken different actions. She was a whistleblower in a broad sense in that she suffered the same fate that befalls most whistleblowers.

The U.S. government was awarded a record $875 million in another Medicare fraud case. That whistleblower received $77 million for his efforts and retired to Florida.

In 2002, the rights of whistleblowers were increased by the passage of the Sarbanes-Oxley Act. Contained within this statute is a whistleblower provision that affords protection for employees of publicly traded companies who provide "information, cause information to be provided, or otherwise assist in an investigation regarding any conduct which the employee reasonably believes constitutes a violation of the Securities and Exchange Commission, or any provision of Federal law relating to fraud against shareholders. . . ." In other words, if an employee discovers that her employer is not following the securities laws, she may inform the Department of Labor of these violations, may be protected from losing her job, and may share any financial recovery that results.

Congress also creates whistleblower protections in specialized statutes. For instance, after a number of violent pipeline explosions that killed innocent bystanders, Congress passed the Pipeline Safety Improvement Act of 2002. In the past, pipelines were not regularly inspected. Over time pipelines can fracture, allowing seepage of dangerous products into the earth, which then migrate to the surface. When employees filed reports or raised cautionary flags, they were demoted, moved, or fired. This statute now makes it illegal to discharge or discriminate against any employee who provides information to the federal government about violations of pipeline safety.

Today, businesses that service or sell to the federal government must avoid fraudulent activities. Ethically, this standard has always held true. As a result of being overcharged and defrauded by businesses, the federal government now makes fraud explicitly illegal and rewards the whistleblower.

The following case involved a government employee who brought an action under the federal False Claims Act. The real issue was whether this employee could be regarded as a whistleblower because she obtained the information in the course of her employment.

CASE 2.3

United States Court of Appeals
Tenth Circuit, 2003
318 F.3d 1199

UNITED STATES v. CONSUMER INSURANCE GROUP

BACKGROUND AND FACTS Holmes served as the postmaster in Poncha Springs, Colorado. In October 1995, employees of defendant Consumer Insurance Group (CIG)—Benbrook, Benton, and Modrejewski—inquired at the Poncha Springs post office about the cost of bulk mailing. After Holmes calculated the per-piece cost of CIG's intended mailing, the employees told Holmes that they were being charged a lower rate per pound at the Howard, Colorado, post office.

The per-pound rate, which is significantly lower than the per-piece rate, applies if each individual piece of mail weighs in excess of 3.3062 ounces. Each individual piece being mailed by CIG, however, weighed only 0.3 ounces, which was significantly less than the required weight. Holmes informed the defendant of her conclusion that CIG should be charged by the piece. The employees responded that CIG could not afford to use the per-piece rate because it was prohibitively expensive. The meeting between Holmes and the CIG's employees ended.

Nearly two years later, in August 1997, Holmes was training an acting postmaster at the Howard post office. Holmes discovered that CIG was still being charged the per-pound rate. Holmes did some calculations and determined that CIG was being undercharged for the mailings by about $200,000 per year. Holmes also discovered that CIG had been falsely certifying that its bulk mailings weighed in excess of 3.3062 ounces per piece. Holmes reported her findings concerning CIG's bulk mailings to her manager, who oversaw both the Poncha Springs and Howard post offices.

Hearing nothing, she reported the problem in December 1997 to the Inspector General's Office in Washington, D.C. The case was investigated and referred to the U.S. Attorney's Office in August 1998. A subpoena was issued to obtain records from CIG. From December 1998 through 1999, the U.S. Attorney's Office and the Postal

Inspection Service continued jointly to build a case against CIG by analyzing the documents produced by CIG pursuant to the subpoena.

On April 2, 1999, Holmes filed this *qui tam* action under the federal False Claims Act (FCA). The term *qui tam* action means that anyone who brings a successful action for a civil wrong will share in the recovery.

The government moved to dismiss Holmes, which was granted by the district court. Holmes appealed the dismissal of her case. The term *relator* is used in the case. A *relator* is a person who brings an action on behalf of the federal government under the False Claims Act.

Circuit Judge BRISCOE

. . . .

Section 3730(e)(4) provides:

> *(A) No court shall have jurisdiction over an action under this section based upon the public disclosure of allegations or transactions in a criminal, civil, or administrative hearing, in a congressional, administrative, or Government Accounting Office report, hearing, audit, or investigation, or from the news media, unless the action is brought by the Attorney General or the person bringing the action is an original source of the information.*
>
> *(B) For purposes of this paragraph, "original source" means an individual who has direct and independent knowledge of the information on which the allegations are based and has voluntarily provided the information to the Government before filing an action under this section which is based on the information.*

. . . .

We conclude the government employee who discovers fraud under these circumstances is a "person" entitled to bring suit under the FCA. The fact that an employee learns of fraud in the course of his or her employment and has a duty to report fraud does not bar the government employee's FCA action.

The term "public disclosure" is not defined in the FCA. In order to be publicly disclosed, the allegations or transactions upon which a *qui tam* suit is based must have been made known to the public through some affirmative act of disclosure. The mere possession by a person or an entity of information pertaining to fraud, obtained through an independent investigation and not disclosed to others, does not amount to "public disclosure." Rather, public disclosure occurs only when the allegations or fraudulent transactions are affirmatively provided *to others not previously informed thereof.*

Applying these principles to the case at hand, we conclude that a public disclosure did not occur when, during the course of their administrative investigation, government investigators questioned Benbrook, Benton, and Modrejewski. It is uncontroverted that all three individuals participated, to some degree, in the alleged fraudulent scheme, and thus were "previously informed" of the fraudulent scheme prior to their respective interviews with government investigators.

. . . .

. . . Holmes has direct and independent knowledge of the fraud allegedly committed by CIG, since she is the person responsible for ferreting it out in the first place.

. . . .

. . . [T]he government argues that a federal employee who discovers fraud in the course of his or her employment and who is required to report it, is not a "person" entitled to bring a civil action . . . because the acquisition of such information within the scope of a federal employee's job eliminates the critical distinction between the government and the individual *qui tam* plaintiff. This argument finds no support in the ordinary meaning of the word "person." In particular, we fail to see how the word could rationally be construed to exclude some, but not all, government employees, and under some, but not all, conditions. Further, we find no support for this argument in principles of agency law, which control the relationship between a federal employee, such as Holmes, and the government. For example, it is apparent that Holmes, in filing her complaint in this matter, was not acting within the scope of her employment and was therefore not acting "as the government" since she was not employed to file suit under the FCA and there is no indication that the preparation or filing of her suit occurred substantially within the time and space limits imposed on her employment by the government.

. . . .

DECISION AND REMEDY The Court concluded that Holmes was entitled to proceed as a relator under the False Claims Act and that there had been no public disclosure.

CRITICAL THINKING: ETHICAL CONSIDERATION Was it ethical for a government employee to institute a claim under the federal False Claims Act when he or she discovers the facts giving rise to the action while employed by the government?

The Community

When a business operates in a community, its treatment of employees, of the government, of the community, and of its supply chain is known in that community. One test of whether this is a respected company is whether people want to work for this company. Communities demand that local companies abide by government regulations. A community is unlikely to tolerate a company's pollution of the air, water, or land.

Most major businesses engage in philanthropic activities. They routinely donate to hospitals, the arts, and universities by giving money, employee time, and access to special assets, such as a supercomputer. Businesses screen charitable requests and determine which organizations are deserving of charitable contributions.

INFOTRAC RESEARCH ACTIVITY

InfoTrac has numerous articles reporting on business scandals. Select one company and search for two articles written about that company. Determine what problems caused the scandal. Write a report as to your conclusions and support your position by citing the articles you have read.

InfoTrac has numerous references to Enron. Select two articles and determine what went wrong with Enron in addition to the problems written about in this chapter. Write a report as to your conclusions and support your position by citing the articles you have read.

Strategy for Ethical Decision Making

When confronted with a problem, a person can take any number of actions. Some actions may be useful, whereas others may create more problems. Philosophers have developed various ethical decision-making models to help a person to resolve a dilemma. Some models are more complex than others.

The following is a decision-making model that can use to resolve the ethical problems found near the beginning of each chapter. This model consists of the following six steps:

1. *Facts* Gather all the necessary facts, including whether any state or federal statutes or whether any administrative regulations apply. Once the

facts have been determined, the problem can be defined.

2. *Stakeholders* List all the stakeholders that may be affected by the decision.

3. *Values* List all personal and work-related values involved in the particular case. These values may include one or more of the following:

   a. Personal values:

      Religious values or idea of good.

      Honesty, such as truth-telling, candidness, or openness.

      Integrity, such as acting on convictions, courageous acts, advocacy, or leadership by example.

   b. Institutional values:

      Responsible citizenship, such as respect for law or social consciousness.

      Pursuit of excellence, such as quality of work.

      Accountability, such as responsibility or independence.

   c. Interpersonal values:

      Promise-keeping, such as fulfilling the spirit of commitments.

      Loyalty, such as fidelity or confidentiality.

      Fairness, such as justice, equal treatment, diversity, or independence.

      Caring for others, such as compassion or kindness.

      Respect for others, such as human dignity or uniqueness.

4. *Alternative Actions* List all the possible alternative actions.

5. *Prioritization* Choose and prioritize by answering the following questions:

   a. Which stakeholder is believed to be the most important in this situation?

   b. Which value is believed to be the most important in this situation?

   c. Which of the choices will cause the greatest good or the least harm?

6. *Potential Action* Make a decision as to which stakeholder should prevail and determine a strategy (course of action) to carry out the decision.

A SAMPLE CASE

Using the Model for Ethical Decision Making

A secretary who has worked for your business for fifteen years is involved in a car accident in which she permanently loses the use of her right hand. Thus, she can no longer effectively type, file, or perform many of the other functions that she previously had performed and that are included in her job description. Your business has a very tight budget and does not have sufficient funds to pay for an additional secretary without reallocating budget items. The company has not had any experience with any employees who have a disability. The secretary has been very loyal to your business, and you have been very satisfied with her work and dedication. She wants to stay at her job. Moreover, she does not believe that she could find other employment at this time. Should your business fire her, lay her off with compensation, or find a way to retain her? The following steps apply the model to this case.

1. *Facts* These items need to be reviewed: the secretary, the job description, the statutes, the administrative regulations, the budget, disability insurance, and the impact on other employees. The Americans with Disabilities Act and its regulations may apply. Review with the injured secretary the specific duties that she can and cannot do under her current job description. Determine if the budget can be modified by allocating funds from another category to the secretarial category in case you decide to retain the worker. Determine if there is any disability insurance on which the secretary may rely. Determine the impact on other employees if the job duties are shared with other employees.

   In your interview with the secretary, you must find out if any rehabilitation or treatment programs would allow her to regain the use of her right hand. Find out if a technological device, such as voice recognition software, would allow her to use a computer and to perform other tasks with one hand. Ascertain her current financial position and her wishes. Learn how the remaining secretarial staff feels about performing the additional duties once performed by the injured secretary. Determine how other companies utilize employees who have suffered similar injuries. Contact government offices that may have information which will assist you in retaining the secretary.

After reviewing the above, based on the medical facts, you determine that the secretary cannot physically perform many of the essential duties of her job description. There is no way to reasonably accommodate her. If you terminate her, the Americans with Disabilities Act would not be violated because she cannot perform the essential functions of her job and your business cannot reasonably accommodate her. The budget is very tight but would allow a shift of funds among some categories. The problem is whether to retain the secretary, even though she cannot perform many of the required duties. You may resolve this problem by using the rest of the decision-making model.

2. *Stakeholders* The stakeholders that may be affected by the decision are:

   a. Your business
   b. The injured secretary
   c. The secretarial staff
   d. The management staff
   e. The general community.

3. *Values* The personal and work-related values involved in the particular case are:

   a. *Loyalty* As the secretary has given her loyalty to your company, so the business should demonstrate its loyalty to her.
   b. *Fairness* The rest of the secretarial staff will have to perform many of the secretary's former duties.
   c. *Respect* Although she now has a disability, the secretary is still a very talented individual who has contributed a great deal to your business.
   d. *Integrity* Your business should be in the forefront of making room for long-term loyal employees who have disabilities.
   e. *Accountability* The managerial staff is responsible for using business funds wisely and for providing essential services within the financial resources of the business.

4. *Alternative Actions* The possible alternative actions from which you could choose are:

   a. Do not retain the injured secretary because of the budget.
   b. Do not retain the injured secretary because of

the budget, but offer her an attractive severance package.

   c. Retain the secretary even though the budget does not accommodate the salary of an additional secretary. Restructure the duties so that the remaining secretarial staff will assume many of her previous duties.
   d. Retain the secretary by changing the budgetary priorities to accommodate the salary of an additional secretary.

5. *Prioritization* Choose and prioritize by answering the following questions:

   a. Which stakeholder do you believe is the most important in this situation? The injured secretary.
   b. Which value do you believe to be the most important in this situation? Integrity that includes leadership by example.
   c. Which of the choices do you believe will cause the greatest good or the least harm? Finding a means to increase or restructure the budget to be able to retain the injured secretary and to hire additional secretarial help.

6. *Potential Action* Retaining the secretary by increasing or restructuring the budget is the most desirable action. Consider working with rehabilitation specialists from an insurance company, a health-care provider, or the state's workers' compensation office. This action will create an affirmative atmosphere among the employees, who will see your business as treating a fellow employee with respect when she was confronted with the potentially devastating combination of paralysis and unemployment. This action also will provide stability in the workplace.

The above solution represents one analysis of an ethical problem. Another decision with different results could be reached if, for example, the budget were not able to accommodate the retention of the secretary. No perfect answer exists.

Legal Ethics

Legal ethics involve the moral and professional duties that lawyers owe other lawyers, their clients, the courts, and the public. Although the legal profession is the butt of many jokes concerning ethical issues, most lawyers are ethical. Lawyers face legal and ethical issues every day.

Courts increasingly are becoming irritated by frivolous lawsuits. It is true that some lawyers, just to earn a fee, will take cases knowing that they cannot win on the merits (facts) while leading the clients to believe otherwise. The state's highest court has the authority to suspend or disbar attorneys who engage in this conduct. Furthermore, courts will force the lawyer to bear all the expenses of such frivolous suits.

The following U.S. Supreme Court case involves the issue of whether an attorney or his firm should be liable for instituting a groundless action. Federal court rules and many states permit the recovery of expenses from an attorney or a client who files a worthless claim. This recovery is commonly called a Rule 11 sanction in the federal courts. Rule 11 is so called because it comes from the federal court rules. The following case decides whether an attorney or his firm should pay the Rule 11 sanction.

CASE 2.4

Supreme Court of the
United States, 1989
493 U.S. 120, 110 S. Ct.
456, 107 L. Ed. 2d 438
http://caselaw.findlaw.com

PAVELIC & LEFLORE v. MARVEL ENTERTAINMENT GROUP

BACKGROUND AND FACTS Northern J. Calloway sued Marvel Entertainment Group for willful copyright infringement of his motion picture script. The original complaint was signed and filed by Calloway's attorney, Ray L. LeFlore. The complaint alleged that Calloway had developed an idea and written a script for a motion picture and that Marvel had begun to develop Calloway's work without his permission.

Marvel filed a motion to dismiss, pointing to a series of documents annexed to the complaint that gave the production company the right to develop the work commercially. The district court dismissed the complaint (with leave to refile the complaint with the court), not on the ground that the documents authorized the alleged infringement, but on the ground that Calloway's complaint had failed to specify the registration number of his copyright and the dates on which the alleged acts of infringement had occurred.

Several weeks later an amended complaint, again signed by LeFlore, was filed. At the trial the jury found in favor of Marvel on all claims. After the original case was completed, Marvel brought a Rule 11 motion and sought sanctions in the amount of $100,000 against both the law firm and Ray L. LeFlore. The Supreme Court took jurisdiction to decide whether a Rule 11 sanction should apply to the law firm or only to the individual lawyer, LeFlore.

Justice SCALIA delivered the opinion of the Court.

. . . .

But in any event it is not at all clear that respondents' strained interpretation would better achieve the purposes of the Rule. It would, to be sure, better guarantee reimbursement of the innocent party for expenses caused by the Rule 11 violation, since the partnership will normally have more funds than the individual signing attorney. The purpose of the provision in question, however, is not reimbursement but "sanction" and the purpose of Rule 11 as a whole is to bring home to the individual signer his personal, nondelegable responsibility. It is at least arguable that these purposes are better served by a provision which makes clear that, just as the court expects the signer personally—and not some nameless person within his law firm—to validate the truth and legal reasonableness of the papers filed, so also it will visit upon him personally—and not his law firm—its retribution for failing in that responsibility. The message thereby conveyed to the attorney, that this is not a "team effort" but in the last analysis yours alone, is precisely the point of Rule 11. Moreover, psychological effect aside, there will be greater economic deterrence upon the signing attorney, who will know for certain that the district court will impose its sanction entirely upon him, and not divert part of it to a partnership of which he may not (if he is only an associate) be a member, or which (if he is a member) may not choose to seek recompense from him. To be sure, the partnership's knowledge that it was subject to sanction might induce it to increase "internal monitoring," but one can reasonably believe that more will be achieved by directly increasing the incentive of the individual signer to take care. Such a belief is at least not so unthinkable as to compel the conclusion that the Rule does not mean what it most naturally seems to say.

DECISION AND REMEDY The United States Supreme Court found that the individual attorney, not her or his firm, is liable individually when a groundless lawsuit is filed by the attorney.

CRITICAL THINKING: ETHICAL CONSIDERATION If Microsoft Corporation is successfully sued, the chief executive officer would not have to pay the judgment out of his personal funds. The Microsoft Corporation would be liable for the judgment. Should a law firm be treated the same as a corporation? Why should a lawyer be personally liable instead of the law firm?

Lawyers charge fees for their professional services. Several methods are used to determine the fee. One common fee arrangement is the contingency fee, which is based generally on a percentage, typically between 20 and 40 percent, of an award granted by a court. This fee arrangement is used in cases such as automobile accidents.

Lawyers and clients can agree to an hourly fee arrangement. When a lawyer charges by the hour, law firms divide the hour into segments. At $200 to $300 per hour, this can add up. Some firms use fifteen-minute segments. Thus, a person who consults with a lawyer for ten minutes, is charged for fifteen.

Lawyers may charge a flat fee. For example, an attorney may charge a flat fee for a simple will.

The American Bar Association drafted a code of

LEGAL HIGHLIGHT

Steal Secrets, Go to Jail

Said Farraj, 28, a law student, worked for a law firm that represented the plaintiffs suing Philip Morris, R.J. Reynolds Tobacco Co., and others. The lawsuit alleged the tobacco companies contributed to asbestos-related illnesses. Some experts believed the damage award could have exceeded $1 billion; thus, this lawsuit was a high-stakes case.

Farraj downloaded a copy of the trial plan of his employer. The 400-page plan included the closely guarded strategy of the trial portion along with other information that would eventually be made available

to the opposition, such as copies of depositions and exhibits. Farraj then sent an e-mail to the law firm representing the defendants offering to sell the plan for $2 million. The defense attorneys immediately contacted the plaintiffs' lawyers, who called the Federal Bureau of Investigation (FBI). An investigation was conducted, resulting in Farraj's arrest.

Confronted with the evidence, Farraj pled guilty to conspiracy to commit fraud, to interstate transportation of stolen property, and to unauthorized access of a computer. He was sentenced to two and one-half years in federal prison.

ethics for attorneys that is in effect in almost every state.[10] Attorneys must follow the code's standards of professional ethics to be allowed to practice law. Ethics boards, usually an arm of the state's highest court, investigate complaints of alleged attorney misconduct and recommend to the appropriate authorities any corrective action.

CYBERLAW

Internet Ethics

The Association of Ethical Internet Professionals®[11] promotes ethical standards. Its members recognize a moral and ethical obligation to the public, to other members, and to the association itself.

The members have adopted an ethical code that emphasizes the following:

1. To treat Web site visitors with honesty and respect.

2. To not violate the confidential and private information obtained from Web site visitors.

3. To properly exercise the authority and privileges provided them by their customers.

4. To protect customers' interests and provide them information needed to make informed decisions.

5. To protect information as private and confidential by providing secure servers for transmission of credit card, Social Security, and other personal information.

6. To not participate in, link to, or promote so-called "adult" material, exploitation of women, children, racial and ethnic division, or violence or hate groups.

7. To not use any client resources for personal advantage unless prior permission is given, not to take personal advantage of inexperienced customers, and to avoid conflicts of interest.

8. To not misrepresent or withhold facts about business policies, warranties, or quality of service or product.

---

[10]The Code of Ethics published by the American Bar Association can be found at http://www.abanet.org/cpr/links.html.
[11]The Association of Ethical Internet Professionals has a Web page at http://www.aeip.com.

Potential shoppers on the WWW are skeptical, for good reason, because of the number of scams and ripoffs. Web shoppers need help in discovering and recognizing Web sites where they can shop in safety. Several Web businesses provide seals of approval for members who agree to act in an ethical manner, such as the Internet Bureau of Business Ethics[12] and the Better Business Bureau.[13] Others concerned about ethics and the Internet are Computer Professionals for Social Responsibility,[14] Internet Legal Services,[15] a legal site that combines legal ethics and the Web, and Better Ethics Online.[16]

International Consideration

Codes and Guidelines that Emphasize Ethical Conduct

The United Nations has drafted a code of conduct to regulate the relations among transnational corporations, multinational corporations, host countries, and home countries. These relationships involve a dynamic combination of economic, political, historical, sociological, and cultural issues. While developing countries seek protection from the predatory business practices of multinational or transnational businesses, the businesses, in turn, seek protection from arbitrary government seizures in developing nations.

The Organization for Economic Cooperation and Development (OECD)[17] was created in 1961 as an intergovernmental institution for Western nations. Its purpose is to achieve the highest sustainable economic growth and employment, to maintain financial stability, and to contribute to the expansion of world trade. The OECD has adopted the *Guidelines for Multinational Enterprises*,[18] which is used as a model by the United Nations. A multinational enterprise is to operate within the general policy objectives of the OECD members and to refrain from interfering with

---

[12]The Internet Bureau of Business Ethics is found at http://www.clickit.com/ezcommerce/theinternetbusinessbureau.htm.
[13]The Better Business Bureau is at http://www.bbb.org.
[14]The Computer Professionals for Social Responsibility is found at http://www.cpsr.org.
[15]Internet Legal Services is at http://www.legalethics.com/ethics.law.
[16]Better Ethics Online is at http://www.isp.cc/better-ethics-online/index.html.
[17]The Web site for the OECD is http://www.oecd.org.
[18]Search for the guidelines at http://www.oecd.org/search.

the host country's political activities. Businesses must consider the needs of the developing nation as an important factor when making decisions about investment opportunities that arise.

The transfer of technology from developed nations to developing nations is one example of an ethical issue facing the international community. In the past, large investments that transferred advanced technology to areas where people were impoverished have often failed to assist the host country because the local people did not benefit from the technology. A steel manufacturing plant in Egypt might provide jobs to a few thousand people, for example, but the employees would not earn enough to stimulate the country's economy.

Would it not be better to encourage business opportunities that would improve conditions for the general population? Devices such as low-cost water pumps, windmills, solar heaters, and steam-driven turbines would benefit far more people in most developing countries than would factories involving advanced technology.

PRACTICAL TIPS

When Should You Blow the Whistle?

You are employed by a company that processes large amounts of hazardous material. In the past, the company was very careful to dispose of it in accordance with government guidelines. The company has recently been sold to another business, but you retain your job.

On several occasions recently, you have observed your immediate superior and other managers disposing of hazardous material by flushing it down the sewer or by dumping it on the ground in remote areas. These practices are not only illegal, but will result in pollution that may last for hundreds of years.

You are concerned about the environment and about possible civil or criminal liability if you do not inform the appropriate governmental officials. You still need your job, however, to pay the bills. The following checklist may provide you with some guidance.

Checklist

✔ *Attorney* Contact an attorney who will contact the appropriate law enforcement authorities on your behalf.

✔ *Documentation* Document illegal activity with a camera if possible. You would need a very small camera, so that the individuals involved do not know you are taking their picture.

✔ *Paperwork* Document paperwork by making copies if possible.

✔ *Work with Others* Attempt to convince other employees to go with you to the law.

Chapter Summary

Ethics is the study of human behavior as it relates to right and wrong conduct. Ethics also is a system of moral standards that serve as guidelines for right behavior.

The two broad philosophies in ethical decision making are deontology and utilitarianism. Ethics based on universal duties is deontology. A deontologist applies universal duties without exception to a situation. Ethics based on consequences is utilitarianism, which advocates that people should seek their own happiness in the happiness of others. An act is ethical if it benefits society.

Top management is responsible for embracing and disseminating ethical standards. Any business, when making decisions, must take into consideration various stakeholders, such as the owners, employees, its supply chain consisting of customers and suppliers, government, and community.

When making a business decision, a person should use an ethical decision-making model. One model consists of six points: facts, stakeholders, values, alternative actions, prioritization, and potential action. Use of these steps helps a person to reach a decision based on ethical thinking rather than by making a rash decision.

The legal profession also is responsible for incorporating ethical standards into the practice of law. Legal ethics incorporate the moral and professional duties that lawyers owe to each other, their clients, the courts, and the public. The courts and bar associations increasingly monitor the behavior of lawyers.

Using the World Wide Web

A variety of academic and government sites include discussions about ethics on their Web pages. For *Web Activities*, links to Web sites mentioned in the chapter, and additional Web sites that relate to the chapter topics, go to **http://bohlman.westbuslaw.com**, click on "Internet Applications," and select Chapter 2.

Web Activities

Go to **http://bohlman.westbuslaw.com**, click on "Internet Applications," and select Chapter 2.
2–1 Students and Ethics
2–2 Business and Ethics

Key Terms

deontology
False Claims Act

legal ethics
stakeholder

utilitarianism

whistleblower

Questions and Case Problems

2–1 Ethics and Morals Define and distinguish among ethics, morals, and law.

2–2 Ethics To what extent should businesses be concerned with social or ethical goals in comparison with short-term, profit-making goals?

2–3 Ethics To what extent does marketplace competition increase or reduce the need for standards of business ethics?

2–4 Stakeholders Should ethics be solely a concern of top management or should it be a shared concern of all stakeholders?

2–5 Stakeholders Discuss the ethical issues that surface in the following situation. A retailer orders in large volume from a carpet manufacturer and is viewed as a major purchaser. One major expense is transportation of the heavy rolls of carpet. The retailer normally accepts nine out of ten carpet shipments. However, in approximately every tenth shipment, the retailer finds a minor flaw in several rolls of the carpet, such as a slight change in the color dye lot. The carpet could be—and is—sold in the ordinary course of business at full price. The retailer informs the manufacturer that it refuses to accept the shipment and is returning the shipment. The manufacturer is confronted with shouldering shipment costs both ways. The retailer then offers to accept the shipment at a 50 percent discount. The manufacturer agrees in order to keep a good customer and to avoid the transportation expense. The retailer does this with all its suppliers. What ethical issues do these facts present?

2–6 Stakeholders Various retail stores lobby the state legislature to pass a statute that allows retailers to sue in civil court for $500 whenever a person is convicted of shoplifting. The statute is passed. The theory underlying this statute is that a business incurs expenses, such as providing witnesses who are employees, whenever a shoplifter is prosecuted. The goods usually are recovered when the shoplifter is arrested. If a person is convicted of shoplifting but the goods are not recovered, she or he may be ordered by the court to pay restitution for the value of those goods. Once the person is convicted, the retailer can then sue for $500 in civil court. If the shoplifter is unable to pay the $500 but is employed, her or his salary can be garnished until the $500 has been paid. Consider that sometimes shoplifters steal food for themselves or their families. Is it ethical for the retailer, in addition to recovering the goods or their value, to recover an additional $500 in civil court without proof of real expenses? Should the retailer sue every shoplifter for the amount stolen?

2–7 Stakeholders The Roths purchased a 1988 Volkswagen Fox GL from Wheeler Motor Company (Wheeler) on October 2, 1989. The vehicle was the last 1988 model in stock. The Roths purchased the car for $8,000, reduced from the $9,813 sticker price. Although the Roths were the first owners of the vehicle, the car had been test driven 590 miles. The key ring submitted into evidence indicated that the car was "new," as did the sales contract. Within the first two weeks after purchase, the steel belt on the right front tire burst through the tread. A crack was found in the right front fender, the right headlight became loose, the right front suspension made a noise, and the right speaker blew out. Wheeler repaired each problem. These problems persisted throughout the twenty-three months during which the Roths drove the car. Matters came to a head when the Roths took the car to a car wash. Paint came off, revealing a primer that was not a Volkswagen primer. The Roths brought action against Wheeler requesting damages, including punitive damages to punish them. The jury awarded $10,000 punitive damages and Wheeler appealed. What was the result and why? [*Wheeler Motor Co., Inc. v. Roth,* 867 S.W.2d 446 (1993)]

2–8 Whistleblower Rodriguez was formerly the assistant superintendent for curriculum and program accountability for the Laredo Independent School District (LISD). She sued the LISD and Superintendent Paul Cruz. She alleged that she was disciplined and demoted for her advocacy of strict compliance with testing procedures and her consistent reporting of testing irregularities, actions that conflicted with Cruz's goal of raising standardized scores. In the past, the teachers would assist students taking the tests. After she stopped this procedure, test scores declined. Cruz's primary interest was to increase test scores, but to do so he had to ignore compliance issues. Cruz denied Rodriguez permission to attend a meeting, typically attended by administrators at her level. Cruz subsequently removed Rodriguez from her position as assistant superintendent. Rodriguez filed this suit alleging a violation of the Texas whistleblower law. Defendants filed a motion to dismiss Rodriguez's claim, asserting failure to state a claim on which relief can be granted. Who should prevail and why? [*Rodriguez v. Laredo Independent School District,* 82 F. Supp. 2d 679 U.S. District Court (S.D. Tex. 2000)]

2–9 Consumers Audrey E. Volkes, 51, was a widow who wanted to become an accomplished dancer. On several occasions, an instructor and other salespeople for Arthur Murray, Inc., told her that she had great dance potential and could reach her goal. In reality, she had difficulty hearing the beat of the music. With continued assurance of her progress, she contracted for more than $31,000 in dance lessons. At one time, she had more than 1,200 unused hours of credit when she was induced to buy an additional 175 hours of instruction at a cost of $4,472.75 to obtain a free trip to Mexico. Eventually, Vokes became disillusioned with her progress and sued Arthur Murray, Inc., for misrepresentation. The trial court dismissed her case because she had failed to state facts that would allow a court to grant her relief. Vokes appealed. Is she entitled to have her day in court? [*Vokes v. Arthur Murray, Inc.,* 212 So. 2d 906 (Fla. 1968)]

2–10 Internet Go to the home page of a Fortune 500 company that has published its code of ethics on the World Wide Web. What ethical concerns does it cover? Is it a detailed document or general in its terms?

Chapter 3

The Judicial System and Litigation

Litigation is a contest authorized by law in a court of justice for the purpose of enforcing a right.

> *Summerour v. Fortson*, 174 Ga. 862, 164 S.E. 809 (1932)

Chapter Outline

Ethical Consideration

To Play or Not to Play Hardball

You are the president of ABC Insurance Company, which insures elevator manufacturers and elevator maintenance companies. One of the company's clients is in the business of installing and maintaining elevators across the country. Most elevators have two braking systems, mechanical and electrical. If the primary brake fails, the secondary braking system becomes operative.

As a routine matter, you receive copies of all complaints filed against your insureds. You receive a copy of a complaint filed by a woman seeking unspecified damages for injuries suffered when an elevator fell in an uncontrolled manner from the fourth floor to the second floor, then abruptly stopped. This fall is similar to jumping from the roof of a two-story building. It is obvious that the plaintiff suffered serious injuries.

Your insured had the elevators installed when the building was remodeled and hired a company to maintain the elevators in the building where the incident took place. You call in the chief legal counsel for the insurance company, who has reviewed the complaint. He informs you that engineers hired by his office to investigate the claim have filed a report stating that the elevator was improperly maintained and, as a result of that negligence, the elevator fell. He also tells you that the law office handling the lawsuit for the injured woman is quite small and inexperienced. He suggests assigning a group of attorneys to the case. These attorneys will generate so much legal paperwork that the plaintiff and her attorneys will be overwhelmed. The plaintiff will be forced to give up or to take a small settlement. If this approach does not work, your counsel will be able to intentionally postpone the trial for several years. This tactic will wear the plaintiff out financially, if not emotionally. It also will deter anyone else from trying to bring a legal action against your client.

Since you believe that the elevator caused the alleged injuries, what course of action should you follow? Use the ethical model presented in Chapter 2 and reprinted on the inside front cover to develop your answer.

Introduction

In this society, most businesspeople will be involved in litigation at some point in their careers. Litigation involves the person filing the lawsuit, the person defending against the suit, and a neutral party called the *judge*.

Everyone needs a basic working knowledge of the court system, at both the state and federal levels. This knowledge leads to a better understanding of how the system operates, and to the discovery of flaws that need correction. As taxpayers, businesspeople have an interest in the legal system working as efficiently as possible without sacrificing any legal protections. Businesspeople need to have an understanding of what they will confront when litigation occurs.

This chapter looks at both the state and federal court systems. The court must determine whether it has the power to decide a particular case. A sample case is followed through a state trial court. The different methods that attorneys use to set their fees are reviewed. Finally, the chapter concludes with a study of how judicial appointments are made.

Artiste Login. Carlo and Carlotta know that their business, Artiste Login, will sooner or later be involved in a lawsuit. Anyone who owns a business knows that not all contracts are fully performed and a lawsuit may arise. Lawsuits involve time, money, and energy that could be used by the business, but some disputes are worth going through the turmoil of a lawsuit. Artiste Login will be involved in a lawsuit concerning a copier later in this chapter.

Court Systems in the United States

At least fifty-two separate court systems function within the United States. Each of the fifty states, the District of Columbia, and the federal government have their own fully developed and independent court systems. Each state's constitution and statutes determine how a court system will work in that particular state.

The federal court system is authorized by Article III, Section 1, of the U.S. Constitution. The federal courts are not superior to the state courts; they are simply an independent system. The United States Supreme Court is the final controlling voice over all the court systems when questions arise concerning the U.S. Constitution, treaties, and federal statutes or regulations.

Whether it is a state or federal court system, there are three basic levels. The first level is the *trial courts*, where cases are heard and decided in trials. The person who loses in these cases can appeal the decision to a higher court, called an *appellate court*. Decisions from an appellate court can be reviewed by the highest court, usually called a *supreme court*.

Regardless of the level of the court, the court must have **jurisdiction**, that is, the power to hear the case. *Juris* means "law." *Diction* means to "speak." Thus, "the power to speak the law" is the literal meaning of jurisdiction. The court must have jurisdiction before it is authorized by law to hear the case. Thus, the court has the power to decide a case.

Trial Courts

On the lowest tier are the trial courts, which are called by many names, such as *county, district, superior*, or *circuit courts*. For example, in Ohio the trial court is called the court of common pleas, whereas in New York the trial court is called the supreme court. Various trial courts have different types of jurisdiction.

Trial courts that have **general jurisdiction** can hear cases on a variety of subject matters. Other trial courts have **limited jurisdiction** and can hear only cases on a specific subject matter. For example, a probate court, family court, criminal court, municipal court, or small-claims court has limited jurisdiction and cannot hear cases that go beyond its stated jurisdiction.

Trial courts have **original jurisdiction**, that is, cases first come before a trial court to be resolved. The trial court determines both questions of facts and questions of law. A jury (if no jury, the judge) determines all questions of facts and is referred to as the *trier-of-fact*. Questions of law, however, are determined by the judge in most jurisdictions.

A case that is filed with a trial court must involve a real case or controversy. Courts do not hear hypothetical cases. If the reason for the case has resolved itself, such as the item in controversy was destroyed in an earthquake, the case will be dismissed. Courts do not hear cases that have become moot. The judicial system is based on courts deciding real controversies between two or more persons with lawyers acting as advocates for their respective parties. The lawyers try to persuade the judge or jury to decide the case in favor of their client with facts and legal logic.

When a trial court exercises jurisdiction, it does so based on its having power both over the person against whom the suit is brought and over the property or subject matter of the case. Without jurisdiction, a court has no power to act. Any judgment the court renders when it does not have jurisdiction is null and void.

Determining proper jurisdiction ensures that a judgment obtained in one state is enforceable in all other states where the defendant may be located or may own property. The **full faith and credit clause** of the U.S. Constitution (Article IV, Section 1) mandates the enforcement of valid judgments made in other states.

Jurisdiction over the Person. To consider a case, a trial court must have power over the person against whom a suit is brought. A state court's power is limited to the territorial boundaries of the state in which the court is located, whereas a federal court has personal jurisdiction throughout the United States. Jurisdiction over the person is known as ***in personam* jurisdiction** or **personal jurisdiction**.

A court, whether city, county, state, or federal, has personal jurisdiction in the following situations. First, a court has personal jurisdiction over any resident of the judicial district even if he is temporarily out of the area on a business trip. Second, personal jurisdiction extends to any business within the judicial district, even if the business has its main plant or office elsewhere. Third, a court has personal jurisdiction over anyone served with a **summons** in the judicial district.

Fourth, the court can exercise jurisdiction over a nonresident person or business by using the **long-arm statute**. This statute allows a court to obtain jurisdiction over a defendant who lives outside the state. If a person or business commits an act or acts within the state, which gives rise to minimum contacts within the state, the court has jurisdiction because the *traditional notions of fair play and substantial justice are not offended* (violated).

The phrase "traditional notions of fair play and substantial justice" is implied in the **due process clause** guaranteed in both the Fifth and Fourteenth Amendments. The phrase means that the person or business has had some contacts, although minimal, within the state. The court has jurisdiction over the person or business if it serves the person or business with the appropriate court papers that provide actual notice of the proceeding and an opportunity to be heard.

When a person is provided with both notice and the opportunity to be heard, the traditional notions of fair play and substantial justice, implicit in the due process clause, are satisfied. The defendant's conduct and connection with the place of litigation are such that he should reasonably anticipate that he can be brought into court, if sued. A person cannot bring a legal action in one state, however, if the defendant has never had contact with that state. Two examples follow.

Example 1. A business located in one state sends 100,000 mailers advertising a watch to residents of a different state. The business receives more than 5,000 responses to purchase a watch. One customer is dissatisfied and sues the business. The business, after being served the appropriate court papers (usually a summons and complaint), can request that the lawsuit be dismissed because the court does not have jurisdiction over the business. The court can find that the business has committed an act within the state by mailing 100,000 mailers, has sold 5,000 watches, and that these mailers and sales constitute the minimum contacts within the state. The court can decide it has jurisdiction over the business and the traditional notions of fair play and substantial justice are not offended because the court papers provided the business with the actual notice of the proceeding and an opportunity to be heard.

Example 2. A business's Internet server is located in one state. The business sends 100,000 mailers electronically (e-mails) to residents of a different state. Where does a dissatisfied customer sue? Can she sue in the state in which she is located if she is dissatisfied with the watch?

Does this example have any facts that are really different from the example using the postal system? What if, however, the business, its server, and the watches are all located outside the United States? What if the e-mails were accidentally sent into a state? Do these changes in facts alter whether the court has jurisdiction?

An inescapable fact of modern commercial life is that a substantial amount of business is transacted using the federal mails, private package carriers, telephone, and the Internet across state, national, and international boundaries. Thus, the need for a physical presence no longer exists when business is conducted. The long-arm statutes will become more important in the future.

In all cases in which a court exercises personal jurisdiction, the defendants must be served with actual notice that they are being sued (usually by service of a summons and complaint). If the defendants are from out of state, the summons and complaint may be served either by a person or by certified mail containing the summons and complaint, for which the defendant must sign. Some states, however, are moving away from this rigid system. States allow the out-of-state defendant to be sent the paperwork by regular mail. This procedure allows the defendant to sign an acceptance of service, thus saving money on litigation fees.

In the following case, the federal district court is confronted with the question of whether the court had personal jurisdiction over the defendant and subject matter jurisdiction. The court discusses the concept of due process of the law when determining the court's jurisdiction.

CASE 3.1

United States District
Court, Eastern District,
Louisiana, 2000
2000 WL 108870

BILGER v. PEREIRA

BACKGROUND AND FACTS Plaintiff Bilger and defendant Pereira were visiting New Orleans, Louisiana, in an attempt to reconcile. One evening, while exiting a restaurant in the Vieux Carre, they began to argue. Plaintiff claimed that when she bent down to retrieve a souvenir that had fallen, defendant threw an unopened bottle of wine to the sidewalk, which shattered and injured plaintiff's wrist and forearm. Bilger went to a hospital and underwent surgery. Afterwards she was given drugs for her pain. In the meantime, Pereira obtained a marriage license. He took Bilger while she was in a drugged state and against her will to Metairie, where he "wrongfully" married her.

When Bilger recovered and was able to travel, Pereira took her to Sacramento, California, where he effected a "wrongful arrest" upon her by keeping her drugged and by denying her access to money. Bilger claimed that, during the "arrest," Pereira ridiculed, verbally assaulted, and threatened her. She finally escaped from Pereira when a friend wired her money. Pereira continued to threaten and harass her by repeatedly calling her and sending her e-mails and regular mail, and by hiring a private investigator to track her in Tennessee, where she had resided since March 1999. Bilger claimed that since she extricated herself from the situation, she had repeatedly requested that Pereira return plaintiff's property, which he refused to do.

On November 5, 1999, Bilger instituted legal action in Louisiana against Pereira alleging among other things negligent and intentional acts in violation of Louisiana, California, and Tennessee tort law. She sought compensatory and punitive damages, return of her personal property, injunctive relief, and costs.

Pereira moved to dismiss this case on the grounds that the federal court lacked subject matter jurisdiction, because both plaintiff and defendant were residents of California, and because the court lacked personal jurisdiction over the defendant.

Judge VANCE

. . . .

A. Subject Matter Jurisdiction. This Court has federal question jurisdiction over this matter under . . . diversity jurisdiction. Defendant alleges that there is incomplete diversity because both plaintiff and defendant are residents of California, even though plaintiff states in her verified complaint that she is a resident of Tennessee. Defendant claims that although plaintiff has resided in Tennessee since March of 1999, she has failed to meet the six-month residency requirement of Tennessee law, because she traveled to California for a period of twelve days. Defendant has failed to cite any law or evidence to support this allegation, and his argument is meritless. In order for this Court to exercise diversity jurisdiction in this case, plaintiff must be "domiciled" in Tennessee. . . . The Fifth Circuit has stated that "residence in fact and the intention of making the place of residence one's home are essential elements of domicile."

Although a plaintiff's statements of intent are entitled to little weight when they conflict with facts, there is no conflict in this case. Plaintiff states in her verified complaint that she resides in Tennessee, and defendant must come forward with more than his bald allegation that plaintiff is not a legal resident (in motion to dismiss for lack of subject matter jurisdiction, court accepts as true all allegations on the face of complaint). The parties agree that plaintiff resides in Tennessee, and there is simply no evidence that she did not intend to remain there when she filed this suit. Thus, this Court has diversity jurisdiction over the case. . . .

B. Personal Jurisdiction. When, as here, a nonresident defendant moves to dismiss for lack of personal jurisdiction, the plaintiff shoulders the burden of establishing jurisdiction over that defendant. Because this Court will rule on the issue without a full evidentiary hearing, the plaintiff need only make a *prima facie* [show a fact that will presumed to be true unless disproved by contrary evidence] showing of jurisdiction. . . . In determining whether plaintiff has made a *prima facie* showing of jurisdiction, the Court must accept as true all uncontroverted allegations in plaintiff's complaint, and resolve any factual disputes in her favor.

A court has personal jurisdiction over a nonresident defendant if (1) the forum state's long-arm statute confers personal jurisdiction over that defendant; and (2) the forum state's exercise of such jurisdiction complies with the due process clause of the Fourteenth Amendment. Under the Louisiana long-arm statute, jurisdiction is proper if the cause of action arises out of "injury or damage by an offense or quasi offense committed through an act or omission in this state." In addition, Louisiana's long-arm statute extends jurisdiction to the full limits of due process; thus, the Court must determine whether the exercise of jurisdiction satisfies the due process clause.

1. Due Process. The exercise of personal jurisdiction over a nonresident defendant satisfies due process when (1) the defendant has purposefully availed himself of the benefits and protections of the forum state by establishing "minimum contacts" with that state; and (2) exercising personal jurisdiction over the defendant does not offend "traditional notions of fair play and substantial justice."

(a) Minimum Contacts. The minimum contacts prong of the due process inquiry is satisfied if a court may exercise specific jurisdiction over the defendant. To determine whether specific jurisdiction exists, courts must examine whether the defendant purposefully availed himself of the privileges of conducting activity in the forum state, and whether the cause of action arises out of or relates to those activities. The defendant's connection with the forum state must be such that he "should reasonably anticipate being haled [sic] into court" there. A single act by the defendant directed at the forum state can be enough to confer *in personam* jurisdiction over him, if the cause of action arises out of that act.

In order to determine whether defendant purposefully availed himself of the privilege of conducting activities within this forum, the Court must consider factors such as the quality, nature and extent of defendant's activities in this forum, and the relationship between the cause of action and the contacts.

Here, plaintiff's claims against defendant arise, in part, out of defendant's activities in Louisiana. Plaintiff alleges in her verified complaint that defendant hurled an unopened wine bottle at the sidewalk upon which she was crouched, injuring her wrist and arm, and that following her surgery to deal with these injuries, he married her against her will while she was in a drugged state. Through these allegedly tortious acts, defendant certainly availed himself of the privileges of this state and should have reasonably anticipated being sued here. Thus, plaintiff has satisfied the minimum contacts prong of the due process analysis.

(b) Fair Play and Substantial Justice. In order to determine whether the exercise of personal jurisdiction over a nonresident defendant comports with traditional notions of fair play and substantial justice, this Court must consider the following factors: (1) the burden on the defendant; (2) the forum state's interests; (3) the plaintiff's interest in convenient and effective relief; (4) the judicial system's interest in efficient resolution of controversies; and (5) the state's shared interest in furthering fundamental social policies. Once minimum contacts are satisfied, the defendant must present a compelling case that conducting the litigation in this Court would impose severe hardship on him such that he would be at a considerable disadvantage in comparison to the plaintiff. In this case, defendant has failed to do so.

Pereira claims that he has very little money and will soon be unemployed and that the travel and lodging expenses of witnesses residing outside Louisiana would unduly burden him. By contrast, plaintiff states in her verified complaint that defendant has considerable resources. As stated above, this Court must resolve all factual disputes in plaintiff's favor. In any event, some of the witnesses involved in the case reside in Louisiana and, possibly, Tennessee, so that defendant would have to deal with the expense of deposing out-of-state witnesses even if the case were in California. Thus, this Court does not find that conducting the litigation in Louisiana overly burdens defendant. As to the second factor, the forum state clearly has an interest in trying the dispute that partially arose out of tortious activity within the state. Further, the plaintiff has submitted to jurisdiction in this state, and has an interest in convenient and effective resolution of this dispute. A substantial part of her claims against Pereira occurred in Louisiana, and many of the sources of proof are in this state, including her treating physician and other health care professionals who saw her when she received medical care at Tulane Medical Center, her medical records, the officer who married the parties and the marriage records. These factors also satisfy the judicial interest in convenient and effective relief in resolving this dispute in Louisiana. Finally, the state has a shared interest in discouraging violent and abusive acts toward other persons, and, in particular, women. Thus, the second prong of the due process analysis is satisfied, and the exercise of personal jurisdiction over defendant in Louisiana comports with traditional notions of fair play and substantial justice.

Because this Court finds that it has subject matter jurisdiction over this case, and that it may exercise specific jurisdiction over defendant, defendant's motion to dismiss must be denied.

DECISION AND REMEDY Federal courts do not have jurisdiction over the marriage, only state courts have that jurisdiction. Although this federal court could not grant a divorce, it could consider the civil torts of fraud and assault once it found it had jurisdiction over the defendant.

CRITICAL THINKING: PUBLIC POLICY What are the elements of jurisdiction?

A person can assert a defense that the court does not have personal jurisdiction when that person's presence was obtained by fraudulent means. An example of fraudulent means is seen in the following illustration: A husband and wife plan to divorce. The wife moves to another state. She writes her husband to join her because she wants to reconcile. He immediately flies to the state where she lives. When he gets off the airplane, he is served the divorce papers. Because his presence was obtained by fraudulent means, the court does not have personal jurisdiction over him. The court could grant a divorce because the court has jurisdiction over the marriage and the wife who lives in that state. The court does not have jurisdiction over him and, therefore, has no power to order him to pay spousal support or to order any property in his name to be divided.

Jurisdiction over Property. Distinctions exist between *in personam* jurisdiction and ***in rem* jurisdiction** or *quasi in rem* **jurisdiction**. When a court's jurisdiction is based on its authority over the defendant's person, the action and judgment are called *in personam* jurisdiction. With this kind of jurisdiction, a court can impose a personal obligation on the defendant in favor of the plaintiff.

If jurisdiction is based on the court's power over property located within its territory, the action is called *in rem* or *quasi in rem* jurisdiction. The effect of a judgment in such a case is limited to the property that supports the jurisdiction. No personal liability can be imposed on the property owner, because she is not under the court's jurisdiction.

A judgment *in rem* affects the interests of all persons in the designated property. A judgment *quasi in rem* affects the interests of particular persons in the property. For example, before a person purchases property that the government sells for unpaid taxes, the purchaser wants to be certain that no one else has an interest in the property. He can determine the property's previous owners through public records, which contain addresses that were valid at the time the entries were made. These addresses, however, may be out of date when the records are searched years later.

These previous owners are specific persons whose current whereabouts may be unknown. They might be deceased and their heirs may have a claim to the property. The new owner should file a suit to clear title to the property. The court has *quasi in rem* jurisdiction over the specified persons, the prior owners. As to the unknown heirs, the court has *in rem* jurisdiction. In either case, when the person's whereabouts are unknown, the jurisdiction is obtained by publishing appropriate notices in a newspaper of general circulation in the county where the property is located.

Subject Matter Jurisdiction. Subject matter jurisdiction imposes a limitation on the types of cases that a court can hear. The limitation is set by the constitution or statute creating the court. A court's subject matter jurisdiction can be limited not only by the subject of the lawsuit, but also by the monetary amount in controversy, by the type of criminal case, or by whether the proceeding is a trial or an appeal. Probate courts (which handle only matters relating to wills and estates) and small-claims courts (which handle cases involving small amounts of money) are examples of courts with limited subject matter jurisdiction.

Venue. Jurisdiction is concerned with determining a court's authority over a specific subject matter or individual. **Venue** is concerned with the particular geographic area within a judicial district where a suit should be brought. The concept of venue reflects the policy of convenience. A trial court should be in the geographic neighborhood where the incident leading to the suit occurred or where the parties involved in the suit reside.

Pretrial publicity or other factors may require a change of venue, that is, moving the trial to another community. A change of venue is used frequently in criminal cases if the defendant's right to a fair and impartial jury appears to be impaired within the current trial location.

CYBERLAW

Cyber Jurisdiction

The Internet creates problems for the courts concerning jurisdiction over the parties. A business that has a Web site reaches the entire world twenty-four hours a day. What happens if dissatisfied customers residing in China, Italy, or Russia decide to institute legal action in their respective countries? Does a business operating out of New York have to defend itself in a courtroom in another country that operates under a different legal system and is located thousands of miles away? A foreign country may have jurisdiction to hear the case. But is it reasonable to expect to be sued in another state's court located hundreds or thousands of miles away from the business or in a foreign country if the business does not have a physical location or operations there? These questions have no standard answer at this time. These issues are currently working their way through the court system and the legislature.

LEGAL HIGHLIGHT

Using a Small-Claims Court

Disputes often occur over small sums of money. For example, your former roommate owes you for last month's rent. To hire the services of a lawyer is expensive and not practical for such a small sum. States have small-claims courts that handle such claims in an expeditious manner.

You can sue your former roommate by filing a complaint in small-claims court. Normally, the service of the summons and complaint is completed by sending them to the defendant using certified mail. The mailing of the documents eliminates the expense of paying a person to personally serve the summons and complaint on your roommate.

Your roommate, as the defendant, must file a written answer to your complaint with the court. If your roommate fails to respond to the court summons, you can file for entry to obtain a default judgment.

If your roommate files an answer, the case proceeds to trial before a judge. In small-claims courts, a jury is not allowed and lawyers are not allowed to represent either party. Usually the hearing is very informal, with each party presenting her side of the case. The judge decides the case based on the facts as determined by the judge.

Most decisions by small-claims courts cannot be appealed to a higher court. Small-claims courts provide a quick and inexpensive way to resolve minor disputes involving money damages.

Res Judicata

Once a case has been fully litigated, neither party may institute another action based on the same facts or circumstances. This rule is known as the doctrine of **res judicata**. A final judgment on the merits by a court of competent jurisdiction is conclusive as to the rights of the parties. A settlement of a dispute within the court system, such as judicial arbitration, is treated as a final judgment or decree. Although not technically correct, some courts use the term *res adjudicata* to mean the same thing.

Appellate Courts

In some states, trial courts of general jurisdiction also have limited jurisdiction to hear appeals from the lower judiciary, such as small-claims courts or traffic courts. Generally, the term *appellate court* refers to the higher reviewing courts and not to trial courts.

Appellate courts also are called **courts of appeal** or courts of review. Every state has at least one appellate court. Most states have multiple intermediate reviewing courts and one supreme court. Often, the intermediate reviewing court is called the *court of appeals*, and the highest court of the state is called the *supreme court*. The highest court in New York and Maryland, however, is call the *court of appeals*.

The losing party has the legal right to appeal the case to an appellate court. The prevailing party may also appeal, if all requested relief were not granted. The appellate court has **appellate jurisdiction**; that is, the justices examine the written record of the case on appeal to determine if the trial court committed an error of law. The only time an appellate court reviews

findings of facts is when the findings are clearly erroneous or when no evidence supports the finding. The appellate court can remand (send back) the case for further findings of fact. Otherwise, all questions of fact remain within the trial court's jurisdiction.

The losing party of an appellate court's decision may appeal to the state supreme court. In all questions of state law, the decisions of each state's highest court are final. When issues of the federal Constitution, treaties, or laws are involved, the decision by the state's highest court is subject to review by the U.S. Supreme Court.

A Typical State Court System

Most court systems, including the federal system, are based on a three-tiered model. Exhibit 3–1 depicts the levels of a typical state court system. It has three main tiers: (1) the trial court of either general or limited jurisdiction, (2) the appellate court, and (3) the supreme court. The flow of appeal cases from the lower courts to the higher courts varies from state to state.[1]

The Federal Court System

The federal court system is similar in many ways to most state court systems. Also three tiered, it consists of (1) trial courts, (2) intermediate courts of appeal, and (3) the U.S. Supreme Court. The federal government also has special courts. Exhibit 3–2 shows the organization of the federal court system in some detail.

Article III of the U.S. Constitution creates the Supreme Court and empowers Congress to create any other inferior courts that it deems necessary. Inferior courts include the district courts; the other courts of limited, or specialized, jurisdiction; and the U.S. courts of appeal.

District Courts. At the federal level, the trial court of general jurisdiction is the district court. Every state has at least one federal district court within its borders. Congress has divided the states and territories into ninety-four federal judicial districts. The number of judicial districts varies over time primarily because of population changes and corresponding caseloads.

Most federal cases originate in the U.S. district courts. Whenever two or more district courts are

---

[1]Find information about specific state courts at http://www.ncsconline.org. Other excellent sites are http://www.courts.net and http://www.firstgov.gov.

Exhibit 3–1   Hypothetical State Court System

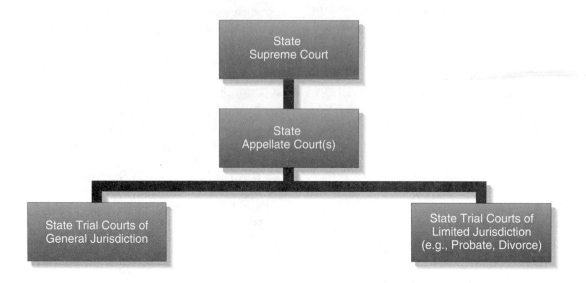

within a single state, each court is limited to its geographic boundaries. The state of Florida, for example, has courts for northern, middle, and southern districts. Thus, a case that arises in the southern Florida district cannot be tried by a court in the northern district, unless a motion for a change of venue has been granted. A **motion** is an application made to the judge by a party to the lawsuit seeking relief for a wrong committed or asserting a procedural right. If the motion is granted, the judge issues an order to grant the relief sought. If the motion is denied, the relief sought is not granted.

U.S. district courts have original jurisdiction in federal matters; that is, federal cases start in the district courts. Other trial courts with original, limited jurisdiction include the U.S. Tax Court, the U.S. Bankruptcy Court, and the U.S. Claims Court, the court that hears claims against the United States on federal contracts. Certain administrative agencies and departments with quasi-judicial power also have original jurisdiction. These agencies and departments are listed in Exhibit 3–2.

Courts of Appeal. Congress has established twelve judicial circuits (regions), including the D.C. Circuit. The courts located within a judicial circuit are called *courts of appeal* or *circuit courts*. Each circuit court

hears only appeals from the district courts located within its respective circuit. A thirteenth circuit, the Federal Circuit, has national jurisdiction and hears cases involving patent laws and cases appealed from both the Court of International Trade and the Court of Federal Claims. Exhibit 3–3 shows the judicial circuits.

Appeals from decisions made by federal administrative agencies, such as the Federal Trade Commission, also are heard by the U.S. courts of appeal. The decision of a court of appeals is final unless the Supreme Court accepts the case.

Supreme Court of the United States. The highest level of the federal court system is the Supreme Court of the United States. The Supreme Court has nine justices. Although this number is not set by the Constitution, it has remained constant since the Civil War (1861–1865).

The Supreme Court has original, or trial, jurisdiction in rare instances as set forth in Article III, Section 2. Most of the time, it operates as an appellate court. The Supreme Court reviews cases decided by any of the federal courts of appeal. It also has appellate authority over cases decided in the state supreme courts that involve the federal Constitution, treaties, or laws.

Exhibit 3–2   **Organization of the Federal Court System**

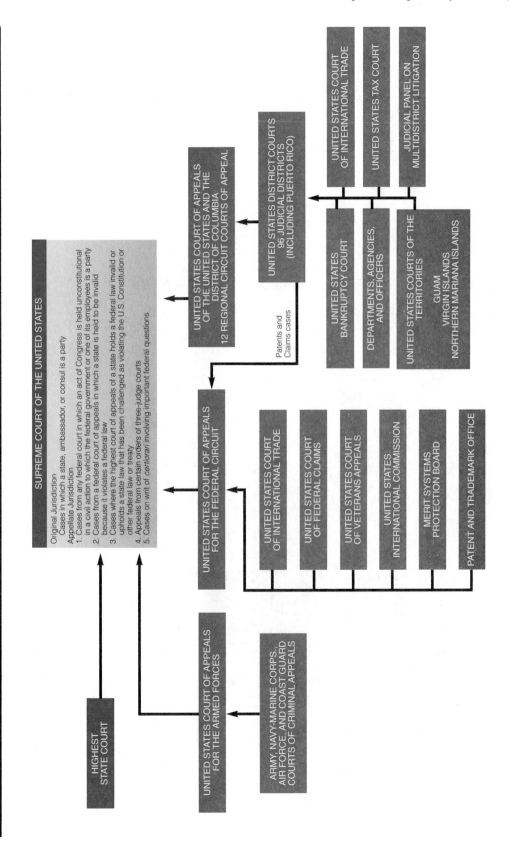

SUPREME COURT OF THE UNITED STATES

Original Jurisdiction
  Cases in which a state, ambassador, or consul is a party
Appellate Jurisdiction
1. Cases from any federal court in which an act of Congress is held unconstitutional in a civil action to which the federal government or one of its employees is a party
2. Cases from a federal court of appeals in which a state is held to be invalid because it violates a federal law
3. Cases where the highest court of appeals of a state holds a federal law invalid or upholds a state law that has been challenged as violating the U.S. Constitution or other federal law or treaty
4. Appeals from certain orders of three-judge courts
5. Cases on writ of *certiorari* involving important federal questions

UNITED STATES COURT OF APPEALS OF THE UNITED STATES AND THE DISTRICT OF COLUMBIA
12 REGIONAL CIRCUIT COURTS OF APPEAL

UNITED STATES DISTRICT COURTS
96 JUDICIAL DISTRICTS
(INCLUDING PUERTO RICO)

UNITED STATES COURT OF INTERNATIONAL TRADE

UNITED STATES TAX COURT

JUDICIAL PANEL ON MULTIDISTRICT LITIGATION

UNITED STATES BANKRUPTCY COURT

DEPARTMENTS, AGENCIES, AND OFFICERS

UNITED STATES COURTS OF THE TERRITORIES
GUAM
VIRGIN ISLANDS
NORTHERN MARIANA ISLANDS

Patents and Claims cases

UNITED STATES COURT OF APPEALS FOR THE FEDERAL CIRCUIT

UNITED STATES COURT OF INTERNATIONAL TRADE

UNITED STATES COURT OF FEDERAL CLAIMS

UNITED STATES COURT OF VETERANS APPEALS

UNITED STATES INTERNATIONAL COMMISSION

MERIT SYSTEMS -PROTECTION BOARD

PATENT AND TRADEMARK OFFICE

HIGHEST STATE COURT

UNITED STATES COURT OF APPEALS FOR THE ARMED FORCES

ARMY, NAVY-MARINE CORPS, AIR FORCE, AND COAST GUARD COURTS OF CRIMINAL APPEALS

Exhibit 3–3 Geographical Boundaries of U.S. Courts of Appeal and U.S. District Courts

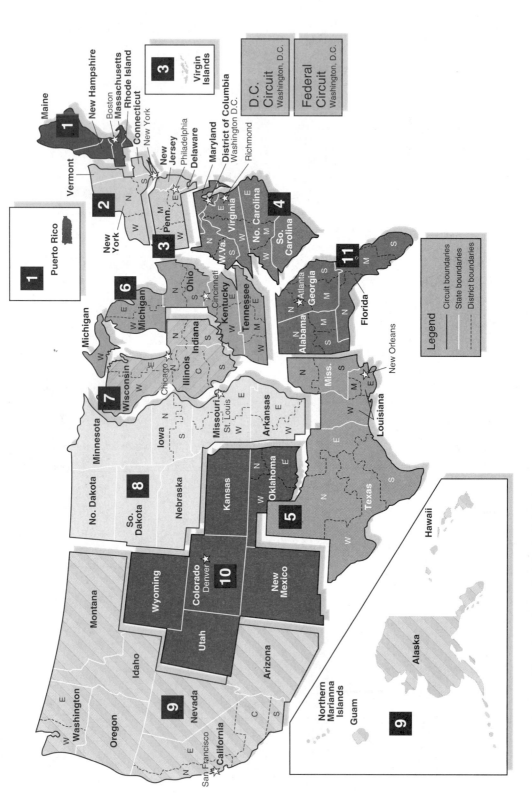

Number and composition of circuits set forth by 28 U.S.C. § 41.

LEGAL HIGHLIGHT

The Friday Conference

On Friday mornings, promptly at 9:30 A.M., a buzzer summons the nine justices of the United States Supreme Court to an all-day meeting. Entering the conference room, each justice shakes hands with the other eight, a ritual started in the 1880s to symbolize harmony. The nine justices are William H. Rehnquist, chief justice of the United States (1972), John Paul Stevens (1975), Sandra Day O'Connor (1981), Antonin Scalia (1986), Anthony M. Kennedy (1988), David H. Souter (1990), Clarence Thomas (1991), Ruth Bader Ginsburg (1993), and Stephen G. Breyer (1994).

A custom started in 1907 is that no one else is allowed in the room—no law clerks, no secretaries, no pages, no security personnel—once the door is shut. The junior justice takes care of the coffee, answers the door (should anyone dare to knock), and handles all messages and documents.

The justices have assigned seats based on seniority. The chief justice sits at the east end of the table, and the senior associate justice sits at the west end. Behind each justice is a cart that holds his or her books and papers. The volumes of the *United States Reports*, containing every decision made by the body since its first decision, line the walls.

The Friday conference has two purposes: to vote on the cases already argued during the week and to select new cases for the Court to review. Only a few cases make it to the Discuss List. Every justice has already screened each case, so the cases are processed quickly. Of the cases originally on the Discuss List, rarely more than six survive to be heard by the Court. During these conferences, each justice tries to persuade the others to her or his point of view. In effect, the other justices serve as a jury. It is this persuasion process that eventually produces the consensus for a coherent Court decision.

Although much is known about the procedure of the Friday conference, the heart of the conference—the exchange of ideas and arguments among the justices—is not revealed. The justices customarily destroy their conference papers and they rarely talk about the sessions.[a]

[a]Additional informational about the justices of the United States Supreme Court can be found at the Oyez Project at Northwestern University's U.S. Supreme Court Multimedia Database Web site at http://er.library.northwestern.edu/detail.asp?id=34363.

Writ of *Certiorari*. The United States Supreme Court has appellate jurisdiction over cases involving a federal question, including the Constitution, "with such Exceptions, and under such Regulations as the Congress shall make" (Article III, Section 2, of the U.S. Constitution). Thousands of cases are filed with the Supreme Court each year, but it accepts and decides an average of only sixty to eighty cases annually.

Civil cases reach the Supreme Court when a party requests the Court to issue a **writ of *certiorari***. If the Court issues the writ, the case will be reviewed, but issuance of the writ is entirely at the Court's discretion. No set circumstance requires the court to issue a writ of *certiorari*.

When a writ of *certiorari* is issued, the Supreme Court orders a lower court to send the record of the case to it for review. The Court is more inclined to issue a writ in the following situations:

- When a state supreme court decides a substantial federal question that has not been decided by the Supreme Court

- When two federal courts of appeal disagree

- When a federal court of appeals decides an important federal question not yet addressed by the Supreme Court or has departed from the accepted and usual course of judicial proceedings

- When a federal court of appeals holds a state statute invalid because it violates federal law

- When a federal court holds an act of Congress unconstitutional and the federal government or one of its employees is a party.

The Supreme Court denies most petitions for writs of *certiorari*. A denial is not a decision on the merits of a case, nor does it indicate agreement with the lower court's opinion. Denial of the writ has no value as precedent. The Court will not issue a writ unless at least four justices approve it. Typically, only petitions for cases that may raise important constitutional questions are granted writs of *certiorari*.

Jurisdiction of Federal Courts

Because the federal government is a government of limited powers, the jurisdiction of the federal courts is limited. Although the Constitution sets the outer limits of federal judicial power, Congress sets other limits on federal jurisdiction. The courts themselves also can establish rules that limit their jurisdiction over the types of cases that have certain characteristics. The following subsections examine these characteristics.

Federal Question Lawsuits. Whenever a plaintiff's cause of action is based, at least in part, on the U.S. Constitution, a treaty, or a federal law, a federal question arises. A case with a legal question that involves the federal Constitution, treaty, or statute is called a **federal question case**. The federal courts have jurisdiction over such cases. For example, all bankruptcy cases must be brought in federal court. No minimum dollar amount in controversy is required when a case involves a federal question.

Diversity of Citizenship Lawsuits. Diversity of citizenship cases involve controversies between (1) citizens of different states, (2) a foreign country as plaintiff and citizens of the same or different states, and (3) citizens of a state and citizens of a foreign country. In diversity of citizenship cases, however, the amount in controversy must be $75,000 or more before a federal court can have jurisdiction. Although diversity of citizenship lawsuits need not involve a federal question, the federal courts cannot hear matters that are exclusively a state matter, such as a divorce.

Consider the following example. Smith is driving from his home state, New York, to Florida. In Georgia, he runs into a car owned by Able, a citizen of Georgia. Able's new Mercedes is demolished and, as a result of the personal injuries she sustained in the accident, Able is unable to work for six months. The property damage is $85,000, and her loss of income for the six months is $35,000; thus, this case involves more than $75,000 worth of damages. Able can sue Smith either in a Georgia state court or in the federal district court. Georgia has *in personam* jurisdiction over Smith through its long-arm statute. By driving on Georgia's highways, Smith has consented to Georgia jurisdiction. If Smith were sued in Georgia, he can have the suit removed to a federal district court on the basis of diversity of citizenship.

Even though most automobile accident cases are litigated in state courts, two reasons exist to take any case to federal court under the diversity of citizenship doctrine. First, the state courts may be prejudiced against the nonresident. This factor may be particularly relevant in smaller communities. Second, depending on the location, it may be faster to have the case heard in federal district court.

At one time, the federal judiciary created its own common law. At times, this body of law would conflict with the law that was applied by a state court. The end result was two court systems in the same state that were at times applying different law. This result caused litigants to look for a court that had law upholding their position so they could file their action in that particular, favorable court. This practice continued until the following landmark case declared that a federal court must apply the state's law when confronted with a factual situation not involving a federal question based on the federal constitution, statutes, and regulations.

LANDMARK CASE

CASE 3.2

Supreme Court of the United States, 1938
304 U.S. 64, 58 S. Ct. 817, 82 L. Ed. 1188
http://caselaw.findlaw.com
http://www2.law.cornell.edu

ERIE R. CO. v. TOMPKINS

BACKGROUND AND FACTS On a dark night Tompkins, a citizen of Pennsylvania, while walking along the railroad's right of way (located in Pennsylvania) was injured by a passing freight train owned by the Erie Railroad Company. He claimed that the accident occurred through negligence of the railroad. He brought an action in the federal court for Southern New York, which had jurisdiction because the company was a corporation formed in New York. Erie Railroad denied liability. The case went to trial where it was heard by a jury.

The question was which law would apply in this case, state or federal law? If the law of Pennsylvania applied, Tompkins would be denied recovery because he was a trespasser. Under federal law, Tompkins could recover because the federal law looked to the railroad's willful and wanton actions in injuring Tompkins and not to whether Tompkins was a trespasser. The federal trial court applied federal law. The court found for Tompkins and awarded him $30,000. This judgment was upheld by the Circuit Court of Appeals. The railroad appealed and the U.S. Supreme Court accepted jurisdiction.

Justice BRANDEIS delivered the opinion of the Court.

. . . .

First. *Swift v. Tyson*, held that federal courts exercising jurisdiction on the ground of diversity of citizenship need not, in matters of general jurisprudence, apply the unwritten law of the state as declared by its highest court; that they are free to exercise an independent judgment as to what the common law of the state is—or should be.

. . . .

Second. Experience in applying the doctrine of *Swift v. Tyson*, had revealed its defects, political and social; and the benefits expected to flow from the rule did not accrue. Persistence of state courts in their own opinions on questions of common law prevented uniformity; and the impossibility of discovering a satisfactory line of demarcation between the province of general law and that of local law developed a new well of uncertainties.

. . . .

The injustice and confusion incident to the doctrine of *Swift v. Tyson* have been repeatedly urged as reasons for abolishing or limiting diversity of citizenship jurisdiction. Other legislative relief has been proposed. If only a question of statutory construction were involved, we should not be prepared to abandon a doctrine so widely applied throughout nearly a century. But the unconstitutionality of the course pursued has now been made clear, and compels us to do so.

. . . .

Third. Except in matters governed by the Federal Constitution or by acts of Congress, the law to be applied in any case is the law of the state. And whether the law of the state shall be declared by its Legislature in a statute or by its highest court in a decision is not a matter of federal concern. There is no federal general common law. Congress has no power to declare substantive rules of common law applicable in a state whether they be local in their nature or 'general,' be they commercial law or a part of the law of torts. And no clause in the Constitution purports to confer such a power upon the federal courts.

. . . .

DECISION AND REMEDY The railroad contended that under the common law of Pennsylvania, the only duty owed to the plaintiff was to refrain from willful or wanton injury. In support of their respective contentions, the parties cited decisions of the Pennsylvania Supreme Court. The case was returned to the trial court to determine what the law of Pennsylvania was at the time of the accident.

CRITICAL THINKING: ETHICS Should there be just one body of law for the entire United States?

Concurrent versus Exclusive Jurisdiction. Concurrent jurisdiction exists when both federal and state courts have the power to hear a case (such as in diversity of citizenship cases). When the subject matter of a case can be tried only in federal or only in state courts, there is **exclusive jurisdiction**. Federal courts have exclusive jurisdiction in cases involving federal crimes, bankruptcy, patents, copyrights, and lawsuits against the United States. States have exclusive jurisdiction in other types of legal matters, such as divorce, probate, and adoption cases.

Following a Case through the Courts

American courts use the **adversary system** of justice where the judge acts as the decision maker between the opposing sides, the plaintiff and the defendant, at trial. Ideally, the judge plays an unbiased and mostly passive role. Each party's lawyer functions as the client's advocate, presenting the client's version of the facts in an attempt to convince the judge, the jury, or both that the client's version is true.

Judges need not be entirely passive. They are responsible for the appropriate application of the law and do not have to accept the attorneys' legal reasoning. Instead, they can base a ruling on their own study of the law. Additionally, if a defendant chooses to act as his own counsel, the judge will often play more of an advocate role, intervening during the trial to assist the defendant and to preserve the record of the proceedings.

Procedure involves the way in which disputes are handled in the courts. Procedural law establishes the rules and standards for resolving disputes. The rules are complex and vary from court to court. The federal court system has rules of procedure that may differ from those of the various state court systems. In addition, rules of procedure differ between criminal and civil cases.

A SAMPLE CASE

Artiste Login Products, Inc. v. Acme Copiers, Inc.

A dispute over a contract has arisen between Artiste Login Products, Inc. (Artiste), and Acme Copiers, Inc. (Copiers). Artiste hires Paul L. Lakin, a lawyer, to represent it.

Artiste and Copiers have entered into several business transactions over several years. On one contract, Copiers alleges that it sold Artiste a copy machine and that Artiste has failed to pay the money owed on the contract. Artiste and Copiers are unable to agree on a settlement out of court or through any alternative dispute resolution methods, which are discussed in Chapter 4.

Copiers files a lawsuit against Artiste in state court. Normally, the paperwork is physically delivered to the clerk of the court either in person, by messenger, or by mail. Many courts allow electronic filing, file transfers through the Internet, or in some instances via CD-ROM using an Internet browser interface. Because Copiers filed the suit, Copiers is the plaintiff and Artiste is the defendant. Lawyers represent each party.

Pleadings and Process. A **pleading** is a document written by one of the parties to the lawsuit and sent to the other party (or parties) and to the court so it can be included in the judge's case file, which is a public record. The purpose of a pleading is to provide information to the other party, to seek information from the other party, or to seek a judicial ruling. Any person who is a party to a lawsuit typically has the opportunity to **plead** (present) her case before a trial court. The following are the more well-known pleadings:

- Complaint or petition
- Answer or response
- Counterclaim
- Reply to counterclaim
- Cross–claim
- Answer to cross–claim
- Third-party complaint
- Third-party answer.

We briefly examine each of these types of pleadings. Some of these pleadings are discussed in more detail later in this section.

A **complaint** is filed by the plaintiff and sets out the legal and factual basis for the suit. For some types of legal action, the plaintiff files a **petition**. For example, in some states, a person who is seeking a divorce files a petition instead of a complaint. A statute or the court rules determine the name of the pleading to be filed in the court.

If the defendant is served with a complaint, he will file an **answer** to the complaint that sets out the defendant's position on the lawsuit. If a petition were filed, the defendant files a response to the petition.

A **counterclaim** is essentially another lawsuit filed within the original lawsuit by the defendant seeking

LEGAL HIGHLIGHT

The Virtual Courtroom

The judiciary is often viewed as stodgy and lagging behind new technology by using procedures that date back to previous centuries. The motto seems to be "We have always done it that way, why change it?"

But change is coming to the judicial system. Transformations can be seen on television when a high profile case is being tried. Started in 1991, Court TV[a] broadcasts interesting court cases over cable and satellite. The programming is determined by "how important and interesting the issues in the case are; the newsworthiness of the case and the people involved; the quality and educational value of the trial; and the expected length of the trial."[b]

Standing contrary to the trend of television cameras in the courtroom are the U.S. Supreme Court and most federal courts. One strong exception exists at the federal level. The U.S. Court of Appeals for the Armed Forces[c] has invited cameras into its courtroom. Oral arguments before this court can be seen on C-SPAN.

The U.S. Supreme Court for the first time allowed audio tapes of oral argument to be released immediately because of the great national interest in the Election 2000 cases of *Bush v. Palm Beach County Canvassing Board*[d] and *Bush v. Gore*.[e] The normal procedure is to release the tapes after several months to the National Archives and Record Administration.

Today, in a trial courtroom a court reporter transcribes everything that is said in real time so the transcription can be viewed on a screen for the jury and the public to read. A monitor may be available for each member of the jury. In some states, all proceedings are video recorded, which removes the requirement of having a court reporter.

One problem that occurs during a trial involves written documents. A witness will be called to the stand. He will be handed a document and the attorney will have the witness testify about the document. The jury, however, does not know what the document contains until it is admitted into evidence by the judge. After the document is admitted into evidence, it is then circulated among the members of the jury. This passing of the document from one member to another is normally done while another witness is testifying. The document being passed from one to another causes the members of the jury either to not listen to the current testimony being given or to ignore the circulating document.

Today, many courtrooms have an electronic podium that includes a camera that sends a photocopy of the document to a computer and in turn back to the monitor directly in front of each juror. When this system is available, the jury member may see the document while testimony is given about it.

Another innovation is in the soliciting of evidence from a witness at a crime lab or another place instead of listening to the expert on the witness stand. A camera is taken into a crime lab where jurors can see how a DNA analysis or a blood alcohol test is conducted. This form of videoconferencing alleviates the need for the expert to appear in court, which really means sitting in the hall outside the courtroom or in a separate witness room. A witness may sit outside and not be called to the witness chair for many hours, if not days. Now the witness can continue working, but remain available for testifying. Instead of requiring a person to come to court (and often waste long periods of time), the courtroom is now going to the witness.

One advantage of videotaping is that attorneys can obtain a copy of the trial videotape to review before the next day. In the past, it was possible to obtain a copy of the transcript by the next day, but this was very expensive. It meant that a court reporter would work additional hours to have it prepared for use the next day. This inconvenience is no longer necessary.

Money and time are also saved when people accused of crimes are arraigned in jail. In the past, those in jail had to be transported to and from the courthouse. This travel was not only costly, but the danger of escape was always present. Today, a room in the jail building can be set up for videoconferencing; the accused remains in jail while the judge is located in the courthouse miles away.

Innovation, new technologies, and imagination are bringing the stodgy courtrooms to life. The virtual courtroom is ready for the twenty-first century.

---

[a] Court TV can be found through cable and satellite listings. The Web page is http://courttv.com.
[b] See http://courttv.com/about/ctvfaq.html.
[c] The Web site for the U.S. Court of Appeals for the Armed Forces is http://www.armfor.uscourts.gov.
[d] *Bush v. Palm Beach County Canvassing Board*, 531 U.S. 70, 121 S. Ct. 471, 148 L. Ed. 2d 366 (2000).
[e] *Bush v. Gore*, 531 U.S. 98, 121 S. Ct. 525, 148 L. Ed. 2d 388 (2000).

damages against the plaintiff. For example, Geoffrey sues for injuries received when Sean's automobile ran a red light and crashed into Geoffrey's automobile. Sean files a counterclaim against Geoffrey because Geoffrey allegedly attacked Sean with a tire iron after the accident. Since a counterclaim, in effect, is a lawsuit, the plaintiff must file a **reply** to the counterclaim setting out his defenses.

A **cross-claim** is brought by one defendant against a codefendant. Normally, a cross-claim comes from the same facts that are the basis for the plaintiff's complaint. For example, an airplane crashes. In a subsequent lawsuit, the airline, the airplane manufacturer, and various builders of parts of the airplane are sued. The defendant airplane manufacturer may file a cross-claim against the codefendant engine manufacturer because the engine was defective. When the codefendant, the engine manufacturer, is sued, it files an answer to set out its defenses in this case. Whenever a cross-claim is filed, the other party should file an answer to the cross-claim.

A **third-party complaint** is filed when another party, who was not an original party to the lawsuit, is sued. Once the third-party complaint is served, the new defendant files an answer. For example, a customer purchases a hamburger from a restaurant, bites into it, and breaks his tooth. He finds a drill bit in the hamburger. He lets the restaurant manager know about this problem, but the manager refuses to settle the case. The manager claims that he purchases prepared hamburger patties in large quantities from a wholesaler. The restaurant merely cooks the hamburger patties. The customer sues the restaurant, not the wholesaler, because the customer does not have a contractual relationship with the wholesaler. The restaurant files a third-party complaint against the wholesaler. The wholesaler should file an answer to the third-party complaint.

Process is a document that comes from the court and is signed by the judge or other judicial official, such as the clerk of the court. The actual document subject to process goes through three steps: it is issued, served, and filed.

A judge or other judicial officer issues a process document that orders a person affiliated with a case to take some action. A copy of the process is served on the person by a *process server*—usually a marshal or sheriff, but sometimes an authorized private party. In most states a party to the lawsuit personally cannot serve any papers involved with that suit. The process server files the process by returning it to the court case file, having noted when, where, and how the piece of process was served.

The following is a partial list of documents that are known as process:

- A summons informs the defendant of the claim brought by the plaintiff.
- A **subpoena** requires the attendance of a witness at a hearing.
- A **subpoena** *duces tecum* requires that evidence be brought to court by its custodian.
- Writ of attachment.
- Writ of garnishment.
- Writ of execution.

A complaint is one type of pleading, whereas a summons is one type of process. In this case, Copiers' lawsuit (or action) against Artiste will start when Copiers' lawyer files a complaint. The complaint is filed with the clerk of the trial court in the proper venue, which is the appropriate geographic area. Copiers will file the lawsuit in the superior court located in Maricopa County, Arizona. The court then issues a summons to the defendant.

The complaint informs Artiste of the reason for which it is being sued. The summons notifies Artiste of the time and place where it must file an answer or response.

The complaint contains (1) a statement alleging the facts necessary for the court to take jurisdiction, (2) a short statement of the facts necessary to show that Copiers has been harmed by Artiste and that Copiers is entitled to a remedy, and (3) a description of the remedy that Copiers seeks. Exhibit 3–4 illustrates a typical complaint. The complaint states that Copiers is a duly organized corporation within the state and that Artiste also is a duly organized corporation of the state. Next, the facts are recited: Artiste agreed to purchase the copier, and it has not paid the monies it owes for the copier. The complaint states that Copiers is entitled to $15,000 to cover the cost of the copier.

After the complaint has been filed, Lakin, on behalf of Artiste, will be served a summons and a copy of the complaint by a process server, certified mail, or electronically. In most states, Lakin is allowed to voluntarily accept service. The service of a summons and

Exhibit 3-4   A Typical Complaint

IN THE SUPERIOR COURT OF THE STATE OF ARIZONA
IN AND FOR THE COUNTY OF MARICOPA

ACME COPIERS, INC., an Arizona corporation;	)))	No. _____
Plaintiff,	))	COMPLAINT
	)	(Contract)
vs.	))	
ARTISTE LOGIN PRODUCTS, INC., an Arizona corporation	)))	
Defendant.	)))	
_____	)	

COMES NOW, the Plaintiff, ACME COPIERS, INC., by and through its attorney, I. M. Goodguy, and for its cause of action against the Defendant claims and alleges as follows:

I

The Defendant, ARTISTE LOGIN PRODUCTS, INC., is a duly organized corporation under the laws of the state of Arizona. The said Defendant caused events to occur within Maricopa County, Arizona, which gave rise to this Complaint. The Plaintiff is a duly organized corporation within the State of Arizona.

II

The Defendant, ARTISTE LOGIN PRODUCTS, INC., contracted with the Plaintiff to purchase a copy machine for $15,000.00. The copy machine was delivered by Plaintiff to the Defendant. Plaintiff then billed the Defendant on May 15, 2004, in the amount of $15,000.00. No payments have been received, which conduct constitutes breach of contract by the Defendant, ARTISTE LOGIN PRODUCTS, INC.

III

Plaintiff has made all demands or performed all other acts necessary to mature or accelerate the aforesaid amount. The Defendant is liable for the Plaintiff's reasonable attorney fees under Arizona Revised Statutes, Section 12-341.01.

WHEREFORE, Plaintiff respectfully demands judgment against Defendant as follows:
1. For the sum of $15,000 as compensatory damages.
2. For reasonable attorney fees under Arizona Revised Statutes, Section 12-341.01, plus Court costs in bringing this action.
3. For interest on all said sums from May 16, 2004, until paid.
4. For such other relief as the Court deems just and proper.

DATED this _____ day of _____, 2005.

_____
I. M. GOODGUY
2001 N. Winning Trial Lane
Tempe, Arizona 85281
Attorney for Plaintiff

complaint is the only time a pleading is served by a process server. Usually, other pleadings, such as an answer, are sent by the parties to each other and to the court. Delivery is by mail, messenger service, or electronic transfer.

A typical summons is shown in Exhibit 3–5. A summons notifies Artiste that it is allowed to prepare an answer to the complaint.

A copy of the answer must be filed with the court and sent to the plaintiff's attorney within a specified time period, usually twenty to thirty days after the summons has been served. If Artiste does not file an answer within the time period, Copiers may obtain a **default judgment**. A default judgment occurs when the defendant fails to file the answer or **response** within the specified amount of time. In a default judgment, the defendant automatically loses the lawsuit.

Choices Available after Receipt of the Summons and Complaint.
Once the defendant is served with the summons and a copy of the complaint, the defendant should file a responsive pleading or motion. This filing must be done within the stipulated time period.

Among the defendant's choices are to file (1) a motion to dismiss, (2) an answer containing any affirmative defenses, (3) a counterclaim, (4) an answer containing both affirmative defenses and a counterclaim, or (5) any of these documents as well as a cross-claim or a third-party complaint. If the defendant does nothing, a default judgment may be entered against him or her. An exception is made for military personnel under the Soldiers and Sailors Civil Relief Act of 1943. A person serving on active duty is entitled to request the court to **stay**, that is, stop, the proceedings until the person is able to return and defend against the lawsuit.

Motion to Dismiss. If the defendant decides to challenge the plaintiff's complaint, the defendant can present to the court a **motion to dismiss**, also called a **demurrer**. The motion to dismiss contends that even if the facts presented in the complaint were true, no legal reason exists to go further with the suit and no need exists for the defendant to file an answer. If, for example, Copiers' complaint alleges facts that exclude the possibility of any breach of contract by Artiste, it

---

LEGAL HIGHLIGHT

Singing the Courthouse Blues

When they appeared at a concert in Portland, Oregon, on November 9, 1981, the Beach Boys—Al Jardine, Bruce Johnston, Mike Love, and Dennis Wilson— were provided security by off-duty deputies. Three of these deputies—Fred Byler, Donald Kerr, and Kevin McVicker—later sued the Beach Boys for $5.4 million. The deputies claimed they were battered and falsely imprisoned when they tried to take photographs of the musicians.

The Beach Boys were served properly with a summons and a copy of the complaint at another concert that they were playing in Portland in February 1983. No appearance was made, and no answer was filed. In August 1984 a default judgment was entered against the Beach Boys for $5.4 million. Each deputy was granted an award of $300,000 in general damages and $1.5 million in punitive damages. That award was

upheld in December 1985 by a judge in the Multnomah County Circuit Court.

The lesson: Never ignore a summons and complaint because the defendant may be held fully liable for the amount of damages alleged in the plaintiff's complaint.

Rules governing the service of a summons vary. Usually, service is made by handing the summons and complaint to the defendant personally or by leaving these documents at either the defendant's residence or place of business.

When the defendant cannot be reached, special rules sometimes permit serving the summons by publishing it in the newspaper or by leaving it with a designated person, such as the secretary of state. If service is obtained in this manner, the court usually will not have personal jurisdiction over the defendant but will have authority over the defendant's property located within the court's jurisdiction.

Exhibit 3-5   A Typical Summons

IN THE SUPERIOR COURT OF THE STATE OF ARIZONA
IN AND FOR THE COUNTY OF MARICOPA

ACME COPIERS, INC., an Arizona corporation;	)))	NO. _____
Plaintiff,	)))	SUMMONS
vs.	))	
ARTISTE LOGIN PRODUCTS, INC., an Arizona corporation,	)))	
Defendant.	))	

WARNING: THIS IS AN OFFICIAL DOCUMENT FROM THE COURT THAT AFFECTS YOUR RIGHTS. READ THIS CAREFULLY. IF YOU DO NOT UNDERSTAND IT, CONTACT A LAWYER FOR HELP.

FROM THE STATE OF ARIZONA TO: PAUL L. LAKIN, statutory agent for ARTISTE LOGIN PRODUCTS, INC.

1. A lawsuit has been filed against you. A copy of the lawsuit and other court papers are served on you with this Summons.

2. If you do not want a judgment or order taken against you without your input, you must file an Answer or a Response in writing with the Court, and pay the filing fee. If you do not file an answer or Response, the other party may be given the relief requested in his or her Petition or Complaint. To file your Response or Answer, take or send the Answer or Response to the Office of the Clerk of the Superior Court, 201 West Jefferson Street, Phoenix, Arizona 85003-2205, or the office of the Clerk of the Superior Court, 222 East Javelina Drive, Mesa, Arizona 85210-6201. Mail a copy of your Response or Answer to the other party at the address listed on the top of this Summons.

3. If this Summons and the other court papers were served on you by a registered process server or the Sheriff, within the State of Arizona, your Response or answer must be Pled within TWENTY (20) CALENDAR DAYS from the date you were served, not counting the day you were served. If this summons and the other papers were served on you by a registered process server or the Sheriff outside the State of Arizona, your Response must be filed within THIRTY (30) CALENDAR DAYS from the date you were served, not counting the day you were served. Service by a registered process server or the sheriff is complete when made. Service by Publication is complete 30 days after the date of the first publication.

WARNING. If you signed an Acceptance/Waiver of Service, you must file your Response or Answer within 60 days from the date the Notice and Request to Accept Service was sent to you. You should see a lawyer to help you make sure that you have complied with the Service and Response or Answers rules.

4. You can get a copy of the court papers filed in this case from the Petitioner's attorney at the address at the top of this paper or from the Clerk of the Superior court at the address listed in Paragraph 2 above.

5. Requests for reasonable accommodation for persons with disabilities must be made to the office of the Judge or Commissioner assigned to the case five days before your scheduled court date.

SIGNED AND SEALED this date:

_____

MICHAEL K. JEANES
Clerk of Superior court

By _____
Deputy Clerk

can move to dismiss. If its motion were granted, Artiste is not required to file an answer.

If the court grants the motion to dismiss, the judge is saying that the plaintiff has failed to state a recognized cause of action. The plaintiff generally is given time to correct the problem and to file an amended complaint.

If the plaintiff does not file an amended complaint, a judgment is entered against the plaintiff solely on the basis of the pleadings. The plaintiff will not be allowed to bring suit on the same matter again.

If the court denies the motion to dismiss, however, the judge is indicating that the plaintiff has stated a recognized cause of action, and the defendant is given an extension of time to file a further pleading. If the defendant does not file an answer, normally a default judgment will be entered for the plaintiff.

Answer and Counterclaim. If the defendant chooses not to file a motion to dismiss or files a motion to dismiss that is denied, he must file an answer with the court. In most answers, the defendant admits to part of the allegations (such as admitting venue), denies other parts of the complaint (such as denying any breach of contract), and sets out any defenses.

If Artiste admits all of Copiers' allegations in its answer, a judgment will be entered for Copiers. If Artiste denies Copiers' allegations, the matter proceeds to trial. Artiste may admit the facts but deny owing the money; in which case, no actual trial of the facts will take place.

A trial's purpose is to determine the facts. If no facts are in dispute, the judge hears only arguments on the legal issues in this case, the legal determination of whether Artiste breached the contract. If a breach of contract occurred, Artiste owes the money. Artiste can prevail in the case, however, by successfully raising an affirmative defense.

Artiste can admit the truth of Copiers' complaint but raise new facts that may result in the action's dismissal. This action is called an **affirmative defense**. For example, Artiste could admit liability but would avoid judgment by stating that the time period for raising the claim had passed. If proven, the judge would dismiss Copiers' complaint based on the statute of limitations.

Artiste may take the following tactic. Artiste files an answer that admits to the purchase of the copy machine. Artiste then alleges as an affirmative defense that Copiers' copy machine failed to perform properly and that Artiste was forced to rent a similar copy machine

from another supplier. This allegation is called, appropriately, a *counterclaim*. If Artiste files a counterclaim, Copiers must answer it with a pleading, normally called a *reply*, that has the same characteristics as an answer.

Discovery. Before a trial begins, the parties can use a number of procedural devices to obtain information and to gather evidence about the case. Copiers, for example, should establish that Artiste received the copier and should determine the reason for neglecting payment. If Artiste alleges the reason to be the copier's malfunction, Copiers would want to determine the specific malfunction and whether renting a replacement was necessary. The process of obtaining information from the opposing party or from witnesses is known as **discovery**.

Discovery includes gaining access to witnesses, documents, records, and other evidence. The rules governing discovery are designed to make sure that a witness or party is not harassed unduly, that privileged material is safeguarded, and that only matters relevant to the case at hand are subject to the discovery.

Discovery serves several purposes. It preserves evidence from witnesses who might not be available to testify at the trial or whose memories will fade as time passes. It also establishes a witness's testimony so that the witness's credibility can be challenged at trial if that testimony changes.

If discovery reveals that both parties agree on all the relevant facts, a motion for a **summary judgment** may be made. A summary judgment means that one side requests a decision from the judge. The party making the request for the summary judgment writes legal arguments, called *legal briefs*, and may make oral arguments to the judge as to the reasons for which the party should prevail based on the law.

The other side may oppose the request for summary judgment or may make its own request for a summary judgment. The judge reviews the pleadings filed in the case and the legal briefs to decide if a summary judgment should be granted. To warrant a summary judgment no relevant facts can be at issue. If relevant facts are disputed, a trial is the means to resolve the dispute. A summary judgment can be issued if only the law is being contested and not the facts.

If one party finds that the opponent's case is too strong to challenge, discovery can lead to an out-of-court settlement. Even if the case does go to trial, discovery prevents surprises by providing parties access to evidence that might otherwise be hidden. Also, discovery serves to narrow the issues so that trial time is spent examining those issues.

Discovery can involve the use of *depositions, interrogatories*, or both. A **deposition** is sworn oral testimony by the opposing party or any witness that is recorded by a court reporter. The person being deposed appears before a court reporter to be placed under oath. The person answers questions asked by attorneys from both sides. A court reporter records and later transcribes the questions and answers.

Today, depositions may be videotaped. Even satellite transmissions are used to allow busy witnesses to stay at their jobs while answering questions for attorneys a continent away.

Interrogatories consist of a series of written questions normally sent to the opposing party. That party, with the aid of an attorney, prepares written answers that are then signed under oath.

Parties are obligated to answer questions even if the answers involve the disclosure of information from their records and files. Uniform interrogatories for specific types of cases, such as automobile accidents, have been developed to make the process more efficient.

Other discovery procedures exist. A party may file a **request to produce**, which requires the other party to make available the physical evidence that it has in its possession. For example, if the defendant claims it paid a debt with a check, a request to produce the check may be sought by the plaintiff.

Requests for physical or mental examination often are used in cases, such as automobile accidents, if the health of one of the parties is at issue. If the plaintiff is seeking monetary damages for injuries, the defendant may request that the plaintiff submit to an examination by the defendant's doctor to determine the type and extent of the injuries.

Dismissals and Judgments before Trial. Following the pleadings and discovery process, either party can file pretrial motions. The use of motions can shorten a lawsuit or avoid a trial. In fact, most lawsuits never come to trial. Numerous procedural avenues are available for resolving a case without a trial. Usually, the defendant attempts to have the case dismissed through the use of pretrial motions.

Either party may move for a summary judgment after discovery is completed. Artiste, for example, can bring in the sworn statement of a witness that Artiste did not purchase a copier or that Copiers has served the wrong person. Unless Copiers can bring in other evidence raising the possibility that Artiste was the purchaser, Artiste will be entitled to dismissal on a motion for summary judgment. Motions for summary judgment can be made before a trial but will be granted only if the lack of factual disputes is truly obvious.

Before a judge will grant a pretrial motion that would avoid a trial, he or she must determine that no genuine issues of fact exist in the case. The only question must be one of law. Only a fact finder, a jury or a judge sitting alone (if the parties do not want a jury), can decide the facts of the case. If the judge denies the summary judgment, the case proceeds to trial.

A judge may grant a dismissal when the case is completely frivolous or is based on false evidence. The following case involves the issue of evidence that was probably false. The court discusses Rule 11 sanctions and Rule 38 appellate court sanctions. Rule 11 sanctions are ones that the trial court may impose and Rule 38 sanctions may be imposed by the appellate court. Both rules are directed toward keeping out of court those cases that are not based in law or fact. If the case is found to be frivolous, the trial court or the appellate court may impose sanctions.

CASE 3.3	**JIMENEZ v. MADISON AREA TECHNICAL COLLEGE**
United States Court of Appeals, Seventh Circuit, 2003 321 F.3d 652 http://www.ca7.uscourts.gov/op3.fwx?submit1=showop&caseno=01-3423.PDF	**BACKGROUND AND FACTS** Plaintiff Elvira Jimenez filed an action against her former employer Madison Area Technical College (College), alleging that the College had discriminated against her on the basis of race, ethnic origin, and sex. In support of these allegations, Jimenez produced inflammatory letters and e-mails allegedly written by various colleagues and supervisors during the term of her employment. After its investigation of the matter, the College, through its lawyer, advised Jimenez's counsel, Nunnery, that the alleged authors of the derogatory letters and e-mails had denied writing the communications attributed to them. The College

requested that Nunnery produce the original documents for its review. Neither the attorney, nor his client, complied with the request.

After finding that Jimenez had relied on falsified documents to support her civil rights claims, the district court sanctioned Jimenez, under Rule 11(c) of the Federal Rules of Civil Procedure, and dismissed her suit. The trial judge labeled Jimenez and Nunnery's actions the most blatant example of a Rule 11 violation that she had ever seen. Jimenez claims that imposition of such a harsh sanction amounts to an abuse of discretion in that she could not proceed with her case. The district court also imposed monetary sanctions on Jimenez's attorney, Nunnery, in the amount of $16,473. Nunnery did not appeal from the court's imposition of such sanctions. Accordingly, the monetary sanctions are not at issue in this appeal.

COFFEY, Circuit J.

. . . .

Perhaps because an attack on the district court's finding of fraud would be futile, Jimenez instead argues that the *severity* of the district court's sanction of such behavior—*i.e.,* its dismissal of her amended complaint—was an abuse of its discretion. She claims that "[t]here is nothing in the Court's record to indicate . . . that [her claims of denial of equal protection and retaliation] were fraudulent." Though her precise reasoning is difficult to comprehend, Jimenez apparently argues that the district court's sanction (dismissal) should have been less harsh because not *all* of her civil rights claims were based on the fraudulent documents. We disagree.

Jimenez's equal protection and retaliation claims are inseparable from the fraudulent allegations of discrimination underlying those claims. Indeed, Jimenez's *entire* cause of action rests on her claim that the College allegedly discriminated against her based on her race and origin—the very allegation she sought to bolster with a bevy of falsified documents.

We recognize that dismissal is a harsh sanction. Thus, we understand why we have uncovered no prior instance in which this Court has reviewed such an obvious and serious Rule 11 sanction for an abuse of discretion. Nonetheless, it is proper for the trial court to impose a severe sanction where the sanction is sufficient to deter repetition of the misconduct or to deter similar conduct by third parties. And, in all cases, we are to give the trial court "*significant discretion* in determining *what* sanctions . . . should be imposed for a [Rule 11] violation." . . .

. . . .

The sanction of dismissal meets the requisite criteria in this case, given the egregious nature of Jimenez's conduct. Jimenez's claim was so unmeritorious and her behavior so deceptive that the filing of her baseless claim amounted to a veritable attack on our system of justice. Although Jimenez believes the district court's order of dismissal was an abuse of discretion, the only abuses ascertainable in this case were those committed by her counsel and Jimenez herself. By bringing "false, fraudulent and salacious charges of discrimination" against Defendants, Jimenez exploited the judicial process and subjected her former colleagues and employer to unnecessary embarrassment and mental anguish. . . . .

The College has filed a Motion for Appellate Sanctions under Rule 38 of the Federal Rules of Appellate Procedure. Pursuant to Rule 38, we may award just damages and single or double costs to Appellee as a sanction against Appellant for filing a frivolous appeal. An appeal is "frivolous" if its "result is foreordained by the lack of substance to the appellant's arguments."

The appeal in the instant case is patently frivolous. In spite of the trial judge's finding that they had submitted "obviously fraudulent documents" to the court, and had perpetrated "the most blatant example of a Rule 11 violation that [she had ever] seen," Jimenez and Nunnery had the audacity to file an appeal from the trial court's sanction. The "foreordination" of Jimenez's failure on appeal could not have been more obvious. Not only did Jimenez cite to the wrong legal standard in her brief before this Court, she presented only *one page* of legal argument in her favor. In light of the flagrancy of Jimenez's Rule 11 violation, and the lack of support for her position on appeal, when considering the direct and castigating language reciting parts of the record by the trial judge, we conclude that appellate sanctions are appropriate in this case.

As far as the amount of attorneys' fees is concerned, the College has presented affidavits attesting that its counsel has incurred $17,156.99 in costs and expenses since the filing of this appeal. The College's counsel has not, however, given a specific breakdown of those fees and costs. Despite its claim to have spent over 125 hours dealing with legal matters connected to this appeal, counsel has made no effort to inform the Court exactly *what* was done during those 125 hours. Indeed, such time estimates are surprisingly high in light of the simplicity of the legal issues presented to this Court.

We are not satisfied with the vague documentation of costs and expenses heretofore provided by the College's counsel. Thus, we order counsel to submit, within the next fifteen days, a more detailed schedule of its time allocation and other expenses incurred in connection with this appeal.

DECISION AND REMEDY The trial court's imposition of sanctions under Rule 11 of the Federal Rules of Civil Procedure was affirmed and the Motion for Rule 38 Appellate Sanctions was granted.

CRITICAL THINKING: PUBLIC POLICY Why should the courts have authority to dismiss cases without a trial when one side to the controversy would like to have her or his day in court?

Pretrial Hearing. Either party or the court can request a **pretrial hearing**, sometimes called a *conference*. Usually, the hearing follows discovery and consists of an informal discussion among the judge and the opposing attorneys.

The hearing serves to identify and narrow the subject matter that is in dispute and to plan the course of the trial. The pretrial hearing is not intended to compel the parties to settle their case before trial, although judges may encourage them to settle out of court if circumstances suggest that a trial would be a waste of time.

The Trial. A trial procedurally consists of several steps from start to finish. It results when the parties are unable to reach a settlement outside of court. Although many lawsuits are filed, about 95 percent of these are settled out of court, mainly because of the time and expense of trying a case. Furthermore, of those cases that finally do reach trial, about 97 percent are resolved at the trial court level. Relatively few trial court decisions are appealed.

Jury Selection. A trial can be held with or without a jury. Most federal trials are held without a jury. Either party may request a jury, but many cases are tried without one. If there is no jury, the judge determines the truth of the facts alleged in the case. In most states and in federal courts, one of the parties in a civil trial must request a jury; otherwise the right to a jury is waived. Remember, when a person is suing for monetary damages, he or she is entitled to a jury. If the lawsuit is for equitable relief, no jury is allowed. See Chapter 1 on the differences between courts of law and courts of equity.

If a party or parties request a jury, the jury members are selected from a panel of citizens who have been ordered by the court to jury duty. The jury panel members (prospective jurors) are subject to *voir dire* (questions) from the judge and from the attorneys for the parties. The questions are asked to determine if any potential jury member has a bias toward one side, has any connection with the parties, or is unable to serve for the length of the trial. In significant cases, attorneys may use a psychologist or jury consultant to help them select jury members. Jurors who are selected to hear the case are paid a small daily fee and mileage. Normally, the losing party pays these costs.

As a result of the questions asked during *voir dire*, prospective jury members may be dismissed from serving on a jury for a particular trial. For example, if a prospective jury member admits that she has read about the case in the newspaper and has formed an opinion about it, the juror may be **challenged for cause**. A challenge for cause means that one party objects to a particular prospective jury member for a justifiable reason. Unlimited challenges for cause are allowed for each party.

A **peremptory challenge** occurs when a juror is dismissed without a stated reason. The number of peremptory challenges allowed varies from state to state but usually is around three. Each side is limited to the same number of peremptory challenges. These challenges, however, must be exercised with caution, because excluding minorities is unconstitutional.

In the case between Copiers and Artiste, both parties want a jury trial. After the jurors are selected, they are impaneled and sworn in. Then the trial is ready to begin.

Opening Statements. Both attorneys are allowed to make opening statements concerning the facts that they expect to prove during the trial. The plaintiff's attorney gives the first opening statement, followed by the defendant's opening statement. Opening statements are not evidence.

Rules of Evidence. Formal rules of evidence adopted by the courts ensure a fair hearing. The judge rules on the admissibility of all evidence, which must be material, relevant, and reliable. For example, Copiers cannot introduce evidence that Lakin has been married five times, has fifteen children, and was convicted of jaywalking twenty years ago because none of this information is material or relevant to the issue of whether Artiste purchased and paid for the copier.

Cases are decided by both direct and circumstantial evidence. Direct evidence shows the existence of facts in question without the need for additional evidence. A witness may testify, for example, that she saw Lakin using the copier at Artiste's main office. Circumstantial evidence consists of facts or circumstances from which the existence or nonexistence of a fact at issue may be inferred. Proof that Artiste mailed out 100,000 copies of an advertisement produced on a copy machine would be circumstantial evidence that the copier was functioning properly.

Information can be kept out of the trial if it qualifies as one of several types of exceptions, such as *hearsay evidence* or *privileged information*. **Hearsay evidence** is out-of-court information given by someone other than the witness to prove the truth of a contested fact. For example, as a witness for Copiers, Jose may be asked while he is on the stand to testify that he had a conversation with Liz, Lakin's neighbor, who said that Lakin told her that he was "going to get the copier for Artiste without having to pay for it." Liz's words, as quoted by Jose, are hearsay. The proper person to call as a witness would be Liz, who can testify as to her own conversation with Lakin.

Information also can be kept out of a trial if it can be categorized by the court as **privileged information**. By recognizing a privilege, the court protects a relationship in which confidential communication is very important. The best example of privileged information is the attorney–client relationship. Most communications between a person and her or his lawyer cannot be disclosed in court or anywhere else. Only the client may waive this right. This privilege encourages full communication between lawyers and clients so that attorneys can represent their clients to the best of their abilities during legal proceedings.

InfoTrac Research Activity

A large volume of business is conducted using e-mail. Go to InfoTrac and type in "electronic mail systems." Find articles concerning a business's liability for e-mail that involves racial or sexual harassment. Discuss the liability issues and how a business can limit its liability.

The common law has long recognized the physician-patient privilege, the husband–wife privilege, and the priest–penitent privilege. Other privileges are based on rules adopted by the court or by statute, such as the accountant–client or the media reporter–

LEGAL HIGHLIGHT

Attorney–Client Privilege or What You Cannot Tell Your Attorney

Our judicial system has long recognized the attorney-client privilege. This privilege protects communications between a lawyer and a client so that the lawyer may represent the client with full knowledge of all the facts. These private conversations cannot be disclosed in court without the client's consent. A major exception to this rule exists, however.

Communications by the client that she or he is about to engage in a crime can be disclosed in court if the discussion occurs prior to the wrongful act. For example, a conversation with a lawyer in which a client sought advice about how to hide assets fraudulently before filing bankruptcy would not be a privileged conversation. This communication could be introduced into evidence against the client in a subsequent trial. In other words, the attorney–client privilege applies to conversations that occur after the wrongdoing. It does not allow persons to include their attorneys in making plans to carry out crimes and then claim the attorney-client privilege regarding what was said during the planning sessions. Attorneys who do not report such conversations are ethically impaired and are subject to criminal prosecution as accessories to the crime.

---

informer privilege. During the past decade, many exceptions to the privilege rules have been made by statutory provisions or court rules.[2]

Now that we have examined some rules of evidence, it is time for the trial to begin.

Plaintiff's Case. Since Copiers is the plaintiff, it carries the burden of proving its case. After opening statements, Copiers' attorney calls the first witness for the plaintiff and then examines the witness in what is called *direct examination.* After Copiers' attorney has finished, the witness may be *cross-examined* by Artiste's attorney. After cross-examination, Copiers' attorney has an opportunity to ask the witness further questions, called *redirect examination.*

When both attorneys have finished with the first witness, Copiers' attorney calls the succeeding witnesses in its case. Each witness is first examined by Copiers' attorney and then is subject to cross-examination by Artiste's attorney (and redirect, if necessary). Witnesses normally do not hear each other testify to prevent collusion or to prevent the tainting of the evidence being presented.

The rules of evidence govern the types of questions that the attorneys can ask and the way in which they can be asked. After the last of the plaintiff's witnesses has been examined, the plaintiff rests its case.

[2]The Federal Rules of Civil Procedure and the Federal Rules of Evidence can be found at http://www.law.cornell.edu.

Defendant's Case. Artiste's attorney then presents the evidence and witnesses for its case. Witnesses for the defense are called and examined, and the attorney for Copiers has a right to cross-examine them. Artiste's attorney has the right to redirect each witness. Evidence favorable to Artiste is introduced. After all evidence has been presented and all witnesses dismissed, Artiste rests its case.

When the defendant's attorney has finished the presentation of evidence, the plaintiff's attorney can present, within certain bounds, additional evidence to refute the defendant's case in a rebuttal. The defendant's attorney can meet that evidence in a rejoinder.

Burden of Proof. During any trial, the plaintiff has the burden of proof, which is a measure of the quality of evidence presented by the plaintiff. Two standards of proof are used in civil courts, while only one standard is used in criminal courts. When thinking of the burden of proof, think of the scales of justice held by the Statue of Justice.

The burden of proof differs for each of the two types of civil courts, courts of law and courts of equity. For example, Copiers sues in a court of law seeking monetary damages. Copiers' burden of proof is to establish its case by a **preponderance of the evidence**. The plaintiff presents enough evidence that the defendant has not overcome, such that the scales of the Statue of Justice are tipped slightly toward the plaintiff.

In a court of equity, Copiers seeks an equitable remedy. Copiers is required to prove its case with a higher degree of evidence, sometimes called **clear and convincing evidence**. The plaintiff must present more evidence than needed by a preponderance of the evidence, but less than that needed in criminal cases. The plaintiff must prove its case with evidence that goes beyond a well-founded doubt. The scales of the Statue of Justice are tipped clearly toward the plaintiff.

In a criminal case, however, the prosecution must prove the defendant guilty **beyond a reasonable doubt**. The jury must be fully convinced the defendant committed the crime, not that he is probably guilty or is likely guilty. The scales of the Statue of Justice do not need to tip all the way toward the prosecution, but nearly all the way.

Motions for Directed Verdicts. After the plaintiff's case has been presented, the defendant's attorney may ask the judge to direct a verdict on the grounds that the plaintiff has failed to present a sufficient case for jury consideration. Thus, there can be only one verdict as a matter of law—for the defendant. This motion for a directed verdict rarely is granted at this stage of the trial.

After the defendant's case has been presented, either attorney may move for a directed verdict. If the judge determines that the evidence presented by either side is so persuasive that a reasonable jury could only decide for that party, the motion will be granted. Typically, these motions are denied, and the case proceeds to a jury verdict.

Closing Arguments. After both sides have rested their cases, each attorney presents a closing argument, urging a verdict in favor of her client. The plaintiff has the burden of proof and therefore is the first party to present its closing argument. The defendant follows and makes its closing argument. The plaintiff then may rebut the defendant's closing argument.

Jury Instructions and Deliberations. The judge instructs the jury (if it is a jury trial) in the law that applies to the case. The instructions to the jury are called *charges*. Then the jury retires to the jury room to deliberate and deliver a verdict (that is, to make and present the decision).

Jury Verdict and Judgment. In *Copiers v. Artiste,* the jury will have to weigh the evidence and not only decide the case but also, if it finds for the plaintiff, decide the amount of money owed. The jury delivers its verdict, which is converted into a judgment once the judge signs the document that names the prevailing party and the amount to be paid.

Motion for a Judgment Notwithstanding the Verdict (J.N.O.V.). After the jury returns the verdict, a motion for a judgment notwithstanding the verdict (j.n.o.v.) can be filed with the trial judge to overturn the jury's verdict. This motion gives the judge the opportunity to decide as a matter of law that after consideration of all the evidence, the jury erred in its decision. This motion usually is denied by the trial judge. If granted, however, a judgment will be entered for the party filing the motion.

Motion for New Trial. At the end of the trial, the losing party can move to set aside the adverse verdict and to have a new trial. The motion will be granted if the trial judge is convinced, after looking at the evidence, that the verdict was in error. A new trial also can be granted on the grounds of newly discovered evidence, misconduct by the participants during the trial, or judge's error.

The Appeal. A notice of appeal must be filed within the prescribed time. If Copiers is the losing party at the trial and decides to appeal, Copiers becomes the **appellant** (the party appealing the case to a higher court) and Artiste becomes the **appellee** (the party defending the appeal).

Copiers' attorney will file the record on appeal with the court of appeals. The appeal contains (1) the pleadings, (2) a transcript of the trial testimony and copies of the exhibits, (3) the judge's rulings on motions made by the parties, (4) the arguments of counsel, (5) the instructions to the jury, (6) the verdict, (7) the post-trial motions, and (8) the judgment or order being appealed.

The state usually requires the person appealing, here Copiers, to post a bond, that is, to pay money or property as one of the steps to file the appeal. If the person appealing prevails at the appellate court, the money is returned. If the person loses the case, the money is paid over to the court or to the other party, depending on law, as reimbursement for the expenses incurred.

Appellate courts do not hear any evidence. Their decision concerning a case is based on the abstracts, the record, and the briefs. The attorneys can present oral arguments, after which the case is taken under advisement. When the court has reached a decision, the decision is written. The writing contains the opinion (the court's reasons for its decision) and the rules of law that apply.

In general, the appellate courts do not reverse findings of fact unless the findings are unsupported or contradicted by the evidence. Rather, these courts review the record for errors of law. If the reviewing court believes that an error was committed during the trial or that the jury was instructed improperly, the judgment will be reversed. Sometimes the case will be remanded for a new trial. Most decisions of the lower court are affirmed, resulting in enforcement of that court's judgment.

Enforcement of Judgments. Once a judgment has been finalized, the party who has been awarded the judgment wants to be able to collect or enforce it. Several procedures exist for the successful party to enforce the judgment against the losing party, if it does not comply. These procedures are discussed in Chapter 14.

Attorneys' Fees and Other Costs

A lawsuit involves a number of expenses. The parties must pay court costs of filing fees, service of process fees, discovery costs, expert witness fees, and fees for the court reporter. These costs are in addition to possible attorneys' fees.

Attorneys' Fees

In our judicial system, people can represent themselves, but that option is not recommended. Most people involved in a lawsuit hire an attorney. Three basic ways to pay attorneys are by the hour, by the type of work performed, or on a contingency fee basis. Fees per hour depend on the location and type of work being performed. Generally, fees range from $100 to $500 per hour. Contracts, probate, and defense are types of work for which lawyers normally charge by the hour.

Lawyers also can charge for the type of work performed, such as for a standard will. An attorney drafts the will based largely on standard clauses that are stored on the computer and arranges for the clients to sign the will in front of witnesses. The attorney may charge a flat rate of $150 for anyone who needs only the standard-form will. Another common variation of a flat fee is a law firm's pricing by units of work. For example, a firm may charge $500 for the preparation of an initial complaint involving a simple commercial problem or may charge $10 per question to answer interrogatories.

Some attorneys are hired on a contingency fee basis. If the plaintiff is successful at trial, she pays a percentage of the judgment to the attorney. Normally, this percentage is one-third of the judgment. The plaintiff is not responsible for compensating the attorney if the case is lost. The plaintiff is responsible, however, for paying all court costs, such as filing fees and discovery costs.

Contingency fee arrangements are used particularly in negligence lawsuits, such as those involving an automobile accident. The plaintiff retains a lawyer by agreeing to pay the lawyer one-third of any recovery made through settlement or from any judgment in the plaintiff's favor if the lawsuit goes to trial. Normally, the defendant who caused the accident is represented by attorneys hired by the defendant's insurance company. These attorneys are paid by the hour, whether the defendant prevails or loses the lawsuit.

The concept of contingent fees has been criticized. This criticism is particularly directed to the large settlements in class action cases. These cases are filed on behalf of a large number of potential victims. In the 1990s, large awards were paid to lawyers who initiated class actions on behalf of victims. For example, one case against Toshiba alleged a defect in the floppy disk controllers of their computers. The consumers each received an individual payment ranging from $210 to $440. The lawyers were paid $147.5 million.

In another example, a law firm received $70 million to handle just one state's claims against the tobacco companies. The state, however, will eventually receive 2.9 billion from this litigation. The justification for these fees is that the lawyers are not paid, unless the case is successful in court. Contingency fees level the playing field so a person without money can file a lawsuit against a billion-dollar corporation and hold it accountable for the injuries or damages it caused.

Other Costs

In any lawsuit, one of the most expensive procedures is that of conducting discovery. Sometimes the cost of discovery is more than the amount being litigated. Some law firms make it a standard practice, in both large and small cases, to request from the opposing side answers to a thousand or more written interrogatories. Depositions are held with witnesses who have only minimum knowledge of the facts. The end result is a delay in trials because of the time required for discovery. These delays increase costs.

To correct this situation, several state supreme courts have adopted two measures: *limited discovery* and *full disclosure*. With limited discovery, the depositions are restricted to the parties and, sometimes, essential witnesses. The length of a deposition is limited to a maximum of four to six hours. The number of expert witnesses for each issue is limited to one per side. An expert witness is a specialist in a particular field and is able to testify about matters relating to her expertise at trial. Finally, only a limited number of interrogatories are allowed, usually thirty to fifty questions.

All parties are required to fully disclose evidence, even when that evidence might be damaging to them. To ensure compliance, the court penalizes the party failing to fully disclose by not allowing its witnesses and exhibits to be presented during the trial. The federal court system is experimenting with full disclosure between the parties.

The Judiciary

On center stage in any trial or appeal is the judge, the person responsible for overseeing the proceedings and for making the final decision in the case. The following sections discuss the selection procedures for the state and federal judiciary.

State Judicial Selection Procedures

Judicial selection varies from state to state. All judges, however, are selected either by election or by merit for a specific term, usually four to six years.

Many states still elect judges to the bench. Opponents of this process claim that it introduces politics into the judiciary. Supporters, however, claim that elections make the judiciary accountable to the public.

Judicial merit selection systems were created as an alternative to elections to ensure a more independent judiciary. Under a judicial merit selection system, applicants apply for an opening on the bench. After a committee reviews the applications, several names are sent to the governor, who then appoints one person from the list.

Judges who are appointed under the merit system stand for **retention** at regular elections. To stand for retention means that the judge's name appears on the ballot unopposed. If the judge is retained, he or she continues on the job. If the judge is not retained, a new judge is selected through the judicial merit selection system.

Federal Judicial Selection Procedures

No formal requirement, such as being a lawyer, exists for a person who wants to serve as a judge at the federal level. When a vacancy occurs in the federal court system, U.S. senators and others recommend candidates for the position to the president. The president selects from a list of candidates and appoints one. That person's name is forwarded to the Senate for confirmation. The Senate holds hearings and either confirms or denies the appointment.

Under Article III, federal judges "hold their Offices during Good Behavior," and not for life as commonly believed. Congress does have the power to impeach judges, but rarely has this been done. Federal judges (with few exceptions, such as bankruptcy court judges who are appointed for a fifteen-year time period) hold virtually lifetime appointments.

U.S. Magistrate Judges

The concept of a magistrate was established in the federal judiciary with the Judiciary Act of 1789. Today, a U.S. magistrate judge is a special jurisdiction judge. He or she holds a position created by the Federal Magistrates Act of 1968. A magistrate is now officially called a *magistrate judge*.

A magistrate judge is a judicial officer appointed by the federal district court to assist in administering some of its functions. The magistrate judge has the authority to conduct many pretrial proceedings and to try minor federal criminal offenses and certain civil cases. For example, a person arrested for speeding in a national park would fall under a magistrate judge's jurisdiction.

International Consideration

Different Legal Systems in Foreign Trade

Procedures to enforce an individual's legal rights internationally differ greatly from country to country. Today, most European countries operate under the civil law system. The civil law system is based on statutes that can be traced back to the Roman emperor, Justinian 1, in A.D. 500.

Under the civil law system, if no statute covers a given topic, the judge acts more like an attorney in developing a case. The legislature—or, in some countries, the executive—is the dominant force in a civil law system. A civil law judge cannot create law, as judges do under the common law system.

The common law system developed in England is the legal system used in many of the former English colonies such as Australia, Canada, and the United States. Under the common law system, the judge is neutral and independent of the parties suing before the court. The judge makes law that must be followed. The legislature also adopts statutes, but in the United States these statutes are subject to judicial interpretation.

Other countries, such as Iran and Saudi Arabia, follow Islamic law. These countries have adopted commercial law codes, but these laws must be interpreted in light of the Koran, a religious document similar in comprehensiveness to the Bible, and by the Sharia, which interprets the Koran. These interpretations have not been changed in nearly a thousand years. Non-Islamic businesspeople must be sensitive to religion's role in Islamic countries.

Businesspeople must appreciate that different cultures have different ways of making, deciding, and applying laws. In addition, the laws may be applied differently to foreigners than to natives before the courts. Foreign legislative and judicial bodies often operate differently from those of the American legal system.

Any country in the world community may utilize the **International Court of Justice (ICJ)**. Located at the Hague in the Netherlands, the ICJ is the principal judicial organ of the United Nations. The ICJ does not handle private disputes between citizens, such as commercial disputes, but matters between countries, which may involve individual citizens.

The ICJ decides cases submitted by U.N. members and renders opinions on legal questions at the request of authorized international organizations. The court is composed of fifteen judges elected by the U.N. General Assembly and the Security Council. Judges serve a nine-year term, with one-third of the judges elected every three years. The jurisdiction of the court depends on the consent of the nations that are the parties to the cases before it. The ICJ has jurisdiction over a sovereign nation only if, and only to the extent that, the nation has agreed that the ICJ shall have jurisdiction covering that particular factual situation.

PRACTICAL TIPS

How to Find an Attorney

How do you find a competent attorney when you need one? The best method, and the oldest one, is to ask your friends and acquaintances. A good attorney has a good reputation. Word-of-mouth recommendations, even in this age of high technology, still are very reliable.

The Yellow Pages of your telephone directory provide a second source. Most attorneys specialize in a certain legal area, such as real estate, bankruptcy, or taxation. Many lawyers indicate their bar specialty in advertisements. A licensed attorney can place her or his name under most specialty headings without having passed any special examinations and without having experience in that particular field. You will have a better chance of finding a knowledgeable attorney if you identify a bar-certified lawyer who is listed only under the heading of the specialty that you need.

Most local bar associations have a referral service. Attorneys register their area of expertise with the bar association. You can have an initial interview with these attorneys for a small fee.

Finally, certain books, such as the *Martindale-Hubbell Law Directory*, often available in local libraries, list attorneys and their specialties.[3] They list the lawyer's specialty, age, gender, and years of practice; the schools from which the lawyer was graduated; and a list of the partners in the law firm.

A good practice is to speak with several attorneys before deciding to retain one. It is very important that you and the attorney have a good working relationship. Ask about the attorney's fees and other costs involved, the time required to resolve the case, whether the case will go to court or be settled, and the anticipated settlement terms. When you interview a lawyer, be prepared with a list of questions, just as you would for any other business appointment. Before you retain an attorney, clarify payment procedures and have them reduced to a signed agreement.

[3]The *Martindale-Hubbell Law Directory* is available on the Web at http://www.martindale.com.

Checklist

✔ *Recommendations* Check with friends and acquaintances who might have had a similar legal problem. Ask for the name of their attorney and whether they were satisfied with the representation. If they were dissatisfied with the attorney's services, find out the name of the opposing attorney.

✔ *Yellow Pages* Look in the Yellow Pages of your telephone directory under the area of expertise that you need.

✔ *Bar Association* Call the state or local county bar association to obtain names of lawyers who are certified in that special area or who handle a large number of cases in that area of the law.

✔ *Library* Go to your local library and look in directories that list attorneys by their specialties.

Chapter Summary

Before a court can act, it must have jurisdiction over the person or the property to be acted on. The court may have *in personam* jurisdiction (personal jurisdiction) of a person or business. *In rem* jurisdiction or *quasi in rem* jurisdiction provides the court with jurisdiction over property located within its jurisdiction.

Within the United States, there are at least fifty-two separate court systems including one for each of the fifty states, for the District of Columbia, and for the federal government. The U.S. Constitution provides for the Supreme Court and any other federal courts as Congress shall designate. Congress has created the federal system with at least one federal district court in each state and U.S. courts of appeal to handle their appeals. To fall under the jurisdiction of the federal courts, a case must involve either a federal question or diversity of citizenship involving $75,000 or more in controversy.

Actions begin by filing a complaint and having a summons issued by the court. Once these are served on the defendant, the defendant must file an answer within a specific time period or have a default judgment rendered against her. The defendant also may bring a counterclaim against the plaintiff, which, in turn, requires a reply. During the course of the lawsuit, either party may bring appropriate motions.

Prior to trial, discovery occurs by either oral depositions or written interrogatories. The plaintiff carries the burden of proof at the trial. The plaintiff always introduces evidence first. Once both parties have presented all the evidence, the case is submitted to the jury for a verdict or to the judge if there is no jury.

The jury or judge is the trier of fact. The losing party may appeal the decision. The reviewing court usually will not reverse the trial court's decision unless an error of law occurred in the trial process.

Filing a lawsuit involves many different types of expenses. These costs involve attorneys' fees, filing fees, service of process fees, discovery costs, expert witness fees, and fees for the court reporter. An attorney may be paid by one of three methods. The attorney may charge by the hour or by the type of work performed. In some types of cases, the attorney is paid on a contingency fee basis; thus, if the plaintiff is not successful at the trial, the attorney does not receive any compensation. If the plaintiff prevails at the trial, the attorney is paid based on a percentage of the judgment under a contingency fee contract.

Two methods are used to select state judges: election or merit. Federal judges are nominated by the president and are confirmed by the senate for a term of good behavior.

Using the World Wide Web

The United States Supreme Court has its own Web page that contains information concerning its history, visiting the Court, and other related sites. Supreme Court cases are available for Web site publication immediately after finalization by the Court. The cases are also published in unofficial form on a number of Web sites including Findlaw and media home pages.

Each federal court of appeals, specialized courts, and district courts has its own Web site. The content varies for each court. To access the district courts, use the Web site for the Federal Judiciary home page.

For *Web Activities*, links to Web sites mentioned in the chapter, and additional Web sites that relate to the chapter topics, go to **http://bohlman.westbuslaw.com**, click on "Internet Applications," and select Chapter 3.

Web Activities

Go to **http://bohlman.westbuslaw.com**, click on "Internet Applications," and select Chapter 3.
3–1 Federal Court of Appeals
3–2 State Supreme Court

Key Terms

adversary system
affirmative defense
answer
appellant
appellate jurisdiction
appellee
beyond a reasonable
   doubt
challenge for cause
clear and convincing
   evidence
complaint
concurrent jurisdiction
counterclaim
courts of appeal
cross-claim
default judgment
demurrer

deposition
discovery
diversity of citizenship
due process clause
exclusive jurisdiction
federal question case
full faith and credit
   clause
general jurisdiction
hearsay evidence
in personam (personal)
   jurisdiction
in rem jurisdiction
International Court of
   Justice (ICJ)
interrogatories
jurisdiction
limited jurisdiction

long-arm statute
motion
motion to dismiss
original jurisdiction
peremptory challenge
personal jurisdiction
petition
plead
pleading
preponderance of the
   evidence
pretrial hearing
privileged information
process
quasi in rem jurisdiction
reply
request for physical or
   mental examination

request to produce
res judicata
response
retention
stay
subject matter
   jurisdiction
subpoena
subpoena *duces tecum*
summary judgment
summons
third-party complaint
venue
voir dire
writ of *certiorari*

Questions and Case Problems

3–1 Court System The U.S. court system has two types of courts: courts with original jurisdiction and those with appellate jurisdiction. Describe the differences between the two systems.

3–2 Jurisdiction Discuss the differences among *in personam* jurisdiction, *in rem* jurisdiction, and *quasi in rem* jurisdiction.

3–3 Federal Jurisdiction Discuss the two types of lawsuits heard in federal courts.

3–4 Appellate Review Discuss the most common method of appellate review exercised by the Supreme Court.

3–5 Civil Procedure Discuss the differences between pleadings and process.

3–6 Judiciary In state judicial systems, judges serve specific terms in office, whereas federal judges serve for a term of good behavior. Compare the two systems. Based on constitutional and public policy grounds, which system seems better?

3–7 Jurisdiction Marvin, a resident of Alabama, was walking near a busy street in Birmingham when a large crate fell off a passing truck and hit him. Marvin received numerous injuries that resulted in large medical expenses and a great deal of pain and suffering. He lost six months of work. He wants to sue the trucking firm for $300,000. The firm's headquarters is in Mississippi, although the company does business in Alabama. Should Marvin bring his lawsuit in an Alabama state court, a Mississippi state court, or a federal district court located in Alabama or Mississippi? Explain your answer.

3–8 Jurisdiction In late 1993, Mid-America Tablewares, Inc., decided to produce and sell a dinnerware line to accompany its Harvest Festival table linen line. In May 1994, Mid-America entered into a contract with Mogi Trading Company, Ltd., whereby it was to provide dinnerware for Mid-America. Mogi was a Japanese corporation with its main place of business in Japan. It was in the business of contracting for the manufacture of ceramic dinnerware from several manufacturers. Prior to entering the contract, the parties exchanged a considerable number of communications and one visit was made by Masaichi Tsuchiya, a Mogi representative, to Mid-America's place of business. In one exchange, Mid-America emphasized the importance of complying with the Food and Drug Administration's (FDA) lead regulations. Tsuchiya faxed a response, discussing the lead issue, and specifically represented that Mogi's goods always met FDA standards. Shortly after Mogi purchased the Harvest Festival dinnerware from a manufacturer, it was shipped to Mid-America. In July 1994, the FDA determined that the dinnerware had unacceptably high lead levels and thereby exceeded FDA regulatory guidance levels. On being informed of the FDA's test results, Mid-America stopped selling it and began the process of recalling all the dinnerware. Mid-America sued Mogi in U.S. District Court, invoking the court's diversity jurisdiction. Mogi claimed that the court lacked jurisdiction. What was the result and why? [*Mid-America Tablewares, Inc. v. Mogi Trading Co.*, 100 F.3d 1353 (7th Cir. 1996)]

3–9 Jurisdiction Rudzewicz, an experienced and sophisticated businessperson, signed a twenty-year franchise contract in 1979 with Burger King Corporation to operate a restaurant in Michigan. He obligated himself to pay $1 million over the twenty-year period. At first business was steady, but when a recession hit, patronage declined, and Rudzewicz fell behind in his payments. After extended negotiations, Burger King filed a lawsuit in 1981. Burger King is a Florida corporation with its main offices in Miami. The franchise contract provided that the franchise relationship was established in Miami and governed by Florida law. All fees and notices were to be sent to the Miami headquarters. Rudzewicz claimed that he was a Michigan resident, that he had not been to Florida, that the claim did not arise in Florida, and that, therefore, the district court lacked personal jurisdiction. Should the case be dismissed in Florida? Explain your answer. [*Burger King Corp. v. Rudzewicz*, 471 U.S. 462, 105 S. Ct. 2174, 85 L. Ed. 528 (1985)]

3–10 Internet The Arizona judicial branch has a comprehensive Web site. Under the section of Public Information & Assistance is a link to jury duty. Which three courts can call a person to jury duty? Who is eligible for jury duty? Can a person be automatically excused from jury duty? When is person exempt from jury duty? The Arizona Web site is found at **http://www.supremestate.az.us**. Find your own state court Web site by using the Web site **http://www.firstgov.gov** and answer the questions for jury duty in your state.

Chapter 4

Alternative Dispute Resolution Procedures

All disputes (if unhappily any should arise) shall be decided by three impartial and intelligent men, known for their probity and good understanding, two to be chosen by the disputants, each having the choice of one, and the third by those two, which three men thus chosen shall, unfettered by law or legal constructions, declare their sense of the testator's intention, and such decision is, to all intents and purposes, to be binding on the parties as if it had been given in the Supreme Court of the United States.

> **George Washington, 1732–1799**
> First president of the United States of America, 1789–1797
> Last Will and Testament

Discourage litigation. Persuade your neighbors to compromise whenever you can. Point out to them how the nominal winner is often a real loser— in fees, expenses, and waste of time. As a peace-maker the lawyer has a superior opportunity of being a good man. There will still be business enough.

> **Abraham Lincoln, 1809–1865**
> Sixteenth president of the United States of America, 1861–1865
> "Notes for a Law Lecture," *The Collected Works of Abraham Lincoln*, edited by Roy P. Basler, Vol. II (July 1, 1850), p. 81

Chapter Outline

Ethical Consideration

Full Disclosure in Arbitration?

A homeowner signed a contract with a builder to build a new home. A dispute arose between the homeowner and the building contractor. Among the many items under dispute, the homeowner claimed that the contractor failed to install below-surface drains as specified in the building plans. She came to you because she wanted to file a lawsuit against the contractor.

You reviewed the contract between the builder and your client. A clause in the contract required that all disputes be resolved by arbitration.

Arbitration is a formal procedure used by parties to resolve disputes. Used in place of a lawsuit, arbitration is a nonjudicial way to quickly and inexpensively resolve disputes. Each party submits its respective evidence in the matter to an impartial third party, called an *arbitrator*.

As you prepared for the arbitration hearing, you came across an old memorandum in the homeowner's handwriting that could be interpreted as acknowledging that she knew the drains had not been installed correctly and that she had relieved the contractor of liability for the drainage system in exchange for some additional work on the new house. When you talk with the homeowner, she states that it is the only copy, and she is sure that the contractor has forgotten about it because it was written during a particularly hectic part of the construction project.

You are aware that discovery procedures prior to arbitration hearings are either nonexistent or are so limited in scope that you probably will not have to involuntarily provide this document to the other side. If this matter were before a regular court, you most likely would be required to turn over a copy of this document to the attorney representing the contractor. Do you have any duty to supply this document to the other side prior to the hearing or at least to present it at the proceeding? Use the ethical model presented in Chapter 2 and reprinted on the inside front cover to develop your answer.

Introduction

Court trials make good material for books, movies, and television shows. Litigation, however, is not the only course of action companies can take when they believe they have a good cause for a lawsuit. Litigation is a stressful ordeal. Companies may find themselves harboring negative feelings toward the opposing party, with whom they may have to continue to do business during the course of the litigation. Of benefit to the company would be a system that allows the company to carry out its business with the opposing party while the dispute is being resolved quickly and inexpensively.

This chapter examines a number of alternative methods of dispute resolution. These different methods each have their strengths and weakness.

Artiste Login. Artiste Login Products, Inc., the online business owned by Carlo and Carlotta, has been involved in several lawsuits during the past few years. They have discovered that lawsuits are unwieldy in terms of money and time for their business. As a litigant, Artiste has had to expend money on attorneys' fees, court fees, and evidence development. Carlo and Carlotta decide to explore methods to resolve disputes that are less expensive and more expeditious than litigation.

Advocates of Alternative Dispute Resolution

The various advocates of **alternative dispute resolution (ADR)** all share the same basic goal: a speedy and just determination of the dispute at a reasonable cost to both parties. The judiciary is one of the strongest advocates of ADR procedures. The late Warren E. Burger, former chief justice of the United States, advocated the development of "mechanisms that can produce an acceptable result in the shortest possible time, with the least possible expense and with a minimum of stress on the participants."

Average citizens' rights are compromised when they must spend thousands of dollars and several years in litigation to obtain a decision, especially for routine cases, such as those involving an automobile accident. More often than not, the case is settled literally in front of the courtroom door after considerable expense, frustration, and years in the judicial system.

The business sector is another strong proponent of alternative dispute resolution procedures. Businesspersons need expeditious justice at a reasonable cost. They often need to be able to maintain a business relationship with the opponent while resolving a particular dispute. Most disputes between businesses involve a contractual problem. People in business accept that disputes are inevitable. Even when a written contract is drawn carefully, problems will arise over the interpretation of a clause or over a disputed set of facts. Disputes over manufacturing delays, merchandise quality, contract performance, and other such misunderstandings are bound to arise.

Once a dispute occurs, most businesspeople prefer to resolve the dispute quickly, privately, inexpensively, and informally. Maintaining a business relationship while involved in litigation is very difficult, if not impossible. To preserve goodwill, most businesspeople are in favor of alternative dispute resolution procedures that will be fair, inexpensive, and quick, but that also will arrive at a just result.

The public has a great interest in reducing the caseload handled by the judiciary. Most cases in court are routine in nature and rarely involve great legal issues. Like businesspeople, the public wants fair, inexpensive, and quick procedures to settle routine legal problems. The field of ADR is evolving, and parties facing disputes may create new forms of ADR. The next sections look at the various types of ADR.

Negotiation, Conciliation, and Mediation

The most common form of ADR is negotiation, which is the foundation for conciliation and mediation. Arbitration, minitrials, short trials, and the use of private judges are more formal procedures that result in a decision. Discussed first are the three informal types of ADR: negotiation, conciliation, and mediation.

Negotiation

Negotiation is the process in which two or more persons meet to discuss their differences and attempt to arrive at a settlement acceptable to both. Negotiation is a technique used to resolve a dispute, not to win an argument. Although reasonableness cannot be ensured by using negotiation, people can use it to engage in joint problem solving through cooperative behavior and to arrive at a mutually acceptable agreement.

All parties should win in a successful negotiation. If only one party gains and the other loses completely, the loser has no vested interest in making sure that the agreement will work. In fact, it is human nature to try to sabotage a forced agreement. Negotiation is both a skill that can be learned and an art form to be practiced.

Negotiation is an integral part of all alternative dispute resolution procedures. It is not, by itself, an ADR procedure in any formal sense. No ADR procedure, however, could exist without negotiation. In fact, the act of filing a lawsuit may in itself be a negotiating technique. Negotiation is by far the best dispute resolution technique because the parties arrive at a solution that they design themselves.

Negotiation Skills. As important a skill as negotiation is, many people are inexperienced at it. Primary or secondary schools rarely teach bargaining or negotiating and these skills often are not addressed even at the college or university level. As a result, people generally have poorly developed negotiating skills.

American businesses at the retail level have disregarded negotiation skills that otherwise are valuable in purchasing and selling at the commercial level. To set a retail price rather than spend time negotiating a price is more efficient and less costly for the business and for the consumer. The quick purchase of an item frees the consumer to spend his time performing other tasks. While the modern business world values efficiency, other cultures value and develop the skills of social contact and bargaining that go along with negotiations. This personal contact is especially useful when businesses deal with one another.

For example, the price of clothing at a department store, food at a grocery store or restaurant, or a night's stay in a motel is rarely subject to negotiation in the American culture. Prices for these items can be negotiated legally, unless a statute sets a price, which today is rare. Consumers, however, rarely take advantage of this freedom to negotiate.

Negotiating skills are necessary in the business world. For example, a customer purchases merchandise, becomes dissatisfied with it, and decides to return it. The customer would like a full cash refund. The businessperson must decide whether to accept the merchandise back and, if the merchandise is returnable, whether to offer credit toward the purchase of additional products from the store or a full refund. Both parties want different results. But to settle this situation, both parties should expect to agree to less than their initial expectation.

When Negotiation Occurs. Negotiation may occur at any stage of a dispute. If a lawsuit has resulted, this period ranges from the moment the customer purchases the merchandise to the time immediately before the judge renders a decision. In fact, sometimes negotiation of a settlement will occur even after a case has been tried and the judge has entered a judgment.

Most cases filed in any court system are settled through negotiation by the attorneys. Comparatively few cases are litigated fully to the point at which a judge or jury makes the decision. Good-faith negotiation is a necessity; without it, the judicial system would collapse, even if only one-fifth of the lawsuits filed actually went to trial.

Artiste Login. Carlo receives an order to design and create a 100-place set of chinaware with all the serving pieces. The design includes a number of flowers in a variety of colors. The design is approved and the sample pieces are painted, then fired in the kiln. A dispute arises over the color intensity and hues in the newly created pieces. Carlo makes several attempts to satisfy the customer. This type of dispute might be resolved through negotiation.

Conciliation

Conciliation occurs whenever a third party successfully gets conflicting parties to accept an agreement. A conciliator does not take an active part in the negotiations but rather attempts to limit all parties' passions and negative rhetoric. Conciliation is one method for obtaining a negotiated settlement from the parties.

Although conciliation is not used as extensively in this country as in other cultures, it is part of the federal labor law and is used widely in labor disputes. Conciliation is used in many states in divorce actions. When a divorce is filed, one of the parties may request a conciliation hearing, which is similar to marriage counseling.

Mediation

Conciliation brings parties together so that they may reach a settlement through negotiation. A conciliator takes no active role in the negotiation. In **mediation**, an impartial third person, called a mediator, also tries to persuade the parties to discuss their issues and come to a resolution.[1]

If the parties cannot agree on the issues, the mediator will not take an active role in helping the parties come to an agreement. The mediator has no formal position and can be discharged at any time by either party. The mediator does not have the power to make a decision or to force the parties to accept any suggestions or recommendations. Only when the parties come to a final settlement of their differences is mediation successful.[2]

Early mediation intervention allows for a quick solution to the problem before the positions taken by the parties become polarized. Mediation is a first step that allows the parties to proceed to arbitration or even to a lawsuit if they cannot work out their differences. Often the parties sign a contract that in case mediation fails, the parties are required to deposit funds to cover the expenses of future arbitration or litigation. Thus, the parties have an incentive to resolve their differences. Mediation does not work when the problem is intractable or the parties are unreasonable. Mediation services are available online.[3]

Judges can use mediation to settle cases before them. First, a judge can send the case to a mediation process that is integrated into the court system. Normally, a non-lawyer mediator is part of the court staff and is trained in facilitating mediation. Second, in a pretrial conference, the judge acts as a mediator to attempt to bring the parties together to reach a negotiated settlement.

The Better Business Bureau uses mediation techniques when it handles complaints between businesses

---

[1]For an excellent discussion of mediation go to http://www.freeadvice.com/law/559us.htm.

[2]Several companies offer mediation and other alternative dispute resolution procedures. One of the largest is JAMS, which can be found at http://www.jamsadr.com.

[3]Go to the Mediation Information & Resource Center to see how mediation works on the Internet. The address is http://www.mediate.com.

and customers. It attempts to bring the two parties together to reach a settlement of their differences. The Magnuson–Moss Warranty Act of 1975 authorizes mediation when a dispute occurs between a consumer and a business over a malfunctioning product or poor quality service.

The Federal Mediation and Conciliation Service (FMCS) provides experienced mediators who serve in disputes between labor and management. If direct negotiations between labor and management on a labor contract break down, the FMCS sends mediators to mediate the dispute. If the parties still are unable to reach an agreement, a strike usually occurs.

Newspapers and radio and television stations may have teams devoted to resolving disputes that their readers or listeners have with a business. Often a person will contact the media to report a problem. A reporter will contact the business with whom the customer has a dispute. Because the media have extensive resources and are very visible, reporters often can contact the person within the business who has the power to resolve the dispute. To avoid bad publicity, most businesses are willing to participate when approached by the media.

Arbitration

Arbitration is a procedure in which the parties to a dispute submit the dispute to an impartial third person, called an **arbitrator**. An arbitrator frequently specializes in arbitrating disputes in a particular area, such as real estate or labor. This person is selected by the parties to make a decision based on evidence that they both submit.[4]

Any and all types of disputes can be arbitrated. Most arbitration situations arise as a result of commercial, construction, employment, insurance, labor, international transactions, and security disputes.[5]

On the surface, arbitration seems to be similar to the judicial system, with a third person resolving the dispute between opposing parties. Major differences do exist, however. Let's compare the two systems.

[4]The Free Advice Web site covers arbitration in great detail: http://www.freeadvice.com/law/557us.htm.
[5]VGIS Communications, Inc., maintains a Web site at http://www.seclaw.com/centers/arbcent.shtml. The name used on this Web site is SEC LAW.com. The site provides a source and rules for conducting arbitration involving disputes between customers and their security brokers.

LEGAL HIGHLIGHT

Code of Ethics for Arbitrators

Arbitrators undertake a serious responsibility to the public, as well as to the parties involved. If the arbitrators do not discharge their duties in good faith and in a diligent manner, the whole system becomes suspect, and the public could lose faith in arbitration. Therefore, arbitration associations have adopted codes of ethics for their arbitrators.

The **American Arbitration Association (AAA)** is one of many private organizations that educates, promotes, researches, and provides the administrative framework for those parties wanting to use ADR methods. The AAA developed the following seven canons in the code of ethics:

1. The arbitrator will uphold the integrity and fairness of the arbitration process.

2. If the arbitrator has an interest or relationship that is likely to affect her or his impartiality or that might create an appearance of partiality or bias, it must be disclosed.

3. An arbitrator, in communicating with the parties, should avoid impropriety or the appearance of it.

4. The arbitrator should conduct the proceedings fairly and diligently.

5. The arbitrator should make decisions in a just, independent, and deliberate manner.

6. The arbitrator should be faithful to the relationship of trust and confidentiality inherent in that office.

7. In a case for which a board of arbitrators is used, each party may select an arbitrator. The arbitrator must ensure that she or he follows all the ethical considerations in this type of situation.

Generally, the arbitrator's decision is final and cannot be appealed. Thus, these canons of ethics help to maintain trust, integrity, and honesty in the arbitration system.

Comparisons between Arbitration and the Judicial System

Few studies comparing arbitration and the judicial system have been made. A potential user of arbitration can consider six factors when comparing arbitration with the judicial system: financial costs, time costs, privacy, formality, selection of the decision maker, and the choice of forum.

Financial Costs. The first comparison between arbitration and the judicial system involves the monetary cost. Government expenditures for running the judicial system vary widely. The cost of a jury trial, including judge, jury members, court reporter, bailiff, clerk, secretary, and physical facilities can average more than $10,000 a day. A person bringing an action in court does not have to pay all of these expenses. But she must pay certain court costs like the filing fee, subpoena and discovery costs, and jury fees, if she is not the prevailing party.

The taxpayers, however, pay a majority of the costs because the court fees paid by the litigants do not cover the actual cost of running the judicial system, such as paying for the construction and maintenance of the courthouses and the salaries of the court personnel, including the judges, clerks, and bailiffs. The time from the filing of a lawsuit to the final disposition of the case always is uncertain and usually is measured in years. As a result, the memories of the witnesses fade and evidence may be destroyed or lost.

Likewise, the cost of arbitration can be expensive. The cost to initiate an arbitration case can be much greater than that for filing a legal action. For example, the filing fee for a court case in Chicago, Illinois, is a flat fee of $221, which does not depend on the value of the case. The cost to start an arbitration case in the same city through the National Arbitration Forum, however, is $800 for a consumer case involving $80,000.

Because the prehearing activities are not as great in arbitration, the attorney fees should be less. In a court case, many pretrial proceedings, such as interrogatories, depositions, and motions, precede the trial. In arbitration, few, if any prehearing activities are conducted. Because of the lack of legal activities, the legal expenses should be lower.

Time Costs. The second comparison between arbitration and the judicial system is the cost factor measured in time. Extremes exist in the processing time of a case, which is measured from the date a lawsuit is filed to the date of its final disposition. In Arizona, this period is less than two years. Contrast Connecticut where the courts were backlogged beyond a five-year period, with more than 60,000 tort cases alone waiting for trial. Half of these cases were pending before the courts in just four cities.

Reasons for Time Lag. Why is the time lag so long in a lawsuit? During a lawsuit, a continuing debate takes place between the attorney representing the plaintiff and the attorney representing the defendant. For example, in a personal injury case, the plaintiff's attorney argues that he or she has little reason to encourage delay. An injured plaintiff must receive and pay for medical care and is often out of work while recovering.

In many cases, the plaintiff's attorney receives compensation from the amount recovered on behalf of the client based on a contingency fee agreement. Therefore, it is in the attorney's best interest to dispose of the case quickly. A practice has developed, however, that once the plaintiff's medical condition has stabilized and the attorneys have finished the discovery stage, each attorney waits for the other attorney to act because neither wants the other to think he or she is afraid of litigating the case.

Unless the judge forces the case to move along, it stalls at this stage until the plaintiff's attorney or the court sets the trial date. Even if the trial date is set early in the case, it will be affected by a rule most courts have: that a lawsuit (including criminal proceedings) must go to trial within a specific time period. As cases pile up, many are in danger of going beyond that time period. Thus, those cases take preference on the trial calendar.

Both sides have a tendency to polarize their positions as the case is processed through the court system. As the case proceeds, the attorneys for the plaintiff and the defendant evaluate the evidence. Often one attorney will make an offer to settle the case. The other attorney will consider the settlement offer and make a recommendation to the client. The party must weigh the settlement offer (money paid now) against the potential of winning or losing a higher amount in a trial held at a later time.

Typically, the first offer is rejected and a counteroffer is made. Between each offer, the attorneys often wait for extended time periods before making the next offer. Only when faced with the decision of actually preparing for trial is a settlement seriously pursued, and even then attorneys usually wait to see if the judge will force early case preparation. A judge can force early case preparation by controlling the court calendar, refusing to allow continuances (postponement) of the case, limiting discovery to a reasonable level, and promoting pretrial settlement conferences.

ADR Time Periods. Statistics on the time it takes for alternative dispute resolution procedures are hard to find because of the wide range of procedures that may be used. The time spent in the court system, however, may be contrasted with the time spent in arbitration where cases can be finalized within 160 days.

Privacy Factor. A third comparison between arbitration and judicial procedures is privacy. Civil court procedures become public record. Anyone can observe many of the pretrial and all of the trial procedures. As a result, information that people or businesses would prefer to keep private is available for anyone to read. The disclosure factor becomes critical when a business must reveal trade secrets, budget planning, marketing strategies, or other sensitive information in court.

Most alternative dispute resolution procedures are private and not open to the public. Nonjudicial procedures allow for confidentiality of most information, whereas judicial proceedings, by law, rarely are closed to the public.

Formality. A fourth comparison between the two is the difference in formality. A judicial proceeding is very formal in nature. The judge wears a black robe and his entry into the courtroom is announced in a formal manner by the bailiff. Only attorneys and the litigants are allowed beyond the railing that separates the public area from the formal courtroom area.

Courtroom decorum has developed through the centuries and is strictly adhered to by judges. During the trial itself, court rules and the rules of evidence are closely followed. Although the rules have a definite purpose, their application often seems meaningless and confusing to the litigants.

Alternate dispute resolution procedures are informal in their setting. This informality allows the parties to be more relaxed, reducing stress from the level that the parties feel in a courtroom. Do not confuse an informal setting with a sloppy or inadequate presentation of material, however. As in a courtroom, the better prepared the parties in alternative dispute resolution procedures are in presenting their cases, the better the chance of resolving the dispute in a manner acceptable to both sides.

Selection of the Decision Maker. A fifth comparison is the selection of the decision maker. In the judicial system, the parties have very little control over which judge is selected for their case. Most alternative dispute resolution procedures, however, allow the participants to have a say in deciding on the decision maker. When people have a voice in choosing the decision maker, they usually are more ready to accept his or her final decision.[6]

Choice of Forum. A sixth comparison is the choice of the forum (place of litigation or hearing). The parties in a lawsuit have little control over where their case will be heard. The judicial system has limited the right of the parties to "forum shop," that is, to shop around for a sympathetic judge.

Arbitration allows the disputing parties the opportunity to select a common forum in advance. This selection opportunity is important, particularly when there are business arrangements between the parties in more than one state.

Because the disputing parties are not subject to a court system, they can decide the best place to hold the arbitration hearing. Some organizations that offer alternative dispute resolution services operate in many or all of the states, and a few even have offices in other countries. As a result, the disputing parties are not restricted by the jurisdictional limits that they would encounter in a court system.

American Arbitration Association

The American Arbitration Association[7] was founded in 1926 as a private, not-for-profit organization as an outgrowth of two earlier arbitration associations.

---

[6]Many professional arbitrators have sites on the Internet. For example, Stephen R. Marsh maintains a Web site at http://adrr.com where he explains quite well the differences between arbitration and mediation.
[7]The Web page for the American Arbitration Association is http://www.adr.org.

LEGAL HIGHLIGHT

Arbitration and Baseball

The first person who submitted his pay dispute to arbitration was Dick Woodson, a player for the Minnesota Twins, a baseball club. He was offered $23,000 to play in the 1974 season, but he wanted $29,000. This case established the manner in which baseball arbitration is followed today. Baseball arbitration is a little different than regular arbitration. The player and the team sign a contract but one item is left blank. The contract provision reads "For the _____ season the player will be paid _____." The arbitrator may be informed separately as to the amount the baseball club is willing to pay and the amount the player requests. In other cases, the arbitrator does not know the figures.

After the hearing, the arbitrator fills in the contract with one of the amounts. In doing so, the arbitrator takes the difference between the two offers and if one side is one dollar over or under the difference, he will prevail. For example, the player wants $1 million, but the club wants to pay $400,000. The difference between the two figures is $600,000. If the arbitrator awards $550,000, the player will be paid $400,000. If the arbitrator awards $850,000, the player will be paid $1 million.

Sometimes the parties modify the above approach. They do not inform the arbitrator about the amounts being offered but agree that once the arbitrator makes an award, they will follow the above procedure.

This type of arbitration is known by either of two names: *high-low* or *baseball*. This procedure is not restricted to baseball salary disputes and can be used by others in their disputes. The advantage of this arbitration method is that both parties are forced to be realistic with their numbers to settle the dispute.

Within both associations were two groups that held different philosophies concerning arbitration. One group was made up of business leaders and trade association executives. They viewed arbitration as a businessperson's court, much like the trade and guild courts of the Middle Ages. The other group was composed of attorneys who, although they believed in arbitration, also believed in the fundamental concepts of due process and fairness.

To satisfy these two groups, the AAA adopted as its purpose "to foster the study of arbitration in all of its aspects, to perfect its techniques under arbitration law, and to advance generally the science of arbitration for the prompt and economical settlement of disputes." Besides the administration of arbitration, the AAA's other functions include education, promotion, and research into the uses of arbitration for settling all types of disputes. Its slogan is "Speed, Economy, and Justice." AAA's performance has shown repeatedly that justice does result when there is speed and economy. The AAA handles more than 90,000 cases annually and maintains thirty-six offices throughout the United States.

Federal Legislation

Congress passed the **Federal Arbitration Act (FAA)**[8] in 1925 and, by doing so, declared a federal policy favoring arbitration. The act withdraws the states' power to require a judicial forum to resolve disagreements when the parties have agreed by contract to solve disputes by arbitration. In the following case, the Supreme Court upholds the intent of Congress to have the parties abide by their contract when it requires the arbitration of any subsequent disputes.

[8]A copy of the Federal Arbitration Act is available at http://www4.law.cornell.edu/uscode/9.

CASE 4.1

Supreme Court of the
United States, 1995
513 U.S. 265, 115 S. Ct.
834, 130 L. Ed. 2d 753
http://supct.law.cornell.
edu/supct

ALLIED-BRUCE TERMINIX COMPANIES, INC. v. DOBSON

BACKGROUND AND FACTS The Gwins owned a house in Birmingham, Alabama. In 1987, they purchased a lifetime "Termite Protection Plan" (Plan) from the local office of Allied-Bruce Terminix Companies, a franchise of Terminix International Company. Both Allied-Bruce Terminix and Terminix International were multistate businesses and shipped materials interstate.

The Plan promised to protect the house against termites, to provide periodic reinspections, to provide further treatment as necessary, and to repair up to $100,000 worth of damage caused by new termite infestations. The Plan also contained an arbitration clause. Alabama had a state statute that made written, predispute arbitration clauses invalid and unenforceable in court, although the rest of the contract would be enforceable. Parties to a contract could agree to arbitration only after a dispute arose.

In the spring of 1991, the Gwins were to sell their house to the Dobsons. Prior to the transfer of title, Allied-Bruce reinspected the house and certified the house to be free from termites. Immediately after the house was sold and the Termite Protection Plan transferred to the Dobsons, the house was found to be swarming with termites. Allied-Bruce attempted to treat and repair the house, but the Dobsons found Allied-Bruce activities inadequate. They sued the Gwins, Allied-Bruce, and Terminix in state court.

Allied-Bruce and Terminix asked the court to dismiss the lawsuit because the contract had an arbitration clause. Under the clause, the dispute was to be submitted to arbitration. Both the trial court and the Alabama Supreme Court refused to dismiss the lawsuit and both enforced the Alabama statute that made written predispute arbitration clauses unenforceable. The case then was appealed to the United States Supreme Court.

The basis of the appeal is Article I, Section 8, Clause 3, of the U.S. Constitution, which is the interstate commerce clause. Section 2 of the Federal Arbitration Act provides that a contract with an arbitration clause involving commerce is valid, irrevocable, and enforceable in court. Since both Allied-Bruce and Terminix were interstate businesses, they wanted the lawsuit dismissed and the arbitration clause enforced. The issue is whether the Federal Arbitration Act would preempt state law, prohibiting predispute arbitration clauses when the contract involved the interstate commerce clause.

Justice BREYER delivered the opinion of the Court.

. . . .

The Federal Arbitration Act, § 2, provides that a "written provision in any maritime transaction or a contract *evidencing* transaction *involving* commerce to settle by arbitration a controversy thereafter arising out of such contract or transaction shall be valid, irrevocable, and enforceable, save upon such grounds as exist at law or in equity for the revocation of any contract." 9 U.S.C. § 2 (emphasis added).

. . . .

. . . [Section] 2 gives States a method for protecting consumers against unfair pressure to agree to a contract with an unwanted arbitration provision. States may regulate contracts, including arbitration clauses, under general contract law principles, and they may invalidate an arbitration clause "upon such grounds as exist at law or in equity for the revocation of *any* contract." 9 U.S.C. § 2 (emphasis added). However, states may not decide that a contract is fair enough to enforce all its basic terms (price, service, credit), but not fair enough to enforce its arbitration clause. The Act makes any such state policy unlawful because that kind of policy would place arbitration clauses on an unequal "footing," directly contrary to the Act's language and Congress's intent.

DECISION AND REMEDY The Court found that the Federal Arbitration Act pre-empted the Alabama state law that invalidated arbitration clauses in contracts. The subject matter of the contract, however, must involve interstate commerce before the Federal Arbitration Act can preempt state law. The arbitration clause in the Plan was upheld, and the case was returned to the lower court to have the lawsuit dismissed.

CRITICAL THINKING: PUBLIC POLICY Why are Congress and the United States Supreme Court supportive of arbitration?

In 1998, Congress adopted the **Alternative Disputes Resolutions Act**. This act mandates that all federal courts, including bankruptcy courts, send litigants in proceedings before the courts to an ADR procedure.

State Legislation

The **Uniform Arbitration Act**[9] was drafted by the National Conference of Commissioners on Uniform State Laws[10] in 1955. The American Bar Association[11] approved it. The act is designed to make legislation on arbitration more uniform throughout the country. The act covers standards of procedure and rules to be used in the arbitration process. It also provides for judicial enforcement of the agreements to arbitrate.

The stated purpose of the act is to "validate voluntary, written arbitration agreements, make the arbitration process effective, provide necessary safeguards, and provide an efficient procedure when judicial assistance is necessary." This act has been adopted in thirty-five states and the District of Columbia. (See Exhibit 4–1.) The states that did not adopt the act normally follow many of the procedures suggested by it.

In 2000, the National Conference of Commissioners on Uniform State laws promulgated the **Revised Uniform Arbitration Act (RUAA)**. By 2003, only three states had adopted the revised act. It is anticipated that more jurisdictions will adopt the revised act into law in the future.

The original act failed to address many issues which were finally dealt with in the RUAA. In the following case of *Howsam v. Dean Witter Reynolds, Inc.*, the U.S. Supreme Court reviewed the RUAA as to whether a judge or an arbitrator should decide an issue involving the statute of limitations.

[9]A copy of the Uniform Arbitration Act, which currently is under revision, is available at http://www.law.upenn.edu/bll/ulc/ulc_frame.htm.
[10]The National Conference of Commissioners on Uniform State Laws has a Web site at http://www.nccusl.org. The National Conference was formed in 1891 to draft proposals for uniform and model laws on subjects where uniformity is desirable and practicable, and work toward their enactment in legislatures.
[11]The Web page for the American Bar Association is http://www.abanet.org.

Exhibit 4–1   States that Have Adopted the Uniform Arbitration Act

Alaska	Indiana	Missouri	South Carolina
Arizona	Iowa	Montana	South Dakota
Arkansas	Kansas	Nebraska	Tennessee
Colorado	Kentucky	Nevada★	Texas
Delaware	Maine	New Mexico★	Utah
District of Columbia	Maryland	North Carolina	Vermont
Florida	Massachusetts	North Dakota	Virginia
Idaho	Michigan	Oklahoma	Wyoming
Illinois	Minnesota	Pennsylvania	

★Has now adopted the new Revised Uniform Arbitration Act along with Hawaii.

<table>
<tr><td>

CASE 4.2

Supreme Court of the
United States, 2002
537 U.S. 79, 123 S. Ct.
588, 154 L. Ed. 2d 491

</td><td>

HOWSAM v. DEAN WITTER REYNOLDS, INC.

BACKGROUND AND FACTS This case arose out of investment advice that Dean
Witter Reynolds, Inc. (Dean Witter), provided its client, Karen Howsam, some time
between 1986 and 1994. Dean Witter recommended that she buy and hold interests in
four limited partnerships. Howsam says that Dean Witter misrepresented the virtues of
the partnerships.

This case focuses upon an arbitration rule of the National Association of Securities
Dealers (NASD). The rule states that no dispute "shall be eligible for submission to arbi-
tration . . . where six (6) years have elapsed from the occurrence or event giving rise to
the . . . dispute."

The Court had to decide whether a court or an NASD arbitrator should apply the
rule to the underlying controversy. The resulting controversy falls within the Dean Witter
standard Client Service Agreement's arbitration clause, which provides:

> *"all controversies . . . concerning or arising from . . . any account . . ., any transaction . . .,
> or . . . the construction, performance or breach of . . . any . . . agreement between us . . . shall be
> determined by arbitration before any self-regulatory organization or exchange of which Dean
> Witter is a member."*

The agreement also provides that Howsam could select the arbitration forum. Howsam
chose arbitration before the NASD.

</td></tr>
</table>

Justice BREYER delivered the opinion of the Court.

. . . .

This Court has determined that "arbitration is a matter of contract and a party cannot
be required to submit to arbitration any dispute which he has not agreed so to submit."
Although the Court has also long recognized and enforced a "liberal federal policy
favoring arbitration agreements," it has made clear that there is an exception to this
policy: The question whether the parties have submitted a particular dispute to arbitration, *i.e.,* the "*question of arbitrability,*" is "an issue for judicial determination [u]nless the
parties clearly and unmistakably provide otherwise." We must decide here whether
application of the NASD time limit provision falls into the scope of this last-mentioned
interpretive rule.

. . . .

At the same time the Court has found the phrase "question of arbitrability" *not*
applicable in other kinds of general circumstance where parties would likely expect
that an arbitrator would decide the gateway matter. Thus "'procedural' questions
which grow out of the dispute and bear on its final disposition" are presumptively *not*
for the judge, but for an arbitrator, to decide. So, too, the presumption is that the arbitrator should decide "allegation[s] of waiver, delay, or a like defense to arbitrability."
Indeed, the Revised Uniform Arbitration Act of 2000 (RUAA), seeking to "incorporate the holdings of the vast majority of state courts and the law that has developed
under the [Federal Arbitration Act]," states that an "arbitrator shall decide whether a
condition precedent to arbitrability has been fulfilled." And the comments add that "in
the absence of an agreement to the contrary, issues of substantive arbitrability . . . are
for a court to decide and issues of procedural arbitrability, *i.e.,* whether prerequisites
such as *time limits,* notice, laches, estoppel, and other conditions precedent to an obligation to arbitrate have been met, are for the arbitrators to decide."

. . . .

DECISION AND REMEDY The Court concluded that the NASD's time limit rule fell within the class of gateway procedural disputes that should be answered by the arbitrator and not by a judge.

CRITICAL THINKING: PUBLIC POLICY Which decision maker, comparatively, can provide more expertise in deciding this type of question, a judge or an arbitrator?

Arbitration occurs in one of two settings: *judicial* or *contractual*. The following sections discuss these two settings.

Judicial Arbitration

Compulsory (court-mandated) arbitration is called **judicial arbitration**. Only civil lawsuits for money damages can be submitted to arbitration. The arbitrator is appointed by the judge overseeing the lawsuit.

In some courts, after the lawsuit has been filed, the parties can volunteer to have their case arbitrated. If the parties do not volunteer, they may be ordered by the judge to submit their case to arbitration. In other jurisdictions, cases under a certain amount, such as $50,000, are required by law to be submitted to arbitration first. If the arbitration fails, the parties can proceed with the lawsuit.

The actual hearing for a compulsory arbitration is the same as if the arbitration were a contractual one. No judge or jury is involved, and the arbitrator does not submit a written decision that sets out the reasons for the decision. Instead, only an **award** (decision) is issued, which is similar to a judgment.

In the hearing, the parties may use depositions, interrogatories, and certified documents to save the cost of a person's testifying at the hearing. Because the time spent to resolve the case is shorter than if the case went to court, the attorneys' fees usually are less.

The following case involves a dispute that went to arbitration. The court had to decide whether a party to a judicial arbitration was required to cooperate in a meaningful manner.

CASE 4.3

Supreme Court of Nevada, 1996
911 P.2d 1181, 112 Nev. 132

CASINO PROPERTIES, INC. v. ANDREWS

BACKGROUND AND FACTS David DelRossi, his wife, four children, and adult niece, Andrews, stayed in two adjoining rooms at the Hacienda Resort Hotel and Casino (Hacienda) in Las Vegas for a week. The assistant hotel manager, O'Donnell, reviewed a computer report that indicated that the bill for the rooms exceeded DelRossi's credit card limit.

O'Donnell made several attempts to reach DelRossi to discuss payment terms but was unsuccessful. O'Donnell then ordered the security guards to perform a "lock-out" on both rooms. A lock-out is a procedure whereby the security guards lock the guest out of the room and deny the guest access to his personal belongings therein. This forces the guest to come to the front desk to pay his bill.

The security guards successfully locked out DelRossi's room and then attempted to do the same on the second room where Andrews and all of the children were staying. The security guard informed Andrews that there was a problem with the bill and that he was to escort her to the front desk so that she could straighten out the problem. Andrews refused to go because one of the children was ill and the others were allegedly near hysteria due to the guard's intrusion into the room.

Despite Andrews' concerns, the security guard forced Andrews to accompany him to the front desk, but he allowed the children to remain in the room. At the front desk, Andrews told O'Donnell that she was not responsible for the payment of the bill, and O'Donnell eventually located DelRossi, who paid the bill in full.

DelRossi sued the Hacienda for negligent and intentional infliction of emotional distress, invasion of privacy, and failure to provide protection from its abusive employees. The case was sent to judicial arbitration.

DelRossi's attorney delivered his prearbitration statement in a timely fashion to Hacienda. Hacienda, on the other hand, refused to share information about its employee and security handbooks and only supplied a statement one day before the arbitration hearing. Hacienda made O'Donnell, a key witness, available for questioning via telephone instead of in person.

The arbitrator awarded DelRossi $15,000 plus attorney's fees. Hacienda filed a motion (request) for a trial *de novo* (new trial). The district court held that Hacienda failed to defend the arbitration action in good faith, thereby waiving its right to request a trial *de novo*.

Hacienda filed this appeal. The Nevada Supreme Court reached a unanimous decision. The decision was written by the whole Court and not by one judge. Such an opinion is called *per curiam*.

PER CURIAM

The purpose of Nevada's Court Annexed Arbitration Program "is to provide a simplified procedure for obtaining a prompt and equitable resolution of certain civil matters." In *Gilling v. Eastern Airlines, Inc.,* a federal court dealing with the issue of good faith participation in arbitration equated "good faith" with "meaningful participation," and determined that if the parties did not participate in a meaningful manner, the purposes of mandatory arbitration would be compromised. We agree with this proposition and conclude that appellants did not defend the case in good faith during the arbitration proceeding because they did not participate in a meaningful manner.

The purposes of . . . mandatory arbitration are "to provide the parties with a quick and inexpensive means of resolving their dispute while, at the same time, reducing the court's caseload."

DECISION AND REMEDY Because Hacienda had failed to participate in a meaningful manner, the arbitrator's award of $15,000 plus attorney's fees in favor of DelRossi was upheld.

CRITICAL THINKING: PUBLIC POLICY The Seventh Amendment preserves the right to a jury trial. If a person does not participate in a judicial arbitration, should a person be denied the right to a jury trial? Please discuss fully.

Contractual Arbitration

The **contractual agreement to arbitrate** may be reached before or after the dispute arises. The parties may include a dispute arbitration clause in their initial contract, ensuring that they will submit any future disputes to arbitration. If a dispute arises, the party making the complaint serves the Demand for Arbitration notice on the opposing party. (See Exhibit 4–2.)

If the parties fail to include an arbitration clause in the contract, however, when a dispute arises they still may mutually agree to submit the problem to arbitration. This agreement is called a Submission to Dispute Resolution and is signed by both parties. (See Exhibit 4–3.)

The two requirements for voluntary arbitration are that the agreement must be entered voluntarily and the agreement must be in writing to be enforceable in a

Exhibit 4–2   **Sample Demand for Arbitration**

American Arbitration Association
Commercial Arbitration Rules

To institute proceedings, please send two copies of this demand *and the arbitration agreement,* with the filing fee as provided in the rules, to the AAA. Send the original demand to the respondent.

DEMAND FOR ARBITRATION

DATE: _____

TO: Name _____

Address _____

(of the Party on Whom the Demand Is Made)

City and State _____   ZIP Code _____

Telephone (   ) _____   Fax _____

Name of Representative _____

(if Known)

Representative's Address _____

Name of Firm (if Applicable) _____

City and State _____   ZIP Code _____

Telephone (   ) _____   Fax _____

The named claimant, a party to an arbitration agreement contained in a written contract, dated _____ _____ and providing for arbitration under the Commercial Arbitration Rules of the American Association, hereby demands arbitration thereunder.

THE NATURE OF THE DISPUTE:

THE CLAIM OR RELIEF SOUGHT (the Amount, if Any):

DOES THIS DISPUTE ARISE OUT OF AN EMPLOYMENT RELATIONSHIP?   ☐ Yes   ☐ No

TYPE OF BUSINESS CLAIMANT _____   Respondent _____

HEARING LOCALE REQUESTED _____

(City and State)

You are hereby notified that copies of our arbitration agreement and this demand are being filed with the American Arbitration Association at its _____ office, with a request that it commence administration of the arbitration. Under the rules, you may file an answering statement within fifteen days after notice from the AAA.

Signed _____   Title _____

(May Be Signed by a Representative)

Name of Claimant _____

Address (to Be Used in Connection with This Case) _____

City and State _____   ZIP Code _____

Telephone (   ) _____   Fax _____

Name of Representative _____

Name of Firm (if Applicable) _____

Representative's Address _____

City and State _____   ZIP Code _____

Telephone (   ) _____   Fax _____

☐ MEDIATION is a nonbinding process. The mediator assists the parties in working out a solution that is acceptable to them. If you wish for the AAA to contact the other parties to ascertain whether they wish to mediate this matter, please check this box (there is no additional administrative fee for this service).

Form C2-3/99

Source: Reprinted with permission of the American Arbitration Association.

Exhibit 4–3   Sample Submission to Dispute Resolution

American Arbitration Association

SUBMISSION TO DISPUTE RESOLUTION

Date: _____

The named parties hereby submit the following dispute for resolution under the _____
_____ Rules* of the American Arbitration

Association.

Procedure Selected: ☐ Arbitration   ☐ Mediation Settlement
                         ☐ Other _____
                                        (Describe.)

FOR INSURANCE CASES ONLY:

_____   _____ to _____   _____
Policy Number   Effective Dates   Application Policy Limits

_____   _____
Date of the Incident   Location

Insured: _____ Claim Number: _____

Name of Claimants	**Check if a minor.**	**Amounts Claimed**
_____	☐	_____
_____	☐	_____

Nature of Dispute and/or Injuries Alleged (Attach additional sheets if necessary.):

Place of Hearing: _____

We agree that, if binding arbitration is selected, we will abide by and perform any award rendered hereunder and that a judgment may be entered on the award.

To Be Completed by the Parties

_____	_____
Name of Party	Name of Party
_____	_____
Address	Address
_____	_____
City, State, and Zip Code	City, State, and Zip Code
( ) _____	( ) _____
Telephone Fax	Telephone Fax
_____	_____
Signature†	Signature†
_____	_____
Name of Party's Attorney or Representative	Name of Party's Attorney or Representative
_____	_____
Name of Firm (if Applicable)	Name of Firm (if Applicable)
_____	_____
Address	Address
( ) _____	( ) _____
Telephone Fax	Telephone Fax
_____	_____
Signature† (may be signed by representative)	Signature† (may be signed by representative)

Please file three copies with the AAA.

*If you have a question as to which rules apply, please contact the AAA.
†Signatures of all parties are required for arbitration.

Source: Reprinted with permission of the American Arbitration Association.

court. Initially, this second requirement may seem to contradict the first. It is necessary, though, because even when there is a written agreement to arbitrate, one of the parties may refuse to participate in the arbitration proceedings or may file a lawsuit, as in the *Allied-Bruce Terminix* case. The other party may request that the court order the first party to arbitrate.

An oral agreement to arbitrate will not suffice. The written agreement is required because that agreement forfeits the parties' right to trial as guaranteed by the federal Constitution. The Seventh Amendment preserves the right to a trial by jury for civil cases at common law exceeding $20.

The modern view is that arbitration is binding on the parties once they have agreed to it. This agreement is called **binding arbitration**. In other words, a legal action cannot be brought when the parties have agreed to submit a controversy to arbitration. The parties are required to utilize arbitration procedures to the fullest extent prior to filing a court action. The only exception would be when both parties refuse to arbitrate after initially agreeing to it.

If one party refuses to arbitrate, the other party may file a lawsuit and seek a court order to compel arbitration. The only defense is that there was no written agreement to arbitrate. The court will order arbitration and stay (stop or delay) any other proceeding if it is presented with a contract that has an arbitration clause. The terms are enforced when the parties have voluntarily agreed to them and provided that the terms are legal and consistent with public policy.

Contractual Arbitration Procedure

Just as a lawsuit follows a series of steps, so does arbitration. Some parts of an arbitration procedure are similar to those of a judicial proceeding, whereas other parts are unique to arbitration. The terms that describe the process are peculiar to arbitration.

Tribunal Administrator. The American Arbitration Association maintains offices around the country. The regional office has the responsibility of providing a **tribunal administrator**. This person manages the administrative matters and all communications between the parties and the arbitrator. The advantage is that the administrative burden of managing details and arrangements is not placed on the arbitrator, who may be located some distance from the parties and the

place of the hearing. The arbitrator will be in direct communication with either of the parties only at the hearing. This arrangement prevents one side from making arguments, presenting evidence, or making suggestions to the arbitrator without allowing the other side an opportunity to be heard as well.

Selection of the Arbitrator. Parties determine the method of appointing arbitrators in the arbitration agreement. The arbitration agreement can specify the procedure to be followed in selecting an arbitrator. In the judicial system, this control cannot be exercised in selecting a judge. Usually, the parties must accept whichever judge is assigned to their case.

Some parties, however, do not have the foresight to include the method of selecting the arbitrator in the contract. In business arbitrations under $50,000, the American Arbitration Association directly appoints the arbitrator.

In cases between $50,000 and $1 million, the parties agree to an arbitrator. A prepared list of proposed arbitrators who have expertise on the disputed topic is sent to each party who then chooses and prioritizes several names. Each party then sends its list to the tribunal administrator who compares the prioritized names to see which arbitrators are mutually acceptable and their order of preference. Finally, an arbitrator is agreed on by the parties. In large, complex disputes of more than $1 million, a panel of arbitrators usually is selected.

Preparation for the Hearing. The parties determine a mutually convenient day and time for the hearing. Written notice of the hearing is provided to each party by the tribunal administrator. Each side prepares for the hearings as it would for a trial. All documents and papers to be submitted into evidence are assembled and ordered logically. Proper arrangements are made if the arbitrator needs to visit a place for an on-the-spot investigation.

Before the hearing, witnesses are interviewed by each party. Each party studies the case from the opposition's viewpoint so that the opposition's evidence and arguments can be addressed. If a transcript of the hearings is needed, arrangements are made with the tribunal administrator for a court reporter to be present.

The Hearing. An arbitration proceeding is very similar in form to a trial but should not take on the adversarial tone of a trial. A cooperative attitude is necessary for effective arbitration. Ordinary rules of courtesy and decorum are encouraged. Exaggeration, overemphasis, concealing of facts, and use of legal technicalities to disrupt or delay the hearing are discouraged.

Each party presents its case to the arbitrator in an orderly and logical manner. Just as in a trial, each side starts with a clear, concise opening statement. The complaining party usually presents first, telling the arbitrator its view of the dispute and the remedy it seeks. The second party then makes its opening statement. Both parties present documents and other materials to the arbitrator. If there are witnesses, they are examined to help each party establish its case. Finally, each side makes a closing argument. The closing argument includes a summary of the evidence, a refutation of the points made by the opposition, and a concluding argument to influence the arbitrator's decision. Following the closing arguments, the arbitrator declares the hearing closed.

The arbitrator hears the controversy and determines the decision based on the evidence produced, even if one party fails to appear, as long as the party received notification of the hearing. Either party to the case may have an attorney present, but representation is not required. Witnesses can be compelled to appear at an arbitration hearing through the use of subpoenas. The hearing can be adjourned to another time if the first meeting is not sufficient time to hear all evidence.

The Award. The arbitrator must make her decision within thirty days after the hearing. If two or more arbitrators hear the case, the majority decision is binding, unless the parties agree beforehand that only a unanimous decision will be binding. The arbitrator's award is based on the facts presented at the hearing.

Once the award is made, the arbitrator cannot change it. Only if the parties both agree to reopen the proceedings and restore power to the arbitrator can the award be changed. The award merely states which party prevailed and, when appropriate, the amount awarded. No supporting reasons are given. For certain types of arbitration, such as an arbitration over an employment dispute, the arbitration association may require the arbitrator to set the reasons for the award.

The award is final and binding on the parties. If the arbitration has been court ordered, the award is submitted to the court. Once the court accepts the award, it becomes the same as a judgment.

The Appeal. The losing party may appeal an award in contractual arbitration. Some of the grounds are:

1. The award was obtained through corruption, fraud, or other misconduct by the arbitrator.

2. Misconduct or partiality was exhibited by the arbitrator.

3. The arbitrator exceeded her or his powers.

4. The arbitrator refused to postpone the hearing or to hear evidence material to the controversy, which substantially prejudiced the rights of one of the parties.

5. The parties did not have a written arbitration agreement and the issue of whether to take the dispute to arbitration was not determined in a court action to compel arbitration.

If the court does find one of these five grounds applicable to the case, it orders either a rehearing in front of the same arbitrator or a new hearing with a different arbitrator. The court has the right to modify the award under the following circumstances:

1. A miscalculation of figures was evident.

2. A mistake in the description of any person or property referred to in the award was evident.

3. The facts determined by the arbitrator were not those submitted to arbitration.

4. The award was not in the proper form.

A court is not allowed to modify an award in contractual arbitration on any other grounds. In judicial arbitration, however, either party may appeal to the court. Normally, no grounds are required for the appeal other than that the appealing party does not accept the decision of the arbitrator. The appeal is treated by the court as a completely new case, and a trial *de novo* will be ordered. A trial *de novo* means that the decision of the arbitrator is not binding and the parties have to start over again. The case proceeds as a lawsuit, as it normally would have, if the arbitration never happened.

Differences

The following nine differences exist between a judicial arbitration and a contractual arbitration:

1. Under the contract arrangement the proceedings are private, but they are public for a judicial arbitration.

2. Under judicial arbitration full discovery rights are preserved, whereas discovery usually is very limited under the contract arrangement.

3. Subpoena power is fully preserved under court arbitration, whereas none exists in the contract arrangement unless provided by statute. A subpoena is issued ordinarily by a court, not by an arbitrator.

4. The rules of evidence apply in a judicial arbitration but not in the contract arrangement.

5. The award is binding under the AAA arbitration rules, whereas in the judicial arbitration the award is binding only if it is not appealed. Judicial arbitration cannot be binding, because the Seventh Amendment to the Constitution guarantees the right to a jury trial.

6. Appeal rights are preserved fully in a judicial arbitration. If an appeal is granted, the parties have a right to a trial in the court. Under the AAA arrangement, the arbitrator's decision is binding and final. Appeals may be made only on very limited grounds.

7. In the judicial arbitration setting, the arbitrator is usually an attorney with little or no arbitration experience, selected at random from the legal community. Under the contractual arrangement, the arbitrator is selected because of subject matter expertise.

8. The cost to the client is less under the contract arrangement, because no lawsuit is filed. Under the judicial arrangement the cost is more, because the case is pending before the courts. The cost, however, usually is less than that of a full court trial.

9. The stress on the parties is greater under judicial arbitration because the case is already in the court system. The stress is reduced under the contract arrangement because the arbitration has been agreed to by both parties.

People entering into contracts should consider whether arbitration clauses should be included. If arbitration is not agreed to in the contract, arbitration may still be imposed by the courts. Although arbitration has many advantages, it is not a perfect alternative to a lawsuit. Disadvantages do exist.

Disadvantages of Arbitration

Arbitration has inherent disadvantages when compared with a judicial proceeding. These seven major disadvantages need to be considered:

1. In most cases the arbitrator's award cannot be appealed except on the five grounds previously listed. Those grounds involve the lack of an arbitration agreement or involve the conduct of the arbitrator. The award itself cannot be appealed even though the arbitrator misapplied the law, as we will see in the next case. A judgment made by a court, in contrast, is appealable if the law is misapplied.

2. Arbitration lacks full discovery and full disclosure requirements. (See Chapter 3.) In arbitration, discovery is very limited. Information disclosure is not required.

3. The formal rules of evidence used in a courtroom trial do not apply in arbitration. These rules were developed to ensure justice to all parties. At times, evidence rules are technical, but they do promote fairness when presenting evidence. Evidence in court, for example, cannot be based on gossip or prejudices and must include relevant material. Often an arbitrator will hear evidence that would not be allowed in a court under its strict rules of evidence. The arbitrator must be careful to consider only evidence that has a bearing on the case.

4. A party may agree to arbitration without realizing it. An arbitration clause is often buried in the fine print within a contract. Even if the party were to read and understand the arbitration clause, he still may be coerced to agree to arbitration because the clause may appear in all contracts used by a particular industry.

5. A party usually is unaware of an arbitrator's background. All arbitrators have biases or prejudices.

6. Arbitrators tend to compromise when making awards rather than making clear-cut decisions for one party. Judicial decisions most often decide for or against one of the parties based on the case's merits.

7. After arbitration, future parties lose the use of prior written decisions as precedent. Written judicial opinions are one of the foundations of American law.

In summary, a person who agrees to arbitration waives the right to a jury trial, the right of appeal, and other protections of due process that are mandatory in the judicial setting. The arbitration proceeding is conducted privately. No written record exists, as is required for judicial proceedings. Finally, the person requesting the arbitration has the same burden of proof as for a trial. Without adequate discovery proceedings, the plaintiff may have a more difficult time proving her case before an arbitrator.

The next case illustrates the power of an arbitrator's award. The court had to decide if the party had the right to appeal an award when the arbitrator made an error as to the law.

CASE 4.4 Court of Appeals of Arizona, 1986 151 Ariz. 418, 728 P.2d 288	# HEMBREE v. BROADWAY REALTY AND TRUST COMPANY, INC.

BACKGROUND AND FACTS Broadway Realty and Trust Company, Inc., sold Hembree a home. The purchase contract had an arbitration clause requiring arbitration of any controversy or claim between the parties. The home had a defective roof. The case was arbitrated, and an award was given to Hembree based on breach of implied warranty, that is, a warranty imposed by law. The decision was appealed on the basis that (1) the arbitrator acted beyond his scope of authority and (2) the law of implied warranty should not have been applied. The trial court confirmed the award, and Broadway Realty appealed.

Chief Judge HATHAWAY

. . . .

I. SCOPE OF AUTHORITY . . . [T]he superior court will not confirm an arbitrator's award if the arbitrator exceeded his authority. An arbitrator's powers are defined by the agreement of the parties. The contract between appellees and appellants states that arbitration will be available for any controversy or claim "arising out of or *relating to this contract*" (emphasis added). . . . [O]nce an implied warranty comes into existence by reason of the circumstances of the sale, the law conceives such a warranty as being a term of the contract. Appellants argue that appellees' implied warranty claim does not arise out of or relate to "this contract." The gist of appellant's argument is that implied warranty can only apply to the sale of a home by a builder/vendor, and since appellant is a developer/vendor, the arbitration clause does not encompass this breach of implied warranty allegation. Appellants' argument, however, is legal rather than jurisdictional. The dispute between these parties relates to the sale of the home and the allegedly defective roof. In their lawsuit, appellees alleged a number of theories including implied warranty. Whether or not that theory was viable under these circumstances was a legal question for the arbitrator. The dispute, however, clearly arose out of and related to this contract for the sale of a home. Therefore, we find the arbitrator was within his authority in addressing the implied warranty claim.

II. MISTAKE OF LAW As stated above, appellants argue that parties who are not builders may not be held liable for breach of an implied warranty of habitability. It is settled case law that upon application to confirm an arbitration award, the superior court may not inquire as to whether errors of law were made by the arbitrator in reaching his decision. The power of this court is likewise severely circumscribed. Therefore this court may not review whether or not the arbitrator was correct in his application of the law. . . .

DECISION AND REMEDY The court upheld the award of the arbitrator. Although noting that the arbitrator might have been mistaken as to the legal issues on the implied warranty, the court held that it could not inquire into legal errors made by an arbitrator.

CRITICAL THINKING: PUBLIC POLICY When a trial judge, trained in the law, makes an error of law, her or his decision can be reversed on appeal. Why should an award based on an error of law by an arbitrator, who is not trained in the law, not be appealable?

Arbitration has both advantages and disadvantages. Only after a number of years of experience will the public and law makers be able to decide which method is preferred, those held in a public forum or those decided in a private forum.

INFOTRAC RESEARCH ACTIVITY

On InfoTrac, read three articles on ADR and summarize what they stated. Find articles that are supportive of using ADR procedures and ones that are not supportive of nonjudicial proceedings.

CYBERLAW

Online ADR

Business is conducted worldwide and naturally legal conflicts will arise that require physical travel to resolve these disputes. Depending on the amount in controversy, travel may be simply too expensive and time consuming. Web sites exist that employ different alternative dispute resolution methods.[12] The most common methods used are mediation and arbitration. The cases submitted to online services tend to be those involving routine claims where only the amount of the claim is in dispute.

One party to the dispute contacts an online

---

[12]These firms have Web addresses: Cybersettle http://www.cyber-settle.com; National Arbitration and Mediation Corp. http://www.clicknsettle.com; Onlinemediators http://www.onlinemediators.com; Internet Neutral http://www.internetneutral.com; and the Mediation Information and Resource Center http://www.mediate.com. These sites also often offer more conventional ADR services.

---

service, which, in turn, notifies the other party. If both parties are willing, settlement discussions may take place via e-mail, chat conference rooms, and faxes. The only requirement is for the parties to be online during the mediation session. The parties are not bound by anything said during these sessions.

Each side sends in an offer to settle the case to a secure, password-protected site. A party can check the site to see the status of the case. Each side is allowed to submit a limited number of offers, usually three. This method forces each side to evaluate the case in a realistic manner.

Just as in face-to-face discussions, in online mediation, the mediator has no authority to make a binding decision. It is only binding when all parties agree to be bound by the decision they reach. Mediation is a voluntary process that any participant may end for any reason. Until the parties agree to be bound, no one is bound.

Although a cost is associated with this type of online service, it is far less expensive than litigating a dispute. Approximately 85 percent of the cases submitted to mediation over the Web have been settled.

Other Forms of ADR

New forms of alternative dispute resolution are being developed constantly. Most of them blend the concepts underlying conciliation and mediation. The following sections examine a few of the more recent developments in ADR.

Hybrid Mediation and Arbitration (Med/Arb)

Commercial agreements today use a hybrid system of combining mediation and arbitration, called **med/arb**, to resolve disputes. If a dispute arises, mediation is used first. The mediator will attempt to help the parties to find their own solution to the problem. Meeting with the parties separately, the mediator tries to bring the parties to agreement. The effect is to guide the parties to a resolution by building momentum in that direction. The resolution is an agreement mutually reached by the disputing parties.

The parties may have several issues that are disputed. They may reach an agreement on several of them under the guidance of a mediator, but cannot reach an agreement on the remaining issues. When that happens, the parties take the remaining issues to arbitration. The person who served as mediator often fulfills the role as arbitrator. The arbitrator's award is binding on both parties.

A modified med/arb procedure is often used by automobile manufacturers when customers have disputes with dealerships. The arbitrator's award is binding on the dealership but is not binding on the customer, who can file a lawsuit if dissatisfied with the arbitrator's solution. A combination of mediation and arbitration is used extensively in the construction industry.

Exhibit 4–4 compares arbitration procedure with court procedure. The chart summarizes those distinctions among the various dispute resolution procedures discussed thus far.

Fact Finding

Used in complex commercial disputes, **fact finding** is an investigative process in which an independent third party investigates the issues and makes findings of fact. Courts use fact finders when confronted with a highly technical and involved fact situation requiring a high degree of expertise in a given area.

Frequently, a fact finder's role is solely that of making a recommendation. Having an independent person to determine certain facts often assists parties in reaching a settlement. If nothing else, the conclusions reached by the fact finder indicate to the parties the probable result of judicial litigation. This indication by itself often helps the parties to reach a negotiated settlement.

A recent example was the appointment of Harvard law professor Lawrence Lessig as a special master (fact finder) by the trial judge in the Microsoft antitrust lawsuit by the Department of Justice. Microsoft objected to his appointment because of his alleged bias. The court of appeals suspended him from the case. If he had remained, he would have advised the judge on the legal issues affecting the lawsuit.

Minitrial

A **minitrial** is another voluntary procedure in which all parties must agree to its use. The primary purpose of a minitrial is to resolve questions of fact and law in complex, commercial disputes. It may be used in addition to fact finding.

No judge presides over a minitrial. Instead, the parties agree on an adviser. Normally, the adviser has had considerable experience with the subject matter that is the basis of the dispute. The parties determine the amount of authority that the adviser can exercise.

On being appointed, the adviser establishes an abbreviated discovery process that requires exchanging the documents, exhibits, written arguments, and names of witnesses that will be used by the parties. On conclusion of the discovery phase, the adviser meets with the parties, issues rulings on discovery matters, and attempts to resolve procedural questions.

Cases are settled more easily when all parties know the facts. When parties have full knowledge of the facts and the legalities that the case entails, the parties are better able to reach a settlement. Minitrials attempt to expedite discovery of the facts. Another advantage of the minitrial is the confidentiality of its procedures. Many businesses prefer to withhold some information from the general public. The minitrial provides a procedure that limits the amount of information made public.

Minitrials have been used in cases of patent infringement, product liability, unfair competition, and antitrust violations. The minitrial is not considered an appropriate mechanism for cases involving constitutional law issues. It also is not appropriate for cases involving a large number of parties or legal questions.

Private Judge

A few states, particularly California, will allow the parties in a dispute to hire a **private judge**, called a *referee*. Normally, the referee is retired from the judiciary. The parties obtain a referee with expertise in the subject matter of the litigation. The referee is given the full powers of a judge, except the power to find someone in contempt of court.

The procedure is the same as that of a regular courtroom proceeding. The proceedings take place

Exhibit 4–4   Arbitration and Court Procedure Comparison Chart

Distinguishing Features	Arbitration Procedure		Court Procedure	
	Negotiation—Mediation	Contractual Arbitration	Court-Ordered Judicial Arbitration	Court Litigation
Dispute types	Any negotiable matter in the civil area	Civil matters of any type or complexity, unless prohibited by law, but only what parties provide for/agree to in writing	Civil matters for monetary relief only; usually a limit on the monetary amount of the claim	Civil and criminal cases heard; money damages and equitable remedies available
Private or public proceedings	Private	Private	Public	Public
Discovery rights	None provided by statute	Usually none or very limited under arbitration statutes; parties can provide for/agree to discovery in writing	Full rights as available under law or statute	Full rights as available under law or statute
Subpoena power	None provided by statute	Arbitrator has power to issue subpoenas in accordance with arbitration statutes; enforcement power rests with the court	Court has power to issue and enforce subpoenas	Court has power to issue and enforce subpoenas
Formal rules of evidence	None provided by statute	Do not apply unless provided by statute or unless parties provide for/agree to in writing	Do apply as provided for by statute and by court rules of procedure	Do apply as provided by statute and by court rules of procedure
Decision finality and enforcement	Verbal or written statement agreement may be enforceable through a judicial process	Final binding; enforceable by an appropriate court on the entering of a judgment based on the award	Final and binding, unless appealed; if not appealed, enforceable by the court on the entering of a judgment based on the award	Final unless reversed on appeal
Appeal rights	Only available through a judicial process	Usually very limited under arbitration statutes unless parties provide/agree otherwise	Trial *de novo* (new trial) and full appeal rights as available under law	Full appeal rights as available under law
Relative speed from initiation to settlement or decision (not including appeal time)	Fastest (days to months); settlement occurs in 60 to 90 percent of cases mediated, depending on the type of case surveyed	Faster or fast (weeks to year); settlement occurs in 50 percent of cases submitted to AAA arbitration; parties can agree how fast or slow process will be	Fast (months to years); settlement occurs in 50 percent of these cases; the percentage of cases going to trial *de novo* is unknown	Slowest (one or more years); settlement occurs in 95 percent of all civil cases, generally right before trial
Who pays cost?	Parties	Parties	Taxpayers and parties	Taxpayers and parties

Source: American Arbitration Association.

The Women at Hooters

On April Fool's Day, 1983, Hooters Restaurant was incorporated by the six men who wanted a restaurant with finger foods and 1950s and 1960s music. The name *Hooters* came from Steve Martin's comedy sketch. The creative menu and the irreverent humor combined with beautiful and vivacious young women, known as the Hooters Girls, to make the first restaurant so popular that within ten years it expanded across the country. But amid all the fun, there was a dark side.

Annette Phillips was employed as a bartender by Hooters in Myrtle Beach, South Carolina. She sued Hooters under Title VII of the Civil Rights Act alleging sexual harassment and a hostile work environment. Among the allegations were that she and other employees had to play sexually degrading games to determine to which restaurant area they would be assigned. She also alleged that Hooters managers exposed their genitals and underwear to female employees, and one manager offered bounty money to anyone who would find reasons to "write up" less attractive female employees, in order to fire them. It was alleged that the final straw was when the brother of the principal owner sexually harassed her by grabbing and slapping her buttocks. After appealing to her manager for help and being told to "let it go," she quit.

Prior to resigning from her position with Hooters, she signed an arbitration agreement, known as the Hooters Rules. After the lawsuit was filed, Hooters requested the court to dismiss the case and send it to arbitration.

But wait, said the court to Hooters. The Hooters Rules when taken as a whole, however, were so one sided that their only possible purpose was to undermine the neutrality of the proceeding. The rules required the employee to provide the company notice of her claim at the outset, including "the nature of the Claim" and "the specific act(s) or omissions(s) which are the basis of the Claim." Hooters, on the other hand, was not required to file any responsive pleadings or to give the plaintiff any notice of its defenses. While the employee was required to provide the company with a list of all witnesses with a brief summary of the facts known to each, the company was not required to reciprocate.

The Hooters Rules provided a mechanism for selecting a panel of three arbitrators that was crafted to ensure a biased decision maker. The employee and Hooters each selected an arbitrator, and the two arbitrators in turn selected a third. Sounds fair until the employee found out that both the employee's arbitrator and the third arbitrator had to be selected from a list of arbitrators created exclusively by Hooters. Thus, Hooters had total control and the rules placed no limits whatsoever on whom Hooters could put on the list. Hooters was free to list people who had existing relationships, financial or familial, with Hooters. In fact, the rules did not even prohibit Hooters from placing its managers on the list. Further, nothing in the rules restricted Hooters from punishing arbitrators who ruled against the company by removing them from the list.

The court struck down the Hooters Rules and wrote the following:

> Given the unrestricted control that one party (Hooters) has over the panel, the selection of an impartial decision maker would be a surprising result. Nor is fairness to be found once the proceedings are begun. Although Hooters may expand the scope of arbitration to any matter, "whether related or not to the Employee's Claim," the employee cannot raise "any matter not included in the Notice of Claim." Similarly, Hooters is permitted to move for summary dismissal of employee claims before a hearing is held whereas the employee is not permitted to seek summary judgment. Hooters, but not the employee, may record the arbitration hearing "by audio or videotaping or by verbatim transcription." The rules also grant Hooters the right to bring suit in court to vacate or modify an arbitral award when it can show, by a preponderance of the evidence, that the panel exceeded its authority. No such right is granted to the employee.
>
> In addition, the rules provide that upon 30 days notice Hooters, but not the employee, may cancel the agreement to arbitrate. Moreover, Hooters reserves
>
> the right to modify the rules, "in whole or in part," whenever it wishes and "without notice" to the employee. Nothing in the rules even prohibits Hooters from changing the rules in the middle of an arbitration proceeding.
>
> We hold that the promulgation of so many biased rules—especially the scheme whereby one party to the proceeding so controls the arbitral panel—breaches the contract entered into by the parties. The parties agreed to

submit their claims to arbitration—a system whereby disputes are fairly resolved by an impartial third party. Hooters by contract took on the obligation of establishing such a system. By creating a sham system unworthy even of the name of arbitration, Hooters completely failed in performing its contractual duty.

Phillips would have her day in court. By not creating an ethical and fair arbitration agreement, Hooters lost its case.[a]

[a] *Hooters of America, Inc. v. Phillips,* 173 F.3d 933 (1999).

---

before the referee, no jury is allowed, and all trial procedures and rules of evidence are followed. A record is maintained for appeal purposes. The formality and judicial nature of this procedure differentiate it from arbitration.

The advantage of a private judge is that the parties are not controlled by the local court calendar. The case will be heard prior to cases filed earlier, because it will not be heard by the judges in the local court system. This procedure allows expeditious treatment of the case before a referee who has both experience as a judge and special expertise in the subject matter.

The parties pay most, if not all, of the costs for this type of litigation. It can be expensive and, therefore, is available only to parties who can afford it. Because of this expense, the use of private judges has been criticized as creating a legal system for the wealthy that may result in a dual system of justice (that is, one for the rich and one for the less advantaged). The wealthy can have their cases decided rather quickly before

LEGAL HIGHLIGHT

Electrical Companies Zap the Media

Three electrical utility companies (the plaintiffs) were building the William H. Zimmer Nuclear Power Plant. They contracted with General Electric Company (GE) to do construction work in the plant. A dispute occurred, and the three electrical companies brought a lawsuit against GE for breach of contract. From the outset of this litigation, the parties recognized the need for confidential treatment of many documents. They stipulated that these documents would not be released. This agreement was confirmed by a court order.

The court required this case to be heard in a minitrial, the results of which were not binding on the parties. The proceeding was closed to the general public. The local news media objected to the closed hearing and filed a lawsuit to enforce their First Amendment rights of freedom of the press. In the meantime, the minitrial was held and the case was settled without going to a formal trial. In the media lawsuit, the judge refused to modify the original order, and the documents were not released to the news media. The news media appealed.

The U.S. Court of Appeals upheld the trial judge's order. The appeals court held that restrictions could be placed on information release when an alternative dispute resolution (ADR) proceeding is used.

Some types of ADR procedures, including minitrials, have been used for more than a decade. A conflict arises, however, between the right of access by the press and the public policy that encourages the use of ADR procedures. The court concluded that the law should favor the ADR proceeding.

If public access were allowed by the media, parties to lawsuits would have little incentive to try to settle the case in an ADR procedure. The public has no right to observe negotiations leading to a traditional case settlement. Thus, the public has no right to papers and other information used in an ADR proceeding that leads to a settlement.

judges with specialized experience, who devote full time to their cases, whereas the thousands of other parties to lawsuits must wait months and often years before their cases reach the court calendar.

Recently, relatively low-cost alternative private courts have been created as for-profit businesses. These private courts allow both parties to determine the hearing dates, location, presiding judge, and whether the judge's decision is binding. Each party is charged a filing fee, as well as a set fee for each half-day hearing session. Obviously, the longer the hearing, the more costly the procedure becomes.

Short Trial

A few states have developed a blend between arbitration and a judicial trial. This procedure is called a **short trial**. The idea is to retain the jury format but have it binding on all parties. The number of jurors is reduced to no less than four. If three members out of the four agree, then that is the verdict. Before the trial, the parties agree that they will not appeal the decision of the jury.

All short trials are concluded in one day with each side having two hours to present evidence. These trials are placed on the court calendar in between regular trials. People called for jury duty like this procedure because they only have to be in court one day. The parties like this approach because they get their day in court within months of filing the lawsuit instead of years.

Partnering

The Army Corps of Engineers created the concept of **partnering** in order to finish projects in a timely manner and to avoid time-consuming lawsuits. Partnering creates teams of key decision makers from each of the contracting parties, such as the general contractor and the subcontractors to name a few. When potential problems arise, they are referred to the partnering team that makes decisions to prevent or solve problems as they arise in large construction projects. Partnering attempts to create a sound working relationship. The decision to include a clause mandating the partnering process is made during the contract negotiations.

In partnering, key decision makers from each contracting party and a neutral facilitator meet in retreats and workshops before the job starts. The individuals become acquainted with one another. The workshops allow each to learn the priorities, needs, and interests of the other project partners.

Partnering creates a framework for team building and requires creating good communication lines, building trust relationships, working through problems, exploring options, and fashioning solutions. The idea is to prevent disputes or, if a dispute does arise, to resolve it as quickly as possible. The goal is to complete the project in a timely manner.

Partnering implements total quality management principles to which all parties should dedicate themselves in order to build a quality project. The partners meet both on a regular basis and an irregular basis when urgent problems require attention throughout the construction period.

The costs of the partnering meetings and of the neutral facilitator are built into the budget of the project. By preventing disputes that might otherwise result in costly delays and lawsuits, all the parties save money. A problem solved costs less than a problem that is ignored or passed off to another party to the contract only to later become a larger and more expensive problem to solve.

Partnering has been so successful in the construction industry that businesses are inserting partnering clauses in long-term supply contracts, purchasing contracts, and other nonconstruction contracts. Partnering is not really an alternative dispute resolution process but rather is an effective management tool that uses ADR methodology.

International Consideration

Arbitration in International Situations

Judicial procedures are used frequently in the United States to resolve disputes at all levels. Some cultures consider the need to resolve a dispute in court to be a personal failure. Thus, many international contracts provide for mediation, arbitration, or both.

The world community favors alternative dispute resolution procedures over the judicial forum. The **United Nations Convention on the Recognition and Enforcement of Foreign Arbitral Awards**,[13] commonly called the **New York**

---

[13]See the Web site at http://www.uncitral.org. A copy of the United Nations Convention on the Recognition and Enforcement of Foreign Arbitral Awards is available at http://www4.law.cornell.edu/uscode/9.

Convention, has been signed by seventy-three countries, including the United States, Canada, and Mexico. This convention allows the enforcement of arbitrated awards in any of the signature countries. Thus, international business associates may have disputes decided by arbitration. That arbitral award may be enforced in the country where the loser resides.

Additionally, the United States, Mexico, and ten Latin American countries have signed the **Inter-American Convention on International Commercial Arbitration (Panama Convention)**.[14] In this agreement, the twelve countries agree to submit their disputes about commercial transactions to arbitration.

With the North American Free Trade Agreement (NAFTA) in effect, trade among the United States, Canada, and Mexico has steadily increased. The contracts negotiated among businesses should consider including mandatory mediation or arbitration clauses. Drafters of the contracts can look to many sources for model clauses, including those recommended by the United Nations or the American Arbitration Association.

One provision of NAFTA requires disagreements to be submitted to an arbitration panel. The three-person panel uses arbitration procedures established by the World Bank. Just as in other arbitration proceedings, there is no appeal from its decisions.

The **United Nations Commission on International Trade Law (UNCITRAL)**[15] has developed model arbitration clauses. The commission has created rules for use in arbitration related to international trade that are known as the UNCITRAL Model Law on International Commercial Arbitration.[16]

The American Arbitration Association follows international arbitration rules. These rules have provisions to determine the place and language of the arbitration, to authorize arbitrators to issue interim orders, and to appoint independent experts if necessary. Both arbitration and mediation provisions can be included in international commercial contracts.

Several organizations worldwide handle arbitration matters. The American Arbitration Association and the United Nations Commission on International Trade Law have already been mentioned. The London Court of International Arbitration[17] and the International Chamber of Commerce[18] (located in Paris, France) are among the other better known organizations. The Danish Institute of Arbitration is a permanent arbitration institution that has been in existence in Copenhagen ever since 1894. This organization has assisted in the settlement of numerous conflicts of a varied nature and accumulated a considerable fund of knowledge on arbitration procedures and the establishment of arbitration tribunals.

[14]See the Web site at http://www.oas.org. A copy of the InterAmerican Convention on International Commercial Arbitration is available at http://www4.law.cornell.edu/uscode/9.

[15]See the UNCITRAL Web site at http://www.uncitral.org.
[16]The Model Law is found at http://www.jus.uio.no/lm/un.arbitration.model.law.1985.
[17]See the London Court of International Arbitration Web site at http://www.lcia-arbitration.com.
[18]See the International Chamber of Commerce Web site at http://www.iccwbo.org.

PRACTICAL TIPS
Arbitration of Disputes Involving "Lemons"

You have purchased your first new automobile. On the way home, it suddenly stops. This event is just the beginning of your nightmare. After twelve trips to the dealership in a six-week period, you realize that you own a true lemon. A good preventive law strategy is to study the law that applies in these types of cases. Here is a checklist that may provide some assistance.

Checklist

✔ *State Statutes* Check to see if your state has a "lemon law." Usually, a modified arbitration procedure is authorized. If your vehicle meets the criteria for the lemon classification, you may be entitled to a replacement automobile or to an appropriate cash refund. If you are dissatisfied with the arbitrator's decision, you can take your case to court. The automobile manufacturer, however, is bound by the decision.

✔ *Documentation* If your state has a lemon law, make sure you follow the statutory provisions. Document every trip to the automobile dealer and make sure that the documentation relates to the problem. Ensure that the documentation is consistent. For example, one document relates to electrical problems, but the next trip states only that the oil was changed. In fact, the automobile was returned for an oil change and for electrical problems. The statute requires that the automobile be returned for the same problem for a specific number of trips. You need to document the number of trips the automobile was returned to the automobile

dealership for the same problem, otherwise, you will not meet the statutory requirement.

✔ *Predispute Arbitration Clause* If your state does not have a lemon law, check to see if your contract has a clause that requires arbitration for any problems that arise.

✔ *Postdispute Arbitration Clause* If your state does not have a lemon law, check to see if the dealer will agree to arbitration if the contract is silent on the matter.

✔ *Lawsuit* If these options are not available, check to see if filing a lawsuit against the manufacturer and dealer is worth the time and expense to compensate you for your loss. You know, however, that this option would be very expensive, and months or years could pass before you finally have your day in court.

Chapter Summary

The judicial system is overburdened with litigation that results in long and expensive delays from the time of filing a complaint to the case conclusion. The judiciary, businesspeople, and the public have a real interest in finding alternatives to formal court procedures. These alternative dispute resolution procedures include negotiation, conciliation, mediation, arbitration, med/arb, fact finding, minitrials, hiring of private judges, short trials, and partnering.

In negotiation, the parties to the dispute resolve their differences by engaging in cooperative behavior to arrive at an agreement acceptable to all. Successful negotiation is an important skill that is not often taught in schools. Negotiations can occur at any stage of a dispute.

Conciliation involves a neutral third party. The conciliator facilitates the negotiations between the parties to help them to arrive at a mutually acceptable agreement. The conciliator does not actively participate in the negotiations and does not impose a decision on the parties. The parties must reach an agreement on their own.

Mediation also involves a neutral third party who facilitates the negotiations between the parties. The mediator helps the parties to negotiate their differences. The mediator has no power to make a decision. The parties must reach an agreement on their own.

In arbitration, the parties submit their dispute to an

impartial third person. The arbitrator usually specializes in the subject area that the dispute is about. In 1925, Congress passed the Federal Arbitration Act, and federal policy favors arbitration. Arbitration is more favorable than litigation, having fewer financial costs, shorter time costs, maintenance of privacy, less formality, a wider choice in decision-maker selection, and choice of the forum.

Arbitration occurs in one of two settings: contractual or judicial. A contractual agreement is voluntary and thus becomes binding arbitration. Many states require that lawsuits be sent to judicial arbitration when the amount requested is for less than a specified amount. If the parties agree with the decision of the judicial arbitrator, the case is settled. If one party disagrees, the case will be heard by the court. Arbitration has several disadvantages, one of which is that when the award is not written, prior precedent is lost.

The field of ADR is evolving. Fact finding is an investigative process used in complex commercial disputes. Minitrials are used in courts where an adviser conducts an abbreviated discovery process. At the completion of discovery, the adviser helps the parties to reach a settlement. A few states allow parties to hire a private judge. The parties are able to hold the trial quickly rather than waiting for the case to be placed on the regular court calendar. Short trials are a combination of arbitration and judicial trials. Partnering is a process used in large construction projects to prevent disputes, or if a potential dispute develops, to resolve the matter quickly. Cyber-mediation is the use of Web sites to be realistic about settlements concerning damage claims.

Using the World Wide Web

Registering a domain name is as simple as filling out a form and sending in the fees. Or is it? If the domain name you have selected has not been taken, generally there is no problem. But what if someone has taken the domain name? The Domain Name Dispute Resolution Service gives effect to the Uniform Domain Name Dispute Resolution Policy adopted by the Internet Corporation for Assigned Names and Numbers.

The Federal Trade Commission (FTC) has published a pamphlet in hard copy and on the Internet concerning arbitration and mediation. Go to the FTC site and answer the following questions:

- How would you find a dispute resolution program in your neighborhood?

- What questions should you ask about the program before you decide to use it?

- How should you prepare for an alternate dispute resolution program?

For *Web Activities*, links to Web sites mentioned in the chapter, and additional Web sites that relate to the chapter topics, go to **http://bohlman.westbuslaw .com**, click on "Internet Applications," and select Chapter 4.

Web Activities

Go to **http://bohlman.westbuslaw.com**, click on "Internet Applications," and select Chapter 4.
4–1 JAMS
4–2 Federal Mediation Web Site

Key Terms

alternative dispute
    resolution (ADR)
Alternative Disputes
    Resolutions Act
American Arbitration
    Association (AAA)
arbitration
arbitrator
award
binding arbitration
conciliation

contractual agreement to
    arbitrate
fact finding
Federal Arbitration Act
    (FAA)
InterAmerican
    Convention on Inter-
    national Commercial
    Arbitration (Panama
    Convention)
judicial arbitration

med/arb
mediation
minitrial
negotiation
partnering
private judge
Revised Uniform Ar-
    bitration Act (RUAA)
short trial
tribunal administrator
Uniform Arbitration Act

United Nations
    Commission on
    International Trade
    Law (UNCITRAL)
United Nations
    Convention on the
    Recognition and
    Enforcement of
    Foreign Arbitral
    Awards (New York
    Convention)

Questions and Case Problems

4–1 Mediation Do you think that mediation should be used before a civil case goes to trial? If so, should the judge, who may be trying the case later, first serve as the mediator? What advantages and disadvantages do you see in such a situation?

4–2 Arbitration With a few exceptions, parties arbitrate their disputes because they have agreed to do so. Even with an agreement to arbitrate, one of the parties frequently changes his mind, deciding against arbitrating the dispute. Why do you think people want to avoid arbitration?

4–3 ADR You are the president of a medium-sized company that manufactures air conditioners. Recently you have noticed a substantial increase in legal expenses because of legal actions brought against your firm. Most, if not all, are brought by former employees and customers. In all cases, you believe the actions are not justified, but you want to decrease the cost of formal litigation. What types of cases would you allow to be handled through alternative dispute resolution procedures? What types of cases would you not allow to be handled through alternative dispute resolution procedures? Which alternative dispute resolution procedures would you use?

4–4 Arbitration Describe the advantages and disadvantages of arbitration over a judicial proceeding.

4–5 Arbitration The Southland Corporation is the owner and franchiser of 7-Eleven convenience stores. An arbitration clause within its franchise agreement requires arbitration for any controversy or claim arising from the agreement. California has a franchise statute that allows legal actions to be brought in the courts. Some of the franchisees brought action against Southland Corporation based on violations of the California franchise law, along with other claims for fraud, misrepresentation, and breach of contract. Southland moved to force arbitration. What should the court hold? [*Southland Corp. v. Keating,* 465 U.S. 1, 104 S. Ct. 852, 79 L. Ed. 2d 1 (1984)]

4–6 Arbitration Alexander argues that he was discharged from his job because of his race. He had his case arbitrated but lost because the arbitrator found that Alexander's discharge was for just cause. Alexander appealed to a federal court to have the arbitration award overturned. On appeal, his ex-employer argued that Alexander had waived his rights under federal law to have the case heard by a court. Should Alexander have a new trial over the same issues and facts decided by the arbitrator? [*Alexander v. Gardner-Denver Co.,* 415 U.S. 36, 94 S. Ct. 1011, 39 L. Ed. 2d 147 (1974)]

4-7 Arbitration Eastern Associated Coal Corp. (Eastern), the employer, and United Mine Workers of America, the union, were parties to a collective bargaining agreement with arbitration provisions. The clause provided that the arbitrator's decision was final. The arbitration agreement specified that Eastern must prove "just cause" in order to discharge an employee. Smith, a union member, worked for Eastern in a job that required him to drive heavy vehicles on public highways. He tested positive for marijuana. Eastern sought to discharge Smith. The union defended Smith's rights. The arbitrator found that Smith's positive drug

test did not amount to "just cause" for discharge. The arbitrator ordered Smith's reinstatement provided that he (1) accept a suspension without pay; (2) reimburse the costs; (3) participate in a substance-abuse program; (4) undergo random drug testing; and (5) provide Eastern with a signed, undated letter of resignation, to take effect if Smith again tested positive within the next five years. Easter appealed. Did Smith get to keep his job? Explain your answer. [*Eastern Associated Coal Corporation v. United Mine Workers of America,* 531 U.S. 57, 121 S. Ct. 462, 148 L. Ed. 2d 354 (2000)]

4–8 Arbitration Beers, while in Craft Warehouse's (Craft) store, was detained, then arrested by police for shoplifting. Beers was prosecuted and found not guilty. Afterwards, Beers' attorney wrote two identical letters to the store owner and store manager demanding $4,000 to settle plaintiff's claim for damages caused by the store's actions. Craft refused to settle. Beers filed two lawsuits seeking $4,000 for false imprisonment and $4,000 for malicious prosecution and attorney fees for each. The two lawsuits were consolidated and it was submitted to mandatory arbitration. The arbitrator awarded $4,000 and no attorney fees. The state statute required that in suits for $4,000 or less, reasonable attorney fees were to be awarded. Was the arbitrator correct in not awarding attorney fees? What was the result and why? [*Beers v. Jeson Enterprises,* 165 Or. App. 722, 998 P.2d 716 (Or. App. 2000)]

4–9 Arbitration AMF, Inc., and Brunswick Corporation compete nationally in the manufacture of bowling center equipment. In an earlier lawsuit, each of the two companies alleged that the other had advertised its products falsely. As part of the case settlement, AMF and Brunswick each agreed to submit to an advisory third party any further dispute involving an advertised claim to determine if there was valid support for the advertisement. The decision of the advisory third party was not binding on either party. Two years later, Brunswick advertised its new laminated bowling lanes as being superior to the wooden lanes AMF produced. AMF demanded that Brunswick's claims be submitted for independent validation by the advisory third party. Brunswick refused and argued that only binding arbitration clauses are enforceable. Is Brunswick's position correct? Why or why not? [*AMF Inc. v. Brunswick Corp.,* 621 F. Supp. 456 (D.C.N.Y. 1985)]

4–10 Internet The Federal Mediation and Conciliation Service assists private businesses by providing workplace mediation and grievance mediation. Discuss the differences between these two mediation services. See the Federal Mediation and Conciliation Service Web site at **http://www.fmcs.gov**.

Chapter 5

The Constitution and the Regulation of Business

The Constitution of 1789 deserves the veneration with which the Americans have been accustomed to regard it. It is true that many criticisms have been passed upon its arrangements, upon its omissions, upon the artificial character of some of the institutions it creates. . . . Yet, after all deductions, it ranks above every other written constitution for the intrinsic excellence of its scheme, its adaptation to the circumstances of the people, the simplicity, brevity, and precision of its language, its judicious mixture of definiteness in principle with elasticity in details.

The American Commonwealth, 3 vols.
(London: Macmillan and Co., 1888),
Vol. 1, p. 34
Viscount James Bryce, 1838–1922
British Ambassador to the United
States of America, 1907–1913
Regius Professor of Civil Law, Oxford
University

Chapter Outline

Ethical Consideration

Good Advertising?

As advertising manager for a local television station, you select which commercials will be aired and when. Just arrived in your office is an advertisement for a lawyer in town. The commercial depicts a casually dressed man who looks into the television camera and announces firmly that he was an accident victim and that this lawyer "got me $155,000, even though the police report said that I was totally at fault." The next scene shows another accident victim relaxing near a pool. This person states that the same lawyer recovered $1 million "from an insurance company that said I didn't even have a claim."

Although you are aware that freedom of speech is an important right, you are personally disgusted by this type of advertisement, which you believe has an insidious negative effect on the image of lawyers and on the judicial system as a whole. Should you reject or air the commercial? Use the ethical model presented in Chapter 2 and reprinted on the inside front cover to develop your answer.

Introduction

The U.S. Constitution governs both personal and business lives as the supreme law in this country. All statutes passed by Congress or by a state legislature, all decisions made by judges in the federal and state courts, and all actions by the president or by the governor of a state must be in accordance with the Constitution. If a conflict arises between the state and federal constitutions, the U.S. Constitution prevails. The Constitution serves as a limitation on the power of the government.

The Constitution needs to be read to understand court decisions and the reasons that govern whether Congress can or cannot adopt laws. Third, every businessperson should appreciate the impact of the interstate commerce clause and other provisions affecting business contained in the Constitution.

Artiste Login. Carlo and Carlotta know that the U.S. Constitution and their state constitution create the two levels of governments that provide them as individuals—and, by extension, to their business—with constitutional protections from certain government actions. Knowledge of the Constitution can aid them when Artiste Login has any interaction with governmental agencies.

Articles of the U.S. Constitution

The Constitution has two functions.[1] First, it creates the government. Second, it establishes an individual's rights in relation to the federal government.

The first three articles of the Constitution establish the framework for the federal government. Article IV gives direction to the states through the supremacy clause, the full faith and credit clause, and the privileges and immunities clause. Article V establishes the methods for amending the Constitution. Article VI ranks the order of the laws, giving highest priority to the Constitution itself and lowest priority to the laws of local government. Article VII, the last article, provides for the Constitution's ratification.

Separation of Powers Clause

The main body of the Constitution creates the federal government and establishes the three branches: the **legislative branch**, the **executive branch**, and the **judicial branch**. The rights, duties, and powers of the legislative branch are set forth in Article I. Article II creates the executive branch and establishes the powers of the president. The federal judicial system is created by Article III.

Each government's branch fulfills a separate function. Although no branch can exercise the authority of another branch, each branch has some power to limit the actions of the other two branches. This scheme creates a system of **checks and balances** among the

---

[1]A complete copy of the Constitution is found in Appendix A. The Constitution and founding documents, such as the Declaration of Independence and the Magna Carta, may be viewed at Exhibit Hall on the National Archives and Records Administration Web site at http://www.archives.gov. The Northwestern University Web site has a multimedia database of Supreme Court decisions found at http://er.library.northwestern.edu/detail.asp?id=34363. Supreme Court cases can be found at the Cornell Law School Legal Information Institute Web site at http://supct.law.cornell.edu/supct.

branches, so that no single branch can accumulate too much power.

For example, the executive branch is responsible for foreign affairs, but treaties with foreign governments require the advice and consent of the Senate. Congress has the power to tax, but the president can veto a tax bill. Congress determines the jurisdiction of the federal courts. The specific powers granted to Congress are listed in Article I, Section 8. Among those powers are the powers to regulate commerce, the taxing power, and the spending power.

Judicial Review. The Supreme Court exercises a power not specifically granted to it. This power is called the doctrine of **judicial review**, which allows the court to determine if acts of the other two government branches are in conflict with the mandates of the Constitution. Congress may pass, on rare occasions, a statute contrary to the Constitution, or the president may act, although rarely, counter to the Constitution. If the acts are in conflict, the Supreme Court can find them unconstitutional. The authority for judicial review is found in ancient English law.

The power of judicial review was first established in 1803 in the case of *Marbury v. Madison*. The Supreme Court determined that it had the power to decide whether a law passed by Congress violated the Constitution. Thus, the power of judicial review resides in the judicial branch and is part of the system of checks and balances. The following case creates the doctrine of judicial review.

LANDMARK CASE

CASE 5.1

Supreme Court of the United States, 1803
5 U.S. (1 Cranch) 137, 2 L. Ed. 60
http://supct.law.cornell.edu/supct/cases/name.htm
http://www.ourdocuments.gov/content.php?page=transcript&doc=19

MARBURY v. MADISON

COMMENTARY Cranch was the second reporter of decisions and served from 1801 to 1815. The reporter of decisions is a Court position responsible for editing the Court's opinions and for supervising their printing and publication. During the time Cranch served, the Court issued oral opinions, which he wrote down. Cranch's reports were praised for their accuracy and clarity. The Court began to issue written opinions to supplement its oral opinions only for important cases during Cranch's service. Because Cranch was not paid, he was allowed to sell his reports to the public to earn a living. The U.S. Reports were published privately by different reporters of decisions who followed Cranch. In 1882, the U.S. Government Printing Office (GPO) assumed the duties of printing the Court's decisions. The GPO has republished these privately published decisions, citing the name of the reporter of decisions.

BACKGROUND AND FACTS After George Washington[a] became president, a political division appeared between those who favored a strong federal government and those who favored a weak federal government. The Federalist Party, led by Alexander Hamilton,[b] was in favor of a strong federal government and tended to reflect the views of the North and banking and manufacturing interests. The Democratic-Republican Party, led by Thomas Jefferson,[c] favored a weak federal government, advocated states' rights, sought a strict interpretation of the Constitution, and represented the views of the South and farmers.

As a result of the national elections of 1800, President John Adams,[d] a Federalist, lost his bid for reelection to Thomas Jefferson. The political party controlling both the presidency and Congress changed from the Federalist Party to the Democratic-Republican Party.

[a] George Washington (1732–1799), a Virginian, was the first president of the United States (1789–1797).
[b] Alexander Hamilton (1755–1804) from New York served as the first secretary of the treasury under President George Washington. Hamilton created the nation's central banking system.
[c] Thomas Jefferson (1743–1826), a Virginian, was elected as the third president of the United States (1801–1809). Jefferson and Adams died within hours of one another on July 4, 1826. Each died believing the other lived. They were the last two signers of the Declaration of Independence, signed fifty years earlier to the day.
[d] John Adams (1735–1826) from Massachusetts was elected as the second president of the United States (1797–1801).

Believing that the Democratic-Republicans would weaken the national government, Adams, during the final hours of his administration, made fifty-nine midnight appointments to the judiciary. One way to extend political influence after leaving office was to appoint people to judiciary terms, since those terms last well beyond an administration. He hoped to pack the courts with loyal Federalists before Jefferson took office. Adams nominated William Marbury as a justice of the peace for Washington, D.C.

The U.S. Senate ratified Marbury's appointment, and Adams signed the commission. To make the appointment complete, the commissions had to be delivered to the appointee. Adams' secretary of state, John Marshall,[e] delivered forty-two of the fifty-nine appointments before he left office. After Jefferson became president, his newly appointed secretary of state, James Madison,[f] refused to deliver the commission to Marbury. Marbury, along with three others, decided to sue.

While Adams was still president, the Congress (dominated by the Federalists) passed a law (the Judiciary Act of 1789) concerning, in part, the issuance of a writ of *mandamus*, which was a writ to enforce the performance of a public duty. The Judiciary Act required the United States Supreme Court to issue the writ, effectively making it a trial court. This statute greatly expanded the powers of the Supreme Court. It was on the basis of this new law that Marbury sued.

In an unusual turn of events, John Marshall had gone from being secretary of state under Adams to chief justice of the United States (appointed by Adams prior to leaving office and confirmed by the senate). Today, any judge would remove herself or himself from the case because of conflict of interest, but Marshall heard the *Marbury* case and wrote the following opinion, which still stands today.

Chief Justice MARSHALL delivered the opinion of the Court.

. . . .

The act to establish the judicial courts of the United States authorizes the Supreme Court, "to issue writs of *mandamus*, in cases warranted by the principles and usages of law, to any courts appointed or persons holding office, under the authority of the United States." The secretary of state, being a person holding an office under the authority of the United States, is precisely within the letter of this description; and if this court is not authorized to issue a writ of *mandamus* to such an officer, it must be because the law is unconstitutional.

. . . .

The question, whether an act, repugnant to the constitution, can become the law of the land, is a question deeply interesting to the United States; but, happily, not of an intricacy proportioned to its interest. It seems only necessary to recognize certain principles, supposed to have been long and well established, to decide it. That the people have an original right to establish, for their future government, such principles, as, in their opinion, shall most conduce to their own happiness is the basis on which the whole American fabric has been erected.

. . . .

It is emphatically the province and duty of the judicial department to say what the law is. Those who apply the rule to particular cases, must of necessity expound and interpret that rule. If two laws conflict with each other, the courts must decide on the operation of each.

---

[e] John Marshall (1755–1835) served as the fourth chief justice of the United States (1801–1835) appointed by President John Adams. In addition to deciding *Marbury v. Madison,* he also wrote the opinion of *McCullock v. Maryland* (1819), which decided that Congress had implied powers and that in a conflict between federal law and state law, federal law would prevail. See footnote 3 in this chapter.
[f] James Madison (1751–1836) from Virginia was elected as the fourth president of the United States (1809–1817). He was a Democratic-Republican.

So if a law be in opposition to the constitution; if both the law and the constitution apply to a particular case, so that the court must either decide that case conformably to the law, disregarding the constitution; or conformably to the constitution, disregarding the law; the court must determine which of these conflicting rules governs the case. This is of the very essence of judicial duty.

If, then, the courts are to regard the constitution, and the constitution is superior to any ordinary act of the legislature, the constitution, and not such ordinary act, must govern the case to which they both apply.

Those, then, who controvert the principle that the constitution is to be considered, in court, as a paramount law, are reduced to the necessity of maintaining that courts must close their eyes on the constitution, and see only the law.

This doctrine would subvert the very foundation of all written constitutions. It would declare that an act which, according to the principles and theory of our government, is entirely void, is yet, in practice, completely obligatory. It would declare that if the legislature shall do what is expressly forbidden, such act, notwithstanding the express prohibition, is in reality effectual. It would be giving to the legislature a practical and real omnipotence, with the same breath which professes to restrict their powers within narrow limits. It is prescribing limits, and declaring that those limits may be passed at pleasure.

. . . .

Thus, the particular phraseology of the constitution of the United States confirms and strengthens the principle, supposed to be essential to all written constitutions, that a law repugnant to the constitution is void; and that courts, as well as other departments, are bound by that instrument.

DECISION AND REMEDY The Court held unconstitutional the provision of the Judiciary Act of 1789 that gave original jurisdiction to the United States Supreme Court to issue writs of *mandamus*. Thus, Marbury never became a justice of the peace.

COMMENT Marshall was faced with a dilemma. If he exercised the authority given the Court by Congress to issue the writ of *mandamus* and thus ordered Madison, the new secretary of state, to deliver the commissions, Madison could refuse. The Court has no way to enforce its orders, because it has no enforcement machinery. The decisions of the Supreme Court even to this day rely on its moral authority. If Marshall did not issue the order, the secretary of state would be allowed to choose the acts that he would perform.

Marshall took another approach altogether. He found the act of Congress unconstitutional. The Constitution clearly delineates the cases over which the Court has original jurisdiction. The Constitution did not grant Congress the power to expand the Court's original jurisdiction as set out in Article III.

Because Congress did not have that power, the congressional act was declared unconstitutional by the Supreme Court. Marshall went on to say that Jefferson and Madison had acted incorrectly in refusing to deliver Marbury's commission, but the Supreme Court issued no order because it did not have the power to do so.

The Court's decision was a masterpiece of judicial navigation. Marshall avoided a confrontation with the president by not ordering him to do anything, found that the president had acted incorrectly, and firmly established the doctrine of judicial review. The case also illustrates that a situation revolving around an insignificant fact, such as an appointment of a justice of the peace, can lead to a monumental judicial decision—in this case, the establishment of the doctrine of judicial review.

CRITICAL THINKING: POLITICAL CONSIDERATION Discuss whether a judge should have the power to declare a statute unconstitutional when the act was passed by an elected legislative body and signed into law by either the president or a governor. Would your answer differ if the position of judge were elected or appointed? Can you find a recent case discussed in a newspaper or magazine in which a court declared a legislative act to be unconstitutional?

The Supreme Court still uses the doctrine of judicial review. When a congressional statute is challenged on the basis of constitutionality, the Court retains its power, as it has since *Marbury v. Madison*, to determine if Congress has exceeded its authority under the Constitution.

The United States Supreme Court has overturned fewer than 150 statutes during the past two centuries. In 1997, however, the Court overturned three statutes in one week.

LEGAL HIGHLIGHT

A Funny Thing Happened on the Way to Amend the Articles of Confederation

After winning independence from England, the original thirteen colonies created a government of states. This government was called the Confederation of the United States of America, a name used in the Declaration of Independence. The Articles of Confederation, adopted in 1781, created the confederation and set out the government powers. It would last only a few short years until 1789.

Although a federal government existed, all the powers were held by the states. Unfortunately, the states did not work together. Each state based its decisions on its own best interests and not on the best interests of the unified thirteen colonies. Dissatisfaction arose and by 1786 five states proposed that the Articles be reformed. Although reform was needed, many people vehemently opposed the idea of a strong central government. Nevertheless, the Congress, operating under the Articles of Confederation, called for a convention to amend the articles. Of the seventy-four delegates named to the convention, only fifty-five delegates from twelve states attended. Rhode Island disagreed with the procedure and sent no delegates.

The convention started on May 14, 1787, in Philadelphia. The delegates labored through a hot, humid Pennsylvania summer. Working secretly, they wrote guarded letters to friends and rarely spoke of the business at hand during their leisure hours. Instead of amending the Articles of Confederation, the delegates

drafted a completely new constitution that would replace the articles. The document created the strong central government so feared by many. Of the fifty-five delegates who started the work, forty-one were present when the convention ended on September 17, 1787. Only thirty-nine signed the document, the Constitution of the United States of America.

The Constitution then was submitted to the states for ratification. Three-fourths of the states (nine out of thirteen) had to ratify the Constitution before it could take effect. Heated debates in newspapers and in meetings followed. A series of newspaper articles, known today as the *Federalist Papers*, written by James Madison, Alexander Hamilton, and John Jay, argued for the adoption of the Constitution.

After intense debate, the ninth state, New Hampshire, ratified the Constitution on June 21, 1788. Article VII of the proposed constitution stipulated that the Constitution would become effective (for those who ratified it) when ratified by nine states. In 1789, the Constitution went into effect. By 1791, all thirteen states had ratified the Constitution. This document is now the oldest constitution in the world in continuous use. The genius of the writers lay in creating a mechanism that could translate theory into reality.

Many people observed that the Constitution listed no personal freedoms. Before ratifying the Constitution, a number of states made it clear that amendments containing the rights of the people in relation to the government would be necessary. The first ten amendments, known as the Bill of Rights, were adopted in 1791.

The Commerce Clause

Congress has the power "to regulate Commerce with foreign Nations, and among the several States, and with the Indian Tribes" (Article I, Section 8). This clause is known as the **commerce clause**. No other clause in the Constitution has a greater impact on business. Because the federal government has the power to regulate commerce, the rules governing the movement of goods through the states are uniform.

Federal Regulation of Commerce. Congress holds the power to regulate any activity, interstate or intrastate, that substantially affects interstate commerce. For example, a federal regulation allows only a maximum number of acres of wheat to be grown. A farmer cannot plant more than the allowed acreage, even though the additional amount is for the farmer's own consumption. If enough farmers grew excess wheat for home consumption, they would reduce the overall wheat demand. A federal law must consider its cumulative effect on the entire economy. Thus, even one farmer may have a substantial economic effect on interstate commerce. If one farmer could grow excess wheat, others could too, and the goal of the federal regulation would be defeated.[2]

[2]*Wickard v. Filbert*, 317 U.S. 111, 63 S. Ct. 82, 87 L. Ed. 122 (1942), and http://www.findlaw.com/casecode/supreme.html.

State Regulation of Commerce. States have a strong interest in regulating activities within their borders. States possess **police powers**, which give them the authority to regulate private activities in order to protect or promote the health, safety, morals, or general welfare of their citizens. For example, states have a strong interest in assuring the safety of privately owned trucks and automobiles using state highways in order to protect the rest of the traveling public.

Most state regulations place some burden on interstate commerce. When a state regulation encroaches on interstate commerce, the courts must balance the state's interest, reflected in the merits and purposes of the regulation, against the burden the regulation places on interstate commerce. A state law enacted pursuant to a state's police powers and affecting the health, safety, and welfare of local citizens, for example, carries a strong presumption of validity.

Courts balance the interests between the state and federal governments. The regulated activity, however, must involve commerce, that is, the exchange or trade of goods or property. The following case discusses whether documents generated by the county government are prohibited to be released to the opposing party under a federal statute in a lawsuit in state court.

CASE 5.2 Supreme Court of the United States, 2003 537 U.S. 129, 123 S. Ct. 720, 154 L. Ed. 2d 610	## PIERCE COUNTY, WASHINGTON v. GUILLEN **BACKGROUND AND FACTS** Ignacio Guillen's wife, Clementina Guillen-Alejandre, died in an automobile accident that occurred at an intersection in Pierce County, Washington (County). Several months before the accident, the county had requested funding to improve this intersection, but the request had been denied. County renewed its application for funding and the second request was approved three weeks after the accident occurred.

Guillen sought to obtain from the county any information about accidents that had occurred at the intersection where the accident occurred. County declined to provide any responsive information, asserting that any relevant documents were protected by federal law citing 23 U.S.C. Section 409. After informal efforts failed to resolve this discovery dispute, Guillen filed an action alleging that County's refusal to disclose the relevant documents violated the state's Public Disclosure Act (PDA). The trial court granted summary judgment in favor of Guillen and ordered County to disclose five documents and pay respondent's attorney's fees. County appealed.

The Washington Supreme Court upheld the trial court's order for a summary judgment. The court considered whether Section 409 was a proper exercise of Congress' power under the spending, commerce, and necessary and proper clauses of Article I of the U.S. Constitution. With respect to the spending clause, the court found that "barring the admissibility and discovery in state court of accident reports and other traffic and accident materials and 'raw data' that were originally prepared for routine state and local purposes, simply because they are 'collected' for, *among other reasons,* federal purposes pursuant to a federal statute" did not reasonably serve any "valid federal interest in the operation of the federal safety enhancement program."

With respect to the commerce clause, the court concluded that Section 409 was not an "integral part" of the regulation of the federal-aid highway system and, thus, could not be upheld under federal law. Finally, with respect to the necessary and proper clause, the court ruled that, although Congress could require state courts to enforce a federal privilege protecting materials "that would not have been created but-for federal mandates such as . . . [§]152," it was "neither 'necessary' nor 'proper' for Congress in 1995 to extend that privilege to traffic and accident materials and raw data created and collected for state and local purposes, simply because they are *also* collected and used for federal purposes."

Section 409 modified Section 152, which was the original statute that provided local governments with funding to improve the most dangerous sections of roads. The modification was adopted to protect local governments against possible liability issues.

From this decision of the state Supreme Court, the County sought review by the U.S. Supreme Court.

Justice THOMAS delivered the opinion of the Court.

. . . .

It is well established that the Commerce Clause gives Congress authority to "regulate the use of the channels of interstate commerce." In addition, under the Commerce Clause, Congress "is empowered to regulate and protect the instrumentalities of interstate commerce, or persons or things in interstate commerce, even though the threat may come only from intrastate activities."

. . . Congress adopted § 152 to assist state and local governments in reducing hazardous conditions in the Nation's channels of commerce. That effort was impeded, however, by the States' reluctance to comply fully with the requirements of § 152, as such compliance would make state and local governments easier targets for negligence actions by providing would-be plaintiffs a centralized location from which they could obtain much of the evidence necessary for such actions. In view of these circumstances, Congress could reasonably believe that adopting a measure eliminating an unforeseen side effect of the information-gathering requirement of § 152 would result in more diligent efforts to collect the relevant information, more candid discussions of hazardous locations, better informed decision making, and, ultimately, greater safety on our Nation's roads. Consequently, both the original § 409 and the 1995 amendment can be viewed as legislation aimed at improving safety in the channels of commerce and increasing protection for the instrumentalities of interstate commerce. As such, they fall within Congress' Commerce Clause power. Accordingly, the judgment of the Washington Supreme Court is reversed and the case is remanded for further proceedings not inconsistent with this opinion.

DECISION AND REMEDY The Court found that it was proper for Congress to limit what evidence could be disclosed under the commerce clause of the Constitution.

CRITICAL THINKING: POLITICAL QUESTION When the Constitution was drafted did our founding fathers consider evidentiary issues when they drafted the commerce clause provision?

The Taxing Power

The **taxing power** comes from the constitutional clause that states that Congress has the "[p]ower to lay and collect Taxes, Duties, Imposts and Excises . . . but all Duties, Imposts and Excises shall be uniform throughout the United States" (Article I, Section 8). *Imposts* are taxes levied on imports. *Excises* are taxes placed on the sale or use of goods or service within a country and generally are paid by the buyer. For example, sales taxes are a form of excise tax.

All states must be treated equally for purposes of taxation. The courts examine whether Congress is actually attempting to regulate an area indirectly through taxation. If Congress is empowered to regulate an area, the tax is valid. If Congress attempts to regulate an area over which it has no authority, however, the tax law is void.

Federal taxes can be supported as a valid exercise of federal regulation. The Supreme Court has upheld statutes that impose taxation on income derived from both legal and illegal sources. For example, the Supreme Court has decided that taxes can be imposed on the transfer of firearms, on the transfer of marijuana, and on gambling income.

Taxing measures generally are found to be valid by the Supreme Court. The Court has held these tax laws to be within the national taxing power of Congress. Moreover, the Supreme Court has interpreted the commerce clause broadly to uphold various types of federal taxes imposed by Congress.

Artiste Login. Carlo and Carlotta own Artiste Login, which is able to create many types of works of art. One unique ability is manufacturing speciality cloth. A movie studio located in the United Kingdom has placed a special order with Artiste Login. The studio needs Artiste Login to weave a bolt of cloth using fine gold. The project is accepted. After months of work, the bolt of cloth is ready to be shipped to the movie studio. The bolt, valued at $5 million, will be insured for shipping. Carlo and Carlotta need to know if Artiste Login is required to pay an export tax on this valuable cloth because the bolt will be shipped from the state in which they live to the studio in the United Kingdom. Fortunately, the Constitution (Article I, Section 9) forbids export taxes on goods exported from the United States to other nations.

The Spending Power

Congress has the power "to pay the Debts and provide for the common Defense and general welfare of the United States" (Article I, Section 8). Thus, Congress is authorized to spend the monies collected under the taxing power. The **spending power** involves policy choices. Some taxpayers object to the government spending money on a particular program, such as Congress spending money to support national defense. It is, however, nearly impossible to object to specific government spending through the legal system because of the **standing to sue** requirement.

In any legal case, the doctrine of standing to sue requires a litigant to demonstrate a direct and immediate personal injury due to the challenged action. With respect to the government, a litigant must show an injury directly related to him that was caused by a particular government spending program and that the court can give him relief from the harm alleged. Rarely is a taxpayer directly harmed by any government spending program. As a result, the spending power seldom is challenged successfully. Communicating directly with members of Congress is a more efficient method of influencing spending policies. The voters also can speak through the ballot box.

The Supremacy Clause

Article VI provides that the Constitution, laws, and treaties of the United States are "the supreme Law of the Land." This **supremacy clause** governs the relationship between the states and the federal government.

When the Constitution specifically delegates a power to the federal government, any state law that conflicts with a federal law in that area is prohibited. If the conflict in the laws is taken to court, the state law will be rendered invalid. For example, under the Constitution only the federal government has the **exclusive power** to coin money, regulate immigration and naturalization laws, or implement bankruptcy laws. Other areas of the law are exclusive to the states, such as laws governing marriage, divorce, child custody, wills, or probate (distribution of property after death).

In other areas, the state and federal governments have **concurrent powers**, when they share powers. For example, robbery of a federally insured bank is both a state and federal crime.

When Congress chooses to act exclusively in an area, it must do so under a provision of the Constitution. Congress has this power under the **preemption doctrine**. When Congress decides to exercise exclusive jurisdiction over a particular area not stated in the Constitution, Congress is said to have preempted the area. Once Congress has acted, the state government no longer has authority to regulate the preempted area. Congress preempts areas that have national importance and where one uniform law is necessary. For example, the federal government has preempted the areas of aviation, labor, and nuclear power.

Congress rarely preempts an entire subject area by prohibiting state regulation. If a state law and a federal law conflict in an area of concurrent powers, and if the congressional intent is unclear, the courts must determine if Congress intended to exercise exclusive dominion over the given area.

Not all congressional powers are stated explicitly in the Constitution. Congress has the implied power under Article I, Section 8, to enact those laws necessary to carry out the enumerated powers vested in Congress and the government by the Constitution.[3]

[3]In *McCullock v. Maryland* (1819) the United States Supreme Court, with John Marshall presiding as chief justice of the United States, had to decide whether Congress had the power to create the First Bank of the United States, a central bank, today known as the Federal Reserve Board.

Alexander Hamilton, secretary of treasury under President George Washington, had persuaded Congress to pass the statute creating the First Bank of the United States. Thomas Jefferson opposed it because the Constitution did not specifically create or authorize the creation of a central bank by the federal government. Hamilton argued that the federal government had implied powers to create a central bank. Hamilton's implied powers argument prevailed when the United States Supreme Court upheld the legislation that created the First Bank of the United States.

Chief Justice Marshall laid down two doctrines that prevail today. First was the implied powers doctrine. James McCullock, cashier of the Baltimore branch of the First Bank of the United States, refused to pay a tax imposed by Maryland on the bank. The court upheld the implied power of the Congress to create a bank, because Congress needed a bank to exercise its specific powers. The court ruled that Congress has implied powers in addition to those expressly set out in the Constitution. The decision was based on the section of the Constitution called the "necessary and proper" clause (Article I, Section 8). This clause gives Congress power "to make all laws which shall be necessary and proper" to carry out its other powers.

The second doctrine is that federal power must prevail over state power in cases of conflict. The tax was declared unconstitutional because it interfered with an instrument of the federal government. Chief Justice Marshall stated that the American people "did not design to make their government dependent on the states."

Federalism is the organizational system of the U.S. government. Under this system, state governments share powers with the federal government. Neither the state nor the federal government is superior to the other except within the particular area of authority granted to it by the Constitution.

Federalism acknowledges that society is best served by distributing various functions among local governments and the national government depending on which government is best able to perform each function. For instance, the federal government can best handle national defense and foreign relations, whereas state and local governments are best able to handle domestic relations, probate, and traffic violations. Exhibit 5–1 depicts this division of powers.

Full Faith and Credit Clause

Article IV, Section 1, reads, "Full Faith and Credit shall be given in each State to the public Acts, Records, and judicial Proceedings of every other State." The Constitution requires every state, through the **full faith and credit clause**, to recognize and enforce the judgments and other public actions of sister states. For example, if you obtain a divorce in one state, all other states must recognize your divorce.

Limitations do apply. For instance, if the original court did not have jurisdiction, the judgment may be challenged in the state where the plaintiff tries to enforce the judgment.

Privileges and Immunities Clause

Article IV, Section 2, provides that "the citizens of each State shall be entitled to all Privileges and Immunities of Citizens in the several States." As a result of the **privileges and immunities clause**, one state cannot discriminate against the citizens of another state solely on the basis of their residency.

Limitations on this clause have evolved during the past 200 years. A state may pass a statute that protects "legitimate local interest." Under this protection, state-supported colleges and universities may charge higher tuition to nonresident students than to resident students. The justification is that the state's residents pay taxes that support the public university system.

Exhibit 5–1   **The American Federal System: Division of Powers between the Federal Government and the State Governments**

Powers Granted by the Constitution and Amendments

FEDERAL GOVERNMENT	FEDERAL AND STATE GOVERNMENTS	STATE GOVERNMENTS

Implied

"To make all laws which shall be necessary and proper for carrying into execution the foregoing powers, and all other powers vested by this Constitution in the Government of the United States, or in any Department or Officer thereof."

(Article I, Section 8:18)

Concurrent

- To levy and collect taxes
- To borrow money
- To make and enforce laws
- To establish courts
- To provide for the general welfare
- To charter banks and corporations

Reserved to the States

- To regulate intrastate commerce
- To conduct elections
- To provide for public health, safety, and morals
- To establish local governments
- To ratify amendments to the federal constitution

Enumerated

- To coin money
- To conduct foreign relations
- To regulate interstate commerce
- To levy and collect taxes
- To declare war
- To raise and support military forces
- To establish post offices
- To establish courts inferior to the Supreme Court
- To admit new states

Powers Denied by the Constitution

Federal

- To tax articles exported from any state
- To violate the Bill of Rights
- To change state boundaries

Federal and State

- To grant titles of nobility
- To permit slavery
- To deny citizens the right to vote

State

- To tax imports or exports
- To coin money
- To enter into treaties
- To impair obligations of contracts
- To abridge the privileges or immunities of citizens or deny due process and equal protection of the law

Bill of Rights and the Other Amendments

The **Bill of Rights** was added to the Constitution in 1791.[4] Most of the first ten amendments contain specific protections for persons from the federal government. Guarantees provided by the Bill of Rights include the following:

1. The First Amendment protects religion, speech, press, assembly, and redress of grievances.

2. The Fourth Amendment offers provisions regarding arrest and unreasonable search and seizure.

3. The Fifth Amendment provides:

    a. protection from **double jeopardy**. A person cannot be tried by the same level of government more than once for the same crime.

    b. freedom from **self-incrimination**. A person cannot be forced to testify against herself or himself.

    c. right to due process. A person has the right to timely notice of a trial and to a fair hearing.

[4]Go to the following Web address to find other sites that discuss the Constitution and its amendments: http://www.constitution.org/cs_found.htm.

4. The Sixth Amendment guarantees the rights to a speedy and public trial by jury, to an attorney, to confront witnesses, and to cross-examination in criminal prosecutions.

5. The Seventh Amendment preserves the right to a jury trial in civil suits.

6. The Eighth Amendment provides for bail and prohibits cruel and unusual punishment.

Delegated Powers

The Tenth Amendment delegates certain **enumerated (delegated) powers** to the federal government and reserves all other powers to the states or to the people. This amendment limits the power of the federal government by stating that "the powers not delegated to the United States by the Constitution, nor prohibited by it to the States, are reserved to the States respectively, or to the people." The federal government has no powers apart from those specified in the Constitution and holds only powers enumerated in the Constitution. Thus, the government can exercise only those enumerated or delegated powers that are expressly or implicitly granted to it.

The phrase *expressly delegated* was not included in the Tenth Amendment because of the history of its use under the Articles of Confederation (1781–1789), the first governing document after the Revolutionary War

LEGAL HIGHLIGHT

Twenty-Seven of 10,000 Proposed Amendments

The delegates to the constitutional convention held in 1787 in Philadelphia did not believe that any protections of individual freedoms should be included in the document. Basically, the constitution should create the government, nothing more. Very shortly after the proposed constitution was circulated among the states, it became evident that the people had other ideas. Indeed, they demanded constitutional protections for the people against actions by the federal government.

More than 10,000 amendments have been proposed during the past 200 years. The first 10 amendments came as a package and were adopted in 1791,

but only 17 amendments were added between 1798 and 1995. Of those 17 amendments, one canceled an earlier one; the Twenty-First Amendment repealed the Eighteenth Amendment on liquor prohibition.

One early proposed amendment intended to use the Constitution to prohibit the act of dueling. Another, which would have been the Thirteenth Amendment, attempted to prohibit Congress from abolishing slavery. Ironically, the Thirteenth Amendment that eventually was adopted abolished slavery.

More than 200 proposed amendments attempted to stop the Civil War. More recent proposals include the Equal Rights Amendment, the Right to Life Amendment, the Term Limits Amendment, a Balanced Budget Amendment, and the Anti-Flag-Burning Amendment.

(1775-1782), which was fought between the prior colonies and England. The term *expressly delegated* was interpreted to mean that the federal government could not exercise any powers beyond those precisely stated in the Articles of Confederation. As a result, the government could not handle new situations that the Articles did not anticipate at the time of drafting.

After a few years, those serving in government knew the Articles needed to be amended. In the end, the men who were sent to amend the Articles dropped the pretense of amending them and drafted the U.S. Constitution, which is still in use. The drafters of the Bill of Rights deliberately omitted the term *expressly delegated* from the Tenth Amendment. (See *Legal Highlight: A Funny Thing Happened on the Way to Amend the Articles of Confederation.*)

Because of the omission of the term *expressly delegated*, the Supreme Court has stated that federal government also has implied federal powers. Thus, the Constitution implicitly allows the federal government to take necessary action to follow through on the specific and implied powers granted to it. The government can take action in areas that did not exist when the Constitution was adopted under the implied powers, such as in the areas of aviation and nuclear power.

The following U.S. Supreme Court case discusses a number of constitutional issues. The commerce clause and the Tenth Amendment are discussed in this case.

CASE 5.3

Supreme Court of the United States, 2000
528 U.S. 141, 120 S.Ct. 666, 145 L.Ed. 2d 587
http://supct.law.cornell.edu/supct/cases/name.htm

RENO v. CONDON

BACKGROUND AND FACTS Congress passed the Driver's Privacy Protection Act of 1994 (DPPA or Act). This Act regulates the sale by state motor vehicle departments (DVMs) of personal information contained in drivers' licenses and motor vehicle registration records. Congress found that many states sold this personal information to individuals and businesses. Those sales generated significant revenues for the states. The DPPA also regulates the resale of this information.

The DPPA's ban on disclosure of personal information does not apply if drivers have consented to the release of their data. States must obtain a driver's affirmative consent to disclose the driver's personal information for use in surveys, marketing, solicitations, and other restricted purposes.

The DPPA's prohibition of nonconsensual disclosures is also subject to a number of statutory exceptions. The DPPA requires disclosure of personal information concerning matters of motor vehicle or driver safety; theft; emissions; motor vehicle product alterations, recalls, or advisories; performance monitoring of motor vehicles and dealers by motor vehicle manufacturers; and removal of nonowner records from the original owner records of motor vehicle manufacturers to carry out the purposes of the Anti-Car Theft Act, the Automobile Information Disclosure Act, and the Clean Air Act. South Carolina law conflicted with the DPPA's provisions.

Under that law, the information contained in the state's DMV records was available to any person or entity that filled out a form listing the requester's name and address and stating that the information would not be used for telephone solicitation.

Following the DPPA's enactment, South Carolina and its attorney general, Condon, filed suit alleging that the DPPA violated the Tenth and Eleventh Amendments to the U.S. Constitution. The district court concluded that the Act is incompatible with the principles of federalism inherent in the Constitution's division of power between the states and the federal government. The Court of Appeals for the Fourth Circuit affirmed, concluding that the Act violates constitutional principles of federalism.

Chief Justice REHNQUIST delivered the opinion of the Court.

. . . .

We of course begin with the time-honored presumption that the DPPA is a "constitutional exercise of legislative power."

The United States asserts that the DPPA is a proper exercise of Congress' authority to regulate interstate commerce under the Commerce Clause, U.S. Const., Art. I, § 8, cl. 3. The United States bases its Commerce Clause argument on the fact that the personal, identifying information that the DPPA regulates is a "thin[g] in interstate commerce," and that the sale or release of that information in interstate commerce is therefore a proper subject of congressional regulation. We agree with the United States' contention. The motor vehicle information which the States have historically sold is used by insurers, manufacturers, direct marketers, and others engaged in interstate commerce to contact drivers with customized solicitations. The information is also used in the stream of interstate commerce by various public and private entities for matters related to interstate motoring. Because drivers' information is, in this context, an article of commerce, its sale or release into the interstate stream of business is sufficient to support congressional regulation.

. . . .

But the fact that drivers' personal information is, in the context of this case, an article in interstate commerce does not conclusively resolve the constitutionality of the DPPA. . . .

. . . .

South Carolina contends that the DPPA violates the Tenth Amendment because it "thrusts upon the States all of the day-to-day responsibility for administering its complex provisions," and thereby makes "state officials the unwilling implementors of federal policy." South Carolina emphasizes that the DPPA requires the State's employees to learn and apply the Act's substantive restrictions, . . . and notes that these activities will consume the employees' time and thus the State's resources. South Carolina further notes that the DPPA's penalty provisions hang over the States as a potential punishment should they fail to comply with the Act.

We agree with South Carolina's assertion that the DPPA's provisions will require time and effort on the part of state employees, . . .

. . . .

. . . [T]he DPPA does not require the States in their sovereign capacity to regulate their own citizens. The DPPA regulates the States as the owners of databases. It does not require the South Carolina Legislature to enact any laws or regulations, and it does not require state officials to assist in the enforcement of federal statutes regulating private individuals. We accordingly conclude that the DPPA is consistent with the constitutional principles. . . .

As a final matter, we turn to South Carolina's argument that the DPPA is unconstitutional because it regulates the States exclusively. The essence of South Carolina's argument is that Congress may only regulate the States by means of "generally applicable" laws, or laws that apply to individuals as well as States. But we need not address the question whether general applicability is a constitutional requirement for federal regulation of the States, because the DPPA is generally applicable. The DPPA regulates the universe of entities that participate as suppliers to the market for motor vehicle information—the States as initial suppliers of the information in interstate commerce and private resellers or redisclosers of that information in commerce.

. . . .

DECISION AND REMEDY The court found that the DPPA regulation was involved with interstate commerce and, therefore, the sale or release of that information in interstate commerce was a proper subject of congressional regulation. The court went on to declare that the statute was not a violation of the Tenth Amendment.

CRITICAL THINKING: POLITICAL CONSIDERATION Why do you think the federal government should ever pass this type of a law?

Bill of Rights in a Business Context

The Bill of Rights guarantees persons certain protections from the government. Does the Bill of Rights protect only individuals or does it also protect businesses?

A business may be conducted by one person operating under her own name or under a fictitious name. Other types of businesses are conducted by partnerships or by corporations. These businesses exist in the eyes of the law as legal entities separate from the individuals who own them.

A **legal entity** can sue and be sued in a court, pays taxes, and holds title to property. Thus, a legal entity includes individuals and various forms of business. As a legal entity, businesses are entitled to some of the same rights and privileges as an individual. The United States Supreme Court has held that since many of the amendments use the word *person* instead of *citizen* (which is used in other parts of the Constitution), illegal (undocumented) aliens and business entities are protected by many constitutional provisions.

The Supreme Court recognizes business entities as persons in very specific areas of the Constitution. In other areas, however, business entities do not qualify for constitutional protection. The following sections discuss portions of the First, Fourth, Fifth, and Fourteenth Amendments. The Fourteenth Amendment, although adopted later than others mentioned, needs to be explored first.

Fourteenth Amendment

Passed after the Civil War (1861–1865), the Fourteenth Amendment applies only to actions by state governments. Until the adoption of the Fourteenth Amendment, the original ten amendments to the Constitution applied only to the federal government.

Through a series of cases over the decades, the Supreme Court has applied selective clauses found in the Bill of Rights to the states. The Court developed the **doctrine of selective incorporation** to apply, not the whole amendment, but specific clauses. These clauses provide people constitutional protections from certain types of activities committed by both the federal and state governments.

Fourteenth Amendment—Selective Incorporation

Today, very few clauses in the Bill of Rights are not applicable to state governments. These clauses are the Fifth Amendment due process clause, the Fifth Amendment grand jury clause, and the Seventh Amendment right to a trial by jury.

With respect to the Fifth Amendment grand jury clause, the Supreme Court found that the states can use methods other than indictment by a grand jury to bring to trial those accused of crimes. The right to a jury trial is included in all state constitutions. Thus, the right to a trial by jury in state lawsuits derives from the state constitution, not the Seventh Amendment. Specific protections for people found in the First, Fourth, Fifth, Sixth, Seventh, and Eighth Amendments are now applicable to both federal and state government actions.

Fifth and Fourteenth Amendments— Due Process Clause

Under our Constitution, no person shall be deprived "of life, liberty, or property, without due process of law." This clause is contained in both the Fifth and the Fourteenth Amendments and thus is applicable to both the federal and state governments.

Adopted as part of the original Bill of Rights, the due process clause found in the Fifth Amendment applies only to the federal government. The Fourteenth Amendment's due process clause, however, has played an indispensable role in providing people the same protections against the actions of state governments that they enjoy under the Bill of Rights against actions by the federal government.

Due process is a basic principle that requires fairness in the government's dealing with persons. Because the Supreme Court interprets this clause on a case-by-case basis, it has generated more cases than any other clause in the Constitution. Most of the basic rights discussed in this chapter are applicable to both government and private employers. But because the Fifth and Fourteenth Amendments apply explicitly to both federal and state governments, public employees have more due process rights than private employees.

The due process clause has two aspects: procedural and substantive. **Procedural due process** requires that safeguards be taken before any government decision can be made to take a person's life, liberty, or property.

Substantive due process focuses on the content, or substance, of legislation. Every statute, regulation, and government act must comply with the Constitution. Otherwise, substantive due process is violated.

For example, Congress passes a statute imposing a $1-million fine and mandatory five-year prison term without a trial on any university professor who appears as an expert on a television news program. This law would be unconstitutional on both substantive and procedural grounds. A court would invalidate this legislation because it abridges freedom of speech, a violation of the First Amendment. A denial of substantive due process requires a court to overrule any state or federal law that violates the Constitution. Procedurally, the law is unfair because the penalty is imposed without giving the accused a chance to defend her or his actions. A court will invalidate any statute or court decision that lacks procedural due process.

Fourteenth Amendment—Equal Protection Clause

The Fourteenth Amendment has the **equal protection clause**, not found in any other part of the Constitution. A state government may not "deny to any person within its jurisdiction the equal protection of the laws." Equal protection means that the government must treat similarly situated individuals in a similar manner. Thus, a state government is prohibited from favoring one class of people at the expense of another. The federal government is not covered by the equal protection clause, but is prevented from favoring a particular group of people by the Fifth Amendment's due process clause.

The government has created a number of protected classes, each of which can be categorized into one of three levels of protection. Receiving the highest level of protection are the classes of race, religion, national origin, and color. If discrimination is alleged by a person falling into one of these classes, the courts use the **strict scrutiny test**.

This test has two requirements that must be met before this type of discrimination is allowed: (1) a compelling governmental interest and (2) use of the least restrictive means available to satisfy that interest. For example, in Iran in the 1970s a number of Iranians occupied the U.S. Embassy. In partial response to this crisis, all Iranians in the United States who were not U.S. citizens were ordered to report to the U.S. government. This requirement would meet the ele-

ments of the strict scrutiny test, even though international visitors from other countries were not required to report. Most government regulations involving protected classes, however, fail.

When a person alleges discrimination based on gender or age, the courts use the **intermediate scrutiny test**. This test requires that there be (1) an important governmental objective and (2) a substantial relationship between the means and the end before the court will approve discrimination on the basis of gender or age. For example, sixteen-year-olds are not allowed to purchase tobacco or alcohol products. The governmental objective is to keep minors from harmful substances and one method is to prohibit them from purchasing tobacco and alcohol. Thus, this discrimination is lawful. If the government prohibited anyone over age thirty from being employed as police officers, however, the first requirement would not be met, because no important governmental objective could be stated.

If a person complains about discrimination on the basis of economic discrimination or any other government classification that does not involve a protected class, the courts use the **rational basis test**. The two requirements of this test are (1) a legitimate governmental interest and (2) a rational relationship between the governmental interest and the means used to accomplish that interest. For example, a state government passed a law requiring everyone in the front seats of motor vehicles to use their seat belts. The courts have upheld such laws. The governmental interest is to protect motor vehicle occupants from serious injuries resulting in the need for medical treatment, often hospitalization, and time off from work. The seat belt law is a rational means to achieve the goal of lessening or preventing harm. Most regulation of businesses comes under the rational basis test.

First Amendment

The First Amendment to the Constitution states:

> *Congress shall make no law respecting an establishment of religion, or prohibiting the free exercise thereof; or abridging the freedom of speech, or of the press; or the right of the people peaceably to assemble, and to petition the government for redress of grievances.*

This section will examine two areas from the First Amendment: freedom of speech and freedom of religion.

Freedom of Speech

The founders believed that the ability to generate and then to exchange ideas allowed for the development of a free and open society. Armed with knowledge, a citizen has the ability to make better decisions.

Although the First Amendment requires Congress (as well as state governments because of the Fourteenth Amendment) to avoid regulating free speech, a business can control speech. For example, the owners of a professional basketball team can require a player to stand when the national anthem is played prior to the game.

Speech is broadly defined as communication, and includes oral, written, and symbolic speech. Speech can be categorized as *protected speech, partially protected speech*, and *unprotected speech*. These categories determine whether speech can be restricted and regulated by the government.

Artiste Login. Artiste Login has a manual for its employees. One restriction printed in the manual is that employees may not pass out flyers for their personal pursuits. Prohibited flyers would include soliciting for a charity, selling puppies and kittens, or advocating for a political position. Carlotta wonders if this prohibition impinges the free speech of the employees. In fact, the prohibition is legal because Artiste Login is a private business. The Constitution restricts Congress from abridging the freedom of speech. Artiste Login must be consistent in applying the restriction, however, even to favorite solicitations, such as the sale of Girl Scout cookies.

Protected Speech. Protected speech cannot be restricted or regulated in any manner by the government, thus allowing a full exchange of ideas to take place. Political speech is an example of protected speech.

In this country's early years, Congress passed a statute forbidding any criticism of the president. The statute was later repealed. Today, such a law would never be passed because it is clearly unconstitutional. Another example is the case that involved the burning of the nation's flag in front of the building where a national political convention was meeting. The act of flag burning was protected as symbolic speech in a case decided by the United States Supreme Court. This decision has led to efforts by Congress to adopt a constitutional amendment prohibiting burning or otherwise defacing the nation's flag.

Partially Protected Speech. Partially protected speech cannot be regulated by the government, but it can be restricted as to time, place, and manner. Two types of speech that fall into this category include offensive speech and commercial speech.

Offensive Speech. Offensive speech (without obscenity) is protected speech. Offensiveness alone does not justify suppression; however, restriction as to time, place, and manner must be reasonable. For example, speakers who use offensive speech may be restricted to a portion of a public park where they may speak freely. Thus, the offensive speech is restricted, but not regulated.

The Federal Communications Commission (FCC) may restrict offensive language on broadcast television to late-night time periods when children generally are not watching. Broadcast television is beamed over public air waves, which the government regulates. Cable television, however, is not subject to such restrictions, since cable companies own the cable that delivers the medium. Cable may carry shows that cannot appear on broadcast television because of their offensive nature.

Over a period of decades, the federal government created and built what is now known as the Internet. Its early use, however, was very restricted. With the demise of the Union of Soviet Socialist Republics and the end of the Cold War in 1991, the government lifted its restrictions and by 1995 turned over control of the Internet to private enterprise.

In 1993, the World Wide Web, one part of the Internet, was created. The WWW makes information accessible to laymen in a variety of formats. Some examples include graphic user interfaces (GUIs), such as interactive text, still photographs, moving videos, streaming videos (such as listening to a congressional debate in real time), telephony (a telephone-like connection that may use live video), and push technology (instead of the user going to the server located at another site, push technology "pushes" the information to a server, with the information always updated), to name just a few services.

The WWW has been very successful and attracted many businesses. Businesses that publish and sell sexually explicit material were quick to take advantage of the lack of regulations on this new medium.

Congress, concerned over the explosion of sexually explicit material on the WWW, passed the

Communications Decency Act (CDA) of 1996. After President William J. Clinton[5] signed the bill into law, a

[5]William Jefferson Clinton (1946 to present) was president from 1993 to 2001. See the official Web site at http://www.archives.gov or http://clinton.archives.gov.

lawsuit was immediately filed. This case was eventually appealed to the United States Supreme Court to determine if the CDA violated the First Amendment. The following case is the decision from the Supreme Court.

CASE 5.4

Supreme Court of the United States, 1997 521 U.S. 844, 117 S.Ct. 2329, 138 L.Ed. 2d 874 http://www.findlaw.com/casecode/supreme.html

RENO v. AMERICAN CIVIL LIBERTIES UNION

BACKGROUND AND FACTS Congress passed the Communications Decency Act in 1996, which became law upon the president's signature. The CDA sought to protect minors from harmful material on the Internet.

One section criminalized the "knowing" transmission of obscene or indecent messages to any minor under the age of eighteen. Providers, which are located both within and outside the United States, were to restrict minors' access by requiring proof of age, such as a verified credit card or an adult identification number. Immediately after the CDA became law, twenty parties filed suit.

A three-judge panel sitting on the district court heard the case. Based on the Act's special review provisions, the case was appealed directly to the United States Supreme Court.

Justice STEVENS delivered the opinion of the Court.

. . . .

Sexually explicit material on the Internet includes text, pictures, and chat and "extends from the modestly titillating to the hardest-core." These files are created, named, and posted in the same manner as material that is not sexually explicit, and may be accessed either deliberately or unintentionally during the course of an imprecise search. "Once a provider posts its content on the Internet, it cannot prevent that content from entering any community."

. . . .

. . . Neither before nor after the enactment of the CDA have the vast democratic fora of the Internet been subject to the type of government supervision and regulation that has attended the broadcast industry. Moreover, the Internet is not as "invasive" as radio or television. The District Court specifically found that "[c]ommunications over the Internet do not 'invade' an individual's home or appear on one's computer screen unbidden. Users seldom encounter content 'by accident.'" It also found that "[a]lmost all sexually explicit images are preceded by warnings as to the content," and cited testimony that "'odds are slim' that a user would come across a sexually explicit sight by accident."

. . . .

The vagueness of the CDA is a matter of special concern for two reasons. First, the CDA is a content-based regulation of speech. The vagueness of such a regulation raises special First Amendment concerns because of its obvious chilling effect on free speech. Second, the CDA is a criminal statute. In addition to the opprobrium and stigma of a criminal conviction, the CDA threatens violators with penalties including up to two years in prison for each act of violation. The severity of criminal sanctions may well cause speakers to remain silent rather than communicate even arguably unlawful words, ideas, and images. As a practical matter, this increased deterrent effect, coupled with the "risk of discriminatory enforcement" of vague regulations, poses greater First Amendment concerns than those implicated by the civil regulation reviewed in *Denver Area Ed. Telecommunications Consortium, Inc. v. FCC.*

. . . .

We are persuaded that the CDA lacks the precision that the First Amendment requires when a statute regulates the content of speech. In order to deny minors access to potentially harmful speech, the CDA effectively suppresses a large amount of speech that adults have a constitutional right to receive and to address to one another. That burden on adult speech is unacceptable if less restrictive alternatives would be at least as effective in achieving the legitimate purpose that the statute was enacted to serve.

In evaluating the free speech rights of adults, we have made it perfectly clear that "[s]exual expression which is indecent but not obscene is protected by the First Amendment."

. . . .

The breadth of the CDA's coverage is wholly unprecedented. Unlike the regulations upheld in [previous cases], the scope of the CDA is not limited to commercial speech or commercial entities. Its open-ended prohibitions embrace all nonprofit entities and individuals posting indecent messages or displaying them on their own computers in the presence of minors. The general, undefined terms "indecent" and "patently offensive" cover large amounts of nonpornographic material with serious educational or other value. Moreover, the "community standards" criterion as applied to the Internet means that any communication available to a nation-wide audience will be judged by the standards of the community most likely to be offended by the message.

. . . .

We find . . . [the government's] argument singularly unpersuasive. The dramatic expansion of this new marketplace of ideas contradicts the factual basis of . . . [the government's] contention. The record demonstrates that the growth of the Internet has been and continues to be phenomenal. As a matter of constitutional tradition, in the absence of evidence to the contrary, we presume that governmental regulation of the content of speech is more likely to interfere with the free exchange of ideas than to encourage it. The interest in encouraging freedom of expression in a democratic society outweighs any theoretical but unproven benefit of censorship.

DECISION AND REMEDY The government was enjoined from enforcing the criminal sections of the Act, that is, to knowingly transmit obscene or indecent messages to minors. The Act's content-based blanket restrictions on speech abridged the freedom of speech protected by the First Amendment.

CRITICAL THINKING: PUBLIC POLICY Why should communications over the Internet be treated differently from communications made through radio and broadcast television over which the government does exercise control through the Federal Communications Commission?

Many organizations dedicated to the concept of freedom of speech can be found on the Internet. One of the more prestigious ones is the Freedom Forum,[6] which "is a nonpartisan, international foundation dedicated to free press, free speech and free spirit for all people." The foundation pursues its priorities through conferences, educational activities, publishing, broadcasting, online services, fellowships, partnerships, training, research, and other programs. The Freedom Forum funds only its own programs and related partnerships. Unsolicited funding requests are not accepted.

[6]The Freedom Forum's Web address is http://www.freedomforum.org.

Operating programs by the Freedom Forum are the Newseum,[7] the First Amendment Center at Vanderbilt University in Nashville, Tennessee, the Media Studies Center in New York City, and the Pacific Coast Center in San Francisco. The Freedom Forum also has operating offices in Cocoa Beach, Florida; Buenos Aires; Hong Kong; Johannesburg; and London.

The Cyberspace Law Institute (CLI) is involved with freedom of speech along with other cyber problems.[8] The CLI has posted many papers written about cyber issues. The American Civil Liberties Union is involved with freedom of speech issues and also has a Web presence.[9]

Commercial Speech. In the past, the United States Supreme Court distinguished between an individual's freedom of speech versus freedom of speech in the commercial area. For example, political speech could not be restrained, but commercial advertising was subject to government control. This view continued until the case of *Virginia State Board of Pharmacy v. Virginia Citizens Consumer Council, Inc.*[10] This case, along with

several others, challenged a legal ban on advertising the price of prescription drugs. The Court held, "It is clear . . . that speech does not lose its First Amendment protection because money is spent . . . as in a paid advertisement."

After this case, several cases arose confronting the issue of commercial speech, that is, advertising. One of the leading cases was *Bates v. State Bar of Arizona.*[11] The state bar of Arizona refused to allow any attorney to advertise services or the price of those services. Advertising was considered unprofessional. Two attorneys advertised, quoting prices for routine legal work. The advertisements did not include anything that might commonly be called trade puffing. Because of this advertisement, the state bar of Arizona suspended the attorneys from practicing law. The United States Supreme Court held that the attorneys' freedom of speech had been violated.

Although commercial speech is protected by the First Amendment, advertisements must not be deceptive, misleading, or fraudulent. In addition to advertising their services, businesses also may want to establish their positions on various social, political, trade, and economic issues. In the following case, the United States Supreme Court discusses commercial speech.

---

[7]The Newseum Web site is http://www.newseum.org. The Newseum plans to open in Washington, D.C., in late 2006.

[8]The Cyberspace Law Institute's Web site is http://www.cli.org.

[9]The American Civil Liberties Union's Web site is http://www.aclu.org.

[10]Virginia State Board of Pharmacy v. Virginia Citizens Consumer Council, Inc. 425 U.S. 748, 96 S. Ct. 1817, 48 L. Ed. 2d 346 (1976), and http://www.findlaw.com/casecode/supreme.html.

[11]Bates v. State Bar of Arizona, 433 U.S. 350, 97 S. Ct. 2691, 53 L. Ed. 2d 810 (1977), and http://supct.law.cornell.edu/supct/cases/name.htm.

CASE 5.5

United States Supreme Court, 2003
538 U.S. 600, 123 S. Ct. 1829, 155 L. Ed. 2d 793

MADIGAN v. TELEMARKETING ASSOCIATES, INC.

BACKGROUND AND FACTS Telemarketing Associates, Inc. (Telemarketers) was an organization of for-profit fund-raising corporations all owned by Richard Troia. In particular, one of these corporations raised money for Vietnam veterans. The corporation received eighty-five percent of the proceeds, while the remaining fifteen percent went to a veterans not-for-profit charity called VietNow.

In the course of the telephone solicitations, the callers from Telemarketers misleadingly represented that "funds donated would go to further VietNow's charitable purposes." Prospective donors were told their contributions would be used for specifically identified charitable endeavors. Typical examples included "food baskets given to vets and their families for Thanksgiving," paying "bills and rent to help physically and mentally disabled Vietnam vets and their families, job training, and rehabilitation and other services for Vietnam vets." One person asked what percentage of her contribution would be used for fund-raising expenses. She was told ninety percent or more goes to the vets. Another person stated she was told her donation would not be used for "labor expenses" because "all members are volunteers." Written materials Telemarketers sent to each donor represented that contributions would "be used to help and assist

VietNow's charitable purposes." The donor's list that was developed remained the property of Telemarketers.

The question presented is whether the above facts stated a claim for relief that could survive a motion to dismiss. In accord with the Illinois trial and appellate courts, the Illinois Supreme Court held they did not. In other words, the plaintiff lost.

Justice GINSBURG delivered the opinion of the Court.

. . . .

We reverse the judgment of the Illinois Supreme Court. Our prior decisions do not rule out, as supportive of a fraud claim against fundraisers, any and all reliance on the percentage of charitable donations fundraisers retain for themselves. While bare failure to disclose that information directly to potential donors does not suffice to establish fraud, when nondisclosure is accompanied by intentionally misleading statements designed to deceive the listener, the First Amendment leaves room for a fraud claim.

. . . .

The First Amendment protects the right to engage in charitable solicitation. But the First Amendment does not shield fraud. Like other forms of public deception, fraudulent charitable solicitation is unprotected speech.

The Court has not previously addressed the First Amendment's application to individual fraud actions of the kind at issue here. It has, however, three times considered prophylactic statutes designed to combat fraud by imposing prior restraints on solicitation when fundraising fees exceeded a specified reasonable level. Each time, the Court held the prophylactic measures unconstitutional.

In *Schaumburg,* decided in 1980, the Court invalidated a village ordinance that prohibited charitable organizations from soliciting contributions unless they used at least 75 percent of their receipts "directly for the charitable purpose of the organization." The ordinance defined "charitable purposes" to exclude salaries and commissions paid to solicitors, and the administrative expenses of the charity, including salaries. The village of Schaumburg's "principal justification" for the ordinance was fraud prevention: "[A]ny organization using more than 25 percent of its receipts on fundraising, salaries, and overhead," Schaumburg submitted, "is not a charitable, but a commercial, for-profit enterprise"; "to permit [such an organization] to represent itself as a charity," the village urged, "is fraudulent."

The Court agreed with Schaumburg that fraud prevention ranks as "a substantial governmental interes[t]," but concluded that "the 75-percent requirement" promoted that interest "only peripherally." Spending "more than 25 percent of [an organization's] receipts on fundraising, salaries, and overhead," the Court explained, does not reliably indicate that the enterprise is "commercial" rather than "charitable." Such spending might be altogether appropriate, *Schaumburg* noted, for a charitable organization "primarily engaged in research, advocacy, or public education [that uses its] own paid staff to carry out these functions as well as to solicit financial support." "The Village's legitimate interest in preventing fraud," the Court stated, "can be better served by measures less intrusive than a direct prohibition on solicitation," "Fraudulent misrepresentations can be prohibited and the penal laws used to punish such conduct directly."

Four years later, in *Munson,* the Court invalidated a Maryland law that prohibited charitable organizations from soliciting if they paid or agreed to pay as expenses more than 25 percent of the amount raised. Unlike the inflexible ordinance in *Schaumburg,* the Maryland law authorized a waiver of the 25 percent limitation "where [it] would effectively prevent the charitable organization from raising contributions." The Court held that the waiver provision did not save the statute. "[No] reaso[n] other than financial necessity warrant[ed] a waiver," *Munson* observed. The statute provided no shelter for a charity that incurred high solicitation costs because it chose to disseminate information as part of its fundraising. Nor did it shield a charity whose high solicitation costs stemmed from the unpopularity of its cause.

. . . .

Third in the trilogy of cases on which the Illinois Supreme Court relied was our 1988 decision in *Riley.* The village ordinance in *Schaumburg* and the Maryland law in *Munson* regulated charities; the North Carolina charitable solicitation controls at issue in *Riley* directly regulated professional fundraisers. North Carolina's law prohibited professional fundraisers from retaining an "unreasonable" or "excessive" fee. Fees up to 20 percent of the gross receipts collected were deemed reasonable; fees between 20 percent and 35 percent were deemed unreasonable if the State showed that the solicitation did not involve advocacy or dissemination of information. Fees exceeding 35 percent were presumed unreasonable, but the fundraiser could rebut the presumption by showing either that the solicitation involved advocacy or information dissemination, or that, absent the higher fee, the charity's "ability to raise money or communicate would be significantly diminished."

Relying on *Schaumburg* and *Munson,* the Court's decision in *Riley* invalidated North Carolina's endeavor to rein in charitable solicitors' fees. The Court held, once again, that fraud may not be inferred simply from the percentage of charitable donations absorbed by fundraising costs.

The opportunity to rebut the unreasonableness presumption attending a fee over 35 percent did not bring North Carolina's scheme within the constitutional zone, the Court explained. Under the State's law, "even where a prima facie showing of unreasonableness ha[d] been rebutted, the factfinder [still had to] make an ultimate determination, on a case-by-case basis, as to whether the fee was reasonable—a showing that the solicitation involved . . . advocacy or [the] dissemination of information [did] not alone establish that the total fee was reasonable."

Training on that aspect of North Carolina's regulation, the Court stated: "Even if we agreed that some form of a percentage-based measure could be used, in part, to test for fraud, we could not agree to a measure that requires the speaker to prove 'reasonableness' case by case based upon what is at best a loose inference that the fee might be too high." "[E]very campaign incurring fees in excess of 35% . . . [would] subject [fundraisers] to potential litigation over the 'reasonableness' of the fee," the Court observed; that litigation risk, the Court concluded, would "chill speech in direct contravention of the First Amendment's dictates." Especially likely to be burdened, the *Riley* opinion noted, were solicitations combined with advocacy or the communication of information, and fundraising by small or unpopular charities. The Court cautioned, however, as it did in *Schaumburg* and *Munson,* that States need not "sit idly by and allow their citizens to be defrauded." We anticipated that North Carolina law enforcement officers would be "ready and able" to enforce the State's antifraud law.

Riley presented a further issue. North Carolina law required professional fundraisers to disclose to potential donors, before asking for money, the percentage of the prior year's charitable contributions the fundraisers had actually turned over to charity. The State defended this disclosure requirement as a proper means to dispel public misperception that the money donors gave to professional fundraisers went in greater-than-actual proportion to benefit charity.

This Court condemned the measure as an "unduly burdensome" prophylactic rule, an exaction unnecessary to achieve the State's goal of preventing donors from being misled. The State's rule, *Riley* emphasized, conclusively presumed that "the charity derive[d] no benefit from funds collected but not turned over to it." This was "not necessarily so," the Court said, for charities might well benefit from the act of solicitation itself, when the request for funds conveyed information or involved cause-oriented advocacy.

. . . .

The Court's opinions in *Schaumburg, Munson,* and *Riley* took care to leave a corridor open for fraud actions to guard the public against false or misleading charitable solicitations. As those decisions recognized, and as we further explain below, there are differences critical to First Amendment concerns between fraud actions trained on representations made in individual cases and statutes that categorically ban solicitations when fundraising costs run high. Simply labeling an action one for "fraud," of course, will not carry the day. For example, had the complaint against Telemarketers charged fraud based solely on the percentage of donations the fundraisers would retain, or their failure to alert potential donors to their fee arrangements at the start of each telephone call, *Riley* would support swift dismissal. A State's Attorney General surely cannot gain case-by-case ground this Court has declared off limits to legislators.

. . . .

We do not agree with Telemarketers that the Illinois Attorney General's fraud action is simply an end run around *Riley's* holding that fundraisers may not be required, in every telephone solicitation, to state the percentage of receipts the fundraiser would retain. It is one thing to compel every fundraiser to disclose its fee arrangements at the start of a telephone conversation, quite another to take fee arrangements into account in assessing whether particular affirmative representations designedly deceive the public.

. . . .

Just as government may seek to inform the public and prevent fraud through such disclosure requirements, so it may "vigorously enforce . . . antifraud laws to prohibit professional fundraisers from obtaining money on false pretenses or by making false statements." High fundraising costs, without more, do not establish fraud. And mere failure to volunteer the fundraiser's fee when contacting a potential donee, without more, is insufficient to state a claim for fraud. But these limitations do not disarm States from assuring that their residents are positioned to make informed choices about their charitable giving. Consistent with our precedent and the First Amendment, States may maintain fraud actions when fundraisers make false or misleading representations designed to deceive donors about how their donations will be used.

DECISION AND REMEDY The Court found that the First Amendment did not bar fraud claims where a high percentage of charitable gifts went to the professional fundraiser after misleading statements like the money is for food baskets for veterans, paying rent for veterans, the money would go to help physically and mentally veterans and their families, and that ninety percent or more went to the veterans, when in fact fifteen percent or less went to them.

CRITICAL THINKING: POLITICAL CONSIDERATION Should there be any restrictions by the government on how a charity may raise donations? Please provide possible restrictions and discuss fully.

At times, determining whether a business's intention is to advocate a public or political position or to use commercial speech is difficult. For example, a bank opposes a referendum approving a graduated personal income tax. The bank wants to spend its money to present an opposition view to the public. A business has as much right to publicize its views as does an individual, even though these ideas will increase the potential for a business to increase its profit. Moreover, the public is enriched by being exposed to all views, whether generated by an individual or a business.

Unprotected Speech. Unprotected speech is not protected by the First Amendment. During the past two centuries, six types of speech have been denied protection: Dangerous speech, fighting words, speech that incites violence or revolution, defamatory speech, obscenity, and child pornography.

Dangerous speech is that which endangers the public. An example provided by the United States Supreme Court is yelling "Fire" in a crowded theater when in fact no fire exists. That word can create a stampede of people, thus placing others in harm's way.

Fighting words are intended to provoke a violent or hostile response from an ordinary person. Usually this type of speech is aimed at an individual.

Defamation is discussed in greater detail in Chapter 8. It is defined as the act of making an untrue statement that impinges on the integrity or character of another person or corporation. Historically, defamation has never been protected by the First Amendment. During the civil rights movement of the early 1960s, the *New York Times* printed articles of a defamatory nature against an elected southern official. When the official brought suit against the newspaper, the United States Supreme Court held that public officials seeking to recover for defamation relating to their performance of official duties must prove **actual malice**.[12] Actual malice means that a statement must be made with the knowledge that it is false or with reckless disregard of whether or not it is false.

The First Amendment covers public figures and officials. A public official is a person who is elected or appointed to government service. A public figure is a person, such as an actor or an athletic coach, who seeks public recognition or a person who is thrust into the limelight, such as a person accused of a crime or a survivor of an airplane crash.

As seen in the case of *Reno v. American Civil Liberties Union*, discussed previously, obscene speech and child pornography are not protected by the First Amendment. Obscene speech is defined by the United States Supreme Court as speech that (1) appeals to the prurient interest, (2) depicts sexual conduct in a patently offensive way, and (3) lacks serious literary, artistic, political, or scientific value. An example is child pornography that uses children for sexual purposes.

The problem with the freedom of speech lies in establishing limits. We all favor freedom of speech for ourselves; however, we also recognize potential reasons to limit others' freedom of speech. Should the American Nazi Party be allowed to hold a parade in a predominantly Jewish neighborhood? Should antinuclear demonstrators be allowed to block nuclear plant entrances?

Freedom of speech limitations have varied over the years. More than 200 years after the 1791 adoption of the First Amendment, society still is defining freedom of speech and limits that should be placed on that freedom.

Freedom of Religion

The government can neither establish any religion nor prohibit the free exercise of religious practices. Any government action, federal or state, must be neutral toward religion. An individual statute, however, may impact religion. As long as it does not promote or place a significant burden on religion, the statute is constitutional.

Sunday closing laws, for example, forbid the performance of certain business activities on Sunday. The closing laws are constitutional because the government has a legitimate interest in providing workers a day of rest. Originally religious in nature, closing laws now have a secular purpose of promoting workers' health and welfare. Even though closing laws admittedly facilitated Christian attendance at religious services, the United States Supreme Court viewed this effect as an incidental, not a primary, purpose of Sunday closing laws. Today, the few closing laws that remain generally allow businesses to be open on Sunday, so long as they do observe a day of rest.

Title VII of the Civil Rights Act of 1964 prohibits government and private employers and unions from discriminating against individuals because of their religion. Instead, businesses must make reasonable accommodations for their employees on the basis of religious beliefs.

The United States Supreme Court addressed this issue in *Estate of Thornton v. Caldor, Inc.*[13] The Court

---

[12]New York Times Co. v. Sullivan, 376 U.S. 254, 84 S. Ct. 710, 11 L. Ed. 2d 686 (1964), and http://supct.law.cornell.edu/supct/cases/name.htm#Case_Name-N-O.

[13]Estate of Thornton v. Caldor, Inc., 472 U.S. 703, 105 S. Ct. 2914, 86 L. Ed. 2d 557 (1985), and http://www.findlaw.com/casecode/supreme.html.

held that a Connecticut statute granting employees the absolute right not to work on their Sabbath had the effect of advancing religious practices in violation of the establishment clause of the First Amendment. The establishment clause prohibits the government from establishing a religion. The Connecticut type of statute discriminated against employees who might want a day off during the weekend for secular reasons.

In *Trans World Airlines, Inc. v. Hardison,*[14] the United States Supreme Court reviewed the case of a former airline clerk who brought a lawsuit against the airline and the union, claiming religious discrimination. The clerk sought to have Saturday, his Sabbath, off. Neither the union nor the airline could work out a solution to the problem because the clerk had low seniority, and those of higher seniority also wanted Saturdays off. Eventually he was fired for refusing to work on Saturday. The Supreme Court held that the airline and the union had made reasonable efforts to accommodate the clerk's religious beliefs and that the proposed solutions to his problem worked an undue hardship on the airline, the union, and his fellow employees. The operation of the seniority system was agreed to by both the airline and the union. As long as the seniority system did not have a discriminatory purpose, it was not an unlawful employment practice, even though the operation of the seniority system was discriminatory in its effect.

Fourth Amendment

The Fourth Amendment reads as follows:

The right of the people to be secure in their persons, houses, papers, and effects, against unreasonable searches and seizures, shall not be violated, and no Warrants shall issue, but upon probable cause, supported by Oath or affirmation, and particularly describing the place to be searched and the persons or things to be seized.

This next section reviews two elements. First, the clause on search and seizure applies in criminal actions. Second, the implied right of privacy is reviewed.

Search and Seizure

Before any governmental agency can search a place, that agency must obtain a search warrant from the

court. The Supreme Court has found some exceptions, such as limited searches of automobiles or places where a suspect may reach for a weapon. Also excluded is the right of the government to search persons coming into the country. The search warrant must be based on probable cause. **Probable cause** requires law enforcement officials to have objective evidence that would convince a neutral magistrate that the proposed search is justified.

The warrant must specifically describe the place to be searched and the persons to be arrested or the items to be seized. General search warrants are prohibited. For example, a general search through a person's belongings is impermissible. The officer executing a search warrant has no authority to extend the search beyond that described in the warrant.

Constitutional protection against searches and seizures is important to businesses and professionals. With increased federal and state regulation of commercial activities, frequent and unannounced government inspection to ensure compliance with the law would be extremely disruptive.

In *Marshall v. Barlow's, Inc.,*[15] the Supreme Court held that government inspectors have no right to enter business premises without a warrant. In that case, the purpose of the law (Occupational Safety and Health Act of 1970) was to provide a safe workplace. If the business were found to be in violation of the government requirements, the government could impose fines for violations. Businesses have a right to require the government to obtain a warrant from a neutral magistrate before conducting a search. This case is discussed in greater detail in Chapter 6.

Right of Privacy

The right of privacy is not spelled out in the Constitution or the Bill of Rights. This right was initially advocated by Samuel D. Warren and Louis D. Brandeis[16] in an 1890 article in the *Harvard Law Review.* They argued that an individual has a personal right to be left alone. In 1965, the United States Supreme Court finally recognized the right to privacy as a constitutional right.

The basis of this right is found in the Fourth Amendment, which states that people should "be secure in their persons, houses, papers, and effects,

---

[14]*Trans World Airlines, Inc. v. Hardison,* 432 U.S. 63, 97 S. Ct. 2264, 53 L. Ed. 2d 113 (1977), and http://www.findlaw.com/casecode/supreme.html.

[15]Marshall v. Barlow's, Inc., 436 U.S. 307, 98 S. Ct. 1816, 56 L. Ed. 2d 305 (1978), and http://www.findlaw.com/casecode/supreme.html.
[16]Louis Dembitz Brandeis (1856–1941) served as associate justice of the Supreme Court of the United States from 1916 to 1939.

LEGAL HIGHLIGHT

So Where Is My Royalty?

Moving day comes and off you go to your new residence. Change-of-address forms are filed with the U.S. Postal Service, the insurance company, magazine companies, and other businesses that need to know you moved. In your new mailbox, you find welcoming letters containing advertisements for local services. People even come to your front door to welcome you.

At the new supermarket, you are offered a membership in a frequent-buyer-bonus program. You sign up because items are discounted for club members, and for every $500 of purchases you will receive a gift. While at the market, you purchase a toaster oven and four frozen diet-food dinners. Once home, you fill out and mail in the product warranty for your toaster oven. You rip the proofs-of-purchase from the four diet-food containers, fill in your name and address for the $1 back on product purchase, and mail these items.

Calling the 800 telephone number you learn how to cook your frozen dinners. After popping the frozen dinners into the toaster oven, you call the 900 telephone number to check on tomorrow's weather report. Using a cordless telephone, you tell your best friend that you will be out of town for the next three days. Telephoning your travel agent, you make airline, hotel, and car rental reservations. Finally, you grab the wireless laptop computer, log on, and check into work. In an e-mail message to a coworker, you complain about the boss's bad attitude. Logging on the Internet, you surf to a grocery store Web site and order goods, such as gallons of water, boxes of soap, and cleaning materials. The Internet provider provides service at a cheaper rate if it can track your Internet activities.

Are these activities protected from legal or illegal snoopers? The only possibly illegal "snooping activity" is listening in on cordless or cellular telephone calls.

The product warranty form asks for lots of personal information. This information is logged into computer databanks and resold. The dollar-off coupon information is resold to other marketers, who now know that you are on a diet.

Although it has been illegal under federal law since 1986 to listen to cordless phone conversations, no way exists yet to know when someone is listening. The manufacture, import, sale, or possession of scanners, electronic devices that monitor or listen, was not made illegal until 1995. If a thief were listening, she or he would know that you would be gone for three days. If a break-in occurs, your laptop computer certainly is a target. After all, it probably contains more personal information about you and your business.

The airline computer reservation system has your travel plans and that information is resold to direct marketers. And those 800 and 900 numbers all have caller ID (identification); that is, when you call in, your telephone number shows up on the computer screen. If the firm has enhanced caller ID, the operator can read on the screen the history of your purchases. That is more information about you to be sold. How about your e-mail messages? Employers legally can screen your e-mail. A survey shows that more than one-half of employers monitor their companies' e-mail. And what about the electronic ordering from the grocery store? The store has electronically collected information about you and can now sell it. At least the Internet provider was upfront and honest about the lower rate in exchange for giving up your privacy.

Virtually no government regulation exists in the privacy area to protect you from having all this information about you placed in databanks. The information in databanks is sold to businesses that engage in an activity called *data mining*. The question is this: If all these people are making money from information generated by you, why aren't you receiving royalties?

against unreasonable searches and seizures." The right of privacy implies more than the right to be protected against unreasonable searches and seizures. The right includes a zone of privacy that protects against government intrusion, particularly against electronic eavesdropping and inspections by administrative agencies. Other protections include government prohibition against the release of your Social Security number, tax records, or census information unless statutory authority exists.

Both federal and state privacy statutes prohibit the respective government from releasing information to third persons. One federal law prohibits video stores from disclosing videotape rental or purchase records. The statute was passed in reaction to Judge Robert Bork's nomination hearing for the Supreme Court in 1987 before the U.S. Senate. During those proceedings, a local newspaper published a list of videos that Bork had rented. Congress's reaction to the published list was to pass the 1988 Video Privacy Protection Act.

The **Children's Online Privacy Act of 1998 (COPA)** is a federal law pertaining to Internet operators and children. Internet operators are prohibited from collecting information about children while they are on the Internet. The law applies to all children under the age of thirteen. If the child's parents consent, then the Internet operator can obtain information. If, however, this information is to be used by third parties, the parents must sign a written statement granting permission before any information is gathered.

The **Electronic Communications Privacy Act (ECPA)** involves the privacy of employees and the general public. It is unlawful for any person to reveal to another person the contents of an electronic communication that is sent or stored. Of special importance in employment situations, the law prohibits employers from intentionally intercepting electronic communications or intentionally disclosing or using this information. The employer has a right to monitor employee's conversations as long as the conversation involves business. An employer does not have a right to monitor a private conversation. Employees can consent to monitoring.

The **Gramm-Leach-Bliley Act (GLBA)** provides consumers with privacy rights. This federal statute requires a business involved in the financial area to inform customers that it may share nonpublic information with others. The customer has a federal right to require financial institutions not to share any gathered information with affiliated or nonaffiliated businesses with the financial institution. This right is known as the **opt-out provision**. This clause means that the customer must take affirmative action in order to have his name excluded from data banks to be shared with others. No action means that the customer allows his name to be included in the data bank to be shared (usually sold) to others. The law requires that privacy notices be sent annually by financial institutions to their customers.

The **Health Insurance Portability and Accountability Act of 1996 (HIPAA)** is the first statute to provide federal privacy standards to patients. In 2003, the law extended privacy protection to medical records, pharmacy records, hospital records, and health information provided to health plans, doctors, hospitals, and other health-care providers. Patients now have access to their medical records and more control over how their personal health information is used and disclosed. The standards represent a uniform, minimum floor of privacy protections for consumers across the country. Violations of these standards may result in a $250,000 fine and ten years in prison.

The **Right to Financial Privacy Act of 1978** restricts the power of the federal government to obtain a person's financial records. The law provides a customer the right to know who has accessed his or her financial records. The Privacy Act was amended by the **USA Patriot Act of 2001**.[17] Under the act, the federal government can obtain financial records, intercept e-mail, and conduct wiretaps without notice to the individual.

INFOTRAC RESEARCH ACTIVITY

Log on InfoTrac and type in "Anti-terrorism Act of 2001," also called the Patriot Act. This act was passed weeks after the September 11, 2001, attacks on the nation. Study four articles. Discuss whether any of the provisions are unconstitutional. Justify your reasons. If you think some provisions are unconstitutional, in what way should the Act be changed to ensure that the questionable provisions comply with the Constitution? Remember, the goal of this statute is the protection of this country while complying with the Constitution.

Many privacy rights issues have come to light because of the Internet. One nonprofit organization that campaigns for the right of privacy is the Center for Democracy and Technology (CDT).[18] Its mission

---

[17]The formal name is *Uniting and Strengthening America by Providing Appropriate Tools Required to Intercept and Obstruct Terrorism Act* (USA Patriot Act) adopted on October 25, 2001.
[18]The Center for Democracy and Technology has a Web site at http://www.cdt.org.

statement states that it "works to promote democratic values and constitutional liberties in the digital age. With expertise in law, technology, and policy, CDT seeks practical solutions to enhance free expression and privacy in global communications technologies. CDT is dedicated to building consensus among all parties interested in the future of the Internet and other new communications media."

CYBERLAW

Privacy

The World Wide Web has stirred serious concerns about privacy. Recently, Georgetown University prepared a report to the Federal Trade Commission on the privacy topic. They sampled of 361 dot.com addresses from a total of 7,500 top Web sites used by consumers.

The survey revealed that 98.8 percent of the sites collected at least one type of personal information; 56.8 percent collected information about gender, zip codes, and other demographic information; and 56.2 percent collected both personal identifying and demographic information. These statistics are just one indication as to the ability to gather private information.

Personal and demographic information often is placed in data banks. This information then is sold to companies seeking to market products and services to individuals or businesses. These purchasers then conduct data mining activities that provide a profile of individuals or businesses. Armed with this information, the purchasers can target information that interests the individual and encourages the person to purchase goods or services.

The real problem is that this personal information is collected and sold without the consent of the consumer. For example, the Web site Toysrus.com used a marketing service from a marketing company called Coremetrics to assist in evaluating information about visitors to the Toysrus.com site. Coremetrics used technology, such as Web bugs and cookies, to track a visitor's whereabouts online as the visitor surfed the Web. The problem that developed was that Toysrus.com had no control over what Coremetrics did with this information. After several legal actions, Toysrus.com terminated its relationship with Coremetrics.

How do you protect your privacy on the Internet? First, do not reveal personal information inadvertently. Do not give your name, address, and other personal information unless you really want to. If you meet a person on the Internet remember that you do not really know this person.

Watch out for *cookies*. A cookie is placed on your computer without your knowledge to collect information about all the Web sites you visit, the time spent on the Web site, if you return to that Web site on a different visit, and whether you make any purchases. You can delete cookies from your computer.

Do not use your computer at work for personal reasons. Most companies have a policy against this. Your employer has a right to monitor the information on the company's computer at your workstation. This right includes monitoring your e-mail and which Web sites you visit.

Do not respond to spammers. They send unsolicited bulk e-mail usually to thousands of persons. Forget about clicking on the remove line. The click just verifies the Web address and you will not be removed from their list.

Review the privacy policies of businesses that sell items on the Internet. Legitimate businesses have written policies about privacy that can be reviewed before you purchase anything. The policy should clearly state whether your name or identity will be sold to other businesses.

Even then you cannot rely on the company's assurances about never selling private information. Toysmart.com was a company that made such assurances. When the company was about to go into bankruptcy, it tried to sell its database, which contained the customer's credit card numbers along with the ages and names of children. A suit was filed by the FTC on behalf of consumers. The case was resolved when the majority shareholder (Disney Corporation) paid $50,000 for destruction of the database.

One reason why the issue of privacy has become so important is the manner in which the European Union (EU) handles privacy concerns. Over many centuries persons in Europe have suffered from tyrannical governments ranging from feudal lords in medieval times to the Nazis and Communists in the twentieth century.

Based on its past, European governments are very concerned with maintaining the privacy of their citizens. One protection measure was the passage by the

EU of the **Personal Data Protection Directive.** This directive adopted what is known as the **opt-in provision**. This clause means that the customer must take affirmative action and request to have his information available in a data bank that is shared. Any business that does not comply with its provisions cannot do business within the EU. The opt-in provision is the opposite of the opt-out provision discussed previously under the U.S. law called the Gramm-Leach-Bliley Act

As a result of the two incompatible provisions of opt-in and opt-out, the U.S. Department of Commerce has issued what is known as the **Safe Harbor Privacy Principles**. The EU has agreed to allow companies to conduct business within the EU if they have adopted these principles. One business that was caught between the U.S. and EU differences was the airline industry, which finally achieved a compromise on passenger lists that was accepted by both governments in 2003.

The Commerce Department requires organizations to comply with seven safe harbor principles. The principles require the following:

1. *Notice* Individuals must be notified about the purposes for which information is collected and used.

2. *Choice* Individuals must be provided the opportunity to choose (opt out) whether their personal information will be disclosed to a third party or when the purpose for collection is changed.

3. *Transfers to Third Parties* Before information can be transferred to a third party, they also must apply the notice and choice principles.

4. *Access* Individuals must able to access their personal information and be able to correct, amend, or delete inaccurate information. Exceptions are provided when the burden or expense of providing access is disproportionate to the risks to the individual's privacy or where the rights of other persons would be violated.

5. *Security* Organizations must take reasonable precautions to protect personal information from loss, misuse and unauthorized access, disclosure, alteration, and destruction.

6. *Data integrity* Personal information must be relevant for the purposes for which it is to be used. An organization should take reasonable steps to ensure that data are accurate, complete, current, and reliable for their intended use.

7. *Enforcement* To ensure compliance, there must be (a) readily available and affordable independent recourse mechanisms so that each individual's complaints and disputes can be investigated, resolved, and damages awarded when appropriate; (b) verification procedures that the commitments companies make to adhere to the safe harbor principles have been implemented; and (c) the ability to remedy problems arising out of a failure to comply with the principles.

LEGAL HIGHLIGHT

Street Cameras

Tampa, Florida, installed thirty-six cameras to watch persons walking the streets, the first city to do so. The employees watch for wanted felons and missing children. The cameras transmit the pictures to computers, which use face scanning technology by targeting eighty reference points on the face ranging from the forehead to the chin. An alarm is set to ring when fourteen of these reference points are made on a face that may belong to a known criminal or a missing child. In three years of use, only one criminal was identified.

Critics believe these cameras to be an invasion of privacy. They assert that the government should not be watching the activities of normal citizens. Critics also raise the issue as to how long the images should be kept in the computer.

The use of cameras in this manner is being adopted in a number of private and public spaces. Face recognition software has not been shown to be relatively accurate at this time and is considered to be cutting-edge technology. The question society must answer is whether the intrusion of cameras is worth the additional loss to a person's privacy.

Sanctions ensure compliance by organizations with these safe harbor principles. Organizations must provide annual self-certification letters; otherwise, they no longer appear in the list of participants and safe harbor benefits are not available. If a business is not listed, it cannot conduct business within the EU.

Fifth Amendment— Self-Incrimination

The Fifth Amendment guarantees against forced self-incrimination by stating that no person "shall be compelled in any criminal case to be a witness against himself." The federal government cannot force an accused person to confess or to give any evidence that might be used against him in any criminal prosecution.

The Fourteenth Amendment's due process clause incorporates the Fifth Amendment provision against self-incrimination and protects an accused from any illegal action by the state government. Accused people, however, have this protection only for themselves. They may be required to testify against others.

The Fifth Amendment's guarantee against self-incrimination extends only to natural people (humans) and not to legal entities. Corporations, partnerships, and other business forms are legal entities and, as such, do not have the protection of that Fifth Amendment clause. When the court orders these organizations to produce their records, they must comply, even when the evidence is incriminating.

What are the rights of businesspeople when they turn over incriminating papers to an accountant or lawyer? This question is answered in the following case.

LANDMARK CASE

CASE 5.6

Supreme Court of the United States, 1976
425 U.S. 391, 96 S. Ct. 1569, 48 L. Ed. 2d 39
http://www.findlaw.com/casecode/supreme.html

FISHER v. UNITED STATES

BACKGROUND AND FACTS Two taxpayers were under investigation for possible civil or criminal liability under the federal income tax laws. One taxpayer obtained from his accountants certain documents relating to the accountants' preparation of the tax returns and transferred these documents to his attorneys.

The Internal Revenue Service attempted to obtain these documents by serving summonses on the taxpayer's attorneys. The attorneys refused to comply, based on their client's Fifth Amendment rights against self-incrimination and the attorney–client privilege.

Justice WHITE delivered the opinion of the Court.

In these two cases we are called upon to decide whether a summons directing an attorney to produce documents delivered to him by his client in connection with the attorney–client relationship is enforceable over claims that the documents were constitutionally immune from summons in the hands of the client and retained that immunity in the hands of the attorney.

. . . .

. . . [P]etitioners' appeal raised only their Fifth Amendment claim, but they argued in connection with that claim that enforcement of the summons would involve a violation of the taxpayers' reasonable expectation of privacy and particularly so in light of the confidential relationship of attorney to client. . . .

. . . .

All of the parties in these cases . . . have concurred in the proposition that if the Fifth Amendment would have excused a taxpayer from turning over the accountant's papers had he possessed them, the attorney to whom they are delivered for the purpose of obtaining legal advice should also be immune from subpoena. Although we agree with this proposition, we are convinced that . . . it is not the taxpayer's Fifth Amendment privilege that would excuse the attorney from production.

The relevant part of that Amendment provides:

"No person . . . shall be compelled in any criminal case to be a witness against himself" (emphasis added).

The taxpayer's privilege under this Amendment is not violated by enforcement of the summonses involved in these cases because enforcement against a taxpayer's lawyer would not "compel" the taxpayer to do anything—and certainly would not compel him to be a witness against himself. The Court has held repeatedly that the Fifth Amendment is limited to prohibiting the use of "physical or moral compulsion" exerted on the person asserting the privilege. In *Couch v. United States*, we recently ruled that the Fifth Amendment rights of a taxpayer were not violated by the enforcement of a documentary summons directed to her accountant and requiring production of the taxpayer's own records in the possession of the accountant. We did so on the ground that in such a case "the ingredient of personal compulsion against an accused is lacking."

Here, the taxpayers are compelled to do no more than was the taxpayer in *Couch*. The taxpayers' Fifth Amendment privilege is therefore not violated by enforcement of the summonses directed toward their attorneys. . . .

. . . .

Confidential disclosures by a client to an attorney made in order to obtain legal assistance are privileged. As a practical matter, if the client knows that damaging information could more readily be obtained from the attorney following than from himself in the absence of disclosure, the client would be reluctant to confide in his lawyer and it would be difficult to obtain fully informed legal advice. However, since the privilege has the effect of withholding relevant information from the fact finder, it applies only where necessary to achieve its purpose. Accordingly it protects only those disclosures— necessary to obtain informed legal advice—which might not have been made absent the privilege. This Court and the lower courts have thus uniformly held that preexisting documents which could have been obtained by court process from the client when he was in possession may also be obtained from the attorney by similar process following transfer by the client in order to obtain more informed legal advice. . . . It is otherwise if the documents are not obtainable by subpoena *duces tecum* [subpoena used to obtain evidence in the hands of another] or summons while in the exclusive possession of the client, for the client will then be reluctant to transfer possession to the lawyer unless the documents are also privileged in the latter's hands. . . .

. . . .

A subpoena served on a taxpayer requiring him to produce an accountant's work papers in his possession without doubt involves substantial compulsion. But it does not compel oral testimony; nor would it ordinarily compel the taxpayer to restate, repeat, or affirm the truth of the contents of the documents sought. Therefore, the Fifth Amendment would not be violated by the fact alone that the papers on their face might incriminate the taxpayer, for the privilege protects a person only against being incriminated by his own compelled testimonial communications. The accountant's work papers are not the taxpayer's. They were not prepared by the taxpayer, and they contain no testimonial declarations by him. . . .

. . . .

Whether the Fifth Amendment would shield the taxpayer from producing his own tax records in his possession is a question not involved here; for the papers demanded here are not his "private papers[.]"

DECISION AND REMEDY The Supreme Court held that nontestimonial (evidence that is not oral) business records not prepared by the taxpayer that are in the custody of third parties, including lawyers and accountants, must be surrendered when a search warrant is issued for them.

CRITICAL THINKING: LEGAL CONSIDERATION Discuss whether personal business records prepared solely by the taxpayer should be required to be surrendered. Explain.

International Consideration

Must a Court Recognize a Foreign Judgment?

Over the decades, the United States Supreme Court has implemented various well-recognized principles of international law, including those of comity, the act of state, and sovereign immunity.

Comity means courtesy or a willingness to grant a privilege, not as a matter of right but out of deference and goodwill. The principle of comity means that one nation recognizes the legislative, executive, or judicial acts of another nation. This doctrine is not based on any international legal obligations but rather on respect for the laws of another country. Under the principle of comity, a judgment from a foreign country is enforceable within the courts of the United States.[19] The foreign judgment must be based on having proper jurisdiction. The effect of comity is similar to the full faith and credit clause of the Constitution, which requires states to recognize the judgments coming from sister states.

The **act of state doctrine** means the courts cannot interfere with the acts of another nation within its boundaries. The effect of this doctrine is that U.S. courts normally are precluded from hearing cases in which a sovereign nation has expropriated or confiscated the assets of an American business.

Expropriation occurs when a government seizes privately owned goods or a privately owned business for a proper public purpose and awards just compensation. A **confiscation** occurs when the other country takes the privately owned goods or business without a proper public purpose and with no award of just compensation. The only exception to the principle regarding an act of state is when a treaty exists between the two countries that permits a legal action in the United States.

In 1976, Congress passed the Foreign Sovereign Immunities Act (FSIA), which codifies the doctrine of sovereign immunity. **Sovereign immunity** means that a person cannot sue the government without its permission. For the purposes of this doctrine, a *foreign state* includes both the state and any agency of the foreign state, such as a state-owned bank.

The FSIA exclusively governs the circumstances under which an action may be brought against a foreign state in a U.S. court. Attachment of a foreign nation's property, for example, is provided for by the FSIA. Attachment is a court order to bring the debtor's (in this case the foreign state's) property under the control of the court during the lawsuit.

One of the primary purposes of the FSIA is to ensure that federal courts, rather than the Department of State, determine claims of foreign sovereign immunity. By removing the claims to federal court, the Department of State is relieved from political pressures to make diplomatic decisions that might be legally correct but politically unpopular. For example, a foreign ship or its cargo may be attached under a court order.

Section 1605 of the FSIA establishes the major exceptions to the jurisdictional immunity of a country. A foreign state is under the jurisdiction of the courts of the United States when the foreign government has waived its immunity. The foreign country also is under the jurisdiction of the courts when the action is based on a commercial activity carried out by the foreign nation within the jurisdictional limits of the United States.

---

[19]Chapter 4 described how the New York Convention requires nations that have signed the convention to recognize foreign arbitration awards. The principle of comity refers to judgments coming from courts.

PRACTICAL TIPS

Stopping Employee Theft

You are the security officer for a large private business that is not unionized. Lately, lost inventory has risen sharply. This type of loss indicates that employees are pilfering items. You have no idea who these employees may be, how many are involved, or if a criminal ring has infiltrated your company. After considering this problem, you develop a checklist.

Checklist

✔ *Notification* Notify all employees that telephone conversations will be monitored. Conversations are monitored routinely in most large businesses.

✔ *Monitoring* Install discreetly hidden video cameras to monitor employees' activities in the warehouse and docking area to discover theft from the inventory.

✔ *Scanning* Scan voice mail and e-mail.

✔ *Searching* Check lockers and desks occasionally since the business owns them. Employees

should be notified that such checks may be conducted with and without the employees' knowledge or permission to detect employee misconduct. Personal belongings may not be searched.

Chapter Summary

The U.S. Constitution is the oldest active constitution in the modern world. It has lasted so long because our founders had the insight to produce a document that accomplishes three major objectives. First, the Constitution creates three branches of government, each independent of the other but with the ability to limit the powers of the other two branches through a system of checks and balances.

Second, the Constitution creates a central government that is supreme, but that derives its power from the states. Federalism is the basic structure of our government. Certain powers are given to the federal government, whereas other powers are shared with the states. The Constitution delegates certain powers or rights, called *enumerated powers*, to the federal government. For example, the commerce clause of the Constitution allows the federal government to regulate all interstate and foreign commerce. Any commerce, considered cumulatively, which has a substantial economic effect, is considered interstate commerce and subject to regulation. Occasionally, conflicts arise between federal and state law. The federal law is upheld under the Constitution's supremacy clause.

Third, the Constitution guarantees the people certain basic rights that neither local nor federal governments can abridge. The first ten constitutional amendments, called the Bill of Rights, set out these rights in detail. These amendments have particular applications to business. For example, under the First Amendment, commercial speech is protected as long as it is not false, deceptive, or misleading. The Fourth Amendment protects businesses from illegal search and seizures in the absence of a valid warrant. Business entities, however, are not protected from self-incrimination under the Fifth Amendment.

Businesses are protected by the due process clause in the Fifth and Fourteenth Amendments. The distinction between substantive and procedural due process is that procedural due process involves the methods used in protecting legal rights, while substantive due process involves protecting the basic legal rights themselves. The equal protection clause applies to both federal and state governments, which must give equal protection of the laws to all people.

Using the World Wide Web

Remember the documents you were supposed to have read in high school civics: the Magna Carta, the Declaration of Independence, the Articles of Confederation, and the Constitution? Today, with only a few keystrokes, people can access those documents on the Internet.

The National Archives and Records Administration provides a variety of interesting documents on its Web pages. Its Exhibit Hall Web page offers a glimpse of our past. Use the search function on the home page to find other interesting information.

For *Web Activities*, links to Web sites mentioned in the chapter, and additional Web sites that relate to the

chapter topics, go to **http://bohlman.westbuslaw. com**, click on "Internet Applications," and select Chapter 5.

Web Activities

Go to **http://bohlman.westbuslaw.com**, click on "Internet Applications," and select Chapter 5.
5-1 World Constitutions
5-2 Magna Carta

Key Terms

act of state doctrine

actual malice

Bill of Rights

checks and balances

Children's Online
   Privacy Act (COPA)

comity

commerce clause

concurrent power

confiscation

defamation

doctrine of selective
   incorporation

double jeopardy

Electronic Communica-
   tions Privacy Act
   (ECPA)

enumerated (delegated)
   powers

equal protection clause

exclusive power

executive branch

expropriation

federalism

full faith and credit
   clause

Gramm-Leach-Bliley
   Act (GLBA)

Health Insurance Porta-
   bility and Account-
   ability Act (HIPAA)

intermediate scrutiny
   test

judicial branch

judicial review

legal entity

legislative branch

opt-in provision

opt-out provision

partially protected
   speech

Personal Data Protection
   Directive

police powers

preemption doctrine

privileges and immuni-
   ties clause

probable cause

procedural due process

protected speech

rational basis test

Right to Financial
   Privacy Act

Safe Harbor Privacy
   Principles

self-incrimination

sovereign immunity

spending power

standing to sue

strict scrutiny test

substantive due process

supremacy clause

taxing power

unprotected speech

USA Patriot Act

Questions and Case Problems

5–1 Judicial Review Discuss the doctrine of judicial review.

5–2 Constitutional Rights A business has a backlog of orders. To meet its deadlines, management is considering running the firm seven days a week, eight hours a day. What issues of constitutional law should management consider in making this decision? Can management terminate an employee for refusing to work more than forty hours a week? Can management terminate an employee for refusing to work on a religious holy day?

5–3 Commerce Clause Unlike all other states in the West and Midwest, Iowa had a statute that prohibited the use of sixty-five-foot double-trailer trucks on its highways for safety reasons. The use of fifty-five-foot trailer trucks and sixty-foot double-trailer trucks was allowed. Consolidated Freightways, a Delaware corporation, owned sixty-five-foot double-trailer trucks. These trucks, which carried commodities, could not use the interstate highways that passed through Iowa. Consequently, Consolidated filed suit, alleging that Iowa's statutory scheme unconstitutionally burdened interstate commerce. Does Consolidated have a valid case? Explain your answer. [*Kassel v. Consolidated Freightways Corp. of Delaware,* 450 U.S. 662, 101 S. Ct. 1309, 67 L. Ed. 2d 580 (1981)]

5–4 Preemption A Wisconsin statute prohibits people or firms that have violated the National Labor Relations Act (NLRA) three times within a five-year period from conducting business with the state. For this reason, Gould, Inc., was not allowed to conduct business with the state. The NLRA has substantive requirements that conflict with the Wisconsin statute. Is this statute constitutional under the supremacy clause or displaced by the NLRA? [*Wisconsin Department of Industry v. Gould, Inc.,* 475 U.S. 282, 106 S. Ct. 1057, 89 L. Ed. 2d 223 (1986)]

5–5 Commercial Speech Drug compounding is a process by which a pharmacist or doctor combines, mixes, or alters ingredients to create a medication tailored to the needs of an individual patient. Compounding is typically used to prepare medications that are not commercially available, such as medication for a patient who is allergic to an ingredient in a mass-produced product. It is a traditional component of the practice of pharmacy. The Federal Drug Administration instituted new regulations that disallowed the advertising or promotion of these drugs. A group of licensed pharmacies that specialize in drug compounding brought legal action to stop the implementation of these regulations. In the past, these pharmacies had prepared promotional materials that they distributed by mail and at medical conferences to inform patients and physicians of the use and effectiveness of specific compounded drugs. Fearing that they would be prosecuted if they continued to distribute those materials, the pharmacies filed a complaint, arguing that the regulations requiring that they refrain from advertising and promoting their products violated the free speech clause of the First Amendment. How would you hold in this situation? [*Thompson v. Western States Medical Center,* 535 U.S. 357, 122 S. Ct. 1497, 152 L. Ed. 2d 563 (2002)]

5–6 Civil Rights A motel owner who refused to rent rooms to African Americans, despite the Civil Rights Act of 1964, brought an action to have the act declared unconstitutional. The motel owner alleged that Congress, in passing the act, had exceeded its power to regulate commerce. The statute was upheld. What legal arguments were used to validate it? [*Heart of Atlanta v. United States,* 379 U.S. 241, 85 S. Ct. 348, 13 L. Ed. 2d 258 (1964)]

5–7 Privileges and Immunities In the early 1970s, an oil pipeline was built across Alaska. In 1972, the Alaska legislature passed an act that became known as the Alaska Hire. The act had a provision requiring the employment of qualified Alaskan residents over non-residents. To qualify for the preference, a person had to have lived in Alaska for one year. The reason for the act was to reduce unemployment. Some individuals who wanted jobs but who did not qualify for preference as Alaskan residents brought suit, challenging the act under the privileges and immunities clause. Who should win this case—the plaintiffs seeking jobs or Alaska seeking to reduce unemployment? Explain. [*Hicklin v. Orbeck,* 437 U.S. 518, 98 S. Ct. 2482, 57 L. Ed. 2d 397 (1978)]

5–8 Separation Clause The plaintiffs, Americans United for Separation of Church and State, Inc., as tax-payers, brought an action to challenge a conveyance of land from the Department of Health, Education, and Welfare (HEW) to Valley Forge Christian College, the defendant. The plaintiffs alleged that such a conveyance violated the establishment clause of the First Amendment. The district court dismissed the complaint on the ground that the plaintiffs lacked standing to sue. What was the result on appeal? [*Valley Forge Christian College v. Americans United for Separation of Church and State, Inc.,* 454 U.S. 464, 102 S. Ct. 752, 70 L. Ed. 2d 700 (1982)] (Note that HEW was later divided into two separate departments, the Department of Education and the Department of Health and Human Services.)

5–9 Interstate Commerce New Jersey enacted a law prohibiting the importation of most wastes into the state. Some of the landfill operators in New Jersey, however, had agreements with out-of-state residents to dispose of their solid and liquid waste. Philadelphia brought an action claiming that this statute violated the commerce clause because it discriminated against interstate commerce. New Jersey asserted that its statute was justified because its landfills were inadequate to dispose of its own waste, and importation had a significant and adverse potential effect on the environment. Is this state regulation of interstate commerce permissible? [*Philadelphia v. New Jersey,* 437 U.S. 617, 98 S. Ct. 2531, 57 L. Ed. 2d 475 (1978)]

5–10 Internet Who was the youngest signer of the Declaration of Independence, who was the oldest, and which state had the largest representation when it was signed? You can go directly to a site that will provide answers to these questions by going to **http://www.archives.gov**, click on "Exhibit Hall," "Charters of Freedom," "Declaration of Independence," "Join the Signers of the Declaration of Independence," and "The Signers Gallery."

Chapter 6

Administrative Agencies and the Regulation of Business

The rise of administrative bodies probably has been the most significant legal trend of the last century and perhaps more values today are affected by their decisions than by those of all the courts, review of administrative decisions apart. They also have begun to have important consequences on personal rights. . . . They have become a veritable fourth branch of the Government which has deranged our three-branch legal theories as much as the concept of a fourth dimension unsettles our three-dimensional thinking.

Federal Trade Commission v.
Ruberoid Co.
343 U.S. 470, 487; 72 S. Ct. 800, 810; 96
L. Ed. 2d 1081, 1094 (1952)
http://www.findlaw.com/casecode/
supreme.htm

Chapter Outline

Ethical Consideration

Conflicts between Freedom of Speech and Ethics

You are a government employee working for the Nuclear Regulatory Agency. Already overwhelmed with requests for various reports, you have received still another request. A congressional committee needs information on the training level required for personnel who work in the various reactors around the country. You have no idea when you will have time to write this report. The agency requires all congressional inquiries to be answered within ten working days. You do not even know how to obtain this information, because the agency does not require that it be kept.

As often happens, you are visited by a lobbyist from a company involved in the manufacture of nuclear power plants. She wants to discuss some pending legislation. In the course of the conversation, you explain your dilemma, and she volunteers to find the information for you. You know that obtaining information from lobbyists is a common practice and that their information generally is reliable.

Should you accept or decline this offer? Use the ethical model presented in Chapter 2 and reprinted on the inside front cover to develop your answer.

Introduction

Generally, when people think about law enforcement, they think about the courts. Actually, few people ever see the inside of a courtroom for any offense more serious than a traffic violation. Businesses infrequently have occasion to be involved in lawsuits.

Instead, businesses more often have contact with a variety of administrative agencies. Congress and state legislatures create administrative agencies to enforce specific statutes that they have passed. For example, the Internal Revenue Service administers and enforces the tax laws passed by Congress. *Administrative agencies* are also called *regulatory agencies* or *bureaucracies*. These three terms are used interchangeably.

This chapter first reviews the areas of business that administrative agencies regulate. Second, the features of administrative agencies that allow them to handle problems more effectively than the legislature or the courts are discussed. Third, the chapter explores the Administrative Procedure Act, its amendments, and the three types of power of an administrative agency: quasi-legislative, quasi-executive, and quasi-judicial. Fourth, the constitutional, statutory, and judicial limits of an administrative agency's power are examined. Fifth, the deregulation process is summarized.

Artiste Login. Carlos and Carlotta have an online business, Artiste Login Products, Inc. Artiste is regulated by a number of federal and state administrative agencies, which do not always issue compatible regulations for Artiste to follow.

Artiste has a number of employees whose employment is regulated by both federal and state labor agencies. The processes that Artiste uses to create its metal and glass sculptures are regulated by agencies that deal with safety practices. Toxic materials fall under the regulation of environmental agencies. Of course, Artiste must comply with federal and state taxing agencies. Even though most of its business is conducted online, Artiste must comply with a myriad of administrative rules issued by these agencies.

Areas of Regulation

Since the late 1960s, the regulation of business has shifted dramatically from the courts, which apply statutory and common law to resolve problems, to administrative agencies, which use more direct and comprehensive controls to resolve problems. The current constraints placed on business transactions by regulatory authorities greatly impact the economy. (See Exhibit 6-1 which shows how administrative agencies fit into the organizational structure of the federal government.)

Today's business decisions are constrained both by congressional statutes and by the interpretation and enforcement of those statutes through rules made and enforced by administrative agencies. The study of the powers, procedures, and practices of these administrative agencies is called *administrative law*.

Administrative agencies handle two areas of public concern: economic regulation and public welfare. An

Exhibit 6–1   ## Organization Chart of the Government of the United States

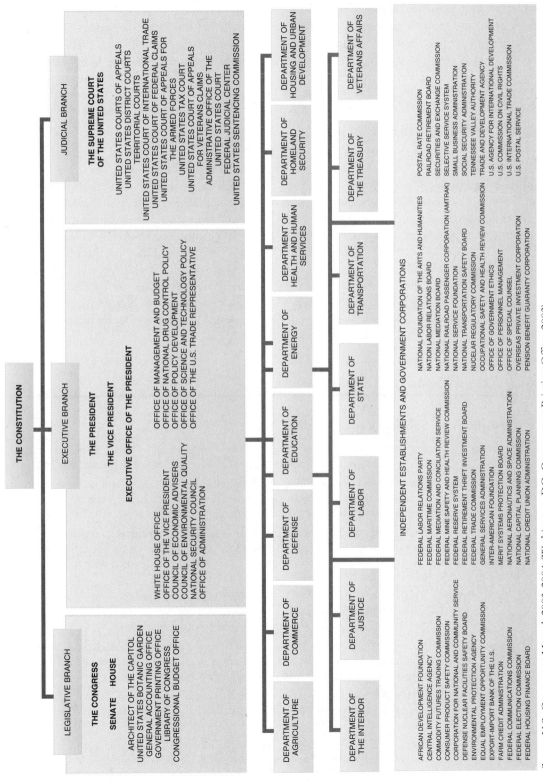

THE GOVERNMENT OF THE UNITED STATES

THE CONSTITUTION

LEGISLATIVE BRANCH

THE CONGRESS

SENATE   HOUSE

ARCHITECT OF THE CAPITOL
UNITED STATES BOTANIC GARDEN
GENERAL ACCOUNTING OFFICE
GOVERNMENT PRINTING OFFICE
LIBRARY OF CONGRESS
CONGRESSIONAL BUDGET OFFICE

EXECUTIVE BRANCH

THE PRESIDENT

THE VICE PRESIDENT

EXECUTIVE OFFICE OF THE PRESIDENT

WHITE HOUSE OFFICE
OFFICE OF THE VICE PRESIDENT
COUNCIL OF ECONOMIC ADVISERS
COUNCIL OF ENVIRONMENTAL QUALITY
NATIONAL SECURITY COUNCIL
OFFICE OF ADMINISTRATION

OFFICE OF MANAGEMENT AND BUDGET
OFFICE OF NATIONAL DRUG CONTROL POLICY
OFFICE OF POLICY DEVELOPMENT
OFFICE OF SCIENCE AND TECHNOLOGY POLICY
OFFICE OF THE U.S. TRADE REPRESENTATIVE

JUDICIAL BRANCH

**THE SUPREME COURT
OF THE UNITED STATES**

UNITED STATES COURTS OF APPEALS
UNITED STATES DISTRICT COURTS
TERRITORIAL COURTS
UNITED STATES COURT OF INTERNATIONAL TRADE
UNITED STATES COURT OF FEDERAL CLAIMS
UNITED STATES COURT OF APPEALS FOR
THE ARMED FORCES
UNITED STATES TAX COURT
UNITED STATES COURT OF APPEALS
FOR VETERANS CLAIMS
ADMINISTRATIVE OFFICE OF THE
UNITED STATES COURT
FEDERAL JUDICIAL CENTER
UNITED STATES SENTENCING COMMISSION

DEPARTMENT OF AGRICULTURE

DEPARTMENT OF THE INTERIOR

DEPARTMENT OF COMMERCE

DEPARTMENT OF JUSTICE

DEPARTMENT OF DEFENSE

DEPARTMENT OF LABOR

DEPARTMENT OF EDUCATION

DEPARTMENT OF STATE

DEPARTMENT OF ENERGY

DEPARTMENT OF TRANSPORTATION

DEPARTMENT OF HEALTH AND HUMAN SERVICES

DEPARTMENT OF HOMELAND SECURITY

DEPARTMENT OF THE TREASURY

DEPARTMENT OF HOUSING AND URBAN DEVELOPMENT

DEPARTMENT OF VETERANS AFFAIRS

INDEPENDENT ESTABLISHMENTS AND GOVERNMENT CORPORATIONS

AFRICAN DEVELOPMENT FOUNDATION
CENTRAL INTELLIGENCE AGENCY
COMMODITY FUTURES TRADING COMMISSION
CONSUMER PRODUCT SAFETY COMMISSION
CORPORATION FOR NATIONAL AND COMMUNITY SERVICE
DEFENSE NUCLEAR FACILITIES SAFETY BOARD
ENVIRONMENTAL PROTECTION AGENCY
EQUAL EMPLOYMENT OPPORTUNITY COMMISSION
EXPORT-IMPORT BANK OF THE U.S.
FARM CREDIT ADMINISTRATION
FEDERAL COMMUNICATIONS COMMISSION
FEDERAL ELECTION COMMISSION
FEDERAL HOUSING FINANCE BOARD

FEDERAL LABOR RELATIONS PARTY
FEDERAL MARITIME COMMISSION
FEDERAL MEDIATION AND CONCILIATION SERVICE
FEDERAL MINE SAFETY AND HEALTH REVIEW COMMISSION
FEDERAL RESERVE SYSTEM
FEDERAL RETIREMENT THRIFT INVESTMENT BOARD
FEDERAL TRADE COMMISSION
GENERAL SERVICES ADMINISTRATION
INTER-AMERICAN FOUNDATION
MERIT SYSTEMS PROTECTION BOARD
NATIONAL AERONAUTICS AND SPACE ADMINISTRATION
NATIONAL CAPITAL PLANNING COMMISSION
NATIONAL CREDIT UNION ADMINISTRATION

NATIONAL FOUNDATION OF THE ARTS AND HUMANITIES
NATION LABOR RELATIONS BOARD
NATIONAL MEDIATION BOARD
NATIONAL RAILROAD PASSENGER CORPORATION (AMTRAK)
NATIONAL SERVICE FOUNDATION
NATIONAL TRANSPORTATION SAFETY BOARD
NUCLEAR REGULATORY COMMISSION
OCCUPATIONAL SAFETY AND HEALTH REVIEW COMMISSION
OFFICE OF GOVERNMENT ETHICS
OFFICE OF PERSONNEL MANAGEMENT
OFFICE OF SPECIAL COUNSEL
OVERSEAS PRIVATE INVESTMENT CORPORATION
PENSION BENEFIT GUARANTY CORPORATION

POSTAL RATE COMMISSION
RAILROAD RETIREMENT BOARD
SECURITIES AND EXCHANGE COMMISSION
SELECTIVE SERVICE SYSTEM
SMALL BUSINESS ADMINISTRATION
SOCIAL SECURITY ADMINISTRATION
TENNESSEE VALLEY AUTHORITY
TRADE AND DEVELOPMENT AGENCY
U.S. AGENCY FOR INTERNATIONAL DEVELOPMENT
U.S. COMMISSION ON CIVIL RIGHTS
U.S. INTERNATIONAL TRADE COMMISSION
U.S. POSTAL SERVICE

Source: U.S. Government Manual, 2003–2004 (Washington, DC: Government Printing Office, 2003)
Retrieved November 12, 2003, from http://www.gpoaccess.gov/gmanual.

example of economic regulation is the Federal Reserve Board, which regulates the banking industry. Public welfare, in turn, is divided into two parts: protection programs and entitlement programs. A protection program is one that protects the public, usually in the health and safety areas. An **entitlement program** is a program that administers benefits to which a person is entitled, such as Social Security, which is discussed in more detail later. (See Exhibit 6–2 for some examples of various types of regulations.)

Economic Regulation

Economic regulation covers three basic areas. First, administrative agencies authorize the operation of certain types of regulated businesses and may be involved in accrediting their equipment. The Federal Aviation Administration (FAA), for example, certifies airlines and airports for operation and certifies specific aircraft for airworthiness. Second, administrative agencies regulate securities and financial businesses. The Securities and Exchange Commission regulates the securities industries. Third, some business activities are entirely subject to regulation, such as the broadcast media, which are regulated by the Federal Communications Commission (FCC).

Other agencies have regulatory powers that regulate all types of businesses. For example, the Equal Employment Opportunity Commission (EEOC) has responsibility for all compliance and enforcement activities that work to eliminate discrimination in business, labor unions, and government.

Public Welfare

For regulation purposes, the term **public welfare** refers to protection and entitlement programs that benefit the public at large. Its jurisdiction is not limited to government aid to lower income people.

The protection programs protect the health and safety of people. The Occupational Safety and Health Administration (OSHA) provides for the public welfare of all by ensuring safety in the work area. All citizens benefit if workers have a safe workplace because time and money losses as a result of injuries and death decrease.

Exhibit 6–2   Types of Regulation

Type of Regulation	Subject Matter of the Regulation
Advertisements	Cigarette, cigar, and liquor advertisements and sexually explicit material are controlled by the Federal Communications Commission as it applies to the broadcast media.
Contracts	Private contracts must follow certain regulations, such as the format for interest-rate disclosures, language requirements, and the consumer's right to rescind a contract within three days in some situations as regulated by the Federal Reserve Board.
Disclosure	Disclosure regulations issued by various regulatory agencies require health and nutritional information on food labels, fuel consumption labels on automobiles, and warning labels on dangerous products. Information about securities must be filed with the Securities and Exchange Commission.
Licensing	Bank charters are issued by the state banking departments; insurance business charters are issued by the state insurance departments; and certificates of operation to railroads, trucking companies, and bus lines are issued by the federal government.
Materials and processes	Materials and processes for some types of manufacturing are regulated. The Food and Drug Administration can ban the use of additives in food. The Environmental Protection Agency regulates the use and disposal of hazardous chemicals.
Quotas	The importation or exportation of certain products is limited. The sale of computer components to terrorist countries is not allowed. The importation of oil is subject to quotas.
Standards	Standards are set by various agencies. The Department of Agriculture sets the standards for meat and poultry. The Federal Aviation Administration sets the standards for airplane certification.

With an entitlement program, the applicants qualify for a program based on a set of criteria. If a person meets certain qualifications, he is entitled to participate in the program.

The most popular of the entitlement programs is the Social Security Insurance program. Employed people are taxed on a portion of their wages for Social Security. The administrative costs for this program that covers millions of people are 1 percent.

Social Security has three programs: retirement, disability, and life insurance. If a person retires and meets the eligibility criteria, she is entitled to receive Social Security benefits. If she dies, Social Security pays benefits to her surviving spouse and minor children. If a beneficiary becomes disabled, he can receive Social Security benefits during the period of disability.

Social Security benefits are not based on income. Millionaires may receive Social Security if they have contributed to it during their working days; however, they must pay income taxes on it.

Features of Administrative Agencies

Regulatory agencies deal with problems more effectively than legislatures. First, because an agency regulates only a specific subject matter area, it develops expertise in that area and adopts detailed regulations. The legislature authorizes an agency to develop the detailed logistics needed to implement and monitor all of the policies it establishes.

Second, a regulatory agency consists of a very well-developed hierarchy. A government employee can work for a particular agency for long periods of time, if not for an entire career. The employee is promoted and rewarded within that structured bureaucracy. In contrast, the legislature consists of elected representatives and thus has little continuity in its personnel.

Third, an agency has more flexibility than a legislature. If an industry wants Congress to pass a law, the process is tedious and the results are tenuous at best. In contrast, Congress has granted agencies the authority to change regulations in a quick and efficient manner. Regulations can be redrafted by an agency as soon as it recognizes the need for change. Some regulations take longer to change because of the requirement to hold formal, public hearings. Even under this requirement, however, an agency's procedure for adopting or amending regulations is faster than that used by Congress to adopt, amend, or delete a statute.

Lobbyists

A **lobbyist** is a person or private interest who attempts to influence government before decisions are made. Lobbyists try to influence both members of Congress and influential employees of administrative agencies. A lobbyist may be a full-time employee of a labor union or trade organization or may be paid by private clients to work on behalf of the clients' interests. An ordinary private citizen may write legislators or attend public meetings with the intent to influence legislators. Lobbyists are required to register, to report the individuals or groups that they represent, and to report contributions and expenditures.

Businesses have an interest in influencing Congress and administrative agencies. That influence helps to determine whether statutes or regulations are adopted or, if adopted, what areas are covered. Businesses can represent themselves, but more often hire lobbyists or are represented by trade associations. For example, more than 2,500 trade associations are located in the Washington, D.C., area. Representatives attend hearings proposing regulations, write position papers, and visit with people. Trade associations hold training sessions for their members so they can participate in the regulatory process. These associations keep members informed of pending regulatory actions and the political developments.

When statutes or regulations are adopted, businesses must comply with the new requirements. Usually, compliance means that businesses need to spend money to be compliant with these regulations. For example, the Federal Aviation Administration issued rules requiring airlines to install intrusion-resistant doors between the cockpit and the main body of the airplane. Not only did the airlines pay for the purchase and installation of the doors, but the additional weight of the doors increased fuel costs.

Artiste Login. Carlo and Carlotta are interested in environmental issues. Carlo is a sculptor who works in metal for many of his projects and Carlotta works with oil-based paints. They need to be concerned with regulations issued by both the federal Environmental Protection Agency and the appropriate state agency. If the regulations governing the disposal of metal scraps and oil-based paints are unreasonably restrictive, the cost of disposal may be prohibitive. Acting alone, Artiste may not have much influence, but by joining a trade association, Artiste can have its views represented.

Criticism

Despite the speed and efficiency with which administrative agencies work compared to legislatures, they are criticized by those who believe that agencies have lim-

ited the ability of elected officials to effect change. The legislative and executive branches of government hold political power and influence, but over the years, some of this power has shifted to the bureaucracy. Thus, to a substantial degree, quasi-permanent, unelected, nonpartisan administrative officials wield political power and influence. The administrative agencies are recognized by some as the fourth branch of the government. (See Exhibit 6–3, which shows the distribution of federal employees for the years 1989, 1995, 1998, and 2002.)

Exhibit 6–3   Distribution of Employees in the Federal Government

Branch of Government	1989	1995	1998	2002
Government (total)	2,875,866	3,123,731	2,789,495	2,710,684
Legislative (total)	39,710	37,690	30,474	29,552
Judicial (total)	15,178	21,090	31,742	33,647
Executive Departments (total)	1,716,970	2,065,038	2,727,279	2,645,700
Agriculture	129,139	122,062	105,664	100,120
Commerce	48,563	45,091	50,041	37,755
Defense	960,116	1,075,437	717,901	667,693
Education	7,364	4,696	4,677	4,626
Energy	21,557	17,130	16,156	15,853
Health and Human Services[a]	155,662	122,250	59,813	64,501
Housing and Urban Development	16,964	13,544	10,063	10,097
Homeland Security[b]	0	0	0	0
Interior	77,357	77,545	72,434	69,067
Justice	56,327	79,667	122,759	128,707
Labor	23,400	18,125	15,894	37,755
State	23,497	25,327	24,713	28,292
Transportation	72,361	65,615	64,859	66,227
Treasury	124,663	152,548	140,873	156,660
Veterans Affairs	228,285	245,992	240,398	223,786
Independent Agencies (total)[c]	1,102,122	997,511	1,070,245	1,024,359
Environmental Protection Agency	14,715	15,590	18,787	17,905
Equal Employment Opportunity Commission	3,515	2743	2,571	2,863
Federal Deposit Insurance Corporation	3,520	9,031	7,778	6,283
U.S. Postal Service	660,014	826,886	871,467	834,558

[a]Changes are sizable because the Social Security Administration separated from the DHHS to became an independent agency in April 1995.
[b]The Department of Homeland Security was created in 2003.
[c]Includes agencies not shown separately.

Source: Office of Personnel Management, http://www.opm.gov/feddata/html/empt.asp.

The Nature of Administrative Agencies

Administrative agencies are the primary interpreters and enforcers of congressional statutes. Created by Congress, an agency derives its authority from its enabling legislation. Four types of agencies can be created: line agencies, independent agencies, government agencies, and quasi-official agencies.

Line Agencies, Independent Agencies, Government Agencies, and Quasi-Official Agencies

An agency under the direct control of the president is known as a **line agency** or as an **executive agency**. A line agency is headed by one person, who is appointed by and serves at the pleasure of the president but who must be confirmed by the Senate. "At the pleasure of" means that the president can release an appointed person at any time, with or without a good reason. For example, the appointee, although doing a good job, may become a political embarrassment because of public statements. The president may request the person's resignation or fire him or her.

The members of the president's cabinet head the line agencies. Like other appointees, the secretary of the Department of Commerce (a line agency), for example, is a cabinet member who serves at the president's pleasure. Exhibit 6–4 shows a sample line agency's structure.

Congress has created a number of administrative agencies that are independent of the legislative and executive branches. An agency that is freestanding from the president and Congress is known as an **independent agency**. The Federal Trade Commission (FTC) and the National Aeronautics and Space Administration (NASA) are examples of independent agencies.

These agencies usually are headed by a commission whose members are appointed by the president and confirmed by the Senate. Commissioners do not serve at the pleasure of the president as do line agency appointees. The president cannot remove them unilaterally. A commissioner can be impeached and if the Senate convicts the person, she is removed from office.

A commission ranges in size from three to fifteen people; the number is determined by Congress. Each commissioner is equal to the others. The chair of the commission runs the daily operations.

LEGAL HIGHLIGHT

An Agency Is Born

A new agency is a rare occurrence. The newest line agency is the Department of Homeland Security (DHS) created in the wake of the terrorist attacks on September 11, 2001. Created in 2003, it consolidated twenty-two former agencies and is staffed by at least 190,000 employees. This agency is the third largest cabinet department.

The mission of the Department of Homeland Security is to (1) prevent terrorist attacks within the United States, (2) reduce America's vulnerability to terrorism, and (3) minimize the damage and recovery time from an attack if one should occur.

DHS is responsible for securing the nation's borders and transportation systems. The goal is to oversee everyone entering the United States. All goods that enter the homeland by sea, train, bus, or truck come under the jurisdiction of the DHS. The prime objective is to prevent the entry of terrorists and their weapons.

DHS is responsible for emergency preparedness and response. The purpose is to ensure the preparedness of the nation's emergency response and to provide aid to the population if terrorists should attack again. Chemical, biological, radiological, and nuclear countermeasures come under the jurisdiction of this department. It leads the federal government's efforts in preparing for and responding to the full range of terrorist threats involving weapons of mass destruction.

Information analysis and infrastructure protection also fall under DHS. This office merges under one roof the capability to identify and assess threats to the homeland, map those threats against current vulnerabilities, inform the president about these problems, issue timely warnings, and take effective appropriate preventive action.

Exhibit 6–4   A Line Agency: Department of Commerce

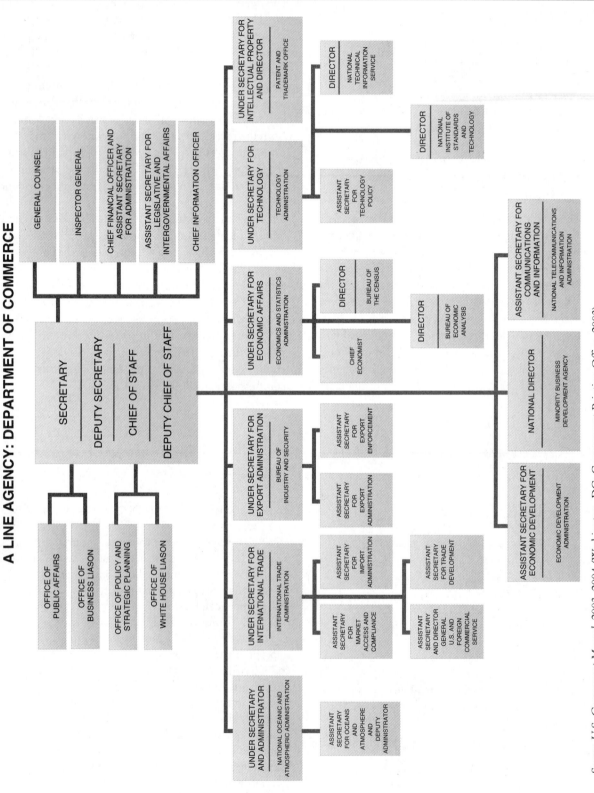

Source: U.S. Government Manual, 2003–2004 (Washington, DC: Government Printing Office, 2003) Retrieved November 12, 2003, from http://www.gpoaccess.gov/gmanual.

When appointing people to the commission, the president is required to be bipartisan, which means that both political parties must be represented. The length of service on the commission varies from agency to agency. Each member is appointed for a specific time period. All terms are staggered, however, and are longer than the four-year presidential term.

Congress creates a **government agency** to administer a quasi-business venture. *Quasi* is a Latin word meaning "as if," so the government agency administrates a program as if it were a private business. These agencies have three similar elements: (1) Each conducts a business-like activity that (2) produces revenue to continue its own existence and, as a result, (3) needs greater flexibility than usually is given to other types of agencies. The major government agencies are the Tennessee Valley Authority (TVA), the Federal Deposit Insurance Corporation (FDIC), the Pension Benefit Guaranty Corporation, and the U.S. Postal Service.

A **quasi-official agency** is created by Congress but does not have the same authority as other agencies. These agencies must publish notices and information in the *Federal Register*.[1] The members of the agency are appointed by the president, subject to Senate approval. The quasi-official agencies are the Legal Services Corporation,[2] National Railroad Passenger Corporation (Amtrak),[3] and the Smithsonian Institution.[4]

C Y B E R L A W

The Internal Revenue Service

Thanks to Congress, every federal administrative agency receives funds to create and support its own Web site. Eventually, all of the state and local administrative agencies will have a Web presence. One federal agency touches all businesses: the Internal Revenue Service (IRS).

The IRS looks for ways to cut its costs; thus, it is very involved with electronic filing of returns and providing electronic access to forms with online instructions on when to use and how to prepare the various IRS forms. One of the early electronic methods used by the IRS was the touch-tone telephone. By filing the form over the telephone, a business saved approximately two-thirds of the time that would have been expended if the business had filed the form by mail.

Today, a popular method of filing a return is to use a personal computer. The business first obtains off-the-shelf tax preparation software. The business applies for a personal identification number (PIN) by completing the letter of application included in the software. The business files the Letter electronically using a third-party transmitter. The third-party transmitter will batch other letters of application and electronically transmit the batch to an IRS center. The IRS will send the business a PIN by mail. The PIN is used in lieu of the business filer's signature.

The goal of the IRS is to increase the use of electronic filing by requiring large businesses to file electronically. For example, partnerships with more than 100 members can only file electronically.

A business or individual may obtain any necessary tax forms over the Internet. In the past, little-used forms were not distributed widely. Someone needing a little-used form had to drive to an IRS center to physically obtain the form. Every form the IRS has is now available for downloading on its Web site.[5] The Internet assists the IRS in two ways. The IRS is able to provide prompt services to the public while reducing its costs.

Enabling Legislation

Administrative agencies are created when Congress passes an **enabling act**. This act creates the agency; sets out its structure; gives it the authority to make rules, investigate problems, and adjudicate cases; and defines any other powers that it will have. Congress decides whether the agency will be a line agency in the executive branch, an independent agency, or a quasi-official government agency.

Congress controls the agencies. First, Congress creates and defines the agency's powers. Second, the Senate

---

[1]The *Federal Register* is a component of the National Archives and Records Administration. The *Federal Register* publishes public laws, presidential documents, and administrative regulations and notices. The *Federal Register* has a Web site at http://www.archives.gov.

[2]The Legal Services Corporation's Web site is found at http://www.lsc.gov.

[3]Amtrak's official Web page is http://www.amtrak.com.

[4]The Smithsonian's Web page is found at http://www.si.edu.

[5]The Internal Revenue Service's Web site is http://www.irs.ustreas.gov.

confirms the appointments of the head of the agency and the commissioners. Third, although the president sends the budget to Congress, only Congress, through its constitutional ability to tax and spend, controls appropriations to an agency. Fourth, Congress may reorganize or abolish the agency. Congress has passed deregulation legislation abolishing some agencies.

After an agency is created, it must adopt a **general policy statement**. The statement sets out, in broad terms, that particular agency's philosophy and its mission and objectives. For example, the general policy statement for the FTC reads that "[i]t is responsible for the administration of a variety of statutes which, in general, are designed to promote competition and to protect the public from unfair and deceptive acts and practices in the advertising and marketing of goods and services."[6]

The statement must be politically astute. It must satisfy both the political atmosphere that created the agency and opponents who might desire to curb its powers or abolish it outright. In 1995, Congress abolished the Interstate Commerce Commission, but was not successful in closing the Department of Commerce or the National Oceanic and Atmospheric Administration.

The authority of different agencies occasionally overlaps. The courts allow this overlapping provided that the agencies' actions are consistent with their respective enabling statutes.

Administrative Procedure Act

The **Administrative Procedure Act (APA)**[7] of 1946 standardized agency practices and governs procedures by which all federal agencies must conduct their business. The APA allows for differences among the agencies, however, because each agency's enabling act differs.

The APA sets out the procedures that an agency must follow when making rules, when acquiring and investigating information, and when adjudicating. The APA ensures that the agency adheres to constitutional requirements.

Three Areas of Power

Administrative agencies have three prime responsibilities: to make rules, to acquire and act on information,

[6]16 C.F.R. § 0.1 (1995 edition).
[7]The Administrative Procedure Act is found at the Legal Information Institute Web site at http://www4.law.cornell.edu/uscode/5/pIch5.html.

and to judge cases. These activities are carried out using the agency's legislative, executive, and judicial powers. An agency may possess one or a combination of three types of power. Congress determines which powers an agency will possess and has not authorized every agency to have all three powers.

These powers really are quasi-powers. For example, an agency with quasi-legislative power does not have the actual power to pass legislation. Only Congress has legislative power. The agency does, however, have the power to adopt rules that are very similar to legislative power, thus, the name *quasi-legislative power.*

Agencies are able to promulgate rules that have the effect of law (a **quasi-legislative function**). They have policing powers to ensure compliance with those rules by acquiring information through record keeping and investigations (a **quasi-executive function**). They prosecute violators, render judgments, and impose penalties in an administrative hearing (a **quasi-judicial function**).

Quasi-Legislative Function. An administrative agency's quasi-legislative function operates in a manner similar to a legislative body. The administrative agency adopts and publishes rules so that the public knows how to conduct its business when dealing with the items regulated by the agency. For example, the Environmental Protection Agency (EPA) has rules on methods to remove and dispose of asbestos found in a building. Any contractor who remodels a building containing asbestos must follow those rules or face penalties.

Purpose of Rule Making. A rule adopted by an administrative agency is similar to a statute passed by Congress. A rule is designed to implement, interpret, or define an agency's law, policy, or practice. A rule is based on future standards of conduct rather than on a past or current act. A business is notified of the standards so it can conduct its business practices in ways that comply with the rule.

Ministerial Powers. When an agency exercises its ministerial powers, the agency must act in obedience to a statute or regulation after the agency ascertains specified facts exist. This action does not involve the exercise of judgment, discretion, or policymaking. These powers are a very important part of an agency's activities. The only contact most members of the public have with an agency occurs when it is exercising its ministerial powers. For example, when a person visits a Social Security office or goes to its Internet site for information, the agency uses its ministerial powers.

Misinformation. The public relies on the agency to provide correct information. Based on that information, individuals and businesses carry out plans, knowing that their action complies with the agency rules. What happens, however, if an agency employee provides inaccurate information? Public policy dictates that an agency is not bound by, or liable for, incorrect information given by its employees. The real meaning of this policy is that a person cannot successfully sue the government.

Why is an agency not liable for the misinformation given by an employee? If it were, an agency could assume powers that Congress had not authorized nor did Congress want the agency to have. If the agency were held liable, the courts would be ordering government money to be spent in a manner not authorized by Congress. Under the Constitution, only Congress has the power to appropriate money.

The agency also is responsible for spending the public monies entrusted to it in accordance with the law. Even if one individual is devastated by incorrect information given by the agency, the government's duty is to the public and to the protection of the public's trust and monies.

The agency rules are available to the public through the *Federal Register*. The courts have held that ignorance of an agency's rules or reliance on the agency's information is no excuse for an individual to not know, not understand, or not comply with those rules. A person may be able to alleviate the harshness of the penalty that results from ignorance of the law, however, if one of the following categories fits the situation:

1. Congress can authorize an agency to stand behind the advice it provides in specific situations. For example, the Internal Revenue Service may issue a binding-opinion letter to a business about a question on a specific tax issue. The IRS must stand by the advice provided in that type of letter.

2. A person may incur a debt to the government because he relied on incorrect information given by an agency employee. The harmed person is not able to sue the government, but may ask the government to forgive the debt based on hardship and poor advice.

3. A person who has been harmed by incorrect advice provided by a government employee also may apply to Congress for a private bill of relief. The person's congressional representative drafts and submits a bill to Congress to compensate the person for the government's error. This route is long, difficult, and not often successful.

Discretionary Rule-Making Powers. Congress has authorized administrators to formulate rules and guidelines under a general (discretionary) authority granted to administrative agencies. For example, the commissioner of Social Security has the discretionary authority to make rules that specify who is eligible for Medicare benefits. This rule-making authority, authorized by Congress, grants quasi-legislative powers to administrators.

The three types of agency rules are *procedural rules,* *interpretive rules,* and *substantive rules.* **Procedural rules** govern an agency's internal practices. An agency inherently has the power to determine its own governance. In accordance with the APA, procedural rules must be published in the *Federal Register.* An agency must follow its own procedural rules. A court may overturn any action that violates a procedural rule.

Remember that an agency is created by a statute. An **interpretive rule** allows the agency to interpret the statute that it is charged with administering. When an agency issues an interpretive rule, the only public action it must take is to publish the rule in the *Federal Register.* For example, the Federal Reserve Board is charged with enforcing the Truth-in-Lending Act. The Federal Reserve Board published in the *Federal Register* an interpretation of the criteria for determining when a late charge would be considered a finance charge. No prior notice or opportunity to comment was given to the public. An agency's definition of a term is considered an interpretive rule.

A **substantive rule** is based on a specific statutory authority to issue rules that create and manage programs. All rules that are not procedural or interpretive in nature are deemed substantive. APA procedural requirements for rule making vary, depending on whether an agency engages in *informal rule making* or *formal rule making.*

Informal and formal rule making are applied when an agency adopts a substantive rule. In **informal rule making**, the agency must publish notice of the

LEGAL HIGHLIGHT

"Governmentese" and Plain English

The contorted language used by regulators has jokingly been called "governmentese." For instance, in the 1970s, the Occupational Safety and Health Administration published standards concerning the ability of a ladder to hold a "live load unit ascending and descending the ladder with additional weights." Translated, this passage was referring to a person—the "live load unit"—climbing up and down a ladder with something in his hand. Regulators now are required to write in plain English. Here is the Consumer Product Safety Commission's description of a book of matches.

§ 1202.3 Definitions.

In addition to the definitions given in section 3 of the Consumer Product Safety Act (15 U.S.C. § 2052), the following definitions apply for the purpose of this standard:

(a) "Bookmatch" means a single splint, with a matchhead attached, that comes from a matchbook.

(b) "Bridge" means the matchhead material held in common by two or more splints.

(c) "Broken bridge" means a bridge that has become separated.

(d) "Caddy" means a package of two or more matchbooks wrapped or boxed together at a production plant.

(e) "Comb" means a piece of wood, paper, or other suitable material that has been formed into splints, that remain joined at their base, and that are designed to have matchheads attached to their tips.

(f) "Cover" means the paperboard or other suitable material that is wrapped around and fastened to the comb(s).

(g) "Friction" means the dried chemical mixture on the matchbook cover used to ignite the bookmatch.

(h) "Match" means a single splint with matchhead attached.

(i) "Matchbook" means one or more combs with matchheads attached and a cover that is wrapped around and fastened to those combs.

(j) "Matchhead" means the dried chemical mixture on the end of a splint.

(k) "Splint" means the support for the matchhead or that portion normally held when using the bookmatch.

§ 1202.4 Matchbook general requirements.

A matchbook shall meet the following general requirements:

(a) The friction shall be located on the outside back cover near the bottom of the matchbook.

(b) The cover shall remain closed without external force.

(c) No friction material shall be located on the inside of the cover where possible contact with the matchheads may occur during ordinary use.

(d) There shall be no bridge(s) or broken bridge(s).

(e) No matchhead in the matchbook shall be split, chipped, cracked, or crumbled.

(f) No portion of any matchhead shall be outside the matchbook cover when the cover is closed.

(g) No part of a staple or other assembly device for securing the cover and combs shall be within or touching the friction area.

(h) A staple used an assembly device for securing the cover and combs shall be fully clinched so that the ends are flattened or turned into the cover.

§ 1202.5 Certification.

Certification shall be in accordance with section 14(a) of the Consumer Product Safety Act (15 U.S.C. § 2063(a)). Under this provision, manufacturers and private labelers of products subject to safety standards must certify that their products conform to the standard, based on either a test of each product or on a reasonable testing program.

§ 1202.6 Marking.

(a) The manufacturer's or private labeler's name and city or a symbol which will identify the name and city shall appear on the matchbook. In addition, every private labeler must label the matchbook with a code which enables it to identify, if requested, the manufacturer of the product.

(b) Boxes or cartons in which two or more caddies are shipped shall be marked "For safety, store in a cool, dry place."

Source: 16 C.F.R. §§ 1202.3–1202.6. Ch. II (1-1-97 edition).

proposed rule, provide interested people an opportunity to participate in the rule making, and incorporate in the rule a concise, general statement of its basis and purpose. Informal rule making is frequently referred to as notice-and-comment rule making.

In **formal rule making**, an agency must conduct a hearing before it can adopt a rule. The parties for and against the rule are entitled to present their case or objection, to submit oral and documentary evidence, to present witnesses, and to conduct examinations of the various witnesses who testify before the agency. Although the parties do not have a right to an attorney, most parties employ an attorney to represent them. In many respects, a formal rule-making hearing is similar to a trial.

Agency rules have the same legal effect as a statute. In other words, these rules become law. Ignorance of these rules is no excuse when a person is accused of violating an administrative rule. These rules are made available to the public in the *Federal Register* and in the *Code of Federal Regulations*.[8] Once a rule has been adopted, the agency later can rescind it.

Quasi-Executive Function. Through the executive function, administrative agencies can ensure that their rules are followed.

Acquisition of Information. The bureaucracy is an information-gathering instrument of the government. Information acquisition enables an agency to become an expert on the subject matter it regulates.

[8]Web sites for the *Code of Federal Regulations* are at http://www.archives.gov and http://www.access.gpo.gov/nara/cfr/cfr-table-search.html.

Most of the information that an agency gathers is obtained voluntarily. On occasion, information must be obtained through compulsion. Agencies gather information in one of three ways: record keeping and periodic reports, subpoena power, and power to conduct physical inspections. The first method obtains information through voluntary cooperation, whereas the latter two methods use compulsion to obtain the information.

Record Keeping and Requirements. Businesses that are regulated by agencies are required to maintain specific records and to make periodic mandatory reports based on those records. For example, a whiskey manufacturer must maintain records for the Bureau of Alcohol, Tobacco, and Firearms. This information allows the agency to study problems and to promulgate, amend, or delete rules as necessary.

Advise. Often, a business will request an agency's opinion as to whether an action contemplated by the business will be legal under a certain regulation. The agency gives an opinion and offers the business informal advice. The agency may issue an *opinion letter* that applies only to the specific business that requested the letter. The business can rely on that letter and conduct business within the guidelines of the letter.

Investigatory Powers. Other executive functions performed by an administrative agency are investigations and prosecutions. When performing these functions, an agency follows procedural rules prescribing its conduct.

Sometimes an agency must seek the assistance of the judicial branch of government to obtain information. The following case involves such a situation.

CASE 6.1

United States Court of Appeals, Seventh Circuit, 2002

288 F.3d 332

UNITED STATES v. CRUM

BACKGROUND AND FACTS Ellis Crum owed federal income taxes for 1991, 1992, and 1993, and his wife Norma owed taxes for 1993. In 1994, the Crums created separate, comanaged trusts in which they placed their primary residence, their rental property, and their music business.

The Internal Revenue Service (IRS) assigned Revenue Officer John Dietrich to investigate possible administrative or judicial collection against the trusts. Dietrich served summonses on the Crums to testify and produce financial records relating to their tax liabilities. When the Crums refused to produce any of the records and failed to appear at the time and place designated in the summonses, the United States filed petitions to enforce the summonses. After consolidating both cases, the court granted the petitions and subsequently denied the Crums' joint motion for postjudgment relief.

The Crums argue that the district court lacked jurisdiction to enforce the summonses in this case. The Crums acknowledge that the U.S.C., title 26, § 7602(a) vests summons authority in the Secretary, which is defined as "the Secretary of the Treasury or his delegate." The term *delegate* is defined further to include "any officer, employee, or agency of the Treasury Department duly authorized by the Secretary of the Treasury."

The Crums rely on the absence of statutory provisions expressly authorizing delegation to IRS employees or expressly locating the IRS in the "Treasury Department." They suggest that employees of the IRS are members of a body called the "Department of the Treasury," which, they say, Congress intended to be distinct from the "Treasury Department."

FAIRCHILD, Circuit Judge.

. . . .

Congress has established a statutory structure that endows the IRS with extensive authority to conduct effective tax investigations. For instance, . . . the IRS Commissioner, as the Secretary's delegate, [has] "a broad mandate to investigate and audit" persons to ensure compliance with federal tax laws. As a necessary incident to this investigatory power, Congress gave the Commissioner expansive authority to summon any person to provide information relevant to a particular tax inquiry. Indeed, the Supreme Court has described § 7602 as the "centerpiece" of a much larger congressional design to expand the IRS's information-gathering authority in order to facilitate tax investigations. . . . [The] district courts have jurisdiction to enforce an administrative summons in an adversarial proceeding commenced by the filing of a petition.

Federal regulations trace the delegation of summons authority. First, the Secretary of the Treasury has delegated summons authority to the Commissioner of the IRS. As authorized by the Secretary, the IRS Commissioner has redelegated this authority to certain IRS employees, including revenue officers such as Officer Dietrich. Courts consistently have recognized that IRS officers have the delegated authority to issue administrative summonses. Officer Dietrich had authority to issue the summonses.

The Crums rely on an alleged distinction between the "Treasury Department" and the "Department of the Treasury." They assert that the "Treasury Department" and the "Department of the Treasury" are "distinct statutory entities, each with a separate identity, history, stature, location, composition, function, and authority"; that Officer Dietrich is a revenue officer who works for the Department of the Treasury but not the Treasury Department; and that no statute authorizes delegation of summons authority to revenue officers of the Department of the Treasury. In an attempt to prove that the IRS is part of the "Department of the Treasury" (delegation to officers of which has not been authorized) and not the "Treasury Department" (to officers of which summons authority can be delegated), the Crums rely on isolated references in the Internal Revenue Code suggesting that IRS officers belong to and perform functions for the Department of the Treasury.

This semantic argument strains credulity. It is true that there are Congressional enactments which refer to a "Department of the Treasury" and others which refer to a "Treasury Department." But we are not persuaded that Congress intended to create separate departments concerning the Treasury, nor does any purpose in doing so appear.

To the contrary, there is only one department and it is referred to by different names. The executive departments are listed at 5 U.S.C. § 101, and that list includes only the "Department of the Treasury." 31 U.S.C. § 301 introduces a subchapter dealing with the organization of the "Department of the Treasury." Subsection (a) says that the Department of the Treasury is an executive department, and (b) says that it is headed by the Secretary of the Treasury.

. . . .

DECISION AND REMEDY The court held that the Internal Revenue Service had broad authority to investigate tax matters. Further, the court found no difference between the Department of the Treasury and Treasury Department.

CRITICAL THINKING: POLITICAL QUESTION Why should the Internal Revenue Service have investigative powers?

Enforcement Powers. Agencies have enforcement powers. All final orders issued by an Administrative Law Judge (ALJ) may result in civil penalties if violated. If criminal penalties are sought, a federal agency must refer the case to the Department of Justice, which is the only agency authorized to file criminal cases. Civil penalties are enforceable unless a reviewing court reverses the agency's decision.

Failure to comply with the penalties is treated like any other violation of the law. In most cases, violations are considered to be a civil matter. For example, the agency requires the installation of pollution control equipment by electrical utility companies to control the pollution created by burning coal, but Ace Electric Company fails to comply by the deadline. The administrative law judge (ALJ) may impose civil penalties, such as fines, on businesses or individuals that fail to comply with the agency's rules.

The following case examines a business's right to a jury trial when the ALJ might levy fines as punishment against it.

CASE 6.2	**ATLAS ROOFING CO. v. OSHA**
Supreme Court of the United States, 1977 430 U.S. 442, 97 S. Ct. 1261, 51 L. Ed. 2d 464 http://www.findlaw.com/casecode/supreme.html	**BACKGROUND AND FACTS** Two firms were cited by the Occupational Safety and Health Administration (OSHA) for having unsafe workplaces. The first firm was fined $7,500 for failing to have the sides of trenches shored. The second firm was fined $600 for failing to have roof-opening covers installed to prevent accidents. Both appealed the fines.

After a hearing before an administrative law judge (ALJ), the findings of the OSHA inspectors were affirmed. The fine of $7,500 was reduced to $5,000. The $600 fine was not reduced. Both firms appealed to the court of appeals, challenging the constitutionality of OSHA's enforcement procedures. The court of appeals found the procedures to be constitutional. Both appealed to the United States Supreme Court. The defendants argued that they were entitled to a jury trial under the Constitution.

Justice WHITE delivered the opinion of the Court.

. . . .

We granted the petitions for writs of *certiorari* [requests for review] limited to the important question whether the Seventh Amendment prevents Congress from assigning to an administrative agency, under these circumstances, the task of adjudicating violations of OSHA. . . .

The Seventh Amendment provides that "[i]n Suits at common law, where the value in controversy shall exceed twenty dollars, the right of trial by jury shall be preserved. . . ." The phrase "Suits at common law" has been construed to refer to cases tried prior to the adoption of the Seventh Amendment in courts of law in which jury trial was customary as distinguished from courts of equity or admiralty in which jury trial was not. . . . Petitioners claim that a suit in a federal court by the Government for civil penalties for violation of a statute is a suit for a money judgment which is classically a suit at common law . . . and that the defendant therefore has a Seventh Amendment right to a jury determination of all issues of fact in such a case. . . .

. . . [W]hen Congress creates new statutory "public rights," it may assign their adjudication to an administrative agency with which a jury trial would be incompatible, without violating the Seventh Amendment's injunction that jury trial is to be "preserved" in "suit at common law." Congress is not required by the Seventh Amendment to choke the already crowded federal courts with new types of litigation or prevented from committing some new types of litigation to administrative agencies with special competence in the relevant field. This is the case even if the Seventh Amendment would have required a jury where the adjudication of those rights is assigned to a federal court of law instead of an administrative agency. . . .

More to the point, it is apparent from the history of jury trial in civil matters that fact finding, which is the essential function of the jury in civil cases, was never the exclusive province of the jury under either the English or American legal systems at the time of the adoption of the Seventh Amendment; and the question whether a fact would be found by a jury turned to a considerable degree on the nature of the forum in which a litigant found himself. Critical fact finding was performed without juries in suits in equity, and there were no juries in admiralty [a field of law dealing only with maritime legal problems], nor were there juries in the military justice system. The jury was the fact finding mode in most suits in the common-law courts, but it was not exclusively so: Condemnation was a suit at common law but constitutionality could be tried without a jury[.] . . .

Thus, history and our cases support the proposition that the right to a jury trial turns not solely on the nature of the issue to be resolved but also on the forum in which it is to be resolved. Congress found the common-law and other existing remedies for work injuries resulting from unsafe working conditions to be inadequate to protect the Nation's working men and women. It created a new cause of action, and remedies, therefor, unknown to the common law, and placed their enforcement in a tribunal supplying speedy and expert resolutions of the issues involved. The Seventh Amendment is no bar to the creation of new rights or to their enforcement outside the regular courts of law.

DECISION AND REMEDY The decision of the court of appeals was affirmed, and the fines for both firms were upheld. More important, the Supreme Court found that Congress had the power to create statutory rights without providing that juries be available to decide facts. Congress is free to create new methods to resolve problems between disagreeing parties.

CRITICAL THINKING: JUDICIAL CONSIDERATION Discuss fully whether a person should be denied a jury trial when confronted with sanctions for wrongful conduct.

Quasi-Judicial Function. Any problems that a person has with an agency usually can be resolved within the agency's administrative courts. The ability of the administrative agency to resolve internally most of the disputes that arise relieves the judicial court system of many cases. Not all agencies have this function, however.

Purpose of Adjudication. Administrative agencies develop policy through adjudication, as well as through rule making. **Adjudication** is another term for a decision from a court or from an agency's administrative court. Adjudication often is appropriate when a decision relates to specific facts and to particular parties or when an agency is not ready to announce a rule and wants to take a more cautious, case-by-case approach. The number of decisions each year is substantial.

Rule making is a legislative power, whereas adjudication is a judicial power. Agencies use either rule making or adjudication, depending on the circumstances. If the future consequences of conduct are to be established and the application will be general, rule making is proper. If liability is to be determined based on present or past acts by a specific individual or business, the case is subject to adjudication.

Administrative Law Judge. Cases brought by an agency against a business are heard by an administrative law judge (ALJ) assigned to the agency. As an employee of the agency, an ALJ is not a member of the federal judiciary. Thus, an ALJ is not an Article III judge as are federal judges, but an Article I judge, because Congress creates the administrative agencies.

The ALJ performs a variety of judge-like functions in the hearing. For example, an ALJ issues subpoenas, administers oaths to witnesses, conducts hearing conferences, regulates the conduct and course of the hearing, rules on admissibility of evidence, and makes other procedural rulings.

Outside the hearing, an ALJ may not talk with anyone on any issues before the administrative law court. The judge is able to remain as insulated as possible from external influences. After the hearing, the ALJ issues a decision with the findings and conclusions that support it, similar to a court judgment.

Procedures for Administrative Adjudication. A case begins with the issuance of a complaint to a business or person after the agency has conducted an investigation, developed evidence, and concludes a violation of a particular regulation has occurred. After a complaint is served on an alleged wrongdoer, the party has an opportunity to answer. Eventually, the complaint is heard by an administrative law judge, who conducts the hearing, rules on motions, and decides both the facts and the law. In an agency hearing, an accused party has no right to a jury.

The hearing is conducted in a manner similar to a trial, but a hearing is more informal. The rules of evidence that apply in a judicial trial are not strictly followed in a hearing. For example, many agencies can determine whether hearsay evidence can be used in hearings. Hearsay is evidence that does not come from

the witness's personal knowledge, but from information that the witness has heard another person say. Evidence based on hearsay testimony is not allowed in a judicial trial. If the agency rules, however, allow hearsay evidence, the ALJ must allow a witness to testify as to what another person said.

Either before or during the hearing, the party and the government can enter into an informal settlement process. The parties also can agree to a **consent decree**. A consent decree is an agreement that is signed by the ALJ so that the agreement carries the court's sanction.

When the parties cannot come to an agreement, a hearing will be held. The ALJ, after considering all the evidence and the law, issues an order. An **order** is the final disposition of the case and is similar to a court judgment. The order is subject to review by the head of the administrative agency.

After the hearing, the party that lost the case may appeal. Most agencies have an appeal route built into the administrative system. The party must follow all administrative review procedures. This process is called the **doctrine of exhaustion of remedies**. This doctrine is deeply rooted in history and provides a reasonable balance between a person's and the government's rights. Only after a person has exhausted all administrative remedies may the case be appealed to the judicial courts for review, if the statutes authorizes court review.

Artiste Login. Artiste Login is under investigation for improper disposal of paints. Carlo and Carlotta cooperate with the investigator and demonstrate that they followed the disposal of hazard wastes regulations. The investigator is satisfied and the matter ends.

If the investigator had not been satisfied, Artiste might then receive a letter or other notice that a hearing is being held by the administrative agency. Artiste Login needs to retain a lawyer and not ignore this hearing. Keeping complete records, showing that classes had been taken on adhering to the disposal regulations, and providing other evidence will help to satisfy an investigator from the agency and avoid a hearing.

The courts uphold the administrative agency's decision when there is **substantial evidence** on the record to support the order. Substantial evidence is defined in a negative way by the courts; that is, the administrative agency's decision must not be clearly erroneous or unsupported by credible evidence. As discussed in Chapter 3, civil cases have two burdens of proof. In a court of law, the plaintiff proves its case by the preponderance of the evidence. In a court of equity, the plaintiff proves its case by clear and convincing evidence.

In the following case, the Court was confronted with the issue of substantial evidence and whether the administrative agency had complied with it.

CASE 6.3

United States Court of Appeals, Ninth Circuit, 2002

320 F.3d 1061

MELKONIAN v. ASHCROFT

BACKGROUND AND FACTS Petitioner Arout Melkonian, an ethnic Armenian, lived in Abkhazia, an autonomous region within Georgia, from his birth in 1959 until September 1992, when he fled across the Russian border to escape kidnapping by ethnic Abkhaz Separatists. He subsequently left Russia and in early 1994 entered the United States illegally and applied for asylum and withholding of deportation under the Immigration and Nationality Act (INA). The immigration judge (IJ) denied his application and the Board of Immigration Appeals (BIA) affirmed. Melkonian appealed.

Abkhazia enjoyed full republic status within the Soviet Union until February 1931, when it was incorporated into Georgia as an autonomous republic. During the Soviet era, Abkhazia was home to ethnic Abkhaz, along with a large number of ethnic Georgians, Armenians, Russians, and Greeks.

After Georgia achieved independence from the Soviet Union in 1991, ethnic tension in Abkhazia increased. Demands by ethnic Abkhaz for greater autonomy led to armed combat between the Georgian National Guard and Abkhaz Separatists (the Separatists) in August 1992. Intense fighting continued until September 1993, when the Separatists succeeded in driving out the Georgian forces and in achieving *de facto* independence.

Since gaining control, the Separatists have engaged in a campaign of ethnic cleansing in Abkhazia. Their main target has been ethnic Georgians, but all non-Abkhaz have suffered. It was reported in 1992 that the Separatists moved through captured towns with prepared lists and addresses of ethnic Georgians, plundered and burned homes, and executed designated civilians. The Separatists are credibly reported to have tortured, raped, killed, expelled, and imprisoned hundreds of Georgians and other non-Abkhaz.

By the end of 1993, the Abkhaz reign of terror had produced dramatic results. Virtually the entire Georgian population of Abkhazia had fled the region, along with most of the rest of the non-Abkhaz population (approximately 250,000 people). The U.S. State Department reported that those fleeing Abkhazia made highly credible claims of atrocities, including the killing of civilians without regard to age or sex. Corpses recovered from Abkhaz-held territory showed signs of extensive torture. The conflict between the Abkhaz Separatists, who continue to control the region, and the Georgian government remained unresolved as of the date of the court's decision.

Both Melkonian and his wife testified at the hearing before the IJ. Melkonian also offered a written declaration in support of his application for asylum.

Before hostilities between Abkhaz Separatists and the Georgian military intensified in August 1992, Melkonian was living in Gagra, Abkhazia, with his wife, Angela (also an Armenian), their eleven-year-old son, Gegam, and Angela's parents. They had a home, a large farm and farmhouse, and a herd of cattle. Life had been relatively calm during the Soviet era, but when the Soviet Union began to disintegrate, living in Abkhazia became difficult. Ethnic groups began to fight among each other, particularly the Abkhaz and the Georgians. As Armenians, Melkonian's family felt bound to side with the Georgians. Melkonian's family demonstrated its loyalty by supplying the Georgian fighters with fruit and with money for weapons.

In the early summer of 1992, Abkhaz fighters descended from the mountains and took control of Gagra. Initially, Melkonian could protect his family simply by giving the Separatists money. Then, when fighting broke out with Georgian troops, the Separatists began to round up Armenian men to fight on the front lines. The Separatists would grab young men off the street and take them to the front. Melkonian explained that the "[Abkhaz fighters] would come in the middle of the night and take the Armenian men at gunpoint." Neighbors and friends he had gone to school with were taken to war and never returned. Angela, Melkonian's wife, testified that the Separatists "were beating Armenians up, threatening them and holding them in fear."

Melkonian's father-in-law, whom Angela described as the head of the family, openly refused to fight for the Abkhaz cause. One day in September 1992 he spoke out against the Separatists' tactics. That night, a group of armed Separatists came to Melkonian's house with shotguns, demanding to see Melkonian and his father-in-law. Angela and her mother were able to convince them that the men were not at home. Immediately thereafter, Melkonian and his father-in-law fled to Russia. Angela, Gegam, and Angela's mother stayed behind to protect their property.

Melkonian hoped things would normalize soon so that he could return home. He explained at the hearing: "We had our farm, we had our house, we had everything." But the situation in Gagra got worse. The Separatists returned to Melkonian's home demanding to know where he and his father-in-law were. This time, Angela and her mother convinced them that the men had only gone across the border to Russia for supplies and would return.

The Separatists continued to pursue Melkonian and his father-in-law, repeatedly breaking into their house at night to search for the men. They stole all of the family's meat and cheese and violently beat Melkonian's cheese maker. They took all of Melkonian's cows and murdered an elderly woman who was trying to protect the herd. They took the family's possessions, including the washing machine, the couch, and the doors, shot the windows and ceiling, and then burned Melkonian's farmhouse and farm. The Separatists placed a man in a car trunk to die, mistaking him for Angela's father.

After an Armenian mother and daughter were burned to death in a home not far from Melkonian's, Angela and Gegam decided that they risked death if they remained in Abkhazia. They crossed over the Russian border and reunited with Melkonian in December 1992. In Russia, the family was safe from the violence of the Separatists, but Melkonian was unable to work without registration. Obtaining registration required knowing someone who could be bribed, and Melkonian knew no one.

To survive, Melkonian and Angela got divorced, and Angela married a Russian man with two children. This allowed her to obtain registration and, ultimately, two B-2 Visitor's Visas. In November 1993, Angela and Gegam left for the United States; both have been granted asylum. Just fifteen days before her departure, Angela divorced her Russian husband and remarried Melkonian. Melkonian was forced to stay in Russia for an additional several months, however, until he was able to purchase travel documents that allowed him to fly to the United States. He arrived in early 1994.

Melkonian believes that if he were sent back to Abkhazia he would be killed by Abkhaz. They would kill him immediately, he believes, because he supported the Georgians and because he is an ethnic Armenian.

WILLIAM A. FLETCHER, Circuit Judge.

. . . .

We review factual findings of the IJ and BIA under the "substantial evidence" standard That is, we must sustain factual findings if supported by reasonable, substantial, and probative evidence in the record. We review questions of law regarding the INA *de novo,* but give deference to the BIA's interpretation of the statute. The BIA must, however, follow the decisions of our court, and we will not defer to BIA decisions that conflict with circuit precedent. To the extent that the BIA adopted the findings of the IJ as its own, we treat the decision of the IJ as that of the BIA.

. . . .

But even if we accepted the IJ's finding that Melkonian left Abkhazia in part to seek better economic fortune (which constitutes a gross mischaracterization of his testimony), it would not preclude eligibility for asylum. Our case law makes clear that a fear of persecution need not be the alien's only motivation for fleeing. Furthermore, given that Melkonian seeks asylum based on a well-founded fear of *future* persecution, his motivations for leaving—while probative—are not the ultimate issue. Rather, the proper inquiry is whether Melkonian's refusal *to return* to Abkhazia is based on a credible subjective fear of persecution by Abkhaz Separatists (a group no party disputes the Georgian government is unable to control); whether the persecution he fears is on account of a statutorily-protected ground; and whether that fear is objectively reasonable.

. . . .

A review of the evidence compels the conclusion that Melkonian established a well-founded fear of future persecution at the hands of Abkhaz Separatists on account of his ethnicity, were he to return to Abkhazia. We remand to the BIA to determine whether, under all of the circumstances, it is reasonable to expect Melkonian to relocate to another region within Georgia.

DECISION AND REMEDY The court reversed the decision of the immigration judge. Melkonian had a subjective fear of future persecution if he should return to his farm in the Separatists-controlled area of Georgia.

CRITICAL THINKING: POLITICAL CONSIDERATION Should the United States allow any immigrant to remain in this country when he enters illegally?

Limitations on Administrative Agencies' Powers

Most limitations on administrative agencies' powers arise from one of three sources: (1) the Constitution, (2) congressional statutes, (3) sunset laws, and (4) judicial review. Constitutional limitations typically relate to administrative agency behavior. Any procedural inadequacies are subject to judicial review.

Major Constitutional Limitations

The Constitution provides the most important limitations on administrative agency actions. Although most constitutional rights, such as due process and unreasonable search and seizure, are regarded primarily as individual rights, businesses also have some constitutional rights.

Both procedural and substantive due process protect businesses against arbitrary, capricious, and unreasonable administrative agency actions. Substantive due process applies when issues arise that involve property or other rights affected by government. Procedural due process focuses on notice and hearing procedures. In most cases people or businesses must be given prior notice of any hearing that might directly affect them.

Enforcement of due process rights through the Fifth and Fourteenth Amendments, however, follows a double standard. Whenever government action directly affects economic activity, courts usually find it to be constitutional. In contrast, courts generally are suspicious of government actions that might limit basic human freedoms.

Fourth Amendment Limitations. The Constitution protects people from unwarranted intrusions into their personal privacy. In civil and criminal cases, businesses also are protected from unreasonable searches. The Fourth Amendment has been used to prohibit building inspectors from looking for building code violations against the desires of the owner of the premises when the inspectors have no warrant. An agency, however, may make an unannounced inspection of those businesses that traditionally have been heavily regulated, such as the alcoholic beverage industry, the

firearm industry, the fishing industry, and the meat-packing industry.

In the case that follows, the United States Supreme Court held that government safety inspectors must have a warrant to make a routine inspection of work areas in a private business.

CASE 6.4

Supreme Court of the
United States, 1978
436 U.S. 307, 98 S. Ct.
1816, 56 L. Ed. 2d 305
http://www.findlaw.com/
casecode/supreme.html

LANDMARK CASE

MARSHALL v. BARLOW'S, INC.

BACKGROUND AND FACTS Prior to this case, inspectors of the Occupational Safety and Health Administration (OSHA) were not required to obtain permission to enter the work areas of firms under OSHA's jurisdiction. OSHA's rules authorized inspections without a search warrant. In 1975, an OSHA inspector entered the customer service area of Barlow's, Inc., an electrical and plumbing installation business. After showing his credentials, the inspector informed the president and general manager, Barlow, that he (the inspector) would be conducting an inspection of the business's working areas.

On inquiry, Barlow learned that no complaint had been received about his company. The inspection simply resulted from random selection. The inspector had no search warrant. Barlow refused to permit the inspector to enter the working area of his business, relying on his rights guaranteed by the Fourth Amendment.

OSHA filed suit in the U.S. District Court. The court issued an order compelling Barlow to admit the OSHA inspector for purposes of conducting an occupational safety and health inspection. The OSHA inspector, now armed with a court order, went back to Barlow's, Inc. Barlow again refused him admission.

This time, Barlow went to the same district court, seeking an injunction to prohibit the inspector from making a warrantless search on the ground that the OSHA inspection violated the Fourth Amendment. This time the district court ruled in Barlow's favor. The district court held that the Fourth Amendment required a warrant for the search involved and that the authorization for warrantless inspections under the OSHA statute was unconstitutional.

A permanent injunction against such searches or inspections was entered on Barlow's behalf. A permanent injunction is a final court order granting relief, in this case forbidding the OSHA inspector from conducting any further searches or inspections of Barlow's premises. The Supreme Court granted a writ of *certiorari* after OSHA challenged the validity of the injunction.

Justice WHITE delivered the opinion of the Court.

. . . .

The Warrant Clause of the Fourth Amendment protects commercial buildings, as well as private homes. To hold otherwise would belie the origin of that Amendment, and the American colonial experience. . . .

. . . [U]nless some recognized exception to the warrant requirement applies, . . . a warrant [is required] to conduct the inspection sought in this case.

. . . Certain industries have such a history of government oversight that no reasonable expectation of privacy could exist for a proprietor over the stock of such an enterprise. Liquor and firearms are industries of this type; when an entrepreneur embarks upon such a business, he has voluntarily chosen to subject himself to a full arsenal of governmental regulation.

. . . The element that distinguishes these enterprises from ordinary businesses is a long tradition of close government supervision, of which any person who chooses to enter such a business must already be aware. . . . "A central difference between [previously discussed] cases . . . and this one is that businessmen engaged in such federally licensed and regulated enterprises accept the burdens as well as the benefits of their trade, whereas the petitioner here was not engaged in any regulated or licensed business. The businessman in a regulated industry in effect consents to the restrictions placed upon him."

The clear import . . . is that the closely regulated industry . . . is the exception. . . .

. . . .

The critical fact in this case is that entry over Mr. Barlow's objection is being sought by a Government agent. Employees are not being prohibited from reporting OSHA violations. What they observe in their daily functions is undoubtedly beyond the employer's reasonable expectation of privacy. The Government inspector, however, is not an employee. Without a warrant he stands in no better position than a member of the public. What is observable by the public is observable, without a warrant, by the Government inspector as well. The owner of a business has not, by the necessary utilization of employees in his operation, thrown open the areas where employees alone are permitted to the warrantless scrutiny of Government agents. That an employee is free to report, and the Government is free to use, any evidence of noncompliance with OSHA that the employee observes furnishes no justification for federal agents to enter a place of business from which the public is restricted and to conduct their own warrantless search.

. . . .

Whether the Secretary proceeds to secure a warrant or other process, with or without prior notice, his entitlement to inspect will not depend on his demonstrating probable cause to believe that conditions in violation of OSHA exist on the premises. Probable cause in the criminal law sense is not required. For purposes of an administrative search such as this, probable cause justifying the issuance of a warrant may be based not only on specific evidence of an existing violation but also on a showing that "reasonable legislative or administrative standards are conducting an . . . inspection are satisfied with respect to a particular [establishment]."

A warrant showing that a specific business has been chosen for an OSHA search on the basis of a general administrative plan for the enforcement of the Act derived from neutral sources such as, for example, dispersion of employees in various types of industries across a given area, and the desired frequency of searches in any of the lesser divisions of the area, would protect an employer's Fourth Amendment rights. We doubt that the consumption of enforcement energies in the obtaining of such warrants will exceed manageable proportions.

. . . .

. . . The authority to make warrantless searches devolves almost unbridled discretion upon executive and administrative officers, particularly those in the field, as to when to search and whom to search. A warrant, by contrast, would provide assurances from a neutral officer that the inspection is reasonable under the Constitution, is authorized by statute, and is pursuant to an administrative plan containing specific neutral criteria. Also, a warrant would then and there advise the owner of the scope and objects of the search, beyond which limits the inspector is not expected to proceed. These are important functions for a warrant to perform, functions which underlie the Court's prior decisions that the Warrant Clause applies to inspections for compliance with regulatory statutes. We conclude that the concerns expressed by the Secretary do not suffice to justify warrantless inspections under OSHA or vitiate the general constitutional requirement that for a search to be reasonable a warrant must be obtained.

DECISION AND REMEDY The Supreme Court upheld the permanent injunction. OSHA inspections conducted without warrants are unconstitutional when the business to be inspected is not one that otherwise is regulated by close government supervision.

CRITICAL THINKING: PUBLIC POLICY CONSIDERATION In this case, the United States Supreme Court articulated a different standard than that used for criminal law when seeking a search warrant. Explain reasons why a different warrant-procurement process should be applied for criminal law and administrative agency searches.

Fifth Amendment Applications. Under the Fifth Amendment, a person cannot be forced to testify against himself in a criminal case. The Supreme Court has held that a business, however, is not a person within the meaning of the Constitution, and thus a business is ineligible for protection under this Fifth Amendment clause.

Administrative agencies may require businesses to create and maintain records. Because a business is not a person, these records are not included under the self-incrimination clause and, therefore, may be disclosed in criminal or civil cases. These types of business records become, in effect, quasi-public records. Because the agency requires the business to maintain these records, the agency can inspect these records to ensure the accuracy of the reports it receives periodically.

Although these records are quasi-public, the disclosure requirement is not tantamount to public disclosure. Businesses legitimately have secrets concerning their products or services. They may have secret marketing strategies or trade secrets, as well as sensitive personnel records.

Congress provides protection in two ways. First, the enabling act specifically may prohibit records from being made public and may prohibit the agency's employees from disclosing certain information. Second, in 1966, Congress passed the Freedom of Information Act. Although this act promotes information access and availability to the public and individuals, certain information is restricted from disclosure. This act will be examined in detail in the next section. In short, business records are protected from public disclosure under restricted circumstances.

Liability of Agencies and Federal Employees. Occasionally, an agency's employee violates a person's constitutional rights, for which the individual federal employee can be held personally liable. For example, agents, while searching a house without a warrant, tear down walls looking for hidden drugs. In this case, the individual agents may be held liable in a court of law by the people whose rights were violated.

The agency, however, cannot be held liable for any constitutional rights violations by its agents. An agency cannot authorize the constitutional violations of persons. To allow an agency to be held liable for the actions of its agents who act in an unconstitutional manner would create a potentially enormous financial burden on the federal government. More important, the deterrent effect would be lost if the victim had a choice of suing the agency or the employee. The victim would choose the agency to sue because it has more money than an individual employee. If the employee knew that the chances of being sued were slim because the agency would be held liable, prospective violators would be undeterred.

Congressional Statutes

When Congress creates an agency, its statutory scheme includes congressional limitations on that agency. Although certain general rules apply to all agencies, a person dealing with a specific agency must be aware of these congressional limitations. Some statutes amend the Administrative Procedure Act and thus affect all agencies. Other statutes apply only to one agency.

Freedom of Information Act. The **Freedom of Information Act (FOIA)** is an amendment to the Administrative Procedure Act. All administrative agencies are subject to the FOIA, which makes all information held by federal agencies available to the public.

Exemptions do exist, however, if information falls within certain categories. Information may be disclosed under the FOIA in one of three ways. First, the *Federal Register* publishes information, such as agencies' policy statements and procedural and substantive rules. Second, agencies must make available for public inspection and copying certain information not printed in the *Federal Register.* Reprints of the opinions of administrative law judges, public statements, interpretive rules, staff manuals, and directives are sold to the public for a nominal fee. Third, if the information is not published under either of these methods and it is not exempt, each agency has established reasonable procedures for the public to follow when requesting a copy of that information. The **Electronic Freedom of Information Act** makes it possible for the public to have free electronic access to these documents on the Internet without having to make a formal request under the Freedom of Information Act.

The significant exempt categories are those that contain information in the following areas: information relating to national defense or foreign policy, internal personnel rules, information protected by another statute that prohibits disclosure, business trade secrets and privileged or confidential business information, and any information that violates personal privacy. Even though certain information may be classified in one of the exempt categories, the agency is not prohibited automatically from disclosing that information. The FOIA gives the agency discretion as to whether to disclose the information.

When an agency decides not to disclose information under the FOIA, the agency must disclose its reasons to the requester. After exhausting the administrative remedies, the requester has the right to file a lawsuit in district court to force the agency to disclose the information.

The agency has the burden of proof to support its action. The burden of proof is the obligation of a party to the case to demonstrate to the court that the evidence favors that party's side. The agency proves its case by substantial evidence in order to support the decision. If an agency has established substantial evidence, a district or an appellate court will not reverse it. The administrative decision will not be set aside unless it is clearly erroneous or unsupported by any credible evidence.

Privacy Act. The **Privacy Act** is a 1974 amendment to the Administrative Procedure Act. The Privacy Act protects only individuals who are citizens or legal aliens. By statutory definition, business entities are not covered.

Agencies accumulate tremendous amounts of information on individuals. If a person requests all of the personal information that an agency has on her, the agency must provide it. The information maintained must be correct, accurate, and current. If this information is stale, inaccurate, or incomplete, the individual can make corrections.

The Privacy Act does not require an agency to disclose information it has on an individual under certain circumstances. For example, if a person is being investigated for a crime, the investigating agency does not have to disclose that an investigation is ongoing even if the individual requests it.

The agency cannot disclose information that it has on an individual to others unless the conditions of the

LEGAL HIGHLIGHT

No Jargon, Please!

The Social Security Administration mails more than 200 million letters a year to people receiving disability and retirement benefits. Most letters routinely inform the person that the amount they receive will be increased or decreased because of an adjustment.

Some letters, however, are written by the bureaucratic monster. For example, one woman received a letter stating, "We are sending you a check for $0. This is money due to you for December 4, 1990. You should receive this check no later than [a blank space].

After that, you will receive your regular check of $0 around the first day of each month." In other words, her claim for disability had been denied. Other Social Security recipients who have grave illnesses have been sent forms suggesting that they find part-time work.

The Social Security Administration now has a writing standard requiring notices to be written at the sixth-grade reading level, to contain no jargon, to have an average of fifteen to twenty words per sentence, and to be written in a "courteous, personal, nonthreatening tone."

Privacy Act are met. For example, if information is requested from an agency on a particular person, the agency cannot provide that information because it is protected under the Privacy Act.

Equal Access to Justice Act. An individual or a small business lacks the financial resources to defend against an unjustified action by a governmental agency. In 1982, Congress passed the **Equal Access to Justice Act**. An administrative law judge or a court may award legal fees (limited to $75 an hour), expert witness fees, or reasonable costs of studies and engineering reports to individuals or small businesses. These fees are awarded if the judge decides that the government agency was substantially unjustified in bringing the action.

The act applies to individuals whose net worth does not exceed $2 million and to small for-profit and not-for-profit organizations with no more than 500 employees and a net worth of no more than $7 million. This act allows an ordinary person to challenge an incorrect legal position held by the government.

Sunshine Act. The **Sunshine Act** of 1976 also amended the Administrative Procedure Act. This act prohibits agencies from holding secret meetings. An agency must give notice of the time and place of its meetings and provide an agenda.

Even though not all meetings are open to the public, a meeting notice must be posted indicating that the meeting is open or closed. The Sunshine Act prevents secret, not closed, meetings.

If a person believes that an agency erred in its decision to close a meeting, the person can sue the agency in district court. The court may grant an injunction against future violations of the Sunshine Act. The court, however, may not overturn any action taken by the agency behind closed doors solely because the Sunshine Act was violated. Overturning the action taken by the agency must be based on other legal grounds.

Regulatory Flexibility Act. In 1980, Congress amended the Administrative Procedure Act with the **Regulatory Flexibility Act**. This act takes into account the differences among the various businesses subject to regulation. In particular, a regulation may have a different effect on a small business than it has on a large corporation.

The act requires a special regulatory flexibility agenda to be printed in the *Federal Register* twice a year, in April and October. An agency must publish in the regulatory flexibility agenda a list of all rules that the agency is considering during the next few months. The rules listed are the ones likely to have a significant economic impact on small businesses.

Cost–Benefit Analysis. Administrative agencies have broad discretionary powers to carry out congressional statutes. Businesses must comply with the administrative regulations, but the cost of compliance is expensive. The cost needs to be compared with the benefits that result from that compliance and projects are made as to whether the expense is worth the benefit, which is called a **cost–benefit analysis**.

This type of analysis began in the early 1800s. The process was formalized in the 1980s when President Reagan issued several executive orders requiring agencies to conduct cost–benefit analyses. When an agency contemplates issuing new regulations, an analysis for the specific project must be included.

The agencies have parameters that help to estimate the costs, but benefits are more difficult to project. For example, if utilities are required to install equipment that cleans the air before it is released, the cost of the air cleaning equipment can be determined. If, however, the manufacturer now has a number of orders for the air scrubbing equipment, the cost in future years may be greatly reduced.

The benefit of cleaner air can result in fewer hospitalizations and deaths from air pollution. With few or no irritants in the air, the corrosion of buildings and historical monuments will end. With clearer air, tourism to the area may boom. The benefits may include the development of a new industry, such as an air cleaning expertise, which leads to developing businesses that aid other regions or countries to clean their air. Although the benefits of fewer hospitalizations, deaths, and less damage to buildings may have been predicted, the benefit of a new industry may not have been predicted.

Sunset Laws

Each of the statutes discussed previously was passed by Congress as separate statutes. **Sunset laws** are included in a variety of statutes that created specific agencies. A sunset law sets an automatic expiration date for the agency in order to force regular legislative review. In the past, some administrative agencies have outlived their purpose or usefulness but continued to exist because the agency's enabling act had not been repealed.

Today, for an agency to continue, Congress must take affirmative action to retain the agency. Knowing that Congress periodically evaluates it, the agency is more likely to be responsive to the public will. At reviewing time, Congress can make known its concerns about the agency by manipulating its budget or by threatening to reorganize or dismantle it.

Judicial Review

Administrative decisions can be appealed to the courts because the judiciary has the power and the duty to interpret the law. Congress's province is to formulate legislative policy, to mandate programs and projects, and to establish their relative national priority. Once Congress has exercised its legislative power by creating a new administrative agency and providing it a mandate, the agency then administers the law, and the judiciary interprets and enforces it.

In a judicial review of an agency's decision, the court reviews whether the person appealing has exhausted the administrative remedies as discussed previously. Failure to exhaust administrative remedies is the most common reason for dismissing a case. If administrative remedies are exhausted, the court determines whether the agency has any authority to make these specific rules.

Congress delegates broad discretionary powers over a specialized subject matter to each administrative agency. As a result, a court gives **judicial deference** to agency decisions. Judicial deference means that the court does not reverse an agency action unless the court finds that the agency violated a condition set out by the Administrative Procedure Act.

The court considers the record created by the administrative agency. This record resembles a court record and contains all the evidence and testimony provided during the administrative hearing. The court upholds the agency's decision if substantial evidence, as discussed previously, supports the decision. The court also determines whether the delegation from Congress was appropriate. If the agency has rule-making authority, the court must determine whether the agency exceeded its authority. For example, the Securities and Exchange Commission does not have the authority to adopt rules involving civil rights.

InfoTrac Research Activity

Several articles about judicial deference are listed in InfoTrac. Find several articles and review them. Discuss whether they have a common theme. Write up your conclusions discussing the common theme you found.

Deregulation

Congress and the president have imposed restraints on agencies by limiting the number of ineffective or potentially harmful rules they can make. In 1978, President Jimmy Carter[9] issued an order requiring agencies to determine the impact of regulations on the economy. The order was issued with an eye to deregulation. Every president since then has worked to make government work more efficiently by abolishing or combining agencies and deregulating businesses.

President Carter's administration, although in office for only four years, made dramatic strides toward deregulation. Deregulation can mean either the elimination of specific agencies or the elimination of specific programs within agencies in order to reduce government regulation. Congress passed many deregulatory acts that took effect after President Ronald Reagan[10] took office. The deregulation occurred mainly in the agencies responsible for economic regulation.

President Reagan issued two executive orders that further limited administrative regulations. These executive orders had several purposes: to establish regulatory priorities, to increase the accountability of agency officials, to provide for presidential oversight of the regulatory process, to reduce the burdens of existing and future regulations, to minimize duplication and conflict of regulations, and to enhance public and congressional understanding of the regulatory objectives.

Each agency must submit annually to the Office of Management and Budget a statement of its regulatory policies, goals, and objectives for the coming year. The agency also must submit information concerning all significant regulatory action under way or planned.

[9]Jimmy Carter (1924 to present) was president from 1977 to 1981. His presidential Web site is found at http://www.jimmycarterlibrary.org.
[10]Ronald Reagan (1911 to present) was president from 1981 to 1989. His presidential Web site is found at http://www.reagan.utexas.edu.

Each agency must prepare a regulatory impact analysis of major rules. These executive orders apply only to the agencies in the executive branch and not to independent agencies. Many independent agencies, however, have chosen to comply voluntarily.

To make the government more available to the public, Congress and the president have mandated that all government resources be published on the Internet. The intent is that in the future, the government will not print much information in a hardcopy format since it will be available electronically.

International Consideration

Use of Administrative Law in Assisting International Transactions

The United Nations[11] has developed various administrative agencies to help it function. The six major agencies created to carry out the United Nations' work are (1) the General Assembly, (2) the Security

[11]The Web page for the United Nations is http://www.un.org.

Council, (3) the Secretariat, (4) the Economic and Social Council, (5) the International Court of Justice, and (6) the Trusteeship Council. Other agencies help the United Nations carry out its mission. These include the United Nations Development Program; the United Nations Educational, Scientific, and Cultural Organization (UNESCO); and the United Nations International Children's Emergency Fund (UNICEF).

The United Nations also has developed an international civil service based on administrative rules. Civil service employees are government workers who are not elected or appointed. They are hired, promoted, and dismissed in accordance with rules based on professional standards.

The civil service standards allow administrative hearings to be held when the employee believes the rules have not been applied properly in his or her case. These hearings are held to interpret these rules and develop case law. Decisions based on these hearings protect employees from such arbitrary actions as dismissal because of alleged national disloyalty. The United Nations civil service rules are only one example of an international organization that has many administrative agencies.

PRACTICAL TIPS

Facing Zoning Problems

You want to open a small video rental store that offers movies that appeal to college students. You find a perfect location with low monthly rent near the dormitories and other student housing. Before signing the lease, however, your prospective landlord insists that you contact the local municipal zoning agency to make certain that this type of business activity is permitted.

Wanting to open the store as soon as possible, you go to the proper city office and discover that the zoning ordinance does not allow the rental of products, only the sale of products. You ask whether there are any exceptions to this ordinance. The zoning official states that you can either (1) obtain a use permit or a variance to the zoning ordinance or (2) attempt to have the city council change the zoning ordinance.

This venture is your first contact with administrative law. To obtain a variance or use permit, you must

submit an application to the zoning board. A zoning board usually is made up of citizens who are appointed to the board. The job of the board is to determine the acceptable use of property within a particular area, such as a city. The board determines in which areas multifamily dwellings (apartments), light industry, parks, and so on are allowed.

An appointed official will review the application and either grant or deny it in a summary manner. If the application is denied, you have a right to appeal the official's decision to a board of adjustment. Normally, the members of the board of adjustment are appointed by the elected officials, either the members of the city council or the mayor. If the board of adjustment denies the request, you then can take your appeal to the judicial system. In some states you would appeal to the city council.

You also may try another administrative route. You can file a petition for a zoning change with the city planning department. The department will make a recommendation to the planning and zoning commission. This commission also is appointed by elected officials. Unlike the board of adjustment, which has the power to make a final administrative decision, however, the actions of the planning and zoning commission are simply advisory to the city council. Once a recommendation is made, it must be adopted by the city council, which acts in a legislative manner when deciding zoning issues.

You probably should file a petition for a change because the ordinance seems to be rather arbitrary in excluding rental businesses but allowing commercial sales. No doubt the restriction was just an oversight when the ordinance initially was adopted and it needs to be changed.

When you are interested in starting a business, first check with local authorities. Do your research. Here is a checklist that provides guidance.

Checklist

✔ *Zoning* Does the zoning law allow the operation of this type of business at your location?

✔ *Signs* What type of signs will be allowed on the premises? An important consideration is whether you can advertise your business on the premises.

✔ *Handicapped Accessibility* Make certain that the building has appropriate facilities for persons with disabilities.

✔ *Hazardous Material* Make certain no prior tenants have left hazardous material on the premises.

Chapter Summary

Administrative agencies handle two areas of public concern: economic regulation and public welfare. Economic regulation takes several forms. An agency may control entry into the marketplace by controlling license procedures, setting rates, or setting standards. Public welfare includes the protection of the public, as well as entitlement programs. Public welfare has two meanings. The broad meaning covers regulation that is for the benefit of the public at large; the secondary meaning covers programs for lower income people. Entitlement programs, such as Social Security, benefit those people who meet the programs' eligibility requirements.

Federal regulatory agencies have several features that allow them to deal with certain problems more effectively than the legislatures or the courts. First, an agency develops expertise in a particular area. Second, a regulatory agency consists of a very well-developed hierarchy that helps to ensure continuity of personnel and experience. Third, an agency has more flexibility than the legislature.

When an agency is under the direct control of the president, it is known as a line agency and is headed by a member of the president's cabinet. Congress also has established independent agencies, which are freestanding from the president and from Congress. Government agencies are created by Congress to administer a quasi-business venture. Quasi-official agencies also are created by Congress but lack the same authority as official agencies.

Administrative agencies engage in three prime areas of activity: they make rules, they acquire and act on information, and they judge cases. These activities are carried out through the quasi-legislative, quasi-executive, and quasi-judicial powers that agencies possess. The Administrative Procedure Act (APA) standardized procedures that agencies must use when exercising their powers. In addition, agencies must not violate a person's constitutional rights.

The APA has been amended several times. The Freedom of Information Act makes all the information held by federal agencies available to the public unless the information falls within an exempt category. The Electronic Freedom of Information Act makes it possible for the public to have free electronic access to these documents on the Internet.

The Privacy Act protects U.S. citizens and legal aliens but not corporations. A person is entitled to see personal information that an agency has concerning him or her. The Equal Access to Justice Act allows recovery of legal fees and court costs by individuals and small businesses when an agency initiates an unjustified action. The Sunshine Act prohibits agencies from holding secret, not closed, meetings. If the topics do not qualify under the closed meeting rules, the meeting must be open.

The Regulatory Flexibility Act takes into account differences in the way a regulation affects a small business versus a large business. The rules that affect small businesses must be published in the *Federal Register*.

The sunset acts are not part of the APA but are included in the statutes that create the agencies. A sunset act sets an automatic expiration date for the agency.

Actions taken by administrative agencies can be appealed to the courts. The courts investigate first whether the authority delegated by Congress to that agency is valid. If a court finds that the agency has the authority to act, the court then determines if the agency has exceeded its properly delegated authority.

Because an agency is given broad discretionary powers over a specialized subject matter, a court gives judicial deference to agency decisions. To reverse an agency action, a court must find that the agency violated a condition set out by the Administrative Procedure Act.

Deregulation has taken place since the late 1970s. Two executive orders limit administrative regulations of line agencies. Each agency must submit to the Office of Management and Budget each year a statement of the goals of the upcoming year and set out major planned programs. Each agency also must prepare a regulatory impact analysis of its major rules.

Congress requires the federal executive agencies and

Using the World Wide Web

independent agencies to maintain Internet sites. Information about Congress also is available on the WWW. The Web pages for agencies, although not uniform, generally are easy to use.

For *Web Activities*, links to Web sites mentioned in the chapter, and additional Web sites that relate to the chapter topics, go to **http://bohlman.westbuslaw. com**, click on "Internet Applications," and select Chapter 6.

Web Activities

Go to **http://bohlman.westbuslaw.com**, click on "Internet Applications," and select Chapter 6.
6–1 National Historic Preservation Program and National Trust for Historic Preservation
6–2 General Accounting Office and Office of Management and Budget

Key Terms

adjudication
Administrative Procedure Act (APA)
consent decree
cost-benefit analysis
doctrine of exhaustion of remedies
economic regulation
Electronic Freedom of Information Act

enabling act
entitlement program
Equal Access to Justice Act
executive agency
formal rule making
Freedom of Information Act (FOIA)
general policy statement
government agency

independent agency
informal rule making
interpretive rule
judicial deference
line agency
lobbyist
order
Privacy Act
procedural rule
public welfare

quasi-executive function
quasi-judicial function
quasi-legislative function
quasi-official agency
Regulatory Flexibility Act
substantial evidence
substantive rule
sunset law
Sunshine Act

Questions and Case Problems

6–1 Separation of Powers Find the authority in the U.S. Constitution for government to establish administrative agencies.

6–2 Fourth Branch of Government Administrative agency law has been described as the government's

"headless fourth branch." What does this expression mean? Explain why you agree or disagree with this terminology.

6–3 Substantial Evidence An appellate court will affirm the findings of the administrative law judge when those findings are supported by "substantial evidence on the record." When an administrative agency conducts a quasi-judicial hearing, it records all the evidence and testimony presented at the hearing. The Federal Trade Commission (FTC) accused the Adolph Coors Co. of engaging in certain price-fixing agreements in violation of the Sherman Antitrust Act. After a hearing, the FTC concluded that Coors had in fact engaged in illegal price fixing. Substantial evidence was presented at the hearings in support of the findings. Coors also presented substantial evidence that it had never entered into price-fixing arrangements. Should an appellate court uphold the FTC's findings? [*Adolph Coors Co. v. Federal Trade Commission,* 497 F.2d 1178 (10th Cir. 1974)]

6–4 Procedural Due Process An agency must provide notice and a hearing before it can deprive a party of his or her property or rights. New York State and New York City officials administered various federally assisted welfare programs. Some welfare recipients filed a complaint in court alleging that the state and city terminated, or were about to terminate, the aid without prior notice and a hearing, thereby denying the plaintiffs due process of law. The state and the city, however, adopted procedures, posted notice, and had a hearing after these suits were brought. Does the failure to provide a welfare recipient with a notice of termination before the aid is stopped violate procedural due process? [*Goldberg v. Kelly,* 397 U.S. 254, 90 S. Ct. 1011, 25 L. Ed. 2d 287 (1970)]

6–5 Agency Authority In 1995, the Food and Drug Administration (FDA) published a proposed rule concerning the sale of cigarettes and smokeless tobacco to children and adolescents. In 1996, the FDA issued a final rule entitled "Regulations Restricting the Sale and Distribution of Cigarettes and Smokeless Tobacco to Protect Children and Adolescents." The FDA determined that nicotine is a "drug" and that cigarettes and smokeless tobacco are "drug delivery devices," and therefore it had jurisdiction under the Food, Drug, and Cosmetic Act (FDCA) to regulate tobacco products as marketed. The FDA found that tobacco products "'affect the structure or any function of the body'" because nicotine "exerts psychoactive, or mood-altering, effects on the brain" that cause and sustain addiction, have both tranquilizing and stimulating effects, and control weight. A group of tobacco manufacturers, retailers, and advertisers filed suit challenging the regulations. They claimed that the FDA lacked jurisdiction to regulate tobacco products as customarily marketed, the regulations exceeded the FDA's authority, and the advertising restrictions violated

the First Amendment. The case was appealed to the United States Supreme Court. How did the court rule and why? [*Food and Drug Administration v. Brown & Williamson Tobacco Corporation,* 529 U.S. 120, S. Ct. 1291, 146 L. Ed. 2d 121 (2000)]

6–6 Acquisition of Information Congress passed the Marine Mammal Protection Act (MMPA) to protect porpoises during commercial fishing operations. Captains of fishing boats can take porpoises only if the captains allow government observers to board and accompany vessels on regular fishing trips either to do research or to observe and collect data on the fishing operations for enforcement proceedings by the National Marine Fisheries Service. These inspectors collect data on the captains' fishing practices for later inclusion in any quasi-judicial proceeding against the captains if they have failed to follow the government regulations. The captains of two fishing vessels object. You are the judge. On what will you base your decision as to whether government scientific observers should be required to be aboard the fishing vessels? Will your decision differ if the fishing boat is out for one day or for a six-month trip? [*Balelo v. Baldridge,* 724 F.2d 753 (9th Cir. 1984)]

6–7 Review of Nonaction by Agency The National Traffic and Motor Vehicle Safety Act of 1966 states that if the secretary of transportation makes a determination that a safety-related defect exists, the secretary, through the National Highway Transportation Safety Administration (NHTSA), must order the manufacturer to recall and remedy the defect. The Center for Auto Safety alleged that between 1966 and 1979, defects in automatic transmissions built by the Ford Motor Company caused cars to disengage from "park" and to roll without warning. A 1982 NHTSA investigation ended without a final determination on the existence of a defect because NHTSA and Ford entered a settlement agreement that required Ford to notify owners about the possibility of a defect. NHTSA explicitly reserved the right to commence a new proceeding on the alleged defect if additional acts warranted. In March 1985, the Center for Auto Safety, a nonprofit organization, petitioned NHTSA to reopen the hearing because of additional evidence. The NHTSA administrator denied the petition after reviewing the administrative record. This petition was denied. Center for Auto Safety appealed. Was this denial appealable? Why or why not? [*Center for Auto Safety v. Dole,* 828 F. 2d 799 (1987)]

6–8 Due Process The claimant testified that her employer's vice president continually made comments of a sexual nature to her against her wishes and that this conduct caused her to resign from her job. A hearing was held before the Industrial Claims Board to determine whether she should receive unemployment benefits. At the hearing she introduced into evidence her personal diary, which included entries concerning the incidents. The employer introduced conflicting evidence and objected to the introduction of the diary. The hearing officer offered to allow the employer additional time to review the diary, but the employer did not request a continuance (postponement). The board awarded unemployment benefits to the claimant. The employer appealed the decision to the court, claiming that it did not have a fair hearing. Do you believe that the employer was correct? Why or why not? [*QFD v. Industrial Claim Appeals Office,* 873 P.2d 32 (Colo. App. 1993)]

6–9 Procedures for Administrative Adjudication

This case involved hearsay evidence. Evidence based on hearsay generally is not allowed because hearsay evidence does not come from the witness's own knowledge, but is based on what the witness heard someone else say. Evidence comes from a witness's own knowledge. Hause, while riding his motorcycle, was weaving erratically across two lanes of traffic. A police sergeant stopped Hause and smelled alcohol on his breath. The sergeant called a deputy officer to the scene. The deputy performed a sobriety check. The sergeant then left. Hause then told the deputy that he had between four and seven vodka and grapefruit drinks. The deputy asked Hause if he were feeling the effects of the vodkas. Hause said, "You bet I do." The blood test came back showing a blood alcohol level twice as high as the law allowed. Hause's driver's license was revoked. He requested a hearing to reinstate his license. At the hearing, the hearing officer allowed the deputy to testify as to what the sergeant said he had seen. Hause objected, alleging that these statements were hearsay. The hearing officer, however, overruled the objection. The hearing officer heard other evidence in the case, such as the blood alcohol test evidence and Hause's testimony that he may well have been weaving. The Motor Vehicle Department did not reinstate Hause's license. Hause appealed. Should the revocation of Hause's license be upheld? Why or why not? [*Hause v. MVD,* 873 P.2d 374 (Or. App. 1994)]

6–10 Internet The Internal Revenue Service (IRS) has sent you a notice that you may owe taxes. Go to the Web site of the IRS at **http://www.irs.gov**, click on "Individuals" link. On the new Web page, click on "Taxpayer Advocate." What is a taxpayer advocate? Who may use the services of a taxpayer advocate? How do you reach a taxpayer advocate?

Chapter 7

The Regulation of Business through Criminal Law

Small crimes always precede great ones. Never have we seen timid innocence pass suddenly to extreme licentiousness.

**Jean–Baptiste Racine, 1639–1699
French dramatic poet and
historiographer**

Chapter Outline

Ethical Consideration

Beyond the Insurance Policy

You are the president of Shop' n Serve Mini Markets, a regional chain of all-night mini-markets. Several months ago, an armed robber threatened a clerk's life in one of your stores. Although the clerk was not harmed physically, he was severely traumatized.

The company's medical policy allows for 20 hours of psychological counseling. Since the robbery, the employee has already used the 20 hours and still is too afraid to return to work. The therapist has recommended a regimen of treatment that will exceed 100 additional hours. The employee does not have the money for the supplementary sessions. Should the company pay for the additional treatment? Use the ethical model presented in Chapter 2 and reprinted on the inside front cover to develop your answer.

Introduction

Most businesspeople are basically honest and truthful and act with integrity. Unfortunately, not all businesspeople act ethically, and some commit unethical acts. If the behavior is egregious, the legislature will conduct investigations. Based on the recommendations developed from the investigations, Congress and state legislatures can regulate specific business activities by passing criminal statutes.

Certain business activities, especially economic and environmental enterprises, that once were considered legal are deemed to be criminal today. An example of an economic venture that was lawful, but now is criminal in nature, is the securities laws. By 1911, a few state legislatures regulated the sale of stock (shares in a corporation) through criminal statutes. Two decades later, the federal government passed the first federal statute, the Securities Act of 1933, regulating the sale of new stock. Today, stockbrokers, accountants, lawyers, businesspeople, and others operate under these laws and suffer criminal penalties when these laws are violated.

Before discussing specific criminal acts, the distinction between civil and criminal law needs to be addressed. When a person has been harmed, she brings a civil lawsuit against the person who allegedly caused the harm. If she wins the lawsuit, she usually obtains a monetary award.

When there is a violation of criminal law, only the government—city, county, state, or federal—can prosecute the accused person. All criminal actions are brought in the name of the government, for example, *United States of America v. John Doe, Defendant*. The defendant must have violated a specific law, for which a punishment generally is prescribed. The accused may be incarcerated, fined, or both. The harm here is not to a specific individual but to society as a whole.

The same wrongful act may give rise to both criminal and civil litigation. For example, a person who intentionally kills another is guilty of the crime of murder. He also is liable to the victim's estate for the civil tort of wrongful death.

Two major differences exist between a criminal trial and a civil trial. First, the burden of proof differs. In Chapter 3, the various types of burdens of proof were discussed. A criminal trial requires a higher burden of proof, beyond a reasonable doubt, than in the two types of civil cases. In a civil case, the burden of proof in a court of law is met by preponderance of the evidence, and in a court of equity, the burden is met by clear and convincing evidence.

Second, the Fifth Amendment right against self-incrimination does not apply in a civil case. With the exception of these two issues, the procedures involved in a criminal and a civil action are similar in the basic flow of a case.

This chapter discusses the classification of crimes and the elements of crimes in general. It then focuses on criminal activities that apply directly to the business world.

Artiste Login. Carlos and Carlotta have an online business, Artiste Login Products, Inc. Both owners want to ensure that Artiste does not commit any criminal acts. They are not concerned that Artiste will engage in typical criminal activities, but that they may commit what is known as an economic crime, which can occur when administrative regulations are violated. They know that they must study the regulations to keep themselves informed. Additionally, both want to keep Artiste from being the victim of criminal activities.

Artiste has employees. Carlo and Carlotta want to ensure that the employees do not engage in criminal activities and do not target Artiste for criminal activity. Even though most of its business is conducted online, Artiste must comply with the criminal statutes.

Classification of Crimes

A crime is classified as a *felony, misdemeanor,* or *petty offense,* according to its seriousness. Some states may use other terms for petty offense, such as *civil offense.* The definitions of these classifications vary greatly among the states and the federal government.

A **felony** is more serious than a misdemeanor or a petty offense and is punishable by imprisonment in a federal or state penitentiary for more than one year, by a fine, or even by death. The Model Penal Code[1] distinguishes among the following four types of felony, based on their seriousness:

1. Capital offenses are punishable by death.
2. First-degree felonies are punishable by a maximum penalty of life imprisonment.
3. Second-degree felonies are punishable by a maximum of ten years' imprisonment.
4. Third-degree felonies are punishable by up to five years' imprisonment.

These classifications set the maximum penalties. The actual sentence delivered by the judge to the convicted defendant usually is less than the maximum penalty authorized.

A **misdemeanor** is a crime punishable by a fine, by confinement for up to one year, or both. People convicted of misdemeanors are incarcerated in a city or county jail instead of in a state penitentiary. Disorderly conduct and trespassing are common misdemeanors. Misdemeanors generally are tried in city or other lower courts, whereas felonies are tried in state or federal courts that have general jurisdiction.

A **petty offense** often is not classified as a crime but as a civil matter. These offenses include many

---

[1]Model codes are drafted by the National Conference of Commissioners on Uniform State Laws, which was discussed in Chapter 4. To avoid the potentially wide variety of statutes on a particular topic that could result from each state trying to draft its own legislation, the model code provides a single statutory scheme. The model code is sent to the fifty states for possible adoption into statute. A state may choose to adopt all or part of the model code, to modify parts of it, or to not adopt any part of it at all.

traffic or building code violations. Even for petty offenses, a guilty party may be incarcerated for a few days, fined, or both. The burden of proof for a petty offense is normally a preponderance of evidence, not beyond a reasonable doubt.

Crimes also can be classified according to their nature. For example, there are crimes against the person (murder, assault, rape), crimes against property (theft, burglary, arson), and crimes against the government (perjury, which is lying under oath). These classifications are used to group crimes within a statutory code.

The criminal code is structured to punish acts. The criminal code defines the criminal elements, the levels of seriousness, and the minimum and maximum punishments that can be imposed by the judge on the convicted defendant.

Criminal Statutory Law

Originally, criminal acts were defined by the judiciary under the common law instead of by legislative statutes. Today, all crimes are based on statutes. Judges, however, still use the original common law definitions when interpreting these criminal statutes.

Each criminal statute prohibits a certain behavior. The statute sets out the specific elements of the crime. The prosecutor must prove each element of the crime before a person can be convicted. Most crimes require an act of commission; that is, a person must do something to commit a crime. In some cases, an act of omission can be a crime, but only if the person has failed to carry out a legal duty. Failure to file a tax return is an example of an omission that is a crime.

Criminal statutes are interpreted narrowly by the courts; that is, the courts limit their application. Courts take into consideration the statutory language, the legislative history, and the statute's purpose in order to determine the prohibited type of behavior.

Constitutional Safeguards

The criminal justice system operates on the premise that it is far worse for an innocent person to be punished than for a guilty person to go free. A person is innocent until proven guilty beyond a reasonable doubt. The procedures of the criminal legal system are

LEGAL HIGHLIGHT

Ponzi or Pyramid—It Is Still a Criminal Scheme

Ponzi, pyramid, multilevel marketing plans, network marketing, or matrix marketing—many are the criminal schemes to part a fool from her money. Just who was Ponzi and how do these plans work?

Charles Ponzi developed a loan investment system that has become known as the Ponzi scheme. In 1903, at age twenty-one, he immigrated to the United States from Italy. Working at various low-paying jobs, he finally stumbled on a money-raising scheme. He promised people who invested money with him 50 percent interest on their money if he could keep it for thirty days and 100 percent if he could keep it for ninety days.

By word of mouth, news of this fantastic investment spread. People invested large sums of money, and Ponzi paid the first people with the money coming in from the later investors. More than $250,000 a day rolled in; soon his worth grew to more than $8.5 million. Given time, he could no longer pay everyone what they had been promised. After millions were lost, he eventually was tried, convicted, and served five years in prison. He died in a charity ward in Brazil in 1949 with only $75 to his name, which was used to bury him.

Today, similar scams exist. The criminal operator contacts people by mail, telephone, or e-mail. In 1997, the Federal Trade Commission (FTC) charged that Fortuna Alliance marketed a pyramid scheme through its home page on the World Wide Web and with printed materials.[a]

[a] See the FTC Web page, which has information on Fortuna and information and publications concerning a variety of wealth-building schemes. The FTC Web page is http://www.ftc.gov. Use the search function to find information on Fortuna.

Using fabulous earnings claims, Fortuna Alliance induced tens of thousands of consumers in more than sixty countries to pay between $250 and $1,750 to join the plan. Fortuna Alliance claimed that members would receive more than $5,000 per month in profits as others enrolled in the plan. The company provided members with advice for recruiting others to join the pyramid, both through direct contact and by setting up their own Web sites.

Closed down in the same year by the FTC, it was estimated that more than 95 percent of the people who invested in Fortuna Alliance would have lost money had the scheme continued. The FTC and Fortuna Alliance entered into a consent agreement. Under the agreement terms, Fortuna Alliance set aside $2.8 million to make full refunds to the consumers. Bookkeeping and monitoring provisions were included to allow the FTC to track compliance with the settlement terms.

As for the victims in the sixty countries in which Fortuna Alliance had operated via the Internet, the FTC used legal counsel in London, Belize, and Antigua for the foreign litigation. The Department of Justice's Office of Foreign Litigation was instrumental in reaching settlements for the foreign actions.

Because this is a consent judgment for settlement purposes only, the defendant did not admit to a law violation. Consent judgments have the force of law after they are signed by a judge.

designed to protect individual rights and to preserve the presumption of innocence.

Criminal law brings the weighty force of the government, with all its resources, to bear against the individual. The Constitution provide safeguards for all persons, including those accused of crimes. The United States Supreme Court has ruled that most of these safeguards apply not only in federal courts, but also in state courts by virtue of the Fourteenth Amendment's due process clause.

In past years, the U.S. Supreme Court has been active in interpreting these constitutional rights. The case of *Miranda v. Arizona*[2] established that the police must advise suspects of their constitutional rights prior to interrogation. Suspects must be warned prior to any questioning that they have the right to remain silent, that anything they say can be used against them in a court of law, that they have the right to the presence of an attorney, and that if they cannot afford an attorney one will be appointed for them prior to any questioning. The *Miranda* case has been criticized over the years. The United States Supreme Court upheld the *Miranda* warnings in the following case.

[2]384 U.S. 436, 86 S. Ct. 1602, 16 L. Ed. 2d 694 (1966), or go to http://www.findlaw.com and type in the case name.

CASE 7.1

Supreme Court of the United States, 2000
530 U.S. 428, 120 S. Ct. 2326, 147 L. Ed. 2d 405

DICKERSON v. UNITED STATES

BACKGROUND AND FACTS Petitioner Dickerson, under indictment for bank robbery and related federal crimes, moved to suppress a statement he had made to agents of the Federal Bureau of Investigation, on the grounds that he had not received the *Miranda* warnings before being interrogated. The federal district court granted his motion and the government appealed.

The Fourth Circuit reversed the trial court but acknowledged that Dickerson had not been given his *Miranda* warnings. It held, however, that the federal statute was satisfied because his statement was voluntary. The federal statute provided that a confession could be used if it were voluntary. The Fourth Circuit concluded that *Miranda* was not a constitutional holding and that, therefore, Congress could by statute have the final say on the admissibility question. The United States Supreme Court granted a writ of *certiorari*.

Chief Justice REHNQUIST delivered the opinion of the Court.

In *Miranda v. Arizona,* we held that certain warnings must be given before a suspect's statement made during custodial interrogation could be admitted in evidence. In the wake of that decision, Congress enacted 18 U.S.C. § 3501, which in essence laid down a rule that the admissibility of such statements should turn only on whether or not they were voluntarily made. We hold that *Miranda,* being a constitutional decision of this Court, may not be in effect overruled by an Act of Congress, and we decline to overrule *Miranda* ourselves. We therefore hold that *Miranda* and its progeny in this Court govern the admissibility of statements made during custodial interrogation in both state and federal courts.

. . . .

DECISION AND REMEDY The Court refused to reverse its holding in *Miranda v. Arizona.* All law enforcement officers must give the standard warnings before questioning the accused.

CRITICAL THINKING: POLITICAL CONSIDERATION Over the decades since *Miranda* was first decided, many people have argued that the *Miranda* warnings have resulted in guilty persons being set free without any negative consequences of their criminal behavior. Why should law enforcement officers be required to give these warnings? Why did the U.S. Supreme Court not change this requirement after so much criticism of the original decision?

Criminal Procedure

A criminal prosecution differs from a civil case in several respects. These differences reflect the efforts at safeguarding the individual's rights against actions of the state.

Before a warrant for arrest can be issued, *probable cause* must exist for believing that the individual in question has committed a crime. **Probable cause** is defined as a substantial likelihood (not just a possibility) that the individual has committed a crime. Sometimes arrests may be made without a warrant when there is no time to get one. The action of the arresting officer, however, still is judged by the standard of probable cause.

Individuals must be formally charged with committing specific crimes before they can be brought to trial. Two ways are used to bring a person to court: the use of grand jury or the action of a magistrate.

A grand jury is made up of sixteen to twenty-four members who are citizens in the court's jurisdiction.

The court assembles the grand jury to hear evidence and to determine if an accused should be charged with a crime. This charge is called an **indictment** when issued by a grand jury. Once indicted, the accused can be tried for his crimes in court.

A magistrate is similar to a judge but has less authority. If the magistrate determines that a person should be tried for criminal acts, the charge is contained in a **bill of information**. Some states use other judicial officers, instead of magistrates, such as justices of the peace, to perform these functions.

At the trial, the accused person has to prove nothing. The entire burden of proof is on the prosecution (the government). The prosecution must show that, based on all of the evidence, the defendant is guilty beyond a reasonable doubt.

A jury can come to one of two decisions: guilty or not guilty. Either the prosecution has or has not met its burden of proof. Contrary to media jargon, a verdict of not guilty is different from a statement of

Exhibit 7-1   Major Steps in Criminal Procedure

Offense. Someone commits a crime in violation of the criminal statutes.

Probable Cause Hearing. Police take evidence of crime to magistrate for probable cause hearing; search warrant granted based on probable cause.

Investigation. Police conduct investigation and develop evidence and link to suspect; arrest warrant granted based on probable cause.

Arrest. Suspect is arrested (at scene of crime, after hot pursuit, or pursuant to an arrest warrant) and booked into jail.

Booking. Suspect's name and crime are entered into the books. Suspect is fingerprinted, photographed, and allowed one telephone call.

Initial Appearance. Within one to three days after arrest, this procedure must occur. Suspect informed of charges and bond is set if eligible. Suspect is released on own recognizance (OR), released on bail, or stays in jail. Complaint is filed.

Either

Preliminary Hearing. This hearing is based on a bill of information. Prosecutor establishes probable cause crime has been committed and that suspect that committed the crime.	*Grand Jury.* Same as preliminary hearing, except suspect is not present. The grand jury either issues or does not issue an indictment.

Arraignment. Suspect pleads guilty or not guilty. Case is set for trial.

Plea Bargain. Prosecutor and suspect's attorney may enter into a plea bargain agreement, avoiding a trial.

Trial. Trial can be by a judge alone or with a jury. Jury finds defendant guilty or not guilty. If the jury cannot reach a decision, it is said to be a hung jury.

Appeal. If the defendant is found guilty, the defendant may appeal. If the defendant is found not guilty, the government has no right of appeal.

the defendant's innocence. It merely means that the prosecution failed to present enough evidence to the court to prove the accused guilty beyond a reasonable doubt.

Courts have complex rules about the types of evidence allowed and procedures for presenting that evidence, especially in jury trials. These rules are designed to ensure that evidence in the trial is relevant, reliable, and not unfairly prejudicial to the defendant. The defense attorney cross-examines the government's witnesses who present evidence against the attorney's client in an attempt to show that those witnesses' testimony is unreliable. Of course, the government also may cross-examine witnesses presented by the defense. The prosecutor's responsibility is to prove beyond a reasonable doubt that the defendant is criminally responsible for the crimes charged.

Basic Elements of Criminal Responsibility

The two requirements for many crimes are criminal intent (**mens rea**) and criminal conduct (**actus reus**). Thinking about embezzling funds or about stealing a computer program may be morally wrong, but these thoughts in themselves are not criminal until they are translated into action. A person can be punished for attempting to commit a crime, but only if she takes substantial steps toward the criminal objective, as discussed later in this section.

Criminal Intent

The Model Penal Code recognizes four categories of *mens rea*:

1. *Purpose* What did the accused intend to do? What was his conscious objective?
2. *Knowledge* Did the accused act knowingly with respect to the result?
3. *Recklessness* Did the accused act in such a wanton manner—that is, with knowledge and conscious disregard—that she created a considerable and unjustifiable risk to others?
4. *Negligence* Did the accused act so negligently—that is, deviate so substantially from the standard of care that a reasonable person would exercise under the circumstances—that he created a substantial and unnecessary risk to others?

In most cases, a wrongful mental state is required along with the wrongful act to establish criminal liability. In these cases, the mental state of the accused is important in determining the degree of wrongfulness of the crime. For example, the same criminal act that causes the death of another can be committed by different defendants with varying mental states.

LEGAL HIGHLIGHT

Ford and the Pinto

Ford designed the Pinto to compete with Volkswagen, a German automobile manufacturer whose name translates into "People's Car." The Pinto was to be an efficient, economical automobile.

In an effort to keep the costs down, a decision was made not to include an $11 safety improvement that would have lessened the likelihood of an automobile fire in case of collision. For years following the Pinto's introduction, injury and wrongful death lawsuits totaled more than $1 billion. Ford lost several civil lawsuits and made headlines when a judgment for negligence was awarded against it for $128.5 million, later reduced to $2.5 million.[a]

In 1980, Ford went on trial on criminal charges brought by the state of Indiana for reckless homicide as a result of the deaths of three people. Reckless homicide is a crime in which the accused is aware of and consciously disregards substantial and unjustifiable risk. The jury did not believe that Ford had acted recklessly or intentionally. Ford was found not guilty, but only after spending $1 million to defend itself.

[a]Grimshaw v. Ford Motor Co., 119 Cal. App. 3d 757, 174 Cal. Rptr. 348 (1981).

One person may kill in cold blood with premeditation, called *murder in the first degree.* A second person may kill in the heat of passion, which is *voluntary manslaughter.* A third person may kill as the result of negligence. This killing is *involuntary manslaughter,* such as when someone dies as a result of extreme carelessness involving an automobile.

In each of these situations, the law recognizes a different degree of wrongfulness and the punishment differs accordingly. The greater the degree of *mens rea,* the more reprehensible the crime and, thus, the greater the punishment.

Criminal Conduct

Some statutes require no criminal intent, only criminal conduct. For example, a person shoots a rifle in the air to help the neighborhood celebrate the new year. The person intends no harm. Her conduct, however, the shooting of a rifle, violates a statute, and that conduct constitutes the crime.

Some criminal statutes target business and employee behavior in particular by requiring not criminal intent, but only criminal conduct by the business. These statutes avoid the old legal problem which says that a business cannot form a mental intent and, therefore, cannot be guilty of a crime.

Likewise, the statutes apply to individuals responsible for business management. For example, a person owns a restaurant that sells beer and wine. An employee sells beer to a person below the legal drinking age. The owner can be criminally charged with providing liquor to a minor.

The following case involves a statute that does not require *mens rea.*

LANDMARK CASE

CASE 7.2

Supreme Court of the
United States, 1975
421 U.S. 658, 95 S. Ct
1903, 44 L. Ed. 2d 489
http://www.findlaw.com/
(Type in case name in
search box.)

UNITED STATES v. PARK

BACKGROUND AND FACTS The defendant was the president of Acme Markets, Inc. Acme, a large national food chain, employed 36,000 employees and operated 874 retail outlets, twelve general warehouses, and four special warehouses. During 1970, Acme's president received a letter from the Food and Drug Administration (FDA) concerning rodents in a Baltimore warehouse where his firm stored a considerable amount of food. The rodents adulterated the food, making it unfit for consumption. The vice president in charge of the warehouse responded to the FDA letter.

In 1971 and 1972, similar conditions were observed. The defendant did not have direct control over the Baltimore warehouse but was convicted on five counts of causing adulteration of food that had been bought and sold in interstate commerce. He was fined $50 for each of the five convictions under the Federal Food, Drug, and Cosmetic Act.

Chief Justice BURGER delivered the opinion of the Court.

. . . .

The Act does not . . . make criminal liability turn on "awareness of some wrongdoing" or "conscious fraud." The duty imposed by Congress on responsible corporate agents is, we emphasize, one that requires the highest standard of foresight and vigilance, but the Act, in its criminal aspect, does not require that which is objectively impossible. The theory upon which responsible corporate agents are held criminally accountable for "causing" violations of the Act permits a claim that a defendant was "powerless" to prevent or correct the violation to "be raised defensively at a trial on the merits." If such a claim is made, the defendant has the burden of coming forward with evidence, but this does not alter the Government's ultimate burden of proving beyond a reasonable doubt the defendant's guilt, including his power, in light of the duty imposed by the Act, to prevent or correct the prohibited condition. Congress has seen fit to enforce the accountability of responsible corporate agents dealing with products which may affect the health of consumers by penal sanctions cast in rigorous terms, and the obligation of the courts is to give them effect so long as they do not violate the Constitution.

. . . .

Although we need not decide whether this testimony would have entitled respondent to an instruction as to his lack of power had he requested it, the testimony clearly created the "need" for rebuttal evidence. That evidence was not offered to show that respondent had a propensity to commit criminal acts[;] its purpose was to demonstrate that respondent was on notice that he could not rely on his system of delegation to subordinates to prevent and correct unsanitary conditions at Acme's warehouses, and that he must have been aware of the deficiencies of this system before the Baltimore violations were discovered. The evidence was therefore relevant since it served to rebut respondent's defense that he had justifiably relied upon subordinates to handle sanitation matters.

DECISION AND REMEDY Even though the defendant had no actual criminal intent, he still was convicted of a crime. For conviction, only the wrongful conduct of producing adulterated food that was in interstate commerce was required.

CRITICAL THINKING: MANAGERIAL POLICY Assume that you are a high-level executive in a major corporation that employs more than 20,000 people. The company manufactures a toxic product that, if misused, could result in criminal prosecution of the top executives. Discuss fully how you would protect the corporation and yourself from criminal prosecution.

Attempts and Conspiracies

Two separate offenses can occur prior to a planned criminal act. One is called an *attempt*. The other is called a *conspiracy*.

A person can plan a crime and commit an **overt act**, that is, any act toward committing the crime, but not commit the crime. Legally, the overt act is considered to be an **attempt** to commit the crime. For example, a person plans to rob a bank, buys a gun, steals a getaway car, drives to the bank, and enters it. After yelling "Holdup," however, the person turns around and flees the scene. The crime, the bank robbery, was unsuccessful, but the person is guilty of attempted bank robbery.

A **conspiracy** arises when a person agrees (conspires) with one or more persons to commit a crime. They plan the crime and perform overt acts. Whether or not the crime is carried out, the people are guilty of conspiracy to commit a crime. In the previous bank robbery example, if two or more people plan the robbery and purchase guns (the overt act) to carry out their plan, they are guilty of conspiring to commit bank robbery.

Crimes Affecting Business

Crimes can be committed against businesses and businesses can commit crimes. Criminal offenses that involve businesses are divided into three general areas: crimes against property, white-collar crimes (generally committed by individuals), and crimes committed by businesses. These distinctions are artificial, but they assist in studying specific offenses. For example, crimes listed in the *White-Collar Crimes* section that follows can be committed not only by individuals, but also by businesses. Conversely, crimes listed in the *Crimes Businesses Can Commit* section also can be committed by individuals.

Offenses against Property

Businesses are often victims of crimes against property. This section examines the following offenses against property: burglary, larceny, robbery, and arson.

Burglary. Burglary is defined as entering into or remaining in another's building with the intent to commit a crime. For example, Ace breaks into a ware-

LEGAL HIGHLIGHT

Beware of the Talk Show Expert

Throughout the country, television and radio talk shows provide investment advice. Most are informative and provide objective advice. A few talk shows, however, pitch dubious investments such as stamps, coins, wireless cable, and second mortgages.

For example, the Federal Trade Commission (FTC) brought an action against World Wide Classics, Inc., for fraudulently misrepresenting the value of stamps. The FTC alleged that the talk show host did not reveal that her guest, who gave advice about the investment quality of stamps, actually was her husband. The prices of the stamps were between two and ten times the true market value. World Wide Classics entered into a consent decree, in which it agreed to pay a $10 million fine to the FTC and to liquidate the company. A consent decree is an agreement by the parties (World Wide Classics and the FTC) that carries the court's sanction.

A paid information program must carry a notice to that effect when it airs on television. Radio shows must carry the disclaimer that the program is a paid advertisement. Because it is radio, however, anyone who tunes in after the announcement has been made will miss that information. The listener would not know that the program is a paid announcement because the format is the same as that of an objective show on the same topic. Morris D. English, sentenced to eighteen years for fraud, money laundering, and other charges relating to his second-mortgage scam, had a radio program that touted the worthiness of investing in second mortgages. Nearly 1,500 investors lost $30 million after relying on this advice.

The FTC continually investigates paid programs that are in fact mere fronts for criminal activity. New laws to curb this type of fraud may be passed by Congress. In the meantime, remember the adage, "If it looks too good to be true, it probably is."

Go to the FTC Web site, **http://www.ftc.com**, which is updated frequently with information on current fraudulent activity.

---

house and intends to steal a truckload of videotape recorders. Before he can load his truck, the burglar alarm goes off and he flees the scene. Ace is guilty of burglary because he broke into the premises and intended to commit the felony of theft. Aggravated burglary, which is defined as burglary with the use of a deadly weapon or burglary of a dwelling, receives a heavier penalty.

Larceny. A person's wrongful or fraudulent taking and carrying away of another's personal property is **larceny**. Generally, the person also must intend to deprive the owner of his property permanently. Many business-related larcenies entail fraudulent conduct, that is, actions by the criminal that deceive the victim, the businessperson. Generally, the place from which physical property is taken in a larceny is immaterial, although statutes usually prescribe a stiffer sentence for property taken from buildings, such as banks or warehouses.

As society has become more complex, the definition of *property* has changed. In most states, the list of items considered property that is subject to larceny statutes have been expanded. Stealing computer programs may constitute larceny even though the programs consist of magnetic impulses. Trade secrets can be subject to larceny statutes. The acts of stealing the use of telephone wires with a blue box device or thefts of cellular telephone codes are subject to larceny statutes. Often special larceny statutes cover the theft of natural gas or electricity.

Robbery. **Robbery** is defined as taking another's personal property from his person or in his presence by force or intimidation, with the intent to deprive him of it permanently. The use of force or intimidation is necessary for an act of theft to be considered a robbery.

While robbery involves force or intimidation, larceny does not. Therefore, picking pockets is larceny, not robbery.

Typically, states impose more severe penalties for aggravated robbery (robbery with the use of a deadly weapon). Liquor stores, all-night convenience stores, and banks are especially vulnerable to robbery.

Arson. The intentional, willful, and malicious burning of another's building (and, in some states, of personal property) constitutes the crime of **arson**. Arson statutes apply to the burning of all kinds of buildings. If arson results in a person's death, the arsonist can be charged with murder.

Every state has a special statute that covers burning a building to collect insurance. If Akin owns an insured apartment building that is falling apart and burns it himself or pays someone else to set fire to it, Akin is guilty of arson to defraud insurers. Of course, the insurer pays no claim when insurance fraud is proved.

White-Collar Crime

White-collar crime is defined by the Department of Justice as a nonviolent offense involving corruption, deceit, or breach of trust. This type of crime generally is committed by individuals. More than 30 percent of the criminal filings in federal district courts involve white-collar crimes.

The large range of white-collar crimes includes receiving stolen goods, forgery, obtaining goods or money by false pretenses, embezzlement, use of the mails to defraud, and computer crimes.

Receiving Stolen Goods. In the crime of **receiving stolen goods**, the recipient of the goods does not need to know the true identity of the owner or of the thief. All that is necessary is that the recipient knows or should have known that the goods were stolen. This knowledge implies an intent to deprive the owner of those goods.

Forgery. The fraudulent making or altering of any writing that changes the legal liability of another is **forgery**. If Smith signs Gomez's name without authorization to the back of a check made out to Gomez, Smith has committed forgery. Forgery also includes counterfeiting trademarks, falsifying public records, and altering any legal document.

Most states have a special statute, often called a *credit card statute*, to cover the illegal use of credit cards. Thus, the state's attorney can prosecute a person who uses a forged credit card for violating either the general forgery statute or a statute specifically targeting credit card forgeries.

Artiste Login. Carlotta is an artist who paints in oil. Her work is very much in demand because of its high quality and distinctiveness. She signs all her paintings. A friend shows her an oil painting with her signature. Carlotta immediately recognizes it as a forgery and files a complaint with the police. Forgery is not restricted to paper documents.

Obtaining Goods or Money by False Pretenses. The crime of **obtaining goods or money by false pretenses** consists of obtaining title to another's property by an intentionally false statement of a past or existing fact with intent to defraud another. Statutes covering such illegal activities vary widely from state to state. Almost all states have created a separate crime prohibiting the giving of a no-account or insufficient funds check with the intent to defraud.

In 1984, Congress passed the **Trademark Counterfeiting Act**, which makes dealing in goods or services under a counterfeit trademark a federal crime. The federal **False Statement Act** provides that intentionally making a false statement to the U.S. government to obtain a monetary return is a crime.

Embezzlement. The fraudulent conversion of another's property or money by a person in lawful possession of that property is **embezzlement**. Typically, this crime involves an employee who fraudulently appropriates money. Banks and other businesses face this problem when officers of the business or accountants "jimmy" the books to cover up the fraudulent conversion of money for their own benefit.

Embezzlement is not larceny because the wrongdoer does not physically take the property from the possession of another. It is not robbery because the thief uses no force or intimidation.

Whether the accused takes the money from the victim or from a third person is immaterial. If, as the comptroller of a large business, Saunders pockets a certain number of checks from third parties that were given to her to deposit into the account of another company, she has committed embezzlement.

Another version of embezzlement occurs when the owner of a property provides payment to a contractor specifically to pay various people who have worked on the owner's building. A contractor who does not use the money for this purpose commits a special form of embezzlement called **misapplication**

of trust funds. The funds are entrusted to the contractor for a specific purpose and that trust is violated. The fact that the accused may intend to replace the embezzled property eventually is not a sufficient defense.

INFOTRAC RESEARCH ACTIVITY

Embezzlements are probably the most common white-collar crime. Go to InfoTrac and see what is currently occurring in the business world. You will find at least 64 articles and 618 periodicals. Look for the most recent articles and summarize the most recent embezzlements.

Use of the Mails to Defraud. Use of the mails to defraud the public is a federal crime. Illegal use of the mails involves (1) mailing a writing for the purpose of executing a scheme to defraud or (2) an organized scheme to defraud by false pretenses. For example, if Daniel Webster mails an advertisement offering for sale a cure for baldness that he knows to be fraudulent, he can be prosecuted for use of the mails to defraud.

Computer Crimes. Governments and businesses have used computers since the 1940s. The real explosion of computers for government, business, and home use, however, began in the late 1970s and continues in the 2000s. Computer crimes are an unfortunate result of this widespread use.

LEGAL HIGHLIGHT

Recent Computer Crimes

Every day criminals develop new methods of obtaining money or property illegally through the use of computers and the Internet. Most of the recent activities have centered on the use of credit cards and stolen identities.

One of the more dangerous criminal snares recently used to lure victims occurs when someone sends an official-looking e-mail to the victim requesting personal information. For example, thousands of e-mails were sent to Discover Card customers attempting to obtain their account numbers. The message stated that because the customer's account was dormant, it was being placed on hold. To remove the hold status, the customer was required to log on the Web site provided in the e-mail, then type in the Discover Card account number, expiration date, and other personal information. The linked Web site had the Discover logo and looked official. In fact, the Web site belonged to the criminal who captured the victim's personal information. He would use the Discover Card until the account was closed, usually after tens of thousands of dollars had been charged fraudulently to the account.

Some persons in Indonesia, as well as in other parts of the world, have made computer fraud a way of life.

They go to international chat rooms involved with credit fraud. They obtain user names and with computer programs that banks use input random numbers until they have a person's credit card numbers and expiration dates. The situation has gotten so bad that many companies refuse to ship to Indonesia. That has not stopped them. They have the goods shipped to such places as Java West, India. Someone in the postal service in India will think that a mistake has been made and ships the package on to Java West, Indonesia. Similar activities have occurred frequently in Romania and the Ukraine.

To offset these activities, United Parcel Service, through a partnership with DoUWantIt.com and Mail Boxes Etc., has devised a partial solution to reduce these types of fraud. A person purchases an item from, say, Amazon.com or eBay. The customer pays by credit cards and the retailer waits to ship the goods until the transaction goes through on the credit card. Then the goods are shipped to one of the locations operated by either Mail Boxes Etc. or DoUWantIt.com. When the customer picks up the merchandise, she must have the credit card with her plus two other identifications.

As international business increases, businesses will need to keep up with these ingenious illegal schemes. There will always be people who want to get something for nothing.

Computer crimes can be delegated to three groupings. The first type is the sabotage of the computer or its programs. This type of crime is committed by a disgruntled current or former employee or by a hacker using the telephone or cable wires or through the Internet. The second type is computer or software theft. These activities fall into the category of crimes against property.

The third type involves computers being used to commit a wide range of crimes. Computers can commit crimes in record time—as little as three milliseconds. Detection often is difficult. Companies, and even the government, have discovered multimillion-dollar electronic thefts, but only after a significant period of time. Some electronic thefts include causing a computer to write extra paychecks, to transfer monies, or to shave cents off interest accounts and place the money into personal accounts.

The law involving computer crime is still developing. To counter the rising computer crime activity, Congress has passed several statutes. The **Counterfeit Access Device and Computer Fraud and Abuse Act**[3] was passed in 1984. This act makes it a federal crime to access a computer with a counterfeit or unauthorized card or device with the intent to obtain (1) restricted federal government information, (2) financial records from financial institutions, and (3) consumer files from consumer reporting agencies.

The **Electronic Communications Privacy Act**[4] was passed in 1986. Under this act, it is a federal crime to intercept an *electronic communication* at the point of or during transmission, when transmitted through a router or server, or after receipt by the intended recipient. An electronic communication includes any electronic transfer of signals, writings, images, sounds, data, or intelligence of any nature.

The **Information Infrastructure Protection Act**[5] was passed in 1996. Congress made it illegal to intentionally transmit a computer virus or to trespass into an Internet-connected computer.

Under these statutes, any unauthorized person who seeks entrance into another's computer systems, including electronic mail, computer-to-computer data transmissions, remote computing services, and private video conferences, commits a crime.

The statutes also prohibit the establishment of bulletin boards that list the passwords of individuals or businesses. They apply to governmental computers, computers of federally insured institutions, cellular car telephones, and computer access that crosses state lines. The penalties vary but can be as much as ten years in prison plus a $100,000 fine.

Congress passed the **Identity Theft and Assumption Deterrence Act** in 1998, with needed amendments in 2000.[6] The act makes it a federal crime to steal a person's identity. The Federal Trade Commission manages and tracks the victims. Since passage of the act, the FTC has recorded more than 170,000 victims. The FTC maintains a database that is accessible by both federal and state agencies. The information generated by this act has assisted greatly in the prosecution of criminals who have committed identity theft.

The full extent of computer crime in business is not known. Firms victimized by computer crime rarely publicize the fact. They are afraid that their customers will doubt the accuracy of their computer-generated material.

Trials of apprehended computer criminals are rare. The affected business usually allows the case to be plea-bargained instead of going to trial. A plea bargain occurs when the defense attorney negotiates with the prosecutor that the accused will plead guilty in return for something, such as pleading guilty to a lesser crime or a statement by the prosecutor to the judge for a lighter sentence. Sometimes, for fear of publicity, the business will not even report the crime and may be blackmailed into giving the person who committed the crime a reference for another job.

---

[3]The Counterfeit Access Device and Computer Fraud and Abuse Act is found in two code sections at the Legal Information Institute. The prohibition against access devices is found at http://www.law.cornell.edu/uscode/18/1029.html. The prohibition concerning computers is at http://www.law.cornell.edu/uscode/18/1030.html. You can start your search at the Cornell University law site at http://www.law.cornell.edu.

[4]The Electronic Communications Privacy Act is found at the Legal Information Institute under the section on Unlawful Access to Stored Communications at http://www.law.cornell.edu/uscode/18/2701.html. You can start your search at the Cornell University law site at http://www.law.cornell.edu.

[5]For more information on this statute and the statute itself, go to http://www.usdoj.gov/criminal/cybercrime/1030_anal.html.

[6]This act may be obtained at http://www4.law.cornell.edu/uscode/18/1028.html.

LEGAL HIGHLIGHT

Protection from Identity Theft

Identity theft tops the list of complaints filed with the Federal Trade Commission and is the fastest growing criminal activity. Protect yourself from having your identity stolen. The following list provides some actions you can take.

1. *Checks* Use initials and not your full name on checks. The bank has your signature on file, which should be different from the name printed on the check. The person who steals checks will not know that the signature is different. The bank should reject payment of the check with a different signature and notify you. Do not put your home address on checks. If possible, use a P.O. box or use an office address.

   A driver's license has a date of birth written on it. If stolen, the identify thief will have your full name, address, date of birth, and a Social Security number, which is all the information needed to engage in identity theft. So it is a good idea to not use your Social Security number for a state driver's license identification number. Request the driver's license bureau to assign another number.

2. *Credit Cards* Your credit card company furnishes you with an address and telephone number to notify them of lost or stolen cards. Make copies of both sides of all your credit cards. If any card is stolen, a copy has the information needed to make a more complete report to the credit card company. Place the copies in a very safe place, such as a safety deposit box.

3. *Reports* File a police report if your cards are lost or stolen. Send the report to your creditors and others who require proof of the crime.

   Contact the fraud departments of one major credit bureau to place a fraud alert on your file. As soon as the fraud alert is placed, the other credit bureaus will be notified. You will be notified if any attempt is made to open an account in your name.

   Close any accounts that have been tampered with or any unauthorized new accounts. File an ID Theft Affidavit available at the Federal Trade Commission's Web site to dispute new unauthorized accounts.

   File a report with the Federal Trade Commission. The FTC maintains a database of identity theft cases that is used by law enforcement agencies.

   Take precautions. Do not let carelessness on your part help an identity thief wreak havoc on your credit record and cause you to spend weeks, months, even years to straighten out this problem. Update your knowledge by using the Federal Trade Commission Web site at **http://www.ftc.gov**.

CYBERLAW

Fraud

The new frontier for criminal fraud activity is the World Wide Web (WWW). Government prosecutors have obtained a number of convictions for computer fraud.

In one type of fraud, a person offers an item for sale, but the seller uses various fictitious names and addresses. A buyer sees an item on a Web site and sends in a payment. The purported seller accepts the pay-ment, but no merchandise is sent. In a variation, the seller sends merchandise, but it is not what was ordered. Or the items sent are different than what the seller represented.

Sometimes goods are placed on an auction Web site, such as eBay. Although it is against the auction house rules, the seller bids on the item to drive up the price, making the ultimate price paid by an authentic buyer artificially high. The seller also can use an alias to post a message on the seller's page at the auction house stating that the seller (posing as a buyer) was completely satisfied with prior dealings. This posted information is seen by other legitimate prospective buyers and gives them false confidence about the seller.

Other cases involve counterfeit merchandise, such as counterfeit Beanie Babies. On a Web auction house, a seller posts for sale a number of hard-to-find Beanie Babies. A buyer makes a winning bid, but when the merchandise arrives, the Beanie Babies are reproductions or knock-offs, instead of authentic items.

The sellers are not the only ones who perpetuate fraud. A buyer can win a bid on an auction house Web site, then pay for it by using a stolen credit card.

Investment schemes also use the WWW to entice consumers to invest in nonexistent funds. The investment company promises to pay high rates of return with no risk. The company is vague about the nature of the investment, while stressing the rates of return. Many of these investment company offerings are really

LEGAL HIGHLIGHT

The Barbie Doll Web Caper

Americans lose $40 billion a year to fast-talking swindlers on the other end of the telephone. Other swindlers use the World Wide Web. Ripoffs are as varied as the imagination. Let's look at this case that used the Web to sell Barbie dolls.

Debbie Ann Amyot, who lives in Maryland, collects Barbie dolls. While surfing the Web, she came across an advertisement for the sale of a "mint" collection of ninety-five Barbie dolls in their original boxes. The advertisement further stated that the dolls and boxes were all in "collector's condition." Intrigued, Ms. Amyot e-mailed and also telephoned the seller, Mary Jean Cain, who lives in Georgia. Ms. Amyot agreed to purchase the entire doll collection for $6,140. Ms. Amyot mailed the check. After Ms. Cain received the check, she shipped the doll collection.

Upon Barbie's arrival, Ms. Amyot joyously opened the box to see her new purchase. Joy turned to dissatisfaction when she saw only thirty-six dolls in poor condition, contained in boxes that were also in poor condition. She called Ms. Cain and requested to return the dolls. Ms. Cain terminated all contact with Ms. Amyot and had her telephone disconnected.

Disgusted and infuriated, Ms. Amyot complained to the police. Eventually, Ms. Cain was charged in Maryland with one count of theft by deception of property with a value over $300.[a] Ms. Cain moved to dismiss the charge on the ground that Maryland lacked territorial jurisdic-

[a] State v. Cain, 360 Ms. 205, 757 A.2d 142 (2000).

tion. The issue before the Court of Appeals of Maryland was whether it had jurisdiction over Ms. Cain in Georgia. The court started its decision with this statement:

This case appears to present a cutting-edge issue, because it involves a prosecution for theft by means of deception across state lines perpetrated partly via the Internet. But in reality, the case turns on principles developed by common-law courts long ago, in connection with business done by mail.

The court held that it did have jurisdiction under the following well established doctrine:

The principle that an accused, acting from outside a jurisdiction through an innocent agent inside the jurisdiction, is liable to prosecution in the jurisdiction, has often been applied in cases in which the innocent agent is a common carrier, and the accused acts through the common carrier by inducing a victim to deliver property to the common carrier, to be shipped from inside to the accused outside.

In other words, the accused, Ms. Cain, acting from outside Maryland, is liable for prosecution in Maryland because she induced Ms. Amyot to deliver property, her check, to a common carrier, the U.S. Post Office, which delivered the check outside of Maryland, in this case to Georgia.

Although a new technology was used to commit a potential scam, the tried-and-true legal rules still apply. This case was limited as to whether the Maryland court had jurisdiction over an out-of-state accused. Remember that the previous facts are the prosecution's version. Since Ms. Cain has not been tried or convicted, she has the presumption of innocence.

Ponzi schemes. The company normally operates the scam for a short time, takes in the investment money, quickly spends the money, then closes down before the scam is detected.

Anyone who surfs the Web has seen advertisements to correct credit. Many companies operate legitimate businesses. Others, however, are fronts for criminals. The business requires the consumer to make an up-front payment to straighten out her poor credit record. The consumer then discovers that the company has done nothing. The consumer cannot get her money back and the only recourse left is to complain to the police.

Another type of fraud, the vacation ripoff, starts when the consumer receives an electronic certificate congratulating the person on winning a fabulous free vacation. The winner is required, however, to pay a handling fee. Often, the vacationer ends up on a cruise ship that looks more like a tug boat. The hotel accommodations are often shabby, and the advertised ocean view, golf course, and tennis courts are miles away.

Fraud also snares businesses. For example, a business receives a sales pitch to purchase a bulk e-mail list that includes millions of addresses. The addresses are loaded into the purchaser's computer. A sales letter is designed and is attached to the bulk e-mail list. The business sends the letter to the list of addresses. The problem is that the sending of bulk e-mail (also called *spamming*) probably violates Internet service provider (ISP) agreements and can result in the ISP shutting down the business's Web site. The consequences might be even greater. Several states have laws regulating the sending of unsolicited commercial bulk e-mail. Businesses need to check their state laws before using bulk e-mail lists.

In the past, all of these scams were (and still are) committed the old-fashioned way: via the mails and telephones. The technology-savvy criminal uses the Web to snare victims. Consumers and businesses must stay alert to possible criminal scams.

Crimes Businesses Can Commit

Many people believe that a business cannot be convicted of a crime, but in reality businesses are charged with and convicted of committing crimes. Of course, a business cannot be sentenced to serve a prison sentence, but it can be fined and can lose its license.

Arthur Andersen, an accounting firm, is a good example. After Arthur Andersen was convicted of obstruction of justice for impeding the investigation into accounting failures connected with Enron, Arthur Andersen was fined $500,000 and placed on probation for five years. Because it was convicted of a felony, Arthur Anderson could no longer sign any audit documents that were required to be filed with the Securities and Exchange Commission. Further, many state licensing agencies for certified public accountants have taken steps to cancel its licenses to practice accounting. Arthur Anderson had to dissolve its certified public accounting firm and operates as a much smaller company today.

Criminal statutes do not specify corporate crimes. *Corporate crime* is a generic term that covers crimes that businesses or businesspeople commit. Many times criminals pose as businesspeople and use the business to commit crimes. During the past decades, criminal liability has expanded beyond the traditional types of crimes.

Businesses are held criminally liable for antitrust violations, such as fixing prices on goods or services, failing to issue and trade stock in accordance with securities laws, failing to meet safety standards set by statute, or failing to pay taxes. Business managers, such as officers and directors, who are in a position to prevent the crime may be prosecuted and, if found guilty, can be fined, incarcerated, or both.

Businesses are responsible criminally for the conduct of their employees. The Model Penal Code recognizes that a business can be guilty of a criminal offense through the actions of its employees if one of three situations occurs. First, the legislative purpose of the statute in question is to impose criminal liability on a business for its employees' acts when those acts are committed within the scope of employment. Second, the business has a legal statutory duty to perform a specific function, such as keeping accurate accounting records, but it fails to perform that function. Third, the criminal act is authorized, requested, dictated, performed, or recklessly tolerated by the higher levels of business management.

Businesses need to be aware of the following criminal areas: offenses under the Racketeer Influenced and Corrupt Organizations Act (RICO), extortion, violations of the Foreign Corrupt Practices Act, bankruptcy fraud, regulatory offenses, obstruction of justice, and currency offenses, including money laundering. The following sections review each of these areas.

RICO Crimes. Congress passed an amendment to the Organized Crime Control Act of 1970, known as the **Racketeer Influenced and Corrupt Organi-zations Act (RICO)**[7] of 1970. The policy behind the amendment intended to control organized crime's investments in legitimate business and to force forfei-ture of any profits resulting from criminal activity. Any offenses that violate this statute are called RICO crimes.

RICO has two major sections: criminal and civil. Many states have followed the federal example and have adopted "little RICOs" that are similar to the federal statute.

Criminal RICO. The criminal provisions in RICO require a "pattern of racketeering activity" that is defined as two or more racketeering acts within ten years of each other. Generally, racketeering means extorting money by threat or engaging in an illegal profit-making enterprise.

The statute lists more than fifty specific federal crimes that constitute racketeering acts under RICO. These racketeering acts include mail fraud, wire fraud, fraud in the sale of securities, bankruptcy fraud, extor-tion, interstate transportation of stolen property, arson, murder, gambling, robbery, and drug dealing. A con-viction of any two of these offenses within a ten-year period can lead to a conviction under RICO's crim-inal provisions. If convicted, a person is subject to a $25,000 fine, twenty years in prison, and forfeiture of all property obtained through the criminal activity to the federal government.

Civil RICO. In addition to RICO's criminal provi-sions, Congress also included civil provisions. Civil RICO lawsuits can be brought in a civil court of law by either the government or a private party, which can be a business or a person. The purpose behind RICO's civil provisions is simple: The government has insuffi-cient resources to prosecute every RICO violation. This statute allows private individuals who have been harmed to sue.

The person bringing a civil RICO action must have been harmed by a business's illegal actions. In addition to proving the harm suffered, the plaintiff must show the court evidence that the business committed two

RICO violations within the last ten years. The person does not need to show that the business was convicted in criminal court of the RICO violation. Civil RICO cases have been filed against firms such as General Motors, Merrill Lynch, American Express, and Pru-dential Insurance Company of America.

The penalties that the court can impose are the unique part of civil RICO. If the party is unable to prove the defendant's two prior RICO violations, the plaintiff receives only the amount of the damages proven. If the person is able to prove the two prior RICO acts, the person is entitled to treble damages, which equal the amount of the actual damages multi-plied by three.

The penalties that the court can impose differ for a case brought by a private party than for a case brought by the government. The government can seek penal-ties that include divestiture, dissolution, or reorganiza-tion of the business, as well as seeking an injunction (a court order to prevent an action) against future racket-eering activities. **Divestiture** means to take away from the defendant something of value, such as ille-gally gained profits or property used in the commis-sion of the crime. **Dissolution** is a drastic measure the state takes to terminate the business entity so that it no longer exists. **Reorganization** means that the busi-ness's structure or management is restructured in a manner that will prevent its future participation in such criminal acts.

Although each year the number of lawsuits filed under RICO statutes increases, the chance of a busi-ness being sued under RICO still is very slight. In 1989 less than one-half of 1 percent of the federal courts' entire caseload involved RICO allegations. Even so, many groups, including manufacturers, var-ious chambers of commerce, and certified public accountants, wanted the law changed. In the late 1980s, legislation was moving through Congress to lessen substantially RICO's impact when the scandal with the savings and loan associations became public. Congress quickly and quietly let the proposed change to the statute drop in an effort to appear strong against business crime.

In the following case, the United States Supreme Court considered whether the act required two sepa-rate persons or entities before there can be a civil RICO cause of action.

---

[7]The RICO statutes can be found at http://www4.law.cornell. edu/uscode/18/1961.shtml.

CASE 7.3

Supreme Court of the
United States, 2001
533 U.S. 158, 121 S. Ct.
2087, 150 L. Ed. 2d 198.
http://caselaw.lp.findlaw.
com/cgi-bin/getcase.pl?
court=US&navby=case&
vo l=000&invol=00-549

CEDRIC KUSHNER PROMOTIONS, LTD. v. KING

BACKGROUND AND FACTS Cedric Kushner Promotions, Ltd., is a corporation that promotes boxing matches. Cedric Kushner Promotions, Ltd., sued Don King, the president and sole shareholder of Don King Productions, a corporation, claiming that King had conducted the boxing-related affairs of Don King Productions in part through a RICO pattern, i.e., through the alleged commission of at least two instances of fraud and other RICO crimes. The district court dismissed the complaint. The court of appeals affirmed that dismissal. The case was heard by the U.S. Supreme Court.

Justice BREYER delivered the opinion of the Court.

The Racketeer Influenced and Corrupt Organizations Act (RICO or Act), 18 U.S.C. § 1961 *et seq.,* makes it "unlawful for any person employed by or associated with any enterprise . . . to conduct or participate . . . in the conduct of such enterprise's affairs" through the commission of two or more statutorily defined crimes—which RICO calls "a pattern of racketeering activity." The language suggests, and lower courts have held, that this provision foresees two separate entities, a "person" and a distinct "enterprise." This case focuses upon a person who is the president and sole shareholder of a closely-held corporation. The plaintiff claims that the president has conducted the corporation's affairs through the forbidden "pattern," though for present purposes it is conceded that, in doing so, he acted within the scope of his authority as the corporation's employee. In these circumstances, are there two entities, a "person" and a separate "enterprise"? Assuming, as we must be given the posture of this case, that the allegations in the complaint are true, we conclude that the "person" and "enterprise" here are distinct and that the RICO provision applies.

. . . .

DECISION AND REMEDY An employee who conducts the affairs of a corporation through illegal acts comes within the terms of the RICO statute. The act forbids any person to unlawfully conduct a criminal enterprise. The statute explicitly defines a person as "any individual . . . capable of holding a legal or beneficial interest in property" and defines an enterprise including "a corporation." Linguistically speaking, the employee and the corporation are different "persons," even when the employee is the corporation's sole owner.

CRITICAL THINKING: PUBLIC POLICY The RICO statute was passed in an attempt to control organized crime. Why are such companies as American Express, General Motors, Merrill Lynch, and other legitimate businesses prosecuted under the RICO statute?

Extortion. Extortion is a white-collar crime in which a public official misuses his office to force monetary or property payment from another so that the official will carry out his official duties. Often an extortionist threatens or uses actual force or induces fear. In the past, extortion was committed only by public officials, for example, a restaurant paying a health inspector to provide a passing inspection. If the restaurant did not pay, the inspector would close it down for failing the health inspection.

Extortion commonly is called a crime of **bribery**. Some states limit bribery to public officials receiving money or property for doing their official duty. Other states have broadened the definition to include both public officials and private individuals. In those states, bribery and extortion are the same. In the private sector, extortion/bribery includes kickbacks and pay-offs from an individual working for one company to an individual working for another. The payments are made for various reasons; for example, to obtain proprietary information, to cover up an inferior product, or to secure new business.

Foreign Corrupt Practices Act. Until the 1970s, bribery of foreign officials to obtain business contracts rarely, if ever, was discussed. Indeed, payments in cash or in-kind benefits to government officials for such purposes were considered normal business practice, although not necessarily legal.

A business might make cash payments to a foreign official so the business would be awarded lucrative contracts or so the foreign government would keep competitors out. In-kind benefits involve the exchange of property or services instead of cash. For example, instead of paying the official in cash, an all-expenses-paid week to attend the Super Bowl activities is provided. As a result of documented cases of U.S. businesses bribing corrupt dictators, Congress in 1977 passed the **Foreign Corrupt Practices Act (FCPA)**.

The FCPA consists of two major parts. The first part prohibits all U.S. companies and their directors, officers, shareholders, employees, or agents from offering bribes to foreign government officials for which the purpose is to obtain or retain business for the U.S. company.

The second part of the FCPA applies to all businesses registered with the Securities and Exchange Commission (SEC), even if the business operates only in the United States. It requires all registered companies to keep detailed records that "accurately and fairly" reflect the company's financial activities. These companies must have an accounting system that provides "reasonable assurance" that all transactions entered into by the company are accounted for and are legal. In fact, the second part has nothing to do with bribery or foreign corrupt practices. This part of the FCPA is directed toward accountants and financial officers because previous bribes often were concealed in business financial records.

Employees are prohibited from making false statements to accountants. No one can make false entries in any record or account. Violations of the act may result in a fine of up to $1 million and the incarceration of convicted officers or directors for a maximum of five years. Those officers and directors also can be fined up to $10,000, which cannot be paid with company funds.

Federal Sentencing Guidelines. The federal *Sentencing Guidelines for Organizations*[8] enacted in 1991 gave both profit and nonprofit businesses an incentive to police themselves. Under these guidelines, if an organization has a compliance program in place and is then found guilty of a crime, the organization will receive greatly reduced penalties compared to those that would be levied if no program were in place. A company must monitor and audit its records and accounts. The systems must be reasonably designed to detect criminal conduct by all employees.

Bankruptcy Fraud. The U.S. Constitution, Article I, Section 8, provides all persons protection from creditors through **bankruptcy**. It has two goals: (1) to forgive the overwhelming debts owed by a person and (2) to distribute the debtor's assets to the creditors.

The federal **Bankruptcy Reform Acts** of 1978 and 1994 govern bankruptcy law. This act is discussed in more detail in Chapter 14. **Bankruptcy fraud** takes place when a person involved in bankruptcy misleads the bankruptcy court. The following are examples of white-collar crimes that can be perpetrated during a bankruptcy proceeding.

False Claims of Creditors. Creditors are required by the bankruptcy law to file their individual claims against a debtor who is in bankruptcy proceedings. A creditor who files a false claim commits a crime. For example, A is going into bankruptcy. A's friend, B, makes an agreement with A that she will file a false claim in bankruptcy court against A's assets. The claim is for payment for engineering work that was never done. When B is successfully paid, she returns the money to A. Both A and B have committed federal bankruptcy fraud.

Transfer or Concealment of Property. Prior to bankruptcy proceedings, a debtor has an incentive to transfer assets to favored parties before or after the petition filing for bankruptcy. For example, a company-

---

[8]Information on the federal *Sentencing Guidelines for Organizations* can be found at http://www.corporatecompliance.com/ and at http://www.ussc.gov.

owned automobile worth $15,000 can be sold at a bargain price of $1,000 to a trusted friend or relative.

Closely related to the crime of fraudulent transfer of property is fraudulent concealment of property. The number of ways in which debtors fraudulently, but cleverly, have concealed assets would require several books to outline.

Scam Bankruptcies. In a **scam bankruptcy**, perpetrators swindle creditors by purchasing goods in advance while planning a bankruptcy proceeding. The perpetrators purchase a legitimate business that sells highly movable goods, such as jewelry or electronic home entertainment equipment. *Movable goods*, as the term is used here, refers to personal property that can be sold easily but cannot be traced easily. The scam begins when the swindlers pose as new owners of a business and purchase numerous items on credit from a seller. The swindlers pay off initial debts quickly.

This activity continues until the creditors are willing to offer larger and larger amounts of credit to the new owners. Finally, the swindlers order a very large amount of merchandise on credit. They sell the goods immediately at whatever price is necessary to unload the merchandise quickly for cash. Then the swindlers close down the business and disappear. Of

LEGAL HIGHLIGHT

Cybercrime

Cybercrime refers to crimes committed using high technology, for instance, a computer with a modem connected to the Internet. Add a cellular telephone and a cryptographic manual and the criminal has all the necessary tools. Online crimes cost the 40 million Internet users around $350 million per year. Here are some examples.

1. *White-Collar Crime* Nearly every white-collar crime can be committed using technology. Hackers can break into computers holding sensitive information, such as a bank computer, change the codes, and transfer money to the hacker's bank account. They can change criminal files located on police computers. It is estimated, however, that about 80 to 85 percent of computer crime losses are committed by insiders. Most businesses suffer losses not to hackers, but to disloyal employees.

2. *Espionage* Spies can work from the comfort of their computer rooms. No one has to break into the business office to photograph strategic plans of the company. Business research materials and passwords are available in computer files. With the correct keystrokes and the right software, a business spy can break into the business victim's computer system. In a nanosecond, the files are copied and the thief logs off. Or the thief can leave a program on the computer that logs everything the computer does. The thief then reenters the computer later to check it.

3. *Theft* Analog cellular telephones leave an electronic fingerprint when used. Thieves station themselves near airports or other busy areas to capture those fingerprints by the hundreds and immediately sell the numbers. The result is that the cellular telephone user receives a bill from the telephone company that can run to hundreds of thousands of dollars. Thieves can also break into a business telephone system, steal its long-distance access code, and, again, when the bill arrives it might document hundreds of thousands of dollars worth of telephone calls that have been made illegally.

These crimes are but a few that take advantage of high-end technology. Businesses need to install a security system to keep hackers out and to monitor their employees. Passwords and codes need to be treated as top secret. Sloppy security measures allow the criminal access to the businesses' confidential and secret information.

For more information, see the National Fraud Information Center Web site located at **http://www. fraud .org** and the Better Business Bureau Web site at **http://www.bbb.org**.

course, the business is bankrupt. The amount that those creditors will recover typically is very small and the scam operators are nowhere to be found.

Regulatory Offenses. Congress has created administrative agencies that regulate businesses, such as the Occupational Safety and Health Administration, the Environmental Protection Agency, the Securities and Exchange Commission, and the Food and Drug Administration. These agencies were discussed in detail in Chapter 6.

Administrative agencies enforce statutes that have civil provisions. In the past decade, more violators have been assessed civil and administrative penalties than prosecuted criminally under the provisions of some statutes. In an administrative hearing, the burden of proof is less, no right to a jury exists, and settlements can be reached more easily. At the same time, administrative penalties may amount to more than $1 million a day per violation.

If an agency finds that a business has committed egregious criminal acts, the agency may refer the case to the Department of Justice for prosecution. The Department of Justice is the federal agency that has criminal jurisdiction. Administrative agencies do not have the authority to prosecute criminal cases.[9]

Obstruction of Justice. Executives may be prosecuted for destroying or hiding business records, such as e-mails, required under a subpoena by a grand jury, a court, or an investigative agency. The crime of obstruction of justice is independent of any other criminal violation. Even if a business is guilty of no other criminal act, it can be found guilty of obstruction of justice.

Currency Offenses. Criminals hide their illegally gained money by using schemes involving currency. Many types of crimes involve the hiding or misuse of currency, ranging from the violent world of narcotics trafficking to the crime of income tax evasion. To make it harder for criminals to deal in currency, Congress passed two separate laws; one statute is aimed at money laundering and the second makes currency reporting mandatory. The following sections describe these two laws.

---

[9]The Department of Defense does have criminal jurisdiction over military service members, but it is beyond the subject matter of this book on the legal environment of business.

Money Laundering. Criminals can use legitimate businesses to make it appear that money gained from illegal activities was earned through legal business activities. Criminals operate small businesses that generate cash flow, such as fast-food restaurants or dry cleaners. Such an operation can conduct business, but in reality serves as a front for the deposit of large amounts of cash through business accounts. This is one type of money laundering.

Congress made money laundering a crime by passing the **Money Laundering Control Act.** The act includes not only cash transactions, but also wire transfers of money, including transactions over the Internet.

Currency Transaction Report. A federal statute requires that financial institutions and businesses file a **Currency Transaction Report (CTR)** with the Internal Revenue Service under two different circumstances. First, a bank is required to file a CTR when it suspects criminal activity by a customer who is involved in a financial transaction of $1,000 or more. For example, if a customer does not appear to have a business and makes only cash deposits into his account, the bank may suspect criminal activity.

Second, when a single transaction or a series of related transactions of cash amount to more than $10,000, the merchant or financial institution must file a CTR. Cash is broadly defined by the statute to include currency, cashier's checks, bank drafts, traveler's checks, and money orders. Regular checks are not included in this area because they are in the banking system, where suspected illegal transactions can be documented.

A person purchases a house for $100,000 and pays for it with eleven cashier's checks, each made out in the amount of $9,990.90. The real estate broker must file the CTR, because the series of transactions contributed to one purchase, even though no single cashier's check was $10,000 or more. The act covers real estate brokers, insurance brokers, stock brokers, and all types of retailers, such as automobile, truck, airplane, and motorcycle dealers; boat dealers; jewelers; antique dealers; home entertainment businesses; and travel agents, to name a few.

USA Patriot Act

As a result of the terrorist attacks that brought down the twin World Trade towers in New York City, the damage inflicted on the Pentagon, and the loss of an aircraft in a field in Pennsylvania, with the attendant loss of thousands of lives on September 11, 2001, the USA Patriot Act was passed by Congress. The act amended provisions of various federal statutes and created legislation in new areas.

The act expanded what information may be obtained in surveillance and investigative situations by law enforcement agencies. For example, amendments to the Electronic Communications Privacy Act now cover normal telephone conversations. To listen in on these communications, all the government must certify in the application for a search warrant is that the "information likely to be obtained by such installation and use is relevant to an ongoing criminal investigation." A judge does not have any discretion to decide whether this assertion is based on probable cause. Prior to the Patriot Act, the government had to establish before a judge that based on the facts probable cause existed that a crime had or would be committed. Many object to parts of the act as unconstitutional.

The statute provides for a greater sharing of information among law enforcement agencies. The penalties for terrorism are increased and the definition of a terrorist act is broadened to include the harboring of a terrorist. The act strengthens laws concerning illegal aliens and provides more authority to the agencies charged with protection of the nation's borders.

Defenses

The prosecutor bears the burden of proving to a jury (or judge, if both the prosecutor and the defense agree to no jury) that the accused is guilty beyond a reasonable doubt. The accused, however, has no responsibility to put on a defense; the government must respect the protection that the Constitution guarantees every defendant. For example, the government cannot torture a confession from a person because the Fifth Amendment protects people from being forced to testify against themselves. The constitutional protections are found in the Fourth, Fifth, Sixth, and Eighth Amendments.

Other defenses exist that a person or business may use if accused of a criminal act. Some of these are of historical origin and others have been created by statute.

Double Jeopardy

The Fifth Amendment to the U.S. Constitution provides that: "[N]or shall any person be subject for the same offense to be twice put in jeopardy of life or limb." This clause prevents both more than one prosecution and more than one punishment for the same offense by the same level of government.

A problem occurs, however, when different crimes are committed at the same time. For example, a person holds up a store with a gun. In doing so, the criminal forces the clerk to move to the other side of the store and then takes $1,000 from the cash register. These simple facts involve several crimes: armed robbery, grand theft, assault with a deadly weapon, and even possibly kidnapping. The kidnapping occurred when the clerk was forced to move without consent.

To determine whether a single act constitutes a violation of more than one distinct statutory provision, the court must determine whether each provision requires separate proof of wrongdoing. For example, in the previous situation grand theft is established by the taking of $1,000, whereas assault with a deadly weapon is proven through the use of a gun.

The Constitution was designed to prevent double jeopardy, that is, the defendant's being tried twice by the same level of government. A person, however, can be convicted in both state and federal court for the same wrongful conduct. A person who commits a robbery at a national bank, for example, may be prosecuted in both federal and state courts.

Double jeopardy requires the case to have reached a final conclusion. A case is not final, for example, if it is appealed to higher courts or if the jury could not reach a verdict. Such a jury is referred to as a *hung jury*.

In the following case, the United States Supreme Court was confronted with the problem of whether double jeopardy should apply when property had been forfeited to the government under a civil procedure. The government had seized the defendant's property under civil law and prosecuted him for his conduct under criminal law.

CASE 7.4

Supreme Court of the
United States, 1996
518 U.S 267, 116 S. Ct.
2135, 135 L. Ed. 2d 549
http://supct.law.cornell.
edu

UNITED STATES v. URSERY

BACKGROUND AND FACTS Michigan police found marijuana growing adjacent to
Guy Ursery's house and then discovered marijuana seeds, stems, stalks, and a growlight
in his house. The U.S. government instituted civil forfeiture proceedings against the
house, alleging that the property was subject to forfeiture because it had been used for
several years to facilitate the unlawful processing and distribution of a controlled substance (marijuana).

Ursery ultimately paid the United States $13,250 to settle the forfeiture claim in full.
Shortly before the settlement was completed, Ursery was indicted for manufacturing
marijuana. A jury found him guilty, and he was sentenced to sixty-three months in
prison. He appealed his conviction, alleging that the forfeiture of his house and the conviction violated his Fifth Amendment rights. The Sixth Court of Appeals reversed his
conviction, holding that it violated the double jeopardy clause of the Fifth Amendment.

Chief Justice REHNQUIST delivered the opinion of the Court.

. . . .

. . . First, in light of our [previous] decisions . . . and the long tradition of federal statutes
providing for a forfeiture proceeding following a criminal prosecution, it is absolutely
clear that *in rem* civil forfeiture has not historically been regarded as punishment, as we
have understood that term under the Double Jeopardy Clause. Second, there is no
requirement in the statutes that we currently review that the Government demonstrate
scienter in order to establish that the property is subject to forfeiture; indeed, the property may be subject to forfeiture even if no party files a claim to it and the Government
never shows any connection between the property and a particular person. Though
both [statutes] contain an "innocent owner" exception, we do not think that such a
provision, without more indication of an intent to punish, is relevant to the question
whether a statute is punitive under the Double Jeopardy Clause. Third, though both
statutes may fairly be said to serve the purpose of deterrence, we long have held that
this purpose may serve civil as well as criminal goals. Finally, though both statutes are
tied to criminal activity, . . . this fact is insufficient to render the statutes punitive. It is
well settled that "Congress may impose both a criminal and a civil sanction in respect to
the same act or omission." By itself, the fact that a forfeiture statute has some connection
to a criminal violation is far from the "clearest proof" necessary to show that a proceeding is criminal. We hold that these *in rem* civil forfeitures are neither "punishment"
nor criminal for purposes of the Double Jeopardy Clause.

DECISION AND REMEDY The United States Supreme Court found that the government has the authority to confiscate property under the civil law and to criminally prosecute the wrongdoer. These two government actions do not violate the Fifth
Amendment's guarantee against double jeopardy.

CRITICAL THINKING: MANAGEMENT ISSUE Although this case does not involve
a business, the principle is applicable to business situations. If a person is hired who
later is caught selling marijuana from a company vehicle or on the business property,
what are the potential outcomes? Discuss how a business can control its employees'
conduct to protect company property from forfeiture.

Self-Defense

The **self-defense** doctrine gives a person the absolute right to defend his person. People may use deadly force if they are afraid for their own lives or those of another. The fear must be based on a reasonable belief that death or great physical harm is imminent if they do not use force.

Deadly force may not be used, however, except in response to the threat of deadly force. For example, if a person is involved in a fight in which both parties are of equal physical condition, neither party has a right to use a weapon on the other. A person also cannot use deadly force in protecting her property except when confronted with threat of deadly force. In other words, a person has no right to shoot another who is, for example, siphoning gas from her vehicle.

Entrapment

On occasion, the police or other government agencies have actively encouraged a defendant to participate in a criminal act. This encouragement is referred to as *entrapment*. For an accused to use this defense, he must fully admit to committing the crime. The jury must decide if the government agent's active pressures or suggestions precipitated the crime or if the crime would have occurred anyway. In other words, the entrapment occurs if the defendant was not predisposed to committing the crime.

Incapacity

One of the most common defenses is that a defendant lacks the mental ability to be held responsible for her actions. This defense is defined differently from one state to another. Most states excuse criminal conduct if the defendant lacks the capacity to differentiate between right and wrong.

A few states follow the irresistible-impulse theory, which means that, in spite of recognizing the wrongness of an act, the defendant could not control his actions.

Many states have adopted statutes that allow a jury to find a person mentally incompetent. Under these statutes the defendant is placed in a mental hospital, but on recovery must serve the full sentence for the criminal act.

In the case of John Hinkley, who attempted to assassinate President Ronald Reagan, the law at that time imposed on the government the burden of proving that Hinkley was sane. Hinkley's long history of mental illness prevented the government from meeting that burden, so Hinkley was found not guilty. He was hospitalized, however, for his mental condition. The law was changed so that the government no longer has to prove that the defendant is sane. A defendant may defend herself by proving that she is insane.

Intoxication

Intoxication involves the voluntary consumption of either alcohol or drugs, legal or illegal. Although a person cannot drink two beers, commit a crime, and then claim that his intoxication caused the crime, the very heavy consumption of either drugs or alcohol may serve as a defense for a crime that requires *mens rea*. For example, a person consumes a quart of whiskey and then picks a fight with and kills another person. Can intoxication be used as a defense?

Intoxication may be a defense against a first-degree murder charge, but it probably would be an insufficient defense for manslaughter. First-degree murder requires intent to take another person's life. Manslaughter requires reckless conduct on the part of a person that results in the death of another. The question would be whether the person was so intoxicated that she or he could not form the intent.

Punishment for Criminal Activity

Congress and state legislatures have the authority to specify the type of conduct that is criminal and determine the punishment for its violation. Of course, criminal statutes cannot violate the U.S. Constitution. Once a person or business entity has been convicted, federal judges must follow the sentencing guidelines, as discussed previously in this chapter.[10]

The Eighth Amendment to the Constitution states that "excessive bail shall not be required, nor excessive fines imposed, nor cruel and unusual punishments inflicted." This amendment applies both to criminal actions and forfeiture situations.

Excluding capital cases, very few cases have found criminal punishment to be cruel and unusual. Successful challenges have been exceedingly rare. In one

---

[10]You may want to review what the penalties are for violating federal criminal law. Go to the following site for this information: http://www.ussc.gov/guidelin.htm.

case, the U.S. Supreme Court did reverse the sentence which involved a person who was found guilty of falsifying a public document. He was sentenced to a twelve-year term, required to wear a chain at the ankle and wrist at all times, subjected to hard and painful labor, and not allowed assistance or contact with any friends or relatives. The Court found this to be cruel and unusual punishment. The U.S. Supreme Court has held that state legislatures have the responsibility of establishing the length of sentences. The length of sentence should not be left to the courts as seen in the following case.

CASE 7.5

United States Supreme Court, 2003
538 U.S. ___, 123 S. Ct.1179, 155 L. Ed. 2d 108
http://laws.findlaw.com/us/000/01-6978.html

EWING v. CALIFORNIA

BACKGROUND AND FACTS On parole from a nine-year prison term, Gary Ewing walked into the pro shop of the El Segundo Golf Course in Los Angeles County on March 12, 2000. He walked out with three golf clubs, priced at $399 apiece, concealed in his pants leg. Ewing was arrested in the parking lot.

Ewing was no stranger to the criminal justice system. In 1984, at the age of twenty-two, he pleaded guilty to theft. In 1988, he was convicted of felony grand theft auto. After Ewing completed probation, however, the sentencing court reduced the crime to a misdemeanor, permitted Ewing to withdraw his guilty plea, and dismissed the case. In 1990, he was convicted of petty theft with a prior conviction. In 1992, Ewing was convicted of battery. One month later, he was convicted of a second theft.

In January 1993, he was convicted of burglary. In February 1993, he was convicted of possessing drug paraphernalia. In July 1993, he was convicted of appropriating lost property. In September 1993, he was convicted of unlawfully possessing a firearm and trespassing. In October and November 1993, Ewing committed three burglaries and one robbery at a Long Beach, California, apartment complex over a five-week period. On another occasion, Ewing accosted a victim in the mail room of the apartment complex. Ewing claimed to have a gun and ordered the victim to hand over his wallet. When the victim resisted, Ewing produced a knife and forced the victim back to the apartment itself. On December 9, 1993, Ewing was arrested on the premises of the apartment complex for trespassing and lying to a police officer. The knife used in the robbery and a glass cocaine pipe were later found in the back seat of the patrol car used to transport Ewing to the police station. A jury convicted Ewing of first-degree robbery and three counts of residential burglary. Sentenced to nine years and eight months in prison, Ewing was paroled in 1999.

Ten months after his release, Ewing stole the golf clubs at issue in this case. He was convicted of one count of felony grand theft of personal property in excess of $400. As required by the three strikes law, the trial court later found that Ewing had been convicted previously of four serious or violent felonies for the three burglaries and the robbery in the Long Beach apartment complex. In California, if a person is convicted of three serious or violent felonies, the three strikes rule becomes effective. Ewing was sentenced to twenty-five years to life under this statute. The California Supreme Court refused to hear the case and Ewing brought the case to the U.S. Supreme Court.

Justice O'CONNOR delivered the opinion of the Court

. . . .

Our traditional deference to legislative policy choices finds a corollary in the principle that the Constitution "does not mandate adoption of any one penological theory." A sentence can have a variety of justifications, such as incapacitation, deterrence, retribution, or rehabilitation. Some or all of these justifications may play a role in a State's sentencing scheme. Selecting the sentencing rationales is generally a policy choice to be made by state legislatures, not federal courts.

When the California Legislature enacted the three strikes law, it made a judgment that protecting the public safety requires incapacitating criminals who have already been convicted of at least one serious or violent crime. Nothing in the Eighth Amendment prohibits California from making that choice. To the contrary, our cases establish that "States have a valid interest in deterring and segregating habitual criminals." . . . [T]he constitutionality of the practice of inflicting severer criminal penalties upon habitual offenders is no longer open to serious challenge.

. . . .

California's justification is no pretext. Recidivism is a serious public safety concern in California and throughout the Nation. According to a recent report, approximately 67 percent of former inmates released from state prisons were charged with at least one "serious" new crime within three years of their release. In particular, released property offenders like Ewing had higher recidivism rates than those released after committing violent, drug, or public-order offenses. Approximately 73 percent of the property offenders released in 1994 were arrested again within three years, compared to approximately 61 percent of the violent offenders, 62 percent of the public-order offenders, and 66 percent of the drug offenders.

In 1996, when the *Sacramento Bee* studied 233 three strikes offenders in California, it found that they had an aggregate of 1,165 prior felony convictions, an average of 5 apiece. The prior convictions included 322 robberies and 262 burglaries. About 84 percent of the 233 three strikes offenders had been convicted of at least one violent crime. In all, they were responsible for 17 homicides, 7 attempted slayings, and 91 sexual assaults and child molestations. . . . The *Sacramento Bee* concluded, based on its investigation, that "[i]n the vast majority of the cases, regardless of the third strike, the [three strikes] law is snaring [the] long-term habitual offenders with multiple felony convictions . . . ."

The State's interest in deterring crime also lends some support to the three strikes law. We have long viewed both incapacitation and deterrence as rationales for recidivism statutes.

. . . .

DECISION AND REMEDY The Court held that Ewing's sentence of twenty-five years to life in prison, imposed for the offense of felony grand theft under the three strikes law, was not grossly disproportionate and therefore does not violate the Eighth Amendment's prohibition on cruel and unusual punishments.

CRITICAL THINKING: PUBLIC POLICY The taxpayers must pay annually between $16,000 and $35,000 to imprison one person. The amount taxpayers spend annually per student in colleges and universities ranges from $1,000 to $5,000. What arguments can be made to keep the current system of three strikes rule in criminal cases and what arguments can be made against the rule?

Permanent War-Crimes Court

The first permanent war-crimes court was established in 2003. It will hear cases in The Hague, Netherlands. Eighteen judges sit on this court. Eighty-nine countries have backed the establishment of this court.

For centuries, the world has seen unspeakable crimes with victims numbering in millions. Responding to this, in 1998 the Rome Treaty was created, which established this court as the International Criminal Court. This treaty was ratified by the United States during President William Clinton's administration.

But when the court met for the first time, the United States was absent. This absence was a result of September 11, 2001, attacks, the war in Afghanistan, and the war in Iraq, plus other potential conflicts. Because of these events, the United States is not involved with the court.

International Consideration

The World Community versus International Criminals

International criminal law as a definitive body of law is very limited in scope, but it is a growing area. In 1951, the United Nations drafted a proposal for an international criminal court that has been revised in light of international narcotics trade and terrorism. Political considerations, constitutional prohibitions, and divergent cultural backgrounds have kept the proposal in various stages of draft form.

The U.N. Committee on Crime Prevention and Control has adopted various resolutions, including recommendations that the United Nations conduct criminal justice surveys more often, promote technical cooperation in crime prevention and criminal justice, redress the victims of crime and human rights violations, and address illicit drug production and trafficking. It has drafted five model treaties covering prevention of crimes that infringe on cultural heritage, extradition, mutual assistance, and transfer of supervision of foreign offenders.

The United Nations has several agencies working in the area of illicit drugs. The Commission on Narcotic Drugs is responsible for placing drafts and resolutions concerning illicit drugs before the U.N. General Assembly. The U.N. Division of Narcotic Drugs (DND) provides practical, technical, and scientific assistance to member states. It also operates the Drug Abuse Assessment System, which enables the DND to analyze drug abuse data at national, regional, and international levels and to facilitate worldwide cooperation.

The International Narcotics Control Board assesses the adverse national security aspects of drug trafficking. It also studies the direct threat to political institutions and economies from the illicit production, trafficking, and abuse of drugs and escalating drug-related violence.

Economic crime is a relatively new category of crime, and the policies of various nations on this topic remain divergent thus far. The United States was the first country to define antitrust activities, such as monopolies or unfair competition, as both a criminal and a civil offense. Over the decades many other countries have come to recognize antitrust activities as criminal acts, but still other nations officially encourage businesses to participate in antitrust activities. Even the United States now allows some forms of antitrust activities by businesses when they have dealings overseas.

Extradition is the delivery of an accused or convicted person to the country in which the crime allegedly occurred. It has been a political topic for centuries. For extradition to be required, a treaty outlining the extradition rules must exist between the two countries involved. Often these treaties provide that a person cannot be executed if extradited or that a person cannot be extradited if accused of a political crime. What constitutes a political crime, however, is a matter of definition. Defining what is a domestic political crime is difficult for a country internally, let alone for two nations striving to reach an agreement on extradition rules.

PRACTICAL TIPS

Bad Checks

All states have a statute that makes it a crime to write a check against a closed account or one with insufficient funds. Many times these crimes are classified as a felony, and a defendant, if convicted, is sentenced to prison. Each year, businesses lose millions of dollars because of bad checks. A business can reduce its losses by preparing a checklist such as the following one.

Checklist

✔ *Bad Checks* Most bad checks are written on new accounts. If the printed number on the check's upper right-hand corner is low or handwritten, this could signal that the check might not be good.

✔ *Postdated Checks* A business should never accept a postdated check, even though a postdated check is legal—unless it can be shown that the check writer had no intention of making the check good on that date. To convict a person of writing bad checks requires proof that the defendant, at the time of giving the check, intended to defraud the business. When a merchant accepts a postdated check, she acknowledges that currently the account lacks sufficient funds to cover the check. In effect, the merchant grants credit by accepting a postdated check. The check cannot be dishonored until the date on the check, which makes it very difficult to prove fraudulent intent at the time that the check was written.

✔ *Reviewing the Check* The employee of a business always should look closely at a check to confirm that the written and numerical amounts match. The person writing the check may write a number different from the figure on a check. If the figures do not match, a bank should not honor the check and should instead return it to the business. Check processors, however, review hundreds of checks an hour and often look only at the numbers; they may not take time to verify that the words written out match. Generally, the figure written in words is the amount legally posted to the bank account.

✔ *Identification* Merchants should require government-issued identification with a picture, such as a driver's license, for identification of the check writer. Merchants also should record the identifying driver's license number on the check. Both of these actions will help if a trial results.

✔ *Forged Checks* Forged checks may be spotted in several ways. First, each geographic area has a specific two-digit Federal Reserve number that appears twice on the check: as the first two digits of the nine-digit series at the bottom and as the denominator of the fraction at the upper right. If these are inconsistent, the check is not drawn on a bank. A businessperson should know the Federal Reserve number for his area. Second, the nine-digit number has a special magnetic ink that has a dull finish. Third, checks should have one perforated edge. Most forgers use a regular paper cutter that leaves all four sides of the check smooth.

✔ *No Threats* A businessperson should never threaten the check writer with criminal prosecution after receiving a bad check. Making such a threat could result in the merchant's being charged with extortion. The crook might go free and the businessperson might end up serving time! If the businessperson believes that a crime has taken place, she should report it to the police or to the county or district attorney's office.

Chapter Summary

Criminal law affects the business community in many ways. An act may constitute both a criminal and a civil wrong. When criminal conduct occurs, society is harmed. All criminal actions are brought in the name of the government, for example, *United States of America v. John Begone.* Many criminal acts also give rise to a civil action by the injured party.

Crimes may be classified as felonies, misdemeanors,

and petty offenses. A person convicted of a felony may serve a sentence of one year or more in a state or federal prison, be fined, or be put to death. A person convicted of a misdemeanor may serve less than one year in a local jail, be fined, or both. If convicted of a petty offense, a person usually is fined.

When a person is charged with a crime, the government must prove the defendant guilty beyond a reasonable doubt. The Constitution guarantees protection for individuals and businesses accused of crimes.

Historically, most crimes require both criminal intent (*mens rea*) and criminal conduct (*actus reus*). Many crimes require only criminal conduct and not criminal intent. This requirement allows businesses incapable of criminal "intent" to be convicted of crimes. Attempts and conspiracies might occur prior to a planned criminal act. Even if a crime is not committed, people can be charged with an attempt to commit the crime or with engaging in a conspiracy with another for the purpose of committing the crime.

Some important crimes that affect business are offenses against property, such as burglary, larceny, robbery, and arson. White-collar crimes are nonviolent offenses involving corruption, deceit, or breach of trust committed by individuals. A few types of white-collar crimes include receiving stolen goods, forgery, obtaining money or goods by false pretenses, embezzlement, use of the mails to defraud, and computer crimes.

Businesses also can commit crimes. More types of business actions may be regarded as criminal because of the expanding definition of criminal acts. Businesses are subject to the Racketeer Influenced and Corrupt Organizations Act (RICO), extortion, the Foreign Corrupt Practices Act (FCPA), bankruptcy fraud, regulatory offenses, obstruction of justice, and currency offenses including money laundering.

RICO has both criminal and civil provisions. A business that has committed more than two acts of racketeering in ten years may be prosecuted criminally and may be liable for treble damages to the injured party in a civil lawsuit. Racketeering acts involve more than fifty federal statutes and consist of criminal activity such as mail fraud, wire fraud, fraud in the sale of securities, bankruptcy fraud, extortion, interstate transportation of stolen property, arson, murder, gambling, and robbery.

The FCPA consists of two parts. The first part forbids bribe payments to foreign officials. The second part requires businesses to establish and maintain accounting procedures.

Bankruptcy fraud is a crime in which a business perpetuates a fraud on a federal bankruptcy court. These acts typically consist of creditors' false claims, property transfer or concealment, and scam bankruptcy.

Regulatory offenses are committed by businesses when they violate regulatory statutes. Even though some offenses are civil, an administrative agency can impose large fines. Other offenses are criminal but must be prosecuted by the Department of Justice.

Obstruction of justice means interference with court procedures. These offenses usually include business record destruction or concealment in violation of court orders.

Using the World Wide Web

A number of sites are available to the public to look at the activities of law enforcement. For *Web Activities*, links to Web sites mentioned in the chapter, and additional Web sites that relate to the chapter topics, go to **http://bohlman.westbuslaw.com**, click on "Internet Applications," and select Chapter 7.

Web Activities

Go to **http://bohlman.westbuslaw.com**, click on "Internet Applications," and select Chapter 7.
7–1 Searches
7–2 Arrests

Key Terms

actus reus	bankruptcy fraud	burglary	Device and Computer
arson	Bankruptcy Reform Acts	computer crime	Fraud and Abuse Act
attempt	bill of information	conspiracy	Currency Transaction
bankruptcy	bribery	Counterfeit Access	Report (CTR)

dissolution
divestiture
Electronic Communica-
   tions Privacy Act
embezzlement
extortion
extradition
False Statement Act
felony
Foreign Corrupt
   Practices Act (FCPA)
forgery

Identity Theft and
   Assumption
   Deterrence Act
indictment
Information Infrastruc-
   ture Protection Act
larceny
mens rea
misapplication of trust
   funds
misdemeanor
Money Laundering

Control Act
obtaining goods or
   money by false
   pretenses
overt act
petty offense
probable cause
Racketeer Influenced
   and Corrupt Organi-
   zations Act (RICO)
receiving stolen goods
reorganization

robbery
scam bankruptcy
self-defense
Trademark Counter-
   feiting Act
use of the mails to
   defraud
white-collar crime

Questions and Case Problems

7–1 Procedure Civil trials and criminal trials follow essentially the same format. There are, however, several important differences between them. In criminal trials, the defendant must be proved guilty beyond a reasonable doubt, whereas in civil trials, the defendant need only be proved guilty by a preponderance of the evidence. Explain possible reasons for this difference.

7–2 Crime Types The following situations are similar (all involve the theft of Jean's television set), yet three different crimes are described. Identify the three crimes and explain their differences.

a. While passing Jean's house one night, Sam sees a portable television set left unattended on Jean's lawn. Sam takes the television set, carries it home, and tells everyone that he owns it.

b. While passing Jean's house one night, Sam sees Jean outside with a portable television set. Holding Jean at gunpoint, Sam forces her to give up the set. He then runs away with it.

c. While passing Jean's house one night, Sam sees a portable television set in a window. Sam breaks the front door lock, enters, and leaves with the set.

7–3 RICO Compare civil RICO with criminal RICO.

7–4 Criminal Knowledge Lana Acty formed Posters 'N' Things, Ltd., which operated a general merchandise outlet called World Wide Imports. Based on information that World Wide Imports was selling drug paraphernalia, the police obtained a search warrant; executed it on the petitioner's business premises; and seized various items, including pipes, bongs, scales, roach clips, and drug diluents. They also seized catalogs

and advertisements describing products sold by the petitioner. The advertisements offered products such as "Coke Kits," "Free Base Kits," and diluents sold under the names "PseudoCaine" and "Procaine." Among the charges against Acty was that she violated the Mail Order Drug Paraphernalia Act. Acty argued that the statute was vague as to the definition of drug paraphernalia and that the act required specific intent, in other words, the prosecutors had to prove that Acty specifically knew that the products would be used for illegal drug activity by the individual purchasers. Convicted and sentenced to nine years in prison, she appealed her case, which affirmed the convictions. Did the government have to prove that Acty knew her products would be used for drugs? Why or why not? Explain your answer. [*Posters 'N' Things v. United States,* 511 U.S. 513, 114 S. Ct. 1747, 128 L. Ed. 2d 539 (1994) http://supct.law.cornell.edu]

7–5 Civil RICO The plaintiff, Sedima, and the defendant, Imrex, entered into a joint-venture agreement in which Imrex would provide electronic components to Sedima. They were to split the net proceeds when Sedima sold the product. Although $8 million in orders were processed, Sedima became convinced that Imrex was inflating the bills and cheating Sedima out of profits. Sedima filed a lawsuit alleging RICO claims based on mail and wire fraud, because Imrex allegedly had used the mails and wires to overbill Sedima. Imrex's defense was that it had never been criminally convicted of a RICO violation. Must Sedima prove that Imrex was or could have been criminally prosecuted in order to recover civil damages under RICO? Explain. [*Sedima S.P.R.L. v. Imrex Co.,* 473 U.S. 479, 105 S. Ct. 3275, 87 L. Ed. 2d 346 (1985)]

7–6 Arson Joseph Russello committed arson on a building that he owned. Prior to being charged and convicted, he collected the insurance on the building. What type of crime has Russello committed under these circumstances? Explain. [*Russello v. United States*, 464 U.S. 16, 104 S. Ct. 296, 78 L. Ed. 2d 17 (1983)]

7–7 Arson Faulknor was a seaman on the ship *Zemindar*. One night, while on duty, Faulknor went in search of the rum that he knew the ship was carrying. He found it and opened one of the kegs. Because he was holding a match at the time, he inadvertently ignited the rum and set fire to the ship. At the trial, it was determined that even though he had not intended to set fire to the rum, he had been engaged in the unlawful act of stealing it. Does Faulknor's theft of the rum make him criminally liable for setting fire to the ship? Explain. [*Regina v. Faulknor*, 13 Cox Crim. Cas. 550 (Ireland 1877)]

7–8 Forfeiture John Bennis was arrested after the police observed him engaged in a sexual act with a prostitute in his automobile in Detroit, Michigan. He was convicted of gross indecency. The state of Michigan brought a civil action against John and his wife Tina, who jointly owned the automobile, to have it declared a public nuisance and forfeited to the state. Tina objected because she did not know of her husband's activities and asserted that if the automobile was forfeited she was entitled to one-half of its value. The automobile was an eleven-year-old sedan purchased by the Bennises for

$600. Who prevails and why? [*Bennis v. Michigan*, 526 U.S. 442, 116 S. Ct. 994, 134 L. Ed. 2d 68 (1996)]

7–9 Constitutional Rights Rushton's twelve-year-old neighbor notified the sheriff's office that Rushton had been growing marijuana at his house. The sheriff had time to obtain a search warrant; however, he did not obtain it because of overtime costs to pay his deputies to prepare and review the warrant application and to find the county attorney or justice of the peace, neither of whom were readily available that night. After Rushton went to bed, the sheriff and four deputies knocked at the door. Rushton's wife admitted them into the home. Without giving the *Miranda* warnings, a deputy interrogated Rushton, who implied that he was growing marijuana. He asked if he needed a lawyer, but his question was not answered. The sheriff obtained Rushton's signature on a search consent form. Based on the consent form, the officers conducted the search and seized eighteen plants and other material. Was it necessary for the sheriff to give the *Miranda* rights in order to use Rushton's statements against him in a criminal trial? Explain. [*State v. Rushton*, 870 P.2d 1355 (Mont. 1994)]

7–10 Internet In the aftermath of Enron and other high-profile corporate fraud cases, the U.S. Department of Justice (DOJ) created the Corporate Fraud Hotline. Why was the hotline established? What are the initiatives of the Corporate Fraud Hotline? Go to **http://www.usdoj.gov** and, using the search function, type in "corporate fraud hotline."

Unit 2

Business and Private Law

Chapter 8

Torts

I am charmed with many points of the Turkish law; when proved the authors of any notorious falsehood, they are burned on the forehead with a hot iron.

**Lady Mary Wortley Montagu, 1689–1762
English writer**

Chapter Outline

Ethical Consideration

Media's Responsibility When Reporting about Families of Public Figures

Senator Big Success had a teenage son, Small Success. The son, who otherwise had a spotless record, recently was arrested for shoplifting some small items from a grocery store. When he was arrested, Small Success had ample money in his wallet to pay for the items. He told the police that he had come into the store without the intent to steal. He said that he was tired of the pressure to live up to the many expectations placed on him because of his father's prominence and that, while in the store, he had a sudden whim to do something "bad." The items he took were of an insignificant monetary value. The city attorney decided not to prosecute out of respect for the senator and because the store was paid in full for the items.

You are the editor of the *Morning Glory*, the local newspaper. One of your reporters wants to write up this story focusing on the failure of celebrities and politicians to take the time to be good parents who teach their children right from wrong. Although you have no problem running stories about Senator Big Success, who is a public figure, you consider the fairness of putting such a public spotlight on the actions of his young son. In addition, by bringing up the city attorney's decision not to prosecute, the story might force the prosecution of Small Success, resulting in negative publicity and a blemish on his record. Do you let your reporter go ahead with the story or assign her to another project? Use the ethical model presented in Chapter 2 and reprinted on the inside front cover to develop your answer.

Introduction

Tort is a French word for "wrong." Society is interested in protecting its members' personal physical safety and in preventing property damage. Tort law provides remedies for acts that cause harm. Society also recognizes intangible interests in things, such as personal privacy, family relations, reputation, and dig-

nity. Tort law provides remedies for the invasion of these protected interests, too.

Tort law is a part of the civil law. Injured parties may file civil lawsuits in an attempt to seek compensation for their injuries. An act that is a tort also can be a crime; thus, criminal law and tort law overlap. This chapter examines different types of torts, different situations where tort law imposes liability on a person or business, and different types of damages.

Artiste Login. Carlo and Carlotta own Artiste Login, an online company. They have a number of employees and the company owns several motor vehicles. Artiste has recently found itself in the middle of a tort case. Last night, Cal drove an automobile while under the influence of alcohol. He ran a red light and while driving through the intersection impacted and wrecked a truck owned by Artiste and driven by Pat, an employee. Pat was injured.

Cal has committed a crime, driving under the influence of alcohol, and has committed a tort, negligent driving. Artiste needs to decide whether it will retain an attorney and sue Cal in a civil court for damages to the truck or settle with Cal's insurance company.

Pat needs to decide whether he will file a civil lawsuit for the accident or settle with Cal's insurance company. The local prosecuting attorney will decide whether to prosecute Cal for any criminal acts, such as driving under the influence of alcohol, running a red light, and reckless driving.

Some tort actions result solely in civil lawsuits with no criminal prosecution. The burden of proof in a criminal action is higher (beyond a reasonable doubt) than the burden of proof in a civil tort case (by a preponderance of the evidence). *Preponderance* means that the plaintiff presented the greater weight of the evidence, which was more convincing than that presented by the defendant. Thus, Cal might be found not guilty of a crime, but may be found liable in a civil lawsuit for injuries to Pat and for the damage caused to the truck.

Types of Torts

Torts are divided traditionally into three categories. **Intentional torts**, as the name implies, are injuries caused by intentional acts. For example, when a movie star hits a photographer, he commits the intentional tort of assault and battery. **Negligence** consists of harm caused by careless acts or failure to perform a legal duty. Most automobile accidents are the result of negligence.

Strict liability requires the person causing the harm to compensate the injured party without regard to fault. Generally, this liability is imposed by law. A person who harbors wild animals is strictly liable for any harm they may cause. The following sections examine these three types of torts in more detail.

Intentional Torts

An intentional tort arises from an act that the defendant consciously performs. She either intends to harm another or knows with substantial certainty that injury to another could result. The intent to perform the act is this tort's distinguishing element. The actual nature of the damage ultimately caused is irrelevant in determining wrongdoer's intent.

For example, if Sean intentionally pushes Lil and she falls to the ground and breaks her arm, it does not matter that Sean never intended to break Lil's arm. Sean did intend to push Lil, and that in itself is a tortious act of battery. Sean is liable for the consequences, including injury to Lil's arm. If the push had been accidental, no intentional tort would exist.

Liability might be imposed for negligent conduct, however. Intentional torts are subdivided into two categories: wrongs against the person and wrongs against property. Further discussion of some specific intentional torts follows.

Wrongs against the Person

Intentional torts against a person include assault, battery, false imprisonment, infliction of mental distress, invasion of privacy, defamation (including disparagement of goods, slander of title, and defamation by computer), and fraud or deceit. If the person suffers an injury as a result of any of these torts, the term personal injury, or PI, applies.

Assault and/or Battery. An intentional act (that is not excused or allowed on grounds of self-defense or defense of others) that creates in another person a reasonable, imminent apprehension or fear of harm is an **assault**. If the harm results from physical contact and the victim experienced apprehension, either before or after the physical contact, **battery** occurs.

For example, Foster threatens to hit Heise with a baseball bat during an argument. The threat is an assault. Taking this example one step further, if Foster strikes Heise and she sees the strike coming, an assault and battery has occurred, because Heise has apprehension. On the other hand, assume Foster had not threatened Heise, but instead hits her with the baseball bat, rendering her unconscious. When she wakes up in the hospital, she has fear. A battery occurred because of the unlawful physical contact and the apprehension, even though the apprehension arose after the blow.

Physical injury does not have to occur. Receiving an unwelcome kiss or being escorted from a person's apartment with your arms pinned can constitute an assault, battery, or both.

False Imprisonment. False imprisonment, frequently associated with false arrest, is the intentional confinement or restraint of a person without justification and the interference with the person's ability to move about freely. Physical barriers, physical restraints, or threats of physical force can constitute intentional confinement. For false imprisonment to apply, it is essential that the person being restrained resist the restraint. A person is under no duty to risk personal harm in trying to escape, however.

Almost all states have adopted **merchant protection legislation** that allows a merchant to detain any suspected shoplifter, provided that reasonable cause for suspicion exists and that the detention is executed in a reasonable way. Merchants thus are given statutory protection from being sued successfully for false imprisonment. Because the loss to business from shoplifting is estimated to exceed $10 billion a year, this protection is important for businesses.

The following case first provides a discussion of whether an employer can be liable to an employee for false imprisonment. Second, the court discusses whether a business is protected under the merchant protection statute.

CASE 8.1

Supreme Court of Rhode
Island, 2003
814 A.2d 320

BOURQUE v. STOP & SHOP COMPANIES, INC.

BACKGROUND AND FACTS The plaintiff Lois Bourque was detained by the Defendant Stop & Shop Companies, Inc., for allegedly shoplifting. She was innocent of this charge. Before the defendant would allow her to leave, she had to sign a written document It specified that she acknowledged "appropriating" merchandise without paying for or intending to pay for it, and that, in consideration for Stop & Shop's agreement to "release" her and "permit" her to leave the premises, she released, waived, and discharged her right to sue Stop & Shop for any claims resulting from her apprehension and questioning.

She brought legal action for false imprisonment, false arrest, and willful and malicious conduct on the part of Stop & Shop by detaining plaintiff until she signed the release. There was a Rhode Island statute that stated the following:

> *A merchant may request a person detained for shoplifting to sign a statement waiving his or her right to bring a civil action arising from the detention in return for a signed statement from the merchant waiving the right to bring criminal charges based upon the alleged shoplifting. Any statement shall state in writing in large print at the top of the form that the person detained has a right to remain silent and a right not to make or sign any statement and a right to call an attorney.*

Concluding that the supermarket had coerced Bourque into signing a release by threatening to detain her until she did so, a Superior Court jury returned a civil verdict against the supermarket, finding it liable for damages. The defendant supermarket, Stop & Shop Companies, Inc., appealed the judgment.

PER CURIAM.

. . . .

Stop & Shop raises several issues on appeal. First, it argues that the trial justice erred by denying its motion for judgment as a matter of law on the basis that plaintiff waived her right to sue Stop & Shop when she signed a written waiver that Stop & Shop provided to her after its security personnel apprehended her for suspected shoplifting. . . . In addition, it purported to afford Stop & Shop the right to detain her if she did not sign the release. Furthermore, he ruled, because plaintiff did not voluntarily sign the waiver, her signature was coerced and, therefore, the waiver was invalid.

. . . .

With respect to the written waiver, we agree with the trial justice that the language used in Stop & Shop's waiver form exceeded what (Rhode Island Statute) allowed because it included a confession of wrongdoing on the part of the detained customer. Any person signing this document waived the right to sue the store for false arrest, negligence, and other similar claims for damages, and Stop & Shop in return waived its right to bring criminal charges. But, in addition, the waiver form also required the person signing it to acknowledge misappropriating certain merchandise from the store without paying or intending to pay for it. Thus, the form included the following statement: "I have acknowledged appropriating certain merchandise for my own use without paying for or intending to pay for the merchandise." (The statute) does not allow the merchant to include this type of statement in the waiver document. Upon reading the statute, it is clear to us that this type of acknowledgment is not consistent with the law.

. . . .

DECISION AND REMEDY The law does not permit or authorize a merchant to say, "You must sign this paper and then we'll let you leave the room." It is unlawful to continue to detain a person even if the initial stop was proper and if the initial detention was done lawfully.

CRITICAL THINKING: MANAGERIAL CONSIDERATION A merchant is allowed by statute to use reasonable restraint against a customer if it is believed that a theft has occurred. Define the point at which a reasonable restraint becomes unreasonable.

Infliction of Mental Distress. People have a right to be free from imposed mental distress. The tort of **infliction of mental distress** is defined as a party's intentional act that amounts to extreme and outrageous conduct resulting in another person's severe emotional distress. For example, a creditor telephones Paul every hour during the night in an attempt to collect a debt. As a result, Paul suffers intense mental anxiety. The courts have found such acts by the creditor to be extreme and outrageous conduct that exceeds the bounds of decency accepted by society. The person committing these acts may be liable in a tort action. These acts also may be in violation of the Fair Debt Collection Practices Act, which is described in Chapter 14.

Invasion of Privacy. Closely allied to infliction of mental distress is the separate tort of the invasion of a person's privacy. A lawsuit based on **invasion of privacy** does not involve injury to a person's property or character, but rather concerns an intentional invasion of a person's intangible right to be left alone. The use of two-way mirrors in women's fitting rooms that allow the store manager and others to observe women changing clothes has led to liability under this tort. The unauthorized commercial use of a person's picture is another example of invasion of privacy, as is publishing information about a person on the Internet without permission.

Defamation. **Defamation** occurs when someone makes false and malicious statements to others about another person or business. This tort, discussed in Chapter 5 under free speech, imposes a general duty on all people to refrain from making defamatory statements about others. Breaching this duty verbally is the tort of **slander**. Breaching it in writing is the tort of **libel**.

The basis for the tort of defamation is the publication of one or more statements that hold up an individual or business to contempt, ridicule, or hatred. Publication means that the defamatory statements are

LEGAL HIGHLIGHT

What Your Grocery Store Won't Tell You

Many grocery stores offer customers special discounts if they will register their names, addresses, and preferences. Those who sign up are provided a card to use in the future when making purchases. The card has a bar code. Every time the card is swiped in the machine, the grocery computer is able to track all of the purchases by that individual customer. Although disclosed in the registration material, most customers are oblivious to the tracking features, but well aware of the discount program.

To help ensure customer loyalty, the computer prints special coupons for products that the customer normally purchases. If a customer has not made any purchases within a specific time, coupons are sent to the customer that provide special discounts next time he makes an in store purchase.

A few cases have involved these purchase records being entered into evidence in court. For example, purchases of excessive alcohol might be introduced into evidence to throw light on a customer's behavior. Or, if a person is denied medical insurance and brings a lawsuit, the fact that the customer purchases cartons of cigarettes and alcohol could be introduced by the insurance company to show why insurance coverage was denied. In the computer age, people are losing their right to privacy, not to the government, but to private businesses.

made to, or within the hearing of, people other than the defamed party.

In the case of a writing, the publication occurs when a third person reads a defamatory document without the consent of the person who is defamed. If Thompson writes Andrews a private letter accusing him of embezzling funds, that letter does not constitute libel unless someone reads it without the consent of Andrews. If Peters calls Gordon dishonest, unattractive, and incompetent when no one else is around, that act does not constitute slander. Because neither message was communicated to a third party, neither qualifies as defamation.

Disparagement of Goods, Slander of Title, and Defamation by Computer. These torts involve defamation of a business or its products. A false statement made about a business's product is a tort called **disparagement of goods**.

An example of this tort is a recent case involving the magazine *Consumer Reports* and the Suzuki Samurai automobile manufacturer. *Consumer Reports* tested the Suzuki Samurai to determine whether the vehicle would roll. At first, the automobile did not roll over, but when the course was modified, the vehicle did tip over. *Consumer Reports* published its findings. Suzuki sued *Consumer Reports* claiming the report was a disparagement of goods. The U.S. Court of Appeals for the Ninth Circuit held that the case should be presented to a jury to determine whether *Consumer Reports'* conduct was reckless and disregarded the falsity of the test by predetermining the result.[1]

Defaming the title (proof of ownership) that a business has to its property may prevent a business from selling the property. The tort that outlaws this is called **slander of title**.

Erroneous information from a computer about a business's credit standing or reputation can impair that business's ability to obtain credit. If the computer information's owner fails to correct erroneous information in a timely manner, the company may be liable to the victim. This tort is called **defamation by computer**. The company also is responsible under the Fair Credit Reporting Act, discussed in Chapter 14, for reporting correct information.

Libel actions have involved agricultural products. Many farmers and ranchers have convinced state legislatures to pass food-libel laws.[2] One provocative case involved the Oprah Winfrey show. Winfrey stated on national television that many cattle sold in the United States had the potential to cause "mad cow" disease. The Texas Beef Group brought an action against her. The appellate court held in her favor stating that she had a right of free speech. Other states, however, have similar laws. In Colorado, it is a criminal offense to disparage agricultural products, even a lemon. The future of these statutes is yet to be determined.

Defenses. A person who is sued for defamation may assert several defenses. First, truth is normally a complete defense against a defamation charge. For example, in the scenario given previously, let's say Thompson publishes his letter stating that Andrews was an embezzler. If Andrews had been convicted in court for embezzlement, truth would be Thompson's defense to any defamation lawsuit.

Second, under the defense of **privilege of immunity**, even if the statement were false, no action can be brought against the speaker or writer. The two types of privileged communications are *absolute* and *qualified*. In general, these privileges are granted if some important and overriding social value in sanctioning a person's conduct exists, even though the conduct may result in defamation.

Absolute privilege applies to judicial and legislative proceedings, but only when relevant to the activities of either governmental body. For example, statements made by an elected representative on the floor of Congress are absolutely privileged communications. These same statements, if made in a different arena, such as a newsletter or a press conference, are not privileged.

Qualified privilege is a common law concept based on the philosophy that a person's right to know or to speak is of equal importance to another person's right not to be defamed. For the communication to have a qualified privilege, the plaintiff must show that the privilege was abused in order to recover.

Examples of a qualified privilege are found in recommendation letters and in employee evaluations. Generally, if a person communicates in good faith and

---

[1]Suzuki Motor Corp. v. Consumers Union of U.S., Inc., 292 F.3d 1192 (9th Cir. 2002).

[2]The Coalition for Free Speech posts a collection of agricultural libel laws at http://www.cspinet.org/foodspeak.

LEGAL HIGHLIGHT

McHamburger v. McVeggies

McDonald's®, a corporation worth millions, sued Helen Steel and Dave Morris, vegetarian activists, for libel in a London court. Ms. Steel, who worked part time in a pub, and Mr. Morris, an unemployed postman, were among five activists sued in 1990. Three apologized, but Ms. Steel and Mr. Morris decided to fight.

It all began in 1985 when a group decided to expose the nutritional reality behind McDonald's products. They circulated leaflets, criticizing McDonald's practices, such as meat purchasing practices and employment practices. Undercover private investigators, hired by McDonald's, infiltrated the activist group. The corporate spies took notes of the meetings, befriended the activists, stole letters from the group, and determined where they lived. Later these investigators would testify for McDonald's.

Libel laws in England are very strict and differ from those in the United States. In the United States, a plaintiff who is a public official (like the president or a congressperson) or a public figure (such as an actress or a business) must prove that the defendant published a story with the knowledge that it was false or with a reckless disregard of the truth. This high standard makes libel a very difficult case to prove. In England, the defendant has the burden of proving the truth of her statements. Furthermore, although the poor in England have access to legal aid, public legal assistance is not available in libel cases.

The trial began on June 28, 1994, and ended on December 13, 1996, lasting 313 court days. The previous record for a libel trial was 101 days. More than 130 witnesses testified, generating 40,000 pages of documents and 20,000 pages of transcripts. Mr. Justice Rodger Bell of the High Court in the Royal Courts of Justice presided over the trial. Mr. Justice Bell did not allow a jury, ruling that the central issues were too complex and scientific for a jury to follow.

In a David and Goliath battle, Ms. Steel and Mr. Morris, both inexperienced in the courtroom, dressed casually, often wearing denim, while Mr. Richard Rampton, the attorney for McDonald's and a Queen's Counsel, dressed formally in his wig and robe. (The designation of Queen's Counsel indicates that the attorney is among the top 10 percent of the legal profession in England.) Ms. Steel and Mr. Morris often prepared for the day's trial while riding the Underground (subway) and waited a week to obtain trial transcripts when the price decreased.

Judge Bell ruled in favor of McDonald's on most of the issues and granted a judgment of $98,000 against Ms. Steel and Mr. Morris. He did find that certain aspects of the leaflet were truthful. He found that McDonald's had paid lower wages and had sent workers home early to further lower their wages, had treated chickens cruelly, and had exploited children through advertising.

Estimates place the cost of the trial to McDonald's at $16 million dollars (the price of about 6.8 million Big Macs) and caused worldwide unfavorable publicity. As far as collecting the judgment against Ms. Steel and Mr. Morris, McDonald's announced that it did not intend to pursue collection procedures. After all, their joint income was less than $12,500 a year. The case resulted in international media coverage; a book, *McLiable: Burger Culture on Trial* (Macmillan, 1997); and a British television documentary. A World Wide Web (WWW) home page on the Internet contains a history along with documents.

And where is that leaflet that caused this great stir? It is accessible on the WWW, of course. Well, at least a shorter version is—in seven languages and as PDF files, of which two million were circulated in five years.

You can view the legal documents and other information on this case at **http://www.mcspotlight.org/case/index.html**. The verdict is located at **http://www.mcspotlight.org/case/trial/verdict/verdict0_sum.html**.

limits publication to those who have a legitimate interest in the communication, the statement falls within the qualified privilege.

Fraud or Deceit. The tort of **fraud** or **deceit** involves (1) a misrepresentation of material facts, (2) the intent to deceive or the reckless disregard of the facts' truthfulness, (3) the knowledge that the facts are false, (4) the victim's justifiable reliance on these facts, and (5) damages. Sometimes failure to disclose material facts is a form of deceit.

For example, a homeowner knows that the roof has started to leak even though it is not evident. The house is for sale. The owner should inform any potential buyer of this latent (hidden) defect. If he fails to disclose this fact to a potential buyer, the seller may be held liable under the tort of fraud for any future damages that the buyer suffers as a result of the leaky roof.

Wrongs against Property

Intentional torts that are wrongs against property include trespass, conversion, and nuisance. In these types of torts, the property is said to be damaged.

Trespass to Land. Any time a person enters another's land or causes something to enter onto the land or to remain there without consent or privilege, a tort of **trespass** to land has been committed. The person committing the tort of trespass is called a **trespasser**. Once the trespass is established, certain rights, duties, and privileges flow to both the owner and the trespasser. Some of these follow.

1. A trespasser is liable for any damage that she causes to the property.

2. A trespasser can be removed from the premises by use of nondeadly reasonable force without the property owner's being liable for assault, battery, or both.

3. The trespasser generally assumes the risks of the premises (that is, a trespasser cannot complain of personal injuries that occur as a result of the condition of the premises). This rule, however, does not permit the owner to lay traps. The owner may be required to post warnings on the property. Under the attractive nuisance doctrine, young children are exempt from assuming the risks of premises if the condition of the premises

attracts them to it (such as a swimming pool or large sand piles on construction sites).

Trespass to Personal Property. Trespass to personal property, such as an automobile, is similar to trespass to real property. In either type of trespass, a trespasser claims an intent to use the property rather than ownership interest.

A person's single act can result in two types of legal action. For example, a person takes an automobile without the intent to permanently keep it, but to drive to another city where eventually the car is abandoned. The trespasser did not intend to keep the automobile, but only to temporarily use it without the owner's permission. The trespasser can be charged with the crime of joy riding and may be civilly sued by the automobile owner for trespass to personal property.

Conversion. Whenever personal property is taken from its rightful owner or possessor and placed in the service of another, the tort of **conversion** occurs. Conversion is the civil side of crimes related to stealing. A store clerk who steals merchandise from the store commits the crime of embezzlement and the tort of conversion at the same time. Of course, when conversion occurs, the lesser offense of trespass to personal property usually occurs as well.

If the initial taking of the property was unlawful, trespass has occurred. If the initial taking of the property was lawful, but the property, however, has been retained beyond the time period agreed to, then the retention of that property is conversion. Even if the initial taking of the property had been permitted by the owner, failure to return the property may be conversion. For example, you lend a friend the use of your car over the weekend. Two weeks later he has not yet returned the car. Although he initially possessed the car with your permission, he is now liable to you for conversion.

Nuisance. A person can commit a tort through the unreasonable use of his own property. A **nuisance** is an improper activity (that may involve the use of a person's own property) that interferes with another's enjoyment or use of his property. Nuisances can be either public or private. This topic is discussed in detail in Chapter 24.

A **public nuisance** disturbs or interferes with the public in general and is generally a crime. A **private nuisance** interferes with the property interest of a limited number of individuals and is a tort. Reasonable limitations on property use prevent the owner from unreasonably interfering with the health and comfort of neighbors or with their right to enjoy their own private property.

For example, Rick cannot keep chickens in his townhouse because this would constitute a nuisance, even if no city ordinances prohibited such activity. Lin cannot set up a speaker system in her backyard and play rock-and-roll or symphonic music at a volume that disturbs her neighbors. Lin's act also may be a crime (public nuisance) if, for instance, a city ordinance specifies that no sound exceeding 100 decibels shall be audible within 100 feet of another's property between 11 P.M. and 7 A.M.

Negligence

Intentional torts involve a particular mental state. In negligence, however, the perpetrator neither intends to bring about the consequences of the act nor believes that the consequences will occur. The perpetrator's conduct merely creates the risk of such consequences. Without the creation of a risk, negligence cannot occur. The risk, moreover, must be foreseeable in that a reasonable person would anticipate the risk and guard against it.

Many of the actions discussed in the section on intentional torts would constitute negligence if they were committed carelessly and without intent. For instance, carelessly bumping into someone who then falls and breaks an arm constitutes negligence. Likewise, carelessly (as opposed to intentionally) flooding another's land constitutes negligence. In a sense, negligence describes a way of committing a tort rather than constituting a distinct category of torts.

Negligence occurs when a person is injured or her property is damaged because someone else's conduct falls below the required duty of care. Negligence requires three elements: (1) breach (failure) of duty of care, (2) injury, and (3) causation. Various defenses may be available to a person accused of negligence.

Breach of Duty of Care

The first element of negligence, breach of duty of care, can be determined based on a two-part question:

1. Is there a duty of care?
2. Did the defendant's action breach (fail to live up to) that duty?

Tort law recognizes several standards for the duty of care, depending on the particular situation. First, the standard of care may be measured by an **objective standard of care**, one of reasonableness, known as the "reasonable person" standard. In determining if a tort has been committed, the courts ask, "How would a reasonable and prudent person have acted in the same or similar circumstances?"

The reasonable person standard is objective. Reasonableness does not necessarily describe the way in which a particular person would act; it describes society's judgment as reflected by a jury as to the way in which people should act in the same situation. If the reasonable person existed, he would be careful, conscientious, even tempered, and honest. This hypothetical, reasonable person frequently is discussed in law.

Many times the standard of care is determined by the profession, industry, or business. Trade and professional organizations often determine the standard of care. The government may set the standard of care, such as when the government requires a recall of defective products.

Innkeepers and common carriers, such as motels and trucking firms, are held to a higher standard of care than that of reasonableness. For example, if your baggage is lost by an airline, you are able to recover damages up to an amount set by the government without proving negligence. If the passenger needs higher coverage than that, the passenger can purchase insurance coverage.

Excluding common carriers and innkeepers, the injured person must prove that the business did not act in a reasonable manner. In the following case, the court reviews the standard of care based on a reasonable and prudent business owner.

CASE 8.2

District Court of Appeal
of Florida, First District,
2000
764 So. 2d 637

MOULTRIE v. CONSOLIDATED STORES INTERNATIONAL CORPORATION

BACKGROUND AND FACTS Mrs. Moultrie and her two sons went to Big Lots Store #505, owned by the defendant Consolidated Stores International Corporation (Consolidated), to buy a vacuum cleaner. Mrs. Moultrie walked down an aisle of the store to the back wall, to an area where vacuum cleaners were displayed.

Mrs. Moultrie pointed to a vacuum cleaner she wanted her son to take down from the shelf. When her son reached up to get the vacuum cleaner, Mrs. Moultrie took a step backward to give him more room. As she did so, she tripped and fell on an empty wooden pallet that had been left in the aisle. The pallet was approximately six inches in height.

Mrs. Moultrie acknowledged that if she had looked to the right and left sides of the floor as she traversed the aisle of the store, she would have seen the pallet. Mrs. Moultrie explained that when she enters any store, she assumes the aisles are clear and does not examine them for obstructions.

Consolidated filed a motion for summary judgment alleging that the pallet was an open and obvious condition and, due to the open and obvious nature of the pallet, she could not recover for her injuries. At the hearing conducted on the motion for summary judgment, Consolidated's counsel argued that a storekeeper is entitled to assume that a customer will perceive that which would be obvious to him upon the ordinary use of his senses.

Moultrie urged the pallet was not open and obvious, because "open and obvious" denotes knowledge of the existence of the condition or activity and an appreciation of the danger it involves. The trial court granted Consolidated's motion for summary final judgment, presumably persuaded that the pallet that resulted in Mrs. Moultrie's injury constituted an open and obvious condition. Consolidated is the appellant and Mrs. Moultrie is the appellee.

JOANOS, J.

. . . .

The well settled principles governing motions for summary judgment provide: "[t]o establish entitlement to a summary judgment, the moving party must demonstrate conclusively that no genuine issue exists as to any material fact, even after all reasonable inferences are drawn in favor of the party opposing the summary judgment." . . . On review of the trial court's grant of summary judgment, this court must resolve all doubts as to the existence of a genuine issue of material fact against the moving party. . . .

In actions involving premises liability, a "business invitee is one who is 'invited to enter or remain on land for a purpose directly or indirectly connected with business dealings with the possessor of the land.'" A business owner owes an invitee a duty—to use reasonable care in maintaining the premises in a reasonably safe condition and to give the plaintiff timely notice and warning of latent and concealed perils, known to the defendant or which by the exercise of due care should have been known to him, and which were not known by plaintiff or which by the exercise of due care could not have been known by him.

In this vein, an owner is entitled to assume the invitee will perceive that which would be obvious to the invitee through the normal use of his senses, and is not required to give the invitee notice or warning of an obvious danger.

Known or Obvious Dangers. A possessor of land is not liable to his invitees for physical harm caused to them by any activity or condition on the land whose danger is known or obvious to them, unless the possessor should anticipate the harm despite such knowledge or obviousness. In [a previous case] the supreme court instructed: "'In any case where the occupier [of land] as a reasonable person should anticipate an unreasonable risk of harm to the invitee notwithstanding his knowledge, warning, or the obvious nature of the condition, something more in the way of precautions may be required.'"

At the core of the duty element is the requirement that each defendant who creates a risk must exercise prudent foresight whenever others may be injured as a result of the risk. Thus, "duty exists as a matter of law and is not a factual question for the jury to decide." "As to duty, the proper inquiry for the reviewing court is whether the defendant's conduct created a foreseeable zone of risk, not whether the defendant could foresee the specific injury that actually occurred."

When we view all favorable inferences in favor of appellants, application of the foregoing principles to the record in this case shows that appellee created a foreseeable zone of risk by leaving an empty wooden pallet in the aisle of its store. The height of the pallet was such that it might not fall within the line of vision of adult invitees who entered the Big Lots Store to purchase items placed on counters and shelves. Further, the diagram sketched by appellant at the request of appellee's counsel shows the pallet was in a main aisle of the store, placed to the left side, rather than centered in the aisle. In these circumstances, we believe reasonable persons could differ as to whether the wooden pallet was open and obvious.

The cases cited by appellee involving uneven pavement, traffic bumps, and steps within business premises or residences, were decided in favor of the respective defendant on the ground that the conditions were a matter of common knowledge or every day life. Such is not the case here. Although appellee argued the pallet was "open and obvious," appellee has not asserted, nor could it do so, that it is customary or common practice for relatively large, empty wooden pallets to be placed in store aisles, with no elevated pennant or other type of warning device to alert customers or store employees of its presence.

. . . .

DECISION AND REMEDY The facts did not present a condition that was so open, obvious, and ordinary that it could be held as a matter of law that the pallet did not constitute a foreseeable risk of harm to individuals either patronizing or working in the store. Rather, there appeared to be material issues of fact as to whether the pallet was "open and obvious" and, if so, whether the defendant should have anticipated that, as a general rule, adult shoppers do not focus on the floor of a store aisle when moving toward merchandise they propose to buy. The motion for summary judgment was reversed and the case was returned to the trial court for a trial.

CRITICAL THINKING: PUBLIC POLICY Why should there be any legal difference when a person falls because of a crack in the sidewalk versus falling due to an item being left in an aisle?

A second standard of care may be imposed by a statute. Everyone driving a vehicle, for example, has a **statutory duty** not to proceed through an intersection when the traffic light is red. Reasonableness is not relevant under this standard of care.

For example, a person receives a traffic ticket for running a red light. He may tell the judge that at 3 A.M. he was rushing his pregnant wife to the hospital, that he stopped at the red light, that he looked both ways and determined that no cross traffic was coming from either direction, and that he then proceeded through the signal. The judge in his wisdom may dismiss the ticket. If the driver struck someone in the intersection, however, reasonableness as to his action could not suffice as a defense in the civil case. The statutory duty to stop at the red light is the standard of care. Because someone was harmed, he would be liable in civil court for the harm he caused, even though the judge does have the discretion to dismiss the ticket.

Injury

The plaintiff must suffer some loss, harm, wrong, or invasion of a protected interest to recover damages for a negligent act. The reason for the requirement of injury is obvious. Without an injury, the plaintiff lacks damages for which the defendant is required to compensate.

A defendant pays compensation in an effort to make the plaintiff "whole" again. Essentially, the purpose of the tort of negligence is to compensate the victim for legally recognized injuries resulting from the wrongdoer's acts. The intent is not to punish those acts.

Causation

Causation is the last element necessary to prove negligence. If a person breaches her duty of care, that breach must cause damage, and the person's negligent act must be linked closely with the damage for the person to be liable. The courts have limited the monetary amount of a person's liability if her negligent act is not wholly responsible for the resulting harm.

In deciding whether there is causation, the court must address two issues. First, was the act the cause in fact? Did the injury occur because of the defendant's act

or would it have occurred anyway? Causation in fact usually can be determined by the "but for" test: but for the wrongful act, the injury would not have occurred.

If Carl carelessly leaves a campfire burning and the fire burns down the forest, causation in fact exists. The forest would not have burned but for Carl's negligent act. Therefore, Carl may be liable for the damages he caused.

If Carl carelessly leaves a campfire burning, but it burns out, and lightning causes a fire that burns down the forest, there is no causation in fact. In both examples, there is a wrongful act (Carl's leaving the campfire burning) and there is damage. In the second example, however, no causal connection exists between the wrongful act and the damage. Thus, Carl is not liable.

The second issue answers this question: Was the act the *proximate cause* of the injury? **Proximate cause** is the reasonable, causal relationship between the defendant's unreasonable conduct and the plaintiff's injury or damage. The purpose of proximate cause is to limit the defendant's liability as a result of his misconduct.

How far should a defendant's liability extend for a wrongful act that was a substantial factor in causing injury? For example, Carl's fire not only burns down the forest, but also sets off an explosion in a nearby ammunition plant that levels the entire plant, destroys the marshmallow factory located next door, and severely damages houses and businesses in the nearby community. Should Carl be liable to the ammunition plant owners, the marshmallow factory owners, and the people harmed in the nearby community?

The limitations on a person's liability are the issue when the courts consider proximate cause. Proximate cause is a question of public policy. The courts must ask whether the connection between an act and an injury is strong enough to justify imposing liability.

The courts use **foreseeability** as the test for proximate cause. If the act's consequences or the victims' harm were unforeseeable, no proximate cause exists. Carl was negligent, but for how much is he liable? How far along the chain of events could Carl reasonably foresee? In the next case, the court reviews the issue of foreseeability.

CASE 8.3

Court of Appeals of New
York, 1928
248 N.Y. 339, 162 N.E.
99, 1928 N.Y. LEXIS
1269, 59 A.L.R. 1253
http://www.wooster.edu/
economics/js/law_
archive/Palsgraf.html

LANDMARK CASE

PALSGRAF v. LONG ISLAND RAILROAD COMPANY

BACKGROUND AND FACTS Palsgraf, plaintiff, was standing on a platform of the Long Island Railroad Co., defendant, after buying a ticket to go to Rockaway Beach. A train stopped at the station, bound for another place. Two men ran forward to catch it. One of the men reached the platform of the car without mishap, though the train was already moving. The other man, carrying a package, jumped aboard the car, but seemed unsteady, as if about to fall. A guard on the car, who had held the door open, reached forward to help him in, and another guard on the platform pushed him from behind.

He dropped the package and it fell to the rails. It was a small-sized package, about fifteen inches long, and was covered by a newspaper. In fact, it contained fireworks, but there was nothing in its appearance to give notice of its contents. The fireworks exploded when they fell. The shock of the explosion toppled some scales at the other end of the platform, many feet away. The scales struck the plaintiff, causing injuries.

Judge CARDOZO, Ch.

. . . .

The conduct of the defendant's guard, if a wrong in its relation to the holder of the package, was not a wrong in its relation to the plaintiff, standing far away. Relatively to her it was not negligence at all. Nothing in the situation gave notice that the falling package had in it the potency of peril to persons thus removed. Negligence is not actionable unless it involves the invasion of a legally protected interest, the violation of a right. . . . "Negligence is the absence of care, according to the circumstances." . . .

A different conclusion will involve us, and swiftly too, in a maze of contradictions. A guard stumbles over a package which has been left upon a platform. It seems to be a bundle of newspapers. It turns out to be a can of dynamite. To the eye of ordinary vigilance, the bundle is abandoned waste, which may be kicked or trod on with impunity. Is a passenger at the other end of the platform protected by the law against the unsuspected hazard concealed beneath the waste? If not, is the result to be any different, so far as the distant passenger is concerned, when the guard stumbles over a valise which a truckman or a porter has left upon the walk? . . .

. . . The range of reasonable apprehension is at times a question for the court, and at times, if varying inferences are possible, a question for the jury. Here, by concession, there was nothing in the situation to suggest to the most cautious mind that the parcel wrapped in newspaper would spread wreckage through the station. If the guard had thrown it down knowingly and willfully, he would not have threatened the plaintiff's safety, so far as appearances could warn him. His conduct would not have involved, even then, an unreasonable probability of invasion of her bodily security. Liability can be no greater where the act is inadvertent.

Negligence, like risk, is thus a term of relation. Negligence in the abstract, apart from things related, is surely not a tort, if indeed it is understandable at all. Negligence is not a tort unless it results in the commission of a wrong, and the commission of a wrong imports the violation of a right, in this case, we are told, the right to be protected against interference with one's bodily security. But bodily security is protected, not against all forms of interference or aggression, but only against some. One who seeks redress at law does not make out a cause of action by showing without more that there has been damage to his person. If the harm was not willful, he must show that the act as to him had possibilities of danger so many and apparent as to entitle him to be protected against the doing of it though the harm was unintended. . . .

The law of causation, remote or proximate, is thus foreign to the case before us. The question of liability is always anterior to the question of the measure of the consequences that go with liability. If there is no tort to be redressed, there is no occasion to consider what damage might be recovered if there were a finding of a tort. We may assume, without deciding, that negligence, not at large or in the abstract, but in relation to the plaintiff, would entail liability for any and all consequences, however novel or extraordinary. There is room for argument that a distinction is to be drawn according to the diversity of interests invaded by the act, as where conduct negligent in that it threatens an insignificant invasion of an interest in property results in an unforseeable invasion of an interest of another order, as, e.g., one of bodily security. Perhaps other distinctions may be necessary. We do not go into the question now. The consequences to be followed must first be rooted in a wrong. . . . .

DECISION AND REMEDY The court found that the plaintiff in a legal action for negligence must show that the act as to that person had possibilities of danger so many and apparent as to entitle him to be protected against the harm. In other words, the damages or injuries must have been foreseen when there was a breach of duty of reasonable care owed to the plaintiff.

CRITICAL THINKING: PUBLIC POLICY Why does the law require that damages must be foreseeable when there is a breach of reasonable care by one person to another? Why should a person who causes a loss not be liable for the full damages that may result?

Res Ipsa Loquitur

Some types of accidents occur only when someone is negligent. For example, you are walking on a sidewalk next to a building that is under construction. Pedestrians are allowed to walk there. Suddenly, a hammer falls from the building and strikes you on the shoulder and breaks several of your bones. This accident normally occurs only as a result of someone's negligence. But you have no idea who lost the hammer or why it fell from the building.

The doctrine of *res ipsa loquitur* (the thing speaks for itself) is used in these types of cases. This doctrine applies under the following conditions:

1. The event that caused the damage must not occur in the absence of negligence.

2. The conduct of the plaintiff or any other third party could not have caused the event.

3. The defendant owes the plaintiff a duty of reasonable care.

In the case just mentioned, the event of the hammer falling happens only as a result of someone's negligence. Neither you nor any other third party caused the hammer to fall. The construction company owed a duty of reasonable care to protect the pedestrians in the street below from harm. The area where you walked should have been covered. Additionally, the hammer should not have been in a position where it could fall to the street. Instead, it should have been anchored by a cord so that it could not have fallen.

The plaintiff cannot prove negligent conduct by the defendant because the plaintiff lacks access to all the information. Instead of trying to prove negligence, the plaintiff can prove the elements of *res ipsa loquitur*. The burden of proof shifts to the defendant to prove itself not negligent. In this case, the defendant may try to prove that an act of God caused a violent wind to rip the hammer from its secured place, causing it to fall to the street.

Defenses to Negligence

Defenses to negligence are (1) *superseding (intervening) forces*, (2) *assumption of risk*, and (3) *contributory negligence*, and (4) *comparative negligence*. We next look at each of these defenses.

LEGAL HIGHLIGHT

McDonald's Hot Coffee Case

Early one cold February morning in 1992, Mrs. Liebeck, age seventy-nine, and her grandson went to the drive-through window at the local McDonald's® where she ordered coffee. She rarely went to a fast-food restaurant; thus, this was a new experience for her. Her grandson parked the car so that she could add cream and sugar to her coffee. She placed the styrofoam cup between her knees to remove the plastic lid. When she pulled up on the plastic lid, the hot coffee spilled into her lap.

The sweatpants she was wearing held the hot coffee next to her skin. She suffered third-degree burns (a burn that goes completely through the skin) over 6 percent of her body, including her inner thighs, buttocks, and groin areas. She was hospitalized for eight days where she endured skin grafting and other medical treatments.

She sought to settle the case for $20,000, but McDonald's refused, so she filed a lawsuit. During discovery, McDonald's revealed that more than 700 claims had been filed by people who had been burned between 1982 and 1992. Some of them had suffered third-degree burns, similar to Mrs. Liebeck's burns.

McDonald's served its coffee between 180 and 190 degrees Fahrenheit, approximately 20 degrees higher than the industry standard. The McDonald's quality assurance manager testified that a burn hazard exists with any food or liquid above 140 degrees. He also admitted that coffee served at 180 degrees or more was unconsumable since it would burn the mouth and throat.

Experts for Mrs. Liebeck testified that liquids above 180 degrees will produce third-degree burns in two to seven seconds. If a 155-degree liquid were spilled, the extent of the resulting burn would be decreased significantly. In other words, Mrs. Liebeck would have suffered some burning if the coffee had been 155 degrees, but she would have avoided the serious third-degree burns.

McDonald's argued that many buyers intended to drink the coffee at work or home, even though its own customer survey indicated that buyers intended to drink the coffee while driving. McDonald's asserted that customers know that coffee is hot, but admitted in court that most did not know that they could suffer third-degree burns. The company also admitted that the warning statement "Hot" printed on the cup actually served as a reminder and not a warning that third-degree burns could result, since the customers were not informed of the hazard of serious burning.

In an on-camera interview after the verdict, one juror stated that when she was selected to hear the case, she thought the case was silly, but agreed to keep an open mind. She changed her mind after she heard the testimony of the various witnesses. The jury awarded Mrs. Liebeck $200,000 in compensatory damages, but reduced it to $160,000 because the jury found her to be 20 percent at fault for the spill. The jury also awarded her $2.7 million in punitive damages, which equals about two days of McDonald's coffee sales. The court later reduced the punitive award to $480,000 (three times the compensatory damages), but stated that McDonald's conduct was reckless, callous, and willful.

A **superseding (intervening) force** may break the causal connection between a wrongful act and injury to another. If so, it cancels the wrongful act. For example, Jed takes his automobile to a mechanic to repair his brakes. After repairing the brakes and replacing the tires, the mechanic fails to tighten bolts. Jed is driving along when he hears a terrible rattle coming from the automobile. As he is stopping his car along the shoulder of the freeway, the wheel comes off. Just then a drunk driver hits the car, injuring Jed. The drunk driver is an intervening force and may break the connection between the mechanic's negligent act and the damage to Jed and his automobile that resulted from the accident.

A plaintiff who voluntarily enters into a risky situation, knowing the risk involved, is barred from legal recovery. This defense is called **assumption of risk**. For example, a driver who enters an officially sanctioned automobile race accepts the risk of being killed or injured in a crash. The driver has assumed the risk of injury. Knowledge of the risk and voluntary assumption of that risk are the two requirements for this defense that disallow any recovery.

All individuals are expected to exercise a reasonable degree of care in looking out for themselves. In some jurisdictions, an injured person who has failed to exercise such care over herself is prevented from recovery for injury resulting from negligence. The defense of **contributory negligence** is available when both parties have been negligent and their combined negligence has contributed to cause the injury. When the plaintiff sues a defendant for the tort of negligence to recover damages, the defendant can assert that the plaintiff was contributorily negligent. When the defendant proves that the plaintiff also contributed to the accident by being negligent, the plaintiff will not be allowed to recover damages from the defendant.

The modern legal trend is moving away from the assumption of risk and contributory negligence defenses. Instead of allowing these defenses to completely prevent a plaintiff from recovering in a negligence lawsuit, an increasing number of states allow recovery based on the doctrine of **comparative negligence**. This doctrine enables computation of both the plaintiff's and the defendant's negligence. The plaintiff's damages are reduced by a percentage that represents the degree of his contributing fault. In some states, comparative negligence is used to reduce damages when the assumption-of-risk doctrine applies.

For example, Mario is driving his automobile. Although it is equipped with safety belts, he is not wearing his. Mario approaches an intersection with a green light. Peter, approaching in his car from the opposite direction, turns left in front of Mario's automobile. The cars collide, and Mario is thrown from his automobile and severely injured.

Subsequently, Mario files a lawsuit against Peter alleging negligence. Peter defends by using the comparative negligence defense. Through expert witnesses, Peter shows the jury that Mario's nonuse of his seat belt is a factor that the jury may use to reduce Mario's claim to damages. Mario may not recover damages for the full extent of his injuries. His failure to wear a safety belt was an act of negligence that contributed to the extent of his injuries. Data demonstrate that motorists suffer fewer and less severe injuries from accidents when they wear seat belts.

Strict Liability

The final category of torts is called *strict liability*, or *liability without fault*. Negligent torts involve an act that departs from a standard of care and causes an injury. Under the doctrine of strict liability, liability for injury is imposed for reasons other than fault.

When a person engages in abnormally dangerous activities, that person will be liable under strict liability if any harm occurs to others. An abnormally dangerous activity has three characteristics:

1. The activity involves potentially serious harm to persons or to property.

2. The activity involves a high degree of risk that cannot be guarded against completely by exercising reasonable care.

3. The activity is not performed commonly in the community.

Strict liability is applied because of the activity's extreme risk. Although an activity, such as blasting with dynamite, is performed with all reasonable care, innocent people still risk injury; thus, unless a person voluntarily and with knowledge enters a posted work site in which blasting work is being carried out, the dynamiter is liable for any damage to property or injury to a person caused by the blasting.

Because of the risk of harm, public policy requires that the person engaged in the dangerous activity be held liable for injuries caused by the activity. Responsibility is imposed because of the activity's nature, not because any fault exists. It is reasonable to require the person engaged in the activity to carry insurance or otherwise to be prepared to compensate anyone who suffers harm.

Applications of the strict liability principle are found in workers' compensation acts and in the area of product liability. Product liability is discussed in Chapter 11. In workers' compensation and product liability, either the employer or the manufacturer bears the liability as a matter of public policy. Such liability is based on two factors:

1. The employer and manufacturer are better able to bear the cost of injury than the injured person because they can spread it out to society through an increase in the cost of goods and services. For example, a toy manufacturer normally would sell a toy to a million customers for $20. The price can be raised to $21 (an increase of 5 percent) in

order to pay for the liability claims ($1 million) for injuries to customers.

2. The employer and manufacturer profit from their activities and, therefore, as a matter of public policy, should bear the cost of injury as an operating expense.

Specific Torts Related to Business

Several torts have a direct application to the business environment. First, a business can be harmed when another business wrongfully interferes with a contractual or business relationship. Second, a business's trademarks, trade names, patents, and copyrights can be infringed. Finally, a business can have its trade secrets stolen.

Wrongful Interference with a Contractual or Business Relationship

In an **intentional interference with a contractual or business relationship** case, the plaintiff must prove that the defendant intentionally induced the breach of a valid contractual or business relationship, not merely that the defendant reaped the benefits of the broken relationship. For example, Alicia has a one-year contract to deliver to Eat-Rite Restaurants all the doughnuts Eat-Rite requires for its breakfast menu. Frank's Doughnut Hole had unsuccessfully bid for the contract earlier. Frank's offers Eat-Rite a special price, much lower than Alicia's, if Eat-Rite will change suppliers immediately. Frank's further offers to pay for any costs Eat-Rite incurs in making the change. Eat-Rite breaks its contract with Alicia.

Based on this scenario, Frank's will be liable for wrongful interference with a contractual relationship.

LEGAL HIGHLIGHT

Mass Torts

The media often talk about *mass torts*. In a mass tort, an act has harmed a number of plaintiffs, with the number sometimes in the hundreds or even thousands.

A specific mass tort often gives rise to a class-action lawsuit. In this type of lawsuit, a large number of people each have a claim against the same defendant arising out of the same wrongful act allegedly committed by the defendant. In a class-action suit, the judge allows one or more plaintiffs to represent the class in a lawsuit against one or more defendants. Once a court has certified a class-action suit, the eventual case disposition binds all the parties. Some examples of class-action suits involving mass disasters include the following cases.

In 1981, the skywalks in the Hyatt Regency Hotel in Kansas City collapsed, killing more than 100 people and injuring hundreds more. The federal court certified two class-action suits. The claims were eventually settled.

A. H. Robins manufactured the Dalkon Shield, an intrauterine device (IUD), from 1971 to 1974. Between 1974 and 1986, more than 12,000 women filed damage suits. Robins went into bankruptcy court in 1986. More than 130,000 claims eventually were filed with the bankruptcy court against Robins.

In 1980, a fire swept through the lobby of the MGM Grand Hotel in Las Vegas, Nevada, killing 84 hotel guests and injuring more than 500. In addition to helicopters from the Las Vegas area, helicopters from a U.S. Air Force reserve unit located in Phoenix, Arizona, responded. The final settlement was in excess of $205 million.

In 1992, Pfizer, Inc., established a $500-million settlement plan to compensate 55,000 people or their estates who received defective heart valves. The valves had a history of fracturing, resulting in patients' trips to emergency rooms. Some people died as a result of the fracturing.

Businesses should monitor their activities to prevent or lessen these catastrophic events. It is cheaper to have a risk management program than to pay substantial damages.

For more information about mass torts, visit the Rand Corporation Web site covering this area of interest. It may be found at **http://www.rand.org/publications/RB/RB9021/RB9021.word.html**.

Suppose, however, that Frank's merely advertises a special price and further states that it will beat any valid price offered by a competitor. Eat-Rite reads the advertisement, breaks its contract with Alicia, and contracts with Frank's Doughnut Hole. Although Frank's will reap the benefits of Eat-Rite's breach of contract with Alicia, Frank's will not be liable for the tort of wrongful interference with a contractual relationship.

The best known case of wrongful interference is *Texaco v. Pennzoil*.[3] The Getty family wanted to sell its business, Getty Oil Company. After negotiations, the chief executive officer (CEO) of Pennzoil reached an oral agreement with the representatives of Getty Oil for the two companies to merge. Both sides shook hands. Even though this contract involved millions of dollars, the law did not require this type of contract to be in writing to be enforced in court. The CEO for Pennzoil flew to New York that evening. The next day he heard that Texaco had purchased Getty Oil.

Pennzoil sued Texaco for wrongful interference with Pennzoil's contract with Getty Oil. The trial jury found that Texaco had wrongfully interfered with the planned merger (the contract) between Pennzoil and Getty Oil Company. The jury found that the three elements required for a wrongful interference with a contractual relationship were present. These requirements follow:

1. A valid contract existed between Pennzoil and Getty.

2. Texaco knew that this contract existed.

3. Texaco intentionally induced the breach of the contract by Getty, resulting in an economic or pecuniary gain.

The trial judgment was the largest in U.S. history, $7.53 billion in actual damages and $3 billion in punitive damages.[4]

Infringement of Trademarks, Trade Names, Patents, and Copyrights

A **trademark** is a distinctive mark, motto, device, or implement that a manufacturer stamps, prints, or otherwise affixes to its goods. The trademark identifies

[3]1729 S.W.2d 768 (Tex. Ct. App. 1987).
[4]The case was settled in 1988 for $3 billion. On the day of the payment, Texaco completed its reorganization and emerged from twelve months of bankruptcy proceedings. In 2000, Getty Petroleum Marketing Inc., was purchased by LUKOIL, a Russian oil company.

and vouches for the origin of goods on the market. Thus, trademark law affects every business. For example, Corel® WordPerfect®, a software word-processing program, is a registered trademark of Corel Corporation.

Trademarks are filed with the U.S. Patent and Trademark Office,[5] which has issued more than 2,500,000 trademarks. Trademarks may be registered prior to use or after the trademark has been used. Legal protection is afforded to businesses that have made the effort and spent the time and money to develop a trademark.

Clearly, if a person uses another's trademark, consumers will be misled into believing that the goods are genuine instead of what they really are—counterfeit goods. The law seeks to avoid this kind of confusion. An example of a trademark is the computer company, Gateway™.

A **service mark** is similar to a trademark, but is used by the service industry to distinguish the services of one business from those of another. For example, each airline has a particular mark or symbol associated with its name. Titles or character names used in radio and television frequently are registered as service marks. An example of a service mark is one from Gateway,™ which is found in its advertisements, "A better way."SM

Once a trademark or service mark has been registered with the federal government, the registering firm is entitled to its exclusive use for marketing purposes. Whenever another intentionally or unintentionally copies a trademark or service mark to a substantial degree or uses it in its entirety, the trademark or service mark has been infringed. The trademark need not be registered with the government in order to be granted protection from the tort of trademark infringement. Registration does furnish proof of the date of inception of its use, however.

A **patent** is a government grant that conveys and secures to an inventor the exclusive right to make, use, and sell an invention for twenty years from the date the application was filed. Patents for a lesser period are given for designs, as opposed to inventions. For either a regular patent or a design patent, the applicant must demonstrate to the satisfaction of the U.S. Patent Office that the invention, discovery, or design is gen-

[5]The U.S. Patent and Trademark Office's Web page is http://www.uspto.gov.

uine, novel, useful, and not obvious in light of the technology of the time. A patent holder provides notice to all that an article or design is patented by placing on it the word *Patent* or the abbreviation *Pat.* plus the patent number.

If a firm uses a device that is substantially similar to someone else's patented device, the tort of patent infringement exists. Patent infringement may exist even though only some features or parts of an invention are copied.[6]

A **copyright** is a right granted by statute to the author or originator of literary or artistic productions, performing arts works, visual arts works, sound recordings, serial and periodicals, and computer programs.[7] Most works created after January 1, 1978, automatically received statutory copyright protection

for the life of the author plus seventy years. An idea, however, cannot possibly be copyrighted. What is copyrightable is the particular way in which an idea is expressed.

Artiste Login. Carlotta produces at least one oil painting a year. To protect her works, Carlotta files for copyright protection for each of her paintings. Artiste has retained an attorney who specializes in copyright issues to ensure that all Carlotta's works are protected to the fullest extent of the law.

Whenever the form of expression of an idea is copied, an infringement of copyright has occurred. The infringement neither has to be exactly the same as the original nor must the original be reproduced in its entirety. If a substantial part of the original is reproduced, a copyright infringement exists. Limited copying is permitted under the "fair use" doctrine. The following case shows how the fair use doctrine has been applied in the music field.

[6]Patents are used in international business. The status of European patents is available at the European Patent Office at http://www.european-patent-office.org.

[7]Copyrights are issued by the U.S. Copyright Office. Its Web page is http://www.copyright.gov.

CASE 8.4

Supreme Court of the United States, 1994
510 U.S. 569, 114 S. Ct. 1164, 127 L. Ed. 2d 500
http://supct.law.cornell.edu/supct/html/92-1292.ZO.html

CAMPBELL v. ACUFF-ROSE MUSIC, INC.

BACKGROUND AND FACTS Roy Orbison and William Dees coauthored "Oh, Pretty Woman" and assigned their rights in the song to Acuff-Rose Music, Inc., in 1964. Acuff-Rose copyrighted the song in that same year.

Luther R. Campbell, Christopher Wongwon, Mark Ross, and David Hobbs are known collectively as 2 Live Crew, a popular rap music group. In 1989, Campbell wrote a song entitled "Pretty Woman," which he intended, based on its comical lyrics, to satirize the original work. On July 5, 1989, 2 Live Crew's manager wrote to Gary Teifer of Acuff-Rose, informing him that 2 Live Crew intended to parody "Oh, Pretty Woman." Full credit would be given to Orbison and Dees as owners and authors. Acuff-Rose would be paid the rate required by statute for the song's use. Teifer responded on July 17, denying the license because "we cannot permit the use of a parody of 'Oh, Pretty Woman.'"

On July 15, two days before Teifer's letter, 2 Live Crew released its version of "Pretty Woman" on record albums, tapes, and compact discs, all entitled "As Clean As They Wanna Be." Both the compact disc cover and the compact disc itself acknowledged Orbison and Dees as the authors of "Oh, Pretty Woman" and Acuff-Rose as the publisher.

Almost a year later, after nearly a quarter of a million copies of the recording had been sold, Acuff-Rose sued 2 Live Crew and their record company, Luke Skywalker Records, for copyright infringement, among other allegations. Acuff-Rose contended that the lyrics of "Oh, Pretty Woman" as sung by 2 Live Crew "are not consistent with good taste or would disparage the future value of the copyright."

Moving for summary judgment, 2 Live Crew argued that "Pretty Woman" was a parody that constitutes fair use under the Copyright Act. The district court granted the summary judgment, which was appealed. The court of appeals reversed the action of the district court and found that the rap group's parody was not fair use of a copyrighted song. Campbell filed a writ of *certiorari* with the Supreme Court of the United States. The writ was granted.

Justice SOUTER delivered the opinion for a unanimous Court.

. . . .

It is uncontested here that 2 Live Crew's song would be an infringement of Acuff-Rose's rights in "Oh, Pretty Woman," under the Copyright Act of 1976, but for a finding of fair use through parody. . . .

The germ of parody lies in the definition of the Greek *parodeia*, . . . as "a song sung alongside another." Modern dictionaries accordingly describe a parody as a "literary or artistic work that imitates the characteristic style of an author or a work for comic effect or ridicule," or as a "composition in prose or verse in which the characteristic turns of thought and phrase in an author or class of authors are imitated in such a way as to make them appear ridiculous." For the purposes of copyright law, the nub of the definitions, and the heart of any parodist's claim to quote from existing material, is the use of some elements of a prior author's composition to create a new one that, at least in part, comments on that author's works. If, on the contrary, the commentary has no critical bearing on the substance or style of the original composition, which the alleged infringer merely uses to get attention or to avoid the drudgery in working up something fresh, the claim to fairness in borrowing from another's work diminishes accordingly (if it does not vanish), and other factors, like the extent of its commerciality, loom larger. Parody needs to mimic an original to make its point, and so has some claim to use the creation of its victim's (or collective victims') imagination, whereas satire can stand on its own two feet and so requires justification for the very act of borrowing.

. . . .

While we might not assign a high rank to the parodic element here, we think it fair to say that 2 Live Crew's song reasonably could be perceived as commenting on the original or criticizing it, to some degree. 2 Live Crew juxtaposes the romantic musings of a man whose fantasy comes true, with degrading taunts, a bawdy demand for sex, and a sigh of relief from paternal responsibility. The later words can be taken as a comment on the naivete of the original of an earlier day, as a rejection of its sentiment that ignores the ugliness of street life and the debasement that it signifies. It is this joinder of reference and ridicule that marks off the author's choice of parody from the other types of comment and criticism that traditionally have had a claim to fair use protection as transformative works.

. . . .

It was error for the Court of Appeals to conclude that the commercial nature of 2 Live Crew's parody of "Oh, Pretty Woman" rendered it presumptively unfair. No such evidentiary presumption is available to address either the first factor, the character and purpose of the use, or the fourth, market harm, in determining whether a transformative use, such as parody, is a fair one. The court also erred in holding that 2 Live Crew had necessarily copied excessively from the Orbison original, considering the parodic purpose of the use. We therefore reverse the judgment of the Court of Appeals and remand for further proceedings consistent with this opinion.

Appendix A to the Opinion of the Court

"Oh, Pretty Woman" by Roy Orbison and William Dees
Pretty Woman, walking down the street,
Pretty Woman, the kind I like to meet,

Pretty Woman, I don't believe you, you're not the truth,
No one could look as good as you
Mercy
Pretty Woman, won't you pardon me,
Pretty Woman, I couldn't help but see,
Pretty Woman, that you look lovely as can be
Are you lonely just like me?
Pretty Woman, stop a while,
Pretty Woman, talk a while,
Pretty Woman give your smile to me
Pretty Woman, yeah, yeah, yeah
Pretty Woman, look my way,
Pretty Woman, say you'd stay with me
Cause I need you, I'll treat you right
Come to me baby, Be mine tonight
Pretty Woman, don't walk on by,
Pretty Woman, don't make me cry,
Pretty Woman, don't walk away,
Hey, O.K.
If that's the way it must be, O.K.
I guess I'll go on home, it's late
There'll be tomorrow night, but wait!
What do I see
Is she walking back to me?
Yeah, she's walking back to me!
Oh, Pretty Woman.

Appendix B to the Opinion of the Court

"Pretty Woman" as Recorded by 2 Live Crew
Pretty woman walkin' down the street
Pretty woman girl you look so sweet
Pretty woman you bring me down to that knee
Pretty woman you make me wanna beg please
Oh, pretty woman
Big hairy woman you need to shave that stuff
Big hairy woman you know I bet it's tough
Big hairy woman all that hair it ain't legit
'Cause you look like 'Cousin It'
Big hairy woman
Bald headed woman girl your hair won't grow
Bald headed woman you got a teeny weeny afro
Bald headed woman you know your hair could look nice
Bald headed woman first you got to roll it with rice
Bald headed woman here, let me get this hunk of biz for ya
Ya know what I'm saying you look better than rice a roni
Oh bald headed woman
Big hairy woman come on in
And don't forget your bald headed friend
Hey pretty woman let the boys

Jump in
Two timin' woman girl you know you ain't right
Two timin' woman you's out with my boy last night
Two timin' woman that takes a load off my mind
Two timin' woman now I know the baby ain't mine
Oh, two timin' woman
Oh pretty woman

DECISION AND REMEDY 2 Live Crew's "Pretty Woman" would have been an infringement of the original copyrighted material unless the song was a parody under the fair use exception. The Supreme Court found that "Pretty Woman" was a parody. The Court remanded the case to be heard by the district court as to whether there was a threat of harm to the Acuff-Rose market for "Oh, Pretty Woman" by the parody version sold by 2 Live Crew.

Amici curiae (friends-of-the-court) briefs were filed in this case. People are allowed by the court to file *amici curiae* briefs to provide the court with information, even though they are not party to the lawsuit. In this case, the entertainment industry split between the two sides. Dolly Parton, Michael Jackson, and the Nashville Songwriters' Association supported Acuff-Rose's position. On the other side, *Mad* magazine, the *Capitol Steps*, and television shows, such as *Comedy Central, Saturday Night Live,* and *Monty Python,* sided with 2 Live Crew.

The Web site **http://www.benedict.com/** compares copyrighted music and unauthorized versions. Included are "Oh, Pretty Woman" and "Pretty Woman."

CRITICAL THINKING: PREVENTIVE LAW Plagiarism is the unauthorized use of another's work and presenting it as one's own work. Discuss the difference between a parody and plagiarism.

Theft of Trade Secrets

Those processes or items of information that are neither patented nor patentable are nevertheless protected by law against a competitor's appropriation. Businesses generally protect their trade secrets by having all employees who use the process or information agree in their contracts never to divulge the trade secret. If a salesperson tries to solicit the company's customers for noncompany business or if an employee copies the employer's unique method of manufacture, he or she has appropriated a trade secret and also has broken a contract—two separate wrongs.

When a thief steals confidential data, his crime is also a tort called **theft of trade secrets**. This theft occurs when a business, for instance, wrongfully taps into a competitor's computer. The victim can sue the thief in a civil court for damages.

CYBERLAW

Cyber Liability

Buying and selling on the Internet is now a part of daily business. In addition to the everyday risks businesses face, however, doing business on the Internet presents new risks. Business losses are incurred as the result of viruses, hackers, power outages, and electronic problems. If a business's Web page is not available, the business cannot place orders or receive orders and can suffer additional losses.

Businesses usually keep their records on a computer, thus, they need to be prepared for computer crashes during which data could be lost. All businesses need to back up their data frequently.

Without the data, businesses cannot file the mandatory government reports with the various governmental agencies, pay current bills, or collect on the accounts receivables.

Businesses need to protect confidential information collected by their customers. Liability may result if the business makes an unauthorized disclosure of a customer's private information to third parties. Often e-businesses will post their privacy statements on their Web page to notify customers that any information collected will be placed in a database. As such, the database is an asset that may be sold. If the e-business has informed its customers about its practice, the e-business will not have liability unless a statute requires the e-business to keep specific information confidential.

Defamation suits can be filed as a result of postings of untruthful statements in e-mails, Web sites, chat rooms, or bulletin boards. Many businesses have guidelines to prevent defamation lawsuits.

Many insurance companies exclude coverage for cyber liability. If a business needs coverage, it must purchase specific coverage to cover cyber losses. Several insurance companies offer broad coverage for any potential loss from cyberspace while other companies offer limited coverage. When a company has a Web business, it needs to consider purchasing a business interruption policy or lost income policy.

Damages

People who have been harmed may choose to file a lawsuit against the person who caused the damages. The following sections review the different types of damages that may be sought.

Damages for Intentional Tort

An intentional tort occurs when a person intentionally harms another. If Greene deliberately hits Levy's car intending to harm her, Levy can sue for compensatory damages and for pain and suffering, but also for **punitive damages** (sometimes called **exemplary damages**).

Punitive damages are quasi-criminal in nature. Many intentional torts are also crimes. The criminal system lacks the resources to process effectively all of these types of crimes, so most states allow the plaintiff to seek punitive damages in a civil lawsuit. Instead of being based on the amount of harm the plaintiff has endured, these damages are based on the defendant's worth and the amount of wrongful conduct. As the name implies, punitive damages are intended to punish the defendant for his intentional tort and to prevent others from committing a similar act.

The question arises as to whether the amount of punitive damages should be related to the type of intentional act committed. The United States Supreme Court answered this question in the following case.

CASE 8.5

Supreme Court of the United States, 1996
517 U.S. 559, 116 S. Ct. 1589, 134 L. Ed. 2d 809
http://supct.law.cornell.edu/supct/html/94-896.ZS.html

BMW OF NORTH AMERICA, INC. v. GORE

BACKGROUND AND FACTS In 1983, BMW of North America, Inc. (BMW), had a nationwide policy to repair and sell as new the cars that were damaged in the course of manufacture or transportation. The dealers were advised that repairs had been made only when repair costs exceeded 3 percent of the suggested retail price.

Gore purchased a black BMW sports sedan for $40,750.88 from an authorized BMW dealer in Birmingham, Alabama. He drove the car for nine months without noticing any flaws in its appearance. To make it look "snazzier than it normally would appear," he took the car to "Slick Finish," an independent detailer. Slick Finish detected that the car had been repainted.

In fact, the top, hood, trunk, and quarter panels had been repainted in BMW's vehicle preparation center in Brunswick, Georgia. The original damage apparently had been caused by acid rain exposure during transit between the manufacturing plant in Germany and the preparation center. Because the $601.37 cost of repainting Gore's car was only about 1.5 percent of its suggested retail price, BMW did not disclose the damage or repair to the Birmingham dealer. Testimony by a former BMW dealer placed the value of a repainted car at 10 percent below that of a car that had not been repainted.

Gore sued BMW, alleging that BMW's intentional failure to disclose that the car had been repainted constituted suppression of a material fact. He sued for $500,000 in compensatory and punitive damages, and costs. The jury found BMW liable for compensatory damages in the amount of $4,000. The jury also assessed $4 million in punitive damages based on a determination that the nondisclosure policy constituted "gross, oppressive or malicious" fraud. BMW appealed.

The Alabama Supreme Court upheld the punitive damage award, but found that the jury had improperly calculated the amount and thus reduced the punitive damages to $2 million. BMW appealed the Alabama Supreme Court's decision.

Justice STEVENS delivered the opinion of the Court.

. . . .

Punitive damages may properly be imposed to further a State's legitimate interests in punishing unlawful conduct and deterring its repetition. In our federal system, States necessarily have considerable flexibility in determining the level of punitive damages that they will allow in different classes of cases and in any particular case. Most States that authorize exemplary damages afford the jury similar latitude, requiring only that the damages awarded be reasonably necessary to vindicate the State's legitimate interests in punishment and deterrence.

. . . .

Perhaps the most important indicium of the reasonableness of a punitive damages award is the degree of reprehensibility of the defendant's conduct. As the Court stated nearly 150 years ago, exemplary damages imposed on a defendant should reflect "the enormity of his offense." This principle reflects the accepted view that some wrongs are more blameworthy than others. Thus, we have said that "nonviolent crimes are less serious than crimes marked by violence or the threat of violence." . . .

In this case, none of the aggravating factors associated with particularly reprehensible conduct is present. The harm BMW inflicted on Dr. Gore was purely economic in nature. The presale refinishing of the car had no effect on its performance or safety features, or even its appearance for at least nine months after his purchase. BMW's conduct evinced no indifference to or reckless disregard for the health and safety of others. To be sure, infliction of economic injury, especially when done intentionally through affirmative acts of misconduct or when the target is financially vulnerable, can warrant a substantial penalty. But this observation does not convert all acts that cause economic harm into torts that are sufficiently reprehensible to justify a significant sanction in addition to compensatory damages.

DECISION AND REMEDY The Court overturned the $2 million award, which the Court noted to be 500 times Gore's actual harm. The Court refused, however, to set out a mathematical formula for calculating punitive damages. Instead, the Court held that the amount of punitive damages must be proportionate to the type of wrong inflicted on the victim.

CRITICAL THINKING: PUBLIC POLICY Should the Court have established a mathematical formula to provide clearer legal guidelines? Explain.

Damages for Negligence

Lana is driving her car through an intersection on a green light. Gastin, approaching the same intersection, fails to stop at the red light, striking Lana's car and injuring her. She is taken to the hospital for treatment of her injuries. Lana decides to file a lawsuit to seek two types of damages: compensatory damages and damages for pain and suffering.

Compensatory damages reimburse the plaintiff, Lana, for the expenses she incurred resulting from the accident. Typically, such costs include hospital bills, doctors' bills, physical therapy bills, and lost wages during the period for which her personal injuries made her unable to work. Compensatory damages also cover the car repair bills, which are called property damages. These costs can be calculated relatively easily using the bills submitted.

Damages for pain and suffering are not as easy to quantify. These damages are awarded to compensate Lana who has endured pain and suffering caused by the automobile accident.

Both compensatory damages and damages for pain and suffering are determined by the amount of harm that Lana has suffered. Lana proves the amount of injury incurred through documents, such as medical and hospital bills. Lana can also put forth evidence as to the amount of pain and suffering she has endured. If the case is not settled and proceeds to trial, the jury will decide the amount to be awarded for both types of damages.

Current Tort Controversy

The American Tort Reform Association[8] is a broad-based, bipartisan coalition that is involved in reforming the civil justice system. The Association of Trial Lawyers of America[9] defends the current system. The issue is whether the tort system should be modified.

In 1998 and 2003, Congress considered bills that would place a cap on pain and suffering damages and punitive damages; require the loser to pay all the court costs and attorneys' fees for the prevailing party; and abolish the contingent fee system. This fee payment system allows plaintiffs to arrange to pay an attorney a percentage of the damages awarded. This percentage usually ranges from 20 to 50 percent, depending on the case's difficulty. The attorney receives payment only if recovery of damages occurs.

In 2003, the House of Representatives passed legislation limiting noneconomic damages to a maximum amount of $250,000 in medical malpractice cases. Noneconomic damages include pain and suffering compensation. The House passed the bill after the premiums for medical malpractice insurance increased greatly. Many states over the past decade placed limits on medical malpractice damages.

Do the facts verify that a problem really exists? Or is it a situation where the insurance companies have lobbied successfully to increase their profits?

State courts handle more than 98 percent of all litigation in the United States. A study conducted by the National Center for State Courts (NCSC) showed that 98 million new cases were filed, of which 17.3 million were civil cases. Civil cases were defined as all contract cases, estate and probate matters, small claims court filings, and domestic relations cases. The actual number of tort cases filed in a recent year was 447,374, less than one-half of 1 percent of all cases filed. Included in the tort filings were all motor vehicle cases, which make up the majority of tort cases. Malpractice cases are a very small percentage of tort claims.

When the NCSC compared the tort filings with previous years, it found these to be increasing at more modest rates than in previous years. The NCSC concluded that tort filings were not increasing at a faster rate than other major categories of civil filings.

The NCSC findings were consistent with research conducted by the University of Wisconsin Law School, which examined twenty years of federal court data. It identified the major change to be a great increase in lawsuits among businesses. Most national and multinational business lawsuits are filed in the federal courts.

The RAND Corporation's Institute for Civil Justice conducted a similar study. It surveyed 70,000 individuals who had been injured. Most had been injured on the job or in motor vehicle accidents. Ten percent received compensation through the court system. Only a few people injured through defective products sought compensation through litigation.

In 1975, California was the first state to limit recovery in medical malpractice cases to $250,000 for

[8]The American Tort Reform Association's Web site is http://www.atra.org/about.

[9]The Association of Trial Lawyers of America is found at http://www.atla.org/index.aspx.

noneconomic damages. Between 1975 to 1987, the cost of malpractice premiums went up 190 percent with an average premium of $27,570, which was eight percent higher than in states that had no caps on recovery. No insurance company will state that premiums will stay the same or decrease in states that have passed this type of legislation or are considering passing such legislation. Congress considered in 2003 imposing a limit of $250,000 for noneconomic damages, citing the California experience, without considering that the $250,000 limit had been imposed over a quarter of a century earlier.

The argument over tort reform continues into the new century. If any tort reform is needed, it must be based on facts, not perceived inequities.

INFOTRAC RESEARCH ACTIVITY

Numerous articles on InfoTrac discuss tort reform. Both sides on this issue are presented in various articles. Go to Info-Trac and review four articles that present different views on tort reform. Write a paper that either supports tort reform or defends the current tort system.

International Consideration

Combining Criminal and Civil Law

Differences exist between the common law system used in the United States and the civil law system used in Europe. For example, a drunk driver causes an accident that harms a person. In this situation, driving while under the influence of alcohol is both a tort and a crime. In the common law system, the lawsuit for the tort is handled separately from the criminal prosecution in the court system. The victim of a tort must file the lawsuit, while the government exclusively pursues the criminal prosecution.

The civil law system allows great latitude in compensating victims of wrongful acts. For example, the French civil law code, which is followed by a large number of countries, reads "every human act that causes damages to another obliges the one through whose fault it has occurred to pay damages." The French code allows the courts to combine civil and criminal proceedings. The victim of a drunk driver is represented by an attorney in criminal proceedings. In the same procedure, the court determines if the drunk driver is guilty of the crime of driving under the influence of alcohol. If the driver is found guilty, the judge imposes the sentence. Additionally, the judge has the authority to calculate civil liability on the victim's behalf.

Some jurisdictions in the United States take the same approach. For example, a person is assaulted and sustains injuries. After the criminal is convicted, the judge has the authority to order the defendant to pay the victim's expenses, such as medical costs, hospital bills, and lost income. But the statutes do not allow the judge the authority to order payment for pain and suffering. This is one example in which the differences between the common law system and the civil law system are shrinking.

PRACTICAL TIPS

Duties Owed to the Insurance Company

Insurance provides protection for businesses. If the business sustains a loss, the insurance reimburses the business for part or all of its losses, based on what type of coverage was purchased. A business should consider these three types: property insurance, product liability insurance, and motor vehicle and aircraft insurance.

Property insurance has two components. Property insurance covers the business premises for potential losses from disasters, such as fire, tornadoes, and hurricanes. Usually, damage from floods and earthquakes is not included in the basic coverage and must be covered specifically by additional insurance. Property insurance also covers liability for a business's legal duty or obligation. This type of insurance covers the liability the business owes to a person injured as a result of a negligent act of the business. For example, a person slips, falls, and is injured on the business's premises as a result of the business's negligent act (allowing the floor to be dirty and slippery). A business also may purchase business interruption insurance. This insurance compensates the business for profit loss for the time period during which it is unable to function, such as after a fire.

Product liability insurance provides liability coverage if a business's manufactured or sold item harms someone or damages property. Not all losses or damages lead to liability, however. This topic is partially covered in this chapter and in more detail in Chapter 11.

Motor vehicle and aircraft insurance consists of three types: liability coverage, collision coverage, and comprehensive coverage. If a business employee, within the scope of her duties, negligently harms someone or damages property while using the business-owned motor vehicle or aircraft, the liability portion of the insurance will cover the claims. If the business's motor vehicle or aircraft is damaged, the collision portion covers vehicle or aircraft repair or replacement. The comprehensive coverage will repair or replace the business's vehicle or aircraft that was damaged as an act of God or that has been stolen.

Insurance policies generally have deductibles that range from $50 to millions of dollars. For example, a typical deductible for automobile insurance is $250. The insured (the person purchasing the insurance) pays the first $250 dollars of any damage. If the damage exceeds $250, the $250 must be paid by the insured before the insurance company pays the excess. Insurance premiums are based on the insured's prior losses.

The policy requires the insured to report all losses, including out-of-pocket losses. For example, a business employee has an accident that results in $100 worth of damage to its automobile. The business pays for the repair, but does not report the repair cost to its insurance company. By not informing the insurance company, the business has breached a term in its insurance policy.

Another reason for which a business has a duty to report any losses promptly to the insurance company is that prompt notification allows the insurance company to immediately investigate the circumstances surrounding the loss. The insurance company can send an investigator to view the scene of the loss and to take photographs. Potential witnesses can be interviewed while their memories are fresh.

Cases have been filed in which the initial damages appeared to be minor, but months later an injured party filed a lawsuit for thousands of dollars. By that time the insurance company cannot adequately prepare a defense. Because of these situations, if the business fails to report the accident, and thus breaches the terms of the insurance contract, the insurance company has the right to decline to represent the business in the lawsuit or to pay any judgment rendered against the business.

To be in a better position in dealing with the insurance company, the business should take the following actions before any loss occurs. Keep insurance policies in a safe-deposit box or safe place. One person should review the policies annually to ensure that the business is receiving the best coverage for the amount of premiums being paid. Photographs or videotapes of all property should be taken and placed in a safe place. A detailed inventory with receipts should be kept and updated on a regular schedule. Funds should be set aside to cover the deductible and other expenses in case of a disaster. Finally, the information should be stored on computer disks or tapes that are kept off the business premises so if the premises are damaged, the information needed to substantiate a claim with the insurance company will be available.

A business should develop a checklist to follow. Here is a sample checklist that can provide guidance.

Checklist

✔ *Reporting* Immediately contact the business's insurance agent by telephone and follow up on that contact with written notification

✔ *Prevention* If possible, make temporary repairs to prevent further loss. For example, place a tarp over the holes on the roof created by high winds.

✔ *Records* Collect all business records that have not been destroyed. These records include canceled checks, receipts, invoices, computer disks, and contracts that confirm the amount of the losses.

✔ *Documentation* Contact all witnesses to the accident or event creating the loss. Detailed notes of conversations need to be taken and kept in a safe place. Photographs or videotapes of the destroyed property or the accident scene need to be taken and safely stored.

✔ *Inventory* Prepare a detailed inventory of destroyed personal property.

✔ *Computers* Download daily all business records from the computer, remove the backup disks or tapes from the business site, and keep them in a safe place.

Chapter Summary

A tort is a wrong committed by a person that inflicts injury to another or damage to his property. Tort law is part of the civil law. A person can commit a wrong that is both a crime and a tort. First, intentional torts are injuries caused by intentional acts. Second, negligence is a tort under which careless acts can result in liability. Third, strict liability is imposed by law without regard for fault.

Intentional torts are wrongs against a person or a business, such as assault and battery, false imprisonment, infliction of mental distress, invasion of privacy, defamation (disparagement of goods, slander of title, and defamation by computer), and fraud. Intentional torts also can be wrongs against property, such as trespass to real and personal property, conversion, and nuisance. All of these actions are based on the concept that the person or property was intentionally harmed.

The concept underlying negligence is that the defendant did not intend to harm another, but through her carelessness, a person was injured or property damage occurred. The first element of negligence is a breach of the duty of care. This duty is the objective standard of care that we all owe one another. The duty of care is breached when someone fails to act as a rea-

sonable and prudent person would act when confronted with similar circumstances or fails to act in accordance with the duties defined by statutes. The second requirement of negligence is that an injury or damage has taken place. The last requirement is causation, in other words, did the breach of the duty of care cause the damages?

A limiting factor to liability based on negligence is the doctrine of foreseeability—could the defendant foresee the injury or damages to persons in the plaintiff's position when he or she breached the duty of care? Defenses to negligence include superseding intervening forces, assumption of risk, contributory negligence, and comparative negligence.

Strict liability is based on the idea that certain dangerous activities automatically create liability if damages or injuries result. The law imposes this liability because of public policy.

Certain torts apply only in a business situation. For example, a business cannot wrongfully interfere with other businesses' contractual or business relationships. A business can never infringe on another's trademark, patent, or copyright, nor use another's trade secrets without incurring liability for infringement.

Using the World Wide Web

The WWW has a variety of information on it concerning patents and trademarks. Both domestic and international sites are available for research. For *Web Activities*, links to Web sites mentioned in the chapter, and additional Web sites that relate to the chapter topics, go to **http://bohlman.westbuslaw.com**, click on "Internet Applications," and select Chapter 8.

Web Activities

Go to **http://bohlman.westbuslaw.com**, click on "Internet Applications," and select Chapter 8.
8–1 Current Tort Cases
8–2 Mass Torts

Key Terms

absolute privilege	conversion	false imprisonment	intentional tort
assault	copyright	foreseeability	invasion of privacy
assumption of risk	damages for pain and	fraud	libel
battery	suffering	infliction of mental	merchant protection
causation	deceit	distress	legislation
comparative negligence	defamation	intentional interference	negligence
compensatory damages	defamation by computer	with a contractual or	nuisance
contributory negligence	disparagement of goods	business relationship	objective standard of care

patent
private nuisance
privilege of immunity
proximate cause
public nuisance
punitive (exemplary)
   damages

qualified privilege
res ipsa loquitur
service mark
slander
slander of title
statutory duty
strict liability

superseding (intervening)
   force
theft of trade secrets
tort
trademark
trespass
trespasser

Questions and Case Problems

8–1 Comparison Compare and contrast intentional and unintentional torts.

8–2 Merchant Protection Statute Fermino was employed as a salesclerk at Fedco, Inc. She was summoned by the store's personnel manager, who was joined by the store's loss prevention manager and two security agents. She was conducted to a windowless room and interrogated about an alleged theft of $4.95. One security agent told Fermino that a customer and an employee, who were waiting in the next room, had witnessed the theft. She was told that the interrogation could be handled in two ways: the "Fedco way" or the "system way." The "Fedco way" was to award points each time she denied her guilt. When she reached fourteen points, she would be handled the "system way," that is, handed over to the police. After each of Fermino's repeated and vehement denials, the security agent said "one point." The loss prevention manager "hurled profanities" and demanded that she confess.

Fermino's repeated requests to leave the room and to call her mother were denied. When she walked toward the door in an attempt to leave, a security guard threw up his hand and gestured her to stop. She was physically compelled to remain in the room for more than one hour. Fermino filed a lawsuit for unspecified physical injuries, shock and injury to her nervous system, and intentional and negligent infliction of emotional distress. A merchant protection statute allows an arrest for shoplifting. Did Fedco go beyond the protection of this type of statute? [*Fermino v. Fedco, Inc.,* 7 Cal. 4th 701, 872 P.2d 559, 30 Cal. Rptr. 2d 18 (1994)]

8–3 Conversion Mr. and Mrs. Bhattal checked into the Grand Hyatt–New York. Shortly after arriving at their room with their luggage, they left to have lunch. They remembered to lock the door. On returning to their room, they discovered that their luggage was missing. As a result of a computer error made at the front desk, the Bhattals' luggage had been taken from their room and sent to the airport, along with the luggage of the previous occupants of the room, who were crew members of a Saudi Arabian airline. The Bhattals' luggage was never recovered. The Bhattals sued for conversion and intentional infliction of mental anguish. Who should prevail? Explain. [*Bhattal v. Grand Hyatt–New York,* 563 F. Supp. 277 (1983)]

8–4 Negligence Bigbee, the plaintiff, was in a telephone booth on Century Boulevard in the area of Los Angeles, California. Looking up, he saw an automobile coming toward him and realized that it was going to hit the telephone booth. He attempted to flee, but the door to the booth jammed, trapping Bigbee inside. Roberts, the driver of the automobile, was intoxicated. Evidence showed that the telephone booth had been demolished by an automobile crash twenty months before. Bigbee sued the driver and the businesses that served the driver alcoholic beverages. The case was settled as to those defendants. Bigbee also sued Pacific Telephone and Telegraph Company for negligence and strict liability for the design, location, installation, and maintenance of the telephone booths. Pacific Telephone was granted a summary judgment that, in effect, dismissed the case. Bigbee appealed. What result and why? [*Bigbee v. Pacific Telephone and Telegraph Co.,* 34 Cal. 3d 49, 665 P.2d 947, 192 Cal. Rptr. 857 (1983)]

8–5 Intentional Tort Over a ten-year period, a series of break-ins occurred at a farm home that was used to store miscellaneous items. No one lived in this home during that time period. The couple who owned it decided to place a 20-gauge shotgun in such a manner that it would discharge when the interior door was opened. Katko knew that the place was unoccupied and believed it to have been abandoned. Katko kept a collection of old bottles from the surrounding area. In search of bottles, he decided to enter the house by removing a panel covering a window that had no glass. He looked around the inside of the house for old bottles. When he pulled the interior door open to leave, the gun went off and injured his leg severely. He was convicted later of misdemeanor larceny and paid a fine. He sued the owners for his leg injury. Should he prevail? Explain. [*Katko v. Briney,* 183 N.W.2d 657 (Iowa, 1971)]

8–6 Negligence Kmart Enterprises sold a rifle to William Knuck, who was a heavy marijuana user and was under indictment for a felony. Federal law prohibits the sale of any firearm to such a person. Kmart was supposed to question potential customers about marijuana use or felony indictments prior to a sale. This was not done. William Knuck's brother, a heroin addict and alcoholic, took the rifle while drunk and assaulted his estranged wife and a police officer. The police officer brought a negligence action against Kmart, which defended on the grounds of intervening circumstances. Discuss whether Kmart was successful. Why or why not? [*Kmart Enterprises v. Keller,* 439 So. 2d 283 (Fla. Dist. Ct. App. 1983)]

8–7 Negligence Charles and Patricia Keas were on vacation when their nineteen-year-old daughter, Kimberly, had a visitor, Kenneth Maxwell, at her parents' home, where she lived. After consuming alcoholic beverages, Kimberly became angry, grabbed a knife, and stabbed Kenneth to death. His estate brought a lawsuit against Kimberly's parents based on negligence because the parents failed to prevent their daughter from gaining access to alcohol when they knew, or should have known, that she was addicted to it. Were the parents negligent? Why or why not? Explain your answer. [*Maxwell v. Keas,* 639 A.2d 1215 (Pa. Super. 1994)]

8–8 Negligence The Kveragas rented a motel room at the Scottish Inns. That night, three intruders kicked open the door, shot and injured them, and robbed them of $3,000. The Kveragases filed a lawsuit alleging that the motel owners failed to adequately provide for the motel guests' safety. The room was equipped with a hollow-core door that fit poorly into the door frame. The only door lock was incorporated into the handle, a grade-three lock, although a security chain also was provided. The plaintiffs had both locked and chained the door. A single kick applied to the door, however, opened it. Dead-bolt locks, which are considerably stronger than the type of lock employed at this motel, and other security devices were easily available and used throughout the motel industry. A dead-bolt lock could have withstood the force that was applied to the door. The trial court directed the jury to return a verdict for the Scottish Inns, which the jury did, on the grounds that the motel owners and operators had no duty to protect their guests from sudden criminal acts. The plaintiffs appealed. Should the jury had been given the right to determine negligence? Why or why not? [*Kveragas v. Scottish Inns, Inc.,* 733 F.2d 409 (1984)]

8–9 Negligence William H. Jordan was the principal of a middle school in Tulsa, Oklahoma. He brought an action for negligence against a local newspaper that had published a "letter to the editor" falsely attributed to him. The letter, on school stationery and enclosed in a school envelope, contained racist statements. Jordan claimed that he did not write the letter, did not sign the letter, and did not know anything about the letter until it was published. Jordan admitted that he was a public figure. Was the newspaper negligent in publishing the letter without verifying its authenticity? Does Jordan's position as a public figure have any bearing on the decision? Why or why not? (*Hint:* Refer to the sections on public figures in Chapter 5.) [*Jordan v. World Publishing Co.,* 872 P.2d 946 (Okla. App. 1994)]

8–10 Internet The U.S. government is sued often for committing torts. According to the statute, how will the United States be treated? Is the United States liable for punitive damages? Go to the Law Information Institute at **http://www.law.cornell.edu/uscode/28/2674.shtml**.

Chapter 9

Contract Formation

An acre of performance is worth the whole world of promise.

> *Familiar Letters,* 1650
> J. B. Howell, 1594–1666

Chapter Outline

Introduction

People and businesses enter into and perform millions of contracts daily. A **contract** is an agreement between two or more parties that can be enforced in a court of law or a court of equity. In the legal environment of business, questions and disputes about contracts arise daily. Answering those questions and resolving those disputes are the essence of contract law.

The legal framework provides the stability and the structure within which businesses can plan and carry out their contracts. When adverse business conditions occur, a businessperson cannot rely on good faith that the other party to the contract will perform simply out of a sense of duty. The enforceability of contracts in courts of law and equity ensures the promised performance or entitles the person harmed to some form of relief.

This chapter discusses the sources of commercial law, contract formation, and some contractual terms and elements.

Artiste Login. Carlo and Carlotta own the online business, Artiste Login Products, Inc. They need a working knowledge of contract law because the fundamental method of exchanging goods, services, property, and money is accomplished through contracts. Good contracts are essential to good business.

Comparing Torts with Contracts

The previous chapter discussed tort law. Occasionally, tort law and contract law arise out of the same set of facts. Torts, such as fraud and misrepresentation, can originate within a contract's context. A tort also results when someone intentionally interferes with an existing contract.

Contract and tort, however, are different branches of law. Contract law[1] exists to enforce legally binding agreements between parties; tort law is designed to vindicate social policy. Contract law exists to protect promises that have been made, whereas tort law exists to protect people from certain kinds of harms.

Conduct that breaches a contract becomes a tort when it also violates a specific principle of tort law. Besides fraud and misrepresentation, a major tort action tied directly to contract law is the tort of intentional interference with contractual relationships. This tort arises when a third party intentionally causes or attempts to cause a contract party to breach a contract. The laws of torts and contracts overlap in such an action.

Sources of Commercial Law

Commercial or *business law* is the body of law that governs commercial transactions. Commercial law covers such topics as contracts, partnerships, corporations, and agencies. Many principles of commercial law developed centuries ago from what was known as the **law merchant**.

---

[1] A general overview of contract law can be found at the Cornell Law School Web site at http://www.law.cornell.edu. Once there, on the left side, click the bar "Law About . . ." and find contracts. The Web site provides an overview of contract law. Another Web address that provides a considerable amount of information on contract law is http://www.freeadvice.com.

The Law Merchant

The Magna Carta (which means the Great Charter) is a charter granted in 1215 by King John to the barons at Runnymede, England. The Magna Carta is regarded as the foundation of the U.S. Constitution. One chapter particularly made special provisions for merchants, stating that all merchants should "have safe and secure conduct, to go out of, and to come into England, and to pass as well by lands as by water, for buying and selling by the ancient and allowed customs."

A system of mercantile courts developed in England and throughout Europe long before the advent of the common law courts. These mercantile courts administered the law merchant, which set out the rules that governed the contract process. These rules evolved from merchants' customs. The merchants themselves administered these mercantile courts.

The law merchant was important during the Middle Ages, during which time the fair, or market, was the primary commercial event. As the merchant traveled from place to place, he reasonably could be assured that the law would be similar, no matter where he conducted his business. The law merchant became part of the common law and eventually was brought to the United States and incorporated into U.S. law.

Codification of Commercial Law

From its very beginning, the United States adopted the English common law, which covered commercial transactions. When early U.S. commerce was just developing, many gaps in the body of this law existed. States took opposing positions on many commercial issues, leaving New York's businesspeople, for example, uncertain as to Connecticut's law. Over the years, both the legal and the business professions realized the necessity for uniform laws covering commercial transactions.

To achieve this uniformity, the legal profession, through the National Conference of Commissioners on Uniform State Laws[2] in conjunction with the American Law Institute (ALI), developed uniform codes of commercial law. Once a uniform code is completed, it is sent to each state. The state may choose to adopt the uniform code completely, may change parts of it to make it compatible with local law,

or may choose not to consider or adopt the uniform code. Today, these codes are continually being developed to correspond with changing business needs. Of all the uniform codes, the most important to businesses is the **Uniform Commercial Code (UCC)**.[3] The UCC is discussed in Chapter 11.

Contract Terms

A *contract* is an agreement between two or more parties to perform—or to refrain from performing—some act now or in the future. When valid, this agreement is enforceable. A contract is based on a promise, but not all promises are legally enforceable. A contract is created when there is an offer and an acceptance of that offer along with several other requirements.[4]

An **offer** is a promise that can be met with **acceptance** (a return promise) or with **rejection**, that is, the person receiving the offer refuses it. Every offer involves at least two parties. The **offeror**, or the party making the offer, promises to do—or not to do—an act. The **offeree** is the party to whom the offer is made and who has the power to accept or reject the offer. If the offeree accepts (by performing an act or by returning a promise), the contract is formed because promises have been exchanged. The offeree's rejection terminates the offer.

During the offer stage, negotiations occur. Negotiations may take years, as in the purchase of a large land tract, or may be over quickly, as in the decision to purchase a soft drink.

CYBERLAW

Electronic Contracts

Electronic commerce (e-commerce) involves electronic contracts (e-contracts) using one of two methods. First, closed networks are used among businesses. For several decades, business-to-business (B2B) and government-to-business (G2B) contracts have

[2]One Web page for the National Conference of Commissioners on Uniform State Laws is found at http://www.law.upenn.edu/bll/ulc/ulc_frame.htm.

[3]The Uniform Commercial Code is found at http://www.law.cornell.edu/ucc.ucc.table.html.

[4]Contract law is rather complicated. One of the best sources for answers to contract questions is http://www.findlaw.com.

used the electronic data interchange (EDI). Second, the World Wide Web (WWW) open environment has cleared the way for business-to-consumer (B2C) contracts and for B2B and B2G contracts to expand.

EDI was created in the 1960s when large department stores, such as Sears and J.C. Penney, were expanding rapidly. Dealing with hundreds of suppliers for hundreds of thousands of types of goods led to an overwhelming amount of paperwork for the purchaser and supplier. Necessity drove the purchaser to look for a more efficient method. Each retailer decided on its own computer system and had software designed for the system. Each retailer used its own standard contract forms and these forms were placed on the computer. The suppliers to each retailer adapted their business practices and used several computers that were compatible with the various computer systems operated by different purchasers.

If a supplier dealt only with one purchaser, the supplier had efficiencies built in because the computer system replaced the labor-intensive paperwork. If a supplier did business with a number of purchasers, a major problem arose. The supplier needed to purchase a number of computer systems that were compatible with the different computers and software systems of the various purchasers. For example, a wholesale dress supplier may sell to ten different purchasers. The supplier needed a number of different computer systems to communicate with all ten purchasers. The suppliers clearly needed a better method.

Suppliers and purchasers held a series of meetings and agreed on a set of standards that became the electronic data interchange. The EDI has an internationally agreed set of standards under UN/EDIFACT (United Nations Electronic Interchange for Administration, Commerce and Trade).[5] EDI transactions represent a paperless business information exchange that is independent of either business partner's unique business processes, computer software, or hardware. EDI provides flexibility, but does not impose the requirement of common hardware, software, business processes, or terminology on the diverse participants, only common data usage and transmission formats.

As stated on the UN/EDIFACT Web page, implementing EDI is not a goal in and of itself. The adoption of EDI should be part of a larger effort to improve business practices. When EDI is used to replace paper while leaving the existing business processes in place, it brings benefits, including reduced data entry and mailing costs, more accurate information, faster communications, and decreased paperwork and reproduction. Fully exploiting the potential of EDI, however, requires reengineering the business to bring about the greater advantages of

- faster processing of actions,

- availability of timely and accurate data for decision makers,

- lower personnel requirements, and

[5]UN/EDIFACT can be found at http://www.unece.org/trade/untdid.

LEGAL HIGHLIGHT

The Tow Truck and Mud Wrestling

Ron's car got stuck in the mud in a swampy area behind a local bait shop in rural Maryland. He called a tow truck to haul the car out of the mud and then went fishing. The tow truck came and it too got stuck in the mud. The driver contacted another tow truck, which promptly got stuck in the mud as well. The two drivers called a third tow truck, which also got stuck.

A bulldozer was called in. It too got stuck in the mud. Next called was a construction company. Through the efforts of four dump trucks, the company constructed a dirt road. With a solid base in place, the bulldozer, the three tow trucks, and Ron's car were rescued from the mud.

The bill was $4,740. Who shall pay? Ron agreed to pay for one tow truck. The first tow truck driver contended that Ron told him to get the car out and that Ron's father would pay for it. Ron's father said, "No way."

As in many cases of this type, the dispute was settled out of court. Only the parties know how it ended. All in all, it was a muddled contract case.

- a responsive environment that supports innovations, such as direct vendor delivery, flexible manufacturing, rapid distribution, and central pay.

Businesses form contracts by communicating electronically among their respective computers. EDI allows parties to send standardized forms such as purchase orders, invoices, and shipping notices back and forth. EDI has become both a convenient and an efficient substitute for transmitting conventional paper documents between parties.

Terms Used with Contracts

Contract law uses specific terms to describe various contractual situations. Three sets of terms describe the contract's formation, the contract's enforceability in court, and the contract's performance.

Formation. The following terms define the various situations under which a contract is formed.

Bilateral and Unilateral Contracts. A **bilateral contract** is a "promise for a promise." A bilateral contract is created when the offeror makes an offer (promise) and wants the offeree to give his acceptance in the form of a return promise to perform. The offeree's return promise is the acceptance. Most contracts are bilateral.

For example, Miguel offers to sell his residence to Katrina for $100,000. When Katrina agrees (gives a return promise) to purchase Miguel's residence at that price, a bilateral contract results. In a sale of land, a statute (called the **statute of frauds**) requires that for the contract to be enforceable in a court of law, this type of contract must be in writing.

Whether a contract is bilateral or unilateral depends on the offeror's requirement of the offeree in accepting the offer. If the offeror's promise requires the offeree to complete the performance with a return act (and not with a promise), the contract is called a **unilateral contract**. The person making the promise wants the other person to perform an act in return. An example is the reward situation. A person offers a cash amount for the return of a lost dog, as indicated by the following advertisement. The person offering the reward requires action (the return of Useful), not a promise.

$500 REWARD
Return of two-year-old female border terrier.
Responds to name Useful.
Call 555-555-5555

Express and Implied Contracts. In an **express contract**, the terms of the offer and the acceptance are specifically stated, either orally or in writing. If the terms are not exactly set out, but are implied, a valid contract exists that is called an **implied-in-fact contract**. Implied contracts are created by the parties' conduct. When individuals act as if a contract were made, even though no words were spoken or written to that effect, the law implies a contract. For example, when a person visits the doctor's office to be treated for a cold, the person, by her conduct, agrees to pay for the doctor's services.

Formal and Informal Contracts. Statutes set out the provisions for a **formal contract**, requiring it to be in a special form to be valid. All formal contracts must be written, but not all written contracts are classified as formal contracts. An example of a formal contract is a bail bond to obtain someone's release from jail. Other examples are negotiable instruments and letters of credit (see Chapter 12). If the contract is not a formal contract, it is classified as an **informal contract**. Today, most contracts are either oral or written informal contracts.

Enforceability. Another way to describe contracts is according to their enforceability by a court, using the terms *valid, voidable,* and *unenforceable contracts* or *void agreements.* A **valid contract** meets the elements required for the contract to be enforced in a court. These elements are discussed in detail in the next section.

In a **voidable contract**, one party to the contract is bound, but the other party may disaffirm (or avoid) it. For example, a **minor** (a person under a specified age, generally under age eighteen) has the right to disaffirm contracts, that is, she can avoid performing the contract. Occasionally, both parties may have the right to disaffirm the contract, such as when two minors have entered into a contract.

An **unenforceable contract** is one that started out as a valid contract, but for some legal reason, now cannot be enforced in court against the other party. In other words, statutes forbid the courts to enforce the contract. Consider, for example, a person entering into a valid contract to buy a stereo system on credit. Later the person goes into bankruptcy and the contract debt is discharged (forgiven) by the bankruptcy court. The valid contract has been converted into an unenforceable contract by the bankruptcy statute as applied by the bankruptcy court. Now the creditor cannot sue the debtor to collect the money owed on the contract because it has been discharged.

The term *void contract* is an oxymoron (a combination of contradictory words). If a contract is void, the law will not enforce the agreement. For example, if the purpose of a contract is illegal, it is a **void agreement**. In these cases, the word *agreement* is used because, by definition, a contract is legal.

Performance. Contracts can be described based on the performance status of each of the parties—*executed* versus *executory* contracts. These terms can apply in two situations. First, they can refer to the contract's status, considered as a whole. An **executed contract** is a fully performed contract. An **executory contract** has not been performed.

Second, these terms can refer to the state of performance by one party in relation to the other. For example, Ann hands over a textbook to a friend with the understanding that she will receive twenty dollars for it. Ann's performance is fully executed, whereas the friend's performance is executory. In this case, the contract is partially performed. Because the contract still is not fully performed, it is an executory contract. Exhibit 9–1 summarizes the contract terms covered in this section.

Elements of a Contract: Part 1

All legally enforceable contracts must satisfy these requirements:

Exhibit 9–1   Contract Terms

Contract Formation

1. The manner by which the offeree is required to accept the offer determines this classification of contract.
   a. *Bilateral* A promise for a promise.
   b. *Unilateral* A promise for an act (completed act is acceptance).

2. The parties' manner of expression determines this classification of contract.
   a. *Express* Formed by words (oral, written, or both).
   b. *Implied-in-fact* Formed by the conduct of the parties.

3. A court decision determines this classification of contract.
   a. *Quasi-contract* Imposed by law to prevent unjust enrichment.

4. The form determines this classification of contract.
   a. *Formal* Required by law to be in special written form to be valid.
   b. *Informal* No special form is required; may be oral or written.

Enforceability

1. *Valid* The contract has the necessary contractual elements of offer, acceptance, consideration, parties with capacity, and a legal purpose. It can be enforced in court.

2. *Voidable* A contract exists, but one party, by law, has a defense to avoid performing its contractual obligation. That party can elect to perform its obligation and can enforce the contract against the other party.

3. *Unenforceable* A contract exists, but it cannot be enforced by either party in a court because of a legal defense.

4. *Void* No contract exists. The agreement cannot be enforced in court.

Performance

1. *Executed* A fully performed contract.

2. *Executory* A contract not performed.

3. *Partially executed* A contract not fully performed by one or both parties.

1. *Offer* An offer is a promise. An offer must be made by the offeror to the offeree.

2. *Acceptance* An acceptance is the return promise or act. The offeree either makes a return promise or performs the act requested in the offer. The offer and acceptance constitute mutual assent.

3. *Consideration* Consideration is the main reason for entering the contract. Two elements form consideration. First, the promises must be bargained for and exchanged. Second, the promises must have legal value. The consideration must be legally sufficient to support the offer and acceptance so the contract will be enforceable in court.

4. *Capacity* The parties must have the legal ability (capacity) to form a contract.

5. *Legality* The subject matter of the contract must be legal for the contract to be enforceable in court.

6. *Writing* Some types of agreements must be in writing to be enforceable in court.

The first three elements are discussed in this chapter. The last three are examined in Chapter 10.

Requirements of the Offer

An offer is a promise to do—or to refrain from doing—some specified thing now or in the future. Three elements are necessary for an offer to be effective: (1) *objective intent* by the offeror to be bound by her offer, (2) terms of the offer must be *reasonably definite*, and (3) offer must be *communicated* to the offeree. For a valid contract to exist, an offer must have been made.

Intent. An offeror must objectively intend to be bound by her offer. Objective intent is determined from the words and actions of the parties as interpreted by a reasonable person. In a dispute, an offer is interpreted as the expectation of a reasonable and prudent person if she heard or read the offeror's promise. Contract law is not concerned with the subjective (secret) intent of the offeror, that is, the offeror's real intent. The issue, instead, is whether the offeror intends to be bound by her offer if the offeree accepts it. Statements made in obvious anger, jest, or excitement do not meet the objective intent test.

Definite. An offer must have reasonably definite terms so that the parties can specifically determine the acts necessary to perform their part of the contract. If a dispute arises, a court must be able to determine if the promises by the parties have not been performed and, if so, to decide on an appropriate remedy.

Communication. The third requirement for an effective offer is communication. A person cannot agree to a contract without knowing that the contract exists. Suppose Jones advertises a reward of $100 for the return of her lost dog. Garcia, not knowing of the reward, finds the dog and returns it to Jones. Garcia

LEGAL HIGHLIGHT

Opera, Dinner, and Court?

In San Francisco, Bill, a certified public accountant, asked Ann to join him in attending the opera and for dinner afterward. They agreed to the date three months in advance of the date of the opera. Late on the afternoon of the performance date, Ann called Bill to break the date because her old boyfriend was in town. Since Ann notified him so late in the afternoon, Bill was unable to find anyone else to accompany him. Bill decided to get even.

He sued Ann for breach of contract in small claims court. He requested the court to grant him the following damages: (1) the cost of one opera ticket, (2) one-half of the mileage cost to purchase and pick up the ticket in advance, and (3) the cost of his time to find someone to take in her place.

The small-claims court dismissed Bill's case, stating that a promise to go on a date was not a legally enforceable contract. Social promises are not legally enforceable. Life is not always fair.

cannot recover the $100 in a court, because he did not know that it was offered and, therefore, no contract existed to be enforced. Jones may still give the reward to Garcia, but a court will not force Jones to do so.

Termination of the Offer

An effective offer provides the offeree the power to transform that offer into a contract by accepting it. This power of acceptance, however, does not continue forever. Either an action by one of the parties or an operation of law can cancel an offer.

Termination of the Offer by Action of a Party.

An action of one of the parties can end the offer by (1) revocation of the offer by the offeror, (2) rejection of the offer by the offeree, or (3) counteroffer by the offeree. In determining a contract's validity, a court must determine if the offer is still open.

Revocation of the Offer by the Offeror. **Revocation** is the offeror's withdrawal of the offer. Even if the offeror promises to keep the offer open, she can inform the offeree of the revocation before the offeree accepts. The offeror revokes the offer in one of two ways. First, the offeror specifically repudiates the offer. For example, the offeror says, "I withdraw my offer of October 17." Second, the offeror acts in a manner inconsistent with the offer. In this case, the offeror makes an offer to sell a clock to Gabriel. The next day, while Gabriel is deciding, the offeror sells the clock to Amanda.

The offeror, however, must inform the offeree of the revocation before the offer is accepted. If the revocation follows the offeree's acceptance, the revocation normally is ineffective. A valid contract already has been formed because an acceptance usually is effective at the time it is made. Most states follow the general rule that a revocation is effective only on the offeree's actual knowledge of the revocation.

For example, an offer is made on April 1. When the offeree accepts the offer on April 3, a contract is formed. If the offeror sends a revocation on April 2 that is delivered to the offeree on April 4, the revocation is not effective. If the revocation had reached the offeree on April 2, however, before the offer was accepted, the offer would have been terminated.

Although most offers are revocable, certain offers can be made irrevocable. Two common types of irrev-

ocable offers are (1) those involved in option contracts and (2) offers made irrevocable by virtue of promissory estoppel. In a contract dispute, the court must consider whether the offer is revocable.

Option Contracts. An **option contract** is a separate contract that removes the offeror's right to revoke the offer for the time period specified in the option. If an offeror promises to hold an offer open for a specific time period, and the offeree pays for the promise, an option contract has been created. If no time is specified, a reasonable period of time is implied.

For example, Beverly plans to purchase twelve acres at a prime location. She needs time to determine if she can obtain financing. If she cannot obtain financing, she does not want to buy the property. Beverly pays the landowner $1,000 to give up his right to sell the land to someone else and to take the property off the market for a specified time period, such as 180 days. An option contract has been created. During the 180 days, the landowner cannot revoke his offer to Beverly. At the end of the 180 days, the option expires. If she does not obtain financing, Beverly is not obligated to purchase the land under this option contract.

Promissory Estoppel. Estoppel means "to bar, to impede, or to stop." **Promissory estoppel** means that the offeror cannot revoke the offer if the offeree changes his position by relying on the promises made in the offer. In such cases, revocation is considered unjust to the offeree.

For example, Dan (the offeree) owns a grocery business and the store building. Big Chain (the offeror) offers him a manager's position in a new store that it plans to build but tells Dan that he must sell his business and store building to be hired as manager. Relying on this offer, Dan sells his business and store building. Big Chain then revokes its offer, saying that it no longer plans to build its store and thus does not plan to employ Dan. Had the offer not been made, Dan still would have his store building and grocery business. Dan has a case based on promissory estoppel. Big Chain cannot revoke its offer because the offeree, relying on the offer, changed his situation.

The following case involves promissory estoppel. The court compensated a person even though no enforceable contract was present.

CASE 9.1

Supreme Court of Kansas,
2003
275 Kan. 157, 61 P.3d 669

PAVING, INC. v. CITY OF DEERFIELD

BACKGROUND AND FACTS Ritchie Paving, Inc., sued the city of Deerfield, Kansas, seeking to recover its expenses in preparing the low, but unsuccessful, bid for a Deerfield street improvement project. Deerfield's bid documents stated "the successful bidder as the lowest, qualified, responsible, and responsive bidder to whom owner makes an award."

On April 17, 2000, Deerfield let bids for a street improvement project. The bid form required a bidder to supply commencement and completion dates within the calendar year 2000 for the project, with the commencement date no later than October 17. The project was to be completed within 75 days.

Ritchie Paving submitted a timely bid for $760,502.20 and specified a commencement date of October 1, 2000. Ritchie Paving's bid was the lowest bid by more than $31,000, but it was rejected. The bid documents also stated: "If the contract is to be awarded, award will be to the lowest, responsible, responsive bidder whose evaluation by owner indicates to owner that the award will be in the best interests of the project."

The following reasons were given on behalf of Deerfield for not accepting Ritchie Paving's bid:

1. A high probability that bad weather could delay the completion of the project;

2. That the grant from the federal government would be lost if the project were not completed by April 1, 2001;

3. That a dirt hauling agreement between Deerfield and Kearny County required that the project be completed before the end of the summer 2000; and

4. That Deerfield might have to pay a higher interest rate on their bonds because of a later completion date.

Deerfield's bid documents did not indicate that any of these factors were to be considered by bidders. The lawsuit ensued.

The district court granted Deerfield's motion to dismiss for failure to state a claim upon which relief may be granted. Ritchie Paving appealed. This appeal was transferred from the court of appeals to the Kansas Supreme Court.

The opinion of the court was delivered by ALLEGRUCCI, J.

. . . .

In *Swinerton & Walberg Co. v. City of Inglewood-L.A. County Civic Center Authority,* the unsuccessful bidder alleged in addition to a tort cause of action for breach of statutory duty a cause of action in promissory estoppel. The California court concluded that the unsuccessful bidder, Argo Construction Co., Inc. (Argo), stated a cause of action in promissory estoppel based on *Restatement of Contracts,* § 90, which states: "A promise which the promissary should reasonably expect to induce action or forbearance of a definite and substantial character on the part of the promisee and which does induce such action or forbearance is binding if injustice can be avoided only by enforcement of the promise."

. . . .

It would have been simple for the City, which put great store by having the street improvements made during the summer of 2000, to have stated that preference in its bid documents. Instead, Deerfield specified that commencement date for the project could be no later than October 17. By setting the deadline for starting the project in mid-October and expressing no preference for an earlier commencement, Deerfield promised to award the contract to the lowest responsible bidder that gave project dates within the specifications. Ritchie Paving reasonably relied on the promise to its detriment in incurring the expenses of bid preparation. Thus, the theory of promissory estoppel . . . fits the circumstances of this case.

DECISION AND REMEDY The city failed to show that Ritchie Paving was not the low responsible bidder; thus, the city had no reasonable justification for rejecting Ritchie Paving's bid. The court recognized promissory estoppel as a proper remedy for an unsuccessful responsible low bidder to recover bid preparation costs. The recovery was based on reasonable detrimental reliance on Deerfield's promise.

CRITICAL CONSIDERATION: MANAGEMENT What reasons are valid for a public authority to reject the lowest bid?

Rejection of the Offer by the Offeree. An offeree may reject the offer, in which case the offer ends. A rejection, by conduct or by words, shows an intent not to accept the offer and terminates the offer. Rejection is effective as a termination of the offer when the offeror learns of the rejection.

For example, Fatima offers to sell her used personal computer printer to Hans for $45. On May 1, Hans responds that the offer appears to be a little high and asks Fatima to lower her price. Fatima cannot treat these words as a rejection, because Hans' words did not indicate an intent not to accept but merely an inquiry as to whether Fatima would modify her offer. Fatima, however, refuses to modify her offer. On May 3, Hans mails a rejection letter to Fatima. Before Fatima receives Hans' letter, Hans calls Fatima and accepts her offer. Because Fatima received Hans' call accepting the offer before she received his letter of rejection, the contract is valid and enforceable.

Counteroffer by the Offeree. A **counteroffer** is a rejection of the original offer that, at the same time, constitutes a new offer. Any subsequent attempt by the offeree (now the offeror) to accept the expired offer is construed as a new offer, giving the original offeror (now the offeree) the power of acceptance.

Suppose Arnold offers to sell his used computer to Dale for $500. Dale responds, "Your price is too high. I offer to purchase your computer for $250." Dale's response is termed a *counteroffer* because it constituted

Exhibit 9–2   The Dynamics of a Rejection and Counteroffer

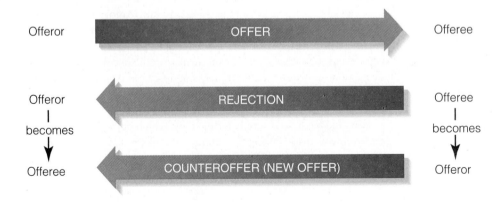

Offeror	OFFER	Offeree
Offeror | becomes ↓ Offeree	REJECTION	Offeree | becomes ↓ Offeror
	COUNTEROFFER (NEW OFFER)	

a rejection. The counteroffer ended Arnold's offer to sell at $500 and, at the same time, created a new offer by Dale to purchase at $250.

Exhibit 9–2 illustrates the relationship reversals of offeror and offeree when a counteroffer is made.

The following case involves a counteroffer. When trying to settle a case before proceeding to trial, attorneys will make offers and counteroffers, such as in this case.

CASE 9.2

Missouri Court of Appeals, 2000
18 S.W.3d 8

BECK v. SHRUM

BACKGROUND AND FACTS Lillian L. Shrum, defendant, appeals from a judgment and order granting a motion to enforce settlement in favor of Betty Anne Beck, plaintiff. The issue on appeal is whether Shrum's $7,500 offer had been rejected by a counteroffer.

The case was for personal injuries sustained in an automobile accident involving Shrum and Beck. Prior to trial, Susan Horowitz was the attorney for Shrum. On the day set for trial, the trial court granted Horowitz's motion to withdraw from the case. Crystal Smith, an attorney, entered her appearance for Shrum. James Whitney, Jr., remained Beck's counsel at all times.

At the hearing on the motion to enforce settlement, Whitney and Smith advised the trial court of the following. After the petition and answer were filed, a pretrial settlement conference was held. At this conference, Beck wanted $50,000. Shrum's insurance company offered to settle the case for $7,500. At some point after the settlement conference, Whitney told Horowitz that "If I could get $15,000 I could maybe talk [Plaintiff] into settling, although [Plaintiff] had never given [Whitney] any indication of another figure for which [Plaintiff] would settle." After talking with Shrum's insurance company, Horowitz indicated that "They couldn't, but the $7,500 was still available." Horowitz did not appear at the hearing because she was on maternity leave.

Whitney knew that Smith was reassigned to the case six days before the hearing. Four days before the hearing, Smith was present at Whitney's office for another matter. At that time, Whitney said to Smith, "If I could get a little more money, I could settle it. . . ." Smith indicated that she would talk to the appropriate people, and Whitney replied, "How about ten thousand, some more money will settle it." After this conversation, Whitney spoke with Beck, and she agreed to accept the $7,500 if she could not get more money.

While going through security at the courthouse with Smith on the day of the hearing, Whitney accepted the $7,500 offer of settlement. Smith replied, "I don't know how that you can do that, because you made a demand of ten." After calling Shrum's insurance company, Smith told Whitney that the company said, "There wasn't $7,500 on the table" because the offer had been rejected when Whitney said, "[I]f you can get me ten, we can make this thing go away." In granting plaintiff's motion to enforce settlement, the trial court took "judicial notice of the custom and practice that an offer is on the table until it is withdrawn, and the attorney is advised that it is withdrawn."

SHERRI B. SULLIVAN, Judge

. . . .

The basic elements of a contract are offer, acceptance and consideration. Any acceptance that includes new or variant terms from the offer amounts to a counteroffer and a rejection of the offer, which may become open again only if renewed by the offeror. However, although a request for a change or modification of a proposed contract made before an acceptance thereof amounts to a rejection of it, a mere inquiry as to whether the offeror will alter or modify its terms, made before acceptance or rejection, does not amount to a rejection. *Jaybe Construction Co. v. Beco, Inc.* (concluding that the following statement was an inquiry: "The plaintiff stated that the bid to the state was a 'close' one, and if possible the plaintiff would like to have the defendant 'shave' its figure. . . ."); *Foster v. West Pub. Co.* (concluding that the following statement, made subsequent to certain suggestions by the speaker, was an inquiry: "This, I say, would be my idea of a square deal; but, if you are not disposed to take the same view, I suppose there is nothing for me to do. . . ."). Consequently, if the offer has not been withdrawn, it may be accepted within a reasonable time to create a binding contract.

The issue, then, is whether Whitney's discussion with Smith at his office constituted an inquiry or a counteroffer. Both Smith and Whitney testified that Whitney used conditional language, *i.e.*, "if," in the discussion. The language is not a clear rejection of the original offer, but rather it inquires about a larger amount of money while still keeping the original offer under consideration. Therefore, because the $7,500 offer had not been withdrawn and because Whitney made an inquiry about $10,000, not a counteroffer, his acceptance of the $7,500 offer at the courthouse created a binding contract.

DECISION AND REMEDY The court found that the mere inquiry as to whether the insurance company was willing to pay more to settle the case was not a rejection of the original offer. The original offer was never withdrawn prior to acceptance.

CRITICAL THINKING: PREVENTIVE LAW How can defendants protect themselves in similar situations?

Mirror-Image Rule. At common law, the **mirror-image rule** requires the offeree's acceptance to match the offeror's offer exactly. In other words, the acceptance must mirror the offer. Any change in, or addition to, the original offer's terms automatically ends that offer and constitutes a counteroffer. The original offeror (now the offeree) can accept the counteroffer's terms, creating a valid contract. The acceptance is effective when sent unless otherwise stated.

Termination of the Offer by Operation of Law. Operation of law is a broad concept used by the court or statute to impose rights or liabilities on a party to a contract without any action taken by the party. The offeree's power to accept an offer and to form a contract can be ended by operation of law.

Four types of operation of law can end the offer: lapse of time, destruction of the offer's specific subject matter, either party's death or incompetence, and the offer's illegality. Often an offer will have a time limitation stated. For example, this offer ends at 12:00 P.M., noon, Pacific Standard Time, tomorrow. At 12:00:01 the offer has terminated. If no time is stated, the offeree has a reasonable time within which to accept. A reasonable time can vary from a few seconds, such

as on a stock market, to over a year in a slow-selling real estate market.

The remaining three ways may occur between the time the offer is made and before the offer is accepted or rejected. The subject matter of the offer may be destroyed between the time the offer was made, but before it was accepted or rejected. If so, the offer is terminated. For example, you offer to purchase the stock car that won a national race. The owner of the stock car takes it on a final tour of the United States. While showing off the car at a race track, the driver hits the wall at a tremendous speed. The car bounces off with parts flying everywhere. The driver has few injuries, but the car is destroyed, thereby terminating the offer.

Either party may die or become mentally incompetent after an offer is made. The offer is terminated unless the offer is irrevocable, such as an option contract. The last type of operation of law occurs after an offer has been made. The legislature passes a statute or a court declares the subject matter of the offer to be illegal, thereby ending the offer. For example, Congress passes a law making it illegal to sell computer chips to terrorist countries. Any outstanding offers to sell computer chips to a firm in a terrorist country end by operation of law.

Exhibit 9–3 summarizes the ways in which an offer can be terminated.

Acceptance

Acceptance is an offeree's voluntary agreement to the terms of the offer and is usually indicated by either words or conduct. The acceptance must be unequivocal and communicated to the offeror.

Except in certain circumstances, only the person to whom the offer is made, or that person's authorized agent, can accept the offer and create a binding contract. Part of the offer identifies the offeree as one of the offer's conditions. For example, Jones offers to sell his motorcycle to Hanley. Hanley rejects the offer, but Hanley's friend, Smith, attempts to accept the offer. No contract is formed.

Silence as an Act of Acceptance. Ordinarily, silence does not constitute acceptance, even if the offeror states, "By your silence and inaction you will be deemed to have accepted this offer." An offeree carries no burden of performing some act in order to reject an offer unless the offeree has accepted a "duty to speak" by agreement or the offeree solicited the offer.

Book and video clubs have a contract with their members. The clubs will automatically send a book or video selection unless the member returns a card indicating that she does not want the selection in the upcoming month. Silence acts as an acceptance because the contract between the club and the member establishes silence as an acceptance method. These clubs fall under the Federal Trade Commission's **Negative Option Rule**, which requires the clubs to give members enough time to respond if they want to decline the monthly selection.

Communication of Acceptance. At common law, whether the offeror must be notified of the acceptance depends on the nature of the offer. In a unilateral contract, generally it is not necessary to notify the offeror because the act of acceptance is evident The offer calls for the full performance of the act. Acceptance is not completed, therefore, until the act has been fully performed. In the example used previously to illustrate a unilateral contract, the contract is complete only when someone returns the lost dog for the reward.

In a bilateral contract involving real property or services, the offeree must communicate the acceptance to the offeror. The acceptance takes the form of a promise (not an act), and the contract is formed when the return promise (the acceptance) is made (rather than when the act is performed).

The acceptance is effective when sent by the same manner in which the original offer was made. For example, if the offer is sent by e-mail, the acceptance, if sent by e-mail, is effective when sent, even though the offeror never receives the e-mail containing the acceptance. This rule is known as the **mailbox rule**.

Exhibit 9–3   Termination of an Offer

1. *By acts of the parties:*
   a. *Revocation* Unless the offer is irrevocable, it can be revoked by the offeror at any time before acceptance without liability. The revocation is effective when received by the offeree. Irrevocable offers are (i) option contracts or (ii) when an offer becomes irrevocable because of promissory estoppel.
   b. *Rejection* Accomplished by words or actions that demonstrate a clear intent not to accept or consider the offer further. A rejection is not effective until known by the offeror.
   c. *Counteroffer* A rejection of the original offer and a new offer constitutes a counteroffer.

2. *By operation of law:*
   a. *Lapse of time* The offer terminates (i) at the end of the time period specified in the offer or (ii) if no time period is stated in the offer, at the end of a reasonable time period.
   b. *Destruction* The offer terminates when the specific subject matter of the offer is destroyed. Destruction automatically terminates the offer.
   c. *Death or mental incompetence* If either party dies or becomes incompetent, the offer is terminated, unless the offer states it is binding on the deceased or incompetent party's heirs or the offer is irrevocable.
   d. *Illegality* If the court or a statute makes the subject matter of the offer illegal after the offer has been made, that supervening illegality terminates the offer.

LEGAL HIGHLIGHT

What Happens When the Marriage Ceremony Does Not Occur

A nurse and a lawyer who had been married twice before became engaged.[a] Everything was going normally until the couple had a big disagreement and decided not to get married. She had sent out wedding invitations, paid a down payment for the facilities, bridal gowns, photographers, florists, etc. totaling

[a] DeFina v. Scott, 755 N.Y.S.2d 587 (2003).

$16,000. He had conveyed one-half interest in a condominium apartment to his future wife before she had spent the $16,000.

After the breakup, the lawyer wanted to cancel his conveyance to his former fiancee and wanted her to return the expensive engagement ring that he had purchased from Tiffany & Co. She wanted to be reimbursed the $16,000. A lawsuit ensured.

The court held that he was entitled to the ring and to have the conveyance canceled, but the court placed a lien on the condominium in the amount of $16,000 until she was reimbursed for her expenses.

The offer can state the method to be used to return the acceptance. For example, the offer is made by mailing it to the offeree who is instructed to e-mail back the acceptance. If the offeree uses a method of communication authorized by the offeror, the acceptance is effective when sent. If the offeror states no specific method of responding, such as by mail, the rule is to mail the acceptance. The acceptance will be effective when mailed.

Exhibit 9–4 summarizes the requirements for contract acceptance.

INFOTRAC RESEARCH ACTIVITY

Many articles on InfoTrac discuss offer and acceptance. Some articles discuss in detail the problems a business may face when contracting. Review four articles and write a paper that discusses four problems that may arise.

Genuineness of Mutual Assent

The offeror and the offeree must have a meeting of the minds, called **mutual assent**. In other words, the offer made by one party must be the offer accepted by the other party. The terms of the offer must be the terms of the acceptance. Mutual assent means that both sides contract for the same item or service.

Factual disputes occur when a meeting of the minds was apparent, but in reality the parties did not reach an understanding. No genuine assent exists as to the contract terms when fraud, misrepresentation, certain forms of mistake, duress, or undue influence take place. A party to the contract can use these situations to prove to the court why he should not be ordered to perform the contract.

Fraud and Misrepresentation. When fraud occurs, the injured party can void the contract. The five requirements that establish fraud are as follows:

1. A misrepresentation of a material fact exists.
2. The guilty party makes the contract with the knowledge that the material fact is false or with reckless disregard as to its truthfulness.
3. The guilty party intends to deceive.
4. The innocent party justifiably relied on the misrepresentation.
5. The innocent party has suffered damages.

Fraud is difficult to prove because the other party's knowledge and wrongful intent must be established. Because of the difficulty in proving fraud, many injured parties sue for **misrepresentation** instead. To establish a claim for misrepresentation, one need not prove that the guilty party intended to deceive or had knowledge of falseness. Obviously, this makes misrepresentation

Exhibit 9–4   Acceptance of a Contract

1. Agreement can be made only by the offeree or the offeree's authorized agent.
2. *Mirror-image rule* Terms must be unequivocal. Under the common law, terms of acceptance must be same as terms of offer.
3. Acceptance of a bilateral offer can be communicated to the offeror by an authorized mode of communication and is effective upon dispatch. Unless the mode of communication is expressly specified by the offeror, the following methods are implicitly authorized:
   a. The same or a faster mode than used by the offeror.
   b. By mail, when the two parties are at a distance.

much easier to prove, but may result in a lesser remedy. The court usually awards greater damages if fraud is proved.[6]

Mistake, Duress, and Undue Influence. Mistakes occur in two forms. A *unilateral mistake* is made by only one of the contracting parties. A *mutual* (also called a *bilateral*) *mistake* is made by both parties.

Unilateral Mistake. A **unilateral mistake** does not affect the contract, which is still valid and enforceable, unless the mistake is so obvious that the other party recognized or should have recognized it. A person cannot take unfair advantage when she knows or should have known that the other party is mistaken.

For example, a court was faced with this set of facts. Jean ran a retail camera store. Jim, a salesperson for a printing company, obtained an order from Jean for return address labels. Jean needed 4,000 labels. She, however, was busy at the time she filled out the form and inadvertently wrote "4,000 m.m." in the blank quantity space. The initials *m.m.* to a person who uses cameras mean millimeter, which is a unit of measurement used when taking photographs. Jean was used to writing "m.m." after numbers and did not realize her mistake. Jim looked at the order but did not recheck it with Jean. He returned to the office elated that he had a sale for four million million (four trillion) labels. Neither he nor his company had ever had such a large order. In fact, a special printing run was made and a freight company made the delivery. The usual method of sending labels to the customer is by mail. This time, however, two trucks

backed up to Jean's business and the drivers asked where to unload the four trillion labels. Jean refused to accept delivery because she wanted only 4,000 labels. In this case, the court held that Jim should have known that Jean had made a unilateral mistake because of the unusual nature of the order. He easily could have telephoned Jean to recheck the order before going to the trouble and expense of having the labels printed and delivered. The court ruled that Jean did not have a contract to purchase four trillion labels.

In contrast, had Jean filled out the form for "4,900" labels (with intent only to order 4,000), the burden of her unilateral mistake would fall on her, and she would be held liable for the purchase of 4,900 address labels. The mistake would not have been obvious; thus, Jim would not have been held responsible for recognizing it.

Mutual Mistake. No contract is formed in the case of a **mutual (bilateral) mistake** under two circumstances: (1) when the parties disagree as to the identity of the contract's subject matter or (2) when they are mistaken as to the existence of the subject matter. If one of these two conditions occurs, a meeting of the minds has not occurred and a court will not find a binding contract. If a court finds, however, that a mutual mistake has occurred as to the value of the contract's subject matter, the contract generally will be fully enforceable against both parties.

For example, Shu-Jen contracts to sell Tyrone a painting for $5,000. Both believe the painting's artist to be Tory, but they learn, instead, that the artist is Lori. Because the mutual mistake affected the subject matter's identity, there is no meeting of the minds and neither can enforce the contract. Had the mistake been related to the value—not the artist—of the painting, the contract would have been fully enforceable.

---

[6]Recent acts of fraud are posted on the Internet. Go to http://www.lectlaw.com/tcos.html and look for the heading "Swindles, Scams, & Rip-offs." Posted are a long list of phony scams ranging from fraudulent student scholarships to living trusts.

In the following case, the court was confronted with the issue of whether the jury should have been instructed about the requirement for a meeting of the minds. The case illustrates why it is important to be very clear and to follow up an oral conversation with a letter confirming the contents of the conversation.

<table>
<tr>
<td>

CASE 9.3

Court of Appeals of
Missouri, 1986
718 S.W.2d 207

</td>
<td>

FLO-PRODUCTS CO. v. VALLEY FARMS DAIRY CO.

BACKGROUND AND FACTS The plaintiff, Flo-Products Company, gave a telephone quote of "fifteen thirty-six" for certain cylinders to be used in the defendant's dairy packaging machine. The defendant's maintenance supervisor testified that the oral quote was "fifteen thirty-six," which he thought was $15.36. The cylinders were shipped to the defendant and billed at $1,536. The defendant refused to accept delivery because of the price discrepancy.

Flo-Products sued Valley Farms. The trial court did not instruct the jury to consider whether the parties had ever achieved a meeting of the minds. The plaintiff won a judgment in the trial court. Valley Farms appealed because the court did not instruct the jury concerning the meeting-of-the-minds element.

Judge DOWD

. . . .

. . . The jury was instructed . . . to find for plaintiff if they believe[d] plaintiff furnished the cylinders at defendant's request and that the charges for the cylinders were reasonable. Defendant requested the court to instruct the jury that "meeting of the minds" was a necessary element of plaintiff's case but the court refused the instruction.

Defendant alleges the trial court erred in refusing to give defendant's requested instruction on "meeting of the minds."

. . . "Meeting of the minds" is a necessary element to the making of a contract[.] . . . [A] meeting of the minds' as to price was a controverted [disputed] issue. For a verdict-directing instruction in favor of plaintiff to be acceptable, it must require the jury to find all the necessary elements of plaintiff's case except for uncontroverted facts. It is reversible error for an instruction to assume or ignore a controverted fact.

The discrepancy in the parties' understanding of the price term remained a controverted fact throughout the trial. Plaintiff Flo-Products Co. chose to submit its case to the jury[.] . . . [T]he jury [is required] to find for plaintiff if they believe: 1) Defendant requested plaintiff to furnish the goods, 2) Plaintiff furnished the goods to defendant, and 3) Plaintiff's charges were reasonable. Instructing the jury . . . under these circumstances resulted in a directed verdict for plaintiff without the only controverted issue of the case ever being before the jury.

DECISION AND REMEDY The trial court erred in not giving the jury an instruction on the requirement that the parties must have a meeting of the minds to have a valid contract. The discrepancy in the parties' understanding of the price remained the contested issue throughout the trial, yet the jury never made a decision on these contested facts. The trial court's judgment was reversed and the case was remanded to the trial court.

CRITICAL THINKING: PUBLIC APPLICATION Assume you are a jury member who was impaneled to hear this case. Assume that the jury was not provided the jury instruction that you knew to be tantamount to the decision. Discuss how you would vote as to the defendant's liability and discuss the arguments you would make to the other jury members.

</td>
</tr>
</table>

Duress. **Duress** occurs when one party is forced into a contract by fear. The courts allow the party who was under duress to rescind the agreement. For example, if Piranha Loan Company threatens to harm Chang unless he signs over to Piranha his $10,000 car in order to secure a $100 loan, Piranha is guilty of using duress, so Chang could rescind the agreement.

Duress may involve the threat of physical or economic harm, such as the loss of a job. The threatened act must be wrongful or illegal. When a party is threatened with physical harm, any agreement signed while the party is subject to such a threat is void (that is, it is without any legal effect). When a person signs an agreement under threat of economic harm, the person may choose to carry out the agreement or to disaffirm it.

Undue Influence. **Undue influence** arises from special kinds of relationships in which one party can greatly influence another party, thus overcoming that party's free will. Minors and elderly people are often under the influence of close relatives. If, for example, Shady influences an elderly person who is under his legal care to enter into a contract that benefits Shady, undue influence has been exerted.

Undue influence can arise from a number of fiduciary (founded on trust) or confidential relationships, such as attorney–client, doctor–patient, guardian–ward, parent–child, husband–wife, or trustee–beneficiary. The essential element of undue influence is that the party of whom advantage is being taken does not, in reality, exercise free will when entering into the contract. This contract is voidable by the person who was unduly influenced.

Exhibit 9–5 summarizes the defenses that a party to a contract can use to contest mutual assent.

Consideration

The third requirement of a legally enforceable agreement is **consideration**. Consideration is divided into two elements: (1) One party must exchange something of legal value for the other's promise and (2) the parties must bargain for and exchange the promises. Legal value may consist of a return promise or a performance.

Exhibit 9–6 summarizes the legal elements of consideration.

Exhibit 9-5   Problems of Assent

Fraud	When fraud occurs, usually the innocent party can enforce or avoid the contract at his option. The five elements necessary for a court to find fraud follow: 1. Misrepresentation of a material fact exists. 2. Contract is made with knowledge that the fact is false. 3. Contract is made with the intent to deceive. 4. Innocent party justifiably relies on the misrepresentation. 5. Innocent party is damaged.
Misrepresentation	The elements in preceding items 2 and 3 are not required for the court to find misrepresentation. Usually in misrepresentation cases, the innocent party can rescind the contract but cannot seek damages.
Mistake	*Unilateral* Generally, the mistaken party is bound by her mistake and the other party can enforce the contract unless the other party knows or should have recognized the mistake. *Mutual* When a mistake made by both parties involves the identity or existence of the contract's subject matter, either party can avoid performing the contract.
Duress	Duress is defined as forcing a party to enter an agreement under fear induced by a threat (for example, the threat of violence or economic pressure). The party forced to enter the contract can rescind the agreement.
Undue Influence	Undue influence arises from special relationships, such as fiduciary or confidential relationships, in which one party's free will has been overcome by the undue influence exerted by the other party. Usually, the contract is voidable.

Exhibit 9-6   Elements of Consideration

1. *Legal value* Does not mean economic value.
   a. *Legal detriment* To promisee, who promises to do (or refrain from doing); no prior legal duty to perform (or to refrain from performing).
   b. *Legal benefit* To promisor.
2. *Bargained for and legally sufficient* The promisee's performance or promises to perform must be given in exchange for the promisor's promise. Adequacy of consideration relates to how much consideration is given and whether a fair bargain is reached. Courts inquire into the adequacy of consideration (if the consideration is legally sufficient) only when fraud, undue influence, or duress may be involved.

Requirements of Consideration. To create a binding contract, the elements of consideration not only must exist but also must be legally sufficient. To be legally sufficient, consideration for a promise must be *legally detrimental* to the **promisee**—the one receiving the promise—or *legally beneficial* to the **promisor**—the one making the promise. In every bilateral contract, each party (offeror and offeree) is treated as both a promisor and a promisee because each makes a promise. Neither *legal detriment* nor *legal benefit* is synonymous with actual economic detriment or benefit.

Note the language change from *offeror* and *offeree* to *promisor* and *promisee*. The former two words describe the parties during the contract formation. Once the parties exchange promises, they become the *promisor* and *promisee*.

Legal detriment occurs when a person does, or promises to do, something that he had no prior legal duty to perform or when the person gives up a legal right. Conversely, **legal benefit** occurs when a person obtains something that he had no prior legal right to obtain. In most cases, each party to a contract suffers a legal detriment and receives a legal benefit.

For example, Fine Gravel Company owns and mines a gravel pit. The land owned by Fine Gravel is adjacent to a school, but the actual mining takes place on the land furthest from the school. The school is one mile away from the mining site. After many years, Fine Gravel decides to mine within a few hundred yards of the school. It also plans to build a road for its trucks next to the school fence. The school board objects because of the danger to the children and the noise that the construction will produce. The school board offers $150,000 to Fine Gravel Company to refrain from building the road and from mining near the school.

The gravel company agrees. The consideration flowing from the gravel company is the promise to refrain from an act that it is legally entitled to do, that is, to earn profits by mining gravel. The consideration flowing from the school board to Fine Gravel is the promise to pay a sum of money that it is not otherwise legally required to pay. In other words, the school board's legal benefit was the maintenance of conditions conducive to learning near the school grounds. Its legal detriment was to pay $150,000. The benefit to Fine Gravel was the $150,000. Its legal detriment was to give up the right to build the road and the right to mine land that it owned.

In the following case, one of the classics of contract law, the court found that refraining from certain behavior at the request of another was sufficient consideration to support a promise to pay a sum of money.

CASE 9.4

Court of Appeals of New York, Second Division, 1891

124 N.Y. 538, 27 N.E. 256

HAMER v. SIDWAY

BACKGROUND AND FACTS William E. Story, Sr., was the uncle of William E. Story II. In the presence of family members and guests at a family gathering, Story, Sr., promised to pay his nephew $5,000 to refrain from drinking, using tobacco, swearing, and playing cards or billiards for money until he reached the age of twenty-one.

The nephew agreed and fully kept his promise. When he reached age twenty-one, he wrote his uncle that he had kept his part of the agreement and was entitled to $5,000. The uncle replied by letter that he was pleased with his nephew's performance and that he was keeping his nephew's promised money in the bank to earn interest. The nephew agreed that his uncle should keep the money according to the terms and conditions of the letter.

The uncle died about twelve years later without having paid his nephew any part of the $5,000 or interest. Sidway, the executor of the uncle's estate (the defendant in this action), did not want to pay the $5,000 plus interest to the nephew, claiming that the nephew had not given valid consideration for the promise. In the meantime, the nephew sold his interest (his right to collect the $5,000 if the court ruled in his favor) to Hamer. Hamer sued Sidway to collect the $5,000. The court disagreed with the executor and reviewed the doctrine of detriment-benefit as valid consideration under the law.

Justice PARKER

. . . The defendant contends that the contract was without consideration to support it, and therefore invalid. He asserts that the promisee, by refraining from the use of liquor and tobacco, was not harmed, but benefitted; that which he did was best for him to do, independently of his uncle's promise—and insists that it follows that, unless the promisor was benefitted, the contract was without consideration—a contention which, if well founded, would seem to leave open for controversy in many cases whether that which the promisee did or omitted to do was in fact of such benefit to him as to leave no consideration to support the enforcement of the promisor's agreement. Such a rule could not be tolerated, and is without foundation in the law. The exchequer chamber [a type of court] in 1875 defined "consideration" as follows: "A valuable consideration, in the sense of the law, may consist either in some right, interest, profit, or benefit accruing to the one party, or some forbearance, detriment, loss, or responsibility given, suffered, or undertaken by the other." Courts "will not ask whether the thing which forms the consideration does in fact benefit the promisee or a third party, or is of any substantial value to any one. It is enough that something is promised, done, forborne, or suffered by the party to whom the promise is made as consideration for the promise made to him. In general a waiver of any legal right at the request of another party is a sufficient consideration for a promise." . . . Now, applying this rule to the facts before us, the promisee used tobacco, occasionally drank liquor, and he had a legal right to do so. That right he abandoned for a period of years upon the strength of the promise of the testator that for such forbearance he would give him $5,000. We need not speculate on the effort which may have been required to give up the use of those stimulants. It is sufficient that he restricted his lawful freedom of action within certain prescribed limits upon the faith of his uncle's agreement, and now, having fully performed the conditions imposed, it is of no moment whether such performance actually proved a benefit to the promisor, and the court will not inquire into it; but, were it a proper subject of inquiry, we see nothing in this record that would permit a determination that the uncle was not benefitted in a legal sense. . . .

DECISION AND REMEDY The court ruled that the nephew had provided legally sufficient consideration by giving up smoking, drinking, swearing, and playing cards or billiards for money until the age of twenty-one and, therefore, he was entitled to the money promised him. In the late 1800s, when this case took place, a minor could legally do these things.

Under the doctrine of detriment-benefit, the court looks at the party who suffered a detriment (harm) and the party who received a benefit (right). In this case, the nephew suffered a detriment of giving up his rights to drinking, smoking, swearing, and playing cards or billiards for money. The uncle received the benefit of the satisfaction that his nephew was not engaging in these activities.

COMMENT The *Hamer v. Sidway* case is a good illustration of the distinction between a benefit to the promisor and a detriment to the promisee. Here the court did not inquire as to whether a benefit flowed to the promisor but required only that a legally sufficient detriment to the promisee occurred.

CRITICAL THINKING: LEGAL APPLICATION This chapter covers the basic concepts of legal consideration. The key to understanding legal consideration is to recognize a bargain for exchange and a legal sufficiency of consideration. The most difficult aspect of determining these is identifying the detriment and benefit that occurred as applied to each party. In buying your textbook for this course from the local bookstore, you were involved in a contract. Explain the benefit and detriment of each party to this contract.

Although the previous case was decided more than 100 years ago, the principal rule on consideration remains the same. To have consideration each side must have a legal detriment and each is entitled to a legal benefit.

Sometimes, in spite of the appearance that each side has made a binding promise, actually the promise cannot be found. The words may sound good, but in reality are **illusory promises**. If a person has not made a promise that can be enforced in a court, that person is not a promisor; thus, no contract exists.

Unliquidated Debts. Consideration is important when settling a disputed debt, or **unliquidated debt**. If the parties reach an amicable settlement for an unliquidated debt, the debt, at that point, becomes liquidated. A **liquidated debt** is one that is not disputed. Legal consideration comes into play whenever an unliquidated debt becomes liquidated.

For example, Steve is in his automobile when Brandon's truck strikes it in the rear. Steve suffers a whiplash injury, resulting in great pain and suffering. Steve believes that he should recover at least $100,000 for his automobile damage, injury, and pain and suffering. Brandon's insurance company believes that

$2,000 is adequate to cover Steve's injury and to repair his automobile. To avoid a lawsuit, both parties agree that Steve will receive $10,000. Legal consideration is present in this case. Steve's legal detriment is giving up his legal right to sue for $90,000 more. His benefit is the settlement increase of $8,000. The reverse is true for Brandon. His benefit is Steve's reduced request from $100,000 to $10,000. His legal detriment is to pay $10,000 instead of $2,000. The debt was unliquidated originally but became liquidated when the parties reached a settlement.

Prior Existing Duty. In addition to parties experiencing bargaining difficulties involving unliquidated debts, problems concerning consideration often arise when a prior duty under an existing contract exists. The prior existing debt rule applies to resolving this problem. Every loan is due on demand unless the parties have an agreement that indicates a specific repayment arrangement. Payment on demand means that you can demand repayment at any time.

For example, let's assume that you loan a friend $100. When you see your friend at a football game, you ask him for the $100, but he insists that he only has $25. He offers to pay you the $25 if you will forget about the remaining $75. You know that your friend is unemployed and you probably will never recover the money that you loaned to him. As a result, you accept the $25 from him. The next day you find out that your friend won a $1 million lottery. You go to your friend and ask for the remaining $75, but your friend refuses to pay it, contending that the $25 payment discharged the remaining $75 he owed you. If you filed a lawsuit, a court would find in your favor. Your agreement to accept $25 in return for discharging the remaining $75 lacked legal consideration. Your friend owed you a liquidated debt of $100 and cannot discharge it by paying only $25. By paying you $25, your friend did not suffer a legal detriment, because he was under a prior legal duty to pay you the full $100. You did suffer a legal detriment by giving up $75, but you did not obtain a legal benefit because you were entitled to $100 and not just $25. Each person must obtain a legal benefit and must suffer a legal detriment. The fact that your friend won the lottery is irrelevant as to whether your friend still owed you the $75. Once the friend had money to repay the loan, you are legally justified to collect the $75. Without the lottery winnings, the $75 is merely uncollectible.

Promissory Estoppel. Earlier in this chapter, the doctrine of promissory estoppel was discussed. In that context, if a court found that promissory estoppel existed, the court would hold that the offer was irrevocable. The offeror did not have the right to revoke the offer and the offeree had the right to accept the offer.

The courts also use the doctrine of promissory estoppel as a substitute for legal consideration. If legal consideration is not present, this doctrine can be used by the courts to find a contract when the facts satisfy the requirements of promissory estoppel. The requirements are summarized by Section 90 of the *Restatement of Contracts,* which states, "A promise which the promissary should reasonably expect to induce action or forbearance of a definite and substantial character on the part of the promisee and which does induce such action or forbearance is binding if injustice can be avoided only by enforcement of the promise."

Adequacy of Consideration. Adequacy of consideration refers to a bargain's fairness. A court normally will not question the consideration's adequacy if it is legally sufficient. If a person buys an item at too high a price, she may have buyer's remorse, but the court will

not set the contract aside unless a reason, such as fraud or mistake, exists.

Quasi-Contracts

Occasionally, a person is unjustly enriched at the expense of another. No express contract exists, and no conduct occurs to imply a contract, yet for one individual to be enriched at the expense of the other is unjust. The law will imply a promise to pay. This type of conduct creates a contract by operation of law, an **implied-in-law contract** (more commonly called a **quasi-contract**).

In a quasi-contract, the parties make no promise by word or conduct, but the law will impose a promise on the party who benefited. To recover, the plaintiff needs to prove three elements. First, a benefit was conferred on the defendant by the plaintiff. Second, the defendant appreciated or knew of the benefit. Third, the acceptance or retention by the defendant of the benefit was done under circumstances that unjustly enriched the defendant at the expense of the plaintiff.

A quasi-contract is distinguishable from an implied-in-fact contract. An implied-in-fact contract is a true contract made between the parties and is enforceable in court. In contrast, only a court can declare that a quasi-contract exists, because it is a legal fiction. The court creates a quasi-contract (that is, a fictional contract) for reasons of social policy, that is, to prevent a person from being enriched unjustly at the expense of another.

The following example shows a situation in which the court can grant the remedy of a quasi-contract. Joel, a salesperson, returns home at 10 A.M. to find a work crew ready to paint his house. He knows that they are supposed to paint his neighbor's house. He says nothing and leaves. When he returns to his house at 5 P.M., the house is painted. Under a quasi-contract, the painting company's remedy is to sue Joel for a reasonable amount for the paint job. He has received a benefit and to retain that benefit without paying for it would be unjust. Joel had a chance to stop the painting and he failed to do so. Until he pays, he has been unjustly enriched at the expense of the paint company.

The following case represents another application of the doctrine of quasi-contract. The case involves a house purchase, an insurance company, the buyer and seller, and a violent weather storm.

CASE 9.5

Missouri Court of
Appeals, 1990
799 S.W.2d 632

PETRIE v. LE VAN

BACKGROUND AND FACTS The Petries purchased a house from Le Van. The deed to the house was transferred on September 24, 1986. Unknown to either party, a severe storm had damaged the roof the night before the deed was recorded in the Petries' name. Because the title to the house was still in Le Van's name, only he could have a homeowner's insurance policy in case the house suffered any property damage.

The Petries asked Le Van to make a claim against his homeowner's insurance policy. The insurance company issued Le Van a check in the amount of $2,176.22. He refused to turn the money over to the Petries, who had made the roof repairs at a cost in excess of the $2,176.22. The Petries filed this lawsuit against Le Van, claiming that Le Van was unjustly enriched.

When a person unfairly holds money or property that belongs to another, the person who holds the money or property is said to hold it in trust for the real owner. The court uses the term *constructive trust* to describe a remedy when unfairness is involved, because the court constructs the trust.

Judge SHANGLER

. . . .

A person who has been unjustly enriched at the expense of another is required to make restitution to the other. The principle against unjust enrichment emerged against the grain of the common law forms of action then available for remedy and with the aid of the restitution devices of the equity court. The common law courts overcame this limitation on remedies imposed by the forms of action through the fiction of quasi contract. The law gave to a plaintiff against a defendant under an obligation, from the ties of natural justice, to refund, an action as if it were upon a contract. The equity courts independently developed restitution remedies against unjust enrichment. The fiction of constructive trust was used in cases of fraud or breach of fiduciary duty to reach the gains that, in conscience, belonged to another by treating the fraudulent procurer as a trustee. The constructive trust also became the means for restitution from one unjustly enriched by the mistake of another, even though the mistake was not induced by fraud or misrepresentation.

. . . .

The right to restitution for unjust enrichment presupposes: (1) that the defendant was enriched by the receipt of a benefit; (2) that the enrichment was at the expense of the plaintiff; (3) that it would be unjust to allow the defendant to retain the benefit.

. . . .

In that assessment, it is not the power of equity to order specific performance, injunction, or some variant of equitable conversion by contract as to the insurance proceeds that is invoked. It is equitable principle and good conscience that govern. In this case, it is the equitable principle against double recovery that disallows Le Van from retention of both the insurance proceeds and the full purchase price of the property and that good conscience requires that Le Van pay over to the Petries. If Le Van may keep the proceeds of the insurance and also the full purchase price, he has a windfall. Le Van is compensated for that which he did not lose and the Petries pay for that which they did not receive.

DECISION AND REMEDY The court found that Le Van was enriched at the expense of the Petries. The trial court was directed to enter a judgment in the amount of $2,176.22 against Le Van.

CRITICAL THINKING: LEGAL CONCEPTS In the last chapter you reviewed the concept of tort law, including the tort of conversion. Discuss whether the plaintiff should have sued under the quasi-contract theory or under the tort theory of conversion.

This chapter discussed the first part of contract law. The next chapter will complete the review of basic contract law.

International Consideration

Variations in Terms of Sale When Dealing Internationally

For international commerce to thrive, governments must establish standard contract criteria. For example, should contracts be in writing and, if so, what constitutes "in writing"? Does a videotape, DVD (digital versatile disc), CD (compact disc), e-mail, or a fax qualify for a writing, or is the term limited to conventional hard copy? People who negotiate, draft, and adopt treaties and conventions confront many problems of this type.

The **United Nations Commission on International Trade Law (UNCITRAL)**[7] developed model laws that cover commercial transactions. These codes include the 1974 **Convention on the Limitation Period in the International Sale of Goods**.[8] This convention established unified rules for and set the statute of limitations at four years, that is, the period within which a lawsuit must be brought. The purpose is to harmonize the differences between the common law and the civil law approaches of various countries.

[7]The United Nations Commission on International Trade Law is found at http://www.uncitral.org.
[8]Documents on International Sale of Goods and Related Transactions are found at http://www.uncitral.org/english/texts/sales/index.htm.

In 1980, the **Convention on Contracts for the International Sale of Goods (CISG)** was adopted. The rules provide guidance for contract formation, performance, warranty provisions, interpretation, and remedies.

In many Western countries, in a contract for the sale of goods, the price often is left open when the delivery is not close in time to when the contract is signed. The price in an open-price sale is set by the market at the time when the vendor delivers the goods. The market price is assumed to be the reasonable price. Some non-Western nations require that sellers state the price within a detailed written contract. The CISG has adopted the market price in an open-price sale. The parties, however, can include in their contract another method of setting the price.

The CISG establishes the time period for acceptance. This period begins at the moment the seller hands the telegram for dispatch; on the date shown on the seller's letter; or if no date appears, then on the postmarked date. If the seller makes the offer by telephone, fax, or other means of instantaneous communication, the period begins at the time the offer reaches the offeree. The acceptance is effective when it reaches the offeror. The contract is made at the moment an offer's acceptance becomes effective. Note that the time when the acceptance becomes effective according to the CISG is very different from the time established in the UCC. Under the UCC, the acceptance is effective when it is sent under most conditions.[9]

[9]More information about international contract law can be found at the Pace University School of Law site at http://cisgw3.law.pace.edu.

PRACTICAL TIPS

Making Sure You Are Insured

A common problem that businesses confront involves the handling of consumer complaints about the provided product or service. For example, you go to Jim

Onest Insurance Agency to purchase automobile liability insurance coverage. Onest obtains the necessary information to bind your vehicle for coverage and records this information in his computer. You pay the initial premium and leave his office. Shortly after you leave, a power failure causes the computerized information to be lost.

As you drive down the street, you fail to stop at a stop sign and collide with a vehicle that had the right of way. No personal injuries are sustained, but extensive property damage occurs to the other vehicle. You contact Onest to inform him of the accident. He attempts to verify coverage but cannot do so because the information in the computer has been lost. He forgets about your check and informs you that you have no coverage.

This simple example illustrates some of the aspects of contract law. When you went to the insurance agency, you made an offer to purchase insurance, which Onest accepted. Legal consideration was present because the promises were bargained for and exchanged. Each party received a legal benefit and suffered a legal detriment. Lack of capacity or having an illegal contract is not at issue here. Most states do not require this type of contract to be in writing to be enforceable. You have proof of this contract in your canceled check. By not recognizing your contract, Onest has breached it.

To avoid a lawsuit, you could have done several things. The following checklist provides guidance as to what information you need.

Checklist

✔ *Specifics* Determine the specifics of who, what, when, where, and how much insurance pertaining to the insurance company and insurance policy.

✔ *Names* Ascertain the name, address, telephone number, and e-mail address of the company issuing the insurance policy.

✔ *Policy Number* Obtain the policy number.

✔ *Receipt* Request a copy of the receipt of payment instead of relying on your check, credit card, or debit card receipt as your receipt. Remember to keep the check (or its copy) or the receipts as evidence that you purchased the policy.

Chapter Summary

Today's basic contract law has replaced the old law merchant with case law and statutes called uniform laws that the states may adopt. Contracts are divided into three elements: formation, enforceability, and performance. The following terms describe the types of contract formation: unilateral and bilateral contracts, express and implied-in-fact contracts, quasi-contracts (implied-in-law contracts), and formal and informal contracts. Contract enforceability can be described as valid, voidable, or unenforceable. Some types of agreements are void, such as illegal contracts.

A contract's performance status is either executed or executory. To have a valid and enforceable contract, the parties must ensure that the following items are present: offer, acceptance, and consideration. The remaining elements of contact law are discussed in the next chapter.

Using the World Wide Web

The federal government has developed several initiatives to promote and develop electronic commerce. The Federal Electronic Commerce Program "coordinates, monitors, and reports on the development of Electronic Commerce (e-commerce) within the Federal Government." E-commerce is the preferred way of doing business with the federal government.

Federal agencies are buying and paying for most products and services electronically. Universities and research centers can seek grants and deliver reports online. Citizens are using smart cards to receive a range of benefits. Suppliers have real-time access to government business opportunities. Federal government buyers find what they need using electronic catalogs.

E-commerce is doing business electronically through the exploitation of the Web to improve commerce. E-commerce uses many core technology tools, the Web, electronic data interchange (EDI), electronic mail (e-mail), electronic funds transfer (EFT), electronic benefits transfer, electronic catalogs, credit cards, smart cards, and other techniques. The growing availability of sophisticated technology and easy-to-use Web tools is helping e-commerce flourish throughout government.

The Defense Logistics Agency (DLA) is the buying agent for all branches of America's military service and a number of other federal civilian organizations. DLA annually purchases and distributes nearly $11 billion of food, clothing, electronics, medical supplies, construction supplies, spare parts, and fuel. Its Defense Contract Management Command supervises contracts and provides contract administration services for more than 360,000 contracts per year—worth more than $900 billion—by private companies for military services and federal organizations. The DLA uses the Web to make routine purchases, thus saving the taxpayers money.

[10]The E-Commerce Guide is found at http://e-comm.internet.com/.

E-Commerce Guide[10] features a comprehensive list of links to hundreds of World Wide Web sites. These resources are devoted to the evolving electronic commerce industry.

For *Web Activities*, links to Web sites mentioned in the chapter, and additional Web sites that relate to the chapter topics, go to **http://bohlman.westbuslaw. com**, click on "Internet Applications," and select Chapter 9.

Web Activities

Go to **http://bohlman.westbuslaw.com**, click on "Internet Applications," and select Chapter 9.
9–1 Student Loans
9–2 Auctions

Key Terms

acceptance
bilateral contract
consideration
contract
Convention on
    Contracts for the
    International Sale of
    Goods (CISG)
Convention on the
    Limitation Period in
    the International Sale
    of Goods
counteroffer
duress
executed contract

executory contract
express contract
formal contract
illusory promise
implied-in-fact contract
implied-in-law contract
informal contract
law merchant
legal benefit
legal detriment
liquidated debt
mailbox rule
minor
mirror-image rule
misrepresentation

mutual assent
mutual (bilateral) mistake
Negative Option Rule
offer
offeree
offeror
operation of law
option contract
promisee
promisor
promissory estoppel
quasi-contract
rejection
revocation
statute of frauds

undue influence
unenforceable contract
Uniform Commercial
    Code (UCC)
unilateral contract
unilateral mistake
United Nations
    Commission on
    International Trade
    Law (UNCITRAL)
unliquidated debt
valid contract
void agreement
voidable contract

Questions and Case Problems

9–1 Type James is confined to his bed. He calls a friend who lives across the street and offers to sell her his watch next week for $100. If his friend wants to accept, she is to put a red piece of paper in her front window. The next morning, she places a red piece of paper in her front window. Is this contract bilateral or unilateral? Explain.

9–2 Consideration Ingram started to work for Central Adjustment Bureau, Inc. (CABI). A week after starting

work, his supervisor gave him an employment contract to sign. The contract contained a provision that restrained him from competing against CABI if he quit the company. He signed the contract because he was told that he would be fired if he did not sign it. Seven years later, he quit and started a competing business. CABI sued Ingram to prevent him from competing. Ingram defended on the basis that the contract lacked consideration because he signed it after he was working.

Who prevailed and why? [*Central Adjustment Bureau, Inc. v. Ingram*, 678 S.W.2d 28 (Tenn. 1984)]

9–3 Undue Influence Conrad purchased a farm in 1945 for $23,500. He had thirteen children. In 1975, he conveyed his farm to his eldest son for the same amount as he had paid, although the farm was currently worth about $150,000. At the time of the conveyance, Conrad, at age eighty-two, was in extremely poor health and had been hospitalized often for various ailments. Eventually, a person called a conservator was appointed by a court to take care of Conrad's affairs. Conrad, through his conservator, filed a lawsuit to rescind the conveyance of the farm. At the trial, the eldest son testified that his father trusted and relied on him. Should this conveyance be set aside? If so, why? [*Schaneman v. Schaneman*, 206 Neb. 113, 291 N.W.2d 412 (1980)]

9–4 Offer–Acceptance The Olivers mentioned to Southworth, a neighbor, that they planned to sell off some of their ranch land. Southworth expressed interest in purchasing the property and later notified the Olivers that he had the money available to buy it. The Olivers told Southworth that they would let him know shortly about the details concerning the sale. The Olivers later sent a letter to Southworth—and (unknown to Southworth) to several other neighbors—giving information about the sale including the price, the property location, and the amount of acreage involved. When Southworth received the letter, he sent a letter to the Olivers "accepting" their offer. The Olivers stated that the information letter had not been intended as an "offer" but merely as a starting point for negotiations. Southworth brought suit against the Olivers to enforce the "contract." Did a contract exist? Explain. [*Southworth v. Oliver*, 284 Or. 361, 587 P.2d 994 (1978)]

9–5 Offer–Acceptance James desired to sell some timber that he owned. He sent notices to numerous potential buyers for bids (offers) for the timber. Eames responded by submitting the highest bid. James, however, refused to go through with the transaction, and Eames sued. Describe potential legal arguments for both James and Eames. [*Eames v. James*, 452 So. 2d 384 (La. App. 1984)]

9–6 Duress Laemmar was an employee of J. Walter Thompson Co. During the years of his employment, he purchased shares of common stock from the company. Laemmar's stock was subject to repurchase by the company if Laemmar's employment were terminated for any reason. The company's officers and directors decided to

increase their control and demanded that Laemmar and several other employees sell their stock back to the company or lose their jobs. Although Laemmar did not want to sell his stock, he did so in order to keep his job. The officers and directors made no physical threats or suggestions of physical harm to Laemmar. Later, Laemmar instituted a lawsuit to rescind his sale of the stock on the basis of duress. Can Laemmar rescind? Explain. [*Laemmar v. J. Walter Thompson Co.*, 435 F.2d 680 (7th Cir. 1970)]

9–7 Misrepresentation Campbell (the plaintiff) was a high school dropout and was employed as a sheetmetal worker before he entered into negotiations with the defendant, Southland Corp., to purchase a 7-Eleven convenience store franchise. Southland Corp. operated more than 7,000 convenience stores. Southland Corp. required Campbell to prepare a business plan showing that he needed to receive a monthly income of $3,400 to meet both business and personal expenses. Southland Corp. did not inform Campbell that the store's average monthly income was $1,340, but Southland Corp. did inform Campbell that the average net income in his approximate location ranged from $1,400 to $3,100 per month. After operating the store for nineteen months, Campbell's store was below the franchise agreement's net worth requirement. Southland Corp. terminated Campbell's franchise (contract). Campbell filed a lawsuit alleging misrepresentation. The trial judge granted Southland Corp.'s motion for summary judgment because the projected profits were opinions and opinions normally do not constitute fraud. Should the judge's decision be upheld? Explain your decision. [*Campbell v. Southland Corp.*, 871 P.2d 487 (Or. App. 1994)]

9–8 Offer–Acceptance Treece, the defendant, was a vice president of Vend-A-Win, Inc., a corporation that was in the business of distributing punchboards (a gambling device). The Washington State Gambling Commission was investigating various aspects of gambling. Treece spoke before the commission on behalf of Vend-A-Win's application for a temporary license to distribute punchboards. During his appearance, which was televised, he stated, "I'll pay a hundred thousand dollars to anyone to find a crooked board. If they find it, I'll pay it." The statement brought laughter from the audience. Barnes, the plaintiff, watched a television news report of Treece's statement and also read a newspaper account. Barnes telephoned Treece, asking him if his statement was serious. Treece restated that he meant it and that the money was being held in escrow. Barnes was in possession of two crooked punchboards. Following Treece's instructions,

Barnes brought one of the punchboards into Vend-A-Win's offices for inspection. He turned the other board over to the Washington State Gambling Commission. Treece and Vend-A-Win each refused to pay Barnes. Barnes filed a lawsuit. What result and why? [*Barnes v. Treece*, 15 Wash. App. 437, 549 P.2d 1152 (1976)]

9–9 Misrepresentation The Richardsons were moving and needed to purchase a new residence. Richardson viewed the Hardins' home on two occasions and both times, Hardin did not make any statements that influenced Richardson's decision to purchase. The buy/sell contract, a standard form, contained language that buyers were accepting the house "as is, where is" without any reliance on any representations of the sellers. After moving into the home, the Richardsons discovered foundation defects. They hired a civil engineer who reported that the foundation had failed and would continue to degrade, ultimately to the point of collapse. The only option was to remove the home from the foundation, reconstruct a properly designed new foundation, and reset the home. He believed that the problems were known to the Hardins because he had found some caulking in the cracks behind the paneling. The Richardsons did not have the property inspected because they asked Hardin about whether she had ever had any problems with the home. They claimed that Hardin answered that she had never had any problems with the home and that she was sad to leave it. The Richardsons assert fraud because the Hardins had settling problems that Hardin failed to mention. The Richardsons filed suit alleging fraudulent misrepresentation. What result and why? [*Richardson v. Hardin*, 5 P.3d 793, (2000)]

9–10 Internet The federal government is active in engaging and promoting electronic commerce. Go to **http://www.whitehouse.gov/omb/egov**. List the statutes that are related to e-gov and select one statute to discuss.

Chapter 10

Contract Defenses and Remedies

*If a man owe a debt and Adad, the storm god,
inundate his field and carry away the produce,
or, through lack of water, grain has not grown in
the field, in that year he shall not make any
return of grain to the creditor, he shall alter his
contract tablet, and he shall not pay the interest
for that year.*

> Code of Hammurabi
> **Hammurabi**
> **Sixth ruler of the First Amorite dynasty
> of Babylon, reigning 1792–1750 B.C.**

Chapter Outline

Ethical Consideration

The Value of a Handshake: The Statute of Frauds as a Sword

After being graduated from college, you find your first job. After working for a while, you saved enough money for a down payment on a new sports car and decide to sell your old Peugeot, which served you well while you were in college. You place an advertisement in the newspaper asking $3,000 for the car, expecting to sell it for around $2,500.

The advertisement generates interest and you invite a prospective buyer to your home to examine the car. After the buyer looks at the car, she offers you $2,700. As a recently divorced, single mother of four children, she needs the car for her family. As you shake her hand in acceptance of her offer, you hear the telephone ring.

The person on the telephone tells you that he is calling from his cellular telephone across the street. He came to buy the car, and as he drove up, he saw you shake hands with the first buyer. He wants the car and offers you $3,000 in cash. When you tell him that you already have agreed to sell the car, he reminds you that the agreement is not legally binding because you have not put anything in writing or signed over the owner's certificate of title. He then says that he will pay an extra $200 above the $3,000 if you sell the car to him. He needs it for a movie.

To whom should you sell the car? Use the ethical model presented in Chapter 2 and reprinted on the inside front cover to develop your answer.

Introduction

In the previous chapter, the first three elements of a binding contract—offer, acceptance, and consideration—were studied. This chapter explains the other two elements: legal capacity and legality.

Once a contract has been created, one of the parties may decide not to perform as promised in the contract. If the other party decides to sue, the party that broke the promise can request the judge to legally excuse him from performing the promise. A *defense* to a contract is a legal excuse. The last two requirements

for a contract, legal capacity and legality, can be used as affirmative defenses to a contract. The chapter also includes discussion of the other potential defenses.

The previous chapter discussed the relationship between the two original parties to a contract. This chapter examines a third party's involvement with the contract. A third party can purchase rights and obtain defenses in the original contract. In a gift situation, a third party may be given rights in the original contract.

Although most contracts are discharged as fully performed, other ways to discharge contracts exist. Finally, the types of damages and the remedies that a person may request in a lawsuit when a party to a contract has been harmed are reviewed.

Artiste Login. The online company, Artiste Login Products, Inc., is owned by Carlo and Carlotta. In order to purchase and sell goods, services, and real property, Artiste will engage in many different types of contracts. Artiste produces a variety of art products and, as a result, has a number of suppliers, such as the one that provides the raw materials for bronze and steel sculptures or the plastic materials for furniture.

A number of products are sold to retail stores. These commercial customers will purchase small items in volume for resale. If a dispute over a contract arises, Artiste needs to be aware of its duties and understand its rights.

Elements of a Contract: Part 2

The last two elements of a contract are legal capacity and legality and they are discussed in this section. These two elements can be used as a defense. This section also examines the statute of frauds requirement for some types of contracts.

Legal Capacity

Legal capacity, the competence (or legal ability) of the parties, is the fourth requirement for a valid contract. Legal capacity has two areas: mental competency and age. In most contracts, both parties have full legal capacity to enter into a contract, to perform the contract, and if they fail to perform, to have the contract enforced against them in a court of law.

When a court judges a party to be mentally incompetent and appoints a guardian over her, however, no legal capacity exists. Such a person has no legal capacity to form a contract and any contract into which she enters is void.

Limited competence exists when one or both parties are minors, are intoxicated, or are mentally incompetent, but not officially judged to be mentally incompetent by a court. These parties have full and legal capacity to enter into a contract, but, if they so desire, they can avoid liability under the contract. This type of contract is said to be *voidable*. Most litigation in this area involves the contracts of minors.

For contractual purposes, the **age of majority** (when a person is no longer a minor) varies from state to state. For the sake of discussion, this text will use eighteen years as the age at which a person becomes an adult. The general rule of law is that a minor can enter into any contract that an adult can enter into, provided that the contract is not one prohibited by law. A contract prohibited by law in most states, for example, is that a person under twenty-one years of age may not purchase alcoholic beverages.

Minors can enter into contracts and they also have the right to **disaffirm** (to avoid) their liabilities under the contracts, subject to certain exceptions, such as necessaries (that is, goods or services needed for the sustenance of the minor, such as food, clothing, or shelter). A minor may disaffirm a contract at any time prior to age eighteen or during a reasonable period of time thereafter.

If, however, by the time the minor becomes an adult (or for a reasonable period of time thereafter), he has failed to disaffirm an executed contract, the contract is ratified. A minor, on reaching the age of majority, has no legal responsibility to act on executory contracts. The minor's inaction, however, does not constitute **ratification** (adoption) of the executory contract. Ratification is the act of accepting and giving legal force to a contract. Only after minors reach adulthood can they ratify contracts made when they were minors.

A contract to purchase necessaries may not be totally disaffirmed by a minor. The rule applicable to contracts for the purchase of necessaries is that the minor is liable to the other contracting party for the reasonable value of the goods or services actually used. This purchase imposes on the minor a quasi-contractual liability to pay for purchases needed to fulfill the minor's basic needs if no parent or guardian is willing and able to furnish the required necessity.

Under Article 2 of the Uniform Commercial Code (UCC), dealing with the sales of goods, a minor cannot recover goods that she sells to an adult once that adult purchaser transfers them to a third party who is a bona fide purchaser (a good-faith purchaser for value). The new buyer needs to know that the items he buys in good faith will not be taken back by the seller as the result of a dispute between the seller and a minor from whom the seller purchased the item.

For example, Mary Minor, who is sixteen, owns a car, which she sells to Al Adult. Al drives the car for six months and then sells it to Ellie Elder, who pays Al's asking price. Seven months have now passed and Mary Minor decides she wants her old car back. Although Mary Minor could disaffirm the contract with Al Adult if he still owned the car, she cannot now recover the car from Ellie Elder. The UCC provision protects Ellie Elder from Mary Minor's change of mind because Ellie Elder is a good-faith purchaser who paid value and was not a party to the contract between Mary Minor and Al Adult.

When disaffirmance occurs and no third party is involved, the adult must return the item to the minor. If the property itself cannot be returned, the adult must pay the minor its equivalent value. If both parties to the contract are minors, each has a right to disaffirm it.

When disaffirmance occurs, the minor also must return whatever he received and still possesses as a result of the contract. In most states, the minor's duty of restoration is only to return goods (or other consideration). If the minor meets this condition, he is not liable for depreciation or nonwillful damage to the goods. In the following case, for example, a minor was not liable for damages to an automobile.

CASE 10.1

Court of Appeals of Utah, 1994
883 P.2d 931

SWALBERG v. HANNEGAN

BACKGROUND AND FACTS In 1990, Hannegan, the defendant, contracted to purchase Swalberg's 1974 Ford truck for $2,500. The fact that Hannegan was a minor apparently was not discussed when the parties entered into the contract. Swalberg, an adult, made no allegation that Hannegan misrepresented his age. Hannegan paid Swalberg $640 on the sale date and agreed to pay the balance of $1,860 three months later.

Rather than paying the balance, however, Hannegan disaffirmed the contract on the basis of his minority. Swalberg filed a complaint asking that the contract be enforced or, in the alternative, that the truck be returned and that defendant be held responsible for the reasonable value of his use of the truck or for its depreciation amount while in defendant's possession. Thereafter, while Hannegan was still a minor, Swalberg gained possession of the truck.

Swalberg filed a motion for summary judgment. Swalberg argued that when Hannegan disaffirmed the contract, he did not properly restore the truck since he purchased it for $2,500 and returned it in a condition worth only $700. The trial court granted Swalberg's motion and awarded him $1,160, which was the remaining balance minus the value placed on the truck in its returned condition. Hannegan appealed the trial court's order.

Judge BENCH

. . . .

The dispositive issue on appeal is whether a minor who disaffirms a contract is required to restore the full value of the property received under the contract. Defendant argues that Utah law does not require a disaffirming minor to restore the other party to his or her precontractual status. We agree. Utah Code Ann. § 15-2-2 (1986) provides:

> *A minor is bound not only for the reasonable value of necessities but also for his contracts, unless he disaffirms them before or within a reasonable time after he obtains his majority and restores to the other party all money or property received by him by virtue of said contracts and remaining within his control at any time after attaining his majority.*

This statute requires only that the property remaining within the minor's control be returned to the other party. The trial court held, however, that defendant was required to return the property in its original condition or be liable for the difference in value. This holding is clearly contrary to the provisions of this unamended nineteenth century statute, as interpreted by controlling Utah case law.

DECISION AND REMEDY By state statute in Utah, the disaffirming minor must only return the property remaining within his or her control. The court allowed the minor to effectively disaffirm the underlying contract without restoring the property to its precontract condition. The Utah state legislature can amend the statute to require a minor to restore property to its precontract condition.

CRITICAL THINKING: PRACTICAL APPLICATION Discuss what steps the plaintiff could have taken to have prevented this legal action.

What happens if a minor lies about his age? The states have not been uniform in handling this troublesome area. The courts have created four different approaches.

Under the traditional view, the minor still may disaffirm the contract because the lack of capacity cannot be forfeited by misstating one's age. The adult who contracts with a minor who has lied can suffer severe consequences because the minor can return to the adult only the remains of the item purchased, if anything is left.

The second approach also allows the minor to disaffirm, but the items must be returned to the adult. The third approach allows the minor to disaffirm, but the minor is liable for fraud. The fourth method of handling this problem does not allow the minor to disaffirm the contract.

Legality

The fifth requirement of a contract is **legality**. A contract encompasses the performance of a legal act by each party. An agreement is illegal if either its formation or its performance is criminal, tortious, or otherwise opposed to public policy.

The reasoning for this requirement is quite simple. If a civil court requires a person to perform a contract that involves the commission of an illegal act, a criminal court could punish that person for committing a crime as a result of a civil court order. This result is not only illogical, but it defies public policy against the courts being party to a crime.

Generally, an illegal agreement is void. Neither party has rights against the other when the agreement's purpose is illegal. The following subsections discuss areas in which the courts have found illegality.

Licenses. Most businesses need some type of license from the government to operate. Licenses can be divided into two categories: regulatory or revenue raising.

Regulatory licensing statutes govern the qualifications of the person or business to conduct specific types of operations. Real estate and construction licenses are examples. If a person lacks this type of license, normally any business contract that she enters into is declared null and void. If an unlicensed pool builder constructs a swimming pool, for instance, the homeowner is not required to pay for it, because the agreement is void.

A good business practice is to verify that the person or business is properly licensed before contracting with it. Most states have established a consumer recovery fund. A consumer may recover damages from the fund if a licensed business fails to perform appropriately. States, however, generally do not protect consumers who have dealt with an unlicensed business.

Revenue-raising licensing statutes, as the name implies, establish licensing requirements solely to raise money. For example, most states have a sales tax. To ensure that the sales tax is collected and remitted to the state department of revenue, the state requires businesses to secure a sales tax license. The state can monitor a business to ensure that it collects the sales tax on its gross receipts and then forwards the monies to the state.

If a business fails to obtain a revenue-raising license, the state can take action against the business. Generally, if a business fails to obtain the appropriate revenue-raising license, however, the lack of the license has no effect on contracts into which the business may enter.

Usury. Usury is the charging of a higher interest rate than the law allows for a loan of money. In a few states, usury is a crime. Usury statutes set the maximum interest rate that may be charged for loaning money. Any higher interest rate is considered usurious.

For example, if a state usury statute sets the interest rate at 24 percent per annum, any rate above 24 percent is usurious and illegal. Any creditor charging above 24 percent may be forced to forfeit both principal and interest. Most states have modified the harsh consequence of total forfeiture of both principal and interest. Today, a business that charges a usurious rate may forfeit all interest but not principal. Other states merely require the forfeiture of the interest amount deemed to be usurious.

Many states abolished usury laws or set a very high interest rate in response to economic conditions of the 1970s and 1980s. In states without usury laws, predatory loans are now on the raise. The interest rates can be as high as 180 percent with exuberant fees and excessive premiums for insurance that the borrower may not know is part of the loan package. The loan agreement usually includes a stiff prepayment penalty, so the borrower cannot pay the loan in full after qualifying for a lower interest rate loan. The loans are written in such a way that the borrower does not understand the true interest rate or the lender may lie about it.

In the late 1990s, a few states readopted the usury laws because of abuses by some businesses. Predatory lenders usually target the non-English-speaking and elderly population. The explosion of these types of loans in some areas is so high that some state bars are forming litigation teams to file lawsuits against the lenders.

Sometimes it is difficult to determine whether an amount charged is interest or whether it is a fee. The next case discusses this problem.

<table>
<tr><td>

CASE 10.2

Court of Appeals of Texas,
2003
114 S.W.3d 561

</td><td>

GARCIA v. TEXAS CABLE PARTNERS

BACKGROUND AND FACTS Javier Garcia entered into a consumer lease with Time Warner Communications covering cable equipment for the purpose of receiving cable services, which the company provided. Pursuant to the cable service contract, Garcia agreed to pay a monthly fee for cable television services. The monthly billing statement notified the customer that a five-dollar administrative late fee would be charged monthly for payments received ten days after the due date. Garcia alleged that Time Warner Communications charged him, and other similarly situated persons, for late fees when the company billed its customers for cable-television services. He sued Time Warner Communications and Time Warner, Inc., alleging the late fee constituted usury under Texas law. He sought class certification for this lawsuit. The trial court held for the defendant and the plaintiff appealed.

</td></tr>
</table>

Opinion by Justice DORSEY.

The issue is whether the late fee constitutes usury under the Texas Finance Code. The essential elements of a usurious transaction are: (1) a loan of money; (2) an absolute obligation that the principal be repaid; and (3) the exaction of a greater compensation than allowed by law for the borrower's use of the money. Usury is defined as "interest that exceeds the applicable maximum amount allowed by law."

Our usury statutes are derived from the Texas Constitution, which provides the following grant of authority to the legislature: "The legislature shall have authority to classify *loans and lenders,* license and regulate *lenders,* define interest and fix maximum rates of interest." Pursuant to this grant of authority, the legislature has enacted a statute addressing maximum rates of interest, which includes a definition of "interest." Therefore, for the usury laws to apply, there must be an overcharge by a lender for the use, forbearance, or detention of the lender's money. The judicial inquiry is whether this has occurred. Whether an amount of money is interest does not depend on what the parties call it but on the substance of the transaction. Because usury statutes are penal in nature, we strictly construe them.

Courts of appeals have held that, because a rental or lease agreement is not a "lending transaction," the usury statute does not apply to late charges assessed on overdue rental payments.

In *Tygrett v. Univ. Gardens Home Owners Ass'n,* the court discussed whether a late payment penalty charge resulting from overdue condominium assessments could be usurious. The court noted that since usury must be founded on an overcharge by a lender for the use, forbearance, or detention of the lender's money, a lending transaction was necessarily required. The court held that the late charge was not within that category because no funds of the condominium association were transferred or loaned to Tygrett. The court concluded that the payment of late charges did not constitute the use, forbearance, or detention of a lender's money within the meaning of the usury statute.

In *Rimco Enters., Inc. v. Texas Elec. Serv. Co.,* Texas Electric Service Company (TESCO) sued Rimco on a sworn account to recover nonpayment of electricity, plus late charges. Rimco counterclaimed for usury, contending that there was a charge of interest in excess of the lawful rate. The trial court entered judgment for TESCO, and denied Rimco's usury counterclaim. In affirming the judgment, the appellate court stated: "We think it obvious that the 'late charges' do not arise from the use, forbearance, or detention of money. It follows that there could be no usury in the demand of TESCO."

A case which does not involve a rental or lease agreement, but which is nevertheless instructive, is *First Bank v. Tony's Tortilla Factory, Inc.* In that case, First Bank imposed NSF fees of $20 per check against Tony's, totaling $47,600. Tony's sued First Bank, alleging that the NSF fees constituted usury. The trial court directed a verdict for First Bank on the usury claim. The issue before the supreme court was whether First Bank's NSF fee for checks drawn on an account with insufficient funds constituted usury. The supreme court stated:

> It is undisputed that each NSF fee was assessed as a processing fee for the additional work required in connection with handling the bad check. . . . There is no dispute that the NSF fee was charged to all customers, in the same amount, regardless of whether First Bank paid or rejected a check. It is undisputed that the amount of the NSF fee had no relationship to the amount of the funds advanced. . . . Thus, the NSF fee was not interest on the amount advanced to cover the bad checks. The NSF fees were charged for the costs of processing a check drawn on an account with insufficient funds. The mere profitability of the NSF fee to First Bank does not make the fee usurious interest.

Each NSF fee was separate and additional consideration for processing each bad check. Thus, the NSF fee was for consideration other than the lending of money. . . . Based on these undisputed facts, we hold that, as a matter of law, the NSF fees charged in this case were not interest.

DECISION AND REMEDY Defendant's business was characterized as cable equipment lending. A contract between parties to "lend" property is a rental agreement and the late fees charged were not construed as "interest" under Texas usury law.

CRITICAL THINKING: PUBLIC POLICY Why should there be any limit on the rate of interest that may be charged for a loan?

Blue Sky Laws. Blue sky laws were passed by states to prevent fraud in investment sales. These laws apply to the sale of securities within a state, that is, intrastate sales. The basic purposes are to prevent dishonest sales practices and to require full, truthful disclosure. Chapter 20 covers this topic in more detail.[1]

[1]Do not confuse blue sky laws with blue laws. Blue laws were statutes that forbid contracts from being created on Sundays. In 1610, Virginia passed the first statute. It stated that "Every man and woman shall repair in the morning to the divine service and sermons preached upon the Sabbath day, and in the afternoon to the divine service, and catechising, upon pain for the first fault to lose their provision and the allowance for the whole week following; for the second, to lose the said allowance and also to be whipt; and for the third to suffer death."

Restraints of Trade. Competition is the basis of the U.S. economic system. First, common law, later followed by state and federal laws, prohibits many types of restraints of trade. For example, if Haught owns a shopping center and agrees with O'Brien, who operates a record store, not to allow any other record stores in the mall, this agreement is void because it is in restraint of trade.

A restraint-of-trade agreement is normally void by itself. Some restraints, however, can become part of a contract in two situations: in a sale of a business contract or in an employment contract.

When a business is sold, one of its major assets is

the seller's goodwill, especially for a small business. The business's value diminishes significantly if the seller opens a new business near the original one.

Trade-restraint situations that involve employment contracts are not as easily defendable. In this case, the employee signs a contract agreeing not to compete against the employer following termination of the employment relationship.

Courts have upheld both types of restrictions, if they are reasonable as to time and geographical area. The theory behind these restrictions is that they allow the buyer and the employer to protect their valuable property rights.

Other trade restraints may be illegal under the Sherman Act, the Clayton Act, and other federal or state antitrust statutes. Chapter 21 discusses these acts.

Gambling and Insurance. Gambling and insurance are two different concepts. All states have some provisions for regulating gambling. At one time gambling was illegal in every state except Nevada. Attitudes have changed over the years and today most states allow some form of gambling. The activity of gambling, however, is regulated. For example, under federal law gambling casinos can operate on federally recognized Indian reservations. While slot machines may be legal in a casino operating on federal lands, local private businesses may be prohibited from having these same gaming machines on their property. A contract involving gambling and gambling machines is illegal unless the state statute specifically allows gambling.

People can be confused as to whether the purchase of an insurance is policy a form of gambling. When a person purchases insurance is she gambling that a loss might occur? The answer is no, because of the concept of insurable interest.

With a life insurance policy, a person must have an insurable interest in the life of another at the time the policy is issued. This insurable interest must be based on love, blood, or business. For example, a spouse has an insurable interest in the life of the other spouse. A parent has an insurable interest in the life of the minor children. A business has an insurable interest in the key employees and a creditor has an insurable interest in the debtor's life.

All people, of course, have an insurable interest in their own lives. A person can take out a life insurance policy on his or her own life and name anyone as the beneficiary. That same person, however, cannot stand at the airport and count every tenth person and take out a policy on that stranger's life. The person does not have an insurable interest in the life of a stranger.

Property insurance is based on a different concept. At the time of the loss, the person must have an insurable interest in the property. A relationship between the person and the property must exist and she needs to have a reasonable expectation of benefiting from its continued existence. For example, Sally owns a home. If it is destroyed by a fire, Sally would suffer a loss, therefore, she has an insurable interest in the residence. If Sally sells her residence, however, she no longer has an insurable interest, even though there may be an insurance policy still in existence naming her as the insured party.

Statute of Frauds

Certain valid contracts, by statute, must be in writing to be enforceable by a court. This statute is called the *statute against the perpetuation of fraud*, or the **statute of frauds** for short.

The writing must be signed by the person against whom it is being enforced. Even without this statute, good business practice requires a written contract. Exhibit 10–1 sets out the contracts covered by the statute of frauds.

The statute of frauds varies from state to state. The following major types of business contracts must be in writing:

1. Contracts involving land interests, such as leases and sales;

2. Contracts that, by their terms, cannot be performed within one year from the date that the contract was formed; and

3. **Collateral contracts**, which are express written contracts made by a third person (called a *guarantor*) in addition to the original contract. A third person (guarantor) makes the same promise to pay a debt or to perform a duty to one party (the creditor) on the original contract if the debtor is unable to do so. A collateral contract between the guarantor and the creditor parallels the original contract between the creditor and the debtor.

Parol Evidence Rule. The **parol** (oral) **evidence rule** also is known as the *best evidence rule* because the courts will not allow into evidence any oral statements

Exhibit 10-1   Contracts Covered by the Statute of Frauds

Contracts to Guarantee the Debt of Another	*Application* Applies only to express written contracts made between the guarantor (third party) and the creditor who is a party in the original contract. The contract terms of the collateral contract make the guarantor secondly liable for the debt of the debtor who is a party of the original contract. The original contract is between the creditor and the debtor. The collateral contract is between the creditor and the third party guarantor who promises (guarantees) to pay the debt or to perform the duty of the debtor in the original contract if the debtor is unable to pay the debtor or to perform the duty.
Contracts Involving an Interest in Real Estate	*Application* Applies to any contract for an interest in real estate, such as sale or lease.
Contracts with Terms That Cannot Be Performed within One Year	*Application* Applies only to contracts that are impossible to perform fully within one year from the date of the contract's information.
Exception to Contracts Otherwise Unenforceable under the Statute of Frauds	*Memorandum* Written evidence of an oral contract signed by the party against whom enforcement is sought. Generally, the writing must name the parties and identify the contract's subject matter. In the sale of goods, the quantity must be stated. In the sale of real estate, the contract requires a land description and price. Exceptions exist under each section.

made prior to or at the time of a written contract's signing. The courts believe that the best evidence is the written contract. Oral evidence cannot change or add to a fully integrated contract.

This rule does allow for some oral testimony. For example, oral testimony can explain terms or clarify ambiguities in the contract. Parol evidence may be used to show misrepresentation, fraud, duress, undue influence, mistake, and lack of contractual capacity. Oral testimony also can clarify a typographical or clerical error that, when corrected, allows the court to reform the contract to the true intentions of the parties.

INFOTRAC RESEARCH ACTIVITY

Go to the InfoTrac Web site and type "statute of frauds" in the search function. Articles that discuss oral contracts and their enforceability are available on the Web site. Summarize four of these articles. When is an oral contract enforceable?

Exculpatory Clauses

On many occasions one party to a contract may want to add a provision that limits any potential liability

based on negligent acts. Courts do not favor these types of provisions. A contract clause limiting liability from negligent acts will be enforced, however, if both parties are of equal bargaining strength. These contract provisions limiting liability are called **exculpatory clauses**. These clauses often are found on ticket stubs to parking lots or sporting events, leases, and contracts for the sale of goods, real property, or services. Any type of contract term that attempts to limit liability for intentional acts, however, will not be enforced.

CYBERLAW

Federal Electronic Signatures Act and Uniform Electronic Transactions Act

The **Electronic Signatures in Global and National Commerce Act** was signed into law by President William J. Clinton in 2000. This law attempts to eliminate legal barriers to using electronic technology to form and sign contracts, collect and store documents, and send and receive notices and disclosures. Consumers must affirmatively consent to doing business electronically.

The act provides that no contract, signature, or record shall be denied legal effect solely because it is in electronic form. This statute allows businesses to contract electronically online in buying and selling their products.

The act does not apply to court proceedings, wills, trusts, mortgage foreclosures, and other similar types of documents. Specific concerns were raised by consumers, so the act also does not apply to insurance and utility cancellation and termination notices.

The statute does not state what a signature must be. Congress did not want to limit new technology, so it declined to provide a definition. States are allowed to define what a signature is by state statute. More likely, the state governments will follow the federal act and not provide a statutory definition. The definition of a signature will be left to technology and what the contracting parties agree to accept as a signature. What concerns the parties is authenticating the signature. In the future, computers may be configured with slots like an automated teller machine (ATM) machine to slide a card through or even possibly the computer could scan a person's eye to authenticate the signature.

The National Conference of Commissioners on Uniform State Laws has issued a draft called the Uniform Electronic Transactions Act for states to consider adopting as law. This proposed act was issued (1) to facilitate electronic transactions consistent with other applicable law, (2) to be consistent with reasonable practices concerning electronic transactions and with the continued expansion of those practices, and (3) to effectuate its general purpose to make uniform the law with respect to electronic business.[2]

Other Contractual Issues

After the original parties to a valid contract meet all contract requirements, other problems may arise.

[2]The Uniform Electronic Transactions Act may be found at http://www.law.upenn.edu/bll/ulc/ulc_frame.htm.

LEGAL HIGHLIGHT

A Fax, Spam, and Do Not Call

Need to drum up business? Why not fax to hundreds or thousands of potential customers at a time? Faxing takes time, but the results may be worth it. If faxes are sent locally, the only cost is the recipient's fax paper. If faxes are sent long distance, the cost is low because of the short time needed to send the fax. But wait a minute!

Have you read your friendly federal statutes lately? In 1992, Congress passed a law prohibiting the sending of unsolicited faxes and requiring the sender to remove from a fax list anyone who requests removal. Congressional members had been inundated with complaints from outraged constituents who had to bear the cost of unsolicited faxes. Even congressional offices were tired of receiving commercial faxes. Congress had the power to act and it did.

The Federal Communications Commission (FCC) oversees the law. Penalties are rare, but when numerous complaints are filed against a company, either the FCC or the state attorneys general can pursue the issue in court.

Faxes can be sent when the sender has established a business relationship with the recipient. The relationship can start when the recipient inquires or applies to, or requests a fax from, the sender. The recipient can request to be removed from the list at any time.

In 2003, Congress, after being pressured by the populace, passed legislation that authorized the Federal Trade Commission to establish a National Do Not Call list. This list was established to cut the number of calls from telemarketers. The Do Not Call list is discussed in more detail in Chapter 15.

Based on the laws restricting faxes, Congress in 2003 passed legislation that banned the spamming of e-mail. *Spamming* is the sending of unsolicited e-mail (also called junk e-mail) to thousands, even hundreds of thousands, of recipients at a time. Some people receive more than 300 spams per day. The time spent sorting the valid e-mails and deleting these spam e-mails is counted in hours. When businesses abuse consumers, Congress often reacts. Congress acted to prohibit spamming as a result of enough presesure by citizens.

First, third parties may have rights based on the contract even though they did not participate in its original formation. Second, if a contract dispute arises, the parties need to know the available remedies.

Assignments and Delegations

Sometimes people who are not directly connected with the initial contract become involved in it. A third party (someone who was not an original party) can acquire an interest in a contract by assuming the rights or duties arising from it. An original party to a contract can transfer its rights or duties to a third person after making the original contract.

Each party to the contract has rights and duties. One party has the right to the performance that the other party promised. The transfer of the rights of a party to a contract to a third person is known as an **assignment**. The original party is known as the **assignor**. The third party who takes the assignment is known as the **assignee**. The assignee takes the place of the original party to the contract. If the original party to the contract has a defense to the contract against the assignor, the defense may also be used against the assignee.

For example, Nancy contracts to purchase a computer for $1,500. She promises to pay Computer Company $150 a month. Computer Company (the assignor) assigns the right to receive the $1,500 to Finance Company (the assignee). Now Nancy must pay the $150 a month to Finance Company until she pays the full $1,500 to complete her performance on the contract. Nancy has a defense for failing to pay if the computer does not work or if Computer Company used fraud to induce Nancy into the contract. Those defenses also may be used against the assignee, Finance Company. Exhibit 10–2 sets out assignments and delegations.

Each party to a contract has a duty to perform. The transfer of duties to another person is called a **delegation**. A contractual duty can be delegated to someone else to perform unless the duty of performance is personal and must be performed by the original party. For example, Enrique has an automobile for sale on which he is still making loan payments. Carrie wants to buy the automobile and assume the note. The note is the evidence of the amount loaned to Enrique to purchase the automobile. Enrique is under a duty to repay the note, but his duty can be delegated to Carrie if she is financially qualified to assume the note. Now she is primarily liable on the note, but Enrique is still liable if Carrie fails to pay the note. A person who owes a duty is not relieved of the duty if he delegates the duty to someone else to perform.

If the contract performance is personal in nature, the duty cannot be delegated. For example, Wong contracts with Happy the Clown to perform at Wong's birthday party. Happy cannot delegate this duty to another entertainer, such as the Scottish Bag Pipers Band, without Wong's consent. These contracts are for services and are not assignable because one person's service may be very different from another's. The payment for the services is assignable.

The following case reviews an assignment clause in a contract.

Exhibit 10–2   Assignment and Delegation

Assignment	An assignment is the transfer of rights under a contract to a third party. The rights of the assignor (the person making the assignment) may be ended and the assignee (the person to whom the rights are assigned) now has a right to demand performance from the other original party to the contract. Generally, all rights are assignable except where the law prohibits this, where the contract prohibits assignment, or where the assignment would materially alter or increase the duties of the original party to the contract.
Delegation	A delegation is the transfer of duties under a contract to a third party. The delegate (the third party) assumes the obligation of performing the contractual duties previously held by the delegator (the one making the delegation). Some duties cannot be delegated because they are personal or because their delegation is prohibited by contract.

CASE 10.3

Supreme Court of
Colorado, 1994
874 P.2d 1049 (Colo.)

PARRISH CHIROPRACTIC CENTERS v. PROGRESSIVE CASUALTY INSURANCE COMPANY

BACKGROUND AND FACTS Colorado has an automobile no-fault insurance law. A no-fault law permits each driver in a traffic accident to collect insurance money from her or his own insurance company regardless of whose fault the accident is.

The defendant, Progressive Casualty Insurance Company, issues insurance policies under Colorado's automobile no-fault law. The personal injury protection (PIP) insurance policy issued by Progressive has the following clause: "Interest in this policy may not be assigned without our written consent." Progressive is the insurer and the patients are the insureds.

The plaintiff, Parrish Chiropractic Centers, P.C. (Professional Corporation), treated many patients injured in automobile accidents who held PIP policies issued by Progressive. Parrish required its patients to sign an assignment of insurance benefits agreement. An assignment in this case means that the patients authorized Progressive to pay the insurance benefits directly to Parrish (instead of paying the benefits to the patients) under the patients' PIP policies.

Progressive routinely honored such assignments until it changed its business practice from paying Parrish the insurance benefits to paying the patients. The reasons were that (1) treatment with Parrish, on average, took considerably longer and Parrish was more expensive than other chiropractors, and (2) the purported assignments of benefits violated the express terms of the policy and, consequently, were void from the beginning. Under the previous assignment method, both Progressive's and the patients' abilities to control the treatment frequency and costs provided by Parrish were diminished.

Under the new system, Progressive paid the PIP benefits directly to the patients and Progressive refused to honor any more assignments sent by Parrish. Although the patients received the insurance benefits, some failed to pay their chiropractic fees as they were supposed to. Parrish filed this lawsuit to recover its unreimbursed chiropractic fees. Parrish lost in both lower courts. The courts held that the assignments to Parrish were invalid as a matter of law in light of the express provision in the policies. If either court had upheld the assignments, Progressive's obligation under the insurance contract would have been materially changed. Parrish appealed to the Colorado Supreme Court.

In its opinion, the court discusses what is called a *chose in action* (a right that can be enforced by a lawsuit). If the insured is entitled to receive benefits and the insurance company does not pay the insured, she or he can sue the insurance company for the benefits. Whoever is entitled to the benefits has a chose in action, that is, a right to sue to enforce the right to receive those benefits. If the benefits have been assigned, then the third person has the chose in action. The assignment, in this case, is a transfer of the entitlement to the insurance benefits from the patient to the medical provider. The assignment is a chose in action.

Assignments were made by the patients directing Progressive to pay their benefits to Parrish. If Progressive fails to pay Parrish, Parrish has the right to file a lawsuit to receive the benefits under the assignment. Generally, public policy supports the transfer of choses in action, but exceptions exist. This court discusses one of those exceptions.

Justice MULLARKEY

. . . .

Contract rights generally are assignable, except where assignment is prohibited by contract or by operation of law or where the contract involves a matter of personal trust or confidence. Where the contract in question specifically prohibits the assignment of rights or interests under the contract without the consent of one or more of the contracting parties, any purported assignment without such consent will not be enforced.

. . . .

A distinction traditionally has been made, however, between an assignment of an insurance policy before a loss has occurred and the assignment of the benefits due to the insured after a loss. Non-assignment clauses are strictly enforced against attempted preloss transfers of the policy itself, because assignments before loss involve a transfer of a contractual relationship and, in most cases, would materially increase the risk to the insurer. By contrast, assignments of post-loss benefits are usually found to be valid regardless of any non-assignment clause in the policy. This rule is explained by the fact that (1) post-loss assignments of the benefits due under the policy are viewed as transfers of a chose in action and public policy favors the free alienability [transferability] of choses in action, and (2) such assignments would not materially increase the insurer's risk or obligation under the policy. . . .

Having set forth the general rules regarding non-assignment clauses in insurance policies, we now turn to an important exception to those rules. In recent years, several courts have concluded that non-assignment clauses in group health care contracts are enforceable against post-loss assignments to health care providers of the insured's right to receive benefits under the policy. . . .

. . . .

. . . To hold otherwise would be to force Progressive to deal with parties with whom it has not contracted, regardless of the fact that its policy contains an express contractual provision requiring its prior consent to any assignment of interests in the policy. The public policy of this state does not dictate such a result.

Accordingly, we reject Parrish's argument that a non-assignment clause in an insurance policy is unenforceable as a matter of law against post-loss assignments of policy benefits.

DECISION AND REMEDY The Supreme Court of Colorado also held that Parrish was not a third-party beneficiary of the PIP insurance contract. The insurance policy specifically forbade an assignment without Progressive's approval. Thus, the purported assignment to Parrish was not enforceable. Parrish was not obligated under any statute or by contract to treat Progressive's insureds. Parrish was merely an incidental beneficiary of Progressive's policy.

CRITICAL THINKING: PUBLIC POLICY Discuss whether any contract should be assignable.

Third-Party Beneficiaries

Third-party beneficiaries fall into two general categories: *intended beneficiaries* and *incidental beneficiaries*. A person's inclusion in one or the other category depends on whether the original parties, at the time of contracting, intended to benefit a third person. If so, that party is an **intended beneficiary**. If not, the party is an **incidental beneficiary**. For example,

commuters on a train are the incidental beneficiaries of the contract between the union and the railroad.

An intended beneficiary generally is either a *creditor beneficiary* or a *donee beneficiary* (although, in some situations, the intended beneficiary may not fall under the heading of either creditor or donee). A **creditor beneficiary** purchases the right to receive money owed under the contract. For example, you owe Alice $100. You are hired to work at a music performance, for which you will earn $100. You request your employer to pay the $100 to Alice instead of to you. Alice is a creditor beneficiary of your contract for services with the music company.

A person is a **donee beneficiary** when the main purpose of the contract is to give a gift to him, even though he is not a party to the contract. The best example is the standard life insurance contract. The contract is between the life insurance company and the insured, but the party who is designated to receive the

insurance proceeds after the insured dies is the donee beneficiary.

What rights does a creditor or donee beneficiary have? Generally, an intended beneficiary may bring a lawsuit on a contract, but an incidental beneficiary may not.

The following case examines whether a hospital was the third-party beneficiary of an agreement between two other parties.

CASE 10.4

Supreme Court of Oregon, 1994
867 P.2d 1377, 318 Or. 370

SISTERS OF ST. JOSEPH OF PEACE, HEALTH, AND HOSPITAL SERVICES v. RUSSELL

BACKGROUND AND FACTS The defendant, Russell, broke his arm and back while at work at a logging mill. The plaintiff, Sisters of St. Joseph of Peace, Health, and Hospital Services, dba (doing business as) Sacred Heart General Hospital, provided medical treatment to Russell. He was uncertain as to who his employer was at the time of the injury.

For that reason he filed four separate workers' compensation claims against four purported employers. At a workers' compensation hearing, the referee held that the employer was insured by Aetna Casualty & Surety Company for workers' compensation purposes. Aetna appealed. While the decision was pending, all four purported employers and their insurance carriers entered into a disputed claim settlement (DCS) agreement with Russell that Aetna would be the insurance carrier. Russell and Aetna dismissed the appeal.

Sacred Heart was not compensated under this agreement and sued Russell and Aetna. Russell testified at the trial that he only agreed to pay the hospital for the treatment that saved his life. Although the jury found that Russell did not have to pay the hospital, it held that Aetna was responsible for paying Russell's hospital bill.

The appeals court reversed the trial court's decision and held that Aetna's liability depended on whether Russell was liable to the plaintiff. The hospital appealed the case, claiming that it was the beneficiary of the DCS between Russell and Aetna and that, therefore, Aetna should pay Russell's hospital bill.

Justice GRABER

. . . .

In this case, plaintiff gave medical care to Russell. Plaintiff billed Russell for that medical care. In other words, at the time the DCS agreement was signed, plaintiff had given something of value to Russell and was asserting that Russell had a duty to pay for it. In those circumstances, plaintiff was a creditor beneficiary of the DCS agreement if the parties intended that contract to benefit plaintiff. To determine whether Aetna and Russell intended to benefit the hospital, we must examine the DCS agreement.

. . . .

. . . Paragraph 5 absolved the four purported employers and their insurers of any further responsibility for Russell's "disputed and denied conditions excepting, however, the terms [that] this agreement provide[,] the parties agree that the sums heretofore set

forth to be the sole responsibility of the carrier Aetna Casualty & Surety Company."
. . . .

Paragraph 5 of the DCS agreement . . . makes "*the sums* heretofore set forth" "the sole responsibility of the carrier Aetna" (emphasis added). One of those *sums* is stated to be *the full and exact dollar amount of plaintiff's bills* for Russell's care. . . . Paragraph 6 refers to the medical providers, including plaintiff, as Russell's "creditors." As a whole, the paragraph suggests that the parties to the DCS agreement recognized that Russell's medical expenses . . . were, in fact, owed.

DECISION AND REMEDY The court upheld the jury's verdict that Aetna was responsible for paying Russell's hospital bill. It found Aetna liable because Sacred Heart was a creditor beneficiary under the various provisions of the DCS agreement between Russell and Aetna.

CRITICAL THINKING: PREVENTIVE LAW Assume there are four separate employers on a construction site. Assume further that an employee, such as Russell, is shared by the four employers over a period of time. Russell works on various problems, keeps track of his time, and is paid by each of the four employers separately. He is injured. Discuss whether the employers can avoid a lawsuit such as the one that occurred here.

Discharge

A contract usually is discharged because it has been fully performed. Contracts can also be discharged in other ways. The following examines the discharge of a contract by performance and then reviews other methods of discharge.

Discharge by Performance

In most cases, a contract is fully performed and is discharged. For example, when you purchased your textbook, you paid the store the price marked on the textbook and you left the store with the book. Assuming the textbook is complete and appropriately printed, the contract was fully performed.

Some contracts, because of their basic nature, cannot always be fully performed. Construction contracts involving many blueprints and other specifications often are not completely performed in every last detail. Even though minor deviations may exist, the contract may be discharged by substantial performance. A door to a classroom may be off by an eighth of an inch from the original plans. This minor deviation does not mean that the contract is breached. The contract can be discharged by substantial performance.

To have substantial performance, the contract must not have been intentionally breached and the performance must be close to that required by the contract. In the case of an intentional material breach, the contractor is not entitled to damages from the property's owner. If the performance were substantial, the contractor would be entitled to payment under the contract terms, less the damages the owner incurred.

Discharge by Agreement

If the contract is not yet fully performed, the parties may agree to discharge the contract. Businesspeople can agree to settle claims or to discharge debts. The following agreements are frequently used: (1) accord and satisfaction, (2) covenant (agreement) not to sue, and (3) novation. Exhibit 10–3 briefly describes these three types of agreements.

Accord and Satisfaction. **Accord and satisfaction** involves a debtor's offer to settle a debt owed to the creditor that is different from the original contract and the creditor's acceptance of the debtor's offer. An *accord* is the agreement in which the parties decide to modify their contract or to settle a disputed debt. *Satisfaction* takes place when the accord, that is, the agreed performance, has

Exhibit 10-3   Discharge of a Contract by Agreement

1. *Accord and satisfaction* The agreement by one party to a contract to perform, and the other party to accept, something different from that which was originally agreed, in satisfaction of the original contract. The agreement is the accord. The execution of the agreement is the satisfaction.

2. *Covenant not to sue* An agreement not to sue on a present, valid, and enforceable claim.

3. *Novation* A valid contract that substitutes a new party for one of the original parties, thereby, discharging the original contract and the previous party.

been completed. At that point, the accord and satisfaction are completed and the debtor's obligation is discharged.

Covenant Not to Sue. A **covenant not to sue** is a contract between the two parties agreeing that one person waives his right to sue, usually in return for a settlement. For example, Brian is involved in an automobile accident caused when Kay failed to stop at a red light. Kay offers Brian $500 to release her from any further liability resulting from the accident. Brian believes that the repair to his car will be less than $400 and signs the release, which includes a covenant not to sue. Later Brian discovers that the repair to his car will cost $600. Can Brian collect the balance of $100? The answer is no. The covenant not to sue limits Brian's recovery to $500 and he no longer has the right to file a negligence lawsuit.

Novation. A **novation** is a contract whereby an outside party is substituted for one of the party's to the original contract. A common type of novation occurs when a debtor is completely discharged from the contract and another debtor is substituted. The discharged debtor (an original party to the contract) no longer is liable under the original contract.

For example, you sell your home to Weinstein. As part of the contract, Weinstein assumes (takes over) the payments on the mortgage note. Without a novation, you still are liable if Weinstein does not pay because you signed the original mortgage note. If the mortgage company agrees to substitute Weinstein for you, however, a novation has occurred. Weinstein now is liable; you are discharged from liability on the original mortgage note. In the following case the court discusses the doctrine of novation.

CASE 10.5	**WELLS FARGO FINANCIAL LEASING, INC. v. LMT-FETTE**
United States District Court, S.D. Iowa, 2003 250 F. Supp. 2d 1120	**BACKGROUND AND FACTS** In June 2001, Nader of Standard Office Systems (SOS) contacted Rubenstahl, president of LMT-Fette, Inc. (LMT), about purchasing an in-house copy machine. Rubenstahl told Nader that LMT was not interested in purchasing the machine. Nader, however, persuaded Rubenstahl to have LMT lease the equipment on a trial basis with no obligation to buy. Rubenstahl agreed to a trial lease only because of Nader's assurance LMT would be under no obligation to buy the equipment.

To secure financing for the lease, Nader presented Rubenstahl with a preprinted Wells Fargo Financial Leasing, Inc. (Wells Fargo), credit application and lease agreement. Based on his prior business experience with Nader, Rubenstahl had no reservations about signing the preprinted documents before Nader entered all the information and terms. Nader explained the documents were merely protocol.

The first page of the lease agreement requested the name and address of the vendor and lessee, description of the equipment, terms of the transaction, and the signatures of the lessor and lessee. The second page had various preprinted clauses detailing the terms of the lease agreement. The credit application called for vendor and equipment information and had a signature block labeled "Delivery and Acceptance Certificate." Rubenstahl signed and initialed the documents allowing Nader to later complete them.

Nader listed SOS as the vendor, LMT as vendee, $5,362.50 as the monthly payment amount, and sixty (60) months as the payment term. Nader submitted the documents, and Wells Fargo approved the lease.

Rubenstahl contacted Nader before the equipment was delivered and told him LMT was no longer in a position to lease the equipment even on a trial basis. Nader told Rubenstahl not to worry, LMT was under no obligation, and SOS would take over the lease. Rubenstahl did not contact Wells Fargo about this arrangement. Rubenstahl denies ever receiving the equipment, although the equipment invoice bears his stamped signature.

Rubenstahl received a Wells Fargo billing statement indicating $5,362.50 was due on the equipment lease. Rubenstahl contacted Nader wondering why LMT received the bill. Nader explained that the mailing address was wrong on the statement; it should have been addressed to SOS. Nader promised to take care of the error. Rubenstahl asked Nader whether SOS was going to maintain the lease or cancel it. Nader explained that SOS was going to maintain and "buy out" the lease. Once again, Rubenstahl did not contact Wells Fargo.

A second bill was received by LMT, and Rubenstahl again contacted Nader. Nader explained the address problem had not been straightened out but assured Rubenstahl that he would resolve the problem. Again, Rubenstahl did not contact Wells Fargo.

LMT received a third bill and a telephone call from a Wells Fargo credit agent inquiring about the delinquent account. Rubenstahl told the agent he cancelled the lease. He explained SOS was the responsible party because SOS was buying out the lease. The agent informed Rubenstahl that Wells Fargo considered LMT responsible for the lease.

Rubenstahl contacted Nader, who reassured him there was nothing to worry about and that it was only a paperwork problem. Nader further explained that he was a "sub-agent" for Wells Fargo and was authorized to transfer leases. Rubenstahl received another telephone call, this time from a Wells Fargo attorney.

Rubenstahl again explained the SOS-LMT arrangement and was again informed LMT was responsible for the lease. Rubenstahl went to Nader's office and told him about the call from the Wells Fargo attorney. Nader divulged that an SOS employee had been "playing games" with the lease and had been fired. Rubenstahl requested a letter from Nader detailing the lease arrangement between SOS and LMT. The letter stated SOS held LMT "harmless" for any debt associated with Wells Fargo Financial Services and that further inquiries should be directed to Nader at SOS. The letter also stated SOS had possession of the equipment and SOS would "continue" to make payments per the terms of the lease. It further promised SOS would indemnify LMT for attorney's fees and costs. Once again Nader assured Rubenstahl there was nothing to worry about because a buyout of the lease was in progress.

A Wells Fargo representative contacted Rubenstahl to inform him LMT was in default and the accelerated balance of $327,199.99 was due. Rubenstahl was also informed that Wells Fargo intended to litigate the matter. At this point, Rubenstahl requested a telephone conference with Nader and Wells Fargo.

During the conference call meeting, Wells Fargo agreed to dismiss the lawsuit if a payment of $50,000 was made by April 30, 2002, followed by a second payment of $275,000. Although it was agreed during this discussion that SOS would make those payments, Wells Fargo made it clear that receipt of payment from SOS did not release LMT from liability on the lease. Wells Fargo received $50,000 but never received the $275,000 payment; and, therefore, Wells Fargo did not dismiss the lawsuit.

Plaintiff Wells Fargo moved for summary judgment, arguing it was entitled to judgment as a matter of law because it is undisputed that defendant LMT had a binding lease agreement with Wells Fargo and defaulted on that agreement. Defendant LMT resisted the motion, pleading the affirmative defenses of fraudulent misrepresentation, negligent misrepresentation, and novation.

GRITZNER, J.

. . . .

C. Novation LMT's final defense is that a novation occurred when Wells Fargo agreed to accept payment from SOS. "A novation is a substituted contract that includes as a party one who was neither the obligor nor the obligee of the original duty."

> "To establish a substitution or novation of a contract, the claimant must show (1) a previous valid obligation, (2) agreement of all parties to the new contract, (3) extinguishment of the old contract, and (4) validity of the new contract." A novation is not easily established. "The burden of proving a novation rests upon him who asserts it, and where a novation is pleaded in defense the burden of establishing it is on the defendant."

LMT suggests there is evidence Wells Fargo agreed to have SOS and Nader assume liability under the lease agreement during the phone conference and that this evidence raises a genuine issue of material fact as to the responsible party. The Court disagrees. LMT must present more than a mere allegation of a novation to survive Wells Fargo's summary judgment motion.

Wells Fargo clearly and repeatedly expressed that LMT was the party responsible for the lease. In the telephone conference between the parties, Wells Fargo told LMT it would dismiss the lawsuit if a payment of $50,000 was received by April 30, 2002, followed by a second payment of $275,000. Only the $50,000 payment was received, so Wells Fargo did not dismiss the lawsuit. In addition, Wells Fargo argues a novation could not occur absent a writing since the lease agreement required any modifications be in writing.

. . . .

DECISION AND REMEDY LMT failed to establish a novation occurred when Wells Fargo agreed to the two payments. Of the four elements necessary to show a novation occurred, LMT had shown only that there was a valid previous obligation. LMT failed to generate a factual issue over whether there was a valid new contract, an extinguishment of the old contract, or an agreement of all parties to a new contract.

CRITICAL THINKING: MANAGEMENT What management mistakes were made in this case?

Discharge by Operation of Law

A contract may be discharged by operation of law. If the terms of the contract were altered by one party without the knowledge of the other party, the contract may be discharged because the parties had no meeting of the minds on the modified part of the contract.

If one party breaches a contract, the harmed party must file a lawsuit during the time period established in a statute of limitations. When the time period during which the harmed party could have sued has passed, the contract is discharged.

Sometimes a contract becomes impossible for a party to perform. The following reasons constitute impossibility of performance:

1. If one party dies or becomes mentally incompetent and that person's performance is essential to the contract's completion;

2. If the specific subject matter of the contract is destroyed, making it impossible to perform; or

3. If one of the parties goes into bankruptcy and receives a discharge from the court.

Remedies and Damages

Breach of contract is a party's failure to perform a duty as promised in the contract. Once the defendant fails to perform or performs inadequately, the plaintiff can choose one or more of several remedies.

A **remedy**, in contract law, is the relief provided for a plaintiff when the defendant fails to perform and therefore breaches the contract. A remedy enforces a right. The remedy is not a part of a lawsuit, but is the end result of the lawsuit. In breach of contract cases, the normal remedy is money damages. Occasionally, the plaintiff is able to request an equitable remedy, such as rescission, restitution, specific performance, or reformation. Let's look at the two types of remedies, legal and equitable.

Legal Remedies

One party breaches the contract. The other party has not breached the contract, but has suffered economic harm and has the right to seek the legal remedy of money damages in a court of law. The money compensates the nonbreaching party (the plaintiff) for the losses incurred because the breaching party (the defendant) failed to perform the promises made in the contract. The harmed party's position is reinstated as if the contract had been fully performed.

When possible, the nonbreaching party has a duty to mitigate (lessen or reduce) the amount of damages. For example, if a person has been wrongfully fired from a job, he has a duty to seek similar employment within the same area, that is, to try to mitigate the damages. By obtaining a new job, the former employee has mitigated the damages. If the new job pays less than the previous job, however, the person can seek damages. The person cannot remain unemployed without seeking a job and then file a lawsuit for all the damages incurred since the firing. He is not obligated to take a job, however, that is very different from the previous job; an accountant does not have to take a housekeeper's position. On the other hand, the previous employer has the right to argue that the

former employee made insufficient attempts to lessen the damages and, therefore, is entitled to only a portion of the damages requested.

The three most common types of damages sought in a breach of contract case are *compensatory damages, consequential damages*, and *liquidated damages*. Discussion of the differences among these types of damages follows.[3]

Compensatory Damages. The injured party seeks **compensatory damages** to make up for the monetary loss caused to her because the other party breached the contract. The economic injury must arise directly from the contract breach.

For example, Farouk had a contract with Luis to purchase 100 flat-screen television sets for $4,500 per set. Luis breaches the contract by refusing to complete the sale. Farouk purchases the 100 sets at $5,000 per set. The compensatory damages that Farouk can seek are $500 per set or $50,000 for the contract. Compensatory damages place the injured party, as nearly as possible, in the position in which she would have been if the contract had been performed.

Consequential Damages. Consequential damages, in contrast, are foreseeable damages resulting from special circumstances beyond the contract itself. The damages arise not directly from the contract breach, but as a consequence of it. The damages must have been foreseeable and the breaching party must have known of the special circumstances.

The court awards consequential damages in addition to compensatory damages. Consequential damages are also called *special damages*. If foreseeable, a business's lost profits that result from a breach of contract are an example of special damages.

The following example includes both compensatory and consequential damages. TV Manufacturer contracts to sell $40,000 worth of wide-screen digital television sets with full Dolby sound to Visual Systems. The delivery date is December 1. Visual Systems plans to resell the television sets immediately and to make a profit of $15,000. TV Manufacturer is aware of Visual Systems' resale plans. On November 25, TV Manufacturer notifies Visual Systems that the television sets will

---

[3]You can review the different types of damages at http://www.freeadvice.com/law/5183us.htm. If this Web site does not respond, go http://www.freeadvice.com and then click on "Contract Law" under the icon for General Practice.

not be delivered and that the contract has been canceled. Visual Systems purchases equivalent televisions from another manufacturer for $50,000. Visual Systems can sue TV Manufacturer for compensatory damages in the amount of $10,000, the difference between the open market price, $50,000, and the contract price, $40,000 (plus any costs incurred because of the breach). In addition, Visual Systems is entitled to consequential damages for any foreseeable loss that it can prove, which in this illustration would be lost profits. TV Manufacturer, however, must know at the time of contracting that, if it breaches the contract, it is responsible for any profit loss.

Liquidated Damages. Liquidated damages are the amount of damages that the parties establish in a clause contained in the written contract. The parties agree to the amount of damages in advance. If one party breaches the contract, all the parties know how to calculate the damages.

Liquidated damage clauses are very common in the construction industry. The contractor promises to complete a building on a specified date. In the event it fails to complete the project on time, the contractor agrees to pay the owner a specific sum for every day the project is not completed.

The court upholds liquidated damage provisions if the damages meet two requirements. First, the amount of liquidated damages must be difficult to assess at the time the contract is signed. Second, the damages specified in the contract must bear some reasonable relationship to the actual damages incurred. A liquidated damage clause is declared null and void if it does not satisfy both requirements.

The amount of damages contained in the liquidated damages clause cannot be so large that it is punitive in nature. Punitive damages are not awarded in a breach of contract case.

Equitable Remedies

The most common equitable remedies available to a nonbreaching party are rescission and restitution, specific performance of a contract, and reformation of a contract. Equitable remedies are available in unusual circumstances.

When a rescission of a contract is ordered, the parties are restored to their original positions before the contract was made. Rescission is available when fraud,

mistake, duress, or failure of consideration occurs. When a contract is rescinded, each party returns all money or items received back to the other party under the contract. The return of the items is called **restitution.** Restitution prevents unjust enrichment.

The remedy of specific performance of a contract is not often allowed. If money damages would be an inadequate remedy because the contract involves land or unique personal property, the court may grant the equitable remedy of specific performance. Each party is ordered to perform the specific promises in the contract. Specific performance is inappropriate for contracts relating to personal services.

Contract reformation occurs when the contract needs to be rewritten (reformed) because of errors in the written document. The court orders the contract to be reformed in accordance with the parties' true, original intentions. Exhibit 10–4 summarizes the remedies available for a breach of contract.

International Consideration

Selling Goods Internationally

As discussed in Chapter 9, the United Nations Convention on Contracts for the International Sale of Goods (CISG)[4] is a comprehensive document that covers all aspects of the sale of goods. Articles in the CISG cover the delivery of the goods and the handing over of the shipping documents or warehouse receipts so that the buyer can take possession of the goods.

The seller must deliver goods of the quantity, quality, and description required by the contract. The seller is liable when the goods fail to conform. The buyer must inspect the goods promptly and give notice of any problems with conformity within a reasonable time period. The buyer loses the right to rely on the lack of conformity if he does not give the seller notice within two years after the goods were "actually handed over to the buyer."

The remedies under the CISG are money damages, avoidance of the contract, and specific performance. The last remedy rarely is allowed in contracts for the sale of goods under U.S. law unless the item is unique, such as the Hope diamond.

[4]CISG is found at http://www.uncitral.org.

Exhibit 10–4   Remedies for Breach of Contract

Equitable Remedies

Recission and Restitution	1. *Recission* An action to cancel the contract and return the parties to the positions they occupied prior to the transaction. Available when fraud, mistake, duress, or failure of consideration is present.
	2. *Restitution* When a contract is rescinded, both parties must make restitution to each other by returning goods, property, or money previously conveyed. Restitution prevents the unjust enrichment of the defendant.
Specific Performance	Requires the performance of the act promised in the contract. Only available in special situations, such as in contracts for the sale of unique goods or land, and where monetary damages would be an inadequate remedy. Specific performance is not available as a remedy in contracts for personal services.
Reformation	Corrects or rewrites a written contract to conform with the original intention of the parties.

Legal Remedies

Damages	A legal remedy designed to compensate the nonbreaching party for the loss of the bargain. By awarding money damages, the court tries to place the parties financially in the position they would have occupied had the contract been fully performed. The nonbreaching party frequently has a duty to mitigate damages incurred. The three broad categories of damages are:
	1. *Compensatory damages* Compensate the nonbreaching party for economic injuries actually sustained and proven to have arisen directly from the breach of contract.
	2. *Consequential damages* Result from special circumstances beyond the contract itself. These damages flow only from the consequences of a breach. The defendant must know at the time of the contract the existence of the special circumstances. Thus, these damages are foreseeable as a breach of the contract. The breaching party knows that the nonbreaching party will suffer two types of damages, compensatory damages and the additional loss of consequential damages.
	3. *Liquidated damages* Compensate the nonbreaching party by setting out the amount of damages in the contract. First, the amount of damages must be difficult to determine at the time the contract is signed. Second, the amount of liquidated damages must be reasonable in relationship to the actual damages and cannot be punitive in nature.

PRACTICAL TIPS

Contractual Capacity

A businessperson may become involved with parties who lack contractual capacity (such as minors or those judged to be mentally incompetent) in several ways. For example, a minor might earn millions of dollars on a successful recording and need to invest this money, or a person who has had a successful business career but now has Alzheimer's disease may be unable to manage his own affairs.

In all states, procedures exist to appoint a person to manage these assets. This person is called either a *guardian* or a *conservator*. In many states, the appointed guardian arranges for the personal care of the person who is incompetent, whereas an appointed conservator manages the protected party's assets. The same person may serve in both roles or two different people may be appointed.

Before appointment, the conservator must post a bond with the court in the amount of the total assets that she will manage. If no bond is posted, all assets must be held in restricted, fully insured bank accounts. The conservator can remove funds from these restricted accounts only by specific court order. In states that have not established the concept of a conservator, the appointed person, or guardian, handles both the protected person's personal care and finances.

The following checklist can provide guidance for protecting yourself when dealing with individuals with impaired capacity to contract.

Checklist

✔ *Background Check* Determine if the guardian or conservator has been privately or court appointed. If this person has been privately

appointed, you should exercise care. If you know or should have known that the guardian was embezzling monies and using the funds for her personal benefit, you will be required to return anything that the dishonest guardian paid or gave you.

✔ *Documentation* If the guardian or conservator has been court appointed, he will have the court documents reflecting the appointment. You should make copies for your business files.

✔ *Verification* Verify that the person has authority to enter into this particular contract with you on behalf of the protected party by requesting to see the court order or the document called a *power of attorney*. The person may have restricted authority.

Chapter Summary

The first three elements of a binding contract, offer, acceptance, and consideration, were described in Chapter 9. The last two elements are legal capacity and legality.

Parties to a contract must have the capacity to contract. Minors and most people who are mentally incompetent can enter into contracts, but these contracts are voidable at their option. A minor is liable for necessary items, but only to the extent of the reasonable value of the property or services actually used. When disaffirmance occurs, a minor must return any items even though they might be in poor condition. If a court determines a person to be mentally incompetent, any contracts made after the court's judgment are void.

A valid contract must have a legal object or subject matter. The general rule is that an illegal agreement is void. In addition, the law requires certain contracts to be in writing to be enforceable.

Contractual rights and duties can be transferred to a third person through assignment of the rights or delega-

tion of the duties. Third parties may be given benefits under a contract. Beneficiaries are either incidental or intended beneficiaries. An intended beneficiary can be categorized as a creditor beneficiary or a donee beneficiary.

Contracts can be discharged by acts or by agreement, such as full performance, accord and satisfaction, covenant not to sue, or novation. Contracts can be ended by operation of the law, which is the unilateral alteration of a written contract, the expiration of the statute of limitations, discharge by bankruptcy proceedings, or impossibility of performance because of a party's death or insanity or because of the destruction of the contract's subject matter.

When a party breaches his contractual commitments, he is liable for the damages caused. The injured party may recover through the equitable remedies of rescission and restitution, specific performance, or reformation, or through the legal remedy of money damages.

Using the World Wide Web

Various Web sites provide information on electronic commerce. The American Institute of Certified Public Accountants (AICPA) has broken new ground by ensuring that Web sites offering electronic commerce

meet standards of consumer information protection, transaction integrity, and sound business practices. In 1997, the AICPA and the Canadian Institute of Chartered Accountants introduced the CPA WebTrust[SM] seal, which CPAs will be able to use to ensure consumers that Web sites bearing the seal are trustworthy and reliable with regard to confidential consumer information.

The United Nations (UN) has developed a model law on electronic commerce that is being submitted to members of the UN for their signature. The U.S. government also has developed initiatives concerning electronic commerce.

For *Web Activities*, links to Web sites mentioned in the chapter, and additional Web sites that relate to the chapter topics, go to **http://bohlman.westbuslaw.**

com, click on "Internet Applications," and select Chapter 10.

Web Activities

Go to **http://bohlman. westbuslaw.com**, click on "Internet Applications," and select Chapter 10.
10–1 Real Estate
10–2 Legal Forms

Key Terms

accord and satisfaction
age of majority
assignee
assignment
assignor
blue sky law
breach of contract
collateral contract
compensatory damages

consequential damages
covenant not to sue
creditor beneficiary
delegation
disaffirm
donee beneficiary
Electronic Signatures in
    Global and National
    Commerce Act

exculpatory clause
incidental beneficiary
intended beneficiary
legal capacity
legality
liquidated damages
novation
parol evidence rule
ratification

remedy
restitution
statute of frauds
usury

Questions and Case Problems

10–1 Restrictive Covenant A major corporation requires you to sign a contract as a condition of your employment. The contract contains a clause stating that you cannot compete directly or indirectly with the employer for a period of one year after your termination. Are these provisions legal? Why or why not? Does this type of covenant constitute duress?

10–2 Usury Mallard was sent a past due water bill, which included a 10 percent late fee. He claimed that this fee was in violation of the usury laws. Mallard was sued and lost in the trial court. He appealed. What result and why? [*Mallard v. Forest Heights Water Works, Inc.*, 260 Ga. App. 750, 580 S.E.2d 602 (2003)]

10–3 Mistake Leydet entered into a written contract with the city of Mountain Home for delivery of treated wastewater over a twenty-year period to irrigate his farmland. Delivery started in 1982 and Leydet paid. The city was never capable of delivering the amount set out in the contract and Leydet could never use more than that which the city delivered from 1982 to 1987. A drought for next two years prevented the city from

delivering the amount of water contracted. Leydet sued, seeking damages. The city defended that the drought excused it from fully performing on the contract. Any other steps taken would have been prohibitively expensive. Thus, performing was impracticable, and nonperformance was excused. Who should prevail and why? [*Leydet v. City of Mountain Home*, 812 P.2d 755 (Idaho App. 1991)]

10–4 Accord and Satisfaction Six Industries, Inc., was a general contractor for the construction of an insurance building. Six Industries entered into a subcontract with Kirk Williams Co. for heating and air-conditioning installations in the building. As a standard practice on projects of this size, the contract between the parties was changed by formal written change orders on several occasions. Near completion of the building, Six Industries submitted two last change orders. Kirk Williams refused to sign or complete the change orders because it claimed that Six Industries had delayed the project to Kirk Williams's detriment. Six Industries issued a check to Kirk Williams for $14,850.04. On the check, the following language appeared: "Endorsement and/or negotiation of the check constitutes a full and complete release of Six Industries, Inc., and acknowledges full payment of all monies due." Kirk Williams received the check and the bookkeeper deposited it. Kirk Williams tried to return the money alleging that he was owed more money. Six Industries asserted that the depositing of the check was accord and satisfaction. Was there an accord and satisfaction through the cashing of the check? Explain. [*Kirk Williams Co. v. Six Industries, Inc.*, 11 Ohio App. 3d 152, 463 N.E.2d 1266 (1983)]

10–5 Capacity In 1982, Webster Street Partnership, Ltd. (Webster), entered into a lease agreement with Sheridan and Wilwerding. Webster was aware that both Sheridan and Wilwerding were minors. Both minors were living away from home, believing that the landlord would allow them to return home at any time. Sheridan and Wilwerding paid the first month's rent, but then failed to pay the rent for the next month and vacated the apartment. Webster sued them for breach of contract. They claimed that the lease agreement was voidable because they were minors. Who will prevail in court and why? [*Webster Street Partnership, Ltd. v. Sheridan*, 220 Neb. 9, 368 N.W.2d 439 (1985)]

10–6 Liquidated Damages Vrgora, a general contractor, entered into a contract with the Los Angeles Unified School District (LAUSD) to construct an automotive service shed and specifically enclosed room outfitted with an electronic vehicle performance tester. The contract provided for liquidated damages in the amount of $100 per day if the project was not completed within 250 days. Vrgora was responsible for purchasing and installing the tester. A dispute between the tester's manufacturer and Vrgora arose. The manufacturer finally delivered the tester over six months later. As a result, Vrgora completed the project several months late. LAUSD now wants Vrgora to pay $20,700 in damages for failing to complete the contract within 250 days. Who should prevail and why? [*Vrgora v. Los Angeles Unified School District*, 152 Cal. App. 3d 1178, 200 Cal. Rptr. 130 (1984)]

10–7 Mistake Alchem, an Israeli corporation, manufactures and sells lightweight, small-sized, halogenated aerosol fire extinguishers. Alchem entered into a contract with the company Gerard owned that made Gerard its exclusive distributor outside of Israel. A contract condition required the approval of the Underwriters Laboratories (UL). A UL approval in the United States is an indication of safety, quality control, and reliability. UL approval is essential if the product is to be marketed in the United States, because most U.S. pur-

chasers require it, but it means very little, if anything, outside the United States. The process of obtaining UL approval takes a long time, ranging from a minimum of three to a maximum of fifteen years. After seven years, Alchem still had not obtained UL approval. Naturally, Gerard sold no extinguishers in the United States. Alchem, however, did sell some fire extinguishers in distributorship areas outside the United States, where UL approvals were not required even though Alchem had given Gerard exclusive dealership in those areas. Gerard sued Alchem. Alchem argued that Gerard could have sold the product outside the United States, and by not doing so, it had acted in bad faith. Gerard argued that it did not have a duty to sell any products prior to UL approval. Which company is correct? Was there a mutual mistake? Explain your answer. [*Gerard v. Almouli*, 746 F.2d 936 (2d Cir. 1984)]

10–8 Beneficiary On April 26, 1984, Stine loaned her daughter and son-in-law, the Stewarts, $100,000 to purchase a home. The Stewarts did not give a security interest or mortgage to secure the note. The Stewarts eventually paid $50,000 on the note, leaving $50,000, together with unpaid accrued interest, due. The Stewarts divorced on October 2, 1992. The couple executed an Agreement Incident to Divorce on October 1, 1992, which disposed of marital property, including the home identified as the Lago Vista property. The agreement provided that he could lease the house, but if he sold it, he agreed that "any monies owing to [Stine] are to be paid in the current principal sum of $50,000.00." The agreement further stated:

The parties agree that with regard to the note to Mary Nelle Stine, after application of the proceeds of the [Lago Vista property], if there are any amounts owing to [Stine] the remaining balance owing to her will be appropriated 50% to NANCY KAREN STEWART and 50% to WILLIAM DEAN STEWART, JR. and said 50% from each party will be due and payable upon the determination that the proceeds from the sale of said residence are not sufficient to repay said $50,000.00 in full.

Stine did not sign the agreement. In November 1995, he sold the Lago Vista property, did not pay any proceeds to Stine, and did not make any further payments on the $50,000 principal. Consequently, on July 27, 1998, Stine sued Stewart for breaching the agreement. The statute of limitations had expired on the original note. Was Stine a creditor or donee beneficiary of the agreement reached during the divorce proceedings? [*Stine v. Stewart*, 45 Tex. Sup. Ct. J. 966, 80 S.W.3d 586 (2002)]

10–9 Parol Evidence Hupy, a lawyer, began purchasing one-page advertisements in the attorney section of the Yellow Pages Directory in 1989. The contract with Ameritech Publishing, Inc., provided:

5. We maintain publishing standards and specifications which change from time to time. . . . We reserve the right to print your Advertising Units on any page and in any position <u>on a page within the specified classified heading</u>.

. . . .

9. <u>This document is our complete agreement. It replaces and supersedes (and you should not rely upon) any prior oral or written representations or agreements</u>. . . . However, any change to this document or to these terms must be in writing, signed by both you and us, and dated by both you and us at least fourteen (14) weeks prior to the Issue Date of the directory.

Ameritech placed Hupy's full-page advertisements at the front of each attorney advertisement section from 1989 to 1999. In 2000, Ameritech began selling two-page advertisements. Although Hupy was told that he would lose his priority position unless he purchased a two-page advertisement, he still purchased a one-page advertisement and lost his priority position. Hupy sued Ameritech for breach of contract. Hupy alleged that, beginning in 1989 and continuously thereafter, Ameritech told Hupy that he would retain his position in front of other advertisers as long as a full-page advertisement was purchased. Hupy argued the importance of maintaining the first position to attract new clients. Ameritech's position was that the parol evidence rule precluded any introduction of oral evidence which would change the written contract. How did the court hold and why? [*Michael Hupy & Associates, S.C. v. Ameritech Publishing, Inc.,* 2003 WL 22331405 (Wis.App. 2003)]

10–10 Internet The national Better Business Bureau's Web site has useful information on a variety of topics including the BBB AutoLine. This service does not handle cases that fall under state lemon car laws, which are aimed at disputes between the car owner and the dealership. The BBB AutoLine offers an arbitration service that attempts to resolve disputes between consumers and automobile manufacturers involving alleged defects in a vehicle's material or workmanship. Once the arbitrator renders a decision, what two options are available to the consumer and what happens under each option? See the Web site at **http://www.dr.bbb.org/autoline/index.asp**.

Chapter 11

Sales Law and Product Liability

To things of sale, a seller's praise belongs.

> *Love's Labour's Lost*, 1598
> **William Shakespeare, English classical writer, 1564–1616**

Chapter Outline

Ethical Consideration

Safe Products—At What Cost?

Motorcycle Runner is a company that manufactures a popular motorcycle called Distance Runner. You are the president and chief executive officer (CEO) of the company. Motorcycle Runner competes with several large businesses in the motorcycle market. The company is very profitable because of its highly successful innovative designs, including a gas tank with double the normal capacity. Although the bike is relatively safe, the large-capacity gas tank is more likely than a normal-sized gas tank to rupture, leading to spilled gas that could cause a fire. The owner's manual discloses this danger in bold print.

A confidential internal report indicates that 5 percent of the motorcycles will probably be involved in accidents. If a fire erupts from a ruptured gas tank, it will probably cause the cyclist's death. Generally, these accidents are caused when the driver exceeds the speed limit and loses control of the motorcycle. The report suggests that if the tank were reduced in size and made safer, the risk of rupture could be reduced to 1 percent. The increased cost of the motorcycle and the loss of the large-capacity gas tank, however, would probably reduce sales by 20 percent.

This large reduction would force a significant number of the employees to be laid off and might jeopardize the company's future. Does the company continue to make Distance Runner with its large-capacity tank or change its construction of the gas tank? Use the ethical model presented in Chapter 2 and reprinted on the inside front cover to develop your answer.

Introduction

The material discussed in the previous two chapters examined contract law in a general fashion. The subject matter of contracts can be services, real property, or goods.[1] **Goods** are defined as all items that are movable at the time they are identified to a specific contract. Goods also include growing crops and the unborn young of animals, plus any other objects that

[1] See UCC 2-105.

may be severed from real estate by the seller. Money, negotiable instruments, and investment securities, however, are not classified as goods.

Contracts concerning goods are covered by a set of statutes called Article 2, Sales, under the Uniform Commercial Code (UCC). Although the UCC covers a range of legal topics, in this chapter the UCC is a shorthand way to refer to Article 2, governing the sale of goods.

The material discussed in the previous two chapters applies to all three types of subject matter: services, real property, and goods. This chapter focuses on additional law that applies only to the sale of goods. When a contract involves goods, the court will look first to the UCC, Article 2, rules. If no specific UCC rule exists, the court turns to other statutes, then to common law.

Many consumers, however, prefer to lease goods rather than purchase them. The UCC, Article 2A, Leases, covers leases such as automobiles and computer equipment leases. The chapter reviews the background of the UCC, then turns to specialized areas, such as title, risk of loss, trial sales, performance, and remedies. The chapter wraps up with a discussion on the legal theories of product liability.

Artiste Login. Artiste Login Products, Inc., is involved in many contracts for the sale of goods. Carlo and Carlotta, the owners, have read the provisions of Article 2, Sales, and notice that the provisions tend to protect the interests of the buyer over those of the seller. In contrast, Carlo and Carlotta know that the laws covering the sale of services or the sale of real property follow the common law, which tends to favor the seller.

Instead of purchasing goods, Artiste might be better off financially if it leased goods. For example, Artiste may prefer to lease an automobile. UCC Article 2A provides legal guidance in the lease of goods. It basically treats the long-term lease of goods in the same manner as a sale. Article 2A has been adopted by a number of states.

Background of the Uniform Commercial Code

During the 1930s, to create uniform commercial laws, some members of Congress proposed a statutory scheme that would cover all interstate commercial transactions. The bills never were passed. Congress, however, cannot control intrastate commerce, because the Constitution gives the individual states control over business conducted within their respective borders.

The National Conference of Commissioners on Uniform State Laws[2] and the American Law Institute[3] began work on the Uniform Commercial Code in 1942. In 1952, they completed the first draft of a uniform act that would apply to both intrastate and interstate transactions. All fifty states, the District of Columbia, and the Virgin Islands have adopted the Uniform Commercial Code, which has been updated several times.[4]

The UCC consists of these articles:

1. General Provisions
2. Sales
2A. Leases
3. Negotiable Instruments
4. Bank Deposits and Collections
4A. Funds Transfers
5. Letters of Credit
6. Repealer of Bulk Transfers
7. Warehouse Receipts, Bills of Lading and Other Documents of Title
8. Investment Securities
9. Secured Transactions; Sales of Accounts and Chattel Paper
10. Effective Date and Repealer
11. Effective Date and Transition Provisions.

The code remains closely consistent with the basic principles of commercial law that derived from the law merchant and common law, yet it expands and comprehensively orders these principles to modernize, clarify, and standardize the rules.

Each article contains sections that establish the rules on a particular topic.[5] Of the articles that make up the UCC, only three, Article 2 (Sales), Article 3 (Negotiable Instruments), and Article 9 (Secured Transactions; Sales of Accounts and Chattel Paper), significantly impact contractual situations. Articles 3 and 9 are discussed in Chapter 12.

General Terms of the UCC

The UCC clarifies the legal relationship of the parties in modern commercial transactions. The code is designed to help determine the intentions of the parties to a commercial contract and to give force and effect to their agreement. Businesspeople are assured that their contracts, if validly entered into, will be enforced. In turn, this assurance encourages further business transactions.

The UCC provides guidance to parties who are involved in a contract for the sale and purchase of goods. The drafters of the UCC wanted it to be a practical guideline for businesspeople to use. The code is flexible enough to provide for expansion of commercial practices under the court's interpretation, whereas the statutory aspects provide a stable framework.

The UCC reinforces the principle of the freedom of contract. The parties to the contract may make whatever arrangements suit them within limits. The obligations of good faith, diligence, and reasonableness are the standards set by specific provisions of the UCC for the courts to use when reviewing a contract that is the subject matter of the dispute. Many UCC sections include the words "unless otherwise agreed," indicating that the parties may set their own terms.

If the parties fail to include certain terms in the contract, the UCC encourages application of the rules of a particular trade to fill in the missing terms or to guide a court in interpreting a clause. This principle is called **usage of trade** [UCC 1-205]. A baker's dozen, for example, means thirteen items, not twelve. A contract for the sale of a baker's dozen of jelly-filled rolls means a purchaser expects thirteen rolls in the box.

The UCC defers to the parties' previous **course of dealing**. The conduct between the parties on previous contracts establishes a basis for understanding and interpreting their promises and conduct in the current contract [UCC 1-205].

Often the sheer number of UCC rules seems overwhelming. Most rules are based on common sense and used by most consumers on a daily basis without them being aware of their knowledge.

---

[2]The National Conference of Commissioners on Uniform State Laws has a Web site at http://www.nccusl.org.

[3]The American Law Institute's Web site is at http://www.ali.org. The ALI was organized in 1923 and its purpose is "to promote the clarification and simplification of the law and its better adaptation to social needs, to secure the better administration of justice, and to encourage and carry on scholarly and scientific legal work."

[4]Note, however, that Louisiana has adopted only Articles 1, 3, 4, and 5 of the Uniform Commercial Code.

[5]The Uniform Commercial Code is constantly being reassessed to ensure that it is current with business practices. To view current provisions and suggested modifications, go to http://www.law.upenn.edu/bll/ulc/ulc_frame.htm.

Artiste Login. Carlotta purchased a new automobile. She picked it up at the car dealership (seller's place of business). If, however, she were to purchase a used automobile from a private party, she would go to the seller's home to take delivery of the automobile, because the UCC states that if the seller does not have a business, the place of delivery is the seller's home [UCC 2-308]. Under the UCC, she also is free to agree that the automobile will be delivered at a place other than the seller's place of business or home, such as Artiste's business office (the buyer's place of employment).

A **merchant** is a person who deals in goods and holds himself out as having knowledge about the goods or skills peculiar to the practices involved in a contract. A contract "between merchants" means that both parties to the contract have the knowledge or skill of merchants [UCC 2-104]. Merchants are subject to special rules under the UCC.

Uniform Commercial Code and Contract Law

A court, when reviewing a contract case, looks first to the contract's subject matter. Once the court determines the subject matter, it reviews any applicable statutes, such as the UCC.[6] If no statute exists, the principles of common law apply.

The material in Chapters 9 and 10 discussed the elements of a binding contract. These elements are (1) offer, (2) acceptance, (3) legal consideration, (4) capacity to contract, and (5) legal objective. The statute of frauds that requires certain types of contracts to be in writing to be enforced in court, if a breach of contract occurs, was discussed in Chapter 10. The basic contract law set out in Chapters 9 and 10 is followed by the Uniform Commercial Code. The UCC modifies some of those rules when the contract involves the sale of goods.

The following are some of the changes made to contract law by the UCC involving the sale of goods: (1) An offer sometimes does not have to be definite and certain, (2) some offers are not revocable, (3) method of acceptance is treated differently, (4) mirror-image

[6]Many contracts contain standard clauses. Contracts involving the sale of goods under the Uniform Commercial Code generally contain these clauses. You can find some of these on the Internet at http://lectlaw.com/formb.htm.

doctrine of the acceptance sometimes does not apply, and (5) legal consideration is not always required. One section requires certain contracts to be in writing when the value of the goods is more than $500.

Missing Terms

As covered in Chapter 9, one element of an offer is that it must be definite and certain. Article 2 has liberalized this rule. Under the UCC, even though one or more of the contract's terms were not agreed to, a court may enforce a contract for the sale of goods. If the parties clearly intended to make a contract, and if a reasonably certain basis exists to find an appropriate remedy, the court will supply or clarify the missing terms [UCC 2-204(3)].

The most common missing terms are price, delivery place, shipment or delivery time, and time of payment. If the price is omitted, the court imposes the reasonable price at the time the goods were delivered [UCC 2-305(1)]. If the place of delivery is unspecified, the court requires delivery at the seller's (not the buyer's) home or business [UCC 2-308(a)]. If the shipment or delivery time is ambiguous, the court establishes a reasonable deadline following the contract formation [UCC 2-309(1)]. If the payment time is unspecified, the court makes the payment due at the time and place of delivery. Unless the purchaser arranged to pay for the goods on credit, she must pay in cash (currency or check) at the delivery time and place [UCC 2-310(a)].

Irrevocable Offers

Although most offers are revocable, certain offers can be made irrevocable. Two of these were discussed in Chapter 9: (1) those involved in option contracts and (2) offers made irrevocable by virtue of promissory estoppel. Under the UCC, offers that meet the definition of a *firm offer* are not revocable.

A **firm offer** is a modification of an option contract and applies only to offers involving the sale and purchase of goods. A firm offer occurs when a merchant makes a written, signed offer either to buy or to sell goods and indicates in the offer that the offer is irrevocable. The merchant's offer is irrevocable even though the offeree does not pay any consideration [UCC 2-205]. The offer remains open for the stated time period. If the time is unspecified, the offer remains open for a reasonable period that cannot exceed three months. Exhibit 11–1 summarizes the requirements for an effective offer.

Acceptance

An offer may be accepted in any manner and by any medium reasonable under the circumstances [UCC 2-206(1)(a)]. This rule is practical for business transactions.

Another rule deems that the acceptance is effective when sent. Under this rule, a contract is formed even though the offeror never received the message of acceptance.

An order to purchase goods may be treated as either a bilateral or a unilateral contract. The offer to buy goods can be accepted by a promise to ship the goods (bilateral contract) or by an actual shipment of the goods (unilateral contract) [UCC 2-206(1)(b)]. For example, Shirts Galore, Inc., receives a purchase order to ship two dozen red shirts to Burton's Men Store, Inc. Shirts Galore can accept by promptly shipping the red shirts to Burton's. If Shirts Galore does not have the red shirts to ship but will have them in three days, Shirts Galore can send a FAX or e-mail (the acceptance) to Burton's that the shirts will be shipped. If Shirts Galore sends the red shirts as promised, the contract is completed. If Shirts Galore, however, sends blue shirts, Shirts Galore is in breach of contract because it shipped nonconforming goods.

The offeree has an obligation to communicate the acceptance to the offeror. If notice of acceptance is not provided after a reasonable time period, the offeror may treat the offer as having lapsed [UCC 2-206(2)].

Acceptance with Added Terms. In contracts for real property and services, the acceptance approves all of the terms of the offer and cannot modify any of the terms. Otherwise, if the acceptance changes any term it becomes a counteroffer. This rule is called the *mirror-image rule*, which was discussed in Chapter 9.

The UCC provisions modify the mirror-image rule. The rule caused considerable problems in commercial transactions for the sale of goods. Normal practice is for commercial sellers and buyers to use standard form contracts involving goods. Buyers send purchase orders forms while sellers usually accept goods on their standard confirmation forms.

Any variations in terms between these two forms violated the mirror-image rule. Two forms drafted by two different companies will vary to some degree and the result is confusion. For example, the confirmation form contains a requirement that any disputes must be submitted to arbitration (see Chapter 4), whereas the purchase order form does not address this topic. This type of conflict is referred to as the "battle of the forms." Under the common law's mirror-image rule, no contract results when terms in the standardized confirmation forms (acceptance) contradict terms of the purchase order (offer). In the commercial world of contracting for the sale and purchase of goods, the mirror-image rule was too rigid and did not reflect business practice.

If, however, a contract is (1) for the sale of goods and (2) both parties are merchants, the contract is formed when the offeree "accepts" the offer, even though the terms of the acceptance (the confirmation form) modify or add to the terms of the original offer [UCC 2-207(1)]. When the contract is between merchants, the new terms become part of the contract automatically. For example, if the confirmation form requires disputes to be arbitrated, this new term becomes part of the contract. To prevent the offeree from forcing terms on the offeror, however, the code has three exceptions to this rule [UCC 2-207(2)].

Exhibit 11-1   Requirements for an Effective Offer

1. *Intent* The offeror must have shown a serious, objective intent to become bound by the offer.
2. *Definite* The terms of the offer must be sufficiently definite to be ascertainable by the parties or by a court. Under the UCC, the court can supply missing terms if the parties clearly intended to make a contract for the sale of goods and if a reasonably certain basis exists for giving an appropriate remedy [UCC 2-204]:
   a. *No price* Reasonable price at time of delivery [UCC 2-305(1)].
   b. *No delivery place* Seller's place of business or, if none, seller's home [UCC 2-308(a)].
   c. *No time set to ship or deliver* Reasonable time after contract is formed [UCC 2-309(1)].
   d. *No time set for payment* Money to be paid on delivery [UCC 2-310(a)].
3. *Communication* The offer must be communicated by the offeror to the offeree.

The first exception places the burden on the offeror. The offer must clearly require the acceptance to be the same as the offer with no variations, that is, a return to the mirror-image rule [UCC 2-207(2)(a)]. The purchase order form can include a statement "Acceptance to be on these terms only." Any additional terms in the confirmation form will not become part of the contract.

Under the second exception, if the acceptance form imposes new duties or materially changes the offeror's duties, those terms will not be part of the contract [UCC 2-207(2)(b)]. The offeror states what duties it is willing to undertake and those duties cannot be materially changed. For example, if the terms in the acceptance increase the prices to the offeror-buyer, that increase will not become part of the contract. The price increase materially alters the offeror's duties.

The third exception provides the offeror an opportunity to read the confirmation form for the new or changed terms. Once found, if the offeror does not agree to the new or changed terms, the offeror must object to (reject) those terms within a reasonable time period [UCC 2-207(2)(c)]. The contract will continue on the original terms set forth in the purchase order.

When one or both parties to the contract are nonmerchants, the UCC has a different rule. In these cases, the contract is formed according to the offeror's terms, not according to the additional acceptance terms. The additional terms are considered to be proposals to the newly formed contract, which the offeror can accept or reject. If the offeror takes no action, the proposed terms are rejected.

The Drafting Committee for Uniform State Laws has recommended a change to UCC 2-207 for merchants and nonmerchants. Under the proposed modification, the new terms in the purported acceptance do not at any time become part of the contract unless the offeree proves that the offeror agrees to the terms or that the offeror knew or had reason to know of the inconsistent terms and did not object to them. If adopted, the proposed rule will eliminate the problem of the battle of the forms that now exists between the buyer and the seller.

Exhibit 11-2 summarizes the rules for acceptance involving goods.

Consideration. The doctrine of consideration has been modified for contracts for goods. A contract involving goods can be modified and the modification does not require additional consideration to be binding [UCC 2-209].

Artiste Login. Carlotta orders one dozen lamps from a manufacturer for Artiste's furniture store at $75 per lamp. After paying for the lamps, she discovers that one of Artiste's competitors sells a similar lamp to the general public for $60. She contacts the manufacturer and explains that competitors are selling a similar lamp

Exhibit 11-2   Acceptance of an Agreement for Sale of Goods

1. Agreement can be made only by the offeree or the offeree's authorized agent.
2. *UCC rule* A definite acceptance of an offer is not a counteroffer, even if new terms modify the terms of the original offer [UCC 2-207]. If either party is a nonmerchant, additional terms are proposals for addition to the contract but not part of it. Between merchants, the additional terms become a part of the contract, with these exceptions:
    i. Offer limits acceptance to its terms [UCC 2-207(2)(a)].
    ii. New terms materially change offer [UCC 2-207(2)(b)].
    iii. New terms are rejected [UCC 2-207(2)(c)].
3. Under UCC 2-206(1)(a), in acceptance of offers for the sale of goods, any medium that is reasonable under the circumstance.
4. Under UCC 2-206(1)(b), an offer to buy goods for prompt shipment means:
    a. the offer can be accepted by shipment of conforming goods, and
    b. the offer can be accepted by promise to ship. The shipper can send conforming or nonconforming goods. If nonconforming goods are sent, the shipper is in breach of contract for failing to ship conforming goods in accordance with the contract.

for $60. The manufacturer and Carlotta reach an agreement that she will pay only $30 per lamp.

The second agreement is enforceable because it involves a modification to a contract for the sale of goods. Neither party provided any new consideration to support this second agreement. Carlotta did not suffer any legal detriment, because she was obligated to pay $75 per lamp. The manufacturer received no legal benefit, because Carlotta already was obligated to purchase the dozen lamps. The modification is enforceable in court because UCC 2-209 exempts this type of modification from requiring new consideration and from the prior existing debt rule.

Writing

Contracts involving the sale of goods for the price of $500 or more must be in writing and signed by the party against whom enforcement is sought [UCC 2-201(1)]. If, however, the signed writing is insufficient because it omits or incorrectly states a term, the contract is still valid up to the amount or quantity of goods stated in the writing.

The UCC does not allow the enforcement of oral contracts, unless they fall under one of its exceptions. The first issue is to determine if both parties are merchants or if the parties are merchants and consumers or if both parties are consumers.

Both parties to an oral contract for goods are merchants. If one party sends a written confirmation to the other, the confirmation is the written evidence of the oral contract. The receiver has ten days to provide its written objection. If this objection is not sent, the terms of the oral contract are enforceable and are presumed to be the terms contained in the written confirmation. The contract is enforceable against either party in a court, even though the party that sent the written confirmation is the only one who signed it [UCC 2-201(2)].

When the parties are not both merchants, three exceptions exist. First, a court may enforce an oral contract up to the amount of payment made or up to the quantity of the goods received and accepted by the buyer [UCC 2-201(3)(c)]. This rule can be seen in the following story about Artiste.

Artiste Login. Sean orally agrees to pay $5,000 for furniture from Artiste's furniture store. Although the furniture is delivered, Sean does not pay for it. Artiste could sue and prove in court that $5,000 worth of furniture was delivered to Sean. The court could find a contract up to the value of the goods received and accepted by Sean, that is, the $5,000.

In another scenario, Sean may have paid for the furniture, but Artiste refuses to deliver it. Sean can sue Artiste and prove that he has paid Artiste $5,000. The court can order Artiste to return the $5,000 or to deliver the furniture. If Artiste refuses to deliver the furniture, Sean can purchase furniture from another store, and if he has to pay more, he can recover the $5,000 plus the additional costs.

Now assume Sean orally agreed to pay $5,000 for two rooms of furniture, $3,000 for the living room and $2,000 for the den. If Artiste delivers the living room furniture, but does not deliver the den furniture, the oral contract is enforceable up to the amount of the goods received and accepted by Sean, that is, the $3,000.

Second, a court can enforce an oral contract up to the amount that a party admits to in court or in court documents [UCC 2-201(3)(b)]. The admissions in written documents or oral admissions in court allows the judge to determine the terms of the contract. Let's continue to look at the contract relationship between Artiste and Sean.

Artiste Login. Sean orally agrees to pay Artiste $5,000 for the furniture. When Artiste sues him, he files a response that he had an oral agreement to pay $5,000. This written response is his admission in writing; the court can enforce the agreement up to $5,000, the amount Sean has admitted to in a court document. Or, if he files a response that does not make any admissions, but he gives testimony in the trial and admits to the agreement to pay $5,000, the court can enforce the agreement.

The UCC allows enforcement of oral contracts that involve specially manufactured goods [UCC 2-201(3)(a)]. This type of good could be furniture specifically made to fit a particular house or golf clubs custom made for a person. Goods of this type are not suitable for sale to others in the ordinary course of business. In the following case, the court examines the requirements of specially manufactured goods.

CASE 11.1

Intermediate Court of
Appeals of Hawai'i, 1994
874 P.2d 1100 (Haw. App.)

CONTOURS, INC. v. LEE

BACKGROUND AND FACTS DiGrandi was the president of Contours, Inc., a custom furniture manufacturer. During a meeting between DiGrandi and Lee, they agreed in writing that DiGrandi would make and deliver several pieces of furniture for $18,000. Lee paid $3,000 down.

Lee needed the furniture by November 28 for several large parties he had planned for December. If the furniture were not delivered on time, Contours agreed to pay Lee $500 for each day delivery was delayed. Minor oral modifications to the original contract reduced the total price from $18,000 to $15,000.

Although work on a dining room table was incomplete and Lee had not yet made any payments to reduce the $12,000 outstanding, Lee requested that the table be delivered by December 5 before his parties with the understanding that Contours would pick it up after the parties for the final finish. After the parties were held, Contours attempted on several occasions to pick up the furniture so it could complete the work required for the final finish, but Lee refused to surrender it. Contours brought a lawsuit to recover $12,000. The trial court reduced this sum by $3,500 because of Contour's seven-day delay in delivering the finished furniture.

Chief Judge BURNS

. . . .

The original contract was in writing. The subsequent oral modification of the contract canceling the order of some goods and changing the order for the remaining goods cannot be enforced against Lee absent an exception to the relevant statute of frauds. Thus, the question is whether the circuit court was right when it implicitly concluded that the oral modifications of the written contract were enforceable. In the absence of an essential finding of fact, we cannot answer this question.

Hawai'i's Uniform Commercial Code, Hawai'i Revised Statutes (HRS) chapter 490 (1985), states in relevant part as follows:

> § 490:2-201 *Formal requirements, statute of frauds.* (1) *Except as otherwise provided in this section a contract for the sale of goods for the price of $500 or more is not enforceable by way of action or defense unless there is some writing sufficient to indicate that a contract for sale has been made between the parties and signed by the party against whom enforcement is sought or by his authorized agent or broker.*

. . . .

> (3) *A contract which does not satisfy the requirements of subsection (1) but which is valid in other respects is enforceable.*

>> (a) *If the goods are to be specially manufactured for the buyer and are not suitable for sale to others in the ordinary course of the seller's business and the seller, before notice of repudiation is received and under circumstances which reasonably indicate that the goods are for the buyer, has made either a substantial beginning of their manufacture or commitments for their procurement.*

. . . .

As used in HRS § 490:2-201(3)(a), the term "specially manufactured," refers to the nature of the particular goods in question and not to whether the goods were made in an unusual, as opposed to the regular, business operation or manufacturing process of the seller. That the seller may be in the business of manufacturing custom designed and made goods does not necessarily preclude his goods from being deemed "specially manufactured" within the meaning of this exception. The crucial inquiry is whether the manufacturer could sell the goods in the ordinary course of his business to someone other than the original buyer. If with slight alterations the goods could be so sold, then they are not specially manufactured; if, however, essential changes are necessary to render the goods marketable by the seller to others, then the exception does apply.

DECISION AND REMEDY The court of appeals sent the case back to the trial court to determine if the furniture manufactured by Contours was specially manufactured goods. If the furniture were specially manufactured goods, the statute of frauds, as found in the Uniform Commercial Code, was satisfied.

CRITICAL THINKING: POLITICAL QUESTION Recently, Great Britain repealed the statute of frauds; thus, contracts no longer need to be in writing to be enforced in court. Discuss whether the United States should do likewise.

If the party is able to use one of the exceptions, the oral contract is enforceable up to the amount or quantity of goods proved in court. Other parts of the oral contract remain unenforceable. Exhibit 11–3 summarizes the statute of frauds and its exceptions under the UCC.

Unconscionable Bargain. The law has long been concerned about the power balance between a strong party in relationship to a weak party in a contract. Chapter 1 discussed the concept of equity. Equity is applied by the courts to obtain fairness in these types of contracts.

The UCC applies the concept of equity both to clauses and contracts for the sale of goods that involve **unconscionability** [UCC 2-302]. The legal test for unconscionability is whether, in the light of the general commercial background and the business needs of the particular trade or case, the clauses in the contract are so one sided as to be harsh and shocking to the conscience of the court under the circumstances. A

court may refuse to enforce a contract or a provision of a contract if it is found to be unconscionable.

In this illustration, a school purchases catsup in large quantities. A provision in the sales contract requires the school to reject each shipment within ten days if the goods fail to meet the contract specifications. After the rejection period passes, the school finds a catsup shipment to be contaminated. This contamination could only be discovered through microscopic analysis of the catsup bottles after the shipping container had been opened. In this case the court would find the ten-day rejection clause to be unconscionable.

In the following case, the court was faced with determining whether a contract was unconscionable. In the facts section, the truth-in-lending law is discussed. This federal statute requires that all financial costs and percentage rates be disclosed to a consumer. The truth-in-lending law will be covered in more depth in Chapter 14.

Exhibit 11–3   Statute of Frauds under the UCC

Contracts for the Sale of Goods Priced at $500 or More	1. *Application* Applies only to the contract for the sale of goods when the purchase price (excluding taxes) is $500 or more [UCC 2-201(1)].
	2. *Exceptions*
	a. Between merchants, where one sends a written confirmation and the recipient does not object in writing within ten days [UCC 2-201(2)].
	b. Admission under oath of an oral contract [UCC 2-201(3)(b)].
	c. Partial performance by buyer's payment or possession creates an enforceable contract up to the amount paid or quantity possessed [UCC 2-201(3)(c)].

CASE 11.2

United States District Court, Western District of Michigan, 2000
91 F. Supp. 2d 1087 (W.D. Mich.)

LOZADA v. DALE BAKER OLDSMOBILE, INC.

BACKGROUND AND FACTS Plaintiffs Nancy Lozada, Bob Warren, A. D. Christian, and Jeanne Uwamaliya were all customers of Dale Baker Olds. They sought to purchase motor vehicles on credit. Because of their respective credit histories, Dale Baker Olds salesmen determined that plaintiffs would not be eligible for conventional auto financing. As a result, the salesmen referred plaintiffs to the Dale Baker Olds special finance department, which, in turn, after the contracts and notes were signed, sold these to Consumer Finance Corporation (CFC).

After selecting a vehicle, each plaintiff was introduced to Assistant Special Finance Manager Stormie Moore to complete the necessary documentation to obtain credit to finance their vehicles in the subprime credit market. At that time, each plaintiff was presented with and signed a retail installment contract, which contained disclosures of the annual percentage rate, finance charge, amount financed, total sale price, and payment schedule. Those disclosures were contained under the heading "TRUTH IN LENDING DISCLOSURES" and placed immediately above the signature line.

While plaintiffs were shown the retail installment contracts at the time they signed them and while those installment contracts contained disclosures, plaintiffs were not given a copy of the contracts or disclosures until some days after they signed their agreements. Plaintiff Lozada received a copy ten days after signing the document. Plaintiff Warren received a copy two days after signing the document. Plaintiff Christian received a copy fifteen days after signing.

On the basis of this history, plaintiffs contended that Dale Baker Olds failed to make the disclosures required by the Truth-in-Lending Act (TILA) and the relevant regulations promulgated by the Federal Reserve Board pursuant to its authority under the TILA. Plaintiffs contended that CFC, as assignee of Dale Baker's contract with plaintiff Christian, was liable both under the federal and state statutes and under the terms of the contract. CFC moved to compel arbitration in accordance with the contract. The arbitration clause was written in very small print on the front of the contract.

HILLMAN, Senior District Judge

. . . .

In order to determine whether a contract is procedurally unconscionable, the court typically considers the relative bargaining power of the parties, their relative economic strength, the alternative sources of supply, "in a word, what are their options?" Having reviewed the verified allegations of the complaint, I am persuaded that plaintiffs have adequately alleged that inclusion of the arbitration provision was procedurally unconscionable.

In their complaint, plaintiffs allege that at the time of signing, Christian, like other consumers managed by the special finance department, was hurried to sign and had no reasonable opportunity to review the agreement. The complaint further alleges that Dale Baker Olds did not provide a copy of the contract to Christian at the time of signing. In fact, Christian was not given copies of any paperwork until two weeks after he had signed and after financing had been finalized through CFC. Plaintiffs further allege that such treatment resulted from the admitted practice of the special finance department to refuse to provide the customer with a copy of the retail installment contract until the contract had been purchased from Dale Baker Olds by a third-party finance company. As a consequence of both circumstances, plaintiffs contend that Christian did not and could not freely accept the arbitration provision.

I conclude that plaintiff has adequately alleged that the arbitration provision at issue was procedurally unconscionable. . . . Where a contract is prepared by one party and offered for rejection or acceptance without opportunity for bargaining under circumstances in which the party cannot obtain the desired product or service except by acquiescing in the form agreement, Michigan courts will conclude that the contract is adhesive and therefore procedurally unconscionable. . . .

. . . .

Further, the consumer protection statutes under which this action was brought were specifically designed to protect unsophisticated consumers from unscrupulous creditors. . . . A party seeking to remedy a contract's failure to comply with legislation designed in part to prevent unconscionable contracts has articulated a sound basis for asserting procedural unconscionability. . . .

Finally, while print size alone would not warrant a finding of procedural unconscionability, the fact that the arbitration clause was written in the smallest print on the front of the contract is somewhat suggestive of procedural unconscionability.

Taken together, I find that plaintiffs have sufficiently alleged . . . unconscionability in the formation of the agreement to arbitrate. . . .

. . . .

DECISION AND REMEDY The court found that the plaintiffs' complaint would not be dismissed and refused to order arbitration. The court determined that the arbitration clause was unconscionable because of the manner in which it was formed when the contract was entered.

CRITICAL THINKING: PRACTICAL APPLICATION Arbitration was discussed In Chapter 4. The courts give great leeway to enforce arbitration clauses. Why did the judge in this case decide that this arbitration provision would not be enforced?

Identification

Goods must exist in order to be identified to the contract. The terms *existing goods* and *identified goods* have separate meanings under the UCC. *Existing goods* means that the goods have been manufactured and are currently in a tangible form. **Identified goods** are existing goods that have been identified to a particular contract. Commonly in a furniture store, a sofa, for example, will have a sign saying, for example, "SOLD to Mr. & Mrs. J. B. Flick." This existing good, the sofa, has been identified to a particular contract. Identification can be made in any manner to which the parties explicitly agree.

For parties who fail to place in their contract the manner in which the identification will occur, the UCC provides guidelines [UCC 2-501]. If the goods exist, the contract automatically identifies them when the contract is made. If you purchase a coat in a store, the coat exists and the contract identifies it at the time you purchase it.

May the seller substitute other goods once the seller has identified particular goods to the contract? The UCC does allow the supplier to substitute other goods until it notifies the buyer that specific goods have been identified to this contract.

When a seller goes into bankruptcy, identification becomes very important if creditors have competing claims to goods. Under the UCC, when the buyer has paid the purchase price of the goods, followed by the merchant filing for bankruptcy within the next ten days, the buyer has a right to obtain the goods identified to the contract in preference to other creditors. When the goods have not been identified to a specific contract, the buyer has no preference to the goods or the money paid for the goods with respect to other creditors or to the seller's bankrupt estate.

Risk of Loss

The seller retains the risk of loss until he has completed all duties with respect to the goods under the contract.

(The risk of loss is covered in more detail later in this chapter.) As long as the seller has a risk of loss, he has the right to obtain insurance to protect himself against such risk. Likewise, the buyer has an insurable risk in the goods once they exist and are identified to the contract. The reason for the UCC rules concerning the manner of identifying the goods is to determine the party who has an insurable interest in the goods.

Future Goods

A contract also may be made for the sale of goods that do not yet exist. This agreement is called a **contract for future goods**. After these goods are manufactured, they are identified to the contract when they are shipped, marked, or otherwise designated by the seller as the goods belonging to this particular contract.

Title

Three concerns arise around the issue of the title (proof of ownership) to goods. The first is **warranty of title**. A warranty is a promise that a particular statement of fact is true. In this case, it indicates the truth of the seller's statement that it has good title. (Later in this chapter warranties are discussed in detail.) The second issue concerns when the title passes from the seller to the buyer. The third problem involves voidable titles; that is, titles that are subject to legal challenge.

Warranty of Title

Sellers must warrant that they have good title to the goods they sell [UCC 2-312]. To **warrant** means to promise that the facts stated in the contract are true. The supplier guarantees the type of title it has. The seller may own a half-interest in the goods, while the other half-interest is owned by someone else. The seller can only sell its half-interest. The seller also must fully disclose any liens held against the goods, unless this disclosure is exempt by law.

A creditor is entitled to place a lien against the title of the goods in order to protect its interests. (Liens are discussed in the next chapter.) The creditor lends money to the debtor–seller to purchase the goods originally. The creditor has an interest in ensuring that the debtor–seller repays the loan. If the debtor–seller fails to repay the loan, the creditor has the legal right to have the item repossessed and sold to repay the loan.

The creditor also wants to make certain that the original buyer notifies the creditor if the goods are resold. A *lien*, which is recorded in a government office, provides notice to other lenders (creditors) that the buyer has already borrowed money from a previous creditor and that the creditor has a legal interest (to be repaid) in those particular items. If the item is to be sold, the seller must notify the creditor of the pending sale, thereby giving the creditor the ability to protect its interest. When the item is sold, the seller repays the creditor, and the seller is entitled to the rest of the money. The following case involves a warranty of title in the sale of an automobile.

CASE 11.3 Court of Appeal of Louisiana, 1990 564 So. 2d 384 (La. App. 3d Cir.)	**BOYER v. TRINITY UNIVERSAL INSURANCE CO.** **BACKGROUND AND FACTS** Edward J. Cop purchased a 1982 BMW from Sunbelt Auto Imports, Inc., and received a Louisiana certificate of title. Cop sold the BMW to Wade B. Randolph, who likewise obtained a Louisiana title. Randolph sold the BMW to James Boyer, who also secured a Louisiana title. Approximately two years later, Reimer-Oberst, a German BMW dealership, repossessed the vehicle. Reimer-Oberst claimed that it had never been paid for the BMW and had never released the original title. Boyer reported this situation to his insurance company, Trinity Universal Insurance Company, filing a claim to be reimbursed for the cost of the BMW. Failing to reach a negotiated settlement, Boyer sued Trinity. Trinity in turn sued Randolph. The trial court granted a judgment in favor of Boyer against Trinity. The court dismissed the action by Trinity against Randolph. Trinity appealed.

Judge KNOLL

. . . .

We first look at the legal relationship between Boyer and his immediate predecessor in title, Randolph. A seller is bound to two principal obligations, that of delivering and that of warranting the thing which he sells. The warranty respecting the seller has two objects: the buyer's peaceable possession of the thing sold, and the second is the hidden defects of the thing sold, or its redhibitory vices.

The peaceable possession of a buyer is disturbed when he is evicted from the totality or a part of the thing purchased, due to the right or claims of a third person. Moreover, Civil Code Article 2501 defines the buyer's warranty against eviction:

> *"Although at the time of the sale no stipulations have been made respecting the warranty, the seller is obliged, of course, to warrant the buyer against the eviction suffered by him from the totality or part of the thing sold, and against the charges claimed on such thing, which were not declared at the time of the sale."*

Louisiana law is clear that an evicted buyer is entitled to the restitution of the purchase price from the seller.

. . . .

We now turn our attention to Trinity's indemnity [reimbursement] claim against Randolph. In *Bewley Furniture Co., Inc. v. Maryland Casualty Co.*, the Louisiana Supreme Court characterized indemnification as follows:

> *"It has long been held in Louisiana that a party not actually at fault, whose liability results from the faults of others, may recover by way of indemnity from such others. The cases have referred to this imposed liability variously as technical, constructive, vicarious and derivative.*

. . . .

> *The rule of indemnity . . . is founded upon the general obligation to repair the damage caused by one's fault and the moral maxim that 'no one ought to enrich himself at the expense of another.'"*

Applying this jurisprudence to the case *sub judice* [case before the court], we find that Trinity, who was found vicariously liable to Boyer under its contract of insurance, sought indemnification from Randolph on the basis that the cause of Boyer's eviction was Randolph's defective title to the BMW. Under this analysis, it is clear that Randolph was the real party at fault, and ultimately should bear the burden for Boyer's loss. Therefore, we find that the trial court clearly erred when it failed to grant Trinity's third-party demand for indemnification against Randolph.

DECISION AND REMEDY The court found that the insurance company was liable to Boyer, who lost his vehicle. The court allowed the insurance company to recover from Randolph, who had sold the BMW to Boyer, for breach of warranty of title.

CRITICAL THINKING: PRACTICAL APPLICATION How can a purchaser of a motor vehicle protect herself or himself in case the title is not valid?

Passing of Title

Passing of title from the seller to the buyer and passing the risk of loss for the goods from the seller to the buyer are not the same thing. Different rules apply as to when a purchaser comes into title and when it assumes risk of loss. The UCC deals with these issues between the seller and buyer in terms of their performance under the contract.

The buyer and seller always can agree as to when the title passes from the seller to the buyer. Most of the time, the parties fail to consider title possession when making a contract. In the absence of an agreement as to when the title passes, the UCC outlines several situations, which will be discussed in the following sections [UCC 2-401]. Title cannot change from the seller to the buyer, however, prior to the identification of the goods to a particular contract [UCC 2-401(1)].

Shipping Contracts. When goods must be moved, title passes at the time the seller completes his duty with respect to the goods' physical delivery. The shipping contracts used most are **free on board, point of shipment** (designated as **F.O.B.**); and **free on board, destination (F.O.B. destination**). In an F.O.B. situation, if the contract requires the seller to ship ten computers to the buyer, the title passes to the buyer at the time and place that the seller physically delivers the goods to the shipper for the shipment [UCC 2-401(2)(a)].

If the contract, however, requires the ten computers to be shipped and delivered to the buyer's place of business, the title changes when the shipper **tenders** (offers) delivery of the computers at the buyer's location. This example is that of an F.O.B. destination contract. The act of the shipper notifying the buyer that the goods are ready to be delivered is called the *tender* of the goods. Think of the word *tender* as meaning "to offer." The shipper tenders the goods for delivery to the buyer at the buyer's location [UCC 2-401(2)(b)]. Exhibit 11–4 summarizes the various types of transportation contracts.

Documents of Title. If the goods do not require shipment, two scenarios may occur. The first scenario between a seller and a buyer involves documents of title. No documents of title are involved in the second scenario. Let's look at these two situations.

When a transportation company or a warehouse is involved, the seller must provide the buyer a document of title [UCC 2-401(3)(a)]. A **document of title** is a paper representing ownership in the goods. The two most common documents of title are the *bill of lading* and the *warehouse receipt*. Exhibit 11–5 summarizes various types of documents of title. A **bill of lading** indicates title to goods in the transportation industry. A **warehouse receipt** indicates title to goods stored by a distributor.[7]

A business uses a bill of lading in the following manner. A manufacturer ships 100 crates of DVD players by truck from City A to a distributor's warehouse located in City B. The shipping company prepares a bill of lading. One copy accompanies the goods while the manufacturer receives the other copies. The manufacturer sends one copy to the distributor, which takes the paperwork to the shipping company's office in City B. The bill of lading is a document of title, indicating the distributor's right to possession of the DVD players.

A warehouse receipt is used in the following situation. The distributor stores videotapes in its warehouse. The buyer, a store that rents and sells videotapes at the retail level, purchases a number of videotapes from the distributor. The distributor provides the store manager with a warehouse receipt. The manager drives to the warehouse located ten miles away, where she presents the warehouse receipt to the warehouse clerk. The warehouse receipt is a document of title that provides proof that the holder is entitled to possession of the videotapes. The clerk turns the videotapes over to the store manager. Title passes to the store manager on the passing of the warehouse receipt.

But what happens if no documents of title control the goods that a third party holds? Title passes at the time and place of contracting once the goods are identified to the contract [UCC 2-401(3)(b)]. In the previous situation, suppose that the seller has no document of title controlling the videotapes. The seller calls the warehouse, provides the buyer's description to the attendant, and authorizes the warehouse to release the videotapes to her. Here, title passes when the buyer contracts with the seller to purchase the videotapes.

If the buyer rejects the goods or otherwise refuses to perform, and if the title has passed to the buyer, the title now revests (returns) to the seller. This revestment occurs by operation of law and is not considered a sale [UCC 2-401(4)].

---

[7]An example of a bill of lading and how to complete one is found at http://www.showtrans.com/bl.htm.

Exhibit 11-4   Types of Transportation Contracts

I. *Point-of-shipment contract*

   A. Seller has duty to:
   1. Contract with a transportation company.
   2. Deliver the goods to the transportation company.

   B. Buyer has the duty to pay shipping costs.

   C. Terms:
   1. Free on board (F.O.B.) [UCC 2-319(1)(a)]. Term used in ground or air transportation.
   2. Free alongside (F.A.S.) [UCC 2-319(2)]. Term used in marine transportation.
   3. F.O.B. vessel, car, or other vehicle [UCC 2-319(1)(c)]. The seller, at its own expense and risk, must load the goods on board. After loading, the goods are treated as F.O.B.

   D. Most contracts are point-of-shipment contracts.

II. *Destination contract*

   A. Seller has duty to:
   1. Contract with a transportation company.
   2. Deliver the goods to the transportation company.
   3. Pay for shipment to the destination.
   4. Retain the risk of loss and the right to insure.

   B. Terms:
   1. Free on board, destination (F.O.B. destination) [UCC 2-319(1)(b)].
   2. Cost, insurance, and freight (C.I.F.) [UCC 2-320(1)].
   3. Cost and freight (C. & F.) [UCC 3-320(1)].
   4. Ex-ship [UCC 2-322]. Requires delivery from a ship which has reached the named port of destination. Risk of loss shifts to buyer once the goods are unloaded from the ship. At that time, buyer must pay seller unless other arrangements have been made.
   5. No arrival, no sale [UCC 2-324]. If the conforming goods do not arrive, no sale has been made.

Exhibit 11-5   Documents of Title

A document of title represents ownership in the goods. The paper or document represents that the person in possession or named in the document has the right to receive, hold, and dispose of the goods listed on the document of title. The document of title may be negotiable or nonnegotiable. Chapter 12 discusses negotiability.

   I. *Warehouse receipt* A warehouse receipt is need to retrieved goods stored in a warehouse [UCC 1-201(45) and UCC 7-201 through 7-210].

   II. *Documents of title* Documents of title used when the goods are transported [UCC 1-201(6) and UCC 7-302 through 7-309].
   A.   *Bill of lading* Used in motor vehicle or rail transportation.
   B.   *Air bill, air consignment note, or airway bill* Used in air transportation.
   C.   *Marine bill* Used in ocean or marine transportation.

   III. *Miscellaneous documents of title*
   A.   *Bill of sale* Method of transferring ownership in goods.
   B.   *Certificate of title* Method of transferring ownership in goods. Used in titles for motor vehicles.
   C.   *Deed* Method of conveying ownership in real property.

Voidable Title

Although the original seller can reclaim goods from the buyer if the buyer committed an illegal act, what happens if the unscrupulous buyer resells the goods to an unsuspecting third party? In three situations, the third-party buyer in the ordinary course of business may obtain valid title if it has no knowledge of the illegal conduct of the original buyer.

In the first situation, assume that an original buyer pays for a lamp with a check that eventually is dishonored by the bank because of insufficient funds. The lamp is in the possession of the buyer. If the buyer sells the lamp to an innocent purchaser who has no knowledge of the bad check, the new buyer obtains valid title to the lamp.

In the second situation, title can be transferred if the seller mistakes an impostor for the buyer and turns over possession of the goods to the impostor. For example, Gabriel, who has excellent credit, purchases a dining room set from a furniture store. The next morning an impostor purporting to be Gabriel arrives early at the delivery dock and convinces the store's employee to load the dining room set on a truck. The employee believes the impostor to be Gabriel. The impostor sells the dining room set to a third party, who knows nothing about this fraudulent transaction. The new purchaser has valid title to the dining room set. The only recourse for the furniture store is to locate the impostor and bring a civil legal action against her. The furniture store may also file a criminal complaint against the impostor with the local prosecuting attorney's office.

In the third situation, the seller, instead of the original buyer as set out in the previous two situations, is the one who creates the problem. If a person leaves an item with a business that sells similar merchandise, the UCC allows the business to transfer valid title. For example, Lee takes his lawn mower in to be repaired. The repair shop also sells new and used lawn mowers. The shop accidentally sells Lee's lawn mower to a person who has no knowledge that Lee owns it. That purchaser has valid title to Lee's lawn mower. Lee, however, can bring a civil action against the repair shop if it fails to reach a settlement with him.

The reasoning behind the three rules is simple. When there are two innocent parties, the person who could have controlled the loss will incur the loss [UCC 2-403].

Risk of Loss

A buyer and seller always can bargain over who carries the risk of loss in the event that the merchandise is damaged or destroyed. Normally, the parties bargain over price, quality of goods, shipment terms, and credit terms. Seldom do they consider the consequences of merchandise damage or loss.

If risk of loss is not covered in the agreement, the Uniform Commercial Code supplies the rules as to who bears the loss. Basically whoever purchases insurance assumes the risk of loss. This underlying principle applies even in situations in which the buyer or seller breached the contractual obligations.

In the absence of contract breach by either the buyer or seller, and if the contract does not require the seller to deliver the goods to a particular place, the risk of loss passes to the buyer when the seller delivers the goods F.O.B. to the carrier. This rule holds even when the goods are shipped on the basis of **collect on delivery (C.O.D.)**. When goods are sent C.O.D., the delivery company collects from the buyer the money owed for the goods when it delivers them. If the buyer does not pay for the goods, the delivery company returns the goods to the seller. If the seller must deliver the goods at a particular destination (F.O.B. destination), the risk of loss passes to the buyer when the goods are tendered. The buyer is entitled to take delivery on payment [UCC 2-319].

If a third person holds the goods and there is a document of title, the risk of loss transfers to the buyer when it receives the document of title. If there is no document of title, the risk of loss passes to the buyer when the seller informs the third person of the sale [UCC 2-509(2)].

In all other cases, if no breach of contract is involved, and if the seller is a businessperson, the risk of loss transfers to the buyer when the buyer takes possession of the goods. If the seller is not in business, the risk of loss transfers to the buyer on the tender of delivery [UCC 2-509(3)]. Assume that you purchase a desk at a yard sale, but because you rode to the sale on your bicycle, you are unable to take possession of the desk. The seller, who is not a merchant, says you can have immediate delivery of the desk. You bicycle home to get your automobile. While you are gone, a rainstorm occurs, and lightning strikes your desk. In this situation, you hold the risk of loss. If the seller had

LEGAL HIGHLIGHT

The Midas Touch

Advanced technology makes the recovery of treasures from ships sunk centuries ago possible. Who has title to these riches? Is it the person who studies the ship's history; makes the careful calculations; finances the project; risks her or his life to search underwater; and recovers the gold, silver, and artifacts? Or is it the original owner, or even the government? Consider the Spanish galleon, *Nuestra Señora de Atocha,* which sunk off the Marquesas Keys in 1622 while en route to Spain, heavily laden with $250 million in cargo (contemporary value). Or consider the U.S.-flagged *SS Central America,* which was sailing from San Francisco carrying three tons of gold (worth $1 billion today) when it was lost in 1857 during a hurricane off the South Carolina coast.

The law had not been clearly established when cases involving these sunken ships reached the courts. In the case of the Spanish galleon, the court ruled that the persons who recovered the treasure could treat the treasure as abandoned and thus had valid title. The rule applied is called the *American rule.* The court noted that under the *English rule,* the treasure would belong to the U.S. government.

In the case of the *SS Central America,* thirty-nine insurance companies claimed ownership of the gold because they paid the claims of the original owners after the ship was lost. Factors beyond the owners' control caused the ship to be destroyed and the cargo to be lost, but the owners never abandoned the gold because salvage attempts were made over the years. Under salvage laws, the insurance companies showed that title was never divested (changed or withdrawn).

At times, the courts protected the rights of the original owner while compensating the party who recovered the cargo. The courts base these decisions, called *salvage law,* on the principle of equity. The person taking the risk to recover the cargo is paid a reasonable amount (based on the difficulty and hazardousness of the salvage efforts), whereas the owner retains title and ownership. The salvagers of the *SS Central America* spent $30 million to recover $22 million in gold. As a result of this expenditure, the court allowed the salvagers possession of most of the gold. The insurance companies shared only a small part of the return.

---

been a merchant, however, she would have retained the risk of loss.

What happens when either the buyer or the seller breaches its contractual obligation? If the seller ships goods in a condition that allows for the buyer to reject them, the risk of loss remains with the seller [UCC 2-510(1)]. Many times a buyer accepts goods inconsistent with the original order and later revokes the acceptance. In that event, the buyer looks first to its insurance company for reimbursement of its losses and may look to the seller to pay the rest of the loss if the insurance does not pay the total amount lost [UCC 2-510(2)].

The seller may look to the buyer when goods have been identified to the contract, but the buyer repudiates the contract and the goods are later damaged. In such cases, the seller, to the extent of any deficiency in the seller's insurance coverage, may treat the risk of loss as the buyer's responsibility for a commercially reasonable length of time [UCC 2-510(3)].

Other delivery terms affect risk of loss. For example, **cost, insurance, and freight (C.I.F.)** indicates that part of the purchase price includes insurance during transportation. In this situation, the insurance company holds the risk of loss once the goods are shipped until the buyer is tendered delivery. If the contract is **cost and freight (C.&F.)**, the rules of F.O.B. contracts apply [UCC 2-320]. C.I.F. and C.&F. shipment terms are used predominantly with international sales.

Trial Sales

In addition to the usual method, goods can also be sold using one of two types of contract clauses. The first type is called a **sale on approval** [UCC 2-326(1)(a)]. When this clause is inserted in a contract, no sale occurs until the potential purchaser is satisfied. If the potential purchaser is not satisfied, the goods are returned to the owner. For example, you want to buy a helicopter. Using this clause, you could use the helicopter for a reasonable time period. If you approve, the owner sells the helicopter to you. If the helicopter does not meet your approval, you return it to the owner. All sales on approval agreements are made to the ultimate consumer.

The second type of clause is called a **sale or return** [UCC 2-236(1)(b)]. This clause is used when the buyer is also a reseller; that is, the buyer purchases the goods for resale. Books and magazines are usually sold under a sale or return clause. If the purchaser does not resell the goods, it can return them to the original seller.

Under either one of these circumstances, the question arises as to which party, the seller or the buyer, has the title and risk of loss. When the goods are sold with a sale-on-approval clause, the seller retains the title and risk of loss until the buyer approves of the goods and the sale is complete. When the goods are sold with a sale-or-return clause, the buyer has actually purchased the items, so the title and risk of loss transfer to the buyer. If the buyer needs to return any items, such as unsold magazines, the title and risk of loss transfer back to the seller.

Performance

Normally, the parties to a contract negotiate the terms of its performance. As we have seen, the UCC supplies many of the necessary terms when the parties neglect to cover certain details. The UCC also assists both the seller and the buyer by providing them with certain rights when the contract neglects to address a particular issue.

Rights of Buyer and Seller

The buyer and seller have several rights. First, a buyer has a right to inspect goods before accepting or paying for them. The buyer can make certain that the goods conform to the specifications established in the contract. In some cases, such as when the goods are sent C.O.D., the buyer can inspect the goods only after paying. The buyer then has a right to revoke his acceptance if the breach of contract substantially impairs the value of the goods [UCC 2-513].

Second, the UCC allows both parties the right to obtain adequate assurance for further performance.

Each party to a contract expects the other person to perform fully. At times, one party may doubt the other person's ability to perform fully. As long as this concern is based on good faith and fair treatment of the other party, the buyer or seller can request further assurances of full performance.

For example, you order 100,000 computer chips from Johnson Industries. In a recent trade journal, an article implies that Johnson's quality control has not been fully effective and that many defective chips have resulted. You could insist that Johnson post a performance bond prior to your acceptance of future chips. Johnson would be required to purchase a performance bond from a bonding company. The bond requires the bonding company to pay you should Johnson fail to perform the contract by selling you inferior chips.

In another example, you granted credit to a buyer, but later discover that the buyer is considering filing for bankruptcy. At that point, you could decide to send future shipments C.O.D. or you could request payment before shipment [UCC 2-609].

Impracticability

When parties enter into a contract, they believe that conditions exist that will allow the seller to perform fully on the contract. Sometimes, however, the seller cannot deliver the products as promised because of factors beyond the seller's control. It becomes impractical for the seller to perform. When the seller has several outstanding contracts with a number of buyers for a limited supply of the products, the UCC allows allocation of the goods by the seller to the buyers in any manner that is fair and reasonable. For example, a seller contracts to provide a unique type of wheat to the buyer. A storm destroys most of the crop. The UCC allows allocation of the wheat among all of the purchasers, so that one buyer could not insist on complete performance.

Another example of impracticability occurs when a contract requires that construction be completed within a certain time frame. Factors beyond the contractor's control, such as a building site being flooded after a dam broke, can delay the completion of the building by several weeks. The court takes these types of factors into consideration when determining whether a breach of contract has occurred. When a court finds impracticability, no breach of contract has occurred. At the time of contracting, however, the

What Happens When Your New Software Crashes Your Computer?

Shopping at your local computer store, you notice a bin of programs on compact disc (CD). Enticed by the advertising material on the box, you purchase the CD. You think the new program will be great. After you install the software on your computer, the computer crashes and you must reinstall all of your programs. What can you do about this? Can you obtain a refund? Can you collect damages for the hours it took to reinstall the other software?

Anyone who owns a computer for any length of time has been confronted with these problems. The seller denies liability because you accepted its licensing agreement when you installed the software. The software included a provision stating the seller is not liable if anything goes wrong.

The computer industry is attempting to provide suppliers with more defenses against consumers. A proposed provision for the UCC is Article 2B. This provision states that when you purchase a program you are not purchasing a product, only the right to use the program, which is a license. If you are not pur-

chasing goods, the consumer protection laws are not applicable.

Until Article 2B is passed by individual state legislatures, most courts hold that programs purchased at a store are a product. Under the UCC, you have a right of inspection under Section 2-513. If you promptly revoke your acceptance of the goods, you may be able to obtain a return of your purchase price.

When you reinstall the other software, you may need to contact the supplier to obtain assistance and sometimes pay a fee for assistance. This fee is an incidental expense that is recoverable under UCC 2-715. You cannot, however, recover for your time spent to reinstall the software.

What about software downloaded from the World Wide Web? In this instance, there is no physical product, just digital product. When starting the download process, you must click on an agreement that almost no one reads. Your click signifies that you agree with it. Once you click, the warranty disclaimer becomes effective. The terms in the disclaimer favor the seller and can be used against you in a legal dispute. In other words, you have no rights because you waived any rights you may have had with a click.

event that now makes the contract impracticable must have been unforeseeable [UCC 2-615].

Remedies

In the event that the other party to a contract for the sale of goods breaches its contractual obligations, the same basic rules govern your rights as in the breach of an ordinary contract, as discussed in Chapter 10. The next section identifies the parties' specific rights when a breach occurs. Keep in mind, however, that the rules are very similar to those that apply to the breach of an ordinary contract.

Remedies of Buyers

Your bakery company ordered 100,000 bushels of wheat to be delivered in sixty days from Growers

Market. You agreed to pay the current market price for the day on which you entered into your contract. Since then, however, the market price increased substantially. Because of this, Growers notifies you that it will not send you the 100,000 bushels of wheat. What are your rights?

Wheat is a type of product that easily is purchased on the open market. Thus, you can secure what is called **cover**. That is, you can obtain goods similar to those required by the contract from other available sources. You then may recover from the original seller the difference between the contract and current market price, plus incidental or consequential damages [UCC 2-711, 2-712].

Incidental damages include items, such as costs for transportation, reasonable charges, and expenses or commissions incurred in connection with obtaining cover. Consequential damages include loss of business profits if your business closes because of the seller's breach. For consequential damages to be available, the supplier must have known at the time of contracting that if it were to breach the contract, your business would close as a result [UCC 2-712, 2-713, 2-715].

Occasionally, the courts will force a seller to perform the contract. This order for specific performance occurs if the goods are unique or if obtaining cover is impossible. For example, one of the best indicators of the overall state of the economy is the health of the construction industry. Concrete is a construction item that normally is available. When the economy is expanding quickly, a shortage of concrete may exist. Concrete production takes large investments in capital goods and plants. Starting a new plant is not very easy or quick. Under certain conditions, a concrete manufacturer might refuse to deliver the amount of concrete for which it contracted. This refusal may be an attempt to secure a higher price from you. You can bring action in court seeking specific performance of this manufacturer to deliver the concrete if you cannot obtain cover from any other reasonable source. If specific performance is impossible, the court may award you appropriate damages [UCC 2-716].

Remedies of Sellers

The major problem that a seller confronts is nonpayment for goods that the buyer accepts. In this situation, the seller is entitled to be paid the contract price.

A more complicated problem occurs when the buyer refuses the goods and repudiates the contract. Normally, the seller may recover the difference between the market price and the unpaid contract price together with incidental damages, less any expenses saved by the buyer's breach. If this rule fails to place the seller in as good a position as if the contract had been performed, the measure of damages is the profit, including overhead, that the seller would have earned if the buyer had fully performed the contract, plus any incidental expenses [UCC 2-708].

A third kind of problem occurs when the seller cannot sell the goods identified to the contract at a reasonable price in the market. In this situation, the measure of damages is the contract price [UCC 2-709].

CYBERLAW

Taxes

In 1999, Congress passed the Internet Tax Freedom Act, which placed a three-year moratorium on state and local taxes on Internet access or on electronic commerce. The act was renewed in 2002. Congress also declared no new federal taxes would be imposed during the same time period. The act created the Advisory Commission on Electronic Commerce to examine the impact of the imposition, collection, and administration of taxes on electronic commerce in other countries and the United States and the impact on global economy.

State and local governments depend heavily on sales tax revenue. As more tax-exempt sales are made over the Internet, state and local governments stand to lose a portion of their income. More than 7,500 jurisdictions in the United States impose a sales tax. It is not the sheer volume of jurisdictions, but the complexity of the various tax codes that presents a real challenge to those selling goods and services over the Internet.

If all 7,500 jurisdictions imposed taxes on Web sales, the growth of the Web and electronic commerce would be significantly impacted. Therein lies the conflict. State governments depend on sales taxes as a substantial portion of their income. If sales over the Internet are not taxed, state revenues will drop. Additionally, retailers located in the state pay taxes; thus, their products are by necessity priced higher than the same product sold over the Web by a business that does not pay sales tax. Sales on the Web and electronic commerce are new and growing and the imposition of numerous sales taxes could stifle growth.

To try to solve the problem, more than thirty-five states have reviewed the state sales tax system. They have created the Streamlined Sales Tax Project (SSTP) with their main goal being simplification. Although this goal sounds easy, it contains many challenges. Some simplification strategies with which the project is concerned are as follows:

• *Centralized Registration* Currently, multistate sellers must register separately in each state.

- *Uniform Exemptions* A buyer, such as a hospital, may be exempt from taxes in one state, but not in another. The goal is to have the purchaser provide a standard set of information and the reason for the exemption.

- *Uniform Definitions* For example, sandals may be taxed as shoes in one state, but not in another. The project is creating a uniform definition of key terms (sale, gross receipts, delivery, tangible personal property) and developing uniform definitions for commonly exempt items, such as food and clothing.

- *Uniform Taxing Source Laws* This goal includes the ability to determine which jurisdiction has the right to tax. The project would limit the frequency of tax rate changes. Currently, state and local governments frequently change rates.

- *Uniform Number of Remittances* The goal is to have a uniform number of remittances per month, uniform electronic funds transfer formats, and uniform rule on remittances due on a legal holiday.

- *Uniform Tax Return and Standardized Remittance Form* The goal is to have a multiseller registered. In turn, it would have a uniform tax form to file and a standardized form with which to make remittance filings to a number of taxing entities.

The states must be neutral in imposing any tax. The tax on products or services must be uniform without regard to the method of sale. A sales tax system cannot provide an advantage to a supplier based solely on whether the sale was made in a store or online. These reforms should reduce the transaction costs to both storefront sellers and online sellers.

The National Governors Association has a Web page on the project.[8] The Electronic Commerce Association can provide additional information.

Product Liability

When a product malfunctions, the buyer can seek remedies under the legal theories of misrepresentation, negligence, strict liability, and breach of warranty. The

[8]The National Governors Association's discussion of the project is at http://www.nga.org.

remainder of this chapter looks at these theories and discusses the liability that a business may incur when a malfunctioning product harms someone.

Increasingly, the courts are combining tort law and contract law when a lawsuit involves products that malfunction and cause injuries. Consumers buy beer, medicine, microwave ovens, hair dryers, sporting goods, automobile tires, and thousands of other items with the complete faith that the product is designed properly, is manufactured for its intended use, is safe for consumption, and is labeled correctly. The Product Safety Commission, however, reported 21,600 deaths and 30 million consumer-product-related injuries from defective products in a recent one-year period.

Losses from injury and death because of defective products can be the result of misrepresentation, negligence, strict liability, or breach of warranty by manufacturers, distributors, or sellers. These legal principles make up an area of the law called **product liability.** It does not fit squarely into any one body of law.

Common law rules of torts and contracts once set the parameters of product safety, but the common law standards applicable to product liability vary greatly from state to state. The Uniform Commercial Code provides the courts some degree of uniformity when determining potential liability for products through warranty law.

Historical Development

A long-established rule holds that the seller of goods has a duty to exercise the care of a reasonable person in ensuring that the goods are safe for the buyer. In the past, courts enforced this rule by using negligence as a basis for liability.

When applying negligence principles to product liability, however, earlier courts required **privity of contract**. The privity requirement meant that the injured party who sued for negligence also had to prove that a contract existed, that is, that she had bought the defective item from the defendant. This requirement imposed a hardship on the injured. For example, a family member used and was injured by a defective item that another family member had purchased. The injured family member could not recover because he was not in privity of contract with the seller. The consumer suffered a disadvantage as a result of the privity of contract rule because only the purchaser could sue, not the ultimate injured consumer, such as a family member or a gift recipient.

This same requirement, found in contract and warranty law, made contract, warranty, and tort laws insufficient in protecting consumers from unsafe products. Because of the privity requirement, the ultimate consumer frequently was not protected. The courts eventually resorted to the law of torts, specifically negligence, and abandoned the privity requirement. Yet negligence, too, proved inadequate in protecting the consumer because the manufacturer could avoid liability by proving that it had exercised reasonable care in producing the goods.

A new theory was developed to deal with the dilemma of the injured, but uncompensated victim. The common law extended the theories of contracts and torts, finally blending them to develop a cohesive doctrine known as *product liability*. Let's examine these four legal principles: misrepresentation, negligence, strict liability, and breach of warranty.

Product Liability Based on Misrepresentation

Misrepresentation occurs when a business misrepresents a material fact concerning the character or quality of the good being sold. The seller is liable for physical harm to the consumer if the consumer justifiably relied on the misrepresentation.

The misrepresentation does not depend on the seller's negligence or whether the seller was committing fraud. The consumer can be anyone who uses the good, not just the item's buyer. For example, an automobile manufacturer advertises that its windshield glass is shatterproof. A driver is injured when a stone strikes the windshield and it shatters. The manufacturer is liable to the driver whether or not the driver purchased the automobile.

Product Liability Based on Negligence

As discussed in Chapter 8, *negligence* is defined as failure to use that degree of care that a reasonable, prudent

---

LEGAL HIGHLIGHT

Bridgestone/Firestone and Ford

In 2000, Bridgestone/Firestone recalled 6.5 million of its ATX, ATX II, and Wilderness AT tires. Before the recall, the National Highway Traffic Safety Administration (NHTSA) received more than 1,400 complaints, including reports of 88 deaths and at least 250 injuries all linked to the ATX, ATX II, and Wilderness AT tires.

Bridgestone/Firestone was a supplier of tires to Ford Motor Company. Ford used these tires on its Ford Explorers, which are sport utility vehicles (SUVs). Most SUVs have a high center of gravity that can cause them to overturn more often than other motor vehicles. A driver of a Ford Explorer would lose control when the tire tread separated, causing blowouts. Most of the accidents frequently occurred in hot weather and at high speeds.

Initially, Bridgestone/Firestone claimed that these accidents happened because the customer was not inflating the tires properly. To lower the center of gravity,

Ford had recommended a lower level of air than what Bridgestone/Firestone had recommended. The chief executive officer of Bridgestone/Firestone, Masatoshi Ono, however, accepted full responsibility for the events.

When the media reported that Bridgestone/Firestone had recalled tires as early as two years previously in other countries, Congress became interested. Apparently Bridgestone/Firestone, when contacted by Ford to report the foreign recalls, replied that it was not required under recall regulations to report foreign recalls.

The publicity led to both the Senate and the House of Representatives holding hearings. Congressional representatives also contacted the Department of Justice to see if any criminal action could be taken because of the failure to notify the government and the failure of both companies to protect their customers and the motoring public. Dozens of product liability actions were filed against Bridgestone/Firestone and Ford in both the United States and in foreign countries.

person would have used under similar circumstances. The manufacturer of a product must exercise due care to ensure that the product is safe to be used as intended. Due care must be exercised in designing the product, in selecting the materials, in using the appropriate production process, in assembling and testing the product, and in placing adequate labeling to warn consumers about dangers of which an ordinary person might not be aware. The manufacturer's duty of care extends to the inspection and testing of items that are used to make the final product that is sold.

The defendant-manufacturer can defend itself by proving its use of due care in the manufacture of its product. The plaintiff's major burden is to tie the defendant-manufacturer's failure to exercise due care to the plaintiff's injury. Between the time that a product is manufactured and the time that the plaintiff uses the product, numerous events involving different people take place. A retailer, for example, often must assemble a product before it can be sold to the consumer. If a manufacturer can show that any such event caused or contributed to the injury, it will assert that it has no liability because of this intervening cause. Other defenses exist, but their application varies from state to state.

Defenses discussed in Chapter 8 are assumption of risk, contributory negligence, and comparative negligence. For example, a person plugs an electric cord into an outlet, then plugs the other end into the electrical cord of a lawn mower that has a bare metal pushbar. If the person tries to mow wet grass, he may be electrocuted. The bare metal pushbar may be a negligent design, but mowing a wet lawn may be contributory negligence.

Likewise, any time a plaintiff misuses, modifies, or alters a product, the manufacturer can claim that the plaintiff contributed to the cause of her injuries. The defense is that the plaintiff's comparative negligence offsets the manufacturer's negligence.

Product Liability Based on Strict Liability

In early English history, a person whose conduct resulted in the injury of another was held liable for damages, even if he had not intended to injure anyone and had exercised reasonable care. Around 1800, the courts abandoned this approach in favor of the fault approach (negligence), in which the act became a tort

only if the defendant was wrong or blameworthy in some respect. Dissatisfaction with the product liability cases led to a return to the English doctrine of strict liability in the United States.

Requirements of Strict Product Liability. The difference between negligence and strict liability is that negligence evaluates the conduct of a supplier, processor, or manufacturer, whereas strict liability focuses entirely on the product's condition. Strict product liability consists of five requirements. First, the defendant must be engaged in the business of manufacturing that product. Second, the defendant must sell the product in a defective condition.

Third, the product must be unreasonably dangerous to the user or consumer because of its defective condition. Fourth, the defective condition must be the proximate cause of injury or damage. Fifth, the goods must not have been substantially changed from the time at which the product was sold to the time at which the injury was sustained.

In any action against a manufacturer or seller, the plaintiff has no obligation to show the reason or manner in which the product became defective. The plaintiff, however, must show that, at the time the injury was sustained, the product's condition was essentially the same as it was when it left the defendant-manufacturer.

In addition, all states have extended the strict liability protection to bystanders who are people near to, but not using, the defective item when they are injured by it. The injured party no longer is required to be a consumer or user of the product.

Most courts allow the application of the strict liability doctrine to cases even when no personal injuries have occurred. When a defective product causes only property damage, the seller also may be liable under the theory of strict liability.

The *Restatement of Torts*, third edition, takes a slightly different approach on product liability cases. Its position is succinct: If a product is defective, there is liability.

A defective product may be the result of a manufacturing error, design defect, or inadequate warnings. A manufacturing defect is one where the product departs from its intended design, even though all possible care was exercised in the preparation and marketing of the product. A design defect is one where the foreseeable risks of harm posed by the product could have been reduced or avoided by the adoption of a reasonable alternative design. Inadequate warnings exist when the foreseeable risks of harm posed by the product could have been reduced or avoided by the provision of reasonable instructions. The *Restatement*, third edition, expands strict liability to include all product liability based on defects or faulty information.

In the following case, the court reviews the use of an expert witness. This type of witness is one who appears in court to testify about his expertise as applied to the facts in a case. In this case, the witness used his expertise to address management's attitude toward safety by using documentary evidence. This type of evidence applies to any type of writing, whether public or private. Here, the expert witness used documents generated by the defendant to show that management knew that the product was unsafe but decided against correcting the defect because of cost considerations.

CASE 11.4

Court of Appeal of California, Fourth District, 1981
119 Cal. App. 3d 757, 174 Cal. Rptr. 348

LANDMARK CASE

GRIMSHAW v. FORD MOTOR CO.

BACKGROUND AND FACTS In November 1971, the Grays purchased a new 1972 Pinto hatchback. The Grays had trouble with the car from the beginning. They returned the car for repairs a number of times, for problems including excessive gas and oil consumption, automatic transmission downshifting, lack of power, and stalling. A heavy carburetor float caused the stalling and excessive fuel consumption.

On May 28, 1972, Mrs. Gray and thirteen-year-old Richard Grimshaw set out on a trip in the Pinto, which was then six months old and had 3,000 miles on it. While on the freeway, Mrs. Gray was driving at sixty miles per hour (which was legal in 1972). As she approached a major exit ramp with congested traffic, she moved from the outer fast lane to the middle lane of the freeway. Shortly after this lane change, the Pinto stalled and coasted to a halt in the middle lane. It was later established that the carburetor float had become so saturated with gasoline that it suddenly sank, opening the float chamber and causing the engine to flood and stall. The Pinto erupted into flames when it was rear-ended by a car proceeding in the same direction. Mrs. Gray suffered fatal burns, and Grimshaw suffered severe and permanently disfiguring burns on his face and entire body.

Grimshaw and Mrs. Gray's heirs, the plaintiffs, sued Ford Motor Company, the defendant. Following a six-month jury trial, verdicts were returned in favor of the plaintiffs. The court awarded the Gray family $559,680 in compensatory damages. It awarded Grimshaw $2,516,000 in compensatory damages and $125 million in punitive damages. The trial court reduced the punitive damages to $3.5 million. Ford appealed the judgment on seven major grounds.

Acting Presiding Justice TAMURA

Ford seeks reversal of the judgment as a whole. . . .

In the ensuing analysis (*ad nauseam*) of Ford's wide ranging assault on the judgment, we have concluded that Ford has failed to demonstrate that any errors or irregularities occurred during the trial which resulted in a miscarriage of justice requiring reversal.

. . . .

[Court's discussion of expert witness who was a former Ford employee]

A party offering an expert witness is enticed to examine him "as to his qualifications and experience so that the full weight to be accorded his testimony will become apparent." Such examination "should not be limited by narrow and stringent rules." It was therefore within the court's discretion to permit plaintiffs to elicit from Mr. Copp testimony as to when he left Ford and why. Evidence as to why he left Ford was part of the background information concerning the witness's professional experience which would assist the fact finder in determining the weight to be given to his testimony.

While the evidence may also have tended to enhance the witness's credibility, the purpose of permitting a party producing an expert to question him as to his educational background, training, and experience in his area of expertise is not only to establish "the competency of the witness to the satisfaction of the court, but also for the purpose of making plain the strength of the witness's [sic] grounds of knowledge and the reason for trusting his belief." Therefore, the fact that the evidence may have enhanced the witness's credibility did not render it inadmissible.

. . . .

. . . The fact that Ford fired a high ranking engineering executive for advocating automotive safety was indicative of Ford management's attitude towards safety in automobile production and was thus relevant to the issue of malice [intent to harm someone deliberately]. It had a tendency in reason to prove that Ford's failure to correct the Pinto's fuel system design defects, despite knowledge of their existence, was deliberate and calculated. Ford's argument that firing Mr. Copp in 1976 for speaking out on safety does not reasonably tend to show that Ford disregarded safety in designing the Pinto some five years earlier lacks merit. The evidence was not that Mr. Copp first took his stand on safety in 1976; he testified that he had been outspoken on auto safety during all the many years he worked for Ford.

Ford complains that since Mr. Copp was permitted to testify to the circumstances surrounding this termination, Ford was compelled to cross-examine him to show that the reason for his dismissal was unexplained absences from work and unsatisfactory work performance; that if the court had not permitted Mr. Copp to give his version of the reason for termination, Ford would have had little or no reason to examine him about his retirement and plaintiffs would not have been able to adduce rehabilitation testimony [testimony that restores the witness's credibility (believability)] highly prejudicial to Ford. The record discloses that Mr. Copp testified only briefly concerning the circumstances of his early retirement from Ford but that on cross-examination Ford engaged in extensive questioning to show that the reason for his termination was not his safety views but unsatisfactory work and absenteeism. Plaintiffs thereafter introduced rehabilitating testimony. Mr. Copp was permitted to testify to his campaign for automotive safety during his entire period of employment with Ford, including a conversation he had with Henry Ford II on the subject, his testimony before a United States Senate Committee concerning the Chevrolet Corvair's unsafe design and his role in exposing Ford's conduct in connection with the emission control program. Ford argues that but for the court's erroneous initial ruling and its consequent cross-examination on the reason for Mr. Copp's retirement, the damaging rehabilitation evidence would not have come in. Since we find no error in the court's initial ruling and since Ford has not advanced any independent reason why the rehabilitating evidence should have been excluded, Ford's complaint concerning the prejudicial nature of that evidence must be rejected.

. . . .

[Court's discussion of documentary evidence]

Ford contends that the court erroneously admitted irrelevant documentary evidence highly prejudicial to Ford. We find the contention to be without merit.

(1) Exhibit No. 125:

Exhibit No. 125 was a report presented at a Ford production review meeting in April 1971, recommending action to be taken in anticipation of the promulgation of federal standards on fuel system integrity. The report recommended . . . deferral from 1974 to 1976 of the adoption of "flak suits" or "bladders" [equipment that would protect the fuel tank and prevent fires] in all Ford cars, including the Pinto, in order to realize a savings of $20.9 million. The report stated that the cost of the flak suit or bladder would be $4 to $8 per car. The meeting at which the report was presented was chaired by Vice President Harold MacDonald and attended by Vice President Robert Alexander and occurred sometime before the 1972 Pinto was placed on the market. A reasonable inference may be drawn from the evidence that despite management's knowledge that the Pinto's fuel system could be made safe at a cost of but $4 to $8 per car, it decided to defer corrective measures to save money and enhance profits. The evidence was thus highly relevant and properly received.

. . . .

(2) Exhibits Nos. 95 and 122:

Ford urges that a report (Exhibit No. 95) and a motion picture depicting Ford's crash test No. 1616 (Exhibit No. 122) should have been excluded because they were irrelevant and highly prejudicial to Ford in that they showed that in a 21.5-mile-per-hour crash of a 1971 Pinto prototype into a fixed barrier the fiber neck of the fuel tank separated allowing fluid to spill from the tank, whereas no such filler neck separation occurred in the Gray vehicle. Under the test for ascertaining relevancy of evidence to which we have previously alluded, we find no abuse of discretion in the court's ruling. Not only did the filler neck separation show the vulnerability of the Pinto fuel system in a 21.5-mile-per-hour fixed barrier test, but crash test No. 1616, as Ford conceded, resulted in a puncture of the fuel tank from the exposed bolt heads on the differential housing. Thus, the exhibits showed the defect in the Pinto's gas tank location and design, the hazard created by the protrusions on the differential housing, and, in addition, they served as evidence of Ford's awareness of those defects. Exhibit Nos. 95 and 122 were properly received in evidence.

. . . .

Ford contends that Grimshaw's counsel committed prejudicial misconduct in referring to Ford's executives meeting in the "glass house" and deciding to approve the Pinto's fuel tank design with knowledge that it was unsafe and would result in the loss of many lives. Ford argues that although there was evidence that the corporate headquarters of Ford was referred to as the "glass house" there was no evidence of management meetings held there in connection with the Pinto design. The record contains substantial evidence from which it reasonably may be inferred that Ford's management knew that the Pinto was unsafe but nevertheless decided not to alleviate the problem because of cost considerations, and thus that those decisions were made in Ford's corporate headquarters.

DECISION AND REMEDY The court of appeals, in a forty-one-page opinion, found against Ford on every issue on appeal. The trial court's judgment was affirmed.

CRITICAL THINKING: ETHICAL MANAGEMENT DECISION MAKING Discuss whether the top officials of Ford took into consideration the possible injuries or death to users of their vehicles when deciding whether to install the flak suit or bladder at a cost of $20.9 million. When should profits versus customer protection be considered in manufacturing a product?

Duty to Warn

A business has a duty to warn when it knows or should have known of any hazards associated with the product use when these hazards are not obvious, reasonably apparent, or as well known to the user as to the manufacturer or seller. Courts use this duty to warn in deciding product liability cases based either on strict liability or on negligence theories.

One example of a manufacturer's duty to warn involved a can of hair spray that contained butane. When the hair spray was used close to a flame, the butane gas would explode, which, in turn, caused serious injuries. In one case, the jury awarded $1.5 million because the container lacked any meaningful warnings. Sellers of a product need to place a conspicuous warning on the product to attempt to limit this form of liability.

INFOTRAC RESEARCH ACTIVITY

Search for product liability on Info-Trac. Review four recent articles and compare the author's viewpoint on product liability.

Defenses to Strict Product Liability. The courts allow the defenses of *assumption of the risk* and *comparative negligence*. When the defendant uses assumption of risk as a defense, it must show (1) that the plaintiff voluntarily proceeded while recognizing the risk, (2) that the plaintiff knew and appreciated the risk created by the defect, and (3) that the plaintiff's decision to undertake the known risk was unreasonable. The doctrine of comparative negligence also applies in these three situations.

The traditional defense of contributory fault, although frequently used in negligence cases, has been rejected by the courts in strict tort liability actions. Because strict liability assumes that the product manufacturer could foresee the danger, in principle, negligence and the defense of contributory negligence are immaterial in an action based on that theory.

Product Liability Based on Warranty

A *warranty* is the seller's assurance to the buyer that goods meet certain standards. If the goods fail to meet those standards, the warranty is breached, and the defendant-seller is liable. The UCC designates several types of warranties that can arise: express warranties [UCC 2-313], implied warranties of merchantability [UCC 2-314], and implied warranties of fitness for a particular purpose [UCC 2-315].

Express Warranties. A seller can create an **express warranty** by making representations concerning the quality, condition, description, or performance potential of the goods. Express warranties arise under three conditions. First, the goods conform to the seller's statements of fact or promise. These declarations are usually promises made during negotiations such as the statement "These drill bits will easily penetrate stainless steel without dulling."

Second, the goods conform to their description. For example, the description states "Crate contains one 150-horsepower diesel engine," or the contract calls for delivery of a "camel hair coat." Third, the goods conform to a sample or model.

To create an express warranty, the seller's promise must become part of the basis of the contract. If the seller merely makes a statement that relates to the value or worth of the goods or makes a statement of opinion or recommendation about the goods, no express warranty is created.

In this illustration, the seller claims, "This is the best used car to come along in years; it has four new tires and a 350 horsepower engine just rebuilt this year." The seller has stated several facts that create a warranty. First, the automobile has an engine, it has 350 horsepower, and it was rebuilt this year. Second, the automobile has four tires and they are new.

The seller's opinion that it is "the best used car to come along in years" is known as "trade puffing" and creates no warranty. Trade puffing is the expression of an opinion by a seller that is not made as a representation of fact. A statement relating to the value of the goods, such as "It's worth a fortune" or "Anywhere else you'd pay $10,000 for it," normally will not create a warranty.

Implied Warranties. The two types of implied warranties are created by law from the facts of the case and are not expressly stated by the parties. An **implied warranty of merchantability** automatically arises in every sale of goods made by a merchant who deals in goods of that kind. A retailer of ski equipment makes an implied warranty of merchantability every time it sells a pair of skis. A neighbor selling skis at a garage sale does not make this type of implied warranty, because the neighbor is not a merchant.

Goods that are merchantable must be reasonably fit for the ordinary purposes for which such goods are used. They must be comparable to the quality of similar goods on the market. The goods must be adequately packaged and labeled and conform to their labels.

Some examples of nonmerchantable goods include light bulbs that explode when switched on, pajamas that burst into flames on slight contact with a stove burner, high heels that break off during normal use, or shotgun shells that explode prematurely.

The implied warranty of merchantability also imposes liability on the merchant for safe product performance. Whether the merchant knew of, or could have discovered, a defect that makes the product unsafe makes no difference. Merchants, however, do not absolutely insure against all accidents arising in connection with the goods. For example, a bar of soap remains merchantable even though a user can slip and fall by stepping on it.

The **implied warranty of fitness for a particular purpose** arises when any seller (merchant or nonmerchant) knows the particular purpose for which a buyer will use the goods and knows that the buyer is relying on the seller's skill and judgment to select suitable goods. A "particular purpose of the buyer" differs from the "ordinary purpose for which goods are used" (merchantability). Goods can be merchantable but still not fit for a buyer's particular purpose. For example, house paints suitable for outside wooden siding are not suitable for painting over stucco walls.

A contract can include both a warranty of merchantability and a warranty of fitness for a particular purpose, which relates to a specific use or to a special situation for which a buyer intends to use the goods. For example, a merchant-seller recommends a particular pair of shoes, knowing that a customer wants mountain-climbing shoes. The buyer purchases the shoes, relying on the seller's judgment. If the shoes were not only improperly made, but were also unsuitable for mountain climbing, the seller has breached both the warranty of merchantability and the warranty of fitness for a particular purpose. Exhibit 11–6 summarizes the three warranty types covered by the Uniform Commercial Code.

Disclaimers or Defenses against Implied Warranty Liability

The Uniform Commercial Code permits a seller to disclaim implied warranties or to defend under certain conditions against implied warranty liability. There are four common disclaimers and defenses. First, the seller (manufacturer) can specifically disclaim either or both implied warranties. To specifically disclaim any implied warranty of fitness, the disclaimer must be in writing and conspicuous. The UCC provides this example: "There are no warranties which extend beyond the description on the face hereof." To specifically disclaim the implied warranty of merchantability, the disclaimer can be oral or written. It must, however, "mention merchantability" and, if in writing, must be conspicuous [UCC 2-316(2)].

Second, the seller can disclaim both implied warranties by selling the goods with expressions such as "with all faults" or sold "as is" [UCC 2-316(3)(a)]. Third, a defense may be available to the seller if the buyer actually examines the goods. The defense is that the buyer accepts responsibility for any defect it finds or should have found [UCC 2-316(3)(b)]. Fourth, implied warranties can be excluded or modified by usage of trade, previous course of performance, or previous dealings between the parties [UCC 2-316(3)(c)]. With the availability of these defenses and disclaimers, implied warranties offer a limited advantage to a buyer in seeking to sue under the warranty theory of product liability.

Magnuson-Moss Warranty Act. The **Magnuson-Moss Warranty Act** of 1975 is designed to prevent

Exhibit 11–6   Three Warranties under the UCC

Type	How Created
Express warranty [UCC 2-313]	1. An affirmation of fact or promise, or 2. A sale by description, or 3. A sample shown as conforming to a finished product.
Warranty of merchantability [UCC 2-314]	1. The seller is a merchant, and 2. The seller deals in goods of the kind.
Warranty of fitness for a particular purpose [UCC 2-315]	1. The buyer's particular purpose or use must expressly or implicitly be known by the seller, and 2. The buyer must purchase in reliance on the seller's selection.

deception in warranties by making them easier for consumers to understand. The act is enforced by the Federal Trade Commission (FTC). To some degree, the Magnuson-Moss Warranty Act modifies the UCC warranty rules regarding consumer sales transactions. The UCC remains the primary statute of warranty rules for commercial (business-to-business) transactions and for consumer transactions not covered by the Magnuson-Moss Warranty Act.

No seller is required to provide a written warranty for consumer goods. If a seller chooses to make an express written warranty, however, and the cost of the consumer goods is more than $10, the warranty must be labeled as "full" or "limited." In addition, if the cost of the goods is more than $15 (under FTC regulation), the warrantor must disclose certain information fully and conspicuously in a single document in "readily understood language." These disclosures include the name and address of the warrantor, what specifically is warranted, enforcement procedures for the warranty, any limitation on warranty relief, and the fact that the buyer has legal rights.

Although a **full warranty** may not cover every aspect of a product, the aspects that it does cover ensure some type of buyer satisfaction in case the product is defective. Full warranty requires free repair or replacement of any defective part. If a part cannot be repaired within a reasonable time, the consumer can choose either a refund or a replacement without charge. The full warranty frequently has no time limit.

A **limited warranty** arises when the written warranty fails to meet one of the minimum requirements for a full warranty. If damage to the product or unreasonable consumer use caused the problem with the product, the warrantor is released from the service obligation under either type of warranty.

When a sales contract grants an express warranty, the Magnuson-Moss Warranty Act prevents sellers from disclaiming or modifying the implied warranties of merchantability and fitness for a particular purpose. Sellers can impose a time limit on the duration of an implied warranty. Such time limits, however, must correspond to the duration of the express warranty.

Federal Preemption in Product Liability Cases.

Congress has passed legislation requiring that information be disclosed when certain products may be unsafe. The question presented is whether these statutes preempt state laws under the supremacy clause of the U.S. Constitution.

The problem of exemption has confronted Congress and the courts, for example, in deciding cases concerning the health hazards in smoking tobacco products. Congress passed legislation requiring health and safety warnings on all tobacco products and restricting the advertisement of these products. The tobacco industry has taken the position that these federal statutory provisions preempt all state laws that might create liability.

International Consideration

Product Liability in the European Union

A major U.S. trading partner is the European Union (EU). The EU has rules that apply to U.S. businesses when products are bought from and sold to the EU.

In 1985, the Council of the European Communities adopted the Product Liability Directive, which addresses problems caused by malfunctioning of products. All member countries of the EU, except France, Ireland, and Spain, adopted this directive.

Article I summarizes its purpose: "The producer shall be liable for damage caused by a defect in his product." Although the directive terminated no prior theories in product liability cases, it did create a new and uniform system in pursuing cases that involve a malfunctioning product. The directive attempts to eliminate economic barriers that may inhibit the free transfer of goods so that all businesses in the EU handle product liability issues consistently.

The directive's primary objective is to compensate consumers for death or injury. It allows recovery for damages to certain noncommercial property, but excludes damage to the product itself. Prior law or the United Nations Convention on Contracts for the International Sale of Goods covers the issues of damages to the product or to commercial property. Pain and suffering compensation is not covered by the directive.

The Product Liability Directive covers damage claims between 500 and 70 million Euros (European currency). All actions must be brought within three years from the time the plaintiff learns of or reasonably could have learned of the injury, defect, and producer identity and within ten years after the product was placed into circulation.

Although several aspects of the directive are similar to the strict liability doctrine in the United States, the directive grants the injured consumer additional rights. Under strict liability in the United States, the injured person must prove that the product is "unreasonably dangerous." Under the directive, the consumer only needs to show the product to be defective. Article 6 defines this requirement as "not providing the safety which a person is entitled to expect, taking all circumstances into account, including: (a) the presentation of the product; (b) the use to which it could reasonably be expected that the product would be put; and (c) the time when the product was put into circulation." The directive creates a "consumer expectation test." In addition, privity is no longer required to bring an action.

An action can be maintained against a producer, which is interpreted very broadly to include (1) the manufacturer of the finished product or any component, the producer of any raw materials, or any person who presents himself as the producer by trademark; (2) any importer of a product for sale, rental, or leasing; and (3) any product supplier, if the producer is unknown. Agricultural products are excluded unless a member state agrees to cover these products.

The directive does allow the producer defenses. The directive does not have a comparative negligence defense, but it does allow recovery to be reduced by the consumer's contributory negligence. It allows the defenses of (1) state-of-the-art product, (2) state of scientific and technical knowledge, (3) compliance with member state design or production regulations, and (4) the development risks defense. A defendant may have the additional defenses that she did not put the product into circulation, that the defect did not exist at the time it was placed into commerce, or that no intent to produce the item for commercial purposes existed.

The European Council of Ministers has adopted the Product Safety Directive. This directive's importance is that it established a high standard of protection for the safety and health of persons by requiring member states to permanently monitor marketed products to ensure that no unacceptable risks occur. Provisions exist for the testing, recalling, and banning of unsafe products. Other directives promote the health and safety of specific consumer products. All of these directives assist consumers in purchasing safe products and in granting them fair compensation if they should be injured.

PRACTICAL TIPS

When a Retailer Becomes Liable

You are the chief executive officer for a company that owns a chain of stores. Retail toys and hobby supplies are sold to a targeted market segment of older children and adults. The company does not manufacture any products, but instead purchases inventory directly from manufacturers throughout the world.

Recently, a competitor lost a case involving a miniature radio-controlled automobile kit and was held liable for $1.5 million. The customer purchased a kit, which exploded because of a short circuit. The customer suffered severe eye damage.

Your firm sells the same type of product and you are concerned that a similar case might arise. Although you sampled the product and found no similar problem, you are curious, however, about legal theories that might surface in this type of case.

A request is sent to the firm's attorney for general information about product liability. She lists several different legal theories that could be used. As a retailer, the company may be liable to the consumer even though the firm did not manufacture or package the product.

First, a plaintiff may bring action based on a breach of express warranty because the product must conform to the description on the box or to the model that you use for demonstration purposes. Second, a plaintiff may rely on the theory of breach of the implied warranties of merchantability and of fitness for a particular purpose.

Third, a plaintiff may base a lawsuit on the legal theory of strict liability. This theory applies whenever a product is unreasonably dangerous and causes an injury. Fourth, an action for negligence might be brought. Normally, however, this would be used against the manufacturer.

Fifth, fraud might exist if the firm intended to deceive the customer about a material fact. To be liable, the deception must be made by a company's representative with the knowledge of its falsity, and the customer must rely on the deceit, which must, in turn, cause injury to the constomer.

How can the firm limit its potential liability? One way is to buy liability insurance. Insurance costs, however, have greatly increased during the last few years. Currently, the firm is a self-insured organization, which means no insurance is carried to protect itself from legal action, and the firms assumes this potential liability.

What else can be done to provide the firm with maximum protection in the absence of insurance coverage? The following checklist provides guidance for some legal routes to consider.

Checklist

✔ *Use Disclaimer Agreements* Obtain from each customer a signed written statement disclaiming any liability for your firm. This approach might be applicable to a small service business, such as a go-cart track. Some courts, however, have held these types of agreement to be against public policy. In other states, courts decide these agreements on a case-by-case basis and only uphold them when the agreements are entered into at arm's length and when the bargaining power between the parties is on a somewhat equal basis. The liability disclaimer does not prevent a consumer who was not the original purchaser from filing a lawsuit. As a practical matter, disclaimer agreements offer little protection for most retail concerns.

✔ *Use the Uniform Commercial Code* Under the UCC, a retailer can bring the manufacturer into the lawsuit when the lawsuit is brought for breach of warranty. The manufacturer must either defend the lawsuit or be bound by the court decision. The practical effect is that the manufacturer ultimately is held liable.

Note, however, that this provision applies only to warranties, not to strict product liability. Remember, too, that because the firm purchases inventory from international sources, enforcing a judgment against a manufacturer outside the United States on inventory bought in Asia, South America, or other parts of the world may be impossible.

✔ *Purchase Insurance* In spite of high insurance rates, insurance may be the only reliable method of protecting the firm. The cost of this protection is passed on to the consumer in the form of higher prices.

In other words, no foolproof method exists to protect retail businesses from lawsuits brought by consumers based on malfunctioning products.

Chapter Summary

The Uniform Commercial Code provides rules that govern the sale of goods. Often the buyer and seller neglect to provide details in their contracts. When a court examines the agreement in a lawsuit, it first determines if particular rules of the trade exist or if the parties have a history of prior dealings in order to supply missing terms. If neither exists, the court applies the UCC rules.

Some of the rules covering contracts have been modified by the UCC. In particular, a merchant can make a firm offer that is not revocable. Legal consideration is not necessary when modifying a contract for the sale of goods. Other changes made by the UCC are practical for business to follow.

For the court to apply any of these rules, the goods must be existing and identified to this particular contract. Placing the customer's name on an existing item is one way to identify goods. Other UCC rules apply to future goods.

Title to goods is important. Unless excluded by specific terms of the contract or by circumstances, the seller always warrants that it has good title and that the goods have no liens against them. The UCC established specific rules as to the point at which the title is transferred from the seller to the buyer. Under certain circumstances, the seller with a voidable title may transfer a valid title to a bona fide purchaser in the ordinary course of business.

Rules for risk of loss are set out in the UCC when the risk is not specified in the contract. In addition, the buyer has the right to inspect goods on delivery. When the goods are sent by the method of collect on delivery (C.O.D.), the buyer loses this right.

Sales contracts can use two types of clauses that affect the passing of title and the shifting of the risk of loss. The first is sale on approval. The other type is called sale or return.

If either side believes that the other may not perform on its promise, the UCC provides for adequate assurances for future performance. The buyer's or the seller's doubt as to whether the other side will perform must be based on good faith and fair dealing. The UCC provides rules for performance and for breach of contract by either party.

Product liability is based on several theories, negligence, strict liability, or warranty. Negligence can apply, but the difficulty is establishing the point when the breach of the duty of care occurred. Under limited circumstances, strict liability may be used. Warranties provided by the seller, such as an express warranty, implied warranty of merchantability, or implied warranty of fitness for a particular purpose, also may provide the basis for liability.

Using the World Wide Web

In 1994, President William J. Clinton signed a new policy on U.S. access to space. The U.S. National Space Transportation Policy, NSTC-4, guides the government efforts to develop a lower cost, reliable launch capability in order to further the commercialization of space. The Department of Commerce keeps a variety of statistics on business.

The International Chamber of Commerce has developed Incoterms, which are standard commercial terms. These terms are used in international sales to define the responsibilities of buyer and seller in contracts.

For *Web Activities*, links to Web sites mentioned in the chapter, and additional Web sites that relate to the chapter topics, go to **http://bohlman.westbuslaw. com**, click on "Internet Applications," and select Chapter 11.

Web Activities

Go to **http://bohlman.westbuslaw.com**, click on "Internet Applications," and select Chapter 11.
11–1 Lemon Law
11–2 Census

Key Terms

bill of lading
collect on delivery
  (C.O.D.)
contract for future goods
cost and freight (C.&F.)
cost, insurance, and
  freight (C.I.F.)
course of dealing
cover
document of title

express warranty
firm offer
free on board, destination (F.O.B. destination)
free on board, point of shipment (F.O.B.)
full warranty
goods
identified goods

implied warranty of
  fitness for a particular
  purpose
implied warranty of
  merchantability
limited warranty
Magnuson-Moss
  Warranty Act
merchant
privity of contract

product liability
sale on approval
sale or return
tender
unconscionable bargain
unconscionability
usage of trade
warehouse receipt
warrant
warranty of title

Questions and Case Problems

11–1 Strict Liability Kerly stands on a street corner, waiting for a ride to work. Beyer has just purchased a new car manufactured by Able Motors. Beyer is driving down the street when suddenly the steering mechanism breaks, causing Beyer to run over Kerly. Kerly suffers permanent injuries. Beyer's total income per year has never exceeded $15,000. Kerly files suit against Able Motors under the theory of strict liability in tort. Able pleads no liability, because (1) due care was used in the manufacture of the car and (2) Able is not the manufacturer of the steering mechanism (Smith is). What is the outcome of Kerly's lawsuit?

11–2 Privity Baxter manufactures electric hair dryers. Garza purchases a Baxter dryer from her local Ace Drugstore. Green, a friend and guest in Garza's home, has taken a shower and wants to dry her hair. Garza tells Green to use the new Baxter hair dryer. As Green plugs in the dryer, sparks fly out from the motor and continue to do so as she operates it. Despite this, Green begins to dry her hair. Suddenly, the entire dryer ignites into flames, severely burning Green's scalp. Green sues Baxter on the basis of the torts of negligence and strict liability. Baxter denies liability, particularly because Green did not purchase the dryer. Discuss the validity of Green's actions and any defense claimed by Baxter.

11–3 Negligence Beech Aircraft Corp. manufactured airplanes. Executive Beechcraft, Inc., owned, operated, and maintained airplanes, one of which was manufactured by Beech Aircraft. One part was to be installed in only one way. If installed backwards, the part would cause the plane, once airborne, to crash. No markings on the part indicated the correct way to install the part. The part, once installed, looks the same whether installed correctly or backwards, but the part functions differently. A plane did crash after Executive Beechcraft installed the part backward. Everyone on board, including Nesselrode, was killed. Nesselrode's estate brought action against Beech Aircraft. Beech Aircraft argued that it was not at fault because it had not installed the part. Was it correct? Explain. [*Nesselrode v. Executive Beechcraft, Inc.,* 707 S.W.2d 371 (Mo. 1986)]

11–4 Strict Liability Ford Motor Co. manufactured and distributed the Ford Cortina, which had only a cardboard shield separating the fuel tank from the passenger compartment. Nanda suffered severe disabling burns when the gas tank in his car exploded upon being struck in the rear by another car. Nanda filed a strict liability action against Ford Motor Co. Discuss who should prevail and why. [*Nanda v. Ford Motor Co.,* 509 F.2d 213 (7th Cir. 1974)]

11–5 Proximate Cause A two-year-old child lost his leg when he became entangled in a grain auger on his grandfather's farm. The auger had a safety guard that prevented any item larger than four and five-eighths inches from contacting the machine's moving parts. The child's foot was smaller than the openings in the safety guard. Was such an injury reasonably foreseeable? Explain. [*Richelman v. Keuanee Machinery & Conveyor Co.,* 59 Ill. App. 3d 578, 375 N.E.2d 885, 16 Ill. Dec. 778 (1978)]

11–6 Strict Liability Larry Colvin, an ironworker, was setting a steel truss on a concrete column while in a squatting position. He reached above his head to pull himself up. He grabbed an I-beam, known as a purlin, eight or ten feet long, that was not yet welded into place. The purlin failed to support Colvin's weight and he fell. The plans for the building called for the purlins to be over forty feet long, but only seven conformed to that length. The remaining purlins were substantially shorter and were welded together to serve their purpose as spacers between the trusses and the roof. Red Steel Co. supplied the purlins. Discuss whether Red Steel is strictly liable for Colvin's injury due to the short length of the purlin. [*Colvin v. Robert E. McKee, Inc.,* 671 S.W.2d 556 (Tex. Civ. App., Dallas 1984)]

11–7 Acceptance Block and Co., Inc., a mail-order business, entered into a contract with Alden Press, Inc., for Alden to print 125,000 copies of a catalog. Later Block discovered that the catalog covers with Block's address labels were fading. Alden Press attempted to resolve the problem, but Block believed that the entire catalog had to be reprinted. Block had Alden Press mail out 20,000 catalogs in spite of the defect because Block had no other choice in order to stay in business. Block ordered catalogs from another source and refused to pay anything to Alden Press. Alden alleged that the catalogs had been accepted. Explain how you would decide this case. [*Alden Press, Inc., v. Block and Co., Inc.,* 527 N.E.2d 489 (Ill. App. 1 Dist. 1988)]

11–8 Risk of Loss Petrosol International, Inc., a wholesale marketer of petroleum products, sold 10,000 barrels of propane to Commonwealth Petroleum Co. This gas was stored in an underground storage facility called the Lake Underground Storage when the title to the propane transferred from Petrosol to Commonwealth. Commonwealth notified the Lake Underground Storage of the transfer and that it owned the propane. Although Commonwealth would not move the gas immediately, they could move it over the next six months. During that period, a wall in the Lake Underground cavern collapsed and the propane was lost. Under these conditions, who should stand the risk of loss—Petrosol or Commonwealth? Did this type of sale involve an F.O.B. contract? Explain your answer. [*Commonwealth Petroleum Co. v. Petrosol International, Inc.,* 901 F.2d 1314 (6th Cir. 1990)]

11–9 Risk of Loss Morauer contracted with Deak & Co., Inc., to purchase several bags of silver and gold coins. The purchase occurred in Washington, D.C., which requires a sales tax. Morauer and Deak decided that Deak would send the coins to Morauer's residence in Maryland to avoid the sales tax. Deak sent the coins by registered mail. At the time of shipment, the seller's insurance would cover any loss. More than two years later, Morauer took an inventory and discovered that half of the shipment had been lost. By that time, the U.S. Postal Service had destroyed its records, and the seller's insurance had expired. Who should assume this loss? Explain. [*Morauer v. Deak & Co., Inc.,* 26 UCC Rep. (D.C. Super. Ct. 1979)]

11–10 Internet Commercial business is growing in outer space. The U.S. Department of Commerce is involved in space development for commercial purposes. Go to the Department of Commerce, Office of Space Commercialization Web site at **http://www.technology.gov/space**. What are the three primary areas in which the office conducts activities? What are the four sectors of commercial space industry?

Chapter 12

Negotiable Instruments and Secured Transactions

We promise according to our hopes, we perform according to our selfishness and our fears.

Maximes, 1665
Duke Francois de la Rochefoucauld, VI, 1613–1680
French classical author

Chapter Outline

Ethical Consideration

Legally Right but Morally Wrong: The Dilemma of the HDC

You are the branch manager of Bell Savings Bank and Trust. The bank stock is owned by local people, some of whom rely on the dividends for a major portion of their income. Bell Savings is more than 100 years old and has a good community reputation.

As the manager, you look for ways to generate income for Bell. On behalf of Bell Savings, you purchase twenty promissory notes from Rosta's Computer Services, Inc., a company that sells computers to small businesses. The manager of Rosta's Computer Services informs you that these promissory notes represent well-paying accounts from its business customers that have purchased computer equipment. You examine the notes and find them in proper order. Bell Savings purchases the notes at the usual discounted price, that is, an amount less than the principal on the note.

Bell Savings receives payments on a regular basis for two months. Within four months, however, your collection manager informs you that many of the notes are in default. When Bell contacted these customers regarding their lack of payments, they told the collection manager that they had not received the promised computer equipment and therefore refused to pay for it. The customers were contacted individually and there does not appear to be any collusion among the disappointed customers. You try to contact Rosta's Computer Services, but find its telephone disconnected. The post office has no forwarding address.

Bell Savings is a holder in due course (HDC) on the notes. To be an HDC means that the holder has the legal right to enforce payment on the notes through a lawsuit. The only defense the note signers, here the customers, have is to identify a physical error in the note itself. In this case, the notes are in proper order and have nothing wrong with them.

As bank manager, you recognize that the customers have received nothing for the notes, and the bank, unknowingly, may be part of a scam. Rosta's Computer Services apparently committed a fraud. Both the bank and the customers, however, are the innocent parties. Under the HDC doctrine, Bell Savings has the right to collect the principal and interest on the customers' notes by filing a lawsuit. The court will order the customers to pay the principal and interest as promised in their notes, even though they received nothing in return. Some of the small businesses may be forced out of business if they must pay.

Is the HDC doctrine ethical in this situation? Should the bank enforce collection on the notes? Use the ethical model presented in Chapter 2 and reprinted on the inside front cover to develop your answer.

Introduction

Contracts are essential for the existence of a market economy. Many contracts are completed simply by the exchange of an item for money. In other contracts, the price is too large to be paid immediately. The purchaser may pay some money immediately and borrow the rest either from the seller or a financial institution. The lender needs to ensure that the money is repaid by taking a lien against the borrower's property.

This chapter reviews some of the more important provisions of the law concerning these transactions. Each of these very complex topics can be reviewed only briefly in a legal environment textbook.

Artiste Login. Carlo and Carlotta own Artiste Login Products, Inc. Their business will need to purchase raw materials to create sculptures, to purchase a studio and an office building, and to purchase computer equipment, such as servers, modems, and software. When Artiste purchases office supplies, it pays the seller in cash. In situations involving large sums, such as the purchase of real property and buildings, contracts are used and money is borrowed.

When Artiste purchased its office building and land, Artiste needed to obtain a loan. In this situation, Artiste is a debtor. The creditor that lends Artiste the money with which to make the purchase needs to ensure that the loan will be repaid. Artiste will sign a note and a lien. The note reflects the amount of money borrowed, whereas the lien allows the creditor to repossess the real property if Artiste fails to repay the loan. This example reflects several areas of the law that have developed over the centuries.

Negotiable Instruments

Negotiable instruments are specialized written documents signed by the debtor acknowledging a debt. These documents contain either an unconditional promise or an order to pay a fixed sum of money either on demand or at a specified future time.

Negotiable instruments have a lengthy history, originating before the age of Hammurabi, king of Babylon, at about 1750 B.C. In thirteenth-century Europe, traveling merchants used some form of negotiable instruments because of the problems of transporting and guarding gold and silver against lost or theft. In the early 1700s, the English Parliament adopted the first statutes on negotiable instruments, which now are the foundation for the current law.

In the United States, the Uniform Commercial Code (UCC), Article 3, entitled Negotiable Instruments, establishes the law of negotiable instruments. Article 3 worked very well to meet business problems, but over time, with changes in technology and business practices, deficiencies became apparent. Article 3 was revised and these revisions have been adopted in most states. The revised Article 3 is used in this chapter.

Functions and Requirements of Negotiable Instruments

Negotiable instruments have the dual purposes of substituting for currency and serving as a credit device. Currency includes legal coins and paper money bills.

A Substitute for Currency. The financial system lacks sufficient currency to meet all of society's needs. For centuries, negotiable instruments have served as a substitute for currency and they still do so today. Few Americans actually use currency to purchase an automobile, a residence, or a business entity. People use negotiable instruments because they are convenient and safe.

A Credit Device. Negotiable instruments are one method by which credit is extended to debtors. When a creditor lends money to a debtor, the creditor needs evidence that a loan has been made. The debtor signs a document reflecting the principal amount of the loan, the interest rate, repayment date and terms, and other clauses that the creditor may use to protect itself.

Requirements for Negotiable Instruments

An instrument is either *negotiable* or *nonnegotiable*. A nonnegotiable instrument is usually a contract. Both the form and content determine whether an instrument is **negotiable**. For an instrument to be negotiable, it must meet these criteria:

1. Be in writing and signed [UCC 3-103(a)(6), UCC 3-103(a)(9)].
2. Be an unconditional promise or order to pay a fixed amount of money [UCC 3-104(a)].
3. Be payable to "**bearer**" (person who has physical possession of the instrument) or to "order" at the time it is issued [UCC 3-104(a)(1)].
4. Be payable on demand or at a definite time [UCC 3-104(a)(2)].

Each of these requirements is reviewed separately. If any requirement is omitted, the instrument is a contract.

In Writing and Signed. Negotiable instruments must be written on something that is portable and permanent, so that they can be freely transferred. The problem with an oral promise is the lack of hard evidence that the promise was made. A written negotiable instrument sets out the amount of liability, is portable and permanent, is freely transferable, and is used as a substitute for currency.

The person creating a negotiable instrument must sign it for it to become negotiable, but extreme latitude is granted in determining the definition of a signature. A signature includes any symbol used by the party with the intention of authenticating the instrument. Various symbols can be used in lieu of the traditional written signature. Initials, the mark of X, or a thumb print will suffice if a person intends it to be a signature.

Unconditional Promise or Order to Pay a Fixed Amount of Money. A negotiable instrument must include an unconditional order or unconditional promise to pay a fixed amount of money. A mere acknowledgment of the debt, which might logically imply a promise, is insufficient for making the instrument negotiable. For example, an IOU (I owe you) is a written document that literally says "I owe you money," but it is not negotiable because it only acknowledges indebtedness. The IOU is usually considered to be a contract.

The payment terms must be included in the writing on the face of a negotiable instrument. The **holder** (person who has possession) of the negotiable instrument must be able to determine its terms by looking only at the instrument. The terms cannot be conditioned on an event or agreement [UCC 3-106]. The instrument cannot be controlled by events beyond the instrument itself. If the holder must conduct an investigation to determine if the condition has occurred, its use as a substitute for currency would be reduced significantly.

Negotiable instruments may refer to collateral that secures debt repayment. This reference does not make the promise unconditional. Many negotiable instruments also reference another writing to clarify the parties' rights concerning acceleration of payments or prepayment of the debt [UCC 3-106].

An instrument may be payable with or without an interest rate. A stated interest rate may be fixed or variable. The variable rate, however, derives from external data, such as a specific bank's prime rate or the Federal Reserve discount rate. Reference to this external data is allowed in a negotiable instrument to determine the variable interest rate.

If the instrument provides for interest, but the amount of interest payable cannot be determined from the description, interest is payable at the *judgment rate* in effect at the place of the instrument's payment and at the time interest first accrues [UCC 3-112]. **Judgment rate** is an interest rate set by statute and used when the parties have failed to set the interest rate.

A negotiable instrument must set a requirement to pay a fixed amount of money, which normally is payable in U.S. dollars. If the instrument allows payment in foreign money, it may be paid either in foreign money or in an equivalent amount of dollars calculated by using the current bank-offered spot rate at the place of payment for the purchase of dollars on the day on which the instrument is paid [UCC 3-107]. A **spot rate** is the exchange rate in effect between currencies at the time and place at which the exchange is made.

An instrument cannot be stated in terms of value of goods or services because it would be too difficult to ascertain the market value. For example, if the value in a ten-year negotiable instrument were stated in computer chips, determination of a Pentium chip's value today would be difficult to compare with its value in ten years.

Payable to Order or to Bearer. One function is to use a negotiable instrument as a substitute for currency; thus, freedom to transfer the instrument is an essential requirement. A negotiable instrument requires that it be "payable to order" or "payable to bearer" or words to that effect. These words acknowledge that another person, unknown at the time that the instrument is made and who is not the original payee, may eventually be the owner of the negotiable instrument.

Except on checks, these words or their equivalents must appear on both the three-party order-to-pay instruments and the two-party promise-to-pay instruments. Except on checks, if these words are absent or deleted, the instrument is nonnegotiable and, therefore, is assignable only as a contract and is governed by contract law, which the chapter addresses later.

Under revised Article 3, a check is still a negotiable instrument, even if the words "payable to order" or "payable to bearer" have been deleted. In the past, people marked out these words when writing a check. Without these words, the check became a nonnegotiable instrument and destroyed the possibility of anyone being a **holder in due course** (that is, a person who not only has possession of the negotiable instrument, but also holds a special status in the eyes of the law concerning it; holders in due course are discussed later in this chapter). The new provisions ensure that a person who accepts a check in good faith and for value will become a holder in due course.

An instrument that states "payable to order" and that names a specific person as recipient is often referred to as **order paper**. When no specific person is designated, so that the instrument essentially is payable to any person holding (bearing) the paper, it is called **bearer paper** [UCC 3-109].

Payable on Demand or at a Definite Time. A negotiable instrument must be payable on demand or at a definite time. Clearly, the person responsible for paying the negotiable instrument must know when she must pay. For an interest-bearing instrument, a person must know the exact interval during which the interest will accrue in order to determine the present value of the instrument.

The instrument's very nature may indicate that it is payable on demand [UCC 3-108]. For example, a check, by definition, is payable on demand. Negotiable time drafts, in contrast, are payable at a definite time that is specified on the instrument's face [UCC 3-108]. The person responsible for paying the negotiable instrument is under no obligation to pay until the specified time has arrived or elapsed.

Categories of Negotiable Instruments and Parties to Negotiable Instruments

Negotiable instruments are divided into two categories: two-party and three-party instruments [UCC 3-104]. The following sections examine these different negotiable instruments.

Two-Party Instruments

A promise to pay is a two-party negotiable instrument between the **maker** and the **payee**. A maker is the person who signs and issues an instrument and who promises to pay a certain sum of money to a payee, that is, the person to whom an instrument is made payable. To **issue** means to sign and deliver a nego-

tiable instrument for the first time. The maker's signature must appear on the face of the promissory instrument for the maker to be liable. The maker is a debtor, usually of the payee (who is the creditor).

Generally, two-party instruments are used by people as credit instruments, where the debtor promises the creditor to repay the amount borrowed with interest over a period of time. The most common two-party instruments are *promissory notes* and *certificates of deposit*.

Promissory Notes. A **promissory note** is a written promise to pay (other than a certificate of deposit) made between two parties, the maker and the payee.

A promissory note, commonly referred to as a note, can be made payable at a definite time or on demand. A promissory note must be payable to bearer or "payable to the order of" a payee. Banks and other financial institutions that lend money commonly use a note to document that a loan of money was made to a borrower (the debtor).

For example, Foster wants to purchase an automobile, but needs to borrow money to finance the purchase. When Foster borrows from a financial institution, the First National Bank of Anywhere, he signs a promissory note. In the note, Foster promises to repay the money he owes. Exhibit 12–1 illustrates a sample promissory note.

Exhibit 12–1   A Sample Promissory Note

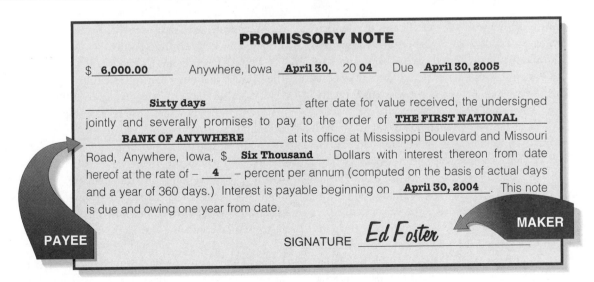

Various types of credit transactions involve the use of notes. Often, the name of the loan type appears in the title of the note. For example, a promissory note to repay money lent to purchase real property is called a **mortgage note**, that is, a note secured by a mortgage.

A mortgage note contains two legal concepts: the note (the negotiable instrument) and the mortgage (the **secured transaction**). A secured transaction secures repayment of the loan by taking a **lien** against real property, such as in this case, or against goods in other situations. In this illustration, a mortgage is a type of secured transaction whereby the debtor agrees to repay money that the creditor lent on the note in order to purchase real property, such as a house and its surrounding land. If the debtor fails to repay on the note, the creditor initiates a legal procedure to take the property, sell it, and use the proceeds to pay the remainder owed on the note. Although the note is not the mortgage, the note notifies others that payment on it is secured (or backed up) by a mortgage.

Similarly, a **collateral note** (a note secured by some type of collateral) indicates that the creditor lent money to the debtor to purchase personal property (goods). The item purchased, such as an automobile, is used to secure the repayment. The automobile serves as collateral to the note. If the debtor fails to pay, the creditor repossesses the collateral, here, the automobile.

An **installment note** is a note payable by installments, such as when a person pays for a computer over a twenty-four-month period. If the computer serves as collateral to secure repayment, the note may be called a **collateral installment note.**

Certificates of Deposit. A **certificate of deposit (CD)** evidences a loan made by a person for a specific period of time to a bank; in return, the bank agrees to repay the principal with interest. Certificates of deposit are either negotiable or nonnegotiable instruments. Most large CDs ($100,000 or more) are negotiable. Their negotiable status allows them to be sold, to be used to pay debts, or to serve as security (collateral) for a loan.

For example, Ross goes to Citizen's Bank, where he has an account, to purchase a certificate of deposit. In buying the CD, Ross lends the bank his money and the bank pays him interest. Ross is considering the purchase of one of three lake lots within the next six months and may need the CD as a down payment. Therefore, Ross wants the CD to be payable to bearer. Citizen's Bank signs the certificate of deposit as a

maker and issues it to Ross, but makes the CD payable to bearer. Ross can now make a down payment to the contractor or the architect with the bearer CD. Exhibit 12–2 shows a sample certificate of deposit.

Three-Party Instruments

An *order to pay* is a three-party negotiable instrument. The three parties are the drawer, drawee, and the payee. A person has funds on deposit with an institution. When the person issues a draft (or check), the institution is ordered to draw down the funds on deposit by the specific amount written on the draft. The **drawer** is the person who has the funds on deposit and who creates and signs an instrument that orders the **drawee** to pay a certain sum of money to the payee. The drawer's signature must appear on the order instrument's face. That way, the drawee can authenticate the signature and then follow the exact order. If the drawee disobeys the order, it can be held liable. The drawee is a debtor of the drawer (who is the creditor).

Generally, three-party instruments are used by people in lieu of currency. All three-party instruments fall into the general category of drafts. Checks, cashier's checks, certified checks, and traveler's checks are specialized forms of drafts.

Drafts. A **draft** is an unconditional written order by the drawer to the drawee to pay money to the payee. The drawer can make the instrument payable to himself. For example, you can make a check payable to yourself. The drawer "orders" the instrument to be paid by the drawee to the payee. The drawer does not "make a promise to pay," which is the language used in instruments between two parties.

The draft represents a debt owed by the drawee to the drawer that has been made either by agreement, such as an agreement between a depositor and a bank, or through a debtor-creditor relationship. Two types of drafts are *time drafts* and *sight drafts*.

A **time draft** is a draft that is payable at a definite future time. A **sight draft**, also called a **demand draft**, is payable on sight (on demand). When the holder presents a sight draft for payment, such as a share draft used by a credit union, the drawee must pay it. Insurance companies use sight drafts to pay claims.

Checks. A depositor draws a **check** on a bank or financial institution, ordering it to pay a sum of money

Exhibit 12-2   A Sample Certificate of Deposit

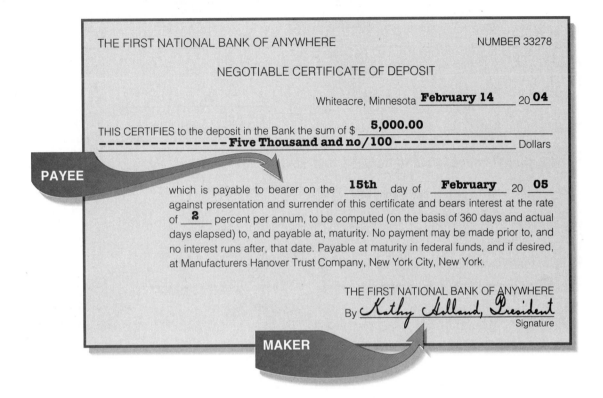

THE FIRST NATIONAL BANK OF ANYWHERE   NUMBER 33278

NEGOTIABLE CERTIFICATE OF DEPOSIT

Whiteacre, Minnesota **February 14** 20 **04**

THIS CERTIFIES to the deposit in the Bank the sum of $ **5,000.00**

---------------- **Five Thousand and no/100** ---------------- Dollars

PAYEE

which is payable to bearer on the **15th** day of **February** 20 **05** against presentation and surrender of this certificate and bears interest at the rate of **2** percent per annum, to be computed (on the basis of 360 days and actual days elapsed) to, and payable at, maturity. No payment may be made prior to, and no interest runs after, that date. Payable at maturity in federal funds, and if desired, at Manufacturers Hanover Trust Company, New York City, New York.

THE FIRST NATIONAL BANK OF ANYWHERE

By *Kathy Holland, President*
                          Signature

MAKER

on demand to a payee [UCC 3-104(f)]. The person who writes the check is called the *drawer* and is a depositor in the bank on which the check is drawn. The person to whom the check is payable is the *payee*. The bank on which the check is drawn is the *drawee*. If Dominic writes a check against his checking account to purchase a boat, he is the drawer, his bank is the drawee, and the boat seller is the payee.

A **cashier's check** is a draft in which the bank is both the drawer and drawee. A person goes to a bank and deposits money with it for the amount of the cashier's check, plus a fee for this service. A bank officer issues the check, authorizing the payee to receive the check's amount on demand. The payee then draws on the bank's own account, instead of on a private person's account. Because it is drawn on a bank, a cashier's check is accepted for many transactions for which a personal check would not be. Because the bank is both the drawer and the drawee, payment is assured (unless the bank goes into bankruptcy before the check clears).

A **certified check** carries a certification that the drawer has sufficient funds to cover payment. A **traveler's check** is a draft from a financial institution. This type of check requires a countersignature and is payable on demand at or through a bank. A traveler's check can be used around the world in lieu of currency if the traveler's check is issued in the local currency. For example, a traveler may be unable to purchase a toy in a London store if her traveler's checks are issued in dollars. The traveler's checks need to be issued in pounds sterling to be accepted in a London store.

A check is the most commonly used three-party instrument. For example, Marilyn Hicks has a checking account at the First National Bank of Anywhere. She plans to purchase her new automobile by check. She signs the check as the drawer and issues it to A-1 Car Company, the payee. On the check's face, she orders the drawee, First National Bank of Anywhere, to pay the amount written on the check's face to the payee, A-1 Car Company. Exhibit 12–3 shows a sample check.

Exhibit 12-3 A Sample Check

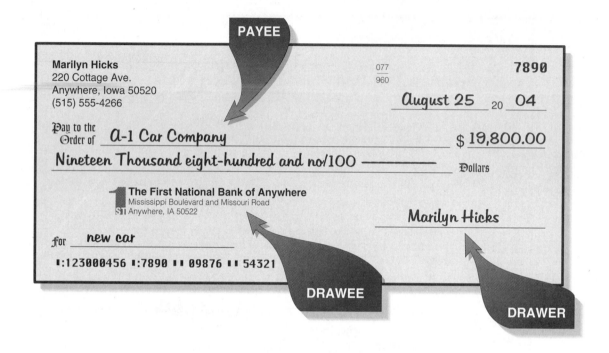

Signature Liability of Makers, Acceptors, and Drawers

A maker is primarily liable on a note or CD. A drawee-acceptor is primarily liable on a draft [UCC 3-412 and UCC 3-413(a)]. An **acceptor** is a drawee that, by its signature, agrees to pay the drawer's instrument.

The instrument is presented by the payee, holder, or drawer to the drawee for payment, and the drawee accepts the instrument. When a maker or acceptor is primarily liable, the maker or acceptor must absolutely pay the face amount of the instrument, assuming that no real defense exists (see later section titled *Defenses*).

On a draft, a drawer is secondarily liable. To hold the drawer absolutely liable on its signature, the holder must properly present the instrument (for example, for a domestic check, within ninety days of date of issue) to the drawee. The drawee may dishonor (not pay) the instrument because the drawer has insufficient funds in the account, has closed the account, or has made an error by dishonoring the draft.

If the drawee rightfully dishonored the instrument (insufficient funds), the drawer is liable to the holder. If

the drawee wrongfully dishonored the instrument, the drawee is liable to the drawer. The holder must provide the proper notice of dishonor to the drawer in order for the drawee to be held liable. The holder is not obliged to notify a drawer of a check that the check has been dishonored because the law presumes that the drawer knows the balance in the checking account.

A person is discharged from liability on an instrument as the result of a payment, cancellation, or material alteration. If the drawer or maker pays the instrument, it is discharged [UCC 3-602]. The payee or holder may cancel the instrument by intentionally marking it paid (when in fact it has not been paid) or by intentionally destroying it [UCC 3-604]. If the instrument has been materially altered as previously discussed, liability on the instrument may be totally or partially discharged [UCC 3-407].

Indorsements

If negotiable instruments are used as a substitute for currency, a method to transfer ownership of an order instrument from the payee to a third person must exist.

This transfer method is simple. The payee indorses (signs) the instrument on the back (or on another document permanently attached to the negotiable instrument) and delivers it to another person. Indorsements are required whenever the instrument being negotiated is classified as order paper.

The indorsement should be identical to the name that appears on the instrument. The payee or indorsee whose name is misspelled can indorse with the misspelled name, the correct name, or both. The payor can require both signatures [UCC 3-204(d)].

The following text first deals with the parties to an indorsement. Then it looks at various types of indorsements and signature and transfer liabilities. Finally, bearer paper is discussed.

Indorsers and Indorsees

The drawer originally makes out the negotiable instrument to a payee or to bearer. If a payee is named, the payee becomes an **indorser**. The person who receives the instrument is the **indorsee**. To *indorse* means to sign on the back of the instrument for the purpose of transferring the ownership.

For example, Marie Holland, a medical doctor, receives a check for $125 from a patient. Holland wants to purchase some software for her computer from Positive Logic Computer Company. She indorses (signs her name) on the back of the check and delivers it to Positive Logic. Holland's name appears both as the payee on the check's front and the indorser on the check's back. As the indorsee, Positive Logic is entitled to the $125. Positive Logic then can indorse the check to someone else and become an indorser in turn.

Four categories of indorsements are recognized: *blank*, *special*, *qualified*, and *restrictive*. Exhibit 12–4 contains examples of these various indorsements.

Blank Indorsement. A **blank indorsement** occurs when a payee or a previous indorser signs his name on the back of the negotiable instrument. If a payee merely signs his name without naming a new payee, it becomes a blank indorsement.

When Marie Holland, in the previous example, indorsed the check on the back with her name, she gave a blank indorsement (see Exhibit 12–4). The check becomes bearer paper that anyone can cash. A person should never indorse a check or other negotiable instrument in blank until she is ready to transfer ownership of that instrument.

Special Indorsement. A **special indorsement** is when the payee or previous indorser signs his name on the back of the negotiable instrument, but names a new payee. For example, Joe Jones receives his paycheck for $400. He wants to purchase a $400 printer from Wang. He can indorse "Pay to Wang, Joe Jones" (see Exhibit 12–4). When Joe Jones named a new payee, he made a special indorsement.

Qualified Indorsement. The blank or special indorser guarantees payment of the instrument to the holder or any subsequent indorser in the event of default (failure to pay) by the maker or drawee [UCC 3-415(b)]. Blank and special indorsements are unqualified indorsements.

In contrast, an indorser uses a **qualified indorsement** to disclaim or limit any liability to this instrument. A qualified indorsement commonly includes the notation "without recourse." The qualified indorser is not guaranteeing any payment, although title is still transferred from the indorser to the holder. An instrument with a qualified indorsement can be further negotiated. See Exhibit 12–4 for a sample qualified blank indorsement.

Restrictive Indorsement. A **restrictive indorsement** is effective as between the indorser and the indorsee. Restrictive indorsements do not prevent the further transfer or negotiation of the instrument [UCC 3-206].

Types of restrictive indorsements are conditional indorsements (pay to Rosemary Porter on condition of her delivery of her blue truck at 100 Green Street by August 7, 2005), prohibiting indorsements (pay to Regina Hildaga only), and trust indorsements (pay to Katherine Burns in trust for David Burns).

A common type of restrictive indorsement is one that makes the indorsee (almost always a bank) a collecting agent of the indorser. For example, "for deposit only" is a very common indorsement (see Exhibit 12–4). This type of indorsement has the effect of locking the instrument (usually a check) into the bank collection process.

Indorsements and Signature and Transfer Warranty Liabilities

Blank, special, and restrictive indorsements are unqualified indorsements. That is, the indorser guarantees payment of the instrument in addition to transferring

Exhibit 12–4   **Indorsements**

A. Checks

Checks deposited must be indorsed in a specific area on the back side of each check. The entire indorsement (whether a signature or a stamp), along with any other indorsements, identification information, driver s license number, etc., must fall within 1½ inches of a check s trailing edge. As you look at the front of a check, the trailing edge is the left edge. When you flip the check over, all indorsement information must be within 1½ inches of the edge.

B. Other negotiable instruments

On the other types of negotiable instruments, an indorsement may legally be placed anywhere.

A Sample Blank Indorsement

A Sample Qualified Blank Indorsement

A Sample Special Indorsement

A Sample Restrictive Indorsement

title to it. Unless an indorser can claim a valid defense against the holder demanding payment, the indorser is liable to the instrument's holder.

The indorser may be liable either on the basis of its signature (guaranty of payment) or on breach of warranties that the indorser made when transferring the instrument. When an indorser's signature makes the indorser liable, the liability is called *signature liability*.

Signature Liability. For signature or contractual liability, the blank and special indorsers have secondary liability. Liability based on a signature is dependent on three things. First, the instrument was properly presented to the person with the responsibility of paying it. Second, the instrument was dishonored. Third, the indorser received timely notice of dishonor [UCC 3-415(a)].

Proper presentment requires the holder to present the instrument to the party responsible for its payment (for example, a note is presented to the maker), in a proper manner (for example, a check at the drawee's bank or at the holder's bank goes through a clearinghouse), on or before the instrument's due date [UCC 3-501].

Most improper presentments result because the holder fails to present the instrument within the appropriate time period. Time instruments must be presented on or before the due date. Demand instruments (other than domestic checks) must be presented within a reasonable period after date of issue. To hold a blank or special indorser liable for its signature on a domestic check, the holder must present the check to the bank for payment within thirty days of the indorser's indorsement [UCC 3-415(e)].

Dishonor usually occurs when the party responsible for payment fails to pay upon presentment. Once the instrument is dishonored, the holder must notify (in any reasonable manner) any secondary party that the holder intends to hold liable.

A bank must provide this notice before midnight of the banking day following receipt. Those other than a bank must provide the notice within thirty days after the instrument is dishonored [UCC 3-503(c)]. Should the holder fail to make proper presentment or to provide the blank or special indorser proper notice of dishonor, the indorser is completely discharged from signature liability [UCC 3-415(c)].

Transfer Warranty Liability. When indorsers receive consideration (something of value as opposed to receiving a gift) from the transferee, the indorsers make five transfer warranties [UCC 3-416(a)]. These five warranties cover all of the instrument's subsequent holders. First, the warrantor is entitled to enforce the instrument. Second, all signatures on the instrument are authentic and authorized. Third, the instrument has not been altered. Fourth, the instrument is not subject to a defense or claim that can be asserted against the warrantor. Fifth, the warrantor has no knowledge of any insolvency proceeding commenced with respect to the maker or acceptor or, in the case of an unaccepted draft, the drawer.

In the case of checks, the indorser cannot disclaim these warranties. The claimant, within thirty days after it has reason to know of the breach and the identity of the warrantor, must notify the warrantor of the breach. If the warrantor receives late notification, the warrantor is discharged to the extent of any loss caused by the delay in notification.

Should any of these warranties be breached at the time of the indorser's transfer, a subsequent holder can hold the indorser liable. This action is independent of presentment and notice of dishonor (signature liability). Even if the holder improperly presents the instrument, a holder could sue for breach of warranty.

A bearer also can transfer an instrument and thus make the same transfer warranties as an indorser. The extent of liability, however, is that these warranties only flow to the bearer's immediate transferee, not to all subsequent holders.

A qualified indorser, who receives consideration, also makes transfer warranties. These warranties are the same as those made by a blank, special, or restrictive indorser, and these warranties also flow to all subsequent holders.

Holders and Holders in Due Course

Negotiable instruments can be held by one of two transferees: the holder or the holder in due course (HDC). Legally, the two have very different rights.

Holder

A *holder* is a person who is in possession of an instrument that is payable to bearer or payable to an identified person [UCC 1-201(20)]. A holder is one of three people.

First, the holder may be the original payee. Second, if the payee has transferred the negotiable instrument to another, that person (also called the *transferee*) is a holder. Third, a person in possession of a bearer instrument is likewise a holder. (A bearer instrument is made out to cash or bearer, or has been converted from order paper to bearer paper by a blank indorsement. Bearer instruments are discussed in more detail later in the chapter.)

All three of these types of holders have the status of an assignee of a contract right. As an assignee, the holder obtains only those rights that its predecessor-transferor had in the instrument. If a conflicting, superior claim or defense to the instrument exists, a holder cannot collect payment.

The holder is usually, but not necessarily, the negotiable instrument's owner. For example, Valdez takes a check made payable to him. He indorses the check on the back in blank, anticipating that he will deposit the check in his bank in the afternoon. He misplaces the check and someone steals it. The thief is a holder under the law. Even though, obviously, not the owner, the thief can legally transfer the check (a bearer instrument because of Valdez's blank indorsement) to another person, and that person can collect the money. This third person now becomes the holder.

Holder in Due Course

A *holder in due course* is a special-status transferee of a negotiable instrument. An HDC has a very special and protected standing within the law. If a holder has acquired the instrument in a manner that meets the UCC requirements, the holder transforms its position from that of ordinary holder to that of holder in due course.

An HDC normally is immune to any defenses (excuses for performance) asserted by the drawer or maker against paying the instrument. This immunity allows these instruments to serve as substitutes for currency because they must be paid, unless there is a real defense against the instrument itself. As discussed later in this chapter, the Federal Trade Commission has modified the HDC doctrine as it applies to consumer transactions.

The law protects an HDC because negotiable instruments are currency substitutes. People who accept negotiable instruments as currency substitutes must have some protection. The law, therefore, does not allow the drawer or maker many reasons to avoid paying the instrument that he signed.

Under revised Article 3, in order to become an HDC, a holder of a negotiable instrument must meet six requirements. The holder must take the instrument

1. for value;
2. in good faith;
3. without notice that it is overdue or defective;
4. without notice that the instrument contains an unauthorized signature or has been altered;
5. without notice of any claim to the instrument; and
6. without notice that any party has a real defense, such as illegality, lack of legal capacity, duress, fraud in the inducement, discharge in bankruptcy, or material alteration [UCC 3-302(a) (2)].

The chapter discusses real defenses later. The underlying requirement for achieving the status of a holder in due course is, of course, that the person must first be a holder of the instrument.

Value. An HDC must provide value for the instrument [UCC 3-303]. A person who receives an instrument as a gift or who inherits the instrument has not met the requirement of value. In these situations, the person remains an ordinary holder, does not possess the rights of an HDC, and is subject to all the contract defenses.

The concept of value in the law of negotiable instruments differs from the concept of consideration in the law of contracts. For example, under contract law, a promise to pay a debt that the person already owes is not consideration. A holder who takes an instrument in payment of a prior debt, however, has provided value.

Likewise, an executory promise (a promise to perform or pay in the future) is valid consideration to support a contract but does not constitute value to qualify a holder as an HDC. A holder takes the instrument for value only to the extent that the consideration actually has been performed or paid. For example, Lori makes out a check for $500 payable to Rory on Sunday. Rory needs funds but cannot cash Lori's check until Monday. Rory negotiates the check to Gary, who pays Rory $200 in cash and promises to pay Rory the balance on Friday, when he gets his paycheck. Gary has provided value in the amount of $200, so he can only qualify as an HDC for that amount.

Good Faith. An HDC must accept the instrument in good faith. The purchaser-holder must act honestly in the process of acquiring the instrument. Good faith is defined as honesty in fact in the conduct or the transaction concerned [UCC 1-201(19)].

The good-faith requirement applies only to the holder. Whether the transferor acts in good faith is immaterial. Thus, a person who in good faith takes a negotiable instrument from a thief can be an HDC.

Without Notice. A person who acquires an instrument knowing, or having reason to know, that it is defective in any one of the following ways forfeits the HDC protection. This protection is lost when an instrument

1. is overdue,
2. has been dishonored,
3. has an unauthorized signature,
4. has been altered, or
5. has any real or personal defenses that might be raised.

A check is presumed to be overdue if the holder fails to present it for payment within ninety days of its issue [UCC 3-304(a)(2)]. A person should examine the instrument before taking it to see if anything is wrong with it (any erasures or words crossed out) and to see if the time for payment has passed.

If nothing is wrong with the face of the instrument, and the person acquiring the instrument has no knowledge of any defect concerning the instrument, the person becomes an HDC. If the acquiring person is an HDC and demands payment on the instrument, the instrument must be paid. The following case discusses this issue.

CASE 12.1

Superior Court of New Jersey, Appellate Division, 2000

329 N.J. Super. 379, 748 A.2d 111

COMMERCE BANK v. RICKETT

BACKGROUND AND FACTS On January 5, 1998, defendant Bruce Rickett, individually and trading as Rick's Auto Sales, deposited a check to Commerce Bank, N.A. (the Bank). The check was issued to him on January 3, 1998, by DeSimone Auto, Inc. (DeSimone), in the amount of $12,000. The Bank credited Rickett's account and shortly thereafter allowed him to draw against same.

The check, dated January 3, 1997, but actually issued on January 3, 1998, was drawn on DeSimone's account at the Bank of Gloucester County for payment of a 1997 Buick LeSabre motor vehicle. The understanding between Rickett and DeSimone was that the check would not be presented for payment if the motor vehicle was damaged. Shortly after issuance of the check, DeSimone inspected the vehicle and found frame damage. DeSimone telephoned Rickett, advising him to pick up the vehicle and return the check. DeSimone returned the vehicle to Rickett, who accepted it. Thereafter, DeSimone issued a "stop payment" on the check.

Contrary to their agreement, Rickett had already presented the check for payment on January 5, 1998, and drawn against it. The check was returned by the Bank of Gloucester County to the Bank as unpaid on January 13, 1998. The amount charged back to Rickett's account by the Bank was $11,016.48.

The Bank filed a complaint against both Rickett and DeSimone, seeking the amount charged back to Rickett's account. Rickett could not be located by the Bank. As to DeSimone, the Bank asserted that it was a "holder in due course" and, therefore, entitled to payment from DeSimone.

DeSimone contended that the erroneous date of "January 3, 1997" placed the Bank on notice that the check might have been overdue, and, accordingly, the Bank could not be a holder in due course because "holder-in-due-course" status attaches at the time the transaction is made. The trial court granted a motion for summary judgment filed by the Bank and DeSimone appealed.

NEWMAN, J. A. D.

. . . .

In granting summary judgment in favor of the Bank in the amount of $11,016.48, Judge Supnick found that the Bank was a holder in due course, largely relying on the fact that DeSimone had admitted that the check was actually issued on January 3, 1998, not January 3, 1997, and on the Bank's proof that "checks presented for negotiation are often misdated in the first few days of a new year with the prior year still being written on the check." . . .

On appeal, DeSimone contends that the application of N.J.S.A. 12A:3-302a(2) negates the Bank's status as a holder in due course. That section reads as follows:

a. Subject to subsection c. of this section and subsection d. of 12A:3-106, "holder in due course" means the holder of an instrument if:

the holder took the instrument for value, in good faith, without notice that the instrument is overdue or has been dishonored or that there is an uncured default with respect to payment of another instrument issued as part of the same series, without notice that the instrument contains an unauthorized signature or has been altered, without notice of any claim to the instrument described in 12A:3-306, and without notice that any party has a defense or claim in recoupment described in subsection a. of 12A:3-305.

DeSimone asserts that the "January 3, 1997" date on the face of the check made it overdue. N.J.S.A. 12A:3-304 provides, in relevant part:

a. An instrument payable on demand becomes overdue at the earliest of the following times:

. . . .

(2) if the instrument is a check, 90 days after its date [.]

DeSimone also cites to N.J.S.A. 12A:3-113, which provides, in pertinent part:

a. An instrument may be antedated or postdated. The date stated determines the time of payment if the instrument is payable at a fixed period after date.

DeSimone reasons that, because the check was dated January 3, 1997, and deposited in early January 1998, the Bank had actual notice that the check was overdue, as defined by the ninety-day period for checks set forth in N.J.S.A. 12A:3-304a(2), and was therefore not a holder in due course under N.J.S.A. 12A-3:302a(2). DeSimone also construes N.J.S.A. 12A:3-113a to mean that the fact that the check was dated January 3, 1997, establishes the check's "date" as January 3, 1997, automatically rendering the check overdue when it was deposited on January 5, 1998.

DeSimone's reliance on N.J.S.A. 12A:3-113a to support its argument that January 3, 1997 must be viewed as the check's "date" for purposes of determining whether the instrument was overdue . . . is misplaced. N.J.S.A. 12A:3-113a refers to an instrument payable at a fixed period of time. A check does not fit within that definition, but rather is a demand instrument. Accordingly, N.J.S.A. 12A:3-113a is inapplicable.

The issue presented is whether, pursuant to N.J.S.A. 12A:3-304a(2), a check becomes overdue ninety days after the date on the face of the check or ninety days after its date of issue. We construe N.J.S.A. 12A:3-304a(2) to mean that a check becomes overdue ninety days after the date it is actually issued. To interpret N.J.S.A. 12A:3-304a(2) otherwise is impractical and inconsistent with other provisions in the Code.

Pazol v. Citizens Nat'l Bank of Sandy Springs is factually similar. There, a check that bore the date "January 4, 1963" was deposited on or about January 9, 1964. The drawer entered a stop-payment order, but the payee-depositor was permitted to withdraw its full value before the depositary bank received notice that the check had been dishonored. The payor bank refused to transfer funds, and the depository bank sued the drawer for the value of the check. The drawer sought a general demurrer on the ground that the depository bank had actual notice that the check was overdue based on the date on the face of the instrument and that it could not claim to be a holder in due course. The court rejected this argument, ruling that, although the date on an instrument is presumed to be correct, "this presumption is not conclusive, and may be overcome by parol evidence that it was in fact made on another date[.]"

The reasoning of the *Pazol* court is persuasive. Here, the Bank has established that the date on the face of the check was incorrect by DeSimone's admission that the check was actually issued on January 3, 1998. Accordingly, the Bank was a holder in due course, as DeSimone only challenges that status on the ground that the Bank had notice that the check was overdue.

. . . .

DECISION AND REMEDY DeSimone was found to be improvident in issuing an otherwise facially valid check for the full price of an uninspected vehicle. The Bank did not bear the loss because DeSimone was careless in filling out the instrument. It was admitted that the check was actually issued on January 3, 1998, thus making the Bank a legitimate holder in due course.

CRITICAL THINKING: LEGAL THEORY Discuss why a person should be held liable when he or she has been defrauded.

The case would have ended differently if a contract had been involved. The following section specifically addresses the differences between the assignment of a contract and the negotiation of a negotiable instrument.

Assignment or Negotiation

Once issued, a negotiable instrument can be transferred by *assignment* or by *negotiation*. The critical distinction is that with an assignment, the contract rights are assigned to a third party who has the status of an assignee and who has no better rights than the transferor-assignor.

A negotiable instrument is negotiated to a third person who, if he has the status of an HDC, can have better rights than the transferor. Again, because negotiable instruments serve as a substitute for currency, a person who accepts an instrument must be reasonably certain that she can collect on it free from any defenses that may be asserted against the holder of a normal contract assignment.

Assignment

Assignment is a transfer of rights under a contract. Recall from Chapter 10 that, under general contract

principles, a transfer by assignment from an assignor (the original party to the contract) to an assignee (the person buying the contract right) provides the assignee only those rights that the assignor possessed.

Any defenses to the contract that can be raised against the assignor also can be raised against the assignee. A nonnegotiable instrument cannot be negotiated but can be assigned. Furthermore, when a transfer fails to qualify as a negotiation, it becomes an assignment.

Negotiation

Negotiation is the transfer of a negotiable instrument in a manner such that the transferee becomes a holder [UCC 3-201]. The holder minimally receives the previous possessor's rights [UCC 3-203(b)]. Unlike an assignment, a transfer by negotiation allows for a holder to become a holder in due course and to receive more rights in the instrument than the prior possessor [UCC 3-306].

Negotiating Order Paper. Order paper initially names a specific payee, who then can indorse the instrument. Two steps required to negotiate (transfer) order paper are (1) indorsement and (2) delivery.

Artiste Login. Carlo issues a payroll check "to the order of Wang." Wang takes the check to the supermarket, signs her name on the back (a blank indorsement), gives it to the cashier (a delivery), and receives currency. Wang has negotiated the check (an order instrument) by a blank indorsement and delivery to the supermarket. The supermarket is now an HDC because it accepted the check for value, in good faith, and without noticing any problems with the check.

Negotiating Bearer Paper. Bearer paper is negotiated by delivery alone. No indorsement is necessary [UCC 3-201(b)].

In an earlier example, Marie Holland indorsed a check in blank. She delivers the check to Ross who goes to the drawee bank to cash the check. In theory, since the check is now a bearer instrument, he should be able to present the check and the bank should pay him the amount of the check. The bank, however, may require Ross to indorse the check. Technically, however, this indorsement on the back is not required for negotiation. The bank may require it for purposes of identification and of verification that Ross received the money [UCC 3-501(b)(2)]. The use of bearer paper involves more risk through loss or theft than does the use of order paper.

Itzak writes a check "payable to cash" and hands it (a delivery) to Latifa. Itzak negotiated the check (bearer paper) to Latifa by delivery alone. Latifa places the check in her wallet, which subsequently is stolen. The thief possesses the check. At this point, negotiation has not occurred because delivery must be voluntary on the part of the transferor. If the thief "delivers" the check to an innocent party who pays the thief the amount on the check, negotiation will have occurred. All rights to the check will be passed absolutely to that party, and Latifa will lose all rights to recover the proceeds of the check from the innocent party [UCC 3-305(c)]. Of course, she can recover her money from the thief if the thief can be found.

Converting Order to Bearer Paper and Vice Versa. The maker or drawer controls whether the instrument has a named payee (order paper) or whether a bearer (bearer paper) is entitled to payment. If it is order paper, the payee's indorsement determines whether the instrument continues as order paper or converts to bearer paper. A blank indorsement converts the order paper to bearer paper [UCC 3-205(b)],

while a special indorsement continues the paper as order paper.

Bearer paper may be converted to order paper if the back of the paper has a special indorsement. For example, a check originally payable to "cash" is bearer paper and is negotiated by delivery. If the check subsequently is indorsed "pay to Jones," it must be negotiated as order paper (by indorsement and delivery), because it names a specific payee [UCC 3-205(a)].

Defenses

Defenses by a party to avoid payment fall into two general categories: *real defenses* and *personal defenses.* **Real defenses** prevent payment to all holders of a negotiable instrument, including an HDC. **Personal defenses** prevent payment to an ordinary holder of a negotiable instrument [UCC 3-305].

Real Defenses

Real (or universal) defenses are valid against all holders, including HDCs or holders who take an instrument through an HDC. (A holder who does not qualify as an HDC but who derives title through an HDC acquires the rights and privileges of an HDC [UCC 3-203(b)]. This is sometimes referred to as the *shelter principle.*) The following are several real defenses.

Forgery. Forgery of a maker's or a drawer's signature cannot bind the person whose name is used unless that person ratifies (formally confirms) the signature [UCC 3-401 and UCC 3-403(a)].

Fraud in Execution. A person may be deceived into signing a negotiable instrument, such as when a person believes that she is signing something other than a negotiable instrument (for example, a receipt). This deception is called *fraud in execution.*

For instance, a consumer unfamiliar with the English language signs a paper presented by a salesperson as a request for an estimate. In fact, it is a promissory note. Even if the note were negotiated to an HDC, the consumer may have a valid defense based on the real defense of fraud in execution. This defense cannot be used if a reasonable person would not or should not have been deceived as to the character of the instrument being signed.

Alteration. An alteration is material if it changes the contract terms in any way. Examples of material alterations include changing the number or relations of the parties, or adding to or removing from the writing after the instrument is signed [UCC 3-407(a)].

A material alteration is a complete defense against an ordinary holder, but is at best only a partial defense against an HDC. A holder cannot recover anything on an instrument that has been materially altered [UCC 3-407(b)]. If the original terms are altered, such as the amount payable, prior to the HDC purchasing the instrument, the HDC can collect the original amount from the maker or drawer. If the instrument is incomplete and later completed in an unauthorized manner prior to the HDC purchasing the instrument, the alteration cannot serve as a defense against an HDC. Furthermore, the HDC can enforce the instrument up to the amount written [UCC 3-407(c)].

Bankruptcy. When a debt that is represented by a negotiable instrument is discharged (forgiven) in bankruptcy, that discharge is an absolute defense against paying the instrument to either a holder or an HDC. The purpose of bankruptcy is to settle and forgive all of the solvent's debts [UCC 3-305(a)(1)].

Operation of Law. When illegal conduct renders an instrument void, payment to either a holder or an HDC is dismissed. If a person were declared mentally incompetent by state proceedings, any instrument issued by that person thereafter would be null and void. The instrument is void from the beginning (time of issue) and unenforceable by any holder or an HDC [UCC 3-305(a)(1)].

Extreme duress is another defense. When a person signs and issues a negotiable instrument under extreme duress, such as an immediate threat of force or violence (for example, at gunpoint), the instrument is void and unenforceable by any holder or HDC [UCC 3-305(a)(1)].

Personal Defenses

All other defenses that are valid in a contract setting, such as breach of contract, breach of warranty, misrepresentation, mistake, undue influence, and economic duress, are considered personal defenses. These defenses are invalid against an HDC but valid against an ordinary holder.

For example, Penny wants to install a digital widescreen television for the patrons at her bar. Penny agrees to purchase the television for $2,800 from an acquaintance, Slick. Slick, knowing his statements to be false, tells Penny that the television is only six months old and is in good working order. In addition, he tells Penny that he owns the television free and clear of all claims. Penny pays Slick $500 in cash and issues a negotiable promissory note for the balance. As it turns out, Slick still owes the original seller $500 on the television purchase, and the television is subject to a security interest (lien) filed by the original seller in the appropriate state office. In addition, the television is three years old. Penny can refuse to pay the note if it is held by an ordinary holder, such as Slick in this case. If Slick has negotiated the note to an HDC, however, Penny must pay the HDC. Of course, Penny can then sue Slick. (Penny cannot use the Federal Trade Commission rule described in the next section because she owns a business and therefore does not qualify as a consumer.)

Federal Limitations on Holder-in-Due-Course Rights

A Federal Trade Commission (FTC) rule has severely limited the preferential position enjoyed by an HDC in a *consumer credit transaction*. A **consumer credit transaction** occurs when a consumer enters into a contract to purchase an item and at the same time receives credit from the seller or financial institution to purchase the item. The consumer signs a note promising to pay for the item. Payment by check is exempt as a credit transaction for purposes of this FTC rule.

Prior to the FTC rule, the law giving preferential treatment to an HDC worked a severe hardship on consumers. For example, Ron, a consumer, buys a new wall-mounted plasma television for his home from Shady TV Dealers for $2,500. Ron signs a promissory note to pay for the television. The payee is Shady TV Dealers. Shady sells the note (negotiates it) at a discounted amount to Better Bank. The bank, having paid value, having taken the note in good faith, and having taken it without notice of any problems, qualifies as an HDC. Ron discovers that the television is defective and never will work properly. This defect is a personal defense and, naturally, he wants to withhold payments for the TV. The note, however, is held now by the bank, an HDC. Prior to the FTC rule, Ron would have to pay the bank on the note. In the past, the defenses Ron had on the contract for the purchase of the defective television were valid only against Shady TV Dealers, not the bank.

Today, under the FTC rule, when a note is part of a consumer credit contract, the note must include a warning to any holder who may qualify as an HDC that the note holder is subject to all contract defenses that the original purchaser may have against the original seller. In other words, in a consumer credit contract, personal defenses are valid even when the holder would otherwise qualify as an HDC. With the warning included, Ron can use the FTC rule as a defense against both Shady TV Dealers and Better Bank. The following case is an example of the application of this doctrine.

CASE 12.2

Court of Appeals of New Mexico, 2002
132 N.M. 459, 50 P.3d 554

JARAMILLO v. GONZALES

BACKGROUND AND FACTS In December 1989, Nicklos Jaramillo purchased a mobile home for his son, Darrell, that was delivered the following January. To finance the purchase, Nicklos executed a retail installment contract and security agreement with the seller, who then assigned the contract and security agreement to a predecessor of the Bank of America (the Bank). The Jaramillos made regular monthly payments on the home and were current on their payments at the time the following incident occurred. Gonzales is not identified in the case, but would be either the seller or a representative of the Bank.

In June 1995, Darrell returned home from work one day to discover that the mobile home had flooded. He attempted to clean up the water and dry out the mobile home. He investigated the cause of the flooding and learned that the seller of the mobile home had gone out of business. After numerous phone calls, he finally traced the manufacturer of his mobile home to a plant in Georgia. The Georgia plant dispatched a local repairman to determine the cause of the flooding. The repairman informed Darrell that the flooding was caused by leaks in the polybutylene used in the plumbing throughout the home and that his "problems were just beginning." The deficiencies of polybutylene are well known throughout the mobile home industry.

Darrell filed a claim with his insurance company to recover for the damage the flooding caused to the mobile home and his personal effects. The insurance company settled the claim for $15,317 and issued a check payable to Darrell and the Bank that held the contract. Darrell deposited the check in his own account without informing the Bank. Darrell did not use the money to repair the mobile home.

In February 1996, the Jaramillos' attorney sent a letter of revocation to the Bank, stating that the flooding had caused considerable damage and had rendered the mobile home uninhabitable. The letter asserted that the Bank, as the assignee of the contract, was subject to all claims and defenses that could have been asserted against the seller. The Bank did not acknowledge the letter of revocation; instead, it sent a routine monthly billing statement showing a past due balance. The Bank followed the billing statement with a collection letter and a phone call to Nicklos. When Nicklos told the Bank that he had revoked acceptance of the mobile home and that he would not be paying on the contract, the Bank advised him of his contractual obligation and the effect of nonpayment on his credit rating. The Bank continued to seek to collect on the contract and reported a delinquent debt to credit agencies.

Thereafter, Nicklos was denied credit twice due to the reports made by the Bank. In April 1996, upon the Bank's continued refusal to accept the revocation, the Jaramillos filed suit.

FRY, Judge.

. . . .

FTC Holder Rule The Bank contends that its status as an assignee of the original sales contract limits the remedies available to Plaintiffs. It argues that the "FTC Holder

Rule" permits affirmative recovery against an assignee of a contract only if the product is of little or no value when it was delivered to the buyer. According to the Bank, Plaintiffs failed to satisfy this condition because the trial court found that the mobile home had substantial value when it was delivered.

. . . The FTC *Holder Rule*, 16 C.F.R. § 433.2 (2002), provides in part that in connection with any sale of consumer goods or services, it is an unfair or deceptive act to take or receive a consumer credit contract that fails to contain the following provision in at least ten point, bold face, type:

NOTICE

ANY HOLDER OF THIS CONSUMER CREDIT CONTRACT IS SUBJECT TO ALL CLAIMS AND DEFENSES WHICH THE DEBTOR COULD ASSERT AGAINST THE SELLER OF GOODS OR SERVICES OBTAINED PURSUANT HERETO OR WITH THE PROCEEDS HEREOF. RECOVERY HEREUNDER BY THE DEBTOR SHALL NOT EXCEED AMOUNTS PAID BY THE DEBTOR HEREUNDER.

In adopting this rule, the FTC abrogated the holder in due course rule in consumer credit transactions, thus preserving the consumer's claims and defenses against the creditor-assignee. The Bank argues, however, that this abrogation applies only if there is a total failure of performance or the like. This argument is based on the official *Statement of Basis and Purpose* published by the FTC with the rule. That statement provides in part:

From the consumer's standpoint, this means that a consumer can (1) defend a creditor suit for payment of an obligation by raising a valid claim against the seller as a set-off, and (2) maintain an affirmative action against a creditor who has received payments for a return of monies paid on account. *The latter alternative will only be available where a seller's breach is so substantial that a court is persuaded that recission and restitution are justified.*

Preservation of Consumers' Claims and Defenses, 40 Fed. Reg. 53,506, 53,524 (Nov. 18, 1975) (emphasis added). The Bank argues that this commentary language limits the consumer's affirmative actions to those situations in which recission is the proper remedy. . . .

Other courts have rejected the notion that this commentary can be used to limit the clear language of the notice required by the rule. . . .

We agree with these courts, and for three reasons we conclude that the Holder Rule does not limit affirmative claims to those instances where recission would be appropriate.

First, the commentary is not a rule, but rather a lengthy explanation of the history and reasoning behind the rule. Second, the rule is unambiguous. It simply mandates the inclusion of specific language in consumer credit contracts. There is nothing in the rule that limits the types of claims or defenses that may be brought against the assignee. Because the rule is unambiguous, there is no basis for referring to commentary to understand the meaning of the language in the rule

Third, even if we were to look to the commentary to determine the meaning of the rule, we note that the commentary is not limited to the narrow statement relied on by the Bank. Rather, the commentary discusses at length the rationale for the rule and concludes that the purpose of the rule is to reallocate the costs of seller misconduct in the consumer market, "compel[ling] creditors to either absorb seller misconduct costs or return them to sellers." In discussing the measures available to the assignee, it is clear the FTC contemplated that consumer claims could be for something less than total recission and that it was for the assignee to determine which mechanisms for allocating costs of seller misconduct best served its purposes. Thus, the whole purpose of the rule is to shift the liability for seller misconduct from the consumer to the seller and assignee. This purpose surely would not be promoted by limiting consumer claims to only those circumstances where recission was appropriate. Viewing the commentary as a whole, we conclude there is no basis to limit the claims that a consumer may bring against the assignee.

Moreover, the FTC *Guidelines for the Holder Rule* state that the required notice under the rule "protect[s] the consumer's right to assert against the creditor *any* legally sufficient claim or defense against the seller. *The creditor stands in the shoes of the seller.*" These *Guidelines* make it clear that affirmative action for recovery, other than complete recission, is contemplated in appropriate cases.

DECISION AND REMEDY The language of the FTC Holder Rule is clear and unambiguous and contains no limitation on the kind of action or defense a consumer may raise against an assignee. Therefore, the Jaramillos were not required to show that the mobile home had little or no value when it was delivered to them before asserting their claim against the Bank.

CRITICAL THINKING: PUBLIC POLICY Why did Congress pass a law that allows consumers the right to disaffirm a contract even after years of product use?

Accord and Satisfaction Doctrine

As discussed in Chapter 10, a contract can be discharged through the doctrine of accord and satisfaction. Most commonly this doctrine is applied to checks.

Assume a dispute exists between two parties over exactly how much is owed. The debtor can settle the dispute by sending the creditor a check with a notation of "in full settlement" or "payment in full." These words indicate that a debtor is attempting to settle a disputed debt. When the creditor cashes the check, an accord and satisfaction results. The creditor cannot bring a lawsuit to recover the remaining debt.

This law worked well when checks were handled manually and the creditor could control the cashing of the check. In the modern world, large businesses handle thousands of checks daily. The creditor's employees rarely see checks because electronic equipment processes them. A check is cashed before the creditor has any actual knowledge of the terms written on it. Only after the check has cleared the bank does the creditor find out about the notice because the debtor refuses to pay any more and references the terms on the check.

Revised Article 3 provides businesses with two protections. First, the creditor can send the debtor a conspicuous statement requiring her to communicate with a designated person, office, or place in case of a

dispute. Delivery of this notice frees the creditor from being bound by any communication sent by the debtor unless it is sent to the specified location. Any check sent with the "paid in full" notation, therefore, is effective only if it is sent to the specified address and the check is then cashed.

Second, even if the business fails to send this notice, it can escape the settlement if it refunds the amount of the check within ninety days of cashing the check. These changes assist businesses confronted with an honest dispute [UCC 3-311].

Checks and the Banking System

Often the banking system handles negotiable instruments and secured transactions. For example, checks (drawn on a bank by a depositor ordering the bank to pay money to a payee) are an integral part of the banking system. People deposit funds into and withdraw funds from their banking accounts using checks and debit cards. The law on deposits and collections appears in the UCC, Article 4, entitled Bank Deposits and Collections.

Checks are the most common kind of negotiable instrument regulated by the Uniform Commercial

LEGAL HIGHLIGHT

Bounce a Check, No Bank Account

For decades, it was easy to open a bank account. When a person applied for a new checking account, the new bank did not review the prior check-writing history or investigate to discover if the applicant had bounced checks in the past.

Today, the attitude of banks has changed. When a person applies for a checking account at a new bank, his or her prior history is reviewed. For example, if a check was bounced or if the bank paid a check and was not immediately reimbursed, the bank may report the customer to ChecSystems and may close the account.

ChecSystems is a national database company that more than 80 percent of U.S. banks have joined. Once a bank sends a person's name to this database, the information remains on a negative list for five years. The customer may not be able to open another checking account during those five years. The banking community is not interested in handling customers who bounce checks, do not immediately repay an overdraft, or do not keep their payments on the bank credit cards current. Customers who engage in this type of behavior costs banks money.

Consider the difficulty of not being able to write or cash checks. People are forced to use to an expensive check-cashing service. These services normally charge 5 to 10 percent of the amount of the check being cashed. Utilities, house payment, groceries, and other bills would need to be paid in cash or with money orders or certified checks.

Code. Checks, credit cards, debit cards, and charge accounts are rapidly replacing currency as a means of paying for goods and services. Approximately 62 billion personal and commercial checks are written each year in the United States. Checks are more than a daily convenience. "Checkbook money" is an integral part of the economic system. A check is a credit instrument treated like cash by the industry.

The Bank–Customer Relationship

Article 4 of the UCC governs modern bank deposit and collection procedures. This article governs the relationships of banks with one another as they process checks for payment. It also establishes a framework for deposit and checking agreements between banks and their customers.

The provisions of Article 3 of the UCC establish the extent to which any party is liable on a check. A check can fall within the scope of Article 3 as a negotiable instrument and also is subject to the provisions of Article 4 while it is in the course of collection. In the case of a conflict between Articles 3 and 4, Article 4 controls [UCC 4-102(a)]. Exhibit 12–5 shows the collection route that a check takes from the time it is issued until it returns to the drawer.

Customer Duties

A checking account holder has a duty to examine the monthly statements and canceled checks for forgeries with reasonable promptness. When the customer's negligence substantially contributes to a forgery, the bank is not obliged to credit the customer's account for the forged check amount.

"Reasonable promptness" means within a few days, but no more than thirty. The court applies comparative negligence rules if a forgery is discovered. If the customer fails to examine the statement or fails to notify the bank of forged checks, the withdrawals from the customer's account based on the forged checks become the customer's responsibility after thirty days [UCC 3-406 and UCC 4-406]. If the checkbook is left where a thief could easily find it, the court may find the customer negligent even if the forged check is discovered within thirty days.

Duties of the Bank

A commercial bank serves its customers primarily in three ways. First, the bank must honor checks for the withdrawal of funds deposited in the customer-drawer's account. Second, the institution must accept

Exhibit 12–5   A Sample Route of a Check

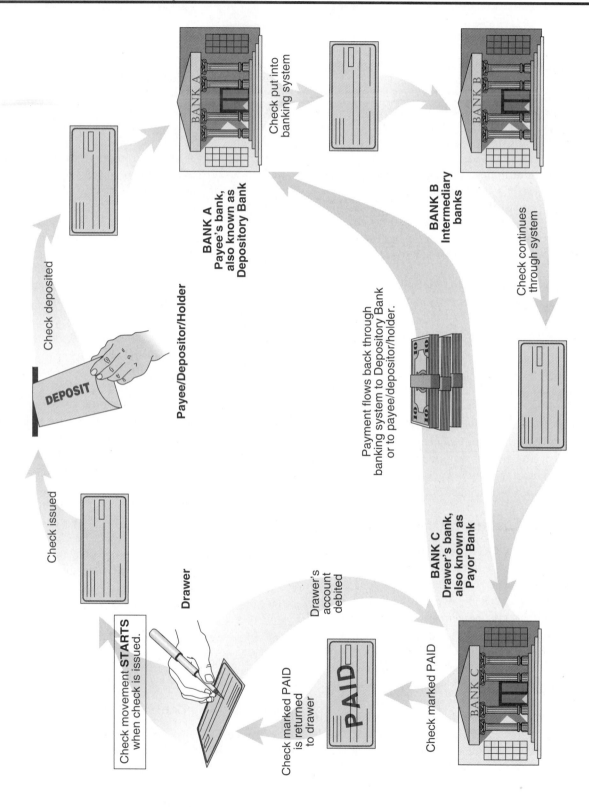

Payee/Depositor/Holder

Check deposited

Check issued

BANK A
Payee's bank,
also known as
Depository Bank

Check put into
banking system

BANK B
Intermediary
banks

Check continues
through system

Payment flows back through
banking system to Depository Bank
or to payee/depositor/holder.

Drawer

Check movement **STARTS**
when check is issued.

Drawer's
account
debited

Check marked PAID
is returned
to drawer

PAID

BANK C
Drawer's bank,
also known as
Payor Bank

Check marked PAID

deposits in currency and must collect on checks written to or indorsed to its customers that are drawn on other banks. Third, the bank must honor *stop-payment orders*.

Honoring Checks. When a commercial bank provides checking services, it agrees to honor the checks written by its customers if sufficient funds in the account cover each check. When a drawee bank wrongfully fails to honor a check, it is liable to its customer-drawer, not to the check holder, for damages resulting from its refusal to pay. The bank contract is with customer-drawer, not the check holder [UCC 4-401].

The bank may agree to accept overdrafts for a customer. An overdraft charges the customer's account for the check amount, even though the account contains insufficient funds to cover the check [UCC 4-401]. Once a bank makes special arrangements with a customer to accept overdrafts to an account, the bank may be liable to the customer for damages caused by any wrongful dishonoring of overdrafts. Today, overdrafts are treated as customer loans that charge interest from the day on which the bank pays the overdraft until the customer deposits funds to cover the overdraft plus the fees for handling the overdraft.

Honoring Stop-Payment Orders. Only a customer can order the bank to pay a check, and only a customer can order the bank to stop a check payment. This right does not extend to holders (such as payees or indorsees) because the drawee-bank's contract is limited to its customer-drawers. A customer cannot issue a **stop-payment order**, however, on a cashier's or teller's check because they are not issued on the customer's account.

The bank has a duty to inform its customers of the requirements for a stop-payment order. A customer can give a stop-payment order orally, usually by phone, and it is binding on the bank for fourteen calendar days unless confirmed in writing. A written stop-payment order is effective for six months, unless renewed in writing [UCC 4-403(b)]. The customer must give the bank a reasonable time to effect a stop-payment order. Until such time, the bank is not liable to its customer if the bank honors the check.

When the drawee bank pays a check after the customer has filed a proper stop-payment order, the bank is liable for the actual loss suffered by the customer-drawer because of the wrongful payment. This amount might be much less than the check amount. For example, JoAnn orders six plants priced at $50 each from Frank's Greenhouse. She pays Frank $300 in advance. Frank delivers only five plants and tells JoAnn that the sixth plant will be delivered in six months. JoAnn immediately stops payment on her $300 check. Inadvertently, the bank honors the $300 check over her stop-payment order. JoAnn can only establish a loss of $50 ($300 − $250 = $50) because she received five plants. The bank is liable for only $50 for the plant that she did not receive.

Paying on Forged Signatures. Signatures of the drawer, maker, or indorser occasionally are forged. Forgery is common with checks. A forged drawer's signature on a check has no effect legally, as a general rule [UCC 3-406]. Banks require the customer's signature on a signature card. Banks, which process thousands of checks each hour, rarely compare the signature on the check with the signature card. The bank is still responsible, however, for determining if the signature on a customer's check is genuine.

Occasionally a forged check will be processed and paid. The general rule is that the bank must recredit the customer's account when it pays on a forged signature. The customer has duties to the bank, however. If the customer's negligence contributed to the forgery or if the customer breached his duty to discover and report the forgery to the bank, the bank is not liable for those forged checks. The following case involves a situation in which the customer failed to check her monthly statement regularly.

CASE 12.3

Supreme Court, Appellate Division, Second Department, 1995
216 A.D.2d 536, 628
N.Y.S.2d 804

MANSI v. GAINES & STERLING NATIONAL BANK & TRUST COMPANY OF NEW YORK

BACKGROUND AND FACTS Mansi, the plaintiff, alleged that substantial sums of money were removed from her accounts with the Sterling National Bank & Trust Company of New York (Sterling). These withdrawals were accomplished by a fraudulent power of attorney and by forged checks. Mansi sued the bank and sought compensatory damages, punitive damages, and attorneys' fees. Mansi submitted an affidavit from a handwriting expert stating that the signatures on eighteen checks were apparently forgeries.

Sterling acknowledged that it honored the eighteen checks but claimed that, pursuant to the bank's business practices, nine of those checks and the respective account statements had been forwarded to Mansi more than one year before she filed the lawsuit. With respect to the remaining nine checks, Sterling asserted that Mansi's claims were barred by UCC 4-406 because Mansi failed to inform Sterling about the nine checks until thirty days had passed.

Sterling noted that at a deposition Mansi stated that she did not review her monthly bank statements. She acknowledged in her answer to interrogatories that she had failed to examine canceled check copies for more than one year. Sterling submitted evidence that its practice was to check the signature on every check filed against the customer's signature card. Portions of the affidavit from Mansi's handwriting expert worked against her when the expert stated that the checks in question bore signatures that were apparently "written by another person who attempted to simulate her signature" and thus were not obvious forgeries.

Judges SULLIVAN, PIZZUTO, SANTUCCI, and GOLDSTEIN

. . . .

Although the evidence in the record indicated that the appellant honored 18 checks which may have been forged, liability with respect to nine of those checks was barred by UCC 4-406(4) since the plaintiff did not report the alleged fraud within one year after those checks and the bank statements with respect thereto were made available to her.

With respect to the remaining nine checks, liability was barred by UCC 4-406(2)(b) since it was established that the plaintiff failed to exercise reasonable care to examine her bank statements and the plaintiff failed to submit any evidence that the appellant failed to exercise ordinary care in paying the items.

DECISION AND REMEDY Mansi lost her lawsuit because she failed to review her bank statements for more than one year. She might have been able to recover if she could have proven the bank to be negligent. In this case she was unable to do so.

CRITICAL THINKING: PREVENTIVE LAW What steps should a business take to prevent this problem?

The Impostor Rule, the Fictitious Payee Rule, and the Dishonest Employee Rule. The *impostor rule*, the *fictitious payee rule*, and the *dishonest employee rule* deal with basic theft using a check. The theft can be carried out in three different ways. The following three examples illustrate these. The problem is to determine who bears the burden of loss created by the theft.

Impostor Rule. The **impostor rule** involves a theft by an impostor. Sanchez works as a consultant for ABC

Distributing Company, but it does not pay her immediately for the work she performed. Ivana Imp goes to ABC Distributing Company and represents herself to be Sanchez. ABC Distributing Company issues a check to Ivana Imp made out to Sanchez. She indorses the check by forging Sanchez's name and deposits the check into her own bank account. Shortly thereafter, Ivana Imp withdraws cash from her account and disappears.

Fictitious Payee Rule. A **fictitious payee rule** involves a theft by an employee who creates a fictitious payee. In one scenario, Fred Fact, an employee, has the authority to make and sign his employer's checks. Fred Fact makes checks out to a fictitious payee, endorses the checks, and deposits them into his own account.

In a second scenario, Fred Fact lacks the authority to sign checks because Fred Fact's employer signs the checks. Fred Fact again makes out the checks to a fictitious payee. If, while he is signing checks, the employer asks about the fictitious payee, Fred Fact tells a good story about the payee's being either an employee or a business with which the employer deals. Again, Fred Fact deposits these checks into his own account.

Dishonest Employee Rule. The **dishonest employee rule** involves a theft by an employee working in the employer's business operations. For example, Dirk Dishonest works in business operations and has the authority to indorse negotiable instruments, to process instruments for bookkeeping purposes, to prepare and process instruments for issue in the employer's name, and to perform other acts on his employer's behalf. Dirk Dishonest indorses his employer's signature on a check made payable to the employer. Instead of depositing the check into the employer's account, he deposits the check into his own account.

Discussion of the Three Rules. In the business world, these three wrongdoers, Ivana Imp, Fred Fact, and Dirk Dishonest, have harmed others and are ultimately liable under the law. In many cases, by the time these people are identified, they are either long gone or under arrest. More important, however, these people often have no money to repay the victims.

These three scams are operated similarly. The wrongdoer cashes the checks or deposits them in his or her bank account. Only the manner in which the check is obtained differs. Once deposited, the check is sent through the banking system until the drawee bank finally pays it. The problem becomes who will bear the burden of the loss.

Revised Article 3 of the UCC states that the forged signature is as effective as the valid signature of the drawer, payee, or indorser. The bank, which in good faith paid the instrument, is not liable. In other words, the forged signature is binding on the drawer. The bank that cashes the check is not liable to pay a second time.

In the impostor theft, ABC Distributing was the drawer and, through its negligence, contributed to the forged indorser's signature. ABC Distributing could have verified that Ivana Imp either was Sanchez or had the authority to act on behalf of Sanchez. Even so, Ivana Imp victimized ABC Distributing. The innocent parties are the drawer, ABC Distributing, and the bank that paid the check. ABC Distributing, even though a victim, had the best opportunity to prevent the fraud. If the bank paid the check in good faith, the bank will not be liable. In the end, ABC Distributing paid on the check to Ivana Imp and also must pay Sanchez, to whom it still owes money [UCC 3-404].

In the case of the fictitious payee theft, the two innocent parties are the employer and the bank. The employer, even though a victim, should know its employees and creditors and should have verified Fred Fact's representations. The rule is that the forged indorsement is effective as the payee's indorsement. The bank paid the check in good faith and will not be liable. In the end, the employer paid on a check made out to a nonexistent party [UCC 3-404].

In the dishonest employee theft, the employer trusted the employee and is responsible for the employee's dishonest actions. The rule is that the forged indorsement is effective as the indorsement of the payee (employer). The bank paid the check in good faith and is not liable. In the end, the employer must bear the loss [UCC 3-405].

These simple rules have a major exception. Under revised Article 3, the comparative negligence rule may apply when a bank pays on a check with a forged signature. If the bank fails to exercise ordinary care in paying the check that results in a loss, the loss is allocated between the drawer, payee, or indorser, who are each partially at fault, and the bank that is also negligent.

Courts decide to apply the comparative negligence rule on a case-by-case basis. In any of the three previously discussed cases, if the bank failed to exercise ordinary care in paying the check and that failure contributed to the loss, ABC Distributing or either employer could assert comparative negligence against the bank. If the bank is at fault, it will have to pay part or all of the loss.

Electronic Funds Transfer Systems

The present basis of the payment-collection process is the check. Banks, however, are finding these billions of pieces of paper increasingly difficult to cope with.

Electronic funds transfer (EFT)[1] systems assist banks by removing the mountains of paperwork formerly necessary to transfer money. The following systems are different ways that funds are transferred electronically.

1. *Automated Teller Machines (ATMs)* Located conveniently in a variety of locations and connected online to the bank's computers, these machines receive payments on loans, receive deposits for or dispense cash from checking or savings accounts, and make credit card advances.

2. *Point-of-Sale Systems* Located in the merchant's store and connected online to the bank's computers, a point-of-sale system immediately debits the customer's checking account and transfers the funds to the merchant's account.

3. *Automatic Payments and Direct Deposits* Advance authorization allows regular electronic fund transfers from an account (for the automatic payment of bills) or into an account (for direct deposit, such as an automatic payroll deposit).

4. *Telecommunications Systems* A customer can order, by computer or telephone, money transfers to and from his or her accounts or for bill payment.

5. *Automatic Clearinghouses* Clearinghouses record customer entries in the form of electronic signals, eliminating check use. Businesspeople use clearinghouses for recurrent payments, such as payroll, Social Security, or pension funds.

EFT technology, however, has created consumer concerns. With the speed of the transmissions, issuing stop-payment orders becomes difficult. Precisely because transmissions are electronic, fewer paper records are available. Electronic systems allow more opportunities for an unauthorized person to tamper

---

[1]The terms *electronic funds transfer* (EFT) and *electronic transfer of funds* (ETF) are used interchangeably in business and government.

---

with an account, with a resulting decrease in privacy. The time between the writing of a check and its deduction from an account (the *float time*) is lost.

A Bank's Liability in EFTs. Federal statutes, such as the Electronic Fund Transfer Act (EFTA), govern electronic funds transfers made by customers. The information concerning the consumer's rights under federal law must be given to every customer who opens an EFT account.

Banks provide a monthly statement for every month in which a customer electronically transfers funds. Otherwise, statements are provided every quarter. The statement specifies the amount and date of the transfer, the names of the retailers involved, the location or identification of the terminal, the fees, and an address and telephone number for inquiries and error notices. Receipts are provided for transactions made using computer terminals, but banks are not obliged to receipts for telephone transfers. The customer has the duty to reconcile his receipts against the statements.

Article 4A. Banks, other financial institutions, and the federal government electronically transfer between $1 billion and $2 trillion on any given day. The UCC, Article 4A, Funds Transfers, sets out a comprehensive scheme that covers the bank's relationship with the fund's originator and with the payee. Typically, the originator sends money via electronic transfer through the bank to the customer (payee). A payment order is sent that debits the money from the originator's account and credits it into the payee's account. Most states have adopted Article 4A.

Transfer of Funds by the Federal Government

The federal government has a financial interest in making electronic funds transfers operate efficiently. In the past, the U.S. Treasury issued millions of checks annually to pay government debts (accounts payable) and it also received millions of checks from those who owed debts to the United States (accounts receivable). The government has converted a significant portion of these transactions from manual transfers to electronic ones.

The Department of Treasury issued rules concerning the electronic payment and collection of funds in compliance with the Debt Collection Improvement Act (DCIA) of 1996. This initiative is known as "Electronic Funds Transfer" or "EFT '99." The initiative's first goal is to convert all federal government payments to electronic form.

Federal payment recipients, such as those receiving Social Security, who have an account at a financial institution are mandated to participate. When filing an application for the federal payment, the recipient must fill out a direct deposit form. The Treasury Department sends these payments electronically. The DCIA includes vendors, Medicare recipients, welfare recipients, and veterans.

Recipients without an account at a financial institution and who would face financial hardship if payments were received electronically are eligible for a waiver receipt of paper checks. For those people without a regular bank account who certify that they have physical disabilities or confront geographic barriers (such as living overseas in a remote area), the payments are transmitted electronically to special accounts, electronic transfer accounts, that permit ATM and point-of-sale access. The agency issuing the payment has the discretion to issue waivers, such as in the case of certain one-time payments, or if the recipient is residing in a foreign country.

Any business that pays more than $20,000 in employment taxes is required to file its payment electronically to the Internal Revenue Service or face a 10 percent penalty.

The government cited several reasons for phasing out checks in favor of electronic payments. First, electronic payments are safer, faster, easier, and less expensive to process than those made by paper check. Paper checks are easily lost, stolen, damaged, or delayed. Second, each year, individuals, businesses, and the government were losing an estimated $65 million dollars as a result of forgery, theft, and counterfeiting of government checks.

Third, problems with electronic payments can be resolved quickly. For example, a lost or stolen paper check can take two weeks to replace, while an electronic transfer problem can be traced and corrected within a single day. Fourth, electronic payments save the federal government more than $100 million a year in processing costs and postage fees. Electronic payments cost the U.S. Treasury less than two cents, compared with the average cost of forty-three cents per paper check. More information about the electronic funds transfer rule is available on the Internet.[2]

CYBERLAW

Electronic Checks

Consumers order merchandise using electronic checks. This type of payment works in several ways as seen with Artiste Login.

Artiste Login. The customer, Artiste Login Products, Inc., can create an account with an online electronic check business, Virtual Monies. Instead of a signature that authenticates a paper check, Artiste and Virtual Monies agree that the verification is Artiste's e-mail address. Artiste has created an account on which it may draw.

Artiste needs to purchase office supplies. Carlo is the person responsible for purchasing these supplies. After searching the Web, he finds what is needed with an online merchant. After filling out the online purchase order, Carlo also supplies the merchant with the account number with Virtual. The merchant forwards the essential information to Virtual, including the account number, the dollar amount, and the date and time of the purchase. Virtual sends an e-mail to Artiste to confirm the purchase. Artiste must respond before the purchase can be completed. Once Artiste replies, Virtual forwards an electronic check to the office supply merchant. The merchant receives the check, which is printed on a laser printer equipped with magnetic toner that will capture the bank account number and routing information on the check, dollar amount, date and time, and the check serial number. The check can be deposited in the same manner as a paper check. Notice that no encryption mechanism was used because the verification was the e-mail.

In another variation, Artiste creates an account with a merchant. Artiste sends a copy of an Artiste check to the merchant who takes all the pertinent information and returns the void check to Artiste. The

[2]See the U.S. Department of Treasury's Web site under "Regulations and Policy" at http://www.fms.treas.gov/eft.

merchant now has an electronic copy of the customer's check. When the customer places an order, the merchant must e-mail Artiste a "check stub." Artiste must reply to the e-mail authorizing the order. The merchant takes the check information, the transaction amount, and initiates an Automated Clearing House (ACH) debit. The debit is processed electronically through the ACH Network. Artiste's bank statement contains all the information from the electronic check, just as if it were a paper check.

The **Electronic Payment Association (NACHA)**[3] is a not-for-profit trade association. Some of its activities include developing operating rules and business practices for the Automated Clearing House Network,[4] and facilitating the adoption of electronic payments for e-commerce, electronic bill payment and presentment (EBPP), financial electronic data interchange (EDI), international payments, electronic checks, electronic benefits transfer (EBT), and student lending. NACHA represents more than 12,000 financial institutions and more than 600 members in its seven industry councils and corporate affiliate membership program. The ACH Network serves 20,000 financial institutions, 2.5 million businesses, and 100 million people.

The Board of Governors of the Federal Reserve System[5] is removing barriers to the development of electronic check presentment. These efforts include reducing legal barriers to the electronic collection or return of checks, while protecting consumers who use paper checks. The board is developing and implementing technical standards for the exchange of electronic checks and for check imaging. The Federal Reserve is partnering with the banking industry to encourage businesses to use and accept electronic checks.

InfoTrac Research Activity

Search for articles about electronic checks on InfoTrac. Review four articles and write a summary of these articles.

[3]Electronic Payment Association's Web page is http://www.nacha.org.
[4]Automated Clearing House information is available at http://www.fms.treas.gov/ach/index.html.
[5]The Board of Governors of the Federal Reserve System's Web page is http://www.federalreserve.gov.

Secured Transactions

Business today relies heavily on *secured transactions*, also called *liens*, which are business arrangements that secure repayments of loans. Secured transactions date back to Roman times (753 B.C. to 476 A.D.) and are nearly as old as negotiable instruments. Even though the concept dates from ancient times, secured transactions are as basic to modern business practice as the concept of credit.

The provisions covering secured financing are found in the revised Article 9 of the UCC, which most states have adopted. Revised Article 9 applies to any transaction that intends to create a security interest in personal property. Transactions involving real property are excluded [UCC 9-109]. Exhibit 12–6 shows a sample security agreement.

Creating a Security Interest

Few purchasers (manufacturers, wholesalers, retailers, or consumers) have the resources to purchase goods or real property with currency. These purchasers need to borrow the money. Creditors, however, rarely lend money to debtors based solely on promises to repay the debt. Creditors need to minimize their risk of loss from nonpayment. A lender has two major concerns should the debtor default on the obligation. First, the creditor will want the debt to be satisfied from specific property (collateral) of the debtor. Second, the creditor will want its secured position in the property to have priority over other creditors' and purchasers' claims to that specific collateral (property).

A secured transaction involves two steps. In the first step, the creditor loans money to the debtor. The debtor and the creditor generally sign a contract or negotiable instrument in which the debtor agrees to repay the money. Although this step is not the secured transaction, it is the fundamental step, because a secured transaction must be created to secure repayment of an underlying debt as documented by a contract or a negotiable instrument.

If the debtor fails to make payments on the loan, the creditor needs to be able to repossess the debtor's item that secures the loan. That is the second step, which entails the security agreement, in which the debtor promises in writing to give up her specific property (personal or real) to the creditor if the debtor

Exhibit 12–6   A Sample Security Agreement

SECURITY AGREEMENT

June 30, 2004

Date

William M. Smith	**1306 37th Street**	**Des Moines**	**Polk**	**Iowa**
Name	No. and Street	City	County	State

(hereinafter called "Debtor") hereby grants to   **Janet Johnson Appliance Corporation**

706 Grand Avenue		**Des Moines**	**Polk**	**Iowa**
No. and Street		City	County	State

(hereinafter called "Secured Party") a security interest in the following property (hereinafter called the "Collateral"):

One 2004 Sony 42-inch plasma screen television set, Serial No. AZ22478

to secure payment and performance of obligations identified or set out as follows (hereinafter called the "Obligations")

$50.00 per month for the next 60 months to be paid on the first day of every month

beginning on the first day of August, 2004.

Default in payment or performance of any of the Obligations or default under any agreement evidencing any of the Obligations is a default under this agreement. Upon such default Secured Party may declare all Obligations immediately due and payable and shall have the remedies of a Secured Party under the Iowa Uniform Commercial Code.
Signed in triplicate.

William M. Smith
Debtor

Janet Johnson Appliance Corporation   **SECURED PARTY**

By *Janet Johnson, President*

---

fails to repay the debt. This written promise forms the secured transaction (agreement). If the debtor defaults on the loan (fails to make an agreed payment), the creditor can repossess and sell the debtor's property, using the proceeds to reduce the debt's balance.

For a creditor to become a secured party, the creditor must be provided by the debtor with a security interest in the debtor's collateral. A creditor must meet three requirements to have an enforceable security interest.

First, unless the creditor has possession of the collateral, the creditor must have a written security agreement signed by the debtor. The security agreement must describe the collateral reasonably so that it can be identified. A description of collateral as "all the debtor's assets" or "all the debtor's personal property" does not reasonably identify the collateral [UCC 9-

108].[6] The security agreement must be in written form and signed and authenticated by the debtor. Authentication includes signing, executing a symbol, or using some type of electronic encryption method that indicates that the debtor desires to be bound [UCC 9-102(a)(7)].

Second, the creditor must have provided something of value to the debtor (as opposed to a gift). Normally, the value provided by the creditor is in the form of a direct loan or involves a commitment to sell goods on credit.

Third, the debtor must have rights in the property used as collateral; that is, the debtor must have some ownership interest or right to obtain possession of that

[6]A financing statement may state that it "covers all assets or all personal property" [UCC 9-504].

property. The debtor's rights can represent either a current or a future legal interest in the collateral. For example, a retail seller-debtor can provide a secured creditor a security interest, not only in existing inventory owned by the retailer, but also in future inventory that the retailer will acquire.

Once these requirements are met, the creditor's rights are said to "attach to" the collateral. Attachment means that the creditor has an enforceable security interest against the debtor. The attachment of the security interest in the collateral establishes the rights and liabilities of the debtor and creditor with respect to the collateral [UCC 9-203].

Perfection

Even though the creditor's security interest has attached to the debtor's property, the secured creditor must take steps to protect its claim to the collateral over claims that third parties may have to the same property. The third parties may be other secured creditors, general creditors, trustees in bankruptcy, or purchasers of the collateral. The procedures to protect the creditor's rights are called *perfection*.

Perfection can be achieved through one of three ways. The first method is attachment. When a purchase-money security interest agreement is used in the purchase of consumer goods (goods used or bought primarily for personal, family, or household purposes), perfection occurs automatically upon creation of the security interest without a filing and without the secured party's taking possession. A purchase-money security interest agreement secures payment of the unpaid balance of the purchase price. The agreement is provided to the creditor by the consumer when he or she purchases consumer goods.

Other forms of collateral may be perfected only by an attachment. For example, a person dies owing a hospital for hospital care. The person's heir who will inherit the estate makes an assignment to the hospital. This assignment is a perfected security interest without filing.

The second method occurs when a secured party's possession of a debtor's collateral is notice of a possible lien and, thus, perfection. For example, a deposit at a financial institution like a certificate of deposit can only be perfected by possession [UCC 9-312].

The third method is the most common method of perfecting a lien against real property or goods. The secured party files the relevant document with the appropriate government office.

In the sale of goods, the most common document is called a *financing statement* [UCC 9-310]. A creditor files a financing statement on a UCC-1 form. A **financing statement** is a document signed by the debtor that briefly describes property used as collateral in a security agreement. This document does not create the security interest, but is filed in a public office to notify the public that a security interest exists in the described personal property. Under prior law, the general rule required the financing statement to be filed where the collateral was located. Revised Article 9 requires that it be recorded in the state of an individual's residence. If there is only one place of business, the financing statement should be recorded in that state. The major change affects a debtor that does business in several locations. In that situation, the creditor must record the financing statement in the state where the business was created, such as the place of incorporation.

Creditors often clash with others as to which creditor has first rights. The priority of lien against other lien holders is subject to state law. As a general rule, the party that perfects its lien has first priority rights to the collateral. One type of purchaser, however, prevails regardless of a secured party's perfection and despite the fact that the purchaser knows of the secured party's interest at the time of purchase. This type of purchaser is anyone who purchases goods in the ordinary course of business [UCC 9-320(A)].

For example, Last Chance Bank has a perfected security interest in the inventory of Gary's retail TV store. Joan purchases a TV set from Gary that is subject to Last Chance Bank's perfected security interest. Joan, as a purchaser, takes the TV set free of Last Chance Bank's security interest (if Gary goes into default, Last Chance Bank cannot repossess the TV from Joan), even if Joan knew of the loan at the time of sale.

In the following case, the court was confronted with the issue of whether a buyer of a motor home, which was sold under consignment, could defeat the interest of a prior secured party. A **consignment** occurs when an owner of goods turns them over to a person in the business of selling this type of goods and who agrees to sell the goods in the ordinary course of business. The consignee does not take title to the goods because the original owner (consignor) retains title.

CASE 12.4

Supreme Court of
Oregon, 1997
325 Or. 81, 934 P.2d 421

SCHULTZ v. BANK OF THE WEST, C.B.C.

BACKGROUND AND FACTS In 1987, defendants (the Muirs) bought a motor home. In 1988, the Muirs borrowed money from Bank of the West (Bank), which took a secured interest (lien) in the motor home. The Bank also perfected its right by filing the lien in the appropriate government office.

Gateleys' Fairway Motors (Gateleys) was in the business of selling motor homes. In 1992, the Muirs contracted with Gateleys to sell the motor home on consignment. Gateleys sold the motor home to plaintiffs, the Schultzes.

Gateleys failed to notify the Schultzes that the motor home was being sold on consignment or that a security interest was attached to it. After Gateleys failed to pay any of the sale money to the Muirs, Gateleys filed for bankruptcy.

After learning of the Bank's security interest, the Schultzes brought this action, seeking a declaration that they owned the motor home free of the security interest. The trial court granted summary judgment in plaintiffs' favor. The Bank appealed, and the Oregon Court of Appeals reversed the trial court, holding that the Bank's security interest remained in force. The Oregon Supreme Court accepted review of the case.

Justice GILLETTE

. . . .

Whether or not a buyer takes goods free of a prior perfected security interest is governed by Article 9 of the Uniform Commercial Code (the UCC). The specific question for decision here is whether plaintiffs are entitled to the special protection afforded to consumers by UCC section 9-307 (codified as ORS 79.3070(1)). That section provides in part:

> "*A buyer in ordinary course of business as defined in ORS 71.2010(9) . . . takes free of a security interest created by the seller even though the security interest is perfected. . . .*"

The cross-referenced section, ORS 71.2010(9), defines "buyer in ordinary course." It provides:

> "'*Buyer in ordinary course of business' means a person who in good faith and without knowledge that the sale to the person is in violation of the ownership rights or security interest of a third party in the goods buys in ordinary course from a person in the business of selling goods of that kind but does not include a pawnbroker.*"

If plaintiffs can show that they come within the terms of ORS 79.3070(1), they own the motor home free of the Bank's security interest. To do so, the parties here agree that plaintiffs must show two things: (1) They were a "buyer in ordinary course" when they bought the motor home from Gateleys, and (2) the seller of the motor home was the one who created the security interest.

. . . .

1. Were plaintiffs buyers in the ordinary course of business?

As always, in construing an Oregon statute, this court's task is to discern the intent of the legislature. In doing so, this court looks first to the text and context of the statute. Here, the relevant text from ORS 71.2010(9) states that a buyer in ordinary course "*buys . . . from a person* in the business of selling goods of that kind." (Emphasis added.) Clearly, the plaintiffs bought from Gateleys, which was in the business of selling goods of that kind. But does the text require that the "person in the business of selling goods" *have title* to the specific goods that the buyer buys, *i.e.,* be the "seller" of the goods. This inquiry is important, because Gateleys disposed of the Muirs' motor home on consignment—it did not have title.

The text does not require that the "person" from whom the goods are purchased have title. This is clear, first, from the text itself. Use of the word, "person," instead of "seller" in a law as carefully crafted as the UCC is a conscious choice. That choice recognizes that there will be those who hold out goods for sale who do not have title, e.g., consignees such as Gateleys, in circumstances in which the stability of the marketplace would be undermined if good faith purchases from those parties were not valid. This point is made even more clear by the textual exclusion of "pawnbroker"—a special kind of consignee—from the definition. Finally, the text of ORS 71.2010(9) recognizes that a sale to a buyer in ordinary course may be "in violation of the ownership rights . . . of a third party." Any ownership rights in a third party would mean that the "person in the business" did not have title to the goods. Thus, the text of ORS 71.2010(9) indicates that "person" does not mean "seller."

. . . .

2. Was the security interest created by the seller?

We now turn to ORS 79.3070(1). It provides that "[a] buyer in ordinary course of business . . . takes free of a security interest created by the seller even though the security interest is perfected and even though the buyer knows of its existence." Here, the Muirs created the security interest, but plaintiffs' dealings were with Gateleys. In order to prevail, plaintiffs must show that, in spite of the fact that they dealt with Gateleys, the Muirs were "the seller" for the purposes of this provision. In our view, that issue turns on whether the seller is the party whose title to the goods was transferred.

On its face, the text is not decisive, because it does not say whether, for the purpose of the provision, the concept of "seller" is limited to the party with legal title to the goods or whether, instead, the seller is simply the party that physically performs the exchange of goods for money with the buyer. Context, however, answers the question. As we have noted elsewhere, ORS 72.1060(1) provides that "[a] 'sale' consists in the passing of title from the seller to the buyer for a price." Nothing in ORS 79.3070(1) suggests that this definition, which specifically states that it is the seller who transfers title, is inapplicable. We hold that "seller," as that term is used in ORS 79.3070(1), refers to the legal owner of the goods purchased by a buyer in ordinary course. Gateleys, with whom plaintiffs dealt, did not itself transfer title to the goods. Thus, it was not the "seller," for the purposes of ORS 79.3070(1). The true seller of the motor home was the party that ultimately parted with title—the Muirs. And, because the Muirs created the security interest, plaintiffs took the motor home free of the Bank's security interest.

. . . .

DECISION AND REMEDY The Oregon Supreme Court found that a person may obtain title to goods that are sold on consignment even though the title owner is not in the business of selling such goods. Because the consignee was in the business of selling the goods, UCC 9-320 is satisfied, and the buyer in the ordinary course of business will obtain clear title to the goods.

CRITICAL THINKING: LEGAL ANALYSIS Two justices drafted a strong dissent to the decision. They basically argued that the title holder was not in the business of selling motor homes. Therefore, UCC 9-320 was not applicable. Do you agree with the majority opinion or with the two dissenters and why?

Default

Article 9 of the UCC defines the rights, duties, and remedies in case a debtor defaults on a secured loan. When a debtor defaults, a secured creditor can protect its claim to the collateral by enforcing its security interest by a court judgment, by foreclosure, or by any other available judicial process [UCC 9-609].

Secured Party's Remedies. A secured party's remedies are divided into two categories. First, a secured creditor can forgo its rights in the security interest and proceed to a court judgment on the debt. Once the secured party has the judgment for the amount of damages, the judgment can be used to take other assets of the debtor to satisfy the judgment debt. This procedure is used when the secured collateral's value has been greatly reduced below the debt amount, such as a wrecked automobile, and the debtor has other assets available to satisfy the debt.

Second, a secured creditor can take possession, called **repossession**, of the collateral covered by the security agreement [UCC 9-609]. On repossession, the secured party can retain the collateral covered by the security agreement for partial or complete satisfaction of the debt [UCC 9-620] or can resell the goods and apply the proceeds toward the debt. The sale must be conducted in a commercially reasonable manner [UCC 9-610].

The creditor's rights and remedies under the UCC are cumulative. When a secured creditor is unsuccessful in enforcing its rights by one method, it can pursue another method. The UCC does not require the secured creditor to choose between remedies, that is, between a lawsuit to obtain a judgment or repossession of the collateral.

The secured party has the right to take peaceful possession of the collateral on default. As long as no breach of the peace occurs, the secured party can simply repossess the collateral. Otherwise, the secured party must use the judicial process [UCC 9-609].

The definition of a breach of the peace is of prime importance to both parties, for such an act can open the secured party (the party repossessing) to lawsuit for tort liability. The UCC fails to define breach of the peace, so the parties must look to the state laws to determine it.

In most states, the secured party must obtain the collateral without breaking and entering, committing assault or battery, or trespassing. Generally, the creditor or the creditor's agent must receive permission to enter a debtor's home, garage, or place of business. For example, if an automobile is the collateral on a defaulted loan and the repossessing party walks onto the debtor's premises, proceeds up the driveway, enters the vehicle without entering the garage, and drives off, this probably will not amount to a breach of the peace. In some states, however, an action for

---

LEGAL HIGHLIGHT

Do I Still Owe on the Car?

People often overextend themselves financially. For example, Katie had an executive position with a large corporation, earning $60,000 per year. She purchased a new car for $40,000. After making a $10,000 down payment, she took a seven-year loan for the remaining $30,000. Four years later, she is downsized out of a job with several hundred other managers. Katie still owes $10,000 on the loan. Unable to meet the loan payments, she decides to return the car to the bank.

If the bank is able to sell the car for $10,000 plus costs of the resale, Katie owes nothing. If the bank sells it for more, she receives the surplus since she is the car owner. Unfortunately, banks often sell cars in this type of situation for less than the amount still owed to the bank. If the bank can obtain $4,000, it can go to court to obtain a deficiency judgment (that is, a judgment for the amount still deficient for the contract to be paid in full) for $6,000.

Returning the car to the bank fails to relieve Katie of her bank debt. If Katie is unable to repay the remaining $6,000, she may be forced to go to bankruptcy court to have her debts forgiven.

wrongful trespass could be the debtor's basis for filing a breach-of-the-peace lawsuit. Thus, most car repossessions occur when the car is parked on a street or in a parking lot.

Proceeds from the Disposition of Collateral. If the secured party sells the collateral on the debtor's default, proceeds from the collateral sale are applied in the following order. First, the creditor's reasonable expenses stemming from the retaking, holding, or sale preparation are paid. These expenses can include reasonable attorneys' fees and legal expenses. Second, the balance of the debt owed to the secured party is satisfied.

Third, written demands for subordinate security interests that were received prior to the completion of distribution of the proceeds are paid. Subordinate security interests are for loans that are second or third liens on the property. Second, third, or even fourth liens are so named for the position they occupy after the first (senior) lien. When the collateral is sold, the first lien holder is paid first. If any money is left, the second lien holder is paid. Each subordinate lien holder is paid in turn as long as the money lasts [UCC 9-615].

For example, Bill buys an expensive antique automobile—one that is known to appreciate in value—and signs a security agreement. He has the car loan nearly paid, but borrows more money by using the equity in the car as collateral for another loan from Bank B to start a small business. Unfortunately, the business fails, and Bill defaults on the original car loan and on the second (business) loan. When the creditor repossesses the car and sells it, first the costs of the whole process of repossession are paid. Next the original loan balance is paid. Finally, the second (business) loan balance from Bank B is paid, assuming that the business loan secured party (Bank B) gave written notice [UCC 9-615].

Any surplus is paid to the debtor. If the loan balances are not paid, the creditor may go to court and obtain a deficiency judgment (a judgment for the amount still deficient to have the contract paid in full).

Termination

When a debtor pays a debt, the secured party must send a **termination statement** to the debtor. If the secured party filed a lien, it must file the termination statement in the same place at which the original financing statement was filed.

The termination statement shows that the debt has been paid. If the secured party fails to file a termination statement at the proper time, the secured party may be liable to the debtor for $500. Additionally, the secured party is liable for any loss caused to the debtor for its failure to file the appropriate release-of-debt documents [UCC 9-625].

International Consideration

Selling Overseas: How Do You Get Your Money?

The United States has signed the **United Nations Convention on International Bills of Exchange and Promissory Notes**. Basically, the convention covers both orders to pay and promises to pay. Bills of exchange were developed during the Middle Ages. The UCC, Article 3, Negotiable Instruments, does not use the term *bill of exchange*; it instead uses the term *draft*. Bills of exchange and bills of lading are commonly used in international trade.

Common carriers, such as ocean vessels, airline companies, and railroad businesses, use bills of lading to keep track of goods being shipped. The shipping company issues a multipart bill of lading. One part stays with the goods and another part is turned over to the seller. Whoever controls the seller's copy of the bill of lading controls the goods. The seller's bill of lading is surrendered to the transport company before the buyer takes possession of these goods. How does the buyer obtain possession of the seller's bill of lading?

A bill of exchange is essentially like a check, but it is not drawn on a bank. Instead, a bill of exchange uses financial institutions as the payee and not as the drawee like on checks. The seller draws it on the buyer. The drawer (seller) signs the bill of exchange ordering the drawee (buyer) to pay the money to the payee (usually a financial institution). The seller sends the seller's copy of the bill of lading and the bill of exchange to its financial institution, typically a bank. The seller's bank forwards the documents to the buyer's bank, which notifies the buyer that the documents are available to be picked up. The buyer accepts (pays for) the bill of exchange and in return receives the bill of lading. The buyer then can obtain possession of the goods from the transportation company. The buyer's bank sends the money, minus a service fee, to the seller's bank.

The UN convention provides unified rules on this complex topic. Whereas the Western world has had centuries of experience in this field, many developing countries have not. This convention provides guidance and ensures uniformity for the creation, interpretation, and performance of bills of exchange and promissory notes.

Normally, a letter of credit that is issued by a financial institution is associated with the transaction just described. Letters of credit will be discussed in more detail in Chapter 13. The rules covering letters of credit are based on treaties. The International Chamber of Commerce originally adopted the **Uniform Customs and Practices for Documentary Credits (UCP)** in the 1930s. The UCP has since been modified to reflect changes in business. The UCP has many provisions involving letters of credit.

PRACTICAL TIPS

The Problem with Postdating a Check

On Wednesday, Sally sees an advertisement to join a health club. The advertisement states "Today only for one-half price." After work she stops by to check out the club. A salesperson shows her all the club features and reminds her of the one-half price sale. Payday is Monday, five days away, but Sally wants to join at the bargain rate. The salesperson agrees to accept a postdated check and assures Sally that the check will not be deposited until Monday.

When Sally arrives home on Tuesday after work, she receives a notice from her bank that her account is overdrawn. Two minutes later, the health club calls concerning her bounced check. On Wednesday, she checks with the bank and finds that the postdated check was deposited on the previous Thursday. The health club threatens Sally with criminal action. Has Sally committed a crime?

Most people believe that postdating or antedating a check is illegal. The truth is that no date is required on a check to make it negotiable, because it is a demand instrument. Thus, to postdate or antedate a check is not illegal. The act of postdating or antedating the check becomes illegal when the drawer intends to defraud the payee by failing to have the money to cover the check in his or her account. Fraud is difficult to prove under these circumstances, however. As you may remember from Chapter 9, to prove fraud, you must prove an objective intent to deceive at the time of the act. Intent is difficult to prove with a postdated check.

In Sally's case, the district attorney will not prosecute because the date on the face of the check clearly shows that the funds would be available on Monday. If Sally can show that the money (her paycheck) was in the account on Monday, the district attorney cannot show intent to deceive.

Many payees, such as the health club, will require that a date be inserted on the check because under UCC 4-404, a check is "stale" if it is not presented to the bank for payment within six months from the check's date. Thus, after six months, the bank can refuse to pay the check in good faith. To ensure that the bank will pay the check, the payee may require that the date be filled in.

If Sally lives in a state that has adopted the revised Article 3 of the UCC, she must give the bank advance written notice that she is writing a postdated check. If she fails to give the bank written notice, it may honor the check prior to the date on the check. If she provides written notice, the bank must honor Sally's request to hold payment on the check before the date. Otherwise, the bank is liable to Sally for problems that arise.

Sally should have followed this short checklist.

Checklist

✔ *Postdated Checks* Never write a postdated check.

✔ *Oral Assurances* Never rely on the oral assurances of a salesperson. Reduce any oral assurances to writing.

Chapter Summary

Negotiable instruments serve two purposes: substituting for currency and serving as a credit device. Two major types of negotiable instruments are promises to pay, which are two-party instruments, and orders to pay, which are three-party instruments. The two-party instruments have a maker who signs and issues an instrument with a promise to pay a certain sum of money to a payee. The three-party instruments have a drawer who creates an instrument that orders the drawee to pay money to the payee.

Revised Article 3 of the UCC lists the types of negotiable instruments: promissory notes, certificates of deposit, drafts, checks, cashier's checks, teller's checks, traveler's checks, and money orders (which are checks). All of these instruments fall into one of two categories: two-party instruments or three-party instruments. For these instruments to be negotiable, they must meet four requirements. A negotiable instrument must be (1) in writing and signed by the maker or drawer, (2) an unconditional promise or order to pay a fixed amount of money, (3) payable to bearer or to order at the time it is issued, and (4) payable on demand or at a definite time.

To negotiate this type of instrument, a payee indorses (signs) on the instrument's back and delivers it to another person. The payee who signs the back becomes an indorser, and the person who receives the instrument is called the indorsee. A bearer is any person who physically possesses an instrument that either is payable to anyone without designation or is indorsed in blank.

Negotiable instruments are held by either a holder or a person who becomes a holder in due course (HDC). The holder may be the original payee or one who has taken a negotiable instrument from another person. A holder takes the negotiable instrument subject to all of the defenses that the maker or the drawer has against paying the instrument. A holder has the status of an assignee of a contract right.

An HDC has a special status, however, and is protected by the law. The only defense the maker or drawer has against paying the instrument held by an HDC is a real defense, that is, when something is wrong with the instrument itself. Defenses based on the contract cannot be used against an HDC. To become an HDC, the person must accept the instrument (1) for value, (2) in good faith, (3) without notice that the instrument is overdue or defective, (4) without notice that the instru-

ment contains an unauthorized signature or has been altered, (5) without notice of any claim to the instrument, and (6) without notice that any party has a real defense.

The Federal Trade Commission limits the rights of an HDC to have the instrument paid. In consumer transactions, every contract must carry a warning that the holder has no greater rights to be paid than the original party to the contract. One way a contract is discharged is through the doctrine of accord and satisfaction. In the past, a dispute could be settled if the debtor sent the creditor a check with a notation of "payment in full" or similar words. The creditor in the modern business world would fail to notice the notation in time to return the check uncashed to keep the dispute alive. Today, the creditor must designate a special office to which a check with such a notation must be sent. Even if a creditor fails to supply an office address, the business can refund the check's amount within ninety days of cashing it to avoid closure on settlement.

The UCC recognizes four types of indorsements: blank, special, qualified, and restrictive. Blank and special indorsers who have received consideration from the transferee make five transfer warranties.

A maker or acceptor has primary liability on an instrument. Primary liability means that this person absolutely must pay the instrument's face amount. A drawer, however, has secondary liability to pay because the drawer orders the drawee to pay. Once the drawee accepts the instrument, the drawee has primary liability. An instrument is discharged by payment, cancellation, or material alteration.

The UCC governs the relationship between a bank and its customers. The bank has a duty to pay checks drawn on a customer's account, to accept deposits, and to honor stop-payment orders. The customer must check its statements every month and check for forged signatures on checks.

Electronic funds transfer systems include ATMs, point-of-sale systems, automatic payments and direct deposits, telecommunications systems, and automatic clearinghouses. Federal laws govern many aspects of electronic funds transfers.

When a merchant extends credit or makes a loan, the merchant wants to ensure debt repayment. The merchant will have the debtor use her or his property as collateral to secure repayment of the monies owed. A secured transaction also is called a lien. The creditor has two major concerns: (1) that if the property used as collateral is sold, the amount of money raised from the sale will pay the debt; and (2) that the creditor's debt will have priority over the claims of other creditors to, and purchasers of, the collateral.

The creditor (secured party) needs to perfect its security interest to protect its claim in the collateral over other creditors' claims. Three methods of perfection are recognized: (1) attachment, (2) possession, and (3) filing documents (usually a financing statement) in the appropriate public office. If the debtor defaults on the loan payment, the secured party can ignore its interest in the property and proceed to a lawsuit for judgment. The secured party can take possession of the collateral to satisfy the debt or to resell the goods and apply the proceeds toward the debt.

The proceeds of the collateral sale are applied (1) to the reasonable expenses of selling the collateral, (2) to satisfy the debt owed to the secured party, and (3) to pay subsequent subordinate security interests if any proceeds are still on hand. Once the debt has been paid, the secured party must file a termination statement in the same public office as the original document evidencing that the security interest had been filed.

Using the World Wide Web

Negotiable instruments and secured transactions are covered by state statutes. If your state government has a Web site for statutes, you should be able to find the statutes dealing with negotiable instruments and secured transactions.

For *Web Activities*, links to Web sites mentioned in the chapter, and additional Web sites that relate to the chapter topics, go to **http://bohlman.westbuslaw.com**, click on "Internet Applications," and select Chapter 12.

Web Activities

Go to **http://bohlman.westbuslaw.com**, click on "Internet Applications," and select Chapter 12.
12–1 Enrolled Agents
12–2 Income Extensions

Key Terms

bearer
bearer paper
blank indorsement
cashier's check
certificate of deposit
   (CD)
certified check
check
collateral installment
   note
collateral note
consignment
consumer credit
   transaction
demand draft
dishonest employee rule
draft

drawee
drawer
electronic funds transfer
   (EFT)
Electronic Payment
   Association
   (NACHA)
fictitious payee rule
financing statement
holder
holder in due course
   (HDC)
impostor rule
indorsee
indorser
installment note
issue

judgment rate
lien
maker
mortgage note
negotiable
negotiable instrument
order paper
payee
payment order
perfection
personal defense
promissory note
qualified indorsement
real defense
repossession
restrictive indorsement
secured transaction

sight draft
special indorsement
spot rate
stop-payment order
termination statement
time draft
traveler's check
Uniform Customs and
   Practices for Docu-
   mentary Credits
   (UCP)
United Nations Con-
   vention on Inter-
   national Bills of
   Exchange and
   Promissory Notes

Questions and Case Problems

12–1 Negotiable Instrument The following is written by Gloria Natale on the back of an envelope: "I, Gloria Natale, promise to pay to Perry Wilson or bearer $1,000 on demand." Is this note a negotiable instrument? Please explain fully.

12–2 Check Jeff draws a check for $1,500 made payable to the order of Kelley. Jeff turns the check over to Kelley. Kelley owes her landlord $500 in rent and transfers the check to her landlord with the following indorsement: "For rent paid. [Signed] Kelley." Kelley's landlord has contracted to have Eric repair the electrical wiring in several apartments. Eric insists on immediate payment. The landlord transfers the check to Eric without indorsement. Later, in order to pay for the electrical supplies at Supply Store, Eric transfers the check with the following indorsement: "Pay to Supply Store, without recourse. [Signed] Eric." Supply sends the check to its bank indorsed "For deposit only. [Signed] Supply Store."

a. Classify each of these indorsements.

b. Was the transfer from Kelley's landlord to Eric without indorsement an assignment or a negotiation? Explain.

12–3 HDC Mansfield issues a ninety-day negotiable promissory note payable to the order of Eastwood. He leaves the note's amount blank, to be filled in by Eastwood when the price of the diamond that Mansfield plans to buy from Eastwood is determined. Mansfield orally authorizes Eastwood to fill in the blank, but the amount is not to exceed $10,000. Eastwood, without authority, fills in the note in the amount of $200,000 and thirty days later sells the note to the First National Bank for $16,000. Eastwood does not buy the diamond for Mansfield and leaves the state. First National Bank had no knowledge that the instrument was incomplete when issued or that Eastwood had no authority to complete the instrument in an amount over $10,000. Does the bank qualify as a holder in due course? If so, for what amount? Explain fully.

12–4 HDC On April 1, Jesse draws a check payable to George for $4,000 to remodel Jesse's house by June 15. George indorses the check in blank to Ronald on July 2 as payment for fireworks that George was buying from Ronald. On July 3, Ronald attempts to cash the check. The bank refuses to pay the check. Ronald tries to collect the amount of the check from Jesse. Jesse claims that his defense—that George never remodeled the house—is valid against Ronald. Ronald claims that the check must be honored because he is an HDC. Who is correct? Explain fully.

12–5 HDC A business advertises freezers, offering purchasers the incentive of the right to purchase frozen food, including meat, at substantial discounts. You visit the business and discover that the cost of the freezer is twice the cost offered by other retailers, but you can finance the freezer by signing a promissory note and security agreement. The business promises that upon signing the documents, you are entitled to purchase all the meat you need over the next year for only ninety-nine cents a pound. You decide to purchase the freezer and sign the documents. The next day, the retailer takes the note to the local bank. The bank purchases the note at a 5 percent discounted rate, which means that the bank purchases the note at 5 percent less than its face value (the principal). The bank sends you a notice that it now holds the note and that you should make your payments to it. The freezer arrives a week later and it works. When the meat arrives, however, it is spoiled. Can you stop making payments to the bank until the retailer supplies edible meat? Explain.

12.6 Dishonest Employee The plaintiff, Globe Motor Car Company, was an automobile dealership located in Fairfield, New Jersey. Globe had an agreement with First Fidelity Bank to finance Globe's inventory. Globe promised to repay the loan upon selling a motor vehicle. The office manager, John Gallo, handled most of Globe's day-to-day finances. Gallo embezzled more than $1.5 million from his employer over a three-year period. On many occasions, Gallo simply retained money paid to Globe. He purchased a vehicle for his own use instead of depositing the proceeds to pay off the bank loans owed on the cars being traded in. On other occasions, Gallo made himself and others the payees on checks signed in blank by the owner. As the embezzlement progressed, Gallo forged the owner's signature to checks payable to himself and others. To conceal his activities, Gallo removed checks made out to him from the monthly checking account statement The plaintiff claimed that the bank should reimburse all funds paid on these forgeries. [*Globe Motor Car Co. v. First Fidelity Bank*, 273 N.J. 388, 641 A.2d 1136 (1993)]

12–7 Check Money Mart Check Cashing Center, Inc., cashed a paycheck for an employee of Epicycle Corp.

Epicycle had placed a stop payment on this check because of claims it had against the employee. Was Money Mart required to verify the check's validity before cashing it? Explain. [*Money Mart Check Cashing Center, Inc. v. Epicycle Corp.*, 667 P.2d 1372 (Colo. 1983)]

12–8 Repossession Wade purchased an automobile that was financed by Ford Motor Credit Co. Wade fell behind in her monthly payments. The vehicle was repossessed from Wade's driveway at 2 A.M. by a Ford Motor Credit agent. Wade testified that she heard a car burning rubber, looked outside, and saw that her vehicle was missing. No other confrontation occurred. Wade claims that this repossession was a breach of the peace and was wrongful. She sought damages from Ford Motor Credit, whereas Ford Motor Credit sought $2,900 as a deficiency. Was this repossession wrongful? Was Ford Motor Credit entitled to a deficiency judgment? [*Wade v. Ford Motor Credit Co.*, 8 Kan. App. 2d 737, 668 P.2d 183 (1983)]

12–9 Risk Trans World Airlines, Inc. (TWA), entered into a sale and lease-back agreement with Connecticut National Bank (CNB). TWA sold ten aircraft to CNB for $312 million and then leased them back. The trans-

action's purpose serves to increase cash flow. In the contract, TWA agreed to pay back $100 million on January 31, 1991. The Persian Gulf conflict in early 1991, however, resulted in decreased air travel and increased oil prices. This curtailed TWA's cash flow, rendering TWA unable to pay the $100 million on January 31. CNB filed a lawsuit for the return of the aircraft. TWA argued that CNB should not repossess the aircraft because the Persian Gulf conflict was an intervening cause excusing TWA from its agreed performance. Who should prevail, and why? [*Connecticut National Bank v. Trans World Airlines, Inc.*, 762 F. Supp. 76 (S.D.N.Y. 1991)]

12–10 Internet The Federal Reserve Board handles the check clearing process. Go to the Federal Reserve Board's Web site at **http://www.federalreserve.gov**. On the left under "Advance Search," click on "Payment Systems." On the next page, in the middle under "Payment Services," click on "Check Services." What is an interbank check? What percentage of interbank checks make up the total amount of checks written? How many check-clearing centers does the Federal Reserve maintain?

Chapter 13

International
Business Law

The manufacturer who waits in the woods for
the world to beat a path to his door is a great
optimist. But the manufacturer who shows his
"mousetraps" to the world keeps the smoke
coming out of his chimney.

O. B. Winters, 1892–1940
American advertising man

Chapter Outline

Ethical Consideration

Monitoring Conditions of Foreign Employees

As the president of a large clothing manufacturer, you recently returned from visiting several suppliers in Asia. Some of the suppliers treated their workers well. Others, however, took unfair advantage of their employees based on your ethical standards.

In some locations, you saw young children and pregnant women performing strenuous work. These workers are paid much less than workers in the United States. Often, they are paid below the minimum wage set in their own countries. Their work generates a substandard living wage. Work hours range from twelve to fifteen hours day, seven days a week. Employers lock the workplace doors during working hours, so that if a fire were to break out, the workers would be trapped inside. The plants were filthy and inadequately ventilated. The smell of strong dyes and other pungent odors permeated the air.

You discuss the situation with upper-level management at your firm. Some of the managers agree that the conditions are terrible. They argue that the company needs to monitor the suppliers more closely. The company, however, needs to keep the product cost down to remain competitive in the global marketplace. Other managers argue that each nation must develop its own standards for employment protection, minimum wage, and child labor laws.

Should you try to monitor the working conditions of your suppliers or simply look for the cheapest manufacturing costs for your products? Use the ethical model presented in Chapter 2 and reprinted on the inside front cover to develop your answer.

Introduction

Since World War II, businesses have become increasingly multinational. Commonly, U.S. businesses have investments or manufacturing plants in various foreign countries and foreign countries have operations in the United States. Because the exchange of goods, services, and ideas on a global level is common, the businessperson must have some familiarity with the laws pertaining to international business transactions.

International law consists of a body of laws that legally bind otherwise independent nations. No sovereign nation can be compelled against its will to obey an external law. Nations, however, can and do voluntarily agree to be governed in certain respects by international law to facilitate international trade and commerce. A nation's laws fundamentally control the relationship between its international business activities (conducted within its borders or conducted by the nation's businesses outside its borders) and the nation's international agreements.

This chapter explores the sources of the international business laws, the sources of the U.S. international business laws, the agencies responsible for implementing these laws, the statutes affecting international businesses, and international business transactions. The *International Considerations* sections at the end of each chapter (except this one) provide further information.

Artiste Login. Carlo and Carlotta are internationally known artists, each in his or her own right. They import materials that are not readily available in the United States. Over the years, they have developed part of their business as an import business that sells the materials to other artists. Another part of their business is the exporting of their art and sculptures. They need to know more about exporting and importing, including the changes in the law since 2001.

Sources of International Law

International, regional, and national laws regulate businesses engaged in international commerce. International law has evolved in three ways: through international customs, through agreements that have the force of law, and through international organizations and conferences. Agreements are developed either by the nations themselves gathering together or by international agencies to which various nations belong.

International Customs

International customs have evolved among nations in response to their relations with one another. The

United Nations International Court of Justice defines international custom (customary law) as "evidence of a general practice accepted as law." Customary law serves as an independent form of law. This definition's application, however, is subject to challenge on a case-by-case basis. The courts must decide, for example, when a particular custom has evolved into a general practice that constitutes a law.

Agreements

Instruments used to bring about an international agreement include a *treaty* or *compact*, a *convention*, a *protocol*, or an *executive agreement*. A **treaty**, or **compact**, is a written international agreement between two or more nations, governed by international law and authorized by each nation's supreme power.

When a country is a party to multiple treaties, conflicts may arise. Under the auspices of the United Nations, the **Vienna Convention on the Law of Treaties**[1] was adopted in 1969 and became legally enforceable in 1980. The entire body of the law of treaties is codified by this convention. It covers issues such as the legal difference between treaties and other types of agreements, constitutional limitations on treaty making powers, terminology, legal designation of parties, and general rules that apply to interpreting treaties.

A **convention** is a code adopted by an international organization, such as the United Nations. The organization circulates the draft convention (or code) among the organization's members, with the hope that it will be adopted by those members.

A **protocol** is an official agreement, but it does not have the force of a treaty. The document reflects issues on which the diplomats agree.

The last important type of international agreement is the **executive agreement** into which a head of state (the executive) enters on reaching an agreement with another head of state. The creation of an executive agreement is simpler and faster than that of a treaty, which is used for more complicated problems. The U.S. Constitution fails to provide for an executive agreement, but the device has a long history in the diplomatic world.

These various types of international agreements affect international business relationships and cover a multitude of areas, such as *exporting*, *importing*, *quotas*, and *tariffs*. **Exporting** is the selling of goods manufactured in, and sent (exported) from, the domestic country to a foreign country. **Importing** is the buying of goods manufactured in a foreign country, which are then brought (imported) into the domestic country.

A **quota** limits the quantity of goods to be imported. For example, the United States at one time had a quota on the number of automobiles that could be imported from Japan. This quota was designed to protect the domestic automobile manufacturers. Other items once subject to quotas include silicon chips and high-technology electronic equipment.

A **tariff** is a tax placed on imported goods. No equivalent tax exists for the same type of domestic goods. A tariff generally is assessed on either an *ad valorem* basis or a *flat-rate* basis. An **ad valorem tariff** is based on a percentage of the value of the imported goods. A **flat-rate tariff** may be based on a unit, such as a barrel of oil. It also may be based on weight, such as a tariff assessed on each ton of material that is imported, such as steel.

International Organizations

More than 3,100 governmental international organizations exist around the world, of which 300 or more deal with economic matters. These organizations normally form as a result of an international agreement.

The organizations or agreements fall into five classifications. First, the United Nations has an array of organizations, the duties of which range from keeping the peace to addressing health concerns. The United Nations operates out of three locations. It is headquartered in New York City; the UN International Court of Justice is located at The Hague in the Netherlands; and the UN European office and several specialized agencies operate out of Geneva, Switzerland.

The second type of organization or agreement includes economic organizations or agreements, such as the World Bank,[2] the International Monetary Fund (IMF),[3] the **World Trade Organization (WTO)**,[4] and the Organization for Economic Cooperation and Development (OECD).[5] Third are the regional

---

[1]All of the entire provisions of the Vienna Convention on the Law of Treaties are available at http://www.ifs.univie.ac.at/intlaw/konterm/vrkon_en/html/doku/treaties.htm#1.0.

[2]The World Bank's Web site is at http://www.worldbank.org.

[3]Information on the International Monetary Fund can be found at http://www.imf.org.

[4]The home page for the World Trade Organization is http://www.wto.org.

[5]The OECD's home page is http://www.oecd.org.

organizations, such as the European Union (EU), the Association of Southeast Asian Nations (ASEAN),[6] the Andean Common Market (ANCOM),[7] the Gulf Cooperation Council,[8] and the Asian-Pacific Economic Cooperation forum (APEC).[9]

Fourth, specialized commodity agreements exist for products like jute, sugar, or cotton. Fifth, specialty agreements and organizations exist that are very narrow in scope, such as the World Intellectual Property Organization, which deals with copyright and patent issues or the American-Mexican Boundary Treaty Act of 1972.

World Trade Organization

After World War II, the United States and other nations recognized the need to avoid the economic mistakes that followed World War I and helped to fuel World War II. Having fought two world wars within a forty-year period, the nations were determined to prevent another war and to build relationships on different levels.

Negotiations among these nations started in 1947 and led to the **General Agreement on Tariffs and Trade (GATT)**, originally signed in 1948. The eighth and latest GATT agreement, called the Uruguay Round,[10] was ratified by the United States in 1995. The Uruguay Round created the World Trade Organization (WTO).

The WTO has three purposes: (1) to help trade flow as freely as possible by removing trade barriers and making the rules transparent and predictable, (2) to serve as a forum for trade negotiations, and (3) to administer the dispute-resolution system. The WTO is an international organization that administers the GATT. The Russian Federation is the only nation with a major economy that has not joined the WTO. it is believed that the Russian Federation will join in the future.

The agreements reached under the WTO cover three areas. The GATT covers international trade of goods. Trade in the services industry, such as securities, banking, and insurance services, is addressed in the **General Agreement on Trade in Services (GATS)**. Protection of intellectual property rights, such as copyrights and patents, is set out in the **Trade-Related Aspects of Intellectual Property Rights (TRIPS)** agreement.

The WTO administers all of these agreements. The WTO facilitates the implementation of trade agreements by requiring full participation of all its member countries in one new trading system and by providing a permanent forum to discuss new issues facing the international trading system. The WTO system is available only to countries that (1) are contracting parties, (2) agree to adhere to the Uruguay Round agreements, and (3) submit schedules of market access commitments for industrial goods and services.

With the complicated trade agreements, disputes will arise. Under the WTO, disagreements are heard by the Dispute Settlement Body. After its decision is rendered, appeals may be made. Members must comply with its findings and rulings. The Dispute Settlement Body follows a strict timetable to prevent case backlogs.

When trading with other member states, each country must abide by two nondiscrimination principles: normal trade relations and national treatment. **Normal trade relations (NTR)**[11] means equal treatment with the other countries granted NTR status, not favorable treatment. The importing country must handle imported goods from another nation the same as those from other NTR countries. NTR status can be granted to a country that is not a member of WTO, such as Vietnam. The United States has granted NTR status to Vietnam, which is reviewed on an annual basis. Any goods, services, or intellectual property

---

[6]The six member states of ASEAN are Brunei, Indonesia, Malaysia, Republic of the Philippines, Singapore, and Thailand. Some information about ASEAN is available through the International Monetary Fund at http://www.imf.org/external/np/sec/decdo/asean.htm.

[7]The five member states of ANCOM are Bolivia, Colombia, Ecuador, Peru, and Venezuela.

[8]The six member states of the Gulf Cooperation Council are Bahrain, Kuwait, Oman, Qatar, Saudi Arabia, and the United Arab Emirates.

[9]The twenty-one member states of APEC are Australia; Brunei Darussalam; Canada; Chile; People's Republic of China; Hong Kong, China; Indonesia; Japan; Republic of Korea (South Korea); Malaysia; Mexico; New Zealand; Papua New Guinea; Peru; Republic of the Philippines; the Russian Federation; Singapore; Chinese Taipei (Taiwan); Thailand; the United States; and Vietnam. The home page for APEC is http://www.apecsec.org.sg.

[10]Since 1947, eight rounds have been completed. Rounds are named after the place where the talks started, this latest time in Uruguay. Negotiations lasted from 1986 to 1993. Between 1995 and 1996, 124 countries had signed the Uruguay Round. In 2001, the talks for the next round started in Doha, Qatar, and will be known as the Doha Round. Most of the agreements will be finished by January 2005.

[11]For policy reasons, the WTO, followed by the U.S. Department of State, in 1998 changed the terminology from most-favored-nation status to normal trade relations.

from Vietnam must be treated as though they origi-nated within a WTO country.

National treatment means that the importing country must treat foreign goods just as it treats domestic goods; that is, once the imported goods clear customs, they become part of the domestic commerce. For example, dresses made in Mexico and imported into the United States must be treated the same as dresses made in the United States. No additional taxes may be attached because the dresses are made in another country. The WTO requires that if one nation grants a trade advantage to another country, it must grant that advantage to all other WTO members.

Two WTO agreements have fostered free trade. The 1997 Information Technology Agreement elimi-nated $600 billion in tariffs on 95 percent of the world's production of computers, telecommunications equipment, and semiconductors. The 1997 Basic Telecommunications Act opened up competition in the communications sector, ranging from satellites to submarine cables.

Occasionally, Congress passes a federal statute that directly opposes a foreign trade agreement that Con-gress has previously ratified. The courts must decide which act has priority. In most cases, the judicial system leaves it to Congress to determine which law should have priority. Problems also may arise when a treaty provision conflicts with state law. When an inter-national agreement has preempted a particular area, no local government can adopt laws to the contrary.

U.S. Agencies Concerned with International Business

This section discusses the U.S. governmental agencies' regulation of international law. Federal authority con-cerned with international law is addressed first.

Federal Lawmaking Authority

The Constitution divides the lawmaking authority concerning international relations between the Con-gress and the president. Article I, Section 8, grants Congress the power "[t]o regulate Commerce with foreign Nations, and among the several States." During the past two centuries, the Supreme Court has reaffirmed Congress's authority to establish economic policy and to impose and collect taxes and duties.

Article I, Section 9, however, specifically forbids export taxes. Article II, Section 2, grants the constitu-tional right to make treaties to the president. The Senate, however, must ratify treaties by a two-thirds vote. During the last century, the president has pre-dominantly dealt with international affairs.

Agencies Regulating International Trade

Four federal agencies and one special court handle trade policy and trade disputes. The following subsec-tions examine these agencies and the court.

Office of the U.S. Trade Representative. Estab-lished in 1963, the **U.S. Trade Representative (USTR)**[12] is a cabinet-level official with the rank of ambassador, directly responsible to the president.

The formulation of trade policy for the United States starts in the office of the USTR, which is also responsible for all bilateral and multilateral trade nego-tiations. The USTR is the chief representative of the United States in all activities concerning GATT.

U.S. Customs and Border Protection. The **U.S. Customs and Border Protection**[13] agency, estab-lished in 1789, is housed in Department of the Home-land Security. The customs section assesses and collects customs duties, excise taxes, fees, and penalties owed on imported merchandise.[14] It detects and apprehends persons engaged in fraudulent practices designed to circumvent customs.

The customs section also enforces copyright, patent, trademark, and maskwork[15] provisions; quotas; and marking requirements for imported merchandise. It collects international trade statistics and cooperates with customs services in other countries.

International Trade Administration. The **Inter-national Trade Administration (ITA)**[16] is part of

---

[12]You can find more information about the U.S. Trade Representative at http://www.ustr.gov.

[13]Formerly known as the U.S. Customs Service, the agency was renamed and moved from the U.S. Department of Treasury. The new name is U.S. Customs and Border Protection, which is housed in the Depart-ment of Homeland Security. Its home page is at http://www.cbp.gov.

[14]Duties of the U.S. Customs and Border Protection are found by exploring http://www.cbp.gov.

[15]Maskwork is discussed in more detail in Chapter 16. A *maskwork* is a series of related images, fixed or encoded, in a three-dimensional pat-tern on a computer chip.

[16]Information about the ITA may be found at http://www.ita.doc.gov.

the Department of Commerce (DOC). Created in 1980 by the secretary of commerce, the ITA promotes world trade and strengthens the international trade and investment position of the United States.

The ITA supports the trade policy negotiation efforts of the U.S. Trade Representative. It also promotes export trading companies and issues them certificates that provide limited exemptions from liability under the antitrust laws. These certificates are discussed later in the chapter.

International Trade Commission. The **International Trade Commission (ITC)**[17] is an independent agency created in 1916. The ITC imposes tariff adjustments and import quotas for industries. It can authorize monetary assistance to workers and firms in industries adversely affected by imports.

The ITC has broad investigatory powers concerning (1) the volume of importation in comparison with domestic production and consumption; (2) the conditions, causes, and effects relating to competition of foreign industries with those of the United States; and (3) all other factors affecting competition between domestically produced and imported articles. The commission advises the president as to the probable economic effect on the domestic industry of any proposed trade agreement involving the increase, reduction, or elimination of a tariff.

The ITC, upon petition by a harmed group, conducts investigations to determine if the increase in quantity of a particular import comprises or poses the threat of a serious injury to a domestic industry that produces a competitive article. If the commission finds that this situation, called *dumping* (examined later in this chapter, but for now it means selling below price), exists, it recommends to the president an action to redress the injury.

U.S. Court of International Trade. Established in 1890 and formerly known as the United States Tariff Commission, the **Court of International Trade (CIT)**[18] became a court in 1980. The court has all the powers in law and equity of a federal district court. It reviews agency decisions involving dumping and countervailing duty matters.

[17]A large amount of information about the ITC is available at http://www.usitc.gov.
[18]Additional information can be obtained at http://www.uscit.gov.

A **countervailing duty** is an import tax equal to the grant extended to an exporter by its home country to encourage exportation or to assist the exporter in meeting competition. Countervailing duties are intended to eliminate the competitive advantage gained by government subsidization of foreign exporters.

The CIT hears all civil actions against the United States that arise from laws governing import transactions. This court also holds exclusive jurisdiction over civil actions resulting from import transactions that are commenced by the United States and that seek penalties for alleged fraud or negligence.

Statutes Regulating International Trade

Congress has the constitutional authority to pass legislation concerning international trade. The following subsections explain some of these federal statutes.

Export Administration Act

The **Export Administration Act** restricts the export of goods and technology in the military field when release of these would be detrimental to the United States. The Export Enhancement Act, which amends the Export Administration Act, liberalized the products that can be exported, stiffened penalties for violating the statute, and increased enforcement.

Under the Export Administration Act, an exporter must determine if the products being considered for sale can be shipped to the specific country in which the exporter hopes to do business. For example, many exports to Cuba, North Korea, and Iran are prohibited. If the act permits trade with a specific country, the exporter must determine if a license is required.

Two types of licenses exist: general and validated. The **general license** is really a misnomer. Many goods can be shipped to specific countries without an official license. The general license is more of a general authority to ship than an actual license. The Department of Commerce classifies foreign countries to indicate if goods being exported to a specific country require a general license.

A **validated license** helps the United States to enforce its foreign policy by restricting the sale of goods involved with high technology. This license prohibits certain types of goods from being shipped to

LEGAL HIGHLIGHT

NAFTA and the Free Trade Association of the Americas

Two important trade agreements in the Western Hemisphere are the North American Free Trade Agreement (NAFTA)[a] and the Free Trade Association of the Americas.

NAFTA

Created in 1993, the North American Free Trade Agreement joined the United States, Canada, and Mexico to form a free trade area. Canada is the largest trading partner of the United States, and Mexico ranks third. (Japan is second.) The agreement among the three countries involves 363 million people and $6.3 trillion in combined gross domestic product.

NAFTA's purpose is to eliminate trade barriers and to facilitate the cross-border movement of goods and services among the three countries. Customs administration within each country's jurisdiction will continue. Goods imported into the three countries must comply with each country's laws and regulations.

The section in NAFTA concerning trade between the United States and Mexico abolished tariffs in stages. More than one-half of the tariff barriers were phased out in 1994. At the ten-year point, most of the goods and services are tariff free. By 2009, tariffs on politically sensitive items will be the last to be eliminated. Examples of these are corn, peanuts, sugar, orange juice, powdered milk, tuna, and used cars.

In 1998, all United States–Canada trade became duty free. The United States–Canada Free-Trade Agreement of 1988 already had reduced the tariffs between these two countries. NAFTA superseded the 1988 agreement.

NAFTA created the North American Made rules of origin to prevent non-NAFTA countries from funneling their goods into the U.S. market and from gaining access to the duty-free area. For example, toys imported from India into Mexico cannot be sent to the United States duty free under NAFTA, because a country outside of the duty-free area would benefit from entering the U.S. market duty free. Goods, in this case toys, made with materials or labor from outside the region, however, can qualify for NAFTA treatment if the goods undergo substantial transformation within NAFTA jurisdiction.

The three official languages of the NAFTA countries are English, French, and Spanish. For a product to be sold in the other two countries, its label must be in the language of the buyer country. Many companies print information in all three languages right on the item. Other manufacturers label the item in the appropriate language.

Prior to NAFTA, foreign ownership of financial services was either prohibited or severely restricted depending on the country. As a result of NAFTA, U.S., Canadian, and Mexican banks and securities firms can have 100 percent foreign ownership by firms from another NAFTA country. Firms may acquire 100 percent ownership in Mexican insurance companies. Investors from the three countries must be legally treated the same within each country.

Under NAFTA, U.S. trucking companies have carried international cargo to the Mexican states contiguous to the United States since 1995 and to all of Mexico since 1999. U.S. companies are able to purchase Mexican trucking firms. Border crossing by commercial truck traffic has increased so much that new customs facilities were built to expedite trade.

Before NAFTA, a traveler needed to purchase three tickets to travel through the three NAFTA countries, Canada to the United States, the United States to Mexico, and then within Mexico. Bus passengers now can purchase one ticket to travel from Canada to Mexico and vice versa. The passengers, however, still need to pass through customs and immigration checkpoints.

The U.S. and Mexican governments each invested $225 million in the new North American Development Bank. With these funds, the bank can borrow up to $3 billion from other sources to lend aid to communities hurt by NAFTA.

Two side agreements to NAFTA cover environmental standards and workers' rights. The Commission for Environmental Cooperation (CEC)[b] is

---

[a]All of the provisions of NAFTA can be obtained at http://www.sice.oas.org/trade/nafta/naftatce.asp.

[b]The home page for the Commission on Environmental Cooperation is at http://www.cec.org.

located in Montréal (Québec), Canada. The CEC facilitates cooperation and public participation to foster conservation, protection, and enhancement of the North American environment. The U.S.–Mexico Border Environmental Commission is authorized to spend up to $8 billion from the North American Development Bank, the World Bank, and the Inter-American Development Bank on various environmental cleanup projects. Environmental problems include air and water pollution and contaminated soil. NAFTA can impose fines or trade sanctions when a country fails to enforce its own environmental laws.

The North American Agreement on Labor Cooperation[c] authorized the establishment of the Commission for Labor Cooperation to investigate plant closures and labor abuses. NAFTA can authorize fines or trade sanctions if a country fails to enforce its worker safety standards, child labor rules, or minimum wage laws.

[c]Find the Northern American Agreement on Labor Cooperation at http://www.naalc.org.

Free Trade Association of the Americas

The Free Trade Association of the Americas (FTAA)[d] has a long-term goal to unite all the countries of North America and Latin America into one free trade area, eliminating all tariffs. Originally, the FTAA planners outlined a twenty- to thirty-year time frame with unification by the year 2030. The time length was shortened considerably after President William J. Clinton (1993–2001) sent emissaries to Latin America in late 1994 to ask each leader what the United States could do that would be most beneficial to their country. One word summed up their collective thoughts: trade.

The Summit of the Americas was planned and held less than six weeks later, in December 1994, in Miami, Florida. For the first time in modern history, the leaders of both North and Latin American countries are marching to the same economic and political tune—open markets and democracy. The single common goal is to create by 2005 a thirty-four member Free Trade Association of the Americas that will stretch from the northern reaches of Canada to the southern tip of Chile. The Summit of the Americas meets on a regular basis.

[d]The home page for the Free Trade Association of the Americas is at http://www.ftaa-alca.org. Information is available through the Organization of American States' Web site at http://www.sice.oas.org/ftaa_e.asp.

countries of concern that may pose a military threat to the United States.[19]

The act authorizes keeping products within the United States when there is a short supply. During the Korean conflict (1950–1953), when copper was in short supply, its export was restricted.

The Export Administration Act controls exports even when the final product is produced outside of the United States. The act's jurisdiction depends on whether the final goods are manufactured either with technical data developed in the United States or with parts originating in the United States. For example, a computer made in South Korea from component parts from the United States, or based on technical information from the United States, must have a validated license when sold by the South Korean company to a buyer in the People's Republic of China. Export laws have extraterritorial applications.

One major problem that exporters face is determining whether their goods will be diverted from one country to another. For example, a U.S. exporter sells a product to Nigeria. Unknown to the exporter, the Nigerian business ships the product to Iran. An exporter can be held liable if it should have known that the product could be sent to an embargoed area.

The penalties for violating the Export Administration Act are substantial. Fines can equal up to five

[19]In 2000, the U.S. Department of State replace the term *rogue state* with the term *country of concern*. No official list of countries classified as rogue states existed, but it was commonly assumed to include Iran, Iraq, Libya, and North Korea. These states were believed to be sponsoring terrorism or developing nuclear, chemical, or biological weapons.

times the value of the exports or $1 million, whichever is greater, for a willful violation. The businessperson responsible for the violation faces five years in prison, plus a $250,000 fine. The law allows for property forfeitures, civil penalties, and revocation of export license privileges.

The following case illustrates the implementation of this act when the defendant was involved in a diversion of goods to a banned country.

CASE 13.1

United States Court of Appeal, Eleventh Circuit, 1989
885 F.2d 775

UNITED STATES v. ELKINS

BACKGROUND AND FACTS This prosecution arose out of an investigation into the 1985 shipment of two Lockheed L-100-30 aircraft to Libya, which, at the time, was subject to strict export controls. Export licenses were required for the export of these two jets. Because of government restrictions on trade with Libya, export licenses would not have been granted to export these planes to Libya.

Elkins owned a company called Armaflex, Inc. He negotiated with Lockheed as a representative of Contrust, a West German oil exploration subsidiary controlled by Badir, a Libyan dealer. Lockheed preferred to sell the aircraft to Armaflex rather than to Contrust.

Elkins created a new corporation, AFI International, which represented Contrust in the negotiations. In negotiations with Lockheed, Elkins maintained that the airplanes were destined for the West African country of Benin. When Lockheed learned of Badir's involvement, Lockheed canceled the negotiations.

Elkins assured Lockheed that Badir represented a legitimate West German concern and that Badir was a Libyan expatriate antagonistic to the Libyan government. Based on this information, Lockheed resumed negotiations.

Elkins withheld from Lockheed the fact that the planes were to be modified with a midair refueling capability and were to be used by the Libyan Air Force. Elkins and Lockheed agreed on the sale of two L-100-30 planes and parts to AFI. The contract provided that AFI had the sole responsibility for obtaining a valid export license. Elkins made a net profit of $7 million.

Lockheed officials accompanied Elkins to the Department of Commerce to obtain an export license. The U.S. government officials knew that Contrust was owned by Libyans. Elkins explained that the planes were destined for Benin. At no time did Elkins inform government officials of the planned refueling modification. The Department of Commerce approved the export license. Lockheed delivered the planes to Benin. They were never seen in Benin again. One plane was found in Cairo. The plane's radio signal and operations manual indicated that the plane had been used by the Libyan Air Force.

Elkins, along with several other individuals, was indicted as a result of an investigation. Elkins was convicted of violating export restrictions. He received a fifteen-year prison sentence and was fined $6.6 million. A $100 special assessment also was imposed. Elkins appealed.

Circuit Judge JACKSON

. . . .

An indictment must set forth the elements of the offense in a manner which fairly informs the defendant of the charges against him and enables him to enter a plea which will bar future prosecution for the same offense. In this case, the indictment charged defendant with conspiracy to commit four substantive offenses against the United States. Although the fraud was charged as the object of the substantive offense of wire fraud rather than as the object of the conspiracy, defendant had clear notice that violations of the substantive offenses constituted fraud against the government. Conspiracy to violate the substantive offenses is conspiracy to defraud the government. Reading the indictment as a whole, we conclude that the indictment adequately charged defendant with conspiring to deprive the United States of its ability to control its foreign policy by concealing material facts from responsible government agencies.

We also conclude that the district court adequately charged the jury on conspiracy to defraud the United States. . . .

. . . The district court clarified and repeated this instruction as follows:

> *What must be proved beyond a reasonable doubt is that the accused planned knowingly and willfully to devise or intending to devise a scheme to defraud the United States of America and its executive agencies out of the right to implement its foreign policy and to conduct its affairs free from stealth, false statement, and fraud and that the use of the interstate wire or foreign wire communications were to be closely related to the scheme.*

. . . Conspiracy to commit wire fraud against the United States contains all of the elements of conspiracy to defraud the United States. Conspiracy to commit wire fraud contains the additional element of use of wire transmission services in furtherance of the scheme to defraud.

. . . .

Defendant was sentenced to five years' imprisonment on the conspiracy conviction, and to a consecutive term of ten years' imprisonment and a $6.6 million fine on the export control violation conviction. Defendant also received a special assessment of $50 on each count. Defendant eventually makes one argument that his sentence violated the Eighth Amendment: "Because the harshness of Appellant's sentence far exceeds the sentences imposed in similar export prosecutions in the Northern District of Georgia and elsewhere, Appellant respectfully submits that this Court should conclude that his sentence is unconstitutionally disproportionate." A sentence is disproportionate for Eighth Amendment purposes if the punishment is grossly disproportionate when compared with the nature of the crime. . . .

In a variety of situations, life sentences with the possibility of parole have been held not to violate the Eighth Amendment. These sentences, five years for conspiracy and ten years for violating export control laws, certainly are not grossly excessive compared to the nature of the crime. Additionally, the ten-year sentence imposed for violating export control regulations is not grossly disproportionate to the sentences imposed in other federal jurisdictions for violations of the same federal laws. Defendant unlawfully sold $57 million worth of high technology aircraft equipment to an unfriendly nation. Although his sentence may have been longer than the sentences normally imposed for this offense, that fact alone does not mean it was grossly disproportionate. . . .

Defendant also challenges the fine imposed on count two. There may be circumstances where an excessive fine constitutes cruel and unusual punishment in violation of the Eighth Amendment. We need not identify those circumstances in this case. Defendant made a gross profit of $13,049,474, a net profit of $7,336,233, and an after-tax profit of $3,368,917 from the sale of these aircraft. Defendant's fine of $6.6 million was less than his gross profit and less than his net profit from the sale of these planes. Although a large amount, we hold that a fine representing an amount less than the net profit of an illegal transaction does not violate the Eighth Amendment absent a showing of severe, particularized hardship suffered by defendant.

DECISION AND REMEDY Elkins's conviction for conspiracy against the United States in violation of the Export Administration Act was upheld.

CRITICAL THINKING: MANAGEMENT CONSIDERATION Assume you are in the position of handling exports for your firm like the one involving Lockheed in the above case. Discuss the steps to take to protect your firm from selling products requiring a validated license to a foreign country that is on the list of possible military threats to this country.

Omnibus Trade and Competitiveness Act

Congress passed an act to enhance the competitiveness of U.S. exports. The **Omnibus Trade and Competitiveness Act (OTCA)**[20] passed in 1988 has four purposes: (1) to authorize the negotiation of reciprocal trade agreements; (2) to strengthen U.S. trade laws; (3) to improve the development and management of U.S. trade strategy; and (4) through these actions, to improve living standards in the world.

Under this act, Congress made it the highest priority to pursue a broad array of domestic and international policies. Congress resolved that maintaining a position of world leadership is in the national interest of the United States. This national policy established the importance of maintaining the vitality of the technological, industrial, and agricultural base of the United States.

Trade Promotion Authority. Working with the president, Congress, through the OTCA, developed a procedure that currently is called **trade promotion authority** (formerly called *fast-track authority*) to use when dealing with other governments. Trade promotion authority means that once the president has signed an agreement with another country or countries, Congress must either approve or disapprove of the agreement as signed. Congress cannot amend it.

Article I of the Constitution gives Congress exclusive authority to set tariffs and to enact other legislation concerning international trade. Article II of the Constitution gives the president exclusive authority to negotiate international agreements. If the president negotiates a trade agreement that requires changes in U.S. tariffs or in other domestic laws, the trade agreement must be submitted to Congress for approval.

In the past, the president would enter into a negotiated trade agreement with a foreign government and then send the agreement to Congress for approval. If

[20]For more information see http://www4.law.cornell.edu/uscode/15/271.html.

approved, Congress would return the bill to the president for a signature. The trade agreement then was binding on the United States, although it did not become part of the domestic statutes.

Occasionally, the president was politically embarrassed when he made a trade agreement and then Congress either adopted the agreement with amendments or refused to adopt it. Foreign nations viewed the need for Congress's approval as "two shakes of the dice." When Congress failed to approve an agreement and passed amendments, the president was forced to reopen negotiations. Foreign countries took a dim view of this process because the original commitment was not honored. To remedy this problem, Congress enacted the former fast-track procedures for adopting trade agreements.

Congress first created fast-track authority in the **Trade Act** of 1974, which adopted the Tokyo Round of the General Agreement on Trade and Tariffs. Congress renewed fast-track authority in 1979, 1984, 1988, 1991, 1993, and passed trade promotion authorization in 2002.

When trade promotion authority is not authorized, Congress can take one of four actions. First, Congress can approve the agreement with no amendments. Second, Congress can reject the agreement. Third, and the most common action, Congress can amend the negotiated agreement and then vote on its approval. Finally, Congress can take no action, and the president would abide by the agreement without formal approval from Congress. This last action allows the president to engage in politically sensitive agreements, such as arms control agreements. Congress does not want to formally approve the agreement, but its inaction frees the president to follow the agreement's terms.

Trade promotion authority, when authorized, has three features. First, the president must consult extensively and coordinate with Congress throughout the negotiating process. Second, the president must notify Congress of his or her intention to negotiate and sign a trade agreement. Public notice of the anticipated trade agreement is published in the *Federal Register*. Finally, Congress approves or rejects the agreement with no amendments.

Trade promotion authority provides the president with credibility to negotiate trade agreements while Congress retains its central role before, during, and after negotiations. This procedure reassures foreign governments that the president can deliver on promises made.

Both NAFTA, which established a free trade zone among Canada, Mexico, and the United States, and the Uruguay Round of GATT were negotiated on the fast-track procedure. Each house of Congress could debate the merits of ratifying NAFTA and GATT, but no member of Congress could amend the legislation. Congress approved both NAFTA and GATT as ordinary bills of legislation, not as treaties, although this point is in litigation.

Export Trading Company Act

The **Export Trading Company Act** of 1982 resulted from legal difficulties arising from violations of antitrust laws by companies conducting business internationally. The act allows a business to file an application for a certificate of antitrust immunity with the International Trade Administration.

The application contains information based on the company's business plans. Once the administration grants the certificate, and as long as the company follows its business plan, the company is immune from antitrust prosecution by the Department of Justice.

Export-Import Bank

The **Export–Import Bank (Eximbank)**[21] provides financial assistance to exporting and importing firms. The primary type of assistance offered consists of the credit guarantees that Eximbank provides to commercial banks. Based on those guarantees, the commercial banks, in turn, make direct loans to exporting companies.

National Export Strategy

The **National Export Strategy** is an expanded and streamlined program to promote U.S. exports by the federal government. The strategy focuses on one central goal: to create a more efficient, effective, and customer-focused set of export promotion and export financing programs. The dynamic global marketplace has more than four billion customers. This market opportunity represents a challenge for U.S. firms able and willing to compete.

The four key elements of the National Export Strategy are the streamlining of programs, leveraging of resources, national allocation of resources, and removal of obstacles. To better assist businesses, the Department of Commerce (DOC) in 1980 established a partnership with myExports.[22] The Small Business Administration administers the Export Assistance

---

[21]The Export-Import Bank Web site is http://www.exim.gov. The statute establishing the bank is found at http://www4.law.cornell.edu/uscode/12/ch6A.html.
[22]The Web site for myExports is http://www.myexports.com.

LEGAL HIGHLIGHT

What Is a BEM?

BEM stands for Big Emerging Market. These markets are Argentina, Brazil, India, Indonesia, Mexico, the People's Republic of China, Poland, South Africa, South Korea, Taiwan, and Turkey.

These countries are expected to account for more than 44 percent of total global imports during the next twenty years, surpassing even Japan and Europe. In the next two decades, almost three-quarters of all global imports are expected to come from the BEMs and other developing countries, which will account for 26 percent. Keep your eyes on the BEMs for future growth.

Centers,[23] a number of which have set up in various cities. These agencies help an export or import business with the myriad of government agencies to gather information, permits, or other necessary government documents before conducting business.

The DOC also is leveraging its key resources by establishing a national network of private-sector intermediaries to provide company-specific resources for small-and medium-sized businesses to ensure their long-term success. Government trade events are oriented toward firms preparing to export. In the future, government support will be withdrawn and these trade events will be privatized.

To allocate government resources rationally, the National Export Strategy developed an effective interagency process to aid businesses. For example, the Department of Commerce, the Department of Energy, and the Environmental Protection Agency have formed an interagency group to review strategies to boost environmental exports.

The last element of the National Export Strategy is to remove obstacles. The DOC identifies government regulations and other barriers to exporting. The DOC helps to remove identified barriers through reform or by suggesting legislation to Congress. Since 1994, the government's licensing and decision-making processes have removed most of the exporting obstacles. The National Export Strategy is helping to make the United States a global leader in exports for the twenty-first century.

Unfair Import Practices

Several unfair import practices can occur. The following subsections examine four types of unfair practices: (1) dumping; (2) infringement of copyright, trademark, and patent laws; (3) government financing of products, called subsidizing; and (4) the sale of gray-market goods.

Dumping

Dumping is the practice of selling goods in the buyer's country below the price charged for them in the seller's country. Its purpose is to drive out competition in the buyer's country. When material injury is sustained by a domestic industry, WTO allows additional duties to be added to equal the price discrepancy.

The **Trade Agreement Act** of 1979, based on the GATT Antidumping Code, regulates dumping in the United States. The International Trade Administration protects domestic industries against economic injury caused by the sale of foreign merchandise at less than fair value in the United States.[24]

The ITA ascertains the types of goods most likely to be sold at less than fair value. If a business believes itself to be injured, it files a complaint with the International Trade Commission. The ITC determines if a threat of material injury or actual material injury to the business exists because the imports are being subsidized or sold at less than fair value. If the ITC finds that dumping has occurred, import duties are assessed against the merchandise. The duties can remain in effect for three to five years after violations of the act have ceased.

INFOTRAC RESEARCH ACTIVITY

Go to InfoTrac and type in "dumping." Read the most recent six articles that take different positions on dumping. Compare and contrast the articles.

Infringement

The ITC likewise is charged with investigating unfair competition methods, including infringement of copyright, patent, trademark, and maskwork laws. For example, a business located in a developing country produces copies of music tapes created by a U.S. recording company that holds the copyright to such works. This copying is done without permission and without paying royalties to the copyright holders. These tapes can be seized by the U.S. Customs and Border Protection agency on request from the ITC.

Subsidies

A third unfair import practice occurs when a government provides subsidies to its local export businesses. Subsidies take different forms, such as low-interest or interest-free loans, rebates on taxes earned from sales to foreign countries, or price guarantees to offset international currency fluctuations.

---

[23]Additional information on the Export Assistance Centers located throughout the country and ways to obtain financing are found at http://www.sba.gov/oit/export/useac.html.

[24]Antidumping information is found at http://ia.ita.doc.gov; also look for the Antidumping Procedures Manual link.

LEGAL HIGHLIGHT

APEC

The Asia-Pacific Economic Cooperation forum (APEC) was formed in 1989 as a loose gathering of Pacific Rim countries without a clear goal. By the end of 1994, APEC had become the most powerful economic region in the world. It represented 40 percent of the world's population and a combined gross regional product of about $14 trillion—more than half of the gross world product.

Twenty-one countries are now members. APEC's goal was clear: the removal of trade barriers. The three members of NAFTA—Canada, Mexico, and the United States—belong to APEC.

APEC adopted the Bogor Declaration, which calls for the industrialized members of APEC to remove trade barriers by the year 2010. Free and open trade for both developed and developing countries is the goal set for 2020. APEC's trade liberalization efforts will complement and harmonize with those of the World Trade Organization.

Any subsidy distorts the true movement of trade in the international community. The ITA is charged with protecting U.S. businesses from foreign businesses that receive subsidies when these subsidies constitute a material injury to an industry. A countervailing duty may be imposed when the ITA determines that the exporting country is subsidizing a business.

Gray-Market Goods

The term **gray-market goods** refers to foreign-manufactured goods for which a valid U.S. trademark has been registered. The goods are purchased legally abroad and imported into the United States, but without the consent of the American trademark holder. The term *gray market*, which at times is used unfairly, implies a nefarious undertaking by the importer. A more accurate term for the goods is **parallel import**. This term is devoid of negative connotations. But *gray-market goods*, for better or for worse, has become the commonly accepted term for such goods. The next case discusses the problem of importing goods from Europe when a company in the United States holds a possible valid trademark.

CASE 13.2	VITTORIA NORTH AMERICA, L.L.C. v. EURO-ASIA IMPORTS, INC.

United States Court of Appeals, Tenth Circuit, 2001
278 F.3d 1076

BACKGROUND AND FACTS Plaintiff-appellee Vittoria North America, L.L.C., (VNA), an Oklahoma limited liability company, alleges that it is the U.S. owner of the trademark Vittoria, which designates a well-known brand of bicycle tires. VNA alleges that defendant-appellant Euro-Asia Imports (EAI), a California sole proprietorship, has purchased Vittoria-branded bicycle tires overseas and imported them into the United States in violation of VNA's trademark rights. VNA sued Euro-Asia Imports and its sole proprietor Robert Hansing (collectively EAI) under Section 526 of the Tariff Act (the Act) seeking damages as well as an injunction to prevent EAI from continuing to import Vittoria bicycle tires into the United States.

In 1992, VNA's predecessor Hibdon Tire Center entered into an agreement (the 1992 Agreement) with Vittoria Italy, an Italian company. Hibdon Tire Center agreed to form VNA as a North American distributor of Vittoria tires, and Vittoria Italy agreed to designate VNA as its exclusive distributor in the United States, Canada, and Mexico. VNA distributed Vittoria-branded bicycle tires in the United States from that time forward. In February 1999, Vittoria Italy entered into an agreement (Assignment Agreement) with VNA purporting to assign VNA "all right, title and interest in and to the United States Trademark 'VITTORIA' and the registration therefore, together with the goodwill of the business connected with the use of and symbolized by said Trademark, as well as the right to sue for infringement of the Trademark or injury to said goodwill." The Assignment Agreement stated that "[t]he purpose of this Agreement is to permit Assignee [VNA] to act against infringers and unauthorized importers of Vittoria trademarked products into the United States." Vittoria Italy retained the right to retake title to the Trademark and its associated goodwill upon giving thirty days' written notice to VNA.

Shortly thereafter, VNA filed suit against EAI alleging that it infringed on VNA's trademark rights by importing Vittoria tires into the United States without first gaining VNA's consent. EAI concedes that it has been purchasing Vittoria-branded tires overseas and importing the tires into the United States since the early 1980s. VNA's suit seeks damages, an injunction to prevent further importation by EAI, and confiscation of EAI's inventory of Vittoria-branded products.

The district court granted VNA's motion for partial summary judgment, holding that undisputed facts in the case established VNA's right to protection under (federal law).

EAI appealed the district court's injunction. EAI contended that the evidence relied on by the district court was insufficient to prove VNA's ownership of the Vittoria trademark in the United States. Further, EAI argued that VNA was not entitled to protection under the Act because it falls under a regulatory exception denying gray-market protection to U.S. companies if they are owned by or subject to common control with a foreign manufacturer of the trademarked goods.

EBEL, Circuit Judge.

. . . .

In this case we are called upon to interpret provisions of the Tariff Act of 1930 designed to protect domestic owners of trademarks affixed to goods produced overseas by foreign manufacturers. The Act states:

> . . . *[I]t shall be unlawful to import into the United States any merchandise of foreign manufacture if such merchandise, or the label, sign, print, package, wrapper, or receptacle, bears a trademark owned by a citizen of, or by a corporation or association created or organized within, the United States, and registered in the Patent and Trademark Office by a person domiciled in the United States, . . . unless written consent of the owner of such trademark is produced at the time of making entry.*

In other words, the Act provides so-called "gray market" protection to U.S. owners of trademarks associated with goods of foreign manufacture, prohibiting any other person or entity from importing goods bearing that trademark into the United States without the consent of the trademark owner. The prototypical gray market victim . . . is a domestic firm that purchases from an independent foreign firm the rights to register and use the latter's trademark as a United States trademark and to sell its foreign manufactured products here.

. . . .

We next consider EAI's contention that VNA is not entitled to gray market protection under the Act. In order to prove entitlement to protection under the Act, VNA must show that it is a corporation or association created or organized within the United States, that it owns the Vittoria trademark in the United States, that the trademark is registered in the Patent and Trademark Office of the United States Customs

Service, and that EAI is, without VNA's consent, importing Vittoria-branded goods of foreign manufacture. The district court found that undisputed evidence sufficiently established each of these points.

EAI contests whether the evidence demonstrates that VNA owns the Vittoria trademark in the United States. First, EAI asserts that the transfer was invalid for purposes of establishing any rights to graymarket protection because the transaction was not at arm's-length and because VNA did not "pay dearly" for the assignment. EAI relies on *K Mart Corp. v. Cartier, Inc.* to support its argument that the Act does not extend protection under such circumstances. *Cartier*, however, does not purport to establish requirements for a valid transfer of a trademark. Rather, it considers an exception to the Act exempting U.S. trademark holders from its protections who are owned by or under common control with a foreign manufacturer of trademarked goods.

. . . .

C. The Common Control Exception

We next consider whether, in spite of a valid transfer of the trademark from Vittoria Italy to VNA, a regulatory exception to the Act removes VNA from the scope of its gray market protections. The regulation in question, 19 C.F.R. § 133.23(d)(1), reads, in relevant part:

> *Gray market goods subject to the restrictions of this section shall be detained for 30 days from the date on which the goods are presented for Customs examination, to permit the importer to establish that any of the following exceptions . . . are applicable: (1) The trademark or trade name was applied under the authority of a . . . trade name owner who is the same as the U.S. owner, a parent or subsidiary of the U.S. owner, or a party otherwise subject to common ownership or control with the U.S. owner. . . .*

EAI does not allege that VNA is the same as Vittoria Italy, is a parent or subsidiary of Vittoria Italy, or that it is subject to common ownership with Vittoria Italy. Rather, EAI argues that the evidence is sufficient to show common control of the two companies or control of VNA by Vittoria Italy.

[C]ommon control is defined as "effective control in policy and operations and is not necessarily synonymous with common ownership. . . ."

In this case, EAI asserts genuine questions of material fact exist with respect to the following allegations: (1) VNA and Vittoria Italy work in concert to design, develop and distribute Vittoria products; (2) VNA and Vittoria Italy make joint decisions as to "present and future product ranges"; (3) Vittoria Italy sells Vittoria-branded products directly to original equipment manufacturers in the United States; (4) Vittoria Italy pays a significant percentage of VNA's advertising budget and exercises some measure of control over VNA's marketing of Vittoria products; (5) Vittoria Italy determines which product lines VNA is allowed to market in the United States; (6) Vittoria Italy reimburses VNA for nearly all of its liability for warranty claims on Vittoria products; (7) Vittoria Italy's catalog lists VNA as its "U.S. distributor"; and (8) the president and CEO of Vittoria Italy, Rudie Campagne ("Campagne"), makes decisions about employees of VNA as well as a sister company of VNA called XLM. Although these allegations show a "close and profitable business relationship," they fall short of establishing common control.

For example, allegations of joint decision making and cooperative efforts to develop and market products for the United States at most give rise to an inference that a close business relationship exists between VNA and Vittoria Italy. Indeed, such cooperative planning is required by the 1992 Agreement. Similarly, Vittoria Italy's reimbursing VNA for warranty liabilities does not give rise to an inference of control.

While Vittoria Italy provides funding to support VNA's advertising, Vittoria Italy has no legal control over how those funds are spent. EAI's evidence that Vittoria Italy controls VNA's employment decisions apparently consists of a single e-mail from Campagne expressing his disapproval with VNA's management team and a "strong request" that it rehire a retired former officer of the company, which it did. Again, this is not evidence of control, but only evidence of VNA's understandable desire to preserve a good business relationship with Vittoria Italy.

. . . .

EAI relies on a concurrence by Justice Brennan in *K Mart Corp. v. Cartier, Inc.,* discussing the legislative history behind the Act and concluding that "Congress did not intend to extend . . . protections to affiliates of foreign manufacturers." Justice Brennan observed that Congress's intent was to protect only domestic interests, and that "[t]he barriers that Congress erected . . . are fragile barriers indeed if a foreign manufacturer might bypass them by the simple device of incorporating a shell domestic subsidiary and transferring to it a single asset—the United States trademark."

We believe EAI reads too much into Justice Brennan's concurrence by attempting to apply the descriptive word "affiliate" to this context. First, extending the common control exception to companies who merely work together under cooperative contractual arrangements would not advance the two policy considerations . . . that Justice Brennan identified in his concurrence. The first of these is that independent U.S. entities which acquire rights to trademarks have significantly greater investment-backed expectations at stake than subsidiaries or other "affiliates" of foreign manufacturers. However, close but independent business allies are also likely to have invested significant financial and human capital into their endeavors, as the record shows to be the case here. Second, Justice Brennan contrasted independent U.S. trademark holders with those covered by the common control exception because, in the latter case, the foreign manufacturer can protect its U.S. marketing efforts simply by restricting who can purchase the product and where those customers can subsequently export it. The same cannot be said of U.S. trademark owners associated with foreign manufacturers only by virtue of a contract or other cooperative arrangement rather than by "common control." While close business allies may hope to persuade their partners to adopt such controls, without more they are not able to force an unwilling foreign manufacturer to protect them from gray market importers. Such is the case here.

Finally, we find no evidence that VNA and Vittoria Italy have engaged in fraud or otherwise have attempted to subvert the limits Congress placed on [those] protections. Although EAI alleges that VNA was created "at the behest" of Vittoria Italy, it points to no evidence that the agreement leading to the creation of VNA was anything but an arm's-length transaction between the Hibdon Tire Center and Vittoria Italy. Further, there is no evidence that Vittoria Italy has any legal authority to control VNA's actions, and no evidence of other connections between them such as interlocking officers or directors.

. . . .

DECISION AND REMEDY The court found that the assignment agreement between the manufacturer and the United States distributor was valid, that the goodwill was transferred with the trademark, and that there was no common control between the parties.

CRITICAL THINKING: MANAGERIAL CONSIDERATION Discuss how the problem represented by this case could have been handled without going to court.

International Business Transactions

A business can be an exporter, an importer, or both. An exporter sells its goods overseas, whereas an importer buys products made in another country. Conducting business internationally involves a few more steps than does a domestic business transaction. Exporting is more complicated than importing. The following sections discuss some steps involved in developing first an export business, then later, an import business.

Developing an Exporting Business

Once a business decides to export its products or services, it must develop a master international business plan. Usually, a business devotes far more time and effort to establishing an overseas business within a foreign market than in developing a U.S. market for its products. Top management must make a long-term commitment to develop an export market.

Planned, orderly growth is necessary. In the beginning, a business should target only one or two geographic areas. It may need to modify its products to meet the regulations imposed by the importing country and the cultural preferences of the people who live there. Information concerning sales messages, warranties, and other important information must be printed in the language of the importing country.

The firm needs to establish contacts with government agencies and with businesspeople who are knowledgeable about the export business. These agencies and people include accountants, attorneys, consultants, **customs brokers** (licensed people who conduct customs business on behalf of others), financial institutions and lenders, **freight forwarders** (businesses that arrange the international transportation of goods), import or export companies, insurance agents, marketing and public relations services, translation and cross-cultural services, international organizations, port authorities, telecommunications systems, and government support resources.

Conducting Business. An exporter can conduct business internationally either indirectly or directly. The two indirect ways are by distributorship or by agent. The direct method is one in which there is

contact between the exporter and the importer with no intermediary. The following sections discuss these three methods.

International Distribution Agreements. One cost-effective way to enter the international market, especially for small to medium-sized firms, is through a distributor. The distributor actually conducts the business overseas. A business must choose an overseas distributor with great care. The complications involved in overseas communications, transportation, and government regulations require the international distributor to act with greater independence than would a domestic counterpart.

The contract with an overseas distributor should be comprehensive and written in the languages of all parties involved. Some of the issues that should be covered include the amount of authority that the agent has, the amount of support that either party will provide, the specific products that are covered and their delivery and service terms, the geographic territory that the distributor will cover, the method of payment, and other essential terms.

The government controls over imports and exports need to be established in the contract, as well as any government restrictions that apply to the products. A clause that specifies if arbitration will be used and, if so, the identification of the arbitration provider should be negotiated. A statement should specify if the contract is assignable. The contract needs to state clearly that it is the sole applicable agreement.

The contract ending date needs to be defined, either by setting a date or by setting out the conditions that will terminate the contract. Any other grounds that will end the contract should be stated. The contract should provide the amount of notice that one party needs to provide to the other in order to end the contract, such as a thirty-day notice or a two-week notice. Finally, the contract should state the damages that can be sought, such as liquidated damages, and any limitations on the amount of damages.

International Agent. An **international agent** can help a business find buyers in another country. Unlike a distributor, which actually conducts business, an agent brings the seller (exporter) and the buyer (importer) together. The agent may live and work both inside and outside the United States.

LEGAL HIGHLIGHT

European Union and the European Community

What is the difference between the European Union (EU) and the European Community (EC)? Basically the EU is a political union rather than a legal one. Its ultimate objective is European integration by promoting economic and social progress. All nationals of the twenty-five member states are now citizens of the EU, which grants them certain rights, such as human rights protection.[a] The EU is founded on international treaties among sovereign states, rather than on a constitution.

The main feature of the European Community is its community market. The citizens within these countries enjoy various freedoms, such as the free movement of goods, workers, services, capital, and payments. The EC also implements various policies, such as commercial, agricultural, competitive, and environmental policies.

The 1957 Treaty of Rome, which is the foundation treaty for the EU, originally created the former European Economic Community (EEC). In 1991, the **Maastricht Agreement**[b] (officially the Treaty on European Unity) was signed in Maastricht, the Netherlands. The Maastricht Agreement amends the Treaty of Rome by replacing the EEC with the European Union and by providing the basis for a political, monetary, and economic union.

The Maastricht Agreement created a single market among the then-fifteen EU countries' 375 million consumers and $7 trillion combined gross domestic product. The EU recognizes eleven languages: Danish,

Dutch, English, Finnish, French, German, Greek, Italian, Portuguese, Spanish, and Swedish.

Air passenger and cargo services are integrated. Citizens of the member states can travel freely within the EU by air, bus, train, or automobile. A traveler who enters the EU or who is a citizen of the EU does not need a passport and is exempt from customs when traveling within the EU.

International shippers have unified guidelines. Because the border controls have been abolished, millions of tons of cargo now move freely. Any EU air carrier can fly directly to any other EU member country instead of being required to land in each country along the way. The EU railways are integrated and a high-speed rail system throughout the EU is planned. All regulations for maritime traffic are integrated. An imposed 15 percent minimum value-added tax (VAT) frees businesses from overlapping taxation of profits.

The EU has integrated its banking, securities, investment services, and insurance sectors. U.S. businesses can open these services in any EU country, if they meet EU standards. Reciprocal national treatment is required by each of the EU countries. The country in which a business originates is called the *home country*. A firm may have branches or sell services in the other EU host countries.

Professional services can be offered across borders. The *Mutual Recognition of Professional Qualifications* for accountants, lawyers, and consultants allows these professionals to practice in other member states.

In the corporate area, however, no uniform decisions have been reached on any rules ranging from disclosure to accounting procedures. No uniformity on minimum wage legislation or layoff restrictions has been agreed on. Although much work lies ahead before the EU really is an integrated union, much has been accomplished during the past forty years.

[a]Information on the member states and applicant states can be found at http://europa.eu.int/abc/governments/index_en. htm#members.
[b]A complete copy of the Maastricht Agreement can be found at http://europa.eu.int/en/record/mt/top.html.

The agent knows the businesspeople in the foreign country, visits the various firms, conducts trade shows, understands the culture, and speaks the language. The agent helps to set up the sales and subsequent contracts by representing the U.S. principal. The importer chooses to deal with an exporter (the U.S. principal) based on the agent's integrity and reputation.

Direct Contact. An exporter can have direct contact between the importer and itself. If all goes well, this contact results in a contract. Neither the exporter nor the importer is represented by an agent.

The exporter and the importer find one another through reputation, trade shows, networking through professional organizations, or any number of other ways. They then negotiate and finally contract with each other directly. These contracts must be evaluated in view of the company's objective in entering the international marketplace.

Contracts Involved in Exporting. Whether a firm uses an agent or distributor, or deals directly with the importer, the export/import contract needs to be negotiated until all details have been considered. The traditional components of a contract, such as the price and types of goods, remain the same. Attorneys familiar with both business and international law, however, should be involved in drafting these contracts. The contract draft needs to be reviewed by all parties prior to reducing the contract to final form. Once the exporter and importer agree on the terms, they have a purchase/sell (export/import) contract.

Usually, this contract will refer to other contracts needed to complete the business transaction. The exporter faces the task of sending and delivering the goods overseas while ensuring itself that it will be paid by the importer. The importer needs assurances that the product delivered is the same as that promised in the contract.

Another type of contract pertains to the financing of the purchase/sell contract. In this contract, the buyer enters into a financing arrangement with a lending institution, whereby credit is extended to the buyer. Another contract involves people who facilitate

exporting and importing, such as freight forwarders and customs brokers. The last type of contract concerns the export transaction documents. Each of these contracts is separate, but they all fit together to complete the total business transaction.

In comparison with domestic contracts, most international contracts involve more people and different means to bring a business deal to a successful conclusion. The following sections address additional clauses to be included in an export/import contract, various financing methods, export facilitators, and export transaction documents.

Clauses within an Export/Import Contract. Although the function of an export/import contract is the same as that of a domestic contract, additional clauses need to be included in international contracts. The following subsections describe provisions for consideration in an export/import contract: choice of law and forum, official-language clause, and risk-of-loss clause.

Choice of Law and Forum. The parties can write into the contract *choice-of-law* and *choice-of-forum* clauses. A **choice-of-law clause** selects the substantive law of a governmental body that will apply. For example, a Florida business contracts with a firm in London. The parties can insert a clause stating that Florida law will apply in case of a dispute. Many countries recognize the validity of the choice-of-law clause and will enforce it in their courts. Before entering into a transnational business contract, it is critical that both parties be familiar with the laws of the foreign countries involved.

If a choice-of-law provision is contained in the contract, it determines the law that will apply. It does not settle, however, where the lawsuit should be filed. A **choice-of-forum clause** designates the forum, or location, in which the case will be heard in the event of any dispute.

Complications occur when the parties are incorporated in different countries and are doing business in other countries. This type of situation complicates the decision as to where to file any court action. The following case considers some of these problems, including the place to file the lawsuit.

CASE 13.3	# CHIQUITA INTERNATIONAL v. FRESH DEL MONTE PRODUCE

District Court of Appeal
of Florida, 1997
690 So. 2d 698

BACKGROUND AND FACTS Chiquita had a long-standing business relationship with a Philippine banana grower, Tagum Development Corporation (TADECO). TADECO provided Chiquita with vast quantities of bananas for Chiquita's Asian market.

At some point in the relationship, TADECO notified Chiquita that it would terminate their relationship. Sometime thereafter, Chiquita realized that TADECO had contracted with Del Monte to provide it with the bananas TADECO had previously sold to Chiquita.

Chiquita filed suit against Del Monte in the Circuit Court of Dade County for tortious interference with its contract and business relationship with TADECO. The complaint alleged that the tortious interference at issue occurred in Coral Gables, Florida. Among the defendants were several subsidiaries of Del Monte. Del Monte filed a motion to dismiss for *forum non conveniens* (not a convenient forum). The trial court granted the motion, which was appealed.

Judge SORONDO

. . . .

The Appellant/Plaintiff, Chiquita, appeals the dismissal of its complaint against Appellees/Defendants, Del Monte (collectively), on grounds of *forum non conveniens.*

. . . .

. . . [T]he Supreme Court of Florida [has] adopted the federal doctrine of *forum non conveniens.* The Court held that in reviewing a *forum non conveniens* motion, the courts must engage in a four-step analysis:

> *[1] As a prerequisite, the court must establish whether an adequate alternative forum exists which possesses jurisdiction over the whole case. [2] Next, the trial judge must consider all the relevant factors of private interest, weighing in the balance a strong presumption against disturbing plaintiff's initial forum choice. [3] If the trial judge finds this balance of private interests in equipoise or near equipoise, he must then determine whether or not factors of public interest tip the balance in favor of a trial in [another] forum. [4] If he decides that the balance favors such a . . . forum, the trial judge must finally ensure that plaintiffs can reinstate their suit in the alternative forum without undue inconvenience or prejudice.*

Chiquita argues that Del Monte failed to establish and the trial judge failed to properly find that an adequate alternative forum exists which possesses jurisdiction over the whole case, the first of the . . . criteria. We agree.

Chiquita International Limited is a corporation organized under the laws of Bermuda. Fresh Del Monte Produce, N.V. is a corporation organized under the laws of the Netherland Antilles. Del Monte Fresh Produce Company is a corporation organized under the laws of the State of Delaware in the United States of America. Del Monte Fresh Produce International, Inc. is a corporation organized under the laws of Liberia. Chiquita is headquartered in Cincinnati, Ohio. Del Monte Fresh Produce International, Inc. is headquartered in Monaco. Chiquita repeatedly asserts throughout its briefs that the other two Del Monte corporations referred to above are headquartered in Coral Gables, Florida. Although Del Monte clearly identifies the headquarters of Del Monte Fresh Produce International, Inc. in its appellate pleadings, it does not identify the corporate headquarters of the other two corporations. Regardless of where their "formal" headquarters may be, however, it is clear that Del Monte has a significant corporate presence in Coral Gables, Florida, where some of the companies' major executives are located. Indeed, as we have previously noted, the alleged plot to tortiously interfere with Chiquita's contract with TADECO was allegedly "hatched" in Coral Gables.

There is nothing in this record that even remotely suggests that a Philippine court would have subject-matter jurisdiction over four foreign corporations, none of which maintains a business presence in the Philippines, in a lawsuit which arises as a result of an intentional tort allegedly committed in Florida. We do not believe that Del Monte has established, as it must, that the country of the Philippines is an "adequate alternative forum" with jurisdiction over this case.

. . . .

In light of our conclusions concerning the first two of the . . . criteria, it is clear that we do not find that the parties are in equipoise or near equipoise, as required by the third criterion, and consequently we do not proceed with the analysis.

DECISION AND REMEDY The court found that the Florida court had the proper jurisdiction to hear the case. The doctrine of *forum non conveniens* was not applicable.

CRITICAL THINKING: MANAGERIAL CONSIDERATION What additional provision should have been included in the contract between Chiquita International and TADECO to avoid this dispute?

Official-Language Clause. A clause in the contract should designate the official language to be used in interpreting the contract's terms. This clause promotes a clear and precise understanding of the contract's terms by each of the parties. For example, in a sale-of-goods contract, the basic contract of sale should include a legal definition of terms, the price and manner of payment, and a provision specifying the acceptable currency for payment.

Risk-of-Loss Clause. Transacting international business involves peculiar risks because thousands of miles often separate buyers and sellers. Sellers want to avoid delivering goods for which they might not be paid. Buyers want evidence that sellers have shipped goods and that insurance has been purchased to cover any loss, damage, or theft. Specific clauses can dictate the exact moment when risk of loss passes from the seller to the buyer. In addition, a *force majeure* clause, which protects the parties from forces beyond their control (such as acts of God), also should be included.

Financing Methods. At least five different methods of financing exports are available for businesspeople: cash in advance, open account, factoring, forfaiting, and letter of credit. In choosing a financing method,

the exporter tries to maximize cash flow, reduce transaction risks, and enhance competitiveness by offering flexible payment terms to the buyer.

When the seller and buyer are in different countries, two problems exist: (1) delivering the goods from the seller to the buyer and (2) ensuring payment from the buyer to the seller. Appropriate financing arrangements ensure that the seller receives payment for the goods sent and the buyer receives the goods.

Cash in Advance or Open Account. When the importer pays cash in advance for goods, the importer takes a chance that the exporter will follow through on the sales contract by sending the quality and quantity of goods on the agreed delivery schedule.

The importer may establish an open account with the exporter. When the seller ships the goods, the exporter sends a statement to the importer as in a domestic credit situation. The problem with this arrangement is that the importer might not pay. The exporter would then have to bring legal action in a foreign country to obtain payment.

Factoring. A **factor** offers credit services. A factor who works for an exporter is known as the *export factor.* When working for an importer, the factor is known as the *import factor*. The factor is placed legally between the seller and the buyer.

An exporter contacts an export factor for a credit check on the importer. The export factor requests credit information from an import factor through an international factors network. Once the importer's credit is approved, the exporter ships the goods and submits the invoice and transportation documents to the export factor, who in turn forwards all the documents to the import factor. The import factor assumes the credit risk and administration and collection of the payment from the importer. The exporter normally has no dealings with the import factor.

The financing arrangement with a factor works in the following manner. The factor pays the exporter, less a commission charge, when the receivables are due (or shortly thereafter), regardless of the importer's financial ability to pay. The cost of the factoring commission charge is fixed. It ranges generally between 1 and 3 percent, depending on the country, sales volume, and amount of paperwork involved. The factor then collects its money from the importer.

Small and medium-sized firms find factoring their export receivables to be the most hassle-free method of financing export sales and of collecting payment from the buyers. With export factoring, the exporter avoids tying up working capital and spending substantial amounts of time in administering accounts receivables. The following limitations, however, do exist:

- Factoring generally is available only to firms that have an established export market and want the flexibility of selling on open accounts.

- A factor does not handle a one-time transaction, because the factor requires access to a certain volume of the exporter's yearly sales.

- A factor works with short-term receivables of 30- to 180-day terms.

- Factors work only in developed countries, because those countries have established legal and financial systems.

- A factor assumes credit risk. The importer still has recourse to the exporter for disputes by the importer concerning merchandise (such as the quality or condition of the goods) and the terms of the contract of sale (such as the timeliness of delivery).

- Exporters working with a letter of credit often receive payment sooner than if they were working with collection factoring alone.

Traditionally, export factoring was limited to textiles, apparel, footwear, and carpeting sectors. U.S. factors now work with more diversified consumer products. Generally, an export factor does not work with an exporter that has a contract that involves capital goods of large projects because the repayment schedules stretch over several years. In some cases, a forfaiter may handle those types of projects.

Forfaiting. Like a factor, a **forfaiter** is in the business of supplying credit. The term *forfaiter* is derived from the French term *forfait*, meaning "having surrendered or relinquished rights to something." The exporter surrenders possession of the export receivables (usually guaranteed by a bank in the importer's country) by selling the receivables at a discount to a forfaiter in exchange for cash. The practice of forfaiting developed after World War II as a means of financing the then West German exports to Eastern bloc countries. These countries were short of hard currency, so forfaiting developed to extend medium-term financing.

In a typical forfaiting transaction, an exporter contacts a forfaiter before finalizing the transaction. Once the forfaiter commits to the deal and sets the discount rate, the exporter incorporates the discount into the selling price. Forfaiters usually work with promissory notes that are unconditional and easily transferable as debt instruments that can be sold on the secondary market.

Forfaiters, except when working with exporters of unquestionable creditworthiness, require a guarantee from a reputable commercial bank in the importer's country or sometimes a guarantee from the government itself. Typically, the guarantee consists of the guaranteeing bank's written endorsement directly on the notes. The guarantee eases the risks to the forfaiter when working with receivables from developing countries.

The exporter's contract with the importer typically involves capital goods, commodities, or large projects. The contract usually has medium- to long-term repayment periods, usually between six months and ten years. Because of high costs, many forfaiters refuse transactions of less than $250,000. Forfaiters often purchase receivables as a one-shot deal, without requiring an ongoing volume of business. Trade finance offices in banks handle many forfait transactions in which exporters already may be customers and have established a working relationship with the bank.

Forfaiting eliminates virtually all financial risk to the exporter. The exporter, however, still remains liable for the contract performance, such as quality of goods and timeliness of delivery. Forfaiting, however, has the following limitations:

- Forfaiting is unavailable for short-term financing of less than 180 days.

- Interest costs and commitment fees may be high.

- Transaction size usually is limited to $250,000 or more.

Export Factoring versus Forfaiting. From the exporter's viewpoint, both export factoring and forfaiting ensure that the exporter will be paid. In both cases, the exporter sells receivables to a third party at a discount for cash. The two methods differ significantly in these primary ways:

- Factors want access to a large percentage of the exporter's factoring business. Forfaiters will work on a one-transaction basis.

- Factors work only with short-term receivables (no greater than 180 days). Forfaiters work with medium- to long-term receivables (180 days to ten years).

- Payment terms tend reflect the type of product involved. Factors work mostly with consumer goods. Forfaiters work with capital goods, commodities, and large projects.

- Factors work in developed countries with strong legal and financial frameworks and where credit information is readily available. Most forfaiters operate in developing regions, even though the country's legal and financial structures are inadequate. Forfaiters usually require a bank guarantee or a guarantee from the developing country's government.

Letters of Credit. A **letter of credit** is an instrument issued by a lending institution in favor of a beneficiary, the exporter. The letter of credit substitutes the bank's creditworthiness for that of the importer, because the bank guarantees the exporter payment for the merchandise sold under the export/import contract.

A letter of credit ensures the seller that it will receive payment, while at the same time ensuring the buyer that payment will be held until the seller complies with the terms of the letter of credit. The letter, thus, protects both the buyer and the seller. If the documents presented by the seller comply with the terms of the letter of credit, the bank must honor the letter. The UN agreement on Uniform Customs and Practices for Documentary Credits[25] provides internationally honored rules, covering letters of credit.

Businesses often use two documents, *bills of exchange* and *bills of lading*, in connection with letters of credit. The **bill of exchange** normally is called a *draft*. A check is a form of a draft. A check, however, always is drawn on a bank, whereas bills of exchange are drawn on the buyer of the goods.

A bill of lading initially is issued by a common carrier, such as a railroad, trucking, airline, or marine shipping company. The bill of lading controls possession of the goods. (Bills of lading were discussed in Chapter 11.)

The common carrier delivers the bill of lading to the seller. Prior to shipment, the buyer obtains a letter of credit from its bank. In the meantime, the seller (drawer) prepares a bill of exchange naming the buyer as the drawee. The payee normally is the seller's bank.

The bill of lading, the bill of exchange, and the letter of credit are sent to the seller's bank, which in turn sends all three documents to the buyer's bank. The buyer's bank pays the bill of exchange under the terms of the letter of credit and provides the buyer with the bill of lading. The buyer's bank must pay the seller through the seller's bank when the seller complies with the terms of the letter of credit. The seller looks to the buyer's bank, not to the buyer, to be paid when the seller presents the documents required by the letter of credit. The buyer takes the bill of lading to the transportation company that has possession of the goods. With the bill of lading, the buyer obtains possession of the goods. The UN Convention on International Bills of Exchange and Promissory Notes[26] provides the rules in this area.

[25]The Uniform Customs and Practices for Documentary Credits was discussed in Chapter 12. More information is available at http://www.uncitral.org.

[26]The UN Convention on International Bills of Exchange and Promissory Notes was discussed in Chapter 12. Its Web site is at http://www.uncitral.org/english/texts/payments/paymentsindex.htm.

Export Facilitators. Exporters may know their own business, but unless engaged in exporting on a large scale, most need assistance in navigating through the various government regulations. Exporters can hire consultants, but most exporters need expert help in the actual transaction. Two common export facilitators are freight forwarders and customs brokers.

Freight Forwarders. An exporter contracts with a freight forwarder to provide three services: freight arrangement, document handling, and information services. A freight forwarder buys cargo space with an airline or marine shipping company. Based on the exporter's needs, the forwarder may purchase either the entire space on a cargo airplane or ship or may combine the cargo with shipments from other exporters to obtain a lower cost based on a consolidated rate.

The basic documentation for shipping goods internationally is the same as for shipping goods domestically. The exporter supplies the freight forwarder with a commercial invoice and a packing list. The rest of the documentation needed to ship goods internationally varies from country to country. For example, alligator handbags entering the United States from Italy require a certificate indicating that the leather does not come from an endangered species. Goods entering Mexico from the United States require a certificate of origin indicating that they were actually manufactured in the United States.

The U.S. Customs and Border Protection and the Department of Commerce must be informed of products being shipped to safeguard U.S. interests and to provide trade statistics. An invoice is required by the destination country for the shipment to pass through that country's customs. The importer may require a quality certificate or an insurance certificate. The freight forwarder ensures that all required documentation accompanies the cargo.

The freight forwarder also has tracking and tracing abilities. It keeps the exporter and importer informed on the cargo's progress across international borders. Once the destination country is reached, the freight forwarder can follow the cargo's movement from the seaport or airport to the destination warehouse or to the importer directly. All appropriate documents accompany the shipment. Both the exporter and the freight forwarder retain copies.

Customs Broker. A customs broker is licensed to conduct customs business on behalf of others. The customs business concerns the entry and admissibility of products through customs and the classification and valuation of those products. The customs broker ensures that duties, taxes, or other assessed charges are paid. The service provides information to the exporter or importer on the cost of clearing merchandise through customs.

A customs broker may be licensed in several countries and may offer other services, such as freight forwarding services. For example, a customs broker may be licensed in both the United States and in Mexico and is authorized to advise clients of customs procedures in both countries. If the broker also handles freight forwarding, it can make transportation arrangements for cargo shipment. A broker can handle the document preparation needed for cargo shipment.

Export Transaction Documents. Many documents are required to export a product. Some documents are required because they are part of normal business procedures, such as shipment documents. The government requires others. The use of accurate and complete export documentation can avoid costly delays.

Shipment Documents. Shipment documents include the bill of lading, marine bill, or airway bill. Land carriers use a bill of lading, ocean carriers use a marine bill, and airlines use an airway bill. All three documents are virtually the same, but the name reflects the type of transportation. The documents establish the contract terms between the shipper (the freight forwarder) and the transportation company. These documents also represent the title to the goods. The contract details that freight is to be moved between two points for a specified price. Although the carrier provides the forms, the shipper prepares them. The bill of lading, marine bill, or airway bill serves as a document of title, a contract or carriage, and a receipt for the goods.

Another shipment document is a warehouse receipt. If the goods are not delivered directly to the buyer, the seller arranges for the goods to be sent to a warehouse. To claim the goods, the seller must send the warehouse receipt to the buyer.

Usually, the seller sends the warehouse receipt through a factor or bank, so the buyer must pay for the goods or have credit extended prior to the release of the warehouse receipt to the buyer. The buyer takes the receipt to the warehouse and claims the goods. A warehouse receipt may be issued prior to or after the goods have been shipped and may serve as a document of title.

Invoices and Certificates. A packing list is sent with the goods to show the detailed contents of the package, such as the number and kind of items being shipped. The invoice shows the buyer and seller, the shipment and payment terms, and the product. The invoice and all packing lists, if more than one carton or item is sent, should conform.

As discussed earlier in this chapter, exportation of certain types of goods may require an export license. A shipper's export declaration (SED) is a form that must be filed with the U.S. Department of Commerce for any shipment valued at more than $500. An export declaration is a formal statement made to the collector of customs at a port of exit declaring the full particulars about

LEGAL HIGHLIGHT

Ethics in International Sales

American businesses must consider the effects of selling their products in foreign markets. A product appropriate to the American market may be unacceptable in other countries. Marketing techniques should always be directed so that a company does not exploit a foreign economy. The following are some examples.

In the United States and the rest of the industrialized world, the consumption of tobacco has decreased in recent years. Meanwhile, the use of tobacco is increasing in developing countries. These countries' governments are very involved in tobacco sales, either through their ownership of the distributor or through their taxation of the products. Because this involvement provides these governments with a positive revenue flow, they refrain from discouraging tobacco use.

After the 1964 U.S. Surgeon General's Report, U.S. tobacco companies moved abroad, entering into marketing arrangements with foreign firms through business agreements and making direct investments in production facilities.

To this day, U.S. trade policy pressures countries, such as the People's Republic of China, to open their markets to our products, one of which is tobacco. U.S. tobacco companies compete for a share of the Chinese market, where the percentage of smokers has increased greatly during the past twenty years. As the number of smokers has increased, the diseases associated with smoking have likewise increased.

Did the tobacco companies employ ethical conduct in moving their production overseas or in trying to open new markets for tobacco? Is it up to foreign governments to regulate this area based on determining the good of their own citizens? Is it ethical, however, for the governments of poorer nations to use valuable foreign exchange on a product that poses serious health hazards? Should the foreign governments, instead, purchase products that would improve their health care standards? Should the U.S. government assist in tobacco sales to these countries for the purposes of balancing foreign trade and assisting U.S. producers?

Whereas tobacco use presents a clear health hazard, other products marketed overseas to developing countries would seem benign at first glance. For example, in this country, no major problems developed from the use of baby formula. In developing countries, serious problems arose. These problems centered on three issues.

First, many people in these countries are illiterate. The directions on the side of the box or package have little value to an unschooled consumer. Second, the foreign consumer often dilutes the formula, resulting in undernourished babies. Their mother's milk would have been less likely to cause malnourishment. Third, formula is made by adding water. In many developing countries, the poor quality of the water supply exposes infants to additional health hazards.

Should American companies sell potentially harmful products to developing countries? In these examples, the products themselves were not defective. What ethical responsibility does a business have to its foreign customers?

the goods being exported. For example, on an export declaration for computers being shipped overseas, exact information about the computers must appear.

A certificate of origin indicates where the product was actually produced or assembled. Every article of foreign origin imported into the United States must be marked with its country of origin in such a manner that the ultimate purchaser, for example, a person shopping for a business suit, can see it. The purpose is to allow the ultimate purchaser to decide if she or he would buy or refuse to buy the item based on its country of origin. An agreement, such as NAFTA, may provide a uniform certificate of origin to be used by exporters in all member countries.

An insurance certificate verifies that coverage was purchased by the seller to protect against loss or damage while the goods are in transit. The exporter can arrange to obtain an open cargo insurance policy that the freight forwarder maintains. The open cargo policy allows the exporter to ship products over a specified time period, so long as the maximum amount of value specified in the insurance policy is not exceeded. The exporter need not purchase insurance for each shipment. The buyer may require a quality certificate to ensure that the product meets certain standards.

Developing an Importing Business

Like an exporter, an importer needs to develop its goals and objectives when deciding to import products. A business that intends to import products should perform a market analysis to determine the expected market demand, the expected repeat sales potential, and the existing and likely competition for marketing the same or similar products. The business should also evaluate the life expectancy, warranties, and quality of the product.

Because its product is located in another country, the importer needs to consider the logistics of importing the product. The U.S. government may have import restrictions. The Food and Drug Administration requirements must be met for food or plant products. Other products may need approval by other government agencies. The product may need to be repackaged in order to be sold at the retail level. U.S. specifications may differ from those of the exporting country, so the importer must determine if modifications need to be made. Transportation costs may be involved to move the goods from the seaport or airport to the final destination. Compliance with each of these steps increases the sales price.

The importer needs to know if the supplier is reliable and has supplies available to meet the importer's expected demand for the product. Once the product is in the United States, the importer must ensure that it meets U.S. safety and durability standards. The importer must consider the product's price, the order lead time needed, installation and maintenance requirements, and likely technical problems.

The importer also needs to determine the classification and duty rate for the imported goods. For this information, an importer refers to the Harmonized Tariff Schedule of the United States (HTSUS). Sometimes the U.S. Customs and Border Protection agency disputes the classification of import goods. The proper classification is critical in determining the tariff rate that is applied to a particular product. Tariff or duty means a tax imposed on imported products. The problem of classification is discussed in the following case.

CASE 13.4	**MARUBENI AMERICA CORP. v. U.S.**
United States Court of Appeals, Federal Circuit, 1994 35 F.3d 530	**BACKGROUND AND FACTS** Marubeni America Corporation imported vehicles manufactured by Nissan in Japan. Nissan began to manufacture a vehicle named the "Pathfinder." This vehicle had two doors, two-wheel or four-wheel drive, and a body that consisted of one unit. This body was configured much like an ordinary station wagon in that it had rear seats that folded forward (but not flat) to create extra cargo space. The spare tire was housed within the cargo space or attached outside the vehicle on the rear hatch, depending on the model. The rear hatch operated like that of a station wagon. The vehicle, however, was built around a frame normally used for a truck. The cab portion from the front bumper to the frame was consistent with that of a truck.

The import duty on passenger vehicles was 2.5 percent, whereas the duty for trucks was 25 percent. U.S. Customs took the position that this vehicle was a truck. Marubeni America Corporation sued. The trial court reversed the position of U.S. Customs, and the government appealed.

Circuit Judge RICH

. . . .

The issue is whether the Pathfinder has been classified under the appropriate tariff provision. Resolution of that issue entails a two step process: (1) ascertaining the proper meaning of specific terms in the tariff provision; and (2) determining whether the merchandise at issue comes within the description of such terms as properly construed. The first step is a question of law which we review de novo and the second is a question of fact which we review for clear error.

The government asserts that the CIT [Court of International Trade] erred by applying improper and inconsistent standards, and that the Pathfinder is not primarily designed for the transport of persons based on the practice of Nissan and the industry.

. . . .

The two competing provisions of the HTSUS [Harmonized Tariff Schedule of the United States] are set forth below.

> *8703 Motor cars and other motor vehicles principally designed for the transport of persons (other than those of heading 8702), including station wagons and racing cars.*

> *8704 Motor vehicles for the transport of goods.*

There are no legally binding notes to these headings that are relevant to the classification of dual-purpose vehicles such as the Pathfinder; therefore, we need only look to the common meaning of the terms as they appear above.

. . . .

The government argues that "the correct standard to be utilized in determining the principal design of any vehicle must be its construction—its basic structure, body, components, and vehicle layout—and the proper question to be asked is whether that construction is uniquely for passenger transportation."

. . . .

. . . "[R]equir[ing] that the resulting product be uniquely constructed for the purpose of transporting persons," to the exclusion of any other use, is a constrictive interpretation of the terms with which we cannot agree.

There is nothing in the statute, legislative history, or prior Customs decisions that would indicate that "principally designed" refers only to a vehicle's structural design as asserted by the government. To answer the question, whether a vehicle is principally designed for a particular purpose, not uniquely designed for a particular purpose, one must look at both the structural and auxiliary design features, as neither by itself is determinative.

The government's exclusionary construction fails on another point. Heading 8703 HTSUS specifically includes "station wagons," which are not uniquely designed for transport of persons, rather, they are designed as dual-purpose vehicles for the transport of goods and persons. The Pathfinder, like a station wagon, is a vehicle designed with a dual-purpose—to transport goods and persons.

. . . .

The CIT also recognized that the Pathfinder was basically derived from Nissan's Hardbody truck, yet the Pathfinder was based upon totally different design concepts than a truck. The CIT correctly pointed out these differences and more importantly, the reasons behind the design decisions, including the need for speed and economy in manufacturing to capture the changing market, a market into which Nissan was a late entrant. Specifically, the designers decided to adopt the Hardbody's frame side rails and the cab portion from the front bumper to the frame just behind the driver's seat so that they could quickly and economically reach the market. The front suspension system was also adopted from Nissan's truck line but the rear suspension was not. The fact that a vehicle is derived in-part from a truck or from a sedan is not . . . determinative of its intended principal design objectives which were passenger transport and off road capability.

. . . Customs has drawn what appears to be a line between two door and four door versions of sports utility vehicles. . . . This line, classifying two door dual-purpose vehicles for the transport of foods while classifying the four door version as principally designed for transport of persons, appears to be arbitrary.

. . . Two door passenger cars are equipped with a seat slide mechanism that effectively slides the front seat forward to provide easier access to the rear seat. The doors of two door passenger cars are generally wider as well. The CIT found that the Pathfinder has both of these features so that passengers can be easily accommodated. Therefore, the two door Pathfinder accommodates passengers in the rear seat as well as two door passenger cars, if not as easily as four door sports utility vehicles. Consequently, the number of doors on a vehicle should not be determinative.

. . . .

We hold that the court applied the correct legal standards, and that the evidence of record supports the CIT's decision that the Pathfinder is principally designed for the transport of persons.

DECISION AND REMEDY The appeals court upheld the trial court's decision. The Pathfinder was principally designed for the transport of people, not cargo. The court discussed the differences between a passenger car and a truck. The decision was that the Pathfinder was a passenger vehicle and, as such, subject to the lower tariff rate of 2.5 percent.

CRITICAL THINKING: POLITICAL QUESTION Discuss why the import duty of an automobile would be ten times lower than that of a pickup truck.

The classification and duty rate can be determined based on the advice of the importer's customs broker and that of the U.S. Customs and Border Protection agency officials. To avoid problems, the importer can obtain a written letter ruling from the U.S. Customs and Border Protection agency determining the proper classification and duty rate for both current and prospective transactions. A **letter ruling**[27] is the official position of the U.S. Customs and Border Protection agency with respect to a particular product. It is valid until revoked or modified.

[27]Letter rulings are issued by many administrative agencies, such as the U.S. Customs and Border Protection agency or the Internal Revenue Service.

A letter ruling prevents a later charge by the U.S. Customs and Border Protection agency that the importer willfully or negligently misclassified the product, subjecting it to civil penalties, criminal punishment, or both. For example, does sweetened molten chocolate in a tank truck qualify for the lower tariff rate of "Chocolate: Sweetened: in bars or blocks weighing ten pounds or more" or for the higher tariff rate of "Chocolate: Sweetened: in any other form"? A written letter ruling would prevent a dispute if the importer misclassified the product. In this case, an importer argued that its molten chocolate was in a block larger than ten pounds. Because the importer's chocolate was molten and not solidified, the former U.S. Customs prevailed in the lawsuit. The court held that the common meaning would be applied, that is, that bars or blocks meant solidified chocolate. The cost of the lawsuit and possible civil and criminal action could have been avoided if the importer had requested a letter ruling from the former U.S. Customs prior to the product's entry into the United States.

CYBERLAW

Electronic Auctions

Electronic auctions help people and businesses buy and sell products using the World Wide Web. Most people are familiar with business-to-consumer (B2C) types of electronic auctions, such as eBay, which is the English-style auction. The English model is familiar because it is used by public auctions and people have seen it on television or in the movies. Businesses, however, use a business-to-business (B2B) auction model, which is the Dutch-style auction. This model is not familiar to most people because it is conducted privately. The two auction models are opposite in nature.

The B2C electronic auction uses the public network, the Web. The auction house sets up an electronic auction business that is open to the public. Neither the buyer nor the seller is qualified. Because neither is qualified, fraud is inevitable so the electronic auction site provides some protections.

The site offers information on the site as to ways to protect against being defrauded, such as a seller making sure a check has cleared before sending items to a buyer. Buyers can purchase insurance in case the items have been stolen and placed on the Web by the seller-thief. Remember, anytime a person believes he or she has purchased stolen merchandise, the person must notify the police. The sale was made electronically and the purchaser can be traced and charged with possession of stolen property. For example, you purchase a digital camera through an electronic auction site. The digital camera works fine, but has a plate attached saying "Property of State High School. ID # 55-555-55. If found, please return. Call 555-555-5555." Because you did not purchase the item from State High School and since the ID plate was not removed,

you have an obligation to call. At some point, State High School will take inventory and discover that the camera was checked out to a student in the journalism department who cannot account for it. It does not take long to check the student's computers at school and at home to determine that you have the stolen digital camera in your possession.

The seller sets the length of time the auction will last, usually four to seven days. Potential buyers can view the product and choose whether to bid. Usually, bidding starts not long before the end of the auction, commonly during the last hour. Anyone really wanting the item will wait to see the bids of others, then in the last fifteen to thirty seconds place a bid, leaving no time for someone to raise the price. The bid price will be higher than the previous bid, so the price goes up. Once the final bid is in, the winning bidder is obligated to purchase the item.

The B2B auction works in a totally different manner. These auctions are conducted on private networks, so the public is not able to see how they are conducted. A business, such as an automobile manufacturer, needs to build 10,000 automobiles. For example, at this particular auction, the manufacturer needs steel, composite materials, seats, and tires. Of course, the manufacturer wants to purchase these items at as low a price as possible.

In this type of auction, both the purchaser and the suppliers are prequalified. The purchaser must have the financial strength to make the purchases. Both domestic and international suppliers must be able to supply the materials in the quantities needed and be able to ship them in a timely manner. The purchaser may have its own network, such as Covisint,[28] the

[28]Covisint is an independent company. Its home page is at http://www.covisint.com. The name Covisint (pronounced KO-vis-int) is a combination of the primary concepts of why the exchange was formed. The letters "Co" represent connectivity, collaboration, and communication. "Vis" represents the visibility that the Internet provides and the vision of the future of supply chain management. "Int" represents the integrated solutions the venture will provide as well as the international scope of the exchange.

The Web allows a manufacturer's production schedule and any subsequent changes to be sent simultaneously and instantly throughout its entire supply chain. This real-time information results in less costly inventory at all levels of the supply chain and increases the ability to respond quickly to market changes. Purchasers and suppliers, regardless of their size and position in the supply chain, are able to communicate with each other in a real-time, virtual way. The result is lower costs to both the buyer and seller.

automotive Internet exchange formed by General Motors, Ford, DaimlerChrysler, Renault, and Nissan, or the purchaser may select an electronic house that specializes in B2B auctions, such as Free Markets.[29] Either way, the network is private.

A B2B auction is open from one to three hours. A supplier must bid and if it does not, the auction house will call. If the supplier still does not bid, the supplier is disconnected from the network and not allowed to participate or watch the rest of the auction. The auction works in the following manner. A supplier wants to sell its products to the purchaser and bids the sale price. A second supplier sees the bid and it also wants the contract, so the second supplier bids a lower price than the first bidder. As a result, the price of the products is reduced. Often the purchaser can save between 10 and 20 percent, which can translate to multimillions of dollars in savings to the purchaser.

In a B2B auction, the purchaser is not obligated to purchase. The purchaser will look at other things besides lowest price. Other factors are the location of the supplier (for instance, in another state or in another country), stability of transportation when shipping from another country, reputation of the supplier, and many other factors.

A B2C auction is commonplace and establishes as nearly a true market price as possible. A B2B auction is commonplace among businesses and aids in lowering costs to the purchaser.

[29]Free Markets' Web site is located at http://www.freemarkets.com.

Increasing Sales through Exports

You are employed by a small company that has grown steadily and hopes to continue to increase sales substantially during the next year. The firm is owned and managed by a family whose grandparents started it. Because you are the first person to be hired into a management position outside of "family," you want to demonstrate that profits can be increased through additional sales.

The family members tend to be hesitant in initiating new ideas. While in college, you studied aspects of international business, joined international organizations, and traveled overseas on vacation. Profits will increase, you believe, if the business exported overseas. The family members may initially oppose exporting, because they lack an understanding of international business procedures. You want to present solid facts in favor of exporting.

One fact is that the United States has only 5 percent of the world's customers. Your firm currently misses out on selling to 95 percent of its potential customers.

You write a paper on the required government documents, the means to finance the production of the additional products, and the methods of ensuring payment from foreign buyers. You develop answers to specific questions involving the countries on which to concentrate.

Most of this information is provided by the federal government. The government lists the specialists in specific areas. Specific agencies assist small businesses in determining potentially successful international business opportunities, obtaining customer leads, arranging financing, and advising in a number of aspects of international business.

The Commercial Service of the U.S. Department of Commerce is one of the best sources of this type of information. This agency can become your business's international advocate.

The Commercial Service has a global network operation of more than 70 offices in the United States and more than 130 offices all over the world with 1,400 employees dedicated to serving American business firms. Through partnerships with other trade promotion organizations—public and private—the Commercial Service can offer your business comprehensive, customized solutions to international trade challenges.

The International Trade Administration, also located in the U.S. Department of Commerce, has created Export Assistance Centers located in most U.S. commercial centers. These centers assist with international market research, trade contacts, overseas contracts, export credit insurance, and short- and long-term financing.

Before you discuss the idea of exporting with the family members, however, you should research the following items:

Checklist

✔ *Opportunities* Study which countries offer the best opportunity for selling your company's products.

✔ *Business Plan* Present a business plan to the family members on exporting.

✔ *Marketing Plan* Develop a marketing plan within the country or countries. Review from this chapter possible alternative plans.

✔ *Financial Plan* Discuss informally your ideas with local financial institutions to ascertain whether you can obtain their assistance in processing the appropriate financial documents to obtain payment for your product. In many small communities, the local bank lacks the resources or knowledge to assist in this area. You may have to contact a financial institution in a major commercial area to obtain this help.

✔ *Pro Forma Statement* Prepare a pro forma statement indicating the total financial results of exporting.

Chapter Summary

Growth in international business relations has led, in turn, to the development of international law. International law consists of a body of laws that are considered to be legally binding among otherwise independent nations. This legal area has developed through three methods: international customs, agreements that have the force of law, and international organizations and conferences. International customs consist of the relationship that nations have developed over the years with one another on particular legal matters. Agreements are reached either by nations acting independently, as in the signing of treaties, or through international organizations and conferences.

The U.S. Constitution grants authority to Congress and the president to regulate commerce with foreign nations. Several administrative agencies and one court assist in this regulation. The Export Administration Act, the Omnibus Trade and Competitiveness Act, and the Export Trading Company Act are the important statutes dealing with import and export activities. The Export-Import Bank is important to the financial aspects.

Four unfair import practices can result in either goods forfeiture or additional import duties. These practices are dumping; infringement of copyright, patent, trademark, and maskwork laws; government subsidizing; and the sale of gray-market goods.

Exporting and importing involve more people and paperwork than domestic business transactions. To conduct business overseas, a firm may contact an importer directly, but this method is extremely risky. Usually, a business will use one of two indirect methods: either an international distribution agreement or an international agent. Financing also differs for financing imports versus financing domestically purchased products. The exporter needs assurances that it will receive payment, and the importer needs assurances that the product order will be delivered. Five common financing methods are cash in advance, open account, factoring, forfaiting, and letters of credit.

The myriad of government regulations and customs rules and the complexity of shipping product procedures compel the exporter to use the services of freight forwarders or customs brokers. Once a business decides to import goods, it must abide by the U.S. Customs and Border Protection agency rules. To determine the tariff (tax) to be paid, the importer must abide by the Harmonized Tariff Schedule of the United States. When the importer is unsure of the classification, it can request a letter ruling from the U.S. Customs and Border Protection agency to prevent civil penalties, criminal punishment, or both.

Using the World Wide Web

A number of international organizations have Web pages. These sites provide updated and in-depth information about the organization's activities, meetings, and reports. The European Union has a Web site that allows a person to stay abreast of current activities.

The Organization of American States (OAS) is the world's oldest regional organization. It is the principal forum in the hemisphere for dialogue on political, economic, and social issues. Every country in the Americas is a member of the OAS. Its headquarters is located in Washington, D.C.

The United Nations has locations throughout the world. It has a well-developed Web site. The countries that have the eight largest economies are called the Group of Eight (G-8). They are Canada, France, Germany, Italy, Japan, the Russian Federation, the United Kingdom, and the United States. The G-8 is often referred to as the G-7 (Group of Seven) when the Russian Federation does not attend.

Developments involving the North American Free Trade Agreement and the Free Trade Association of the Americas can be tracked using the Web. The same is true of the Web sites for the United Nations and the European Union.

These Web sites open with a choice of languages. Choose the language you are most comfortable with and proceed to explore.

For *Web Activities*, links to Web sites mentioned in the chapter, and additional Web sites that relate to the chapter topics, go to **http://bohlman.westbuslaw .com**, click on "Internet Applications," and select Chapter 13.

Web Activities

Go to **http://bohlman.westbuslaw.com**, click on "Internet Applications," and select Chapter 13.
13–1 U.S. Small Business Administration
13–2 U.S. Customs and Border Protection

Key Terms

ad valorem tariff
bill of exchange
choice-of-forum clause
choice-of-law clause
compact
convention
countervailing duty
Court of International
    Trade (CIT)
customs brokers
dumping
executive agreement
Export Administration
    Act
Export-Import Bank
    (Eximbank)
Export Trading
    Company Act
exporting
factor

flat-rate tariff
forfaiter
freight forwarders
General Agreement on
    Tariffs and Trade
    (GATT)
General Agreement on
    Trade in Services
    (GATS)
general license
gray-market goods
importing
international agent
international custom
international law
International Trade
    Administration (ITA)
International Trade
    Commission (ITC)
letter of credit

letter ruling
Maastricht Agreement
National Export Strategy
national treatment
normal trade relations
Omnibus Trade and
    Competitiveness Act
    (OTCA)
parallel import
protocol
quota
tariff
Trade Act
Trade Agreement Act
trade promotion
    authority
Trade-related Aspects of
    Intellectual Property
    Rights (TRIPS)
treaty

U.S. Customs and
    Border Protection
U.S. Trade Representa-
    tive (USTR)
validated license
Vienna Convention on
    the Law of Treaties
World Trade Organiza-
    tion (WTO)

Questions and Case Problems

13–1 Export You own a small manufacturing business and are considering exporting products to increase sales. Your major concern is receiving payment once the goods have been shipped. What methods are available to ensure that you receive payment? Explain how your choice of method would depend on the type of product that is sold. What other factors should you consider in making your final decision?

13–2 Imports XYZ, Inc., desires to import goods from a business in Haiti. It wants to be certain that the goods it receives are those that it ordered and that the goods are received in acceptable condition. The Haitian business wants payment if the goods are shipped. Describe the procedures that should be followed.

13–3 Conflict between Federal Law and a Treaty Congress passed a poultry inspection statute, called the Poultry Products Inspection Act (PPIA). The statute contained a provision mandating that all imported poultry products be subject to the same inspection, sanitation, quality, species verification, and residue standards applied to poultry products produced in the United States. The Department of Agriculture and the Food Safety and Inspection Services (Agency) adopted a regulation that required foreign producers to have inspection procedures "at least equal to" those applicable to local producers. The Mississippi Poultry Association, which represented the local poultry associations, took exception to the language "at least equal to" because it differed from statutory language of "be subject to the same" standards. The Agency took the position that this interpretation would place the regulation in violation of a GATT provision. Who prevailed? Explain your answer. [*Mississippi Poultry Association v. Madigan*, 992 F.2d 1359 (1993)]

13–4 Import Duty Sears, Roebuck & Co. imported from Japan electronic merchandise consisting of tuners, amplifiers, turntables, and dual cassette decks, as well as wooden racks. Its speakers were manufactured in the United States. Sears put these items into three boxes and sold them as the model 9291 stereo rack system. One box contained the speakers, one contained the rack, and the last contained the electronic merchandise. Sears took the position that this was an entire system that should be taxed at a 4.2 percent rate. The government argued that the three individual components should be taxed at different rates ranging from 4.2 to 7.7 percent.

Testimony was given that all of the components were advertised and sold as one complete system. Most of the items, however, could be used with other products with little or no modification. Should these items be treated as one complete commercial entity or should they be taxed individually? Explain your answer. [*Sears, Roebuck & Co. v. United States*, 723 F. Supp. 805 (Ct. Int'l Trade, 1989)]

13–5 Antidumping and Countervailing Duty The plaintiffs represented the domestic prestressed concrete steel wire stand industry. They believed the wire stand manufactured in Spain, France, and Brazil was being subsidized by those governments and sued the foreign manufacturers. Prior to the court's ruling, the plaintiffs' domestic production increased steadily over several years and employment in the industry likewise increased. The International Trade Commission (ITC), based on this information, found that the importers' actions did not create a material injury to the domestic producers. The ITC did not apply the antidumping and countervailing duty provisions. The plaintiffs argued that their net profits had decreased because of the subsidies. Should the court reverse the findings of the ITC based on reduced profits? Support your reasons. [*American Spring Wire Corp. v. United States*, 590 F. Supp. 1273 (Ct. Int'l Trade, 1984)]

13–6 Gray-Market Goods Lever Brothers Company (Lever US), an American company, and its British affiliate, Lever Brothers Limited (Lever UK), both manufacture deodorant soap under the "Shield" trademark. The trademark was registered in each country. The products were formulated differently to suit local tastes. The U.S. version lathered more and the two soaps smelled different. A third party unrelated to either Lever US or Lever UK purchased the Lever UK-made Shield and imported Shield into the United States. Numerous complaints about the product were filed by persons who had purchased the Lever UK Shield, thinking it was the U.S. product. Lever US wanted the U.S. Customs Service to stop these imports. Customs refused, because it had a regulation that allowed the importation of goods with the same trademark if they were manufactured by a subsidiary company. Lever US sued the U.S. Customs Service and sought an order from the court to stop the importation of the gray-market goods that were physically different from the U.S. goods. Neither Lever US nor Lever UK authorized the importation by the third party and they wanted the importation terminated. What result and why? [*Lever Brothers Co. v. United States,* 981 F.2d 1330 (1993)]

13–7 International Agreement Charles T. Main International brought an action to recover assets that had been lost because of the shah's overthrow in Iran. To obtain the release of hostages, President Jimmy Carter signed an agreement to submit all claims by either Iran or the United States to binding arbitration. The plaintiff wanted to recover assets from Iran that had been frozen in the United States. Main claimed that the president's agreement, freezing Iranian assets, exceeded the president's authority and violated his company's constitutional rights because the freeze amounted to the taking of company property without just compensation. Explain the result. [*Charles T. Main International v. Khuzestan and Power Authority,* 651 F.2d 800 (1st Cir. 1981)]

13–8 Arbitration Mitsubishi Motor Corp. and Soler Chrysler-Plymouth entered a contract that required binding arbitration. A dispute occurred and Mitsubishi wanted to arbitrate it. Soler Chrysler-Plymouth claimed that Mitsubishi had violated the U.S. antitrust laws, which made the parties' contract illegal and thus not subject to arbitration. Who prevailed in this case? Explain. [*Mitsubishi Motor Corp. v. Soler Chrysler-Plymouth,* 473 U.S. 614, 105 S. Ct. 3346, 87 L. Ed. 2d 444 (1985)] (See Chapter 4, concerning arbitration.)

13–9 Import Hasbro Industries imported G.I. Joe action figures that could be manipulated. Hasbro advertised G.I. Joe as a doll. G.I. Joe also appeared in doll collector books. Letters from purchasers referred to the figure as a doll. Hasbro requested U.S. Customs to classify the G.I. Joe action figures as "toy figures," that is, as a modern update of a toy soldier. This classification would allow G.I. Joe to be imported duty free (tax free). If classified as a doll, Hasbro would have to pay duties. The U.S. Customs office determined that the G.I. Joe action figures were dolls because the figures were individually named and provided with specific biographical information, thus inviting play. Because U.S. Customs found that the G.I. Joe action figures were not comparable to toy figures, G.I. Joe was subject to a tariff. Do you think that a G.I. Joe is a doll or a toy figure that should be imported duty free? Explain. [*Hasbro Industries v. United States,* 879 F.2d 838 (Fed. Cir. 1989)]

13–10 Internet Explain the difference between the Trade Information Centers and the Export Assistance Centers. Go to **http://www.ita.doc.gov** and to **http://www.sba.gov/oit/export/useac.html** for information about each organization.

Chapter 14

Rights of Consumers, Debtors, and Creditors

Creditors have better memories than debtors, they are a superstitious sect, great observers of set days and times.

Benjamin Franklin, 1706–1790
American statesman, scientist, and public leader

Chapter Outline

Ethical Consideration

Can You Be Required to Have Credit Life Insurance?

You are the sole owner of both Fine Automobiles Dealership and Cheap Rates Insurance Company. When Fine Automobiles Dealership sells an automobile on credit, it requires all purchasers to acquire credit life, credit disability, and credit unemployment insurance. This type of insurance guarantees the monthly automobile payment in case of death, disability, or unemployment. Fine Automobiles Dealership has a serious, legitimate concern regarding continued payment of the automobile loan in case of death, disability, or unemployment. Under federal law, the cost of this insurance must be treated as an interest expense.

The Fine Automobiles Dealership sales force is required to recommend only Cheap Rates Insurance Company, which earns a substantial premium from selling this insurance. In fact, Cheap Rates Insurance Company has a low claim rate and a high income over expenses. Thus, Cheap Rates Insurance Company can pay its shareholders high dividends.

Is it ethical for Fine Automobiles Dealership to require such insurance from its credit customers through Cheap Rates? Is it ethical for Fine Automobiles Dealership to recommend to its customers only Cheap Rates Insurance Company rather than advising them to shop around to determine if Cheap Rates Insurance Company actually does provide the best coverage for the lowest rates? Use the ethical model presented in Chapter 2 and reprinted on the inside front cover to develop your answer.

Introduction

Purchase on credit is a basic element of our business community. In the last fifty years, the United States has converted from a cash to a credit society. Consumer credit card use led this transformation. Consumer credit has increased from $2.5 billion at the end of World War II to $1.4 trillion by 2002. Major consumer products, such as automobiles, stereos, televisions, and furniture, are almost always purchased on credit. Consumer credit rests on two assumptions: the debtor's willingness to pay and the debtor's ability to pay.

By the mid-1960s, the tremendous increase in credit unfortunately had led to a rise in consumer abuse. Consumers were insufficiently informed about shopping comparatively for interest rates. They were misled into signing installment contracts. Few regulations protected consumers from harassment by debt collectors. They were denied access to their credit reports. Worst of all, the consumer had little recourse from computer billing errors. State law failed to adequately protect consumers.

The U.S. Congress became concerned and, in 1968, adopted the Consumer Credit Protection Act, which has been amended several times. After a discussion of this act and its amendments, the chapter ends with sections on the rights of creditors and a review of some bankruptcy laws.

Artiste Login. Carlo and Carlotta's business, Artiste Login Products, Inc., deals with consumer credit on a daily basis. People send paper checks and money orders through the mail. They also use electronic checks. Most of their consumers, however, purchase online using a credit card through the company's secured Web site.

Consumer Credit Protection Act

The **Consumer Credit Protection Act (CCPA)** is the primary source of federal law covering credit transactions. Numerous federal agencies enforce the CCPA. Individual consumers also can use the act to protect their rights when a business fails to fully comply with the CCPA's provisions. The legal consequences vary for each provision violated, but both criminal and civil sanctions result if a business fails to comply.

The Consumer Credit Protection Act has been amended over the decades. These amendments are known by their popular names, which are listed here:

1. Consumer Credit Cost Disclosure Act, commonly known as the Truth-in-Lending Act;
2. Fair Credit Billing Act;
3. Fair Credit Reporting Act;

4. Equal Credit Opportunity Act; and

5. Fair Debt Collection Practices Act.

The Electronic Fund Transfer Act discussed in Chapter 12 also is part of the Consumer Credit Protection Act.

Consumer Credit Cost Disclosure: Truth-in-Lending Act

During hearings in 1968, Congress discovered that financial institutions stated interest rates and the loan's total dollar cost in a variety of ways. Rates of interest were based on recognized, but varying, financial methods of calculation. No uniform method of stating an interest rate existed. Congress heard considerable debate as to whether charges for insurance, credit reports, discount points, and other items should be classified as interest charges. Prior to 1968, a consumer could not shop for credit because of the difficulties in comparing one lending institution's charges with another.

To resolve this problem, Congress passed the Consumer Credit Protection Act. Title I of the act is known as the **Consumer Credit Cost Disclosure Act**, more commonly called the **Truth-in-Lending Act (TILA)**. The TILA deals with deceptive credit practices and requires notice and disclosure to prevent sellers and creditors from taking unfair advantage of consumers. Through disclosure, the purchaser can compare more easily the available credit terms. The act applies to most consumer credit transactions.

Disclosure Requirements of the TILA. The disclosure requirements apply to credit transactions in which a finance charge is imposed or in which payment is made in more than four installments. The most important information that a lender must disclose includes (1) the cash price; (2) the down payment or trade-in allowance, if any; (3) the unpaid cash price (the cash price minus the down payment) that is to be financed; (4) the **finance charge** (the total amount of interest and other charges, such as filing fees and insurance premiums); and (5) the **annual percentage rate** (the true rate of interest charged on a yearly basis) by which the finance charge is calculated.

The creditor also must tell the debtor the date on which the finance charge begins to accumulate; the number, amounts, and due dates of payments; the late-payment charges; and whether there is a prepayment penalty. A prepayment penalty is an amount that the debtor pays if he pays off the debt early. In the past, the prepayment penalty often was a substantial amount of the debt. For example, Harris borrows $5,000. Over time, he has paid back $4,000 in monthly installments. He now wants to pay the remaining $1,000 early in one last payment. According to the terms of the contract, in order to pay the loan early, the prepayment penalty is calculated to be $2,000. In other words, he would have to pay a total of $3,000 in order to pay off the loan early. Today, many states ban prepayment penalties.

The provisions of the Truth-in-Lending Act apply to both sales and leases of personal and real property. Two key terms summarize the act's disclosure philosophy: finance charge and annual percentage rate. Armed with this information, the consumer can comparison shop for a loan or for credit.

The Federal Reserve Board issues the administrative rules that implement the TILA. Known as Regulation Z,[1] these rules include model forms for businesses to follow when selling goods. The forms, if used correctly by a business, fully comply with the statute. Exhibits 14–1 and 14–2 provide examples that come from the Code of Federal Regulations.

The **Consumer Leasing Act** requires full disclosure of all financial terms in consumer leasing contracts. The Federal Reserve Board's Regulation M governs this area. It requires disclosures to consumers similar to those required by Regulation Z.

Creditors Subject to the TILA. The Truth-in-Lending Act applies to businesses that, in the ordinary course of their operations, lend money, sell on credit, or arrange for the extension of credit to consumers. The TILA protects only human debtors; that is, business entities and governmental agencies are not protected by the act. Furthermore, sales or loans made between two consumers do not come under the act's jurisdiction.

Transactions involving purchases of property (real or personal) for personal, family, household, or agricultural use come under the terms and provisions of the act if the amount being financed is less than $25,000. Transactions covered by the act typically

---

[1] Regulation Z can be found at http://www.federalreserve.gov/regulations/default.htm.

Exhibit 14-1   Loan Model Form Supplied by the Federal Reserve Board

ANNUAL PERCENTAGE RATE The cost of your credit as a yearly rate.	FINANCE CHARGE The dollar amount the credit will cost you.	AMOUNT FINANCED The amount of credit provided to you or on your behalf.	TOTAL OF PAYMENTS The amount you will have paid after you have made all payments as scheduled.
%	$	$	$

You have the right to receive at the time an itemization of the Amount Financed.
❑ I want an itemization.   ❑ I do not want an itemization.

Your payment schedule will be:

Insurance

Credit life insurance and credit disability insurance are not required to obtain credit, and will not be provided unless you sign and agree to pay the additional cost.

Credit Life		I want credit life insurance.	_____ Signature
Credit Disability		I want credit disability insurance.	_____ Signature
Credit Life and Disability		I want credit life and disability insurance.	_____ Signature

You may obtain property insurance from anyone you want that is acceptable to   (creditor)   . If you get the insurance from   (creditor)   . You will pay $ _____ .

Security: You are giving a security interest in:
❑ The goods or property being purchased.
❑ (Brief description of other property).

Filing Fees $ _____   Non-filing insurance $ _____

Late Charge: If payment is late, you will be charged $ _____ / _____ % of the payment.

Prepayment: If you pay off early, you
❑ may   ❑ will not   have to pay a penalty.
❑ may   ❑ will not   be entitled to a refund of part of the finance charge.

See your contract documents for any additional information about nonpayment, default, any required repayment in full before the scheduled date, and prepayment refunds and penalties.

e means an estimate

Source: 12 *Code of Federal Regulations,* Section 226, Appendix H-2, 2000.

include retail and installment sales, installment loans, car loans, home improvement loans, and certain real estate loans. Real estate loans of more than $25,000 on a debtor's residence are not covered by the act.

Penalties. A creditor who fails to comply with the disclosure requirements may be liable to the consumer for any actual damages plus twice the amount of the finance charge and attorneys' fees. Damages may not

Exhibit 14-2   Credit Sale Model Form Supplied by the Federal Reserve Board

ANNUAL PERCENTAGE RATE The cost of your credit as a yearly rate.	FINANCE CHARGE The dollar amount the credit will cost you.	AMOUNT FINANCED The amount of credit provided to you or on your behalf.	TOTAL OF PAYMENTS The amount you will have paid after you have made all payments as scheduled.	TOTAL SALE PRICE The total cost of your purchase on credit, including your downpayment of $ _____
%	$	$	$	$

You have the right to receive at the time an itemization of the Amount Financed.
   ❏ I want an itemization.   ❏ I do not want an itemization.

Your payment schedule will be:

Insurance
Credit life insurance and credit disability insurance are not required to obtain credit, and will not be provided unless you sign and agree to pay the additional cost.

Credit Life		I want credit life insurance.	Signature _____
Credit Disability		I want credit disability insurance.	Signature _____
Credit Life and Disability		I want credit life and disability insurance.	Signature _____

You may obtain property insurance from anyone you want that is acceptable to   (creditor) . If you get the insur-

ance from   (creditor) . You will pay $ _____.

Security: You are giving a security interest in:
   ❏ The goods or property being purchased.
   ❏ (Brief description of other property).

Filing Fees $ _____   Non-filing insurance $ _____

Late Charge: If payment is late, you will be charged $ _____ / _____ % of the payment.

Prepayment: If you pay off early, you
   ❏ may   ❏ will not   have to pay a penalty.
   ❏ may   ❏ will not   be entitled to a refund of part of the finance charge.

See your contract documents for any additional information about nonpayment, default, any required repayment in full before the scheduled date, and prepayment refunds and penalties.

e means an estimate

Source: 12 *Code of Federal Regulations,* Section 226, Appendix H-1, 2000.

exceed $2,000. The total liability for a class action is $500,000 or 1 percent of the creditor's net worth, whichever is less.

The consumer has one year from the date of the violation to bring suit against a creditor who failed to provide the disclosure statement. A creditor who willfully and knowingly violates these provisions is liable criminally and may be fined $5,000, imprisoned for up to one year, or both. In addition, the debtor can rescind the transaction at any time up to three years from the date of the transaction.

Other Provisions of the CCPA

Over the years, Congress has added statutes to the CCPA's initial provisions. These provisions cover real estate improvements, credit and debit card usage, credit billing errors, equal credit opportunities, and debt collection practices.

Real Estate. A consumer wants to improve her residence. She enters into a contract with a creditor to borrow the money and, in turn, provides the creditor a security interest in the residence to secure payment for the improvement.

The TILA gives the consumer-borrower the right to rescind the contract by midnight of the third business day following the signing of the contract even though all disclosure provisions of the TILA have been followed. This protection is called the *three-day rescission rule*. A consumer must be given notice of this right to rescind along with the material disclosures of annual percentage rate, the finance charge, the amount financed, the total payments, and the payment schedule.

For example, Sandy wants to have a pool built. She signs a contract with Pool Company to have the pool built for $20,000. Sandy does not have $20,000, so she signs a note to repay the $20,000 and provides Pool Company a security interest in her home. If she fails to repay the note, Pool Company can go to court to force the sale of Sandy's house to recover the loan amount that has not been repaid. For a creditor to have this right, however, the contract must state clearly Sandy's right to rescind the contract within three business days after the signing of the contract. Further, it must include all disclosure requirements.

If Sandy rescinds the contract within the three business days, the security interest in her residence is void and she pays no finance charge. The Pool Company must return any money or property that it received (such as a down payment) and Sandy must return anything that she received (in this example, probably nothing). If the return is impracticable, the consumer must pay the reasonable value of what has been received.

The three-day rescission rule does not apply in two situations. The first involves an emergency situation in which the customer needs to have his home repaired immediately, as in the case of damage resulting from a fire or storm. The second situation concerns the purchase money lender. The rule does not apply to a creditor that lends money in order for a consumer to purchase a residence if the creditor takes a lien (mortgage). The following case illustrates the need for businesses to comply with the Truth-in-Lending Act requirements.

CASE 14.1	## STUTSMAN COUNTY STATE BANK v. FEDERAL DEPOSIT INSURANCE CORPORATION

United States Court of Appeals, Eighth Circuit, 2000

207 F.3d 464

BACKGROUND AND FACTS During a period of nearly two years beginning in August 1996, Stutsman assessed and collected a one-time processing fee for each credit account opened pursuant to a particular open-ended credit plan, without disclosing the processing fee in the Initial Disclosure Statement.

The parties stipulated, among other things, that the processing fees in question varied from $27 to $59 and that they cumulatively affected approximately 25,640 active accounts, for a total of approximately $1,470,938. Stutsman presented evidence to show that it had disclosed the processing fee in a script read to credit applicants over the telephone and in written credit approval letters and that a third party had generated and mailed the Initial Disclosure Statements pursuant to a contract with Stutsman.

The administrative law judge (ALJ) concluded that Stutsman had engaged in a clear and consistent pattern or practice of violations, requiring reimbursement of the affected customers under 15 U.S.C. § 1607(e)(1), and that waiver of the reimbursement requirement was not warranted under any of the exceptions in 15 U.S.C. § 1607(e)(2)(A)–(D) (the Truth-in-Lending statutes). Upon review of the ALJ's findings and recommendation, the Federal Deposit Insurance Corporation Board of Directors (Board) affirmed and adopted the ALJ's conclusions.

PER CURIAM

. . . .

We have carefully reviewed the ALJ's findings and recommendations, the Board's decision and order, the record on appeal, and the arguments of the parties. We deny the petition for review because the Board's factual findings are supported by substantial evidence on the record as a whole and because the Board has thoroughly examined the relevant data and has articulated a satisfactory explanation for its legal conclusions, including a rational connection between its findings of fact and the remedy imposed.

Stutsman's petition for review of the Board's decision and order is denied.

DECISION AND REMEDY Charging a fee for a consumer open credit account and not informing the consumer about the fee in writing prior to the credit being granted was a direct violation of the Truth-in-Lending Act and Regulation Z. The bank was required to make a full refund of these fees.

CRITICAL THINKING: MANAGERIAL CONSIDERATION As a bank manager, should you have been concerned about the letter of the law or its main purpose? Did the bank attempt to comply with the purpose of the law? If so, why then did the bank not prevail?

Credit Cards. The TILA has specific provisions that cover the issuance and use of credit cards.[2] First, an individual or a business must request that an initial credit card be sent. Any unauthorized use of an unrequested card cannot be charged to the named cardholder. Renewal credit cards, however, can be sent without a specific request.

Second, if a credit card is lost or stolen, $50 is the limit of the cardholder's liability for the unauthorized card use. The $50 limit is for each card, so if a consumer loses ten cards, the actual loss to the consumer could be $500.

Debit Cards. Debit cards are used to debit the customer's bank account immediately through the use of electronic transfer of funds. People often use debit cards at automatic teller machines or in stores when making purchases. To use a debit card, the user must provide a PIN (personal information number) at the time of the transaction.

If a debit card is lost or stolen, the consumer is liable for an unauthorized transfer of up to only $50 if he takes reasonable steps to notify the financial institution within two business days after the loss or theft. After the two-day period, the consumer's liability increases to $500. If the consumer fails to report the card loss or theft or any unauthorized charges within sixty days, the consumer has unlimited liability. If a person is unable to notify the institution of a loss or theft because of extended travel or hospitalization, he has a reasonable time to notify the institution.

Cards are being developed to take advantage of technology. For example, MasterCard is currently issuing what is known as PayPass cards. These cards work like a wand, which is waived in front of a sensor. Cards of this nature are particularly beneficial when the merchant must handle a large number of customers quickly. For persons who work but do not have a bank account, the payroll card is being developed and tested. The employer places a worker's earnings on a payroll card, which the employee can use as a debit card. Another type of card uses a radio-frequency identification system. The radio-frequency card was used at the Salt Lake City Winter Olympics by the athletes to pay for vending machine purchases. The future

[2]The Truth-in-Lending Act is found at http://www.law.cornell.edu/uscode/15/1601.html. The Federal Trade Commission has various consumer protection acts on its Web site at http://www.ftc.gov.

LEGAL HIGHLIGHT

Who Really Loses in Cases of Credit Card Fraud?

Popular credit card companies have advertised that they will protect consumers if their credit cards are misused or if they are defrauded. A $50 limit on losses is mandated by federal law when credit cards are lost or stolen and then misused. But what happens when a person purchases an expensive item that costs more that $50 over the Web or through a mail-order firm and then the consumer never receives the goods? Do the credit card companies live up to their advertisements that they will protect the consumer in these types of cases?

Credit card companies will assume the loss if the seller is dishonest or goes out of business. These companies do not assume the liability if the credit card is lost or stolen and then misused by a third person. In those situations, the credit card companies go back to the merchants who took the lost or stolen credit card and allowed the charges to be made. The credit card companies send warnings to their merchants. If they fail to heed the warning list and allow the credit card to be used, the credit card companies reverse the charges back to the merchant. An additional fee is imposed for the cost of charging the costs back to the merchant. The end result is the retailer incurs the loss, not the credit card company.

---

will bring more changes to credit/debit cards to make them more user friendly. As these changes are being made, one question is whether the current law is sufficient to cover these changes or whether the law will need to be updated to reflect future issues.

Fair Credit Billing Act. Even computers make errors on charge accounts. The experience of correcting these errors can be unnerving. An amendment to the TILA, the **Fair Credit Billing Act**, requires creditors to correct errors promptly and without damage to a person's credit rating. See Exhibit 14–3 on page 424 for a sample notice of billing error rights.

A person who believes that her charge account statement is in error must notify the creditor in writing with a statement explaining the perceived error. The customer must pay the undisputed amount while waiting for an answer from the business on the amount in question. Within thirty days, the creditor must acknowledge the inquiry and within ninety days the creditor either must correct the account or provide an explanation as to why the creditor believes the account to be correct. During this time, the creditor is not allowed to give an unfavorable credit report or to attempt to collect the amount in dispute.

INFOTRAC RESEARCH ACTIVITY

InfoTrac offers many articles about the Fair Credit Billing Act. Some of these describe problems that have occurred involving billing mistakes and what a person can do about the mistake. Go to InfoTrac and type in "Fair Credit Billing Act." Read the most recent five articles and summarize them.

Fair Credit Reporting Act. At one time, consumers had no access to the contents of credit and investigative reports kept on them by credit reporting agencies. Consumers also had no control over the use of these reports. Inaccuracies, once reported, were almost impossible to uncover, much less to correct.

In 1970, Congress enacted the **Fair Credit Reporting Act**. Consumers are entitled, on request, to be informed of the nature and scope of a credit investigation, the kind of information that is compiled, and the names of people who will receive the report.

Any inaccurate or misleading material must be reinvestigated and, if not verified, removed from the file. Consumers have the right to include in the file

LEGAL HIGHLIGHT

Identity Theft—the Financial Institution's Role

Identity theft is the fastest growing white-collar crime. Roughly 100,000 identities are stolen each year. This crime costs financial institutions more than $2.4 billion a year.

To battle this problem, banks and credit unions have initiated new procedures. Some banks require a thumb print on the back of checks from noncustomers who want to cash a check. Other banks obtain a credit report before opening a new account. If the new cus-tomer balks, the account is not opened. Other banks call the residence of a new customer and also verify the telephone number with the telephone company. Social Security numbers or the mother's maiden name, once used for identification, are no longer effective in the Internet age, because this information is easy to obtain. Some banks now require the customer to change his or her password every sixty or ninety days.

In the future, voice, iris, retina, or finger scans will become standard procedure for identification. This information will be embedded in a chip on a smart card. The financial institutions need to be aggressive in this area because they cannot continue to lose $2.4 billion a year.

---

their own 100-word statement describing their position with regard to any disputed matters. The law also provides for updating information. Information more than seven years old must be deleted. Information regarding any bankruptcy more than ten years old must be removed.

The original act was modified in 1996 by the passing of the Consumer Reporting Reform Act.[3] This act requires all credit bureaus to make an employee, not recordings, available when a consumer calls the company. The credit bureaus must provide a toll-free number during normal working hours. The credit bureaus must verify the information within thirty days. Consumers must consent to a prospective or new employer obtaining their credit report. Before any personal medical information is released, the consumer must authorize it.

[3]The Consumer Reporting Reform Act is available at http://www.ftc. gov/os/statutes/fcra.htm.

In 2003, Congress once again amended the Fair Credit Reporting Act. Consumers are able to obtain a free credit report and their credit score once a year from each of the credit bureaus. Businesses are required to black out Social Security numbers, parts of credit card numbers, and parts of debit card numbers on receipts. Medical information must be coded when included in credit reports. A national system of fraud detection was established in order to track identity theft quickly. Creditors must notify consumers before reporting negative information to credit bureaus. The federal law, however, prohibits states from passing stronger consumer-protection laws.

A consumer credit reporting agency that fails to comply with the terms of the Fair Credit Reporting Act can be held liable for actual damages, for punitive damages, and for attorneys' fees and court costs. The following case involved a credit reporting agency and one of its reports.

<table>
<tr><td>

CASE 14.2

United States Court of
Appeals, Third Circuit,
1997
115 F.3d 220

</td><td>

CUSHMAN v. TRANS UNION CORPORATION

BACKGROUND AND FACTS In the summer of 1993, an unknown person, possibly a member of Cushman's household, applied under her name for credit cards from three credit grantors: American Express (Amex), Citibank Visa (Citibank), and Chase Manhattan Bank (Chase). The person provided the credit grantors with Cushman's Social Security number, address, and other identifying information. Each company issued a credit card to that person in Cushman's name, and that person accumulated charges totaling approximately $2,400 on the cards between June 1993 and April 1994. These charges occurred without Cushman's knowledge.

In August 1994, a bill collector informed Cushman that Trans Union Corporation (TUC) was publishing a consumer credit report indicating that she was delinquent on her payments. Cushman notified TUC that she neither had applied for nor used the three credit cards in question, and suggested that a third party had fraudulently applied for, obtained, and used the cards.

In response, a TUC clerk called Amex and Chase to determine if the verifying information (such as Cushman's name, Social Security number, and address) in Amex's and Chase's records matched the information in the TUC report. The TUC clerk also asked if Cushman had opened a fraud investigation with the credit grantors. Because the information matched and because Cushman had not opened a fraud investigation, TUC published the information in its report.

Because TUC failed to contact Citibank, it deleted the Citibank entry from the report. TUC's investigations were performed by clerks who were paid $7.50 per hour and who were expected to perform ten investigations per hour. No evidence indicated that TUC obtained access to pertinent documents from the credit grantors that would enable TUC to perform a handwriting comparison.

TUC allowed Cushman the opportunity to complete and sign a form requesting that a special handling statement be placed on her report. A TUC employee testified, however, that the form would not have been used for a handwriting comparison had Cushman completed it. TUC advised consumers in Cushman's position to communicate and to complete signature verifications and fraud affidavits with the credit grantors.

When TUC sent Cushman a copy of the updated report still containing the Amex and Chase delinquencies, she sent a second letter to TUC reiterating her disagreement with the facts contained in the report and offering to sign affidavits for TUC to the effect that the delinquencies were not hers. TUC subsequently performed a reinvestigation identical to the first one. The credit report remained unchanged. At no time did TUC provide Cushman with a description of its reinvestigation procedures.

Cushman brought this action in the district court, alleging violations of the Fair Credit Reporting Act (FCRA). Subsequently, in April 1995, TUC verified the information with Citibank and placed the Citibank entry back onto Cushman's report. TUC notified Cushman of the reinsertion through her attorneys.

That September, Cushman, for the first time, disputed the delinquencies with the three credit grantors. A Citibank employee, comparing a handwriting sample provided by Cushman with the credit card application, determined that the card had been fraudulently obtained. The other two credit grantors came to a similar conclusion. TUC has since deleted the entries from Cushman's report.

By this time, TUC had been granted a summary judgment. Cushman appealed.

Circuit Judge COWEN

. . . .

As this Court recently wrote: The FCRA was enacted in order to ensure that "consumer reporting agencies adopt reasonable procedures for meeting the needs of

</td></tr>
</table>

commerce for consumer credit, personnel, insurance, and other information in a manner which is fair and equitable to the consumer, with regard to the confidentiality, accuracy, relevancy, and proper utilization of such information." The FCRA was prompted by "congressional concern over abuses in the credit reporting industry." In the FCRA, Congress has recognized the crucial role that consumer reporting agencies play in collecting and transmitting consumer credit information, and the detrimental effects inaccurate information can visit upon both the individual consumer and the nation's economy as a whole.

Title 15 U.S.C. § 1681i(a) provides in relevant part:

If the completeness or accuracy of any item of information contained in [her] file is disputed by a consumer, and such dispute is directly conveyed to the consumer reporting agency by the consumer, the consumer reporting agency shall within a reasonable period of time reinvestigate and record the current status of that information unless it has reasonable grounds to believe that the dispute by the consumer is frivolous or irrelevant. If after such reinvestigation such information is found to be inaccurate or can no longer be verified, the consumer reporting agency shall promptly delete such information.

. . . .

. . . According to TUC, it is never required to go beyond the original source in ascertaining whether the information is accurate. This position has been rejected [by the courts].

. . . .

. . . [T]he plain language of the statute places the burden of reinvestigation on the consumer reporting agency.

. . . .

A reasonable jury weighing this evidence . . . could have rendered a verdict for Cushman. The jury could have concluded that after TUC was alerted to the accusation that the accounts were obtained fraudulently, and then confronted with the credit grantors' reiteration of the inaccurate information, TUC should have known that the credit grantors were "unreliable" to the extent that they had not been informed of the fraud. Similarly, the jury could have concluded that seventy-five cents per investigation was too little to spend when weighed against Cushman's damages. It was for "the trier of fact [to] weigh the[se] factors."

. . . .

DECISION AND REMEDY The district court abrogated its role by granting the motion to dismiss the action on behalf of the credit reporting company. The judgment of the district court, therefore, was reversed and the case remanded for a jury trial.

CRITICAL THINKING: POLITICAL CONSIDERATION Without this federal law, a consumer could still bring legal action for defamation against a credit reporting agency if inaccurate information were in a credit file. Why does the government require credit reporting agencies to verify information contained in their credit reports?

Equal Credit Opportunity Act. In 1974, Congress enacted the **Equal Credit Opportunity Act**,[4] which forbids certain forms of discrimination. If a person can

, repay a loan, she cannot be denied credit on the basis of race, color, religion, national origin, sex, marital status, age, or the fact that her income is derived from public assistance. Discrimination against a person by denying her credit on any of these bases is illegal. The

[4]The Equal Credit Opportunity Act is at http://www4.law.cornell.edu/uscode/topn.

Exhibit 14–3   Sample Notice of Billing Error Rights

BILLING ERROR RIGHTS

YOUR BILLING RIGHTS

KEEP THIS NOTICE FOR FUTURE USE

This notice contains important information about your rights and our responsibilities under the Fair Credit Billing Act.

Notify us in case of errors or questions about your bill.

If you think your bill is wrong, or if you need more information about a transaction on your bill, write us on a separate sheet at 1400 South Cactus Road, Swiftrace, California 99999-5555 or at the address listed on your bill. Write to us as soon as possible. We must hear from you no later than sixty (60) days after we send you the first bill on which the error or problem appeared. You can telephone us, but doing so will not preserve your rights.

In your letter, give us the following information:
Your name and account number.
The dollar amount of the suspected error.

Describe the error and explain, if you can, why you believe there is an error.
If you have authorized us to pay your bill automatically from your savings or checking account, you can stop payment on any amount you think is wrong. To stop the payment, your letter must reach us three (3) business days before the automatic payment is scheduled to occur.

Your rights and our responsibilities start after we receive your written notice.

We must acknowledge your letter within thirty (30) days, unless we have corrected the error by then. Within ninety (90) days, we must either correct the error or explain why we believe the bill was correct.
After we receive your letter, we cannot try to collect any amount you question, or report you as delinquent. We can continue to bill you for the amount you question, including finance charges, and we can apply any unpaid amount against your credit limit. You do not have to pay any questioned amount while we are investigating, but you are still obligated to pay the parts of your bill that are not in question.
If we find that we made a mistake on your bill, you will not have to pay any finance charges related to any questioned amount. If we didn't make a mistake, you may have to pay finance charges, and you will have to make up any missed payments on the questioned amount. In either case, we will send you a statement of the amount you owe and the date on which it is due.
If you fail to pay the amount that we think you owe, we may report you as delinquent. However, if the explanation does not satisfy you, write to us within ten (10) days telling us that you still refuse to pay. We must tell anyone we report you to that you have a question about your bill. We must tell you the name of anyone we reported you to. When the account is finally settled, we must tell anyone we report you to that the matter has been settled.
If we don't follow these rules, we can't collect the first $50 of the questioned amount, even if your bill was correct.

LEGAL HIGHLIGHT

Earth Calling Computer, Earth Calling Computer, Do You Read Me?

When Congress considered passing the Fair Credit Billing Act, the members of Congress heard horror stories about computers that sent incorrect bills to consumers. Here are some of the complaints of people struggling to receive an accurate bill.

• A women in Yonkers, New York, bought furniture from Gimbels. One piece arrived damaged and beyond repair. The furniture piece was returned. The replacement piece did not match and was returned. After five months, the third piece had not arrived. The woman paid for the delivered pieces but not for the undelivered piece. The woman was in constant contact with the Gimbels credit department, but apparently the credit personnel failed to talk to the computer. The computer billed her for one year, then turned the unpaid bill over to a debt collection agency. The letter to her read, "The good things of life are obtainable by many people through their recorded credit reputation." In frustration, she wrote to the debt collection agency, three Gimbels executives, the attorney general for New York, the Federal Trade Commission, Consumers Union, Senator William Proxmire (Democrat, Wisconsin, who was holding hearings on the

passage of the act), and the New York State Consumer Protection Board. She received replies from all except the debt collection agency and Gimbels.

• BankAmericard sent an unsolicited credit card to a man in the Bronx, New York. He never received the card because it was stolen. Despite his repeated efforts to inform the credit card issuer that these charges were not his, the computer continued sending him the bill, including interest and late-payment charges.

• A couple from Monaghan, New York, ordered furniture from Macy's. They owed $1,217. Macy's twice delivered the wrong furniture. After ten months, Macy's finally delivered the correct furniture and the bill was paid. The couple was in contact with Macy's during this period, but the personnel failed to correct the computer. It billed them for finance charges for the ten months, plus 6 percent sales tax, although the sales tax in that area was only 3 percent. Finally, the couple wrote to the chairman of the board of Macy's. He expressed concern. Within three days, however, an attorney for Macy's called and gave them five days to pay the bill or be taken to court. They contacted the New York State Consumer Protection Board, which resolved the problem. In the meantime, they were denied a house loan because of this "unpaid" bill.

civil liabilities for violation of this act include actual damages as well as punitive damages up to $10,000, plus attorneys' fees and court costs.

CYBERLAW

Protecting Your Credit

Credit! Without good credit, businesses and people cannot borrow money to purchase a business, buildings, computer systems, vehicle, or any other large purchase. The ability to obtain credit requires a good credit history.

Any number of things can occur to adversely affect a credit rating. For example, you may not discover someone has stolen your identity until it is too late to stop the thief from using your good credit to obtain money or property. Or a former landlord might file an unfavorable report with a credit reporting firm. You would not know about this negative information in your credit report until you or your prospective creditors review your credit report.

How do lenders make a decision as to whether to lend money to a specific borrower? Most lenders use a

LEGAL HIGHLIGHT

Can You Trust Your Parents?

Some students have had the misfortune to discover that their parents have used their (the students') name and identity to obtain credit cards. The parents unfortunately were struggling financially, sometimes because of a divorce, a job loss, or a poor business decision.

In these situations, parents who have ruined their own credit history are tempted to obtain credit using their children's names. The parent knows all the correct information to complete a credit application. They do not plan to damage their children's credit history, but desperation drives the parents.

When young persons start to work, they, no matter how young, should check their credit record. They need to obtain a copy of their credit report at least once a year to catch identity theft early. Credit reports can be accessed online.

---

scoring system. To obtain a good score, you need to have different types of accounts, for example, mortgages on your house and your business property, unsecured loans, or credit cards, and always pay those accounts on time.

A lower score is not achieved solely because you pay your bills late or are delinquent. Having a large number of credit cards will lower your score. Inactive credit cards hinder your score. Credit cards used to pay other accounts will impede your score. A number of credit card accounts opened within a short period of time results in points being deducted from your score.

If you or your creditors check your credit report more than three times in a month, these actions negatively impact your score. Although you may have been shopping for lower rates for a loan, creditors view it as a precursor to credit delinquency. These actions of yours may be innocent. Creditors, however, view these actions negatively and use them as warning signs that you are about to abuse your credit.

You can check your credit report in a couple of ways. If you have Internet access, you can type in "free credit report." Numerous firms on the Web offer free credit reports. Many will provide you with tips on correcting errors and mistakes. Often, you do not pay for this service for the first thirty days. If you are satisfied with their service, you can subscribe to the service primarily to have the company alert you if negative information is filed. Another way to check is to use the Federal Trade Commission's Web site. The FTC has listed the major credit reporting bureaus.

Each bureau charges a nominal fee to view your credit report.

If you are denied credit, however, a free credit report may be obtained from the reporting company that provided the potential creditor negative information.

Only you can protect your good credit rating. Check your credit report annually at a minimum. If the actions of others have impaired your credit report, you can then take immediate, corrective action.

Fair Debt Collection Practices Act. In 1977, Congress passed the **Fair Debt Collection Practices Act**. This act applies to anyone who is in the business of consumer debt collection for others (collection agencies). Even without federal statutory provisions, however, invasion of a person's privacy or intentionally causing a person emotional distress is illegal.

For example, under the Fair Debt Collection Practices Act, Ace, a debt collector, cannot contact Dan, a debtor, before 8 A.M. or after 9 P.M. Repeatedly calling Dan on the telephone is prohibited. If Dan's employer has a policy against debt collectors contacting employees at work, the debt collector cannot call his place of employment. Ace can contact a third party one time for Dan's address, but cannot tell the third party that Dan owes a debt. Dan can write a letter advising Ace to stop communicating with him. If Dan notifies Ace that he has an attorney, the debt collector must make subsequent communications with Dan's attorney. The return address on Ace's postcards or envelopes must conceal that Ace is a debt collector. Ace cannot threaten to use physical violence and cannot threaten

LEGAL HIGHLIGHT

Gossip, Gossip, Gossip

What type of information was placed in people's credit files prior to the passage of the Fair Credit Reporting Act? Here are a few examples.

- A man who applied for automobile insurance was denied coverage. He later found this statement in his file: "Subject's son is a hippie type."

- A woman's application for automobile insurance was denied. In her file was a notation that she was a topless dancer who was divorced.

- A man who applied for life insurance was denied. In his record was a statement based on gossip from an unknown source that his former boss had "suspected him of taking money from the till." No charges had ever been filed.

- Another man was fortunate. His file contained the statement: "We learn of no connection with any Peace movement or other serversice [sic] type organization. He is regarded as a normal loyal american [sic]."

- A man who applied for life insurance was denied. His file included a false statement that he kept "unsavory company." A second statement, more than fifteen years old, said that he had destroyed property. The truth was that he had accidentally broken a neighbor's plate-glass window while playing softball. When he went to the credit bureau and told his story, the credit bureau agreed

to correct his file for a fee. The fee to check out his story was $10 an hour, with a fifteen-hour minimum, payable in advance.

- A man in Atlanta had immigrated to the United States from his native Hungary. He arrived in the United States penniless and knowing little English. Twelve years later he had a thriving business. When he went to borrow money, however, he was denied credit again and again. Finally, he found that his record noted that he had been involved in a $200 lawsuit, had bad debts, had gone bankrupt, and had skipped town. In fact, he had a business, had lived in the same house for twelve years, had not been involved in a $200 lawsuit, had no bad debts, and had never filed for bankruptcy.

  After two personal visits to the credit reporting bureau and letters to the Justice Department, the Federal Trade Commission, President Richard M. Nixon, and the man's hometown newspaper—and with lawyers talking directly to the credit reporting bureau—the man still failed to clear the false information from his file. The problem began in 1966. Finally, in March 1972, he was told that the incorrect information had been expunged from his file. When he applied for credit cards from Standard Oil and Sears in May 1972, however, credit was denied. Both companies cited the same source of their negative information: the credit reporting agency with which he had been fighting for years.

---

to harm Dan's reputation or property. He also must refrain from using obscene or profane language.

Ace cannot imply that he is collecting the debt under government authority and cannot wear a badge or uniform. Ace cannot claim to be an attorney unless admitted to practice law. Because Ace is not the original creditor, he must notify Dan that he is attempting to collect a debt and that any information that Dan provides may be used for that purpose. Ace must include this warning in any written correspondence to Dan. Ace cannot misrepresent that nonpayment of the

debt will result in Dan's arrest or imprisonment. The threats of the seizure, garnishment, attachment, or sale of any of Dan's property or wages is forbidden unless Ace intends to file a lawsuit against Dan and informs Dan of the remedies that Ace may use to collect if it wins.

If a debt collector violates a provision of the act, the collection agency must pay actual damages plus additional damages up to $1,000 and attorneys' fees. The following case considers possible violations of the Fair Debt Collection Practices Act.

<table>
<tr><td>

CASE 14.3

United States Court of
Appeals, Seventh Circuit,
2003
323 F.3d 534

</td><td>

SCHLOSSER v. FAIRBANKS CAPITAL CORPORATION

</td></tr>
</table>

BACKGROUND AND FACTS Fairbanks purchased the Schlossers' mortgage from ContiMortgage as part of Fairbanks's acquisition of 128,000 subprime mortgages, 10 percent of which were identified as in default. According to ContiMortgage's records, the Schlossers' mortgage was delinquent at the time of the transfer, and Fairbanks treated it as such. It sent a letter to the Schlossers, identifying itself as a debt collector, notifying the Schlossers that they were in default, and attempting to collect:

DEMAND LETTER—YOU COULD LOSE YOUR HOME!

> *This letter constitutes formal notice of default under the terms of the Note and Deed of Trust or Mortgage because of failure to make payments required. . . .*
>
> *This letter is a formal demand to pay the amounts due. In the event that these sums are not paid to Fairbanks Capital Corp. "Fairbanks" within 30 days of this letter the entire unpaid balance, together with accrued interest, legal fees and expenses, WILL BE ACCELERATED and foreclosure proceedings will be instituted. . . .*
>
> *You have the right to bring a court action if you claim that the loan is not in default or if you believe that you have any other defense to the acceleration and sale. . . .*
>
> *This letter is from a debt collector and is an attempt to collect a debt. Any information obtained will be used for that purpose.*

When the Schlossers tried to make their regular monthly payment to Fairbanks, Fairbanks refused, again asserting that the loan was in default, and instead instituted foreclosure proceedings. The Schlossers sent letters insisting that they weren't in default and eventually Fairbanks caused the foreclosure action to be dismissed.

The Schlossers filed suit against Fairbanks for violation of the Fair Debt Collection Practices Act (FDCPA), claiming (on behalf of themselves and a class of similar debtors) that Fairbanks's letter did not notify them of their right to contest the debt in writing, which would have required Fairbanks to verify the debt before continuing collection activity. The district court granted Fairbanks's motion to dismiss the FDCPA claim, denied as moot the Schlossers' motion for class certification, and declined to take supplemental jurisdiction over the state law claim. The district court concluded that, because the debt was not actually in default when Fairbanks acquired it, Fairbanks was not a debt collector within the meaning of the FDCPA. The Schlossers appealed.

WILLIAMS, Circuit Judge.

. . . .

As the district court recognized, the FDCPA distinguishes between "debt collectors" and "creditors." Creditors, "who generally are restrained by the desire to protect their good will when collecting past due accounts," are not covered by the Act. Instead, the Act is aimed at debt collectors, who may have "no future contact with the consumer and often are unconcerned with the consumer's opinion of them." In general, a creditor is broadly defined as one who "offers or extends credit creating a debt or to whom a debt is owed," whereas a debt collector is one who attempts to collect debts "owed or due or asserted to be owed or due another."

For purposes of applying the Act to a particular debt, these two categories—debt collectors and creditors—are mutually exclusive. However, for debts that do not originate with the one attempting collection, but are acquired from another, the collection activity related to that debt could logically fall into either category. If the one who acquired the debt continues to service it, it is acting much like the original creditor that created the debt. On the other hand, if it simply acquires the debt for collection, it is acting more like a debt collector. To distinguish between these two possibilities, the Act uses the status of the debt at the time of the assignment:

> *(6) The term "debt collector" means any person who . . . regularly collects or attempts to collect, directly or indirectly, debts owed or due or asserted to be owed or due another. . . . The term does not include—*
>
> > *(F) any person collecting or attempting to collect any debt owed or due or asserted to be owed or due another to the extent such activity . . . (iii)* concerns a debt which was not in default at the time it was obtained by such person.

In other words, the Act treats assignees as debt collectors if the debt sought to be collected was in default when acquired by the assignee, and as creditors if it was not.

. . . .

Fairbanks's interpretation, which exempts its collection activities from the statute if the debt was not actually in default when acquired, produces results that are odd in light of the conduct regulated by the statute. For example, §1692g, upon which the Schlossers' suit is based, requires debt collectors to notify the debtor that she may contest the debt in writing, and that if she does, the collector will obtain verification of the debt. This validation provision is aimed at preventing collection efforts based on mistaken information. Yet Fairbanks's interpretation makes its mistake about the status of the loan irrelevant. So those like Fairbanks that obtain a mix of loans, only some of which are in default, would be subject to the FDCPA if they fail to provide the required notice of the mechanism for correcting mistakes when they attempt to collect a loan they assert is in default—but only as to those loans about which they are *not* mistaken. And the same would be true for professional debt collectors in the business of acquiring defaulted loans for collection; debtors correctly asserted as being in default when the loan was acquired could challenge the failure to provide notices aimed at correcting mistakes, while those mistakenly identified as in default would have no recourse under the statute. We cannot believe that Congress intended such implausible results, and therefore, even if Fairbanks's reading is the most straightforward, it is not necessarily the correct one.

. . . .

DECISION AND REMEDY The court held that when an entity or person has a debt transferred to it which is allegedly in default, the Fair Debt Collection Practices Act is applicable. All of the terms of this statute must then be complied with.

CRITICAL THINKING: POLITICAL CONSIDERATION Why do you think Congress was so specific in requiring notice to debtors of their right to contest a debt?

Other Consumer-Oriented Laws

At the federal and state levels, a variety of consumer protection laws exist. These laws regulate a range of activities from the operation of dance studios and health clubs to used automobile sales and even funeral sales. The following sections discuss two major laws.

Uniform Consumer Credit Code

In 1968, the National Conference of Commissioners on Uniform State Laws promulgated the **Uniform Consumer Credit Code (UCCC)**. The UCCC has been controversial and only a few states have adopted it. It is a comprehensive body of rules governing the most important aspects of consumer credit. Sections of the UCCC, for example, focus on truth-in-lending,

LEGAL HIGHLIGHT

Consumer Prevails over Credit Reporting Agency

Judith L. Upton had the misfortune to have a name that was similar to that of another person—Judy C. Upton. To further the confusion, her Social Security number was only one number apart and they both had the same date of birth. Judith L. Upton lived in Oregon and Judy C. Upton lived in Washington.

Judith L. Upton discovered this problem in 1996 when her credit report included many unpaid debts. On investigation, she discovered the mistake of having a Judy C. Upton negative credit report attached to her credit report.

She contacted all creditors who sent the proper information to the credit reporting agency but it was never corrected in her credit file. When she went for a mortgage, all the negative information was still there. She again went to the creditors and obtained documentation of the mistake.

After she was able to finally obtain her mortgage, she filed legal action. A federal jury in Portland, Oregon, returned the largest verdict ever of $5.3 million for violating the Fair Credit Reporting Act.

---

door-to-door sales, referral sales, and maximum credit interest rate ceilings.

The UCCC also addresses creditor remedies, including deficiency judgments. The UCCC applies to most types of sales, including real estate. It also covers installment loans, retail installment sales, and usury (charging more than the maximum rate of interest allowed by state law).

Real Estate Settlement Procedures Act

Congress passed the **Real Estate Settlement Procedures Act** in 1974. The act governs the purchase of a house and the borrowing of money to pay for it. The time between when the contract is signed by both the buyer and the seller and the time when the property is titled in the buyer's name is approximately six weeks. At time of settlement, the buyer and seller are informed of all the costs and resolve any problems.

After a person applies for a mortgage loan, the lender, within three business days, sends him a booklet prepared by the U.S. Department of Housing and Urban Development. The booklet outlines the applicant's rights and explains settlement procedures and costs. The lender provides the buyer an estimate of most of the settlement costs within that three-day period. If the loan is approved, the lender must provide a truth-in-lending statement that shows the annual percentage rate on the mortgage loan.

Creditors' Rights

A creditor has the right to payment. When the debtor fails to fulfill his obligation to make timely payments, state laws establish procedures by which a creditor can secure debt payment or recovery of the goods for which the debt was incurred.

Writ of Execution

A debt must be past due in order for a creditor to commence legal action against a debtor. If the creditor is successful, the court awards the creditor a judgment against the debtor (usually for the amount of the debt plus any interest and legal costs incurred in obtaining the judgment). If the debtor still does not or cannot pay the judgment, the creditor can return to the court to obtain a writ of execution.

A **writ of execution** is an order, issued by a judge or the clerk of the court, directing the sheriff to seize and sell any of the debtor's nonexempt real or personal property that is within the court's geographic jurisdiction (usually the county in which the courthouse is located). **Nonexempt property** is property that the creditor can have seized from the debtor and sold. The proceeds of the sale are used to pay off the judgment and the costs of the sale itself. This procedure is known as a **judicial sale**. Any excess of the proceeds is paid to the debtor who owned the property.

LEGAL HIGHLIGHT

Women and the Credit Revolution

The Equal Credit Opportunity Act was passed in 1974. Until this act was adopted, most single working women could not obtain credit or buy homes or automobiles in their own names without a cosigner.

A woman whose marriage had ended either in divorce or by the death of her husband also could not obtain credit. A married couple's credit was maintained in the husband's name, even if only the wife worked. If the marriage ended, the woman had no credit rating. Financial institutions would deny her a loan, a credit card, or a bank card. Worse, if her former husband had good credit, it did not follow her; if he had a bad credit rating, it did follow her. Here are some more examples:

- A woman received $250,000 in a divorce settlement. From 1970 to 1972, she repeatedly applied for a bank card with a $500 limit; she was denied credit because she was divorced.
- In 1973, a married female attorney who had had a law practice for ten years was denied a department store credit card in her own name.
- In 1969, a widow of six years received a credit card in her deceased husband's name after being denied credit in her own name.

Congress heard many similar stories. Recognizing that women had become a stable part of the nation's workforce, Congress passed the Equal Credit Opportunity Act.

As a side note, prior to this law, both single women and single men found it nearly impossible to purchase a house. Financial institutions determined single people to be unstable. Today, more than one-fourth of all houses, condominiums, and townhouses are sold to single people.

At any time before the sale takes place, the debtor can pay the judgment and can redeem the nonexempt property. **Exempt property** is specifically named in statutes as property that can be kept by the debtor and is protected from the creditor. Such property may include the debtor's furniture and other essentials for living.

Attachment

A **writ of attachment** is a court-ordered seizure by which the sheriff takes the defendant's specified property into custody. The writ of attachment is normally a prejudgment remedy, requested by the creditor either when the lawsuit is filed or sometime after the filing, but before the entry of a final judgment. The remedy assists the creditor in collecting the debt owed if the judgment is made in the creditor's favor, because the sheriff, not the debtors, has custody of the property.

By statute, the restrictions and requirements concerning a creditor's right to attachment before judgment are very specific. The due process clause found in the Fifth and Fourteenth Amendments of the U.S. Constitution limits a court's power to authorize seizure of a debtor's property without notice to the debtor or a hearing on the facts.

To use attachment as a remedy, the creditor must follow certain procedures. He must file an affidavit with the court. An affidavit is a short written statement of facts given under oath and is used as evidence in a court. The **affidavit** states that the debtor is in default and states the statutory grounds under which attachment is sought. A bond must be posted by the creditor to cover court costs, the loss of the use of the goods as incurred by the debtor, and the value of the property attached.

When the court is satisfied that the creditor has met all the requirements, it issues a writ of attachment. This writ directs the sheriff or other officer to seize nonexempt property. If the creditor prevails at trial, the seized property then can be sold to satisfy the judgment.

Garnishment

A **garnishment** is a statutory procedure in which a debtor's property, currently in another's possession, is applied to the payment of that person's debts. For example, the wages owed to a debtor by his employer might be garnished. The court can issue a writ of garnishment for these wages, addressed to the employer, requiring that a portion of the employee's paycheck be paid to the creditor.

Garnishments are regulated by federal and state law. Congress determined that debtors needed some protection. Congressional hearings showed that the lack of laws protecting debtors encouraged lenders to extend credit to people who could not afford it. The federal law sets out the maximum amounts that can be garnished. Before the federal law was passed, many states allowed the creditor to garnish (that is, to take) the debtor's entire paycheck.

State laws today frequently set even lower limits on the amounts set by federal law. Federal agencies that try to collect debts, however, are not subject to the limits placed by the states. For example, when the Internal Revenue Service (IRS) tries to collect debts owed to it, it allows reasonable amounts for food, housing, housekeeping supplies, apparel and services, personal care products and services, and transportation. Federal law determines the amounts based on the debtor's location. Under these regulations the employee retains at least some of his paycheck.

An employer cannot discharge an employee for garnishment of his paycheck. If the debtor is fired, the employer may be fined $1,000, imprisoned for one year, or both.

In addition to the protections offered by federal or state statutes, the United States Supreme Court declared that a consumer has a right to a hearing before wages can be garnished. The following case established this right. This decision was based in part on the Constitution's due process clause.

CASE 14.4

Supreme Court of the United States, 1969
395 U.S. 337, 89 S. Ct. 1820, 20 L. Ed. 2d 349
http://www.thelawengine.com

LANDMARK CASE

SNIADACH v. FAMILY FINANCE CORPORATION

BACKGROUND AND FACTS Family Finance Corporation garnished Mrs. Sniadach's wages after it alleged that she failed to make timely payments on a loan. No trial or hearing was held to determine that Mrs. Sniadach had defaulted on the debt or that the garnishment was otherwise authorized. Her only notice was served on her at the same time that her wages were garnished.

Mrs. Sniadach contended that the finance company's failure to give her notice that the wages would be seized violated her right to due process. Both the trial court and the Wisconsin Supreme Court upheld the procedure allowed by Wisconsin law to garnish wages without prior notice to the consumer. Mrs. Sniadach took her case to the United States Supreme Court.

Justice DOUGLAS delivered the opinion of the Court.

[Family Finance Corporation] instituted a garnishment action against [Sniadach] as defendant and Miller Harris Instrument Co., her employer, as garnishee. The complaint alleged a claim of $420 on a promissory note. . . .

. . . .

. . . She . . . claims that the Wisconsin garnishment procedure violates that due process required by the Fourteenth Amendment, in that notice and an opportunity to be heard are not given before the . . . seizure of the wages. What happens in Wisconsin is that the clerk of the court issues the summons at the request of the creditor's lawyer; and it is the latter who by serving the garnishee sets in motion the machinery whereby the wages are frozen. They may, it is true, be unfrozen if the trial of the main suit is ever held and the wage earner wins on the merits. But in the interim the wage earner is deprived of his enjoyment of earned wages without any opportunity to be heard or to tender any defense he may have, whether it be fraud or otherwise.

Such summary procedure may well meet the requirements of due process in extraordinary situations. But in the present case, no situation requiring special protection to a state or creditor interest is presented by the facts; nor is the Wisconsin statute narrowly drawn to meet any such unusual condition. [Sniadach] was a resident of this Wisconsin community and in personam jurisdiction was readily obtainable.

. . . In this case, the sole question is whether there has been a taking of property without that procedural due process that is required by the Fourteenth Amendment. We have dealt over and over again with the question of what constitutes "the right to be heard" within the meaning of procedural due process. . . . [W]e said that the right to be heard "has little reality or worth unless one is informed that the matter is pending and can choose for himself whether to appear or default, acquiesce or contest." . . .

A prejudgment garnishment of the Wisconsin type is a taking which may impose tremendous hardship on wage earners with families to support. . . . Over and beyond that was the great drain on family income. As stated by Congressman Reuss:

> The idea of wage garnishment in advance of judgment, of trustee process, of wage attachment, or whatever it is called is a most inhuman doctrine. It compels the wage earner, trying to keep his family together, to be driven below the poverty level.

. . . .

The result is that a prejudgment garnishment of the Wisconsin type may as a practical matter drive a wage-earning family to the wall. Where the taking of one's property is so obvious, it needs no extended argument to conclude that absent notice and a prior hearing this prejudgment garnishment procedure violates the fundamental principles of due process.

DECISION AND REMEDY The Court ruled that the Wisconsin statute was unconstitutional. As a result of this decision, today a court must determine that a valid debt exists before wages can be garnished. The debtor also must receive proper notice and be offered a hearing before garnishment can take place.

CRITICAL THINKING: POLITICAL CONSIDERATION The case failed to discuss the issue of terminating employees if their wages are garnished. As discussed prior to this case, federal law does not allow businesses to terminate employees when their wages are garnished. Discuss whether the federal government should allow a business to terminate an employee when his or her wages are garnished.

Mortgage Foreclosure on Real Property

Chapter 12 reviewed the procedure by which a secured party (a creditor) repossesses personal property. The same basic format applies for the repossession of real property, with some differences. Liens on real estate have various names depending on the way in which the lien was created. For this discussion, the term *mortgage* is used since it is a familiar term.

Creation of the Mortgage. A real estate mortgage is a lien against real property to secure payment of a loan given (usually) to secure the purchase of the real property. For example, to purchase a house, Jane enters into a purchase agreement. She arranges with a lender to borrow money over a thirty-year period at a 9 percent interest rate. She signs a note with the lender in which she, the debtor-borrower, agrees to pay back the money in monthly installments to the creditor-lender during the next thirty years. At this point, the unsecured note is the only evidence of the debt. If Jane were to default on the note, the creditor could only sue her in court on the note.

The creditor wants something to back up the note, that is, the creditor wants a secured note (sometimes called a *mortgage note* as explained in Chapter 12). In real estate, the note is secured by a lien against the home (real property), called a **mortgage**. Jane, the debtor-borrower, creates a mortgage on the real estate and becomes the **mortgagor**. The creditor-lender is the beneficiary of the mortgage and is the **mortgagee**.

Default and Foreclosure. If Jane (the mortgagor or debtor-borrower) defaults by failing to pay the note, the real estate mortgage agreement provides that the mortgage company (the mortgagee or creditor-lender) can declare the entire loan due immediately. The mortgagee can have the loan paid by seeking a lawsuit called a **foreclosure**.

In this suit, the real estate that is covered by the mortgage is sold at a court-ordered sale (a foreclosure sale) under a writ of execution. If the proceeds of the sale are sufficient to cover both the costs of the foreclosure and the loan, any surplus is paid to the debtor. Jane is entitled to the surplus money because she owned the property. The creditor holds only a lien against her property. The creditor is entitled to have only the loan repaid and is not entitled to make a profit. The creditor only can collect the amount of the unpaid loan plus costs.

Deficiency Judgment. If, however, the sale proceeds are insufficient to cover the foreclosure costs and to repay the loan, in most states the mortgagee can seek to recover the difference from Jane (the mortgagor) by obtaining a *deficiency judgment*. A **deficiency judgment** represents the deficiency amount, that is, the difference between the loan along with the foreclosure costs and the amount actually received from the foreclosure sale's proceeds.

A deficiency judgment normally is obtained in a separate legal action that the creditor files after the foreclosure, because she only knows of a deficiency after the sale is complete. The creditor can recover the amount of the deficiency judgment from other property owned by the debtor.

Only nonexempt property (property that is subject to execution or garnishment) can be used to satisfy the deficiency judgment. In many states, the creditor cannot obtain a deficiency judgment at all against a debtor when the foreclosure involves the debtor's residence.

Between the time of default and the time of the foreclosure sale, Jane can redeem her property by paying the full amount of the loan still outstanding plus any interest and other costs that have accrued. In some states, Jane may even redeem her property within a statutory period after the judicial sale.

Protection for the Debtor

In most states, certain types of real and personal property are exempt from execution or attachment. Probably the most familiar of these exemptions is the **homestead exemption**. Each state permits the debtor to retain the family home, either in its entirety or up to a specified dollar amount, free from unsecured creditors or trustees in bankruptcy claims. The purpose is to ensure that the debtor will retain or be able to obtain some form of shelter. A homestead exemption, however, is not valid against a purchase-money lender.

For example, Dan owes Carey $40,000 as the result of a contract. The debt is the subject of a lawsuit. The court awards Carey a judgment of $40,000 against Dan. At some time before, during, or in some states even after the judgment has been awarded, Dan can file a homestead exemption. Dan's home is valued at $180,000, but he owes $30,000 on the purchase-money lender's mortgage. To satisfy the judgment debt, Dan's family home is sold at public auction for $175,000. Assume that the state law allows a homestead exemption of $125,000. The proceeds of the sale are distributed as follows:

- The purchase-money lender is paid $30,000.
- Dan is paid $125,000 as his homestead exemption.
- Carey is paid $20,000 toward the judgment debt.
- A $20,000 debt is still owed.

Carey now has a deficiency judgment for $20,000. This deficiency judgment can be satisfied from any other nonexempt property (personal or real) that Dan may have if allowed by state law.

Personal property that often is exempt from satisfaction of judgment debts includes the following:

- Household furniture, such as beds, dining tables, and chairs, usually up to a specified dollar amount;
- Clothing and certain personal possessions, such as family pictures, books, tools, and Bibles; and
- A vehicle for transportation (at least up to a specific dollar amount).

If Dan is unable to repay the rest of the $20,000, he may seek protection from his creditors. The following sections discuss **bankruptcies** (a debtor's public declaration that his bills or debts exceed his assets) and **reorganizations** (a plan formulated between a debtor and creditor under which the debtor pays a portion of his debts and is discharged of the remainder and under which the debtor can remain in business).

Bankruptcies and Reorganizations

The U.S. Constitution, Article I, Section 8, provides that

The Congress shall have power . . . To establish . . . uniform Laws on the subject of Bankruptcies throughout the United States.

Federal law governs bankruptcy proceedings. Congress passed the Bankruptcy Act, which has been amended over the decades. The Bankruptcy Act often is referred to as the Bankruptcy Code or just the code.

Bankruptcy courts are special federal courts. The U.S. court of appeals appoints bankruptcy judges for fourteen-year terms. Each federal judicial district has a **U.S. trustee** who monitors the administration of bankruptcy cases. Appeals of bankruptcy cases go to the Bankruptcy Appellate Panel or a federal district court before they can be heard by the appropriate U.S. circuit court of appeals.

Goals of Bankruptcy

Bankruptcy is designed to accomplish two main goals. The first is to provide relief and protection (a fresh start) to debtors who are deeply in debt and cannot recover financially without help.

The second major goal of bankruptcy is to provide a fair means of distributing a debtor's assets among all creditors. Although the bankruptcy acts are federal laws, state laws on secured transactions, liens, judgments, and exempt property play a role in federal bankruptcy proceedings.[5]

[5]A good Internet link where you can locate answers to questions involving bankruptcy is http://www.agin.com/lawfind. The American Bankruptcy Institute's Web site contains information involving bankruptcy and legislative updates. The Web address is http://www.abiworld.org.

Bankruptcy Chapters

The Bankruptcy Code, comprised of several chapters, is contained in the *United States Code*. Chapters 1, 3, and 5 include general definitions and provisions governing the case administration, the creditors, the debtor, and the estate. These three chapters apply generally to all bankruptcies.

Several chapters set forth different types of bankruptcy relief. Chapter 7 provides for liquidations. Chapter 9 governs the adjustment of debts of a municipality. Chapter 11 allows for reorganizations of individual and business debtors. Chapter 12 provides bankruptcy relief for family farmers. Chapter 13 provides for the adjustment of debts for individuals with regular income.

Chapter 7, Liquidations. The most familiar type of bankruptcy proceeding is referred to as a *straight bankruptcy*. Put simply, a debtor in a **straight bankruptcy** lists her debts and turns her assets over to a trustee. The trustee sells the assets and distributes the proceeds to creditors. The debts then are discharged (forgiven) so that the debtor is relieved from the obligation to pay these debts.

Any person—defined here to include individuals, partnerships, and corporations—may be a debtor under Chapter 7. The term *corporation* as used here includes unincorporated companies and associations, as well as labor unions. Chapter 7 does not apply to railroads, insurance companies, banks, savings and loan associations, or governmental units. Other chapters of the Bankruptcy Act or other federal and state statutes apply to them.

Bankruptcy Procedure. A straight bankruptcy begins when a debtor or creditors file a petition on the bankruptcy court's official forms. The debtor can file a voluntary petition, or unsecured creditors whose aggregate claims equal $5,000 or more can file an involuntary petition against the debtor. The petition lists both secured and unsecured creditors, their addresses, and the amount owed to each; states the debtor's financial affairs; and lists all of the debtor's property, including property that the debtor claims as exempt.

These official forms must be completed accurately, sworn to under oath, and signed by the debtor. To conceal assets or knowingly supply false information on these schedules is a federal crime and can result in the debtor's discharge in bankruptcy being denied.

The filing of a petition operates as an **automatic stay**, which stops or suspends all civil litigation against the debtor. In other words, creditors cannot start or continue legal actions against the debtor to recover claims against her, nor can creditors take any action to repossess the debtor's property. All actions against the debtor then must go through the bankruptcy court.

Trustees. A court-appointed trustee is distinguished from a U.S. trustee. The U.S. trustee is an administrative position within the bankruptcy court. A **regular trustee** (interim or permanent) is appointed by the court to represent the creditors.

The court appoints an interim trustee to preside over the debtor's property until the first meeting of creditors. At this first meeting, a permanent trustee is elected by the creditors. The trustee's principal duty is to collect the debtor's property, reduce it to money, and close up the estate as soon as possible, keeping in mind the best interests of all parties. Trustees are entitled to compensation for services rendered, plus reimbursement for expenses.

A trustee steps into the debtor's shoes and has specific powers to rescind the debtor's obligations. This power is called **avoidance**. Any reason that a debtor can use to obtain the return of his property can be used by the trustee as well. These grounds include fraud, duress, incapacity, and mutual mistake.

For example, Ben sells his boat to Frank. Frank gives Ben a check, knowing that he has insufficient funds in the bank account to cover the check. Frank has committed fraud. Ben can cancel the contract and recover the boat from Frank. If Ben has filed for bankruptcy, his trustee can exercise the same right to recover the boat from Frank.

The trustee's power of avoidance includes setting aside liens that are granted by statutes, called **statutory liens**, such as a landlord's lien. In some states, if the renter does not pay, the landlord can keep and even sell the tenant's personal property.

The trustee also can set aside **preferential payments**, that is, payments that the debtor made to favored creditors, but not to other creditors, within ninety days prior to the filing of the bankruptcy. Payments that the debtor made to an insider (a relative, partner, officer, or director) within one year can be set aside.

The same rules apply to a preferential lien that the debtor granted prior to filing bankruptcy. A **preferential lien** (as opposed to a statutory lien just mentioned) is one that the debtor made voluntarily, such as a lien placed on land that is owned free and clear, to enable a favored creditor to receive payments over the other creditors.

One reason the debtor would make a preferential lien is to gain favor with a creditor so that, after the bankruptcy, the creditor will continue to deal with the debtor. Another reason is to protect property by giving a preferential lien to a family member. The court, however, will not recognize the family member's property right because after bankruptcy, the family member could return the property to the debtor. These types of preferential liens operate to the detriment of the other creditors and are not allowed. The purpose of setting these payments and liens aside is to ensure that all creditors are treated equally.

Exemptions. An individual debtor is entitled to choose to keep certain property as exempt from bankruptcy. An individual debtor can choose between the exemptions provided under the state law or federal law if the state law allows this choice. The following list shows some of the property exempt under federal law:

1. Equity interest in a debtor's residence up to $15,000;

2. One motor vehicle up to $2,400;

3. Household furnishings and apparel up to $8,000 with no more than one item worth more than $400;

4. Jewelry up to $1,000;

5. Professional books or tools of no more than $1,500;

6. Life insurance contracts;

7. Professionally prescribed health aids;

8. Miscellaneous property up to $800;

9. Social Security, profit sharing, disability, alimony, and other funds for the support of the debtor or of his or her dependents; and

10. Amounts paid to the debtor under a crime victim's law or wrongful death award, and amounts up to $15,000 (not including pain and suffering) for a personal injury.

Property Distribution. After reducing the debtor's assets to money, the trustee must pay the debts to those unsecured creditors who appropriately filed claims. Bankruptcy law establishes an order-of-priority list for certain classes of debts owed to unsecured creditors. Each class must be fully paid before the next class on the list is entitled to any proceeds.

If there is insufficient money to pay a class, the money is prorated among the creditors of that class, and all classes lower in priority receive nothing. If all classes are fully paid, any remaining balance goes to the debtor.

Examples of the order of priority among classes of unsecured creditors are as follows:

- All bankruptcy costs (top priority);

- Claims for unpaid wages, salaries, or commissions due to employees that were earned within ninety days of the bankruptcy petition (limited to $2,000 per employee);

- Claims for funds that creditors prepaid to the debtor for goods or services that the debtor failed to deliver (limited to $900 per claim); and

- Certain taxes (and penalties) owed to government entities.

All of these creditors and others must be paid before any unsecured creditor receives proceeds from the debtor's estate. Some debts, however, are not dischargeable.

Nondischargeable Debts. From the debtor's viewpoint, the primary purpose of a Chapter 7 liquidation is to obtain a fresh start through the **discharge** (excused from paying) of debts. In certain circumstances, however, a debt will not be discharged.

Debts that are not dischargeable include claims for back taxes accruing within three years prior to bankruptcy, claims against property or money obtained by the debtor under false representations, claims for alimony and child support, claims for certain student loans, and judgments or consent decrees awarded against a debtor for liability incurred as a result of the debtor's operation of a motor vehicle while legally intoxicated.

These debts are nondischargeable because of statutes. Other debts are reviewed on a case-by-case basis and found to be nondischargeable as discussed in the next case.

CASE 14.5

United States Bankruptcy Court, Northern District of New York, 2002
288 B.R. 36, 173 Ed. Law Rep. 608

STERN v. EDUCATION RESOURCES INSTITUTE

BACKGROUND AND FACTS James E. Stern (Debtor) matriculated at Bates College in Lewiston, Maine, in 1984. He was graduated in 1988 with a joint interdisciplinary major of philosophy, psychology, and anthropology. In 1990, Debtor entered Syracuse University College of Law as a full-time student, being graduated with a Juris Doctorate in 1993. He passed the New York State Bar examination and was admitted to practice in New York. To finance his education, he incurred approximately $150,000 in student loans.

He was a solo practitioner from 1995 until 2001, specializing in civil rights, and supplementing his income by handling criminal defense work and cases for the Teamsters Legal Benefit Panel and assigned counsel program. Although successful in defending two malpractice claims filed against him, the malpractice insurance premium increased in 2001 to a level that he was unable to afford to practice as a solo practitioner.

Without malpractice insurance, he was unable to participate in certain programs, such as the Teamsters Legal Benefit Panel. As a result of his inability to obtain affordable malpractice insurance and the resultant decrease in earnings, he decided to close his practice in July 2001. In August 2001, he and his wife moved to France to be with her father, who had suffered a stroke.

Debtor testified that in France he was not even qualified to be a street sweeper because of his inability to speak the language, although he was taking language classes. He was collecting residual income from his prior law practice of approximately $2,000, which he expected to cease in the near future. He did not believe he would be able to get a position as a lawyer in either the government or the private sector because of his debt and his history of default on his student loans. He testified that he intended to allow his license to lapse as he no longer had an interest in pursuing a legal career.

According to the Debtor's tax returns, his annual business income from 1995 to 2000 amounted to $11,500, $11,700, $12,831, $16,965, $17,183, and $33,774. That between 1996 and 2001, Debtor's wife earned annually $5,722, $15,896, $8,606, $19,145, $25,829, and $32,666, respectively.

According to Schedule J, filed with his petition in June 2001, his monthly expenses totaled $1,870, exclusive of any payments on his student loans. This included $550 in rent, $175 in utilities, including telephone, $300 for food, $150 for clothing, $50 for laundry, $50 for medical and dental, $100 for transportation, $50 in recreation, and $395 for insurance. His current monthly expenses total $2,155.

Debtor argued that his financial circumstances warrant a discharge of his student loan debt. He contended that "I'm never going to be able to get a house, I'm never going to be able to have a car, and I won't—you know, I want to have kids. I want to be responsible, and I can't—I can't possibly pay this amount and have a life, not with what I expect I'll be able to earn." He argued that amortization of a nearly $150,000 debt over 50 years, accruing at least 8 percent interest per year, would require him to pay approximately $14,000 per year over a fifty-year period. Debtor contended that it would be impossible to make those payments without imposing undue hardship upon him. Additionally, Debtor took the position that he was unemployable in the legal profession because of his inability to afford adequate malpractice insurance coverage.

STEPHEN D. GERLING, Chief Judge.

. . . .

Code 523(a)(8) is applicable to loans "made, insured, or guaranteed by a governmental unit, or made under any program funded in whole or in part by a governmental unit or nonprofit institution. . . " There appears to be no dispute among the parties that the loans obtained by the Debtor in this case fall within the parameters of the statute. Congress, in enacting the statute, was cognizant of the fact that educational loans are different from most loans. They are made without business considerations, without security, without cosigners, and rely for repayment solely on the debtor's future increased income resulting from the education. In this sense, the loan is viewed as a mortgage on the debtor's future.

The Second Circuit Court of Appeals in *Brunner* established a three-prong test for a debtor seeking an undue hardship discharge under Code § 523(a)(8). The Debtor must prove

> *"(1) that the debtor cannot maintain, based on current income and expenses, a 'minimal' standard of living for [himself] and [his] dependents if forced to repay the loans; (2) that additional circumstances exist indicating that this state of affairs is likely to persist for a significant portion of the repayment period of the student loans; and (3) that the debtor has made good faith efforts to repay the loans."*

Furthermore, all prongs of the three-prong "undue hardship" test must be met in order for the debt to be discharged. If the Debtor fails to prove one of the elements, the Debtor's educational loans cannot be discharged.

. . . .

Minimum and Maximum Analysis

The first prong of the test requires the Court to examine whether the Debtor has demonstrated, based on his current income and expenses, that he cannot maintain a minimal standard of living for his family and repay his educational loans. It is clear from the evidence and testimony elicited at the trial that the Debtor is presently struggling financially. . . . The Court concludes that the Debtor's current income prevents him from repaying his student loans at this time.

Duration of Inability to Repay Loans

The second prong of the test requires that the Debtor prove more than his present inability to pay his student loan obligations. . . .

In this case, the Debtor possesses both a bachelor's degree and a Juris Doctorate. While unable to gain full-time employment since quitting his law practice in Syracuse and moving to France, it is evident to the Court that he is bright, articulate, well educated and suffers from neither physical nor mental disability that would prevent him from earning a living in the future which would permit him to repay his student loans. The Debtor apparently has decided that he no longer wishes to pursue a legal career. . . . The Debtor has failed to convince the Court that factors exist beyond his reasonable control that would prevent him from improving his financial situation. Accordingly, the Court concludes that the Debtor has failed to meet his burden of proof with respect to the second prong of the test.

Good Faith

Because the Court has determined that the Debtor has failed to meet his burden of proof with respect to the second prong, it need not address whether the Debtor made a good faith effort to repay his student loans in reaching the conclusion that the Debtor is not entitled to a full discharge of his student loan obligations pursuant to Code.

. . . .

DECISION AND REMEDY The court did not allow a discharge of student loans based on his inability to repay them. Normally, a student must wait seven years to obtain a discharge of these loans.

CRITICAL THINKING: POLITICAL CONSIDERATION Why should student loans be treated differently from other financial obligations? Explain your answer.

Discharges are granted only to individuals as debtors, not to corporations or partnerships. The latter may use Chapter 11 or, where appropriate, Chapter 12 bankruptcy proceedings.

Reaffirmation. A debtor can reaffirm (renew) his old debts through a reaffirmation agreement; that is, the debtor can agree to repay the debt. The debtor must agree to these repayments before he is granted a discharge.

The agreement must be filed with and approved by the court. The debtor must be counseled by his attorney and must file a declaration stating that the debtor knows the consequences of the voluntary agreement and that the agreement imposes no hardship on the debtor or on his dependents.

The debtor can rescind the agreement at any time prior to discharge or within sixty days of filing the agreement, whichever is later. This rescission period must be stated clearly and conspicuously in the reaffirmation agreement.

Chapter 11, Reorganizations. Chapter 11 reorganization is used most commonly by a corporate debtor. Essentially, in a reorganization the creditors and the debtor formulate a plan under which the debtor pays a portion of its debts and is discharged of the remainder. The debtor may continue in business. Proceedings may be initiated by either a voluntary or involuntary petition. A fast track for reorganization is provided for small businesses that have debts of less than $2 million and that are not engaged in owning or operating real estate.

The same principles that govern the filing of a Chapter 7 petition apply to Chapter 11 proceedings and to the court's entry of the order for relief. The

LEGAL HIGHLIGHT

A Lesson on Reaffirmation

Sears, Roebuck and Co. (Sears) has its own credit card system, which is used by 60 million customers. The credit card operation is very profitable and in recent years has accounted for nearly one-half of Sears' net income.

Bankruptcies, in the meantime, have been climbing. In 1992, approximately 900,000 personal bankruptcies were filed. In 1999, more than 1,354,376 were filed.

These bankruptcies affected Sears' credit card business. Approximately 500,000 customers had charged more than $400 million in merchandise between 1992 and 1997. During that time, Sears made 500,000 reaffirmation (repayment) agreements with bankrupt credit card customers. If the person signed the reaffirmation agreement and paid the debt down to a predetermined level, Sears then would extend a small line of credit, usually $500. This offer was very enticing to the bankrupt person because it helped her reestablish credit after bankruptcy.

When a person filed for bankruptcy, the creditors were notified. Sears then sent a nonlawyer representative to attend the public creditor meetings. The representative later approached the customer about repaying the Sears debt. Most reaffirmations followed this model.

A reaffirmation agreement must be filed with the bankruptcy court, which then must approve the agreement. Sears failed to file the reaffirmation agreements with the various bankruptcy courts.

A bankruptcy judge in Massachusetts discovered the reaffirmation plans when a bankrupt man requested that the Sears debt be discharged after he signed a reaffirmation agreement. Finding that Sears had failed to file or gain court approval of the agreement, the judge ordered a hearing.

Sears decided not to contest the allegations, to conduct an audit of its records from 1992 to 1997, and to return, with interest, money paid by customers whose reaffirmation agreements were not filed with the court. The cost: $400 million, plus a stain on its reputation as a good corporate citizen.

automatic stay and adequate protection provisions previously discussed apply in reorganizations.

The debtor generally continues to operate its business as a "debtor in possession." The court may appoint a trustee to operate the debtor's business if it finds gross mismanagement of the business or if trustee appointment is in the debtor's best interests.

The debtor files a Chapter 11 plan that must be "fair and equitable." Classes of claims, such as those by secured and unsecured creditors, must be designated under the plan. The court provides the same treatment for each claim within a particular class. Once the plan has been developed, it is submitted to each class of creditors for acceptance. Each class is required to accept the plan.

The plan must be in the best interests of the creditors. On confirmation, the debtor receives a Chapter 11 discharge for all claims not protected under the plan. Those debts protected by the plan are paid in part according to the plan, but the remainder of those debts is discharged.

Chapter 13, Adjustment of Debts of an Individual with Regular Income. The Bankruptcy Act provides for the formulation of plans to allow people with regular income to pay off their debts free from the harassment of creditors. Under these plans, people avoid the stigma of being adjudicated bankrupt.

Who May File. Individuals (not partnerships or corporations) with regular income who owe unsecured debts of less than $250,000 and secured debts of less than $750,000 may take advantage of Chapter 13. The act includes individual business proprietors and individuals on welfare, Social Security, fixed pensions, or investment income. Many small business debtors can choose between filing a plan under either Chapter 11 or Chapter 13.

Several advantages of filing a Chapter 13 plan include that it is less expensive and less complicated than a Chapter 11 proceeding or a Chapter 7 liquidation. A Chapter 13 case can only be initiated by the voluntary filing of a petition by the debtor. Any eligible debtor who is presently in a Chapter 7 or Chapter 11 bankruptcy proceeding can convert it to a Chapter 13 case.

Bankruptcy Proceedings. When a debtor files a Chapter 13 petition, the automatic stay previously discussed takes effect. The debtor may propose a plan that provides for either full or partial payment of his debts. A Chapter 13 plan must provide for the turnover of the debtor's future earnings or income to the trustee as is necessary to carry out the plan. Full payment of all claims entitled to priority must be included in the plan.

The full payment is made by paying smaller amounts over a longer time period than would have been allowed under the original creditor–debtor agreement. Each claim within a particular class must be treated equally. Each secured debt, for example, must be paid in the same method as all other secured debts. The time for payment under the plan may not exceed three years, unless the court approves an extension. The plan, with extension, may not exceed five years.

The plan must be confirmed by the court as long as all of the debtor's projected disposable income will be applied to making payments. Disposable income is all income less amounts needed to support the debtor (and dependents), amounts needed to meet ordinary expenses to continue a business operation, or both.

The debtor must make "timely payments," which must begin under the proposed plan within thirty days after the plan has been filed. A debtor's failure to make timely payments or to commence payments within the thirty-day period allows the court to convert the case to a Chapter 7 liquidation or to dismiss the petition.

After completion of all payments under a Chapter 13 plan, the court discharges all debts for which the plan provided. Taxes, alimony, and child support debts cannot be discharged.

Even if the debtor fails to complete the plan because of circumstances beyond the debtor's control and if the property distributed by the plan was greater than would have been paid in a Chapter 7 liquidation, a hardship discharge may be granted. For example, if the debtor were seriously injured in an accident and became permanently disabled, the debtor's income

would be severely reduced; therefore, he would be unable to complete the plan. In such a case, a discharge of the remaining debts might be granted.

Chapter 12, Adjustment of Debts of a Family Farmer with Regular Annual Income. The Family Farmer Bankruptcy Act defines a family farmer as one whose gross income is at least 50 percent farm dependent and whose debts are at least 80 percent farm related. The total debt must not exceed $1.5 million. A partnership or closely held corporation (at least 50 percent owned by the farm family) also can take advantage of this law.

A Chapter 12 filing is very similar in procedure to a Chapter 13 filing. The farmer-debtor must file a plan not later than ninety days after the order of relief. The filing of the petition acts as an automatic stay against creditors and co-obligor actions against the estate.

The plan's content and confirmation are basically the same as for a Chapter 13 filing. The plan can be modified by the farmer-debtor, but except for cause, must be confirmed or denied within forty-five days of the filing of the plan's filing. The plan must provide for payment of secured debts at the collateral's value. If the secured debt exceeds the collateral's value, the remaining debt is unsecured.

For unsecured debtors, the plan must be confirmed either if the value of the property to be distributed under the plan equals the amount of the claim or if the plan provides that all of the debtor-farmer's disposable income received in a three-year period (or longer, by court approval) will be applied to making payments.

Disposable income includes all income received less amounts needed to support the farmer-debtor and family and to continue the farming operation. Completion of payments under the plan constitutes the discharge of all debts for which the plan provided.

International Consideration

Consumer Credit Protection in Foreign Countries

The Organization for Economic Cooperation and Development (OECD) was started in 1961 as an intergovernmental institution for Western countries. Its aim is to achieve the highest sustainable economic growth and employment, to maintain financial stability, and to contribute to the expansion of world trade.

No direct equivalents to the consumer protections set out in this chapter, however, have been adopted in the international setting. In 1977, the OECD recognized the importance of consumer credit. A recommendation was made to its member countries to adopt internal legislation that includes the following protections.

Consumers should be provided with credit information through advertisements, a recommendation that is very similar to the Truth-in-Lending Act. The documents should clearly establish full disclosure of all credit terms. Legislation should provide for the consumer's privacy. Regulation of door-to-door sales, abolishment of the consumer holder-in-due-course concept, prohibition of unfair trade practices, and regulation of debt collection agencies are a few of the consumer protections recommended by the OECD. Notice that most of these provisions are already a part of the U.S. Consumer Credit Protection Act.

PRACTICAL TIPS

The Proper Way to Grant Credit

You are a manager of a medium-sized manufacturing firm that sells predominantly to retail consumers. Your average sale is $2,500, which necessitates that your firm grant credit.

No problems arise when your customers pay in accordance with your agreement and your customers normally pay on time. You, however, must plan ahead to give your company the best position possible under federal and state laws in the event that a customer does not pay.

Checklist

Before granting credit, the following checklist can be used for guidance.

✔ *Credit Application* Obtain a detailed credit application that lists the consumer's assets and liabilities. Included on this form are the names and addresses of creditors and the consumer's relatives. The information about the relatives may help you to determine assets that are available for attachment, execution, or garnishment. It also may help you to locate the debtor, if he or she moves.

✔ *Social Security Number* Although you cannot require it, ask for a Social Security number. This information is helpful for identification purposes, especially when the consumer has a common name, such as Gomez, Nguyen, or Smith. With this information, you can verify credit information with reporting agencies or with the listed creditors.

If you will receive more than four payments, you must comply with the truth-in-lending laws.

✔ *Government Forms* Be sure to use the forms drafted by the Federal Reserve Board and published in the *Code of Federal Regulations*. You will save time and conform with the law.

If your product is sold door to door, federal and state law apply.

✔ *Cooling Off Period* State clearly in the contract the three-business-day cooling-off period.

✔ *Revocation Notice* State clearly in the contract where the customer should send a revocation notice if she or he exercises that option.

If you sell personal property (goods), decide whether to secure your interest under the Uniform Commercial Code, Article 9. This procedure is covered in Chapter 12.

✔ *Signed Written Agreement* Obtain a written security agreement signed by the debtor when the consumer-debtor has possession of the product.

✔ *File Lien* File a financing statement (UCC-1) with the appropriate public office to protect your interest.

If an account becomes delinquent, follow federal regulations when collecting.

✔ *Written Policy* Establish a written policy concerning debt collection.

✔ *Review the Law* Review the provisions of the Fair Debt Collection Practices Act.

✔ *Investigate and Respond* Investigate and respond to a debtor's inquiry if he or she contests a bill.

✔ *Do Not Threaten* Never threaten criminal prosecution, even if the debtor has committed a criminal act, such as giving a bad check or committing fraud on the credit application. These threats could be considered duress in a civil action and the threats themselves could result in you being charged with the crime of extortion.

✔ *Contract* If you decide to hire a debt collection agency, write a contract with the collection agency that includes its agreement to conform with federal law.

At times, your firm will have to write off a debt as uncollectible and take a tax loss, if allowed. The old saying "You can't get blood out of a turnip" has application today. If the consumer is unemployed, is in prison, has a disability, or is suffering some other catastrophe, your firm should take the loss as soon as possible. In fact, if you have no losses on credit sales, possibly your credit policies are too rigid. Your firm might be able to increase sales by relaxing those policies.

Be prepared for a debtor to file for bankruptcy. Having knowledge of the bankruptcy chapters available to the debtor and your rights as a creditor under each chapter is important in establishing your credit policy.

Chapter Summary

The Consumer Credit Protection Act has five sections that apply directly to businesses and consumers. The Truth-in-Lending Act requires the disclosure of the price owed, the finance charges, and the annual percentage rate of interest for the privilege of paying off the debt over a period of time. It also allows a three-business-day cooling-off period for credit transactions involving liens on residences (except first liens). The Federal Reserve Board has prepared forms that allow businesses to comply with this act. Under this act, a consumer normally can incur no more than $50 of liability on a stolen or lost credit card for its unauthorized use.

The Fair Credit Billing Act was enacted to assist debtors in correcting billing errors. The law allows any debtor who believes that a billing statement is in error to notify the creditor in writing explaining the error. The debtor does not have to pay the disputed amount at that time. The creditor must acknowledge receipt of the error inquiry and within ninety days correct the account or justify to the debtor the reason why the amount is correct.

The Fair Credit Reporting Act establishes certain rights for consumers. The consumer can obtain the information contained in the credit records. In the event that the debtor contests this information, the reporting agency must investigate and correct misinformation and/or allow the debtor to file explanations. Only information from the last seven years may be maintained. Information regarding bankruptcies over ten years old must be deleted from the record.

The Equal Credit Opportunity Act prohibits the creditor from discriminating against credit applicants based on race, color, religion, national origin, gender, marital status, age, or income receipt through public assistance.

The Fair Debt Collection Practices Act was adopted to protect consumers from overzealous collection agencies. Debt collectors must refrain from certain practices that would cause an invasion of the debtor's privacy and from the intentional infliction of emotional distress or duress.

Creditors use three judicial methods to try to collect on judgments owed them: writ of execution, writ of attachment, and writ of garnishment. Writs of attachment and execution are directed against nonexempt property in the debtor's possession. The writ of garnishment is directed against the debtor's property that is in the possession of a third party.

Chapters 7, 11, 12, and 13 of the Bankruptcy Code are of major importance to businesses. Chapter 7 allows a discharge of most debts. Chapter 11 provides for reorganization. Chapters 12 and 13 permit family farmers and individuals, respectively, to readjust their debts with a payout plan over a three- to five-year period. Some debts are not dischargeable by bankruptcy. In addition, certain assets are exempt from bankruptcy by law, meaning that the debtor may keep these assets.

Using the World Wide Web

Founded by the U.S. Congress in 1913, the Federal Reserve is the central bank of the United States. Congress charged the Federal Reserve with providing the nation with a safe, flexible, and stable monetary and financial system.

As stated on its Web page, "The Federal Reserve's duties fall into four general areas: (1) conducting the nation's monetary policy; (2) supervising and regulating banking institutions and protecting the credit rights of consumers; (3) maintaining the stability of the financial system; and (4) providing certain financial services to the U.S. government, the public, financial institutions, and foreign official institutions."

For *Web Activities*, links to Web sites mentioned in the chapter, and additional Web sites that relate to the chapter topics, go to **http://bohlman.westbuslaw.com**, click on "Internet Applications," and select Chapter 14.

Web Activities

Go to **http://bohlman.westbuslaw.com**, click on "Internet Applications," and select Chapter 14.
14–1 Reestablishing Credit
14–2 Credit Card

Key Terms

affidavit
annual percentage rate (ARP)
automatic stay
avoidance
bankruptcy
Consumer Credit Cost Disclosure Act
Consumer Credit Protection Act (CCPA)
Consumer Leasing Act Consumer Reporting Reform Act

deficiency judgment
discharge
Equal Credit Opportunity Act
exempt property
Fair Credit Billing Act
Fair Credit Reporting Act
Fair Debt Collection Practices Act
finance charge
foreclosure
garnishment
homestead exemption

judicial sale
mortgage
mortgagee
mortgagor
nonexempt property
preferential lien
preferential payments
reaffirm
Real Estate Settlement Procedures Act
regular trustee
reorganization
statutory liens
straight bankruptcy

Truth-in-Lending Act (TILA)
Uniform Consumer Credit Code (UCCC)
U.S. trustee
writ of attachment
writ of execution

Questions and Case Problems

14–1 Bankruptcy The East Bank was a secured party on a loan of $5,000 that it made to Sally. Sally later experienced financial difficulty. Creditors other than the East Bank petitioned her into Chapter 7 involuntary bankruptcy. The value of the secured collateral had decreased substantially. On sale, the debt to East Bank was reduced only to $2,500. Sally's estate consisted of $100,000 in exempt assets and $2,000 in nonexempt assets. After the bankruptcy costs and back wages to Sally's employees were paid, no funds remained for unsecured creditors. Sally received a discharge in bank-

ruptcy. Six years later she decided to go back into business. By selling a few exempt assets and getting a small loan, she could buy a small but profitable restaurant. She went to East Bank for the loan. East Bank claimed that the balance of its secured debt was not discharged in bankruptcy. Sally signed an agreement to pay East Bank the $2,500, because the bank was not a party to petitioning Sally into bankruptcy. Because of this, East Bank made a new unsecured loan to Sally.
a. Discuss East Bank's claim that the balance of its secured debt was not discharged in bankruptcy.

b. Discuss the legal effect of Sally's agreement to pay East Bank $2,500 after the discharge in bankruptcy.

c. If, one year later, Sally went into voluntary bankruptcy, what effect would the bankruptcy proceedings have on the new unsecured loan?

14–2 Credit Card Liability Green receives two new credit cards on May 1. One was solicited from the King Department Store. The other was unsolicited from Flyways Airline. During May, Green makes numerous credit card purchases from King, but she does not use the Flyways Airline card. On May 31, a burglar breaks into Green's home and steals both credit cards, along with other items. Green notifies the King Department Store of the theft on June 2, but she fails to notify Flyways Airline. Using the King credit card, the burglar makes a $500 purchase on June 1 and a $200 purchase on June 3. The burglar then charges a vacation flight on the Flyways Airline card for $1,000 on June 5. Green receives the bills for these charges and refuses to pay them. Discuss Green's liability in these situations.

14–3 Bankruptcy Procedures Prior to filing for bankruptcy, Bray made loan payments to his company's credit union through payroll deductions. Bray's employer continued to deduct the loan payments from Bray's paychecks after being notified of the bankruptcy petition. Is this a violation of the Bankruptcy Code? [*In re Bray*, 17 B.R. 152 (Bkrtcy. N. D. Ga. 1982)]

14–4 Fair Credit Reporting Act In 1976, Zeller and Samia jointly purchased a beach cottage. Zeller signed a note promising to pay Samia $3,333.33, which was his share of the $10,000 down payment. In 1985 the relationship between the two parties deteriorated. In 1986, Samia sued Zeller for the balance due on the note. In 1987, after Zeller failed to pay, Samia reported a charge-off of $11,000 (unpaid principal, interest, and costs) to Credit Data. A charge-off is a bookkeeping entry that occurs when a creditor believes a debt to be no longer collectible. As a result, two mortgage companies and a credit card company rejected Zeller's credit requests. Zeller filed an action alleging violations of the Fair Credit Reporting Act (FCRA) and sought actual and punitive damages. Did Samia's action of filing the charge-off with Credit Data violate the Fair Credit Reporting Act? Explain. [*Zeller v. Samia*, 758 F. Supp. 775 (D. Mass. 1991)]

14–5 Truth-in-Lending Two salespeople from Capitol Roofing visited the plaintiffs, Norman and Judy Cole, to sell them siding for their home. After a sales pitch, the salespeople estimated the cost to be $4,900. Before the salespeople left, the Coles signed a number of documents, including a work order, a home improvement retail installment contract, a security agreement and disclosure statement, a loan application, a notice of right to cancel, and a deed of trust. The only document the Coles fully read was the work order. They only saw the signature block on the other papers. The salespeople misrepresented to the Coles the real nature of the paperwork. The Coles were told that they had signed a work order, credit application, and insurance papers. Shortly thereafter, the Coles decided to hold off on the work so that they could obtain estimates from other companies. Mrs. Cole called Capitol Roofing the next morning and said they had decided to wait. She was told that the papers had been processed, the workers would be out at the end of the week, and she could do nothing. She went to work, and when she returned, she found the crew installing the siding. The contract was assigned by Capitol Roofing to United Companies Mortgage (UCM). The Coles experienced problems with the siding. After eleven payments, the Coles became frustrated and discontinued payment to UCM. They brought legal action to recover the payments that they did make. Did they prevail and why? [*Cole v. Lovett*, 672 F. Supp. 947 (1987)]

14–6 Truth-in-Lending Harold Grey signed an installment contract as payment for membership in European Health Spas, Inc. The disclosure documents that accompanied the installment loan contract were printed in regular type, with the exception of the following words, which were printed in capital letters: "FINANCE CHARGE," "ANNUAL PERCENTAGE RATE," and "MEMBER ACKNOWLEDGES THAT HE HAS READ AND RECEIVED A FILLED-IN SIGNED COPY OF THIS AGREEMENT." In addition, at the top of the disclosure statement, the words "NOTICE TO BUYER" were printed. Under federal truth-in-lending regulations, the words *finance charge* and *annual percentage rate* must be printed conspicuously in the truth-in-lending disclosure statements. Otherwise, the creditor is deemed in violation of the act. Discuss whether European Health spas met the requirement of conspicuousness. [*Grey v. European Health Spas, Inc.*, 428 F. Supp. 841 (D. Conn. 1977)]

14–7 Truth-in-Lending In the summer of 1972, Robert Martin applied for and was issued an American Express card. Approximately three years later, in April 1975, Martin gave his card to E. L. McBride, a business associate, and orally authorized McBride to charge up to

$500 on it. Martin also wrote to American Express requesting that charges on his account be limited to $1,000. In June 1975, however, Martin received a statement from American Express indicating that the amount owed on his card account was approximately $5,300. Under the Truth-in-Lending Act, for how much will Martin be liable to American Express? [*Martin v. American Express, Inc.*, 361 So. 2d 597 (Ala. App. 1978)]

14–8 Fair Debt Collection Practices Act Telecredit Service Corp. is a computerized check authorization and purchase service. It purchases, on average, 608,959 dishonored checks a year. A customer writes a check to a merchant, who then verifies with Telecredit whether the customer previously has written bad checks. If the customer's record is clean, Telecredit authorizes acceptance of the check. If the check then is dishonored, Telecredit purchases the check and attempts collection of it. Holmes wrote a bad check for $315. Telecredit purchased the check and used various means to collect from Holmes. These procedures possibly violated the Fair Debt Collection Practices Act. Telecredit argued that it owned the check and thus was exempt from the act's restrictions. Is Telecredit subject to the act? Explain. [*Holmes v. Telecredit Service Corp.*, 736 F. Supp. 1289 (D. Del. 1990)]

14–9 Fair Debt Collection Practices Act To pay for groceries, Arsenault wrote a check in the amount of $156.94 to "Copps," a local supermarket. The check, which was subsequently dishonored by his bank because of insufficient funds, was drawn on an account that Arsenault held jointly with plaintiff Bass. In most states, writing a check with insufficient funds is fraud and a crime. To collect on the check, Copps employed defendant law firm, Stolper, Koritzinsky, Brewster & Neider, S.C. (SKBN), which instituted collection activities against Arsenault. The first three collection attempts, to which Arsenault did not respond, were in the form of collection letters addressed solely to Arsenault. Its fourth collection letter, however, was addressed jointly to Arsenault and Bass. This letter, written and signed by defendant Leschensky, a nonattorney employee of SKBN, advised that she drafted and filed lawsuits in collections matters, and that she would "hold off taking any action for 7 days" if Arsenault or Bass would make arrangements to pay. Bass brought an action for statutory damages for defendants' failure to comply with the Fair Debt Collection Practices Act (FDCPA) in its collection letter. Among other complaints, Bass alleged that in the letter Leschensky misrepresented herself as an attorney in violation of the FDCPA and that the letter failed to include language specifically required by the act stating that the letter's purpose was to collect a debt and that any information received would be used solely in collection efforts. SKBN conceded before the district court that the letter lacked this required language. The district court granted Bass's motion for a summary judgment because of the possible fraud and the defendants appealed. What was the final decision in this case and why? [*Bass v. Stolper*, 111 F.3d 1322 (1997)]

14–10 Internet Your business needs two cashiers. An advertisement for workers nets 100 applications. You want to review the credit reports of each applicant because you plan to eliminate those with poor credit histories. As a prospective employer, are you able to view those credit reports? What type of requestors can see a credit record? Go to the Federal Reserve Web site, which addresses this question, at **http://www.federalreserve.gov/**. On the left side, under "Advanced Search," click on "Consumer Information." On the next page, in the middle, under the "Consumer Credit" section, click on "Your Credit Report: What it Says about You."

Chapter 15

Consumer Protection

Caveat emptor: *Let the buyer beware.*

    Latin maxim

Introduction

Earlier chapters addressed ways in which the law attempts to protect consumers' interests. Courts, administrative agencies, and legislatures have prohibited certain business practices because they have been determined to be unfair or deceptive. This chapter discusses laws that attempt to control unfair and deceptive trade practices, to prevent misleading advertising, and to encourage the development of safe products.

Consumer protection statutes promote both safety and fair dealing. They try to prevent injury to a person's body or damage to his property or economic well-being. Although some statutes provide a specific remedy should the consumer suffer an injury, consumer protection statutes aim to eliminate the harm itself. Many of these statutes provide no remedies for injured consumers. Redress for injuries suffered usually involves another area of the law, such as tort or contract law (covered in Chapters 8 through 11).

This chapter will familiarize you with the nature and existence of some of the important statutes. The Federal Trade Commission is the primary enforcement agency at the federal level of consumer statutes.

Artiste Login. Artiste Login Products, Inc., is involved in many contracts for the sale of goods that the business produces. Carlo and Carlotta, the owners, need to be aware of federal and state consumer protection statutes. Often, these statutes stipulate civil and criminal penalties for failing to comply with the statutory requirements. The requirements may be as simple as disclosing information or disclosing it in a specific manner.

Federal Trade Commission

Congress created the Federal Trade Commission (FTC) in 1914 by adopting the **Federal Trade Commission Act**. The purpose of the agency was to prevent unfair methods of competition in commerce to police anticompetitive practices. In 1938, Congress expanded the mission of the FTC to include consumer protection with the **Wheeler-Lea Amendment**, which included a broad prohibition against "**unfair or deceptive acts or practices**." Today, the Federal Trade Commission Act has a dual focus: to regulate anticompetitive business behavior and to provide consumer protection. This chapter examines the consumer protection aspects of the FTC. The antitrust mission is studied in Chapter 21.

Prior to 1938, courts aided only a few purchasers who sued sellers of defective goods by finding that the seller had breached a contract, had breached a warranty, or had violated a duty to the purchaser. As pointed out in Chapter 11, these claims often are difficult to prove.

The Wheeler-Lea amendment enabled the FTC to focus its attention on direct consumer protection. For example, the amendment authorized the FTC to monitor deceptive advertising practices. The FTC does not have to prove to the court that an advertising practice affected the competition, only that the advertisement was unfair and deceptive. The definitions of the two words *unfair* and *deceptive* are left to the FTC. In general, any practice that would tend to mislead consumers is unfair or deceptive.

The FTC has three bureaus: the Bureau of Competition, the Bureau of Economics, and the Bureau of Consumer Protection. The Bureau of Competition handles the FTC's antitrust activities. The Bureau of Economics evaluates the economic impact of the FTC's actions. This bureau provides economic analysis and support to antitrust and consumer protection investigations and rule makings of the FTC. The Bureau of Consumer Protection monitors advertising and labeling practices, investigates complaints, and prosecutes cases involving alleged unfair practices. Exhibit 15–1 shows the FTC's organizational structure.

For every consumer protection statute, society poses three questions:

1. From what harm does the statute protect consumers?

2. Whom does the statute protect?

3. What is the cost of this protection?

Exhibit 15–2 lists statutes and regulations designed to protect consumers. Not all are enforced by the Federal Trade Commission.

Trade Regulation Rules

In 1975, Congress passed the **Magnuson–Moss Warranty–Federal Trade Commission Improvements Act**, which provided the FTC with the authority to adopt trade regulation rules that define unfair or deceptive acts in particular industries. The act is discussed in more detail later in this chapter. A **trade regulation rule** is a statement by the agency that has general applicability. The rule's effect is to implement the agency's law, policy, or practice. In other words, a rule has the force of law.

FTC trade regulation rules apply to an entire industry rather than to a particular seller. The commission can focus on an industry and formulate standards to which all businesses within that industry must conform. In the past, the FTC has investigated household detergents, appliances, office copiers, the title insurance business, the funeral industry, and car rental agencies. Other investigations included entire industries, such as transportation, health-care facilities, nursing homes, agriculture, and energy.

The FTC may institute an action against an alleged wrongdoer either in its administrative law court or in federal court. The FTC first tries to persuade a seller to stop an unfair or deceptive practice. This tactic is effective because most cases are settled by a *consent decree*. The seller and the FTC reach an agreement as to how the seller will conduct its business in the future. This agreement is finalized in the form of a consent decree whereby the seller consents to an order restraining the activity found by the FTC to be unfair or deceptive. A defendant-seller may be required to compensate injured buyers when the seller has violated an FTC rule or order.

If the FTC and the seller do not come to an agreement, the FTC may take the case to an administrative law court and request a **cease-and-desist order**. This order requires the seller-defendant to cease its activities and desist from undertaking those activities in the future. This type of order forces the seller to correct its business operations.

If unable to reach an agreement, the FTC may elect to take the case to a U.S. district court instead of bringing the case to the FTC's administrative law court. At the request of the FTC, the district court can grant an injunction to restrain or prohibit a particular practice. Fines for violations may amount to $10,000 per day. Any person or firm subject to an FTC order or rule may seek a review of the FTC's action in a U.S. court of appeals.

Additional orders that the FTC can issue include *affirmative disclosure orders*, *corrective advertising orders*, and *multiple product orders*. By issuing an **affirmative disclosure order**, the FTC requires the defendant to place affirmative disclaimers into future advertisements.

An affirmative disclaimer states the ways in which the product will not benefit the user. The disclaimers help to remedy past deceptive advertisements. For example, the FTC required the J. B. Williams Company to state in its future advertisements for Geritol that it would not benefit the great majority of people who suffer from tiredness. Geritol had advertised that it was effective for any illness for which tiredness was a symptom. The advertising was deceptive, according to the FTC, because tiredness is symptomatic of many illnesses—including cancer and diabetes—on which Geritol had no effect.

A **corrective advertising order** is very similar to an affirmative disclaimer, but it takes the remedy one step further. This order requires the defendant to place a statement in the advertisements to the effect that its past advertisements were false.

The FTC can order the words "contrary to prior advertising" to be placed in future advertisements if the

Exhibit 15–1   Organizational Structure of the Federal Trade Commission

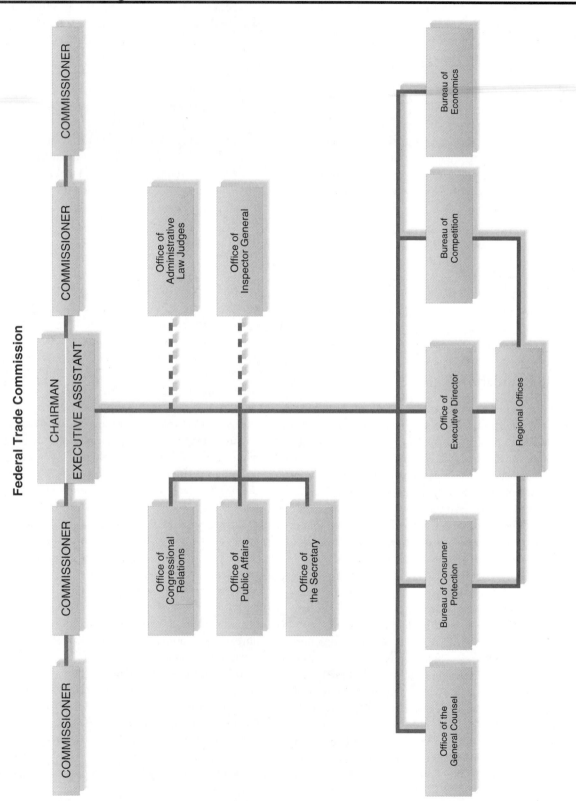

Exhibit 15–2   **Consumer Protection Statutes and Regulations**

Date	Popular Name	Purpose
		Advertising
1938	Wheeler-Lea Act	Amends the Federal Trade Commission Act (1914); prohibits unfair or deceptive acts or practices.
1946	Lanham Act	Prohibits deceptive advertising.
1950	Oleomargarine Tax Repeal Act	Prohibits advertising that oleomargarine is a dairy product.
1969	Public Health Cigarette Smoking Act	Prohibits advertising of cigarettes on television.
1973	FTC Rules of Negative Options	Regulates advertisements for book and record clubs.
1988	Charity Games Advertising Act	Allows advertising of gambling if state run or for charitable purposes.
		Inspection and Certification
1906	Meat Inspection Act	Provides for inspection of meat.
1907	Wholesome Meat Act	Amends Meat Inspection Act.
1938	Food, Drug, and Cosmetic Act	Provides for inspection and regulation of food, drugs, and cosmetics.
1958	Food Additive (Delaney) Amendment to Food Drug, and Cosmetic Act	Requires that food additives not cause cancer and be safe.
1966	Hazardous Substances Act	Regulates hazardous substances
1968	Poultry Inspection Act	Provides for inspection of poultry.
1969	Child Protection and Toy Safety Act	Bans toys that pose electrical, mechanical, or thermal hazards.
1972	Odometer Act	Regulates odometers.
1976	Medical Device Amendments	Requires premarket clearance of medical devices.
1976	Toxic Stubstances Control Act	Regulates certain chemical substances and mixtures.
1994	Hazardous Material Transportation Act	Requires inspection of hazardous materials during transportation.
		Labeling
1906	Jewelers' Liability Act	Prohibits stamping on gold or silver products with "U.S. Assay."
1939	Wool Products Labeling Act	Requires accurate labeling of wool products.
1951	Fur Products Labeling Act	Prohibits misbranding of fur products.
1953	Flammable Fabrics Act	Sets standards and requires labeling for flammable fabrics and products.
1958	Textile Fiber Products Identification Act	Requires accurate labeling of textiles.
1960	Hazardous Substances Labeling Act	Requires accurate labeling of hazardous substances.
1966	Fair Packaging and Labeling Act	Requires accurate names, quantities, and weights on packages.
1966	Child Protection Act	Requires childproof devices and special labeling.
1966	Cigarette Labeling and Advertising Act	Requires labels warning of possible health hazards.
1970	Poison Prevention Packaging Act	Requires labeling of poisonous household substances.
1986	Smokeless Tobacco Act	Requires conspicuous warnings on tobacco products.
1990	Nutrition Labeling Act	Requires labels listing calories and nutritional information.
1990	Dolphin Protection Consumer Information Act	Unlawful to claim that any tuna product is "dolphin safe."
1992	Energy Policy Act	Energy efficiency labeling.
1994	Violent Crime Control and Law Enforcement Act	Sets standards for "Made in America" or "Made in the U.S.A." labels
1996	Telecommunications Act	Defines "pay-per-call service" (currently 900 numbers)
		Sales and Warranties
1968	Interstate Land Sales	Requires full disclosure in interstate land sales.
1973	FTC Rule on Door-to-Door Sales	Regulates door-to-door sales contracts.
1975	Magnuson-Moss Warranty Act	Regulates warranties on consumer products.
1976	Real Estate Settlements Procedures Act	Requires disclosure of home-buying costs.
1980	FTC Rule on Vocational and Correspondence Schools	Regulates contracts with vocational and correspondence schools.
1984	FTC Rule on Used Cars	Regulates warranties in used car sales.
1992	Telephone Disclosure and Dispute Resolution act	Regulates advertising for, operation of, and billing and collection procedures for pay-per-call (currently 900 numbers).
1994	Telemarketing and Consumer Fraud and Abuse Prevention Act	Regulates sales made over the telephone.

defendant engaged in egregious and intentional deception. For example, Novartis Consumer Health produces Doan's pills. The product had been advertised as more effective than other painkillers for back problems. The FTC required the company to spend $8 million over one year in its advertising and packaging to state that "Although Doan's is an effective pain reliever, there is no evidence that Doan's is more effective than other pain relievers for back pain."[1]

Generally, if the FTC finds deceptive advertising, it requires the firm to refrain from making any further

deceptive advertisements. In cases in which a firm sells multiple products, such an order may have little effect. If the FTC finds not only deceptive advertising but also a history of false advertising, it can issue a **multiple product order**. This order requires all future advertisements for all of the firm's products (or for all of the products in a certain category) to be accurate, not just advertisements for the original product that the firm falsely advertised. In the following case, the court of appeals reviews the power of the FTC to issue a multiple product order.

[1]Novartis Corporation v. Federal Trade Commission, 223 F.3d 783 (2000).

<table>
<tr><td>

CASE 15.1

United States Court of Appeals, Ninth Circuit, 1982

676 F.2d 385

</td><td>

SEARS, ROEBUCK AND CO. v. FEDERAL TRADE COMMISSION

BACKGROUND AND FACTS In the early 1970s, Sears formulated a plan to increase sales of its top-of-the-line Lady Kenmore dishwasher. The plan did not call for any reengineering of the dishwasher or other mechanical improvement. Rather, the plan fostered an image change for the Lady Kenmore, or in sales jargon, Sears sought to "reposition" the machine in the marketplace. The advertising objective was to change the consumer image from a "price" (economy) brand to that of a superior product at a reasonable price. Sears hoped that the machine would move from market leadership to market dominance as the market share increased.

Sears recognized that a dishwasher that eliminated the need to prerinse and prescrape dishes would attract new customers and command a premium price. It also knew that a machine's ability to clean dishes on the upper rack as thoroughly as those on the bottom rack would further attract new customers. Based on this knowledge, Sears prepared advertisements claiming that the Lady Kenmore "completely eliminated" the need for prescraping and prerinsing. The advertisements characterized the machine as the "freedom maker."

Advertisements for the Lady Kenmore appeared in print and on television throughout the country over a four-year period at a cost to Sears of roughly $8 million. During the first three years, Lady Kenmore unit sales rose 300 percent. The value of the company's total dishwasher sales rose from $73,470,000 in 1971 to $94,500,000 in 1973.

The "no scraping, no prerinsing" claim was false. Sears had no reasonable basis for asserting the claim. Furthermore, the owner's manual that customers received after purchasing the dishwasher contradicted the claim. A 1973 survey conducted for Sears found that more than half of recent Lady Kenmore purchasers disagreed with the proposition that the Lady Kenmore did not require prerinsing.

The FTC began an investigation of the advertisements in 1975. In 1977, the FTC issued a complaint, charging Sears and its advertising agency, J. Walter Thompson Company, with disseminating deceptive and unfair advertisements. After an extensive administrative hearing, the administrative law judge (ALJ) held Sears liable for deceptive and false advertising. The ALJ issued a multiple product order to Sears not to make any performance claims for any major home appliances without first possessing a reasonable basis consisting of competent and reliable tests. Further, it ordered Sears to keep records for three years. Sears sought review of the administrative law judge's order.

</td></tr>
</table>

Judge REINHARDT

. . . .

A judgment regarding "reasonable relation" in multi-product order cases "depends upon the specific circumstances of the case." "[T]he ultimate question is the likelihood of the petitioner committing the sort of unfair practices [the order] prohibit[s][.]" We answer that question by first examining the specific circumstances present in a particular case. Then, giving due deference to the Commission's expertise and judgment, we determine whether there is a "reasonable relation" between those circumstances and the concern regarding future violations manifested by the Commission's order.

Where a fair assessment of an advertiser's conduct shows a ready willingness to flout the law, sufficient cause for concern regarding further, additional violations exists. Two factors or elements frequently influence our decision—the deliberateness and seriousness of the present violation, and the violator's past record with respect to unfair advertising practices. Other circumstances may be weighed, including the adaptability or transferability of the unfair practice to other products. The weight given a particular factor or element will vary. The more egregious the facts with respect to a particular element, the less important it is that another negative factor be present. In the final analysis, we look to the circumstances as a whole and not to the presence or absence of any single factor.

. . . .

. . . Sears states that advertisements concerning the other covered products, e.g., microwave ovens and trash compactors, are never related to those promoting dishwashers since dishwashers do not perform work similar to the work performed by the microwave ovens or trash compactors, and that, therefore, an order covering these functionally unrelated machines is inherently unreasonable. This argument misses the fundamental point that the Commission is concerned not with how machines work, but with how machines are sold. Thus, the correct question is not whether the machines function in similar ways but whether the machines could be sold with similar techniques. . . .

. . . .

. . . Under [the specific] circumstances, Sears' advertising campaign demonstrates "blatant and utter disregard" for the law. The Commission also considered petitioner's compliance record and concluded that is was "a wash." We see no reason to find otherwise.

Sears' advertisements were no accident or "isolated instance." Rather, they were part of an advertising strategy, with attendant slogans, adopted without regard to the actual performance of the advertised machines. As the Commission pointed out, the covered machines are major ticket items generally purchased infrequently by any particular person. For that reason, their profitability does not depend on repeat purchases as is the case with frequently purchased, low-cost items. A selling strategy based on this purchasing fact, e.g., the making of false and unsubstantiated performance claims as to a major ticket item, would be effective for a considerable period of time, with great benefit to the merchant but at great cost to consumers. This selling strategy could readily be transferred to the marketing of other machines in the home appliance category.

The prevention of "transfers" of unfair trade practices is a fundamental goal of the Commission's remedial work. Justice Brandeis, a draftsman of the 1914 legislation which created the Commission, made this point in *Federal Trade Comm'n v. Gratz*[.] Objecting to the Court's attempt to narrow the Commission's remedial authority, he expressed a view which has since become law.

> *The purpose of Congress [in creating the Commission] was to prevent any unfair method which may have been used by any concern in competition from becoming its general practice. It was only by stopping its use before it became general practice that the apprehended effect of all unfair methods . . . could be averted.*

It is not only pretermitting a "general practice" which is important here, however. The "transfer" to any other single major home appliance could well cause substantial damage to consumers prior to the time that the Commission could again investigate the Acts and obtain the evidence necessary to prove that a similar violation had occurred. By that time, it would be too late to protect the large number of consumers who, in reliance on the truthfulness of the advertised claims, had purchased a major home appliance which they expected to perform the advertised work for many years. This danger is particularly acute where national brands, like Sears' major home appliances, are involved and the advertising campaigns are both widespread and intensive.

In addition, if we were to deny "transfer prevention" authority to the Commission under these circumstances, unscrupulous merchandisers (and we do not imply that Sears falls in that category) might be encouraged to transfer unlawful but successful advertising techniques from product to product, leaving the Commission the job of instituting separate proceedings to secure new orders for each unlawfully advertised product. Because so drastic a limitation on the Commission's enforcement procedure would conflict with the Congressional intent described by Justice Brandeis, would consume enormous resources, and would afford no particular protection to lawful advertisements and little protection to consumers, the Commission need not wait until a "transfer" occurs before issuing multi-product orders in cases like the one before us. It may issue and enforce such orders to avert an "apprehended effect."

To prevent the false and unsubstantiated performance claims strategy from being used in connection with another major home appliance or from becoming Sears' general practice with respect to such appliances, the Commission deemed a broad order necessary. A judgment of this nature depends on detailed knowledge of the major home appliances business and its related advertising techniques. "[D]eceptive advertising cases necessarily require 'inference and pragmatic judgment.'" This sort of knowledge of the commercial world and the ability to make the type of judgment required lie in the realm of the Commission's greater expertise.

We note one other important Act. . . . [T]he order before us is not an all- products order. It is a limited order that applies only to 14 major ticket items. These 14 items constitute a small proportion of the total number of products sold by Sears.

In light of the flagrant and egregious nature of the violation found and the other circumstances present here, and giving the Commission's conclusions the required "great weight," we find no basis for substituting our judgment for the Commission's regarding the necessity for this multi-product order. We hold that the multi-product order is reasonably related to the petitioner's conduct, that a multi-product order is appropriate, and that the inclusion of the "performance claims" provision in that order is supported by the record before us and does not render the order overbroad.

DECISION AND REMEDY The court of appeals upheld the validity of the FTC's multiple product order covering all of Sears' major home appliances, including clothes washers, clothes dryers, disposals, trash compactors, refrigerators, freezers, ranges, stoves, ovens, and stereophonic consoles. As the court pointed out, the FTC's fundamental goal is to prevent the "transfer" of unfair trade practices from one product to another. Congress created the FTC to stop unfair practices before they became a general practice. Thus, the FTC has the power to issue multiple product orders.

CRITICAL THINKING: ETHICS Discuss whether a major corporation today would attempt a sales program similar to Sears' dishwasher advertisements of the 1970s.

Exemptions to FTC Regulation

The major exemptions to FTC trade regulation activities are those firms or industries that are regulated by local, state, or other federal authorities. For example, public utilities are regulated by state authorities. Thus, few public utilities are subject to the FTC's authority.

Industries directly regulated by federal agencies are also outside the scope of FTC investigations. For example, the securities markets are regulated by the Securities and Exchange Commission. Some exceptions exist for which both the FTC and another federal agency have the power from Congress to investigate the same industry. For example, the FTC enforces some credit protection statutes even though the Federal Reserve Board, the Federal Home Loan Bank Board, and other federal agencies regulate credit. Another example is that both the FTC and the Food and Drug Administration regulate the labeling of food and drugs.

These agencies have interagency agreements that set out each agency's specific duties and indicate which will have primary investigative and enforcement powers. Thus, only one federal agency handles the aspects of any given case, rather than two or more federal agencies competing and wasting resources by repeating investigation and enforcement procedures.

Deceptive Advertising

Through its focus on advertising, the FTC can investigate before an injury to consumers occurs. If the investigation uncovers deceptive advertising, the FTC can take the case to its administrative law court. If an advertiser challenges an FTC administrative court ruling in a judicial court, the FTC needs only to prove that the advertisement could deceive consumers, not that it actually did so. Evidence of consumer misunderstanding of the claims made in the advertisement usually is not offered.

The FTC has adopted a policy statement that sets out the guidelines as to the three elements of deceptive advertising.[2] First, the advertising must contain a representation, omission, or practice. Second, the representation, omission, or practice must be found likely to mislead consumers acting reasonably under the circumstances. Third, the representation, omission, or practice must be material (or significant). It also must be likely to mislead. An actual deception need not occur.

Advertisements are frequently challenged based on one of these issues: (1) false statements or claims, (2) failure to disclose important facts, (3) statements that are less than the whole truth, or (4) unsupported claims.

False Statements or Claims

Misrepresentations about the quality, composition, origin, character, or availability of products are illegal. Such misrepresentations need not involve an explicit false statement or claim. An advertisement that creates a false impression is deceptive; no verbal or written statement is required. For example, a cosmetic company advertises a "rejuvenescence cream" that would rejuvenate and restore youth or the appearance of youth to the skin. Unfortunately, medical science knows that virtually nothing can restore skin youthfulness. This type of advertising is false and deceptive.

Failure to Disclose Important Facts

Silence may be considered deceptive when it represents a failure to disclose important facts. Some facts known to the seller are so important that they should be communicated to prospective buyers. Although the FTC does not require that every negative fact about a product be revealed, instances exist when the FTC requires an advertiser either to include additional information or to stop its advertising program.

Even if state law permits a practice (that is, a certain type of advertising or a certain wording used in advertising), an FTC ruling will preempt the state's determination of legality. In the following case, the court reviewed the FTC's allegation that the defendant engaged in deceptive advertising.

---

[2]The FTC regulations on *Guides Against Deceptive Pricing* are located at http://www.ftc.gov/bcp/guides/decptprc.htm.

CASE 15.2

United States Court of
Appeals, Ninth Circuit,
2001
265 F.3d 944

FEDERAL TRADE COMMISSION v. GILL

BACKGROUND AND FACTS The FTC filed this action against Keith H. Gill and Richard Murkey seeking a permanent injunction and consumer redress. The Commission asserted three claims: (1) violation of the Credit Repair Organizations Act (CRO) by charging clients for services that were not fully performed, (2) violation of the CRO Act by making untrue or misleading statements to induce consumers to purchase their services, and (3) violation of the FTC Act by making untrue or misleading statements to induce consumers to purchase services.

Gill was a licensed to practice law in California and worked as a sole practitioner. In addition to a general legal practice, beginning in 1995, Gill offered credit repair services to consumers, ostensibly through his law office, but in reality through the defendant Murkey. Defendants used telephones, the U.S. mail, and radio to advertise their credit repair services to consumers.

Most consumers signed contracts with Gill's law office, and both Gill and Murkey testified that they considered every consumer who signed a retainer agreement with the Gill law office to be Gill's client. Gill testified that his relationship with Murkey was governed by a written contract between the two.

To reach potential credit repair clients, defendants used radio broadcasts, newspaper advertisements, telephone conversations, and personal meetings throughout the United States. During 1997 and 1998, Murkey appeared regularly on a radio talk program broadcast throughout most of Southern California, discussing credit restoration. The format resembled a talk show, and when Murkey was not available, stations replayed the tapes, rather like a radio infomercial. He told consumers that any sort of negative information, including accurate and not obsolete information, could legally be removed from a consumer's credit report, notably, through the use of defendants' services. Murkey repeated the telephone and facsimile numbers and encouraged consumers to call for a free credit evaluation or further information. Examples of claims made during the broadcasts include the following:

1. There are many legal ways under the Federal Fair Credit Reporting Act to fix credit, no matter what type of negative it is, including foreclosure and or bankruptcy, judgments, tax liens . . . even if those [items] are not paid off.

2. Because of the federal laws and the consumers' rights under the federal laws, we still have legal rights as consumers and we can, in fact, knowing the right proper techniques and strategies and procedures that we have perfected in our offices over the years, we can legally remove those negatives from someone's credit report.

3. Most likely, in our offices, we can clean your credit in six weeks to two months.

Beginning in February 1999, Murkey's program was broadcast over Cable Radio Network, which could be heard in, among other places, Rhode Island, Florida, Kentucky, New York, New Jersey, Arizona, Nevada, and possibly Texas.

In fact, defendants' legal process for removing negative information from their clients' credit reports was premised on the obligation of credit reporting agencies (CRAs) to respond to all consumer disputes within thirty days. CRAs must remove any legitimately challenged item that they cannot verify within the thirty-day period. If the CRA does verify the item, even after thirty days have passed, it can (and generally will) restore the item to the credit report.

PAEZ, Circuit Judge:

. . . .

For over thirty years, Congress has sought to balance the need of creditors for accurate credit information with consumers' interests in accuracy and fair use of such data. In

1970, Congress passed the Fair Credit Reporting Act (FCRA) with the express purpose of requiring "consumer reporting agencies [to] adopt reasonable procedures for meeting the needs of commerce for consumer credit, personnel, insurance, and other information in a manner which is fair and equitable to the consumer, with regard to the confidentiality, accuracy, relevancy, and proper utilization of such information in accordance with the requirements of this subchapter." Consumer reporting agencies ("CRAs") like Trans Union, Experian, and Equifax must exercise care in accurately and completely reporting credit information. The FCRA limits the length of time that a CRA is permitted to report an adverse item of information. Generally, bankruptcies may be reported for ten years; all other negative information can remain on a report for up to seven years. Older items are referred to as "obsolete."

The FCRA sets forth a procedure for disputing the completeness or accuracy of an item and obtaining a reinvestigation. When a consumer notifies a CRA of a disputed item, that agency has 30 days to "reinvestigate free of charge and record the current status of the disputed information, or delete the item from the file . . ., before the end of the 30-day period [.]" Upon the creditor's certification that the questioned information is accurate, the CRA can reinsert the information in the consumer's file. . . . Although the FCRA does not mandate reinsertion, the CRA's duty to "follow reasonable procedures to assure maximum possible accuracy of the information concerning the individual about whom the report relates" effectively compels this result.

Throughout the 1990s, Congress attempted to address problems resulting from the continued growth of the credit reporting industry. In Senate Report 103-209, concerning the Consumer Reporting Reform Act of 1994, the Committee on Banking, Housing and Urban Affairs noted that the industry "maintains 450 million credit files on individual consumers and processes almost 2 billion pieces of data per month." As the industry grew, so did the inaccuracies. "From 1990 to 1993, the Federal Trade Commission . . . received more complaints regarding consumer reporting agencies than any other industry." Meanwhile, CRAs had ventured into new areas, "creat[ing] and sell[ing] lists of consumers for general direct marketing solicitations not initiated by the consumer and, through a process known as 'prescreening,' sell[ing] more refined lists of credit worthy borrowers for creditors who use the information to extend offers of credit to such borrowers."

B. The Credit Repair Organizations Act

Enter the credit repair clinic. Congress had recognized the abuses by many of the newly emerging credit repair clinics well before it finally enacted the CRO Act in 1996. In 1988, Representative Frank Annunzio described these businesses as "kin to 'get rich quick' schemes. They promise fast results and newfound wealth in the form of available credit." The House Report on the Consumer Reporting Reform Act of 1994, the immediate predecessor to the Act passed in 1996, explained further:

> *[T]hese credit repair businesses, through advertisements and oral representations, lead consumers to believe that adverse information in their consumer reports can be deleted or modified regardless of its accuracy . . . however, accurate, adverse information may be reported for 7 years, or in the case of bankruptcy, 10 years. Therefore, such representations by credit repair clinics are often misleading. . . .*
>
> *Where credit repair clinics do succeed, however, they often do so through abuse of the reinvestigation procedures . . . consumer reporting agencies must generally delete information that cannot be verified within 30 days of receiving notice of the dispute. Credit repair clinics take advantage of this provision by inundating consumer reporting agencies with so many challenges to consumer reports that the reinvestigation system breaks down, and the adverse, but accurate, information is deleted.*

Thus, the CRO Act's express purposes are twofold: "(1) to ensure that prospective buyers of the services of credit repair organizations are provided with the information necessary to make an informed decision regarding the purchase of such services; and (2) to protect the public from unfair or deceptive advertising and business practices by credit repair organizations."

. . .

The CRO Act became effective on April 1, 1997. Of the prohibited practices listed in the CRO Act, three are involved in the instant appeal prohibiting any person from

> *mak[ing] any statement, or counsel[ing] or advis[ing] any consumer to make any statement, which is untrue or misleading (or which, upon the exercise of reasonable care, should be known by the credit repair organization, officer, employee, agent, or other person to be untrue or misleading) with respect to any consumer's credit worthiness [sic], credit standing, or credit capacity to (A) any consumer reporting agency. . . . prohibits any person from "mak[ing] or us[ing] any untrue or misleading representation of the services of the credit repair organization[.]" Finally, (b) provides that "[n]o credit repair organization may charge or receive any money or other valuable consideration for the performance of any service which the credit repair organization has agreed to perform for any consumer before such service is* fully *performed."*

A violation of the CRO Act is to be treated as a violation of the FTC Act.

C. The Federal Trade Commission Act

Section 5 of the FTC Act, has long prohibited "[u]nfair methods of competition in or affecting commerce, and unfair or deceptive acts or practices in or affecting commerce[.]" Section 5(a) empowers the FTC to prevent such acts or practices. An act or practice is deceptive if "first, there is a representation, omission, or practice that, second, is likely to mislead consumers acting reasonably under the circumstances, and third, the representation, omission, or practice is material."

. . . .

As a preliminary matter, violation of the CRO Act's prohibition against making or using any untrue or misleading representation of the services of the credit repair organization is not only a violation of the CRO Act, but also an unfair or deceptive act or practice in commerce in violation of section 5(a) of the FTC Act. . . . All the FTC must show to establish violations of both acts, then, is an untrue or misleading statement regarding the services of the CRO.

Defendant Murkey's only complaint about the district court's judgment against him in the amount of $1,335,912.14 is that the district court should have taken into consideration "the thousands of consumers who have benefitted from his services over the years." Murkey cites no authority for this proposition, and none exists.

In fact, as the district court correctly noted, [the Act] provides for recovery of "any amount paid by the person to the credit repair organization" if the CRO violated any provision of the CRO Act. Moreover, the CRO Act incorporates the

FTC's authority under the FTC Act to seek monetary remedies. We have held that restitution is a form of ancillary relief available to the court in these circumstances to effect complete justice. In the absence of proof of "actual damages," the court properly used the amounts consumers paid as the basis for the amount Defendants should be ordered to pay for their wrongdoing. Murkey does not contest the district court's calculation of the amount of equitable monetary relief, and we affirm the judgment.

. . . .

DECISION AND REMEDY The court held that representations by the defendants that they could permanently remove negative credit information from their credit files, even if this information was accurate and not obsolete, were clearly false and violated both the Credit Repair Organizations Act and the Federal Trade Commission Act.

CRITICAL THINKING: MANAGEMENT CONSIDERATION Discuss the difference between trade puffing (see the following text) and deceptive acts or practices.

Statements That Are Less Than the Whole Truth

Deception that involves stating less than the whole truth is the counterpart to failing to disclose important facts. Instead of omitting a material fact, the advertiser uses true statements out of context or in a way that deliberately misleads. A product that is "guaranteed for life," for example, is usually construed to mean a guarantee for the consumer's life, not the product's. The FTC restrained the Parker Pen Company from making such guarantees after Parker revealed that it referred to the life of its pens in its lifetime guarantee.

Ocean Spray Cranberry Juice was required by a consent order to explain in future advertisements its statement that "Cranberry Juice Cocktail has more food energy than orange juice or tomato juice." Ocean Spray used "food energy" to mean—not vitamins or minerals—but calories.

Recently, Palm, Inc., settled a complaint with the FTC involving their advertisements that indicated that their handheld devices could do many different functions. Palm, Inc., however, did not inform prospective buyers that they needed to purchase separate devices or software to use these features. The company agreed not to continue these advertisements without informing the consumer about these additional purchases.

Unsupported Claims

Firms must supply reasonable, scientific evidence to substantiate advertising claims. Otherwise, the advertisement makes unsupported claims. If a business claims its product to be faster or safer than similar products, sufficient testing must prove the claim's validity.

Certain statements are considered mere trade puffing rather than deceptive advertising. *Trade puffing* is an opinion stated by the seller of goods. For example, a manufacturer's statement that its product is "the best" would not be regarded as a product claim but merely as puffing. In contrast, a statement that a product lasts three times longer than comparable products must be supported by reasonable evidence. For example, Wonder Bread advertised that its bread contained calcium that would increase a person's intelligence. The FTC asserted that Wonder Bread did not have adequate scientific evidence to support this claim. Wonder Bread agreed in the future not to advertise in this manner. The next case demonstrates the requirement that a product must live up to the claims made about it.

CASE 15.3	**FEDERAL TRADE COMMISSION v. PANTRON I CORPORATION**
United States Court of Appeals, Ninth Circuit, 1994 33 F.3d 1088 http://www.mlmlaw.com/library/cases/mlm/federal/9pantron.htm	**BACKGROUND AND FACTS** Pantron I Corporation (Pantron) marketed the Helsinki Formula (Formula), which supposedly arrested hair loss and stimulated hair regrowth in baldness sufferers. The Formula consisted of a conditioner and a shampoo and sold for $49.95 for a three-month supply. Pantron offered a full money-back guarantee to unsatisfied customers.

Pantron's advertisements (including late-night infomercials hosted by the *Man from U.N.C.L.E.*, Robert Vaughn) featured both Formula claims. The advertisements also represented that recognized scientific studies supported those claims.

In November 1988, the Federal Trade Commission (FTC) filed a suit in U.S. district court. The FTC's complaint alleged that the advertisements, which represented that the Formula was effective, were false and constituted an unfair or deceptive trade practice in violation of Sections 5 and 12 of the Federal Trade Commission Act and that no scientific evidence supported the claims.

The district court conducted a five-day bench trial (judge alone) in November 1989. The FTC presented various evidence to show that the Formula had no effectiveness (other than its placebo effect) in arresting hair loss or in promoting hair regrowth. Dr. Karl Kramer, a dermatologist and expert witness, testified that, based on his knowledge and review of the medical literature, he believed that the Helsinki Formula was useless in treating hair loss.

Dr. Elaine Orenberg corroborated Dr. Kramer's testimony. She stated that the studies on which Pantron relied (by Dr. Schreck-Purola and Dr. Pons) failed to satisfy the generally accepted scientific standards of being randomized, double blinded, and placebo controlled. The "placebo effect" means that even though a product has no inherent merit, it may have some effectiveness in treating the condition based on psychological or other unexplained reasons. For example, a patient who takes a sugar pill believing it to be a strong pain reliever may well experience some pain relief, even though the sugar pill is inherently worthless in treating pain. In this example, the sugar pill is a "placebo" and the relief experienced by the patient is the "placebo effect." Additional research, known as the Groveman study, determined that the ingredients in the Formula were ineffective in stopping hair loss and promoting hair regrowth. The Groveman study was a placebo-controlled, double-blinded, randomized study that appeared in the *Archives of Internal Medicine*, a peer-reviewed journal.

Pantron introduced evidence that users of the Helsinki Formula were satisfied that it was effective. Eighteen users testified that they had experienced hair regrowth or a reduction in hair loss. Pantron conducted a consumer satisfaction survey in late 1988. During routine sales follow-up calls, a Pantron representative interviewed a cross section of 579 Helsinki Formula customers. The Pantron official who conducted the survey could not remember the questions that he asked and the company failed to record these questions. The survey data showed positive results ranging from 29.4 percent of those using the product for less than two months, to 70 percent of those using it for six months or more. More than half of the orders came from repeat purchasers, Pantron received very few written complaints, and less than 3 percent of the customers exercised their rights under the money-back guarantee.

Pantron introduced the results of Finnish studies, for which the Helsinki Formula was named, performed by Dr. Ilona Schreck-Purola. Her uncontrolled, unblinded, unrandomized, un-peer-reviewed study concluded that the Formula was effective in arresting excessive hair loss within two to four weeks and that it led to new hair growth in 60 percent of the subjects within four months.

The district court found no scientifically valid evidence that the Formula was effective for hair loss treatment or for inducing growth. The district court concluded that the FTC had marginally carried its burden of proof that Pantron's claims were false. The court refused to order monetary equitable relief because the FTC failed to establish that defendants' conduct caused actual deception and injury to consumers or that defendant knew or should have known such conduct to be fraudulent. The FTC appealed the district court's refusal to award any monetary equitable relief.

Circuit Judge REINHARDT

. . . .

The Federal Trade Commission brought this suit pursuant to sections 5(a) and 12 of the Federal Trade Commission Act. Section 5(a) of the Act declares unlawful "unfair or deceptive acts or practices in or affecting commerce" and empowers the Commission to prevent such acts or practices. Section 12 of the Act is specifically directed to false advertising. That section prohibits the dissemination of "any false advertisement" in order to induce the purchase of "food, drugs, devices, or cosmetics." It also provides that the dissemination of any such false advertisement is an "unfair or deceptive act or practice in or affecting commerce" within the meaning of section 5. The Act defines "false advertisement" as an advertisement, other than labeling, "which is misleading in a material respect."

. . . .

The district court concluded that the F.T.C. failed to carry its burden of proving that Pantron's efficacy representations were false. It held that "[t]o prevail on its charge that defendant has misrepresented the efficacy of the 'Helsinki Formula,' the F.T.C. must prove that the product is wholly ineffective; i.e., that it does not work at all." The district court held that the F.T.C. had not satisfied its burden of proof. It concluded that, although Pantron's clinical studies did not conform to contemporary American scientific standards, they nevertheless showed that the Formula is effective in reducing hair loss in many people.

We hold that the district court erred in concluding that Pantron's representations regarding the Helsinki Formula's efficacy did not amount to false advertising. Although there was sufficient evidence in the record to support the district court's finding that use of the Helsinki Formula might arrest hair loss in some of the people some of the time, the overwhelming weight of the proof at trial made clear that any effectiveness is due solely to the product's placebo effect.

. . . .

Assessing this evidence, the district court concluded that the F.T.C. had failed to carry its burden of showing that the Helsinki Formula is "wholly ineffective." In essence, the district court held that, as a matter of law, a seller can represent that its product is effective even when this effectiveness is based solely on the placebo effect. We believe that the district court misapprehended the law.

. . . .

Because the district court's refusal to order monetary relief against the corporation was based on the application of erroneous legal principles, and because an application of the proper principles compels an order of monetary relief, we instruct the district court to order the Pantron Corporation to pay monetary equitable relief to the extent of its unjust enrichment.

DECISION AND REMEDY The court decided that for a seller to represent a product as "effective" when its efficacy resulted solely from a "placebo effect" was unlawful. The representation constituted a "false advertisement" under the Federal Trade Commission Act.

CRITICAL THINKING: POLITICAL APPLICATION Should the government interfere in advertisements if product use makes customers feel better, even though the product fails to accomplish the advertisements' claim?

Other Deceptive Practices

Every year complaints flow into the Federal Trade Commission office. By categorizing the complaints, the FTC can determine if patterns develop. Once a pattern of deception evolves, the FTC may issue rules to curb its practice. The following are a few of the more important regulations that the FTC has developed in order to protect the public.

Illegal Multilevel Marketing Schemes

Many legal multilevel marketing (MLM) programs similar to Amway exist. MLM programs survive by making money from product sales, not new recruits. In contrast, "pyramid schemes" reward participants for inducing other people to join the program; over time, the hierarchy of participants resembles a pyramid as newer, larger layers of participants join the established structure. As discussed in Chapter 7, these pyramids are called *Ponzi schemes.*

Pyramids are operated strictly by paying earlier investors with money tendered by later investors. No clear line separates illegal pyramid schemes from legitimate MLM programs. To differentiate the two, regulators evaluate the marketing strategy (e.g., emphasis on recruitment versus sales) and the percent of product sold compared with the percent of commissions granted. The following case is an example of a business conducting an illegal MLM operation.

CASE 15.4	**FEDERAL TRADE COMMISSION v. FIVE-STAR AUTO CLUB, INC.**
United States District Court, S.D. New York, 2000 97 F. Supp. 2d 502	

BACKGROUND AND FACTS The Federal Trade Commission enforces Section 5 of the FTC Act that prohibits unfair or deceptive acts or practices in or affecting commerce. The FTC filed suit against Five Star Auto Club, Inc., and other defendants alleging that they (1) made false and misleading earnings claims to consumers, (2) made false and misleading promises to consumers that their program offered "everyone the opportunity to drive their dream vehicle for free," (3) provided others with the means and instrumentalities to make the same deceptive claims, and (4) failed to disclosed to consumers that Five Star's pyramid structure would not allow many of Five Star's participants to achieve the benefits promised by defendants.

First, defendants promised, both explicitly and by implication, that Five Star made it possible for everyone to drive their dream vehicle for free, or for no more than $100 per month. Second, defendants claimed that Five Star participants could make a substantial income from the sale of Five Star memberships. Participants could join Five Star at three different levels: consultants, members, and members-consultants.

Consultants paid a $95 annual fee to Five Star. In exchange for their dues, consultants had the right to receive commissions from the sale of memberships, but did not have the right to participate in Five Star's Vehicle Incentive Program (VIP), Reverse Value Lease (RVL), or Buyers Assistance Program (BAP).

Members paid a $395 annual fee to Five Star and in exchange received the right to participate in the VIP, BAP, and RVL. Members could not earn commissions. Member-consultants paid a $490 annual fee to Five Star and in exchange received all the benefits of both consultants and members.

The promise that Five Star made it possible for everyone to drive their dream car for free while earning a substantial income lies at the heart of the Five Star advertising scheme. The VIP is the vehicle through which defendants claimed they could fulfill this promise. A letter to all new participants suggesting that they sell Five Star memberships began by asking: "Would you be interested in driving a new car for just $100.00 per month under a new Lease Alternative? Keep it simple by asking them just one question."

To qualify for a VIP lease, Five Star participants were required to pay Five Star $100 per month starting on the 10th of the month after they joined the VIP program. Participants could join the VIP program at three different times. First, defendants encouraged VIP participants to start paying monthly dues on the 10th of the first month after enrollment. This option allowed member-consultants to start earning commissions on the sale of new memberships immediately. Second, VIP participants could start paying $100 per month on the 10th of the month following establishment of a complete primary group. Pursuant to this option, participants could not earn commissions on the sales necessary to establish their primary group. Third, VIP participants could wait until delivery of their VIP vehicle to start paying $100 per month. Under this option, participants would have to pay their own down payment, security deposit, and bank acquisition fees (estimated by defendants at $2,000 to $4,000).

Both Five Star's VIP program and the promise of a substantial income were predicated on the receipt of these monthly dues. The $100 per month dues were the financial backbone of the Five Star program.

To qualify for a VIP lease, a consumer ("A" level) had to establish both a "primary group" and "secondary group" of new members. A member's primary group ("B" level) consisted of those new members whose memberships were purchased directly from the original member. The number of members required in a consumer's primary group depended on the cost of the desired vehicle. For example, in order to qualify to lease a $12,000 vehicle, a consumer had to directly sell three new memberships. To qualify to lease a $40,000 vehicle, a consumer had to sell twenty new memberships.

Additionally, a consumer participating in the VIP program had to establish a secondary group ("C" level) that was three times the size of his/her primary group in order to qualify to lease a vehicle for free or for $100 per month. The secondary group consisted of new members who purchased their membership either directly from the original participant or from an individual in the original participant's primary group.

To sustain the VIP program, it was imperative that VIP participants recruit new members who also participated in the VIP program and/or attempted to earn commissions. Specifically, even if 100 percent of the payments received by a participant's downline were placed in escrow, less commissions paid on those memberships, there would not be enough money placed in escrow to prepay for a VIP lease, unless at least a portion of that participant's downline was paying $100 per month VIP dues. Moreover, Five Star's program anticipated that a consumer's primary group would recruit the consumer's secondary group. The only incentive to recruit new members was to achieve a VIP lease and/or earn commissions; therefore, a consumer's primary group had to establish his/her own downline of recruiters.

Five Star promised to pay consultants a $100 commission for each new membership they sold directly. Additionally, consultants were promised a $20 per month commission for each $100 per month payment made by each member in their secondary group. This $20 commission increased to $40 when a consumer had twenty or more members in his/her secondary group.

Five Star's promotional materials focus on the theoretically large earnings that they claimed could be achieved through the $20 and $40 per month commissions. Defendants made numerous monthly earnings claims ranging from $180 per month to $80,000 per month.

These monthly commissions were dependent on participants' recruiting others who in turn would also attempt to recruit new members, because these commissions were to be paid only if a consumer's downline recruit participated in the VIP program (thus making the $100 per month payments from which monthly commissions are derived).

McMAHON, District Judge

. . . .

II. DEFENDANTS VIOLATED SECTION 5 OF THE FTC ACT

A. In order to establish that Defendants engaged in deceptive acts or practices in violation of Section 5 of the FTC Act, the Commission must demonstrate: (1) a representation, omission, or practice; (2) that is likely to mislead consumers acting reasonably under the circumstances; and (3) that the representation, omission, or practice is material.

B. It is not necessary to prove Defendants' misrepresentations were made with an intent to defraud or deceive, or were made in bad faith to establish a Section 5 violation.

C. The Commission has demonstrated by a preponderance of the evidence that Defendants violated Section 5 of the FTC Act by making the false and material claims that consumers participating in the Five Star program could "Drive [their] Dream Car for Free" and earn a substantial income. The Commission has also shown that Defendants violated the FTC Act by providing others with the means and instrumentalities to deceive others in order to perpetuate the Five Star scheme. The Commission has further demonstrated that Defendants violated the FTC Act by failing to disclose the material information that because of Five Star's structure, the vast majority of participants had not and could not achieve the promised car or income.

. . . .

A pyramid scheme is a mechanism used to transfer funds from one person to another. In the most extreme form of a pyramid scheme, there is no product or service; instead, people are motivated to join by promises of a certain portion of the payments made by those who join later and are placed in one's "downline." If enough additional people join the scheme, a given member could recoup his or her initial payment and even receive additional returns. But, by the nature of the scheme, those at the bottom of the structure at any given time will have lost money, and the number of consumers at the bottom who have lost money will grow exponentially as more people are recruited to join. Moreover, the required number of new members cannot, in fact, be recruited on a perpetual basis, causing the scheme to collapse of its own weight if it does not first falter when a significant number of members are unable to find enough people as gullible as themselves to recruit.

3. A legitimate multi-level marketing ("MLM") firm includes a system of distributing products or services in which each participant earns income from sales of a product to his or her downline and also from sales to the public. The operative question is whether the revenues from sales of the goods and services to consumers is sufficient to cover the production costs or costs of the goods sold, the various marketing expenses, and the promised rewards for recruiting new participants. If the revenue from such sales is sufficient, there is no structural certainty of collapse.

4. Defendants claim that their "retail product" includes the "Buyer's Assistance Program" which was allegedly received by consumers who purchased Five Star memberships, as well as advantages in insurance, long distance rates, and the like. However, even under conditions most favorable to Defendants' position, sale of memberships/BAP was not sufficient to provide the promised rewards of a free car lease and substantial income.

5. Based on a thorough review of Five Star marketing material, the FTC's expert, Dr. Vander Nat, initially concluded that at least 90% of all participants would lose money and would not qualify for a lease. However, as Dr. Vander Nat explained, the higher the value of the car sought by the average participant, the greater the size of the bottom of the pyramid, and therefore the higher the percentage of participants who will lose money, and not receive their dream car.

6. Using the information available in the Five Star Netmark database, and some very conservative (i.e., pro-Defendant) assumptions, Dr. Vander Nat estimated that in fact 97.7% of all participants failed to qualify for a car, and that 95% of all participants lost money on the Five Star scheme. I find Dr. Vander Nat's testimony to be credible and I accept it.

. . . .

DECISION AND REMEDY The Defendants' failure to disclose the limitations of their marketing plan resulted in misleading their customers and violated the law in that this constituted an unfair or deceptive act or practice.

CRITICAL THINKING: MANAGERIAL ISSUE What modifications could Five Star have made to make them a lawful multilevel marketing company?

INFOTRAC RESEARCH ACTIVITY

Many articles discuss multilevel marketing. Go to InfoTrac and type in "multilevel marketing." Review four recent articles and write a summary of them. In doing so, answer the question as to when it is legal to have a multilevel marketing method of sales.

Bait and Switch

In some cases, the Federal Trade Commission has promulgated specific rules to govern advertising. One of its more important rules is called *Guides against Bait Advertising.*[3] This rule is designed to prohibit bait-and-switch advertisements that specify a very low price for a particular item. The low price is the bait to lure the consumer into the store.

The salesperson then tries to switch the consumer to a more expensive item. According to the FTC guidelines, bait advertising occurs if the seller refuses to show the advertised item, fails to have adequate quantities of it available, fails to promise or to deliver the advertised item within a reasonable time, or discourages employees from selling the item.

Deceptive Comparisons

Deceptive comparative advertising is subject to the **Lanham Act** of 1946. This statute prohibits false

[3]The FTC regulations on bait and switch are located at http://www.ftc.gov/bcp/conline/pubs/buspubs/ad-faqs.htm.

descriptions about products or services when people are likely to be damaged by these deceptive advertisements. An inaccurate comparative advertisement is one in which the defendant makes false statements about either the quality or the price of its own product as compared with a competitor's product.

The FTC has ruled that several forms of pricing are deceptive.[4] Stating the price of goods in a way that causes consumers to believe they are getting a bargain or a good deal, when in fact they are not, is unlawful. If the seller compares the current sales price with a higher regular price, the good actually must have been offered by that seller at the higher price in the recent past. It is deceptive to compare the retail price of goods with a "manufacturer's list price" that is not the usual and customary retail price in the area.

The FTC has issued guidelines for the offer of "free" merchandise.[5] If goods are offered "two for the price of one" or "buy one, get one free," the price charged for the two items must not exceed the regular price for the same single item. The seller cannot recover the free item's cost by marking up the regular price of the item to be purchased or by substituting inferior merchandise. In the case that follows, the FTC charged Bristol-Myers Company with inaccurate comparative advertising for their Bufferin and Excedrin products.

[4]See the FTC's site on advertising on the Internet at http://www.ftc.gov/bcp/conline/pubs/buspubs/ruleroad.htm.
[5]*Free* is defined in the FTC regulations and can be found at http://www.ftc.gov/bcp/guides/free.htm.

CASE 15.5	**BRISTOL-MYERS COMPANY v. FEDERAL TRADE COMMISSION**
United States Court of Appeals, Second Circuit, 1984 738 F.2d 554	**BACKGROUND AND FACTS** Bristol-Myers Company (Bristol) petitioned the court of appeals to review an order issued by the Federal Trade Commission (FTC) made in respect to Bristol's advertising of two of its well-known analgesics, Bufferin and Excedrin. The order represented more than ten years of agency work, formally commencing with the FTC's filing of complaints in February 1973 against Bristol and its advertising agencies concerning alleged violations of Sections 5 and 12 of the FTC act. After a hearing, the FTC found that Bristol had misrepresented the analgesic superiority of Excedrin and Bufferin over competing products and further found that such superiority was not established by the use of phrases such as "scientific tests" and "medically endorsed." The FTC found that Bristol made seven false and deceptive claims of this nature. The FTC prohibited Bristol from making comparative

establishment claims asserting the products' superior effectiveness without proof consisting of two or more adequate and well-controlled clinical investigations conducted in accordance with procedures that the order set forth in detail.

The FTC found that Bristol deceptively advertised that its products contained special ingredients even though other over-the-counter drug products commonly use the same ingredients. The FTC found that these special ingredient claims concealed that Bufferin and Excedrin were aspirin based. The deception was based on Bristol's emphasis on the unspecified analgesic ingredients.

Circuit Judge OAKES

. . . .

Whatever the merits [of] the argument that the use of such a presumption violates the First Amendment, it is clear that in this case the FTC made a factual finding, based on its investigation of Bristol's ads, that consumers viewing the ads would believe them to be making claims supported by a reasonable basis. It then found that lacking such a basis the ads were deceptive. A conclusion of this nature is "in the very realm of the Commission's greatest expertise—what constitutes deception in advertising. . . . As such the reviewing court must give the Commission's findings 'great weight.' " We find the conclusion amply supported in this case.

. . . .

DECISION AND REMEDY Bristol had a history of deceptive practices. False claims that consumers are unable to evaluate for themselves and that encourage the unnecessary use of a potentially hazardous product constitute serious violations, which helped to justify the scope of the remedial order. The court found that the FTC had quite carefully worded its remedial order to suit the violations. The order was broad enough to protect the public while narrow enough to permit compliance without undue burden.

CRITICAL THINKING: MANAGEMENT CONSIDERATION Discuss the advertising a company should use when selling over-the-counter drugs.

Deceptive Testimonials and Endorsements

From its inception, the FTC has proceeded with vigor against deceptive testimonials and endorsements used to promote products. This advertising technique convinces consumers that someone other than the seller believes in the product's benefits. Film stars and athletes often endorse products. FTC guidelines require that the endorsements reflect the celebrity's honest opinion about the product. The endorser must be a product user.

If an advertisement represents that the endorser has superior expertise in judging the product, the endorser must have experience or training that qualifies her as an expert. If an advertisement represents that the endorser is a doctor, she must have a medical degree. Some advertisements contain dramatizations involving purported doctors or scientists. Because the public recognizes that these people are actors, these advertisements are allowed.

Telemarketing Fraud

The Telemarketing and Consumer Fraud and Abuse Prevention Act was adopted by Congress in 1994[6] as a result of widespread fraud carried out by persons who victimized consumers to the tune of $40 billion per

[6]For more information on the Telemarketing and Consumer Fraud and Abuse Prevention Act, go to http://www.ftc.gov/bcp/conline/pubs/buspubs/tsr/introduc.htm. The actual FTC rules are found at http://www.access.gpo.gov/nara/cfr/waisidx_00/16cfr310_00.html.

LEGAL HIGHLIGHT

Singing the Refund Blues

Singer Pat Boone appeared in many commercials endorsing Acne-Statin, advertised for acne treatment. Boone promoted the product on television and in printed advertisements, telling the public that all of his daughters used Acne-Statin. Many people relied on his endorsement and purchased the product. When the product failed to work as advertised, consumers filed complaints with the FTC.

An investigation revealed that, in fact, not all of Boone's daughters had used the product and, therefore, that these advertisements were unfair and deceptive. The FTC required Boone to contribute to a fund for making refunds to those purchasers who had relied on his endorsement.

Source: In the Matter of Cooga Mooga, Inc., 92 F.T.C. 310 (1978).

---

year. The act requires the FTC to issue rules to prevent telemarketers from undertaking a pattern of unsolicited telephone calls that a reasonable consumer would consider coercive or abusive and in violation of a person's right to privacy.

Under the FTC regulations, telemarketers can make unsolicited telephone calls from the hours of 8:00 A.M. to 9:00 P.M. The solicitor must disclose promptly and clearly to the person receiving the call that the call's purpose is to sell goods or services and must make other disclosures, including the nature and price of the goods and services. The act authorizes the FTC, attorneys general of individual states, and private persons to bring actions under this act.

The FTC regulates automatic telephone dialing systems or prerecorded voice calls. If a solictior uses an artificial or prerecorded voice message, that message must state, at the beginning, the identity of the business, individual, or other entity initiating the call. During or after the message, the caller must give the telephone number (other than that of the prerecorded message player that placed the call) or address of the business, other entity, or individual that made the call. The telephone number may not be a 900 number or any number where the charges exceed local or long-distance standard rates.

Telephone Consumer Protection Act

The Telephone Consumer Protection Act of 1991 prohibits unsolicited fax advertisements. It sets penalties between $500 and $1,500 for each unwanted solicitation. In recent years, class-action suits have been used to enforce this statute. For example, Hooters restaurant chain sent out 1,000 faxes with coupons. A class-action suit resulted in the jury awarding a $12 million verdict.

Do Not Call List

In 2003, Congress passed a statute authorizing the Federal Trade Commission and the Federal Communications Commission (FCC) to implement a Do Not Call registry for telemarketers. Consumers have a choice as to whether they want to receive telemarketing calls. If they no longer want to receive telemarketing calls, consumers register their phone numbers on a national Do Not Call registry.

Once registered, it is illegal for telemarketers to call that number. The penalty goes up to $11,000 per each call. Telemarketers are required to update their data banks every 90 days. The constitutionality of this act is under litigation.

Excluded from this regulation are charitable organizations, political candidates, the banking industry, insurance companies, and businesses that have had a previous commercial relationship in the past eighteen months. The FCC's authority is limited to regulating financial-services companies, long-distance providers, and airline telemarketers.

Telemarketers, however, can entice consumers to enter contests, where, according to the clauses in fine print, consumers agree to waive their rights. Another way around the registry is for telemarketers to relocate to nearby countries, such as Canada, where they can continue calling into the United States.

Do Not Spam List

In 2003, Congress passed another statute authorizing the Federal Trade Commission to implement a Do Not Spam registry for e-mail addresses. The commercial marketers subject to the law are those who send e-mails to mass lists of consumer e-mail addresses. Consumers who do not want to receive spam can register their e-mail addresses with the FTC. Marketers are prohibited from sending e-mail advertisements to the registered addresses without being subject to penalties of fines and prison terms.

Senders of spam e-mails are prohibited from disguising their identity by used a false return address or misleading subject line. The law prohibits senders from harvesting addresses from Web sites. Spam e-mail will need to include a mechanism so recipients could indicate they do not want future mass mailings. Unwanted or deceptive e-mails can be forwarded to the FTC.[7] These e-mails will be placed in a spam database in order to gather evidence for the FTC to target the most egregious marketers.

Marketing Research

The FTC has not issued specific regulations about marketing research, but has issued a policy statement to guide marketing research firms.[8] The FTC believes that deceptively inducing consumers to provide personal information that they erroneously assumed would be kept confidential is unfair.

For example, the FTC prohibits businesses from using a secret or invisible code on a survey form or return envelope to identify the consumer who provided the information. The FTC did not find the code itself to be unfair and deceptive. A deceptive practice is to use a survey accompanied by a misleading promise of anonymity in order to obtain highly sensitive information about a consumer that otherwise would not have been disclosed. Use of any information for purposes other than those of the market survey is considered deceptive.

[7]The e-mail address is uce@ftc.gov.
[8]Market surveys gather information on consumers. See a speech on consumer privacy at http://www.ftc.gov/speeches/varney/priv&ame.htm.

CYBERLAW

Identity Theft

Advances in computer technology make it possible for detailed information about people to be compiled into a database so it can be shared more easily and cheaply than ever. In many respects, computer technology is good for society as a whole and individual consumers. For example, it is easier for law enforcement to track down criminals, for banks to prevent fraud, and for consumers to learn about new products and services. At the same time, as personal information becomes more accessible, individuals, companies, associations, and government agencies must take precautions to protect against the misuse of that information.

Although identity theft—where someone uses your name and personal information to obtain money or property—has been committed for decades, with the advent of the Web, the incidents of identity theft have skyrocketed.

How does identity theft begin? Thieves can operate alone or an organized effort may be involved. Thieves start collecting information by co-opting your name, Social Security number, credit card number, or other pieces of your personal information for their own use. People leave these pieces of information laying around in abundant number. Here are some ways to protect yourself:

- *Social Security Numbers* Restrict the use of your Social Security number (SSN). For example, do not have your SSN printed on your driver's license. Instead request the driver's license bureau to assign another number. Do not print your SSN on your checks. The thief will have your SSN and your name and address.

- *Credit Card Applications* Shred any credit card application form when you do not intend to apply for that credit card. If you do not destroy the application, someone could fill it in and receive a credit card that is issued in your name.

- *Credit or Debit Cards* When you pay with a credit or debit card, make sure you receive the copy. For example, some people leave the credit card receipts in the gasoline pumping station when purchasing gas. Fortunately, however, recently installed machines do not print out the credit card number. Or you may accidentally drop the credit card receipt instead of placing it in a safe place and keeping track of it.

- *E-Mail Request* If you receive an e-mail request that appears to be from your Internet service provider (ISP) stating that your "account information needs to be updated" or that "the credit card you signed up with is invalid or expired and the information needs to be reentered to keep your account active," do not respond without checking with your ISP first. This request is a common ploy used by identity thieves.

Taking precautions to safeguard your personal information is time consuming. But trying to fight an identity thief is more than time consuming—it is emotionally draining. An ounce of prevention is worth a pound of cure in this situation.

The Federal Trade Commission[9] educates consumers and businesses about the importance of personal information privacy. Its Web site contains updated information including government reports and congressional testimony, law enforcement updates, and links to other sites with helpful information about identity theft.

Other Consumer Protection Laws

Over the years, Congress has passed laws that provide consumers protection from abhorrent business practices. The following subsections examine the more significant of these statutes.

Fair Packaging and Labeling Act

The number of products that are prepackaged has increased significantly since 1950. The packaging often prevents the consumer from inspecting the product, so the label becomes the only source of information about the package's contents. The **Fair Packaging and Labeling Act (FPLA)**[10] was enacted

by Congress in 1966 to give the Department of Commerce the authority to deal with this problem.

The FPLA applies to those who package or label any consumer commodity. It primarily focuses on items sold in supermarkets. Four provisions of the FPLA are mandatory:

- The label must include the name and address of the manufacturer, packer, or distributor.
- The front panel must indicate the net quantity.
- The quantity must be listed in a specific manner.
- If the quantity is stated as a specified number of servings, the size of each serving must be indicated.

These mandatory provisions enable the purchaser to compare competing products. The Department of Commerce, the Federal Trade Commission, and the Food and Drug Administration all issue rules under the FPLA. Other federal statutes that also apply to packaging and labeling include the Wool Products Labeling Act, the Fur Products Labeling Act, the Cigarette Labeling and Advertising Act, and the Flammable Fabrics Act.

Magnuson-Moss Warranty-Federal Trade Commission Improvements Act

Dissatisfaction with automobile warranties led Congress to pass the Magnuson-Moss Warranty-Federal Trade Commission Improvements Act of 1975.[11] This act, also discussed in Chapter 12, establishes standards for consumer warranties.

The act requires that every warranty disclosure contain certain information that is necessary for a consumer to determine the extent of the warranty and the method of enforcing it. If a warrantor refuses to honor the warranty, then the consumer can bring a legal action in either a state or federal court. The government also may bring a court action to prevent a manufacturer from continuing to issue deceptive warranties or for failing to comply with the act.

Food, Drug, and Cosmetic Act

The purpose of the Food and Drug Administration (FDA) is to protect the public from harm caused by

---

[9]Go to the Federal Trade Commission's Web site at http://www.ftc.gov/, then click on "Consumer Protection."
[10]The Fair Packaging and Labeling Act is found at http://www.law.cornell.edu/uscode/15/ch39.html.

[11]An explanation of the Magnuson-Moss Warranty-Federal Trade Commission Improvements Act can be found at http://www.ftc.gov/bcp/conline/pubs/buspubs/warranty/undermag.htm.

LEGAL HIGHLIGHT

Telemarketing Fraud

Most telephone sales pitches are made on behalf of legitimate organizations offering bona fide products and services. Unfortunately, many telephone sales calls are frauds. Consumers lose more than $40 billion a year to telemarketing fraud. Fraudulent telemarketers and sellers can reach you in several ways, such as cold telephone calls, mail, or direct advertisements.

Cold Calls

A telemarketer telephones you at home. Your number is available from telephone directories, mailing lists, or "sucker lists." The latter refers to lists of consumers who have spent (read "lost") money purchasing fraudulent prize promotions or merchandise sales. These lists contain names, addresses, phone numbers, and other information, such as how much money was spent by people who have responded to telemarketing solicitations. "Sucker lists" are bought and sold by unscrupulous promoters. They are invaluable to scam artists who know that consumers who have been deceived once are vulnerable to additional scams. This practice may be reduced as a result of the Do Not Call registry if the courts allow it to be implemented.

Direct Mail

You receive a postcard announcing that you have won cash, an appliance, a diamond, or even an automobile. The postcard represents the items as free except for a small shipping fee. You are tempted to call the toll-free number to check on the prize. If you do, the salesperson will use persuasive sales pitches, scare tactics, and exaggerated claims to separate you from your money.

Once you have called the number, the telemarketer may ask for your checking account number. Without your knowledge, the outfit you called sends a demand draft to your bank. A demand draft is similar to a check, but the customer's signature is unnecessary. A bank does not normally check for authorized signatures and pays the draft; you will only discover the theft after your checks bounce or when you receive your monthly statement. In the meantime, the thief who has posed as a telemarketer changes locations. Remember to treat your checking account number as a secret.

Broadcast and Print Advertisements

You are reading the newspaper, watching television, or surfing the Web. You see an advertisement for a product or a service that prominently features a telephone number. You make the telephone call in response to a television, newspaper, or magazine advertisement or a direct-mail solicitation. Even though these advertisements are usually placed by legitimate businesses, criminals also place advertisements. Although the advertisement appears legitimate, you still need to be cautious about buying or investing over the telephone.

Fight fraud by reporting scam artists to your state attorney general. Many states have a telephone fraud statute that makes this activity illegal. The federal law provides local law enforcement officers with the power to prosecute fraudulent telemarketers when operating across state lines.

Additionally, you can file a complaint with the FTC. Contact the Consumer Response Center by phone: toll-free 1-877-FTC-HELP (382-4357); TDD: 202-326-2502; by mail: Consumer Response Center, Federal Trade Commission, 600 Pennsylvania Avenue, NW, Washington, D.C. 20580; or use the FTC's Web page at **http://www.ftc.gov** to file an online complaint. Although the FTC cannot resolve individual problems for consumers, it can act against a company if it sees a pattern of possible law violations.

food, drugs, cosmetics, therapeutic items, household substances, pesticides, poisons, and other consumer items. The FDA is part of the Department of Health and Human Services. Through its rule-making authority, the FDA attempts to ensure that food is safe, pure, and wholesome; that drugs and therapeutic items are safe and effective; that cosmetics are harmless; and that consumers are not exposed to excessive risks of injury.

The **Food, Drug, and Cosmetic Act** of 1938 prohibits the adulteration or misbranding of various items. The FDA informs the public through press releases about products that pose an imminent danger to health or products that grossly deceive the consumer. Warnings have involved soup, fish, cranberries, fireworks, and baby food.

Although numerous amendments to the act have been passed, none has been more important than the 1962 Drug Amendment. The amendment was adopted after a drug called thalidomide that caused numerous birth defects had been sold extensively in Europe. The 1962 Drug Amendment requires the Food and Drug Administration to follow certain procedures in approving new prescription drugs for marketing.

The FDA has been severely criticized throughout its history. Critics contend the agency takes too long to

---

LEGAL HIGHLIGHT

Fleecing the Small Business

Many schemes abound to defraud businesses, particularly small firms. Rarely do small businesses have the resources to verify sales pitches and they end up losing money on worthless products. The following anecdotes describe some of these frauds.

One scheme is to sell paper and toner for the office copier over the telephone. The caller asks the business for its copier type. The caller just happens to be overstocked with toner and paper for that specific model. The caller claims that the business will receive a very good deal if it purchases this oversupply over the telephone. Once the business agrees, the paper and toner are shipped collect on delivery (C.O.D.), which does not allow the business to inspect the products before paying for them. Later, when the business opens the boxes, it discovers that the poor quality of the paper and toner could ruin the copier and even void the copier warranty. The caller's name is either unknown or fake. The small business is stuck with an unusable product.

The advance loan fee fraud lures in businesses short on cash. A con artist places an advertisement in a local newspaper offering working capital loans at a favorable rate of interest. A business calls the number given and receives a loan application. To process the application, the business pays an origination fee of $1,000 to $2,000, which is submitted with the completed application. Several days elapse before the business attempts to track progress on the loan, at which time the business discovers the telephone number to be disconnected and the address to be a mail drop with no forwarding address.

Charitable solicitation schemes abound because many legitimate businesspeople support causes that help people (for example, research to cure catastrophic diseases like cancer). A con artist will form a company with a name very similar to a legitimate charity or with a name that implies great charitable activities. Small businesses are solicited for donations. In reality very little, if any, of the funds are donated to any charitable cause beyond the con artist's own needs.

An uglier fraud is the blackmail trick. A supplier tells the purchasing clerk of ABC Corporation that he is sending the clerk an expensive television set because ABC Corporation is an outstanding customer. The supplier hopes that the clerk will continue to place large orders. The clerk receives the gift. Later, if the clerk fails to continue placing large orders, the supplier threatens to inform the employer about the clerk's accepting bribes.

The phony invoice scam occurs when a crook makes out a phony invoice for goods never delivered. She presents the invoice to the person in charge of paying the bills. Thinking that management ordered and accepted this item, the person pays the invoice. By the time the accounts payable department discovers that no order was made and the invoice is phony, the crook has disappeared.

Business opportunity frauds rip off the naive person. An advertisement placed in the newspaper's classified section offers the opportunity to buy a franchise or coin-operated machines. The sales pitch touts that you can be your own boss by owning your own business. Actually, the buyer gets very little, if any, monetary return on the hard work and money invested. The buyer needs to be very careful before investing in a franchise or in coin-operated machines.

approve new drug applications, thus keeping the benefits of new scientific discoveries from the consumer for unreasonable periods of time. The FDA, however, now has established a fast track to allow drugs used to fight acquired immune deficiency syndrome (AIDS) to reach the market sooner.

Violations of the Food, Drug, and Cosmetic Act regulations can result in fines or imprisonment. In addition, plaintiffs who allege that they have suffered harm from an adulterated or misbranded product frequently bring civil lawsuits for damages. These plaintiffs generally introduce evidence that the defendant has violated an FDA rule or regulation.

Biosafety Protocol

In recent years, great innovations have been made in farming. The use of seeds with modified genes has resulted in greater yields for farmers. These modifications also permit the plant to resist insects and weeds. Many persons have became alarmed at these changes, especially in Europe.

In 2000, 138 nations, including the United States, signed a protocol sponsored by the United Nations. The protocol states that any genetically engineered food would be clearly labeled "May contain living modified organisms." This label informs consumers that the vegetables or fruits contain these modified genes; thus, consumers determine whether they want to purchase the modified food.

Postal Fraud Statutes

Consumers purchase billions of dollars' worth of products through the mail each year. Of two federal statutes that prohibit mail fraud, one is criminal in nature and the other, civil. Violations of the criminal statute provide for imprisonment and fines.

The civil statute allows the postmaster general to return all mail addressed to, or mailed by, a promoter who has made a false representation. This procedure of intercepting the fraudulent seller's mail is effective in combating deceptive practices. In more serious cases, the postmaster can confiscate the mail instead of returning it. The postal regulations require that unordered merchandise have a clear and conspicuous statement indicating that the merchandise is a free sample. The promoter can take no action to persuade the consumer to pay for unordered merchandise later.

The following case was brought by the U.S. Postal Service to stop the defendants from using the mails to defraud consumers.

CASE 15.6	# UNITED STATES v. WEINGOLD
United States District Court, New Jersey, 1994 844 F. Supp. 1560	**BACKGROUND AND FACTS** Defendant Harold P. Weingold and seven corporate defendants were engaged in the business of direct-mail marketing. They were accused of creating and implementing eleven separate mail fraud schemes by using different names and mailing addresses to solicit orders for such items as procedures to win lotteries, a cosmic protector, and tarot cards.

Three of the promotions were titled respectively the Helen Archer promotion, the Paul Zax, Jr., promotion, and the Holy Trinity Society, Inc., promotion. For example, one solicitation letter from the Helen Archer promotion scheme read as follows:

> *Last night I had a vision about you. It was very powerful. Very vivid. I know for a fact you had won a very large cash prize (something like $211,721.06 or even more) and you were collecting your money from the Pennsylvania State Lottery Director, Mr Charles Kline! This will happen sometime before Friday, August 13, probably in the next several weeks! Every time I've had these visions before, it has always meant a BIG CASH PAYOFF for the person involved.*
>
> *It is very important that I speak with you right away (name of recipient). I will give you my private phone number. This is so important that I've made special arrangements with the phone company so you won't ever have to pay any long distance charges.*

Under oath, Helen Archer, a reputed psychic, acknowledged that the "vision" was about a sum of money, $211,721.06, and that no specific vision of the person to whom she was writing occurred. Instead, she would receive "an impulse" or "feeling" when running her fingers over a computer-generated commercial mailing list that the addressee was the recipient of the generalized vision of the money.

People who responded to the Archer solicitation received a postcard bearing a 1-800 telephone number. A person calling that number would receive a tape-recorded message that would instruct the caller to note and add together the numbers for the time of day, add together the numbers in her or his age, and add together the numbers of her or his Social Security number to obtain the caller's "lucky numbers." The defendants then had the names and addresses of callers and used that information in follow-up contacts to sell them products or services.

In the Paul Zax, Jr., promotion scheme, the solicitation letter specifically cited examples of lottery winners, who supposedly won the lottery because his "secret formula was used." One testimonial in the solicitation letter included the sixteen employees of the Barrington, Illinois, Police Department, representing that they won $8.3 million in the Illinois State Lottery using the Zax method. In fact, the winning individuals had not used the Weingold/Zax secret formula nor any lottery device.

Another scheme was the Holy Trinity Society, Inc., promotion scheme, which offered a personalized communication from a person named "Wilkerson" who told a tale of having received a pendant with the image of the Virgin Mary from an "old man." The pendant's "secret power" provided the old man with good fortune and now required him to pass it on to another person. Wilkerson claimed to be its current owner and offered to provide it to the recipients of the solicitation for the "token sum" of $20. Recipients were to receive at least one "miracle" within six months, or the money would be refunded.

The U.S. Postal Service (USPS) filed a suit in U.S. district court, seeking an injunction against the defendants to stop them from using these types of sales schemes.

District Judge BASSLER

. . . .

To obtain injunctive relief . . . on the grounds of false representations . . . the United States Postal Service must show by a preponderance of the evidence that there is probable cause to believe that the defendants' schemes are "reasonably calculated to deceive persons of ordinary prudence and comprehension." A showing of intent to mislead is, therefore, necessary for the entry of a preliminary injunction.

. . . .

A showing of "probable cause" requires the Government to establish a set of facts which would cause a reasonably prudent and intelligent person to believe that a cause of action . . . exists.

. . . .

Weingold argues that if the solicitations are carefully analyzed there is no basis to conclude that they are misleading. For example, he claims that he did not misspeak when he wrote that the Barrington, Ill. Police Department used his "secret formula," because they, in fact, used the concept behind his formula-pooling; or again, when he said the Pope endorsed the Holy Trinity Pendant, because the Pope did, in fact, thank the Virgin Mary in a public address shortly after he was shot by a would-be assassin.

Weingold cannot hide behind a technical exegesis of consumer solicitations reminiscent of the philosophy of common law pleading. The solicitations must be read as a whole; isolated passages cannot provide immunity from all of the circumstantial evidence indicative of an intent to deceive.

. . . .

In their closing argument, defendants disingenuously argued that this case is about the "beliefs" of the defendants and members of the consuming public. The Government here is not trying to censor any beliefs; quite to the contrary, the Government's purpose here is to protect the public from deceptive solicitations. This case is not about the First Amendment, but about fraud. As the Third Circuit has recognized, defendants possess "no constitutional right to disseminate false or misleading materials."

. . . .

Because the Government has met its burden of proving probable cause to believe that the defendants' solicitations and promotions are intentionally vague, misleading, false, and in light of the precedents . . . , the Court will grant the Government's application for a preliminary injunction.

DECISION AND REMEDY The court determined that the government met the burden of proof because the solicitations were intentionally vague and misleading. The court determined that the letters were intended to deceive persons of ordinary prudence and comprehension.

CRITICAL THINKING: ETHICAL APPLICATION This chapter began with a Latin phrase that stated *caveat emptor*: Let the buyer beware. This maxim represented the law's philosophy for many years. Does the consumer bear any responsibility for buying into these types of schemes?

Unsolicited Merchandise

The Postal Reorganization Act of 1970 makes it illegal to mail products to persons who did not order the product. A person may keep unsolicited product if it was sent unsolicited. A consumer may be sent one of two types of merchandise legally through the mail without the consumer's consent or agreement: (1) free samples that are clearly and conspicuously marked and (2) merchandise mailed by a charitable organization that is soliciting contributions.

Under either scenario, a consumer may consider the merchandise a gift. In all other situations, it is illegal to send merchandise to someone, unless that person has previously ordered or requested it.

A person who does want to pay for unsolicited merchandise or make a donation to a charity may do one of following (with no obligation to the sender): (1) If the package is not opened, mark it "Return to Sender," and the Postal Service will return it with no additional postage to the consumer. (2) If the package is open, a person may keep the item or throw it away.

If a company sends unordered merchandise, it is illegal to follow the mailing with a bill. If a person is aware of violations of the federal law prohibiting the mailing of unordered merchandise, or if a person has personally had difficulty with such items—especially if statements were sent demanding payment for the merchandise—a person should contact his or her local postmaster or the nearest postal inspector.

Mail-Order Houses

Mail-order houses, a growing industry, have annual sales exceeding $80 billion. Consumers buying from mail-order houses typically have less protection than those who purchase items in stores. Many mail-order houses are located in a different state from the purchaser, thus making it more costly for the customer seeking redress for grievances. The FTC and the U.S. Postal Service share enforcement of the laws concerning mail-order houses.[12]

Negative option plans used by book, record, videotape, and compact disc clubs are regulated. Such plans require the member to return a card to decline merchandise to be sent. A negative option plan must disclose all of its terms, must notify the consumer of intent to send the product in enough time for the member to accept or reject, and must include a rejection form for the club member's use.

An FTC rule requires a mail-order house to ship ordered merchandise promptly. If the business is unable to ship the goods within thirty days, it must notify the

---

[12]The FTC regulations on mail-order houses can be found at http://www.ftc.gov/bcp/conline/pubs/buspubs/mailordr/toc.htm.

buyer of her option either to cancel the order and receive a refund or to allow further shipment delay.

Interstate Land Sales Full Disclosure Act

During the 1950s and early 1960s, many older people invested their life savings in real estate, particularly in Florida and the Southwest. Much of this land was marketed through advertisements in magazines and newspapers, through mail and telephone solicitations, and by personal contact in booths set up near convention facilities. The purchasers rarely saw the parcel of land prior to signing the purchase contract and paying for the land. Later, they would discover that the land they had purchased was underwater or was years away from being ready for development.

The **Interstate Land Sales Full Disclosure Act**, passed in 1968 and administered by the Department of Housing and Urban Development (HUD), is intended to decrease the opportunities for fraud and deception that are inherent in these "sight unseen" sales. The Office of Interstate Land Sales Registration within HUD regulates the sale of undeveloped land for homesites. Regulations require developers to disclose fully their financial condition. These rules also govern advertising and sales practices.

Developers must file a registration statement with the agency before commencing sales. If the Office of Interstate Land Sales Registration determines that the disclosure is adequate, the developer can solicit sales. If the disclosure is inadequate, the developer must file additional information to gain approval.

Purchasers must receive a copy of the property report before signing a contract. The act applies to sales and leases of property in subdivisions, as well as to condominium units that will be uncompleted for two years after the purchase date. Congress used its power under the interstate commerce clause to pass this legislation. If the developer fails to follow the statute, the purchaser may be entitled to a full refund.

Consumer Product Safety Act

The **Consumer Product Safety Act** was passed in 1972 to protect consumers from unreasonable risk of injury from hazardous products.[13] The act is administered by the Consumer Product Safety Commission (CPSC), which has sweeping powers to regulate the production and sale of potentially hazardous consumer products. Consumer product safety legislation began earlier with a variety of statutes that sought to improve the safety standards in selected industries.

The act is very comprehensive. The CPSC is charged with regulating "any article, or component part thereof produced or distributed for sale to a consumer for use in or around a permanent or temporary household or residence, a school, in recreation or otherwise, or for the personal use, consumption or employment of a consumer." The CPSC also enforces the Refrigerator Safety Act, the Flammable Fabrics Act, the Child Protection and Toy Safety Act, the Poison Prevention Packaging Act, and the Hazardous Substances Labeling Act.

Congress has charged the CPSC with conducting research on product safety and with maintaining a clearinghouse that collects, investigates, analyzes, and disseminates injury data relating to the causes and possible prevention of death, injury, and illness associated with consumer products. Product manufacturers must inform the CPSC about events that cause injury or death.

The commission has the authority to establish construction standards, as well as performance standards, for the finished product and to issue adequate danger warnings. If the CPSC can isolate a consumer product that is extremely hazardous to consumers, it can ban the product's sale.

Door-to-Door Sales

Door-to-door sales are singled out for special treatment in the laws of most states and by FTC regulation.[14] The FTC regulation requires door-to-door sellers to provide consumers with a written notice of their right to cancel a sale within three business days. The seller must provide the buyer with a written form that can be filled in and mailed back to the seller exercising the right to cancel the contract. If the seller fails to follow these regulations, the customer can cancel within one year.

The door-to-door rule applies in addition to state statutes. Consumers are protected by the most favorable benefits of the FTC rule and of their own state

---

[13]The Consumer Product Safety Act can be found at http://www.cpsc.gov. This site has information about products that were recalled years ago. A consumer can report an unsafe product at this Web site.

[14]The regulation on door-to-door sales is found at http://www.ftc.gov/bcp/conline/pubs/buying/cooling.htm.

laws. The Federal Trade Commission rule requires the seller to provide the notification in the same language in which the sale was negotiated.

This business type has a lengthy history of using high-pressure tactics (such as salesmen staying in the prospective customer's house all night talking until the customer signs) and other systematic consumer abuse (such as businesses sending encyclopedias with blank or missing pages). The special treatment also stems in part from the nature of the sales transaction. A door-to-door seller has the advantage of a captive audience because individuals cannot leave their own homes and they hesitate to ask people to leave. Repeat purchases are less likely with door-to-door sales than they are in stores, because the seller has little incentive to establish goodwill with the purchaser. Furthermore, the buyer is unlikely to comparison shop for alternative products and their prices.

Miscellaneous Consumer Protection Statutes

A variety of other consumer protection statutes exist that will not be examined in depth here. Various state statutes prohibit unfair or deceptive acts or practices (UDAP statutes). These state laws provide private remedies to fight the wide range of consumer abuses. Every state has at least one UDAP statute. Most of these statutes were adopted during the mid-1960s to the mid-1970s. The following consumer areas are regulated by the FTC or other federal agencies and/or by the states' UDAP statutes.

Statutes cover subject matter ranging from automobiles to funeral homes. For example, the federal Odometer Act prohibits odometers from being rolled back. The FTC Used Car Rule governs the sales of used cars. State laws regulate towing company charges

and collection procedures. Many other federal and state laws regulate such areas as mobile home sales, private vocational schools, insurance sales, solar energy equipment, hearing aids, health spas, dancing studios, and carpet sales.

This discussion of statutes and regulations barely taps the volume of consumer protection in force today from both the federal and state governments. As a direct result of consumer abuse by some businesses, all businesses and consumers now pay the price for this protection.

International Consideration

Self-Regulation by Foreign Corporations

Consumer protection proposals originated in the late 1800s in Germany, the Netherlands, Sweden, and the United Kingdom before crossing the Atlantic to the United States. The debate over whether government regulation or business self-regulation is better continues. Over the decades, the European Union has taken a leadership role in this area.

The International Chamber of Commerce, an independent organization, has promoted self-regulation by developing voluntary codes of marketing practices for businesses. The goal is to avoid governmental regulation. In 1976, the Organization for Economic Cooperation and Development (OECD) adopted the *Guidelines on Multinational Enterprises*. This document deals with issues of corporate disclosure and the liability of parent companies for their subsidiaries. No international organization to date specifically deals with consumer protection, however.

PRACTICAL TIPS

Operating a Mail-Order Business

After much consideration, you decide to start a new business. You believe the business should initially involve limited overhead. After reviewing numerous business opportunities, you choose to operate a mail-order business. You can operate it from your home

during your spare time, thus limiting overhead expense.

A mail-order business's largest expense is advertising through magazines, catalogs, and brochures. To be successful, you need repeat sales from satisfied customers. You decide to offer a line of "how-to" books that describe unusual furniture construction, furniture refinishing, and general household repairs. You prepare advertisements to be placed in magazines and newspapers of general interest, such as, *Better Homes & Gardens* and *Reader's Digest*. You also prepare a small catalog offering thirty-two different books or plans.

The business is governed by federal and/or state laws. You must comply with the U.S. Postal Service regulations. If you advertise in a fraudulent manner by misrepresenting your products, the Postal Service will return your customers' mail, and the Department of Justice may bring criminal charges against you. You must make only claims that you can prove. For example, if a customer's testimonial is used, you must be able to prove to the Postal Service authorities that the consumer is real. If you offer a money-back guarantee, any customer who is dissatisfied with your product must be given a full and prompt refund.

The actual mailing of the product is another problem. The Postal Service offers a book rate that is considerably lower than the first-class postal rate. At the book rate, however, you cannot include any advertisements for your other products with the books. Your product must be a book and not merely plans for the construction of certain products. Failure to follow the Postal Service rules may result in the mailing being returned or, worse, confiscated.

The rules of the Federal Trade Commission must be followed. Any promotional material must make true claims, disclose important facts, state the whole truth, and explain unsupported claims. The FTC and the Postal Service cooperate in their investigations when fraudulent materials are involved.

If products are sold through the mail, you must comply with the regulations of other administrative agencies. For example, you must comply with the Fair Packaging and Labeling Act, if the product has a label. The label must disclose at least the minimum required information. If you sell cosmetics through the mail, the regulations of the Food, Drug, and Cosmetic Act apply. The following is a checklist for mail-order business owners:

Checklist

✔ *Sales* Offer several products that allow repeat sales.

✔ *Advertisements* Find the best magazines to ensure you a good response to your advertisements.

✔ *Verification* Verify that the information and graphics contained in the advertisements are completely truthful. Make only claims that you can substantiate.

✔ *Shipping* Use more than one method to ship your product. If the Postal Service or other private carrier goes on strike, you can be out of business.

✔ *Compliance* Comply with all federal and state laws and regulations if you are selling a unique product.

Even a simple business operated from a home can involve compliance with many federal and state laws. These laws are intended to protect the consumers, even though the laws may be troublesome and costly for business.

Chapter Summary

Consumer laws protect the consumer from both financial and bodily harm. Costs associated with this protection eventually are paid by the consumer in the form of higher prices.

The Federal Trade Commission has the primary duty to prohibit "unfair or deceptive acts or practices." The Bureau of Consumer Protection carries out this responsibility by issuing trade regulations that apply to entire industries and by obtaining consent decrees or cease-and-desist orders.

The FTC regulates advertising that makes false statements or claims, fails to disclose important facts, does not relate the whole truth, or makes unsupported

claims. The FTC also enforces rules against bait-and-switch advertisements. These advertisements entice a consumer with an alleged bargain. Then the salesperson attempts to convince the consumer to buy a more expensive product.

Other statutes that protect consumers include the Fair Packaging and Labeling Act, which requires certain information to be disclosed on any package that prevents the consumer from inspecting the product. The Food, Drug, and Cosmetic Act ensures that goods are safe, pure, and wholesome and that pharmaceutical products are therapeutic and not experimental. The U.S. Postal Service has the power to return or confiscate any mail that makes a false representation. The Interstate Land Sales Full Disclosure Act controls the sale of unimproved lots through interstate commerce. Finally, the Consumer Product Safety Act ensures the safety of products that are sold to the public.

Using the World Wide Web

The Federal Trade Commission has adopted many regulations to implement the statutes that it implements. Other federal agencies are also involved in consumer protection, such as the Postal Service and the Food and Drug Administration. All consumer regulations are now available on these government Web sites.

For *Web Activities*, links to Web sites mentioned in the chapter, and additional Web sites that relate to the chapter topics, go to **http://bohlman.westbuslaw. com**, click on "Internet Applications," and select Chapter 15.

Web Activities

Go to **http://bohlman.westbuslaw.com**, click on "Internet Applications," and select Chapter 15.
15–1 Multilevel Marketing
15–2 Advertising on the Web

Key Terms

affirmative disclosure
   order
cease-and-desist order
Consumer Product
   Safety Act
corrective advertising
   order

Fair Packaging and
   Labeling Act (FPLA)
Federal Trade
   Commission Act
Food, Drug, and
   Cosmetic Act
Interstate Land Sales Full

Disclosure Act
Lanham Act
Magnuson-Moss
   Warranty-Federal
   Trade Commission
   Improvements Act
multiple product order

trade regulation rule
unfair or deceptive acts
   or practices
Wheeler-Lea Act

Questions and Case Problems

15–1 Consumer Product Safety Act Joyce, who made toys at home, introduced a new line of home-made dolls. These stuffed dolls were especially appealing because they had real glass marbles for eyes. Three-year old Samantha received one of these marble-eyed dolls for her birthday. Samantha was captivated by the shiny marble eyes. Unfortunately, after a month of use, the glue holding the marbles on the face of the doll disintegrated to the point that Samantha was able to pull the marbles off, put one in her mouth, swallow it, and then choke on it. She was rushed to the hospital, where her stomach was pumped. Samantha's mother feels that Joyce, as the manufacturer, should be regulated by a federal agency. Which agency would regulate and under what act? What can the agency do to regulate the marble-eyed dolls?

15–2 False Advertising Monty advertises a fuel-saving device for automobile engines. The advertisement claims that the device is "an important unique invention," that "every car needs one," and that a typical driver will realize a significant improvement in fuel economy. Jane buys the device and installs it on her automobile. After six months, she checks her maintenance records and finds that she has realized no savings in fuel economy. Discuss fully any rights that Jane may have under consumer protection laws.

15–3 Medical Regulations IRONMED advertises that it can cure "tired blood." One television advertisement states that "If you often have a tired and run-down feeling and if you take vitamins and still feel worn out, remember, your trouble may be due to iron-poor blood.

Vitamins alone can't build up your iron-poor blood. But IRONMED can. Just two tablets daily contain seven vitamins, plus twice the iron in a whole pound of calves' liver. IRONMED starts strengthening your iron-poor blood in 24 hours." Ron begins to take IRONMED daily. After six months, he feels the same—worn out and tired. Ron hears that most people feel tired not as a result of iron-deficiency anemia (iron-poor blood), but for a variety of other reasons that only medical tests can detect. Discuss fully Ron's rights under consumer protection laws. Fully discuss the potential actions of the specific federal agency that would regulate IRONMED.

15–4 Regulation of Food Baby Food, Inc., makes and sells a baby formula from which it has removed all the salt. Ann feeds her baby the infant formula but notices that after being on the formula for a while the baby is sick and weak. Although she takes the baby to a pediatrician, the baby dies six weeks later from a lack of salt. Ann checks the formula's label and sees that salt is a listed ingredient. Later she learns through a magazine article that Baby Food, Inc., had removed the salt from the infant formula two years before her baby was born. The American Academy of Pediatrics Committee on Nutrition found that salt is absolutely necessary for a baby's nutrition. Discuss fully Ann's rights under consumer protection laws. Fully discuss the potential actions of any federal agency that regulates Baby Food.

15–5 Bait and Switch Goldberg entered the Manhattan Ford Lincoln-Mercury, Inc. (Manhattan), showroom to purchase a 1985 Lincoln Town Car, proposing to trade in his 1981 Volvo as part of the deal. Manhattan originally agreed to provide a $10,000 trade-in allowance, subject to appraisal and the sales manager's approval. Goldberg was to keep his Volvo until the Lincoln was ready. Because of slight damage to the Volvo, Manhattan reduced the trade-in allowance to $8,500. Goldberg insisted that the Volvo should not be subject to mechanical inspection at the time of delivery. Manhattan's sales manager refused to sign such a provision. Negotiations ended. Goldberg sued, claiming that each of these stages in negotiation for the used car constituted a "deceptive practice," a bait-and-switch situation. Was this a bait-and-switch situation? Why or why not? [*Goldberg v. Manhattan Ford Lincoln-Mercury, Inc.* 492 N.Y.S.2d 318 (1985)]

15–6 Deceptive Practices In the past, used automobile dealers commonly turned back the odometers on used cars. The federal Odometer Act allows a penalty in the amount of $1,500 for each occurrence. Ohio's attorney general brought action against Hughes Motors. The defense was based on the grounds that (1) the attorney general had no standing without naming the consumers as part of the lawsuit and (2) no judgment could be entered unless the attorney general could prove actual loss. Was the defendant successful in its legal position? Explain. [*Celebrezze v. Hughes*, 18 Ohio 3d 71, 479 N.E.2d 886 (1985)]

15–7 Bait and Switch All-State Industries of North Carolina, Inc., which produced aluminum siding and storm windows, featured in advertisements ADV, a lower cost aluminum. Following the training manual, however, All-State's salespeople always attempted to sell PRO grade to customers because of its better quality. The salespeople received no commission for selling ADV, but they received a substantial commission if they sold PRO. Was this an unfair trade practice of bait and switch? Explain. [*All-State Industries of North Carolina, Inc. v. Federal Trade Commission*, 423 F.2d 423 (1970)]

15–8 Safety Standards The Consumer Product Safety Commission proposed safety standards that mandated placing a warning on swimming pool slides. Research showed that there was one chance in ten million that a spinal injury could occur when using a pool slide. Would you consider a warning standard reasonably necessary? Does the use of a pool slide constitute an "unreasonable risk" of bodily harm? [*Aqua Slide N Dive Corp. v. Consumer Product Safety Commission*, 569 F.2d 831 (1978)]

15–9 Deceptive Comparisons American Home Products Corp. sold one of its products under the trade name Anacin. The company promoted Anacin by claiming that it consisted of a unique pain-killing formula far superior to that of similar products. In reality, Anacin was only aspirin. The Federal Trade Commission issued a cease-and-desist order after finding this claim to be deceptive. American Home Products appealed the decision. Was this trade puffing or was it deceptive advertising? Explain. [*American Home Products Corp. v. Federal Trade Commission*, 695 F.2d 681 (1982)]

15–10 Internet List several current frauds that the U.S. Postal Inspection Service warns against. Go to the U.S. Postal Inspection Service Consumer Tips site at **http://www.usps.com/websites/depart/inspect/consmenu.htm**.

Chapter 16

Property Law and Intellectual Property and Computer Law

Property, or the dominion of man over external objects, has its origin from the Creator, as his gift to mankind.

William Blackstone,1723–1780
English judge, author, and professor

Chapter Outline

To Publish or Not?

You are a student in a research university. As part of a class project, you find a relatively simply method around the copyright protection for digital video discs (DVD). With your method, you can upload a DVD, such as for a movie, to your computer's hard drive. While it is uploading, you can disable the anticopy software by using a simple technique. This technique, although simple, is a difficult one to discover. Once on the hard drive, the DVD can be downloaded by others in a peer-to-peer file-sharing network. You are aware that this research may be a violation of the Digital Millennium Copyright Act that makes it illegal to bypass any technology measures that protect copyrighted material.

To receive credit for your research, you must publish a paper in a scholarly journal. You write your article and submit it to the top research journal in your area of research. The article is sent out for scholarly peer review. The article is accepted for publication. You are familiar with the movie business and are very certain that if the article were to be published, the newspapers will publish your findings. If your findings are disseminated, the businesses involved in the making of the movies, the movie studio that holds the copyright to the movies, the businesses that distribute and sell the DVDs, and the company that sold the encryption software will fall in value on the public stock exchanges.

Do you keep your research to yourself? Do you allow your findings to be published, even if you are certain that various companies value will fall? Although you have discovered how to subvert the copyright protection, you have not used this bypass. Use the ethical model presented in Chapter 2 and reprinted on the inside front cover to develop your answer.

Introduction

In our culture, individual rights and property rights are so interwoven that any discussion of one must include both. We place a premium on individual rights, but property rights also are protected whenever that protection does not conflict with individual rights.

The recognition of property rights allows Americans to have the economic system that exists today. Our business community exists based on the concept of property rights and the law that protects these rights. Business organizations own or control property that, with the addition of labor, produces a final product or service. The end result of any successful business is profit based on the sale of these products or services. Property rights are the foundation of our free enterprise system.

The Constitution specifically recognizes and protects property rights. The Fifth Amendment provides that "[n]o person shall be . . . deprived of life, liberty, or property, without due process of law; nor shall private property be taken for public use, without just compensation." Similar language is found in the Fourteenth Amendment: "No State shall . . . deprive any person of life, liberty, or property, without due process of law."

The distinction between real property and personal property is important because different laws apply to each category. In particular, the law of taxation and the methods of property transfer vary depending on whether property is real or personal. This chapter addresses (1) the classifications of property, (2) property rights and ownership title, (3) real property, (4) methods to acquire ownership over personal property, (5) bailments, and (6) intellectual property law and its effects on computers.

Artiste Login. Carlo and Carlotta operate an online business. Both are artists and sell many products on the Internet. Special orders are also taken online. Every business has property rights recognized by both the federal and state governments. Artiste owns real property consisting of land, an office building, and several artists' studios. It owns personal property, such as its computer system, office furniture and supplies, raw materials from which sculptures are created, and finished products. Carlo and Carlotta need to understand the various laws that apply to their various property holdings.

Classifications of Property

Property is divided into these classifications: real or personal, tangible or intangible, and fixtures. The following sections discuss these different types of property.

Real and Personal Property

Real property (sometimes called *real estate* or *realty*) means the land surface, the airspace, those materials below the surface, and those items attached permanently to the land. **Personal property** is any item that is not land or attached permanently to land. Real property is conveyed by a **deed**. Personal property is sold by the use of a **bill of sale**, especially when transferring ownership of an expensive item.

At different times, the same article may be real property or personal property. For example, a growing tree is considered real property. When it is cut down and turned into lumber, the tree becomes personal property. The tree becomes real property again when it is transformed into a house frame.

Tangible and Intangible Property

All property is classified as tangible or intangible. **Tangible property** is visible and has physical existence, such as land, cattle, buildings, sheep, automobiles, or computers. **Intangible property** has invisible value. Examples are annuities, checks, copyrights, patents, common stock, debts, or bonds. The value of any of these properties is invisible. The rights these papers represent are recognized by the law.

Fixtures

A **fixture** is personal property that becomes so closely associated with the real property to which it is attached that the law views it as real property. Personal property becomes a fixture when it is attached to the realty by roots; embedded in it; or permanently attached by means of cement, plaster, bolts, nails, or screws. For example, a tree and a rosebush grow in the ground at a nursery. Once they are dug out of the ground, they become personal property. A homeowner purchases the tree and the rosebush. When the homeowner plants them in the ground, they become fixtures because they are reattached permanently to real property.

Gravity even can be the method of attachment, if the item is large enough. A two-ton statue, for example, qualifies as a fixture. The fixture can be physically attached to real property, can be attached to another fixture, or can even be without any actual physical attachment to the land, as long as the owner intends the property to be a fixture.

Fixtures are included in the sale of land unless the sales contract provides otherwise. The sale of a house includes the land and the house and garage on it, as well as the cabinets, plumbing, and windows. These items are affixed permanently to the property; thus, they are considered part of it. Unless otherwise agreed, the curtains and throw rugs are not included. Items, such as drapes, metal storage units, and window-unit air conditioners, are difficult to classify. A contract for the sale of a house or commercial realty should indicate the items included or not included in the sale. State law may list items considered fixtures.

To determine if a certain item is a fixture, the court examines several elements. The following case emphasizes some of the problems surrounding fixtures.

CASE 16.1	VALLERIE v. TOWN OF STONINGTON
Supreme Court of Connecticut, 2000 253 Conn. 371, 751 A.2d 829	**BACKGROUND AND FACTS** Norwest and Vallerie brought an application for relief against the town of Stonington. They alleged that the tax assessor's October 1, 1994, and October 1, 1995, valuations of the property they owned were manifestly excessive and contrary to law. The plaintiffs claimed that the tax assessor illegally valued the personal property of floating docks and finger piers as real property. If these items were not classified as real property, the plaintiffs would save a considerable amount in taxes. The trial court rejected the plaintiffs' claim, finding that the finger piers and floating docks were fixtures and, therefore, part of the real estate. The plaintiffs appealed.

PER CURIAM

. . . .

The plaintiffs do not quarrel with the trial court's legal conclusion that "[i]n determining whether the docks and [finger piers] are personalty or realty we must first look at whether the docks and [finger piers] are fixtures. If they are fixtures, the personalty becomes part of the property and they are considered realty. To constitute a fixture, we must look at the character of how the personalty was attached to real estate, the nature and adaptation of the docks and [finger piers] to the uses and purposes to which they were appropriated at the time the annexation was made, and whether the annexer intended to make a permanent accession to the realty. The character of the personal property attached to the real estate is determined at the time that the property is attached to the real estate."

The plaintiffs do, however, contest the trial court's determination that the docks and finger piers are fixtures. We consider that determination a conclusion of fact. "[W]here the factual basis of the [trial] court's decision is challenged we must determine whether the facts set out in the memorandum of decision are supported by the evidence or whether, in light of the evidence and the pleadings in the whole record, those facts are clearly erroneous."

We conclude that the trial court's determination that the floating docks and finger piers are real property was not clearly erroneous. The court found the following facts: "The docks have fresh water and electricity available to boats using the slips. The river has a depth of ten feet at the subject premises. The docks and the slips remain in the water throughout the year. The docks are used to get to the [finger piers] which contain the boat slips. The slips are on open water. The docks and slips float up and down with the tide but are kept in place with seventy to eighty pilings in the river. The docks are attached to bulkheads which are imbedded in concrete. The docks contain utility stanchions with lights that act as street lights. The stanchions also contain lines for water, electricity and telephone service. The water lines are turned off in the winter. There are a total of 133 slips attached to four docks. The docks are periodically removed, repaired and replaced. The economic life of a dock is about fifteen years."

. . . .

The trial court concluded that: "First, there was no evidence presented to us that the annexer ever claimed that the docks and [finger piers] were personalty as did Norwest when it acquired title in 1995. There was also no evidence presented that the annexer meant the docks and piers to be temporary structures. The main business conducted on the subject premises is that of a marina as a going concern. The marina business at the premises is structured on having docks and finger piers attached to the land by bulkheads and concrete walks, running out into the Pawcatuck River, containing stanchions providing amenities such as electricity and water to the slips, supported by pilings driven into the bed of the river. All of these factors cause us to conclude that the intent of the annexer was to make the docks and [finger piers] a permanent fixture to the land."

DECISION AND REMEDY The court concluded that the trial court applied the correct principles of law to the question before it. After examining the trial evidentiary record and exhibits, the Supreme Court of Connecticut concluded substantial evidence existed to support the trial court's factual findings that the docks and finger piers were real estate.

CRITICAL THINKING: LEGAL THEORY Why should society have the doctrine of fixtures?

Property Rights and Ownership Title

Property can be viewed as a bundle of rights. Some of these rights are possession, use, and the right to dispose of the property.

More than one person can hold the same property rights at one time. You may own, with another person, either personal or real property in one of four types of concurrent ownerships. The four types of concurrent ownerships are (1) tenancy in common; (2) joint tenancy with right of survivorship, commonly called joint tenancy; (3) tenancy by the entirety; and (4) community property.

Tenancy in Common

Tenancy in common is co-ownership in which two or more persons own an undivided (equal or unequal) fractional interest in the property, but, on one tenant's death, that interest passes to his heirs. For example, a brother and sister, Michael and Laura, own a farm as tenants in common. Should Michael die before Laura, Michael's interest in the farm would become the property of Michael's heirs. If Michael sold his interest to Patricia before he died, Patricia and Laura would be co-owners as tenants in common. If Patricia died, her interest in the property would pass to her heirs who, in turn, would own the property with Laura as tenants in common.

Joint Tenancy with Right of Survivorship

In a **joint tenancy with right of survivorship**, two or more people own an undivided interest in either personal or real property. If a joint tenant dies, his interest transfers to the remaining joint tenants, not to his heirs. If Michael and Laura are joint tenants and Michael dies before Laura, the entire farm becomes Laura's property. Michael's heirs receive absolutely no interest in the real estate.

If, prior to Michael's death, he sells his interest to Patricia, Patricia and Laura become tenants in common. Michael's sale terminates the joint tenancy. Joint tenancy with right of survivorship can be terminated at any time by gift or by sale before the joint tenant's death. If either Patricia or Laura dies, her interest passes to her heirs, who would own the property as tenants in common.

Tenancy by the Entirety

Tenancy by the entirety is less common today than it used to be. Only a husband and wife can own property in tenancy by the entirety. Typically, it is created by a husband and wife purchasing property. It is distinguished from joint tenancy with right of survivorship because neither spouse can transfer his or her interest separately without the other's consent. Generally, the two must sell the property together. A divorce will end a tenancy by the entirety. Depending on the state in which the property is located, a divorce usually turns the estate into a tenancy in common.

Community Property

The type of ownership known as **community property** applies in Arizona, California, Idaho, Louisiana, Nevada, New Mexico, Texas, Washington, and Wisconsin. The community property laws apply only to the property of married couples. Each spouse owns an undivided one-half interest in most property acquired during the marriage.

Under this type of ownership, when a spouse dies, he or she can give his or her one-half community property interest to someone other than the other spouse through a last will and testament. The deceased, however, cannot deprive the other spouse of his or her own one-half interest.

Several exceptions exist. Property acquired prior to the marriage or property obtained by gift or inheritance during the marriage usually is not classified as community property, but rather as separate property.

Real Property

Real property[1] consists of land, buildings, plants, trees, subsurface and air rights, and fixtures. Whereas personal property is movable, real property is immovable.

Air and Subsurface Rights

The owner of real property has relatively exclusive rights to the airspace above his property. Until one

---

[1]Interested in purchasing your first home? You can obtain current information about purchasing a residence or other real estate at the National Association of Realtors' Web site at http://www.realtor .com. You can also conduct a preliminary search for a new home at this site.

LEGAL HIGHLIGHT

Private Control

Charles H. Keating, Jr., was one of the major participants in the savings and loan scandals of the late 1980s. He was convicted of numerous counts of defrauding small investors by enticing them to buy high-risk bonds. He served time in prison before his convictions were overturned on appeal.

Before being convicted, Keating was involved with the antipornography movement. One investment his firm financed was a subdivision, called Estrella, located near Phoenix, Arizona.

Keating was so opposed to pornography that he placed in the Declaration of Covenants, Conditions, Restrictions and Easements (commonly called deed

restrictions) for Estrella a provision restricting homeowners from having items in their homes that "depict, describe or relate to any Specified Sexual Activity or Specified Anatomical Area and that the Board, in its sole and absolute discretion, deems to be unacceptable or inappropriate due to the indecent or otherwise offensive nature or content." This meant that the homeowners association could come into a home and remove any book, picture, videotape, or similar item that the board found offensive.

After his conviction, the Estrella development went into bankruptcy. The restrictions were modified after the property was sold in bankruptcy to another developer. These deed restrictions were not in force long enough to have a lawsuit determine their legality.

---

hundred years ago, the right to airspace use was irrelevant. Today, cases involving air rights involve questions such as the right of airspace for high-rise buildings, the right of individuals and governments to seed clouds and produce artificial rain, and the right of commercial and private airplanes to fly over property. Flights over private land normally do not violate the property owners' rights unless the flights are low and frequent, causing a direct interference with the enjoyment and use of the land.

In many states, but not all, the owner of the surface of a piece of land is the owner of the subsurface. Subsurface rights can be extremely valuable because they include the ownership of minerals and, in most states, oil and natural gas.

Water rights also are extremely valuable, especially in the West. When the ownership is separated into surface and subsurface rights, each owner can pass title to her rights without the other's consent.

Ownership Interest in Real Property: Estates in Land

Ownership of property is an abstract concept that exists within the legal system. No one actually can possess or hold a piece of land, the air above, the earth below, and all the water contained on it. The legal

system, therefore, recognizes certain rights and duties that constitute the ownership interest in real property. Rights of ownership in real property are called *estates* and are classified according to their nature, interest, and extent. Interests in real property are divided into two classifications: freehold estates and nonfreehold estates.

Freehold Estates. A **freehold estate** is one in which the owner holds the right to the land for an undetermined time period. The two classes of freehold estates are estates in fee and life estates.

Estates in Fee. The three major categories of estates in fee are **fee simple absolute** (the title to the land is held by the owner with virtually no limitations), **fee simple defeasible** (the title to the land is taken away automatically from the owner under certain conditions), and **fee simple subject to a condition subsequent** (the title to the land can be taken away by the original owners if a specified event occurs).

A fee simple absolute (generally called a *fee simple*) encompasses the greatest aggregation of rights, privileges, and power possible. The owner of a fee simple estate has the right to use the land for whatever purpose she sees fit, subject to two restrictions. First, laws prevent the owner from unreasonably interfering with another person's land. Second, the owner is subject to applicable zoning, building, and other regulations. A person can own a fee simple for an indefinite period, then can dispose of it by sale or gift.

The owner of a fee simple defeasible or of a fee simple subject to a condition subsequent estate has fewer rights than the owner of a fee simple. With a fee simple defeasible or a fee simple subject to a condition

LEGAL HIGHLIGHT

Dino Dirt

The Black Hills Institute of Geological Research, Inc., collected and restored fossils for display in museums. In August 1990, Black Hills was excavating fossils in western South Dakota. Sue Hendrickson, a researcher working on the project, made an exciting discovery of a sixty-five-million-year-old *Tyrannosaurus rex* fossil. The fossil is the largest, most complete, and best preserved and, therefore, the most valuable *Tyrannosaurus rex* skeleton ever found. As a tribute to the person who found the fossil, it was named Sue.

Black Hills was excavating with permission on the ranch of Williams, a Native American. Since 1969, the ranch had been held in trust by the United States under federal law for the sole use and benefit of Williams. Two days after the discovery, Black Hills scientists began excavating Sue. Black Hills purchased from Williams the right to excavate Sue for $5,000. After excavation, Black Hills moved the ten tons of bones to Hill City, South Dakota, where scientists began the laborious process of restoring the fossil.

In May 1992, however, federal officers seized Sue and moved her to the South Dakota School of Mines and Technology. The federal authorities contended that under the law the United States, not Williams, owned the property. Because the land was held in trust by the United States for Williams, he had no right to sell any real estate because he did not own the land. A lawsuit was filed.

The federal district court had to decide whether the fossils, before Black Hills excavated it, were personal property (Williams had a right to sell) or real property (he had no right to sell). If it were land within the meaning of the relevant statutes and regulations, the contract between Williams and Black Hills was void.

The court found that the fossil was real property. Sue Hendrickson found the fossil embedded in the land. Under South Dakota law, the fossil was an "ingredient" comprising part of the "solid material of the earth." The bones were a component part of Williams' land, just like the soil, the rocks, and whatever other naturally occurring materials made up the earth of the ranch. The fact that the skeleton was once a dinosaur that walked on the surface of the earth and the fact that a bone was protruding from the ground when Hendrickson discovered it did not make the fossil personal property.

The salient point was that the fossil for millions of years had been an "ingredient" of the earth that the United States held in trust for Williams. The tyrannosaurus rex died nearly sixty-five million years ago and gradually became fossilized and incorporated into land that would eventually become land that was held in trust by the United States. Although the fossil became movable, personal property after a great deal of work to separate the bones from the dirt, at the time Hendrickson discovered the fossil, it was part of Williams' land and was subject to federal law. Because the U.S. government held the land in trust for Williams, it was decided to sell Sue, that is, convert an asset into money, at a public auction.

Later, Black Hills filed a lien in an attempt to recover $209,000 for the expenses it incurred in removing Sue from the Williams land. The court denied Black Hills the right to a lien on the basis that Black Hills had not acted in good faith in excavating the fossil.

Sue was sold at auction in October 1997 by Sotheby's[a] auction house in New York for $8.4 million to the Field Museum of Natural History[b] in Chicago, Illinois. Prior to the auction, experts estimated Sue would sell for no more than $1 million. Sue now is on public display in Chicago and has her own Web site.[c]

---

[a]Sotheby's Web site is found at http://www.sothebys.com.
[b]The Web site for the Field Museum of Natural History is located at http://www.fieldmuseum.org.
[c]Sue has her own Web site at http://www.fieldmuseum.org/sue/default.htm. Since the *Tyrannosaurus rex* was named after its discoverer, Sue Hendrickson, it is referred to in the feminine gender, although the scientists have not determined its gender.

subsequent, the right of ownership can be taken away if specific conditions set out in the deed either occur or fail to occur.

For example, a conveyance from Lincoln "to Tex and his heirs as long as the land is used for a church" creates a fee simple defeasible. In this type of conveyance, Lincoln retains a partial ownership interest. As long as the specified condition occurs (the land is used for a church), Tex maintains other ownership rights. If the specified condition fails to occur (the land ceases to be used for a church), the land reverts (returns) to the original owner, Lincoln, or to his heirs. The interest that Lincoln retains is called a *future interest*, because if it arises, it will arise in the future.

A fee simple subject to a condition subsequent is very similar to a fee simple defeasible, but normally involves additional language in creating it. Added to the language in the previously discussed transfer to a church would be words such as "the grantor or his heirs shall have a right to reenter and take possession whenever the property is not used as a church."

Life Estates. A **life estate** is where the duration of the estate is measured by the life of one or more human beings. A life estate may be created, for example, by a conveyance of the land by the owner to another person (the life tenant) to occupy and use the land during his lifetime. The person granting the life estate has designated someone else (or the owner himself) as the future owner of the land, who holds the land in fee simple absolute after the life tenant. During the life estate, however, the life tenant has the same rights as a fee simple owner except that he must preserve the value of the land for the holder of the future interest.

Nonfreehold Estates. A **nonfreehold estate** occurs when a person can possess real estate without owning the property. This type of estate generally is treated as a personal interest and not as an interest in real property.

Nonfreehold estates commonly are called *leases* or *tenancies*. **Leases** are classified as (1) tenancy for years, (2) tenancy from period to period, or (3) tenancy at will. Another tenancy, however, called tenancy by sufferance, is not actually an estate.

Landlord-Tenant Relationship. Before looking at the types of tenancies, the landlord–tenant relationship must be defined. Many real property owners do not use their property themselves. Instead, others, called **tenants**, occupy and use the property under a lease. A lease is a contract by which the **landlord**—the owner—grants the tenant exclusive right to use and possess the land, usually for a specific time period. The tenant must pay rent and return the premises in good condition at the end of the lease period.

The landlord ensures that the tenant can possess the property at the time the lease period begins. The landlord must not have rented the premises to another or allow others to occupy and remain on the premises. The tenant is entitled to possess the premises in peace and without disturbance. Usually, the lease or state law determines the landlord's obligation to maintain and repair the premises. In absence of agreement, generally the tenant is liable for maintenance and normal repairs, and the landlord is liable for major repairs and improvements.

LEGAL HIGHLIGHT

Whose House Is This?

Edna Snowden of Sunset Beach, California, thought life estates were wonderful. She was the beneficiary of one. In 1928, Snowden moved in with Mrs. Mary Jane McKinley as live-in housekeeper and companion.

When McKinley died in 1946, her two sons inserted a clause into the deed that gave Snowden a life estate. She was to live in the house rent free. The owners of the house were to maintain all the utilities and provide whatever work was necessary to keep the place livable at no cost to her. She was sixty-eight years old at that time.

When she died in the early 1980s, at more than 100 years old, she had outlived the two sons and six more owners of the house. The last owner, a schoolteacher, was the first owner to live in the house in almost forty years.

Types of Tenancies. A *tenancy for years*, a *tenancy from period to period*, and a *tenancy at will* involve the transfer of the right to possession from the landlord (lessor) to a tenant (lessee) for a specified time period. In every lease, the tenant has a qualified right to exclusive possession (qualified by the landlord's right to enter the premises for limited purposes, such as emergency repairs). The tenant can make appropriate use of the land, for example, to grow crops, but cannot injure the land by, for example, cutting down timber for sale or pumping gas or oil.

A **tenancy for years** is created by express contract (which can sometimes be oral) in which the property is leased for a specified time period. For example, signing a one-year lease to rent an apartment creates a tenancy for years. After the period specified in the lease ends (without notice), the right to the apartment's possession returns to the lessor.

A **tenancy from period to period** is created by a lease that does not specify the length of time for which it is to last, but does specify that rent is to be paid at certain intervals, usually monthly. This type of tenancy is renewed automatically for another rental period unless terminated.

Suppose a landlord rents an apartment to a tenant "for as long as both agree." In such a case, the tenant receives a leasehold estate known as a **tenancy at will**. At common law, either party can terminate the tenancy without notice. This type of estate usually arises when a tenant who has rented under a tenancy for years retains possession, with the landlord's consent, after the lease ends. Sometimes the tenant pays no

Exhibit 16–1   Forms of Ownership of Real Property

Forms of Ownership	Types and Definitions
Concurrent ownership	1. *Tenancy in common* Each tenant owns an undivided fractional share of the property. Such interest can be conveyed without consent and, upon death, passes to tenant's heirs. 2. *Joint tenancy with right of survivorship* Each tenant owns an undivided share of the property. Such interest can be conveyed without consent, converting the interest to a tenancy in common. Upon death, interest passes to surviving joint tenant, not heirs. 3. *Tenancy by the entirety* Like a joint tenancy with right of survivorship between husband and wife in common law states. 4. *Community property* In those states that recognize community property, most property acquired during marriage by either or both spouses is owned equally by each spouse.

Freehold estate (held indefinitely)	1. *Estate in fee:*
	  a. *Fee simple absolute* Most complete form of ownership.
	  b. *Fee simple defeasible* Ownership ends automatically if specified condition occurs or fails to occur. Land reverts to original owner.
	  c. *Fee simple subject to a condition subsequent* Ownership may end if the specified condition occurs or fails to occur. Ownership continues in the current owner. Original owner must take affirmative action to reacquire the land.
	  d. *Life estate* A person owns the property during his or her lifetime. Upon death, the property reverts back to the grantor or to someone the grantor has selected.

Nonfreehold estates (possessory interests held for a specified period of time)	1. *Tenancy for years* Lasts for a period of time stated by an express contract. 2. *Tenancy from period to period* Period determined by frequency of rent payments; automatically renewed unless proper notice is given. 3. *Tenancy at will* For as long as both parties agree. No notice of termination is required. 4. *Tenancy by sufferance* Possession of land without any legal right.

rent, but acknowledges that the landlord owns the property. Quite often, this tenancy is converted to a tenancy from period to period, which then is renewed automatically and requires proper termination notice.

Whenever a tenancy for years, tenancy from period to period, or tenancy at will ends and the tenant retains possession of the premises without the owner's permission, a **tenancy by sufferance** is created. This tenancy is not a true tenancy and is not an estate, because it is created by a tenant's wrongfully retaining possession of the property. The tenant is subject to immediate eviction. State statutes must be followed in eviction cases. The landlord files an eviction suit in court. Generally, an eviction action is heard by a judge shortly after the case is filed. State statutes provide that these types of suits will be given preference on the court calender.

Exhibit 16–1 summarizes the forms of ownership described in this section.

Transfer of Ownership

A number of methods exist by which real property ownership can pass from one person to another. These methods include (1) inheritance or will, (2) eminent domain, (3) adverse possession, and (4) conveyance by deed, including selling the property or giving it away.

Transfer by Inheritance or Will. When a person dies with a will, both real and personal property passes according to the will's terms. When the person dies without a will, the real and personal property passes to those relatives listed according to state statues. Any property held in joint tenancy with right of survivorship, however, passes to the remaining tenants outside the will.

Eminent Domain. Even when ownership in real property is fee simple, a superior ownership may limit that fee simple. Called **eminent domain**, the police power of the government allows it to condemn land for public use. The government can acquire real property as authorized by the Constitution and by state law whenever required by public interest.

For example, when a new public highway is to be built, the government must decide where to build it and how much land to condemn. The power of eminent domain generally is invoked through condemnation proceedings. After the government determines that a particular land parcel is necessary for public use, it brings a judicial proceeding to obtain title to the land. Then, in another proceeding, the court further determines the land's fair value, which usually equals its approximate market value. Under the Fifth Amendment, private property may not be taken for public use without just compensation.

In the following case, the United States Supreme Court had to decide whether a city had the right to require a landowner to dedicate part of her property in exchange for a building permit. "To dedicate" means that the city would have the right to use the dedicated property.

CASE 16.2	# DOLAN v. CITY OF TIGARD
Supreme Court of the United States, 1994 512 U.S. 374, 114 S. Ct. 2309, 129 L. Ed. 2d 304 http://supct.law.cornell.edu/supct/html/93-518.ZO.html	**BACKGROUND AND FACTS** In 1973, the state of Oregon enacted a comprehensive land use management program that required all Oregon counties and cities to adopt new comprehensive land use plans consistent with the statewide planning goals. Pursuant to the state's requirements, the city of Tigard developed and codified a comprehensive plan in its Community Development Code (CDC).

The CDC required property owners in the central business district to comply with a 15 percent open space and landscaping requirement. In effect, the structures and paved parking could cover no more than 85 percent of the land site. A transportation study identified congestion in the central business district as a particular problem, so Tigard adopted a plan for a pedestrian/bicycle pathway intended to encourage alternatives to automobile transportation for short trips. The CDC required any new development to advance this plan by dedicating land for pedestrian pathways.

Dolan owned a plumbing and electric supply store located in Tigard's central business district. The store had 9,700 square feet and sat on the eastern side of a 1.67-acre parcel. On the southwestern corner of the lot was Fanno Creek. The year-round flow of the creek rendered the area within the creek's 100-year floodplain virtually unusable for commercial development.

Dolan applied to the city planning commission for a permit to redevelop the site. She planned to build a new store twice the size of the existing one and to pave a parking lot. The existing store, located on the opposite side of the parcel, would be razed in sections as construction progressed on the new building. In the second phase of the project, Dolan proposed to build an additional structure on the northeast side of the site for complementary businesses and to provide more parking. The proposed expansion and intensified use were consistent with the city's zoning scheme in the central business district.

The commission required that Dolan dedicate the portion of her property lying within the 100-year floodplain for improvement of a storm drainage system along Fanno Creek and that she dedicate an additional fifteen-foot strip of land adjacent to the floodplain as a pedestrian/bicycle pathway. The amount of land required for this dedication was nearly 7,000 square feet, or roughly 10 percent of her land.

She could apply the dedicated property to her 15 percent open space and landscaping requirement mandated by the city's zoning scheme. Tigard would bear the cost of maintaining a landscaped buffer between the dedicated area and the new store. Dolan requested variances from the CDC standards, but her request was denied. She filed a lawsuit that she eventually appealed to the U.S. Supreme Court.

Chief Justice REHNQUIST delivered the opinion of the Court.

. . . .

The Takings Clause of the Fifth Amendment of the United States Constitution, made applicable to the States through the Fourteenth Amendment, provides: "[N]or shall private property be taken for public use, without just compensation." One of the principal purposes of the Takings Clause is "to bar Government from forcing some people alone to bear public burdens which, in all fairness and justice, should be borne by the public as a whole." Without question, had the city simply required petitioner to dedicate a strip of land along Fanno Creek for public use, rather than conditioning the grant of her permit to redevelop her property on such a dedication, a taking would have occurred. Such public access would deprive petitioner of the right to exclude others, "one of the most essential sticks in the bundle of rights that are commonly characterized as property."

On the other side of the ledger, the authority of state and local governments to engage in land use planning has been sustained against constitutional challenge. "Government hardly could go on if to some extent values incident to property could not be diminished without paying for every such change in the general law." A land use regulation does not effect a taking if it "substantially advance[s] state interests" and does not "den[y] an owner economically viable use of his land."

. . . .

. . . Under the well-settled doctrine of "unconstitutional conditions," the government may not require a person to give up a constitutional right—here the right to receive just compensation when property is taken for a public use—in exchange for a discretionary benefit conferred by the government where the property sought has little or no relationship to the benefit.

. . . .

. . . [B]ecause petitioner's property lies within the Central Business District, the Community Development Code already required that petitioner leave 15% of it as open space and the undeveloped floodplain would have nearly satisfied that requirement. But the city demanded more—it not only wanted petitioner not to build in the floodplain, but it also wanted petitioner's property along Fanno Creek for its Greenway system. The city has never said why a public greenway, as opposed to a private one, was required in the interest of flood control.

. . . .

Cities have long engaged in the commendable task of land use planning, made necessary by increasing urbanization particularly in metropolitan areas such as Portland. The city's goals of reducing flooding hazards and traffic congestion, and providing for public greenways, are laudable, but there are outer limits to how this may be done. "A strong public desire to improve the public condition [will not] warrant achieving the desire by a shorter cut than the constitutional way of paying for the change."

DECISION AND REMEDY The Supreme Court found that Tigard had violated Dolan's constitutional rights. The city had not carried its burden of demonstrating a reasonable relationship between the need for the dedication of private property for public use and the landowner's proposed development.

CRITICAL THINKING: PUBLIC POLICY Some owners of real property believe that their property should be used entirely at their discretion. For example, an owner may put a junkyard next to a luxury hotel. After all, the person owns the property. Should the government restrict a person's use of his or her own property without paying compensation to the owner?

Adverse Possession. Adverse possession is a means of obtaining title to land without a deed. Essentially, one person possesses the property of another in an open, hostile, notorious manner and for an uninterrupted statutory time period (ranging from three to thirty years, with ten years being most common). Called an *adverse possessor*, that person acquires title to the land and cannot be removed from the land by the original owner.

For example, Bill and Karen find an unoccupied house in the woods. They decide to occupy the house, find the owner, and buy it. After six months, they cannot find the owner. Because the land has two years of back taxes owed, they assume the owner has abandoned the property. Bill and Karen pay the back taxes and for ten years live on the property, fence in the property, remove trespassers, pay taxes and utilities, have mail and other items delivered to it, and invite guests to the house. Suddenly, the recorded title owner, Jerry, appears and demands that Bill and Karen vacate the premises. If Bill and Karen have possessed the property continuously for the required statutory period (assume ten years), they successfully can claim title by adverse

possession. Their possession was open, exclusive as to the others (hostile), and without Jerry's permission.

After the adverse possessor meets all statutory requirements, a quiet title action may be filed in court. If granted, the court's judgment is recorded in the appropriate government office. A **quiet title action** decides who has title to the property; thus, this action settles a dispute over the title and places the title in the true owner's name. The adverse possessor records the judgment and holds title, just as if a conveyance by deed had been made.

Conveyance by Deed. Possession and land title generally pass from person to person by means of a deed, the written instrument of conveyance for real property. A deed is signed by a property owner to transfer title to another person. Deeds must meet certain requirements, such as being delivered from the grantor to the grantee and containing a full description of the property as well as, in some states, an acknowledgment of the grantor's signature by a notary public.

Several types of deeds are used today. The first is a **general warranty deed**. This type of deed provides the buyer the most protection against defects in the title to the land. The seller warrants, first, that he has the right and power to convey the title to the land. Second, the seller warrants that no liens or interests exist or, if they do, that they are listed and/or known to the buyer. Liens and interests include mortgages, tax liens, mechanics' liens, and easements and these usually are recorded in a public office. Third, the seller warrants that the buyer will have "quiet enjoyment" of the property, in other words, that no one with a better title will force the buyer from the property. These warranties apply to any adverse claims that may exist from the original grant from the government through the seller's ownership.

A second type of deed is the **special warranty deed**. The seller warrants only that he did nothing previously to lessen the real estate's value and does not warrant what prior owners have done.

The third type of deed is called a **bargain and sale deed**. This deed does not warrant or guarantee title, but it does convey the title to the purchaser.

The fourth type of deed, called the **quitclaim deed**, conveys less than other types of deeds. This deed transfers to the buyer whatever interest the grantor (who is not necessarily the seller) has, if any. This type of deed can clear interests, if any, in the property. For example, a piece of reality is held in the name of the husband. The husband and wife separate. A prospective property buyer may want a warranty deed from the seller husband and a quitclaim deed from the wife. If the prospective buyer pays a nominal amount of money, the wife will sign a quitclaim deed transferring any interest she may have in the property. In many states, however, a quitclaim deed causes the title to be defective. A court action must clean up the rights of the parties involved. In those states, a person should use a bargain and sale deed instead of a quitclaim deed.

Recording Statutes. Every state has a **recording statute**. The purpose of this type of statute is to provide prospective buyers with a way to check a property's history and to determine any outstanding interests, liens, judgments, or taxes that have been placed against the property's title. Recording a deed (or a lien) provides notice to the world that a certain person owns a particular parcel of real estate and notice that a "cloud" may be on the title. This information is known as **constructive notice**. A buyer

may not know about the recorded document, but the law presumes that the buyer has a knowledge of it, because these are public records.

Anything recorded against the property can act as a cloud on its title for persons interested in purchasing or lending money on it. Tax liens, mortgages, or judgment liens are clouds on the title. Recorded liens prevent owners from selling their land without paying creditors who have liens against the property. By recording your deed, you give the public notice that you are the true owner. In the case of recorded deeds, former owners are prevented from fraudulently conveying the land to other purchasers.

Nonpossessory Interests

Some interests in land do not include rights of possession. One important nonpossessory interest is an **easement**. An easement is the right to make limited use of another person's real property without actually possessing it. Often, an easement is called a *right-of-way*. The right to drive across another's property and the right to place water and sewage pipes, electrical and telephone wires, cables, or fiber optic lines on another's property are examples of easements. Easements can be created by deed, will, contract, or statute. Also, a person may obtain an easement similar to owning property by adverse possession. These easements are called **easements by prescription**.

Acquiring Ownership of Personal Property

Personal property ownership can be accomplished in a variety of ways. Rights can be acquired by possession, purchase, production, gift, will or inheritance, accession, or confusion.

Possession

If you have possession, you normally have ownership. A familiar adage is "Possession is nine-tenths of the law." In reality, this ownership concept is limited in its application. Possession is important in the following situations: wildlife, lost or mislaid property, and abandoned property. One example of acquiring ownership by possession is the capture of wild animals. Wild animals belong to no one in their natural state. The first person

LEGAL HIGHLIGHT

Rails to Trails

Listen as the train's lonesome whistle gives way to the biker's bell. A conversion is taking place that ranges from the Atlantic to the Pacific. Abandoned railroad lines are being converted to hiking and bicycling trails.

In the last half of the nineteenth century, railroad tracks were built across the nation. The land on which the railroad was laid was sometimes purchased outright, so the railroad paid a fee simple interest. In other areas, the railroad had an easement.

By 1916, the United States had the largest railroad system in the world with almost three million miles of track. The railroad reached the smallest villages, tying people together and moving products across the nation. By the 1960s, the railroad system gave way in part to a nationwide freeway system and to the airline transportation system. Both the trucking and airline industries offered cheaper rates for moving freight; thus, they took freight business from the railroads. People decided to travel by passenger automobiles or by airplanes. By the 1990s, less than half of the original 1916 rail system existed.

Slowly, the railroad system gave way. Some easements ended when the railroad line was abandoned. Other easements were broad enough so that when the railroad no longer used the land, the language in the easement allowed other public uses. Still other land reverted to the original grantor's heirs or to the current landowners. In other words, land dispersement arrangements were inconsistent across the nation. In the 1980s the federal government passed the Rails-to-Trails Act that allowed for the conversion of abandoned railroad property to trails. Across forty-nine states (Hawai'i being the exception) the Rails-to-Trails program converted 878 rail property to trails.

Rail-trails, as they are called, are skinny public parks that cross urban, suburban, and rural America. These rail-trails currently function as trails for hiking, bicycling, horseback riding, in-line skating, cross-country skiing, and wheelchair use.

Although rail-trails are popular with the public, owners of private land adjacent to them have successfully sued to prevent such conversions. In some situations, for example, if the easement were written in such a manner that the land reverted back to the land owner, a conversion can be stopped. Land owners argue that the trains traveled across the property at regular intervals and without stopping. Hikers and bikers, on the other hand, often stop and leave the trail, prompting trespassing and private property misuse, such as picking fruits from private orchards. Hundreds of people may pass by where an occasional train ran a decade ago.

But towns that were dying during the last decade also benefit from the boom that hundreds of travelers bring with them. Towns, counties, and states are working together to connect rail-trails. For more information, go to the Rails-to-Trails Conservancy, a nonprofit public charity Web site at **http://www.railtrails.org**.

---

to take possession of a wild animal normally owns it. The killing of a wild animal amounts to assuming ownership of it. A commercial fishing captain, for example, acquires ownership over fish caught in the open seas.

Mislaid or Lost Property. Property voluntarily placed somewhere by the owner, then inadvertently forgotten, is **mislaid property**. When mislaid property is found, the finder does not obtain title to, or possession of, the goods. Instead, the possessor of the place at which the property was mislaid becomes the property's caretaker because it is highly likely that the true owner will return. Suppose you leave your textbook under your chair after class. The textbook is mislaid property. If a school employee finds it, the school becomes responsible for the book's reasonable care.

Property that is not left voluntarily but is forgotten is **lost property**. In the absence of a statutory provision, a finder of lost property can claim title to the property against everyone, except the true owner. If the true owner demands that the lost property be returned, the finder must return it.

INFOTRAC RESEARCH ACTIVITY

There are many articles on InfoTrac that involve lost property. Go to Info-Trac and type in "Lost Articles (Law)." This will present you with many periodical references. Review the four most recent articles and summarize what they contained.

Abandoned Property. Property that the true owner intentionally discards is **abandoned property**. For example, garbage qualifies as abandoned property. Someone who finds abandoned property acquires title to it and such title is good against everyone, including the original owner. The lost property's owner who eventually gives up any further attempt to find the lost property frequently is held to have abandoned the property.

Purchase

Purchase is one of the most common means of acquiring and transferring personal property ownership. The purchase or sale of personal property (called goods) is covered in Chapter 11.

Production

Production, the fruits of labor, is another means of acquiring ownership of personal property. Nearly everyone in the United States today is involved in some sort of production. For example, writers, inventors, and manufacturers all produce personal property and thereby acquire title to it. If you are employed to produce an item, however, your employer will own the produced item.

Gifts

A **gift** is another common means of both acquiring and transferring ownership of personal property. A gift is a voluntary transfer of property ownership. It is not supported by legally sufficient consideration to make a contract, because the very definition of a gift is giving without consideration. A gift must be transferred or delivered in the present rather than in the future and the donor must intend to make a gift.

For example, suppose that your aunt, the donor, tells you, the donee, that she is going to give you a new Corvette for your next birthday. This statement is simply a promise to make a gift. Only when the Corvette or its keys are delivered to you is it considered a gift. Once the gift has been unconditionally delivered, it is irrevocable (cannot be taken back by your aunt).

Will or Inheritance

The law in our society requires that when a person dies (the decedent), title to the decedent's property must *vest in* (deliver full possession to) someone. The decedent can direct the passage of property after her death through the legal instrument known as a will, subject to certain limitations imposed by the state. If the person dies without a will, she is said to have died intestate. State law determines the distribution of her property among her relatives. If no relatives can be found, the property *escheats* (title is transferred) to the state.

In addition, a person can transfer property through a trust. The owner (settler) of the property transfers legal title to a trustee, who has a duty imposed by law to hold the property for the use or benefit of another (the beneficiary).

Accession

Accession means addition or increase, or coming into possession of a right. In property law, accession means that someone has added some improvement to a piece of personal property (owned by another) by either labor or materials. Generally, no dispute exists about ownership of the improved property after accession occurs, especially when the accession is accomplished with the owner's consent.

For example, Michio takes his Corvette to Corvette Customizing Garage. Michio wants a unique bumper placed on his Corvette. Michio simply pays the customizer for the value of the labor for improving his automobile. He retains title to the Corvette with the unique bumper.

Confusion

Confusion occurs when property of the same type, otherwise known as *fungible goods*, is mixed. **Fungible goods** are identical goods (the equivalent of other, like units) by nature or usage of trade. For example, a farmer takes his wheat crop to the grain elevator. Once the wheat is mixed with other farmers' wheat of like grade and quality, the ownership changes. The farmers become owners of the grain as tenants in common. The farmer now owns a percentage of the wheat in the grain elevator. No means or reason exists to separate the farmer's original grain from the other farmers' grain; thus, title can pass without the grain being removed from the elevator.

Bailments

A **bailment** is formed by the delivery of personal property, without transfer of title, by one person (called a **bailor**) to another (called a **bailee**), usually under an agreement for a particular purpose (for example, loan, storage, repair, or transportation). On completion of the purpose, the bailee must return the bailed property to the bailor or a third person, or dispose of it as directed. Individuals and businesses are affected by the law of bailments at one time or another.

Most bailments are created by agreement, but not necessarily by contract, because in many bailments not all of the elements of a contract, such as mutual assent or consideration, are present. For example, let's say you mislay your textbook, which is found by a classmate. Your classmate is a bailee, but not by contract, because no mutual assent or legal consideration occurred. Similarly, if you loan your textbook to a friend so that your friend can read tomorrow's assignment, a bailment is created, but not by contract, because again mutual assent or legal consideration were not present. In contrast, many commercial bailments, such as the delivery of your suit or dress to the cleaners, are based on contract.

A bailment is distinguished from a sale or a gift. In a bailment, possession transfers without passage of title or without intent to transfer title. In a sale or gift, in contrast, title transfers from the seller or donor to the buyer or donee.

Once a bailment is created, the bailee has certain duties and rights concerning the bailed property. Exhibit 16–2 summarizes these rights and duties.

Intellectual Property Law and Computer Law

Intellectual property concerns the creative processes that flow from a person's mind. Inventions, such as the integrated chip or the jet engine, result from creative minds. Or the mind might produce a screenplay, a novel, or a song.

The U.S. Constitution recognizes these creative processes. Article I, Section 8, Clause 8, reads as follows:

Exhibit 16-2   Rights and Duties of a Bailee

Rights
1. A bailee has the right to be compensated or reimbursed for keeping bailed property. This right is based in contract or quasi-contract.
2. Unpaid compensation or reimbursement entitles the bailee to a lien (usually possessory) on the bailed property and the right of foreclosure.
3. A bailee has the right to limit his or her liability. An ordinary bailee can limit risk, monetary amount, or both, provided that proper notice is given and the limitation is not against public policy. In special bailments, such as common carriers or innkeepers, limitations on types of risk usually are not allowed, but limitations on the monetary amount of risk are permitted by regulation.
4. The right of possession allows actions against third persons who damage or convert the bailed property and allows actions against the bailor for wrongful breach of the bailment.
5. The right to an insurable interest in the bailed property allows the bailee to insure and recover under the insurance policy for loss or damage to the property.

Duties
1. A bailee must exercise reasonable care over property entrusted to him or her. A common carrier (special bailee) is held to a standard of care based on strict liability unless the bailed property is lost or destroyed because of (a) an act of God, (b) an act of a public enemy, (c) an act of a governmental authority, (d) an act of a shipper, or (e) the inherent nature of the goods.
2. Bailed goods in a bailee's possession must be returned to the bailor or disposed of according to the bailor's directions.
3. A bailee cannot use or profit from bailed goods except by agreement or in situations where the use is implied to further the bailment purpose.

To promote the Progress of Science and useful Arts, by securing for limited Times to Authors and Inventors the exclusive Right to their respective Writings and Discoveries.

The federal government has exclusive jurisdiction in these areas.

Computer law is not a specific topic, but involves a wide range of statutes and common law. The federal and state governments have concurrent jurisdiction over various aspects of the subject known as computer law. State law generally covers contracts for computers, while patents on computer components are under exclusive federal jurisdiction.

A distinction must be made between hardware and software when discussing computers. **Hardware** is the equipment itself, such as the central processing unit, the video monitor, the keyboard, and the mouse.

Software is the programming involved with a computer system. The two basic kinds of software are system programs, which coordinate the computer's operation, and application programs, such as word-processing programs or spreadsheet programs, which solve particular user problems. Some authorities expand the software's definition to encompass not only the programming, but also the advice, assistance, and counseling in loading the software onto the hardware.

The question for developers is whether a new creation of software or hardware should be copyrighted or patented. These decisions are covered under intellectual property law. The following sections discuss intellectual property law, then computer law.

Protection of Intellectual Property Rights

Intellectual property rights cover a wide range of materials, including those related to the computer industry. Although the computer was developed prior to World War II (1941–1945), the real market expansion started slowly in the late 1970s and early 1980s, with explosive growth in the late 1980s and 1990s. The personal computer (PC) became more affordable with the refinement of semiconductor chips and integrated circuits.

The law has evolved slowly, whereas the pace of technology has accelerated. Congress has amended patent, copyright, and trademark laws and passed new laws dealing with legal issues surrounding computer technology. In Chapter 8 issues involving trademarks and patents were covered but more extensive coverage is warranted.

Trademark Law. A trademark is a distinctive mark, motto, device, or implement that a manufacturer stamps, prints, or otherwise affixes to its goods. But a trademark is a valuable property asset to a business.

The primary purpose of marks is to prevent consumers from becoming confused about the source or origin of a product or service. Marks assist consumers and businesses to determine where the product was made.

The original federal law covering trademarks was the Lanham Act of 1946. The statute had deficiencies. In 1995, Congress passed an amendment called the **Federal Trademark Dilution Act**. This law sets forth guidelines for determining which marks are truly distinctive. This determination is difficult to discern at times as indicated by the following case.

CASE 16.3	**TIMES MIRROR MAGAZINES, INC. v. LAS VEGAS SPORTS NEWS, L.L.C.**
United States Court of Appeals, Third Circuit, 2000 212 F.3d 157	**BACKGROUND AND FACTS** In 1886 the phrase "The Sporting News" was granted federal trademark protection and since that time it has been the banner headline of a weekly publication entitled *The Sporting News*. The mark is now owned by its publisher, Times Mirror Magazines, Inc. Applying the relatively new Federal Trademark Dilution Act of 1995 (FTDA or Act), the district court issued an injunction against Las Vegas Sports News, L.L.C., d/b/a *Las Vegas Sporting News* (LVSN), from using the name on its weekly sports-betting publication. The court concluded that Times Mirror was likely to succeed on the merits of its dilution claim against LVSN, because the mark was famous in its niche market and LVSN's use of the title on its publication diluted the Times Mirror's mark by blurring its distinctiveness. From this decision the defendant appealed.

ALDISERT, Circuit Judge.

. . . .

The Sporting News provides its readers with information on baseball, basketball, football and hockey, and has a weekly circulation of approximately 540,000 in the United States and Canada. *The Sporting News* does not provide any information on gambling, because Times Mirror "believe[s] that there is a portion of the population that is adamantly opposed to gambling and that they would not look favorably on any of [its] products if they thought [the magazine was] promoting gambling in any way." The magazine is advertised on television, in direct mail solicitations, in promotions and occasionally on the radio. It is typically sold for $2.99, but nine special content issues are sold each year for $3.99. Over the last several years, Times Mirror has invested millions of dollars in *The Sporting News* in an attempt to improve the quality of its magazine and to increase readership.

LVSN publishes *Las Vegas Sporting News*, which contains articles, editorials and advertisements on sports wagering "for the sports gaming enthusiasts or individuals that like to take a risk." *Las Vegas Sporting News* is published 45 times a year and generally has a circulation of 42,000, but some special editions have had a circulation of up to 100,000. The publication is sold for $2.99 at several hundred newsstands across the country, but most copies are given away in gambling casinos free of charge.

In 1997, LVSN publisher Dennis Atiyeh changed the name of his publication from *Las Vegas Sports News* to *Las Vegas Sporting News*. The publisher says that he changed the publication's title for two reasons: (1) the previous publisher of *Las Vegas Sports News* had a poor reputation, having fallen into disrepute with gambling casinos and (2) the term "sporting" more accurately reflected the publication's content, because the publication was a "sports gaming" publication, and not purely a "sports publication." Atiyeh admits that at the time he changed the name of his publication, he was familiar with Times Mirror's publication *The Sporting News*. Since the 1997 name change to *Las Vegas Sporting News*, circulation of the publication has increased, but not substantially.

. . . .

Times Mirror retained Glenn Hauze, a private investigator in Pennsylvania, "to gain as much information as possible regarding the availability of the *Las Vegas Sporting News*," in anticipation of litigation. . . . Hauze began his investigation by visiting three newsstands in or around Lehigh Valley, Pennsylvania. The first newsstand he visited was in Plumsteadville, and it carried both *The Sporting News* and *Las Vegas Sporting News*. *Las Vegas Sporting News* "was up on the shelf with the other sporting magazines," but *The Sporting News* "was down amongst the tabloids." The following day, Hauze found copies of *Las Vegas Sporting News* for sale at newsstands in Allentown and Quakerville. At the Allentown newsstand, *Las Vegas Sporting News* and *The Sporting News* were displayed within inches of each other in a bay window in front of the store, along with a large number of other sporting type publications.

. . . .

To establish a prima facie claim for relief under the federal dilution act, the plaintiff must plead and prove:

1. The plaintiff is the owner of a mark that qualifies as a "famous" mark in light of the totality of the eight factors listed in § 1125(c)(1),

2. The defendant is making commercial use in interstate commerce of a mark or trade name,

3. Defendant's use began after the plaintiff's mark became famous, and

4. Defendant's use causes dilution by lessening the capacity of the plaintiff's mark to identify and distinguish goods or services.

. . . .

The district court held Times Mirror established a likelihood of success on the merits of its federal dilution claim against LVSN, because (1) Times Mirror's mark "The Sporting News" was famous; (2) LVSN made commercial use in interstate commerce of the name "Las Vegas Sporting News"; (3) Times Mirror's mark became famous before LVSN began using the name "Las Vegas Sporting News" and (4) LVSN's use of that name diluted the strength of "The Sporting News" mark. Because Appellant only challenges the first and last prongs of Times Mirror's prima facie claim for dilution, we focus our attention on the district court's findings that "The Sporting News" is a famous mark under the Act and that LVSN's use diluted the strength of Times Mirror's mark.

. . . .

The district court determined that Times Mirror and LVSN competed in the same, or at least significantly related, markets—namely, the sports periodicals market. LVSN contends that its readers, who essentially are interested in wagering on sports, are distinct from the readers of *The Sporting News*, who are interested in sports generally. We find such a distinction to be without merit. Surely many, if not the vast majority, of those individuals who gamble on sports in Las Vegas also follow the sports on which they are wagering. We conclude therefore that the district court did not err by finding that LVSN and Times Mirror shared a common market. Because a mark can be famous in a niche market where the mark has a high degree of distinctiveness within the market and where the plaintiff and defendant operate within or along side that market, we hold that the district court did not commit an obvious error by holding that the mark "The Sporting News" was famous in its niche and therefore entitled to protection under the FTDA against LVSN's use of a similar mark in the same market.

DECISION AND REMEDY The Court found that the names *The Sporting News* and *Las Vegas Sporting News* were similar. The owner of the name *The Sporting News* was entitled to have an injunction against the use of the words *Las Vegas Sporting News*.

CRITICAL THINKING: JUDICIAL DETERMINATION If you were the judge in this case would you have held in a similar manner? Support your reasons.

Patent Law. Patents are filed with the U.S. Patent and Trademark Office (USPTO).[2] A patent provides the patent holder the exclusive right to make, use, and market an invention for a nonrenewable period of twenty years.

In 1981, the Supreme Court held that if a "claim containing a mathematical formula implements or applies that formula in a structure or process, which, when considered as a whole, is performing a function which the patent laws were designed to protect (e.g., transforming or reducing an article to a different state or thing), then the claim satisfies the [patent laws]."[3] This case set the stage for software to be patented.

Computer software now is patentable with the USPTO. Although the USPTO accepts software patents, these patents are subject to challenge and difficult to defend. Those who patent computer games have an easier time because the game is unique.

The *algorithm* (a sequence of steps designed for programming a computer to solve a specific problem) used in software is not patentable because an algorithm, like a law of nature, cannot be the subject of a patent. The software process itself can be patented even though some steps, such as the use of the algorithms within the software, are not novel or independently eligible for patent protection. The software must be viewed as a whole to show that it performs a function designed to be protected by the patent laws.

[2]The Web site for the U.S. Patent and Trademark Office is http://www.uspto.gov.
[3]Diamond v. Diehr, 450 U.S. 175, 101 S. Ct. 1048, 67 L. Ed. 2d 155, 169 (1981).

Copyright Law. The U.S. Copyright Office[4] issues copyrights. Copyrights are granted by the government to protect original works from being used by others without compensating the copyright holders.

The Constitution encouraged people to be creative by granting authors exclusive rights to their original compositions. These creative people earned royalties when others purchased their works. During the past two centuries, Congress has passed a number of statutes concerning copyrights.

Copyrights for original works are governed by the Copyright Act of 1976, as amended. A copyright is valid for the author's life plus seventy years. The Internet challenges the centuries-old traditions of copyright and royalties. Music is easily downloadable from the Web, whereas previously the release of music was controlled and made available only in stores. The songwriter, the artist, and the music publishing company were assured of their royalties. Today, music and other copyrighted works are freely available on the Internet and can be accessed without any assurance that royalties will be paid.

Congress in 1984 passed the **Protection of Semiconductor Chip Products Act**. Products in the field of semiconductor chip production, which are called *maskwork*, were allowed to be copyrighted. A **maskwork** is a series of related images, fixed or encoded in a three-dimensional pattern on a chip, that are layered in a series, so that each image has a pattern. Imagine a film negative that is black on clear plastic. As it is processed into a picture, various layers of plastic with images are layered. Eventually, the final product, a colored photograph, is produced. Maskwork is a similar process. This application of copyright law protects the manufacturer from counterfeiters, a prevalent problem in the industry.

The law also gave authority to the secretary of commerce to issue orders extending protection under the Semiconductor Chip Products Act to foreign governments. In the future, treaties and other agreements will be used to achieve international consensus in this area. In 1985, President Ronald Reagan (1981–1989) issued an executive order extending protection against unauthorized duplication of semiconductor chip products to foreign countries.

The Copyright Act was amended in 1990 by the **Computer Software Rental Amendments Act**,

which allows a computer program's copyright holder to control the rental, leasing, or lending of the computer program after the first sale. Prior to the passage of this act, the exclusive right to sell a copy extended only to the first sale of the copy. After the first sale of a copy, the copyright owner did not have any control over the conditions of future sales.

Computer Law

When discussing the legal issues of computer hardware, the general principles of Uniform Commercial Code, Article 2, Sales, and Article 2A, Leases, will suffice. The Uniform Commercial Code (UCC) was previously discussed in Chapters 9 through 12. The sale and purchase of computer hardware is identical to the sale and purchase of many other types of personal property. The sale of hardware, which is a tangible, movable good, is covered by the UCC. Contracts for computer hardware are covered generally by state law.

The unique aspect of computer law involves software and semiconductor chips. These items are usually copyrighted or patented, as discussed previously, and, as such, are covered by federal laws. Once copyrighted or patented, software is sold to consumers.

Is the sale of software loaded on the hardware, such as a PC that is sold with word-processing, spreadsheet, and database software loaded, covered by general contract law or the UCC? Is software that is sold separately from a PC covered by general contract law or the UCC? The importance of this determination is that Article 2 gives very specific rights and obligations to both the buyer and the seller. If Article 2 fails to apply, basic contract law applies. Article 2 is more protective of the buyer, whereas common law tends to give more protection to the seller, for instance, under the doctrine of *caveat emptor* (let the buyer beware).

The courts uniformly have held that when software is sold with or given with the sale of hardware, a sale of goods occurs. Thus, Article 2 of the UCC applies.

The problem occurs when software is sold separately. When the software is purchased from a store, the courts tend to treat it as a sale of goods because it is sold under a sales contract. What happens, however, when a program is written for a specific use instead of for common usage? Is this a sale of goods or the provision of a service?

[4]The U.S. Copyright Office Web site is located at http://lcweb. loc.gov/copyright.

LEGAL HIGHLIGHT

What the Computer Knows about You

In two seconds, you can communicate with a person anywhere in the world, thanks to computers and satellites. In the past, you left a trail of paperwork as a result of your daily activities. Today, you leave an electronic wave of information as various computers monitor your daily activities.

At the job site, your arrival time in the parking lot is electronically noted. The time at which you turn on the computer at your workstation is logged. Your telephone calls are monitored not only for the content of your conversation, but also for the length of time to the second. Your pay is deposited electronically into your bank account, and preauthorized bills are paid.

Your travel agent's computer knows that you are taking a trip. It knows your name, address, telephone number, arrival and departure times, destination, meal preferences, whether you are traveling round-trip or one way, and whether you have excess luggage or are bringing your pet. It knows the rates charged and the time used in automobile rentals and hotel arrangements, your driver's license information, perhaps your Social Security number, and any special requests. The computer knows your credit card issuer, your card number, the expiration date, those authorized to sign, and the number of credit cards you have. It knows your passport number and places that you have visited outside of the United States.

Which information did you voluntarily disclose and which information was gathered with little knowledge or thought on your part? How long does this information remain in the various computer banks? Is this information destroyed or archived? Who accesses it: competitors who may gain access lawfully by purchasing it, or the government, which may request information from parties who control it? How should businesses handle sensitive information? The gradual loss of privacy will continue as more information is gathered and stored on computers.

The Web allows all of this information to be gathered into large databases. Congress passed legislation to cover information gathered by companies on the Web because of complaints by consumers. For example, a dot com called ToySmart went into bank-

ruptcy. The Web site stated that any information gathered at the Web site would not be sold or distributed. Once in bankruptcy, however, the database was seen as an asset to be sold to help pay the creditors. The company placed an advertisement in the *Wall Street Journal*. The Federal Trade Commission, the attorneys general of forty-two states, and others sued ToySmart to keep it from divulging the data, which included names, addresses, and credit card numbers. The Walt Disney Co., a majority owner of ToySmart, paid $50,000 for the toy company to destroy its database. This action by Walt Disney Co. speaks to its high ethics, because the action was not taken for immediate monetary gain.

Another example, in 2000, Amazon, the online retailer, announced that it had changed its privacy policy. The policy printed on the its Web site clearly stated, in fine print, that Amazon reserved the right to change its policy. The policy changed from not sharing any private information and not selling the information it collected to Amazon making the database available for purchase. Customers were not allowed to opt out of being in the database nor could they request specific information be deleted.

Congress adopted the opt-out method over the opt-in method for consumers. The opt-in method means that the customer's protected, unless he signs a permission form so the company that holds the information can sell it to a purchaser. The opt-out method operates in reserve. Any information held by the company is available for sale, unless the customer is proactive. The customer must request the form, sign the form, and return the form stating that he does not give permission to the company to sell any information it holds about him. In other words, the customers must know of their rights, then act on those rights.

The Electronic Privacy Information Center (EPIC)[a] is very active in this field. It has a number of publications on the topic of electronic privacy. After the change in Amazon's privacy policy, the EPIC ended its ties with Amazon. Amazon's old privacy policy and new privacy policy are available through the EPIC's Web site.

---

[a]The Electronic Privacy Information Center's Web page is at http://www.epic.org.

The cases are divided on this issue. Logic dictates that this transaction would be considered a sale of a specialty good based on a transfer of a tape or disc. Under the law, the definition of goods is very broad and should encompass the sale of software.

Some cases hold, however, that the sale of software is a transaction involving a service, not a sale of goods, since the program on the tape or disc is being sold. In those jurisdictions where these cases have been decided, the general principles of contract law are applied, and the protection given to buyers by Article 2 of the UCC is inapplicable.

A large segment of the computer software business involves transfer by either a lease or a license, but not by a sale. The UCC covers the leasing of goods in Article 2A, Leases. Forty-nine states have adopted Article 2A.

Article 2B treats a computer program as a license whenever there is a sale. This article is known as the Uniform Computer Information Act.

CYBERLAW

Web Pages

The business world is facing major changes in selling goods and services over the coming years. Sales over the Internet have mushroomed during the last few years with no limit in sight. E-commerce is conducted through a business Web site. To obtain a Web address, a business must have a domain name, an electronic digital address used by computers. At the present time, between 20,000 and 30,000 names are being registered each day.

Until 1995, names were reserved on a "first come, first served" basis. Now a business must register its domain name through InterNIC, a registered service mark of the U.S. Department of Commerce.[5] Names are not registered directly with the InterNIC. Names are registered with one of the companies appearing in a Registrar Directory that is maintained by InterNIC. A registration is valid for two years and can be renewed every year for up to ten years.

The Internet Corporation for Assigned Names and Numbers (ICANN)[6] is a nonprofit international cor-

poration that determines Internet policy including policy pertaining to domain names. ICANN resolves questions involving domain disputes.

A business cannot hijack the name of another business entity. Court cases have established that when a business has a valid trademark, it cannot be used by another person as a domain name. Names can be registered if not already taken. The name must be used or someone may register it and use it. For example, if a travel business reserves a name that includes the word *travel* that is acceptable. Another business cannot reserve a name that includes *travel*, if travel is not part of that business.

Occasionally, during the Internet's infancy, a person would deliberately register a domain name that reflected the name of an existing business, usually a famous one. The **Anticybersquatting Consumer Protection Act** imposes a penalty, if this occurs. The registrant can be held liable for up to $100,000 under this act. This liability is imposed when a person attempts to use a domain name that is identical or confusingly similar to a trademark.

Software Warranties. The UCC applies to the transfer (sale or lease) of software; thus, specific warranties apply. In particular, the UCC defines an express warranty, the implied warranty of merchantability, and the implied warranty of fitness for a particular purpose. These warranties are covered in Chapter 11. Warranties provide the buyer-user with specific rights that are unavailable through the common law. Often, the software agreement specifically states that no warranties apply. The question that courts now face is whether a manufacturer can sell these new products without warranties. If a state has enacted Article 2B, any software sold within the state does not carry any warranties.

E-Mail and Business. E-mail use by persons and businesses has increased exponentially over the years. The advantage is its speed and ease of use. Misuse of e-mail, however, may result in lawsuits. People routinely send informal messages by e-mail that they normally would not write. E-mail is viewed as a temporary document rather than a permanent one that may be available for years to come.

People assume that once the delete key has been hit, the e-mail message is destroyed, similar to shredding a piece of paper. But this misunderstanding is far removed

[5]The InterNIC's Web address is http://rs.internic.net.
[6]The ICANN's Web address is http://www.icann.org.

from the actuality. Unless e-mail shredding software is installed on the storage server, e-mail remains for years on a server where it is stored. Or the message may be moved to another area of the computer.

When a user presses the delete key, the computer allows the area occupied by the e-mail to now be overwritten. Until overwritten, the message, however, is still retrievable until a new message or document is saved over the same area of the hard drive. The average user cannot instruct the computer to overwrite a given area. The internal operation of the computer determines this procedure. Most deleted messages may be recovered and may be used against a person or business in the event a legal action is instituted.

Under federal and most state laws, e-mail is a discoverable document in the event of a lawsuit. The problem is that e-mail normally is kept informally, like other written business documents. To determine which messages were sent or which were received by e-mail can take numerous hours. For example, when Microsoft was sued by the U.S. Department of Justice, Microsoft had to supply all of its prior e-mails, many more than a decade old.

Businesses should implement a retention policy that maintains important messages that may minimize liability and that may have legal importance at the time of a trial. If evidence is destroyed, the destruction allows the opponent to argue that the business knew of the evidence's potential relevance to the litigation. The best defense is to show the jury a formal retention policy that allowed the destruction of certain types of e-mail.

A business has potential civil and criminal liability when it uses e-mail. For example, if an employee sends child pornography by using the business's e-mail server, the business may have to defend itself in criminal court. At the very least, the business may lose a computer because the government may seize any computer used in the commission of a crime.

Another example is one where one employee uses the business's Internet access to download and send explicit pictures to another employee who finds the material offensive. This act can serve as the basis of a sexual harassment action against the business. Again, the best defense to these types of situations is to establish a written policy against them.

A continuing problem involves the ownership of e-mail. Many employees regard their e-mail messages as private, comparable to mail sent through the U.S. Postal Service and, as such, these e-mail messages should be unavailable to their employers. The courts have denied this argument, finding that e-mail belongs to the business and not the employee and, as such, the employee has no right to expect privacy.

Electronic Theft Act

The Electronic Theft Act of 1997 amended the copyright and trademark laws. This legislation was viewed as "closing a loophole" in the criminal law. Under the prior law, people who intentionally distributed copied software over the Internet did not face criminal penalties if they did not profit from their actions.

Under this act the reproduction or distribution of ten or more copies of one or more copyrighted works that have a total retail value of $2,500 or more constitutes a felony, with a maximum sentence of three years' imprisonment and a fine of $250,000. The reproduction or distribution of one or more copies of one or more copyrighted works that have a total retail value of more than $1,000 constitutes a misdemeanor, with a one-year maximum sentence and a fine of up to $100,000.

The Ever-Developing Field

In an ever-changing society, the concept of personal property, especially in the computer technology area, is expanding. Often, after a new type of property is developed, the courts and legislature must resolve problems that arise from it. For example, the courts have determined that to make illegal duplicate tapes of records, audiotape recordings, videotape recordings, computer programs, compact discs, and DVDs is a crime. The next question is this: Is the law broad enough to cover the developing problems of personal property in outer space, in space laboratories, or during very long space flights?

International Consideration

Protecting Your Assets and Ideas in Foreign Countries

The laws of the host country control investments in businesses and property. Many countries restrict foreigners from owning a majority interest in domestic businesses. Under the **Exon-Florio provision** of the Omnibus Trade and Competitiveness Act of 1988, the U.S. president can prevent the purchase by a foreign business of any U.S. firms, such as airline companies, telecommunications businesses, or defense industries, if the purchase threatens national security.

Some countries require foreign investors to go through a preapproval procedure. The potential investor must submit a proposal to a host country's government for evaluation. Various agencies review the proposal, which occasionally goes through up to 100 agencies, to determine if the potential investor meets government requirements. This procedure may take months, if not years. Ownership in private property is allowed only through a trust by which the foreign business owns up to 49 percent, while a domestic business owns the remaining 51 percent. Usually, these trusts have a limited ten-year period, after which time the trust must end or be renewed.

Other countries encourage international investments by offering preferences and incentives, particularly for high-technology industries. The Eastern European countries that had ties with the former Soviet Union encourage investments to bolster sagging economies. For example, Hungary in 1988 adopted the Investments of Foreigners in Hungary Act. This act encourages investments by streamlining an approval procedure, allowing profits to flow out of the country, providing contract guarantees, and allowing foreign managers. The Russia Federation (Russia) allows private land ownership by foreign businesses. Tax and other incentives are being used to encourage investment in Russia.

A business may protect its intellectual property, such as copyrights and patents, at the international level. The United States signed the **Universal Copyright Convention** in 1952 and the **Berne Convention for the Protection of Literary and Artistic Works** in 1988. The Universal Copyright Convention grants an author copyright protection in every country that has signed when he or she first publishes a work in one of the countries with the prescribed notice. Each country is bound to protect the work according to its laws. The Berne Convention similarly provides the citizens of any other member country

the same copyright protections that it provides its own citizens.

As early as 1883, the United States and others were signatories to a treaty that provided the citizens of other countries the same rights to obtain a patent as were granted to the country's own citizens. This early treaty established the principle of right of priority. If a person applied for a patent in his or her own country and within a year applied for a patent in one of the other countries, the later application was considered as having been made on the same date as the one made in his or her own country.

The **Paris Convention for the Protection of Industrial Property** attempts to achieve uniformity in the patent area by having countries adopt a universal system of granting and recognizing patents. This convention also recognizes the principle of right of priority.

In 1998, the U.S. signed the **Digital Millennium Copyright Act (DMCA)**,[7] which implements two World Intellectual Property Organization treaties. The treaty limits liability of online service providers for copyright infringement. An exception is made under the treaty for making a copy of a computer program by activating a computer for purposes of maintenance or repair. Other provisions cover diverse issues, such as distance education, libraries, and Webcasting of sound recordings.

In the following case, the appellate court was confronted with new subpoena powers that Congress granted to private copyright holders under the DMCA. This act was passed when the only method to share files was to use an Internet service provider (ISP) and prior to peer-to-peer (P2P) file sharing. The act authorized associations organized to protect copyright material to file in court for a subpoena. The subpoena required ISPs to disclose the names and addresses of those named in the subpoena who were suspected of having downloaded the copyrighted material without permission and without paying royalties. The filing for these subpoenas could occur without a case being previously filed.

[7]To see a copy of the Digital Millennium Copyright Act, go to the U.S. Copyright Office's Web page at http://www.copyright.gov/laws.

CASE 16.4

United States Court of
Appeals, District of
Columbia
351 F.3d 1229 (2003)

RECORDING INDUSTRY ASSOCIATION OF AMERICA, INC. v. VERIZON INTERNET SERVICES, INC.

BACKGROUND AND FACTS In the late 1990s using a program called Napster, individuals with a personal computer and access to the Internet began to offer digital copies of recordings for download by other users, an activity known as peer–to–peer (P2P) file sharing. Although recording companies and music publishers successfully obtained an injunction against Napster's facilitating the sharing of files containing copyrighted recordings, millions of people in the United States and around the world continued to share digital .mp3 files of copyrighted recordings using P2P computer programs, such as KaZaA, Morpheus, Grokster, and eDonkey. Unlike Napster, which relied upon a centralized communication architecture to identify the .mp3 files available for download, the current generation of P2P file sharing programs allow an internet user to search directly the .mp3 file libraries of other users; no Web site is involved. To date, owners of copyrights have not been able to stop the use of these decentralized programs.

The Recording Industry Association of America, Inc. (RIAA), began to direct its anti-infringement efforts against individual users of P2P file sharing programs. In order to pursue apparent infringers, the RIAA needed to be able to identify the individuals who were sharing and trading files using P2P programs. The RIAA could readily obtain the screen name of an individual user, and then using the Internet Protocol (IP) address associated with that screen name, could trace the user to his ISP. Only the ISP, however, can link the IP address used to access a P2P program with the name and address of a person—the ISP's customer—who can then be contacted or, if need be, sued by the RIAA.

The RIAA used the subpoena provisions of § 512(h) of the Digital Millennium Copyright Act to compel the ISPs to disclose the names of subscribers whom the RIAA had reason to believe were infringing its members' copyrights. Federal law allows a copyright owner to request the clerk of any United States district court to issue a subpoena to an ISP for identification of an alleged infringer. Some ISPs had complied with the RIAA's § 512(h) subpoenas and identified the names of the subscribers sought by the RIAA. The RIAA sent letters to and filed lawsuits against several hundred such individuals, each of whom allegedly made hundreds, or in some cases even thousands, of .mp3 files of copyrighted recordings available for download by other users. Verizon refused to comply with and instead challenged the validity of two § 512(h) subpoenas it had received.

On July 24, 2002, the RIAA served Verizon with a subpoena issued pursuant to § 512(h), seeking the identity of a subscriber whom the RIAA believed to be engaged in infringing activity. The subpoena was for "information sufficient to identify the alleged infringer of the sound recordings described in the attached notification." The "notification of claimed infringement" identified the IP address of the subscriber and about 800 sound files he offered for trading; expressed the RIAA's "good faith belief" that the file sharing activity of Verizon's subscriber constituted infringement of its members' copyrights; and asked for Verizon's "immediate assistance in stopping this unauthorized activity. Specifically, we request that you remove or disable access to the infringing sound files via your system."

When Verizon refused to disclose the name of its subscriber, the RIAA filed a motion to compel production of the information. In opposition to that motion, Verizon argued § 512(h) does not apply to an ISP acting merely as a conduit for an individual using a P2P file sharing program to exchange files. The district court rejected Verizon's argument based upon "the language and structure of the statute, as confirmed by the purpose and history of the legislation" and ordered Verizon to disclose to the RIAA the names of its subscribers.

The RIAA then obtained another § 512(h) subpoena directed to Verizon. This time Verizon moved to quash the subpoena, arguing that the district court lacked jurisdiction under Article III to issue the subpoena and in the alternative that § 512(h) violates the First Amendment. The district court rejected Verizon's constitutional arguments, denied the motion to quash, and again ordered Verizon to disclose the identity of its subscriber. Verizon appealed the orders.

Chief Judge GINSBURG

. . . .

The issue is whether § 512(h) applies to an ISP acting only as a conduit for data transferred between two internet users, such as persons sending and receiving e-mail or, as in this case, sharing P2P files. Verizon contends § 512(h) does not authorize the issuance of a subpoena to an ISP that transmits infringing material but does not store any such material on its servers. The RIAA argues § 512(h) on its face authorizes the issuance of a subpoena to an "[internet] service provider" without regard to whether the ISP is acting as a conduit for user-directed communications. We conclude from both the terms of § 512(h) and the overall structure of § 512 that, as Verizon contends, a subpoena may be issued only to an ISP engaged in storing on its servers material that is infringing or the subject of infringing activity.

. . . .

We need not, however, resort to investigating what the 105th Congress may have known because the text of § 512(h) and the overall structure of § 512 clearly establish, as we have seen, that § 512(h) does not authorize the issuance of a subpoena to an ISP acting as a mere conduit for the transmission of information sent by others. Legislative history can serve to inform the court's reading of an otherwise ambiguous text; it cannot lead the court to contradict the legislation itself.

In any event, not only is the statute clear (albeit complex), the legislative history of the DMCA betrays no awareness whatsoever that internet users might be able directly to exchange files containing copyrighted works. That is not surprising; P2P software was "not even a glimmer in anyone's eye when the DMCA was enacted." Furthermore, such testimony as was available to the Congress prior to passage of the DMCA concerned "hackers" who established unauthorized FTP [file transfer protocols] or BBS [bulletin board sites] on the servers of ISPs. The Congress had no reason to foresee the application of § 512(h) to P2P file sharing, nor did they draft the DMCA broadly enough to reach the new technology when it came along. Had the Congress been aware of P2P technology, or anticipated its development, § 512(h) might have been drafted more generally. Be that as it may, contrary to the RIAA's claim, nothing in the legislative history supports the issuance of a § 512(h) subpoena to an ISP acting as a conduit for P2P file sharing.

. . . .

DECISION AND REMEDY P2P software was not available when the Digital Millennium Copyright Act was passed by Congress. The act's language was not broad enough to cover new technology. The transfer of copyrighted material is still illegal, but the statute covering subpoenas does not allow a copyright owner to force ISPs to disclose their customers' names and addresses.

CRITICAL THINKING: POLITICAL ISSUE Should a private organization, such as the Recording Industry Association of America, have subpoena powers without a case being filed? Should the federal statute be amended to allow this?

The World Trade Organization (WTO) fosters cooperative methods that allowed for negotiations of the global agreement on intellectual property protection (TRIPS). All WTO members are committed to enact and enforce copyright, patent, and trademark laws.

PRACTICAL TIPS

Protecting Real Property

You decide to purchase a specific parcel of real property, which consists of several vacant buildings located in a suburban area on twenty acres of land. Because the property is rather isolated, numerous illegal intrusions into the buildings have been made by transients in order to stay a night or two and by youths for parties. These individuals have caused considerable damage to the buildings.

You consider several alternatives to deal with these occurrences: (1) placing guard dogs on the premises, (2) hiring a night watchperson, (3) setting up shotguns that would be triggered by a person touching a string close to the floor, or (4) simply letting these people use the premises until you find a tenant to lease the property.

You check with an attorney to identify the best alternative. The attorney tells you that the first alternative is not allowed. Many states, including yours, have adopted laws naming a dog's owner liable for bites when the owner knows the dog to be vicious.

The second alternative is possible. The use of a night watchperson is proper as long as he does not use firearms against trespassers. No one can shoot mere trespassers. Before a person can use deadly force, a clear danger to the shooter or another person must exist.

The third alternative is the worst choice. The property owner who sets up this type of gun arrangement is liable for criminal and civil charges if anyone is injured. According to longtime English and American laws, no one can protect property by this method.

The fourth alternative is also not feasible. If a person, even a trespasser, is injured on your property by falling into a hole or tripping on debris, you may be liable. As the property's owner, you have certain legal duties toward others on the property. Many states require that you act as a reasonable and prudent person would under the same or similar circumstances. Other states require you to make the premises reasonably safe once you are aware that other people are using them.

What should you do? Here is a checklist you should consider.

Checklist

✔ *Insurance* Purchase sufficient liability insurance for any incidents that may occur on the property.

✔ *Signs* Post "No Trespassing" signs prominently. Board up the buildings, making them very difficult for anyone to enter.

✔ *Notification* Inform the police department about the situation and ask the police to watch the premises.

✔ *Guards* Hire security guards, if the expense can be justified.

These alternatives are the safest ones that a real estate owner may exercise.

Chapter Summary

Property rights are of prime importance to our society. In fact, the U.S. Constitution protects property rights.

These property classifications are recognized: real or personal, tangible or intangible, and fixtures. All property constitutes either real estate or personal property. Tangible property has physical existence, whereas intangible property consists of rights. Fixtures are items that are installed in real estate and that become part of the land.

A person may own real property with another person. These joint forms of ownership are tenancy in common, joint tenancy with right of survivorship, tenancy by the entirety, and community property. To own an interest in either tenancy by the entirety or community property, the joint owners must be husband and wife.

Different interests in real property are found in freehold and nonfreehold estates. A freehold estate provides a person ownership for an indefinite period. Freehold estates include the fee simple absolute, fee simple defeasible, fee simple subject to a condition subsequent, and life estates. The nonfreehold estates are leases that govern possessory rights to real property in the relationship between a landlord and a tenant.

Transferring all interest in real property occurs by will, by operation of law (eminent domain), by adverse possession, or by deed. Eminent domain is the right of the government to take a person's property. In doing so, however, the government must pay just compensation

to the owner. Adverse possession means obtaining title to land (without a deed) by the adverse use of real property for a specified time period.

The seven ways to obtain personal property ownership are by possession, purchase, production, gift, will or inheritance, accession, and confusion.

Bailments concern the transfer of possession of personal property without transfer of title from the "owner" to another person. The bailment can be based on a contract or it can be gratuitous.

Intellectual property and computer law are growing areas of the law. Intellectual property covers patents and copyrights. An important question in computer law is whether transfer of a computer program entails a sale of goods or of service.

Using the World Wide Web

A number of Web sites exist where you can find information concerning intellectual property law and computer law. In addition to the sites listed at this book's Web site, performing a search on *intellectual property law* using a major search engine would yield hundreds of hits.

For *Web Activities*, links to Web sites mentioned in the chapter, and additional Web sites that relate to the chapter topics, go to **http://bohlman.westbuslaw. com**, click on "Internet Applications," and select Chapter 16.

Web Activities

Go to **http://bohlman.westbuslaw.com**, click on "Internet Applications," and select Chapter 16.
16–1 Trademarks
16–2 Copyright

Key Terms

abandoned property
accession
adverse possession
Anticybersquatting Consumer Protection Act
bailee
bailment
bailor
bargain and sale deed
Berne Convention for the Protection of Literary and Artistic Works
bill of sale
community property

Computer Software Rental Amendments Act
confusion
constructive notice
deed
Digital Millennium Copyright Act (DMCA)
easement
easements by prescription
eminent domain
Exon-Florio provision
Federal Trademark

Dilution Act.
fee simple absolute
fee simple defeasible
fee simple subject to a condition subsequent
fixture
freehold estate
fungible goods
general warranty deed
gift
hardware
intangible property
joint tenancy with right of survivorship
landlord

lease
life estate
lost property
maskwork
mislaid property
nonfreehold estate
Paris Convention for the Protection of Industrial Property
personal property
production
Protection of Semiconductor Chip Products Act
purchase

quiet title action
quitclaim deed
real property
recording statute
software

special warranty deed
tangible property
tenancy at will
tenancy by sufferance
tenancy by the entirety

tenancy for years
tenancy from period to
 period
tenancy in common
tenant

Universal Copyright
Convention

Questions and Case Problems

16–1 Mislaid Property Sally goes into Meyer's Department Store to shop for the holidays. She has been engrossed in looking over a number of silk blouses when she suddenly realizes that she has a dinner engagement. She hastily leaves the store, inadvertently leaving her purse on a sales counter. Julie, a sales clerk at the store, notices the purse on the counter but leaves it there, expecting Sally to return for it. Later, when Sally returns, the purse is gone. Sally files an action against Meyer's Department Store for the loss of her purse. Discuss the probable outcome of her suit.

16–2 Leases Goodman contracted to lease an apartment near the campus from landlord Lopez for one year, with the monthly rent due and payable on the first of each month. At the end of the year, Goodman fails to vacate the apartment and Lopez does not object. Goodman continues to pay the rent on the first day of the month and Lopez accepts it. Six months later, Lopez informs Goodman that the apartment has been leased to Green and that Goodman must vacate the premises by the end of the week. Goodman refuses to leave; Lopez threatens eviction proceedings. Discuss the parties' rights under these circumstances.

16–3 Mislaid Property Bill Heise is a custodian for the First Mercantile Department Store. While walking to work, Bill discovers an expensive watch lying on the curb. Later that day, while Bill cleans the store aisles, he discovers a wallet containing $500 with no identification. Bill turns over the wallet to his superior, Moe Frances. Bill gives the watch to his son Gordon. Two weeks later, Martin Avery, the watch's owner, discovers that Bill found the watch. Martin demands it back from Gordon. Bill then decides to claim the wallet with its $500, but Moe refuses to turn it over, denying that Bill is the true owner and contending that the money is really the store's property. Discuss who is entitled to the watch and who is entitled to the wallet containing $500.

16–4 Adverse Possession Harold was a wanderer until twenty-one years ago. At that time, he decided to settle down on a vacant three-acre piece of land, which he did not own. People in the area indicated to him that they had no idea who owned it. Harold built a house on the land, married, and raised three children while living there. He fenced the land, placed a gate with a sign, "Harold's Homestead," above it, and had trespassers removed. Harold now is confronted by Joe Moonfeld, who has a deed in his name as property owner. Joe orders Harold and his family off the property, claiming his own title ownership. Discuss who has best "title" to the property. What steps should Harold take to protect his property interest, if any?

16–5 Bailment Kleenco is in the business of providing commercial cleaning services. United is in the business of renting trucks to the general public. Keith Sugioka (Sugioka), an employee of Kleenco, rented a 1987 one-half-ton Toyota pickup truck (the truck) from United for eighteen days. He signed the following standard agreement:

Collision Waiver

By initialing, renter agrees to pay the sum of $_____ per day or fraction thereof additional and the renter will be responsible only for the first $_____ of damage (except cube box) provided vehicle is operated in conformity with rental agreement. Collision waiver does not cover overhead roof damage. Any damage to cube box is not in any way covered by this waiver.

Initial here x_____

The full responsibility provision located below the collision waiver provision stated the following:

Full Responsibility

By initialing, renter agrees to pay United Truck for all loss or damage to vehicle (regardless of negligence).

Initial here x_____

Sugioka did not initial or mark the collision waiver provision. Rather, he initialed the full responsibility provision as evidenced by the initials "K.S." on the "Initial here" line.

Sugioka left the keys in the truck, which was then stolen. Action was brought against Kleenco for the value of the truck. What result and why? [*United Truck Rental Equipment Leasing, Inc., v. Kleenco Corp.*, 929 P.2d 99 (1996)]

16–6 Fixtures A mortgage was placed on a parcel of land. Afterward, the land owner constructed a grain storage facility there. It consisted of a number of steel structures bolted into concrete slabs that were partially embedded into the ground and which included fifty to sixty feet of underground tubing. Air was electronically pumped through the tubing to move grain from the dryer to several storage bins. To remove these structures would take about two weeks. The facility's owner defaulted on the mortgage. The mortgagee (creditor) filed an action to regain the property. The mortgagee argued that the grain facility was a fixture and should remain on the land. Do you agree? Explain. [*Metropolitan Life Insurance Co. v. Reeves*, 223 Neb. 299, 389 N.W.2d 295 (1986)]

16–7 Common Ownership Paul was the owner of real estate located in Putnam County, Florida. In 1982, while Paul was living with Lucille, he executed a deed conveying the property to himself and Lucille as joint tenants with right of survivorship. In 1985, Paul and Lucille stopped living together. Three months later Lucille conveyed her interest in the property to her daughter, Sandra. What type of interest does Sandra possess in the property? Explain. [*Foucart v. Paul*, 516 So. 2d 1035 (Fla. Dist. Ct. App. 1987)]

16–8 Lost Property Danny Smith and his brother discovered a sixteen-foot boat lying beside a roadway in Alabama. Danny Smith informed the police, who immediately impounded the boat and stored it in a city warehouse. Although Smith acquiesced to the police action, he told the police that if the true owner failed to claim the boat, he wanted it. When the true owner failed to come forward, the police department refused to relinquish the boat to Smith and instead told Smith that it planned to auction it to the highest bidder on the city's behalf. Smith sued for custody of the boat. Because Smith never physically held the boat, but rather allowed the police to take possession, should Smith succeed in his claim to title as finder? Could Smith defeat a claim if the true owner sought to retake the boat? [*Smith v. Purvis*, 474 So. 2d 1131 (Ala. Civ. App. 1985)]

16–9 Fixtures A bank installed bank vault doors, night depository equipment, drive-up teller window equipment, and remote transaction systems. The city of Lansing taxed these improvements as real property. The bank took the position that it never intended these items to become part of the real estate. Who should win? Explain. [*Michigan National Bank, Lansing v. City of Lansing*, 293 N.W.2d 626 (1980)]

16–10 Internet On December 21, 1970, Elvis Presley met with President Richard M. Nixon (1969–1974) in the Oval Office located in the White House in Washington, D.C. During that meeting, the White House photographer took twenty-eight photographs. A photograph showing the two men shaking hands is the most requested photograph from the National Archives and Records Administration. For the first time, all of the photographs are available on the Web. Go to **http://www.archives.gov/exhibit_hall/when_ nixon_met_elvis/part_1.html**, then click on "Citations." Are these photographs in the public domain or does a user need to make further inquiries as to the rights to use these pictures?

Unit 3

Business Formation

Chapter 17

Agency Law and Private Employment Law

Employment gives health, sobriety, and morals. Constant employment and well-paid labor produce, in a country like ours, general prosperity, content, and cheerfulness.

> Daniel Webster, 1782–1852
> U.S. congressman (1813–1817, 1823–1827), U.S. senator (1827–1841, 1845–1850), and U.S. secretary of state (1841–1843, 1850–1852)

Chapter Outline

The Hard Decisions Surrounding Medical Insurance

Sam's Clothing Store has been in business for more than twenty years. You are the majority shareholder and chief executive officer. Sam's Clothing has a reputation in the community for its excellent employee benefits. One benefit is the group health insurance plan.

Sam's Clothing's very loyal workforce includes several employees who have worked for the clothing store since its inception. One of the long-time employees has severe medical problems that require very expensive procedures. Although he has been absent a little more than normal, he still performs his job. The cost of his medical bills, however, is beginning to affect the medical plan's cost. The company's medical insurance broker informs you that if this employee continues on the medical plan, the rates for next year will increase significantly.

The broker advises you to be prepared to pay significantly higher rates or to provide each employee with a specific sum of money to help offset the cost of private health insurance for which the broker will assist each employee to enroll. Although the broker's idea of letting each person find his or her own insurance appeals to your business sense, you know that individual medical insurance is very expensive.

You believe that the ill employee will be unable to purchase insurance. What course of action should you take? Use the ethical model presented in Chapter 2 and reprinted on the inside front to develop your answer.

Introduction

Agency law[1] is important because it permeates the entire legal system. Agency law defines the relationship between two parties in which one of them, called the **agent**, agrees to represent or act for the other, called the **principal**. The principal has the right to control the agent's conduct in matters entrusted to the agent.[2]

In **employment law**, the employer can control the time and place at which the employee will work and the type of work to be done. The employer is called the master and the employee is called the servant. If the employee is authorized to enter into contracts on behalf of the employer, the employee is acting in the capacity of an agent, and the employer is also the principal. Some states have moved away from the use of the terms *master* and *servant* because they are seen as insulting to employees.

The rules in agency law are relatively simple and straightforward, although the application of the rules to a specific problem is sometimes difficult. Both agency law and its counterpart, employment law, have evolved over the centuries. The basic concepts, however, remain consistent. This chapter discusses agency law and the private employment law. Other laws that affect employment will be discussed in later chapters.

Artiste Login. Carlo and Carlotta hire employees, agents, and independent contractors to work for Artiste Login. Carlo and Carlotta must be aware of the different laws that apply to each category and must also be alert to tax implications.

Background

The forerunners of agency law were the legal principles developed during Roman times relating to slave ownership. Even in ancient times, an owner was financially liable for the torts of his slaves. The reasoning was that if a person could increase his wealth through the services of slaves, he should be responsible for the slaves' acts.

This concept continued to develop through the Middle Ages. Eventually, a body of law governing the relationship of master and servant evolved. A master could be held liable for the servant's acts committed within the scope of employment, in other words, within the time and area of the work assignment. A servant could not enter into contracts on the master's behalf. The liability of a master, therefore, usually was limited to tort damages. For example, the master was

---

[1]At the Web site for Law Com, http://www.law.com, type in the word "agency." More than 1,100 articles are listed on this topic.

[2]The 'Lectric Law Library has a good general discussion of agency law. You may access it at http://www.lectlaw.com/d-a.htm.

liable if a servant negligently harnessed a carriage and this negligence resulted in damages or injuries to another person.

Today, the same concept is applied to the employer–employee relationship. Under employment law, employers are responsible for the harm caused by the torts of their employees who act within the scope of their employment.

The Industrial Revolution, which started in the mid-1700s, created the need for many contractual relationships. The owners of new industrial plants entered into many contracts to keep the plants operating. The owners purchased raw materials in volume from several sources and sold the manufactured products over a wide territory to many people. No longer would the majority of contracts be between the individual who produced an item and the individual who purchased it.

People who owned industrial plants delegated the responsibility to enter into these contracts to individuals known as *agents*. By using agents, an owner (or principal) could conduct multiple business operations simultaneously in various locations. In addition, the owner of the industrial plant incurred liability on the contracts made on his behalf by the agents. As a result, the concept of agency law developed.

The underlying concept of the employer–employee and principal–agent legal relationship is summarized by a Latin phrase, *qui facit per atium facit per se,* which means "he [or she] who acts through another acts himself [or herself]." This phrase summarizes the theory that has served as the foundation of agency law from Roman times through today. If a person increases business profits through the use of other people, he or she should be liable for the actions of those people.

Formation of the Agency Relationship

Generally, no formalities are required to create an agency. The agency relationship can arise by one of several methods: agreement, ratification, or estoppel.

Agency by Agreement

Agency is a consensual relationship. The agency relationship is created when the principal agrees to have the agent act on behalf of the principal. Most agency relationships are created in this manner.

Agency relationships can be based on oral express agreements. Good business practice, however, dictates that the agreement should be in writing. The agency relationship normally is a contractual one; thus, contract rules apply including the statute of frauds discussed in Chapter 10. This statute requires certain types of contracts to be in writing to be enforceable in a court. For example, the sale of any interest in real estate must be in writing; so, for instance, real estate listing agreements between the seller (principal) and the real estate broker (agent) must be in writing.

A common agency by agreement is a written document called a **power of attorney** that grants a person the authority to perform acts on your behalf, such as signing papers, opening accounts, or making purchases. Assume that you are purchasing a house and will be out of town when the actual purchase takes place. Your spouse needs to sign the papers on your behalf. You can grant your spouse the authority to sign your name to the papers by signing a power of attorney. Most states require this document to be signed by the principal in the presence of a government-sanctioned official, such as a notary public. A power of attorney is signed by the principal (you) granting the agent (your spouse, in this case) either unlimited authority to act on the principal's behalf or limited authority to perform specific acts. The agent is called an *attorney-in-fact*.

Agency by Ratification

On occasion, a person who is not in fact an agent, or who acts outside the scope of her authority as an agent, may make a contract on behalf of a purported principal. No authority from the alleged principal, either express or implied, is present when the professed agent makes the unauthorized contract.

If the principal later approves or affirms that contract by word or by action, an agency relationship is created by ratification. **Ratification** is determined by intent, and intent can be expressed by either words or conduct. Ratification binds the principal to the agent's acts and treats these acts or contracts as if the principal had authorized them. The principal must be aware of all material facts; otherwise, the ratification is not effective.

The principal's ratification can be either expressed or implied from the principal's words or conduct. The creation of the agency by ratification "relates back" to the time of the unauthorized act. By her acceptance, the principal acknowledges that the contract started at the time of the unauthorized act. The principal ratifies both the advantages and the disadvantages of the ratified contract or act.

For example, a person with no connection to an alarm business convinces a ninety-year-old widow to sign a contract for the installation of a burglar alarm.

He guarantees her that the company will pay any losses she may incur because of a burglary. When he presents the contract to the business and it agrees to install the system, it also must be bound by the guarantee made by the salesperson. If a burglary loss occurs, the business must pay the widow.

The following case decides if silence on the part of a purported principal can be construed as ratification.

CASE 17.1

Court of Appeals of Ohio, First District, 2003
2003 WL 1571741

MACEWEN v. JORDAN

BACKGROUND AND FACTS MacEwen and Jordan are brother and sister. In September 1994, Jordan's father moved into her home. She stopped working to take care of her father. Two months later, Jordan's father executed a durable power of attorney naming her as his attorney-in-fact. MacEwen was named as successor attorney-in-fact.

Two years later, in 1996, their father executed a new power of attorney, which expressly granted the following power to his attorney-in-fact: "To make gifts at any time, or from time to time, to anyone, including my Attorney-in-Fact, in such amounts and using such property as my Attorney-in-Fact shall determine." Under the new power of attorney, Jordan remained as attorney-in-fact, but MacEwen was replaced by Jordan's husband, a lawyer, as successor attorney-in-fact. The record is silent as to who prepared the power of attorney.

Their father's will, executed in 1987, left his estate in equal shares to MacEwen and Jordan. The will designated that Jordan was to serve as his executor.

Until her father's death in December 1999, Jordan exercised the powers granted under the power of attorney. She made gifts to herself and to her children, including payments for household expenses, in excess of $100,000. The gifts were made from a checking account and a brokerage account that listed Jordan and her father as joint owners with a right of survivorship.

When, following their father's death, the estate's assets filed with the probate court were substantially smaller than he had expected, MacEwen brought a lawsuit, alleging that Jordan, as executor, had concealed probate assets, and that gifts that Jordan had made to herself and to her family prior to their father's death were fraudulent and were made in breach of her fiduciary duty to her father. He sought from the probate court an order that Jordan return those assets to their father's estate.

Following discovery, including the taking of Jordan's deposition, Jordan moved for summary judgment on MacEwen's claims. The probate court magistrate granted the motion from which an appeal was taken.

GORMAN, Judge.

. . . .

. . . MacEwen contends that the probate court erred in granting summary judgment when a genuine issue of material fact remained as to whether Jordan had breached her fiduciary duty to their father by making gifts to herself pursuant to the . . . 1996 power of attorney. A power of attorney is a written instrument authorizing an agent to perform specific acts on behalf of the principal. The holder of a power of attorney has a fiduciary relationship with the principal. This relationship imposes a duty of loyalty to the principal.

As this court has noted, attorneys-in-fact act outside the scope of their authority when they use a general, durable power of attorney to make gifts to themselves.

This self-gifting raises "a suspicion that undue influence may have been exerted" on the principal by the attorney-in-fact. This rule seems well established in other jurisdictions.

We now hold that a general, durable power of attorney does not authorize attorneys-in-fact to transfer the principal's property to themselves or to others, unless the power of attorney explicitly confers this power. An attorney-in-fact may not make gratuitous transfers of the principal's assets unless the power of attorney from which the authority is derived expressly and unambiguously grants the authority to do so. Where, however, the principal has made an express grant of authority to an attorney-in-fact to make gifts to third persons, including the attorney-in-fact, the attorney-in-fact may, in the absence of evidence of undue influence upon the principal, make such gifts.

While this grant of authority effectively extinguishes any duty the attorney-in-fact has to avoid self-dealing, it does not remove all obligations owed to the principal. The attorney-in-fact remains a fiduciary, subject to a minimal duty of care owed to the principal. Thus, attorneys-in-fact bear the initial burden of proving the validity of a transfer to themselves under the power of attorney, while the party attacking the transfer retains the ultimate burden of proving undue influence by clear and convincing evidence.

In determining the validity of such a transfer, a court must first look to the express grant of authority in the text of the power of attorney. Absent that grant, the transfer is presumptively invalid. A court must next look to other considerations, based upon the unique facts of the case, which may include whether a transfer depleted assets necessary to maintain the principal's lifestyle; whether the principal knew of the gift and authorized it in some manner; whether the recipient of the transfer was the natural object of the principal's bounty and affection; whether the transfer was consistent with the principal's estate plan; whether the gift was a continuation of the principal's pattern of making gifts; and whether the transfer was made for another legitimate goal, such as the reduction of estate taxes.

In this case, pursuant to our de novo review of the record before the probate court, and construing the facts most strongly in favor of MacEwen, Jordan presented uncontroverted evidence that she had acted according to her father's intent pursuant to the express grant of authority to make gifts to third persons and to herself. There was no evidence that Jordan's gifts had depleted assets necessary to maintain her father's lifestyle. He remained in Jordan's care in her home from September 1994 until his death. Their father was named on the checking-account and brokerage-account statements mailed to his home that recorded the transactions in his primary assets. The disputed transfers were to or for the benefit of Jordan and her daughter. Jordan was a primary beneficiary of her father's estate plan, as was MacEwen. Thus, Jordan carried her burden of establishing the validity of the power to transfer assets to herself. And MacEwen presented no evidence that Jordan had exerted undue influence on their father when he granted the power of attorney or at any subsequent time.

. . . .

DECISION AND REMEDY The court held that gifts will not be set aside where there is a power of attorney allowing the agent to make gifts to herself, except upon showing that the gifts depleted assets necessary to maintain the principal's lifestyle.

CRITICAL THINKING: ETHICS Although the court found that the gifts were legal, do you think the daughter acted ethically? Explain your position.

Agency by Estoppel

An **agency by estoppel** occurs when a principal leads a third person to believe that another person is his agent. **Estoppel** means to bar, to impede, to stop. When the third person deals with the presumptive agent, the principal cannot deny the agency relationship. In other words, the principal cannot claim the agency relationship does not exist. In these situations, the principal's actions create the appearance of an agency that does not in fact exist.

For example, Kona is in the insurance business and hires McGant as an agent to solicit and sell insurance. Kona advertises to the general public that McGant is his agent. After a period of time, Kona discovers that McGant is keeping some of the premiums paid in cash. Obviously, McGant is dishonest and probably has committed a criminal act. Kona fires McGant immediately, but Kona's advertisements still give McGant the appearance of being Kona's agent. If McGant should contract with an innocent third party after being fired, Kona will be estopped from denying that McGant was his agent. Kona represented McGant to the public as his agent, and an innocent purchaser relied on this representation. Kona, therefore, is not allowed to claim a lack of an agency relationship. To avoid possible future liability, Kona might publish notice that McGant is no longer Kona's agent and personally notify all previous customers who dealt with McGant of this fact.

Agency Relationships

Two types of agency relationships exist. The first is the principal–agent, including professional agents. The second is the employer–employee when the employee is also an agent.

The legal principles developed under either agency law or employment law have similar applications. A person can be both an employee and an agent at the same time. For example, a business may employ a person full time to analyze the real estate market. That person also may have the authority to negotiate the price of, and to purchase or sell, specific pieces of land. Because these two relationships, that is, employer–employee and principal–agent, easily can be intertwined, a clear application of separate legal principles sometimes is impossible.

Exhibit 17–1 summarizes the types of agency relationships recognized by law. Throughout the rest of this chapter, the terms *principal* and *agent* should be construed to also mean *employer* and *employee*, unless otherwise stated.

Relationship between the Principal and Agent

The agent acts on behalf of, and instead of, the principal to negotiate, conduct, and contract business with third persons. The agent has **derivative authority**; that is, she derives the authority to carry out the principal's business from the principal and not from her own acts. The principal is liable to the third party for the agent's acts based on that contract.

Assume that Creative Music Corporation hires Bob, a booking agent, to negotiate and contract with the Super Jazz, the latest jazz group, for a series of appearances and television commercials endorsing Creative Music's products. Contracts made by Bob, the agent, within his authority, are binding and legally enforceable by Creative Music Corporation, the principal. The Super Jazz, the third party, also may enforce the contract against Creative Music Corporation. If Bob had no authority to represent Creative Music Corporation, he could not bind, on his own,

Exhibit 17–1   Legal Relationships in Agency Law

Type of Legal Relationship	Definition
Principal–agent	An agent acts on behalf of, and instead of, the principal and uses a certain degree of his or her own discretion.
Employer–employee	An employee's (servant's) physical conduct is controlled or subject to control by an employer. An employee also can be an agent.

Creative Music Corporation to a contract with the Super Jazz.

The authority must come from the principal. A principal is liable for acts of another only if the principal hires an agent or acts in such a way as to create an agency relationship.

Scope of Agent's Authority. A principal's liability in a contract with a third party arises from the authority given to the agent to enter legally binding contracts on the principal's behalf. An agent's authority to act stems from one of the following sources:

1. Actual authority
   a. Express (or specific).
   b. Implied (or inherent).
2. Apparent authority.

Even if an agent contracts outside the scope of her authority, the principal still may be liable if the principal ratifies the contract, as discussed previously.

Actual Authority. An agent who acts on behalf of the principal either by agreement or by operation of law has **actual authority** that can be either express or implied. Express authority provides the agent specific instructions.

Express authority can be granted orally or in writing. A written agency agreement is a good business practice. A well-drafted instrument clarifies the relationship for both the principal and the agent.

Even the best drafted agency agreement, however, does not cover every aspect of the agent's responsibilities. These responsibilities are part of the agent's **implied authority**, sometimes called *inherent authority*. Often, implied authority is conferred by virtue of the customary practices of that particular agency. Implied authority may be inferred from the position the agent occupies. For example, in a department store, the manager of the men's clothing section has the implied authority to discount the price of a shirt that has a spot on it.

Artiste Login. An agent has implied authority for acts that are reasonably necessary for the agent to carry out her expressly authorized duty. For example, Cherri is employed by Artiste Login to manage one of its stores.

LEGAL HIGHLIGHT

Whose Agent Are You, Anyway?

Television advertisements for insurance may leave you with the impression that the insurance agent is your (the customer's) agent. Legally this is false. The agent represents the insurance company, the principal, not you. The insurance company, not you, pays the agent.

The same is true of travel agents. The travel agent sells you, the third party, a travel package on behalf of his or her principal, which may be a hotel or airline. The travel agent represents and is paid by the hotel or airline, not by you. If something goes wrong with a reservation that a travel agent makes at a hotel, and the clerk tells you that "your travel agent" made a mistake, you might politely inform the clerk that the travel agent is the hotel's agent, not yours. As the principal, the hotel is responsible for its agent's acts.

Real estate agents also confuse customers as to their principals. When you enter a real estate office wanting to buy a house and speak with a very nice real estate broker, remember that she or he earns a commission based on the house's selling price.

Today, in many states, the person representing the buyer must provide a statement that establishes any conflict of interest. Let's say that, you, the buyer, want to purchase a house for the lowest price. The agent's commission depends on the selling price, so he or she has a financial interest in your paying a higher price. The agent actually works for the seller, who pays the commission to both the real estate agent representing her and to the real estate agent representing you. The agent owes you a duty of good faith under state law to represent you when negotiating the price of the house.

Often today, a buyer hires a buyer's representative (another term for a buyer's agent) for a fee. The representative's check is independent of the house's price. The buyer then can be completely assured that the buyer's representative is looking out for the buyer. The bottom line is that, in most commercial transactions, only if you pay the person is he or she your agent.

In the employment contract with Cherri, no clause expressly states Cherri's authority to contract with third persons. The authority to manage a business, however, implies the authority to act as reasonably required in order to operate the business. Cherri's implied authority as a manager includes the right to hire or fire employees, buy merchandise and equipment, and advertise products sold in the store.

Apparent Authority. A principal makes a third party reasonably believe that a particular person is the principal's agent and has the authority to act on the principal's behalf. If the third party relies on the appearance of authority that the principal has apparently given to another person, the person is said to be an agent by **apparent authority**. This agency is based on the principle of estoppel. The apparent authority is a substitute for actual authority when the principal instructs the agent not to perform certain duties even though the agent occupies a position that would appear to have such authority. The principal is stopped from saying that the person had no authority to act on the principal's behalf, even though the agent has no actual authority.

Apparent authority often is considered to be title authority. That is, the authority exists by virtue of the person's business title—general manager, assistant manager, sales manager, and so on. It also depends on the size and scope of the business. For example, not all radio station managers have the authority to promote other station personnel. In a small station, the owner may retain the right to promote personnel, whereas in larger stations, the general manager may have that authority. A person may have apparent authority when no actual authority exists. In the previous example involving Cherri, if her supervisor told Cherri that she could not contract for advertising, Cherri still would have apparent authority to do so.

Anyone dealing with an agent needs to determine the authority of that agent. Does that person have authority to enter into the contract that is proposed? As indicated previously, a person's title is only one factor to consider. Statements by a purported agent alone do not create authority. A person may lie about her authority and be very convincing.

The principal's actions determine the authority. The level of authority is particularly important when a salesperson seeks orders for goods or services. The agent's authority must be ascertained before goods or services are ordered from the agent. The following case discusses the concept of implied or inherent authority.

CASE 17.2	# MENARD, INC. v. DAGE-MTI, INC.
Supreme Court of Indiana, 2000 726 N.E.2d 1206	**BACKGROUND AND FACTS** Dage-MTI, Inc. (Dage), was a manufacturing corporation that owned a thirty-acre parcel. Dage was governed by a six-member board of directors (Board) of which both Kerrigan and Sterling were members. In addition to being a Board member, Sterling had served as president of Dage for twenty years.

For many years, Sterling operated Dage without significant input from or oversight by the Board. During 1993, however, Kerrigan took steps to subject Dage's management to Board control.

In late October 1993, the Dage shareholders held a meeting. During the course of the meeting, Sterling first informed other directors that Menard, Inc. (Menard), owner of home improvement stores, had expressed interest in purchasing a thirty-acre parcel of land owned by Dage.

On October 30, 1993, Menard forwarded a formal offer to Sterling pertaining to the purchase of ten and one-half acres of the thirty-acre parcel. Upon receipt of the offer, Sterling did not contact Menard to discuss the terms and conditions of the offer. Instead, he forwarded the offer to all Dage directors with a cover note acknowledging that Board approval was required to accept or reject the offer. Ultimately, this offer was rejected. This rejection was communicated to Sterling and, although he viewed the offer to purchase favorably, he let the offer lapse. Later, he informed Menard's agent, Gary Litvin, that members of Dage's Board objected to various provisions of the offer.

On November 30, 1993, Sterling called Kerrigan and informed him that Menard would make a second offer for the entire thirty-acre parcel. Sterling presented a two-part proposed resolution to the Board that authorized Sterling to "offer and sell" the thirty-acre parcel. Sterling and Kerrigan discussed the offer and Sterling was told to change the "offer and sell" provision to "to offer for sale." He was instructed that he could only "offer" the thirty-acre parcel to Menard at a particular price. Additionally, Sterling was told that in soliciting offers for the thirty-acre parcel, he was not to negotiate the terms of a sale. Gorinsky, another lawyer hired by Kerrigan to represent his interests concerning Dage, reminded Sterling that any offer from Menard would require Board review and acceptance. He instructed Sterling to forward any offer to the Board for approval or rejection.

Finally, Sterling was told that if Menard submitted an agreement with the same objectionable provisions as the first offer, it would be rejected. Sterling agreed to follow the instructions of the Board. Based on the discussion, Sterling drafted a new resolution, which stated that he was authorized "to take such actions as are necessary to offer for sale our 30 acre parcel . . . for a price not less than $1,200,000."

Piccolo was a member of the board of directors and a financial consultant retained by Kerrigan. On December 6, 1993, Sterling informed Piccolo that Menard had agreed to make another offer. Piccolo reminded Sterling of his obligation to secure Board approval of the offer. Menard forwarded a second proposed purchase agreement to Sterling. This offer was for the purchase of the entire thirty-acre parcel for $1,450,000.

During a week-long series of discussions beginning December 14, 1993, and unknown to any other member of the Dage Board, Sterling negotiated several minor changes in the Menard agreement and then signed the revised offer on behalf of Dage. Menard also signed, accepting the offer. Under a paragraph of the agreement, Sterling, as president of Dage, represented as follows: "The persons signing this Agreement on behalf of the Seller are duly authorized to do so and their signatures bind the Seller in accordance with the terms of this Agreement." No one at Dage had informed Menard that Sterling's authority with respect to the sale of the thirty-acre parcel was limited to only the solicitation of offers.

Upon learning of the signed agreement with Menard, the Board instructed Sterling to extricate Dage from the agreement. Menard filed suit to require Dage to specifically perform the agreement and also for damages.

The trial court ruled in favor of Dage. The court of appeals affirmed, finding that Sterling did not have the express or apparent authority to bind the corporation in this land transaction.

SULLIVAN, Justice

. . . .

Two main classifications of authority are generally recognized: "actual authority" and "apparent authority." Actual authority is created "by written or spoken words or other conduct of the principal which, reasonably interpreted, causes the agent to believe that the principal desires him so to act on the principal's account." Apparent authority refers to a third party's reasonable belief that the principal has authorized the acts of its agent, it arises from the principal's indirect or direct manifestations to a third party and not from the representations or acts of the agent, . . .

" 'Inherent agency power is a term used . . . to indicate the power of an agent which is derived not from authority, apparent authority or estoppel, but solely from the agency relation and exists for the protection of persons harmed by or dealing with a servant or other agent.' "

. . . .

We find the concept of inherent authority—rather than actual or apparent authority—controls our analysis in this case. Menard did not negotiate and ultimately contract with a lower-tiered employee or a prototypical "general" or "special" agent, with respect to whom actual or apparent authority might be at issue. Menard dealt with the president of the corporation, whom "'[t]he law recognizes . . . [as one of] the officers [who] are the means, the hands and the head, by which corporations normally act.'"

. . . .

Distilled to its basics, we find that Sterling had inherent authority here if: (1) first, Sterling acted within the usual and ordinary scope of his authority as president; (2) second, Menard reasonably believed that Sterling was authorized to contract for the sale and purchase of Dage real estate; and (3) third, Menard had no notice that Sterling was not authorized to sell the 30-acre parcel without Board approval.

. . . [T]he trial court entered findings of fact and conclusions of law. Having accepted the findings of fact, we review them to see if they will support a finding that Sterling had the inherent authority as president to bind Dage in this transaction.

As to whether Sterling acted within the usual and ordinary scope of his authority as president, the trial court found that Sterling, a director and substantial shareholder of Dage, had served as Dage's president from its inception; had managed the affairs of Dage for an extended period of time with little or no Board oversight; and had purchased real estate for Dage without Board approval. However, the trial court reached the conclusion that "[t]he record persuasively demonstrates that the land transaction in question was an extraordinary transaction" for Dage, which manufactures electronic video products. Thus, the court concluded that "Sterling was not performing an act that was appropriate in the ordinary course of Dage's business."

. . . .

Given that the trial court found that Sterling, as president of the company since its inception, had managed its affairs for an extended period of time with little or no Board oversight and, in particular, had purchased real estate for Dage in the past without Board approval, we conclude that Sterling's actions at issue here were acts that "usually accompany or are incidental to transactions which [he was] authorized to conduct."

Next, we must determine whether Menard reasonably believed that Sterling was authorized to contract for the sale and purchase of Dage real estate. While Sterling's apparent authority to bind Dage was "vitiated" by Menard's knowledge that the sale of Dage real estate required Board approval, this information did not defeat Sterling's inherent authority as Dage president to bind the corporation in a "setting" where he was the sole negotiator.

. . . [C]onsidering that the "agent" in this case is a general officer of the corporation (as opposed to an "appointed general agent" or "company general manager"), we find that Menard "should not be required to scrutinize too carefully the mandates of [this] permanent . . . agent . . . who [did] no more than what is usually done by a corporate president."

Here, the facts establish that Menard reasonably believed that Sterling was authorized to contract for the sale and purchase of Dage real estate. We begin with the premise that "'the acts of a corporation done through its officers are acts done per se.'" Next, we note that at all times "Sterling held himself out as president of Dage." In fact, "Sterling ha[d] served as president of Dage since its inception"; as noted in the preceding section, he was a substantial shareholder and member of the six-person Board of Directors; he had managed the affairs of Dage for an extended period of time with little or no Board oversight; and he had purchased real estate for Dage without Board approval. And although "early in the transaction, Sterling advised [Menard] that he was required to go back to his 'partners' to obtain authority to sell the entire thirty acres[, Sterling later] confirmed that he had the authority from his Board of Directors to proceed."

. . . .

We also find it reasonable for Menard not to scrutinize Sterling's personal "acknowledge[ment] that he signed the agreement for the purchase and sale of the real estate by authority of Dage's board of directors." We believe this especially to be the case where (1) Sterling himself was a member of the Board, (2) the agreement contained an express representation that "[t]he persons signing this Agreement on behalf of the Seller are duly authorized to do so and their signatures bind the Seller in accordance with the terms of this Agreement," and (3) Menard was aware that Dage's corporate counsel, . . . was involved in the review of the terms of the agreement.

Finally, we consider whether Menard had notice that Sterling was not authorized to sell the 30-acre parcel without Board approval. The record does not indicate that Menard was aware of the existence of the consent resolution, much less that it limited Sterling's authority as president. Nor was there evidence that either the Board or Sterling informed Menard that Sterling's authority with respect to the sale of the 30-acre parcel was limited to only the solicitation of offers. . . .

. . . .

DECISION AND REMEDY The court found that the president of a closely held corporation had inherent authority to bind the company involving the sale of real estate. In an agency relationship, an agent has inherent authority that may subject his or her principal to liability. A president of a corporation has a considerable inherent authority to bind the principal, that is, the corporation.

CRITICAL THINKING: REASONING BEHIND THE LAW Why should there ever be implied or inherent authority in an agency relationship?

Professional Agents. A **professional agent** is in a business that handles contracts in a particular field. Often, the state government licenses professional agents to represent principals in contracts in those fields. Examples of professional agents are insurance agents, real estate brokers, travel agents, attorneys, and entertainment agents.

For example, because real estate brokers are licensed to represent a person who wants to sell his real property, a real estate broker is a professional agent. A "real estate agent" is actually a subagent of the real estate broker and only can represent a person through her employer, the real estate broker. A businessperson needs to learn the lines of authority in a particular business in order to determine the functions of professional agents.

The Employee as an Agent

The law defines an employee as one employed by the employer to perform services. The employer controls the employee's conduct. The employer establishes the time of work, the work to be performed, the location at which the work is performed, and other similar directions.

Agency law may apply under the right circumstances to the employer–employee relationship. The rules governing this relationship arose out of the impact of the Industrial Revolution and, more recently, social legislation. The impact of social legislation will be discussed in Chapters 22 and 23.

The employer–employee relationship is included in this chapter because frequently an employee is also an agent for her employer–principal. For example, Malini is employed by a large department store as a clerk in the jewelry section. When she stocks or straightens inventory, she is an employee. When Malini sells a bracelet, she is an agent who contracts with a customer on behalf of her employer, who is also the principal. In both cases, she is an employee. In contrast, a person employed as an electrician in the department store is strictly an employee and has no authority to transact business on the employer's behalf. The employer is liable, however, for negligent torts that the electrician commits on the job.

CYBERLAW

Uniform Computer Information Transactions Act

A new uniform act, the Uniform Computer Information Transactions Act (UCITA), has been approved by the National Conference of Commissioners on Uniform State Laws. The UCITA, which focuses on computer information, has been passed by several states.

One part of the act is involved with electronic agents. The traditional contract concepts do not function when you have a computer program that sends automated responses to other computers where prices are listed. The UCITA provides rules that validate electronic agents. A business is held liable for contracts entered into by its electronic agent.

Two electronic agents (one representing the purchaser and the other the supplier) may enter into a binding contract without any individual being involved. The agents are programmed to solicit bids for these goods and accept the lowest bid over the Web. Electronic agents are used to purchase routine items from electronic catalogs available on the Web.

INFOTRAC RESEARCH ACTIVITY

Go to InfoTrac and type in "Uniform Computer Information Transactions Act." More than 100 articles are listed on this subject. Many organizations oppose this legislation. Review these articles and determine why so many groups are opposed to it. Which groups are opposed to it and which are in favor of it? Summarize your answer.

Duties of Agents and Principals

Once the principal–agent relationship has been created, both parties have duties that govern their conduct. The agent owes to the principal a high **fiduciary duty**, that is, one based on trust and honesty and a duty to act with the utmost good faith. The principal, however, has very limited duties toward the agent, as will become apparent later in this chapter.

The Agent's Duty to the Principal

The duties that an agent owes to a principal are set out in the agency agreement and are imposed by law. Duties are also implied from the agency relationship itself. Duties exist between the principal and the agent, even if the principal's identity is disclosed to a third party. Generally, by operation of law, the agent owes the principal the following five duties: performance, loyalty, obedience, accounting, and notification.

The Duty of Performance. An implied condition in every agency contract is the agent's agreement to use reasonable diligence and skill in performing the work. When an agent fails to perform the work in this manner, liability for breach of the agency contract can occur. In addition, the principal may be liable to a third party for any negligent act of the agent that occurs within the context of the contract.

For example, a principal hires a real estate broker to sell her house in California. A potential buyer asks how many square feet the house has. The real estate broker negligently answers "2,700 square feet," because he is too lazy to look up the precise footage and he considers himself to be good at guessing. When the buyer finds out that the actual size is 2,500 square feet, the principal is liable for the agent's negligent conduct, because the action is within the context of the contract. Of course, the agent is in turn liable to the principal if the buyer successfully collects money for damages against the principal.

The degree of skill or care required of an agent is that expected of a reasonable person under similar circumstances. Although this standard usually is interpreted to mean "ordinary care," if an agent has presented himself as possessing special skills (such as those of an accountant or an attorney), the agent is expected to exercise the skill claimed. Even if the agent is not paid, he must exercise the same degree of skill or care as a paid agent. Failure to do so constitutes a breach of the agent's duty. When an agent performs carelessly or negligently, then he also is liable in tort.

The Duty of Loyalty. Loyalty is one of the most fundamental duties in a fiduciary relationship. The agent has the duty to act solely for the principal's benefit and not for her own interest or that of a third party. This fiduciary duty is owed only in one direction: from the agent to the principal.

For example, International Business Machines (IBM) has the right to appoint two sales agents to the same territory, unless IBM has specifically contracted with one agent for an exclusive territory. The IBM sales agent, however, has no right to represent more than one computer manufacturer.

An agent must refrain from any personal dealings that detract from the good of the principal. An agent employed by a principal to purchase property, for example, cannot buy that property for herself and then resell the property to the principal. Likewise, an agent employed to sell property cannot purchase the property without the principal's consent. In short, the agent's loyalty must be undivided. Otherwise, the agent has a conflict of interest with the principal.

If the agent would like to purchase the property, he must make full disclosure to the principal. If the principal allows the purchase after full disclosure, no conflict of interest arises. The agent's actions must strictly benefit the principal and must not result in any secret profit for the agent.

The Duty of Obedience. When an agent acts on behalf of the principal, the agent has a duty to obey all lawful and clearly stated instructions from the principal. The agent violates this duty whenever she deviates from those instructions. If the circumstances merit it—for example, during emergency situations when the principal cannot be consulted—the agent may deviate from such instructions without violating this duty. Whenever the principal's instructions are not stated clearly, the agent can fulfill the duty of obedience by acting in good faith and in a reasonable manner under the circumstances.

The Duty of Accounting. The agent has a duty to the principal to keep and make available an accounting of all property and money received and paid out on the principal's behalf. The principal is entitled to receive all gifts from third persons collected by the agent. For example, an airline gives an agent a gift for qualifying as a frequent flyer. Because the agent accumulated the mileage while traveling on business for the principal, the gift received by the agent belongs to the principal.

Commingling of personal and agency funds is not allowed. The agent has a duty to maintain separate accounts, one for personal funds and another for the principal's funds. Whenever a licensed professional, such as an attorney, real estate broker, or insurance agent, violates the duty to account, she may be subject to disciplinary proceedings by the appropriate regulatory institution. These proceedings are in addition to the agent's liability to the principal for failure to account.

The Duty of Notification. A maxim in agency law is "All the agent knows, the principal knows." This expression refers to the duty of notification. The agent must notify the principal of all matters that come to his attention concerning the subject matter of the agency and that are within the agency's scope. When the agent notifies the principal, the principal has **actual knowledge**.

When the agent fails to notify the principal, the common law has adopted what is called a **legal fiction**, which means in this case, that whatever the agent knows, the principal also knows. A legal fiction is an assumption in law; in this case, the law assumes the principal has the same actual knowledge that the agent possesses. Under these circumstances, the principal is said to have **constructive knowledge** of the notice to an agent.

Regardless of the actual incident, the law treats this matter as if it had occurred according to the legal fiction version. Even if the agent has not relayed the information to the principal, the law assumes that the principal knew what the agent knew and holds the principal liable. If the agent failed to inform the principal, the agent generally is liable to the principal for failing to fulfill the duty of notification. The knowledge must have been obtained, however, within the scope of the agency. Serving legal papers on the building custodian does not give constructive notice to the employer.

Problems arise when an officer, director, or employee works for two separate businesses and is involved in a transaction that affects both employers. In the following case, the court was faced with several problems that arose when one person, who was a director and an officer in two different businesses, lent a pickup truck belonging to one business to the other.

CASE 17.3	

Supreme Court of
Montana, 1994
874 P.2d 1225

WILLIAMS v. STATE MEDICAL OXYGEN & SUPPLY, INC.

BACKGROUND AND FACTS Brian Cloutier was an officer and director for Cay Enterprises and an officer and director for State Medical Oxygen & Supply, Inc. On behalf of Cay Enterprises, he had Craig Williams and five other teenagers, all employees of Cay Enterprises, move several truckloads of mattresses.

Cloutier arranged to have a State Medical pickup truck left at his home to be used for the job. He gave the keys to the pickup truck to one of the teenagers, who then drove it. He told the teenagers to move as many mattresses in each load as they could. Cloutier also instructed them not to sit on the tailgate of the pickup truck when moving the load. Cloutier provided no ropes or other items to secure the load.

Williams was sitting on top of a load of mattresses when the pickup truck turned a corner. He fell off the pickup truck and hit his head on the pavement. Williams suffered injuries as a result of this fall. He sued State Medical, as well as Cay Enterprises. State Medical prevailed against Williams, who appealed.

Justice NELSON

. . . .

In the instant case, the District Court ruled that the pickup was under the control of State Medical's officer, Cloutier, before he turned the keys over to the Cay Enterprises' employees. That being the case, it follows then, that because Cloutier had control over the pickup before he turned it over to Cay Enterprises' employees, he also had the power to prevent Cay Enterprises' employees from using the vehicle. Therefore, a question of negligent entrustment . . . remains. Was State Medical, through its officer and director, Cloutier, negligent at the time of providing the pickup to Cay Enterprises' employees, if it knew or should have known that Cay Enterprises' employees would likely use the pickup or conduct themselves in such a manner as to create an unreasonable risk of harm to others?

. . . .

The first principle holds, that an officer of a corporation, when acting within the course and scope of his employment, is an agent of the corporation when dealing with third parties.

. . . .

Turning to the second principle, imputing knowledge to two separate corporations which are dealing with one another through a common officer, we start with the premise that under Montana law, the knowledge of an agent is imputed to the principal. As a general rule, where there are two corporations, dealing with one another through a common officer, the question of whether one corporation is to be charged with notice of what is known to the agent by virtue of his relation to the other corporation depends on the circumstances of each case. "However, [a] common officer's knowledge of the affairs of one corporation will be imputed to the other when such knowledge is present in his mind and memory at the time he engaged in a transaction on behalf of such other corporation, or when such knowledge comes to him while acting for such other corporation in his official capacity, or while acting as an agent of such corporation, and within the scope of his authority. . . ."

Therefore, albeit he was going to supervise and manage the mattress moving project on behalf of Cay Enterprises, the knowledge Cloutier had regarding how he would manage and supervise the mattress moving project, at the time he turned control of the pickup over to the Cay Enterprises employees, must be imputed to State Medical.

DECISION AND REMEDY The court reaffirmed the law that a common officer's knowledge of the affairs of one corporation will be imputed to the other corporation when such knowledge is present in his mind and memory at the time he engages in a transaction on behalf of the other corporation.

CRITICAL THINKING: PREVENTIVE LAW Discuss which rules a business should have concerning the use of property by the directors, officers, or employees when the use is not for the business's benefit.

Principal's Duties to the Agent

The principal's duties to the agent are compensation, reimbursement and indemnification, cooperation, and safe working conditions. These duties may be set out in a contract or be implied by law.

The Duty of Compensation. The principal must pay for the agent's services unless it is a gratuitous agency relationship. A **gratuitous agency** occurs when the agent performs services without compensation. Even though the agent may not be paid, she still owes the principal the duties of performance and loyalty, as discussed in the previous section.

The principal must agree to compensate the agent for his services before the agent is entitled to remuneration. When the amount of compensation is agreed on by the parties, the principal owes the duty to compensate the agent on completion of the specified activities. If no amount is agreed on, the principal usually pays either the reasonable value of the agent's service or can look to the customary amount of compensation for such services. For example, in the auction of horses, the auctioneer normally takes a 10 percent commission.

The Duty of Reimbursement and Indemnification. When an agent enters into a contract with a third party to purchase something, the principal, not the agent, has the ultimate duty to pay the third party. The principal may use one of several methods to pay the third party. The principal may arrange with the third party to pay her directly, the principal may advance the funds to the agent to pay the third party, or the agent may pay the third party out of her own pocket.

In the last case, the principal then has the duty to reimburse the agent for expenses that the agent has incurred while performing her job for the principal. If an agent pays for other necessary expenses in the course of reasonable performance of agency duties, the principal has the duty to reimburse the agent.

The principal has an overlapping duty to indemnify (compensate) the agent for any losses that the agent suffers while performing her duties for the principal. For example, if the agent loses money while performing a contract, the principal must compensate the agent for those losses.

Agents can recover no expenses or losses incurred by their own misconduct or negligence. For example, if an agent has the principal's money on hand to pay a bill on time but negligently fails to pay it, the agent must pay the late penalty. The principal has no duty to reimburse the agent.

The Duty of Cooperation. A principal has a duty both to cooperate with and to assist an agent in performing her duties. The principal must do nothing to prevent such performance. For example, a seller hires a real estate broker to sell a house. The broker finds a buyer who is willing, able, and ready to buy the house. The seller-principal must cooperate with the agent, must sign the papers in a timely manner, and must do nothing to prohibit the buyer from proceeding with the purchase.

The Duty to Provide Safe Working Conditions. The principal must provide safe premises, equipment, and conditions for agents and employees. The principal has a duty to inspect working conditions and to warn agents and employees about unsafe areas. If the agent is also an employee (as in the case of a department store clerk), the employer's liability frequently is covered by workers' compensation insurance, which is the primary remedy for an employee's injury on the job.

If the employer has eleven or more employees, federal law requires the employer to display a poster on job safety and health protection in an area where employees gather, such as in a breakroom. The employer also must post a summary of the injuries and illnesses for that location and must post citations for violations of safety standards.

Liability of Principals and Agents to Third Parties

Because the agent deals with third parties, the following sections examine the rights of the third party. Both the principal and the agent may be liable to a third person based either on contract or tort law.

Principal's and Agent's Liability for Contracts

In their relationships with third parties, principals are classified as *disclosed, partially disclosed,* or *undisclosed.* A **disclosed principal** is a principal whose identity is known by the third party at the time at which he makes the contract with the agent. A **partially disclosed principal** is a principal whose identity is unknown by the third party, but the third party knows that the agent is acting for a principal at the time the contract is made. An **undisclosed principal** is a principal whose identity is totally unknown by the third party, and the third party has no knowledge that the agent is acting in any agency capacity at the time the contract is made.

Liability of Disclosed Principals. If an agent acts within the scope of his authority, a disclosed principal is liable to a third party for a contract made by the agent. In these situations, an agent has no contractual liability for the principal's or the third party's nonperformance.

Liability of Partially Disclosed or Undisclosed Principals. In most states, if the principal is partially disclosed or undisclosed, the principal and agent are both treated as parties to the contract. The third party can elect to hold either the partially disclosed principal or the agent liable if the contract is not performed.

If the principal is undisclosed, the agent is deemed to be dealing directly with the third party. Thus, for an undisclosed principal, the agent is liable as a party on the contract. Once the third party discovers that the previously undisclosed principal exists, the third party can elect to sue either the principal or the agent.

For example, Walt Disney Company decides to build another amusement park. Research shows that in a specific prime tourist area, the land needs for the new park will be met if Disney purchases five parcels of land. Disney, however, knows that if word gets out that it plans to purchase land, the price will be higher. Disney hires five different agents to make the five different land purchases. Disney is the undisclosed principal. The five agents make the purchases over the period of a year, each in his or her own name. The sellers relied on the individual agents' credit and reputation, not on that of Disney.

Because each agent has acted within the scope of his or her authority, the undisclosed principal, Disney, must perform in accordance with the contracts made by each of its agents. Even though Disney's identity was not disclosed to the sellers of each of the five properties, Disney must ensure that each of its agents can perform on the respective contracts with each seller. Disney can enforce contracts against each seller through the respective agent, if Disney decides to remain undisclosed. Or Disney may reveal that it is the principal and enforce the contracts in its own name as a disclosed principal. The seller, however, may bring a legal action against either Disney or the agent, but not both after the seller discovers Disney.

Warranties of the Agent

Occasionally, the agent either will lack authority for an action or will exceed the scope of her or his authority. When this situation occurs, the agent, not the principal, is liable to the third party. The agent's liability to the third party is based on a breach of **implied warranty of authority**, not on breach of the contract itself.

The agent can breach the implied warranty of authority by intentionally breaching the warranty or by making a good-faith mistake. The agent is liable if the third party relied on the agent's status.

In contrast, when the third party knows at the time the contract is made that the agent is mistaken about the extent of his authority, or if the agent indicates to the third party uncertainty about the extent of his authority, the agent is not liable personally for breach of warranty. In these situations, the third party recognizes an irregularity and should have checked further about the agent's authority.

Tort Liability

Tort liability was discussed in Chapter 8. Negligence occurs when a person commits an act that she could foresee as potentially causing harm to another. An intentional act occurs when a person intends to harm another. An agent or employee always is liable for her own torts and crimes.

The question arises: Is the principal or employer liable also for the negligent acts of the agent or employee? If the employee makes a misrepresentation to a third party, is the employer liable? Is the employer liable for the intentional torts of the employee?

In the following discussion, most references will be made to the employer–employee relationship, but the same rules apply to the principal–agent relationship. Three areas will be examined: negligence and the doctrine of *respondeat superior*, misrepresentation, and intentional tort.

Negligence and the Doctrine of *Respondeat Superior*. An employer may be liable for the negligent torts of the employee if the employee commits the torts within the **scope of employment**. The employer's liability is indirect because although the employer is not itself negligent, the employer is responsible for its employee's negligent acts. The employer is liable under the **doctrine of respondeat superior**, which is Latin for "let the master answer." This theory imposes strict liability on the employer. Liability is imposed without regard to the personal fault of the employer for negligent torts committed by an employee in the course of employment.

For example, an employee works for a construction company. Part of her job is to drive the company pickup truck from one job site to another. One day the employee has a traffic accident by negligently turning left in front of an oncoming automobile. The employee is liable because she was negligent, but the company also is liable under the doctrine of *respondeat superior*.

An employer that knows or should have known that an employee is likely to commit torts is liable for the employee's acts even if the torts ordinarily would be considered outside the scope of employment. Of course, the employee is responsible for his torts. For example, a cookie manufacturer has many complaints about the actions of a salesman. The salesman goes to a grocery store, removes the competitors' products, and pushes a store manager who objects. The manufacturer is liable for the salesman's assault and battery. The manufacturer knew or should have known about the employee's acts based on earlier complaints and taken steps to prevent any further acts by the salesperson.

When an employee departs from the employer's business to take care of personal affairs, is the employer liable? It depends. If the employee's activity is a substantial departure equivalent to an utter abandonment of the employer's business, the employer is not liable.

For example, Clint, a traveling salesperson, drives his employer's automobile to call on a customer for a possible sales order. On the way to the customer's place of business, Clint deviates one block from his usual route to mail a letter at the post office. As Clint approaches the post office, he negligently runs into Doug's parked vehicle. Clint's departure from the employer's business to take care of a personal affair is minimal. Clint is still within the scope of his employment, and Clint's employer is liable to Doug.

On the other hand, if Clint picked up a few friends for a party in another city and in the process negligently ran into Doug's vehicle, Doug normally could not hold Clint's employer liable. In this case, Clint's action entails more than a minimal departure from the scope of his employment. Only Clint would be liable in this case.

The court considers the following general factors in determining if an agent's particular tortious act occurred within the course or scope of employment:

1. Did the employer authorize the act?

2. What was the time, place, and purpose of the act?

3. Was the act commonly performed by the employee on behalf of the employer?

4. To what extent was the employer's interest advanced by the act?

5. To what extent were the employee's private interests involved?

6. Did the employer furnish the means or instrumentality (for example, a truck or machine) that caused the injury?

7. Did the employer have reason to know that the employee would do the act in question and had the employee done it before?

8. Did the act involve the commission of a serious crime?

The following case involves problems of defining the scope of employment.

CASE 17.4

Supreme Court of Utah, 1991
808 P.2d 1037

CLOVER v. SNOWBIRD SKI RESORT

BACKGROUND AND FACTS Snowbird Ski Resort employed Zulliger as a chef at the Plaza Restaurant located at the base of the ski resort. The Mid-Gad Restaurant was located halfway up the mountain.

Zulliger's father was head chef at both restaurants. Zulliger's father instructed him to make periodic trips to the Mid-Gad to monitor its operations. Zulliger had made several inspection trips to the Mid-Gad. On one occasion, Snowbird paid him for the trip.

Snowbird preferred for its employees to ski to and from work. Part of Zulliger's compensation included season ski passes. Zulliger was asked to inspect the operation of the Mid-Gad prior to beginning work at the Plaza at 3 P.M.

Zulliger stopped at the Mid-Gad in the middle of his first run down the mountain. At the restaurant, he inspected the kitchen, talked to the personnel for twenty minutes, and ate a snack. He skied four runs before heading down the mountain to begin work.

On his final run, Zulliger jumped from a crest on the side of an intermediate run, a jump he had taken many times before. From this jump, a skier would become airborne because of the steep dropoff. It was impossible for skiers above the crest to see skiers below the crest. Snowbird knew the jump well. Snowbird ski patrol often instructed people not to jump from the crest. Furthermore, Snowbird posted a sign instructing skiers to ski slowly at this point in the run.

Zulliger ignored the sign and skied over the crest at a significant speed. Clover, who had just entered the same ski run from a point below the crest, was in Zulliger's path. As Zulliger jumped, he collided with Clover, who was hit on the head and severely injured.

Clover brought claims against Zulliger and Snowbird. The trial court, in a summary judgment, dismissed the claims against Snowbird by finding that as a matter of law, Zulliger was acting outside the scope of his employment at the time of the collision.

Chief Justice HALL

. . . .

Under the doctrine of *respondeat superior,* employers are held vicariously liable for the torts their employees commit when the employees are acting within the scope of their employment. Clover's *respondeat superior* claim was dismissed on the ground that as a matter of law, Zulliger's actions at the time of the accident were not within the scope of his employment. In a recent case, *Birkner v. Salt Lake County,* this court addressed the issue of what types of acts fall within the scope of employment. In *Birkner,* we stated that acts within the scope of employment are "those acts which are so closely connected with what the servant is employed to do, and so fairly and reasonably incidental to it, that they may be regarded as methods, even though quite improper ones, of carrying out the objectives of the employment." The question of whether an employee is acting within the scope of employment is a question of fact.

. . . .

. . . [T]here is evidence that the manager of both the Mid-Gad and the Plaza wanted an employee to inspect the restaurant and report back by 3 P.M. If Zulliger had not inspected the restaurant, it would have been necessary to send a second employee to accomplish the same purpose. Furthermore, the second employee would have most likely used the ski lifts and ski runs in traveling to and from the restaurant.

. . . .

Under the circumstances of the instant case, it is entirely possible for a jury to reasonably believe that at the time of the accident, Zulliger had resumed his employment and that Zulliger's deviation was not substantial enough to constitute a total abandonment of employment.

DECISION AND REMEDY The court found that a jury must decide whether Zulliger's actions were within the scope of his employment. His actions were not, as a matter of law, outside the scope of his employment with Snowbird. Clover will have her day in court.

COMMENT A similar incident occurred in 1997 in Vail, Colorado. An employee of a ski lift company left when his shift was over. Although an expert skier, he ignored poor snow conditions and safety precautions and was skiing too fast for the conditions. He collided with another skier who was killed as a consequence. In 2000, the expert skier was tried and convicted of negligent homicide.

CRITICAL THINKING: ETHICAL ISSUE A delivery person decides to go fishing while using the business vehicle. While driving to the lake, he causes an accident. Discuss whether the employer should be liable to the injured party.

Misrepresentation. Whenever a third person sustains losses because of the agent's misrepresentation, the principal is exposed to tort liability. The key to a principal's liability is whether the agent actually or apparently was authorized to make representations and whether such representations were made within the scope of the agency.

When a principal has placed an agent in a position to defraud a third party, the principal is liable for the agent's fraudulent acts. For example, Harmon is a loan officer for State Employees Credit Union. In the ordinary course of her job, Harmon approves and services loans and has access to customers' credit records. Harmon calls Lopez, a credit union member who has an outstanding loan. Harmon falsely represents to Lopez that the credit union believes that he is about to default on his loan. She threatens to call in the loan (meaning that Lopez must pay the loan in full) unless he provides additional collateral, such as stocks and bonds. Lopez gives Harmon numerous stock certificates, which Harmon keeps in her own possession. She later uses them to make personal investments and loses money on all these investments.

The credit union is liable to Lopez for losses sustained on the stocks, even though the credit union had no direct role or knowledge of the fraudulent scheme. The principal (the credit union) placed the agent (Harmon) in a position that conveyed to third persons (such as Lopez) that Harmon had the authority to make statements and perform acts consistent with her position's ordinary duties. When an agent appears to act within the scope of the authority that the position of agency confers, but actually takes advantage of a third party, the principal who placed the agent in that position is liable. For example, if a security guard had told Lopez that the credit union required additional security for a loan, Lopez would not be justified in relying on that person's authority to make that representation. Lopez reasonably could expect, however, that the loan officer was telling the truth.

Intentional Torts. The employer may be liable for its employee's intentional torts when the employee commits those acts within the scope of employment. The employer's liability is based on one of four theories: (1)

LEGAL HIGHLIGHT

Good Credit Means a Job

Chapter 14 discussed credit reports and procedures to correct erroneous information that might be in a credit file. A credit report is a major tool on which businesses rely when considering the hiring of a new employee. Employers believe that the way in which a person handles his personal finances indicates his honesty and dependability. When a person has serious financial problems, he may be more likely to take advantage of the employment situation and abscond with cash, inventory, or trade secrets. Employers believe this even though no studies have justified this belief.

Some credit firms specialize in providing relevant information from a person's credit record. Stores Protective Association (SPA) assists many of the large retailers in hiring. It maintains records based on both its subscribers' information and public records.

SPA maintains records on all persons who are terminated for dishonesty by a subscriber. It preserves a copy of any written confession signed by the employee. If no written confession exists, the event causing the termination must have been videotaped or witnessed by at least two individuals, and SPA keeps these. SPA also researches public records for any convictions for felonies or criminal misdemeanors and places this information in the individual's file. It keeps the records for seven years, the maximum time allowed under the federal Fair Credit Reporting Act (FCRA). SPA must comply with the rules under the FCRA that require the applicant to give written permission for her or his credit file to be examined.

A good credit rating and clean criminal record, therefore, can affect people's careers

the employer was negligent in hiring or retaining the employee, (2) the employer is liable for certain types of employees' intentional torts, (3) the employer ratifies the intentional tort, or (4) the employer helps to commit the intentional tort.

In a previous section, we saw that an employer, even though it acted responsibly, could be held liable for the negligent acts of its agent or employee under the doctrine of *respondeat superior.* Usually, an employer is not responsible for the intentional torts of its employees. Third persons harmed by the intentional torts of an employee, however, may bring a legal action against the employer for negligence in hiring or supervising the employee.

The law allows negligent hiring actions even though the employee's wrongful act was outside the course or scope of his employment. The basis of these actions is that the employer knew or should have known that the employee was unfit, the employee caused the injury to another person, and a causal connection existed between the injury incurred and the employment of the employee.

Many laws restrict an employer from inquiring into a potential employee's background. An employer, however, will be held liable if it fails to make the proper background checks or if it fails to investigate and take appropriate action for reported incidents of wrongdoing. For example, in one case, a real estate firm employed a person who had been convicted of passing bad checks. The employer knew of the criminal record. The firm was held liable for negligence in hiring when the employee forged legal documents to obtain a commission from a client of the real estate firm. Another example concerns an apartment manager who murdered a child who was collecting money for her newspaper route. The apartment owner had not conducted an investigation of the manager before hiring him. An investigation would have disclosed that the manager had a history of molesting children and had served prison time. The court held the apartment owner liable for failure to use reasonable efforts to investigate the manager's background.

The employer may be held liable for an employee's intentional torts when the employee commits them within the scope of employment. This responsibility is imposed if the employer should have anticipated the intentional act. The employer's liability, however, is very limited in most states.

For example, Duffy's Tavern hires Vicious Vic as a bouncer, knowing that he has a history of arrests for assault and battery. While working one night within the scope of his employment, Vicious Vic ferociously attacks a patron who "looked at him funny." Duffy's Tavern will bear the responsibility for Vicious Vic's assault and battery, because it knew he had a propensity for committing such acts and because he committed this tort during the normal course of his job.

If the employer ratifies the intentional tort or participates in the intentional tort committed by the employee within the scope of employment, the employer is liable for the harm caused by the intentional tort. This liability is imposed directly because the employer directly engaged in or ratified the intentional act that harmed a third person.

For example, Dishonest John defrauds Widow Green by convincing her to sign a contract to sell her house by promising to trade her house for an ostrich farm located in the Nevada desert. She read that a person can make lots of money raising and selling ostriches. No such ostrich farm actually exists. Dishonest John takes the contract to his employer and explains the transaction in detail. The employer is a land developer who wants to tear down the house and, along with other land he has purchased that adjoins Green's land, he plans to develop a commercial center. John's employer agrees to the contract. By his agreement, the employer has ratified the contract. Green finds out that the ostrich farm does not exist and she sues both Dishonest John and his employer. This liability is imposed even when the original intentional act was committed by an employee.

Termination of the Agency Relationship

An agency can be terminated either by an act by one of the parties or by operation of law. Once the relationship between the principal and agent ends, the agent no longer has the right to bind the principal. The principal must notify third persons when the agency ends to stop an agent's apparent authority.

Termination by Act of the Parties

Usually, the agency agreement sets out the time period during which the agency relationship will exist. The agency ends when that time expires. If no definite time is stated, the agency continues for a reasonable time, depending on the circumstances and the nature of the agency relationship, and can be terminated at will by either party.

An agent can be hired to complete a particular objective, such as the purchase of a computer system for a business. The agency relationship automatically ends after the computer system has been purchased because the reason for the agency relationship no longer exists.

Parties can cancel (rescind) a contract by mutually agreeing to terminate the contractual relationship. For example, Leslie no longer wants Cisco to be her agent, and Cisco no longer wants to work for Leslie. Either Leslie or Cisco can communicate with the other the intent to end the relationship. Agreement to terminate the agency relationship effectively relieves each party of any further rights, duties, and powers inherent in the relationship.

LEGAL HIGHLIGHT

Use of the Internet While at Work

Many businesses have rules for employees using the Internet while at work. The computers are owned by the employer, which allows them to monitor employees' use of them.

Employers recognize that employees must take care of some personal business during normal working hours. Allowing them to use the computer for personal business reduces their need to take time off from work. A business might lose a few minutes a day of the employee's productive time, but save a half or full day if the employee is not able to conduct some personal business over the Internet. For example, employees can check on their children in day care or school via the Internet. Employers need to balance the needs of the business with the employees' personal needs.

LEGAL HIGHLIGHT

How Employers Are Firing Employees

In the past, it was common that the last persons hired were the first ones terminated when the employer needed to reduce the number of employees. This practice arose in part because of labor unions trying to protect the longest-employed workers. Labor unions included this practice is union contracts.

During the past decades, however, fewer employees have joined unions. Businesses have changed their practices in reviewing and terminating employees. Today, management reviews their employees every six to twelve months. Percentages are used to rank employees in three or four categories: superior, excellent, satisfactory, and needs improvement. The managers attempt to protect their employees, but some employees must be placed in the "needs improvement" category. Most companies will allow the employees ranked in the "needs improvement" category six months to improve. When a person is in this category, however, she or he should be looking for a new position.

Termination by Operation of Law

Mental incompetency or death of either the principal or the agent automatically and immediately terminates an ordinary agency relationship. Knowledge of the death is not required. For example, Cassie sends Marco to Mexico to purchase a rare coin. Before Marco makes the purchase, Cassie dies. Marco's status as an agent ends at the moment of death, even though Marco does not know that Cassie has died.

An exception to this rule applies to banks. The Uniform Commercial Code, Section 4-405, allows banks to honor checks up to ten days after their customers' death. A bank does not honor any payment of notes or drafts after death, however.

The durable power of attorney is another exception to the rule that an agency is terminated by the principal's incapacity. A durable power of attorney is specifically worded to allow the attorney–in–fact to act on behalf of the principal when he becomes mentally incapacitated.

When an agency's specific subject matter is destroyed or lost, the agency is terminated. For example, Priscilla employs Mark to sell her house. Prior to any sale, a hurricane destroys the house. Mark's agency and authority to sell Priscilla's house are both ended. In addition, when it becomes impossible for the agent to perform the agency's responsibilities lawfully because of war or because of a change in the law, the agency terminates.

When an event occurs that has an unusual effect on the subject matter of the agency so that the agent reasonably can infer that the principal will not want the agency to continue, the agency terminates. Sima hires Aaron to sell a tract of land for $1 million. Subsequently, Aaron learns that Disney Corporation plans a resort and theme park across the road and the land now is worth $5 million. The agency and Aaron's authority to sell the land for $1 million both are terminated.

Notice Required for Termination

When an agency terminates by operation of law because of a principal's mental incompetency, death, or some other unforeseen circumstance, no duty exists to notify third persons. If, however, the parties themselves have terminated the agency, the principal must inform any third parties who knew of the agency's existence that it is terminated.

The principal is expected to notify directly any third person who the principal knows has dealt with the agent. For third persons who have heard about the agency but have not dealt with the agent, constructive notice is sufficient. In other words, a notice should be published in a newspaper within the general area or in commercial journals for technical employees, stating that the principal no longer employs the agent. Until notice is given, the agent retains apparent authority for a reasonable length of time.

Independent Contractors

An **independent contractor** is not an employee, but may be an agent under certain limited situations. Two major issues arise with independent contractors. The first problem is liability; the second is responsibility for tax payment to the Internal Revenue Service. The tax issue is discussed later in the section titled *Employees or Independent Contractors?*

A person who hires an independent contractor is said to have employed the independent contractor. When the term *employment* is used in connection with an independent contractor, however, its meaning differs from the legal context of employer–employee. The employer of an independent contractor has no control over the details of the independent contractor's performance. Because the employer does not control the independent contractor, the employer normally is not responsible for the independent contractor's torts. The Restatement, Second, Agency in Section 2 defines an independent contractor as "a person who contracts with another to do something for him but who is not controlled by the other nor subject to the other's right to control with respect to his physical conduct in the performance of the undertaking. He may or may not be an agent."

The courts review many elements to determine whether a relationship is one of employer–employee or of employer–independent contractor. The following are some factors considered by the courts:

1. The extent of control exercised by the employer over the details of the work,

2. The type of job, business, or occupation involved and the amount of skill required to perform the job,

3. Who supplies the tools or equipment,

4. The length of employment,

5. The method of payment, and

6. The tax returns filed by both parties.

The construction industry is a good example of an employer–independent contractor relationship. If an owner of raw land wants to build an office building, she hires a general contractor, who is responsible for building the office complex. The general contractor in turn hires subcontractors, such as electrical subcontractors or plumbing subcontractors, who are responsible for specific portions of the building.

The general contractor is an independent contractor, and the property owner does not control this professional's acts. The property owner has no contractual relationship with the subcontractors whom the general contractor hires; thus, the owner is not responsible for the subcontractors' acts.

Some states, however, have changed this rule by statute. The statute makes the general contractor an agent for the owner (principal). When the general contractor enters into contracts with subcontractors, the general contractor acts as an agent for the owner, making the owner liable as the principal.

Consider this example. A property owner hires a real estate broker to negotiate a property sale. The owner not only contracted with an independent contractor (the real estate broker), but also established an agency relationship for the specific purpose of finding a third party who will enter into a contract to purchase the property.

A person retaining an independent contractor's services normally is not responsible for the tortious acts of the independent contractor, because of the lack of control over him. An employer is responsible for the acts of an independent contractor, however, when the independent contractor performs one of the employer's duties, as established by law. For example, a department store is liable when it hires an independent security agency to supply security and a security officer makes an illegal arrest for shoplifting. The store, along with the security agency, is liable to the victim. An employer is liable for acts of independent contractors when the activity involves ultrahazardous conduct, such as handling explosives.

Employees or Independent Contractors?

Workers' classification as employees or as independent contractors is significant for federal income tax and employment tax purposes. Employers withhold income, Social Security, and Medicare taxes from employees' wages to forward to the federal government. The same taxes are collected from independent contractors when they pay estimated taxes.

Workers' classification as employees or independent contractors is also significant for a variety of federal and state labor and worker protection laws. These laws cover only employees, not independent contractors. These protections include unemployment insurance, workers' compensation, wage and hour requirements, and family and medical leave requirements. Additionally, independent contractors have no rights to sick leave, vacation time, pension and profit benefits, and other common employee benefits.

The government rarely questions an employer's classification of a worker as an employee. When an employer hires workers as independent contractors, however, government agencies, especially the Internal Revenue Service (IRS), may challenge the decision. A common law test of the employer–employee classification focuses on whether the employer controls the result of the worker's services and the means by which the worker achieves that result.

In company audits, the IRS can reclassify independent contractors as employees. The employer then is liable for the full amount of income taxes and the employee's share of Social Security and Medicare taxes that it failed to withhold for all years open under the statute of limitations. In addition, the employer remains liable for the employer's share of Social Security, Medicare, and unemployment insurance taxes plus interest on these amounts. The IRS can also assess penalties.

The employer's liability for underwithholding can be abated to the extent that the employer demonstrates that the misclassified worker paid income, Social Security, and Medicare taxes. Data to support the determinations, unfortunately, often are difficult to obtain, especially when the worker no longer provides services to the employer.

After an IRS audit of Microsoft Corporation, the Ninth Circuit Court of Appeals in 1996 upheld a lower court's finding that Microsoft had misclassified workers as independent contractors. Before working for Microsoft, these workers signed agreements indicating knowledge of their responsibilities for paying the federal and state income taxes, Social Security and Medicare taxes, and for providing for their own benefits. The case involved software testers and technical manual writers. They worked for years doing the same kind of work as regular Microsoft employees. Because they were independent contractors, however, they could not participate in the company's stock-purchase plan and its tax-deferred 401(k) plan. The case was appealed by Microsoft, but the U.S. Supreme Court refused to grant the writ of *certiorari*. Notice that the Ninth Circuit's holding is the opposite of that of the *DuPont* case discussed in the later section on *Employee Leasing*.

Employment Law

Federal and state statutes regulate many areas of private employment law. These statutes will be examined in Chapters 22 and 23. A body of common law exists in areas that are not regulated by various statutes. These areas include employment contracts and employee termination.

Employment Contracts

Employer–employee relationships are created by a contract. The contract provides the employer with the right to control the employee's conduct, workplace, work habits, and benefits enjoyed within the scope of employment. An employment contract is a mutual agreement between the employer and the employee. Basic contract rules apply. The parties can include any contract terms, as long as these terms conform with all statutes and public policy. For example, a contract today for an hourly wage of $1 violates the minimum wage rate set by the federal Fair Labor Standards Act and is illegal.

In some written employment contracts, employees agree that, should they ever leave their employment, they will not accept employment with a competitor. This clause in the employment contract is called a **covenant not to compete**. If the scope of the prohibition is reasonable in geographic area and duration, the covenant generally is enforceable.

Employee Leasing

A company known as a professional employer organization (PEO) operates in a manner similar to the personnel administration in large corporations. For a small business, the benefits of working with a PEO can be very attractive.

A PEO handles the myriad of details necessary to employing personnel, including payroll administration, income tax withholding, medical benefits, life insurance, disability insurance, workers' compensation, unemployment insurance, retirement plans, tax deferred retirement plans, and compliance with employment statutes and labor laws. The cost of using a PEO runs between 2 and 8 percent of the total payroll; that is, in addition to the employer's regular costs.

The employer approves of the employee to be hired. The new hire is sent to the PEO, who hires the employee and processes all the paperwork. The PEO then leases the employee to the business employer. Each pay period, the funds are transferred from the employer to the PEO to cover wages, taxes, benefits, and fees. If the business decides to fire or lay off an employee, it notifies the PEO, which handles all the paperwork and payment of the final paycheck.

One benefit of using a PEO is that it can pool the employees of all its clients. With the larger pool, the PEO can negotiate lower insurance rates and can amortize the cost of benefit plans over a broader base.

The disadvantage of leasing employees is that the PEO may collapse. Some are poorly managed, while others operate fraudulently. In one case, several companies paid a PEO, but instead of distributing the payroll among the companies' employees, the money vanished along with the PEO operators. The companies are still liable to pay these workers.

Any business considering using a PEO should take a number of steps. It should obtain a list of the PEO's clients and interview a large number of them to be sure that they are satisfied with the PEO's services. If the business interviews only a few clients, it may miss the clients who have had problems and fail to discover the PEO's weaknesses. The potential client along with its accountant should review the PEO's audited financial statement. If the PEO rushes to sign up a number of new clients, some of whom are risky, the PEO may weaken its financial base.

A business should determine if the PEO has a number of clients in the same field. When a PEO knows the industry, it may be able to help a client improve its operation. The PEO should be able to tailor its program to the company's needs, such as administrating a tax-deferred benefit plan.

A business should refuse a standard contract from the PEO. The contract should be tailored to the needs of the business and its employees. Two important contract items to watch for include (1) identifying the company responsible for certain duties, especially tax withholding, and (2) ensuring that the PEO retains liability under the contract. Any contract should be reviewed by an attorney specializing in employment law.

Why would a business use leased employees? First, the business is relieved of the paperwork that the government requires. Second, if the business provides benefits, the tax laws require that the benefits be offered to all employees, not just the managers. If the business retains a few managers, they may enjoy benefits, but the business is not obligated to provide these benefits to leased employees. Third, leased employees are less likely to organize into labor unions.

In 1997, the Fourth Circuit Court of Appeals ruled that the DuPont Co. was not liable to pay standard employee benefits to leased employees.[3] An engineer, who was leased to the company, performed the same work as DuPont engineers. He worked directly for DuPont, but was laid off in 1970. He signed a contract with a national employee-leasing firm and from 1975 to 1993, he worked for other construction companies that regularly worked for DuPont. On his income tax returns and on an unemployment-benefits application, he listed the employee-leasing firm as his employer. He worked for DuPont as a leased employee until his death. His widow was denied any benefits that she would have received had he been DuPont's direct employee. Notice that the outcome of this case differed from the independent contractor situation involving Microsoft discussed in the section titled *Employees or Independent Contractors*?

Difference between Independent Contractors and Leased Employees

Differences exist between leased employees and independent contractors. A leased employee is employed by a leasing firm and leased to another employer where the person actually works. The leasing firm handles all the paperwork, such as withholding all the income and other taxes, and remits the taxes to the appropriate government agencies. Depending on the leasing arrangements, the leasing firm can establish a tax-deferred retirement plan and can purchase a health plan for the benefit of the leased employee. The leased employee usually works for long periods for one employer.

Independent contractors pay their own income and other taxes. They establish their own tax-deferred retirement plans and purchase their own health plans. Independent contractors can work for several employers at once and make their own time schedules. The less independence an independent contractor has, the more likely the IRS will find that an employment relationship exists and not an independent contractor relationship.

[3]Clark v. E.I. DuPont De Nemours, 105 F.3d 646 (4th Cir. 1997).

Modern View on Termination of Employees

If termination of the employment breaches the employment contract, the employee can seek damages. Most employment situations, however, are created without a written employment contract and are called **employment at will**. Employment at will can occur with a written contract if the employer retains the right to terminate the employee at any time either for a good reason or for no reason at all. An employee has no claim against the employer for the termination because an employee has no right to the job.

Employee-at-will situations have led to abuses by employers. Some states passed specific statutes to protect an employee from an arbitrary termination after he has been employed for a specified period of time.

Specific grounds must be established before a person can be fired. States will not allow an employer to terminate an employee who, after being ordered to commit a crime, refuses to do so.

Other states without statutory provisions have attempted through the courts to create certain rights for employees. For example, in the absence of a contract an employee manual given to all employees may be interpreted to be the employment contract. If an employer establishes certain procedures in the manual, these procedures must be followed before an employee can be fired. Otherwise, the employer is liable for breach of contract.

Many states recognize that an implied covenant of good faith and fair dealing is inherent in every employment contract. In other words, the law requires a business to treat its employees fairly, as the next case shows.

CASE 17.5

United States Court of Appeals, Ninth Circuit, 1996
82 F.3d 327
http://laws.lp.findlaw.com/getcase/9th/case/9415748.html

HUEY v. HONEYWELL, INC.

BACKGROUND AND FACTS Honeywell hired John Huey as an hourly employee to work in its shipping and receiving department. He consistently received high job performance ratings and letters of recommendation in recognition of his outstanding job performance.

Honeywell's hourly employees turned in time cards only when they worked more or less than forty hours a week. Huey's supervisor instituted a flextime policy allowing workers to work more or less than forty hours in any week as long as they made up the time. The human resources representative for the shipping and receiving department knew of this policy.

Honeywell's standards of employee conduct and disciplinary procedures were established in the company's personnel manual, but the manual was not distributed to its employees. Honeywell relied on its supervisors to inform its employees of the company's personnel manual and disciplinary procedures.

Honeywell's disciplinary procedures provided that Honeywell would give its employees a series of verbal and written warnings, along with opportunities to be heard and to improve, before they were terminated. The disciplinary procedures further provided that employees be given the benefit of any doubts during the investigation of disciplinary charges, that any termination for violation of a company policy must be supported with documentation, and that discipline was to be mitigated when an employee violated a company policy in reliance on a supervisor's representation of that policy.

One provision in the personnel manual that Honeywell's supervisors routinely failed to relay to employees was the following disclaimer: "Employment at Honeywell, Inc., is voluntarily entered into and employees are free to resign at any time. Similarly, Honeywell may terminate the employment relationship where it believes it is in the Company's best interests. The policy statements contained in this manual do not intend to negate this principle." Acting in accordance with company practice, Huey's supervisor failed to communicate this disclaimer to Huey.

Huey was one of many Honeywell employees in the shipping and receiving department to utilize the flextime policy. In doing so, Huey never claimed or received payment for any hours which he did not actually work. Huey's coworkers informed Honeywell's personnel department that they suspected Huey of falsely reporting his time. Honeywell's security division conducted an investigation.

The comparison of Huey's gate and time records revealed five inconsistencies. One inconsistency was due to Huey's attendance at a work-related seminar. The other four inconsistencies were due to the flextime policy.

Huey was suspended, pending further investigation. Further investigation failed to include any discussions with Huey or his supervisor who had created the flextime. Rather than speaking with Huey, Honeywell hired a private investigation firm, Pinkerton, Inc., to investigate.

Pinkerton engaged in the following activities. It followed Huey on his way home from work; it established surveillance points at Huey's home; it videotaped Huey's activities; and at Honeywell's request, it obtained personal information relating to Huey, his wife, and other members of Huey's family.

Honeywell's management finally called Huey in for an interview two months later. Huey tried to explain that the discrepancies on his time card were due to the flextime policy, but he was told that the decision to terminate him had already been made. Huey was told at this meeting that he was officially terminated. No other employees in Huey's department were terminated or disciplined for utilizing the flextime policy. The federal district court granted a judgment to Honeywell, Inc., and Huey appealed.

Judge FERGUSON

. . . .

Under Arizona state law, a contractual relationship between an employer and an employee with no specified duration is presumed to be "at-will" unless modified by the parties' representations or course of dealing. . . .

Three general exceptions to the at-will employment presumption have developed. First, the public policy exception to the at-will doctrine permits an at-will employee to recover for wrongful discharge upon a finding that the employer's conduct undermined an important public policy. Second, an exception based on contract law allows an at-will employee to recover for wrongful discharge upon proof of an implied-in-fact promise of employment for a specific duration. Such an implied-in-fact promise can be found in the circumstances surrounding the employment relationship, including assurances of job security in company personnel manuals or memoranda. Third, courts have found an implied-in-law covenant of "good faith and fair dealing" in employment contracts and have held employers liable in both contract and tort for breach of this covenant.

. . . .

The following actions by Honeywell created a material question of fact as to Huey's employment status as an at-will employee: (1) Honeywell developed written policies and a personnel manual adopting a progressive disciplinary program; (2) Honeywell relies on its supervisors to orally explain its personnel policies to other employees; (3) Honeywell's written policies and personnel manual were not distributed to its employees; (4) Although the personnel manual contained a disclaimer which stated that no portion of the manual was to be interpreted as altering Honeywell's at-will employment contracts, this waiver was not orally relayed to Huey and he was not given a copy of the manual; and (5) Huey was aware of other employees at Honeywell who were progressively disciplined, rather than terminated, for violating company policies.

. . . [I]f an employer does choose to issue a policy statement, in a manual or otherwise, and, by its language or by the employer's actions, encourages reliance thereon, the employer cannot be free to only selectively abide by it. Having announced a policy, the employer may not treat it as illusory. Honeywell clearly chose to issue a policy statement that it would practice progressive discipline by setting forth such a policy in its manual and relying upon its supervisors to relay this policy to other employees. Therefore, Honeywell may not treat this policy as illusory.

DECISION AND REMEDY The court reversed the granting of the judgment for the defendant and sent the case back for trial. The real question was whether Honeywell had followed its own procedures when it terminated Huey.

CRITICAL THINKING: MANAGERIAL CONSIDERATION Would you recommend that a business have a personnel manual? If so, what should be included in it? Should the employee be provided a copy? Should a business be able to terminate an employee for any reason?

Government Regulation of Employment Law

Many aspects of employment law today are controlled by government regulation. Federal and state laws govern the relationship between management and labor. Discrimination on the basis of gender, race, national origin, religious beliefs, and other invidious classifications is forbidden by statutes. We will examine the government's role in employment law in Chapters 22 and 23.

International Consideration

Decision Making by Employees

U.S. companies operate in a fairly free environment concerning employee relations. Employees rarely serve on boards of directors or have input into the business decision-making process. Other countries, especially European countries and Japan, have a different attitude toward employees.

In other industrialized countries, a distinctive management style exists. Often a two-tiered board of directors governs the corporation. One level supervises the day-to-day activities, whereas the other deals with long-range planning. Substantial employee representation on the supervisory board of directors is required. Both boards of directors must agree to employee layoffs.

American companies that invest in overseas businesses must adhere to the host countries' traditional and legal procedures affecting employee rights. Knowledge of those arrangements is essential to conducting business overseas.

PRACTICAL TIPS

What You Should Do Before Hiring an Employee

As an employer, you can incur substantial liability for hiring the wrong person. This liability may be based on your employees' actions or on your own negligence in hiring a person. The following are some items to keep in mind prior to hiring:

Checklist

✔ *Signed Application* The application form should cover at least the last seven years. Have the applicant sign an authorization form so that you can make a thorough background check, including prior employers, criminal records, educational records, and references.

✔ *Detailed Application* On the application form, request both months and years worked on prior jobs. A substantial gap between jobs may indicate that a person was incarcerated.

✔ *Information Needed* Ignore arrests, but consider convictions.

✔ *Investigation* Investigate given references, including prior employers. Recognize that many prior employers will volunteer little information for fear of a defamation action.

✔ *Credit Report* A credit report also can provide useful information. A poor credit rating may indicate that the person is under serious financial pressure, which, in turn, might result in her or him misappropriating property from the employer or third persons.

Chapter Summary

The body of law that conceals the private relationships within the employment sphere originates in the legal principles concerning slave ownership. During the Middle Ages, the principles expanded to cover the employer–employee relationship. With the Industrial Revolution, the law developed the concepts of principal and agent. The distinction between an employer–employee and principal–agent relationship is that an employee enters into no contracts on behalf of his or her employer, whereas an agent does. The same rules generally apply to both relationships.

The concept underlying these relationships is summarized by the phrase here, which has been translated from the Latin: "He [or she] who acts through another acts himself [or herself]." If a company increases its business through the use of employees, the company is responsible for those employees' acts. An agency can be created by agreement, ratification, or estoppel.

Three types of agency relationships exist: (1) principal–agent, (2) employer–employee, and (3) employer's or principal's relationship with an independent contractor. In a relationship between the principal and agent, the agent has derivative authority to act on the principal's behalf. The agent's authority to act stems from one of the following two sources: (1) actual authority, whether express or implied, or (2) apparent authority.

When an employer and employee relationship exists, the employer can regulate the employee's conduct. An employee commonly acts as an agent for the employer. An independent contractor may be hired by an employer to do specific work or by a principal to assist with a contractual relationship with a third person. These relationships are sometimes unclear. The court reviews several factors to determine if a relationship is one of employer–employee or independent contractor.

The principal and agent each owe the other a set of duties. The agent owes the principal the duties of performance, loyalty, obedience, accounting, and notification. The principal owes the agent the duties of compensation, reimbursement and indemnification, cooperation, and safe working conditions.

In a contract situation, the principal may be a disclosed principal, a partially disclosed principal, or an undisclosed principal. The principal is liable on the contract when the principal is disclosed. If the principal is partially disclosed, both the agent and principal are liable. If the principal is not disclosed, the agent is liable. When the agent acts, she or he gives the implied warranty of authority; that is, she or he has the authority to act on behalf of the principal on the contract.

In a tort situation, the employer is liable for the negligent acts of the employee when those acts are committed within the scope of the employee's employment. Even though the employer has not acted negligently, the employer is liable for the employee's acts under the doctrine of *respondeat superior,* which is Latin for "let the master answer."

Normally the employer is not liable for an employee's intentional torts. Liability is expanding, however, in this area. The employer may be liable under one of four theories: (1) The employer was negligent in hiring or retaining the employee, (2) the employer is liable for certain types of employees' intentional torts, (3) the employer ratifies the intentional tort, or (4) the employer helps to commit the intentional tort.

An agency relationship can be ended by an act of the parties or by operation of law when either the principal or agent becomes mentally incompetent or dies, when an agency's subject matter is destroyed or lost, or when an event occurs that has an unusual effect on the agency's subject matter.

An employment relationship is a contractual agreement. Most types of employment are employment-at-will situations. An employee handbook may be the basis for a written contractual relationship. Employees can be leased on a temporary basis from a company that is a professional employer organization.

Although the employment relationship is a private one, the government controls some aspects. An employer cannot discriminate on the basis of gender, race, national origin, religious beliefs, and other invidious classifications. The government statutes also govern the relationship between management and labor.

Using the World Wide Web

A businessperson should be aware of the positions that the Internal Revenue Service takes on different issues. The IRS's Web site has a list of publications which you can read online or download. No Web site exists specifically dedicated to agency law.

For *Web Activities*, links to Web sites mentioned in the chapter, and additional Web sites that relate to the chapter topics, go to **http://bohlman.westbuslaw. com**, click on "Internet Applications," and select Chapter 17

Web Activities

Go to **http://bohlman.westbuslaw.com**, click on "Internet Applications," and select Chapter 17.
17–1 Employment Rights
17–2 Tax Considerations

Key Terms

actual authority
actual knowledge
agency by estoppel
agency law
agent
apparent authority
constructive knowledge
covenant not to compete
derivative authority

disclosed principal
doctrine of *respondeat superior*
employment at will
employment law
estoppel
express authority
fiduciary duty
gratuitous agency

implied authority
implied warranty of authority
independent contractor
legal fiction
partially disclosed principal
power of attorney
principal

professional agent
ratification
scope of employment
undisclosed principal

Questions and Case Problems

17–1 *Respondeat Superior* Roy makes deliveries for a local pizza restaurant, driving the company car with the restaurant's telephone number printed on the side. One day, after a delivery, but while still on duty, Roy picks up three friends, who need a ride into the next town. Figuring that the restaurant is so busy that he will not be missed, he agrees to take them. While in the next town, Roy accidentally backs into Mr. Phillip's truck, putting a small dent in the truck's bumper. Because it is such a small dent and because Roy needs to get back to work, he leaves without writing a note to the truck's owner. When he arrives back at work, Tony, the restaurant's

owner, is waiting for him. Mr. Phillip had been watching his truck from his apartment window. He saw the accident and the telephone number on the side of the car. When he called the telephone number, he reached Tony. Who is responsible for the cost of fixing Mr. Phillip's bumper? Explain.

17–2 Fiduciary Duty Peters hires Ahmed as a traveling salesperson. Ahmed not only solicits orders but also delivers the goods and collects payments from his customers. Ahmed places all payments in his private checking account and, at the end of each month, withdraws sufficient cash from his bank to cover the payments made. Peters is unaware of this procedure. Because of an economic slowdown, Peters tells his salespeople to offer 20 percent discounts on orders. Ahmed solicits orders, but he offers only 15 percent discounts, pocketing the extra 5 percent. Ahmed has lost no orders by this practice, and Peters rates him as one of his top salespeople. When Peters learns of Ahmed's actions, what are his duties and rights in this matter?

17–3 Employment Law Vijay, a pilot for the Big Canyon Tour Company, flies passengers into the canyon to photograph the view. During the past few years, Big Canyon has honored him with all but one of its outstanding employee service awards. The state legislature passes a law prohibiting all aircraft from flying below the canyon's rim. Wayne, the owner of Big Canyon Tour Company, tells the pilots to ignore the new law because the quality of the view without flying below the canyon's rim is poor. Vijay refuses to break this law even though he will lose his job if he fails to follow company orders. Vijay, an at-will employee, is fired. Is Vijay entitled to damages of any kind? Explain.

17–4 Scope of Employment Dependable Trucking Company has a contract with the U.S. Postal Service to haul mail from a large metropolitan area, Large City, to a small rural community, Small Town, six days a week. The communities are located 100 miles apart. A semitruck that bears no insignia or logo hauls the mail. The semi-truck leaves Large City by 6 A.M., reaches Small Town by 8 A.M., and returns at 5 P.M. The driver receives payment for the two-hour trips and the layover time between 8 A.M. and 5 P.M. Small Town offers few diversions. After making the mail run on Monday and Tuesday a new driver has fully explored the town. On Wednesday, after dropping the trailer off at the Post Office, he drives the tractor to the nearest bar, located ten miles from town, and consumes ten beers. By 4:00 P.M. he starts the drive back to the Post Office. Five miles from Small Town, he fails to stop at a stop sign, and broadsides a car, killing the three occupants. Who is liable? Explain.

17–5 Ratification In 1974, Mrs. Crawford executed a power of attorney naming her daughter, Mrs. Howe, as her agent. She restricted the power of attorney to the agent borrowing money for Mrs. Crawford's benefit. Mrs. Howe and her husband operated a dairy farm. Mrs. Crawford took no part in managing the dairy business and received no benefits from it. In 1980, the

Howes experienced severe financial difficulties in operating their farm and needed to refinance their debt. A few days before the new loan for more than $2 million dollars closed, Mrs. Howe advised the attorney handling the transaction that she would sign the loan instruments as her mother's agent under the 1974 power of attorney so that her mother could avoid coming to town for the closing. The attorney examined the power of attorney, approved it, and prepared the loan papers. Mrs. Howe acted as an agent for Mrs. Crawford in this matter without Mrs. Crawford's knowledge or consent. Mrs. Crawford testified at the trial that she knew nothing about the loan transaction. Mr. and Mrs. Howe were unable to pay the debt and went into bankruptcy. The bank sued Mrs. Crawford to collect the loan, alleging that Mrs. Crawford had ratified the agreement. The trial court entered a judgment for Mrs. Crawford. The bank appealed. What result and why? [*First National Bank of Shreveport v. Crawford*, 455 So. 2d 1209 (1984)]

17–6 Employment Law Sargent, a former bank auditor for Central National Bank & Trust Co., was fired for refusing to destroy or alter a report to the audit committee. Several statutes prohibited the acts that his superiors had allegedly urged him to commit. Sargent brought an action to recover for wrongful discharge. Who prevails? Explain. [*Sargent v. Central National Bank & Trust Co.*, 809 P.2d 1298 (Okla. 1991)]

17-7 Independent Contractor Hansen, nineteen years old and a professional driver, entered the Sunnyside Honda Fall Classic motocross race that was held in the city park. The promotor of the race, Squisher Racing, found sponsors, arranged prizes, hired employees to promote and conduct the race, and arranged with the city for the park rental. The city required the sponsor to provide medical services, and Squisher Racing complied by contracting with Tri-City Aid Service to provide those services. The flyers and posters advertising the race used Sunnyside Honda's logo and two telephone numbers, one of which was Honda's business phone. When a person called the telephone number, a Honda employee answered questions regarding the race. Honda received no money from the race, paid no employees involved in the race, and had no control over the race. Its benefit was the advertising value of sponsoring the race. Hansen broke his neck during the race and was paralyzed as a result. He was treated at the scene by volunteer emergency medical technicians from Tri-City Aid Service, who, he alleged, removed his helmet improperly and exacerbated his injury. Hansen sued Squisher Racing, Sunnyside Honda, the city, and Tri-City Aid Service. Who prevails? Explain. [*Hansen v. Horn Rapids O.R.V. Park*, 932 P.2d 724 (Wash. App. Div. 3 1997)]

17–8 Apparent Authority Alaska Mack Trucks of Fairbanks is a dealer and franchisee of Mack Trucks, Inc., of Allentown, Pennsylvania. As part of the franchise agreement, Mack permitted Alaska Mack to use the name "Mack." Alaska Mack was listed in the telephone directory under the heading "MACK TRUCKS"; the Mack bulldog was displayed on the Alaska Mack building; and the Mack logo was on Alaska Mack's posters, printed Mack brochures, and promotional materials. Furthermore, a distributorship agreement existed between Alaska Mack and Mack Trucks, Inc.; Mack provided training for the distributorship's employees; Mack engaged in national advertising programs and in joint advertising with the distributor; and Mack established sales quotas and required reports as to the use of the vehicles sold. The city of Delta Junction, Alaska, entered into a contract with Alaska Mack Trucks for a fire truck. Alaska Mack modified the truck to carry a 5,000-gallon gas tank. After delivery, the truck exceeded the specifications for total gross weight and it was dangerous to drive. The city brought action against Alaska Mack and Mack Trucks, Inc. Did Alaska Mack have apparent authority to act as an agent for Mack Trucks, Inc.? Did the act of modifying the truck exceed the possible limits of any apparent authority? Explain. [*City of Delta Junction v. Mack Trucks, Inc.*, 670 P.2d 1128 (Alaska 1983)]

17–9 Negligent Hiring Don went to the defendant's racetrack to pay a debt he owed to Bill, whom the defendant employed. Bill began a fight with Don, resulting in injuries to Don. Don brought legal action against the racetrack on the basis of negligent hiring. Bill had been involved in an earlier altercation that the defendant racetrack could have discovered if it had checked with the police department. No conviction occurred, however, because the other victim failed to prosecute. Bill held a license issued by the Oklahoma Horse Racing Commission. Is the racetrack liable for negligent hiring under these facts? Explain. [*Jackson v. Remington Park, Inc.*, 874 P.2d (Okla. App. 1994)]

17–10 Internet You are starting a new business that you have set up as a corporation and will have two employees. Concerned about tax matters, you go to the Web site of the Internal Revenue Service at **http://www.irs.gov**. You click on the "Businesses" link. On the new Web page, you click on "Small Bus/Self-Employed." What is an EIN? Is an EIN required for your business? How do you apply for an EIN?

Chapter 18

Business Enterprises: Noncorporate Business Entities

It is a socialist idea that making profits is a vice.
I consider the real vice is making losses.

Sir Winston Churchill, 1874–1965
Prime Minister of Great Britain,
1940–1945, 1951–1955

Chapter Outline

Ethical Consideration

If I Am Only for Myself, What Am I Getting Out of a Limited Partnership?

You are a limited partner in High Return Real Estate Partnership. High Return owns several apartment buildings and is paying, as promised, a high rate of return to all of the limited partners.

You become suspicious of the lofty return, however, at a time when there appears to be a high vacancy rate in most apartment buildings. After some investigation, you find that, in fact, many of the apartments owned by High Return are vacant. Many of the buildings need significant repair. Neither the exteriors nor the interiors of the apartment buildings are being maintained. You talk with several of the tenants, who complain that High Return has neglected basic plumbing and electrical repairs.

You conclude that High Return, to keep up its image, has decided to forgo making repairs and, instead, to use its cash to pay investors. It is only a matter of time, you believe, before this policy will ruin the properties being held by High Return and jeopardize the value of the partnership.

You approach the general partner and demand a return of your limited partnership investment. The general partner will return your money on the condition that you keep the information you know to yourself. Do you take your money on that condition? Use the ethical model presented in Chapter 2 and reprinted on the inside front cover to develop your answer.

Introduction

Many people consider owning a business at some point in their lives. Unfortunately, the sad truth is that most small businesses fail.

Many reasons exist for the large number of failures among small businesses. These failures include a lack of planning, sufficient financing, effective marketing strategies, good management structures, appropriate accounting systems, and lack of appreciation of the legal issues. Statistics show that businesses employing fewer than twenty employees have an almost 91 percent chance of failure in the first ten years.[1]

This chapter examines five different forms of businesses: *sole proprietorship, partnership, limited partnership, limited liability company*, and *limited liability partnership*. A **sole proprietorship** is a business owned by one person. A **partnership** is a business that is run for profit in which two or more people have an undivided (and sometimes unequal) ownership interest. In a **limited partnership**, two or more people own the business. At least one person, called the **general partner**, has unlimited liability, whereas the **limited partner** has limited liability. This type of business entity often is used as an investment vehicle and for tax benefits.

A **limited liability company (LLC)** is very similar to a corporation in that it affords the owners limited liability, but the LLC can be treated as a partnership for tax purposes. The LLC has become one of the more popular forms of business entity in recent years. At least fifty jurisdictions recognize this form of organization today. The **limited liability partnership**, also known as a *registered limited liability partnership*, protects partners from personal liability for partnership debts. Otherwise, the limited liability partnership is treated as a regular partnership. This form has become popular with professional organizations, such as accounting and law firms.

The limited partnership, the limited liability company, and the limited liability partnership must be authorized by state statute. Sole proprietorships and general partnerships exist without any specific authorization of state law.

In 1994, the National Conference of Commissioners on Uniform State Laws issued the Revised Uniform Partnership Act, discussed later in this chapter. In 1996, the National Conference added the Limited Liability Partnership Act and Foreign Limited Liability Partnership Act to the 1994 act. The Foreign Limited Liability Partnership Act applies to a partnership that is formed in one state and does business in another state.[2]

---

[1] The Edward Lowe Foundation is a not-for-profit organization dedicated to championing the entrepreneurial spirit in this country. It provides information, research, and education about entrepreneurships and financially assists new businesses. The Web address is http://peerspectives.org. One of the major reasons for failure of a business is lack of funding and location. This site may assist you in these areas.
[2] The 'Lectric Law Library offers considerable information about different forms of business entities. This information is available at http://www.lectlaw.com/bus.html.

Artiste Login. Carlo and Carlotta have been fortunate to start a small business that is partially Web based. Although a common belief is that business owners set their own hours, are their own bosses, and make a comfortable living, Carlo and Carlotta know that it takes hard work and long hours. Both are willing to commit themselves to the building of their family business.

Comparing Business Enterprises

Knowing about the different forms of business entities helps a businessperson make decisions when starting a business. The four entities considered most often are the sole proprietorship, general partnership, limited partnership, and corporation. A corporation is by far the most complex business entity. Chapter 19 discusses corporations in detail.

In deciding which form to adopt, the businessperson needs to consider the following factors:

- Difficulty of forming the organization,
- Liability,
- Tax considerations,
- Continuity of existence and ability to transfer ownership,
- Management and control,
- Financing,
- Licenses, and
- Location.

Each of these factors has legal, as well as business, ramifications. Examining each of these issues and making decisions about them will help the owner determine the business form that best suits his or her needs because each type of business organization has advantages and disadvantages.

Difficulty of Forming the Organization

Some business organizations are easier to create than others. A sole proprietorship is the easiest, because a person merely starts doing business. The person may have to obtain a business license from the state or city before starting a business. State governments do not have statutes regulating the formation of a sole proprietorship.

All state governments require a **fictitious name filing** if an owner decides to use a business name other than his own. A form is filed with the state, requiring the proprietor to give his real name and address, and then the fictitious name under which the business will be conducted. This filing notifies the public that a particular person is participating in this business. The state may refuse to grant the use of a particular fictitious name if it is the same or similar to a name already in use.

A general partnership similarly is easy to form. Two or more people simply conduct a business for profit. A person may even be in a partnership without realizing it. Again, besides obtaining a business license or filing for the use of a fictitious name, state governments do not mandate any legal formalities when creating a general partnership.

All states, however, set legal requirements for creating a limited partnership, limited liability company, limited liability partnership, or corporation. All of these business entities must file appropriate documents with some state agency, such as the secretary of state or a corporation commission.

Liability

Financial liability often stems from negligent acts of the businessperson. Perhaps a customer injured herself because the business failed to properly maintain and repair a stairwell or a product failed, resulting in product liability (discussed in Chapter 11).

Sole proprietors and general partners have unlimited liability. If the sole proprietor, partnership, or partner is sued successfully, the person who obtained the judgment seeks to have the judgment paid out of the business's assets and, if the judgment is not fully paid by business assets, then out of the sole proprietor's or general partner's personal assets. Hopefully, the business has insurance so the assets of the business or the personal assets of the owner are not needed.

Personal liability is limited in the case of a limited partnership, limited liability company, limited liability partnership, or corporation. Of these business forms, only the limited partnership is required to have at least one person, the general partner, who has unlimited liability. The liability of investors in the other entities is limited to the amount of their investment.

Personal liability is not limited, however, for people who hold professional licenses, such as lawyers, accountants, and medical doctors who commit malpractice (negligent acts in the professional practice). For example, in the practice of law, regardless of the type of business organization, the attorney has unlimited liability for negligence in handling a client's affairs. Professionals have limited personal liability for all other business matters.

Tax Considerations

A businessperson must consider the federal and state tax laws when deciding on the type of business organization. The income tax law usually is the most important. A business operated as a sole proprietorship receives no tax advantages. Because it is not a legal entity separate from the owner, it files no separate tax returns. The sole proprietor reports and pays the individual tax rate on the income earned.

Partnerships, limited partnerships, limited liability companies, and limited liability partnerships are subject to the income tax reporting laws, but generally do not pay income tax. Each must file an income tax informational return with the government. The income or deductions pass from the legal entity to the investor, who is subject to income tax laws.

A corporation is taxed as a separate entity on its income. In addition, stockholders who receive dividends are subject to individual income tax laws. Depending on the current tax laws and the amount of income involved, the income tax rates for individuals may be higher or lower than the tax rates for corporations (called C corporations under the federal tax laws). Federal tax laws currently allow corporations that meet specific guidelines, called S corporations, to qualify for various tax breaks. The tax status of corporations is discussed in more detail in Chapter 19. Some states have more favorable tax laws for businesses than other states.

Continuity of Existence and Ability to Transfer Ownership

A sole proprietorship usually exists as long as the owner is able to work. Once the person becomes incapacitated or dies, the business ends. Any sale of the business normally occurs only after a probate case is opened in court. Even if the owner is alive and capable, the business may be hard to sell for any number of reasons, including whether a market for this type of business exists. Often, only the business's assets are salable.

A partnership or a limited liability partnership dissolves whenever a new partner is added or a current partner dies or otherwise leaves the business. Although the partnership is technically dissolved, the business may continue under the new entity formed by the personnel change. A death of a member of a limited liability company or a limited partner does not automatically cause a dissolution of the entity.

Selling an interest in any of these organizations, however, may be difficult. The sale of corporate ownership, on the other hand, usually occurs by the selling of the owner's stock shares. If a corporation's shares are listed on a major stock exchange, the transfer of the shares is relatively easy because a structured market exists.

For a corporation that does not offer its shares on a stock exchange, selling the stock may be difficult. In this situation, people are often more willing to buy the corporation's physical assets rather than an ownership interest in the corporation. A purchaser may be reluctant to buy an ownership interest because of a corporation's outstanding liability. For example, an employee is at fault in an accident with a company automobile in January 1998. The corporation is sold in July 1998. A lawsuit is filed against the corporation in December 1999. The corporation is found liable in an amount that bankrupts it. If the person had purchased only the corporation's assets, she would not be liable for the harm caused by the automobile accident.

Management and Control

A sole proprietor has total management and control over his business. With a general partnership or a limited liability partnership arrangement, in the absence of an agreement, each partner has equal management and control responsibilities. Thus, each partner has one vote in management matters, regardless of the proportionate size of her partnership interest. Major problems can result if the partners disagree on business strategy.

In a limited partnership, the general partners have the responsibility of management and control. In a limited liability company, the matter of control is determined by the **operating agreement**. This document spells out the rights of the owners (called **members**) and **managers**.

In a corporation, the shareholders elect a board of directors, which, in turn, hires officers to manage the corporation's activities. The shareholders, through the

Refinancing Your Home: Is This the Way to Raise Capital?

You purchased your house for $85,000 several years ago. Over the years, you have added improvements that have increased the value of the house. Fortunately, the property values in general have increased in your town.

You locate a small business that you think would be a good investment. Your problem is that you have little cash to invest. Watching television, you see advertisements that explain the benefits of a home equity loan. Benefits range from low interest rates that are tax deductible to putting your hidden wealth, that is, your home equity, to good use now.

You apply for a home equity loan to purchase this business. The appraisal places the house's value at $235,000. According to the advertisement, the bank will lend you 100 percent of the equity at a 8 percent rate of interest. You decide to borrow $150,000.

You go to the bank and fully disclose that you intend to use this money to purchase a small business. The bank agrees to lend you the money without even asking for a business plan. You sign a negotiable note agreeing to repay the $150,000 at 8 percent over twenty years, and place a second mortgage on your house to secure the loan. As you sign the loan papers, the loan officer rushes you through the transaction and you fail to read all the documents. The papers include all the disclosures that the bank must make under the federal home equity loan amendments to the Truth-in-Lending Act. Later that month you purchase the business for $150,000.

During the next three years, you deduct the interest paid on the $150,000, along with the interest on the first mortgage, on your federal individual income tax return. One day you receive in the mail greetings from the friendly Internal Revenue Service (IRS). You have been selected for a random audit on home deductions.

During the audit, the IRS auditor informs you that only the interest paid on the first $100,000 of the home equity loan was deductible. You must file amended income tax returns for the past three years, pay the taxes owed, plus interest, plus late payment penalties.

Feeling down and out, you return home to open a letter from your mortgage company. You find the interest rate has jumped from 8 to 10 percent. The 8 percent rate was effective for only the first thirty-six months of the loan. The interest rate is readjusted to the prevailing interest rate after the first three years and is subject to review every third year.

Your business did not borrow the money, therefore, it did not receive any tax deductions for this loan. Is raising capital to purchase a business by mortgaging your home a good idea? What other methods of financing the purchase of a business are available?

election of the board of directors, control and manage the corporation.

Financing

A sole proprietor obtains loans based on his personal worth, which includes the business's assets. The same may be true of the other forms of organizations. If the business has a lengthy record, loans may be made on the strength of the business assets and abilities rather than on the creditworthiness of the individual investors. Some investors, like limited partners, will not sign personal guarantees; in this way, they limit their liability to their investment amount.

Corporations raise money by selling shares. A corporation also may obtain loans based on the strength of its assets and business record. A lending institution, however, dealing with a new corporation or a corporation with few shareholders, may require the individual shareholders or officers to be personally liable for the corporate loans in case the corporation fails. For example, a ten-year-old corporation is owned by a family. The bank may require each shareholder personally to guarantee the corporation's operating line of credit.

Licenses

A businessperson must consider which licenses are needed to conduct business. Almost all states require some type of sales or use tax license, because a business must collect taxes from its customers, which, in turn, are remitted to the state. In addition, many businesses, such as insurance agents, real estate brokers, contractors, and pest exterminators, are subject to specific regulations. Sellers of regulated products, such as alcohol, guns, or explosives, are subject to regulations. Operators of businesses such as pawnshops, funeral homes, nursing homes, day-care centers, and food preparation businesses, require separate types of licenses. Most regulated businesses must obtain a specific license.

The importance of having a license cannot be overemphasized, especially when the purpose of the licensing statute is to regulate and not to raise revenues. Any contract entered into by an unlicensed individual, whose business is required to have a license, may be declared void by a court when the purpose of the statute is to regulate the business or profession. In addition, if an individual should conduct business without a license under these circumstances, she may face criminal prosecution and civil liability, including the inability to collect amounts owed on contracts that the business has completed. The following case reviews the reasons for which a license is required and the repercussions when a person fails to obtain one.

CASE 18.1	**W & N CONSTRUCTION COMPANY, INC. v. WILLIAMS**

Supreme Court of South Carolina, 1996
322 S.C. 448, 472 S.E.2d 622

BACKGROUND AND FACTS W & N Construction Company contracted for and performed approximately $60,000 worth of commercial work at respondents' building in Seneca. After completion, W & N brought a mechanic's lien action to collect an unpaid balance of $30,481.89.

In South Carolina, a person called a master handles this type of situation instead of a judge. The master found that the contract was illegal and unenforceable, because W & N was not a licensed general contractor. Prior to entering into this contract, W & N's license had been revoked when its secretary failed to pay its taxes.

FINNEY, C.J.

. . . .

It is illegal for general contractors who undertake construction in excess of $30,000.00 to do so without first obtaining a license in this state. Nothing in Chapter 11 of Title 40, however, specifically prohibits an unlicensed general contractor from bringing suit to enforce a contract entered into without a license. The master found, notwithstanding the absence of an express statutory prohibition against its maintenance of suit, that W & N had acted illegally in entering into the contract such that it was void and unenforceable. Accordingly, respondents were granted summary judgment.

In *Berkebile v. Outen*, we recognized the general rule that courts will not enforce a contract which is violative of public policy, statutory law, or provisions of the constitution. Similarly, the Court of Appeals recently held: It is a well-founded policy of law that no person be permitted to acquire a right of action from their own unlawful act and one who participates in an unlawful act cannot recover damages for the consequence of that act. This rule applies at both law and in equity and whether the cause of action is in contract or in tort.

A number of jurisdictions adopt the view that an unlicensed contractor may not recover on a contract even though the relevant licensing statute contains no express provision relating to the enforceability of the contract. The rationale is that such licensing statutes protect the public and to permit unlicensed contractors to circumvent licensing requirements by payment of a small fine would defeat the legislative intent. We concur with these authorities.

Accordingly, we affirm the ruling of the master.

DECISION AND REMEDY The plaintiff did not have a contractor's license, so any contract that the business entered into was null and void. In other words, the W & N Construction Company lost $30,000 because it lacked a license.

CRITICAL THINKING: POLITICAL CONSIDERATION Why have states passed legislation requiring construction companies to have a license?

Location

The location of the new business is an important decision, regardless of its form. Numerous legal restrictions may affect the location choice. When reviewing a prospective location, an owner should consider the business's visibility, including signs that promote the business. Most local ordinances control the size, location, and type of signs that a business can display.

Zoning laws are the classification, regulation, and restriction of property use by local government. Owners must be certain that the zoning regulations allow their type of business, along with appropriate signs, to be established in a particular location. Obtaining *use permits* and *variance permits* from local governmental bodies may be required. A **use permit** grants permission to operate a given type of business. A **variance permit** allows an exception to the zoning laws. Chapter 16 discussed other legal issues concerning property that relate to business.

INFOTRAC RESEARCH ACTIVITY

Problems always arise in obtaining a variance permit to a zoning law. Go to InfoTrac and type in "variance" and "zoning." Some of the largest businesses have had major objections to their requests for variance permits to change zoning. What were some of the most recent examples?

CYBERLAW

Web Businesses

All the *Fortune* 1000 companies and many small businesses are on the World Wide Web, which connects more than 100 million people around the world. With new innovations being developed, the Web assists both large and small companies to either start a business or increase the sales of established businesses. The Web market is growing steadily.

Most business organizations are created under state law, even if they are strictly a Web-based business. Many pitfalls await those establishing themselves on the Web. First, you need to select among the hundreds of Internet service providers (ISPs) offering access to the Web. The ISP needs to be stable, be able to support your needs, and be able to provide assistance. Second, you need a Web designer to assist you in developing and designing your Web page.

Once the Web page is designed and developed, it needs to be publicized. You need to register your Web page with an Internet search service that allows surfers to find it. For the search engines, you need to choose words that a customer might use. You can post your Web site with news groups and also e-mail information about it to specific organizations that have a need for your Web page. You can link your Web site with permission to other Web sites. You can always advertise your Web URL in the traditional media, such as newspapers, other periodicals, radio, and other media.

Partnerships

The **Uniform Partnership Act (UPA)** establishes the law on general partnerships. The term *partnership* means general partnership. If a partnership agreement exists but omits certain matters, the UPA supplies the missing provisions. Most sections of the UPA have no application when the partners have made provisions in the agreement addressing that particular area.

A general partnership is defined as "an association of two or more persons to carry on as co-owners a business for profit" [UPA Section 6]. A partnership agreement is a contract. State statutes do not regulate the formation of a partnership.

Although most partnerships are formed pursuant to a partnership contract among the parties, a partnership also may arise as a result of the conduct of the parties. A sharing of profits from a business, for example, raises a presumption of a partnership [UPA Section 7(4)].

If the conduct of the parties leads third parties to believe that a partnership exists, a partnership may be found to exist legally by a court or an arbitrator. This association is known as a **partnership by estoppel** [UPA Section 16].

No law requires a partnership agreement to be in writing. A court will find that a partnership exists if two or more people decide to operate a business as co-owners for profit.

Although a written document is not legally required, a partnership agreement should be prepared. Partners participate in a very close relationship that is not unlike a marriage. Both relationships are based on trust, confidence, and mutual reliance. Misunderstandings, frustrating situations, and disagreements are bound to occur. Through a written partnership agreement, many of these problems can be resolved before they escalate.

The statute of frauds (discussed in Chapter 10) requires the agreement to be in writing if the partnership is to last more than one year. Without a written agreement, the relationship is called a *partnership at will*, which means that it can be dissolved by a partner at any time.

A partnership is treated as a legal entity for certain purposes. For example, partnership property can be held and transferred in the partnership name [UPA Section 8]. In most situations, the partnership is treated as a collection of individuals. Property can be held and transferred in the name of the individual partners [UPA Section 10], the partners can each be sued individually [UPA Section 15], and the partners each have unlimited individual liability.

The **Revised Uniform Partnership Act (RUPA)** of 1994 was sent to state legislatures for possible adoption. At least thirty states have either adopted the new act completely or substantial parts of it. More states are expected to adopt the RUPA.

The RUPA includes major changes to current partnership law. One change is that a partnership is treated as an entity rather than as a collection of individuals. For some purposes though, such as the liability of individual partners and tax issues, the partnership is not treated as an entity. Property acquired by a partnership, however, is the property of the partnership and not of the partners individually. A creditor of the business must exhaust the assets of the partnership before seeking recovery against the personal assets of the individual partners. Under the RUPA, partners are granted greater authority to contract on behalf of the partnership. Reference to the major provisions of the RUPA will be made in footnotes.

Partnership breakups also are changed under the RUPA. The term **dissociation** replaced *dissolution*, that is, the end of a relationship with the partnership. Two methods for partnership breakups are provided. One procedure allows the business to be terminated, whereas the other allows the business to continue. These proposed changes reflect methods by which businesses want partnerships to be treated by legislatures and the courts.

Capital Requirements and Funding of a Partnership

A partnership generally is funded through each partner's capital contributions. The partnership itself also may be able to obtain credit and loans based on its own creditworthiness and that of all of the partners. In addition, the partners may make loans to the partnership.

Partnership Management and Control

Each partner has an equal right to manage and control the partnership [UPA Section 18(e)] and to use partner-

LEGAL HIGHLIGHT

Historic Perspective of Uniform Acts

The constitution of the American Bar Association (ABA), formed in 1878, established as one of its objectives the promotion of the uniformity of legislation among the states. To promote this goal, the ABA created a committee on uniform laws. The committee convened a study of interstate laws to achieve uniformity.

The study group's report showed almost unanimous agreement that "desired uniformity could be secured best by concurrent legislative action in the various states." This report led to the establishment in 1892 of the National Conference of Commissioners on Uniform State Laws.

Since its initial organization, the National Conference has drafted more than 200 laws on numerous subjects and various fields of law, many of which have been widely enacted. The National Conference recommends both uniform acts and model acts.

Uniform acts address matters that are appropriate for state legislation and have substantial interstate implication. An example is the transactions covering the sale of goods in Article 2 of the Uniform Commercial Code.

Model acts, on the other hand, cover subjects that only indirectly affect relationships among the states, but that involve problems common to many states, such as water rights. The National Commissioners specifically state that uniformity is unnecessary for model acts but "helpful if a state desires legislation on the subject."

The earlier part of this text addressed the Uniform Commercial Code. This chapter discusses the application of several additional uniform acts. The next chapter will address the model corporation act.

---

ship property for an appropriate purpose [UPA Section 25(2)(a)]. These rights can be altered by an agreement among the partners. Each partner is an agent for the partnership and for every other partner [UPA Section 9]. Each partner is in a fiduciary relationship with the other partners. Each partner has a fiduciary duty to act in good faith for the benefit of the partnership and to consider the mutual welfare of all partners. For example, unless an agreement states otherwise, a partner cannot engage in outside activities, such as holding a second job, when it involves the partnership's time.

The partners generally receive no compensation for their management of the partnership's business [UPA Section 18(f)]. Instead, the partners share in the business's profits. In the absence of an agreement, profits and losses are shared equally. If an agreement exists, profits and losses are shared in the proportions established by the agreement [UPA Section 18(a)]. The amount of the partners' capital contributions has no application in the sharing of profits and losses unless a contrary agreement has been made.

The partners may agree to delegate day-to-day management responsibilities to one or more of the partners. Each partner, however, has one vote in management matters regardless of his capital contribution. A majority vote usually is required for such partnership decisions [UPA Section 18(b)].

The unanimous consent of all the partners, however, is required in matters significantly altering the nature of the partnership business or property. Other actions requiring the consent of all of the partners include an act by a partner that makes it impossible to carry on the partnership's business in the usual way, the disposition of the goodwill of the business, and the submission of a partnership dispute to arbitration [UPA Section 9(3)].[3]

Any act of a partner that appears to carry on the partnership's business as usual will bind the partnership to that act. This principle does not apply when the partner has no authority and the person with whom

[3]The RUPA follows a similar approach: A majority vote decides any act in the ordinary course of business or in the absence of an agreement, and a unanimous agreement is required for an act outside of the ordinary course of business or to amend the partnership agreement [RUPA § 401], but no provision of arbitration exists in the RUPA as it does in the UPA.

the partner deals knows that the partner has no authority to act [UPA Section 9(1)].[4]

Liability of Old and New Partners

Each partner personally is liable for the entire amount of the partnership's debts. A partner is liable for any act by another partner, even if the act is wrongful, that results in liability for the partnership [UPA Section 13]. This liability exists because, when a partner acts,

she acts as the partnership's agent. Such liability can result from either a contract or a tort [UPA Section 15]. A partner, however, is not liable for other partners' debts that are not connected with the business.[5]

In satisfying their claims based on partnership liabilities, creditors can look to the assets of the individual partners after the partnership assets have been exhausted. If a person joins an existing partnership, his capital contribution is subject to the claims of prior creditors, but he is not liable personally for the prior debts of the partnership [UPA Section 17]. The new partner is liable personally for debts incurred after he joins the partnership, just as an original partner would be. The following case discusses a new partner's potential liability for debts of the partnership that he had joined.

[4]Some conflict appears in this area under the RUPA. Section 301 states that each partner is an agent of the partnership. If the partner has no authority and the third party knows this, the third party cannot hold the partnership liable. Section 303 provides that a partnership may file a statement of partnership authority with a public official that can include limitations on the power of a partner. This seems to indicate that all persons dealing with a partnership must first check the recorded documents. Section 305 states, however, that a partnership is liable for any loss caused to a person when the partner acts in the ordinary course of business.

[5]Under the RUPA, a creditor must first seek the partnership assets before seeking the assets of the individual partners. The liability of a partner is joint and several [RUPA §§ 306, 307].

CASE 18.2

United States District Court, E.D. Virginia, 1995
874 F. Supp. 705

CITIZENS BANK OF MASSACHUSETTS v. PARHAM-WOODMAN MEDICAL ASSOCIATES

BACKGROUND AND FACTS Citizens Bank of Massachusetts and Parham-Woodman Medical Associates, a Virginia general partnership, entered into a construction loan agreement and a note dated April 30, 1985. The note, in the principal amount of $2 million, was to fund construction of a medical office building, Parham-Woodman's principal asset. Nilda R. Ante and Larry E. King were the general partners of Parham-Woodman when the construction loan agreement and the note were executed. Ante and King also executed a guaranty (guaranteeing repayment of the note) in favor of Citizens Bank on April 30, 1985.

As contemplated by the documents, Citizens Bank made advances from time to time during the building's construction. The advances as of June 3, 1986, totaled $1,457,123.15.

Dr. Richard L. Hunley, along with Joseph and Nada Tas, husband and wife, became general partners in Parham-Woodman on June 25, 1986. From July 2, 1986, through November 17, 1986, Citizens Bank made eight additional advances in the amount of $542,876.85. Subsequently, Kenneth E. Brown became a general partner in Parham-Woodman.

The medical office building was built, and the partnership made numerous payments, but ultimately defaulted. On December 15, 1993, a foreclosure sale brought $912,000, which yielded net proceeds of $890,195.12 to Citizens Bank.

Judgment was entered against Parham-Woodman in the amount of $1,218,244.98. The liability of Ante and King was eliminated by their respective bankruptcy discharges. The parties agreed that Brown had no personal liability for partnership debt. The court considered the liability of Richard L. Hunley and Joseph and Nada Tas.

District Judge PAYNE

. . . .

Resolution of the dispositive issue also requires consideration of the Uniform Partnership Act and its effect on the nature and extent of the liabilities of incoming partners. This necessitates an examination of the language of the Act, the intent of the Act's drafters and the interpretation of the Act by other jurisdictions.

Section 17 of the Act . . . makes an incoming partner liable for "all the obligations of the partnership arising before his admission," but provides that "this liability shall be satisfied only out of partnership property." Section 17 altered slightly the common law because, at common law, admission of a new partner dissolved the old partnership and created a new one. New creditors, then, were preferred over creditors of the old partnership when partnership assets were sought to cover unpaid partnership debts. To remedy this unfairness to creditors, drafters of the Act removed the preference with respect to partnership assets. "So as to preserve the present law as nearly as possible," however, and presumably to continue the common law's fair treatment of incoming partners, the drafters provided that for pre-existing debts, "liability of the incoming partner shall be satisfied only out of partnership property." . . . . "It, therefore, results that existing and subsequent creditors have equal rights as against partnership property and the separate property of all the previously existing members of the partnership, while only the subsequent creditors have rights against the separate estate of the newly admitted partner."

Decisions before and after adoption of the UPA suggest the reason why the law restricts an incoming partner's personal liability, a restriction maintained by the Act. Specifically, where a partnership undertakes a debt before a new partner is made, "[t]he credit of [the] new member . . . does not enter into the consideration of the creditors of the old firm, and it would be manifestly unjust to hold the new partner liable." These decisions and the long-standing principle which they confirm support the view that a partnership obligation arises, within the meaning of Section 17, when the creditor extends the credit to the partnership. In this instance, that occurred on April 30, 1985 and not on the occasion when the bank disbursed each advance.

. . . .

DECISION AND REMEDY An incoming partner's personal assets are exempt from satisfying postadmission advances under a preadmission contract's terms. The court found that all of the partners were liable for the debt owed the bank, but that the liability of Kenneth E. Brown, Richard L. Hunley, Joseph Tas, and Nada Tas could be satisfied only with partnership assets.[a]

CRITICAL THINKING: LEGAL CONSIDERATION Should an incoming partner be treated any differently than an original partner or partners with respect to his or her financial responsibility?

[a]A similar result would occur under the RUPA § 306.

Duration and Termination of the Partnership

A partnership has indefinite duration, unless the partnership agreement states a specific time period. The members of the partnership may change; no person, however, can become a partner without the consent of all of the existing partners, unless the partnership agreement states otherwise [UPA Section 13(g)].

Ending a partnership is a three-step process: *dissolution, winding up,* and *termination.* **Dissolution** means that the partnership union is discontinued. The partnership business continues in order to proceed through the stages of winding up and termination. A new partner, a transfer of a partner's interest in the partnership, a partner's decision to withdraw, or unanimous consent by all the partners will dissolve the original partnership. A partnership also is dissolved if the business of the partnership becomes unlawful; if the business can only be carried on at a loss; if the partnership becomes bankrupt; if a partner dies, becomes mentally ill, or becomes bankrupt; or if a court orders a dissolution [UPA Sections 31 and 32].

Dissolution does not mean that the business is terminated automatically [UPA Section 30]. Depending on the circumstances, the business may continue, conducted by a new partnership entity.

When dissolution occurs and a new partnership is not formed, then **winding up** of the business takes place. All the partners must be notified. At this point, the partners no longer can create any new liabilities on behalf of the partnership. The only authority they maintain is to complete the transactions begun, but not yet finished, at the time of the dissolution and to wind up the business [UPA Section 35]. Winding up includes collecting and preserving partnership assets, paying debts, and accounting to each partner for the value of her partnership interest.[6]

Both creditors of the partnership and creditors of the individual partners can make claims on the partnership's assets. In general, partnership creditors have priority on the partnership's assets. Individual creditors have priority on the personal assets of the partners.[7]

When the business has been wound up, it is then terminated. In **termination**, the assets, if any, are distributed in the following order.

1. Debts owed to creditors other than partners,

2. Debts owed to partners for loans made to the partnership,

3. Amounts owed to partners for capital, and

4. Amounts owed to partners as profits [UPA Section 40].[8]

The following case discusses some of the problems that can arise when a partnership dissolves. Notice that the business mentioned in the case continued after dissolution.

---

[6]The RUPA recognizes that the dissociation of one partner who leaves the partnership does not dissolve the partnership. Many dissociations result in a buyout of the withdrawing partner's interest. A dissolution can result for these reasons: if the partnership was at will, was established for a specific time period, had a business that became illegal, could not make a profit, or encountered other similar occurrences [RUPA § 801].

[7]The Bankruptcy Code changed this rule. Thus, the RUPA partnership creditors share pro rata with the partners' individual creditors in the assets of the partners' estate.

[8]The RUPA does not have a similar list as in the UPA. The same theory applies, however, as to the distribution of assets and the payment of obligations [RUPA §§ 401, 807].

CASE 18.3

Court of Appeals of
Nebraska, 2003
2003 WL 718412

CLEVENGER v. REHN

BACKGROUND AND FACTS In August 1998, Clevenger and Rehn, who are sisters, decided to open an antique shop that would include a lunchroom or tearoom. They decided to form an equal partnership and to share equal responsibilities and equal profits in the business they called Porcelain Rose. They prepared a written partnership agreement; however, it was never signed by either party.

In November 1998, Clevenger and Rehn rented two small rooms for their business. The front room was the sales room, where the parties sold antiques, and the back room was where the parties served dinners.

In addition to purchasing inventory for the business, Clevenger also provided utensils, pans, and cookbooks and purchased a deep freeze, a buffet, a kitchen sink, faucets, and other miscellaneous items for the kitchen out of her own personal bank account. On February 2, 1999, the sales portion of the Porcelain Rose opened.

On February 16, 1999, the tearoom section of the Porcelain Rose opened. Approximately two days later, on February 18, Clevenger and Rehn got into an argument regarding who would be the cook and who would deal with the customers. Clevenger walked out of the kitchen on two separate occasions that day to cool off.

The next day, on February 19, 1999, when Clevenger came back to work, both parties were still upset about the previous day's argument, so Clevenger decided to leave and stated to Rehn, "I'm going home."

Rehn testified that during the day on which Clevenger walked out, strong winds blew the front door of the shop back and into an antique trunk situated at the front of the store. This accident caused the key, which was in the door, to snap off. Rehn replaced the locks that evening. Clevenger testified that later on that night, she returned to the shop and found that the locks had been changed and that she could not obtain entry into the store.

On February 22, 1999, Rehn closed the Porcelain Rose bank account and transferred the entire balance, $3,096.83, to her personal account to prevent Clevenger from incurring any additional liabilities. Rehn continued to operate the business until May 1999 and then closed the business.

On November 4, 1999, Clevenger filed a petition in district court seeking to dissolve the Porcelain Rose partnership, recover her capital contribution to the partnership, share one-half of all partnership profits and inventory, have an accounting of the partnership, and sell any remaining partnership property, with the proceeds to be divided equally between the parties. Rehn answered and counterclaimed for essentially the same relief.

A trial was held in August 2000. Clevenger testified that after she walked out of the store on February 19, 1999, she had absolutely no involvement in the Porcelain Rose, but she felt she still had an interest in the Porcelain Rose. She also testified that Rehn solely retained the entire shop inventory after February 19, and therefore Clevenger should be entitled to approximately $10,000 after the dissolution and termination of the partnership.

The trial court found that Clevenger and Rehn formed a partnership; that each contributed time and property to the partnership; that the business opened on February 2, 1999, and on February 19, 1999, Clevenger walked out of the business effectively terminating the partnership; that Rehn continued to operate the business until May 1999, and closed the business during that month; that Rehn published a notice of the partnership termination, showing that the partnership terminated on February 19, 1999, and was operated as a sole proprietorship after that date; and that the partnership was terminated as of February 19, 1999, and that is the date to be used for determining each party's share. Clevenger appealed.

SIEVERS, Judge.

. . . .

Partnerships are formed by the mutual agreement of all partners, and may be altered, modified, or dissolved by like agreement. In the present case, Clevenger and Rehn orally agreed to form the Porcelain Rose as an equal partnership in which they would each work, and they would share equally.

The first step in the analysis of this case involves the dissolution of the Porcelain Rose. Under Nebraska law, the term "dissolution" does not signify the end of a partnership's legal existence. Dissolution . . . is simply a change in the relationship of the partners "caused by any partner ceasing to be associated in the carrying on as distinguished from the winding up of the business." This is clearly an apt description of Clevenger's departure from the Porcelain Rose, regardless of reason or fault, and we do not need to fix blame for this situation in order to decide the case. Upon dissolution, the partnership is not terminated but continues until the winding up of partnership affairs is completed.

The evidence reveals that there was no definite term or particular undertaking . . . which would have restricted either Clevenger or Rehn from dissolving the partnership at will. Therefore, . . . the partnership between Clevenger and Rehn in the Porcelain Rose dissolved on February 19, 1999.

. . . .

One of the keys to this appeal is the fact the terms "dissolution," "winding up," and "termination," as employed by the Nebraska UPA, are not synonyms and have different meanings. Dissolution neither terminates the partnership nor completely ends the authority of the partners. The order of events to end a partnership as a business entity is (1) dissolution, (2) winding up, and (3) termination. It is not until "termination," after the "winding up" of the partnership is completed, that the partnership's legal existence ends and authority of the partners is extinguished. Therefore, the trial court's finding that the partnership was "effectively terminated" on February 19, 1999, does not accurately reflect partnership law, because there was simply no evidence that the partnership was also wound up on that date. In fact, the evidence shows that the two parties got together with their attorneys several weeks after Clevenger's departure and tried to resolve the outstanding issues (i.e., wind up), but they were unsuccessful.

The Nebraska UPA refers to "winding up" in several sections, but neither Nebraska case law nor the Nebraska UPA defines the term "winding up" of partnership affairs; but it is a concept which we think largely "speaks for itself." Winding up is the process by which the business affairs of the partnership are brought to an end, which would involve such things as paying creditors, collecting accounts payable, disposing of inventory and the property used in the business, including converting such to cash and then dividing any remaining property or cash among the partners, or if there were no equity, arranging for the payment of the debts of the partnership. All of these things needed to be done when Clevenger left on February 19, 1999. The district court's decision fails to recognize this reality. Because the record reveals, . . . that the Porcelain Rose partnership dissolved on February 19, . . . both Clevenger and Rehn were entitled to an accounting at that time.

. . . .

It appears that Clevenger was of the mistaken impression that if she "bowed out" of the business, that Rehn would simply "buy her out" as of February 19, 1999, when Clevenger "quit" the Porcelain Rose partnership. However, the winding up of a partnership is not that simple, unless the remaining partner agrees to such, which did not happen. Moreover, it appears to us that the trial judge's decision rests in no small part on the notice published in late April, in which Rehn said that as of February 19, she was operating the Porcelain Rose as a sole proprietorship. But, in the notice sent to Clevenger at the same time, Rehn said she was winding up. But, again, a partnership does not terminate (and convert into another legal entity such as a sole proprietorship) unless it has first been wound up and terminated.

. . . .

Thus, the notice of April 30 was of no real meaning unless the Porcelain Rose partnership had been wound up, which it obviously had not. To the extent that Rehn thought the business was now hers, that notion was as faulty as Clevenger's thought that if she abandoned the enterprise, Rehn would have to "buy her out." By the time of trial, Rehn's testimony was that she was winding up during the time after February 19 until the closing on May 31. At trial, Rehn made no claim that the business was being operated as a sole proprietorship after February 19. The fact that after February 19, Rehn purchased more inventory and food supplies for the store, continued merchandise sales, obtained the help . . . to assist, including serving meals, is simply evidence that the business had not terminated, and we take it simply as evidence of the windup process.

Admittedly, she changed the locks on the business and created a new business bank account and transferred funds to it from the old partnership account, but these things to us simply show that Rehn (as is likewise true of Clevenger) was unaware of the legal ramifications of the entity which the parties created and did not know how to legally end what the parties had started. Rehn closed the Porcelain Rose on May 31, and the remaining inventory of the partnership ended up in her garage—where it remained as of the time of trial.

DECISION AND REMEDY The court found that this was a partnership at will allowing either partner to withdraw without penalty. Further, the court stressed the difference between dissolution and termination. The court held that there had to be a winding up of the affairs of the business before it is terminated.

CRITICAL THINKING: PRACTICAL APPLICATION What steps should Rehn have taken to protect her interest when Clevenger left?

Limited Partnerships

A limited partnership consists of at least one general partner and one or more limited partners. The person who accepts the position of general partner agrees to manage the day-to-day activities of the business. Others want to invest while limiting their liability to the amount invested. The investing partners find a limited partnership attractive for two reasons. First, a limited partnership limits the liability of its limited partners to the amount of their contributions. Second, tax advantages exist. Tax benefits, especially in certain industries, such as oil and lumber, make limited partnerships attractive investments.

The limited partners, as such, are not bound by the obligations of the partnership and cannot have any day-to-day management responsibilities. The general partner or partners have total responsibility for the partnership's management and unlimited liability for its debts.

A limited partnership is only authorized by statute. Failure to comply with the statutory requirements changes the limited partnership into a general partnership. The **Uniform Limited Partnership Act (ULPA)** of 1916 and the **Revised Uniform Limited Partnership Act (RULPA)** of 1976, with 1985 amendments, include the current law on limited partnerships. The RULPA updated the original ULPA to resolve current problems with limited partnerships.

The ULPA and the RULPA require the limited partnership to file a certificate (see Exhibit 18–1) that becomes part of the public record. The certificate is similar to the articles of incorporation for a corporation.

A partnership certificate contains basic information, such as the name, location, and business of the partnership; the name and residence of each partner (general or limited); the term for which the partnership will exist; and the amount of cash and property contributed by each limited partner.

In addition to the certificate of limited partnership, the partners often enter into a more detailed partnership agreement that is not filed as part of the public record, but that covers such items as each partner's share of the profits. The general partners normally share the profits and losses evenly, but may agree to other ratios.

Limited partners share the profits in accordance with the agreement. Limited partners, however, share in the losses of the limited partnership only up to the amount of their capital contribution.

Limited partnership interests are considered to be securities (like stock certificates or corporate bonds). First, one person (the limited partner) pays money to another (the general partner). Second, the money is invested in a common enterprise from which the investor is led to expect profits. Third, the profits arise primarily from the effort of people other than the investor. The issuance, sale, and transfer of a limited partner's interest, therefore, are subject to federal and state securities laws (discussed in detail in Chapter 20).

Sources of Funding for Limited Partnerships

The general and the limited partners contribute to the capital of the limited partnership and also may make

Exhibit 18-1   Sample Certificate of Limited Partnership

CERTIFICATE OF LIMITED PARTNERSHIP

The undersigned, desiring to form a Limited Partnership under the Uniform Limited Partnership Act of the State of _____ , make this certificate for that purpose.

§ 1. Name. The name of the Partnership shall be " _____
_____ ."

§ 2. Purpose. The purpose of the Partnership shall be to [describe].

§ 3. Location. The location of the Partnership's principal place of business is _____
_____ County, _____.

§ 4. Members and Designation. The names and places of residence of the members, and their designation as General or Limited Partners, are:

_____	[Address]	General Partner
_____	[Address]	General Partner
_____	[Address]	Limited Partner
_____	[Address]	Limited Partner

§ 5. Term. The term for which the Partnership is to exist is indefinite.

§ 6. Initial Contributions of Limited Partners. The amount of cash and a description of the agreed value of the other property contributed by each Limited Partner are:

[Name]	[Describe]
[Name]	[Describe]

§ 7. Subsequent Contributions of Limited Partners. Each Limited Partner may (but shall not be obliged to) make such additional contributions to the capital of the Partnership as may from time to time be agreed upon by the General Partners.

§ 8. Profit Shares of Limited Partners. The share of the profits which each Limited Partner shall receive by reason of his contribution is:

[Name]	_____	%
[Name]	_____	%

Signed _____ , 20 _____

_____
_____
_____
_____

Signed and sworn before me, the undersigned authority, this _____ , 20_____.

Notary Public

_____ County, _____

loans to it. The partnership agreement may provide for additional contributions and voluntary or involuntary assessments of the partners after the partnership's formation. The liability of the limited partners is restricted to the amount of their contributions. The ability of the partnership to obtain loans from third parties will be based on the partnership's assets and the creditworthiness of the general partner or partners who have unlimited liability.

Control of the Limited Partnership

The control and management of the limited partnership is vested in the hands of the general partner. Control does not necessarily follow ownership interest, as it does in a corporation. A general partner may have a very small ownership interest, yet still retain the right to control the entity. Unless there is an agreement to the contrary, the general partner has absolute discretion as to when profit distributions are made.

The general partner has all of the rights and powers and is subject to all of the restrictions and liabilities of a partner in a general partnership. The general partner lacks the authority to act in a manner that contravenes the partnership certificate.

A limited partner has the same rights as any general partner to access partnership books and records, to have an accounting of the partnership business, to dissolve and wind up the partnership by court order, to receive the share of profits or compensation stipulated in the partnership certificate, and to have a return of her contribution on dissolution and distribution of the partnership assets, subject to the rights of creditors.

Exhibit 18–2 illustrates the basic comparisons of a general partnership, a revised limited partnership, and a limited liability company.

Liability in Limited Partnerships

A limited partnership must have at least one general partner, who has unlimited liability. Most states now allow the general partner to be a corporation or a natural person.

Generally speaking, the limited partners' liability is limited to their capital contributions. This contribution also includes the amount of capital that limited partners have pledged to contribute, but have not yet actually paid.

Limited partners can lose their limited liability if they participate in the management and control of the partnership's business. For example, if another party (often called a third party) has knowledge of a limited partner's involvement, the limited partner can lose the limited liability protection. A third party that has a legal complaint against a limited partnership that now has few or no assets would therefore look to see if a limited partner has participated in the management of the partnership. If so, then that limited partner loses the limited liability protection and is treated as a general partner with unlimited liability. Certain state statutes specify that the right of a limited partner to demand that the general partner be expelled from the partnership will not be considered as taking part in the control of the business.

The following case examines the question of whether a limited partner had lost his limited liability status. This case was decided under the ULPA.

CASE 18.4	**GONZALEZ v. CHALPIN**
Court of Appeals of New York, 1990 564 N.Y.S.2d 702	**BACKGROUND AND FACTS** Chalpin hired Gonzalez to be the superintendent and maintenance worker at Excel Associate's apartment building. Excel was a limited partnership that had one individual general partner, Lipkin; one corporate general partner, Tribute Music, Inc., a valid corporation; and one limited partner, Chalpin. Chalpin was also Tribute's president, sole shareholder, and director. Gonzalez was not paid for much of the work he performed. He sued Chalpin individually, as well as Excel Associates and its limited and general partners, for breach of contract.

Judge BELLACOSA

. . . .

The general restriction on the liability of limited partners is not controlling here because, if the partner in addition to the exercise of [the partner's] rights and powers as

Exhibit 18–2 **Basic Comparison of Partnerships and Limited Liability Companies**

Characteristic	General Partnership	Revised Limited Partnership	Limited Liability Company

Creation	• By agreement of two or more persons:
	
	  • Informal agreement (determined by actions of the people), or
	
	  • Formal written agreement.
	
	• Purpose is to carry on a business as co-owners for profit.
		• Must be allowed by state law.
		
		• Must file a certificate of limited partnership in the appropriate state office.
		
		• By agreement of two or more persons.
		
		• Partners (one or more general partners and one or more limited partners).
		
		• Purpose is to carry on a business as co-owners for profit.
			• Must be allowed by state law.
			
			• Must file articles of organization in the appropriate state office.
			
			• Two or more persons.

Sharing of profits and losses	• By agreement.
	
	• In absence of agreement:
	
	  • Profits and losses are shared equally by partners.
	
	  • If agreement covers only profits but not losses, then losses are shared in the same ratio as profits.
		• General partners by agreement.
		
		• Limited partners:
		
		  • Share profits by agreement.
		
		  • Share losses only up to their capital contribution.
			• By operating agreement.

Liability	• All partners have unlimited personal liability.	• All general partners have unlimited personal liability. • Limited partners are liable up to the amount of their investment.	• All members are liable up to the amount of their investment.
Capital contribution	• No minimum or mandatory amount by law; the amount is set by agreement or actions.	• Set by agreement (cash, property, or past services) and any obligation, including future services.	• Set by agreement (cash, property, or past services) and any obligation, including future services.

(continued)

Exhibit 18–2   **Basic Comparison of Partnerships and Limited Liability Companies (*continued*)**

Characteristic	General Partnership	Revised Limited Partnership	Limited Liability Company

Management	• By agreement.
	• In absence of agreement, all partners have an equal voice.
		• General partners:
		  • By agreement or
		  • In absence of management clause in agreement, each has an equal voice.
		• Limited partners have no voice, or
		  • If they are active in management, they have general liability as general partners, if third party has knowledge of such involvement.
		  • Limited partner may act as an agent or employee of the partnership and vote on amending the certificate or sale or dissolution of the partnership.
			• Members may be the managers.
			• Members may hire outsiders as managers.

Duration	• By agreement.
	• Can be dissolved by the following:
	  • Action of partner (withdrawal).
	  • Operation of law, death, or bankruptcy.
	  • Court decree.
		• General partners:
		  • By agreement in the certificate.
		  • By withdrawal, death, or insanity of a general partner in the absence of the right of other general partners to continue the partnership.
		• Limited partner's death does not terminate the partnership, unless he or she is the only remaining limited partner.
			• By the articles of organization:
			  • Date set, and/or
			  • Any events that would cause a dissolution.
			• When fewer than two members remain.

Priorities (order) upon liquidation	• Outside creditors. • Partner creditors. • Capital contribution of partners. • Profits of partners.	• Outside creditors. • Partner creditors. • By agreement, amounts before withdrawal to which partners are entitled.	• Outside creditors. • Member creditors. • By the operating agreement.

a limited partner takes part in the control of the business, the limited partner becomes liable as a general partner. . . . Chalpin cannot challenge the trial court's affirmed factual determination that he took part in the control of Excel's business. Instead, he attempts to skirt the individual and general responsibility imposed [by the law] by claiming that he acted at all times solely in his capacity as an officer of Tribute.

Irrefutably, individual liability should not be imposed on a limited partner merely because that person happens also to be an officer, director and/or shareholder of a corporate general partner. . . . But that is not this case. Moreover and conversely, a limited partner who takes part in the control of the limited partnership's business should not automatically be insulated from individual liability merely by benefit of status as an officer and sole owner of the corporate general partner. That is this case.

A limited partner who assumes such a dual capacity rightly bears a heavy burden when seeking to elude personal liability. For once a plaintiff meets the threshold burden of proving that a limited partner took an active individual part in effectuating the limited partnership's interests . . . , the fulcrum shifts. The limited partner in such a dual capacity must then, at least, prove that any relevant actions taken were performed solely in the capacity as officer of the general partner.

Defendant in this case failed to adjust to the shift and did not overcome the proof of involvement and responsibility for his actions undertaken in his individual capacity.

DECISION AND REMEDY The court rejected Chalpin's limited liability defense because he failed to prove that he acted only as an officer of the general partnership. He was held individually liable to Gonzalez.

CRITICAL THINKING: PREVENTIVE CONSIDERATION What actions could Chalpin have taken to avoid being held liable for the debts of the limited partnership?

Tax Consequences for a Limited Partnership

The limited partnership itself is not a taxable entity. The tax status of a limited partnership is the same as that of a general partnership, that is, both are pass-through organizations. The limited partnership makes an informational filing, reporting the allocation of profits and losses and other tax items to the various partners. Individual partners, both limited and general, report their allocated profits or losses on their own tax returns.

Profits and losses pass through the limited partnership to the individual partners before the income is subject to federal taxation. This arrangement is called **pass-through tax treatment**.

Because limited partnerships are used extensively as tax shelters, their tax status as partnerships often is challenged by the IRS. For federal income tax purposes, the IRS regulations provide that a limited partnership will be classified as a "partnership," rather than as "an association taxable as a corporation," if it possesses fewer corporate than noncorporate characteristics. The IRS looks for six corporate-like characteristics:

1. It has two or more associates.

2. It carries on a business for profit.

3. Management is centralized.

4. The business's debts are limited to its assets, and creditors cannot look to the personal assets of the owners for payments.

5. The business has unlimited life on its own and will continue in existence after the original shareholders or partners die.

6. It has free transferability of interest in the business.

If a business entity lacks any two of these corporate characteristics, the IRS will classify it as a partnership rather than as a corporation for tax purposes. The two easiest characteristics to avoid are free transferability of interests and continuity of life. Nearly all limited partnership agreements and limited liability companies provide for a termination date and impose restrictions on transferability of interest to avoid two of the corporate characteristics. If they do not, they will be taxed as a corporation.

Limited Liability Companies

The limited liability company (LLC) is a hybrid form of business organization that provides the limited liability protection of a corporation while retaining sufficient partnership characteristics to qualify for partnership status for federal income tax purposes. Nearly every state has a statute that authorizes the creation of LLCs. More important, the IRS recognizes LLCs.

The LLC form of organization was first developed in Germany and then spread to Latin America. Businesspeople from the United States traveling to Europe and Latin America eventually brought the concept home. In 1977, Wyoming was the first state to adopt legislation to allow this type of entity to cover mining leases. Businesspeople soon recognized the advantages of LLCs and the concept quickly expanded from mining leases to all types of businesses.

Once the IRS recognized this form of organization, states quickly adopted statutes authorizing it. Legislatures, wanting to encourage small businesses, had two goals for the LLC: (1) favorable tax treatment, as if the LLC were a partnership, and (2) limited owner liability, as if the LLC were a corporation.

The LLC differs from either a partnership or a corporation, but has aspects of both. The following sections look at the formation, tax treatment, management, limited liability, and continuity of existence of the LLC.

Formation of an LLC

A limited liability company is no more difficult to form than a limited partnership. All statutory provisions must be followed. Specific provisions vary from state to state. The owners of the LLC are called members. The managers of the LLC, those who manage the LLC from day to day, may be either the members or nonowners.

One or more persons must file the **articles of organization** and pay the appropriate fees at the designated public office. Exhibit 18–3 shows an example of the articles of organization for an LLC. Included within the articles are the name of the company, the date when the company will be dissolved, restrictions on trading the shares, whether the company will be managed by members or nonowners, the name and address of the statutory agent who receives legal papers, and other required information.

A limited liability company is required to use the words *limited liability company* or *limited company*, or the abbreviations LLC or LC. Many states forbid an LLC to use the following words and their abbreviations: *association, corporation,* or *incorporated.*

Tax Consequences

As discussed previously, partnerships and limited partnerships are not subject to federal income tax, even though they must file informational tax returns. The partnership passes income, credits, and losses through to its partners. The partners pay tax on the income received from the partnership.

Income generated by corporations is subject to what some call double taxation. The corporation must pay federal income tax on its taxable earnings. Part of the corporate income may be paid to shareholders as dividends. If the corporation pays dividends to the shareholders, they must report the dividends as income on their federal income tax returns.

The IRS allows small business corporations to apply for an S corporation tax status, which means that the corporation is treated as if it were a partnership for tax purposes. If the business meets all the IRS regulations, the corporation's income is not subject to federal income tax, although an income tax return must be filed. The income, credits, and losses may pass through the corporation to the shareholders. The income is subject to taxation when received by the shareholders. The income is taxed only once, just as it is in a partnership arrangement.

The IRS treats the LLC as a partnership instead of as a corporation if the LLC possesses no more than four of the six corporate-like characteristics discussed previously. The two attributes easiest to limit are continuity of life and free transferability of interests. The articles of organization can set an ending date for the LLC, and the operating agreement can restrict the transferability of interests.

The IRS has issued check-the-box regulations. On the income tax return filed by unincorporated associations, such as limited partnerships or limited liability companies, businesses can check a box indicating their partnership status.

Exhibit 18-3 Sample Articles of Organization

STATE OF ARIZONA
OFFICE OF THE CORPORATION COMMISSION

WORLD AMUSEMENT, L.L.C.

ARTICLES OF ORGANIZATION

Pursuant to A.R.S. § 29-632 the undersigned states as follows:

1. The name of the limited liability company is World Amusement, L.L.C.

2. The address of the registered office in Arizona is 206 N. Campo Avenue, Phoenix, Arizona 85881, which is located in the county of Maricopa.

3. The name and address of the statutory agent is John Lawyer, 100 East Loyola, Tempe, Arizona 85283.

4. There are two or more members at the time the limited liability company is formed.

5. The latest date on which the limited liability company is to dissolve is December 31, 2010.

6. Management of the limited liability company is vested in a manager or managers. The names and addresses of each person who is a manager and each member who owns a twenty percent or greater interest in the capital or profits of the limited liability are:

    Hiley Banks   [x]   member [x]   manager
    Shirley Banks   [x]   member [x]   manager

Signed _____ Date _____

Signed _____ Date _____

The persons executing this document need not be members of the limited liability company at the time of formation or after formation has occurred.

I, John Lawyer, having been designated to act as Statutory Agent, hereby consent to act in that capacity until removed or resignation is submitted in accordance with the Arizona Revised Statutes.

                                         _____
                                         Statutory Agent

Managing an LLC

A limited liability company is managed either by the members or by managers. The managers need not be members of the LLC. The members decide on the management.

If managed by members, the LLC has a management similar to that of a general partnership and is not considered to be centralized. If managed by nonowner managers, the LLC may practice centralized management similar to that of a corporation.

The members' operating agreement establishes their rights and responsibilities as members. The operating agreement may indicate whether a member's interest can be transferred and, if so, the circumstances and method of transfer. The agreement can be as broad or as limited as the members decide.

Limited Liability

The limited liability company affords its members protection of their personal assets from the claims of the LLC's creditors. The members are liable only up to the amount that they invest. That investment may be in the form of contributed property, services, cash, or a promissory note to the LLC in exchange for an LLC interest. The members have greater protection than is offered to general partners in any type of partnership. As discussed previously, in a limited partnership, all general partners have unlimited personal liability. In a general partnership, all partners are personally liable for business debts.

Continuity of Existence

One characteristic of a corporation is that it exists in perpetuity, unaffected by the death, retirement, insanity, or bankruptcy of its shareholders. One way to avoid being taxed as a corporation is to establish a termination date. On termination, if desired, the owners can merely form another LLC.

A problem occurs when a member dies. To keep the partnership aspect that qualifies the LLC for the pass-through tax treatment in the event of a death, the IRS requires an LLC to obtain an agreement not to dissolve signed by a majority of the remaining members and by all of the remaining managers.

The following case discusses limited liability companies and how they are treated as separate entities.

CASE 18.5	GEBHARDT FAMILY INVESTMENT, L.L.C. v. NATIONS TITLE INSURANCE OF NEW YORK, INC.
Court of Special Appeals of Maryland, 2000 132 Md. App. 457, 752 A.2d 1222	**BACKGROUND AND FACTS** The Gebhardts purchased 31.6707 acres of land in Prince George's County on September 1, 1987. They simultaneously purchased title insurance from Nations Title Insurance of New York, Inc. The policy named Joseph and Faye Gebhardt as the insureds.

In 1995, the Gebhardts learned that someone else was paying property taxes on 4.75 acres of the property. They reported to Nations that there was a cloud on the title as to the 4.75 acres. They demanded that Nations correct the situation by negotiating a purchase from person alleging ownership and by obtaining a quitclaim to the 4.75 acres in favor of the Gebhardts.

On December 18, 1996, before the matter was resolved, and apparently to facilitate their estate planning, the Gebhardts executed a special warranty deed conveying all 31.6707 acres in fee simple to Gebhardt Family Investment, LLC, a limited liability company created under Virginia law. The Gebhardts were the sole members of the LLC. The deed stated that the LLC paid consideration of $160,990.00 for the property.

On November 13, 1997, the Gebhardts and the LLC sued Nations for breach of contract for failing to resolve the cloud on title. Trial was held on July 22, 1999, and the sole issue before the court was whether the Gebhardts and/or the LLC were insured under the title insurance policy. The parties apparently reached a settlement agreement as to the amount of damages that Nations would pay in the event that the court found there was coverage.

Joseph Gebhardt was the only witness called. He testified to the effect that he and his wife formed the LLC and conveyed the property in question to it as part of their estate planning. Gebhardt stated that they did not pay any consideration and the consideration of $160,990.00 recited on the deed was written so Virginia would transfer taxes from them as individuals to the LLC. Gebhardt added that he and his wife still owned the property and paid all of the taxes.

The title insurance policy issued by Nations to the Gebhardts in 1987 states, in pertinent part:

> The coverage of this policy shall continue in force as of Date of Policy in favor of an insured so long as such insured retains an estate or interest in the land, or holds an indebtedness secured by a purchase money mortgage given by a purchaser from such insured, or so long as such insured shall have liability by reason of covenants of warranty made by such insured in any transfer or conveyance of such estate or interest, provided, however, this policy shall not continue in force in favor of any purchaser from such insured of either said estate or interest or the indebtedness secured by a purchase money mortgage given to such insured.

Paragraph 2(a) of Conditions and Stipulations to Policy of Title Insurance. The policy defines "insured" as

> the insured named [in the policy] and, subject to any rights or defenses the Company may have had against the named insured, those who succeed to the interest of such insured by operation of law as distinguished from purchase including, but not limited to, heirs, distributees, devisees, survivors, personal representatives, next of kin, or corporate or fiduciary successors.

The court thus determined that the LLC was not insured under the policy because it obtained the property by way of purchase rather than by operation of law. It determined that the Gebhardts' coverage terminated when they conveyed the property to a separate entity. The court directed that judgment be entered in favor of Nations.

MARVIN H. SMITH, Judge

. . . .

The appellants argue that because the Gebhardts are the sole members of the L.L.C. the conveyance was, in effect, to themselves and they still retain an interest in the property within the meaning of Paragraph 2(a) of the policy's Conditions and Stipulations.

The argument is based on a misunderstanding of the nature of limited liability companies. It is widely recognized that:

> [t]he allure of the limited liability company is its unique ability to bring together in a single business organization the best features of all other business forms—properly structured, its owners obtain both a corporate-styled liability shield and the pass-through tax benefits of a partnership. General and limited partnerships do not offer their partners a corporate-styled liability shield. Corporations, including those having made a Subchapter S election, do not offer their shareholders all the pass-through tax benefits of a partnership. All state limited liability company acts contain provisions for a liability shield and partnership tax status.

. . . .

As the trial court recognized, when the Gebhardts conveyed their interest in the property to the L.L.C., they effected a "transfer from one entity or person to another." The Gebhardts and the L.L.C. are separate entities. The Gebhardts may not file suit in their own names on behalf of the L.L.C. Nor may they be held individually liable for wrongful conduct of the L.L.C. While the Gebhardts have an interest in the L.L.C., they no longer have an interest in the property. Rather, it is the L.L.C. that has the interest in the property. To hold otherwise would be to disregard the nature and viability of limited liability companies.

. . . .

By conveying the property under special warranty deed, moreover, the Gebhardts covenanted to protect the L.L.C. only against claims made "by, through, or under" the Gebhardts, as grantors. They did not warrant title against a claim of superior title made by someone else. There is no suggestion that the alleged cloud on title was created by any action or inaction on the part of the Gebhardts while the property was titled in their names. The Gebhardts thus transferred from themselves to the L.L.C. the problem of the cloud on title as to the 4.75 acres. Should the other persons claiming title to the 4.75 acres bring an action to quiet title, the L.L.C, rather than the Gebhardts, would be required to defend and the Gebhardts could not be held personally liable.

. . . .

The appellants admit in their brief that "[t]here has, as yet, been no monetary loss." They nevertheless contend that they suffered a loss in that "a title which has a known overlap cannot be said to be 'undamaged.'" Presumably, the appellants believe, as Mr. Gebhardt testified at trial, that such property is unmarketable. Assuming arguendo that there is a "known overlap"—and the record is unclear in that regard—the fatal flaw in this reasoning is that the Gebhardts successfully conveyed the entire property, including the 4.75 acres in question, to the L.L.C. by way of a special warranty deed. . . . If any loss is suffered because of the cloud on title, it will be suffered by the L.L.C., which was not an insured under the policy either before or after the conveyance.

DECISION AND REMEDY A limited liability company is a separate legal entity. The problem involving the cloud on title became the problem of the LLC and not the Gebhardts once the property was conveyed to it. The title policy only covered the Gebhardts and not the LLCs.

CRITICAL THINKING: LEGAL THEORY Assume for the moment that you own an LLC. You have a contract that restricts the transfer of the contract to another person or entity. The contract prohibits the LLC from transferring the contract from the LLC to you. Why does the law not allow you to combine your individual rights with the rights of the LLC when you are essentially the LLC?

Limited Liability Partnerships

Many states have passed legislation to permit the creation of limited liability partnerships (also called registered limited liability partnerships). The collapse of the savings and loan associations caused the need for this type of business entity.

When the savings and loan associations declared bankruptcy, injured people looked to the law firms and accounting firms of the savings and loan associations. People brought lawsuits against these firms to recover losses that had been incurred as the result of

malpractice acts (negligent acts) by a partner in the law or accounting firms. Many of these organizations were general partnerships that were national or international firms with hundreds of partners. For example, a partner in Hong Kong could be held liable personally for negligent actions of a partner in California even though the partner in Hong Kong did not have any knowledge of the California partner's activities.

These organizations did not want to form corporations or limited liability companies because they would then be subject to the public reporting requirements of the Securities and Exchange Commission

(SEC) and their finances would become public information. The solution was the creation of the limited liability partnership entity. This type of partnership has no general partners, so any judgment is limited to recovery from the partnership assets. If the judgment is for malpractice (negligence), recovery can be made from the partnership's assets and from the individual partner's assets who committed the malpractice. Currently, public disclosure of the partnership's business is not required. The SEC or the courts still must determine if this type of entity protects against information disclosure.

A state statute must authorize a limited liability partnership's creation. Normally these statutes require a public filing containing the name and the address of the partnership, the number of partners in the partnership, and a brief description of the business in which the partnership engages. If the partners follow the statutory provisions, they are not liable personally for the business's debts. In 1996, the National Conference of Commissioners on Uniform State Laws adopted proposed statutes on limited liability partnerships and foreign limited liability partnerships as part of the Uniform Partnership Act.[9]

---

[9]Family businesses can present unique problems. Some of these issues and how to solve them are discussed at Northeastern University's Center for Family Business's Web site at http://www.fambiz.com/. Occasionally, these problems develop because the family is using the wrong form of organization.

International Consideration

Business Entities Overseas

When a business decides to enter international markets, it must determine the type of organization to use overseas. Although a business can sell products through normal export procedures, it may need to establish a permanent office or staff in another country, especially if its products will be manufactured in the foreign country.

Most Western countries recognize two forms of organizations that provide limited liability to the owners. One form is called a corporation for profit, and the second is the limited liability company. Most countries require a minimum amount of capital to start and run the business. They require a larger amount of capital for a corporation than for a limited liability company. For example, Germany recognizes business entities that are similar to U.S. corporations and limited liability companies. In Germany, the creation of a limited liability company requires the investment of a minimum of 50,000 deutsche marks, whereas 100,000 deutsche marks are required for a corporation. Other countries of the European Union have similar provisions. Just as requirements for minimum amounts of capital investment vary among the fifty states, the amounts vary from one country to another in the European Union.

PRACTICAL TIPS

Drafting a Partnership Agreement

You and a friend decide to go into partnership to sell a new product. The following are some of the considerations to be included in your written partnership agreement:

1. Names and addresses of the general partners and the designation of partnership status
2. Name of the partnership and address of the principal place of business
3. Character of the business
4. Duration of the partnership
5. Contributions of the partners:
   a. Form of contribution
   b. Interest on contribution
   c. Additional contribution requirements
6. Assets of the partnership:
   a. Identification of the assets
   b. Valuation of the assets
   c. Control of the assets and accountability for them
   d. Distribution of the assets
7. Duties of the partners
8. Distribution of profits and losses
9. Compensation, benefits, and expenses of the partners
10. Policy and management of the business

11. Accounting practices and procedures
12. Liability and insurance requirements
13. Indemnity clause (to compensate for loss or to reimburse expenses)
14. Changes in the partners by withdrawal, retirement, death, mental illness, bankruptcy, or admission of additional partners
15. Sale or assignment of the partnership interest
16. Arbitration provisions
17. Amendment provisions
18. Dissolution, winding up, and termination of the partnership
19. Date of the agreement
20. Signatures of the partners.

With a well-drafted agreement, you should also be able to answer questions that frequently arise. Use these questions as a checklist.

Checklist

✔ *Time* How much time should each partner spend doing partnership business?

✔ *Time Away* What happens if one partner fails to spend the required time in the business? For example, what happens if your partner goes to Europe for a six-month vacation?

✔ *Disability* What happens if one partner becomes disabled or dies?

✔ *Sharing* How will the profits and losses be shared?

✔ *Capital* What happens if the business requires additional capital?

✔ *Financial* Who should sign the checks, make the deposits, and authorize electronic payments and deposits?

✔ *Termination* If one partner decides to leave the partnership, how does the partnership end?

Chapter Summary

Six forms of business organizations exist: sole proprietorship, partnership, limited partnership, limited liability company, limited liability partnership, and corporation. Concerns in selecting a type of business entity include the difficulty in forming it, limited liability, tax considerations, continuity of existence, transferability, management and control, financing, licenses, and location.

The sole proprietorship is the most informal business organization. A business's sole owner has unlimited liability and the business may cease to operate upon the owner's death or incapacity. No tax advantages exist for this form of ownership. It does, however, give maximum control of the business to the owner.

A general partnership allows people to join together to operate a business. No formal requirements exist to create a general partnership. Each partner has an equal right to manage the business. In the absence of an agreement, partners share profits and losses equally. Partners have unlimited liability for the partnership's debts. If a partner dies, becomes incapacitated, or otherwise leaves the partnership, the partnership dissolves.

Dissolution means that the partnership union is discontinued, but the business continues through the stages of winding up and termination.

The limited partnership must be organized in accordance with statutory provisions. All limited partnerships must have at least one general partner who manages the business's operation and one limited partner. If a limited partner takes an active role in managing, that limited partner assumes unlimited liability for the business's debts. Otherwise, a limited partner's only liability is his or her capital contribution. In a limited partnership, the general partner has unlimited liability. Profits are shared in accordance with the limited partnership certificate. If a partner dies, the limited partnership is not dissolved.

Like the limited partnership, the limited liability company and the limited liability partnership must follow state statutes when they form. Limited liability companies are treated as a partnership for tax purposes if they do not have the characteristics of a corporation. Both the LLC and the limited liability partnership have limited liability, which means that the investor's liability is limited to the amount that the person invested.

Using the World Wide Web

Commerce Clearing House (CCH) Incorporated, a major publisher of business material, maintains one of the more informative Web sites that covers the different forms of organizations and the problems in forming a new business. It details considerations important to starting or purchasing a business.

The Small Business Administration (SBA) maintains a Web site to aid small businesses. At its Web site, you learn about the SBA and where its offices are located in the United States. The SBA maintains an online library.

For *Web Activities*, links to Web sites mentioned in the chapter, and additional Web sites that relate to the chapter topics, go to **http://bohlman.westbuslaw.com**, click on "Internet Applications," and select Chapter 18.

Web Activities

Go to **http://bohlman.westbuslaw.com**, click on "Internet Applications," and select Chapter 18.
18–1 Starting a Business
18–2 Selling a Business

Key Terms

articles of organization
dissociation
dissolution
fictitious name filing
general partner
limited liability company (LLC)
limited liability partnership

limited partner
limited partnership
manager
member
operating agreement
partnership
partnership by estoppel
pass-through tax treatment

Revised Uniform Limited Partnership Act (RULPA)
Revised Uniform Partnership Act (RUPA)
sole proprietorship
termination
Uniform Limited

Partnership Act (ULPA)
Uniform Partnership Act (UPA)
use permit
variance permit
winding up

Questions and Case Problems

18–1 Choice of Business Organizations Lisa, Amy, and Mary are college graduates. Lisa has an idea for a new product that she believes could make the three of them very wealthy. Her idea is to manufacture beer dispensers for home use. Her goal is to market them to consumers throughout the Midwest. Lisa's personal experience qualifies her to be both first-line supervisor and general manager of the new firm. Amy is a born salesperson. Mary has little interest in sales or management, but would like to invest a large sum of money that she has inherited from her aunt. Based on this information, which form of business organization should Lisa, Amy, and Mary consider adopting?

18–2 Limited Liability Assume that Mary, in Question 18–1, is willing to put her inherited money into the business, but that she wants no further liability should the beer dispenser manufacturing business fail. The bank will lend capital at a 9 percent interest rate, but only if certain restrictions are placed on management decisions. The restrictions are unsatisfactory to

Amy and Lisa, so the two decide to bring Mary into the business instead of using the bank. Under these circumstances, discuss the types of business organizations best suited to meet Mary's needs.

18–3 Limited Liability The limited liability aspect of the corporation or limited partnership is one of the most important reasons that firms choose to organize as corporations or limited partnerships rather than as general partnerships or sole proprietorships. Limited liability means that if a corporation or limited partnership is unable to meet its obligations with corporate or partnership assets, creditors will not be allowed to look to the owners (stockholders) of the corporation or the limited partners to satisfy their claims. Assume that Lisa and Amy (from Question 18–1) do not have a wealthy friend like Mary who wants to go into business with them and that therefore they must borrow money from a bank to start their business. Lisa and Amy decide to incorporate. What do you think a bank will ask them to sign when they seek a loan? What effect does this bank loan have on the "advantage" of limited liability under corporations?

18–4 Partnership Able, Baker, and Carlton have formed a twenty-year partnership to purchase land, develop it, manage it, and then sell the property. The partnership agreement calls for the partners to devote full time to the business. Assume that each of the following events takes place:

a. After two years, Baker and Carlton agree that the partnership's working hours will be from 8:00 A.M. to 6 P.M. rather than the previously established schedule of 9 A.M. to 5 P.M. Able refuses to work before 9 A.M. and quits promptly at 5 P.M.

b. After two years, Able quits the partnership.

c. After two years, Able becomes insolvent.

d. After two years, Able dies.

Discuss fully which of these acts constitutes a dissolution and what types of liability, if any, Able faces.

18–5 Limited Partnership Zhang and Zook form a limited partnership, with Zhang as the general partner and Zook as the limited partner. Zook puts up $15,000. Zhang contributes some office equipment that he owns. They properly file a certificate of limited partnership and begin business. One month later, Zhang becomes ill. Instead of hiring someone to manage the business, Zook takes over complete management himself. While Zook is in control, he contracts with Abba for a large sum of money. Zhang returns to work. Because of other commitments, the Abba contract is breached. Abba contends that he can hold Zhang and Zook personally liable if the amount owed him cannot be satisfied out of the assets of the limited partnership. Discuss this contention.

18–6 Dissolution Lange and Bartlett worked together for several years on a part-time basis installing swimming pools. In 1972, they verbally agreed to form the partnership "Pool Boys" and began operating the business full time. This arrangement continued until April 1975, when Lange told Bartlett that he wanted to dissolve the partnership. Bartlett eventually offered Lange $3,000 in payment for Lange's share of the partnership. Lange refused this offer. Neither Bartlett nor Lange obtained an accounting, nor did Lange accept any money. Between 1975 and 1978, Bartlett worked hard and as business increased, the partnership became more profitable. In 1978, Lange sued to recover his interest in the partnership, claiming that he was entitled to one-half of both the assets and the profits from the business

subsequent to April 1975. The trial court entered a judgment that gave him one-half of the assets, but not the profits. Lange appealed, asserting that he was also entitled to one-half the profits. Was he entitled to the profits? Why? [*Lange v. Bartlett*, 121 Wis. 2d 599, 360 N.W.2d 702 (1984)].

18–7 What Is a Partnership? Oddo and Ries entered into a partnership agreement in March 1978 to create and publish a book describing how to restore F-100 pickup trucks. Oddo was to write the book and Ries was to provide the capital. Oddo supplied Ries with the manuscript, but Ries was dissatisfied and hired someone else to revise the manuscript. Ries published the book, which contained substantial amounts of Oddo's work. Did Ries's actions constitute a dissolution of the partnership? Can Oddo require Ries to account formally for the profits on the book? Explain. [*Oddo v. Ries*, 743 F.2d 630 (9th Cir. 1984)]

18–8 Liability Southland Construction, Inc., brought action against Thomas Richeson, individually as an engineer, and also against his business, Richeson, LLC, for negligence and breach of contract in failing to design a wall in a manner conforming to professional engineering standards. As the general contractor for the apartment project, Southland hired the firm of Richeson, LLC, to design a retaining wall. Richeson, individually, drew the engineering drawings and signed them for his LLC. Southland alleged that the wall's design was inconsistent with proper procedures, resulting in its cracking. Southland spent $188,000 to repair the damaged wall. The trial court dismissed Richeson as an individual from the case and Southland appealed. Was only the LLC liable for the cracked wall or were both the LLC and Richeson liable? Explain your answer. [*Southland Construction, Inc. v. Richeson Corporation*, 642 So. 2d 5 (Fla. App. 1994)]

18–9 Partnership by Estoppel Paramount Steamship Company owned the *Courtney D*, a seagoing vessel. Paramount Petroleum Corp. was in the oil business. Both companies belonged to the same shareholders, operated out of the same address, and had the same accountant. Receptionists at either company answered the telephones by saying "Paramount." The *Courtney D* required extensive repairs. Taylor Rental Center extended credit on equipment to make these repairs. When Taylor was not paid, it sued both Paramount corporations. Can both Paramount corporations be held liable under the theory of partnership by estoppel? Explain. [*Paramount Petroleum Corp. v. Taylor Rental Center*, 712 S.W.2d 534 (Tex. Ct. App. 1986)]

18-10 Internet A person wants to start a new business, He or she can use the Small Business Administration (SBA), which has a Web site that offers information to anyone wanting to start a business. Go to **http://**

www.sba.gov/managing/leadership/ethics.html and review what is written on business ethics. What are the three questions a person should ask when faced with an ethical dilemma?

Chapter 19

Corporate Law and Franchising Law

A corporation is an artificial being, invisible, intangible, and existing only in contemplation of law.

> Dartmouth College v. Woodward
> 17 U.S. (4 Wheat.) 518, 4 L. Ed. 629, 1819
> Chief Justice John Marshall, 1755–1835
> Fourth chief justice of the United States of America, 1801–1835

Chapter Outline

Ethical Consideration

Corporate Giving: Whose Money Is It? The Corporation's or the Shareholders'?

As the president of a highly successful business, you believe that business leaders have a civic duty to take significant leadership roles in community affairs. Involvement as a community leader helps to promote goodwill for businesses, although the benefit is difficult to measure. In addition to taking time from your business duties to attend meetings and appear at functions, your office staff and management team support community activities. The business also donates significantly to public programs.

At a recent shareholders' meeting, several shareholders questioned your right as the president to use work time, staff, and business funds to assist in community endeavors. They believe that you should use your free time for community work and donate to charities from your own assets. These shareholders believe that rather than the business donating time and money, it should pay larger dividends. They also believe that each shareholder should decide the charities, if any, they prefer the company to support. Do you continue your community involvement on company time and keep the company's donation programs? Use the ethical model presented in Chapter 2 and reprinted on the inside front cover to develop your answer.

Introduction

The corporate form is the most important type of business organization in the United States. Although corporations are the most formal type, they offer many advantages over other forms of business entities.

A **corporation** is a separate legal entity owned by shareholders. Corporations generally are characterized by two or more persons carrying on a business for profit, with centralized management, continuity of existence, limited liability for the shareholders, and freely transferable shares.

The corporate organizational structure today is used by businesses that plan to have a public offering of securities and a listing on a stock exchange. Any publicly offered securities are subject to federal and/or state securities laws, which is discussed in Chapter 20. Small businesses today do not form corporations, but instead use one of the business forms discussed in Chapter 18.

In the past centuries, individuals owned most businesses. A person who wanted to create a corporation had to obtain a charter from the state legislature. Even in the early 1800s, states did not look fondly on corporations and placed many restrictions on them. During the twentieth century, the states became more flexible, not only in creating corporations, but in allowing corporations to conduct a variety of businesses.

Artiste Login. Carlo and Carlotta need to review all the choices of business entities. Although Artiste is doing a good business, the corporate form of business probably will not be the first choice. Today, a business most often elects to incorporate if it will be selling its shares to the public.

Ease of Formation

Corporations are formed under state law. Most states have adopted one of two model provisions into statutes. Some states use the **Model Business Corporation Act (MBCA)**, while others use the **Revised Model Business Corporation Act (RMBCA)**. No state has adopted all the original provisions in either act.

The MBCA was originally proposed in 1933 and modified in 1969. The RMBCA was introduced in 1984 in response to demands for different forms of corporations and for simpler procedures. Most state legislatures, however, greatly modified the MBCA or RMBCA to reflect their respective state's history. Although the major provisions of the MBCA and RMBCA have been adopted by many states, the corporate statutes vary greatly from state to state. The following discussion references the RMBCA.

Incorporators are the people who start the corporation. They choose the state in which to charter their corporation. Most states allow a business to incorporate in one state but to locate its principal place of business elsewhere, as long as the corporation maintains a registered office in the state in which it is incorporated. A corporation is a **domestic corporation** in the state in which it originally incorporated. A corporation files as a **foreign corporation** in all other states in which it will

LEGAL HIGHLIGHT

The Model Business Corporation Act and the Revised Model Business Corporation Act

The Model Business Corporation Act (MBCA) is a codification of modern corporation law. A model statute is created with the understanding that it may need amendments or changes to reflect local interests, needs, or problems, but it is presented for various jurisdictions to draw on in forming their decisions concerning corporate law.

The MBCA first was published in its complete form in 1933 by the Committee on Corporate Laws of the American Bar Association. It was patterned after the Illinois Business Corporation Act of 1933. The act was drafted, in part, in response to the tumultuous history of corporations in the United States prior to that time. The corporate form of business organization is common today, but it was rare until after the Civil War (1861–1865). Until the late 1800s, the states granted the corporate status sparingly and only when the grant seemed necessary to procure some specific benefit for the community.

The corporate form was limited because people distrusted the sheer size of a corporation. People feared the disastrous effects on the community's economic life, because corporations embody a concentration of economic power. People believed that corporations could easily swallow up small individual businesses, could virtually enslave labor, and, thus, dominate the state.

Even when the use of the corporate structure eventually was permitted for more general business purposes, the states placed severe restrictions on the size and scope of its use. The states limited the scope of the corporation's powers and activities, established a maximum duration for corporations, and required state residence as a prerequisite to incorporation.

By the turn of the century, however, a number of states removed these safeguards from their incorporation statutes to capture the significant revenue raised by charging fees to grant corporate charters. If a state had permissive corporate laws, more corporations would incorporate in the state. For example, New Jersey permitted a New York corporation to incorporate under New Jersey's more permissive laws and yet operate principally in New York.

The constant rivalry among the states competing for revenues and control created notable inconsistencies in corporate law among the states and substantial confusion in the courts.[a] The MBCA filled the need for uniformity in corporate law. Since 1933, the act has undergone several changes and was last revised and renumbered in 1969.

The Revised Model Business Corporation Act (RMBCA) of 1984 served as a convenient guide for the states to revise their respective state corporation acts. It was designed for use by both publicly held and closely held corporations and includes provisions for the rights and duties of shareholders, management, and directors. A number of states have amended their corporation laws, to a limited degree, based on the RMBCA.

Neither the revised and renumbered 1969 act nor the 1984 act has been adopted totally by any state. These acts, however, have influenced the codification of corporate statutes in most states. Considerable variation exists among the state statutes based on these two acts. When making a business decision, the corporation must rely on the individual state statutes and not on the model acts as published by the National Conference of Commissioners on Uniform State Laws.

[a] The intense competition among the states to attract corporate charters is vividly described by Justice Louis Brandeis (1856–1941), associate justice (1916–1939), in *Louis K. Ligget Co. v. Lee*, 288 U.S. 517, 548–564; 53 S. Ct. 483, 490–496; 77 L. Ed. 929, 944–953 (1933).

do business. An **alien corporation** is one that comes from outside the United States to do business within the United States.

Incorporators look for favorable state corporate and tax codes and also consider how the state's case law has interpreted its corporate code. The more developed the state's law, the more the corporation can anticipate the legal consequences of its actions.

Incorporators frequently hire a **promoter**, who makes contacts for and takes preliminary steps to organize the corporation. Unless a promoter specifically limits his liability in the contract by requiring parties to look to the corporation yet to be formed, the promoter bears personal liability for all preincorporation contracts. These contracts can include the purchase or lease of land, contracts to construct buildings, the purchase of equipment and inventory, and even financing agreements with third parties. Even after the corporation forms, the promoter remains personally liable until the corporation, through its board of directors, assumes responsibility for the contracts by adopting them as contracts of the corporation.

Articles of Incorporation

The first step in formalizing a corporation's creation is a public filing. As part of the initial incorporation process, the incorporators must file **articles of incorporation** with a designated state office, such as the office of the secretary of state. Once the state approves the articles of incorporation, it issues a corporate charter. The charter may be a separate piece of paper issued by the state; most states today return the articles of incorporation stamped "incorporated" and the stamped articles serve as the charter.

The articles provide basic information about the corporation and serve as the primary source of authority for its future operations. The articles of incorporation are analogous to a constitution for the corporation. Specific requirements vary somewhat from state to state. Basically, however, the articles of incorporation include the following:

1. The name of the corporation;
2. The purpose of the corporation, which may be stated in a general way in order to include all lawful business;
3. The duration of the corporation, which is almost always perpetual;
4. The date and time of the commencement of corporate existence, which usually starts with the filing of the articles with the secretary of state or which may be set by statute;
5. The number of shares that the corporation has the authority to issue, which often includes a list of the various classes of shares, their rights and limitations, and the capital allowed to start business;
6. The address of the corporation's registered office and the name of its registered agent in the state;
7. The number of members on the first board of directors and, where required, their names and addresses and the name and address of each incorporator; and
8. The shareholders' preemptive rights (the rights of existing shareholders to purchase newly issued stock to maintain their position of control and financial interest in the corporation, if any).

In many states, only one incorporator is required, and the incorporator may be a natural person, a corporation, a partnership, a limited partnership, or a limited liability company. The corporation's name must include the word *corporation, incorporated, company, limited*, or an abbreviation of one of these words. Exhibit 19–1 shows sample articles of incorporation.

Bylaws

After the charter has been issued, the corporation is formed. The incorporator or incorporators elect the board of directors. In many states, the board of directors may consist of only one person. The initial board then meets and, among other things, adopts the corporation's **bylaws**. The bylaws must conform with the state corporate code and its articles of incorporation.

If the articles of incorporation are considered to be equivalent to a constitution, the bylaws are equivalent to statutes. Just as the constitution (articles of incorporation) is the basic governing document and is hard to change, statutes (bylaws) carry out the constitution's guidelines and are easier to change.

The bylaws set forth the internal management rules for the corporation, typically including what constitutes a quorum (minimum number of members who must be present at a meeting in order to take valid actions), voting requirements for shareholders and directors, the requirements for election of the **directors** and **officers** and the terms for which each will serve, the officers' duties, and similar provisions.

Source of Funding

A corporation can raise money in several ways. The two most common are (1) to sell a part ownership in the corporation by issuing equity securities and (2) to borrow money by issuing debt securities.

A corporation commonly acquires funds by accepting offers to buy an interest in it. The corporation

Exhibit 19-1   Sample Articles of Incorporation

State *of* Delaware

Certificate *of* Incorporation

A Stock Corporation

- **First:** The name of this Corporation is _____

_____

- **Second:** Its registered office in the State of Delaware is to be located at _____

_____ Street, in the City of _____

County of _____ Zip Code _____.

The registered agent in charge thereof is _____

_____

_____

- **Third:** The purpose of the corporation is to engage in any lawful act or activity for which corporations may be organized under the General Corporation Law of Delaware.

- **Fourth:** The amount of the total authorized capital stock of this corporation is

_____ Dollars ($ _____) divided into _____ shares of

_____ Dollars ($ _____) each.

- **Fifth:** The name and mailing address of the incorporator are as follows:

Name _____

Mailing Address

_____

_____ Zip Code _____

- **I, The Undersigned,** for the purpose of forming a corporation under the laws of the State of Delaware, do make, file and record this Certificate, and do certify that the facts herein stated are true, and I have accordingly hereunto set my hand this _____ day of _____, A.D. 20_____.

BY: _____

(Incorporator)

NAME: _____

(Type or Print)

---

sends to the purchaser either paper or electronic stock certificates that represent an ownership interest. Usually, an individual never sees the stock certificates, because they are held by a brokerage firm. This ownership interest in a corporation, represented by stock, is known as an **equity security**.

A corporation also may raise money by borrowing it. Often, a corporation issues **bonds** (which represent a long-term debt). Bonds may be secured by the business's assets or the bonds may be unsecured. Unsecured bonds are called **debentures**. Bonds are **debt securities** that represent a corporate obligation.

Equity Securities versus Debt Securities

Differences exist between equity securities (shares in the corporation) and debt securities (evidence of borrowed money). With an equity security, if the value of the shares increases, the shareholders can profit from the increased valuation as owners of the corporation. If the value of the shares decreases, the shareholders lose the equity and may even lose their entire investment.

A debt security is treated like any loan. With a debt security, the holder knows that she will receive interest paid at a specific rate, such as 10 percent, on the loan.

If the corporation dissolves, the debt holders always have a higher priority for repayment than the equity holders when the assets are sold.

Equity Securities

Equity securities are represented by share certificates in a corporation. Equity securities represent ownership and, usually, voting rights. Over the centuries, a wide variety of equity securities have developed. Exhibit 19–2 lists most of the different types of equity securities. The following sections discuss two types of stock, common and preferred, in more detail.

Common Stock. The most commonly held equity security is **common stock**. The owners of common stock generally have the right to vote to elect directors; to amend the articles of incorporation; to amend the bylaws, if the articles so provide; and to decide other major corporate matters. The shareholder also has a right to a share of the corporation's profits proportionate to the number of shares owned, if the board of directors declares a dividend. Common stock generally has no fixed dividend rate and does not carry with it any inherent right to have a dividend declared, even when the corporation is profitable.

On dissolution and liquidation of a corporation, the shareholders have a right to a proportionate share of the assets after the creditors' claims have been satisfied. Unless stock is redeemed (repurchased) by the corporation, the shares have an indefinite duration.

Preferred Stock. Although **preferred stock** generally is considered an equity security, from an investment standpoint it also bears certain similarities to a debt security. Preferred stock offers various designated preferences that the articles of incorporation establish.

Exhibit 19–2   Types and Definitions of Equity Securities

Types	Definitions
Common stock	Owners of common stock receive the lowest priority with respect to dividends paid and to the distribution of assets on dissolution of the corporation.
Preferred stock	Shares of preferred stock have priority over common stock shares as to payment of dividends and distribution of assets on corporate dissolution. Dividend payments are usually a fixed percentage of the face value of the share.
Cumulative preferred stock	With this type of preferred stock, a required dividend not paid in a given year must be paid in a subsequent year before any common stock dividends are paid.
Participating preferred stock	Owners of participating preferred stock first receive agreed to dividends and then receive the same distribution of dividends that is paid on common stock.
Convertible preferred stock	Convertible preferred stock gives holders the option to convert their shares into a specified number of common shares either in the issuing corporation or, sometimes, in another corporation.
Redeemable (callable) preferred stock	Redeemable preferred shares are issued with the express preferred stock condition that the issuing corporation has the right to repurchase the shares as specified.
Authorized shares	Authorized shares are allowed to be issued by the articles of incorporation.
Issued shares	Issued shares are transferred to shareholders.
Outstanding shares	Authorized and issued shares that are still held by shareholders are outstanding shares.
Treasury shares	Treasury shares are authorized and issued but are not outstanding (reacquired by the corporation).
No par value shares	No par value shares are issued without any stated value. The price usually is fixed by the board of directors or the shareholders.
Par value shares	Par value shares are issued and priced at a stated value per share.

Generally, payment of preferred stock dividends carries a preference over dividends paid to common stockholders and often pays dividends at a fixed rate. When a corporation is dissolved and the assets sold and converted to money, preferred shareholders often have priority over common shareholders.

When the corporation is not profitable and preferred dividends cannot be paid, some preferred stock, called **cumulative preferred stock**, carries the right to accumulate the unpaid dividend. This right means that if, in the future, a dividend is declared, the preferred stockholder receives the previous unpaid dividend before any common stockholders receive payment of dividends.

Preferred stockholders may or may not have voting rights on some corporate issues. Usually, voting rights are reserved strictly for common shareholders; if dividends have not been paid to the preferred shareholders, however, then they have a right to vote in many situations. On liquidation, the debt securities and other debts of the corporation are paid first. Then, depending on provisions in the articles of incorporation, the value of the preferred stock may be paid to its holders before holders of common stock receive any payments. Preferred stock dividends paid by the corporation are not deductible as an interest expense (treated as an equity security) for corporate income tax purposes.

A corporation must be careful not to sell more stock than is authorized in its articles of incorporation. In the following case, the officers and directors of the corporation were found liable after the corporation issued too many shares of stock.

CASE 19.1	**AGOSTA v. SOUTHWEST BREEDERS, INC.**
Court of Appeals of Oklahoma, 1991 810 P.2d 377	**BACKGROUND AND FACTS** The articles of incorporation for Southwest Breeders, Inc., allowed the corporation to issue no more than 50,000 shares of its stock at $1.00 per share. On March 31, 1986, Agosta purchased 15,000 shares.

Agosta later discovered that on December 27, 1985, the officers and directors of Southwest Breeders had issued 1,370,000 shares at below-par value to themselves. These shares were clearly in excess of the amount allowed by the articles of incorporation.

Sometime after March 31, Southwest Breeders filed an amendment to its articles of incorporation with the secretary of state, which authorized it to increase the number of shares from 50,000 to 50 million. The state issued an amended certificate of incorporation.

Agosta filed suit to rescind the contract, seeking $6,000 in damages for purchase of the overissued stock. The trial court determined that the sale of the overissued stock to Agosta constituted a sale of nonexistent stock for which the directors were personally liable.

Chief Judge HUNTER

. . . .

A corporation whose capital is limited by its charter either in amount or in the number of shares, cannot issue valid certificates in excess of the limit prescribed. . . . Certificates of stock issued in violation of statute are wholly valueless and void, without regard to the intent of the parties to the overissue.

. . . .

Generally, officers of a corporation are not liable to third persons for corporate acts where they do not purport to bind themselves. . . . However, it is also true that officers and agents of the corporation may be held personally liable by the purchaser for a fraudulent issue of stock or stock issued in violation of the law. 18A [American Jurisprudence, 2d] Corporations, section 515, states, in part:

> It is said that in authenticating and issuing certificates the officers represent that the stock is not spurious and is not invalid by reason of fraudulent or known acts or omissions of such officers, and such representations are addressed to whoever should thereafter purchase the certificate.

In this case, the participation of these officers by their acts in negotiating the sale of the stock and by signing the certificates represented to Agosta that the stock was valid and bound them by their false representations.

DECISION AND REMEDY The court found that the officers personally were liable for the overissued stock that later was found to be invalid.

CRITICAL THINKING: MANAGEMENT CONSIDERATION In this case, the articles later were amended to allow the sale of a larger number of shares. Why then should the members of the board of directors be held personally liable when they would not have been liable if they sold the stock after the articles were amended?

Debt Securities

Different forms of debt exist, including secured bonds and debentures. Both represent a long-term commitment to repay the creditor. The loan is made to the corporation based on its ability to repay the debt. A secured bond or debenture does not carry with it any right to control the corporation's management and usually does not offer any voting rights on other matters.

These obligations earn interest at fixed or variable rates of interest that is payable regardless of the corporation's profitability. They mature at a specified date, when the corporation must repay the principal. Generally, owners of these obligations have first claim against the corporation's assets on its liquidation. The holder of secured bonds has first claim against the assets that have been pledged.

Liability

The corporate form of business entity is favored because liability is limited for shareholders, directors, and officers. Liability may stem from creditors' claims or from a judgment against the corporation. The limit on liability offered by a corporation is not absolute, however.

Liability of Shareholders

When a creditor has a claim against a corporation, the claim must be satisfied from corporate assets. As a general rule, the shareholder has limited liability to the extent of her investment in the corporation. In other words, shareholders can lose, at the most, the amount that they have invested in stock, but their personal assets are insulated from the corporation's liabilities.

In some circumstances, especially with smaller corporations, when the corporation obtains a loan or enters into a contract, the creditor may require, in addition to the corporation's liability, a personal guarantee from the shareholders or officers. A personal guarantee means, of course, that the guarantor's personal assets are at risk if the corporation fails to meet its obligations.

In some circumstances, a court may **pierce the corporate veil** (ignore the corporate structure) and look to the shareholders' personal assets to satisfy corporate obligations. Several reasons exist as to why this might occur. First, the shareholder may have ignored the corporation's existence by failing to comply with the corporate formalities, such as holding meetings of the board of directors or keeping corporate minutes.

Second, the shareholder may have commingled personal and corporate assets. The corporation may be regarded as merely the alter ego of the shareholder (that is, one cannot distinguish between the shareholder and the corporation). Third, the shareholder initially may have undercapitalized the corporation to such an extent that creditors are unable to collect against the corporation. **Undercapitalization** means that the corporation has insufficient capital (money and property) for a successful operation unless it is a bona fide loan.

Fourth, the shareholder, rather than investing capital, may make a loan and take a security interest in the corporate assets. By loaning money to the corporation, the shareholder becomes a creditor and has the same standing as outside creditors. The courts will not allow a shareholder to circumvent the other creditors of the corporation.

Finally, any evidence that the corporation was used to perpetrate a fraud, to circumvent the law, or to accomplish some illegal objective may lead a court to disregard the corporate existence. In the following case, the court had to decide whether to disregard the corporate entity (pierce the corporate veil) and hold the shareholders' personally liable.

CASE 19.2

Court of Appeals of
Tennessee, 2003
2003 WL 1191196

OCEANICS SCHOOLS, INC. v. BARBOUR

BACKGROUND AND FACTS Barbour formed Operation Sea Cruise, Inc. (OSC), under the laws of Panama in 1965 for the purpose of acquiring ownership of, repairing, and operating the sailing vessel *Antarna*. Barbour owned 100 percent of the shares of OSC, which purchased the sailing ship in 1967 and extensively repaired and restored it. In 1971, the plaintiff, Oceanics Schools, Inc., chartered the *Antarna* from OSC for use as a school ship. In exchange, Oceanics Schools would provide repairs and supplies to make the vessel operational.

Oceanics Schools invested approximately $630,000 in repairs and supplies for the *Antarna* and began using the vessel in its school program. In March 1972 , OSC reclaimed possession of the vessel in the Panama Canal Zone and subsequently sold the *Antarna* to a third party, who sailed the ship out of Panamanian waters to the Azores, Portugal. The proceeds of that sale were paid by OSC to Barbour in repayment of "a portion of the loans to the corporation by Barbour."

The Oceanics Schools filed suit against OSC and the vessel by writ of attachment in the District Court of Ponta Delgada, Azores, Portugal, for breach of contract and obtained a judgment against OSC for $929,815.55 plus interest. This judgment was filed in Tennessee where Barbour resided. Barbour was not named in the original judgment, but Oceanics Schools wanted to enforce it against him. The trial court found that Barbour was the alter ego of OSC and then pierced the corporate veil. Barbour appealed this decision.

CHARLES D. SUSANO, JR., J.

. . . .

A corporation is presumptively treated as a distinct entity, separate from its shareholders, officers, and directors. A corporation's separate identity may be disregarded or "pierced," however, "upon a showing that it is a sham or a dummy or where necessary to accomplish justice." A corporation's identity should be disregarded "with great caution and not precipitately." The determination of whether to disregard the corporate fiction depends on the special circumstances of each case, and "the matter is particularly within the province of the trial court."

. . .

. . . Factors to be considered in determining whether to disregard the corporate veil include not only whether the entity has been used to work a fraud or injustice in contravention of public policy, but also: (1) whether there was a failure to collect paid in capital; (2) whether the corporation was grossly undercapitalized; (3) the nonissuance of stock certificates; (4) the sole ownership of stock by one individual; (5) the use of the same office or business location; (6) the employment of the same employees or attorneys; (7) the use of the corporation as an instrumentality or business conduit for an individual or another corporation; (8) the diversion of corporate assets by or to a stockholder or other entity to the detriment of creditors, or the manipulation of assets and liabilities in another; (9) the use of the corporation as a subterfuge in illegal transactions; (10) the formation and use of the corporation to transfer to it the existing liability of another person or entity; and (11) the failure to maintain arms length relationships among related entities.

It is not necessary that all of these factors weigh in a plaintiff's favor in order to justify the piercing of the corporate veil. . . .

. . . .

The trial court found that, (1) at all relevant times, OSC's corporate office was Barbour's private residence; (2) the *Antarna* was OSC's principal asset; (3) its sale effectively liquidated the corporation; and (4) the "transfer of the proceeds from the sale of *Antarna* to Barbour's personal account rendered OSC without assets."

The trial court further found that "[a]t all material times, OSC was undercapitalized." While a mere $2,000 was paid into the corporation as capital, the alleged debt OSC owed to Barbour was in excess of $800,000. Essentially all of OSC's funds came through "loans" from Barbour. In addition, the court noted that OSC "failed to completely observe corporate formalities."

. . . .

DECISION AND REMEDY The court upheld the judgment and found that Barbour was the alter ego of his solely owned corporation. Because of a lack of capital, very few shareholder's and director's meetings, and the fact that all of the assets where paid to him, the court pierced the corporate veil and held Barbour personally liable.

CRITICAL THINKING: MANAGEMENT CONSIDERATION One of the advantages to forming a corporation is that the owner has limited liability. Why should a court ever hold a person personally liable when the third person contracted with the corporation?

LEGAL HIGHLIGHT

Some Costs of Conducting Business

Starting a business can involve significant costs. As you consider the following costs, remember that these are only the basic ones.

1. *Lawyers' Fees* Fees can range from a minimum of $250 to $25,000 or more if the business is a corporation that must meet securities law requirements before issuing stock.
2. *Filing Fees* The fees for filing the incorporation papers can range from a few dollars to several hundred dollars. Often, businesses other than corporations (such as limited partnerships) must pay fees associated with the filing of appropriate forms in various state or federal offices.

Once a business has been established, ongoing costs are significant. A few of these costs follow:

1. *Employer's Contribution to Social Security* Payment of the nonrefundable employer's contribution to the federal Social Security system for all employees is mandatory. A self-employed person must pay the equivalent of both the employer's and employee's Social Security contributions.
2. *Worker's Compensation* All businesses must provide coverage for their employees in the event that they are injured on the job.
3. *Unemployment Insurance Taxes* Payment of state unemployment insurance taxes for all employees is mandatory in all states.
4. *Annual Legal and Accounting Fees* Businesses must keep accurate books both for tax purposes and as a good business practice. The books should be audited by a certified public accountant (CPA). Audit costs can range from several hundred dollars to thousands of dollars. Various forms must be filed on a monthly, quarterly, and annual basis. Corporate records and minute books must be maintained, usually by an accountant or a lawyer. Annual fees for such services can run into hundreds or thousands of dollars.
5. *Retirement Plans* Although no state requires a business to provide retirement plans for its employees, if the business adopts such a plan, it must comply with the applicable federal and state requirements.

Liability of Directors and Officers

The directors and officers of a corporation are fiduciaries of the corporation and of its shareholders. A fiduciary relationship is based on trust and confidence. Directors are elected by the shareholders to the **board of directors**. The board is responsible for the corporation's overall policies and management. The board of directors hires officers to implement the management's policy and to oversee the corporation's daily operations. Directors and officers have three principal duties: obedience, loyalty, and care.

Duty of Obedience. The duty of obedience requires directors and officers to follow all statutes and regulations that govern the corporation's business. Further, they must abide by any limitations established in the articles of incorporation and the bylaws. Case 19.1, *Agosta v. Southwest Breeders, Inc.,* provides an example of a situation in which officers failed to obey the articles of incorporation. In that case, officers personally were held liable for failing to obey the limitations set out in the articles.

Duty of Loyalty. All employees, officers, and directors owe a fiduciary duty to the corporation. This duty prohibits them from making any secret profits at the corporation's expense.

The corporate personnel cannot take advantage of information obtained concerning business contracts or involving the potential purchase by the corporation of real estate or other assets. They cannot purchase property, then sell it to the corporation without full disclosure. Upon leaving the corporation, they cannot use trade secrets obtained while they were involved with the corporation.

Duty of Care. Directors and officers also have the duty of care to the corporation. They must act (1) in good faith, (2) with the care of an ordinary prudent person in a comparable position and under similar circumstances, and (3) in a manner that is reasonably believed to be in the corporation's best interests. If a director or officer possesses special qualifications, such as certification as a public accountant, she must exercise the higher standard required by the professional designation.

Applications of Duties. Directors and officers must perform their duties in good faith and in a manner that they reasonably believe to be in the corporation's best interest. Although the officers and directors of the corporation are not guarantors of its success, they must perform their duties.

In performing their duties, they are entitled to rely on information presented by officers or employees of the corporation whom they reasonably believe to be reliable and competent in the matters presented. Directors of corporations that must register with the Securities and Exchange Commission (SEC) have a greater exposure to liability, because they are ultimately responsible for compliance with SEC rules.

Directors may not rely on information provided by officers and employees if the directors have knowledge or expertise that would make such a reliance unwarranted. Directors must diligently seek information. They must act with the care that a reasonably prudent person in a comparable position would use under similar circumstances. If a director complies with this standard, he will not be held liable simply for holding the position of director.

Directors and officers must deal honestly and in good faith in guiding the corporation. The law allows them wide latitude in making valid business decisions. The law will not hold directors and officers liable for honest errors in business decisions if they made these decisions with the correct motives and in good faith. This law is referred to as the **business judgment rule**. The decisions must be within the powers of the corporation and the resulting actions must be exercised with due care.

The test of the decisions made by directors and officers is objective. They must exercise the same degree of care that reasonably prudent people use in the conduct of their own business affairs to avoid personal liability. To satisfy this test, the directors and officers must act in good faith and on an informed basis. They must believe that their action was in the best interests of the corporation.

Directors must act in the best interests of the corporation as a whole, rather than on behalf of any individual or group of shareholders. Because they are fiduciaries, the directors and officers of a corporation may not usurp business opportunities that legitimately belong to the company itself. When a business opportunity would be of interest to the company, the directors or officers, in good faith, may take advantage of the opportunity only if the company is unable to do so and only if the directors or officers are not in direct competition with the company.

The business judgment rule has been reexamined by several courts because of mergers and buyouts of large corporations. The following case applied the business judgment rule.

CASE 19.3 Supreme Court of Delaware, 1990 571 A.2d 1140	# PARAMOUNT COMMUNICATIONS, INC. v. TIME, INC. **BACKGROUND AND FACTS** In the early 1980s, the Time, Inc., executive board began considering expansion of Time's operations into the entertainment industry. By 1987, Time had established a special committee to consider and propose corporate strategies for the 1990s. First, Time wanted better control over the quality and price of the film products delivered to its subsidiaries, Home Box Office and Cinemax. Second, Time was concerned with the increasing globalization of the world economy.

By late spring of 1987, representatives from Time and Warner Brothers met to discuss the possibility of a joint venture. In July 1988, Time's board of directors met to consider expansion into the entertainment industry on a global scale and heard profiles for Warner, Disney, 20th Century Fox, Universal, and Paramount.

The board approved the strategic plan for Time's expansion. The board gave management the right to continue discussions with Warner about a possible merger. After extensive negotiations, on March 3, 1989, Time's board unanimously approved a stock-for-stock merger with Warner and a new name, Time-Warner, Inc.

On June 7, 1989, Paramount Communications, Inc., made a surprise all-cash offer to purchase all outstanding shares of Time for $175 per share. Time's stock rose the next day from $126 to $170 per share. After many meetings and negotiations, Time's board, on June 16, formally rejected Paramount's offer. At the same meeting, Time's board decided to acquire Warner for all cash for 51 percent of Warner's outstanding stock at $70 per share. This action did not require shareholder approval. To provide the funds, Time agreed to assume $7 billion to $10 billion worth of debt.

On June 23, Paramount raised its all-cash offer to $200 per share. On June 26, Time's board formally rejected this second offer. The board believed Paramount's offer to be inadequate and that the Warner transaction offered a greater long-term value for the stockholders. It also perceived Paramount's offer to be a threat to the "Time Culture" and its editorial freedom because Time would be the acquired company. During the negotiations with Warner and with Paramount, Time was adamant about preserving the "Time culture" and its editorial freedom.

Paramount and some of Time's shareholders instituted this lawsuit. In the lower court, the chancellor (judge) wrote a fifty-page opinion in which he refused to enjoin Time's purchase of Warner's stock. Paramount appealed.

Justice HORSEY

. . . .

The principal ground for reversal, asserted by all plaintiffs, is that Paramount's June 7, 1989 uninvited all-cash, all-shares, "fully negotiable" (though conditional) tender offer [offer to purchase] for Time triggered duties under *Unocal Corp. v. Mesa Petroleum Co.*, and that Time's board of directors, in responding to Paramount's offer, breached those duties. As a consequence, plaintiffs argue that in our review of the Time board's decision of June 16, 1989 to enter into a revised merger agreement with Warner, Time is not entitled to the benefit and protection of the business judgment rule.

. . . .

We turn now to plaintiffs' *Unocal* claim. We begin by noting, as did the Chancellor, that our decision does not require us to pass on the wisdom of the board's decision to enter into the original Time-Warner agreement. That is not a court's task. Our task is simply to review the record to determine whether there is sufficient evidence to support the Chancellor's conclusion that the initial Time-Warner agreement was the product of a proper exercise of business judgment.

. . . .

In *Unocal*, we held that before the business judgment rule is applied to a board's adoption of a defensive measure, the burden will lie with the board to prove (a) reasonable grounds for believing that a danger to corporate policy and effectiveness existed; and (b) that the defensive measure adopted was reasonable in relation to the threat posed. Directors satisfy the first part of the *Unocal* test by demonstrating good faith and reasonable investigation. We have repeatedly stated that the refusal to entertain an offer may comport with a valid exercise of a board's business judgment.

. . . .

Plaintiffs' position represents a fundamental misconception of our standard of review under *Unocal* principally because it would involve the court in substituting its judgment as to what is a "better" deal for that of a corporation's board of directors.

The usefulness of *Unocal* as an analytical tool is precisely its flexibility in the face of a variety of fact scenarios. *Unocal* is not intended as an abstract standard; neither is it a structured and mechanistic procedure of appraisal. Thus, we have said that directors may consider, evaluating the threat posed by a takeover bid, the inadequacy of the price offered, nature and timing of the offer, questions of illegality, the impact on constituencies other than shareholders, the risk of nonconsummation, and the quality of securities being offered in the exchange.

. . . .

We turn to the second part of the *Unocal* analysis. The obvious requisite to determining the reasonableness of a defensive action is a clear identification of the nature of the threat. As the Chancellor correctly noted, this "requires an evaluation of the importance of the corporate objective threatened; alternative methods of protecting that objective; impacts of the 'defensive' action, and other relevant factors." It is not until both parts of the *Unocal* inquiry have been satisfied that the business judgment rule attaches to defensive actions of a board of directors. As applied to the facts of this case, the question is whether the record evidence supports the Court of Chancery's conclusion that the restructuring of the Time-Warner transaction, including the adoption of several preclusive defensive measures, was a reasonable response in relation to a perceived threat.

. . . Delaware law confers the management of the corporate enterprise to the stockholders' duly elected board representatives. The fiduciary duty to manage a corporate enterprise includes the selection of a time frame for achievement of corporate goals. That duty may not be delegated to the stockholders. Directors are not obliged to abandon a deliberately conceived corporate plan for a short-term shareholder profit unless there is clearly no basis to sustain the corporate strategy.

. . . .

We affirm the Chancellor's rulings as clearly supported by the record. Finally, we note that although Time was required, as a result of Paramount's hostile offer, to incur a heavy debt [$7 billion to $10 billion] to finance its acquisition of Warner, that fact alone does not render the board's decision unreasonable so long as the directors could reasonably perceive the debt load not to be so injurious to the corporation as to jeopardize its well being.

DECISION AND REMEDY Time prevailed in this case. A tender offer is made by a group of investors to purchase the stock of a particular company at a fixed price per share in order for the group to gain control over the company. In this case, the court found that Paramount's tender offer was reasonably perceived by Time's board to pose a threat to Time and that the board's response to that threat was reasonable. The court rejected the argument that the only corporate threat posed by an all-shares all-cash offer was the possibility of inadequate value. The threat was to the very life of "Time culture" and editorial freedom.

COMMENT In January 2000, Time-Warner merged with America Online, Inc., (AOL) the world's leading interactive services company. At the time of the merger, AOL's stock had a higher value ($163 billion) than Time-Warner's ($100 billion). The new business, called AOL Time Warner, was the world's leading media and entertainment company. It included filmed entertainment, interactive services, television networks, cable systems, publishing, and music.

When the stock market declined shortly after the merger, AOL lost most of its value. Although the company had plenty of strong leaders, no one exercised leadership. The Securities and Exchange Commission required AOL to restate its earnings. In 2003, AOL was dropped from the name and the company was once again called Time-Warner.

CRITICAL THINKING: MANAGEMENT CONSIDERATION Assume that you are a member of a board of directors for a large corporation. How would you protect yourself from potential liability because of your position?

Control

In theory, one of the characteristics of a corporation is centralized management. Directors set policy for the corporation and hire the officers to run the corporation on a day-to-day basis. An officer also can be a director of the corporation.

The usual officer positions are the president, at least one vice president, the secretary, and the treasurer. Under the MBCA, a person may hold more than one office, but cannot serve as both president and secretary. Corporate officers can be removed by the board of directors at any time, with or without cause and without shareholder approval. A wrongful dismissal can result in liability for breach of contract. The RMBCA, however, does not require any specific officers and leaves it to the corporation to determine this issue.

Shareholders' Control

The shareholders elect the directors and have voting rights on major corporate matters, such as amending the articles of incorporation, deciding to merge or consolidate with another corporation, opting to sell all or substantially all of the corporate assets, or dissolving the corporation. The controlling shareholders, also called majority shareholders, own enough of the stock to control actions that the corporation will take through their voting rights. Minority shareholders have insufficient voting shares to control the corporation.

When transferring their shares, majority shareholders have a fiduciary duty to the corporation and to the minority shareholders, a duty similar to that of directors and officers. A controlling shareholder may dispose of his stock and receive a premium price for the ability to control. The controlling shareholder, however, may not sell control of the corporation if a reasonably prudent person would foresee the possibility of mismanagement by the purchaser.

Generally, in the absence of extraordinary circumstances, such as fraud or detriment to the corporation, courts hold that directors, officers, and controlling shareholders may buy and sell their shares without including, or even making disclosures to, minority shareholders.

Minority shareholders receive some protection through bylaws or restrictions stamped on the stock certificate. This protection may include requiring a majority shareholder, director, or officer to give notice of sale or purchase to minority shareholders, or providing the right of first refusal (to be discussed later) to purchase the shares being sold to the minority shareholders or the corporation.

Close Corporation Control

Shares of a **close corporation** are closely held by family members or by comparatively few persons. Close corporations often are referred to as *closed, closely held, family,* or *privately held corporations.* The members know one another personally. Because the number of shareholders is so small, frequently no trading market exists for these shares. In practice, these corporations operate like partnerships.

In a close corporation, the question of who controls the business is very important. To maintain control, it is said that a person always should try to obtain 51 percent, accept 50 percent, but should never accept 49 percent or less of common stock. In a close corporation, the board of directors can be one person. That person controls the corporation, because the board of directors appoints officers and establishes the budget, including the amount to be paid in salaries and fringe benefits.

Some rights are reserved to the minority shareholder. One is the right to receive information about the business's value if the minority shareholder sells her interest to the majority shareholder. The following case considers this problem.

CASE 19.4 Supreme Court of Colorado, 1994 867 P.2d 892	**VAN SCHAACK HOLDINGS, LTD v. VAN SCHAACK** **BACKGROUND AND FACTS** The Van Schaack Corporation (VSC) owned 29,000 acres of Colorado farmland known as the Box Elder land. Mrs. Van Schaack owned 750 shares of VSC stock. She was not on VSC's board of directors but did receive the annual shareholder letter that included VSC's audited financial statements. In 1982, she wanted to sell her stock, the value of which was almost exclusively determined by the value of the land. She was interested in the present per-acre value and future events that might affect that value, particularly the new Denver International Airport, which would be located on or near the Box Elder land. One director told her that "no way" would the new airport be located on Box Elder land.

Mrs. Van Schaack did not know that at a VSC board of directors meeting in 1980, the board concluded that the Box Elder land would benefit from the relocation of the Denver airport, and by 1981, the board believed that 6,500 acres of Box Elder land would be condemned for the project. VSC sold some land in 1982 at $8,000 per acre. In 1983, VSC purchased 40 acres of land contiguous to its property for $2,750 per acre.

In 1983, Mrs. Van Schaack sold her stock for $1.5 million dollars at $2,000 per share. In 1985, Denver announced the relocation of the airport and the relocation of a major highway to a portion of the Box Elder land. In 1988, Mrs. Van Schaack sued, alleging a breach of fiduciary duty in connection with the sale of stock because the board misrepresented material facts and failed to disclose material facts relating to the value of the Box Elder land, the airport relocation, and the relocation of the highway. Although she was the largest individual stockholder, she was a minority stockholder because her 750 shares represented only 16 percent of the stock. The jury returned a verdict for her in the amount of $750,000. The judgment was appealed.

Chief Justice ROVIRA

. . . .

We have previously recognized that corporate directors owe a fiduciary duty to shareholders in exercising their responsibilities. This duty encompasses the requirement that directors of a corporation and its controlling shareholders act with an extreme measure of candor, unselfishness, and good faith in relation to remaining shareholders. In addition, it is widely recognized that the fiduciary duty imposed on corporate directors and officers dealing with minority shareholders is enhanced in the context of closed corporations.

The duties previously recognized in this jurisdiction applicable to corporate directors dealing with shareholders include exercise of complete candor with minority shareholders in the negotiation of stock transactions. In our view, this duty encompasses the obligation to fully disclose all material facts and circumstances surrounding or affecting a proposed transaction.

Imposition of such a duty is particularly justified in the context of closed corporations because shares of closed corporations are not publicly traded and information affecting the value of such shares is not generally known. While the value of publicly traded securities presumably reflects the marshalling and analysis of all information known by "the market," including information which is required to be disclosed under state and federal securities laws, a liquid and efficient market for shares of a closed corporation is, generally speaking, not available. Indeed, one commentator remarks that a closed corporation is, by definition, "a corporation whose shares are not generally traded in the securities markets."

. . . .

We hold, therefore, that it is a violation of a fiduciary duty for an officer or director of a closed corporation to purchase the stock of minority shareholders without disclosing material facts affecting the value of the stock, known to the purchasing officer or director by virtue of his position but not known to the selling shareholder.

. . . Thus, information is "material" if there is a "substantial likelihood that, under all the circumstances, the omitted fact would have assumed actual significance in the deliberations of the reasonable shareholder" and "would have been viewed by the reasonable investor as having significantly altered the 'total mix' of information made available."

DECISION AND REMEDY The court held that the board of directors of a closely held corporation must disclose material facts affecting the value of the corporate stock when purchasing the stock of a minority shareholder.

CRITICAL THINKING: MANAGERIAL CONSIDERATION Assume that you and four friends decide to form a corporation in which each one of you owns 25 percent of the business. As a minority shareholder, how would you protect your interests from the other shareholders?

Directors' Control

The board of directors is authorized to exercise all of the corporate powers, to manage the business, and to set the policy of the corporation. The directors' responsibilities include the declaration and payment of dividends to shareholders and the fixing of compensation for the officers and directors.

In larger corporations, the directors often serve on executive committees that handle management decisions between board meetings. Often, officers are also directors of the corporation and sit on many of the executive committees created by the board of directors. The board of directors delegates much of the responsibility for day-to-day management to the officers. Major policy, financial, and contract decisions involving the management of a corporation, however, cannot be delegated by the board of directors to the corporation's officers.

Transferability of Interest

Another characteristic of corporations is the free transferability of shares. The law generally recognizes an owner's right to transfer property except when valid restrictions on its transferability exist.

Restrictions are imposed by securities laws if the shares are registered with the Securities and Exchange Commission or if insiders (such as directors, officers, or controlling shareholders of the corporation), who have access to inside information, trade their securities on the basis of this information. Other restrictions may be imposed by contract, articles of incorporation, or bylaws.

Restrictions for Close Corporations

Within a close corporation, the need to provide restrictions on the transfer of common shares is greater than in other types of corporations. The interpersonal relationship of the principal shareholders of the close corporation is very intense. In many close corporations, a person spends more time with fellow shareholders than with his own family. This commitment requires mutual respect, trust, and understanding.

The possibility always exists that one of the principal shareholders may die, divorce, resign, or retire. Without restrictions on the transferability of shares, a remaining shareholder might find herself in business with the former associate's ex-spouse or heirs, or even with a stranger. The shareholder may find it impossible to work with, and to be associated closely with, these new parties.

The articles of incorporation or bylaws can restrict the transfer of shares in a close corporation by imposing the option of the right of first refusal. This option means that the shares to be transferred must first be offered for sale to the corporation or to the remaining shareholders. The corporation or shareholders have the first right either to buy or to refuse to buy the shares.

A procedure should be established to determine the price of the stock. For example, the articles of incorporation, the bylaws, or a shareholder agreement states that the corporation or remaining shareholders have a right to purchase the stock upon a shareholder's death, with the value of the shares to be determined by an independent appraiser.

Additionally, the corporation or remaining shareholders need to have the capability to buy the shares. Funds for the purchase of the stock can be provided by a life insurance policy taken out and paid for by the corporation on the shareholder's life.

Notice of Restrictions

Any restrictions on transferability (including the right of first refusal) must appear on the stock certificate. Some state statutes require that restrictions be placed in the articles of incorporation. If no such statute exists, restrictions should be stated in the bylaws and on the stock certificates.

The common law does not like restrictions on transferability. Because of this, the restrictions must be written in very specific language and follow the state law exactly. The articles or bylaws cannot restrict the transferability completely, but they may require the offering of shares to the other stockholders first and may establish a procedure to determine the value of the shares as discussed previously.

Taxes

The corporation, as a separate entity, is also a separate taxpayer. The corporation pays taxes on its earnings in the year earned. When the earnings are distributed to the shareholders as dividends, the shareholders are taxed on the dividends received. The corporation cannot deduct the payment of dividends from its revenue.

Losses are deducted by the corporation. Losses offset corporate revenue rather than passing through to the shareholders to be deducted from their income for tax purposes.

One means of avoiding the double taxation, when the shareholders are also officers or employees of the corporation, is by paying salaries to officers and employees rather than distributing dividends. Salaries are a deduction from revenue for the corporation. This deduction may be disallowed, however, by the Internal Revenue Service (IRS) if the salaries are held to be excessive or unreasonable.

Avoidance of Taxes

Shareholders can receive income in the form of dividends. Shareholders, rather than contributing all of their money to the capital of the corporation by purchasing shares, can become creditors by lending capital to the corporation as a loan. The interest on the loan is a deductible item for the corporation, but the creditor must pay taxes on the interest received.

The IRS pays close attention to undercapitalization of corporations. Generally, a debt-to-equity ratio

LEGAL HIGHLIGHT

Not-for-Profit Corporations

Not-for-profit corporations, also called nonprofit corporations, are of major importance in the business community. Recently, donations to the nonprofit business sector were found to be an average of $1,620 per household. Forty-four percent of American adults volunteered their time, which equates to nine million full-time employees at a value of $239 billion.

Where, however, did nonprofit corporations come from? Who started the idea of donations? The story starts with a sailor on the high seas.

Thomas Coram was an eighteenth-century English sea captain. He was married to Eunice, but they had no children. In 1772, when he was fifty-four years old, he decided to retire. No longer going to sea, he began to notice a large number of abandoned children in London. These children lived in appalling conditions in the slums of London. The government failed to do anything for these children, and religious organizations were unable to help because of limited financial resources.

Although wealthy, he did not have near the financial resources that were required to aid so many needy children. He convinced his aristocratic friends and acquaintances to obtain a charter from King George II that would allow the creation of a nonprofit corporation. Until this time, charters issued by the king were for profit corporations. Coram and his friends lobbied many people over a number of years before the king was convinced to grant the charter.

This first charter granted the right to construct a hospital for these impoverished street children. The London Foundling Hospital became the first incorporated nonprofit corporation. The hospital was the first in a long line of nonprofit organizations in England and later in the United States.

---

greater than three-to-one may be challenged by the IRS. This type of undercapitalization also endangers the shareholders' limited liability.

Only when the corporation's earnings are distributed to the shareholders as dividends does the shareholder pay tax. Often, the corporation will accumulate earnings rather than distribute them. The IRS rules, however, will impose a tax on the corporation for excessive accumulated earnings. The IRS rules encourage the distribution of earnings to shareholders rather than the retention of earnings not needed for the business.

S Corporation

The label **S corporation** refers to the tax status of a corporation, not to a type of corporation. The promoters apply to the state government for incorporation. Once the state creates the corporation, the shareholders determine if the corporation will apply to the IRS to grant it an S corporation tax status.

The letter S refers to the subchapter in the IRS statutes that set out the qualifications for meeting the S corporation requirements. An S corporation is a voluntary tax status for a close corporation. The shareholders must elect to apply to the IRS for the S corporation status. If the corporation meets all the IRS requirements, the IRS will grant the S status. The S corporation will remain in that status as long as it meets the IRS regulations.

The S tax status allows the corporation to be treated as a partnership (yet retain the advantages of a corporation, such as limited liability) and to pass all losses and gains through the corporation to the individual shareholders without being taxed at the corporate level. In an S corporation, the profit is passed through to the shareholders for tax purposes regardless of whether it actually is distributed to them in the form of dividends.

To qualify, an S corporation can have no more than seventy-five shareholders. An S corporation can have only one class of stock. Only domestic corporations can qualify for this status. Many technical requirements must be met for a corporation to become and to maintain an S corporation status.

The IRS has the authority to audit an S corporation and to revoke the S corporation status if the statutory requirements are not met. The IRS's audit can cover several previous years to determine the year when the corporation first failed to meet the conditions. The corporation then owes back taxes, interest, and late penalties. To maintain the S corporation status, the shareholders' agreement must provide that shares can be transferred only to qualified shareholders (many corporations, partnerships, trusts, and foreigners cannot be shareholders).

CYBERLAW

International Taxes

Many complaints are heard that a person buying items on the Web escapes paying sale taxes. As previously discussed in Chapter 11, states are losing a large source of revenue from sales taxes. One state, Maryland, attempted to obtain from businesses that sell on the Internet the names and addresses of customers and what they purchased to attempt to recover some of the lost revenue. The Internet Tax Freedom Act passed by Congress imposes a moratorium on state and local taxes for transactions on the Web.

Today, we have a worldwide economy. The individual European countries and the European Union (EU) rely heavily on the value-added tax (VAT). It is a form of a sales tax imposed at every level of the sale of goods and services, from raw material to final disposal. The percentage varies from one country to another, but provides 44 percent of the European Union's budget. Luxembourg has the lowest VAT rate at 15 percent in contrast to Sweden and Denmark at 25 percent. EU firms must charge the VAT to other businesses in the EU, but the non-EU countries do not charge this tax. Luxembourg has requested permission to require the payment of this tax from any business whether or not it is an EU business. This proposal is currently under study by the Commission on Directives. The EU is the first to attempt to tax items purchased on the Web.

Duration

Unless otherwise specified in the articles of incorporation, a corporation has perpetual existence. In theory, the death of a shareholder, director, or officer has no effect on the corporate entity. As a practical matter, in many close corporations, the death of the major shareholder, who happens also to be a director or an officer, effectively brings an end to the business, if not the corporation. In such instances, the estate of the deceased shareholder may attempt to find a buyer for the corporation to continue the operation. If a buyer cannot be found, the corporation may have to be dissolved.

A corporation may be *dissolved* and *liquidated*. To **dissolve** means that the corporation ceases its business, except those operations that are necessary to complete the termination of the business. **Liquidation** means that the assets are sold and converted to cash proceeds. The debts are paid and, if any proceeds remain, they are distributed to the shareholders.

The board and a majority of the shareholders adopt a resolution called the **articles of dissolution**. The corporation then proceeds in one of two ways. The corporation on its own may end its business and liquidate assets. Or the corporation may apply to the court to supervise the liquidation. The court has the power to appoint a receiver, who, with the powers and duties specified by the court, will end the business and liquidate the assets.

The articles of dissolution are filed with the state. A dissolved corporation continues to exist to liquidate its business. It must notify all creditors that it is dissolved. The creditors have 120 days in which to file a claim. For unknown creditors, a corporation must publish the notice of dissolution in a newspaper of general circulation. All claims against the dissolved corporation are barred after five years. The prior shareholders are liable up to the amount they received from the dissolved corporation during this five-year period. Finally, the dissolved corporation ceases to exist.

Dissolution also can occur by means other than the voluntary filing of the resolution for articles of dissolution. For example, any of the following may result in dissolution:

1. An act of the legislature in the state of incorporation (such as making the activities of the corporation illegal);

2. Expiration of the time of existence specified in the charter without a renewal;

3. A court decree through an action brought by the state attorney general when the actions of the corporation justify dissolution (such as procurement

of the charter by fraud, abuse of corporate powers, abandonment of operations, or continued violation of criminal statutes);

4. Merger (a legal combination of two or more corporations by which one corporation is absorbed into the surviving corporation, thus dissolving the other corporation);

5. Consolidation (a combination of two or more corporations by which the corporations are joined to form a new corporation, dissolving the original corporations); and

6. The nonpayment of taxes or annual fees owed to the state.

LEGAL HIGHLIGHT

Quality Standards

Today, the marketplace is more global, competition is tougher, and buyers demand higher quality standards than in the past. Regardless of the form of business chosen, management needs to be concerned with the quality of its products, services, and, indeed, the quality of the system that the company uses to conduct its business.

Businesses can look to one or both well-known quality measures, the Malcolm Baldrige award in the United States[a] and the International Standards Organization (ISO) 9000 series standards originating in Europe.[b] Businesses can use the standards as guidelines to improve their own business operations.

The Baldrige award and the ISO 9000 registration differ in focus, purpose, and content. The focus of the Baldrige award is to enhance competitiveness. The award has three purposes: (1) to promote awareness and understanding of the importance of quality improvement to our nation's economy, (2) to recognize companies for outstanding quality management and achievement, and (3) to share information on successful quality strategies. The Baldrige award is a one-time event and not an ongoing process. A business can reapply and be awarded the Baldrige award a second time, but the two awards are separate.

[a]Information on the Baldrige award is available at http://www.quality.nist.gov and http://www.nist.gov/public_affairs/results/res-qual.html.
[b]Information on ISO is located at http://www.iso.ch.

The ISO 9000 series standards focus on enhancing and facilitating trade. The ISO 9000 standards consist of five separate standards found in ISO 9001 to 9005. These standards represent an international consensus on the essential features of a quality system to ensure the effective operation of any business, whether a manufacturer or a service provider, whether in the public or the private sector. A company applies to the ISO for registration. The application can be limited, such as for a product or a service or can be for the total management system.

The company submits documents to be reviewed by the ISO registrar. A preassessment by the registrar identifies potential problems. Two to three auditors spend several days on the premises assessing the application. It the company meets the requirements, it will receive a registration. If the company does not receive the registration, it has a period of time within which it can correct the problems found. After a company receives a registration, the ISO conducts periodic reaudits to verify conformity with the practices and systems registered. ISO 9000 registration ensures that the registrant's practices conform with its quality systems.

The two awards are not similar. The Baldrige award looks to continuous improvement in overall operations. ISO registration, on the other hand, looks to conformance with practices established in the registrant's own quality systems. More businesses are requiring that their suppliers evidence quality by being registered. Many businesses hold ISO registrations, and governments that are purchasing items often will not deal with a business that has not received its ISO registration. Quality can no longer be ignored.

Franchising

The Federal Trade Commission defines a **franchise** as an arrangement between a **franchisor**, who owns a trademark, a trade name, or a copyright, and another person, known as the *franchisee*. The franchisor licenses the **franchisee** (the holder of the franchise) to use the trademark, trade name, or copyright in marketing the goods or services under specified conditions or limitations. Most franchisees are corporations, but ownership is not limited to the corporate form.

The franchise system also has been described as an organization composed of distributive units established and administered by a supplier as a means of expanding and controlling the market for its products. Each franchise dealer is a legally independent, but economically dependent, unit of the integrated business system. The individual franchisee operates as an independent business. It obtains affiliation advantages with the regional or national organization, however, which supplies the products, advertising, and other services.

The use of franchises has expanded rapidly in recent years. Between 1910 and 1940, franchising was used primarily in the automobile industry, sports, and the soft drink bottling industry. Now, franchises account for about 34 percent of all retail sales. The franchise pattern of business development is a particularly appealing form of capitalist enterprise, because it enables groups of individuals with small amounts of capital to become entrepreneurs.

Types of Franchises

The three types of franchises are the **distributorship franchise**, **business format franchise**, and **manufacturing or processing plant franchise**.

1. *Distributorship Franchise* A manufacturing concern (the franchisor) licenses a dealer (the franchisee) to sell its product. The franchise outlets serve merely as conduits through which the trademarked goods of the franchisor flow. The trademark in a distributorship franchise represents the end product marketed by the system. Often, a distributorship covers an exclusive territory. Beer distributorship's are an example of this.

2. *Business Format Franchise* This franchise is the typical chain-style business for which the franchisor merely provides the trademark. The franchisee is responsible for the manufacture and sale of the end product. The franchisee operates under the franchisor's trade name and is identified as a member of a select group of dealers that engage in the franchisor's business. The franchisee generally must follow standardized operations methods. Often, the franchisor requires minimum prices and quality standards to be maintained. Examples of this type of franchise are McDonald's and most other fast-food chains.

3. *Manufacturing or Processing Plant Franchise* The franchisor transfers to the franchisee the essential ingredients or formula to make a particular product. The franchisee then markets it on either a wholesale or retail basis in accordance with the franchisor's standards. Examples of this type of franchise are Coca-Cola and other soft drink corporations.

The Law of Franchising

The growth in franchise operations has outdistanced the law of franchising. The courts interpret franchising statutes when a state has them. If no acts have been adopted by the state, the courts apply general common law principles. Although the franchise agreement itself is a contract, the franchise relationship exhibits characteristics associated with agency and employment law, as well as ordinary contract law.

A franchise purchaser can suffer substantial losses if the franchisor fails to provide complete information regarding the franchisor–franchisee relationship, as well as the details of the contract under which the business will operate. Only a few states that have enacted legislation concerning franchising have included disclosure provisions.

California was the first state to enact a franchise disclosure law. This law serves as a model for other disclosure statutes. The California Franchise Investment Law identifies twenty-two items that must be disclosed in a registration filed with the state. Some of the items to be disclosed follow:

1. The name and business address of the franchisor,

2. The business experience of any people affiliated with the franchisor,

3. Whether any person associated with the franchisor has been convicted of a felony,

4. A recent financial statement,

5. A typical franchise agreement,

6. A statement of all fees that the franchisee must pay, and

7. Other information that the commissioner of corporations may reasonably require.

When misrepresentation permeates a franchise operation's initial sale, the common law remedy of fraud provides inadequate relief. In most cases, the franchisee already has paid the franchise purchase price and also may have incurred substantial losses in the business's initial operating phases. The elements of fraud are exceedingly difficult to prove. The franchisee has a great burden to show that the franchisor's original offer was fraudulent.

The FTC Franchise Rule[1] of 1978 was promulgated in response to widespread evidence of deception and unfair practices in connection with the sale of franchises and business opportunity ventures. This rule requires that within a specified time, franchisors and franchise brokers (sellers of franchises) must furnish the information that prospective franchisees need to make an informed decision about entering into a franchise relationship. The rule establishes the circumstances under which a franchisor or broker can make claims about the projected sales income or profits of existing or potential outlets. The rule also imposes requirements that concern the establishment and termination of the franchise relationship.

INFOTRAC RESEARCH ACTIVITY

Numerous articles and periodicals are available on InfoTrac when you type in "franchising." Franchising offers an opportunity to go into business. Review six articles and summarize which ones would offer the best business opportunity.

The Franchise Agreement

A contract defines the relationship between the franchisor and the franchisee. Each franchise relationship and each industry has its own characteristics, creating a broad range of details that a franchising contract may

[1]To view the FTC Franchise Rule, go to http://www.ftc.gov/bcp/franchise/netrule.htm.

include. The following sections, however, define the essential characteristics of the franchise relationship.

Payment for Franchise. The franchisee ordinarily pays an initial fee or lump-sum price for the franchise license (the privilege of being granted a franchise). This fee is separate from the fees for various products that the franchisee purchases from or through the franchisor. In some industries, the franchisor relies heavily on the initial sale of the franchise to realize a profit. In other industries, the continued dealing between the parties brings profit to both.

In most situations, the franchisor receives a stated percentage of the annual sales or annual volume of business done by the franchisee. The franchise agreement also may require the franchisee to pay a percentage of advertising costs and certain administrative expenses incurred throughout the franchise arrangement.

Location and Business Organization. Typically, the franchisor determines the territory to be served by the franchise. The franchise agreement can specify whether the premises for the business must be leased or purchased outright. In some cases, construction of a building is necessary to meet the terms of the franchise agreement.

In addition, the agreement specifies whether the franchisor or the franchisee bears responsibility for supplying equipment and furnishings for the premises. When the franchise is a service operation, such as a motel, the contract often provides that the franchisor will establish certain standards for the facility and will inspect to ensure that the standards are maintained to protect the franchise name and reputation.

The business organization of the franchisee greatly concerns the franchisor. Depending on the terms of the franchise agreement, the franchisor may specify particular requirements for the business's form and capital structure. The franchise agreement can provide that certain standards of operation, such as sales quotas, quality considerations, or record keeping, must be met by the franchisee.

Furthermore, a franchisor may retain stringent control over the training of personnel involved in the operation and over administrative aspects of the business. Although the day-to-day operation of the franchise business normally is left to the franchisee, the franchise agreement can provide for whatever amount of supervision and control the parties desire.

One area of franchises that causes a great deal of conflict is the territorial exclusivity of the franchise. Many franchise agreements define the territory allotted to a particular franchise, but specifically state that the franchise is nonexclusive. Nonexclusivity allows the franchisor to establish multiple franchises in the same territory.

Price and Quality Controls. Franchises provide the franchisor with an outlet for the firm's goods and services. Depending on the nature of the business, the franchisor may require the franchisee to purchase products from the franchisor at an established price. A franchisor cannot set the prices at which the franchisee will resell the goods, because this violates state or federal antitrust laws. A franchisor can suggest retail prices but cannot insist on them. The franchisor can restrict the franchisee from selling above a maximum price, however.

Although a franchisor can require franchisees to purchase supplies from it, requiring a franchisee to purchase exclusively from the franchisor may violate state or federal antitrust laws. The implications of antitrust violations on territorial restrictions, restrictions on products sold, resale price fixing, and price discrimination are discussed in Chapter 21.

As a general rule, no question exists as to the validity of a provision permitting the franchisor to enforce certain quality standards. Because the franchisor has a legitimate interest in maintaining the quality of the product or service in order to protect its name and reputation, it can exercise greater control in this area than would otherwise be tolerated.

Termination of the Franchise Arrangement

The franchise's duration is negotiated between the parties. Generally, a franchise starts out for a short period, say, a year, so that the franchisee and the franchisor can determine whether they want to stay in business with each other. The franchise agreement usually specifies that termination must be for cause, such as death or disability of the franchisee, insolvency of the franchisee, breach of the franchise agreement, or failure to meet specified sales quotas. Most franchise contracts provide that notice of termination must be given.

Much franchise litigation arises over termination provisions. Because the franchise agreement normally is a preprinted contract prepared by the franchisor, and the bargaining power of the franchisee rarely equals that of the franchisor, the termination provisions of contracts are generally more favorable to the franchisor. The lack of statutory and case law in this area affects the franchisee most keenly. Franchisees in automobile dealerships and gasoline stations have some statutory protection under the Automobile Dealers' Day in Court and the Petroleum Marketing Practices Act.

The franchisee normally invests substantial time and money into the franchise operation to make it successful. Despite this fact, the franchisee may receive little or nothing for the business on termination. The franchisor owns the trademark and hence the business.

Franchisee's Relationship to Franchisor: Agent or Independent Contractor?

The mere licensing of a trade name does not create an agency relationship. The courts have determined that certain other factors in the franchisor–franchisee relationship may indicate the existence of an agency relationship:

1. The terms of the agreement create an agency relationship.

2. The franchisor exercises a high degree of control over the franchisee's activities.

3. A third person looking at the relationship between the franchisor and the franchisee would reasonably believe that an agency relationship exists.

4. The franchisor derives an especially great benefit from the franchisee's activities. The greater the benefit, the more likely an agency relationship will be found.

If these factors show a very close relationship between the franchisor and the franchisee, their relationship will be deemed to be that of an employer–employee or principal–agent in dealings with third parties. If the factors show a high degree of independence between the franchisee and the franchisor, the franchisee will be deemed an independent contractor.

The characterization of the relationship has tax implications and implications for the regulatory treatment of the business organization. In addition, if an agency relationship is found, the franchisor is liable for the franchisee's improper actions or injuries to third parties both in tort and in contract.

How to Expand without Investing

U.S. corporations often do business overseas through the use of licensing or franchising agreements. Licensing agreements can be divided into two categories: *patent licensing* and *know-how licensing*. With a **patent license**, the foreign licensee has access to and use of the patent, and the U.S. licensor receives the royalties. With **know-how licensing**, the U.S. licensor has a trade secret or knows how to use certain technology that no one else knows how to use. The U.S. licensor sells the foreign licensee the right to use the trade secret or know-how.

Franchising is a specialized form of licensing. The franchisor (supplier) licenses the franchisee (foreign firm) to use the franchisor's marketing knowledge, product, and services in exchange for fees. This agreement allows the franchisee to use the franchisor's trademark and copyrights. Examples include the International Hilton Hotel chain, McDonald's, and Coca-Cola.

Foreign companies can, of course, conduct business in the United States under the same arrangements. Examples include foreign automobile dealerships and distributorships of electronic equipment, such as computers, video cameras, and compact disc players.

Choosing the Best Form of Business Organization

Your friend has developed a new oil filter for use in internal combustion engines that enables the engine to use the same oil up to ten times as long as is currently possible. She believes that a market exists for such a product, but being totally unfamiliar with business matters, she comes to you for advice.

After reviewing her developed materials and hearing her explanation of the product, you believe that the project is worth pursuing. The two of you would like to begin a business to produce and sell the product.

Good business practice would suggest that you consult an attorney before proceeding with your plans. A good business lawyer can discuss your goals with you, offer alternative courses of action to meet those goals, and evaluate the probable consequences of each alternative.

To take maximum advantage of the time spent with your attorney, you should prepare certain information. Be prepared to provide information on the assets that will be part of the business and in whose name the assets are currently held. You will transfer real property to the business and your friend may transfer patent or other rights. You will need to discuss the tax consequences of those transfers.

Both you and your friend also will want to collect information on your individual financial and tax statutes that may impact the decision about which form of business entity is appropriate for you. How much money will you need to bring to your business in order to carry it through the first year? You should have an idea as to how you will raise this money. Can you and your friend provide it personally from your savings or through a bank loan or will you bring in other equity investors? If you bring in other investors, the questions of liability and business control will become more complex. Even if you and your friend provide the capital, however, the issues of liability and control of day-to-day operations and long-term policy are critical.

You also must consider the degree of freedom with which your business's ownership interests can be transferred. Your friend may implicitly trust your business judgment, but would she accept being in business with your heirs if you should die? Would you proceed if she sold her interest in the business to a stranger without her technical skills? Perhaps both of you will want the option to buy the other's interest in the business in case of death. Alternatively, you both may want a right of first refusal if one of you decides to transfer your interest during your lifetime.

Obviously, the answers to these questions will impact the form of business organization that you should use. Be sure to consider these questions in advance. When you meet with the lawyer be prepared with a checklist for guidance.

Checklist

✔ *Cash Flow Projections* Bring the cash flow projections, as well as tax and other relevant information to the meeting.

✔ *Assets* Determine the assets that must be initially obtained and their cost.

✔ *Future Actions* Consider actions if one of you should die or decide to leave the business.

✔ *Limited Liability* Decide whether limited liability is of prime importance to you both.

✔ *Research* Research methods to raise the initial funds required for this investment.

Chapter Summary

A corporation is the most formal type of business entity. The first step in formalizing a corporation is to file articles of incorporation with the appropriate state agency. Among the items included in this document are the name, address, and general purpose of the corporation, its duration, the number and classes of shares, the number of directors, and the names of the incorporators.

The next step is the adoption of bylaws by the board of directors. The bylaws control the business's internal operation. In addition, any business must have funds with which to operate. Funds are obtained by issuing securities. The two broad classes of securities are equity securities and debt securities.

The most frequently held equity securities are common stock and preferred stock. Debt securities are secured bonds and debentures. On dissolution, debt securities are paid ahead of equity securities.

Generally, in the absence of a personal guarantee, shareholders are immune from liability for the corporation's debts. If the corporation's business is not properly conducted, however, the courts may allow the corporate veil to be pierced to hold shareholders liable.

As long as directors and officers perform their fiduciary duties, they are not personally liable for the debts of the corporation. They can, however, be held liable for mismanagement in carrying out their responsibilities. Under the business judgment rule, they are protected from legal actions based on losses brought about by their making honest errors in business decisions.

The shareholders own the corporation and elect the board of directors. The board of directors establishes corporate policy and appoints the officers. All corporations must have officers who conduct the corporation's day-to-day activities. These officers are normally a president, at least one vice president, a secretary, and a treasurer.

A corporation reasonably can limit the transferability of securities. The limitations also must be known (placed on the security) to the holder and prospective purchaser. Whenever a business decision is made, its effects on taxes must be considered. Special tax advantages occur if S corporation status is elected instead of the normal tax status of a corporation. All losses and profits pass through the corporation to the shareholders if a corporation elects to be taxed under the S corporation provisions of the Internal Revenue Code.

A franchise exists when one party owns a trademark, trade name, or copyright, and another party contracts to use this right under specified conditions or limitations. Three different types of franchises have been developed: (1) distributorship, (2) business format, and (3) manufacturing or processing plant.

The law of franchising is developed through cases and through state and federal statutes. The Federal Trade Commission's disclosure rules specify information that must be given to all franchisees before they sign franchise agreements. This information enables franchisees to analyze the potential business success of the venture.

The franchise agreement establishes the rights of the franchisor and franchisee. Among the items that may be included are the required payments, the location of the business, the business organization of the franchisee, pricing and quality control provisions, and how the franchise can be terminated.

Using the World Wide Web

The state most famous for incorporating is the state of Delaware. More than 293,000 companies have incorporated within that state. Fifty percent of the corporations listed on the New York Stock Exchange have a Delaware charter and 60 percent of the *Fortune* 500 likewise are organized in that state.

It is possible to incorporate in Delaware via the Web. Different fees are charged depending on the form of organization and how fast the incorporation needs to be finalized. You will discover that it is very simple to create a corporation in Delaware.

For *Web Activities*, links to Web sites mentioned in the chapter, and additional Web sites that relate to the chapter topics, go to **http://bohlman.westbuslaw. com**, click on "Internet Applications," and select Chapter 19.

Web Activities

Go to **http://bohlman.westbuslaw.com**, click on "Internet Applications," and select Chapter 19.
19–1 Incorporation
19–2 Baldrige Award

Key Terms

alien corporation	cumulative preferred	franchisee	officer
articles of dissolution	stock	franchisor	patent license
articles of incorporation	debenture	incorporator	pierce the corporate veil
board of directors	debt securities	know-how licensing	preferred stock
bond	director	liquidation	promoter
business format franchise	dissolve	manufacturing or	Revised Model Business
business judgment rule	distributorship franchise	processing plant	Corporation Act
bylaws	domestic corporation	franchise	(RMBCA)
close corporation	equity securities	Model Business	S corporation
common stock	foreign corporation	Corporation Act	undercapitalization
corporation	franchise	(MBCA)	

Questions and Case Problems

19–1 Franchise Blake is interested in becoming a service station dealer. He contacts Esco Oil Company and obtains a franchise contract in which Esco agrees to furnish Blake with all gasoline, oil, and related products necessary to run the service station. In addition, Esco provides Blake with Esco signs and promotional material. A sign reading "Blake's Esco Service" is provided for the front of the station. In return for supplying all the necessary products, promotional materials, signs, and other services, Esco will receive a percentage of receipts on all products sold. Esco advertises that it stands behind its dealers. The relationship between Blake and Esco is challenged. Discuss whether the association is strictly a franchisor–franchisee relationship or a principal–agent (employer–employee) relationship.

19–2 Fiduciary Duty Morad, Thomson, and Coupounas were officers, directors, and shareholders of Bio-Lab. While serving as officers and directors of Bio-Lab, Morad and Thomson incorporated and operated a competing business, Med-Lab. Coupounas brought a suit on behalf of Bio-Lab against Morad, Thomson, and Med-Lab, alleging that they had usurped a corporate opportunity of Bio-Lab. Who prevails? Explain. [*Morad v. Coupounas*, 361 So. 2d 6 (1978)]

19–3 Board of Directors' Authority The Boston Athletic Association (BAA) is responsible for organizing the Boston Marathon. This activity is the corporation's principal business. The board of directors granted Cloney, the president, authority to negotiate and execute agreements to promote the marathon. Cloney entered into a contract with International Marathons, Inc. (IMI), as the exclusive promoter of the Boston Marathon. IMI was granted all rights, title, and interest to the exclusive use of the Boston Marathon and its logo. The board later learned of the exclusive contract. It brought a lawsuit to declare the contract void based on improper delegation of the board's authority. Should this contract be declared null and void? Explain. [*Boston Athletic Association v. International Marathons, Inc.,* 467 N.E.2d 58 (1984)]

19–4 Usurping Corporate Opportunity

Klinicki and Lundgren founded Berlinair, a closely held Oregon corporation, to provide air transportation out of West Germany. Klinicki, who owned 33 percent of the company stock, was the vice president and a director. Lundgren and his family owned 66 percent of Berlinair, and Berlinair's attorney owned the last 1 percent of stock. One of Berlinair's goals was to obtain a contract with BFR, a West German consortium of travel agents, to provide BFR with air charter service. Later Lundgren learned that the BFR contract might become available. Lundgren then incorporated Air Berlin Charter Company, of which he was the sole owner, and bid for the BFR contract. Lundgren won the BFR contract for Air Berlin while using Berlinair working time, staff, money, and facilities without the knowledge of Klinicki. When Klinicki learned of the BFR contract, he filed a suit as a minority stockholder against Lundgren and Air Berlin for usurping a corporate opportunity. Should Klinicki recover against Air Berlin? If so, what damages should Klinicki be awarded? [*Klinicki v. Lundgren,* 67 Or. App. 160, 678 P.2d 1250 (1984)]

19–5 Personal Liability of Shareholder

Salem Tent & Awning Company was a corporation in the business of renting awnings and tents. Dusty Schmidt came into the office to rent seven tents to cover his Christmas trees during the four weeks before Christmas. Although Schmidt and another person owned Western Oregon Christmas Trees, Inc., he signed the prepared invoice without indicating that he was part owner of this corporation or that the tents were for the business. The invoice stated "Renter is Responsible for Damages." Schmidt gave Salem Tent a $2,000 down payment check on which was printed "Western Oregon Christmas Trees." He gave no indication that a corporation existed. Schmidt received the tents and began to use them. A sudden storm destroyed several of the tents. When Schmidt refused to pay for the damaged tents,

Salem Tent sued for damages. Are both Western Oregon Christmas Trees and Dusty Schmidt liable for this loss, or just one of them? Explain. [*Salem Tent & Awning Co. v. Schmidt,* 79 Or. App. 475, 719 P.2d 899 (1986)]

19–6 Fiduciary Duty to Shareholders

Atlantic Properties, Inc., had only four shareholders, each of whom owned 25 percent of the capital stock. The bylaws required an 80 percent affirmative vote of the shareholders on all actions taken by the corporation. This provision had the effect of giving any of the four original shareholders a veto in corporate decisions. One shareholder refused to vote for any dividends for seven years although he was warned that his actions might expose the corporation to IRS penalties for unreasonable accumulation of corporate earnings and profits. The IRS did impose such penalties on the corporation. Can the dissenting shareholder be held personally liable for these penalties? [*Smith v. Atlantic Properties, Inc.,* 12 Mass. App. Ct. 201, 422 N.E.2d 798 (1981)]

19–7 Pierce the Corporate Veil

In 1997, RNF Media, Inc. (plaintiff), entered into a written contract with Marketing Ad, Inc. (Corporation). Under this contract, RNF Media purchased advertising space and time for Corporation's client, AST Computers (AST). Corporation was to reimburse RNF Media for the cost of these purchases and to pay RNF Media a 5 percent commission on the total sums. Between October 1997 and December 1998, RNF Media advanced approximately $300,000 for AST's advertising, and Corporation reimbursed RNF Media approximately $174,000, leaving an unpaid balance, including commissions, of approximately $126,000.

In early 1998, RNF Media demanded payment of the remaining sums. Ralph Lee (Lee), one of Corporation's officers and two principal owners, promised RNF Media on several occasions that Corporation would pay RNF Media as soon as AST paid Corporation. On January 5, 1999, Lee told RNF Media that Corporation had initiated a lawsuit against AST, because AST still had not paid Corporation.

Lee's representations that RNF Media would be paid as soon as AST paid Corporation, and that Corporation had sued AST for failure to pay, were false. AST had paid Corporation in full in early December 1998. Rather than use such payment to reimburse RNF Media, however, Lee and Brooks, the other stockholder, diverted some of AST's payment to their own personal use. They then caused Corporation to use the rest of the AST money to pay those obligations of Corporation that they had personally guaranteed, in other words, those debts for which they would otherwise be personally liable. Were Lee and Brooks personally liable for the RNF Media debt? Why or why not? [*RNF Media, Inc. v. Lee*, 2003 WL 2008281 (2003)]

19–8 Alter Ego Pacific Development, Inc., was incorporated in the District of Columbia for the purpose of international relations. Pacific's founder, president, and sole shareholder was Tongsun Park. He made all the corporate decisions. The board of directors played no significant role. Pacific purchased property. The purchase price was financed through Valley Finance, Inc., another of Park's wholly owned corporations. Valley placed a mortgage (lien) against the property to secure loan repayment. Park was a South Korean who improperly influenced Congress to provide economic and military aid to South Korea. His actions led to a scandal that involved members of Congress. A resulting IRS investigation of Park and his corporations revealed that he failed to pay his income taxes, and the IRS assessed $4.5 million in back taxes against Park. The IRS seized the property owned by Pacific by claiming that Pacific was merely an alter ego for Park. Because he totally controlled Pacific, the IRS claimed that it could set aside Pacific's corporate veil and use its assets to help pay off the $4.5 million. Valley claimed that the IRS improp-

erly pierced Pacific's corporate veil. Pacific's property should not be used to pay off Park's personal debt of taxes to the IRS, but should be used to pay the debt owed to Valley. Should the corporate veil be pierced? Explain. [*Valley Finance, Inc., v. United States*, 629 F.2d 162 (D.C. Cir. 1980)]

19–9 Franchise Imperial Motors, Inc., has a franchise agreement with Chrysler. The agreement explicitly provided that Imperial would not have the exclusive right to purchase Chrysler cars for resale in a four-town area of South Carolina. Chrysler allowed another dealer to move into a new showroom seven miles from Imperial's location. Imperial brought legal action against Chrysler. Chrysler filed a motion for summary judgment, claiming that Imperial had not established a cause of action. Should the court grant this motion? Explain. [*Imperial Motors, Inc. v. Chrysler*, 559 F. Supp. 1312 (1983)]

19–10 Internet Regardless of the business form you adopt, you need to establish policies on a number of different topics. For example, there should be a policy on e-mail. The Cyberspace Law Institute has a Web site that offers several different model forms. Does the model form on e-mail policy allow a person to use the business's e-mail server for personal use? Go to **http://www. cli.org/emailpolicy/background**, where you will find a list of clauses. Prepare a policy on e-mail.

Unit 4

Business and Government Regulation

Chapter 20

Securities Law

> *Corporations cannot commit treason, nor be outlawed nor excommunicated for they have no soul.*
>
> *Case of Sutton's Hospital (1625)*
> **Sir Edward Coke, 1552–1634**
> **British jurist and politician, advocate of the supremacy of the common law**

Chapter Outline

Securities Disclosure Requirements: Do the Consumers Really Get the Information They Need?

As a staff attorney, you are assigned to prepare material for prospective investors in a limited partnership that will build and manage an office building. After coordinating the material, you are confident that you have satisfied the legal requirements for appropriate disclosure. You believe, however, that the documents are so complicated that few prospective investors will understand them. The market for office space is soft, and you, personally, would never invest in such a project.

You carefully bring your concerns to your supervising attorney. He reminds you, however, that your obligation is to make sure that the legal requirements are met. When you question him about the financial soundness of building an office building in this economy, he explains that the deal allows for the general partners to receive their money up front and, therefore, to benefit whether or not the deal is successful. The general partners are the clients and their interest is to be protected. Because this initial payout to the general partners is fully disclosed, all the legal requirements have been met.

You are dissatisfied with the explanation and perceive that the law firm is participating in a rather shady deal that will benefit the general partners at the expense of the innocent investors. Do you insist on a meeting with the law firm's senior partner in the hope that the firm will refuse to be a party to such a practice, or do you simply certify that the documents meet all legal requirements and remain silent? Use the ethical model presented in Chapter 2 and reprinted on the inside front cover to develop your answer.

pass the initial legislation, a member of the Kansas legislature claimed that promoters were so shrewd that they could sell anyone a "piece of the blue sky itself." Since then, statutes that regulate the sales of securities within a state have been called **blue sky laws**.

The devastating effects of the Great Depression (1929-1939) led Congress to hold hearings. These investigations tried to search out the causes of the financial system's collapse in 1929 so that legislation could be adopted to prevent another such disaster. These laws regulated securities, financial markets, business practices, and specific industries, such as stockbrokerages.

The federal regulating body is the **Securities and Exchange Commission (SEC)**.[1] Federal statutes dominate in the regulation of securities. This chapter discusses the Securities Act of 1933, Securities Exchange Act of 1934, Securities Investor Protection Act of 1970, Foreign Corrupt Practices Act of 1977, Insider Trading Sanctions Act of 1984, Insider Trading and Securities Fraud Enforcement Act of 1988, Securities Enforcement Remedies and Penny Stock Reform Act of 1990, and Market Reform Act of 1990. Then it reviews more recent legislation passed by Congress: the Private Securities Litigation Reform Act, the National Securities Markets Improvement Act, and the Sarbanes-Oxley Act. Before these statutes can be examined, however, the definition of a security must be established.

Artiste Login. When Carlo and Carlotta formed their online business, Artiste Login Products, Inc., they decided the company was large enough to incorporate and to sell the shares on the public stock exchange. They were fortunate to have the money to purchase the controlling shares. The stock was issued and since going public, the value of the company has continued to increase. Carlo and Carlotta know they must be vigilant about all aspects of the corporation. Their corporation is far more regulated than if they had chosen another form of business entity and had not sold shares to the public.

---

[1]The Securities and Exchange Commission's Web site is http://www.sec.gov. An Internet site that covers most security laws is maintained by the University of Cincinnati College of Law. Its address is http://www.law.uc.edu/CCL. Another site that offers investors, the judiciary, policymakers, and students a careful look into the workings of security litigation and, in particular, class action is one that Stanford University maintains. Its address is http://securities.stanford.edu/about/caveat.html.

Introduction

Not until the twentieth century did the government consider regulating securities. In 1911, the state of Kansas adopted the first law to regulate the sale of securities within the state (intrastate transactions). To

What Is a Security?

Stocks and bonds are two common types of securities that were reviewed in Chapter 19. A security, as defined in the Securities Act of 1933, is very broad, and its exact definition is unclear. The courts have interpreted this language expansively. A **security** is defined as (1) an investment of money or other consideration, (2) in a common enterprise, (3) with the investor expecting a profit, and (4) with the profit derived primarily through the efforts of a promoter or a third party other than the investor.

To meet this criterion, the investor must turn money over to another individual for investment purposes, which must be pooled with the capital of other investors so that each individual owns an undivided interest in the whole. The investor has no day-to-day control over the enterprise. A security owner is passive. An officer or employee who owns stock in her company is considered to be a passive investor.

Securities are created by the issuing party, called the **issuer**, such as a corporation or limited partnership. They can be issued in unlimited amounts and at relatively little cost because the physical representation of a security is nothing more than a piece of paper that represents a financial interest. A security is not used or consumed. Rather, it is a type of currency traded in the "secondary market." A security in the secondary market is bought and sold by people who normally are not the security's issuers.

Securities are more vulnerable to price fluctuation than are other types of investments, such as automobiles or real estate. The economy, interest rates, and information concerning the business influence the value of a security. True, false, and misleading information about the business influences the security's price. This distinctive feature of securities makes it very easy for individuals or brokerage firms to misrepresent an investment's value. Securities laws attempt to protect investors by mandating full and truthful disclosure, by prohibiting fraud, and by prohibiting insider trading.

Securities laws have been applied to various transactions that traditionally have not been thought of as securities. In addition to the traditional stocks and bonds, courts have found investment contracts to be securities. Examples of investment contracts include the sale of interest in land involving orange and pecan groves, the sale of limited partnership interests, and investments in mink and chinchilla farms. The *Legal Highlight* entitled *What Do Earthworm Farms, Salvador Dali Prints, and Life Insurance Policies Have in Common?* provides more examples. The possibility that a business venture may be termed a security must be considered in every transaction, because the legal ramifications of engaging in the buying and selling of securities are far reaching. The following case illustrates this point.

CASE 20.1	**REVES v. ERNST & YOUNG**
Supreme Court of the United States, 1990 494 U.S. 56, 110 S. Ct. 945, 108 L. Ed. 2d 47 http://caselaw.findlaw.com	**BACKGROUND AND FACTS** Farmer's Cooperative of Arkansas and Oklahoma (Co-op) is a 23,000-member agricultural cooperative. To raise money, it sold promissory notes payable on demand by the holder. The notes were not backed with any collateral and they were not insured. The Co-op marketed the notes as an investment program, advertising that more than $11 million in assets stood behind these investments. Several months later, the Co-op filed for bankruptcy, leaving 1,600 people holding notes worth a total of $10 million.

This litigation was instituted against the accounting firms including Ernst & Young for overvaluating a gasohol plant that was one of the biggest assets. The plaintiffs obtained a $6.1 million judgment in the trial court.

This judgment was overturned by the U.S. Eighth Circuit Court of Appeals on the basis that the 1934 Securities Exchange Act did not cover these demand notes. The act excluded, among other things, "any note . . . which has a maturity at time of issuance of not exceeding nine months." In other words, the debt, evidenced by a promissory note, paid before the end of nine months is not a security.

Justice MARSHALL delivered the opinion of the Court.

. . . .

This case requires us to decide whether the note issued by the Co-op is a "security" within the meaning of the 1934 Act. Section 3(a)(10) of that Act is our starting point:

> *"The term 'security' means any . . . but shall not include currency or any note, draft, bill of exchange, or banker's acceptance which has a maturity at the time of issuance of not exceeding nine months." . . .*

The fundamental purpose undergirding the Securities Acts is to eliminate serious abuses in largely unregulated securities.

. . . .

In discharging our duty, we are not bound by legal formalisms, but instead take account of the economics of the transaction under investigation. . . . Congress' purpose in enacting the securities laws was to regulate investments, in whatever form they are made and by whatever name they are called.

. . . .

First, we examine the transaction to assess the motivations that would prompt a reasonable seller and buyer to enter into it. If the seller's purpose is to raise money for the general use of a business enterprise or to finance substantial investments and the buyer is interested primarily in the profit the note is expected to generate, the instrument is likely to be a "security." If the note is exchanged to facilitate the purchase and sale of a minor asset or consumer good, to correct for the seller's cash-flow difficulties, or to advance some other commercial or consumer purpose, on the other hand, the note is less sensibly described as a "security." . . . Second, we examine the plan of distribution of the instrument to determine whether it is an instrument in which there is common trading for speculation or investment. Third, we examine the reasonable expectations of the investing public: The Court will consider instruments to be "securities" on the basis of such public expectations, even where an economic analysis of the circumstances of the particular transaction might suggest that the instruments are not "securities" as used in that transaction. Finally, we examine whether some factor such as the existence of another regulatory scheme significantly reduces the risk of the instrument, thereby rendering application of the Securities Acts unnecessary. . . .

. . . .

. . . [W]e conclude that the demand notes at issue here fall under the "note" category of instruments that are "securities" under the 1933 and 1934 Acts. . . .

DECISION AND REMEDY Whether a promissory note is a security depends on the method by which it was issued. The Court established the four factors to be considered in making this determination and concluded that the notes in this case were securities.

CRITICAL THINKING: POLITICAL CONSIDERATION For many years prior to 1933, the philosophy of security law was to prosecute only those persons who committed actual fraud by intentional wrongful acts. Beginning with the passage of the Securities Act of 1933, the philosophy changed and many new statutes and rules were implemented to protect the investing public. With any regulation comes cost. Should laws protect the investing public or should investors perform their own investigations and take responsibility for their investment decisions?

LEGAL HIGHLIGHT

What Do Earthworm Farms, Salvador Dali Prints, and Life Insurance Policies Have in Common?

Earthworm Farms

Allen J. Gross sent out promotional newsletters on how to make money by purchasing an earthworm farm. The newsletter promised several things. First, growing instructions would accompany the earthworm farm. Second, the time involved to grow the earthworms was similar to that of raising a garden. Third, earthworms multiplied sixty-four times a year. Lastly, Gross would buy back at $2.25 per pound all bait-size earthworms produced.

Gerald Smith responded to the newsletter. Gross told Smith that the work required little time or effort, that Gross needed Smith's help in the common enterprise of supplying worms for the bait industry, and that Gross's agreement to repurchase guaranteed success. Smith purchased the earthworm farm.

Smith soon found that earthworms multiply eight times a year rather than sixty-four times a year. He could make a profit only if worms reproduced sixty-four times a year. The price of $2.25 was ten times greater than dictated by true market conditions. Gross could pay the $2.25 price only by selling worms to new worm farmers at inflated prices. In fact, little market existed for the earthworms in Phoenix, Arizona. Smith sued Gross.

The question facing the court was whether the sale of the earthworm farm was an investment contract type of security. The court found that it was. First, Smith invested money when he purchased the earthworm farm. Second, a common enterprise existed because Smith could receive the promised income only if Gross purchased the earthworm harvest and both Smith and Gross were dependent on others purchasing earthworm farms at inflated prices from Gross. Third, the profits came from the efforts of others. The effort required by Smith was minimal because of the promised high earthworm reproduction rate and the profit depended on Gross reselling the production to new earthworm farmers.

Salvador Dali Prints

Some art galleries had sold fake Salvador Dali prints to customers for several years. Some of these galleries were boiler-room operations in which the seller called potential customers, telling them that they could own an affordable Dali print. The seller purchased the print for $25 to $50 and sold it to the victim for $1,500 to $2,500. The print, however, was really a reproduction and not a genuine limited-edition lithograph. The "Dali prints" were neither authorized nor supervised by Dali.

Although each victim was overcharged a relatively small sum, the total amount was staggering. In New York, a boiler-room operation was convicted of defrauding investors out of $1.3 million. Because the operation's owners had sold the Dali prints to victims over the telephone as investments, they were convicted of securities fraud.

Life Insurance Policies

Normally, life insurance policies are not considered a security. When the AIDS virus became predominant and had no known cure, however, the door was opened to the practice of cashing in an ill person's life insurance policy while still alive. The development of medicines, fortunately, extended the lives of these persons for many years. Instead of surviving a few months, these persons now can look forward to many years of productive life.

But before these medicines were developed, AIDS patients needed money to live on because they were too ill to work. If an AIDS patient had insurance, he could go to a financial institution with his life insurance policy. The financial institution would find potential investors, who would be shown the medical records of the insured that indicated that he had a terminal disease. The investors would then place into escrow enough money to pay the premiums over a three- or four-year period with the expectation that the insured would certainly die during that period. The insured was paid a percentage of the value of the policy. The financial institution would obtain a commission for its part, but did not register these transactions as securities.

As the medications improved, the insured did not die within three or four years. The investors had to continue making premium payments for far more years than originally planned. Eventually, these investors sued the financial institutions on the basis of selling a security. A number of courts found that these transactions constituted selling a security.

The Securities Act of 1933

The first securities regulation statute enacted by Congress, the **Securities Act of 1933**,[2] has two aspects: the disclosure of information and the prohibition of fraud and deceit. This act often is referred to as the "truth in securities" law, because it requires full and truthful disclosure by companies issuing securities.

Every new issue of securities must be registered with the SEC, unless the security qualifies for an exemption, as discussed later. The 1933 act also forbids fraud and deceit in the distribution of the securities and applies even to securities not required to be registered. The statute was designed to prohibit various forms of fraud and to stabilize the securities industry by requiring that all essential information concerning the issuing of securities be made available to the investing public.[3]

Requirements of the Registration Statement

Businesses issuing a security, unless exempt, must file with the SEC a **registration statement** that provides important information, such as the names of directors and officers, as well as financial, economic, and other important information. Businesses must register the security before offering it to the public. In addition, businesses must provide investors with a **prospectus**, which is the document that is utilized to sell the security. The registration statement and prospectus supply sufficient information to enable unsophisticated investors to evaluate the financial risk involved. The prospectus must be written in plain English.[4]

The corporation's principal executive officer, principal accounting officer, principal financial officer, and at least a majority of the members of the board of directors must sign the registration statement. Signing the registration statement makes a person potentially liable for any errors or material omissions in it.

The SEC does not attempt to determine whether an investment is a good one. It only demands that

sufficient information be available to a potential investor so that he can make an intelligent decision.

CYBERLAW

EDGAR

The SEC is moving from paper document filings to electronic filings on the **Electronic Data Gathering, Analysis, and Retrieval (EDGAR)**[5] system. This system performs automated collection, validation, indexing, acceptance, and forwarding of submissions by companies that are required by law to file forms with the SEC.

The SEC requires some corporations to file certain documents electronically on EDGAR. For example, all 8-K, 10-K, 10-Q, and other similar documents must be filed electronically. As a result, the SEC has rid itself of much paperwork. Electronic filings allow the general public to view and search on the computer many of the documents filed by corporations.

Requirements of the Registering Corporation

Before filing the registration statement and prospectus with the SEC, the business can obtain an underwriter to monitor distribution of the new issue. A twenty-day waiting period after registration is mandated before any sale can take place. The SEC may extend this period, or the registration statement may require amendments that start the twenty-day period over again.

During this period, oral offers between interested investors and the issuer concerning the purchase and sale of the proposed securities may take place. The securities cannot be bought or sold legally, however. Exhibit 20–1 sets out the time periods for a new security.

During the waiting period, written advertising is allowed in the form of a **tombstone advertisement**. This advertisement is so named because it is outlined in black and resembles a tombstone. Such advertisements simply tell the investor where and how to obtain a prospectus. Normally, any other type of advertising is prohibited.

---

[2]The Securities Act of 1933 is located at http://www.law.cornell.edu/uscode. Click on "Table of Popular Names." Scroll down to "Part 24 Rhode Island through Sheep." Scroll down until you find "Securities Act of 1933."

[3]A good Web site that discusses security fraud is http://www.securitieslaw.com.

[4]The guidelines the SEC has published concerning plain English are found at http://www.sec.gov/investor/pubs/englishhndbk.htm.

[5]The EDGAR database of corporate information Web site is http://www.sec.gov/edgarhp.htm.

LEGAL HIGHLIGHT

Plain English for Investing?

The Securities and Exchange Commission is making investing more understandable by requiring that information given to consumers be written in plain English. Mutual funds, stocks, and bonds often are sold with high-pressure tactics. Demystifying these investments is a challenge. The SEC created a task force to make recommendations.

The SEC task force addressed the lack of readability of prospectuses and other disclosure documents. Issuers, underwriters, and their lawyers created defensively written documents that utilized legal jargon and overinclusive disclosures. The task force found the language describing even basic information about the issuer's business to be "turgid," "opaque," and "unreadable." The result was that trivial issues sometimes received as much attention as material information and buried points significant to an investment decision. The task force recommended the following:

- The use of plain English principles in the organization, language, and structure of the prospectus's and other documents' cover pages, summary, and risk factors section. These sections should communicate the information clearly to investors.

- The use of pictures, logos, charts, graphs, or other design elements.
- The use of clear, concise paragraphs and sentences, using bulleted lists and short sentences, if possible.
- The avoidance of legal and highly technical business terminology.
- The definition of terms in a glossary when the meanings are unclear from the context.

The Office of Investor Education and Assistance wrote a book for businesses called *A Plain English Handbook: How to Create Clear SEC Disclosure Documents*. This book offers insights into those areas that the SEC considers important to be explained in plain English.

The SEC has a hotline to better serve the investing public. Callers can hear prerecorded messages on investing in general, finding investor's alert pamphlets, filing complaints, requesting SEC publications, accessing public records, and obtaining disciplinary information on brokers. The SEC encourages the public to report people believed to be violating any of the federal securities laws. By reporting suspected violations of the federal securities laws that may be occurring over the Internet or anywhere else, a future victim may be protected from losing her or his life savings.

At this time, a **red herring prospectus**[6] (the preliminary prospectus) may be distributed. The name comes from the red legend printed across it, stating that the registration has been filed but has not become effective. The red legend indicates that the prospectus is not final and not yet approved by the SEC.

Once the registration process is complete, the registrant can issue stock. Two SEC rules help to make the process more efficient and cost effective: the simplified registration process and the shelf registration rules.

Regulation A, Simplified Registration Process. Under **Regulation A**, a seller can sell up to $1.5 mil-

lion in a one-year period with a simplified registration process. Regulation A does not place a limit on the number of purchasers.

Disclosure is not required if the offering is under $100,000. Any offering above $100,000 must disclose material information regarding the investment. The circular containing the information must be filed with the SEC ten days prior to the sale of the securities.

Regulation C, Rule 415, Shelf Registration. Corporations with stock having a minimum value of $150 million may register the new security, but need not sell all the securities they have issued at the same time. **Regulation C, Rule 415**, is popularly called **shelf registration**, because these securities are put "on the shelf" to be sold at a later time.

---

[6]To see initial public offerings (IPOs) go to the Red Herring Web site at http://www.redherring.com.

Exhibit 20–1   **Time Periods for a New Security under the Securities Act of 1933**

Time Period	Actions Allowed	Actions Not Allowed
Prefiling period	Preliminary work, such as consulting with the following: • Attorneys • Investment bankers • Accountants. Preliminary work, such as preparing paperwork for filing the following with the SEC: • Registration statement • Supporting documents. Preparing the preliminary prospectus. Publishing a notice setting out the following: • Name of issuer • Description of the security.	Must not offer the security for sale. Must not contract to sell the security. Must not generate publicity to excite the public about the future security.
	Registration Statement and Supporting Documents Filed	
Waiting period, usually twenty days (SEC reviews registration statement and supporting documents)	Publishing or distributing information through the following: • Tombstone advertisements • Red herring prospectus • Notice of proposed offering. Oral offers are permitted.	Must not contract to sell the security.
	SEC Approves Registration	
Posteffective period	Must try to sell all the newly registered securities. • Exemption: Shelf Registration [Rule 415]. Corporations having a minimum value of $150 million may place part of their new securities "on the shelf" to sell later. Securities may be both offered and sold. Final prospectus is issued. Final prospectus is sent before or with all sales or delivery of securities.	Must not have a red herring prospectus.

Once the registration is approved by the SEC, the only requirement is for the company to amend its registration in case of any major changes. This rule aids efficiency by reducing legal, accounting, and printing costs.

Misrepresentations in Registering with the SEC

A registration statement that contains material untruths or omissions makes the issuer liable for violation of the securities laws. In addition, all individuals who signed, were named, or participated in drafting the registration statement are liable. The **due diligence defense** is available to those who sign a false statement. A defendant who exercised "due diligence" in verifying the truth of the statement may escape liability for false statements made to the SEC. The issuer, however, cannot use the due diligence defense.

In the following case, the court found that the registration statement contained material false statements of fact and material omissions. The individuals who were involved in the issuance of the new securities attempted to use the defense of due diligence.

LANDMARK CASE

CASE 20.2

United States District Court, Southern District of New York, 1968

283 F. Supp. 643

ESCOTT v. BARCHRIS CONSTRUCTION CORP.

BACKGROUND AND FACTS This lawsuit was brought by purchasers of BarChris Construction Corporation debentures (an unsecured bond) under Section 11 of the Securities Act of 1933. In 1961, BarChris filed a registration statement to issue the debentures with the Securities and Exchange Commission. The plaintiffs alleged that the registration statement contained material false statements and material omissions.

The defendants fell into three categories: (1) the people who signed the registration statement, (2) the underwriters (consisting of eight investment banking firms), and (3) BarChris's auditors, Peat, Marwick, Mitchell & Company. Included in the group of defendants who signed the registration statement were (1) BarChris's nine directors, (2) BarChris's controller, (3) one of BarChris's attorneys, (4) two investment bankers who were later named as directors of the BarChris Construction Corporation, and (5) numerous other people participating in the preparation of the registration statement.

BarChris grew from a bowling alley building company that started in 1946. The introduction of automatic pin-setting machines in 1952 sparked rapid growth in the bowling industry. BarChris benefited from this increased interest in bowling and its construction operations expanded rapidly. In 1960, BarChris installed approximately 3 percent of all bowling lanes built in the United States. BarChris's sales increased dramatically between 1956 and 1960, and the company was recognized as a significant factor in the bowling construction industry.

BarChris constantly needed cash to finance its operations, a need that grew more and more pressing as the operations expanded. In 1959, BarChris sold over half a million shares of its common stock to the public. By early 1961, it needed additional working capital and decided to sell debentures.

BarChris sold the debentures. Nevertheless, the proceeds from the sale of debentures provided only temporary relief, and soon it experienced increasing financial difficulties, which in time became insurmountable. By early 1962, BarChris began to fail. In October, BarChris filed for bankruptcy. By November, it defaulted on the interest due on the debentures.

The plaintiffs challenged the registration statement's accuracy. They also charged that the text of the prospectus—including many of the figures—was false and that material information had been omitted.

Judge MCLEAN

. . . .

Materiality

It is a prerequisite to liability under Section 11 of the Act that the fact which is falsely stated in a registration statement, or the fact that is omitted when it should have been stated to avoid misleading, be "material."

. . . .

The average prudent investor is not concerned with minor inaccuracies or with errors as to matters which are of no interest to him. The facts which tend to deter him from purchasing a security are facts which have an important bearing upon the nature or condition of the issuing corporation or its business.

Judged by this test, there is no doubt that many of the misstatements and omissions in this prospectus were material.

The "Due Diligence" Defenses

Section 11 (b) of the Act provides that:

> . . . *"no person, other than the issuer, shall be liable . . . who shall sustain the burden of proof—* . . . .

> *(3) that (A) as regards any part of the registration statement not purporting to be made on the authority of an expert . . . he had, after reasonable investigation, reasonable ground to believe and did believe, at the time such part of the registration statement became effective, that the statements therein were true and that there was no omission to state a material fact required to be stated therein or necessary to make the statements therein not misleading."*

Kircher

Kircher was treasurer of BarChris and its chief financial officer. He is a certified public accountant and an intelligent man. He was thoroughly familiar with BarChris's financial affairs. He knew the terms of BarChris's agreements. . . . He knew of the customers' delinquency problem. . . . He knew how the financing proceeds were to be applied and he saw to it that they were so applied. He arranged the officers' loans and he knew all the facts concerning them.

As to the rest of the prospectus, knowing the facts, he did not have a reasonable ground to believe it to be true. On the contrary, he must have known that in part it was untrue. Under these circumstances, he was not entitled to sit back and place the blame on the lawyers for not advising him about it. Kircher has not proved his due diligence defenses.

Trilling

Trilling's position is somewhat different from Kircher's. He was BarChris's controller. He signed the registration statement in that capacity, although he was not a director.

Trilling was not a member of the executive committee. He was a comparative minor figure in BarChris. The description of BarChris's "management" on page 9 of the prospectus does not mention him. He was not considered to be an executive officer.

Trilling may well have been unaware of several of the inaccuracies in the prospectus. But he must have known of some of them. As a financial officer, he was familiar with BarChris's finances and with its books of account.

As far as appears, he made no investigation. He did what was asked of him and assumed that others would properly take care of supplying accurate data as to the other aspects of the company's business. This would have been well enough but for the fact that he signed the registration statement. As a signer, he could not avoid responsibility by leaving it up to others to make it accurate. Trilling did not sustain the burden of proving his due diligence defenses.

Birnbaum

Birnbaum was a young lawyer, admitted to the bar in 1957, who, after brief periods of employment by two different law firms and an equally brief period of practicing in his own firm, was employed by BarChris as house counsel and assistant secretary in October 1960. Unfortunately for him, he became secretary and a director of BarChris on April 17, 1961, after the first version of the registration statement had been filed with the Securities and Exchange Commission. He signed the later amendments, thereby becoming responsible for the accuracy of the prospectus in its final form.

Although the prospectus, in its description of "management," lists Birnbaum among the "executive officers" and devotes several sentences to a recital of his career, the fact seems to be that he was not an executive officer in any real sense. He did not participate in the management of the company. As house counsel, he attended to legal matters of a routine nature.

It seems probable that Birnbaum did not know of many of the inaccuracies in the prospectus. He must, however, have appreciated some of them. In any case, he made no investigation and relied on the others to get it right. . . . As a lawyer, he should have known his obligations under the statute. He should have known that he was required to make a reasonable investigation of the truth of all the statements in the unexpertised portion of the document which he signed. Having failed to make such an investigation, he did not have reasonable ground to believe that all these statements were true. Birnbaum has not established his diligence defenses. . . .

Auslander

Auslander was an "outside" director, i.e., one who was not an officer of BarChris. He was chairman of the board of Valley Stream National Bank. . . . In February 1961 [he was asked] to become a director of BarChris. . . .

. . . .

Auslander was elected a director on April 17, 1961. The registration statement in its original form had already been filed, of course without his signature. On May 10, 1961, he signed a signature page for the first amendment to the registration statement which was filed on May 11, 1961. This was a separate sheet without any document attached. Auslander did not know that it was a signature page for a registration statement. He vaguely understood that it was something "for the SEC."

Auslander attended a meeting of BarChris's directors on May 15, 1961. At that meeting he, along with the other directors, signed the signature sheet for the second amendment which constituted the registration statement in its final form. Again, this was only a separate sheet without any document attached.

It is true that Auslander became a director on the eve of the financing. He had little opportunity to familiarize himself with the company's affairs. . . .

Section 11 imposes liability in the first instance upon a director, no matter how new he is. He is presumed to know his responsibility when he becomes a director. He can escape liability only by using that reasonable care to investigate the facts which a prudent man would employ in the management of his own property. In my opinion, a prudent man would not act in an important matter without any knowledge of the relevant facts, in sole reliance upon representations of persons who are comparative strangers and upon general information which does not purport to cover the particular case. To say that such minimal conduct measures up to the statutory standard would, to all intents and purposes, absolve new directors from responsibility merely because they are new. This is not a sensible construction of Section 11, when one bears in mind its fundamental purpose of requiring full and truthful disclosure for the protection of investors.

I find and conclude that Auslander has not established his due diligence defense.

Peat, Marwick

. . . .

Berardi was then about thirty years old. He was not yet a C.P.A. He had no previous experience with the bowling industry. This was his first job as a senior accountant. He could hardly have been given a more difficult assignment.

. . . .

Berardi had no conception of how tight the cash position was. He did not discover that BarChris was holding up checks in substantial amounts because there was no money in the bank to cover them. He did not know of the loan from Manufacturers Trust Company or of the officers' loans. Since he never read the prospectus, he was not even aware that there had ever been any problem about loans from officers.

. . . .

Accountants should not be held to a standard higher than that recognized in their profession. I do not do so here. Berardi's review did not come up to that standard. He did not take some of the steps which Peat, Marwick's written program prescribed. He did not spend an adequate amount of time on a task of this magnitude. Most important of all he was too easily satisfied with glib answers to his inquiries.

This is not to say that he should have made a complete audit. But there were enough danger signals in the materials which he did examine to require some further investigation on his part. Generally accepted accounting standards required such further investigation under these circumstances. It is not always sufficient merely to ask questions.

[T]he burden of proof is on Peat, Marwick. I find that that burden has not been satisfied. I conclude that Peat, Marwick has not established its due diligence defense.

DECISION AND REMEDY BarChris Construction Corporation itself, the signers of the registration statement, the debentures, the underwriters, and the corporations' auditors were held liable.

CRITICAL THINKING: MANAGEMENT CONSIDERATION While some of the accused persons in this case actively lied, how could the others have avoided liability?

Exemptions

A corporation can avoid the high cost and complicated procedures associated with registration by taking advantage of certain exemptions to the registration requirement. Two general types of exemption are allowed: exempt transactions and exempt securities.

Exempt Transactions. The 1933 Securities Act exempts three types of transactions involving new securities from the registration requirements. The three **exempt transactions** are *small offering exemptions, private offering exemptions,* and *intrastate offering exemptions.*

These exemptions are very broad; thus, an offering may qualify for more than one exemption. Although the sale may be exempt from registration, the SEC may require that a report be filed.

An exemption is available only for the current transaction and does not cover future transactions. The next transaction must either be registered or be exempt from registration in its own right.

Small Offering Exemptions. The SEC rules outline different types of **small offering exemptions**. These offerings by an issuer are not large enough for the federal government to regulate: (1) certain types of bank loans, (2) privately negotiated sales of securities to large institutional investors, and (3) business-venture promotions by a few closely related persons.

These offers involve a small amount of money or the securities are offered for sale in a limited manner. Small offering exemptions are covered by Regulation D and Section 4(f).

Regulation D. **Regulation D** of the 1933 act sets out exemptions from registration requirements if certain conditions are met. Regulation D distinguishes between an accredited investor and an unaccredited investor.

The **accredited investor** is not likely to need government protection in making its investment determinations. An accredited investor is one of the following:

1. An institutional investor, such as an insurance company, bank, credit union, or pension fund;

2. The seller's directors and officers;

3. An individual investor who has had an annual income of more than $200,000, or a husband and wife with annual income in excess of $300,000, for two consecutive years;

4. An individual with a net worth of more than $1 million; or

5. Any corporation or charitable organization with total assets of more than $5 million.

An **unaccredited investor** does not meet the previously listed requirements for an accredited investor. The unaccredited investor is likely to need protection.

Regulation D, Rule 504. A noninvestment company does not engage primarily in the business of investing or trading securities. The **Rule 504** exemption is for noninvestment companies that do not report to the SEC under the Securities Exchange Act of 1934. Under Regulation D, Rule 504, a noninvestment company can sell up to $1 million in securities that it issues in any one year without registration if the company does not advertise or make any general solicitations.

Although Rule 504 exempts the securities from registration, the seller must file a notice with the SEC. Resale of these securities is restricted. State law, however, may apply. Any amount between $500,000 and $1 million must be registered under the state securities registration law.

Regulation D, Rule 505. Under **Rule 505** of Regulation D, a private, noninvestment company may sell up to $5 million in securities in any one year to any number of accredited investors if the company does not advertise or make any general solicitations.

Unaccredited investors can make purchases, but the number of unaccredited investors is limited to thirty-five. If the sale involves any unaccredited investors, the seller must provide all investors with material information about the offering company, its business, and the securities before the sale. The issuer is not required to believe that each unaccredited investor "has such knowledge and experience in financial and business matters that he [or she] is capable of evaluating the merits and the risks of the prospective investment."

A notice of the sale must be filed with the SEC. This exemption applies to businesses, even if they are covered by the 1934 act.

Section 4(f). An issuer can offer to sell securities exempt from registration solely to accredited investors if the amount is no more than $5 million. No unaccredited investors can participate. No limit, however, is placed on the number of accredited investors.

The company cannot advertise or make any general solicitation for the sale of these securities. A notice of the sale must be filed with the SEC.

Private Offering Exemptions, Regulation D, Rule 506. The federal government is not interested in regulating privately made offerings because the goal of the 1933 act is public protection. Thus, the SEC allows **private offering exemptions**.

Under **Rule 506** of Regulation D, a private, noninvestment company may offer an unlimited number of securities if they generally do not solicit or advertise them. An unlimited number of accredited investors can participate. No more than thirty-five unaccredited investors, however, can be involved.

The seller must determine if each unaccredited investor has enough knowledge and experience in financial and business matters to evaluate the merits and risks of the prospective investment. When there are unaccredited investors, the issuer must provide to all purchasers material information about itself, its business, and the securities before the sale.

A notice of the sale must be filed with the SEC. The Rule 506 exemption applies to businesses, even if they are covered by the 1934 act.

Rule 506 differs from Rule 505 in that Rule 506 requires the issuer to verify that each unaccredited investor has sufficient knowledge or experience to evaluate the risks and merits of the security.

Resales. Securities acquired under a previously discussed exemption cannot be resold without registration under the act, unless they requalify for an exemption. **Rule 144A** provides a safe harbor exemption for resales of such securities. A resale may activate registration requirements unless the seller complies with Rule 144 or Rule 144A. These rules are popularly called the **safe-harbor exemptions**.

Safe Harbor Exemption, Rule 144. **Restricted securities** are securities acquired in unregistered, private sales from an issuer. One way in which investors purchase restricted securities is through private placement offerings, Regulation D offerings, and employee stock benefit plans.

If a person has held the restricted securities for more than one year, the securities can be sold if the following conditions set in **Rule 144** are met. Current adequate public information about the issuer of the securities must be available, which can be found in the reports filed with the SEC under the 1934 Act. The amount allowed to be sold is based on a trading volume formula set out in Rule 144. A notice of sale must be filed with the SEC. Once these conditions are met, the seller is protected from SEC action by the safe harbor exemption.

Safe Harbor Exemption, Rule 144A. **Rule 144A** provides a safe harbor exemption for the sellers from the registration requirements of the Securities Act of 1933. The seller is reselling securities that at the time they were issued were not of the same class listed on a national securities exchange or quoted in a U.S. automated interdealer quotation system. These securities may be sold solely to qualified institutional buyers or registered broker–dealers purchasing as principals.

In general, a qualified institutional buyer is an institutional investor that in the aggregate owns and invests on a discretionary basis at least $100 million in securities of issuers that are not affiliated with the buyer. Registered broker–dealers need only own and invest at least $10 million of securities in order to purchase as a principal under Rule 144A. Accordingly, broker–dealers may purchase privately placed securities from issuers as principal and resell such securities to qualified institutional buyers under Rule 144A.

Intrastate Offering Exemptions, Rule 147. With **intrastate offering exemptions**, the federal government allows each state to regulate securities offerings within its boundaries. An intrastate offering must be made only to resident investors in one state by a seller that resides within that state.

The seller's principal office, 80 percent of its assets, and 80 percent of its gross revenues must be in the state. In addition, 80 percent of the proceeds of the offering must be used within the state. An offer made to an out-of-state resident may result in the cancellation of this exemption.

Exempt Securities. In addition to the exempt transactions, some types of securities are exempt from registration under the 1933 act. **Exempt securities** include securities issued by governments (state and federal). For example, a state government issues bonds to build a classroom building. These bonds are exempt from SEC registration. Banks, savings and loan associations, charitable organizations, and common carriers that are regulated by other federal laws are also exempt.

Corporations issue stock dividends or have stock splits. These types of securities are exempt. Exhibit 20–2 sets out in a chart these different types of exempt securities.

Liability under the 1933 Act

Violations of the Securities Act of 1933 may be dealt with by the Department of Justice (DOJ) filing a criminal action, by the SEC filing a civil action, or by a private party filing a lawsuit. Criminal charges can be filed by DOJ if the defendant has engaged in willful violations of the 1933 act. If convicted, the defendant faces up to five years in prison and a $10,000 fine.

The SEC may file a complaint and seek an administrative hearing before an administrative law judge

Exhibit 20-2   Types of Securities Exempt under the Securities Act of 1933

Classification of Security	Types of Security
Based on the issuer	1. Securities issued or guaranteed by a government, such as a U.S. Treasury bond 2. Securities issued by a nonprofit, religious, or charitable organization
Regulated by other statutes	1. Securities issued by a bank or savings and loan association 2. Insurance policies and annuity contracts
No overriding public reason to require registration	Notes or drafts maturing in nine months or less

(ALJ). Prior to the ALJ's issuing a decision, the SEC and the accused may enter into a consent order, in which the accused agrees to discontinue its unlawful conduct. If the SEC and the accused are unable to reach an agreement, a hearing in an administrative law court can be held and the ALJ may issue a cease-and-desist order to prevent or stop illegal activities.

The SEC may seek an injunction or other relief, such as recovery of profits in a federal district court. The SEC may seek civil money damages ranging from $5,000 to $500,000. A private party who is the investor in a new security may bring an action against the company to recover for damages. The amount of recovery, however, cannot exceed the price paid for the securities.

INFOTRAC RESEARCH ACTIVITY

A number of articles on securities fraud are listed on InfoTrac. Go to InfoTrac and type in "Securities Fraud." Review the most recent five articles and write a summary of recent fraud activity.

The Securities Exchange Act of 1934

The primary purposes of the **Securities Exchange Act of 1934**[7] are (1) to ensure the integrity of stock and securities sold through national stock exchanges and over-the-counter markets, (2) to inform the investing public of the financial condition of a business, and (3) to protect the public from fraudulent activity. The 1934 act has six parts. First, it created the Securities and Exchange Commission.

Second, it provides for the regulation and registration of security exchanges where securities are bought and sold (such as the New York Stock Exchange), all broker–dealers that have interstate operations, and securities associations, such as the National Association of Securities Dealers (NASD). Third, the statute requires market surveillance. Today, the SEC uses computers to engage in market surveillance to regulate such undesirable market practices as fraud, market manipulation, and misrepresentation.

Fourth, similar to the 1933 act, the 1934 act establishes a requirement for registration and continuous disclosure by (1) any business with securities listed on any regulated securities exchange and (2) companies that have assets in excess of $5 million and 500 or more shareholders. The act applies to the exchange of securities issued by these companies. Fifth, the statute regulates the solicitation of proxies (written authorization given by a shareholder to a third party to vote the shareholder's stock). Finally, the statute prohibits insider trading.

Securities and Exchange Commission

The Securities and Exchange Commission is an independent regulatory agency. Congress delegated to the SEC administrative rule-making powers and the responsibility for administering the entire body of federal securities law, including the 1933 act.[8]

---

[7]The Securities Exchange Act of 1934 is located at http://www.law.cornell.edu/uscode. Click on "Table of Popular Names." Scroll down to "Part 24 Rhode Island through Sheep." Scroll down until you find "Securities Act of 1934."

[8]The SEC maintains a page for small businesses at http://www.sec.gov/smbus1.htm.

The SEC is composed of five commissioners who serve staggered five-year terms.[9] They are appointed by the president of the United States. No more than three members may be from the same political party.

Proxy Requirement

A **proxy** is written authorization empowering another person to act for the signer, in this case, at the shareholders' meeting. Before the meeting, the company sends the shareholders materials including a proxy solicitation. The 1934 act regulates proxy solicitation for voting. A company or person can solicit proxies from a number of shareholders in an attempt to concentrate voting power. The SEC reviews the procedures used in obtaining proxies. Its rules require that proposed proxy material be filed in advance for examination. In any solicitation, clear disclosures must be made on all matters on which shareholders are to vote. Shareholders must be afforded the right to vote a simple yes or no on each matter.

Insider Trading and Fraud

One of the most important parts of the 1934 act relates to **insider trading**. Corporate directors, officers, and key employees often obtain in advance inside information about matters that can affect the future market value of the corporate stock. This knowledge can give them a trading advantage over the general public and shareholders. Section 16 of the 1934 act prohibits insider trading.

The 1934 act protects investors by prohibiting fraud and manipulation of the markets. Section 10(b) of the 1934 act and Rule 10b-5, a regulation issued by the SEC that implements the statute 10(b), are the primary laws governing issues of fraud and manipulation.

Section 16. **Section 16** of the 1934 act covers directors, officers, and owners of more than 10 percent of the shares of any one class of stock of a company registered with the SEC. These people are designated as insiders who must file reports of their holdings and transactions with the SEC.

If an insider makes a purchase-and-sale or sale-and-purchase of stock within a six-month period that results in a profit, that profit is known as a *short-swing profit*. Congress made this kind of profit illegal.

The 1934 act authorizes the issuer (corporation that issued the shares) or a shareholder to file a lawsuit against those who have profited. Together or independently, the issuer and shareholder can sue those statutory insiders (officers, directors, or shareholders of 10 percent or more of the stock).

Section 16 is a strict liability statute; in other words, the plaintiff need only show that the action took place. The only proof needed is that an insider purchased-and-sold or sold-and-purchased shares within a six-month period. The damages are found by matching the highest sale-and-purchase or purchase-and-sale within any six-month period. In drafting the statute, Congress decided that the plaintiff did not need to prove that the person had used insider information for personal gain.

The SEC cannot pursue any action against those who have made a short-swing profit. Because violations of Section 16 are not crimes, the Department of Justice (DOJ) cannot file any criminal charges. The SEC, however, may refer any information it may have to the DOJ for possible criminal prosecution when the SEC suspects other types of insider trading violations in addition to the short-swing profit violations.

Section 10(b) and Rule 10b-5. One of the basic tools employed by the SEC to provide and promote investor protection is the prohibition of fraud.[10] The most widely applied section is **Section 10(b)** of the 1934 act which makes it unlawful:

> *to use or employ, in connection with the purchase or sale of any security . . . any manipulative or deceptive device or contrivance, in contravention of such rules and regulations as the SEC may prescribe.*

The SEC adopted **Rule 10b-5** to implement Section 10(b). This regulation makes it:

> *unlawful for any person, directly or indirectly, by use of any means or instrumentality of interstate commerce, or the mails, or of any facility of any national securities exchange to defraud or mislead anyone in the purchase or sale of any security.*

---

[9]The five commissioners of the SEC have a Web page at http://www.sec.gov/about/commissioner.shtml. To see how the SEC is organized, go to http://www.sec.gov/asec/wwwsec.htm. To find the regional offices of the SEC, go to http://www.sec.gov/contact/addresses.htm.

[10]The SEC has a page alerting investors to prior frauds and scams at http://www.sec.gov/investor/alerts.shtml.

The antifraud rule applies to the purchase or sale of any security, regardless of how small or large the amount or whether it is a public or private offering. The exemptions discussed earlier under the 1933 act apply only to registration, not to the antifraud provisions. Section 10(b) and Rule 10b-5 cover virtually every transaction involving a security.

The 1934 act does not define the words *fraud* or *misrepresentation*. As a result, the SEC rules and the courts have broadly defined this offense. Violations generally fit into two categories: (1) insider trading cases and (2) claims arising from corporate misstatements or omissions (such as knowingly inflating earnings projections or manipulating financial records to show profits rather than a real loss) or arising from fraud and manipulation by brokers and dealers in trading stock.

The SEC refers to the DOJ those cases involving willful violations of Section 10(b). Violators, if convicted, face up to ten years in prison for each violation and a fine of $2.5 million when the violator is a corporation or $1 million when the violator is an individual.

The SEC may seek a cease-and-desist order to prevent or stop illegal activities. A consent order is obtained by the SEC when the defendant consents to stop its actions. Finally, the SEC may go to federal district court to seek an injunction to stop the defendant's activities.

Private parties may seek damages. They must have been purchasers or sellers trading shares at the same time as the violators.

The following case concerns a violation of Section 10(b) of a registered representative who worked for a brokerage house. The SEC sought an injunction from federal district court against the trader and a cease-and-desist order from its administrative law court against the stockbroker. The court discusses **scienter** (guilty knowledge that is greater than simple negligence) by the registered representative.

CASE 20.3

Supreme Court of the United States, 2002 535 U.S. 813, 122 S. Ct. 1899, 153 L. Ed. 2d 1

SECURITIES AND EXCHANGE COMMISSION v. ZANDFORD

BACKGROUND AND FACTS Between 1987 and 1991, Zandford (respondent) was employed as a securities broker for a New York brokerage firm. In 1987, he persuaded William Wood, an elderly man in poor health, to open a joint investment account for himself and his mentally retarded daughter. The investment objectives for the account were safety of principal and income. The Woods granted Zandford discretion to manage their account and a general power of attorney to engage in securities transactions for their benefit without prior approval. Relying on his promise to conservatively invest their money, the Woods entrusted him with $419,255. Before Mr. Wood's death in 1991, all of that money was gone.

In 1991, the National Association of Securities Dealers (NASD) conducted a routine examination of respondent's firm and discovered that on over 25 separate occasions, money had been transferred from the Woods' account to accounts controlled by Zandford. In due course, he was indicted on 13 counts of wire fraud. Each of the other counts alleged that he made wire transfers that enabled him to withdraw specified sums from the Woods' accounts. Some of those transfers involved respondent writing checks to himself from a mutual fund account held by the Woods, which required liquidating securities in order to redeem the checks. Respondent was convicted on all counts, sentenced to prison for 52 months, and ordered to pay $10,800 in restitution.

After Zandford was indicted, the SEC filed a civil complaint alleging that respondent violated Section 10(b) and Rule 10b-5 by engaging in a scheme to defraud the Woods and by misappropriating approximately $343,000 of the Woods' securities without their knowledge or consent. The SEC moved for partial summary judgment after respondent's criminal conviction, arguing that the judgment in the criminal case stopped Zandford from contesting facts that established a violation of Section 10(b). Zandford filed a motion seeking discovery on the question whether his fraud had the requisite connection with the purchase or sale of a security. The court refused to allow discovery, entered summary judgment against him, enjoined him from engaging in future violations of the securities laws, and ordered him to pay back the $343,000 in ill-gotten gains.

The court of appeals reversed the summary judgment and remanded with directions for the district court to dismiss the complaint. It first held that the wire fraud conviction, which only required two findings—(1) that respondent engaged in a scheme to defraud and (2) that he used interstate wire communications in executing the scheme—did not establish all the elements of a Section 10(b) violation. Specifically, the conviction did not necessarily establish that his fraud was "in connection with" the sale of a security. The court then held that the civil complaint did not sufficiently allege the necessary connection because the sales of the Woods' securities were merely incidental to a fraud that "lay in absconding with the proceeds" of sales that were conducted in "a routine and customary fashion." Respondent's "scheme was simply to steal the Woods' assets" rather than to engage "in manipulation of a particular security." Ultimately, the court refused to stretch the language of the securities fraud provisions to encompass every conversion or theft that happens to involve securities. Adopting what amounts to a "fraud on the market" theory of the statute's coverage, the court held that without some "relationship to market integrity or investor understanding," there is no violation of Section 10(b).

STEVENS delivered the opinion for a unanimous Court.

. . . .

Section 10(b) of the Securities Exchange Act makes it "unlawful for any person . . . [t]o use or employ, in connection with the purchase or sale of any security . . . , any manipulative or deceptive device or contrivance in contravention of such rules and regulations as the [SEC] may prescribe." Rule 10b-5, which implements this provision, forbids the use, "in connection with the purchase or sale of any security," of "any device, scheme, or artifice to defraud" or any other "act, practice, or course of business" that "operates . . . as a fraud or deceit." Among Congress' objectives in passing the Act was "to insure honest securities markets and thereby promote investor confidence" after the market crash of 1929. More generally, Congress sought "to substitute a philosophy of full disclosure for the philosophy of *caveat emptor* and thus to achieve a high standard of business ethics in the securities industry."

Consequently, we have explained that the statute should be "construed 'not technically and restrictively, but flexibly to effectuate its remedial purposes.'" In its role enforcing the Act, the SEC has consistently adopted a broad reading of the phrase "in connection with the purchase or sale of any security." It has maintained that a broker who accepts payment for securities that he never intends to deliver, or who sells customer securities with intent to misappropriate the proceeds, violates § 10(b) and Rule 10b-5. This interpretation of the ambiguous text of § 10(b), in the context of formal adjudication, is entitled to deference if it is. For the reasons set forth below, we think it is. While the statute must not be construed so broadly as to convert every common-law fraud that happens to involve securities into a violation of § 10(b), neither the SEC nor this Court has ever held that there must be a misrepresentation about the value of a particular security in order to run afoul of the Act.

The SEC claims respondent engaged in a fraudulent scheme in which he made sales of his customer's securities for his own benefit. Respondent submits that the sales themselves were perfectly lawful and that the subsequent misappropriation of the proceeds, though fraudulent, is not properly viewed as having the requisite connection with the sales; in his view, the alleged scheme is not materially different from a simple theft of cash or securities in an investment account. We disagree.

According to the complaint, respondent "engaged in a scheme to defraud" the Woods beginning in 1988, shortly after they opened their account, and that scheme continued throughout the 2-year period during which respondent made a series of transactions that enabled him to convert the proceeds of the sales of the Woods' securities to his own use. The securities sales and respondent's fraudulent practices were not independent events. This is not a case in which, after a lawful transaction had been consummated, a broker decided to steal the proceeds and did so. Nor is it a case in which a thief simply invested the proceeds of a routine conversion in the stock market. Rather, respondent's fraud coincided with the sales themselves.

Taking the allegations in the complaint as true, each sale was made to further respondent's fraudulent scheme; each was deceptive because it was neither authorized by, nor disclosed to, the Woods. With regard to the sales of shares in the Woods' mutual fund, respondent initiated these transactions by writing a check to himself from that account, knowing that redeeming the check would require the sale of securities. Indeed, each time respondent "exercised his power of disposition for his own benefit," that conduct, "without more," was a fraud.   In the aggregate, the sales are properly viewed as a "course of business" that operated as a fraud or deceit on a stockbroker's customer.

. . . .

DECISION AND REMEDY The Court found that this type of embezzlement was a violation of Rule 10(b) of the Securities Exchange Act. The Court reasoned that not only does such an embezzlement prevent investors from trusting their brokers who are executing transactions for their benefit, but it undermines the value of a discretionary account like that held by the Woods. The benefit of a discretionary account is that it enables individuals, like the Woods, who lack the time, capacity, or know-how to supervise investment decisions, to delegate authority to a broker. If embezzlement occurs under these conditions, it constitutes a violation of securities law.

CRITICAL THINKING: MANAGEMENT CONSIDERATION What steps could the Woods have taken to prevent this embezzlement?

Disclosure under Rule 10b-5. Any material omission or misrepresentation of material facts in connection with the purchase or sale of a security may violate Section 10(b) and Rule 10b-5. The key to liability is whether the insider's information is material.

Some examples of material facts under Rule 10b-5 that require disclosure are fraudulent trading in the company stock by a broker–dealer, a dividend change (whether up or down), a contract for the sale of corporate assets, a new discovery of a process or a product, a significant change in the firm's financial condition, or a takeover bid by another firm or individual. Exhibit 20–3 compares the disclosure requirements of the 1933 Securities Act with the Securities and Exchange Act of 1934.

The Supreme Court has expressly adopted the standard of materiality applicable to Section 10(b) and Rule 10b-5. According to this standard, an omitted fact is material if there is a substantial likelihood that its disclosure would be considered significant by a reasonable investor.

Timing of Disclosure under Rule 10b-5. Courts have struggled with determining when information becomes public knowledge. Clearly, when inside information becomes public knowledge, insiders should be allowed to trade without disclosure. Insiders should refrain from trading for a reasonable waiting period when the news is not readily translatable into investment action. Presumably, this time period gives the news time to filter down and to be evaluated by the investing public. What constitutes a reasonable waiting period, however, is not at all clear.

Exhibit 20–3   Comparison of Disclosure Requirements

Disclosure	Securities Act of 1933	Securities Exchange Act of 1934
When is disclosure required?	When new securities are issued	Throughout the life cycle of the security
How often is disclosure required?	One-time disclosure	Periodic disclosure
How is disclosure made?	Filing with the SEC: 1. Registration statement 2. Prospectus	Filing with the SEC: 1. Form 10-K, annually 2. Form 10-Q, quarterly 3. Form 8-K, monthly when a special event occurs

The following is one of the landmark cases interpreting Section 10(b) and Rule 10b-5. The SEC sued Texas Gulf Sulphur Company for issuing a misleading press release. The release misrepresented the magnitude and value of a mineral discovery.

CASE 20.4

United States Court of Appeals, Second Circuit, 1968
401 F.2d 833

SECURITIES AND EXCHANGE COMMISSION v. TEXAS GULF SULPHUR CO.

BACKGROUND AND FACTS Texas Gulf Sulphur Company (TGS) drilled a hole on November 12, 1963, near Timmins, Ontario, Canada, which appeared to yield a core with exceedingly high mineral content. Because TGS did not own the mineral rights in the surrounding regions, it maintained secrecy about the core sample results. It undertook evasive tactics to camouflage the drill site and drilled a second hole. TGS completed an extensive land acquisition program and then began drilling this lucrative site. Rumors spread. By early April 1964, a "tremendous staking rush [was] going on."

On April 11, 1964, an unauthorized report of the extraordinary mineral find hit the papers. On April 12, TGS issued a press release that played down the discovery and stated that it was too early to tell if the ore finding would be significant.

The Securities and Exchange Commission (SEC) filed suit against TGS, which had issued a deceptive press release on April 12, 1964. The trial court judge held that the issuance of the press release was lawful, because it was not issued for the purpose of benefiting the corporation, and no evidence indicated that any insider used the information in the press release to personal advantage. Thus, it was not "misleading or deceptive on the basis of the facts then known." The SEC appealed.

Judge WATERMAN

. . . .

At 3 P.M. on April 12,1964, evidently believing it desirable to comment upon the rumors concerning the Timmins project, TGS issued the press release quoted in pertinent part[:]

Recent drilling on one property near Timmins has led to preliminary indications that more drilling would be required for proper evaluation of this prospect. The drilling done to date has not been conclusive, but the statements made by many outside quarters are unreliable and include information and figures that are not available to TGS. The work done to date has not been sufficient to reach definite conclusions and any statements as to size and grade of ore would be premature and possibly misleading. When we have progressed to the point where reasonable and logical conclusions can be made, TGS will issue a definite statement to its stockholders and to the public in order to clarify the Timmins project.

. . . .

. . . It does not appear to be unfair to impose upon corporate management a duty to ascertain the truth of any statements the corporation releases to its shareholders or to the investing public at large. Accordingly, we hold that Rule 10b-5 is violated whenever assertions are made, as here, in a manner reasonably calculated to influence the investing public, e.g., by means of the financial media, if such assertions are false or misleading or are so incomplete as to mislead irrespective of whether the issuance of the release was motivated by corporate officials for ulterior purposes. It seems clear, however, that if corporate management demonstrates that it was diligent in ascertaining that the information it published was the whole truth and that such diligently obtained information was disseminated in good faith, Rule 10b-5 would not have been violated.

. . . .

We conclude, then, that, having established that the release was issued in a manner reasonably calculated to affect the market price of TGS stock and to influence the investing public, we must remand to the district court to decide whether the release was misleading to the reasonable investor and if found to be misleading, whether the court in its discretion should issue the injunction the SEC seeks.

DECISION AND REMEDY   The appellate court's judgment was favorable to the SEC. It determined that the information contained in the press release was material and violated Rule 10b-5. The questions of whether the press release was misleading and which remedies should be imposed were remanded to the trial court for decision. A trial court is bound to apply the law as enunciated by the court of appeals in making this type of decision.

COMMENT   Texas Gulf Sulphur Company was not only sued by the SEC, but numerous civil actions for damages were brought against it by plaintiff-investors who had sold their TGS stock as a result of the deceptively gloomy press release regarding the corporation's mineral exploration. All these suits were settled in 1972. In a federal lawsuit filed against TGS some two years after the initial case, a court of appeals held that investors who had sold stock relying on the representations in the press release could recover damages from both the corporation and the officers who had drafted the release. The court went on to state that the proper measure of damages was the difference between the selling price and the price at which the investors could have reinvested within a reasonable time after they became aware of TGS's curative press release announcing the strike of 25 million tons.

The court held that a diligent and reasonable investor could have known the information within four days of TGS's curative press release. The investors who sold their stock more than four days after the second press release was made could not recover under the Securities Exchange Act by claiming that they had relied on the earlier, deceptive release.

CRITICAL THINKING: MANAGEMENT CONSIDERATION   How would you have handled this situation if you were in TGS management?

Scienter Requirement under Rule 10b-5. Two elements of a Section 10(b) and Rule 10b-5 violation are required. The first is the use of a manipulative or deceptive device in connection with the purchase or sale of a security, in which a material fact has been misrepresented or omitted. Second, the act must have been committed with scienter. The additional requirement of scienter limited the broad application of Section 10(b) after the *Texas Gulf Sulphur* case. The first case to establish the criterion of scienter follows.

CASE 20.5

Supreme Court of the United States, 1976
425 U.S. 185, 96 S. Ct. 1375, 47 L. Ed. 2d 668
http://caselaw.findlaw.com

ERNST & ERNST v. HOCHFELDER

BACKGROUND AND FACTS First Securities Company, a brokerage firm, retained Ernst & Ernst, a Chicago accounting firm, to audit its books. In addition to the auditing, Ernst & Ernst prepared and filed the necessary reports of First Securities with the SEC. The president of First Securities, Leston B. Nay, manipulated a fraudulent scheme of investment in which Hochfelder and others invested their money. The scheme involved interest rates on low-risk escrow accounts. An escrow account is one in which money is deposited with an impartial third party. Unfortunately for Hochfelder and the other investors, these accounts never existed. For more than twenty years, Hochfelder continued unknowingly to place money into a nonexistent account, because he received official-looking statements.

Nay took the money for his own use. The escrow accounts never appeared in Ernst & Ernst's audits, so it failed to suspect Nay. When Hochfelder wanted his money, Nay committed suicide and left information describing the fraud. Hochfelder filed a lawsuit against Ernst & Ernst for aiding and abetting Nay's fraud. The district court granted a judgment in favor of Ernst & Ernst. The court of appeals reversed the decision. The United States Supreme Court reviewed the issue.

Justice POWELL delivered the opinion of the Court.

The issue in this case is whether an action for civil damages may lie under Section 10(b) of the Securities Exchange Act of 1934, and Securities and Exchange Commission Rule 10b-5, in the absence of an allegation of intent to deceive, manipulate, or defraud on the part of the defendant.

Petitioner, Ernst & Ernst, is an accounting firm. From 1946 through 1967 it was retained by First Securities Company of Chicago (First Securities), a small brokerage firm and member of the Midwest Stock Exchange and of the National Association of Securities Dealers, to perform periodic audits of the firm's books and records. In connection with these audits Ernst & Ernst prepared for filing with the Securities and Exchange Commission (Commission) the annual reports required of First Securities. It also prepared for First Securities responses to the financial questionnaires of the Midwest Stock Exchange (Exchange).

Respondents were customers of First Securities who invested in a fraudulent securities scheme perpetrated by Leston B. Nay, president of the firm and owner of 92 percent of its stock. Nay induced the respondents to invest funds in "escrow" accounts that he represented would yield a high rate of return. Respondents did so from 1942 through 1966, with the majority of the transactions occurring in the 1950s. In fact, there were no escrow accounts as Nay converted respondents' funds to his own use immediately upon receipt.

This fraud came to light in 1968 when Nay committed suicide, leaving a note that described First Securities as bankrupt and the escrow accounts as "spurious." Respondents subsequently filed this action for damages against Ernst & Ernst. . . . As revealed through discovery, respondents' cause of action rested on a theory of negligent nonfeasance [negligently failing to perform a required act]. The premise was that Ernst & Ernst had failed to utilize "appropriate auditing procedures" in its audits of First Securities, thereby failing to discover internal practices of the firm said to prevent an effective audit. The practice principally relied on Nay's rule that only he could open mail addressed to him at First Securities or addressed to First Securities to his attention, even if it arrived in his absence. Respondents contended that if Ernst & Ernst had conducted a proper audit, it would have discovered this "mail rule." The existence of the rule then would have been disclosed in reports to the Exchange and to the Commission by Ernst & Ernst as an irregular procedure that prevented an effective audit. This would have led to an investigation of Nay that would have revealed the fraudulent scheme. Respondents specifically disclaimed the existence of fraud or intentional misconduct on the part of Ernst & Ernst.

. . . .

Section 10(b) makes unlawful the use or employment of "any manipulative or deceptive device or contrivance" in contravention of Commission rules. The words "manipulative or deceptive" used in conjunction with "device or contrivance" strongly suggest that Sec. 10(b) was intended to proscribe knowing or intentional misconduct.

. . . .

. . . When a statute speaks so specifically in terms of manipulation and deception, and of implementing devices and contrivances—the commonly understood terminology of intentional wrongdoing—and when its history reflects no more expansive intent, we are quite unwilling to extend the scope of the statute to negligent conduct.

DECISION AND REMEDY The United States Supreme Court reversed the court of appeals and held that in the absence of scienter, no cause of action for fraud exists under Section 10(b).

COMMENT Scienter is generally defined as a mental state embracing the intent to deceive, manipulate, or defraud. The more difficult question is whether recklessness is enough to satisfy the scienter requirement. In certain areas of the law, recklessness is considered a form of intentional conduct, where conduct is so careless as to evince a total disregard for the welfare of others. This type of recklessness then creates liability.

CRITICAL THINKING POLITICAL CONSIDERATION Under the 1933 Securities Act, any person who signs a business's registration statement may be held liable for a material misstatement of fact or a material omission. An injured investor does not have to prove intent to deceive. Under the Securities Exchange Act of 1934, however, a person must prove scienter, that is, must prove the intent to deceive. Should a difference in proof exist between a new issue of stocks versus stocks that have been issued and are now traded?

Persons Who Have a Duty under Rule 10b-5. The SEC prosecutes insiders who trade a security, based on nonpublic information, for personal financial benefit. The reasoning behind this rule is that an insider should refrain from using nonpublic information to his gain, because such actions are unfair to individual investors who lack such information and have no equal means of acquiring the information. The public will lose faith and stop investing if it believes that insiders have an unfair advantage. The courts and the SEC prohibit insiders from trading, unless information first is disclosed to the general public.

Insider trading rules cover not only corporate officers, directors, and majority shareholders, but also anyone having access to, or receiving, information of a nonpublic nature from an insider on which trading is based. People to whom material information is given are known as **tippees**. The person giving the information is known as the **tipper**.

Before liability can be imposed, a fiduciary duty is owed by the tipper to the regulated company to refrain from disclosing nonpublic information, and the tippee must know of this duty. Once this duty is established, both the tipper and the tippee are liable for any profits made by the tippee, in addition to other liabilities imposed by the 1934 act.

The test is determined by whether a fiduciary duty exists. For example, if someone receives information and passes it on to a family member, who in turn passes this information to another person, the second passing of information does not violate this rule. Merely being related to the person who is the insider does not create a fiduciary relationship. The family member who has no direct inside information can pass the information on to others.

Another legal theory creating liability based on insider information is misappropriation of information. For example, if a person finds out information from a newspaper columnist prior to an article appearing in the paper and trades on this information, the trading will create liability. Likewise, a person may obtain information without computer authorization and may trade on this information. This trading also is misappropriation of information.

Whether the insider information results from an insider's breach of fiduciary duty, a tipper–tippee relationship, or a misappropriation of information, the penalties for insider trading are the same. The SEC may refer criminal charges to the DOJ for prosecution. The SEC may seek an order of **disgorgement**, which means that if the order were granted, the wrongdoer would be required to return the wrongfully obtained profits. Those who profit from insider trading lose all their profits under a disgorgement order. The SEC may also seek civil money penalties up to three times the amount of profit.

The following is a case dealing with insider trading. The government sued on a criminal basis, because the defendant made more than $4.3 million by using insider information.

CASE 20.6

Supreme Court of the United States, 1997
521 U.S. 642, 117 S. Ct. 2199, 138 L. Ed. 2d 724
http://caselaw.findlaw.com

UNITED STATES v. O'HAGAN

BACKGROUND AND FACTS Defendant James O'Hagan was a partner in the law firm of Dorsey & Whitney in Minneapolis, Minnesota. In July 1988, Grand Metropolitan, PLC (Grand Met), a company based in London, England, retained Dorsey & Whitney as local counsel to represent Grand Met regarding a potential purchase of the Pillsbury Company, headquartered in Minneapolis. Both Grand Met and Dorsey & Whitney took precautions to protect the confidentiality of Grand Met's plans. O'Hagan did not work on the Grand Met representation. Dorsey & Whitney withdrew from representing Grand Met on September 9, 1988. Less than a month later, on October 4, 1988, Grand Met publicly announced its offer to purchase Pillsbury stock.

On August 18, 1988, while Dorsey & Whitney still represented Grand Met, O'Hagan began purchasing call options for Pillsbury stock. Each option gave him the right to purchase 100 shares of Pillsbury stock by a specified date in September 1988. Later in August and in September, O'Hagan made additional purchases of Pillsbury call options. By the end of September, he owned 2,500 unexpired Pillsbury options, apparently more than any other individual investor. O'Hagan also purchased, in September 1988, some 5,000 shares of Pillsbury common stock, at a price just under $39 per share. When Grand Met announced its plan in October, the price of Pillsbury stock rose to nearly $60 per share. O'Hagan then sold his Pillsbury call options and common stock, making a profit of more than $4.3 million.

The Securities and Exchange Commission initiated an investigation into O'Hagan's transactions, culminating in a fifty-seven-count indictment. The indictment alleged that O'Hagan defrauded his law firm and its client, Grand Met, by using for his own trading purposes material, nonpublic information regarding Grand Met's planned purchase.

According to the indictment, O'Hagan used the profits he gained through this trading to conceal his previous embezzlement and conversion of unrelated client trust funds. A jury convicted O'Hagan on all fifty-seven counts, and he was sentenced to a forty-one-month term of imprisonment. The appellate court reversed the convictions and the government appealed.

Justice GINSBURG delivered the opinion of the Court.

. . . .

Under the "traditional" or "classical theory" of insider trading liability, §10(b) and Rule 10b-5 are violated when a corporate insider trades in the securities of his corporation on the basis of material, nonpublic information. Trading on such information qualifies as a "deceptive device" under §10(b), we have affirmed, because "a relationship of trust and confidence [exists] between the shareholders of a corporation and those insiders who have obtained confidential information by reason of their position with that corporation." That relationship, we recognized, "gives rise to a duty to disclose [or to abstain from trading] because of the 'necessity of preventing a corporate insider from . . . tak[ing] unfair advantage of . . . uninformed . . . stockholders.' " The classical theory applies not only to officers, directors, and other permanent insiders of a corporation, but also to attorneys, accountants, consultants, and others who temporarily become fiduciaries of a corporation.

The "misappropriation theory" holds that a person commits fraud "in connection with" a securities transaction, and thereby violates 10(b) and Rule 10b-5, when he misappropriates confidential information for securities trading purposes, in breach of a duty owed to the source of the information. Under this theory, a fiduciary's undisclosed, self-serving use of a principal's information to purchase or sell securities, in breach of a duty of loyalty and confidentiality, defrauds the principal of the exclusive use of that information. In lieu of premising liability on a fiduciary relationship between company insider and purchaser or seller of the company's stock, the misappropriation theory premises liability on fiduciary-turned-trader's deception of those who entrusted him with access to confidential information.

The two theories are complementary, each addressing efforts to capitalize on nonpublic information through the purchase or sale of securities. The classical theory targets a corporate insider's breach of duty to shareholders with whom the insider transacts; the misappropriation theory outlaws trading on the basis of nonpublic information by a corporate "outsider" in breach of a duty owed not to a trading party, but to the source of the information. The misappropriation theory is thus designed to "protec[t] the integrity of the securities markets against abuses by 'outsiders' to a corporation who have access to confidential information that will affect th[e] corporation's security price when revealed, but who owe no fiduciary or other duty to that corporation's shareholders."

In this case, the indictment alleged that O'Hagan, in breach of a duty of trust and confidence he owed to his law firm, Dorsey & Whitney, and to its client, Grand Met, traded on the basis of nonpublic information regarding Grand Met's planned . . . offer for Pillsbury common stock. This conduct, the Government charged, constituted a fraudulent device in connection with the purchase and sale of securities.

. . . .

We agree with the Government that misappropriation, as just defined, satisfies §10(b)'s requirement that chargeable conduct involve a "deceptive device or contrivance" used "in connection with" the purchase or sale of securities. We observe, first, that misappropriators, as the Government describes them, deal in deception. A fiduciary who "[pretends] loyalty to the principal while secretly converting the principal's information for personal gain," "dupes" or defrauds the principal.

. . . .

DECISION AND REMEDY The court found that O'Hagan violated the law by failing to disclose his personal trading to Grand Met and Dorsey, which made his conduct deceptive within the meaning of Section 10(b) of the Securities Exchange Act.

CRITICAL THINKING: PRACTICAL APPLICATION Assume you are in a restaurant and overhear a conversation among several people about a planned merger of two large corporations. You check with your broker and from the information he tells you, you conclude that the information you overheard has not been publicly disclosed. You do not mention this to your broker. Can you use this information to buy stocks of either corporations?

Reporting Requirements

Section 18 of the 1934 Securities Exchange Act requires publicly held corporations registered with the SEC to file periodic and intermittent reports.[11] The annual report, Form 10-K, is filed at the end of the corporation's fiscal period. Form 10-K must include audited financial statements, the business's current financial status, and its securities holdings.

The unaudited quarterly report, Form 10-Q, reflects any financial changes that have occurred since the last reporting period. Form 8-K is filed any time a material event occurs, such as a change in management control, a significant judgment against the company, or a bankruptcy. A material event is any occurrence that a reasonably prudent investor would want to know about in order to reevaluate its investment.

If private parties relied on the documents filed, they may sue for damages. The reports on which a private party can rely are the 10-K and 8-K reports and the proxy statements because these are audited and certified. The quarterly 10-Q report is unaudited, so it cannot be relied upon. A plaintiff who claims that she or he relied on the filed documents must prove four elements:

1. False or misleading statements or omissions were made.
2. The plaintiff purchased or sold shares.
3. The plaintiff relied on the statements.
4. The defendant knew that the statements were false or misleading or that omissions occurred.

[11]The SEC provides a short description of the most common corporate filings made with the SEC at http://www.sec.gov/edgarhp.htm.

If the previous items are proven, the plaintiff is entitled to damages.

Other Securities Laws

Over the decades since the 1933 and the 1934 acts were passed, other laws governing securities have been passed. Congress adopted new statutes in reaction to various events that demonstrated a particular weakness in the original statute. The new laws strengthened the controls over the securities markets. Reviews of some of these laws follow.

Securities Investor Protection Act

A series of stockbrokerage houses failed in the 1960s, leading Congress to amend the 1934 act to protect the consumer. The 1970 amendment created the **Securities Investor Protection Corporation (SIPC)**, which manages a fund that protects investors from the financial harm caused when stockbrokerage houses fail. The fund is similar to that administered by the Federal Deposit Insurance Corporation (FDIC), which protects bank depositors.

Foreign Corrupt Practices Act

The **Foreign Corrupt Practices Act (FCPA)** of 1977 also amended the 1934 act. Although part of the FCPA applies to corporations doing business in other countries, the rest of the act applies to all corporations registered with the SEC, whether or not they are engaged in foreign business.

The FCPA requires, for the first time, public corporations to maintain records that accurately reflect their financial activities. All corporations reporting under the 1934 act are required to have an internal accounting system to ensure accurate records.

The act attempts to prevent the concealment of illegal activities. Some activities were criminal acts even prior to the adoption of the FCPA. In the past, corporations engaged in acts that ranged from the purchasing of castles in Ireland for top management to the paying of millions to foreign officials to ensure lucrative contracts. These millions of dollars in payment were not disclosed to the shareholders or to the SEC.

Insider Trading Sanctions Act and Insider Trading and Securities Fraud Enforcement Act

The **Insider Trading Sanctions Act (ITSA)** of 1984 gives additional power to the SEC for violations of insider trading. This act applies to people who use nonpublic information and who purchase or sell through a national securities exchange or a registered broker–dealer. The SEC can recover up to three times the profit made in these situations. Any recovery goes to the government, not to parties who may have been injured by such activity.

In 1988, this ITSA was amended by the **Insider Trading and Securities Fraud Enforcement Act**. The amendment enlarged the scope of people who have civil liability under the act, gave the SEC authority to reward informants in insider trading cases,[12] required securities firms to adopt specific policies and procedures to prevent insider trading, and increased criminal penalties. The award of treble damages against securities firms is available for failing to maintain a proper system of supervision to prevent and detect insider trading violations by employees.

Securities Enforcement Remedies and Penny Stock Reform Act

Congress enacted the **Securities Enforcement Remedies and Penny Stock Reform Act** of 1990 in response to the growing number of fraudulent activities discovered in the stock market. As its name

indicates, the act has two major functions: to strengthen enforcement powers of the SEC and to regulate the penny stock market.

Penny Stock Reform. Low-priced stock, ranging in value from a few pennies to several dollars per share, was the subject of unscrupulous activity during the 1980s. Many investors lost money in this high-risk market. This act authorizes the SEC to adopt rules requiring securities dealers and brokers to provide potential investors with specific information about the penny stock prices and the risks involved in the volatile penny stock market.

Enforcement Remedies. The act grants the SEC (1) new authority to issue cease-and-desist orders and (2) expanded authority to impose civil money penalties. A cease-and-desist order is an administrative remedy that directs a person to refrain from engaging in further violative conduct. Cease-and-desist authority permits swift remedial action in response to illegal conduct without filing a lawsuit for a temporary restraining order in court.

The SEC is authorized to issue cease-and-desist orders against anyone who violates securities laws or who engages in activities that make it likely that a future violation of the securities laws will occur. The alleged violator is served notice and a hearing is held. If the SEC issues the cease-and-desist order, the person can file a lawsuit in federal district court for a judicial review of the order.

Prior to this act, the SEC had the authority to seek only an order of disgorgement. In the absence of a criminal prosecution or a private suit for damages, even though the wrongdoer deliberately violated the law, he or she did not risk monetary sanctions more severe than to return the illegal profit under an order of disgorgement. Violators did not have any personal risk because they were left in the same financial position as they had been prior to the wrongdoing. This act greatly expanded the SEC's authority to seek civil money penalties against wrongdoers. People who engage in wrongdoing are now placed at financial risk.

Penalties are applied to active violators of the securities laws. In one case, a broker–dealer failed to comply with the SEC's customer protection rule. The rule required the broker–dealer to maintain a separate account for a customer's fully paid or excess margin securities. A margin security account is used when the

---

[12]The SEC provides a page that offers a bounty to people who provide information on insider trading: http://www.sec.gov/answers/insider.htm.

broker allows a customer to purchase securities on credit. The customer then pays the amount owed into the account. The broker–dealer failed to comply with this regulation simply because it was unwilling to devote the resources necessary to maintain separate accounts. Although the firm did not actively engage in a scheme to defraud, the customer was exposed to a serious risk of loss in the event that the broker–dealer house failed.

The SEC is authorized to impose civil money penalties, which provide a disincentive to engage in insider trading, market manipulation, and fraudulent financial reporting. These penalties also discourage those who want to maximize profits through cost reduction by failing to comply with the SEC regulations.

Market Reform Act

The **Market Reform Act** of 1990 addresses the stability of U.S. securities markets when extraordinarily volatile situations occur. In October 1987, the market fell 508 points in one day. At that time, the fall amounted to a 23 percent decline. This severe decline resulted in the Market Reform Act. One decade later, in October 1997, the stock market experienced its largest one-day decline in history, a 554-point decline in the Dow Jones Industrial Average. Because the market was higher, this decline meant less than an 8 percent decline in stock prices.

Fundamental changes have occurred since the original securities acts were adopted in the mid-1930s. The marketplace has become increasingly institutional. Significant numbers of institutional portfolio managers utilize indexing strategies that trade the market as a whole (the index) through purchases of portfolios of securities rather than by making judgments on individual stocks. These strategies can cause extraordinary peak volume and volatility and can overwhelm the market's capacity. The Market Reform Act ensures the stability, resiliency, and integrity of the nation's securities markets by granting the SEC broader powers.

Limits are now set on program trading, in which computer-driven programs send sell orders when the market reaches certain benchmarks. In the event of a sudden, large movement in the price of securities (up or down), trading is suspended to control the stock markets until order has been restored.

The SEC prohibits manipulative practices related to market price levels and trading practices. The statute allows increased monitoring of risks posed to firms that are SEC regulated. For example, the financial failure of

Drexel Burnham Lambert Group, Inc., affected its two principal regulated subsidiaries, Drexel Burnham Lambert, Inc., a registered broker-dealer, and Drexel Burnham Lambert Government Securities, Inc., a registered government securities dealer. Large traders are required to keep records and provide information to the SEC. Additionally, the Market Reform Act established a coordinated national system for the safe and accurate clearance and settlement of securities sales and purchases.

Private Securities Litigation Reform Act

The **Private Securities Litigation Reform Act** of 1995 curtails lawsuits against businesses based on securities law violations. Numerous cases filed during the past decades were based on questionable grounds, forcing businesses to incur substantial costs and to expend considerable time defending themselves.

The act places limits on private persons considering litigation. The act allows corporations to make statements or projections provided that they are identified as such in a document called a **forward-looking statement**. This statement must state that actual results may differ materially from the predictions. The corporation will be held liable, however, if it made the statements with actual knowledge of the information being false. Forward-looking statements are not authorized for initial public offerings.

The Private Securities Litigation Reform Act limits personal liability. Any damages awarded must be based on individual actual fault rather than on joint liability with others. Joint liability, however, is available in two instances.

First, when all defendants knew that the statements were false and that investors would be likely to rely on the false statements, the defendants can be held jointly liable. In this situation, all defendants can be held individually liable. Additionally, each defendant may be required to pay the judgment owed by the other defendants if those defendants disappear or are insolvent. The purpose for the policy is to protect the innocent investors and to maximize the penalty amount against a knowing wrongdoer. For example, the plaintiff is awarded $300,000. Defendant A is responsible for $200,000, and Defendant B is responsible for $100,000. Defendant A goes into bankruptcy and cannot pay any portion of the judgment. Defendant B, because of the fraud involved, must pay all of the $300,000.

Second, if the plaintiff has a net worth of less than $200,000 and one or more of the defendants cannot pay the judgment, the SEC can require the remaining defendants to pay up to 150 percent of the amount of their judgment to the plaintiff. For example, a plaintiff is awarded a judgment of $500,000. Defendant A is liable in the amount of $200,000, Defendant B is liable for $200,000, and Defendant C for $100,000. Defendant A goes into bankruptcy and cannot pay any of the $200,000. The SEC can require Defendant B to pay up to $300,000 and Defendant C up to $150,000 toward the $500,000 judgment.

The act requires the plaintiffs to certify that they purchased the security honestly, not merely to bring the lawsuit. Further, they must sign a document stating their willingness to represent all people in their similar position. These plaintiffs cannot accept any payment for serving as the representative beyond the award that everyone else in the class receives.

In a class-action lawsuit, the plaintiffs are restricted in alleging a Racketeer Influenced and Corrupt Organization Act (RICO) violation. The only time a RICO violation may be pursued by a class-action suit is after a defendant has been criminally convicted of security laws violations.

National Securities Markets Improvement Act

The **National Securities Markets Improvement Act** of 1996 significantly impacted state securities laws, especially those laws that regulate investment advisers and those laws governing the filing requirements of mutual funds. The act ended the dual regulation of investment advisers by providing the SEC authority over any adviser who manages $25 million or more of assets. Any adviser whose management load falls below this sum is now regulated by the individual states.

This act is particularly important for investment advisers who trade in mutual funds because they make up a large percentage of the market and are sold nationally. Today, if the SEC approves an issue for sale, the stock issuer is no longer required to have a second review at the state level. Issuers, however, still must pay fees to a state to be permitted to sell within that state. A state must impose requirements similar to those that the SEC requires regarding capital, margin, financial responsibility, making and keeping records, bonding, or operational reporting.

Sarbanes-Oxley Act

The **Sarbanes–Oxley Act**[13] of 2002 made more changes than any other statute since the passing of the Securities Act of 1933 and the Securities Exchange Act of 1934. The act covers a wide range of topics, such as increasing regulation of stock markets, reforming the deterrence of business fraud, and increasing corporate accountability. The intent of the law was to help restore public trust in U.S. business reporting. The act created the Public Company Accounting Oversight Board to oversee the activities of the auditing profession.

The changed rules require the principal executive and financial officers to certify their quarterly and annual reports. Among the things they must certify is that they have reviewed the report and the report does not contain any untrue statement of a material fact or omit a material fact.

Ethics have not been forgotten in this act. It is the first regulation that requires a stated ethical code of conduct or an explanation on why there is no code. In addition, the SEC rules define a code of ethics as a codification of standards that is reasonably necessary to deter wrongdoing and to promote among many things:

1. Honest and ethical conduct, including the ethical handling of actual or apparent conflicts of interest between personal and professional relationships;

2. Full, fair, accurate, timely, and understandable disclosure in reports and documents that a company files with the SEC and in other public communications made by the company;

3. The prompt internal reporting of code violations to an appropriate person or persons identified in the code; and

4. Accountability for adherence to the code.

A company is required to disclose in its annual report whether it has a code of ethics. Companies, other than foreign private issuers and registered investment companies, are required to disclose either on Form 8-K or on their Internet Web sites any changes to, or waivers of, such code of ethics.

The SEC has adopted rules under the act to strengthen auditor independence and require additional disclosures to investors about the services provided to companies by the independent accountant.

---

[13]The full text of the act is available at the University of Cincinnati, College of Law, at http://www.law.uc.edu/CCL/SOact/soact.pdf.

The SEC approved new measures that will among many things:

1. Revise the rules related to the nonaudit services that, if provided to an audit client, would impair an accounting firm's independence;

2. Require that certain partners on the audit engagement team rotate after no more than five or seven consecutive years;

3. Establish rules that an accountant would not be independent from an audit client if any "audit partner" received compensation based on the partner procuring engagements with that client for services other than audit, review, and attest services;

4. Require the issuer's audit committee to pre-approve all audit and nonaudit services provided to the issuer by the auditor; and

5. Require disclosures to investors of information related to audit and nonaudit services provided by, and fees paid to, the auditor.

The act covers the actions of lawyers. Attorneys are required to report material violations of the law to the chief legal counsel or chief executive officer. If they do not respond appropriately, lawyers must report to the audit committee or the full board of directors. If this fails to move the company to react, lawyers are obligated to inform the SEC.

The act makes it a crime to destroy, alter, conceal, cover up, or hinder the investigation of any matter. If convicted, the individual may receive a prison sentence of up to twenty years. Retaliation against informants can bring a sentence of ten years. In addition to a prison sentence, a person may be fined up to $5,000,000 and a business fine may be as high as $25,000,000.

A person cannot discharge certain debts in bankruptcy. Nondischargeable debts are those that arise from violating the securities laws, common law fraud, deceit, or manipulation in connection with the sale of any security and which resulted in a judgment, order, or decree.

State Securities Laws

All states have their own business securities laws that regulate the offering of and sale of securities within individual state borders. Since the adoption of the fed-

eral 1933 and 1934 acts, state and federal governments have regulated securities concurrently. Indeed, both acts specifically allow state securities laws. Certain features are common to all state blue sky laws. For example, they all have antifraud provisions, many of which are patterned after the federal law. Most state corporate securities laws regulate securities brokers and dealers.

Typically, these laws provide for the registration or qualification of securities offered or issued for sale within the state. Unless an applicable exemption from registration is found, issuers must register or qualify their stock with the appropriate state office.

A difference in philosophy exists among the state statutes. Many statutes are similar to the Securities Act of 1933 and mandate certain disclosures before the registration is effective. They may require a permit to sell the securities. Other statutes have fairness standards that a corporation must meet in order to offer or sell stock in the state. A few states require a **merit registration**, whereby the states review the registration for its merits rather than being restricted to reviewing it for disclosures only. The Uniform Securities Act (adopted in part by several states) was drafted to be acceptable to states with differing regulatory philosophies.

International Consideration

Attitudes toward Securities Regulations

At this moment, in some country around the world, a stock market is open, is doing business, and can be monitored from homes via personal computers and television. Each market is operated in accordance with the laws of its host country. No international agreements have been made regarding stock markets.

U.S. law has criminalized violations of the heavily regulated securities markets. Computers monitor the markets to ensure compliance with the laws. Other countries, however, differ in their attitudes toward securities regulation.

Japan has legislation prohibiting securities violations, but the government rarely enforces these laws. In the past, some large Japanese stockbrokerage houses reimbursed large traders in the stock market for losses that they incurred on recommended investments. The public revelation of this news eventually led to a change in the government and promises by the stockbrokers to treat large investors the same as small investors. The Japanese market is not as heavily regulated as the U.S. market.

Members of the European Union (EU) have different views of insider trading. Denmark, France, Great Britain, and Switzerland have insider trading prohibitions, whereas the rest of the member nations do not. Large profits have been made on international stock markets. *Caveat emptor* ("let the buyer beware") applies to any U.S. investor in the overseas market.

In 1990, Congress passed the **International Securities Enforcement Cooperation Act**. It allows the SEC to cooperate with other countries to regulate security markets and transactions. The SEC has entered into memorandums of understanding with several foreign countries, allowing for the exchange of information among countries. An outgrowth of this statute was the creation of the **International Organization of Securities Commissions**. This organization's purpose is to cooperate in the promotion of high standards to maintain just, efficient, and sound markets. It has four regional standing committees: Africa–Middle East, Asia–Pacific, European, and Interamerican. In carrying out its purpose, the organization established, among other programs, a set of international accounting standards.[14]

[14]For more information about the International Organization of Securities Commissions go to http://www.iosco.org.

PRACTICAL TIPS

Purchasing and Selling Securities on the Web

More than 200 securities firms offer online brokerage services with an estimated ten-million-plus online accounts. Not surprisingly, the online brokerage industry is experiencing growing pains. State and national securities regulators have been bombarded with complaints from investors stemming from much-publicized server outages, computer glitches, and fraud.

Many members of the public are currently or in the near future will be purchasing securities using Web resources. If you decide to trade online, you need to think about the following items:

Checklist

✔ *Full Disclosure* Receive full disclosure, prior to opening your account, about the alternatives to buying and selling securities online if the online account is not functional. Have the broker explain how to obtain account information if you cannot access the firm's Web site. Do not be in a hurry. Shop around before you pick an online brokerage firm and do your own investigation. Leading financial publications rate online brokers using criteria such as speed of execution and customer satisfaction.

✔ *Links* Understand that you probably are not linked directly to the market, and that the click of your mouse does not instantly execute the trade. Do not forget that technology can fail and that any system can be overwhelmed by demand. Remember that in volatile markets your order could be delayed and you may not get the price you want.

✔ *Software* Understand how the software works before you make your first trade; find out who to contact or a Web site where you can make corrections if you make a mistake or have a problem.

✔ *Confirm Information* Receive information from the firm to substantiate any advertised claims concerning the ease and speed of online trading. Look beyond the slick advertising. Carefully read the customer account agreement. Know your rights. Seek information before trading about entering and canceling orders (market, limit, and stop loss) and the details and risks of margin accounts (borrowing to buy stocks). Search out information from the firm to see if it has had significant Web site outages, delays, and other interruptions to securities trading and account access.

✔ *Understand Quotes* Determine whether you are receiving delayed or real-time stock quotes and when and how often your account information will be updated.

✔ *Review Policies* Review the firm's privacy and Web site security policies to determine whether your name may be used for mailing lists or other promotional activities by the firm or any other party. Remember, these policies probably have a clause that allows the firm to change the policies such that information that is private today may be made available for sale after the change of policy.

✔ *Payments* Receive clear information about sales commissions and fees and conditions that apply to any advertised discount on commissions.

✔ *Customer Service Representative* Know how to, and if necessary, contact a customer service representative with your concerns and request prompt attention and fair consideration.

✔ *State Agency* Contact your state securities agency to verify the registration/licensing status and disciplinary history of the online brokerage firm. Ask for the firm's CRD record to determine whether it has a regulatory disciplinary history. (CRD stands for Central Registration Depository, a computer database containing information on all registered brokers and brokerage firms in the United States.)

Chapter Summary

Securities are regulated by both federal and state authorities. A security can be something other than a stock or bond. It is any financial transaction in which an investor exchanges money for an interest in a common enterprise with the expectation of making a profit through the endeavors of the promoter or third party.

Two primary federal statutes have been adopted: the Securities Act of 1933 and the Securities Exchange Act of 1934. Both the 1933 and 1934 acts prohibit fraud in the issuance of securities and in the disclosure of information available to the investing public.

The 1933 act regulates new issues of securities and requires, prior to issuance, full disclosure of all material facts. This information is presented in a prospectus, which is based on the registration statement. The registration statement is filed with the Securities and Exchange Commission and must be signed by the corporation's principal executive officer, principal accounting officer, and principal financial officer as well as by a majority of the members of the board of directors. Any person signing the registration statement is personally liable if full and truthful disclosure of all material facts is lacking. Certain transactions and securities are exempt from the registration requirements of the 1933 act.

The Securities Exchange Act of 1934 regulates securities that are traded on national exchanges and securities extensively traded over the counter. In addition, this statute established the SEC.

Under Section 10(b) and SEC's Rule 10b-5, no individual may take advantage of insider information, whether a situation involves new securities or ones actively traded. Most insiders are either directors, officers, key employees, or owners of 10 percent or more of the common stock. Rule 10b-5 applies, however, to both insiders and tippees. Any profits realized from inside information belong to the corporation. Substantial criminal penalties can be assessed.

Over the decades Congress has adopted other securities laws. The Securities Investor Protection Act of 1970 created the Securities Investor Protection Corporation. This corporation manages a fund that protects investors from financial harm if their stockbrokerage fails. The Foreign Corrupt Practices Act requires all corporations registered with the SEC to maintain records that accurately reflect their financial activities, to maintain internal accounting systems that ensure accurate records, and to prevent concealment of illegal activities.

The Insider Trading Sanctions Act of 1984 provides the SEC with additional powers to punish violations of insider trading. The Insider Trading and Securities Fraud Enforcement Act amended this act in 1988. The act enlarged the number of people who are liable for insider trading, provided the SEC authority to reward informants, required firms to adopt policies on insider trading, and increased the criminal penalties for SEC violations.

The Securities Enforcement Remedies and Penny Stock Reform Act of 1990 provided more regulation of the penny stock market and granted the SEC more enforcement remedies. The Market Reform Act of 1990 limited the stock market during volatile situations, placed limits on program trading, and prohibited additional manipulative practices.

To restrict the amount of lawsuits against businesses based on securities law violations, the Congress passed the Private Securities Litigation Reform Act in 1995. This act limited the amount of personal liability. The

National Securities Markets Improvement Act places the SEC the exclusive authority to regulate advisers who manage $25 million or more of assets. The Sarbanes-Oxley Act covers a wide range of topics including the increase regulation of stock markets, deterring fraud, and increasing corporate accountability. States also have business securities statutes.

Using the World Wide Web

Securities are offered over the Internet. The SEC allows a business to reference the SEC Web site on the business's Web site, which must include this statement: "Our SEC filings are also available to the public from our Web site." Thus, the public can review the business's filings with the SEC through the SEC's Web site or the business's Web site. Any registration statement filed with the SEC, however, must include all relevant information and cannot merely refer to the information at the business's Web site.

The SEC offers many educational publications for consumers. A number of these publications are available on its Web site. Web sites for various trading organizations are included at the link mentioned in the *Web Activities* section that follows.

Transparency International is an organization devoted to curbing national and international corruption. This organization supports the position that all information about a business should be open (transparent) and available to the public. Openness helps to deter corruption and other criminal activity. Transparency International's Web site has a list of nations considered to be bribe-takers and another list of nations considered to be bribe-givers.

For *Web Activities*, links to Web sites mentioned in the chapter, and additional Web sites that relate to the chapter topics, go to **http://bohlman.westbuslaw.com**, click on "Internet Applications," and select Chapter 20.

Web Activities

Go to **http://bohlman.westbuslaw.com**, click on "Internet Applications," and select Chapter 20.
20–1 Replacing a Security
20–2 Current News

Key Terms

accredited investor
blue sky law
disgorgement
due diligence defense
Electronic Data Gathering, Analysis, and Retrieval (EDGAR)
exempt security
exempt transaction
Foreign Corrupt Practices Act (FCPA)
forward-looking statement
insider trading
Insider Trading and Securities Fraud Enforcement Act
Insider Trading Sanctions Act (ITSA)

International Organization of Securities Commission
International Securities Enforcement Cooperation Act
intrastate offering
exemption
issuer
Market Reform Act
merit registration
National Securities Markets Improvement Act
private offering exemption
Private Securities Litigation Reform Act
prospectus
proxy

red herring prospectus
registration statement
Regulation A
Regulation C, Rule 415
Regulation D
restricted securities
Rule 10b-5
Rule 144
Rule 144A
Rule 504
Rule 505
Rule 506
safe-harbor exemption
Sarbanes–Oxley Act
scienter
Section 10(b)
Section 16
Section 18
Securities Act of 1933

Securities and Exchange Commission (SEC)
Securities Enforcement Remedies and Penny Stock Reform Act
Securities Exchange Act of 1934
Securities Investor Protection Corporation (SIPC)
security
shelf registration
small offering exemption
tippee
tipper
tombstone advertisement
unaccredited investor

Questions and Case Problems

20–1 Requirement of Registration Maresh, an experienced geologist, owned certain oil and gas leases covering land in Nebraska. To raise money for the drilling of a test well, he undertook to sell fractional interests in the leases. He approached Garfield, with whom he had done business in the past. Garfield had mentioned that he would be interested in investing in some of Maresh's future oil ventures. Garfield had wide business experience in the stock market and in oil stocks. He believed that the investment in Maresh's gas leases could be lucrative. Based on Garfield's promise to wire the money promptly, Maresh began drilling. Soon after, when Maresh realized that the land was dry, Garfield claimed that he could rescind the agreement to invest because the investment offered by Maresh was a security within the meaning of the Securities Act of 1933 and it had not been registered. Did Maresh offer a security within the meaning of the 1933 act? Explain. [*Garfield v. Strain*, 320 F.2d 116 (10th Cir. 1963)]

20–2 Possible False Statements Basic, Inc., was a publicly traded company primarily engaged in manufacturing chemical refractories for the steel industry. Combustion Engineering was in a similar business and was interested in acquiring Basic. In 1976, representatives from both companies met to discuss a possible merger. In 1978, Basic made three public statements denying any merger negotiations. About one month after the last denial, Basic announced the merger. Plaintiffs had sold their stock after Basic issued its first denial. They brought action on the basis that directors had issued three false or misleading statements that violated Section 10(b) and Rule 10b-5. The defendants argued that the misstatements were immaterial and not a violation. How should the court handle this defense? [*Basic Inc. v. Levinson*, 485 U.S. 224, 108 S. Ct. 978, 99 L. Ed. 2d 194 (1988)]

20–3 Insider Chiarella was a printer who handled announcements of corporate takeover bids. Even though the documents concealed the target corporations' identities, he was able to deduce the names of the target companies. He purchased stock in target companies and sold the shares immediately after the takeover attempts were made public. He realized a gain of slightly more than $30,000 over fourteen months. The Securities and Exchange Commission investigated and Chiarella was convicted of insider trading. He appealed his conviction. What was the result? Explain. [*Chiarella v. United States*, 445 U.S. 222, 110 S. Ct. 1108, 63 L. Ed. 2d 348 (1980)]

20–4 Press Releases On September 1, 1971, Ecological Science Corp. issued a press release stating, in part, that it had renegotiated the terms of approximately $14 million in loans from its prime lender and that, under the renegotiated agreement, $4 million was due on demand and the remainder on a specified date. The press release, however, failed to mention that on the same date as the renegotiated loan agreement, an insurance and annuity association refused to provide the corporation with the $4 million loan that it had planned to use to repay the demand loan. Moreover, while discussing its European prospects in the press release, Ecological Science Corp. failed to mention the proposed transfer of voting control among its European subsidiaries. Has Ecological Science Corp. violated any of the provisions of the Securities Exchange Act of 1934? Explain. [*Securities and Exchange Commission v. Koenig*, 469 F.2d 198 (2d Cir. 1972)]

20–5 Insider Trading Emerson Electric Co. owned 13.2 percent of Dodge Manufacturing Co. stock. Within six months of the stock purchase, Emerson sold enough shares to a broker to reduce its holding to 9.96 percent of its former Dodge holdings. One week later (but less than six months after Emerson's initial purchase), Emerson sold its remaining shares of Dodge stock. The sole purpose of Emerson's initial sale of just over 3 percent of its Dodge stock was to avoid liability under Section 16 of the Securities Exchange Act of 1934, which prohibits short-swing trading. Assuming that Emerson made no profit on the initial sale of stock, but made substantial profits when it sold the remaining 9.96 percent of Dodge stock, must it return its profits on the sale? Explain. [*Reliance Electric Co. v. Emerson Electric Co.*, 404 U.S. 418, 92 S. Ct. 596, 30 L. Ed. 2d 575 (1972)]

20–6 What Is a Security? American Breeding Herds, Inc. (ABH), offered a cattle breeding plan, under which Ronnett contracted to buy thirty-six Charolais cows at $3,000 per head and a one-quarter interest in a Charolais bull at $5,000, totaling $113,000. The ABH agreement described itself as a "tax shelter program . . . unlike the purchase of securities such as stocks and bonds." Ronnett entered into the agreement based on investment advice from Shannon, an investment counselor. The cows were tagged and sent to an ABH approved breeding ranch. Ronnett signed a maintenance agreement and paid a monthly maintenance fee.

Was the ABH plan a security? Should it have been registered under the securities law? Explain. [*Ronnett v. American Breeding Herds, Inc.*, 124 Ill. App. 3d 842, 464 N.E.2d 1202, 80 Ill. Dec. 218 (1984)]

20–7 Insider Dirks advised institutional investors on the financial merits of different insurance companies. A former officer of Equity Funding of America told Dirks that Equity Funding had fraudulently overstated many assets in its financial reports. While investigating this information, Dirks openly discussed the matter with reporters and a number of his clients. He did not own any shares. Some of his clients sold their stock based on information received from Dirks. The stock fell from about $26 a share to $15 a share in two weeks. The Securities and Exchange Commission (SEC) censured Dirks, contending that he was an insider or a tippee of an insider. Dirks appealed the censure. Should the SEC censure of Dirks be upheld? Explain. [*Dirks v. Securities and Exchange Commission*, 463 U.S. 646, 103 S. Ct. 3255, 77 L. Ed. 2d 911 (1983)]

20–8 What Is a Security? Adams devised a plan to sell "rabbit kits." For $7,200 per kit, a person would receive twelve female and two male rabbits that should produce 720 breeding females within a year. Part of the sales promotion was that Adams would be available for consultation. Also, Adams requested that all buyers join an association that would purchase pelts. Membership in the association was not part of the "rabbit kit." Adams controlled the association. The state of Florida claimed that Adams was selling an unlicenced security. Was Adams selling securities that should have been registered? Explain. [*Adams v. State*, 443 So. 2d 1003 (Fla. Dist. Ct. App. 1983)]

20–9 Advertising vs. Financial Information Apple Computer developed and marketed the Lisa line of computers. The company promoted this new line of computers as if it would take over the computer market. This release was publicized in the major journals with the following quotation: "Lisa is going to be phenomenally successful in the first year out of the chute." Many critics pointed out that Lisa was not IBM compatible, that it experienced problems with software suppliers, and that it was very expensive. Lisa turned out to be a complete failure, causing a 75 percent drop in Apple stock. Purchasers of Apple stock brought an action against Apple for failure to disclose problems with Lisa. Who prevails? Explain. [*In re Apple Computer Securities Litigation*, 886 F.2d 1109 (9th Cir. 1989)]

20–10 Internet You are cruising the World Wide Web when you find an interesting Web site at which you read about a company and its product. You believe that this company would be a good investment. You follow the instructions on the Web site and purchase 500 shares. Six months later you conclude that you were defrauded. You decide to complain to the SEC. What happens to your complaint once it reaches the SEC? Go to **http://www.sec.gov/complaint.shtml** to research the answer.

Chapter 21

Antitrust Law

Every agreement concerning trade, every regulation of trade, restrains. To bind, to restrain, is of their very essence. The true test of legality is whether the restraint imposed is such as merely regulates and perhaps thereby promotes competition or whether it is such as may suppress or even destroy competition.

> *Board of Trade of the City of Chicago v. United States*
> 246 U.S. 231, 38 S. Ct. 242, 62 L. Ed. 683, 1918
> **Justice Louis Dembitz Brandeis, 1856–1941**
> **Associate Justice, United States Supreme Court, 1916–1939**

Chapter Outline

Introduction

To understand what antitrust laws are, we need to look at the definition of a trust, the history of how business trusts operated, and the antitrust statutes that countered these trusts.

Laws that regulate economic competition are referred to as **antitrust laws**. Their purpose is to prevent businesses from controlling the economy through restraints of trade and monopolies. During the last half of the nineteenth century, trusts controlled the economy. A **trust** is a legal entity that encompasses three parties, the trustor, the trustee, and the beneficiary. The **trustor** creates the trust and names the trustee and the beneficiary. The **trustee** holds title to property and manages the property for the benefit of one or more persons or businesses. The people who benefit are called the **beneficiaries**. The beneficiaries are entitled to income from the property.

After the Civil War (1861–1865), large corporations used trusts to eliminate competition. Corporations engaged in the same type of business combined to create a trust. These corporations designated themselves as both the trustor and beneficiary and then also designated a trustee. Once the trust was created, the corporations transferred their stock to a trustee and received trust certificates in return. The trustee made decisions that fixed prices, controlled production, and determined the control of exclusive geographic markets for the entire industry. Corporations (the beneficiaries) participating in a trust no longer competed with one another. The trusts wielded so much power that corporations outside the trusts were unable to affect the market. Basically, these corporations viewed their competitors as friends and their customers as enemies.

Through these trusts, businesses created economic arrangements either to create a monopoly or to restrain trade. Although **monopoly** is not defined in any statute, the courts find that a monopoly exists when a business has either exclusive control or nearly total control of the market share of a business aspect or even of a whole industry.

Restraints of trade (restraining the competition) are not defined by any statute either. The courts find a restraint of trade when businesses try to affect trade by substantially reducing competition. A business may act alone or with others. It does not need to try to achieve a monopoly; it merely needs to try to substantially reduce competition.

During the nineteenth century, trusts gained control of several major industries, including oil, cotton, whiskey, sugar, and linseed oil. Their activities constituted a monopoly in each geographic area. For example, Standard Oil Trust sold kerosene at a price below its own costs to drive smaller competitors out of business. Once its monopoly position was assured, Standard Oil raised prices to recoup the losses and reap monopoly profits. Whether the trust gained a monopoly or restrained trade, the overall effect was to end competition and to pass on higher prices to consumers.

During this time period, common law protected a business's freedom to enter a market and to conduct trade in any manner. The common law, however, was inadequate in dealing with abuses by the giant corporations and trusts conducting trade. The public became concerned that the trusts controlled an increasing number of industries through unfair methods. Some states attempted to control such restraints in trade by enacting statutes to outlaw trusts.

By the 1880s, the federal government recognized that restraints and monopolies were a national problem. Because state statutes have no jurisdiction over interstate trade abuses, the states could not handle these abuses. Congress needed to find a way to destroy the trusts without destroying free enterprise. Congress, therefore, passed a number of antitrust statutes. The most important statutes are the Sherman Act, the Clayton Act, and the Federal Trade Commission Act. All of these acts have been amended over the years. These statutes are enforced by the Department of Justice[1] and the Federal Trade Commission.[2] Exhibit 21–1 lists the major antitrust laws and provides a brief summary of each.

For more than a century, these antitrust laws have protected the competitive process that is the basis of a free market economy. The laws support a competitive marketplace that lowers prices and a free market that helps to maximize consumer choice. These statutes also stimulate innovation by discouraging anticompetitive conduct by businesses that defeats a free market economy.

Most trusts are legal, and their use flourishes today, particularly in estate planning. Trusts, today, may not form monopolies or restraints of trade as they did in the past.

Artiste Login. Although Carlo and Carlotta's online business, Artiste Login Products, Inc., conducts business in the competitive art world, they still need to be aware of antitrust laws. Artiste needs to avoid common mistakes. For example, they are not allowed to fix the price of their products in agreement with other producers of the similar products. They cannot enter into an agreement that would restrain trade, such as an agreement with the manager of a mall where their retail store is located, in which one clause prohibits the mall manager from renting store space to similar business. Such a clause would be illegal. Additionally, Carlo and Carlotta cannot boycott products, unless certain narrow circumstances are present. Even competitive businesses can violate the antitrust laws if they not careful.

Sherman Act

In 1890, Congress enacted the Sherman Antitrust Act, today called the **Sherman Act**, to promote competition within the U.S. economy. The author of the legislation, Senator John Sherman (1823–1900),[3] argued that the Sherman Act did not announce a new principle of law, but simply applied well-recognized principles of the common law.

The Sherman Act was an attempt by Congress to end monopolies and restraints of trade. Sections 1 and 2 of the Sherman Act contain its main provisions:

> *Section 1. Every contract, combination in the form of trust or otherwise, or conspiracy, in restraint of trade or commerce among the several States, or with foreign*

---

[1] The Department of Justice's Web site is http://www.usdoj.gov. The Antitrust Division's Web site is http://www.usdoj.gov/atr/index.html.
[2] The antitrust division of the Federal Trade Commission is located at http://www.ftc.gov/ftc/antitrust.htm. The antitrust guidelines are located at http://www.ftc.gov/bc/guidelin.htm.

[3] A Republican from Ohio, Senator Sherman served in the U.S. House of Representatives (1855–1861) and U.S. Senate (1861–1877, 1881–1897), and also served as secretary of the treasury under President Rutherford H. Hayes (1877–1881). Senator Sherman was the younger brother of famous Civil War military leader for the Union, General William Tecumseh Sherman (1820–1891).

Exhibit 21–1   Major Antitrust Statutes and Amendments

Date	Name	Description	Enforcement	Civil	Criminal
1890	**Sherman Antitrust Act** (name later changed to Sherman Act)		Department of Justice (DOJ) (civil and criminal)	DOJ sues for treble damages and injunctive relief on behalf of the U.S. when it has been harmed.	• Individuals: $350,000 fine and/or 3 years in prison. • Corporation: $10 million fine.
	Section 1	Bans contracts, combinations, and conspiracies in restraint of trade.	State attorneys general (civil)	State attorney generals sue for treble damages and injunctive relief on behalf of respective states when they have been harmed.	
	Section 2	Bans monopolies, attempts to monopolize, and conspiracies.	Private parties (civil)	Private parties sue for treble damages and injunctive relief when they have been harmed.	
1914	**Clayton Act**		Department of Justice, state attorney generals, private parties	Same as above for DOJ, state attorney generals, and private parties.	Directors and officers liable if they had intent and knowledge the action taken has an anticompetitive effect; $5,000 and/or one year (misdemeanor).
1936	Section 2 amended by the Robinson-Patman Act	Price discrimination: Bans sellers from charging different customers different prices for the same goods where the effect may be to lessen competition substantially.			
	Section 3	Bans exclusive dealing and tying arrangements that may lessen competition substantially.	Federal Trade Commission (FTC)	FTC may issue cease-and-desist order or enter into a consent order when the business agrees to the order.	
1950	Section 7 amended by the Celler-Kefauver Act	Bans mergers that may lessen competition substantially.			
1976	Hart-Scott-Rodino Antitrust Improvements Act	Requires premerger notification to DOJ and FTC.			
	Section 8	Prohibits interlocking directorships and officerships when business has $10 million in capital and profits.			
1914	**Federal Trade Commission Act** Section 5 (original)	Created the Federal Trade Commission. Banned "unfair methods of competition in commerce."	FTC	FTC may issue cease-and-desist order or enter into a consent order when the business agrees to the order.	None
1938	Wheeler-Lea Act	Added words to above, "and unfair or deceptive acts or practices in commerce."			
1975	Magnuson-Moss Federal Trade Improvement Act	Section 5 now reads "Unfair methods of competition in or affecting commerce, and unfair or deceptive acts or practices in or affecting commerce, are declared unlawful."			

nations, is hereby declared to be illegal [and is a felony punishable by fine and/or imprisonment]. . . .

Section 2. Every person who shall monopolize, or attempt to monopolize, or combine or conspire with any other person or persons, to monopolize any part of the trade or commerce among the several States, or with foreign nations, shall be deemed guilty of a felony [and is similarly punishable].

Sections 1 and 2 Compared

Section 1 and Section 2 are relatively vague and cover different commercial activity. Congress left it to the courts to determine acts that violated the Sherman Act. The courts have continued to consider the meanings of these two provisions through the intervening decades.

These two main sections differ considerably from each other. Section 1 requires action by two or more people because, by definition, a person needs a cohort to combine or conspire. The essence of the illegal activity is the act of joining together. Section 2, on the other hand, applies both to an individual person and to several people because it states "[e]very person who . . ." therefore, conduct by one person can result in a violation of Section 2.

The cases brought to court under Section 1 of the Sherman Act differ from those brought under Section 2. Section 1 cases often concern the finding of an agreement (written, oral, or based on conduct) that leads to a restraint of trade. Section 2 cases deal with the structure of a monopoly that exists in the marketplace.

Section 1 focuses on restrictive agreements, that is, agreements that have a wrongful purpose, whereas Section 2 looks at the misuse of monopoly power in the marketplace. Both sections seek to curtail commercial practices that result in undesired pricing, collusion, and other restraints of trade. Any case brought under Section 2, however, already must hold the threshold or necessary amount of monopoly power.

The Sherman Act does not regulate a business's actions. The statute establishes ways in which a business should not act. In this sense, the statute is proscriptive rather than prescriptive and forms the basis for policing rather than for regulating business conduct.

Restraint of Trade, Section 1 Violations

The courts use two doctrines in deciding Sherman Act restraint of trade cases: the *rule of reason* and the *per se rule* (only proof of the agreement's existence is required to prove the illegality). The courts have used these two rules during the past century when examining the activities of businesses.[4]

Business activities are first evaluated under the *per se* rule. If the business behavior is not classified as a *per se* violation, the courts evaluate it under the rule of reason.

Per Se Rule, Section 1 Violations

The United States Supreme Court, over the years, has determined that some types of restrictive agreements are inherently anticompetitive and are an unreasonable restraint on trade. Applying the **per se rule** has advantages. First, the government does not need to demonstrate the business's market power or the business practice's anticompetitive effect. Second, the defendant business cannot use any defense. If the government proves that the act took place, the defendant cannot have any excuse for committing the act. The *per se* rule eases administrative burdens, clarifies the behaviors that constitute illegal acts, and deters business behavior that is anticompetitive.

The *per se* restraints only serve to stifle competition. The *per se* rule applies to agreements made among horizontal competitors (those on the same level), such as competing retailers, wholesalers, or manufacturers. Three types of agreements to restrain trade are Section 1 violations of the Sherman Act and generally are illegal *per se*: *horizontal price fixing*, *horizontal market division*, and *group boycotts*. Group boycotts may involve both horizontal relationships and vertical relationships, such as a wholesaler dealing with a retailer.

Horizontal Price Fixing. **Horizontal price fixing** occurs when two or more potential competitors on

---

[4]The Sherman Act does not define what actions are illegal. Congress left it to the courts to determine what is illegal. Many Web sites have information about the different cases handed down over the years. Yahoo! has listed interesting information at http://dir.yahoo.com/Government/Law/Business/Antitrust.

the same level literally "fix" a "price" for their goods or services. (Later this chapter will address how a manufacturer may fix a price to a retailer because the relationship between a manufacturer and a retailer is vertical.) Under the Sherman Act, an agreement to raise, depress, fix, peg, or stabilize the price of goods or services that are traded interstate is illegal *per se.*

The following case, *United States v. Socony-Vacuum Oil Co.,* is the first case in which price fixing was declared illegal *per se.*[5]

[5]Socony-Vacuum Oil Company was one of the companies in the Standard Oil Trust. Socony-Vacuum Oil Company and Standard Oil of New York became Mobil Oil Company. In 1999, Exxon Corporation and Mobil Oil Company merged into Exxon Mobil Corporation (ExxonMobil). For more history, see http://www.exxon.mobil.com.

CASE 21.1

Supreme Court of the United States, 1940
310 U.S. 150, 60 S. Ct. 811, 84 L. Ed. 1129
http://caselaw.findlaw.com /scripts/getcase.pl?court= US&navby=case&vol=310 &p age=150#150

LANDMARK CASE

UNITED STATES v. SOCONY-VACUUM OIL CO.

BACKGROUND AND FACTS During the Great Depression, more oil was refined into gasoline than consumers could use. Major oil refiners kept ample storage facilities and had the capacity to distribute gasoline to retailers. Smaller, independent refiners lacked storage facilities and sold their gasoline at distressed prices on the *spot market* (a term used in the commodities market to mean current price) for immediate delivery to retailers. The glut of gasoline available in the spot market drove prices down.

The major oil companies embarked on a program of purchasing and storing the "distressed oil." The major companies agreed among themselves that each would buy distressed oil from a particular independent refiner. Although it appeared that the bidding and buying were based on the market price, the major companies, through their bidding, established a floor for gasoline prices that enabled them to prevent prices on the spot market from falling any lower.

Justice DOUGLAS delivered the opinion of the Court.

. . . .

The elimination of the so-called competitive evils is no legal justification for such buying programs. The elimination of such conditions was sought primarily for its effect on the price structures. Fairer competitive prices, it is claimed, resulted when distressed gasoline was removed from the market. But such defense is typical of the protestations usually made in price-fixing cases. Ruinous competition, financial disaster, evils of price cutting and the like appear throughout our history as ostensible justifications for price-fixing. If the so-called competitive abuses were to be appraised here, the reasonableness of prices would necessarily become an issue in every price-fixing case. In that event the Sherman Act would soon be emasculated; its philosophy would be supplanted by one which is wholly alien to a system of free competition; it would not be the charter of freedom which its framers intended.

The reasonableness of prices has no constancy due to the dynamic quality of business facts underlying price structures. Those who fixed reasonable prices today would perpetuate unreasonable prices tomorrow, since those prices would not be subject to continuous administrative supervision and readjustment in light of changed conditions. Those who controlled the prices would control or effectively dominate the market. And those who were in that strategic position would have it in their power to destroy or drastically impair the competitive system. . . .

. . . .

DECISION AND REMEDY The Supreme Court affirmed the judgment of the trial court that illegal price fixing took place when the oil companies agreed to purchase the distressed oil from the independent refiners. Each corporation was fined $5,000; each individual, $1,000. The Court held that to try to fix prices even though the prices seemed to be reasonable is an illegal *per se* violation of the Sherman Act.

CRITICAL THINKING: LEGAL APPLICATION Why did the Court not recognize that purchasing oil at a certain price was reasonable so that refiners could survive economically during the Great Depression?

Horizontal Market Division. Dividing a market (**horizontal market division**) for the sale of a specific product among competitors on the same level is a *per se* violation of the Sherman Act. Market division can be accomplished in many ways, all of which are illegal. The act restricts competitors from allocating among themselves exclusive geographic market divisions, customer allocations, or product types. Even though such agreements might seem reasonable, they eliminate competition.

A **territorial and customer division** operates in this basic fashion. Atec Computers, Bell Computers, and Chipper Computers, all wholesalers, compete against one another in the states of Kansas, Nebraska, and Iowa. Tired of the cut-throat competition, they divided up the territories. Atec sells products only in Kansas, Bell sells only in Nebraska, and Chipper sells only in Iowa. This concerted action reduces costs and allows all three (assuming that no other competition exists) to raise the price of the goods sold in their respective states.

The same violation would take place if they divided the customers instead of the geographic area, such as agreeing that Atec would sell only to institutional purchasers (school districts, universities, state agencies and departments, cities, and so on) in the three states, Bell only to wholesalers, and Chipper only to retailers.

In the following case, the Department of Justice filed an antitrust criminal action against one of the largest U.S. agricultural corporations. The case involved a *cartel* that engaged in blatant price fixing, market division, and restrictions on production. A **cartel** is defined as a combination of producers that join to control the production, sale, and price of goods or services.

CASE 21.2	UNITED STATES v. ANDREAS

United States Court of Appeals, Seventh Circuit, 2000

216 F.3d 645 (7th Cir.)

BACKGROUND AND FACTS Archer Daniels Midland Co. (ADM), based in Decatur, Illinois, is an agriculture processing company. ADM's business involves nearly every farm commodity and the processing of commodities, such as lysine. ADM, the self-professed "supermarket to the world," is a behemoth in its industry with global sales of $14 billion in 1999 and 23,000 employees. ADM has a worldwide sales force and a global transportation network involving thousands of rail lines, barges, and trucks.

The Andreas family had long controlled ADM. Dwayne Andreas, a director and the former CEO, had built ADM into a worldwide agribusiness powerhouse. G. Allen Andreas was the board chairman and president. Defendant Michael D. Andreas was vice chairman of the board of directors and executive vice president of sales and marketing. Defendant Terrance S. Wilson was president of the corn processing division and reported directly to Michael Andreas. Defendant Mark E. Whitacre, the informant in this case, was president of its bioproducts division and answered directly to Michael Andreas.

Lysine is an amino acid used to stimulate an animal's growth and is sold to feed manufacturers who add it to animal feed. Lysine is a highly fungible commodity and sold almost entirely on the basis of price. Pricing depended largely on two variables: the price of organic substitutes, such as soy or fish meal, and the price charged by other lysine producers.

Until 1991, the lysine market was dominated by a cartel of three companies in Korea and Japan, which produced all of the world's lysine until the 1990s. The cartel periodically agreed to fix prices, which at times reached as high as $3 per pound. In 1989, ADM announced that it was building the world's largest lysine plant capable of producing two or three times as much lysine as any other plant. In 1991, ADM started production of lysine and immediately created chaos in the market, igniting a price war that drove the price of lysine down to about 70 cents per pound.

In 1992, Whitacre began working with Wilson. The two attended many meetings of the lysine producers. The first meeting was held in Mexico City, chosen in part because the participants did not want to meet within the jurisdiction of American antitrust laws. Between 1992 and 1995, representatives from the lysine businesses met in Paris, Vancouver, California, Hong Kong, and Hawaii.

At these meetings, the companies discussed price agreements and allocating sales volumes among the market participants, which was critical to raising the price. Without the agreement, the five members tended to cheat, resulting in the price of lysine dropping. The purpose of these meetings was disguised by fake agendas and a fictitious lysine producers trade association, so they could meet and share information without raising the suspicions of customers or law enforcement agencies.

In 1992, shortly after the Mexico City meeting, Whitacre began cooperating with the Federal Bureau of Investigation (FBI) in an undercover sting operation aimed at the price-fixing conspiracy. Most of the meetings and telephone conversations involving Whitacre and other conspirators from 1992 through 1995 were taped. Whitacre made between 120 and 130 tapes for the FBI during the investigation by using recording equipment, tapes, and instruction provided by the government. FBI agents met with Whitacre more than 150 times during the investigation. Whitacre was told to record conversations relevant to the conspiracy, but not to record anything about ADM's legitimate business.

In 1995, the FBI raided the offices of ADM in Decatur. These raids ended the cartel. Criminal charges were brought against the three defendants.

The jury convicted the defendants, Michael Andreas and Wilson, of conspiring to violate Section 1 of the Sherman Act, which prohibits any conspiracy or combination to restrain trade. Each defendant was sentenced to twenty-four months in prison. The defendants appealed the length of their sentences.

KANNE, Circuit Judge

For many years, Archer Daniels Midland Co.'s philosophy of customer relations could be summed up by a quote from former ADM President James Randall: "Our competitors are our friends. Our customers are the enemy." This motto animated the company's business dealings and ultimately led to blatant violations of U.S. antitrust law. . . . The facts involved in this case reflect an inexplicable lack of business ethics and an atmosphere of general lawlessness that infected the very heart of one of America's leading corporate citizens. Top executives at ADM and its Asian co-conspirators throughout the early 1990s spied on each other, fabricated aliases and front organizations to hide their activities, hired prostitutes to gather information from competitors, lied, cheated, embezzled, extorted and obstructed justice.

. . . We find no error related to the convictions, but agree with the government that the defendants should have received longer sentences for their leadership roles in the conspiracy.

. . . .

C. *Per Se* Violations

. . . .

Violations of § 1 require evidence proving that the charged practice had the effect of unreasonably restraining trade under the "rule of reason," except in the limited cases referred to as *per se* violations. *Per se* violations are ones that "always or almost always tend to restrict competition and decrease output" such that the court may dispense with the requirement of economic evidence. *Per se* violations are "naked restraints of trade with no purpose except stifling of competition," and have been characterized as so "plainly anti-competitive" and lacking "any redeeming virtue" that they are presumed illegal under § 1. Courts apply *per se* treatment only after "considerable experience" with a particular business practice has inevitably resulted in a finding of anticompetitive effects.

. . . .

The conspirators began discussing the volume limits at their first meeting in Mexico City when Wilson proposed the idea and explained its vital importance to the overall scheme to control the industry. . . . ADM and the others began haggling over how much each would be allowed to produce. This argument continued until Andreas and Yamada met in Irvine, and Andreas threatened to flood the market. . . . The conspirators left this meeting with an agreement that . . . ADM would sell 67,000 tons, with adjustments for expected growth in the market. This agreement constituted an output limitation, which long has been condemned as a *per se* violation of the Sherman Act. . . .

. . . .

. . . While market demand might not support the full production of . . . companies at a profitable price, this fact does not distinguish lysine from many other markets. ADM's entrance into the market may have resulted in oversupply and lower prices for consumers, but this does not grant a license to violate the antitrust laws.

. . . .

E. Sufficiency of the Evidence

Andreas next asks us to overturn the jury's verdict because of insufficient evidence to support it. We will overturn a jury verdict "only if the record contains no evidence, regardless of how it is weighed, from which the jury could find guilt beyond a reasonable doubt." We view "the evidence in the light most favorable to the prosecution," and decide whether "any rational trier of fact could have found the essential elements of the crime beyond a reasonable doubt."

Andreas attended three meetings of the conspirators and served a vital role in the successful efforts to reach an agreement to implement the price-fixing and volume deals. The jury . . . heard Andreas threaten to flood the market if they did not agree. Evidence at trial indicated that the details of the plan were arranged by upper management, but that all sides recognized that their corporate superiors remained in control of the deal and would be called in to settle any unresolved disputes. . . .

Furthermore, Andreas directly supervised Wilson and Whitacre. They reported the results of the meetings to him, and he on more than one occasion coached them on what to say at an upcoming meeting. . . .

It would require a great leap of imagination to believe that Andreas knew nothing of the illegal deals on price and output carried out by his direct subordinates, yet happened to play a key role in Irvine and at subsequent meetings to facilitate those deals. . . . Based on the overwhelming evidence presented at trial, we cannot conclude that the jury acted irrationally in convicting Andreas of conspiring to restrain trade.

Finally, the Court has reviewed all of the evidence against Andreas and Wilson and can fairly characterize it as overwhelming. . . . The price fluctuated, and cartel members cheated each other when they could, but the evidence soundly supports a volume of commerce influenced by the conspiracy of at least $168 million. . . .

DECISION AND REMEDY The court found overwhelming evidence of antitrust activities, such as price fixing and restrictions on production, and upheld the convictions. This edited case focuses on only two defendants. The case involved ADM and a number of other corporate and individual defendants. The decision discussed at length the sentences of Andreas and Wilson. Each defendant originally was sentenced to two years and fined $350,000. Each lost their jobs with ADM. On remand, the trial court increased Andreas's sentence from two years to three years and Wilson's sentence from two years to two years and nine months. The U.S. Supreme Court refused to grant the writ of *certiorari*.

COMMENT One month before the scheduled sentencing of his son, Dwayne Andreas stepped down as chairman in 1999 after serving in that position since 1970. ADM was worth $100 million in 1970 and valued at his departure at $6.5 billion. As a result of its antitrust activities, ADM paid a civil penalty of $35 million, a criminal penalty of $70 million, and Canada fined ADM $11.4 million (U.S.). The estimated total of litigation costs and fines approached $350 million. The value of the common stock dropped $2.4 billion in the days after the raid in 1995.

Unbeknownst to ADM and the FBI, Whitacre was embezzling from ADM. This crime spree started prior to his involvement with the FBI, continued while he made the tapes for the FBI, and ended only after the FBI raids. In the end, he swindled ADM out of $9 million for which he was sentenced to serve nine years, along with two years and six months for his participation in the price-fixing scheme.

CRITICAL THINKING: PUBLIC POLICY The U.S. government would not have discovered these violations of antitrust laws without the cooperation and assistance of Whitacre who had failed to negotiate a grant of immunity when he agreed to cooperate. What policy should the U.S. government adopt concerning someone like Whitacre who comes forward with evidence of crimes, but are also engaging in other crimes unknown to the government?

Trade Associations. Businesspeople in certain types of associations must be careful to avoid engaging in actions that might be considered violations of the antitrust laws. For example, competitors often organize into **trade associations** to pursue common interests, such as lobbying Congress for favorable laws. These associations disseminate information, represent the members' business interests before governmental bodies, initiate joint advertising campaigns, and attempt to police their own industry.

These exchanges of information among related businesses pose special antitrust problems. Trade association activities are, by their very nature, joint actions and therefore subject to the antitrust laws.

Professional Associations. For many years, professionals were regarded as outside the scope of the antitrust laws

because, it was thought, their activities did not involve trade or commerce. This assumption is no longer valid. **Professional associations** are similar to trade associations in that professionals join to pursue common interests.

Similar to trade associations, professionals must avoid engaging in actions that violate antitrust laws. For example, the Supreme Court held that a minimum fee schedule mandated by a bar association was price fixing. It also held that a maximum fee plan set by a medical association was price fixing.[6]

Group Boycotts. Group boycotts (concerted refusals by groups to deal with another) are a *per se*

[6]Arizona v. Maricopa County Medical Society, 457 U.S. 332, 102 S. Ct. 2466, 73 L. Ed. 2d 48 (1982).

LEGAL HIGHLIGHT

Can a University Violate Antitrust Laws?

Most people would consider universities to be outside the realm of antitrust laws. The Department of Justice (DOJ), however, charged nine Ivy League schools[a] with horizontal price fixing. In 1958, the nine schools formed the Ivy Overlap Group to determine collectively the amount of financial assistance to award to students. The students involved had been accepted and had applied for financial aid at two or more of these schools.

To qualify for federal financial aid, the students and their parents were required to disclose financial information to the College Scholarship Service (CSS). CSS processed this information and forwarded it to the U.S. Department of Education, which used the Congressional Methodology formula to determine the amount of aid that the schools expected the family to contribute. After the department determined the amount of family aid, it returned the information to the CSS, which, in turn, forwarded it to the nine schools.

The Ivy Overlap Group met annually to share the information received from CSS. The schools agreed to share financial information concerning candidates. Collectively, the group developed and applied a uniform analysis to determine needs for assessing family contributions. The only meaningful competition to the Ivy Overlap Group was Stanford University.

In 1991, DOJ alleged that the annual meeting involved horizontal price fixing and was in violation of Section 1 of the Sherman Act. It charged the Ivy Overlap Group with unlawfully conspiring to restrain trade by (1) agreeing to award financial aid exclusively on the basis of need, (2) agreeing to utilize a common formula to calculate need, and (3) collectively setting the family's contribution, not on the Congressional Methodology, but on its own formula. The DOJ sought an injunction to stop the practice. Eight of the nine schools signed a consent decree with the DOJ. The schools did not admit wrongdoing, but agreed to stop sharing student information.

Massachusetts Institute of Technology (MIT), however, refused to sign the consent decree. In the trial, the federal district court found that the agreement among the universities was a per se violation of the Sherman Act and found MIT guilty of price fixing. On appeal, the U.S. Court of Appeals[b] reversed the decision. The court noted that financial aid to students was part of the process of determining tuition, which is a commercial transaction. The Ivy Overlap Group agreements, however, did not reduce any output of students, so the effect of the Overlap agreements differed from the normal economic agreements that fixed prices. In fact, the agreements promoted socioeconomic diversity at the member institutions. The appellate court remanded (returned) the case to the district court. In the retrial, the district court was to apply the rule of reason to determine if MIT, in fact, enhanced rather than restricted competition.

In 1992, Congress passed the Higher Education Amendment, which approved the concept of need-blind admissions and agreements among schools on general principles for determining student aid. The act prohibits discussion of individual aid.[c] This act would have ended the Ivy Overlap Group agreements in any event, because the act made these types of agreements illegal.

[a] The nine Ivy League universities are Brown University, Columbia University, Cornell University, Dartmouth College, Harvard University, Massachusetts Institute of Technology, Princeton University, the University of Pennsylvania, and Yale University.

[b] U.S. v. Brown University, 5 F.3d 658 (3rd Cir. 1993).
[c] Higher Education Amendments of 1992, Pub. L. No. 102-325, 91544, 106 Stat. 448, 837 (codified at 20 U.S.C. Ch. 28).

offense. A boycott often cuts off a firm's access to a supply, facility, or market that is necessary for the boycotted firm to compete. The boycotting businesses frequently possess a dominant position in the marketplace. Generally, this type of boycott cannot be justified as intending to increase the market's overall efficiency and to increase competition.

When two levels of the same industry are involved, the traders on one level agree to deal with businesses on another level. For example, the General

Motors new retail automobile dealers agreed to boycott General Motors, the seller, to prevent it from selling cars to automobile discount outlets. The court found this agreement among the retail car dealers to be a *per se* violation of the antitrust law.

Only group boycotts are illegal, not all boycotts. A business can decide with which other businesses it will deal. A business legally may refuse to deal with a particular firm. The statute prevents agreements among businesses, not unilateral refusals by one business to deal with another.

For example, a newspaper's investigative reporter writes a series of articles on automobile dealers who use fraudulent means to sell automobiles. If one automobile dealership on its own withdraws its advertisements from the newspaper, this decision is legal. If the trade association for automobile dealers, comprised of the local competing automobile dealers, decides that none of its members will advertise in the newspaper, the decision is an illegal group boycott. If the newspaper suffers a drop in revenue that can be traced to the withdrawal of those advertisements, it has been economically damaged. In this situation, even though

the group boycotted against another industry, its purpose is to substantially reduce competition, so the action is illegal.

The Rule of Reason, Section 1 Violations

The **rule of reason** determines the anticompetitive acts that violate antitrust laws. When the business actions do not fall under the *per se* rule, the courts use the rule of reason. A court must review all the circumstances of a case to decide whether the defendant's practice created an unreasonable restraint on competition. Defendants can prove in court a procompetitive business justification for their acts. Defenses of this type are discussed later in the chapter.

The next case, involving Standard Oil Company of New Jersey, is the most important early case interpreting the Sherman Act. The Supreme Court found the oil company guilty of violations of both Sections 1 and 2. Having determined that Congress could not have intended a literal interpretation of every restraint of trade in Section 1, the Court used a standard of reasonableness to analyze the oil company's conduct. This case is the first to set out the rule of reason.

LANDMARK CASE

CASE 21.3

Supreme Court of the United States, 1911
221 U.S. 1, 31, S. Ct. 502, 55 L. Ed. 619
http://caselaw.findlaw.com /scripts/getcase.pl?navby= case&court=US&vol=221 &page=1

STANDARD OIL CO. OF NEW JERSEY v. UNITED STATES

BACKGROUND AND FACTS The government charged the Standard Oil Company of New Jersey (Standard Oil) and thirty-five other corporations, John D. Rockefeller, William Rockefeller, and five other individual defendants with a conspiracy alleged to have been formed around 1870. The government charged that the individual defendants organized the Standard Oil Corporation of Ohio and soon afterward became participants in an illegal plan to acquire substantially all of the oil refineries located in Cleveland, Ohio. Therefore, the government charged the original owners of the company with forming and participating in an illegal combination for the restraint and monopolization of all interstate commerce in petroleum products.

The government charged that a trust agreement existed in which the stock of more than forty corporations was held for the benefit of the members of the combination. The trial court voided the trust agreement as a restraint of trade and ordered the trust dissolved. It is questionable, however, if the trust actually was dissolved because the stock held by the trust apparently shifted among the companies, but ultimately was preserved in the same hands.

Chief Justice WHITE delivered the opinion of the Court.

. . . .

. . . The merely generic enumeration which the statute makes of the acts to which it refers, and the absence of any definition of restraint of trade as used in the statute, leaves room for but one conclusion, which is, that it was expressly designed not to unduly limit the application of the act by precise definition, but, while clearly fixing a standard, that is, by defining the ulterior boundaries which could not be transgressed with impunity, to leave it to be determined by the light of reason, guided by the principles of law and the duty to apply and enforce the public policy embodied in the statute, in every given case whether any particular act or contract was within the contemplation of the statute.

. . . .

[Referring] to the acts done by the individuals or corporations who were mainly instrumental in bringing about the expansion of the New Jersey corporation during the period prior to the formation of the trust agreements of 1879 and 1882, including those agreements, . . . we think no disinterested mind can survey the period in question without being irresistibly driven to the conclusion that the very genius for commercial development and organization which it would seem was manifested from the beginning soon begot all intent and purpose to exclude others which was frequently manifested by acts and dealings wholly inconsistent with the theory that they were made with the single conception of advancing the development of business power by usual methods, but which on the contrary necessarily involved the intent to drive others from the field and to exclude them from their right to trade and thus accomplish the mastery which was the end in view.

DECISION AND REMEDY The Supreme Court upheld the trial court's order to dissolve Standard Oil.

COMMENT This divestiture led to a reorganization of the oil business from which the Seven Sisters, as they became known, arose. Five were American companies. Three of these five companies were known as the Standard Oil Group (Exxon, Mobil, and Socal) because they retained many of the directors from Standard Oil and their principal shareholder was John D. Rockefeller. The other two American oil corporations were Gulf and Texaco. The sixth sister was a British company, British Petroleum. The seventh sister was an Anglo-Dutch company, Shell.

CRITICAL THINKING: POLITICAL CONSIDERATION Why not allow trusts that would control prices?

The Supreme Court in *Standard Oil* reasoned that Congress intended the Sherman Act to apply only to unreasonable restraints on trade that would result in monopolization. With this decision, the Court created the rule of reason. The Court rejected the idea that every business act should be illegal, regardless of its reasonableness. If the Court had not interpreted the act in this way, every conceivable business practice would have violated the Sherman Act.

Vertical Restraints. Vertical relationships involve the various levels of a particular supply chain. Manufacturers by necessity deal with wholesalers and retailers. Wholesalers deal with both manufacturers and retailers.

Agreements that restrain trade involving firms at different levels of the production and distribution processes violate antitrust laws. These violations are called **vertical restraints** of trade.[7] These agreements, however, vary to such a degree that even to define the typical vertical arrangement is sometimes difficult.

Resale Price Maintenance. A **resale price maintenance agreement** is a contract to fix prices when a vertical relationship exists. For example, a wholesaler sells a product to a retailer. The wholesaler (the seller),

[7]For an in-depth discussion about vertical restraints go to http://www.antitrust.org.

however, wants to control the price at which the retailer can sell the item, a tactic that is called *vertical price fixing*. The courts review these types of agreements under the rule of reason to determine if a violation of Section 1 of the Sherman Act has occurred.

In the following case, the Supreme Court reviewed a case involving a manufacturer (the seller) fixing the maximum price at which a product could be sold by its retailer (the buyer). Prior to the following case, vertical price fixing was thought to be illegal *per se*. Follow the Supreme Court's reasoning as it applies the rule of reason, and not the *per se* rule, to this case, which involved price fixing in a vertical relationship.

CASE 21.4

Supreme Court of the United States, 1997
522 U.S. 3, 118 S. Ct. 275, 139 L. Ed. 2d 199

STATE OIL COMPANY v. KHAN

BACKGROUND AND FACTS Respondents, Barkat U. Khan and his corporation, entered into an agreement with petitioner, State Oil Company, to lease and operate a gas station and convenience store owned by State Oil. The agreement provided that Khan would purchase the station's gasoline supply from State Oil at the suggested retail price set by State Oil, less a margin of 3.25 cents per gallon. Under the agreement, Khan could charge any amount for gasoline sold to his station's customers, but if the price charged was higher than State Oil's suggested retail price, the excess was rebated to State Oil. Khan could sell gasoline for less than State Oil's suggested retail price, but any such decrease would reduce his 3.25-cents-per-gallon margin.

About a year after Khan began operating the gas station, he fell behind in the lease payments. State Oil then gave notice of its intent to terminate the agreement and began eviction proceedings in state court. At State Oil's request, the state court appointed a receiver to operate the gas station. The receiver operated the station for several months without being subject to the price restraints in Khan's agreement with State Oil. According to Khan, the receiver obtained an overall profit margin in excess of 3.25 cents per gallon by lowering the price of regular-grade gasoline and raising the price of premium grades.

Khan sued State Oil in the United States District Court, alleging in part that State Oil engaged in price fixing in violation of Section 1 of the Sherman Act by preventing him from raising or lowering retail gas prices. The district court found that the allegations in the complaint failed to state a *per se* violation of the Sherman Act because they failed to establish the sort of "manifestly anticompetitive implications or pernicious effect on competition" that would justify *per se* prohibition of State Oil's conduct. The district court held that Khan had not shown that a difference in gasoline pricing would have increased the station's sales, nor had he shown that State Oil had market power or that its pricing provisions affected competition in a relevant market.

The Court of Appeals for the Seventh Circuit reversed, finding that the agreement between Khan and State Oil did indeed fix maximum gasoline prices by making it "worthless" for Khan to exceed the suggested retail prices. After reviewing legal and economic aspects of price fixing, the court concluded that State Oil's pricing scheme was a *per se* antitrust violation under the Supreme Court ruling in the *Albrecht v. Herald Co.* case, which had been decided in 1968. The Supreme Court granted *certiorari*.

Justice O'CONNOR delivered the opinion of the Court.

. . . .

Although the Sherman Act, by its terms, prohibits every agreement "in restraint of trade," this Court has long recognized that Congress intended to outlaw only unreasonable restraints. As a consequence, most antitrust claims are analyzed under a "rule of reason," according to which the finder of fact must decide whether the questioned practice imposes an unreasonable restraint on competition, taking into account a variety of factors, including specific information about the relevant business, its condition before and after the restraint was imposed, and the restraint's history, nature, and effect.

Some types of restraints, however, have such predictable and pernicious anticompetitive effect, and such limited potential for procompetitive benefit, that they are deemed unlawful *per se. Per se* treatment is appropriate "[o]nce experience with a particular kind of restraint enables the Court to predict with confidence that the rule of reason will condemn it." Thus, we have expressed reluctance to adopt *per se* rules with regard to "restraints imposed in the context of business relationships where the economic impact of certain practices is not immediately obvious."

. . . .

We recognize that the *Albrecht* decision presented a number of theoretical justifications for a *per se* rule against vertical maximum price fixing. But criticism of those premises abounds. . . .

The *Albrecht* Court . . . expressed the concern that maximum prices may be set too low for dealers to offer consumers essential or desired services. But such conduct, by driving away customers, would seem likely to harm manufacturers as well as dealers and consumers, making it unlikely that a supplier would set such a price as a matter of business judgment. . . .

Finally, *Albrecht* reflected the Court's fear that maximum price fixing could be used to disguise arrangements to fix minimum prices which remain illegal *per se.* Although we have acknowledged the possibility that maximum pricing might mask minimum pricing, we believe that such conduct—as with the other concerns articulated in *Albrecht*—can be appropriately recognized and punished under the rule of reason.

Not only are the potential injuries cited in *Albrecht* less serious than the Court imagined, the *per se* rule established therein could in fact exacerbate problems related to the unrestrained exercise of market power by monopolist dealers. Indeed, both courts and antitrust scholars have noted that *Albrecht's* rule may actually harm consumers and manufacturers.

. . . .

In overruling *Albrecht*, we of course do not hold that all vertical maximum price fixing is *per se* lawful. Instead, vertical maximum price fixing, like the majority of commercial arrangements subject to the antitrust laws, should be evaluated under the rule of reason. In our view, rule-of-reason analysis will effectively identify those situations in which vertical maximum price fixing amounts to anticompetitive conduct.

DECISION AND REMEDY The United States Supreme Court overruled a case that had restricted a seller from setting maximum prices. Today, a seller of goods may set a maximum price for which a buyer, such as a wholesaler or retailer, may resell the item provided that the price is reasonable when considering all economic factors.

CRITICAL THINKING: ECONOMIC CONSIDERATION Assume Khan had agreed with other gasoline station operators to set a price below which none of them would sell gasoline. How would a court treat this example differently from its handling of the actual case?

Restrictions in the Vertical Distribution Process. The methods by which manufacturers market their products to wholesalers or retailers vary greatly. A manufacturer may sell directly to retailers or to wholesale distributors, who in turn resell to retailers. The manufacturer may even own the retail outlets where its products are sold.

Regardless of the arrangement selected, both the manufacturer and the retailer seek maximum profits. Some methods that increase profits violate the antitrust laws.

The manufacturer often imposes territorial restrictions on its retailers to prevent competition among themselves. This restriction creates a sales advantage for each retailer, because the desired product cannot be purchased anywhere else in the immediate area. Selling goods of the same make under territorial restrictions may result in less competition, but territorial and customer restrictions generally are lawful unless their use unreasonably restrains trade.

Manufacturers may attempt to prohibit wholesalers or retailers from reselling the products to certain classes of buyers, such as competing retailers, constituting consumer restrictions. See the *Legal Highlight* entitled *Toys "Я" Us* for a story in which the retailer controlled the manufacturer through a vertical agreement.

Monopoly Power, Section 2 Violations

The antitrust statutes do not define the term *monopoly*, but the accepted meaning is that of a business that exclusively controls a business aspect or even an entire industry. The courts determine if a monopoly exists

---

LEGAL HIGHLIGHT

Toys "Я" Us

For several years, warehouse (also called discount) clubs sold toys at nearly two-thirds the price charged by retail toy stores. Toy manufacturers projected that these clubs would have 6 to 8 percent of the market. As the warehouse clubs gained market share, the retail toy chain outlets shrunk. Toys "Я" Us, the only national full-line toy chain, decided to take action.

A powerhouse in the toy business, Toys "Я" Us had 29 percent of the top ten toy makers' sales. With its buying power, Toys "Я" Us managed to pull all the major toy manufacturers, such as Hasbro and Mattel, into vertical agreements to restrict their sales to warehouse clubs.

Toys "Я" Us then orchestrated a series of horizontal agreements among the otherwise competing manufacturers to adhere to sales restrictions in the vertical agreements. Toys "Я" Us enforced the agreements by shopping at the competing warehouse clubs to see if the discount clubs sold products that were also offered in Toys "Я" Us stores. In addition, manufacturers would complain to Toys "Я" Us about competitors' products being sold in warehouse clubs. On finding a manufacturer's toys in a discount store, Toys "Я" Us would contact the manufacturer and threaten to stop buying its toy products. The manufacturer would then apologize and reaffirm the agreement to restrict sales to warehouse clubs.

As a result, Mattel, Hasbro, and other major toy manufacturers stopped selling to Price Club, Sam's, B.J.'s, and other discount clubs. Consumers shopping at a discount club could no longer find toys, forcing them to shop at retail toy stores and pay a higher price.

The Federal Trade Commission charged Toys "Я" Us with violations of the antitrust acts by engaging in both vertical and horizontal restraints of trade agreements. The commission found that Toys "Я" Us entered into vertical agreements with individual manufacturers and coordinated a horizontal agreement among the same manufacturers. The commission also found that in the areas where discount clubs and Toys "Я" Us competed, the toy prices were lower in the Toys "Я" Us stores than in those stores where no competitive discount clubs were located. The commission issued an order prohibiting Toys "Я" Us from entering into these types of agreements for five years.

The commission's order was appealed by Toys "Я" Us. The court of appeals held that substantial evidence existed to support the Commission's findings and also upheld the commission's order.[a]

The ironic part of this story is that when Toys "Я" Us became successful, retailers, such as department stores, tried to prevent toy manufacturers from selling to Toys "Я" Us because its prices were too low!

[a] Toys "Я" Us, Inc. v. Federal Trade Commission, 221 F.3d 928 (2000).

on a case-by-case basis, considering, first, whether a firm has accumulated enough dominance in the marketplace that it has monopoly power. Second, the courts decide if the business accumulated its monopoly power through wrongful actions. The courts concern themselves with only those actions that are wrongful and have led to monopoly power.

To determine if a firm has monopoly power, a court must examine whether the firm has market power. **Market power** is determined if the firm's power is so great that it can force its decisions on others, based on structural analysis. Structural analysis involves two steps: (1) Define the market in which the firm's power should be evaluated, and (2) measure the extent of the firm's share of that market.

Structural analysis involves more than identifying a firm within a market and comparing its sales with those of its competitors. The court also determines the *relevant product market* and the *relevant geographic market*. The **relevant product market** evaluates the market for the product, its competition, and items that can be substituted for the product.

The **relevant geographic market** considers the area where the product is sold, the ease of transportation, and the distance that consumers will travel to purchase the product. The geographical area may be national, regional, or local. After determining these markets, the court compares the sales of the firms within these markets.

Although structural analysis is an inexact science, it is a tool used by the courts to support the inference that monopoly power exists. The court also considers any barriers to entry that may exist and whether acceptable substitutes for the firm's product are available.

Defining the Relevant Market. The relevant market is defined by considering information about the characteristics of the product, its substitutes, its competition, and the geographic area where the product is sold. Because the market share is extremely sensitive to the definition of relevant market, both sides in these cases take considerable care in assembling and presenting evidence to determine the market.

Product Market. Substitutes are available for most products. If General Motors raised the prices for its cars significantly, consumers would purchase more Fords or other brands. Courts would determine if General Motors' Cadillac division had monopoly power by considering the following questions: Should all cars sold in the United States be included in the computation of Cadillac's market share? Should only luxury cars be included? Do Japanese, Korean, Swedish, or German automobile imports compete with Cadillacs for sales? Although General Motors is the sole producer of Cadillacs, it will not have monopoly power as long as substitute products exist because market forces will keep the price of Cadillacs competitive with the price of substitute products.

Courts determine the relevant product market by defining the products that can be substituted for the product that is alleged to be dominating the market to the exclusion of competitors. In some cases, the product market is extremely wide. Including all cars sold in the United States in a measure of Cadillac's market share makes Cadillac's share relatively small. Measuring Cadillac sales against the combined sales of cars and trucks decreases Cadillac's share even further. If only luxury cars are considered, Cadillac has a larger market share. Whenever monopoly power is alleged, courts must decide which products offer competition to the dominant product. The following case illustrates the process by which the court determined if a firm had an illegal monopoly.

LANDMARK CASE

CASE 21.5

United States Court of Appeals, Second Circuit, 1945

148 F.2d 416

UNITED STATES v. ALUMINUM CO. OF AMERICA (ALCOA)

BACKGROUND AND FACTS The United States charged Aluminum Company of America (Alcoa) with monopolizing interstate and foreign commerce in the manufacture and sale of "virgin" aluminum ingot. The government contended that because Alcoa was the sole producer of virgin ingot in the United States, Alcoa had an unlawful monopoly. Alcoa contended that it was subject to competition from imported virgin ingot and from "secondary" ingot (recycled aluminum) and did not have monopoly power.

The district court found that Alcoa had a 33 percent share of the market, which included both the secondary material that had been salvaged from scrap and the new ingot. The lower court found for Alcoa. The court of appeals computed the market share differently and found that Alcoa had 90 percent of the virgin ingot market.

Judge HAND

. . . .

From 1902 onward until 1928 "Alcoa" was making ingot in Canada through a wholly owned subsidiary; so much of this [ingot was] imported into the United States it is proper to include with what it produced here. In the year 1912 the sum of these two items represented nearly ninety-one percent of the total amount of "virgin" ingot available for sale in this country. . . .

. . . .

We conclude therefore that "Alcoa's" control over the ingot market must be reckoned at over ninety percent; that being the proportion which its production bears to imported "virgin" ingot. If the fraction which it did not supply were the produce of domestic manufacture there could be no doubt that this percentage gave it a monopoly—lawful or unlawful, as the case might be. The producer of so large a proportion of the supply has complete control within certain limits.

DECISION AND REMEDY The court of appeals found that Alcoa had monopolized the aluminum industry by having a 90 percent share of the virgin ingot market, along with having an intent to acquire a monopoly of this market.

COMMENT The United States Supreme Court did not hear this appeal. The Court lacked a quorum because too many of the justices had been involved with the case before they were appointed to the Supreme Court. Congress passed a special statute to allow the Second Circuit Court of Appeals to hear the case.

CRITICAL THINKING: MANAGERIAL CONSIDERATION Would you, as a businessperson, want the government to use a broad or a limited definition of the relevant market power?

Geographic Market. The relevant geographic market usually is less difficult to determine than the relevant product market. If sellers within an area can raise prices or reduce the supply of products without quantities of lower priced goods quickly flowing into the area, the sellers have a separate geographic market for their products.

Geographic markets may be local, regional, or national. In determining a geographic market, the courts consider the mobility of both competing sellers and purchasers. The courts consider whether a buyer can easily purchase the goods at a lower price outside of the immediate area or whether a seller in another geographic area can ship goods easily into the area. Because consumers are willing to travel greater distances to make

major purchases than to buy everyday necessities, courts determine the geographic market more broadly for sales of automobiles than for sales of milk.

Determining the Market Share. After defining the relevant product and geographic markets, the court can determine the percentage of the market held by any one firm. This percentage is the firm's market share, that is, the comparison of one firm's position with the positions of all other firms with which it competes. Monopoly power is a matter of degree. In the *Alcoa* case, 90 percent of the relevant market was sufficient for the court to conclude that Alcoa held a monopoly.

Courts have found that no monopoly exists when the firms control less than 65 percent of their relevant markets. In the *Alcoa* case, the court said that two-thirds of the relevant market would questionably constitute a monopoly, but that one-third of the market would not constitute a monopoly situation.

The courts attempt to determine if a firm holds such substantial power over a market that it can engage in actions not associated with natural growth to exclude competitors and to control prices. Market share is the measurement used to make that determination objectively.

Clayton Act

In 1914, Congress strengthened the federal antitrust laws by adopting the **Clayton Act**, which is aimed at specific monopolistic practices. The Sherman Act prohibits activities that eliminate competition or result in monopoly power, but it does not reach activities that merely reduce competition or could lead to monopoly power. The Clayton Act declares these specific activities to be illegal, even though these practices might not constitute the contract, combination, or conspiracy in restraint of trade necessary for a Sherman Act violation.

The important sections of the Clayton Act are Sections 2, 3, 7, and 8. Section 2 prohibits price discrimination, Section 3 prohibits exclusive dealing agreements or tying arrangements, and Section 7 prohibits mergers when these arrangements tend to substantially lessen competition or create a monopoly. Section 8 prohibits interlocking directorships and officerships under specific circumstances.

Section 2, Robinson-Patman Act

The objective of Section 2 is to promote economic equality in the purchasing and selling of goods. Section 2, as originally passed, was very weak. In 1936, Congress passed the **Robinson–Patman Act**, which strengthened that section. The Robinson-Patman Act makes it illegal for any seller to discriminate in the prices charged for goods of the same quality to different purchasers.

Sales at differing prices must have an anticompetitive effect for a violation of the act to have occurred. If a seller engages in interstate commerce, it must sell goods of similar grade and quality to different competing purchasers.

The courts view sales of the same or similar goods at different prices to competing consumers (such as competing retailers) as **price discrimination** under Robinson-Patman. Price discrimination is unlawful even when the firm engaged in it does not have, and does not seek, monopoly power. Later sections discuss the three defenses to price discrimination.

InfoTrac Research Activity

The Robinson-Patman Act has generated a number of articles discussing the act. Search InfoTrac for "Robinson-Patman Act." Select six articles and compare the views of the authors.

Price discrimination can occur at two different levels, the primary level or secondary level. Primary level, or first line, price discrimination occurs when the seller of the goods uses price discrimination to drive its own competition out of business. A seller of goods is prohibited from gaining an unfair advantage over its competitor by offering a better price to (and thus discriminating among) different buyers for similar goods when the effect will substantially lessen competition or when it may create a monopoly. For example, Flour Mill offers flour at a lower price to all the large bakeries in the state than to small bakeries. All the large bakeries purchase from Flour Mill. This practice either drives competitors of Flour Mill out of business or allows them a smaller share of the market, because they sell only to the small bakeries.

A secondary level, or second line, price discrimination occurs when the purchaser of the goods uses price discrimination to drive other competitors out of business. Buyers are prohibited from using their economic power to obtain better prices from the seller to gain an economic advantage over their competitors. For example, Large Purchaser and Smaller Competitor are competitors. Large Purchaser uses its purchasing power to induce Supplier to sell to Large Purchaser at a lower price than to Smaller Competitor. Large Purchaser arranges more favorable payment terms and additional services, because of its large purchasing volume. Smaller Competitor suffers competitive damage when it must purchase the goods at a higher price from Supplier. Additionally, Smaller Competitor is unable to arrange favorable payment schedules or additional services. Thus, Smaller Competitor must resell the goods at a higher price. Smaller Competitor loses business to Large Purchaser, because most customers prefer to buy the lower priced goods from Large Purchaser.

Section 3

Section 3 prohibits *exclusive dealing agreements* and *tying arrangements* when they substantially reduce competition or when they tend to create a monopoly. Under an **exclusive dealing agreement**, the seller of goods requires the buyer to promise not to handle the products of any of the seller's competitors. For example, an oil company requires its dealers to carry only its brand of products, such as gasoline, oil, parts, and batteries. This requirement is an exclusive dealing agreement and is illegal if it reduces competition or creates a monopoly.

A **tying arrangement** occurs when the supplier forces the buyer to purchase an unrelated item (the tied item). Usually, but not always, the tied item does poorly on its own in the marketplace. The tied item is often unwanted by the buyer, or the buyer believes it can purchase the tied item at a lower price. The supplier (seller) either wants to get rid of the tied item or may be profiting from it.

For example, Fast-Food Franchise requires its franchisees to purchase not only its secret recipe mix and specially designed cooking machines, but also all paper products, such as paper boxes, paper bags, and paper napkins, in the franchise colors with its stamped logo. The franchise agreement forbids the franchisee from purchasing paper products from a local supplier and having the colors and logo printed. This requirement is an illegal tying arrangement under Section 3, because the franchise must purchase the paper products to buy the tied product, the secret recipe mix. Paper products have nothing to do with the product sold by Fast-Food Franchise and can be purchased at lower prices from others.

Both tying arrangements and exclusive dealing contracts violate Section 2 of the Sherman Act. Under the Sherman Act, both goods and services are covered, whereas the Clayton Act covers only goods. Once, courts treated tying arrangements as *per se* illegal. Recently, however, courts have required the seller to have economic power in the market for the tying product for such dealings to be illegal. Section 3 provisions are subject to the rule of reason today.

Section 7

The original Section 7 also was weak. In 1950, Congress passed the **Celler-Kefauver Act**, which strengthened and expanded this section. Corporations are prohibited from merging with another corporation if the merger might reduce competition or tend to create a monopoly. Section 7 was amended again by the **Hart-Scott-Rodino Antitrust Improvements Act** of 1976. The act requires businesses that intend to merge to provide both the Federal Trade Commission and the Department of Justice with a premerger notification.

One of the largest settlements occurred after the Federal Trade Commission brought action against The Hearst Trust, Hearst Corporation, and First Databank, Inc., to dissolve a 1998 merger of the nation's two principal vendors of integratable drug information databases. One was operated by Medi-Span and the other by First Databank. The merger dissolved Medi-Span leaving First Databank in a monopoly position. None of the businesses involved complied with the premerger notification requirements. The three defendants agreed to pay $19 million profit disgorgement, plus $4 million in civil damages. While the merger was in place, it earned the defendants $1 million per month in illegal profits for nineteen months.[8]

Section 8

Section 8 prohibits interlocking directorates and officers. The law forbids a person from being a director or officer in two or more competing businesses if one of them has capital, surplus, and profits exceeding $10 million as of 1990. This amount is annually reviewed and is increased or decreased based on the gross domestic product (GDP) (the total value of all goods and services produced within a country). The current maximum amount is $13,813,000.

An exception to this rule, however, allows a person to be a director of a second business if the competitive sales of either corporation are less than $1,381,300, that is, 10 percent, of the larger amount. Section 8 also allows a person to be a director if the total competitive sales of both corporations is less than 4 percent of the corporation's total sales.

Actual monopolization is unnecessary under the Clayton Act, as is any attempt to monopolize. The act does not require that an injury to competition be demonstrated. Therefore, the burden of proof for violations of the Clayton Act is less than for violations of the Sherman Act. In short, the Clayton Act reaches (prohibits) practices before a monopoly actually occurs.

[8]U.S. v. The Hearst Trust, 2001 WL 1478814 (2001); *in re* First Databank Antitrust Litigation, 205 F.R.D. 408 (2002) and 209 F. Supp. 2d 96 (2002).

Federal Trade Commission Act

In 1914, Congress passed the Federal Trade Commission Act, which created the Federal Trade Commission (FTC) as a "trust-busting" agency.[9] This bipartisan, independent administrative agency is composed of five commissioners. At any given time, no more than three commissioners can be from the same political party.

The FTC Act, as originally passed in 1914, was very weak. In 1938, Congress passed the **Wheeler-Lea Act,** which provided the FTC a dual focus: the original focus of regulating anticompetitive business behavior and the additional focus of providing consumer protection (which was covered in Chapter 15). In 1975, Congress amended the FTC Act again with the **Magnuson-Moss Federal Trade Improvement Act**, which broadened the scope of the FTC Act.

The FTC's function is to ensure that the marketplace is competitive, efficient, and free from undue restraints. The FTC's antitrust division has the authority to enforce (1) the Federal Trade Commission Act, which prohibits "Unfair methods of competition in or affecting commerce, and unfair or deceptive acts or practices in or affecting commerce" as unlawful; (2) the Clayton Act, which prohibits arrangements, mergers, and acquisitions that threaten competition; (3) the Robinson-Patman Act, which forbids price discrimination; and (4) the Hart-Scott-Rodino Antitrust Improvements Act, which requires companies to file premerger notifications.

Mergers

A **merger** is the combination of two or more businesses into one. Mergers result in one business gaining greater control of the market. Accordingly, the antitrust laws apply to mergers and prevent consolidations that would substantially reduce competition or end in a monopoly.

Section 7 of the Clayton Act is the principal statute that applies to mergers. The act prohibits "one person," including corporations, partnerships, and sole proprietorships, from acquiring another if the merger would tend to reduce competition substantially or to create a monopoly. Congress feared that a concentration of power, by merger or consolidation, potentially would facilitate collusion among sellers in the market and that such collusion would be difficult to detect.

The Hart-Scott-Rodino Antitrust Improvements Act, in addition to amending Section 7 of the Clayton Act, also provided the FTC with more powers.[10] The act required businesses planning to merge to file a premerger notification with the FTC and the Department of Justice. The FTC can enforce these notification procedures. This notification allows affected agencies to review and determine if a potential merger will violate the antitrust laws. The FTC can sue to enforce the notification procedures. Violations of these procedures subject the firms to fines up to $100,000. Three types of mergers exist: *horizontal merger, vertical merger,* and *conglomerate merger.*

Horizontal Mergers

A **horizontal merger** occurs when two or more companies merge that previously competed with the same or similar products in the same geographic area. This type of merger receives rigorous scrutiny because horizontal mergers lead to a concentration of firms in a relevant market. The FTC and the Antitrust Division of the Department of Justice (DOJ) examine horizontal mergers by reviewing the degree of concentration and market shares of merging firms.

If the merged company will gain an increased market share and at the same time less competition, it can increase its product price and diminish its product quality and service. In a concentrated marketplace, innovation can be stifled. Under these circumstances, the merger will be challenged by the DOJ and the FTC. A merger is allowed, however, when the marketplace is enhanced by increasing its efficiency and the merger does not increase the horizontal concentration of power in the marketplace.

The DOJ and the FTC have jointly issued *Horizontal Merger Guidelines.*[11] An analytical process is used to determine whether a horizontal merger will be challenged. The government uses the guidelines to evaluate the concentration of the relevant market and to determine if there will be an increase in market concentration after the merger. The DOJ also considers

---

[9]The Federal Trade Commission's Web page is located at http://www.ftc.gov.

[10]For more information on premerger and the Hart-Scott-Rodino Antitrust Improvements Act, go to http://www.ftc.gov/bc/hsr/hsr.htm. This page also includes early termination information.

[11]The guidelines for horizontal mergers can be found at http://www.ftc.gov/bc/guidelin.htm.

nonmarket issues, such as ease of entry into the business and competitive strength of the merged firms. The policy is to prevent anticompetitive problems in their incipiency. The government tries to avoid unnecessary interference with mergers that are either competitively beneficial or neutral.

In determining whether a horizontal merger will result in an unacceptable increase in market concentration, the DOJ uses a statistical formula called the **Herfindahl-Hirschman Index**. After considering the other factors and implementing this index, the DOJ determines whether a merger is likely to be challenged. The index is featured in the *Legal Highlight* entitled *Herfindahl-Hirschman Index*.

Vertical Mergers

Vertical mergers occur when a company at one stage of distribution acquires a company at a higher or lower stage of distribution. The acquisition of a tire plant by an automobile manufacturer is called a **backward vertical integration**. The acquisition of a car-rental agency by the same automobile manufacturer constitutes a **forward vertical integration**. The government's approach to vertical mergers depends on a number of factors, including the definition of the relevant product and geographic markets, as well as the characteristics identified as impeding competition.

LEGAL HIGHLIGHT

Herfindahl-Hirschman Index

Businesses are required under the Hart-Scott-Rodino Antitrust Improvements Act to file a premerger notification with both the Department of Justice and the Federal Trade Commission. These agencies determine whether the horizontal merger should be permitted. Mergers that create or enhance market power are not allowed to proceed.

DOJ uses the Herfindahl-Hirschman Index (HHI), which is a commonly accepted measure of market concentration. The HHI takes into account the relative size and distribution of the firms in a market. The index approaches zero when a market consists of a large number of firms of relatively equal size. The HHI increases both as the number of firms in the market decreases and the disparity in size between those firms increases. DOJ determines whether the market is concentrated through the use of the HHI.

If the index is less than 1,000 points, the merger normally will not be questioned. If the index is between 1,000 and 1,800 points, the market is considered to be moderately concentrated. The merger likewise will not be challenged if the index increases by 100 or less after the merger. If the index is above 1,800, the market is considered to be concentrated. Thus, if the merger will increase the HHI by more than 100 points in concentrated markets, antitrust concerns are raised. The DOJ will challenge the merger in most circumstances.

The index is obtained by squaring the market shares and then adding all competitors' shares together. The HHI does not use decimals, so they are multiplied by 100. The following is an example.

The Herfindahl-Hirschman Index

Firm	Market Share	Market Share × 100	Market Share Squared
A	0.30	30	900
B	0.10	10	100
C	0.40	40	1,600
D	0.05	5	25
E	0.15	15	225
HHI Number			2,850

Based on guidelines, a proposed merger of any two firms among those listed would not be allowed. For example, if D and E were to merge, the new market share would be 5 + 15, or 20. This figure squared would result in a market share of 400. Because the market share of D and E before merger would be 250 (25 + 225), the difference of 400 − 250, or 150, would be greater than 100 points on an HHI that exceeds 1,800. This merger, therefore, would be challenged.

The government will attack any vertical merger that keeps competitors of either party from a segment of the market that otherwise would be open to them. The law's current theory of injury to competition in vertical mergers is contained in the concept of foreclosure. For example, a manufacturer can acquire a retailer and force the new retail subsidiary to sell the manufacturer's product. This acquisition would foreclose rival manufacturers from the market. The FTC has found that "foreclosure manifests a particularly anticompetitive character when it occurs as part of a trend toward forward integration in a concentrated market."

Conglomerate Mergers

A **conglomerate merger** is the consolidation of two or more firms dealing in unrelated products and operating in markets not horizontally or vertically linked. For example, a firm that operates motion picture theaters acquires a firm that manufactures automobile parts. Sometimes the products of the merged firms are complementary and a merger permits the marketing of additional products at very little expense.

CYBERLAW

Mergers and Antitrust Concerns

Competition usually spurs firms to achieve efficiencies internally. Nevertheless, mergers, even those involving e-commerce companies, have the potential to generate significant efficiencies by permitting a better utilization of existing assets, thus, enabling the combined firm to achieve lower costs in producing a given quantity and quality than either firm could have achieved without the proposed transaction. Indeed, the primary benefit of mergers to the economy is their potential to generate such efficiencies.

As more firms involved with e-commerce propose mergers, they only will be permitted when efficiencies generated through the merger can enhance the merged firm's ability and incentive to compete. Normally, these efficiencies result in lower prices, improved quality, enhanced service, and new products.

Defenses and Exemptions

Congress and the courts have created certain defenses and exemptions to the antitrust laws. More defenses and exemptions exist, but the following are commonly used.

Defenses

The courts have upheld several defenses for businesses confronted with allegations of creating an illegal monopoly or conspiring to restrain trade. The subsections that follow describe some defenses that the courts have accepted.

Defenses to Price Discrimination. Price discrimination in violation of the Robinson-Patman Act occurs when a seller that operates interstate discriminates in the prices charged to different purchasers for goods of like grade and quality, resulting in injury to a competitor. A seller may have defenses. The three defenses to price discrimination are meeting the competition, cost justification, and changing market conditions.

The Meeting the Competition Defense. The statutory provisions of the Clayton Act allow the reduction of a price made "in good faith to meet an equally low price of a competitor." The **meeting the competition defense** allows a business to sell at a lower price to some customers if it must meet a competitor's price. But the price must be lowered to meet, not to beat, a competitive price. Price lowering must not be made with the intent to drive the competitor out of business. Also, the lower price must be for goods of similar quality to those of the competitor. Finally, the lower price to these customers must be temporary so as not to result in a competitive injury to the seller's other customers. As long as the business meets these three conditions, it may sell at a lower price to certain customers to meet competition.

The Cost-Justification Defense. It is less expensive per unit to manufacture and sell a thousand units of an item than ten units. Lower prices are permitted when the savings result from a particular customer's purchase. The seller must carry the burden of proof when using a **cost-justification defense** to price discrimination. A large-volume purchase alone does not justify a seller charging a purchaser a lower price. The seller must prove with actual evidence that the buyer's large purchase saves the seller money, such as lower transportation costs. Then the seller can pass these savings on to the large purchaser. It may be difficult to determine the proper allocation of overhead and other expenses in order to demonstrate these savings.

The Changing-Market-Conditions Defense. The **changing-market-conditions defense** to price discrimination allows a business to discontinue a product or product line or to offer a fire or bankruptcy sale. In doing so, the business may sell the product at a reduced price. This defense allows a business to discount prices on seasonal goods or goods that will deteriorate.

Other Defenses. The courts have approved various defenses to charges of violations of other parts of the antitrust laws. The following are defenses to vertical restraint, monopoly, and merger cases.

The Colgate *Doctrine.* The *Colgate* **doctrine** comes from *United States v. Colgate & Co.* The United States Supreme Court allowed Colgate to refuse unilaterally to deal with retailers that ignored its suggested retail prices (vertical price fixing). This refusal to deal created a vertical restraint between Colgate and its retailers (purchasers of Colgate's products). The Court emphasized that a firm can choose with whom it deals.

The Thrust-Upon Defense. A business that has a monopoly can use the **thrust-upon defense** by showing that the monopoly might have been created by the production of a superior product; by better business practices; or by events, such as owning the only restaurant in an area where all the other restaurants have closed as a result of economic conditions. For this defense, no wrongful intent to create the monopoly must exist.

The Failing-Company and Inadequate Resources Defenses. When a company confronts complete failure with no other prospective purchasers, the courts have allowed a merger, even if it violates antitrust guidelines. This defense is known as the **failing-company defense**.

Related to this doctrine is the **inadequate-resources defense**. If a company has insufficient financial resources to compete, the courts will allow a merger with another competing company, even though the result violates antitrust guidelines.

Exemptions

Congress passed the Sherman Act and the Clayton Act and provided the Federal Trade Commission Act with antitrust provisions. Congress also passed legislation that provides exemptions from antitrust laws. The courts, when interpreting the statutes that set out the exemptions, read the statutes very narrowly, that is, the courts try to limit exemptions.

Labor. The Norris-LaGuardia Act of 1932 and the National Labor Relations Act of 1935 protect unions from antitrust legislation. Today, unions lawfully can engage in actions, normally prohibited, as long as they act in self-interest without conspiring or combining with nonlabor groups.

Agriculture. The Clayton Act exempts agricultural organizations from the Sherman Act. The law allows many farmers to join together to form an agricultural cooperative to deal with the few purchasers of farm products. A cooperative usually forms to deal with specific types of farm products and generally does not cover every farm product that could be sold. Every member of a cooperative that deals in specific products must be involved in that aspect of farm production for the cooperative to keep the exemption.

Baseball. Although most commercial sports activities are subject to the antitrust laws, baseball is an exception. The United States Supreme Court early in the 1900s held that baseball was not commerce. Baseball's exemption is anomalous, especially because no other professional sport receives such treatment.

Insurance. The **McCarran-Ferguson Act**, enacted in 1945, exempted all activities that involve the insurance business from the antitrust laws. The primary element of the insurance business is the spreading and underwriting of policyholder risk. Strict insurance activities are exempted from the antitrust laws by the McCarran-Ferguson Act. An agreement between an insurance company and pharmacies to set the profit margin in prescription drugs, however, is subject to the antitrust laws.

Exports. Congress exempted certain activities from antitrust actions in the belief that certain goals can be better achieved through **cartelization**, that is, a banding together of competing firms. For example, the **Webb-Pomerene Act** exempts acts or agreements made in the course of export trade by associations of competing producers formed solely for the purpose of engaging in export trade. Cartelization promotes an increased national investment in the covered activities, thereby aiding the nation's balance of payments.

Congress designed the Export Trading Company Act of 1982 to increase U.S. exports of goods and services. Businesses can apply for an export trade certificate of review (ETCR). If approved, the secretary of commerce, with the concurrence of the attorney general, issues the ETCR. Persons named in the ETCR obtain limited immunity from both state and federal antitrust laws for activities that the certificate specifies. The proposed export conduct, however, cannot result in a substantial reduction of competition within the United States or restrain the export trade of any competitor of the applicant.

Political Activities. The **Noerr-Pennington doctrine** derives from two United States Supreme Court cases. Basically, the Court held that "the Sherman Act does not prohibit two or more persons from associating together in an attempt to persuade the legislature or the executive to take particular action with respect to a law that would produce a restraint or a monopoly." In other words, businesses can work with (lobby) Congress to pass appropriate favorable laws.

State Government. In general, state governments (which include city and county governments) may take actions that regulate economic activity; these actions are exempt from antitrust laws. The state government, however, must have a state policy and must actively supervise the regulated activity.

The United States Supreme Court has held that not all state or local government actions are exempt from federal antitrust laws. For example, a city government may not grant a cable company exclusive rights to service the city.

Enforcement of Antitrust Laws

Criminal enforcement of the Sherman Act is handled exclusively by the Department of Justice (as are all criminal actions brought on behalf of the U.S. government). Civil enforcement of the Sherman Act also is the responsibility of the Department of Justice. State attorneys general and private parties may file civil lawsuits when they have been harmed.

The Clayton Act, which has primarily civil provisions,[12] is enforced by the Federal Trade Commission, Department of Justice, state attorneys general, and private parties. The Federal Trade Commission Act is enforced exclusively by the FTC.

Enforcement by the Federal Trade Commission

The FTC enforces the Federal Trade Commission Act and Sections 2, 3, 7, and 8 of the Clayton Act. The FTC will investigate a business's anticompetitive conduct. During the investigation, the FTC sends the business a copy of the complaint and a proposed form of a consent order that contains a cease-and-desist order. If the business agrees, the cease-and-desist order is entered and the proceedings end. The business agrees to cease (stop) committing the unlawful acts and to desist (restrain) from committing the acts in the future.

At any time, the business and the FTC may come to an agreement and a consent order will be entered. If the business has also been sued in a civil lawsuit, the consent order protects the accused business. The plaintiff cannot use the FTC's case against the accused in any civil lawsuit when the business enters into an agreement for a consent order.

If the business fails to reply or responds negatively to the proposed form of the consent order, the FTC issues the complaint. An administrative agency proceeding takes place to determine whether the business violated the antitrust laws.

After hearing all the evidence, the administrative law judge (ALJ) may find in favor of the business. The FTC then must decide whether to appeal the ALJ's decision. If the FTC decides against appealing, the case ends.

If the ALJ agrees with the FTC's position, the ALJ may issue an order, which the business may appeal. An appellate court reviews the order. If the order stands, the business that violates the order in the future is subject to fines up to $10,000 per day for each day of continued violation.

---

[12]Section 14 of the Clayton Act includes the act's only criminal sanctions and is not discussed in this textbook.

Enforcement by the Department of Justice

The Antitrust Division of the Department of Justice enforces the criminal aspects of the Sherman Act and the civil provisions in both the Sherman Act and Sections 2, 3, 7, and 8 of the Clayton Act. The DOJ and the FTC each have authority to enforce the Clayton Act. To use their resources more efficiently, each agency clears proposed investigations with the other.

LEGAL HIGHLIGHT

The Breakup of AT&T

American Telephone and Telegraph (AT&T) was a utility regulated by the various state utility commissions. The first case brought by the Department of Justice against AT&T for antitrust activities began in 1949 and ended with a consent decree in 1956 that was a victory for AT&T. The decree merely enjoined AT&T from engaging in any business other than the furnishing of common carrier communications services, the very area in which it held a near monopoly.

Technology advances combined with AT&T's growth convinced the DOJ to renew its investigation. In 1974, following an investigation, DOJ filed a new antitrust lawsuit against AT&T, Western Electric, and Bell Telephone Laboratories, Inc. At the time the lawsuit was filed, AT&T had three million shareholders, over one million employees, an annual payroll of over $21 billion, and assets worth more than those of General Motors, Ford, Chrysler, General Electric, and IBM combined.

AT&T had a near monopoly on long-distance telephone service and controlled nearly all local telephone operating companies (twenty-two in all), which provided AT&T control of nearly 80 percent of all the country's telephones. Western Electric and AT&T had agreed in 1882 that Western Electric had the exclusive right to supply all of AT&T's telephone equipment. Between 1901 and 1913, Western Electric negotiated exclusive contracts with all the local operating companies to supply them with all telephone equipment. The state utility commissions did not regulate Western Electric's profits.

Bell Laboratories served as the research arm and was owned half by AT&T and half by Western Electric. Bell Laboratories and Western Electric developed and standardized products for use by the local operating companies.

The dispute between DOJ and AT&T was waged for six years over jurisdictional issues and involved an expensive, lengthy process. The trial opened on January 15, 1981, and recessed immediately after opening statements. Negotiations continued, but the parties could not reach a settlement. On March 4, 1981, the trial resumed. The DOJ presented more than 100 witnesses and thousands of documents. AT&T moved to have the case dismissed, but the presiding judge, Judge Green, strongly denied the motion, stating that the DOJ had presented a strong case and that AT&T would have a difficult time overcoming the weight of the evidence. AT&T presented 250 witnesses and thousands of documents. On January 8, 1982, within two weeks of when AT&T estimated its case would end, a settlement was announced.

The nineteen-page consent judgment allowed AT&T to maintain its nationwide long-distance telephone network. AT&T was ordered to divest itself of (sell) the twenty-two local telephone operating companies. They reorganized into what was then called the seven "Baby Bells."[a] Because the seven Baby Bells would not have any loyalty to Western Electric and were free to identify other suppliers, the court refrained from ordering AT&T to divest Western Electric. The court also ordered the seven Baby Bells to allow AT&T's long-distance competitors equal access to the local telephone distribution system. The order also allowed AT&T to enter into communications and computer services and to enter the computer and electronics industries without restrictions, except that AT&T could not engage in electronic publishing.

The settlement and subsequent consent judgment reached between AT&T and DOJ has been reviewed and modified through the years. The effect of the court order, however, still stands. It broke up the largest monopoly ever achieved in the United States.

[a] After the breakup of AT&T, the seven regional telephone companies were Ameritech, Bell Atlantic, Bell South, NYNEX, Pacific Telesis, Southwestern Bell, and US West. A number of these companies have been merged into other telecommunications companies.

The DOJ investigates a business that it (DOJ) believes to be committing violations of the Sherman Act or the Clayton Act. DOJ can decide to pursue criminal or civil action in federal district court. If the DOJ and the business agree, they settle the case out of court. The agreement (settlement) results in a consent judgment issued by the district court judge. The court must find that the settlement is in the national interest.

The issues in antitrust cases are extremely complex and often take years to litigate. Settlements usually can shorten the time period to reach the end of the case and can reduce the cost of enforcement. Settlements can occur at any time prior to or during the trial. Although settlements usually reduce costs, they sometimes are reached near the trial's end. Probably one of the best examples of a settlement that occurred after both a lengthy and costly investigation and a trial is the breakup of American Telephone and Telegraph. See the *Legal Highlight* entitled *The Breakup of AT&T* for details.

If negotiations fail, the DOJ will set the case for trial in federal district court. If the court finds in favor of the business, the DOJ must decide whether to appeal the decision. If the decision is not appealed, the case ends.

If the court finds in favor of the DOJ, it can seek a range of remedies from the court against the defendant, such as injunction, confiscation, divestiture, or dissolution. If the court grants the DOJ's request, a remedy will be ordered. With an injunction, the court orders the business to stop permanently its antitrust conduct. In other types of cases, the court can order confiscation (seizure) of goods that are in interstate commerce.

The defendant business can be ordered to divest (to sell off or withdraw from) another business that it owns. For example, the court ordered a wholesale meat packing business to sell its retail butcher shops.

In an extreme case, a dissolution (to end) order can be issued to terminate the business. The business must file articles of dissolution with the state government that created it, so that the business can be dissolved and then go out of business.

The DOJ can file a lawsuit alleging the U.S. government was harmed as a result of the antitrust activities of a business. In these cases, the statute allows the DOJ to recover up to three times the amount of the harm suffered by the government.

After an investigation, DOJ may decide that the business committed criminal acts. Any person violating either Section 1 or Section 2 of the Sherman Act is subject to criminal prosecution for a felony. In criminal cases, DOJ settles a high percentage of antitrust cases through the use of **nolo contendere** pleas. When a business enters a *nolo contendere* plea, it does not admit guilt, but will not fight the case. The court may treat the plea as if the defendant had pleaded guilty and impose the same penalty as if a guilty plea had been entered. The business may choose this plea because it cannot be used in civil cases that may be pending against it. The plea also saves money that the business would have spent in litigating a lengthy case.

If the defendant fails to use the *nolo contendere* plea, the DOJ will take the case to a criminal trial. The court will find the defendant guilty or not guilty. If the court convicts the person or business, the person can be fined up to $350,000, can be imprisoned for three years, or both. A corporation can be fined up to $10 million.

Enforcement by State Attorneys General and Private Parties

The Hart-Scott-Rodino Antitrust Improvements Act of 1976 amended the Clayton Act. This act authorizes state attorneys general and private parties, for the first time, to file civil lawsuits under the Clayton Act and the Sherman Act. The act authorizes state attorneys general to sue on behalf of the residents of their respective states.

The states can sue for three times the amount of damage caused by a firm that has violated the Clayton Act or the Sherman Act and also to recover attorneys' fees. For example, if 3,000 residents have been harmed, but only by a $10 amount, the individual does not have the economic incentive to file a lawsuit against the antitrust violator. The state attorney general can file an action on their behalf and recover three times the amount of the harm, plus attorneys' fees. This case usually is too small for the FTC or the DOJ to be interested in, but a state attorney general may very well be interested in pursuing this type of case.

The act allows private parties harmed by a firm's anticompetitive acts to recover up to three times their damages and their attorneys' fees. The private party often is another business harmed by a competitor engaging in illegal activity. Usually, if only one or two firms have been harmed, neither the federal nor state government is interested in suing. This act allows the victim to pursue his own case rather than relying on federal or state officials to file a lawsuit.

International Consideration

Parallel Antitrust Lawsuits

The United States has had antitrust laws for more than 100 years. Many nations, however, do not have any history of regulating anticompetitive behavior and some nations encourage and assist businesses in anticompetitive behavior.

The export and import trades account for nearly one-quarter of the U.S. gross domestic product. As the U.S. economy becomes increasingly globalized, the threat to business freedom and consumer welfare from foreign cartel activity increases. The Oil Producing Exporting Countries (OPEC) is an example of a cartel. Cartels range from being very effective, such as when they achieve a monopoly, to less effective, such as when they are unable to control production, sale, or prices.

Congress passed the **International Antitrust Enforcement Assistance Act (IAEAA)** of 1994. The statute provides antitrust guidance to businesses engaged in international operations, concerning the enforcement policies of the DOJ and the FTC. The law improves the ability of law enforcement agencies to gather evidence from abroad for use in U.S. antitrust enforcement cases. The statute also authorizes the DOJ and the FTC to assist foreign antitrust authorities on a reciprocal basis.

The European Union (EU) has had antitrust laws since its inception. Articles 85 and 86 of the Treaty of Rome[13] are modeled after the U.S. antitrust laws. Article 85 prohibits concerted anticompetitive conduct, such as price fixing and limiting of markets. Article 86 aims at monopolistic practices and market domination.

EU regulations implement Article 85 and Article 86. The regulations determine whether a product concentration creates or strengthens a dominant position as the result of effective competition. The question is whether the product concentration significantly impedes the common market or whether it is incompatible with the common market. The EU law also prohibits and regulates the confidentiality requirements of an antitrust investigation. The member states have given the EU sovereign authority to administer or enforce antitrust laws.

The EU recognizes opportunities for cooperation in antitrust investigations between the EU and the United States. One example is the parallel antitrust cases brought against Microsoft Corporation by both the United States and the EU. In these cases, Microsoft was charged with a horizontal restraint.[14] Microsoft required original equipment manufacturers (OEMs), that is, computer hardware manufacturers, to sign contracts to install Microsoft's disk operating system (MS-DOS). The contract indicated two payment methods. The OEM could pay for MS-DOS per installation, but the cost was prohibitive on an individual computer basis. Using the cheaper method, the OEMs paid for MS-DOS on every computer manufactured, rather than just for the computers on which MS-DOS was installed. This type of contract was a disincentive for OEMs to install other operating systems, such as IBM's operating system OS/2, because they would have to pay another fee in addition to that already paid to Microsoft.

The parallel lawsuits were filed at Microsoft's request so that the same rules in both the United States and the EU would apply. The case was settled, and Microsoft revised its contract so that the OEMs pay a fee per computer on which MS-DOS actually is installed. Although the parallel case occurred prior to the 1994 adoption of the IAEAA, it signals unprecedented cooperation between two sovereigns to enforce antitrust laws. The IAEAA will encourage more parallel lawsuits to be filed in the future.

In 1997, the Department of Justice charged Microsoft with violating this agreement. The DOJ alleged that Microsoft violated the court order by requiring OEMs to license and distribute Microsoft's Internet browser, called Internet Explorer, as a condition of licensing Microsoft's operating system. Microsoft also made it almost impossible to delete this program. The Justice Department sought, among other things, the breakup of Microsoft into two companies and a

---

[13]A brief review of the history of the EU follows. In 1957, the Treaty of Rome provided for a common market that eventually led to the European Economic Community (EEC). The Single European Act of 1987, amending the Treaty of Rome, provided for the economic union of the western European nations. During the time period from 1987 to 1994, the name evolved from the EEC to the European Community (EC). In 1993, the Treaty on European Union (commonly called the Maastricht Treaty) amended the Treaty of Rome. The Maastricht Treaty in 1994 created the European Union (EU) and provided for a political union of the western European nations. Many parts of the original Treaty of Rome remain in effect, such as the antitrust provisions.

[14]Information on the *United States v. Microsoft* case is located at http://www.findlaw.com/01topics/01antitrust/microsoft.html.

court order prohibiting Microsoft from requiring OEMs to install Internet Explorer along with Microsoft's operating system.

At the federal district court level, after a lengthy trial the court found Microsoft guilty of violations of Section 2 of the Sherman Act for the maintenance of a monopoly power by anticompetitive means. The court noted that no current products were available for users of personal computers worldwide that could be substituted for the Windows operating systems without incurring substantial costs. As a result, the court inferred that Microsoft could set the price of a license substantially above that which would be charged in a competitive market and leave the price at that level without losing customers.

Microsoft was found guilty of violations of Section 1 of the Sherman Act. Microsoft was liable for illegal tying of the browser, Internet Explorer, with the Windows operating system. This tying action by Microsoft forced its customers to take Internet Explorer as a condition of obtaining Windows.

The court noted first that Microsoft did not concede that any of its business practices violated the Sherman Act and had failed to amend its conduct. Second, Microsoft, despite credible evidence of antitrust violations, continued to do business as it had in the past and indicated that it may operate the same in future markets. Third, the court found Microsoft to be untrustworthy.

In an earlier proceeding a preliminary injunction had been issued. Microsoft's purported compliance with the injunction, the court noted, was illusory and its explanations of its actions were disingenuous. The trial court ordered Microsoft to submit a proposed plan of divestiture, one that would divide Microsoft into two companies. Microsoft appealed the court's findings to the D.C. Circuit Court of Appeals.

The appellate court upheld the trial court's finding that Microsoft had violated the antitrust laws. The appellate court found that while the case was still pending at the trial court level, the trial judge made public statements that indicated that he may have been biased against Microsoft. The appellate court, however, found that Microsoft could not be divided into two companies since Microsoft had been one creation and not one consisting of purchasing other businesses. The appellate court sent the case back to a new trial judge to determine the penalty.

In the meantime, the Department of Justice and Microsoft reached an amicable settlement. The settlement provided consumers more choices and allowed competitors more technical information about Microsoft's Windows operating system.

While this case was working its way through the courts, another case was brought against Microsoft by AOL-Time Warner Inc. This case involved the lengthy Internet browser war between Netscape and Microsoft Internet Explorer. This case was settled in 2003 by Microsoft paying $750 million and agreeing to help develop the technology that would enable both browsers to work together along with developing better instant messaging capabilities.

PRACTICAL TIPS

Avoiding Antitrust Violations

You are the marketing director of a firm that recently patented a revolutionary product similar to plastic, but with the strength of steel, the breathing ability of leather, the smoothness of silk, and the flexibility of rubber. The business goal is to maximize profits without running afoul of the antitrust laws.

In preparing a detailed marketing plan to reach your goal, you recognize one large benefit granted by federal law. A product that is patented by the U.S. government has an automatic exemption to the antitrust laws in the event that the product occupies a monopoly position in the marketplace.

A patent, however, does not exempt the business from other antitrust regulations. The following list itemizes some areas of caution:

Checklist

✔ *Same Price* Sell this product at the same price to competing distributors unless filling large orders creates cost savings.

✔ *Give Distributors Freedom* Refrain from requiring the distributors to sell at a given price unless you have retained title to the product.

✔ *No Price Setting* Refrain from setting the maximum price of the goods.

✔ *No Tying* Do not require the purchase of one product to be based on the purchase of other products.

This checklist provides several examples of how a business must be concerned with antitrust violations even when the law grants it the right to create a monopoly.

Chapter Summary

The three major antitrust statutes are the Sherman Act, the Clayton Act, and the Federal Trade Commission Act. The federal law attempts to prevent anticompetitive acts by businesses, to support an innovative marketplace, and to maximize consumer choice, all of which contribute to a free market economy. Anticompetitive business practices can result in a monopoly, in restraint of trade, or in substantially reducing competition.

In 1890, Congress passed the Sherman Act, which has two sections. The first section makes it illegal to enter into any contract, combination, or conspiracy in restraint of trade or commerce. The second section makes it illegal to monopolize or attempt to monopolize any trade or commerce. Violations of either section may result in a criminal felony conviction. The major defense to the Sherman Act is that business conduct is subject to the rule of reason. Certain conduct, such as price fixing, is conclusively a *per se* violation of the Sherman Act. The Department of Justice can pursue both civil and criminal lawsuits under the Sherman Act. State attorneys general and private parties can seek up to three times the amount of damage caused by violations of the Sherman Act.

The Clayton Act was adopted in 1914. This statute makes specific conduct, including price discrimination, exclusive dealing, tying arrangements, certain types of mergers, and interlocking directorships and officerships, violations of the antitrust law. Violations of the Clayton Act are subject to civil lawsuits.

Sections of the Clayton Act have been modified over the years. The Robinson-Patman Act in 1936 amended Section 2. The Celler-Kefauver Act in 1950 and the Hart-Scott-Rodino Antitrust Improvements Act in 1976 both amended Section 7. The last act also required businesses to provide both the Department of Justice and the Federal Trade Commission with premerger notification. The Department of Justice, the Federal Trade Commission, state attorneys general, and private parties can pursue various remedies for violations of the Clayton Act. The Federal Trade Commission Act also was adopted in 1914.

A number of exemptions to the antitrust laws also exist. These exemptions include labor unions, agricultural organizations, baseball, insurance, certain foreign trade groups, and certain activities conducted by individual states. The Webb-Pomerene Act allows cooperatives to file for an exemption from antitrust laws when competing overseas. The Export Trading Company Act of 1982 allows individual businesses to file for an export trade certificate of review. If approved, the business receives limited immunity from antitrust laws when operating in international markets.

In 1994, Congress passed the International Antitrust Enforcement Assistance Act. The act provides antitrust guidance to businesses that operate internationally. It improves the ability to gather evidence from overseas. The DOJ and the FTC are authorized to provide assistance to foreign antitrust authorities when pursuing antitrust violations.

Using the World Wide Web

The Federal Trade Commission has enforcement and administrative responsibilities under thirty-seven separate acts. They are grouped in three categories: (1) statutes relating to both the competition and consumer protection missions, (2) statutes relating principally to the competition mission, and (3) statutes relating principally to the consumer protection mission. The statutes

are available on the FTC's Web site. Also available at the FTC's Web site is a glossary of terms.

The home page of the Department of Justice's Antitrust Division is responsible for civil and criminal enforcement of the antitrust statutes, with the exception of the Federal Trade Commission Act. Antitrust cases brought by the DOJ can be found at the DOJ Web site.

For *Web Activities*, links to Web sites mentioned in the chapter, and additional Web sites that relate to the chapter topics, go to **http://bohlman.westbuslaw. com**, click on "Internet Applications," and select Chapter 21.

Web Activities

Go to **http://bohlman.westbuslaw.com**, click on "Internet Applications," and select Chapter 21.
21–1 Federal Trade Commission
21–2 Department of Justice

Key Terms

antitrust law
backward vertical
   integration
beneficiary
cartel
cartelization
Celler-Kefauver Act
changing-market-
   conditions defense
Clayton Act
Colgate doctrine
conglomerate merger
cost-justification defense
exclusive dealing
   agreement
failing-company defense
forward vertical
   integration

group boycott
Hart-Scott-Rodino
   Antitrust Improve-
   ments Act
Herfindahl-Hirschman
   Index
horizontal market
   division
horizontal merger
horizontal price fixing
inadequate-resources
   defense
International Antitrust
   Enforcement Assist-
   ance Act (IAEAA)
Magnuson-Moss Federal
   Trade Improvement
   Act

market power
McCarran-Ferguson Act
meeting the competition
   defense
merger
monopoly
Noerr-Pennington
   doctrine
nolo contendere
per se rule
price discrimination
professional association
relevant geographic
   market
relevant product market
resale price maintenance
   agreement
restraints of trade

Robinson-Patman Act
rule of reason
Sherman Act
territorial and customer
   division
thrust-upon defense
trade association
trust
trustee
trustor
tying arrangement
vertical merger
vertical restraint
Webb-Pomerene Act
Wheeler-Lea Act

Questions and Case Problems

21–1 Price Setting Discuss fully whether each of the following situations violates the Sherman Act.

a. Genovese Foods, Inc., is the leading seller of frozen Italian foods in the northeastern United States. Various retail outlets that sell Genovese products compete closely and customers are very price conscious. Genovese conditions its sales to retailers with the retailer's agreement to offer the products within a specific price range. Within this range, the retailer can set any price that the retailer believes to be appropriate.

b. Zimmermann, Inc., Hicks, Inc., and Micro, Inc., compete in the manufacture and sale of microwave ovens sold primarily on the West Coast. As a patriotic gesture and to assist the unemployed, the three competitors agree to lower their prices on all microwave models

by 20 percent for a three-month period, which includes the Fourth of July and Labor Day.

c. Best Beer, Inc., sells beer to distributors all over the United States. Best Beer sends to each of its distributors a recommended price list, explaining that past records indicate that beer sold at these prices should ensure the distributor a reasonable rate of return. The price list clearly states that Best Beer's sale of the beer to the distributor is not conditioned on the distributor's reselling the beer at the recommended price and that the distributor may freely set the price.

21–2 Sherman Act, Section 1 Innovative Appliance Store is a new appliance retail seller in Sunwest City. Innovative's unique sales techniques and financing have caused a substantial loss of sales for the appliance department of Depressed Department Store. Depressed is a large department store that is part of a large chain with substantial buying power. Depressed told a number of appliance manufacturers that if they continued to sell to Innovative, Depressed would discontinue its large volume of purchases from these manufacturers. The manufacturers immediately stopped selling appliances to Innovative. Innovative filed suit against Depressed and the manufacturers, claiming that their actions constituted an antitrust violation. Depressed and the manufacturers can prove that Innovative is a small retailer with a small portion of the market because the relevant market was not substantially affected. They claim that they are innocent of restraint of trade. Discuss fully whether an antitrust violation occurred.

21–3 Clayton Act, Section 7 The partnership of Montoya and Marsh is engaged in the oil wellhead service industry in New Mexico and Colorado. They presently hold about 40 percent of the market for this service. The firm of West, Williams, and Wilson, Inc., competes with the Montoya-Marsh partnership in the same geographic area. The West corporation holds approximately 35 percent of the market. Montoya and Marsh acquire West's stock and assets. Discuss which antitrust law has been primarily violated.

21–4 Sherman Act Harcourt Brace Jovanovich Legal and Professional Publications (HBJ) is the nation's largest provider of bar review materials and lecture services. From 1976 to 1979, HBJ offered a Georgia bar review course in direct competition with BRG of Georgia, Inc. (BRG). In early 1980, both companies entered into an agreement that gave BRG an exclusive license to market HBJ's material in Georgia. Both agreed that HBJ would not compete with BRG in Georgia and that BRG would not compete with HBJ outside of Georgia. Under the agreement HBJ received $100 per student enrolled by BRG and 40 percent of all revenues over $350. The price of BRG's course increased from $150 to $400 following the agreement. After being sued by persons enrolled in the bar review course, both companies defended on the grounds that no *per se* violation occurred under a geographic market allocation theory, because they refrained from dividing the relevant market in which they had previously competed. Who should prevail? Explain. [*Palmer v. BRG of Georgia,* 498 U.S. 46, 111 S. Ct. 401, 112 L. Ed. 2d 349 (1990)]

21–5 Tying Agreement Febco, Inc., manufactured lawn and turf equipment. Colorado Pump and Supply Co. was a wholesale distributor of such equipment in the Colorado area. Colorado Pump distributed a control device for sprinkling systems. Although Febco manufactured one of the better sprinkler controls, a number of other manufacturers competed in the field with competitively priced and satisfactory substitutes for Febco's controllers. In an agreement between Febco and Colorado Pump, Colorado Pump received the right to distribute Febco products, provided that it stocked its complete product line. Industry data proved that in this line of goods, distributors needed to protect the "goodwill" of manufacturers by carrying a complete line of manufacturer's goods or none at all. Does the requirement by Febco that Colorado Pump stock an entire line of Febco products constitute an illegal tying arrangement? Explain. [*Colorado Pump and Supply Co. v. Febco, Inc.,* 472 F.2d 637 (10th Cir. 1973)]

21–6 Rule of Reason Sylvania sold its televisions directly to franchise retailers. Sylvania limited the number of franchises granted for any given area and required each franchise to sell Sylvania products from only the franchise locations. A franchise did not constitute an exclusive territory. Furthermore, Sylvania retained sole discretion to increase the number of retailers in an area, depending on the success or failure of existing retailers in developing their market. Continental TV, Inc., a Sylvania franchisee, withheld payments owed for Sylvania products after a dispute over Continental's bid to add locations. John P. Maguire & Co., the finance company that handled the credit arrangements between Sylvania and its franchisees, sued Continental for payment and for return of secured merchandise (the televisions). In turn, Continental claimed that Sylvania violated Section 1 of the Sherman Act by entering into and by enforcing franchise agreements that allowed the sale of Sylvania products only in specified locations. Was this a violation of the Sherman Act? Explain. [*Continental TV, Inc. v. GTE Sylvania, Inc.,* 433 U.S. 36, 97 S. Ct. 2549, 53 L. Ed. 2d 568 (1977)]

21–7 Sherman Act, Section 1 American Oil Co. produced and distributed oil, gas, and related products. Olson was engaged in bulk distribution and retail sales of oil products. Early in 1967, American decided to acquire control of Olson's bulk distribution operations by purchasing substantially all of Olson's bulk assets. Thereafter, American hired Lawrence McMullin to assume control of the Olson operation for American. Under the agreement, McMullin took charge of the Olson plant and was paid on a commission basis in lieu of salary for the bulk petroleum sales that he procured.

In addition, the contract between American and McMullin imposed certain territorial limitations and price restrictions on sales resulting from McMullin's operations. Could the agreement between McMullin and American Oil that imposed price restrictions and territorial controls on McMullin's operations violate Section 1 of the Sherman Act? Explain. [*American Oil Co. v. McMullin,* 508 F.2d 1345 (10th Cir. 1975)]

21–8 Sherman Act, Section 1 The National Collegiate Athletic Association (NCAA) plays an important role in regulating amateur collegiate sports. As a result of various surveys and reports, the NCAA concluded that telecasting games adversely affected college football game attendance and seriously threatened the athletic system in the United States. The NCAA subsequently imposed regulations that restrained member colleges from negotiating and contracting for the telecasting of college football games. Some member colleges asserted that colleges with major football programs deserved greater input in the formulation of football television policy than they presently had in the NCAA. In addition, NCAA announced that it would take disciplinary action against member colleges that proceeded to enter into a television agreement with the National Broadcasting Company (NBC) on their own. Has the Sherman Act been violated in this case? Does the rule of reason or *per se* analysis apply to the NCAA's television plan? Explain. [*National Collegiate Athletic Association v.*

Board of Regents of the University of Oklahoma, 468 U.S. 85, 104 S. Ct. 2948, 82 L. Ed. 2d 70 (1984)]

21–9 Rule of Reason Thompson Everett, Inc. (Everett), the plaintiff, was an independent advertising representative. In this capacity, the plaintiff bought advertising for its clients. The defendants, however, had exclusive contracts to sell advertising for the cable companies; thus, Everett was forced to purchase cable advertisements for its clients through the defendants. Everett claimed that these exclusive contracts violated Section 1 of the Sherman Act in that they unreasonably restrained trade. The defendants contended that they had independently entered into these contracts, that these agreements should be subject to the rule of reason, and that in the interpretation of this rule the product market should include all media rather than just cable advertising. Who should prevail? Explain. [*Thompson Everett, Inc. v. National Cable Adv.,* 850 F. Supp. (E. D. Va. 1994)]

21–10 Internet The case of *United States v. Microsoft* is available at many Web sites. Compare the information reported at the Department of Justice's Web site with the information reported at the FindLaw Web site. The series of *Microsoft* cases can be accessed at the Department of Justice's Web site at **http://search.usdoj. gov/compass?scope=Microsoft&ui=sr&view-template=dojsimple**. The FindLaw Web site is **http://www.findlaw.com/01topics/01antitrust/microsoft.html**.

Chapter 22

Legislative Control over Labor and Labor Relations

Labor disgraces no man; unfortunately you occasionally find men disgrace labor.

Speech at Midland International Arbitration Union, Birmingham, England, 1877
Ulysses Grant, 1822–1885
Eighteenth president of the United States of America, 1869–1877

Ethical Consideration

Should a Business Have a Pension Plan?

You own a small business that manufactures commercial-grade carpeting. You pay your employees either on an hourly or a commission basis. You always have been concerned about the welfare of your employees and their families. Because of this concern, you provide a pension plan. As you review your financial statements, however, you realize that the expense of the pension plan is 5 percent of the business's gross sales. In the competitive global environment, this cost will impede your ability to remain competitive. You consider whether to increase your employees' pay and eliminate the pension benefits.

Many of your employees believe that they will retire comfortably with income from Social Security, and they are not concerned with retirement benefits. Most of your employees are under forty and do not realize that in 2004 the maximum annual benefit paid by Social Security to persons aged sixty-five who paid the maximum amount into Social Security was $19,920. The average Social Security benefit was far less and was insufficient to support a person beyond a minimum standard of living. As a result of increasing economic costs, many senior citizens are forced onto welfare programs and become an economic drain on taxpayers.

Today, as the population ages, the average number of years between retirement and death is increasing. In 1934, when Social Security was enacted, the retirement age was sixty-five. At that time less than 4 percent of the population was sixty-five or older. Today, 4 percent of the population is more than ninety years old. Predictions suggest that the Social Security system will pay a reduced retirement by the time people who currently are in their twenties or thirties reach retirement age if Congress fails to act to ensure financial security for the Social Security trust fund.

The 1980s saw a major decrease in the benefits offered by businesses to their employees. Employers cut or eliminated pension plans. By the mid-1980s, more than half of all workers were not covered by any pension plan. When these plans were abolished, the employers normally increased the hourly rate paid to employees. Some studies have shown that employees did not take the increase in pay and place it in a retirement plan.

You consider your knowledge about the Social Security system in deciding whether to end the pension plan and increase your employees' wages. What ethical responsibilities do you have for making provisions for the retirement of your youthful employees? Use the ethical model presented in Chapter 2 and reprinted on the inside front cover to develop your answer.

Introduction

In the past, the freedom to contract, as applied to employment, gave rise to perceived inequities in the employer–employee relationship and resulted in abuses, such as child labor, dangerous working conditions, and worker discrimination. These abuses produced two major responses in the United States. First, the federal government passed national legislation setting work standards, prohibiting discrimination, and creating safety laws. Second, workers began to unionize to gain a more powerful position in bargaining with management.

The earliest attempts by Congress to set employment standards were ruled unconstitutional on grounds that the laws infringed on an individual's right to contract. Over time, the courts began to limit employers' power in employment contracts and to recognize Congress' constitutional power to regulate employment practices under the commerce clause of Article I, Section 8, of the U.S. Constitution.

Today, unions make up less than 20 percent of the American workforce. Governmental employees, both federal and state, make up 15 percent of the workforce. Sixty-five percent of all American workers are employed at will (without a written contract covering a period of time). Regardless of the worker's contractual category, the employer must meet certain minimum standards for pay, hours, and working conditions. This chapter discusses the legislation that protects employees. Then it looks at the rights of employees to form unions and describes unions' functions.

Artiste Login. Carlo and Carlotta's online business, Artiste Login Products, Inc., employs a number of employees. Which federal and state laws apply to their business? Should they lease employees for the business or should they hire independent contractors? All businesses need to answer these questions.

Fair Labor Standards Act

The **Fair Labor Standards Act (FLSA)** of 1938 established minimum wage requirements[1] and overtime standards.[2] The act also prohibits certain types of child labor. The Department of Labor[3] (DOL) enforces the FLSA. The department has many record-keeping requirements with which businesses must comply. The DOL also determines if businesses are complying with the FLSA. Failure to file reports or maintain required government-mandated reports can result in criminal prosecution.

Who Is Covered?

The FLSA is an extensive statute based on the commerce clause of Article I of the Constitution. Commerce is the production, sale, and purchase of goods of any type. The commerce clause gives Congress the power to regulate interstate and foreign commerce.

The FLSA affects more than 70 million full-time and part-time workers. The fundamental standards set forth in the act apply to workers employed in government, unions, and private industry. For the FLSA to apply to employees in private industry, the employee must be (1) engaged in commerce, (2) engaged in production of goods to be placed in commerce, or (3) employed in an enterprise engaged in commerce.

The first two categories involve the "employee test," which considers the nature of the employee's work, not the nature of the business. In the third category, the controlling factor is the nature of the business. If the enterprise is covered, all the employees are covered, regardless of the relationship between their duties and commerce.

The FLSA explains that certain employer actions constitute a punishable violation of the statute and the rules promulgated under it. Understanding the meaning of *employer* for purposes of the act is key to determining the actions that violate the statute.

The FLSA's definition of the term *employer* is extremely broad. An employer "includes any person acting directly or indirectly in the interest of an employer in relation to an employee." An individual, such as a corporate officer, who actively participates in the running of a business, including the employment practices of the business, is an employer within the meaning of the statute. Such an individual will be liable personally, along with the corporation, for any violations of the act and, therefore, will be liable for the payment of any fines under the act.

An employer who violates the FLSA is liable in a civil action to the employee, who may recover from the employer unpaid wages, overtime compensation, liquidated damages, and reasonable attorneys' fees. Courts are authorized by the statute to issue injunctions restraining further violations. The employer may be prosecuted criminally by the federal government. If found guilty, the employer may be punished by a fine of up to $10,000 for the first offense and by a fine of up to $10,000, plus imprisonment for up to six months, for subsequent violations.

Exempt Employees

Congress allows exemptions to the act; otherwise, businesses could not function. The statute narrowly defines each exemption.

The employer must meet each element of the statutory exemption. Some of the industries exempted from the FLSA include agriculture, commercial fishing, some retail service businesses, and domestic services. In addition, many white-collar positions are not covered by the act because these individuals are believed to be capable of protecting themselves from the employer abuses that the FLSA prohibits.

Wage and Hour Requirements

Both state and federal statutes govern workers' minimum wage and maximum hour requirements. For the most part, state laws are consistent with the FLSA. Most businesses are subject to the federal act; thus, the FLSA is the most important guarantee of proper treatment for employees.

Wages. The minimum wage was initially $0.25 an hour in 1938. Periodically, Congress has increased this amount. In 1997, the minimum wage was raised to $5.15 an hour. The increases in the minimum wage over the years are shown in Exhibit 22–1.

---

[1] For the history of the minimum wage, go to the following Department of Labor Web site: http://www.dol.gov/esa/minwage/coverage.htm.

[2] For information on overtime standards, go to http://www.dol.gov/dol/topic/wages/overtimepay.htm.

[3] The Department of Labor's home page is http://www.dol.gov/.

Exhibit 22–1   Federal Minimum Wage Chart

Year	Minimum Wage
1938	$0.25
1945	$0.45
1950	$0.75
1960	$1.15
1965	$1.25
1970	$1.60
1975	$2.10
1980	$3.10
1981	$3.35
1990	$3.80
1991	$4.25 ($3.61 was a training wage that could be paid for a maximum of 180 days)
1996	$4.75
1997	$5.15 ($4.25 is a training wage paid to those under twenty years of age during the first 90 days on the job)

The FLSA provides for an exception to the minimum wage in the case of tipped employees, defined as those who customarily and regularly receive more than $20 a month in tips. In such cases, the employer may consider the tips as part of the wages, but the wage credit (tips) must not exceed 50 percent of the minimum wage.

The federal government has not preempted this area. A state or local government can set a higher minimum wage than the current federal minimum wage. The state or local law applies only within that government's jurisdiction. No conflict with federal law exists since the FLSA only sets a minimum wage.

Hours. An employer must pay employees for all hours worked in a week. The definition of working time, however, is not completely clear. Generally, the hours worked—those for which an individual must be paid at least the minimum wage and must be included when computing total hours worked to determine overtime hours—encompass all the time that an employee is actually at work or is required to be on duty and that the employee is not free to use for her own purposes.

For example, police officers are regularly required to be at work twenty minutes ahead of the hour, at 7:40 A.M., to change into their uniforms and be in formation by 8 A.M. The officers must be paid for those twenty minutes in addition to their eight-hour shifts.

The calculation and payment of overtime wages can be confusing and is usually the source of many employer–employee misunderstandings. Violations of the FLSA's requirement for overtime wages can occur easily because the formulas for determining overtime pay are complex and appear at times to be unfair and illogical.

The FLSA stipulates that when an employee has worked in excess of forty hours for one workweek, that employee must be paid no less than one and one-half times his regular hourly rate for any hours worked in excess of forty. Overtime is not one and one-half times minimum wage, but one and one-half times the employee's regular wages.

Changes to FLSA

The Department of Labor proposed changes to the FLSA that have been approved by Congress. These proposed changes make major changes to the payment of time and one-half for overtime. Businesses can use "comp time" to compensate an employee instead of paying time-and-a-half for those who worked more than forty hours per week. The employee must agree to this approach prior to working the forty-plus hours. The employer is prohibited from using threats to force the employee to accept comp time. The employee must use this comp time by the end of the year. If it is not used, then the employer must pay twice the amount of the unused time.

Anyone earning more than $65,000 per year is exempt from the provisions of the FLSA. Under prior regulations, managers earning $8,060 or less were automatically covered at time-and-a-half for overtime. Now that amount has been increased to $22,100.

Investigation and Enforcement Procedures. The Wage and Hour Division (WHD)[4] of the Department of Labor has the primary responsibility for enforcing and administering the FLSA. The WHD has officers throughout the United States who conduct

[4]For information on the Wage and Hour Division of the Department of Labor, see http://www.dol.gov/esa/whd.

LEGAL HIGHLIGHT

Exemptions and Requirements under the Minimum Wage

Certain employees are exempt from both the minimum wage and overtime provisions of the FLSA. Some of the exempt employees include:

1. Executive, administrative, and professional employees, including teachers in elementary or secondary schools
2. Employees of certain enterprises, if the annual gross income of the business is under $500,000
3. Employees of seasonal amusement or recreational businesses
4. Employees of small newspapers that have a circulation of less than 4,000
5. Switchboard operators of small telephone companies with less than 750 stations
6. Sailors employed on foreign vessels
7. Employees engaged in fishing operations
8. Certain farm workers
9. Casual babysitters and people employed as companions to the elderly or infirm.

Employers are required to keep records on their nonexempt workers. The following items must be kept on file for the employees who are subject to minimum wage and overtime provisions:

1. Personal information, including name, home address, occupation, gender, and birth date
2. Hour and day when the workweek begins
3. Total hours worked each workweek and workday
4. Total daily or weekly straight-time earnings
5. Regular hourly pay rate for any week when overtime is worked
6. Total overtime pay for the workweek
7. Deductions from or additions to wages
8. Total wages paid each pay period
9. Date of payment and pay period covered.

investigations and gather data on wages, hours, and other employment conditions.

The FLSA provides several methods for recovering unpaid wages. Methods include supervision by the WHD of the employer's payment of back wages, court action by the secretary of labor to collect unpaid wages, a lawsuit by the employee for unpaid wages and attorneys' fees, and an injunction obtained by the secretary of labor to restrain employers from further FLSA violations.

Child Labor Laws

The FLSA provisions that govern child labor are straightforward and the penalties for violating these standards are severe. The child labor laws are part of public policy. They ensure that each minor has the opportunity to attend school. They also prohibit the employment of children in hazardous jobs or under working conditions that endanger their health or well-being.

An individual who is over seventeen years old falls outside of the statute's child labor provisions. Minors between the ages of sixteen and seventeen can be employed with restrictions. Certain industries are considered to be dangerous and, therefore, off limits to sixteen- and seventeen-year-olds. In addition, children between fourteen and fifteen years old may be employed only in specially approved jobs, including at retail stores, restaurants, and service stations.

Children under the age of fourteen can only work in certain occupations, such as agricultural employment, and are subject to FLSA regulations requiring school obligations. Young actors, actresses, and performers also are exempt, when certain conditions from the FLSA prohibitions against child labor are met.

Retirement and Income Security

Federal and state governments have established programs and laws to cover the financial impact on employees of retirement, disability, death, hospitalization, and unemployment. The Social Security Administration[5] administers many of the laws in this area.

Social Security

The key federal law in this area is the **Social Security Act**[6] of 1935. Social Security is more formally known as **Old Age, Survivors, and Disability Insurance (OASDI)**. Both employers and employees must contribute in equal amounts under the **Federal Insurance Contributions Act (FICA)** to help fund Social Security. The contribution amount is a percentage of the employee's annual wage base. (The annual wage base is the maximum amount of an employee's wages that are subject to the tax.)

Social Security pays a monthly benefit to employees when they retire, if they have contributed to FICA. If a worker takes early retirement between ages sixty-two and sixty-four, Social Security will pay a reduced amount. The percentage increases the longer a worker waits to collect. If a retiree waits until age sixty-five, she is eligible for the full monthly benefit. The age for full retirement, however, is gradually being increased.

Social Security disability benefits are available to workers at any age who become disabled prior to retirement age. If a worker reaches age sixty-five, disability benefits are called retirement benefits and the monthly amount remains the same. Minors with disabilities also may collect disability benefits.

For workers who die, the nonworking spouse and minor children may collect survival benefits. Minor children receive more benefits from Social Security than any other federal program. More than 1.9 million children receive survivor's benefits in any year. Out of 100 parents who die leaving minor children, 98 percent of the children qualify for these benefits.

The nation's largest health insurance program, **Medicare**,[7] covers 37 million people. It provides health coverage for people sixty-five years old and older and for those with disabilities who are under age sixty-five. The **Center for Medicare & Medicaid Services (CMS)**[8] administers Medicare.

Medicare has two parts. One pertains to hospital costs and the other to nonhospital medical costs, such as doctors' office visits. People who have Medicare hospital insurance can obtain additional medical insurance for small monthly premiums that increase as medical care costs increase.

For decades, full-retirement age was sixty-five. Beginning with people born in 1938 or later, however, the full-retirement age increases gradually until it reaches sixty-seven for people born after 1959, as shown in Exhibit 22-2.

Exhibit 22-2   Full-Retirement Age Chart

Year of Birth	Full Retirement Age
1937 or earlier	65
1938	65 and 2 months
1939	65 and 4 months
1940	65 and 6 months
1941	65 and 8 months
1942	65 and 10 months
1943–1954	66
1955	66 and 2 months
1956	66 and 4 months
1957	66 and 6 months
1958	66 and 8 months
1959	66 and 10 months
1960 and later	67

Private Retirement Plans

Employers may offer retirement plans to their employees. These plans supplement Social Security benefits. The **Employee Retirement Income Security Act (ERISA)**[9] of 1974 governs the financing, vesting, and administration of private pension plans for workers. The Department of Labor (through the Pension Benefit Guaranty Corporation and the Labor Management Services Administration) and the Treasury Department enforce ERISA's provisions.

[5]The Social Security Administration's Web site is http://www.ssa.gov.

[6]For information about Social Security, go to http://www.ssa.gov about.htm. For a history of the Social Security Act, see http://www.ssa.gov/history/law.html.

[7]For information about Medicare, see the following Web site: http://www.ssa.gov/mediinfo.htm.

[8]CMS has a Web page at http://cms.hhs.gov/default.asp?fromhcfadotgov=true.

[9]Information on ERISA can be found at http://www.dol.gov/dol/topic/health-plans/erisa.htm.

Unemployment Compensation

The **Federal Unemployment Tax Act (FUTA)** of 1954 established a federal-state partnership to cover unemployed workers. FUTA operates through the state system to provide unemployment compensation to eligible individuals—those who worked a certain minimum number of weeks, earned wages in a certain amount, and are currently involuntarily out of work. Unemployment insurance is funded by employers who pay into the fund. The proceeds are paid to qualified unemployed workers.

The cost of administering the unemployment insurance program is paid by the federal government

---

LEGAL HIGHLIGHT

Social Security and You

Before the government pays you any Social Security benefits, you must have earned credit for a certain amount of work, measured in "quarters of coverage." You earn a maximum of four quarters a year (three months is a quarter). If the Social Security Act covers your job, you have an individual lifetime earnings record established at the Social Security Administration (SSA) headquarters in Baltimore, Maryland. Your earnings are reported under your name and Social Security number. You should check on your Social Security statement every three years to ensure that your record is properly credited.

Use one of these methods to obtain your Personal Earnings and Benefit Estimate Statement (PEBE). First, call the SSA at 1-800-SSA-1213 (1-800-772-1213) and request your PEBE. Second, visit your local SSA office, fill out the "Request for Statement of Earnings," and send it in. Third, you can download the forms used to request your PEBE at the Social Security Administration Web site: **http://www.ssa.gov/**. You then fill out the form and mail it in. Fourth, if you have security software on your computer, you can check your PEBE online. Additionally, the SSA automatically sends a PEBE to people approaching retirement age.

The PEBE provides a summary of your account, listing the last three years individually. You can correct a mistake immediately (yes, by sending in another form along with your W-2 forms). If a mistake appears in your record at retirement, your Social Security check will be reduced because your account inaccurately reflects the amount of money you have actually paid into Social Security.

The following chart indicates the distribution of each dollar that you pay into Social Security.

Distribution of a Dollar Paid into Social Security

Dollar	Distributed
70 cents	Paid into a trust fund that pays monthly benefits to retirees and their families and to surviving spouses and children of workers who have died.
19 cents	Paid into a trust fund that pays for the health care of all Medicare beneficiaries.
11 cents	Paid into a trust fund that pays benefits to people with disabilities and their families.
less than 1 cent	Administrative costs paid from the trust funds.

The Social Security trust fund invests the money not used to pay benefits and administrative expenses in U.S. government bonds, generally considered the safest of all investments. Congress has borrowed from the Social Security trust funds to pay for other services and projects provided to citizens.

Will Social Security be available when you need it? The Social Security's Board of Trustees prepares an annual report on the financial soundness of the Social Security program. As currently structured, Social Security can pay benefits for the next three decades. To correct the long-term funding problem, Congress needs to act.

The media often state that Social Security will be broke in the future. If Congress does nothing, the trust fund will be able to pay benefits for many decades at a reduced rate. To see if Congress has the time needed to make changes to protect Social Security, visit the SSA Web site where you can read the SSA trustees' studies on this topic.

out of the tax collected. This program is not a welfare program in that the unemployed person does not have to show a need to receive benefits. The decision to grant or deny benefits is based on whether the individual is willing and able to work and was involuntarily terminated. The following case concerns whether the employer was entitled to reimbursement on Social Security and FUTA taxes paid.

CASE 22.1

United States Court of Appeals, Sixth Circuit, 2000
215 F.3d 1325

CLEVELAND INDIANS BASEBALL COMPANY v. UNITED STATES

BACKGROUND AND FACTS Major League Baseball Clubs (Clubs) and the Major League Baseball Players Association (MLBPA) were involved in three separate grievances in 1990. The MLBPA claimed that the Clubs breached the collective bargaining agreement (CBA) with respect to free agency rights of the baseball players in 1986, 1987, and 1988. After an arbitration panel issued a series of rulings adverse to the Clubs, the Clubs and the MLBPA settled their grievances. The Clubs were required to contribute $280 million to a custodial account for distribution to affected players.

The Cleveland Indians Baseball Company's (Cleveland) share of the settlement fund was $610,000 for the 1986 season and $1,457,848 for the 1987 season. Cleveland received the funds in 1994 and distributed those funds to the following affected players: eight players employed in 1986 and fifteen players employed in 1987. Unsure as to the tax treatment of these distributions, Cleveland paid FICA and FUTA taxes on the total funds as if the payments were wages for services rendered in 1994. Cleveland paid these tax obligations in 1994 and 1995. None of the affected players, however, performed services for Cleveland in 1994 or 1995.

Cleveland filed this action seeking a refund of the FICA and FUTA taxes paid to the United States. Cleveland claimed the funds constituted nontaxable interest; and the non-interest portion was not taxable because the funds were damages for the wrongful breach and not wages for services rendered. Finally, even if the payments constituted wages for services, Cleveland argued that it should have paid taxes at the 1986 and 1987 tax rates applicable when the services were rendered. Because the 1986 and 1987 FICA and FUTA taxes of each of the affected players had been paid up to the maximum required amount from another source, Cleveland asserted that it was entitled to a full refund if the payments were determined to be wages for services rendered in 1986 and 1987.

The government initially disputed Cleveland's claims. Both parties eventually agreed, however, that $629,000 of the payments from the settlement fund to affected players constituted interest and were not subject to FICA and FUTA taxes. Cleveland was entitled to a refund for taxes paid on the interest portion of the settlement. The parties also agreed that the remaining portion of the payments, approximately $2 million, constituted back-wage payments, earnings that would have been paid in 1986 and 1987 but for the Clubs' breach of the CBA. The court needed to determine the appropriate tax year for the back-wage payments made in 1994 for services rendered in the 1986 and 1987 baseball seasons.

PER CURIAM

. . . .

In the district court, the government and [Cleveland] agreed that our decision in *Bowman v. United States* directly addressed this precise issue. The *Bowman* court held that "a settlement for back wages should not be allocated to the period when the employer finally pays but 'should be allocated to the periods when the regular wages were not paid as usual.'" Following *Bowman,* the district court entered judgment in favor of [Cleveland] and ordered the United States to refund the FICA and FUTA taxes paid on the settlement disbursements designated as back wages, including interest from the dates on which the payments were made.

. . . .

Here, our precedent clearly indicates that the statutory provision in question requires settlements for back wages to be allocated to the period in which they were earned or should have been paid, and not to the period in which the back wages were actually disbursed. The government contends that *Bowman* was wrongly decided, arguing that the plain language, legislative history and applicable FICA and FUTA Treasury Regulations demonstrate that back wages are subject to tax in the year in which payment is made and not in which the services were rendered. In addition, the government cites cases from our sister circuits that are at odds with our *Bowman* holding. Despite these arguments, the government "agrees with taxpayer that the issue presented in this case was decided in *Bowman.*"

Even if we were persuaded by the government's argument, we are bound by the *Bowman* decision.

. . . .

DECISION AND REMEDY The decision of the trial court was upheld. The baseball club was able to recover all sums it had paid for both Social Security and unemployment taxes for the players.

CRITICAL THINKING: POLITICAL CONSIDERATION In the normal course of events, if the baseball club paid the wages to the players in 1986 and 1987, it would have also paid both the Social Security and unemployment taxes. An arbitration panel found that the baseball club violated its own collective bargaining agreement with the players. The result in this case, however, was that this baseball club and other clubs did not have to pay these taxes because these taxes had been paid from another source. Is this a just result?

Other Statutes for Employee Protection

Over the years, a variety of state and federal statutes have provided protection to employees. Workers' compensation laws protect employees and their families financially from the risk of accidental injury, death, or disease resulting from their employment. Employers are required by federal laws to provide their employees with health and safety protection on the job. Employees must be informed by their employers when a plant will permanently close. Workers are entitled to leave when they or their family members are ill. Finally, workers are entitled to some privacy in the workplace. The following sections discuss these statutes.

State Workers' Compensation Acts

Workers' compensation laws provide economic protection for workers who are injured on the job. These laws provide for payment of hospital and medical costs incurred by an injured person. The worker also receives disability pay until he can return to the job. In most cases, this income is much less than the worker's regular pay. If a worker is killed on the job, his family receives death benefits. A state agency with administrative quasi-judicial powers administers workers' compensation laws. All rulings of these agencies are subject to review by the courts.

The right to recover under workers' compensation laws is provided to the injured employee without regard to the negligence or fault of the employer. The right to recover is predicated on the employment relationship and the fact that the injury arose out of the employment. Basically, employers are under a system of strict liability, which was discussed in Chapters 8 and 11. Few, if any, defenses exist for employers in workers' compensation cases.

The simple, two-pronged test for determining employee eligibility for workers' compensation consists of the following questions:

1. Was the injury accidental?
2. Did the injury arise out of and in the course of employment?

Intentionally inflicted self-injuries are not considered accidental and are not covered. In the past, heart attacks or other medical problems arising from preexisting disease or physical conditions were not covered. Recently, however, the courts have started to treat these medical problems as covered under the act. Some states have limited by legislation the recovery possible when an employee suffers a heart attack.

In most cases, an employee cannot bring legal action against an employer while receiving workers' compensation benefits, but can bring action against third persons who may have caused the injuries. The following case discusses the question of whether an employee's injuries were caused by the intentional or reckless conduct of the employer and, if so, whether the employee can obtain damages in addition to workers' compensation.

CASE 22.2 District Court of Appeal of Florida, Fifth District, 1997 689 So. 2d 416	# MYRICK v. LUHRS CORPORATION **BACKGROUND AND FACTS** Myrick, the plaintiff, amputated several of his fingers while operating a cut-off saw for his employer, Luhrs Corporation, the defendant. When Luhrs acquired the saw, it was equipped with various safety devices including (1) a work-presence sensor, which was designed so that the saw could function only if materials intended to be cut were on the saw's cutting table; (2) a double palm button safety interlock, which allowed the saw's activation only if both of the operator's hands were on the palm buttons, which were situated far enough from the cutting mechanism to preclude contact between the operator's hands and the cutting mechanism; (3) numerous safety warnings, prominently displayed on various surfaces of the saw, advising any operator of those aspects of operation most likely to result in serious injury or death; (4) a safety panel enclosing the saw's inner workings to prevent unintended operation of the saw; and (5) a free-swinging saw mechanism, allowing the quick removal of any object contacting with the saw blade. Over a period of time, Luhrs removed all of these safety devices. As a result, Myrick injured himself and suffered from physical pain and suffering, mental anguish, loss of the capacity for the enjoyment of life, loss of future earning capacity, and medical expenses. Myrick appealed a trial court's order that ruled that Myrick was limited to his remedies under the Florida Workers' Compensation Act. Myrick claimed that Luhrs had committed an intentional act.

Judge W. SHARP

The courts have long concluded that intentional acts or torts are not included in the scope of the workers' compensation statute. A potential basis for liability survives the workers' compensation exclusivity provisions, if an employer has engaged in intentional acts designed to result in, or that are substantially certain to result in the injury or death of an employee. The injury suffered must be a virtual certainty, not just a strong probability stemming from the employer's actions.

This is a close case. Myrick has alleged that his employer's removal of the various safety devices from the chop saw created a virtual certainty of injury or death to the operator.

. . . .

Reading Myrick's complaint most strongly in his favor as we must do, he alleged his employer deliberately removed or disabled five essential safety devices designed to allow an operator to run the saw without exposing himself to certain danger. Myrick also alleged that he had no knowledge or warning he was being exposed to danger by merely operating the saw. From these allegations, one can infer some cover-up on the part of the employer. Whether Myrick can sustain these allegations with sufficient proofs at a summary judgment or trial, is a different question, not ripe for our consideration.

DECISION AND REMEDY The court allowed Myrick to proceed in the trial court on his intentional tort claim unrestricted by the workers' compensation act.

CRITICAL THINKING: LEGAL ISSUE If employees can sue an employer for an intentional tort, should employees be able to sue when they are injured as a result of the employer's negligent conduct?

Health and Safety Protection

The **Occupational Safety and Health Act** of 1970 was passed to ensure safe and healthful working conditions for practically every employee in the country. The act created the **Occupational Safety and Health Administration (OSHA)**,[10] the Occupational Safety and Health Review Commission, and the National Institute for Occupational Safety and Health. OSHA promulgates and enforces workers' safety and health standards. It also conducts inspections and investigations, requires employers to keep detailed records of worker injuries and illnesses, and conducts research.

OSHA's enforcement policy is twofold. First, it deals with egregious situations on a case-by-case basis, using violation-by-violation citations. Second, it enforces settlements at the corporate, rather than at the plant, level. Both policies allow OSHA to seek large penalties. In addition to assessing civil penalties, OSHA has the power to close a plant.

OSHA first employed the egregious citation strategy against Union Carbide in 1986 after finding flagrant disregard for record-keeping requirements. Violation-by-violation citations and the corresponding penalties were issued for each of the hundreds of instances of the alleged record-keeping infractions. OSHA also sought penalties for alleged violations ranging from $4 million from John Morrell Corporation for health violations in its meat-packing plants to

$7 million from USX Corporation steel plants for safety violations.

Despite OSHA's efforts, every year more than 6,000 Americans die from workplace injuries, an estimated 50,000 people die from illnesses caused by workplace chemical exposures, and 6 million people suffer nonfatal workplace injuries. Injuries alone cost the economy more than $110 billion a year. Many of these workplace injuries and illnesses are predictable and preventable.

To increase worker health and safety and to decrease paperwork, OSHA is changing its focus. To spur the spread of health and safety programs, employers will be offered a clear choice: partnership or traditional enforcement.

OSHA will work with firms that create and implement strong and effective health and safety programs as a partner. For firms with a history of endangering their employees that indicate an unwillingness to change, OSHA will rigorously enforce the law without compromise to ensure serious consequences for violators.

Most OSHA inspections are initiated as the result of an employee's written complaint. OSHA protects the identity of the complaining employee. As an added protection, the act prohibits the discharge of, or any discrimination against, an employee who, by submitting a formal complaint against an employer, exercises her rights under the statute. An employee who believes that she has been discriminated against for bringing possible violations to OSHA's attention may file a complaint. An investigation will be conducted

---

[10]The home page for the Occupational Safety and Health Administration is http://www.osha.gov.

and, if appropriate, a lawsuit may be filed on behalf of the employee in federal court.

In the following case, the question arose as to whether the business had actual or constructive notice of an OSHA regulation. Actual notice occurs when the person has the information or is aware that he possesses the information. Constructive notice is based on a rule of law and not on the facts of a particular situation. The law deems that a person has constructive notice if he should have known about the information.

CASE 22.3

United States Court of Appeals, Fifth Circuit, 1991
926 F.2d 422

CORBESCO INC. v. DOLE

BACKGROUND AND FACTS Corbesco, Inc., is an industrial roofing and siding installation company that was hired to install flat metal roofs and siding over the skeletal structure of five aircraft hangars at the Chennault Air Base in Lake Charles, Louisiana.

Before the ironworkers could lay the aluminum sheet metal roofing, they had to install insulation. To accomplish this, they would shake the insulation rolls out onto the exposed grid of rafters, just as one might shake out a bedspread over a bed.

The ironworkers had to stand or kneel on the edge of the roof. Because the workers had to maintain their balance while leaning over the edge, high winds were very dangerous. Corbesco regularly sought wind and weather forecasts from the National Weather Service.

On April 2, 1987, Roger Mathew was on his knees shaking out insulation when a gust of wind caught the sheet of insulation that he held and pulled him forward. He lost his balance and fell sixty feet through the open structure of steel to the concrete below. Mathew was killed by the fall. The record did not reveal whether Corbesco had telephoned the National Weather Service that day.

The Occupational Safety and Health Administration regulation required safety nets "when workplaces are more than 25 feet above ground or water surface, or other surfaces where the use of ladders, scaffolds, catch platforms, temporary floors, safety lines, or safety belts is impractical."

The OSHA compliance officer inspected the hangar where Mathew had fallen. The OSHA officer cited Corbesco and assessed a $1,000 penalty for failing to install a safety net under the roof. Both the OSHA compliance officer and Corbesco agreed that only safety nets were practical. After being cited, Corbesco installed a safety net in the unfinished hangar. Corbesco filed a notice of contest with the Department of Labor to dispute the OSHA citation and penalty.

An administrative law judge (ALJ) held a hearing. Corbesco proved that the custom of the industry was that ironworkers did not use safety nets while working on flat roofs. OSHA inspectors had made several inspections of the hangar construction project while roofing work was in progress. None had instructed Corbesco to use safety nets.

Corbesco argued that it had no knowledge of the regulation and had no way of knowing that it was in violation. Corbesco had a good safety program. The ALJ reduced the penalty to $50. Corbesco petitioned the appellate court to review the ALJ's decision.

Although the case fails to clarify the point, Corbesco may have appealed the $50 penalty for any number of reasons including higher insurance rates as a result of the OSHA citation, to have a clean record with OSHA, or to preclude liability to Mathew's estate beyond workers' compensation. The court was bound by the ALJ's finding of fact.

Circuit Judge THORNBERRY

. . . .

. . . [T]he Secretary has the burden to prove that Corbesco had actual or constructive notice [of the regulation that] required it to install a safety net. . . .

. . . .

Falling from the edge of a flat roof is not a common hazard in the roofing industry. Nevertheless, the Commission has frequently held that the regulation requires an employer to furnish either a safety net or one of the other enumerated safety devices if its employees are working near the perimeter of a flat roof more than twenty-five feet above the ground; the roof cannot serve as a temporary floor. . . . Though the wording of the regulation remains imprecise, the Commission has now elucidated its meaning. In the light of these decisions, Corbesco had a duty to at least inquire whether it had to install safety nets under the hangars. Therefore, we find that Corbesco had constructive notice of the duties imposed upon it, and its constitutional rights were not violated.

. . . .

The Secretary did not violate Corbesco's right to due process because Corbesco had constructive notice that it was required to install safety nets under its crew while they were working in the edge of a flat roof some sixty feet above a concrete floor. . . . A reasonable construction company in Corbesco's position would have known about these interpretations of this standard.

DECISION AND REMEDY The court held that because Corbesco had constructive notice of the regulation, it was required to install safety nets while the ironworkers were working on the edge of a flat roof some sixty feet above a concrete floor. Corbesco had a duty to at least inquire of OSHA as to whether it had to install a safety net.

Corbesco did not argue that it was not economically feasible to install safety nets in the aircraft hangars. If any construction company believes the cost of complying with an OSHA standard will outweigh the benefits of enhanced safety, the company can seek a variance from the standard rather than wait until it is cited. In this case, Corbesco failed to pursue this alternative.

CRITICAL THINKING: POLITICAL CONSIDERATION Why should a business be held liable for violating a regulation when the government inspectors failed to bring the regulation to its attention?

C Y B E R L A W

Filing Complaints Online

The employment field actively uses the Internet. Most governmental agencies have a Web site for persons to research a given area of labor law. If employees believe they have a complaint against the employer, they can file an online complaint with the appropriate agency.

For example, a business may be operating in a dangerous condition that affects employee safety and health. An employee may anonymously report this condition to the Occupational Safety and Health Administration using the Internet.[11]

[11]The Web address for reporting dangerous conditions is http://www. osha.gov/as/opa/worker/complain.html.

The problem confronting a business is how to deal with these complaints when they do not have any basis. A disgruntled employee may file a report just to get even with the boss. This report is made with the understanding that the employee's name will never be disclosed. This secrecy is not fair to the businessperson who is following the law. But a rule that allowed disclosure might discourage an employee from reporting a dangerous condition because, otherwise, he might be terminated if his identity were disclosed. Obviously, the employer would ensure that the termination is on other grounds than that of filing the report, because, the employer is liable if the termination is based solely on the filing of the report.

The employee who files the complaint, even if done from his personally owned computer at home, must be aware of a pitfall: If the employer sues the employee for any reason, the employer may request the court to seize the employee's computer in order for the employer's computer expert to examine the hard drive for any e-mails or computer files concerning the matter. Of course, the employee may raise an objection with the court and provide reasons why the court should not issue a seizure order for the computer. If the court does grant the request, however, the employer effectively has access to everything on the employee's computer, including online complaints.

Plant Closing Law

In 1988, Congress passed the **Worker Adjustment and Retraining Notification Act (WARN)**, more commonly called the **Plant Closing Act**, requiring businesses to notify employees sixty days in advance if a plant will close. Businesses also must give workers advance notice of a mass layoff that includes more than one-third of the company's employees. WARN applies to businesses employing more than 100 employees.

Family and Medical Leave Act

Passed in 1993, the **Family and Medical Leave Act**[12] provides that employees can take up to twelve weeks of unpaid leave for the birth or adoption of a child, for the care of an immediate family member, or for a serious health condition. The act requires that the employee must have worked for the employer for at least twelve months and must have worked 1,250 hours before being eligible for leave.

A thirty-day notice must be provided to the employer whenever possible. Accrued paid leave, such as vacation or sick time, may be used as part of the twelve weeks. The twelve weeks may be consecutive or may be taken in blocks of time or by working a reduced workweek. For the birth or adoption of a child, however, the worker must take consecutive leave unless the employer agrees to intermittent leave. This act applies to both private and public employees.

Employers with fifty employees or more are subject to the act. Thus, nearly one-half of the nation's workforce is covered. If a health plan is part of the employee's benefit package, the employer must maintain the health plan during the leave period.

Once the leave is over, the employer must reinstate the worker to the same or an equivalent job. Medical verification of the employee's or the family member's condition may be requested. Key salaried employees who are among the highest paid 10 percent in the company may be exempted by the employer, if the absence would cause the employer substantial and grievous economic harm.

The Labor Department has issued the Birth and Adoption Unemployment Compensation Rule, which provides for partial wage replacement under the unemployment compensation program. This rule is on a voluntary and experimental basis. It offers a parent unemployment compensation if leave is taken or he or she otherwise leaves employment following the birth or adoption of a child.

Medical Coverage

Two federal statutes have protected many persons from losing their medical insurance when they leave their employment. The **Consolidated Omnibus Budget Reconciliation Act (COBRA)** was passed in 1985. Prior to this act's passage, a worker's group health coverage was terminated when the worker lost her job, reduced the hours, or changed employment.

Now, when employees are terminated, change employment, or lose health coverage because of reduced work hours, they may buy group coverage for themselves and their families for a limited time period, usually no longer than eighteen months.

The act requires health plans to notify employees entitled to COBRA benefits of the right to continue benefits provided by the plan. Employees must accept coverage within sixty days or lose all rights to benefits. Once the former employee chooses COBRA coverage, he may be required to pay for the premium. The cost of the insurance is at the same rate as the former employer's contribution, plus a 2 percent surcharge.

InfoTrac Research Activity

In our current mobile society, many persons change jobs due to economic conditions. COBRA grants an employee or a divorced person rights to continue medical coverage after leaving a job. Go to InfoTrac and type in "Consolidated Omnibus Budget Reconciliation Act." Review four articles and write a report on the rights of employees.

[12]Information on the Family and Medical Leave Act is given at the following Web site: http://www.dol.gov/dol/compliance/comp-fmla.htm.

The second statute, the **Health Insurance Portability and Accountability Act (HIPAA)**,[13] passed in 1996, protects employees when they change jobs. The word *portability* is a misnomer because the insurance plan does not move with the employee. When a person moves from one employer to another, she must be accepted and charged the same premium for group health insurance as everyone else covered by the new employer's plan. The new employer's health-care plan must cover the employee and that person's family, including any preexisting medical problems.

HIPAA prohibits insurance companies from immediately discontinuing coverage under a plan. An insurance company must follow a specific and detailed set of regulations before it can stop offering a health plan under COBRA.

Neither statute requires a business to offer medical coverage. If the employer stops offering a group health plan, the employee must be allowed to purchase an individual plan, regardless of his health status.

Privacy Rights of Employees

The right of privacy is not stated explicitly in the U.S. Constitution. In 1928, the United States Supreme Court established the right of privacy. Justice Louis D. Brandeis (1916–1939) wrote that it is "the right to be let alone—the most comprehensive of rights and the right most valued by civilized man." The Court based this right on the Fourth Amendment's prohibition against illegal searches and seizures by the government.

Employees use the right of privacy to oppose testing for acquired immune deficiency syndrome (AIDS) and to limit the distribution of information contained in an employee's employment record. Other areas of privacy include polygraphs, drug testing, and employee records.

Polygraphs. For many years, both the government and private businesses used polygraph tests as a condition for employment, retention, or promotion. These tests presented one major problem: They had to be subjectively interpreted by an individual, so their validity was based on the training and knowledge of the interviewer.

Many innocent persons were denied employment based on inaccurate polygraph test interpretations.

To rectify this situation, Congress adopted the **Employee Polygraph Protection Act**[14] of 1988, making polygraph use unlawful except under restricted conditions. Among these exceptions are (1) national defense; (2) ongoing investigations; (3) drug security, drug theft, or drug diversion investigations; and (4) armored car and security personnel.

The major exception to the act is that of ongoing investigations. To request an employee take a polygraph test, an employer must meet three conditions. First, the test must be administered in connection with an ongoing investigation involving economic loss or injury to the employer's business. Second, the employee must have had access to the property that is the subject of the investigation. Third, the employer must have a reasonable suspicion that the employee was involved in the incident under investigation. The polygraph questions must relate to the incident. The employee can stop the test at any time. An employee must voluntarily take the test and cannot be fired solely for refusing to take a polygraph, without additional supporting evidence establishing that the employee was involved in a theft, embezzlement, or other unlawful activity against the employer.

Drug Testing. Approximately 70 to 75 percent of substance abusers—nearly 10 million people—are employed. One of every twelve full-time employees admits to current use of illicit drugs, while one in every ten admits to abusing alcohol. Drug- and alcohol-related problems are one of the four top reasons for the rise in workplace violence. Substance abuse costs businesses $10 billion annually.

Employers face a real impact on the bottom line when employees abuse substances. Some employers try to screen out a potential problem by testing applicants for drugs prior to hiring. Drug testing prior to hiring is legal.

Employers should have a workplace substance abuse program. An employer can test an employee if the employer believes the employee to be under the influence of alcohol or drugs while at work. Employees who hold sensitive jobs, such as national security employees, are tested randomly. Persons involved with aviation, railroads, trucking, or other jobs involved with public safety also are subject to random drug testing.

---

[13]Also referred to informally as the Kassebaum-Kennedy Act, so named for the act's sponsors in the Senate, Senator Nancy Kassebaum, Republican, Kansas, and Senator Edward M. Kennedy, Democrat, Massachusetts. The act often is incorrectly referred to as the Kennedy-Kassebaum Act. The Republicans held the majority of the seats in the Senate when the act was passed, so the Republican's name is placed before the Democrat's name.

[14]Information concerning employees' rights is located at http://www.dol.gov/asp/programs/guide/eppa.htm.

The real problem with random drug testing lies in testing people who work in nonsensitive jobs. The states are split on this issue, and Congress has not set a public policy. Some courts have found that random testing violates an individual's reasonable and legitimate expectation of privacy because of the personal information obtainable from a person's body fluids.

Employee Records. Two legal theories apply to the use and distribution of information contained in an employee's personnel file: defamation and invasion of the right to privacy. A defamation case is founded on an employer's communicating harmful information about a current or former employee. Courts grant most of these communications a limited privilege. As long as an employer is communicating with a prospective new employer, no legal issue arises unless the employee proves the first employer's comments to have been made maliciously. To limit a claim that an employer released the information with the intent of harming a former employee, an employer should disclose only the basic employment history. This information would be limited to job title, dates of employment, and ending salary.

If, in contrast, an employer communicates to current employees that a terminated employee was fired on the basis of ethical or other reasons, this communication can give rise to legal problems. These statements exceed the limited privilege that the law grants. Further, this communication can be considered an invasion of the right to privacy, even if the disclosure were true.

Labor Laws

Labor relations concern the relationship between management and labor over employment conditions. A union is an organization of employees who join to secure more favorable working conditions, pay, and benefits for the employees. Unions represent employees[15] and often are referred to as organized labor.

Employees vote for a union to represent them during collective bargaining. *Collective bargaining* is a process of negotiating an agreement between an employer and the authorized representative, the union, concerning working conditions, including wages, hours, safety, and other employment working conditions.

[15]A history of labor activities worldwide is located at http://www.iisg.nl/~ialhi/.

The history of labor relations stretches back to the early 1800s. Workers joined to request from management working conditions that were better than those where criminals labored. Workers gradually formed labor unions that advocated better working conditions. Employers discouraged union activity, sometimes forcibly, by employing strike breakers who would physically assault or even kill striking employees. Employers fired union organizers and union members and replaced them with immigrants who worked for cheaper wages.

Early legislation and agencies protecting employee rights, such as the National War Labor Board, which operated during World War I, were often temporary. Congress also restricted early legislation to a particular industry, such as the railroad industry. Congress passed the Railway Labor Act of 1926, which required railroads and their employees to attempt to enter into employment agreements through representatives chosen by each side.

Until the early 1930s, laws at the federal and state levels generally favored management. Beginning in 1932, however, Congress passed a number of statutes that improved the workers' rights to join unions and to engage in collective bargaining.

Today, employees in the public and private sectors have the right to organize and to bargain collectively. With the major exceptions of the military and some law enforcement employees, public employees have a statutory right to organize and bargain collectively, although generally they cannot strike.

The expanded Railway Labor Act covers rail and air carrier employees. Federal statutes fail to cover small businesses that do not affect interstate commerce. This chapter does not cover government employees, employees of small businesses, or rail and air carrier employees.

Four major statutes passed by Congress over a period of thirty years govern labor relations in the private sector. The purpose of these laws is to provide for peaceful and stable labor relations at the national level.

The four statutes are the Federal Anti-Injunction Act of 1932, the National Labor Relations Act of 1935, the Labor-Management Relations Act of 1947, and the Labor-Management Reporting and Disclosure Act of 1959. The following sections review these four statutes.

Federal Anti-Injunction Act

Congress protected peaceful strikes, picketing, and boycotts in 1932 with the passage of the **Federal**

LEGAL HIGHLIGHT

Genetic Testing

Medical biotechnology now can determine genetic information from minute bits of blood and tissue samples. Genetic information can point out certain characteristics in an individual that may lead to a disease process, such as colon cancer, or an inherited disease, such as Huntington's chorea. Carrying a genetic characteristic is not a disability until it develops into a physical disease.

Cases exist in which individuals have been discriminated against on the basis of results of genetic testing. As testing becomes more widely available and less expensive, more problems will arise in the employment field. For a small business, the cost of insurance becomes a financial problem.

Regardless of the size of a business, the employer must be concerned with the employee's privacy. Because federal law prohibits discrimination against people, the employer must take steps to prevent harassment and discrimination within the workplace against a person who has a disease characteristic or an inherited disease.

Employers, employees, and the government are working together to reach a resolution regarding testing employees when genetic information may be found. A recent government study showed that genetic information cannot really be separated from the rest of the employee's medical information. The report recommended that the employee's entire medical file be protected.

Anti-Injunction Act, more commonly known as the **Norris-LaGuardia Act**. The statute restricted the federal courts' power to issue injunctions against unions engaged in peaceful strikes. In effect, the act declared a national policy permitting employees to organize.

National Labor Relations Act

The **National Labor Relations Act (Wagner Act)** of 1935 established employees' rights to engage in collective bargaining and to strike. The Wagner Act created the **National Labor Relations Board (NLRB)**,[16] which is an independent federal agency that administers the act. The functions of the NLRB are discussed in more detail in a later section.

The Wagner Act defined a number of practices by employers as being unfair to labor:

[16]The Web site for the NLRB is http://www.nlrb.gov. A list of NLRB members and general counsel can be found at http://www. nlrb.gov/board.html. Decisions and opinions of the NLRB can be found at http://www.nlrb.gov/decision.html.

1. Interference with employees' efforts to form, join, or assist labor organizations;

2. An employer's domination of a labor organization or financial contribution or other types of support;

3. Discrimination in the hiring of, or awarding of tenure to, employees based on union affiliation;

4. Discrimination against employees for filing charges under the act or giving testimony under the act; and

5. Refusal to bargain collectively with the duly designated representative of the employees.

Until this act was passed, an employer could refuse to bargain with a union. Now, an employer is required to recognize the union as a bargaining power if the employees so decide by a neutral election.

The following case concerns whether the employer committed an unfair labor practice by filing a lawsuit against the union.

CASE 22.4

Supreme Court of the
United States, 2002
536 U.S. 516, 122 S. Ct.
2390, 153 L. Ed. 2d 499

BE&K CONSTRUCTION COMPANY v. NLRB

BACKGROUND AND FACTS BE&K Construction Company (Petitioner), an industrial general contractor, received a contract to modernize a California steel mill. According to BE&K, various unions attempted to delay the project because BE&K's employees were nonunion. BE&K filed suit against those unions in federal district court.

The suit was based on the following basic allegations: First, the unions had lobbied for adoption and enforcement of an emissions standard, despite having no real concern the project would harm the environment. Second, the unions had handbilled and picketed at BE&K's site—and also encouraged strikes among the employees of BE&K's subcontractors—without revealing reasons for their disagreement. Third, to delay the construction project and raise costs, the unions had filed an action in state court alleging violations of California's Health and Safety Code. Finally, the unions had launched grievance proceedings against BE&K's joint venture partner based on an inapplicable collective bargaining agreement.

Initially, BE&K sought damages under the Labor-Management Relations Act (LMRA), which provides a cause of action against labor organizations for injuries caused by secondary boycotts prohibited under federal law. But after the district court granted the unions' motion for summary judgment on BE&K's lobbying- and grievance-related claims, the BE&K amended its complaint to allege that the unions' activities violated Sections 1 and 2 of the Sherman Act. The district court dismissed the amended complaint, however, because it realleged claims that had already been decided.

Two unions lodged complaints against BE&K with the National Labor Relations Board (Board). The Board's general counsel issued an administrative complaint against BE&K, alleging that it had violated Section 8(a)(1) of the National Labor Relations Act (NLRA), by filing and maintaining the federal lawsuit. The act prohibits employers from restraining, coercing, or interfering with employees' exercise of rights related to self-organization, collective bargaining, and other concerted activities.

A three-member panel of the Board addressed cross-motions for summary judgment and ruled in favor of the general counsel. The panel determined that BE&K's federal lawsuit had been unmeritorious because all the claims were dismissed or voluntarily withdrawn with prejudice.

The panel then examined whether BE&K's suit had been filed to retaliate against the unions for engaging in activities protected under the NLRA. The panel first concluded that the unions' conduct was protected activity, and then decided that BE&K's lawsuit had been unlawfully motivated because it was "directed at protected conduct" and "necessarily tended to discourage similar protected activity," and because BE&K admitted it had filed suit "to stop certain union conduct which it believed to be unprotected."

The panel also found evidence of retaliatory motive because BE&K's LMRA claims had an "utter absence of merit" and had been dismissed on summary judgment. After determining that BE&K's suit had violated the NLRA because it was unsuccessful and retaliatory, the panel ordered BE&K to cease and desist from prosecuting such suits and to post notice to its employees admitting it had been found to have violated the NLRA and promising not to pursue such litigation in the future.

The panel also ordered BE&K to pay the unions' legal fees and expenses incurred in defense of the federal suit. The case was appealed to the United States Court of Appeals for the Sixth Circuit, which upheld the Board's decision.

Justice O'CONNOR delivered the opinion of the Court.

. . . .

As we see it, a threshold question here is whether the Board may declare that an unsuccessful retaliatory lawsuit violates the NLRA even if reasonably based. If it may, the resulting finding of illegality is a burden by itself. In addition to a declaration of illegality and whatever legal consequences flow from that, the finding also poses the threat of reputational harm that is different and additional to any burden posed by other penalties, such as a fee award. Because we can resolve this case by looking only at the finding of illegality, we need not decide whether the Board otherwise has authority to award attorney's fees when a suit is found to violate the NLRA.

. . . .

First, even though all the lawsuits in this class are unsuccessful, the class nevertheless includes a substantial proportion of all suits involving genuine grievances because the genuineness of a grievance does not turn on whether it succeeds. Indeed, this is reflected by our prior cases which have protected petitioning whenever it is genuine, not simply when it triumphs. Nor does the text of the First Amendment speak in terms of successful petitioning—it speaks simply of "the right of the people . . . to petition the Government for a redress of grievances."

Second, even unsuccessful but reasonably based suits advance some First Amendment interests. Like successful suits, unsuccessful suits allow the "'public airing of disputed facts,'" and raise matters of public concern. They also promote the evolution of the law by supporting the development of legal theories that may not gain acceptance the first time around. Moreover, the ability to lawfully prosecute even unsuccessful suits adds legitimacy to the court system as a designated alternative to force.

Finally, while baseless suits can be seen as analogous to false statements, that analogy does not directly extend to suits that are unsuccessful but reasonably based. For even if a suit could be seen as a kind of provable statement, the fact that it loses does not mean it is false. At most it means the plaintiff did not meet its burden of proving its truth. That does not mean the defendant has proved—or could prove—the contrary.

. . . .

DECISION AND REMEDY The Court held that an employer's unsuccessful retaliatory lawsuit against unions could not serve as a basis for imposing liability upon the employer unless there was a showing that the employer's lawsuit lacked any objective basis.

CRITICAL THINKING: POLITICAL CONSIDERATION Why are there labor laws?

Labor-Management Relations Act

The **Labor-Management Relations Act (Taft-Hartley Act)** of 1947 amended the Wagner Act. This act contains provisions protecting employers, as well as employees. The act was opposed bitterly by organized labor groups, because it provided a detailed list of unfair labor activities. Moreover, a free speech amendment allowed employers to propagandize against unions prior to any NLRB election. The following are some unfair labor practices by unions:

1. Threatening or committing violence,

2. Fining employees who cross picket lines after they have resigned from the union,

3. Coercing the employer in its selection of representatives for collective bargaining,

4. Discriminating against nonunion workers without legitimate union objectives being served, and

5. Refusing to bargain collectively with an employer.

Both the Wagner and the Taft-Hartley Acts address *closed shops* and *union shops*. A **closed shop** occurs when a business requires union membership from its workers as a condition of employment. The Taft-Hartley Act made closed shops illegal because they put the unions, rather than the employers, in charge of hiring.

A **union shop** does not require membership as an employment prerequisite but can, and usually does, require that workers join the union after a specified amount of time on the job. In an **agency shop**, union membership is not a prerequisite to hiring, and workers are not required to join the union after being hired. Workers, however, can be required to pay an amount equal to initiation fees and union dues, the theory being that these people enjoy the benefits of the union.

The Taft-Hartley Act allows individual states to pass their own **right-to-work laws.** A right-to-work law makes it illegal for union membership to be required for continued employment. Thus, union shops are illegal in states with right-to-work laws.

One of the most controversial aspect of the Taft-Hartley Act was the eighty-day cooling-off period. This provision allows federal courts to issue injunctions against strikes that would create a national emergency. The president of the United States can obtain such a court injunction that will last eighty days. For example, President Dwight D. Eisenhower (1953–1961) applied the eighty-day injunction to striking steelworkers in 1959, President Richard M. Nixon (1969–1974) applied it to striking longshoremen in 1971, President Jimmy Carter (1977–1981) to striking coal miners in 1978, and President William J. Clinton (1993–2001) to striking airline employees in 1996.

Labor-Management Reporting and Disclosure Act of 1959

The **Labor-Management Reporting and Disclosure Act (Landrum-Griffin Act)** of 1959 instituted an employee bill of rights, as well as reporting requirements for union activities. This act regulates internal union business, such as union elections. Elections of officers must be regularly scheduled, using secret ballots. Ex-convicts are precluded from holding union office. Union officials are accountable for union property and for union funds. Members have the right to attend and to participate in union meetings, to nominate officers, and to vote in most union proceedings.

The National Labor Relations Board, Office of General Counsel, and Regional Offices

The National Labor Relations Board enforces all of the statutes just discussed. The NLRB handles nearly all employer and employee labor issues, with the exception of airlines, railroads, agriculture, and government labor issues.

The NLRB has two principal functions: (1) to oversee union elections[17] and (2) to prevent employers or unions from engaging in unfair and illegal anti-union activities and unfair labor practices.[18] The NLRB has two major, separate components. First, the board itself consists of five members who are appointed by the president and confirmed by the Senate. The board members have staggered five-year terms and may be removed only for neglect of duty or malfeasance.

Second, the general counsel is appointed by the president and confirmed by the Senate. The general counsel is independent from the board and is responsible for the investigation and prosecution of unfair labor practice cases and for the general supervision of the NLRB field offices in the processing of cases. Of the approximately 35,000 unfair labor charges filed each year, the general counsel finds nearly one-third to have merit. Of these meritorious cases, over 90 percent are settled.

The board has the usual administrative powers. The NLRB supervises elections with secret ballots in which the employees determine if a union will represent them in collective bargaining. The board then certifies the union selected by the majority of employees as the collective bargaining agent.

The general counsel is responsible for investigating and prosecuting unfair labor practices. All attorneys employed by the NLRB—except administrative law judges and attorneys who are members of the NLRB's staff—are supervised by the general counsel's office. The general counsel represents the NLRB in injunction proceedings in federal courts and in appeals to the circuit courts.

Regional offices of the NLRB are under the direction of a regional director and a regional attorney. The regional director reports to the NLRB on election matters and to the general counsel on unfair labor practice proceedings.

Complaints filed by regional directors are heard initially by ALJs who have delegated authority from the NLRB. If appealed, the ALJ's decision serves as a

---

[17]Information on representative cases is located at http://www.nlrb.gov/tri-rcas.html.

[18]Information on unfair labor practices cases is located at http://www.nlrb.gov/tri-ulp.html.

LEGAL HIGHLIGHT

Organizing Institute

Labor union membership declined sharply during the 1980s, with losses of 200,000 members annually. To stop this decline, the American Federation of Labor and Congress of Industrial Organizations (AFL-CIO) created the Organizing Institute in 1989.

The institute's mission is to promote and foster union organizing. It offers training sessions to interest people in careers as union organizers. Graduates employed with international unions affiliated with the AFL-CIO are full-time, paid union organizers. The institute offers various programs designed to assist unions in the area of external organizing.

The following unions directly participate in the training program by providing intern and apprentice campaigns and by hiring graduates: American Federation of State, County, and Municipal Employees (AFSCME), American Federation of Teachers (AFT),

Communications Workers of America (CWA), Hotel Employees and Restaurant Employees (HERE), International Brotherhood of Teamsters (IBT), International Longshoremen's and Warehousemen's Union (ILWU), Service Employees International Union (SEIU), United Auto Workers (UAW), United Brotherhood of Carpenters and Joiners (UBC), United Food and Commercial Workers (UFCW), United Mineworkers of America (UMWA), United Steelworkers of America (USWA), Laborers International Union of North America (LIUNA), Oil, Chemical, and Atomic Workers (OCAW), and Union of Needletrades, Industrial and Textile Employees (UNITE).

The institute recruits labor organizers not only from members of unions but also from college campuses. Has the Organizing Institute visited your campus? For more information, see the Organizing Institute's Web page at **http://www.aflcio.org/orginst/index.htm**.

---

recommendation to the board. Board decisions may be appealed to the court of appeals and, from there, to the Supreme Court of the United States.

Remedies

The NLRB has broad discretionary authority to fashion appropriate remedies. The courts have held that the board's orders will be overturned only if remedies ordered fail to fairly effectuate NLRA policies.

The board may issue cease-and-desist orders and also may require a person to take an action designed to carry out the purposes of the labor acts. For instance, the board may order reinstatement of an employee who is discharged wrongfully, along with the payment of back wages and the restoration of seniority.

When union election results are contested, the board may order new elections if unfair labor practices are deemed to have influenced the outcome. Alternatively it may, in certain instances, require an employer to bargain with the appropriate union without holding a new election.

Organizing a Collective Bargaining Unit

Section 7 of the Wagner Act guarantees that employees have the right to form, join, or assist labor organizations. The employees or a union that wants to represent the employees may start organization efforts. A collective bargaining unit is composed of the employees who have a community of interest. The union needs 30 percent of these employees to show that they want a representation election, that is, an election to determine if a union will represent the workers, and, if two or more unions seek to be elected as the workers' representative, the union that wins the election.

The most common method used by employees to show they want a representation election is through the use of authorization cards. Employees sign a card authorizing the union to act as their union. Signatures are checked against the company payroll. Once verified that 30 percent of the employees have signed, a petition for an election is sent to the NLRB. In practice, a union will usually petition for an election when it has secured authorization cards from 60 percent or more of those eligible to vote. The NLRB will set a date for the election and then will supervise the election procedure.

The employer has no duty to bargain with the union until after the union is elected and is certified by the NLRB as the employees' bargaining representative. Only one union may represent a bargaining unit of employees at one time. Although a large business may have its workforce represented by several unions, each union represents only a portion of the employees who have a community of interest. Once the union is certified, it can then begin to negotiate a collective bargaining agreement with the employer.

The Collective Bargaining Agreement

The NLRA requires both employers and the unions that represent their employees to bargain in good faith. This obligation requires the employer and union to meet at reasonable times and to confer in good faith with respect to wages, hours, and other terms and conditions of employment.

The obligation to bargain in good faith does not require the parties to come to an agreement. The purpose behind the statute is to encourage parties to negotiate enforceable contracts. Once a contract is reached it is enforceable, as the following case shows.

CASE 22.5

Supreme Court of the United States, 1996 517 U.S. 781, 116 S. Ct. 1754, 135 L. Ed. 2d 64 http://supct.law.cornell. edu/supct/html/95-668.ZS.html

AUCIELLO IRON WORKS, INC. v. NATIONAL LABOR RELATIONS BOARD

BACKGROUND AND FACTS Petitioner Auciello Iron Works had twenty-three production and maintenance employees. After a union election in 1977, the National Labor Relations Board certified as the collective bargaining representative of Auciello's employees Shopmen's Local No. 501, which was associated with the International Association of Bridge, Structural, and Ornamental Iron Workers, AFL-CIO.

During the following years, the company and the union negotiated a series of collective bargaining agreements, one of which expired on September 25, 1988. The employees went on strike. Negotiations continued, nonetheless, and, on November 17, 1988, Auciello presented the union with a complete contract proposal. On November 18, 1988, the picketing stopped, and nine days later, the union telegraphed its acceptance of the outstanding offer.

The very next day, however, Auciello told the union that it doubted that a majority of the employees supported the union and, for that reason, disavowed the collective bargaining agreement. Auciello based its doubt on the facts that nine employees had crossed the picket line, that thirteen employees had given it signed forms indicating their resignation from the union, and that sixteen had expressed dissatisfaction with the union. Auciello knew these facts nine days prior to the union's accepting the contract.

In January 1989, the NLRB's general counsel charged Auciello with violations of the National Labor Relations Act. An administrative law judge found that a contract existed between the parties and that Auciello's withdrawal from it violated the act. The board affirmed the administrative law judge's decision.

Justice SOUTER delivered the opinion of the Court.

. . . .

The object of the National Labor Relations Act is industrial peace and stability, fostered by collective bargaining agreements providing for the orderly resolution of labor disputes between workers and employees. To such ends, the Board has adopted various presumptions about the existence of majority support for a union within a bargaining unit, the precondition for service as its exclusive representative. The first two are conclusive presumptions. A union "usually is entitled to a conclusive presumption of majority status for one year following" Board certification as such a representative.

A union is likewise entitled under Board precedent to a conclusive presumption of majority status during the term of any collective bargaining agreement, up to three years. "These presumptions are based not so much on an absolute certainty that the union's majority status will not erode," as on the need to achieve "stability in collective bargaining relationships." They address our fickle nature by "enabl[ing] a union to concentrate on obtaining and fairly administering a collective bargaining agreement" without worrying about the immediate risk of decertification and by "remov[ing] any temptation on the part of the employer to avoid good faith bargaining" in an effort to undermine union support.

. . . .

We hold that the Board reasonably found an employer's precontractual, good faith doubt inadequate to support an exception to the conclusive presumption arising at the moment a collective bargaining contract offer has been accepted.

DECISION AND REMEDY The Supreme Court found that the employer committed an unfair labor practice by disavowing a collective bargaining contract to which the employer and union had agreed. Even though the employer had a good-faith belief that the union did not have the support of a majority of employees when it made the contract, the contract was still binding.

CRITICAL THINKING: LEGAL ISSUE Was it reasonable for the court to force the employer the keep the agreement that it made with a union when the union may have lost the support of the current employees?

Duty of Fair Representation

Both in negotiating and in administering a collective bargaining agreement, a union has an implied duty of fair representation for the employees it represents. A union must act fairly, impartially, and in good faith. The right to determine eligibility for its own membership remains with the union, but it is nevertheless obligated in collective bargaining to represent nonunion or minority union members without hostile discrimination, fairly, impartially, and in good faith.

The union has the power to exercise its discretion in contract negotiations with management. The union can make reasonable distinctions among types of employees in matters of pay, vacation time, and medical benefits, based on differences, such as seniority, type of work performed, competence, and skill.

Strikes

Of the several types of strikes allowed, two types are common: *economic strikes* and *unfair labor practices strikes*. **Economic strikes**, the most common type of strike, are economic in nature, that is, the employees strike for higher wages and benefits. Management may permanently replace economic strikers. The strikers, however, are entitled to priority when management rehires after the strike. Furthermore, management cannot discriminate against these strikers.

Unfair labor practices strikes occur when management violates the law. Earlier in the chapter unfair labor practices were discussed. When this type of strike ends, management must give the job back to the striking employee. Otherwise, management effectively would be rewarded for committing illegal practices prohibited by the Wagner Act.

Labor Side Agreement to NAFTA

The North American Free Trade Agreement (NAFTA) became effective in 1994, joining the United States, Canada, and Mexico for trading purposes. Part of NAFTA is a supplemental agreement officially entitled the North American Agreement on Labor Cooperation (NAALC).[19] This part of NAFTA legislates protections

---

[19]The text of the North American Agreement on Labor Cooperation is located at http://www.sice.oas.org/trade/nafta/Labor-C1.asp.

for labor in the three countries. The NAALC enforces these protections through a system of cooperation, consultation, and the possibility of monetary penalties.

The NAALC established a Commission for Labor Cooperation. The commission consists of three primary parts. The first and most important is the governing council, which is composed of the labor ministers of the three member countries. The second part is the secretariat, a support organization to the council that consists of an executive director and fifteen staffers. Finally, each country has a National Administrative Office (NAO), which provides technical support within the country.

If a country fails to enforce its own labor laws to protect its workers, the council can apply greater pressure on a case-by-case basis by convening one of two committees, the Evaluation Committee of Experts (ECE) or an arbitral panel. The three-member ECE considers a country's pattern of practice in enforcing a fairly broad range of standards, including occupational safety and health labor standards. The ECE must study the particular problem at hand and issue a report with recommendations. Each party must then submit its written response to the ECE.

An arbitral panel examines alleged persistent patterns of failure by a country to enforce effectively its own labor laws and standards relating to three specific areas only: occupational safety and health, minimum wage, and child labor. The arbitral panel must make findings, determinations, and recommendations.

The panel also may establish an action plan and impose monetary penalties against a country. If a country fails to pay a monetary penalty assessed by the arbitral panel, the complaining countries may reimpose tariffs up to the penalty's limit, but for no more than the equivalent of $20 million (U.S.) for the first year, and for no more than 0.007 percent of the total trade in goods between the countries for any year thereafter. If Canada fails to pay an assessed monetary penalty, it can be forced to pay the fine through its own court system.

The ECE and arbitral panels are not authorized to examine matters relating to three important labor law principles: freedom of association (the right to organize unions), the right to bargain collectively, and the right to strike. If a country fails to enforce its laws governing these principles, no penalties can be assessed, and tariffs cannot be reimposed.

The NAOs serve as contact points through which other government agencies and NAOs may access information and assistance in NAFTA-related labor matters. The NAOs consult with one another periodically about labor laws and market conditions in the other two countries. Reviews are also conducted to determine whether the countries are enforcing their labor laws. The U.S. NAO is housed in the Department of Labor, the Canadian NAO is a division of Labor Canada, and the Mexican NAO is located within the Ministry of Labor.

The NAALC encourages each country to enforce its own labor laws. It does not require any country to pass laws that are not already on the books. Furthermore, no country has the authority to enforce labor laws in another country's territory.

International Consideration

Perspectives on Employment

Under international agreements, many industries move their production facilities from developed nations to countries that have cheap labor. Generally, workers in developing countries lack the protections and benefits that are normal for workers in developed nations. Benefits, such as health and safety protections, union contracts, Social Security, workers' compensation, and unemployment benefits, are unavailable.

Some countries even use prison labor to produce products cheaply. These products are then sent overseas to developed countries and sold at a price below domestic manufacturing costs. International agreements allow confiscation of the illegally imported items if this practice is detected.

In most of the developed world, an employee has a vested right to his job. The 1982 International Labour Organization's[20] Convention on Termination at the Initiative of the Employer recognized this practice. The United States is not a signatory to this convention, although most of the Western European countries have ratified it. The convention recognizes that an employee can be terminated only for cause.

The philosophical belief of the United States is that the employer controls all costs, including that of labor. As a result, an employer can terminate employees in cost-cutting measures aimed at maintaining competitiveness. A employee may be terminated with cause based on the employee's performance or without cause as long as the employer does not have a bad motive.

[20]The Web site for the International Labour Organization is http://www.ilo.org/.

What to Do If You Suspect That Some of Your Employees Want a Union

One of your long-term employees informs you that some of your employees are discussing unionizing. Do not panic. Just because your employees discuss union formation does not necessarily mean a union will form. Even if a union is formed, a strike or other negative actions that historically have occurred with union organization will not necessarily be taken against your firm. In fact, many companies today find that better communications with employees result from union recognition.

One major reason for which employees vote for a union is to achieve better communications between the employees and management. The business fails to keep its employees informed about problems that it confronts. These problems can involve business competition, new governmental regulations, higher taxes, or higher costs to maintain employee benefits.

When confronted with these problems, a business may forget the importance of informing its employees and involving them in making decisions. The employees feel neglected by management. The best way to stop a union's organizational effort is to open communication lines with employees and to make them feel valued. Open communications should be offered on a continual basis to foster a good relationship with employees, not only as a reaction to union-organization activity.

What actions can you take to convince your employees not to organize a union? Here are some suggestions.

Checklist

✔ *Communication* Communicate with your employees. Stress the benefits they presently receive and compare them with the benefits offered by other area businesses.

✔ *Costs* Ensure that your employees know the total cost to them for membership in the union, including initiation fees, assessments to support other unions that strike, and monthly dues.

✔ *Statement* Outline the company's sources of funds.

✔ *Strikes* Stress that an employee strike could take months, if not years, from which to recover financially.

✔ *Replacement* Explain that employers can legally replace strikers with other workers, if the strike involves economic issues.

✔ *Written Communications* Send letters to your employees' residences explaining these issues. Married employees' spouses will be involved in making the union decision. Sending a personal message to your employees' residences also indicates your concern for the worker.

✔ *No Distribution* Prohibit union organizers from distributing material in work areas if the restriction is based on safety factors.

✔ *No Nonemployees* Stop nonemployees from entering your property because they can be considered trespassers.

✔ *Reports* Have employees report union organizers' threats.

Organizing activities are protected by the National Labor Relations Act. The following acts are considered to be unfair labor practices:

Checklist

✔ *No Questions* Do not question individuals about their union activities.

✔ *No Threats* Do not threaten to discharge an employee for union activities or threaten to close the plant if a union is elected.

✔ *No Decreases* Do not state that benefits will decrease or that overtime will be cut if the union wins the election.

✔ *No Increases* Do not offer to increase benefits or income during the period of the organizing drive.

✔ *Allow Distributions* Do not stop the distribution of material in work areas by your own employees during breaks and while at lunch. These periods are considered the employees' free time.

Be honest with your employees. Communicate early and often. Do not wait until the union organizers have arrived. It may be later than you think.

Chapter Summary

Federal law has a significant impact on both the relationship between employers and their employees as well as labor-management relations. The Fair Labor Standards Act (FLSA) establishes a minimum wage per hour for employees, overtime pay provisions requiring time-and-a-half of normal pay for any work over forty hours per week, certain record-keeping requirements, and child labor protection. Although some types of employees are exempt, most businesses are bound by this act. The Department of Labor enforces the FLSA.

Federal and state acts govern other labor-related issues as well. Social Security provisions include Old Age, Survivors, and Disability Insurance (OASDI) and Medicare. Unemployment compensation helps the worker financially until a new job is found. Workers' compensation laws cover employees injured or killed on the job. The Occupational Safety and Health Act (OSHA) helps to ensure safe and healthful working conditions for workers.

The Family and Medical Leave Act allows a worker to take unpaid leave to care for a family member who is ill or for a child's birth or adoption. The Consolidated Omnibus Budget Reconciliation Act (COBRA) requires that a former employee be allowed to purchase health insurance. The Health Insurance Portability and Accountability Act (HIPAA) allows a person who is covered by a group health plan to move to a second job. If the second employer also has a group health plan, the employee is covered in full, including any preexisting medical conditions. Other laws govern employees' privacy rights, including the use of polygraphs, drug testing, and employee records.

Congress passed the following four statutes that govern management-labor relations: Federal Anti-Injunction Act (Norris-LaGuardia Act), National Labor Relations Act (Wagner Act), Labor-Management Relations Act (Taft-Hartley Act), and Labor-Management Reporting and Disclosure Act (Landrum-Griffin Act).

The Federal Anti-Injunction Act declared a national policy permitting workers to organize and their right to peaceful strikes, picketing, and boycotts. The act restricted the power of federal courts to issue injunctions against striking unions.

The National Labor Relations Act established the National Labor Relations Board and defined certain acts by management as unfair labor practices. The NLRB oversees representation elections in which workers vote to determine if they want to be represented by a union. The Labor-Management Relations Act amended the Wagner Act. The act forbids closed shops, but allows union shops and agency shops. States are allowed to adopt right-to-work laws whereby only agency shops are allowed. Unfair labor practices by unions are set out in the statute. The president of the United States can determine that a strike will create a national emergency and can seek a court injunction against it.

The Labor-Management Reporting and Disclosure Act created an employee bill of rights. The act regulates internal union business, such as elections.

The NLRB enforces all four statutes. The NLRB supervises representation elections. The Office of General Counsel handles the investigations of all unfair labor practices charges brought either by management or by the union.

Both management and the union must bargain collectively in good faith. The Wagner Act allows workers to decide if they want to be represented by a union. Usually, employees fill out authorization cards, and if over 30 percent of the employees sign, a petition for an election is filed with the NLRB. Once a union has been elected and certified by the NLRB, the union represents all the employees. The union, both in negotiating and in administering a collective bargaining agreement, has an implied duty of fair representation for the employees it represents, even if an employee is not a union member.

Using the World Wide Web

Information about the government agencies and labor unions is readily available on the Internet. In the labor field, a number of international labor sites also can be found online.

For *Web Activities*, links to Web sites mentioned in the chapter, and additional Web sites that relate to the chapter topics, go to **http://bohlman.westbuslaw.com**, click on "Internet Applications," and select Chapter 22.

Web Activities

Go to **http://bohlman.westbuslaw.com**, click on "Internet Applications," and select Chapter 22.
22–1 Overtime
22–2 ERISA

Key Terms

agency shop

Center for Medicare &
Medicaid Services
(CMS)

closed shop

Consolidated Omnibus
Budget Reconciliation
Act (COBRA) *Minor Removals*

economic strike

Employee Polygraph
Protection Act

Employee Retirement
Income Security Act
(ERISA)

Fair Labor Standards Act
(FLSA) *1938*

Family and Medical
Leave Act

Federal Anti-Injunction
Act (Norris
LaGuardia Act) *1932*

Federal Insurance
Contributions Act
(FICA)

Federal Unemployment
Tax Act (FUTA)

Health Insurance
Portability and
Accountability Act
(HIPAA)

Labor-Management
Relations Act (Taft

Hartley Act) *1947*

Labor-Management
Reporting and
Disclosure Act
(Landrum-Griffin Act) *1959*

Medicare

National Labor Rela-
tions Act (Wagner
Act) *1935*

National Labor Rela-
tions Board (NLRB) *1935*

Occupational Safety and
Health Act

Occupational Safety and
Health Administration
(OSHA) *1970's*

Old Age, Survivors, and
Disability Insurance
(OASDI)

Plant Closing Act

right-to-work laws

Social Security Act

unfair labor practices
strike

union shop

Worker Adjustment and
Retraining Notifica-
tion Act (WARN)

workers' compensation
law

Questions and Case Problems

22–1 Workers' Compensation Workers' compensation statutes cover the injuries, disease, or death of employees while at work. Professor Able is employed by a private university in California. Prior to traveling to a professional meeting, he requests permission and travel money to attend the meeting. The university grants permission, but does not grant travel money. After the meeting, but three hours prior to his airplane trip to return home, he visits a cathedral that is noted for its beauty. When he emerges from the cathedral, he stumbles down the stairs and injures himself. An ambulance transports him to the hospital, where an emergency room physician treats and releases him in time to catch the return flight. Are his injuries covered by workers' compensation? Did the injuries occur while he was at work? Explain.

22–2 Child Labor Hamburger Joint is a nationwide fast-food outlet franchise. The management is interested in teenage unemployment; consequently, it created a program for hiring teens. The program will hire fifty people in each teenage bracket. The fourteen-year-olds will be janitors, the fifteen-year-olds will take orders at the counter, the sixteen-year-olds will cook, and the seventeen-year-olds will drive company vehicles to deliver food orders. Do you see any violations of the child labor laws in this program? Explain.

22–3 Overtime Wages Joseph owns an interstate business engaged in manufacturing and selling boats. Joseph

has 500 nonunion employees. Representatives of these employees approach Joseph, seeking a four-day, ten-hours-per-day workweek. Joseph is concerned that this proposal will require him to pay his employees time-and-a-half after eight hours per day. Discuss fully which federal act concerns Joseph and whether the proposal will require Joseph to pay time-and-a-half.

22–4 Workers' Compensation Bernice Aranda was employed as a secretary and normally worked from eight to five. She was leaving her job for the evening. While she was walking to her vehicle, another automobile driven by an escaped convict and chased by the police suddenly appeared at a high speed and struck Bernice. Because she was still on the employer's property, was she covered by workers' compensation? Explain.

22–5 Labor Organizing Union tried to organize 200 employees at a retail store owned by Lechmere, Inc., located in the Lechmere Shopping Plaza. A grassy strip, which is primarily public property, separates the mall property from a turnpike. Union began its campaign by placing a full-page advertisement in a local newspaper. It drew little response, so nonemployee union organizers entered Lechmere's parking lot and placed handbills on the windshields of cars. Lechmere's manager confronted the organizers, informed them that Lechmere prohibited solicitation or handbill distribution of any kind on its property, and asked them to leave. They did so and the handbills were removed. The organizers relocated to the public grassy strip, from where they attempted to pass out handbills to automobiles entering and leaving the parking lot. For six months, the union organizers returned to the grassy strip and to the picket line. Union filed an unfair labor practice charge against Lechmere on the ground that Lechmere barred the nonemployee organizers from its property. A hearing was held and Lechmere was ordered to cease and desist from barring the union organizers from the parking lot and to post signs in conspicuous places that Lechmere would not prohibit the union from distributing union literature. Lechmere appealed to the United States Supreme Court. What was the result of the appeal and why? [*Lechmere, Inc. v. National Labor Relations Board*, 502 U.S. 527, 112 S. Ct. 841, 117 L. Ed. 2d 79 (1992)].

22–6 Overtime Jiffy June Farms properly paid overtime to its employees. It entered into a collective bargaining agreement with the union that exempted Jiffy from paying time-and-a-half for overtime, but that increased basic wages considerably. The lower court found this contract to be a willful violation of the Fair Labor Standards Act. Can the workers waive their rights to overtime pay? Explain. [*Coleman v. Jiffy June Farms*, 458 F.2d 1139 (5th Cir.1972)]

22–7 Labor Organizing The General Drivers, Warehousemen & Helpers Union attempted to organize the drivers of the Q-1 Motor Express, an interstate trucking company. Supervisors threatened drivers to stay away from the organizers. The president of Q-1, Schroering, confronted organizer Denham. Schroering told Denham that the company attorney told him that to thwart the union, he could fire all the drivers, close the company down, and then reopen seventy-two hours later with new drivers because he was not going to permit a "half-ass union [to] come in and try to tell him how to run his business." The company granted a pay increase during the height of the organizing campaign. Was the employees' right to organize violated under the labor laws? Explain. [*NLRB v. Q-1 Motor Express, Inc.*, 25 F.3d 473 (7th Cir. 1994)]

22–8 OSHA At an REA Express, Inc., shipping terminal, a conveyor belt became inoperative because of an electrical circuit short. The manager called a licensed electrical contractor. When the contractor arrived, REA's maintenance supervisor was in the circuit breaker room. The floor was wet, and the maintenance supervisor was using sawdust to soak up the water. The

licensed electrical contractor attempted to fix the short circuit while standing on the wet floor, and he was electrocuted. Simultaneously, REA's maintenance supervisor, who was standing on a wooden platform, was burned and knocked unconscious. The Occupational Safety and Health Administration wanted to fine REA Express $1,000 for failure to furnish a place of employment free from recognized hazards. What was the result? Explain. [*REA Express, Inc. v. Brennan*, 495 F.2d 822 (2d Cir. 1974)]

22–9 OSHA The Occupational Safety and Health Administration issued a regulation that allowed employees to refuse to perform an assigned task if a reasonable apprehension of death or serious injury in accomplishing it existed. Whirlpool Corp. had a plant that produced appliances. Within the plant the appliances were transported by a conveyor belt that was near the ceiling. To protect employees below, Whirlpool installed a screen to stop any appliances that occasionally fell. To remove fallen parts from the screens, maintenance workers were required to climb out onto the screen. In the past, several workers had fallen through the screen to the floor below and one had been killed. Whirlpool issued an order restricting employees from walking on the screens because the old screens were being replaced by stronger screens. Several weeks after the workers had fallen through the screen, management ordered two workers onto an area that still had the old screens. When they refused the order, they were dismissed from their shift and were issued written reprimands to be placed in their employment files. They filed a complaint with OSHA. The secretary of labor filed suit and sought to have the reprimands removed and to recover the lost pay. Who prevailed in this case? Explain. [*Whirlpool Corp. v. Marshall*, 445 U.S. 1, 100 S. Ct. 883, 63 L. Ed. 2d 154 (1980)]

22–10 Internet Having enough money set aside for retirement is an issue that most people face. Funds can be accumulated by contributing on a regular schedule to a number of different types of tax-sheltered funds, such as accounts designated as a 401(k) (for private employees), 403(b) (for government of not-for-profit employees), or various types of individual retirement accounts (IRAs). At the CNN Money Web site is a calculator that can be used. Go to **http://cgi.money.cnn.com/tools/retirementplanner/retirementplanner.jsp** and see how much you must invest in a given year to reach your desired annual income during retirement.

Chapter 23

Employment Law and Equal Opportunity

Laborin' men an' laborin' women
Hev one glory an' one shame;
Ev'y thin' thet's done inhuman
Injers all on 'em the same.

> *The Biglow Papers,* **Series 1, No. 1,**
> **Stanza 10, 1848**
> **James Russell Lowell, 1819–1891**
> **American poet, critic, essayist, editor,**
> **and diplomat, minister to Spain,**
> **1877–1880, and ambassador to Great**
> **Britain, 1880–1885**

Chapter Outline

Ethical Consideration

The Glass Ceiling

You are the general manager of Spikes Construction Company, a heavy construction firm that primarily builds freeways. Sue Sure is hired to work in the accounting department. As a good employee, she has received raises over the years. She has a nice disposition and is well liked in spite of her outspoken position that men generally treat women poorly in the work environment.

When the director of the accounting department has a heart attack, Sure's name is proposed to take his place. Although you know that Sure is very capable, you are worried about bringing a woman into upper management, which until now has been exclusively male. You believe that your management team likes the current all-male atmosphere that allows for sexual jokes, strong language, drinks, and easy companionship—in other words, the good old boy network. The past behavior of some members of the upper management team, in terms of language and actions, may be viewed by Sure as harassing. Further, you are concerned with her ability to deal effectively with the company's suppliers and with its subcontractors on tough accounting issues, such as denying full payment to an outraged subcontractor because it failed to fully perform its contract.

Do you promote Sure or do you conduct a search that will most likely result in the hiring of a strong male executive to fill the vacancy? Use the ethical model presented in Chapter 2 and reprinted on the inside front cover to develop your answer.

Introduction

At common law, both employment agreements between businesses and their employees and contracts between management and labor unions were considered private contractual matters. Common law provided little or no protection to employees or labor union members against arbitrary and discriminatory actions by employers or labor unions.

Not until the National Labor Relations Act (Wagner Act) of 1935 did employees gain some statutory protection. This act prohibits employers from discriminating against employees or job applicants because of their union activities. Within a decade after the Wagner Act, the U.S. Supreme Court prohibited certain forms of racial discrimination by unions. Statutes passed later broadened the regulations governing labor–management relations.

In the past, discrimination in hiring, retention, promotion, and firing was common in the workplace. Discrimination was based on many factors. Most onerous was discrimination based on race, color, religion, national origin, and gender. In 1964, Congress took legislative action to address these problems.

This chapter examines the federal antidiscrimination laws and the agency charged with enforcing these antidiscriminatory statutes. We also discuss affirmative action.[1]

Artiste Login. Your online business, Artiste Login Products, Inc., has a number of employees. New businesses located on the Web are not usually unionized, but this may change in the future. Even though the employees of Artiste are not unionized, as an employer, Artiste needs to be aware of the federal labor and antidiscrimination laws.

The Civil Rights Act of 1964, Title VII

The cornerstone law on antidiscrimination in the employment field is **Title VII of the Civil Rights Act of 1964.**[2] This act prohibits discrimination in all areas of employment on the basis of race; color; religion; national origin; or sex (gender), including pregnancy, childbirth, or abortion. It also prohibits sexual harassment. Coverage extends to employees of private employers and to employees of local, state, and federal governments. The **Equal Employment Opportunity Commission (EEOC)** was created by the Civil Rights Act.

Title VII does not prohibit discrimination based on immigration status, physical disability, or age. Other

---

[1] A good Web site that reviews all of the law involved with employment discrimination is found at http://www.law.cornell.edu/topics/employment_discrimination.html.

[2] The text of Title VII is located at http://www.eeoc.gov/laws/vii.html.

statutes discussed in the chapter prohibit discrimination on these grounds.

Covered Employment Situations under Title VII

Title VII covers three situations: (1) employers with at least fifteen workers, (2) labor unions with at least fifteen members, and (3) employment agencies. For Title VII to apply, the activities of the employer, labor union, or employment agency must be part of, or must affect, interstate commerce, which the courts interpret very broadly.

Types of Discrimination

The EEOC uses the following two theories when determining if discrimination has occurred: **disparate treatment** (classes are treated differently by design) and **disparate impact** (a seemingly neutral requirement impacts the classes differently). Claims based on these two discrimination types can be combined in the same lawsuit when appropriate.

Disparate Treatment. The simplest form of discrimination involves disparate treatment, that is, treating members of one class differently from members of other classes. This discrimination occurs by design, because the employer intentionally discriminates. In the past, for example, newspapers carried two different help-wanted columns, one for men and one for women.

The plaintiff employee must establish a *prima facie* case of discrimination in cases involving hiring, promotion, or salary increase. A ***prima facie case*** is one in which the evidence presented by the plaintiff will prove the case until contradicted and overcome by other evidence presented by the defendant. For example, a health spa places an advertisement seeking men to work at the spa. A woman applies for the position. Her application is rejected. In a *prima facie* case, she must show that (1) she is a member of a protected class, in this case (she is a woman, which is a protected class), (2) she applied and was qualified for the job, (3) her application was rejected, and (4) the employer continued to seek applicants for the job or that a person in an unprotected class was hired. When she shows this *prima facie* case, the defendant must respond.

The defendant may be successful in rebutting the *prima facie* case if the defendant has a valid legal reason for hiring only men. For instance, the health spa would employ only men to staff the men's locker room.

Disparate Impact. Sometimes employment practices may appear neutral on the surface, but, without any intent to do so, the practices adversely affect a protected class. This unintentional discrimination is the nature of disparate impact discrimination cases. Statistics show the adverse impact of the practice on a protected class and often provide the only way to establish a *prima facie* case.

For example, a woman applies for the position of troubleshooter with an electrical utility company. A troubleshooter determines the cause of a problem and then makes the repairs. Some repairs require digging while others require the climbing of utility poles. The job notice states a number of requirements, one of which requires the applicant to be six feet, two inches tall, and another of which requires two years of field experience. The company turns down the female applicant because she is only five feet, eight inches, although she has the work experience. She must show that (1) she is a member of a protected class, (2) she applied and was qualified for the job, (3) her application was rejected, and (4) the employer continued to seek applicants for the job or a person in an unprotected class was hired.

Once she has established the *prima facie* case, the defendant utility company has the burden of providing legitimate, nondiscriminatory reasons for the applicant's not being hired. For example, the utility company could show that it required the applicant to be six feet, two inches tall because the performance in the position requires a person to reach up to certain heights in order to make repairs without the aid of a ladder.

If the defendant can rebut the *prima facie* case, the plaintiff must prove that the reason articulated by the employer is not legitimate. The plaintiff must convince the judge or jury that the reason is a pretext (not true) to cover up a discriminatory employment practice. She can challenge the height requirement by showing that few women are six feet, two inches tall. Unless the utility company can show a legitimate reason for the height requirement, the plaintiff should prevail in this case. The requirement of a physical height of six feet, two inches appears neutral on its face, but has a disparate impact on women and some ethnic groups.

In the following case, the United States Supreme Court reviews an employment practice that appeared neutral, but in fact had a disparate impact on African-American employees. This case was the first to find a disparate impact. Prior to this case, businesses often required a high school diploma for many positions. The diploma requirement resulted in African Americans being discriminated against because in those days many lacked a high school education. In this case, the company practiced intentional discrimination against African Americans prior to the passage of the Civil Rights Act of 1964.

CASE 23.1

Supreme Court of the United States, 1971 401 U.S. 424, 91 S. Ct. 849, 28 L. Ed. 2d 158 http://caselaw.lp.findlaw. com/scripts/getcase.pl? navby=search&court= US&case=/us/401/424. html

GRIGGS v. DUKE POWER CO.

BACKGROUND AND FACTS Thirteen African Americans brought this class-action suit against their employer, Duke Power Company. Prior to July 2, 1965, the effective date of the Civil Rights Act of 1964, the company had hired African Americans in only one of its five departments, the Labor Department. The highest paying jobs in the Labor Department paid less than the lowest paying jobs in the other departments, in which only whites were employed. In 1955, the company instituted a policy of requiring a high school diploma for initial assignment to any department except labor. When the company abandoned its policy of restricting African Americans to the Labor Department in 1965, Duke Power made completion of high school a prerequisite for transfer from labor to any other department.

In 1965, the company provided alternative methods to qualify for a transfer to new employees in all departments other than labor—satisfactory scores on two tests, one testing general intelligence and the other measuring the ability to learn to perform a particular job. Employees who lacked a high school education now could qualify for transfer to other departments by passing the two aptitude tests.

The district court found that the company had followed a policy of overt racial discrimination prior to the enactment of the Civil Rights Act of 1964, but that its discriminatory conduct had ceased. The court of appeals concluded that no discriminatory purpose in the adoption of the diploma and test requirements existed and, therefore, no violation of the Civil Rights Act occurred. The Supreme Court then reviewed the case to determine if these requirements were unlawful under Title VII if they were not shown to be job related.

Justice BURGER delivered the opinion of the Court.

The objective of Congress in the enactment of Title VII is plain from the language of the statute. It was to achieve equality of employment opportunities and to remove barriers that have operated in the past to favor an identifiable group of white employees over other employees. Under the Act, practices, procedures, or tests neutral on their face, and even neutral in terms of intent, cannot be maintained if they operate to "freeze" the status quo of prior discriminatory employment practices.

The Court of Appeals' opinion, and the pretrial dissent, agreed that, on the record in the recent case, "whites register far better on the Company's alternative requirements" than Negroes. This consequence would appear to be directly traceable to race. Basic intelligence must have the means of articulation to manifest itself fairly in a testing process. Because they are Negroes, petitioners have long received inferior education in segregated schools and this Court expressly recognized these differences in *Gaston County v. United States.* There, because of the inferior education received by Negroes in North Carolina, this Court barred the institution of a literacy test for voter registration on the ground that the test would abridge the right to vote indirectly on account of race. Congress did not intend by Title VII, however, to guarantee a job to every person regardless of qualifications. In short, the Act does not command that any person be hired simply because he was formerly the subject of discrimination, or because he is a member of a minority group. Discriminatory preference for any group, minority or majority, is precisely and only what Congress has proscribed. What is required by Congress is the removal of artificial, arbitrary, and unnecessary barriers to employment when the barriers operate invidiously to discriminate on the basis of racial or other impermissible classification.

. . . The Act proscribes not only overt discrimination but also practices that are fair in form, but discriminatory in operation. The touchstone is business necessity. If an employment practice which operates to exclude Negroes cannot be shown to be related to job performance, the practice is prohibited.

DECISION AND REMEDY The judgment of the court of appeals was reversed. The Supreme Court held that diploma and test requirements had to be job related. Duke Power had to prove that the test and degree requirements were necessary for the job.

CRITICAL THINKING: MANAGERIAL PERSPECTIVE How does a manager assure that a test is job related?

Equal Employment Opportunity Commission

The Equal Employment Opportunity Commission (EEOC)[3] is an independent administrative agency that has five members, each appointed by the president and confirmed by the Senate. No more than three members may be from the same political party. Each serves a five-year term.

The EEOC is responsible for the administration and enforcement of the Equal Pay Act of 1963, Title VII of the Civil Rights Act of 1964, the Age Discrimination in Employment Act of 1967, and the Americans with Disabilities Act of 1990.

EEOC Enforcement

The EEOC can issue interpretive guidelines and regulations, but these do not have the force of law. Rather, they provide notice of the commission's enforcement policy. The EEOC may require employers to keep statistics and records of employment and employment practices.

The EEOC, with its investigatory powers, has broad authority to require the production of docu-

mentary evidence, to hold hearings, and to subpoena and examine witnesses under oath. When a person files charges or when the commission members determine that a pattern or practice of illegal discrimination exists, a lawsuit can be filed. The EEOC has the opportunity to attempt conciliation between the parties prior to filing a suit.

EEOC Procedures

Any person claiming harm may file a charge of discrimination with the EEOC. A member of the EEOC or any person may likewise file a charge and whoever files is called the charging party.

Generally speaking, the charge must be filed within 180 days after the discriminatory action. Within 10 days of the filing of a charge with the EEOC, the agency must notify the employer. Once notified, the employer is prohibited from retaliation against the charging employee.

Once the employer has been notified, the EEOC investigates the charge. If it finds reasonable cause to believe that the federal law has been violated, it attempts to resolve the dispute by informal means. When informal means fail to result in a settlement, the EEOC may bring an action thirty days after the charge is filed.

Even when both the EEOC and the company are willing to accept a settlement, the charging party retains the right to sue. If, however, the EEOC does not find reasonable cause to believe a violation has

[3]The EEOC's Web page is http://www.eeoc.gov. The EEOC's National Enforcement Plan is available at http://www.eeoc.gov/nep.html.

occurred, it notifies the charging party and informs her of the right to pursue the matter in court. The charging party has only ninety days to file a lawsuit.

The 1991 Civil Rights Act[4] provides workers with the right to recover compensatory and punitive damages if harassment or other intentional discrimination occurred. Before the court awards money damages, the employee must demonstrate that the employer engaged in a discriminatory practice with malice or reckless indifference. The act sets limits on the combined compensatory and punitive damages based on a sliding scale: for companies with 14 to 100 employees, $50,000; 101 to 200 employees, $100,000; 201 to 500 employees, $200,000; and more than 501 employees, $300,000.

The 1991 Civil Rights Act limits remedies when hiring is at issue. An applicant can obtain an injunction, attorneys' fees, and court costs. The applicant for a job cannot recover back pay.

Pattern and Practice of Discrimination

The Equal Employment Opportunity Commission will bring a lawsuit against an employer when a pattern and practice of discrimination are evident. Because the government initiates the lawsuit, it bears the burden of establishing a *prima facie* case of discrimination by proving a pattern and practice of discrimination.

The government must show that a protected class suffers from discrimination because of a company's standard operating procedure. For example, the government can make a *prima facie* case by showing large statistical disparities between the general workforce's racial composition and that of the company's employees. The government can strengthen its case by presenting evidence of specific instances of discrimination.

In 1995, the EEOC adopted the National Enforcement Plan, which identifies priority issues and creates a plan for administrative enforcement and litigation of the four laws within its jurisdiction. The EEOC does not pursue every case it receives, but focuses on the cases in which the court decision will receive the business community's attention.

Categories of Discrimination

Title VII prohibits discrimination on a nonjob criterion, such as race or color; religion; national origin; or gender, including pregnancy, childbirth, or abortion; and sexual harassment. The following sections discuss these different categories of discrimination.

Discrimination Based on Race or Color

Discrimination in employment on the basis of race or color has existed in this country for more than 300 years.[5] During the last 100 years, the government has made serious attempts to live up to the Declaration of Independence: "We hold these truths to be self-evident, that all men are created equal."

The Civil Rights Acts of 1866, 1870, 1875, 1964, and 1991, along with the Thirteenth, Fourteenth, and Fifteenth Amendments (called the Civil War Amendments) to the Constitution, make racial discrimination illegal. The Civil Rights Act of 1866 specifically made it illegal to discriminate, contractually or otherwise, based on race. The 1866 Civil Rights Act today is used primarily in nonemployment cases, while Title VII is used for employment cases.

The 1866 act prohibits government officials from discriminating against people "under the color of law." For example, a police officer cannot stop a person solely on the basis of his race. The police officer, by stopping someone, acts under the color of law, that is, as if a legitimate reason existed to stop the person. If the police officer received a report that someone fitting the detained person's description robbed a bank, the stop would be legitimate and on a nondiscriminatory basis.

Discrimination Based on Religion

Of all the categories listed in Title VII, religion is the only one protected under the First Amendment of the U.S. Constitution. It reads in part:

Congress shall make no law respecting an establishment of religion, or prohibiting the free exercise thereof . . . .

Employers may not discriminate against employees on the basis of religion, unless the employer itself is a religious organization. Title VII exempts religious associations and religious educational institutions from the prohibition against discrimination on the basis of religion. For example, a Christian church would not have to hire a Jewish rabbi to officiate at its services. Whenever these organizations hire employees for nonreligious purposes, however, they are prohibited from

---

[4]The 1991 Civil Rights Act is at the same site as Title VII, http://www.eeoc.gov/laws/vii.html.

[5]For facts about race/color discrimination, see http://www.eeoc.gov/facts/fs-race.html.

LEGAL HIGHLIGHT

Discrimination and Education

Like businesses, educational facilities cannot discriminate on the basis of gender, color, race, or national origin, but they are covered by different federal statutes. Title IX of the Civil Rights Act of 1964 bans discrimination involving race, color, or national origin by any school that receives federal assistance. Practices that are prohibited are providing services, financial aid, or other benefits on a discriminatory basis.

Title IX of the Education Amendments of 1972 covers sexual discrimination. It provides that "no person in the United States shall, on the basis of sex, be excluded from participation in, be denied the benefits of, or be subjected to discrimination under any program or activity receiving federal assistance." The law applies to educational facilities. Discrimination in any area, including health, physical education, industrial arts, business, vocational, technical, home economics, music, or adult education courses, is banned.

A few exceptions allow classes to be segregated based on sex. Separate classes for discussing human sexuality, athletic segregation for sports involving bodily contact, or music classes for students whose vocal range or quality is best expressed in all-male or -female choruses are legal.

---

discriminating on the basis of race, gender, or national origin. For example, the religious association may not discriminate on the basis of race, gender, or national origin for the position of fund-raiser.

An employer must make reasonable accommodations to an employee's religious practices, beliefs, or observances, as long as the employer can do so without undue hardship in the conduct of its business.[6] Reasonable accommodation must be made for a person's religious clothing and religious observation day, such as Sunday.

The employer need only accommodate the employee's religious beliefs when the consequence to the employer is minimal. For example, an employee requests a vacation day to observe a religious holiday six months in advance. That request should be approved, especially if other employees do not observe the holiday.

On the other hand, if an employee works for an airline, the airline does not have to allow the employee every Sunday off. The employee knew when he was hired that people are needed to work twenty-four hours a day every day of the year because of the nature of the business. If the airline gave the employee every Sunday off, this schedule would be unfair to other employees who also may want some Sundays off. The employer, however, cannot target an employee by always scheduling the employee on his religious observation day with the intent of getting the person to quit.

Discrimination Based on National Origin

Title VII prohibits discrimination based on national origin,[7] but fails to define the term. By case law, *national origin* refers to the country in which a person is born or from which his or her ancestors came. In 1980, the EEOC issued guidelines that defined national origin discrimination to include denial of equal employment opportunity because of an individual's, or his or her ancestors', place of origin, or because an individual has the physical, cultural, or linguistic characteristics of a national origin group.

Title VII's prohibition of national origin discrimination forbids a foreign corporation that conducts business in the United States from discriminating in favor of its own nationals. This prohibition is waived if such discrimination specifically is permitted by a treaty.

Discrimination Based on Gender

Title VII prohibits discrimination based on gender. Title VII, however, does not prohibit employment

---

[6]For more facts about discrimination based on religion, see http://www.eeoc.gov/facts/fs-relig.html.

[7]For more facts about discrimination based on national origin, see http://www.eeoc.gov/facts/fs-nator.html.

LEGAL HIGHLIGHT

What's in a Name?

The National Organization for Women threatened, in October 1982, to file charges against a local police department in Palm Beach County, Florida. The patrol cars were emblazoned with the word "patrolman," and the local group believed that this discouraged women from applying for police jobs.

Concern with this type of language may seem at first to be misplaced. But language is an important barometer of the society that uses it. For example, if a language contains phrases like *lady lawyer* or *woman doctor*, you can be sure that women are new to these fields in that society. Language also directs and limits thoughts and ideas. When you hear the word *fireman* or *policeman*, it is hard to think of a woman in uniform. But any youngster could grow up to be a firefighter or police officer.

Under Title VII, employers generally may not use advertisements that indicate, through language or otherwise, any preference in hiring for a particular race, color, religion, gender, or national origin. Similarly, the Age Discrimination in Employment Act forbids help-wanted advertisements that imply that older workers

need not apply. An advertisement for a "gal Friday" or for an "ambitious young salesperson," for example, might be unacceptable on both counts.

Are prospective applicants really deterred by these language cues and other indications, such as listing certain help-wanted advertisements under gender-segregated columns that are headed "Jobs—Male Interest?" Some studies show this to be the case.

In one study, fifty-two women were asked to rate their willingness to apply for each of thirty-two jobs.[a] When the jobs were separated and labeled by gender, less than half of the women were as likely to apply for male-interest as for female-interest jobs. When the same advertisements were listed alphabetically with no reference to gender, more than 80 percent of the women preferred the male-interest jobs. This result was not surprising in at least one respect: These jobs averaged higher pay.

[a]Testimony of Sandra L. Bem and Daryl J. Bem, then of the Department of Psychology at Carnegie Mellon University, reproduced in Hearings on Section 805 of H. R. 16098, pp. 892–894, Special Subcommittee on Education of the House Committee on Education and Labor, July 31, 1970.

---

discrimination based on sexual or affectional preferences, nor does it protect transsexuals.

Protective state legislation, such as laws that prevented women from lifting more than twenty pounds of weight or from working at night, have been struck down. The protective state legislation often prevented women from obtaining higher paying jobs. Under EEOC guidelines, state statutes may not be used as a defense to a charge of illegal gender discrimination.

Gender-plus discrimination is also illegal under Title VII. This discrimination involves discrimination based on gender, plus an additional element. For example, in the past women with preschool-age children were refused employment. Title VII makes it illegal for an employer to refuse to hire these women when the employer hires men with preschool-age children. An employer may not require female employees to be single if male employees may be married. In the past,

male teachers could be married, but women teachers were required to remain single to keep their jobs.

Gender Discrimination Based on Pregnancy. Title VII was amended in 1978 by the **Pregnancy Discrimination Act.**[8] This act redefined gender discrimination to include discrimination based on pregnancy, childbirth, or related medical conditions. Based on this amendment, health and disability insurance plans must cover pregnancy, childbirth, or related medical conditions in the same way that they cover any other temporary disability.

An employer must provide leaves of absence for pregnant women on the same terms and conditions as those provided to any other worker who has a temporary disability. A woman who is pregnant cannot

[8]For more facts about pregnancy discrimination, see http://www.eeoc.gov/facts/fs-preg.html.

be forced to take maternity leave for any specified period of time. As long as she can perform her duties, she must be allowed to work. The 1978 amendment applies to both married and unmarried women and to any aspect of employment.

The following case involves disparate treatment, gender discrimination prohibitions, and pregnancy discrimination prohibitions under the 1964 Civil Rights Act and the Pregnancy Discrimination Act.

CASE 23.2 Supreme Court of the United States, 1991 499 U.S. 187,111 S. Ct. 1196, 113 L. Ed. 2d 158	# AUTOMOBILE WORKERS v. JOHNSON CONTROLS, INC. **BACKGROUND AND FACTS** Johnson Controls, Inc., manufactures batteries. In the manufacturing process, the element lead is a primary ingredient. Occupational exposure to lead entails health risks, including the potential harm to any fetus carried by a female employee.

Prior to the Civil Rights Act of 1964, Johnson Controls had not employed any women in battery manufacturing. In June 1977, the company adopted a policy of warning any female employee of childbearing age of the potential hazards of working in such a job and then having the employee sign a statement that she had been advised of the risks. Between 1979 and 1983, eight women became pregnant. Their blood lead levels were regarded as critical by the Occupational Safety and Health Administration (OSHA).

In 1982, Johnson Controls shifted from a policy of warning to a policy of excluding women. In 1984, the United Automobile, Aerospace, and Agricultural Implement Workers of America, United Automobile Workers, and others filed a class-action suit challenging the Johnson Controls fetal-protection policy as gender discrimination that violated Title VII of the Civil Rights Act of 1964.

Justice BLACKMUN delivered the opinion of the Court.

. . . .

The bias in Johnson Controls' policy is obvious. Fertile men, but not fertile women, are given a choice as to whether they wish to risk their reproductive health for a particular job. [T]he Civil Rights Act of 1964 prohibits sex-based classifications in terms and conditions of employment, in hiring and discharging decisions, and in other employment decisions that adversely affect an employee's status. Respondent's fetal-protection policy explicitly discriminates against women on the basis of their sex. The policy excludes women with childbearing capacity from lead-exposed jobs and so creates a facial [outward] classification based on gender.

. . . .

First, Johnson Controls' policy classifies on the basis of gender and childbearing capacity, rather than fertility alone. Respondent does not seek to protect the unconceived children of all its employees. Despite evidence in the record about the debilitating effect of lead exposure on the male reproductive system, Johnson Controls is concerned only with the harms that may befall the unborn offspring of its female employees. . . . Johnson Controls' policy is facially discriminatory because it requires only a female employee to produce proof that she is not capable of reproducing.

Our conclusion is bolstered by the Pregnancy Discrimination Act of 1978 (PDA) in which Congress explicitly provided that, for purposes of Title VII, discrimination "on the basis of sex" includes discrimination because of or on the basis of pregnancy, childbirth, or related medical conditions. The Pregnancy Discrimination Act has now made clear that, for all Title VII purposes, discrimination based on a woman's pregnancy is, on its face, discrimination because of her sex. In its use of the words "capable of bearing children" in the 1982 policy statement as the criterion for exclusion, Johnson Controls explicitly classifies on the basis of potential for pregnancy. Under the PDA, such a classification must be regarded, for Title VII purposes, in the same light as explicit sex discrimination. Respondent has chosen to treat all its female employees as potentially pregnant; that choice evinces discrimination on the basis of sex.

We concluded above that Johnson Controls' policy is not neutral because it does not apply to the reproductive capacity of the company's male employees in the same way as it applies to that of females.

. . . .

DECISION AND REMEDY The Court found that the policy was discriminatory on its face by requiring only women to prove themselves incapable of reproducing. The decision to work is that of the employed woman, not that of the employer.

CRITICAL THINKING: MANAGERIAL PERSPECTIVE How does a business protect itself from liability when employees work with hazardous materials? Can the employer have the employee waive any claims to future illness? Can the employee waive the rights to claims for illness on behalf of his or her unborn children?

Gender Discrimination in Pension Plans and Life Insurance. On the whole, women have a longer life expectancy than men. As a result, virtually all pension and annuity plans formerly required either that women pay into the plan a higher annual amount to receive the same yearly retirement benefits or that women pay the same annual amount but retire with a lower annual income.

Today, pension plans and life insurance plans must treat retirees as individuals rather than as classes of men or women. Even though women as a class live longer than men, many women die earlier than the average man, and many men outlive the average woman. Insurance plans now consider other factors in determining rates and benefits, such as smoking habits.

Gender Discrimination Using Sexual Harassment. By the late 1970s, federal courts began ruling that sexual harassment constituted illegal gender discrimination under Title VII.[9] Although Title VII fails to define sexual harassment, the Equal Employment Opportunity Commission adopted a regulation that defines sexual harassment as follows:

[9]For facts about sexual harassment, see http://www.eeoc.gov/facts/fs-sex.html.

Unwelcome sexual advances, requests for sexual favors, and other verbal or physical conduct of a sexual nature constitute sexual harassment when (1) submission to such conduct is made either explicitly or implicitly a term or condition of an individual's employment, (2) submission to or rejection of such conduct by an individual is used as the basis for employment decisions affecting such individual, or (3) such conduct has the purpose or effect of unreasonably interfering with an individual's work performance or creating an intimidating, hostile, or offensive work environment.

The guidelines recognize two kinds of harassment: (1) *quid pro quo* (Latin for "something for something" or "one valuable thing for another") and (2) hostile environment. The *quid pro quo* harassment occurs when the employee's pay, hours, promotion, termination, or other conditions of employment depend on whether the employee submits to the unwelcome or unsolicited verbal or physical conduct of a sexual nature.

A hostile environment exists when employees are subjected to unwanted sexual innuendos, vulgarity, suggestive conduct or touching, or propositioning for sexual favors by coemployees, supervisors, or customers, even though submission to sexual demands is not a condition of continued employment. If this unwanted conduct interferes with an employee's job performance or creates an intimidating, hostile, or offensive environment, the conduct is illegal.

The courts have held that sexual harassment applies to both male–female and female–male harassment. Unlawful harassment occurs even when the harasser is unaware that his conduct creates a hostile working environment. To prove a sexual harassment case, the employee must show that the conduct was of a sexual nature, that it was unwelcome, and that it was severe or pervasive enough in nature to alter the conditions of employment.

The employer may be held liable for illegal sexual harassment perpetrated in the company. To hold an employer liable for a hostile work environment, the employee must meet a two-part test. First, the

employer must have known or should have known of the sexual harassment in the workplace. Second, on notification, the employer must have failed to take prompt and corrective action. When an employer has a valid sexual harassment policy and procedure in place and responds in a timely and meaningful manner to the claim, the employer will not be held liable. An employer is strictly liable, however, when the case is based on a *quid pro quo* harassment.

The next case involves the behavior of the male president of a business toward a female business manager. The case dealt with whether the conduct was so abusive that it amounted to work environment harassment on the basis of gender, resulting in a violation of Title VII even though she did not claim an economic or tangible injury.

CASE 23.3	## HARRIS v. FORKLIFT SYSTEMS, INC.

Supreme Court of the United States, 1993
510 U.S. 17, 114 S. Ct. 367, 126 L. Ed. 2d 295
http://www.findlaw.com/casecode/supreme.html

BACKGROUND AND FACTS Teresa Harris worked as a manager at Forklift Systems, Inc., from April 1985 until October 1987. Charles Hardy was Forklift's president.

Hardy often insulted Harris because of her gender and often made her the target of unwanted sexual innuendos. In the presence of other employees, Harris made statements such as "You're a woman, what do you know" and "We need a man as the rental manager." At least once, he told her that she was "a dumb ass woman." Once he suggested that the two of them "go to the Holiday Inn to negotiate a raise."

In mid-August 1987, Harris complained to Hardy, who was surprised that Harris was offended and claimed that he was only joking. He apologized and promised to stop. Based on this assurance, Harris stayed on the job.

In early September, however, while Harris arranged a deal with one of Forklift's customers, Hardy asked her in front of other employees, "What did you do, promise the guy some sex Saturday night?"

On October 1, 1987, Harris collected her paycheck and quit. She brought action on the basis that the above comments created an abusive work environment for her because of her gender.

The federal district court found that these statements did not create an abusive environment. The court determined that although these statements offended Harris, they were not so severe as to affect seriously Harris's psychological well-being and should not have interfered with her work performance. The appellate court affirmed this decision, which was appealed to the United States Supreme Court.

Justice O'CONNOR delivered the opinion of the Court.

. . . .

Title VII of the Civil Rights Act of 1964 makes it "an unlawful employment practice for an employer . . . to discriminate against any individual with respect to his compensation, terms, conditions, or privileges of employment, because of such individual's race, color, religion, sex, or national origin." As we made clear in *Meritor Savings Bank v. Vinson,* this language "is not limited to 'economic' or 'tangible' discrimination. The phrase 'terms, conditions, or privileges of employment' evinces a congressional intent 'to strike at the entire spectrum of disparate treatment of men and women' in employment," which includes requiring people to work in a discriminatory hostile or abusive environment. When the workplace is permeated with "discriminatory intimidation, ridicule, and insult," that is "sufficiently severe or pervasive to alter the conditions of the victim's employment and create an abusive working environment," Title VII is violated.

This standard, which we reaffirm today, takes a middle path between making actionable any conduct that is merely offensive and requiring the conduct to cause a tangible psychological injury. As we pointed out in *Meritor,* "mere utterance of an . . . epithet which engenders offensive feelings in a [sic] employee" does not sufficiently affect the conditions of employment to implicate Title VII. Conduct that is not severe or pervasive enough to create an objectively hostile or abusive work environment— an environment that a reasonable person would not find hostile or abusive is beyond Title VII's purview. Likewise, if the victim does not subjectively perceive the environment to be abusive, the conduct has not actually altered the conditions of the victim's employment, and there is no Title VII violation.

But Title VII comes into play before the harassing conduct leads to a nervous breakdown. A discriminatorily abusive work environment, even one that does not seriously affect employees' psychological well-being, can and often will detract from employees' job performance, discourage employees from remaining on the job, or keep them from advancing in their careers. Moreover, even without regard to these tangible effects, the very fact that the discriminatory conduct was so severe or pervasive that it created a work environment abusive to employees because of their race, gender, religion, or national origin offends Title VII's broad rule of workplace equality. . . .

. . . Certainly Title VII bars conduct that would seriously affect a reasonable person's psychological well-being, but the statute is not limited to such conduct. So long as the environment would reasonably be perceived, and is perceived, as hostile or abusive, there is no need for it also to be psychologically injurious.

DECISION AND REMEDY The Supreme Court reversed the decisions of the two lower courts and held that if conduct adversely affected the work environment in such a manner that it would reasonably be perceived, or is perceived, as hostile or abusive, a Title VII violation has occurred.

CRITICAL THINKING: MANAGERIAL PERSPECTIVE How should a business handle a sexual harassment complaint?

The next case involves the sexual harassment of a male by other male coworkers. The question presented to the United States Supreme Court was whether same-sex harassment behavior violated Title VII.

CASE 23.4

Supreme Court of the
United States, 1998
523 U.S. 75, 118 S. Ct.
998, 140 L. Ed. 2d 201

ONCALE v. SUNDOWNER OFFSHORE SERVICES, INC.

BACKGROUND AND FACTS Oncale, the plaintiff, worked for Sundowner Offshore Services, a defendant, on a Chevron U.S.A., Inc., oil platform in the Gulf of Mexico. Oncale was married and the father of several children. He was employed as a roust-about on an eight-man crew, which included the following defendants: John Lyons, Danny Pippen, and Brandon Johnson. Lyons, the crane operator, and Pippen, the driller, had supervisory authority. On several occasions, Lyons, Pippen, and Johnson forcibly subjected Oncale to sex-related, humiliating actions in the presence of the rest of the crew. Pippen and Lyons also physically assaulted Oncale in a sexual manner, and Lyons threatened him with rape.

Oncale's complaints to supervisory personnel produced no remedial action; in fact, the company's safety compliance clerk, Valent Hohen, told Oncale that Lyons and Pippen "picked [on] him all the time too" and called him a name suggesting homosexuality.

Oncale eventually quit, asking that his pink slip reflect that he "voluntarily left due to sexual harassment and verbal abuse." When asked at his deposition why he left Sundowner, Oncale stated, "I felt that if I didn't leave my job, that I would be raped or forced to have sex." Oncale filed a complaint against Sundowner and the others alleging sex discrimination in his employment. The district court held that "Mr. Oncale, a male, has no cause of action under Title VII for harassment by male co-workers." Oncale appealed. The Court of Appeals for the Fifth Circuit affirmed the district court's holding.

Justice SCALIA delivered the opinion for a unanimous Court.

. . . .

We see no justification in the statutory language or our precedents for a categorical rule excluding same-sex harassment claims from the coverage of Title VII. As some courts have observed, male-on-male sexual harassment in the workplace was assuredly not the principal evil Congress was concerned with when it enacted Title VII. But statutory prohibitions often go beyond the principal evil to cover reasonably comparable evils, and it is ultimately the provisions of our laws rather than the principal concerns of our legislators by which we are governed. Title VII prohibits "discriminat[ion] . . . because of . . . sex" in the "terms" or "conditions" of employment. Our holding that this includes sexual harassment must extend to sexual harassment of any kind that meets the statutory requirements.

DECISION AND REMEDY The judgment reversed that of the Fifth Circuit. The Supreme Court concluded that sex discrimination consisting of same-sex sexual harassment was actionable under Title VII. Oncale could pursue his lawsuit against the defendants.

CRITICAL THINKING: MANAGERIAL PERSPECTIVE Will the Supreme Court's decision transform Title VII into a general civility code for the American workplace?

Equal Pay Act

The **Equal Pay Act**[10] of 1963 is an amendment to the Fair Labor Standards Act of 1938. The act is limited in scope because it prohibits gender-based discrimination in matters of wages. Pay for women and men for equal work on jobs that require equal skills, effort, and responsibility and that are performed under similar conditions must be equal. Job content rather than job description controls in all cases.

[10]The text of the Equal Pay Act is located at http://www.eeoc.gov/laws/epa.html.

For the equal pay requirements to apply, the act requires that male and female employees work at the same establishment. The issue is whether the jobs performed by the two employees are substantially equal rather than the equivalence of the employees' skills and training.

Small differences in job content fail to justify higher pay for one gender. The courts look to the primary duties involved in comparable jobs. For example, a "barber" and "beautician" perform essentially equal work, as do a "tailor" and a "seamstress."

Enforcement

The EEOC or private parties may bring suit under the Equal Pay Act. If, however, the government sues on behalf of a particular employee, that employee loses the right to sue, unless the employee already has brought suit.

All suits must be started within two years of the violation, or within three years if the violation is willful. Each payday amounts to a new violation. No employer may retaliate against an employee who brings suit or attempts to enforce her rights under the act.

Employers may not reduce the wages of men in order to be in compliance with the act. Rather, the wages of women must be increased. Back pay for up to two years (three years if the violation is willful) is available to the successful employee. Liquidated damages equal to the amount of back pay, plus attorneys' fees will be awarded, unless reasonable grounds exist for the employer to form a good-faith belief that it acted lawfully.

Exceptions

The Equal Pay Act provides specific exceptions. Pay differentials are allowed when based on seniority systems, merit systems, piecework, production bonus systems, or any considerations other than gender. These systems must be created in good faith and not created with the intention of specifically avoiding the act.

Bona fide training programs also may justify pay discrimination. As with the seniority or merit system, the training program must be formal and communicated to employees. If, however, a training program excludes female employees, payment of a premium to male trainees is indefensible.

INFOTRAC RESEARCH ACTIVITY

InfoTrac offers many articles covering the issue of equal pay. This is a subject that is continuously being reviewed. Go to InfoTrac and review the most recent five articles on this subject. Summarize these articles. In doing so discuss the major theme contained in these articles.

Age Discrimination in Employment Act

Congress passed the **Age Discrimination in Employment Act (ADEA)**[11] in 1967 to protect older workers. Before 1967, employers often refused to hire older workers or would fire longtime workers in their fifties and sixties. Younger workers who worked for lower wages and cost the company less in terms of medical benefits because they were younger replaced these older employees. Additionally, if the employer fired an older worker before he was vested in a retirement program, the employer would benefit by not paying out retirement funds.

Amendments have changed the original act to protect persons forty or older, with no upper age limit. The ADEA applies to employers that have twenty or more nonseasonal employees, labor unions with twenty-five or more members, and any employment agency. Most federal, state, and local government employees also are covered. Government workers in policymaking positions, however, are not covered.

Age discrimination is prohibited in all aspects of employment decisions. Discrimination in hiring, firing, promotions, compensation, privileges, or any other terms or conditions of employment is unlawful. Employment advertisements classified toward younger workers are illegal, although an advertisement can call for persons forty or older. Because persons under forty are unprotected, these advertisements are not discriminatory.

In 1990, Congress amended the ADEA with the **Older Workers Benefit Protection Act (OWBPA)**,[12]

[11]The text of the Age Discrimination in Employment Act is located at http://www.eeoc.gov/laws/adea.html.
[12]The text of the Older Workers Benefit Protection Act is located at the same Web page as the Age Discrimination in Employment Act: http://www.eeoc.gov/laws/adea.html.

which prohibits discrimination in benefits packages. The exception occurs when employers can justify age-based reductions in employee benefits plans by significant cost considerations. For example, a person who accepts early retirement will receive a lower retirement income than a person who works longer and retires at an older age. The person who works longer contributes more to her retirement benefits so is entitled to more income from those retirement benefits.

The EEOC is charged with investigating and enforcing the ADEA and the OWBPA. In addition, the law allows an individual to sue in civil court. This right to sue ends if the EEOC takes action to enforce the individual's right.

Recovery includes back wages, attorneys' fees, and equitable relief, such as hiring, reinstatement to the old job, and promotion. The act requires that the employer raise the wages of the person who suffered discrimination and the employer cannot reduce the wage of any employee to comply with the act. Criminal sanctions can be sought if an employer forcibly resists, opposes, impedes, intimidates, or interferes with EEOC representatives in the performance of their duties.

Americans with Disabilities Act

The **Americans with Disabilities Act (ADA)**[13] of 1990 provides federal civil rights protection to people with disabilities. Congress set a national mandate prohibiting discrimination in business and public settings against people with disabilities. Employers with fifteen or more employees may not discriminate against a qualified applicant with a disability.

The act defines a person with disabilities as any person who (1) has a physical or mental impairment that substantially limits one or more of the person's major life activities, (2) has a record of such an impairment, or (3) is regarded as having such an impairment. This protection extends to persons who have recovered from earlier disabilities, such as a person whose cancer is in remission and who currently is cancer free. In the past, this person would not have been protected. The act also extends protection to persons with acquired immune deficiency syndrome (AIDS) or who are HIV (human immunodeficiency virus) positive.

[13]The Americans with Disabilities Act is located at http://www.eeoc.gov/laws/ada.html. For facts, see http://www.eeoc.gov/facts/fs-ada.html.

LEGAL HIGHLIGHT

A Spouse Can Get Out of a Debt under Federal Law

The Equal Credit Opportunity Act (Chapter 14) forbids creditors from discriminating when granting credit based on gender, age, marital status, race, color, religion, national origin, or a person's income being derived from public assistance. The loan officer must make loan decisions based on a person's creditworthiness. The act's purpose is to prevent discrimination by a lender based on extraneous factors.

Financial institutions generally require both husband and wife to sign loan papers. Under federal regulations, "a creditor shall not require the signature of an applicant's spouse . . . on the credit instrument if the applicant qualifies under the creditor's standards of creditworthiness for the amount and terms of the credit requested" (12 C.F.R. § 9202.7).

Three state supreme courts and several federal district courts have found the statute to be violated when a financial institution requires both signatures when one spouse could obtain credit alone if he or she were single. The practical effect of these decisions is that only the spouse who takes out the loan is responsible for repaying it.

Employers also must make "reasonable accommodations" to facilitate the employment of people with disabilities. These accommodations include making facilities accessible, restructuring jobs, accommodating work schedules, and providing training policies and materials to qualified applicants.

Employers may show undue hardship and thus be excused from making reasonable accommodations. The defense of undue hardship means that significant difficulty or expense is involved in making reasonable accommodations. It includes a review of the employer's overall financial resources.

An explosion of litigation has occurred in this area. Employees' number one complaint is back problems, followed closely by mental disability. The most common mental claim is depression, with the requested accommodation being a flexible schedule or time off. Problems can be caused by other employees who do not claim a disability, but who see a fellow employee receiving a benefit, such as a flexible schedule, that they lack.

A potential liability exists for a business that reacts improperly to a disability claim. An employee must show that he was disabled within the statute's definition, that the employee was qualified to perform the essential functions of the job, and that the employee had suffered an adverse employment action under circumstances giving rise to possible discrimination.

The key issue is whether the employer knew an employee to be disabled or treated the employee as disabled. If so, then the employer must reasonably accommodate the employee.

A business may confront its largest losses in this area. For example, in *Miners v. Cargill Communications, Inc.,*[14] Miners, the employee, was observed on several occasions consuming alcoholic beverages during working hours. Cargill offered her an opportunity to attend a chemical dependency treatment program because her supervisor suspected that she might be an alcoholic. When she refused this program, Cargill immediately terminated her.

The court found that the employee had made out a *prima facie* case of discrimination under the ADA. Cargill regarded her as being an alcoholic, thus making her disabled. She was terminated because her employer believed that she was an alcoholic. The attempted accommodation was invalid because the employer had no real evidence that the employee was an alcoholic. The bottom line is that a business must be careful to avoid unjustified conclusions regarding employee disability. Ironically, Miners could have been terminated without liability if Cargill had a policy restricting employees from drinking while working.

The United States Supreme Court has limited the use of this statute. In *Toyota v. Williams*[15] the Court held that to be disabled must mean that a person must have major difficulty with daily activities, such as brushing his teeth. In doing so the Court stated the following:

> *We therefore hold that to be substantially limited in performing manual tasks, an individual must have an impairment that prevents or severely restricts the individual from doing activities that are of central importance to most people's daily lives. The impairment's impact must also be permanent or long term.*

This same thinking was expressed in the case of *Toyota Motor Manufacturing, Kentucky, Inc. v. Williams.*[16] Williams was hired as a automobile assembly line worker who eventually developed carpal tunnel syndrome. She requested reasonable accommodations but her employer refused her request. The Court found against Williams and held her medical problem did not substantially limit her life activity manual tasks.

If a seniority system is in place, however, the business is allowed to let a person who holds seniority to have preference over a person who has a disability for the job. In this situation, there are two competing interests, that of seniority and that of disability. The preference in this case goes to the person holding seniority.

Statutory Defenses

Prohibitions under Title VII and the other laws against discrimination are subject to the following three main statutory exceptions:

1. Bona fide occupational qualifications (BFOQs),
2. Bona fide seniority or merit systems, or
3. Professionally developed ability tests.

The following sections discuss these defenses.

Bona Fide Occupational Qualifications

Title VII allows discrimination in hiring based on gender, religion, or national origin if certain occupational criteria are met. An employer can never discriminate on the basis

[14]113 F.3d 820 (1997).

[15]534 U.S. 184, 122 S. Ct. 681, 151 L. Ed. 2d 615 (2002).
[16]534 U.S. 184, 122 S. Ct. 681, 151 L. Ed. 2d 615 (2002).

of race. A business can discriminate if it can demonstrate a **bona fide occupational qualification (BFOQ)**, which is a qualification reasonably necessary to that particular business's normal operation.

If the employer is sued for discrimination, the employer can use the defense of a BFOQ. The defendant employer has the burden to establish a BFOQ defense. To do so, the defendant must show the alleged discrimination to be a business necessity.

The courts interpret such a defense very narrowly. For example, courts may allow the BFOQ defense for situations in which gender or national origin is inherently part of the job qualification, such as for a wet nurse or for actor authenticity. Customer preference, on the other hand, is not a BFOQ. For example, if an airline surveys its customers and finds a preference for women flight attendants, the courts will refuse this customer preference as a BFOQ.

Bona Fide Seniority or Merit Systems

Statutes allow differences in the terms, conditions, or privileges of employment based on a **bona fide seniority** or **merit system**. The differences, however, cannot result from an intent to discriminate.

Most collective bargaining agreements between management and labor unions include detailed seniority systems. Indeed, such seniority systems are one of the most important aspects of collective bargaining agreements. A seniority system means that the newest employee would be the first laid off in a workplace reduction.

For a seniority system to qualify as an exception to Title VII, the system must be bona fide. A seniority system needs four factors to be bona fide:

1. The system must apply equally to all persons.
2. The seniority units (that is, occupational groupings for purposes of hiring, promoting, and terminating) must follow industry practices, and the units must constitute separate collective bargaining units.
3. The seniority system must not have its genesis in racial discrimination.
4. The system must not be incorporated for any illegal racial purposes.

Professionally Developed Ability Tests

Employers may give and act on the results of any **professionally developed ability test**. The test measures specific abilities related to job performance. An ability test, its administration, and the actions based on the results must not be intended to discriminate illegally.

If the test eliminates a disproportionate number of protected class members, the employer must meet the burden of proving that the particular test is job related. Validation studies that meet professional standards ordinarily prove job relation. For example, if a business hires a person to research on a computer and the Web, it can test a prospective employee for her computer skills. This job cannot require the applicant to take a graduate school admission test.

Prior to the 1991 Civil Rights Act, confusion existed as to whether a business could use race-norming methods to evaluate tests. To race-norm a test means to vary cutoff scores based on a person's race, color, religion, gender, or national origin. This practice became illegal under the 1991 act.

The 1991 act also prohibits quotas. In the past, quotas set a maximum number of people who could be hired or admitted, such as a quota on the number of Roman Catholics hired or admitted to a university. Quotas traditionally excluded people once the maximum amount was reached. Congress passed acts that require that goals be met (not quotas) in order to ensure that people were included.

Immigration Acts

The **Immigration Reform and Control Act** of 1986 has two purposes. First, the act provides for civil and criminal sanctions for employers. Employers suffer penalties if they (1) fail to verify their workers' employment eligibility and (2) knowingly hire any individual unauthorized to work. Second, employers cannot discriminate against workers based on their national origin or lack of citizenship if they are qualified to work in the United States.

The employer is responsible for verifying the worker's eligibility for work by using Form I-9, Employment Eligibility Verification, supplied by the U.S. Citizenship and Immigration Services (CIS), formerly the Immigration and Naturalization Service, which is part of the Department of Homeland Security. The CIS enforces the verification part of the act.

The form's completion involves a four-step process. First, on the first day of employment, the employer provides a Form I-9 to the new worker. Second, the statute outlines which document a prospective employee must provide to show that he is eligible to work in this country. The employee chooses the documents to present to complete the form. The employer must honor documents that on their face reasonably appear to be genuine. The employer must accept any document designated as acceptable by law.

Third, the employer reviews and completes the form. Fourth, the employer files the form in the employer's office separately from the worker's employment file because it contains information not pertinent to employment decisions.

The usual method is to file these forms in alphabetical order by year because, first, the CIS can easily inspect the files and, second, the employer must retain the form for one year after termination or three years after hiring. This filing method simplifies the determination of when forms may be destroyed.

During the hiring process, an employer may not adopt a blanket policy of preferring qualified citizens over qualified aliens, however, because this practice violates the antidiscrimination laws. The federal government determines eligibility to work and employers may not discriminate against eligible workers. If the federal government authorizes an alien who holds a government issued card, such as an Alien Registration Card ("green card"), to work in the United States, the employer must accept the card as proof of eligibility to work. The Department of Justice, Office of Special Counsel, is charged with investigating the claims of workers who believe they have been discriminated against.

The **Immigration Act** of 1990 was the first comprehensive overhaul of legal immigration in twenty-five years. The previous law favored immigration based on family ties with U.S. citizens or nationals. The new law favors immigrants based on their potential ability to contribute to the economy. Managers, professionals, and skilled laborers have preference under this law.

Affirmative Action

The current scope of **affirmative action** is primarily an outgrowth and continuation of attempts to remedy past legally authorized discriminatory practices that resulted in economic deprivation. Those traditionally discriminated against were women and minorities.

Affirmative action is based on a series of presidential executive orders.

In 1961, President John F. Kennedy (1961–1963) created a Committee on Equal Employment Opportunity. His executive order, which first coined the term *affirmative action*, called for the design of measures to achieve nondiscrimination.

President Lyndon B. Johnson (1963–1969) in 1965 issued an executive order requiring the federal government and federal construction contractors to implement affirmative action to ensure equality of employment opportunity regardless of race, religion, and national origin. In 1968, gender was added to the protected categories.

President Richard M. Nixon (1969–1974) signed an executive order in 1970 extending the plan to all federal contractors. As President Nixon remembered, "A good job is as basic and important a civil right as a good education is necessary and right. We would not impose quotas, but would require federal contractors to show affirmative action to meet the goals of increasing minority employment."

Unfortunately, the term *affirmative action* does not enjoy a clear and widely shared definition. Affirmative action refers to remedial steps taken to improve work opportunities for women and for racial and ethnic minorities who suffered economic harm because as classes they were deprived of job opportunities in the past. Under the Civil Rights Act of 1964, women and racial and ethnic minorities were designated as protected classes. By the same token, the Civil Rights Acts and affirmative action executive orders do not tolerate discrimination against white males based on their color or gender.

In the past, discrimination usually was sanctioned either by laws or by the government failing to prevent these inequities. Affirmative action is a process applied through a set of programs, some of which are required by court orders, some by national and state legislation, and some by administrative regulation.

Today, affirmative action is implemented by the federal government and federal contractors adopting affirmative action plans. The purpose of these plans is to improve job opportunities for protected classes. When measurable improvement in hiring, training, and promoting minorities and females is shown, the object of affirmative action has been met.

Affirmative action plans identify and work toward the elimination of artificial barriers to equal employment. A workforce analysis determines if women and protected minorities are being discriminated against. An affirmative action plan establishes timetables and goals (not quotas) to correct any substantial disparities. If an employer makes a good-faith effort to meet timetables and goals, it meets the requirements of affirmative action.

The employer must publicize the existence of its affirmative action program, both internally and externally. Supervisors and managers must be educated concerning the company's policy and of their responsibilities in implementing it. Recruitment sources also must be advised of the company policy. The company must take active steps to expand its traditional recruitment sources to include those sources likely to result in a higher flow of protected minority and female applicants. Finally, the employer must establish a procedure for monitoring the program's success.

At times, a person with better qualifications was denied a job opportunity when employers hired or promoted a lesser qualified individual from a protected class. The person with the lesser qualifications must be minimally qualified for the job to be selected. Opponents believe that affirmative action is prohibited by Title VII, which prohibits discrimination against anyone based on protected classifications.

Although affirmative action plans are adopted to remedy discrimination, these plans may cause, at times, reverse discrimination, that is, discrimination against a white male occurs. The issue of reverse discrimination was decided by the United States Supreme Court in the following case.

CASE 23.5

Supreme Court of the United States, 1987
480 U.S. 616, 107 S. Ct. 1442, 94 L. Ed. 2d 61

JOHNSON v. TRANSPORTATION AGENCY

BACKGROUND AND FACTS The Santa Clara County Transportation Agency voluntarily adopted an affirmative action plan for hiring and promoting minorities and women in 1978. The plan provided that in making promotions to jobs that traditionally had been segregated, the person's gender and ethnicity could be considered. The plan set short-range goals and annually adjusted these goals so that they could serve as a realistic guide for actual employment decisions. The long-term goal was to have a workforce whose composition reflected the proportion of minorities and women in the local area's general workforce.

In 1979, the agency announced a vacancy for a road dispatcher. Twelve employees applied for the promotion, including Joyce, a woman, and Johnson, a man. Both were deemed qualified for the job after their applications had been reviewed by two panels. Johnson tied for second place, while Joyce ranked next lower by two points. The case fails to explain what happened to the person who placed first or the person who tied with Johnson. At the time, the agency never had employed a woman as a road dispatcher. A panel that reviewed both records recommended Johnson for promotion.

The agency's affirmative action coordinator was responsible for informing the agency's director of opportunities for the agency to accomplish its objectives under the affirmative action plan. The coordinator recommended that Joyce be hired for the job after he reviewed both applications with their respective qualifications, test scores, expertise, and background and considered affirmative action matters.

The director accepted the coordinator's recommendation and promoted Joyce. He considered the two-point difference in her ranking to be insignificant as he looked at the whole picture.

Johnson filed a complaint with the Equal Employment Opportunity Commission based in part on reverse discrimination. In other words, he did not receive the job because he was a man, therefore, he was discriminated against. He received a right-to-sue letter from the EEOC. The district court held for Johnson. The Ninth Circuit Court of Appeals, however, overturned that decision. The U.S. Supreme Court granted *certiorari*.

Justice BRENNAN delivered the opinion of the Court.

. . . .

It is clear that the decision to hire Joyce was made pursuant to an Agency plan that directed that sex or race be taken into account for the purpose of remedying under-representation. The Agency Plan acknowledged the "limited opportunities that have existed in the past" for women to find employment in certain job classifications "where women have not been traditionally employed in significant numbers." As a result, observed the Plan, women were concentrated in traditionally female jobs in the Agency, and represented a lower percentage in other job classifications than would be expected if such traditional segregation had not occurred.

. . . .

We next consider whether the Agency Plan unnecessarily trammeled the rights of male employees or created an absolute bar to their advancement. . . . The Plan expressly states that "[t]he 'goals' established for each Division should not be construed as 'quotas' that must be met." Rather, the Plan merely authorizes that consideration be given to affirmative action concerns when evaluating qualified applicants. As the Agency Director testified, the sex of Joyce was but one of numerous factors he took into account in arriving at his decision. . . . [T]he Agency Plan requires women to compete with all other qualified applicants. No persons are automatically excluded from consideration; and are able to have their qualifications weighed against those of other applicants.

. . . .

We therefore hold that the Agency appropriately took into account as one factor the sex of Diane Joyce in determining that she should be promoted to the road dispatcher position. The decision to do so was made pursuant to an affirmative action plan that represents a moderate, flexible, case-by-case approach to effecting a gradual improvement in the representation of minorities and women in the Agency's work force. Such a plan is fully consistent with Title VII, for it embodies the contribution that voluntary employer action can make in eliminating the vestiges of discrimination in the workplace.

DECISION AND REMEDY The judgment of the court of appeals was affirmed. The agency had appropriately taken into account Joyce's gender as one factor in determining her promotion. The Supreme Court found that the agency's plan was moderate and flexible and that it provided a case-by-case approach to reaching the long-term goal of improvement in the representation of minorities and females in the agency's workforce.

CRITICAL THINKING: MANAGERIAL CONSIDERATION What provisions should be included in a business's affirmative action plan?

Affirmative action covers other activities besides employment. Both federal and state levels of government have attempted to assist minority-owned businesses. The governments provide assistance by giving preference to minority-owned companies. Additional compensation is paid if a contract is entered with such a business. In the following case, the United States Supreme Court decided whether the requirement to prefer a minority-owned company in a federal construction contract was constitutional.

CASE 23.6

Supreme Court of the
United States, 2001
528 U.S. 216, 120 S. Ct.
722, 145 L. Ed. 2d 650
http://www.findlaw.com/
casecode/supreme.html

ADARAND CONSTRUCTORS, INC. v. SLATER

BACKGROUND AND FACTS This case is unique in that the U.S. Supreme Court
heard and decided the case twice, once in 1996 (*Adarand I*) and again in 2000 (*Adarand
II*). The basic facts of this case are as follows. Congress passed the Intermodal Surface
Transportation Efficiency Act of 1991 (ISTEA), which authorizes the Department of
Transportation (DOT) to oversee a balanced transportation system, expand safety programs, and continue transportation building programs. Congress had a long-standing
policy that favored contracting with small socially and economically disadvantaged
businesses when a federal contract was involved. To effectuate that policy, ISTEA
directed 10 percent of the appropriated contracting funds be spent on contracting with
disadvantaged businesses.

To qualify for that status, a business had to be certified as owned and controlled by
socially and economically disadvantaged individuals. DOT relied on certifications from
two main sources. First, the Small Business Administration (SBA) certified businesses
for all types of federal procurement programs. Second, state highway agencies certified
businesses. These agencies automatically certified as socially disadvantaged those who
were black, Hispanic, Asian Pacific, Subcontinent Asian, Native Americans, members of
other groups, and women.

In 1989, the DOT awarded a contract for a Colorado highway construction project
to Mountain Gravel & Construction Company, the prime contractor. The prime contract included a subcontractor compensation clause. This clause was required by the
SBA to be included in all prime contracts entered into by all federal agencies. Under this
clause, the prime contractor was rewarded for subcontracting with disadvantaged business enterprises.

Mountain Gravel solicited bids from subcontractors for the guardrail portion of the
contract. Adarand is a Colorado-based highway construction company specializing in
guardrail work. Adarand, whose principal is a white male, submitted the low bid on the
guardrail portion of the project.

Gonzales Construction Company, certified as disadvantaged by the Colorado
Department of Transportation (CDOT), submitted a higher bid. The prime contract
provided that Mountain Gravel would receive additional compensation if it hired a certified company. Gonzales was certified, but Adarand was not. Mountain Gravel would
have contracted with Adarand except for receiving the additional compensation from
the federal government for contracting with a socially and economically disadvantaged
business.

Adarand sued alleging that the subcontractor compensation clause and, in particular, the race-based presumption that forms its foundation violated its Fifth Amendment right to equal protection. The Tenth Circuit upheld the use of the clause and the
presumption. Adarand appealed to the U.S. Supreme Court. Because DOT's use of
race-based measures should have been subjected to strict scrutiny, the U.S. Supreme
Court reversed the case and remanded it back to the district court for a rehearing based
on the strict scrutiny standard.

The district court re-reviewed the case and held that the presumption that members
of the specified racial groups are socially disadvantaged was both overinclusive and
underinclusive, because it included members of those groups who are not personally
disadvantaged and excluded members of other groups who were. The district court
enjoined DOT from using the clause and its presumption. The case was appealed to the
Tenth Circuit.

While the appeal was still pending, Adarand filed a second suit in the district court,
this time against certain Colorado officials. This suit challenged Colorado's method of
certifying disadvantaged business enterprises for federally assisted projects.

Shortly after the second suit was filed, Colorado altered its certification program in response to the district court's decision in its re-review. Specifically, Colorado repealed its presumption of social disadvantage for certain minorities and women, and in its place required that all applicants certify on their own individual statement that each of the firm's majority owners "has experienced social disadvantage based upon the effects of racial, ethnic or gender discrimination," but did not require any further showing of social disadvantage. Adarand requested and received disadvantaged business certification from CDOT.

Meanwhile, on learning that CDOT had certified Adarand as a disadvantaged business, the Tenth Circuit held that the cause of action was moot and vacated the District Court's judgment favorable to Adarand. A petition for the writ of *certiorari* was filed by Adarand with the U.S. Supreme Court, which granted the writ.

PER CURIAM

. . . .

In so holding, the Tenth Circuit "confused mootness with standing," and as a result placed the burden of proof on the wrong party. If this case is moot, it is because the Federal Government has accepted CDOT's certification of petitioner as a disadvantaged business enterprise, and has thereby ceased its offending conduct. Voluntary cessation of challenged conduct moots a case, however, only if it is "absolutely clear that the allegedly wrongful behavior could not reasonably be expected to recur." And the "'heavy burden of persua[ding]' the court that the challenged conduct cannot reasonably be expected to start up again lies with the party asserting mootness."

Because respondents cannot satisfy this burden, the Tenth Circuit's error was a crucial one. As common sense would suggest, and as the Tenth Circuit itself recognized, DOT accepts only "valid certification[s]" from state agencies. As respondents concede, however, DOT has yet to approve—as it must—CDOT's procedure for certifying disadvantaged business enterprises. . . .

DOT has promulgated regulations outlining the procedure state highway agencies must follow in certifying firms as disadvantaged business enterprises.

As described earlier, those regulations require the agency to presume that "women, Black Americans, Hispanic Americans, Native Americans, Asian-Pacific Americans, Subcontinent Asian Americans, or other minorities found to be disadvantaged by the Small Business Administration," are socially disadvantaged. Before individuals not members of those groups may be certified, the state agency must make individual determinations as to disadvantage. . . . CDOT's new procedure under which petitioner was certified applies no presumption in favor of minority groups, and accepts without investigation a firm's self-certification of entitlement to disadvantaged-business status. Given the material differences (not to say incompatibility) between that procedure and the requirements of the DOT regulations, it is not at all clear that CDOT's certification is a "valid certification," and hence not at all clear that the Subcontractor Compensation Clause requires its acceptance.

Before the Tenth Circuit, respondents took pains to "expres[s] no opinion regarding the correctness of Colorado's determination that [petitioner] is entitled to [disadvantaged-business] status." Instead, they stated flatly that "in the event there is a third-party challenge to [petitioner's] certification as a [disadvantaged business enterprise] and the decision on the challenge is appealed to DOT, DOT may review the decision to determine whether the certification was proper." In addition, DOT itself has the power to require States to initiate proceedings to withdraw a firm's disadvantaged status if there is "reasonable cause to believe" that the firm "does not meet the eligibility criteria" set forth in the federal regulations. Given the patent incompatibility of the certification with the federal regulations, it is far from clear that these possibilities will not become reality. Indeed, challenges to petitioner's disadvantaged-business status seem quite probable now that the Tenth Circuit, by vacating *Adarand II*, has eliminated the sole basis for petitioner's certification in the first place.

. . . .

It is no small matter to deprive a litigant of the rewards of its efforts, particularly in a case that has been litigated up to this Court and back down again. Such action on grounds of mootness would be justified only if it were absolutely clear that the litigant no longer had any need of the judicial protection that it sought. Because that is not the case here, the petition for writ of *certiorari* is granted, the judgment of the United States Court of Appeals for the Tenth Circuit is reversed, and the case is remanded for further proceedings consistent with this opinion.

DECISION AND REMEDY The Court held in the first case that all governmental action, by either the state or federal government, based on racial or other classifications should be subjected to detailed judicial inquiry to ensure that the personal right to equal protection of the laws has not been infringed. Any such classifications must be analyzed by a reviewing court under strict scrutiny and will be upheld only if they are narrowly tailored measures that further compelling governmental interests. In the second case, the Supreme Court found that the issue as to mootness was not sustained in that the DOT may not accept the Colorado approach as to when a company can be certified as being disadvantaged.

CRITICAL THINKING: POLITICAL PERSPECTIVE Should a business owned by a minority or a woman have a preference in obtaining government contracts?

Affirmative action programs apply to more than businesses. They also apply to institutions that are federal contractors, including universities. In 2003, the U.S. Supreme Court heard and decided two cases, one involved admission to undergraduate programs[17] and the other involved admission to law school.[18] Both actions were brought against the University of Michigan. The holdings in both cases effectively apply to all schools receiving federal funding.

The Court in both cases emphasized, as it has in previous cases, the importance of considering each particular applicant as an individual, assessing all of the qualities that individual possesses, and, in turn, evaluating that individual's ability to contribute to the unique setting of higher education. In the case involving undergraduate admissions, the Court found that the admission policy that automatically distributed 20 points (one-fifth of the points needed to guarantee admission) to every single "underrepresented minority" applicant

solely based on race was not narrowly tailored to achieve the interest in educational diversity and violated the Equal Protection Clause of the Fourteenth Amendment. This admission procedure almost guaranteed the admission of minority students who were minimumly qualified. The point system, which amounted to an illegal quota system with no individual review of the applicant, was held to be unconstitutional.

In the law school case, the admissions committee reviewed all issues involving the student file. One of the issues was race along with grades, test scores, recommendations, and other criteria. Race did not guarantee the admission of a student who was a minority but it did assist him or her. No one factor was deemed so important that standing alone made a difference between admission and denial.

The admission policy stressed that no applicant should be admitted unless the committee expected the applicant to do well enough to graduate with no serious academic problems. The purpose was to achieve a level of diversity that had the potential to enrich everyone's education. The policy did not restrict the types of diversity contributions eligible for substantial weight in the

[17]Gratz v. Bollinger, 539 U.S. 244, 123 S. Ct. 2411, 156 L. Ed. 2d 257 (2003).
[18]Grutter v. Bollinger, 539 U.S. 306, 123 S. Ct. 2325, 156 L. Ed. 2d 304 (2003).

admissions process, but instead recognized many possible bases for diversity admissions. The policy did, however, reaffirm the law school's long-standing commitment to one particular type of diversity, that is, racial and ethnic diversity with special reference to the inclusion of students from groups that have been historically discriminated against, such as African Americans, Hispanics, and Native Americans, who without this commitment might not be represented in the student body in meaningful numbers.

The Court deferred to the law school's educational judgment that such diversity is essential to its educational mission. To be narrowly tailored, the Court reaffirmed that a quota system could not insulate each category of applicants with certain desired qualifications from competition with all other applicants. The university could consider race or ethnicity only as a "plus" in a particular applicant's file, without insulating the individual from comparison with all other candidates for the available seats. In other words, the Court said that "an admissions program must be flexible enough to consider all pertinent elements of diversity in light of the particular qualifications of each applicant, and to place them on the same footing for consideration, although not necessarily according them the same weight." The Supreme Court found that the law school's admissions program was constitutional because it was a narrowly tailored plan.

Over the years many states have adopted their own affirmative action plans through either legislation or administrative rulings. The criticism that affirmative action leads to reverse discrimination has existed since its inception.

As a reaction to this criticism, some states have moved to eliminate affirmative action. California is one of these states. The voters amended the California constitution by adopting a measure that removed any statute or regulation that granted preferential treatment to current and prospective state government employees based on race, gender, color, ethnicity, or national origin. This constitutional provision was upheld by the United States Court of Appeals, Ninth Circuit, as conforming with the equal protection clause of the U.S. Constitution. The Supreme Court of the United States refused to hear the case, thus, the California law is valid.

Protection for Members of the Military Reserve Force and National Guard

As the active-duty military force in the United States is reduced in size, more reliance is placed on the members of the military reserve force and the National Guard. Employers who saw their workers called up for active duty in conflicts in Somalia, Haiti, Bosnia, Afghanistan, and Iraq to name a few, learned that the federal law protects those workers.

The Uniformed Services Employment and Reemployment Rights Act (USERRA) provides protection and rights of reinstatement to employees who participate in the National Guard and Reserve.[19] Federal law requires these service members to do two weeks of active duty, commonly called summer camp, and to be called up for active duty during a national or international crisis.

[19]The National Committee for Employer Support of the Guard and Reserve can be found at http://www.esgr.org/.

LEGAL HIGHLIGHT

Posting of Labor Laws

Specific employee information notices must be posted at every separate business location. The federal government requires information to be posted on the Occupational Safety and Health Act, Federal Minimum Wage Notice, Employee Polygraph Protection Act, Equal Employment Opportunity Commission/Age Discrimination, and the Family and Medical Leave Act.

State governments can require other mandatory posters, such as workers' compensation and job safety and health protection information. Failure to do so may result in federal and state penalties. Does your employer comply with these requirements?

An employer cannot discriminate against a person because he serves in the reserve force or the National Guard. An employer, therefore, cannot refuse to hire a person on this basis. An employer must reemploy returning persons without loss of seniority and must restore all benefits to them. Using an escalator as an analogy, an employer must place the returning employee back on the escalator where the employee would have been if she had remained on the job. If the employee's position has been eliminated, the employer must place the worker in a similar position.

If the job changes in the reservist's absence, the reservist must accept the changed job. The returning person is entitled to all cost-of-living pay raises, but not to merit pay. The reservist cannot be discharged without cause for six months after returning to work.

If a business refuses to hire or to reemploy a reserve force or National Guard member, a federal court can order the business to offer the person a job. If an employer refuses to comply with the law, the U.S. attorney can bring appropriate action on behalf of the individual. All back wages and benefits can be sought by the applicant dating back to the time at which the business illegally refused the person the job.

CYBERLAW

Workplace Privacy

Millions of businesses and households use the World Wide Web. Many computers are capable of using a Webcam (camera), downloading and uploading streaming video, and telephony (using the computer as a telephone). Some Web sites are devoted to watching people at work. Up to now, letting people watch you at work through the Web sites has been voluntary.

The computer used at work can be connected to a Webcam that allows the world and supervisors to see what the employees are doing. Employers have the ability to track everything done by employees on their computers. Employers can track the number of hours spent playing computer games or shopping on the Web and time spent using the computer as a telephone talking with family and friends around the world, and, of course, they can read employees' e-mail. Employees wearing badges with encoded stripes can be tracked as they move through the work buildings.

Computers manufactured after 1996 come equipped with microphones. The employer can install a software program that can listen to everything said near the computer.

Technology has progressed to the point where faces can be logged into databases. Faces of people on streets can be recorded by a street camera for later comparison with faces in the database, such as those of criminals. Will your employer be able to track you on your private time, shopping, driving, or visiting a government office to file a complaint?

International Consideration

Progress against Discrimination

In the 1960s, the United States started to develop its antidiscrimination laws. The process has continued as further discrimination patterns have become apparent. Most countries have not developed laws as stringent as those in the United States. Few countries provide protection for alien workers, prevent discrimination based on religious beliefs, or provide help based on race or color. Still, international progress in this area slowly is being made.

The European Union (EU) has adopted nonbinding legislation prohibiting sexual harassment. The code is a guide for employers and unions in all EU member countries. Until this legislation was adopted, individual countries had no laws specifically prohibiting sexual harassment. The EU, however, has laws requiring equal pay for work of equal value for men and women. In addition, EU members have laws providing mandatory paid parental leave and requiring management to hold a woman's position open until she returns from maternity leave. A combination of government, management, and union programs provides child care.

The 1991 Civil Rights Act, Title VII of the Civil Rights Act of 1964, and the Americans with Disabilities Act apply to all U.S.-based companies operating in foreign nations. These statutes apply to U.S. employees working for U.S. companies overseas. Employers must comply with these statutes unless doing so would violate the foreign country's laws.

The United States protects older workers from discrimination. The benefits of hiring and continuing to employ older workers are being discovered by management around the world. For example, a retail firm in Great Britain, annoyed at the high turnover of its younger workers, decided to hire workers over age fifty-five. Much to the firm's surprise, the benefits were immediate. Absenteeism dropped dramatically, losses from employee theft decreased, employee turnover dropped, and fewer workers' compensation claims were reported. Customer satisfaction went up and business increased. The older workers took more interest in knowing the products and explaining them to customers. The workers' politeness was very much appreciated by the customers. The experiment was such a success that the firm plans to hire more older workers in its other stores.

PRACTICAL TIPS

Discriminatory Questions

One of the more important business procedures is the hiring of new employees. Before an individual is hired, most businesses ask the person to fill out standard employment applications or answer standard questions. Some of the information sought may be considered discriminatory in nature. Questions that can be discriminatory can take these forms:

1. What is your maiden name?
2. How old are your children? How old is your youngest child?
3. What is your birth date?
4. Have you ever declared bankruptcy?
5. Are you married? (Single? Divorced? Separated? Widowed?)
6. (A more subtle form of the same question): Is there anyone in your life who strongly influences your decisions?
7. Who will care for your children while you are working?
8. How long have you lived at your present address?
9. What is your father's name?
10. Have you ever had your wages garnished?
11. Where do you bank? Do you have any loans outstanding?
12. Do you own or rent your home?
13. Were you ever arrested?
14. What religious group do you belong to? What is the name of your priest? Rabbi? Minister?
15. Where does your husband (wife, father, mother) work?
16. How did you learn to speak Spanish (German, Russian, and so on)?
17. List for me all the societies, clubs, and lodges you belong to.

Thinking through these questions before they come up will help an applicant to handle them in the best way. They may never come up. If they do, though, there are options. Answering militantly ("I'll see you in court for asking me that!") is a no-win choice. Answering something like "Legally I do not have to provide you with that information" is not the best option either.

Try to answer so as to (1) deflect that line of questioning courteously, (2) give the interviewer some useful, helpful information, and (3) not put him or her in the wrong. Suppose the interviewer has asked, "How will you have your children cared for while you work?" One way to answer is "If you'll show how this question is related to my ability to do a good job for you, I'll be glad to answer." Or applicants can say child care is all taken care of and then refer to their record of low absenteeism in their current job, despite family responsibilities.

Another way is to try to think why the interviewer is asking a particular question—why he or she is worried about how you will have your children cared for—and restate the question behind the question. You might say, "If by asking me that question you really mean is, 'Will I be on the job every day, on time, and ready to give my full attention and energy to the job?' the answer is most definitely 'Yes.'"

A third option is a little riskier but sometimes effective. If the rapport up until that question has been pleasant and if you are pretty sure that you are not talking to an ogre, you might be able to laugh pleasantly and say, "I'll bet you didn't really mean to ask me that question, did you?"

Most often, interviewers will back away from the "don't ask" questions if the applicants show in a low key and courteous way that they want to answer only questions directly related to their qualifications for the job. If the interviewer does not back away, the applicant might reconsider whether he or she really wants to work for this type of organization. Worse than not being hired is being hired by an organization where you would be unhappy. Before the interview, consider these factors:

Checklist

✔ *Questions* Think through all the possible questions, good and bad, that you might be asked.

✔ *Preplan* Determine how you will respond.

✔ *Research* Update your research on the company.

The last part of the interview usually consists of the interviewer's question: "Now what questions do you have that I can answer?" If you have researched the company, you should have a number of questions you can ask to show your interest and knowledge.

Source: Business Correspondence for Today, by J. W. Gilsdorf. Copyright 1989. Reprinted by permission of John Wiley & Sons, Inc.

Chapter Summary

The major federal statutory provisions that seek to prevent discrimination in employment are the Equal Pay Act of 1963, Title VII of the Civil Rights Act of 1964, the Age Discrimination in Employment Act of 1967, Older Workers Benefit Protection Act of 1990, and the Americans with Disabilities Act of 1990. Gender discrimination; pregnancy discrimination; sexual harassment; pension plans and life insurance plans; and discrimination based on religion, national origin, or race are prohibited.

Title VII prohibits discrimination for employment based on race, color, religion, national origin, and gender. It covers employers with fifteen or more employees, labor unions with fifteen or more members, and employment agencies.

Two basic legal theories underlie actions based on Title VII. According to the disparate treatment theory, the treatment of any individual that differs from the treatment of other employees based on background or gender is discrimination. Under the disparate impact theory, although on the surface a certain practice is not discriminatory, its effect can discriminate against a protected class. Under either theory, the employer can be found liable.

The Equal Employment Opportunity Commission (EEOC) is charged with the enforcement of Title VII. A person files a charge with the EEOC, which then attempts to settle the potential dispute.

The employer has three statutory defenses to any action under Title VII: (1) bona fide occupational qualifications, (2) bona fide seniority or merit systems, and (3) professionally developed ability tests.

The Immigration Reform and Control Act of 1986 places the burden on the employer to screen applicants and prohibits discrimination on the basis of citizenship or national origin. The employer records the documents that the applicant provides to show that she or he is a citizen or a qualified alien. Members of the military reserve force and National Guard are also protected against discrimination by federal statute.

Affirmative action is the process of improving work opportunities for women and minorities who have been discriminated against in the past. The idea behind affirmative action plans is that if a member of a protected class has the necessary requirements for a job, that individual should receive preference in hiring, training, and promotion. The United States Supreme Court has approved the concept of affirmative action.

Using the World Wide Web

The legal aspects of employment and labor law are provided on many sites on the World Wide Web. Nearly everyone has worked, so employment law is of importance to many. Type into any search engine the name of a statute within the employment and labor law and a number of Web sites will appear.

For *Web Activities*, links to Web sites mentioned in the chapter, and additional Web sites that relate to the chapter topics, go to **http://bohlman.westbuslaw. com**, click on "Internet Applications," and select Chapter 23.

Web Activities

Go to **http://bohlman.westbuslaw.com**, click on "Internet Applications," and select Chapter 23.
23–1 Sexual Harassment
23–2 Employer Support

Key Terms

affirmative action
Age Discrimination in
    Employment Act
    (ADEA)
Americans with
    Disabilities Act (ADA)
bona fide occupational
    qualification (BFOQ)

bona fide seniority or
    merit system
disparate impact
disparate treatment
Equal Employment
    Opportunity
    Commission (EEOC)
Equal Pay Act

Immigration Act
Immigration Reform
    and Control Act
Older Workers Benefit
    Protection Act
    (OWBPA)
Pregnancy
    Discrimination Act

prima facie case
professionally developed
    ability test
Title VII of the Civil
    Rights Act of 1964

Questions and Case Problems

23–1 Civil Rights Act, Title VII Discuss fully which of the following constitute a violation of the 1964 Civil Rights Act, Title VII, as amended.

a. Causeway, Inc., is a consulting firm with ten employees who travel on consulting jobs in seven states. Causeway has an employment record of hiring only white males.

b. Filmtex, Inc., is making a film about Africa. Filmtex needs to employ 100 extras for this picture. Filmtex advertises in major newspapers in southern California for the hiring of these extras. The advertisement states that only African Americans need apply.

c. Green is a major processor of cheese sold throughout the United States. Green employs 100 employees at its principal processing plant. The plant is located in Windward City, which has a population that is 50 percent white and 25 percent African American, with the balance Hispanic American, Asian American, and other minorities. Green requires a high school diploma as a condition of employment on its cleanup crew. Three-fourths of the city's white population complete high school, compared with only one-fourth of the city's minority population. Green's cleaning crew is all white.

23–2 Age Discrimination in Employment For thirty years, Christine McKennon worked for Nashville Banner Publishing Company (Banner) before being

terminated. She believed she was terminated from her job because of her age. She filed suit in federal district court alleging that her discharge violated the Age Discrimination in Employment Act. In preparation for the case, Banner took McKennon's deposition in which she admitted that she had copied and taken home several confidential documents bearing on the company's financial condition. A few days after the deposition, Banner sent McKennon a letter declaring that removal and copying of the records violated her job responsibilities and advising her again that she was terminated. Banner conceded to discriminating against McKennon because of her age, but her misconduct also provided grounds for her termination. The district court granted the summary judgment, which was affirmed by the appellate court. The case was appealed to the United States Supreme Court. What was the result? Explain.
[*McKennon v. Nashville Banner Publishing Co.*, 513 U.S. 352, 115 S. Ct. 879, 130 L. Ed. 2d 852 (1995)]

23–3 Civil Rights Act, Title VII The state of Connecticut required applicants to take a written examination before being considered for a supervisor position. Of those taking the test, whites had a 79 percent passing rate and African Americans had a 34 percent passing rate. The state of Connecticut showed, however, that more African American than whites were promoted from the eligibility list. The state argued that this "bottom line" was a defense to the discrimination suit.

Was this a valid defense? Explain. [*Connecticut v. Teal*, 457 U.S. 440, 102 S. Ct. 2525, 72 L. Ed. 2d 130 (1982)]

23–4 Affirmative Action The city of Memphis, Tennessee, implemented an affirmative action plan. In 1981, the city confronted severe deficits and had to lay off a considerable number of employees. The city announced that it would follow the last-hired/first-fired rule. This policy was contrary to the city's affirmative action plan in that it would cause a large number of African Americans to be terminated. The district court ordered the city to modify the layoff plan to reduce the number of African Americans adversely affected. The case was appealed to the United States Supreme Court. The issue presented was whether a seniority plan that was not intentionally discriminatory would be upheld when the effect was to lay off large numbers of African Americans. What decision do you think the Court reached? Explain. [*Firefighters Local Union No. 1784 v. Stotts*, 467 U.S. 561, 104 S. Ct. 2576, 81 L. Ed. 2d 483 (1984)]

23–5 Civil Rights Act, Title VII Elizabeth Hishon was employed as an associate attorney for a large law firm in Atlanta, Georgia. The firm had more than 100 lawyers but never made a woman a firm partner. The district court held that Title VII was not applicable to the selection of partners in a law firm because partners are owners, not employees, of a firm. Do you think that the district court was correct? Explain. [*Hishon v. King & Spalding,* 467 U.S. 69, 104 S. Ct. 2229, 81 L. Ed. 2d 59 (1984)]

23–6 Age Discrimination in Employment Western Airlines required all of its pilots to retire at age sixty to conform with the Federal Aviation Administration's regulation. Criswell was physically fit and wanted to continue flying past the age of sixty. When he was required to retire, he instituted action. Was this age requirement a valid BFOQ? Explain. [*Western Airlines v. Criswell*, 472 U.S. 400,105 S. Ct. 80, 86 L. Ed. 2d 321 (1985)]

23–7 Civil Rights Act, Title VII Five employees, white and African American, were terminated by Omni Georgia and replaced by five people of Korean origin.

The supervisor who terminated the employees was of Japanese origin. The five terminated employees brought action based on violation of Title VII. Was the law violated? Explain. [*Bullard v. Omni Georgia*, 640 F.2d 632 (5th Cir.1981)]

23–8 Civil Rights Act, Title VII Hasselman was required to wear a "revealing and provocative" uniform while working as a lobby attendant in a large office complex. She was subjected to repeated sexual harassment by different people. Finally, she refused to wear the uniform and was terminated. Was her termination a violation of Title VII? Explain. [*EEOC v. Sage Realty Corp.*, 507 F. Supp. 599 (S.D.N.Y. 1981)]

23–9 Civil Rights Act, Title VII Velva Wise was employed by Mead Corp. She and another employee were involved in a fight. Prior to this fight, four other reported fights among employees had occurred. Only one person had been fired because of fighting, and this was a male who had been involved in two out of the four fights. Wise claimed that Mead discriminated against her when she was terminated. Was she correct? Explain. [*Wise v. Mead Corp.*, 614 F. Supp. 1131 (M. D. Ga. 1985)]

23–10 Internet As an employer, you are concerned about an investigation being conducted by the Equal Employment Opportunity Commission (EEOC) concerning a sexual harassment complaint. Go to the EEOC's Web page at **http://www.eeoc.gov**. On the right side, under "Laws, Regulations, and Policy Guidance," click on "Enforcement Guidances and Related Documents." Scroll to the bottom until you see "Enforcement Guidance on *Harris v. Forklift Sys., Inc.* Date issued 9/9/93," then click on it. Scroll to the bottom until you see "Charge Processing." What are the three steps investigators should look for in their investigation? *Note:* The "Policy Guidance on Current Issues of Sexual Harassment Date issued 3/19/90" referred to in the "Charge Processing" is available on the previous Web page directly below "Enforcement Guidance on *Harris v. Forklift Sys., Inc.* Date issued 9/9/93."

Chapter 24

Environmental Law

To waste, to destroy, our natural resources, to skin and exhaust the land instead of using it so as to increase its usefulness, will result in undermining in the days of our children the very prosperity which we ought by right to hand down to them amplified and developed.

Message to Congress, December 3, 1907
President Theodore Roosevelt,
1858–1919
Twenty-sixth president of the United States of America, 1901–1909
Nobel Peace Prize, 1906

Chapter Outline

Ethical Consideration

Balancing the Need to Protect the Environment and to Meet Current Exigencies

Your company produces a variety of pesticides, including one that eradicates virtually all insects. This particular product, called Life Protector, is banned in the United States because it is highly toxic and poses dangers to farm workers, the general environment, and consumers who ingest the toxic residue. In spite of these dangers, many developing nations use this highly efficient product because it allows crops to grow in insect-infested locations.

Although your company has placed warning labels on the product that list specific rules for its proper handling and application, environmental organizations inform your company that poor, illiterate farm workers apply Life Protector without wearing gloves, breathing apparatuses, or other protective devices required for safety. Your company also has information that the pesticide is being overapplied in many areas and is seeping into the groundwater, creating the potential for severe and long-lasting environmental damage.

You are disturbed by the many reports of the product's misuse. You consider either stopping production or demanding proof that Life Protector is being used correctly before distributing it in a particular country. When you raise these concerns with foreign purchasers, however, they assure you that they are aware of the dangers and are doing the best they can to regulate the pesticide's use. They also contend that the potential for harm, especially in the future, is greatly outweighed by the current need to feed their vast numbers of citizens. They even say that it is better for a few people to die from Life Protector than for many to starve without sufficient crops. Do you continue to manufacture Life Protector and distribute it as you have done in the past, or do you attempt to control its use? Use the ethical model presented in Chapter 2 and reprinted on the inside front cover to develop your answer.

Introduction

The oil spill of the *Exxon Valdez* tanker in Alaska and the meltdown at a nuclear power plant in Chernobyl, Ukraine (formerly part of the Union of Soviet Socialist Republic), conjure in the mind spectacular environmental disasters. Scientific research has discredited traditional beliefs that air, water, and land can absorb and cleanse waste products without being harmed. As our society and the world become more urbanized, concerns grow about the degradation of the environment.

Economic growth, greater wealth, and the proliferation of synthetic products that resist decomposition have motivated policymakers to seek strategies to clean up, reduce, and finally prevent pollution. Environmental laws focus on protecting nature and restraining the people whose activities upset the earth and its delicate life-sustaining ecosystems. These laws also regulate human pollution of air, water, and land.

This chapter covers past, present, and future methods for handling pollution problems. The chapter reviews federal legislation that covers clean air, water, noise, and toxic substances. Administrative agencies implement most of these federal laws through regulations and criminal prosecutions.

Artiste Login. Carlo and Carlotta's online business, Artiste Login Products, Inc., must comply with the environmental laws. The business uses raw material, such as bronze, for its sculptures. Artiste also uses various types of paints for its canvas paintings and for specially manufactured dinnerware. The bronze material and paints that are left over from these processes must be disposed of in accordance with federal and state statutes. Otherwise, Artiste is subject to civil and criminal penalties. Anyone who orders improper disposal, such as dumping the material in a lake or river, may face prison time. Artiste needs to adopt an environmental policy in order to ensure compliance with federal and state laws.

Historical Background

Environmental concerns are not new. In medieval England, the English Parliament passed a number of laws that regulated the burning of soft coal. In the United States, those harmed could seek common law restitution by suing under one of several theories: private nuisance, trespass, negligence, and strict liability.

Property owners historically were granted relief by the courts under the common law doctrine of private nuisance from pollution. The individual had to be able to identify a pollution source that caused a distinct harm to himself separate from harm affecting the general public. A nuisance occurred when a person used her property in a manner that adversely affected a neighbor's property. Thus, if a factory polluted the air and killed a farmer's crops, the farmer could recover damages from the factory.

Nuisance suits that resulted in specific relief for individuals were inadequate when the harm from pollution could not be identified as affecting specific groups as opposed to the public at large. Under the common law, citizens were denied relief without showing specific harm. If a group of citizens wanted to stop a new development that would cause significant water pollution, the group would be denied any relief under the doctrine of private nuisance on the ground that the harm to the group did not differ from the harm borne by the general public. When the public is harmed, only the government can sue under the common law theory of public nuisance.

Another common law cause of action is trespass. Trespass is defined as the intentional or unintentional intrusion on another's land uninvited, regardless of whether any physical damage is done. Traditionally, to be successful in a trespass suit, the landowner had to prove a direct physical invasion of the land, such as the dumping of debris on the property. Today, trespass occurs often in subtler fashion, for example, through radiation pollution or through permeation by a harmful invisible gas. A trespass suit will provide recovery when these invasions harm plant life or destroy animals. Today, under either the trespass or nuisance theory, courts require the plaintiff to show both invasion and harm.

In addition to the torts of nuisance and trespass, injured parties may file a common law negligence action. The basis for a negligence suit is a business's failure to use reasonable care toward an individual's foreseeable injury. Failure to use pollution controls may give rise to an action for negligence, for example, when contamination of the air produces respiratory illnesses in employees and neighboring residents.

Courts have allowed injured parties to recover under the theory of strict liability in tort. Businesses that engage in ultrahazardous activities, such as blasting operations or transporting of radioactive material, are liable for injuries that these activities cause, even if the businesses exercised the utmost care. With strict liability, the injured party does not need to prove the damages resulted from the party's fault (failure to use due care).

Inherent problems exist in pursuing any of these remedies. Historically, the common law limited relief from pollution to situations in which the harm was caused by two or more independent sources. For example, if a number of firms pollute the air, a harmed individual could sue any individual firm. Until early in the twentieth century, however, the plaintiff was unable to sue all of the factories simultaneously. Thus, specific proof of damages in individual actions often was impossible.

These difficulties in seeking relief in pollution cases, coupled with the fact that tort theory initially only allowed for money damages and thus was ineffective in preventing environmental harms, ultimately gave rise to the federal and state legislation that today regulates and controls activities affecting the environment.

Regulation by State Government

State governments have some authority in regulating the environment. The private tort actions just noted take place under state laws. Federal legislation permits direct state or local governmental control of the environment. Many states have statutes against polluting the air, the water, and the general environment.

State laws range from restricting the amount of emissions from motor vehicles to requiring state environmental impact statements for developments above a certain size or monetary amount and to restricting the disposal of toxic material. These laws vary from one state to another because each state has its own problems. State environmental laws influence business decisions. Many of these state statutes were passed under pressure from the federal government.

Several states, for example, have attempted to regulate the dumping of bottles and cans through the use of what are commonly called "bottle bills." The following case illustrates the implementation of one of the first statutes of this kind of regulation.

<table>
<tr><td>

CASE 24.1

Court of Appeals, Oregon, 1973

15 Or. App. 618, 517 P.2d 691

</td></tr>
</table>

AMERICAN CAN CO. v. OREGON LIQUOR CONTROL COMMISSION

BACKGROUND AND FACTS The state of Oregon adopted a law prohibiting the use of nonreturnable containers for beer and carbonated beverages. The law also prohibited the sale of metal beverage containers that used detachable pull-top opening devices. The American Can Company filed a lawsuit against the Oregon Liquor Control Commission attacking the validity of the statute, claiming violation of equal protection and due process clauses of the Fourteenth Amendment and the commerce clause of the U.S. Constitution. The trial court upheld the law. American Can Company appealed.

Judge TANZER

. . . .

The primary legislative purpose of the bottle bill is to cause bottlers of carbonated soft drinks and brewers to package their products for distribution in Oregon in returnable, multiple-use deposit bottles toward the goals of reducing litter and solid waste in Oregon and reducing the injuries to people and animals due to discarded "pull tops."

. . . .

. . . [T]he introduction of any new circumstance affecting competition will cause economic winners and economic losers throughout the industry as it readjusts to that new circumstance. The evidence is that plaintiffs expect to be among the losers, unless, of course, they are able to make marketing adjustments.

Economic loss restricted to certain elements of the beverage industry must be viewed in relation to the broader loss to the general public of the state of Oregon which the legislature sought, by enactment of the bottle bill, to avoid. The availability of land and revenues for solid waste disposal, the cost of litter collection on our highways and in our public parks, the depletion of mineral and energy resources, the injuries to humans and animals caused by discarded pull tops, and the esthetic blight on our landscape, are all economic, safety and esthetic burdens of great consequences which must be borne by every member of the public. The legislature attached higher significance to the cost to the public than they did to the cost to the beverage industry, and we have no cause to disturb that legislative determination.

The bottle bill is not discriminatory against interstate commerce and is not intended to operate to give Oregon industry a competitive advantage against outside firms. The ban on pull tops and the deposit-and-return provisions apply equally to all distributors and manufacturers whether Oregon-based or from out of state. According to plaintiffs' testimony, the economic burden of the industry's adjustment to the change will be shared by Oregon businesses as well as non-Oregon businesses. . . .

. . . .

Plaintiffs' . . . constitutional challenges having failed, we hold the bottle bill to be a valid exercise of Oregon's police power. In doing so, we acknowledge having had the benefit of an able analysis by the trial court.

DECISION AND REMEDY The appellate court affirmed the trial court's ruling that Oregon legitimately exercised its state police power in passing laws concerning solid waste disposal. It recognized the additional cost to the beverage industry, but the court would not accept that cost as a justification for overturning a legislative enactment. Hence, the bottle bill was upheld.

CRITICAL THINKING: POLITICAL CONSIDERATION Can any business ethically justify opposition to control over bottles and cans?

Regulation by Local Government

County and municipal local governments control certain environmental aspects. Zoning laws adopted by local governments control the land use. Many communities have adopted ordinances controlling the appearance of buildings. Both usage and appearance regulations have a direct impact on the local government.

Currently, Americans generate about 160 million tons of solid waste per year. Packaging is one form of solid waste that rapidly is increasing. Compact discs, for example, are placed in containers that are much larger than the discs themselves in order to prevent theft. Food is packaged in individual servings to provide convenience and to reduce food waste. Both types of packaging result in increased solid wastes. Cities and counties have the primary responsibility for disposing of this and other types of garbage. Landfills take 85 percent of the solid wastes, while only 8 percent is incinerated. The rest, including glass, newspapers, and cans, is recycled.

Ordinances controlling outdoor billboards, antinoise laws prohibiting certain levels of noise from being heard beyond the business premises, and laws banning smoking indoors are examples of local government regulations. Political decisions in these areas often are hard to make. If smoking is banned in restaurants, will the patrons go to restaurants in the next city? Less patronage means less income for businesses, which leads to fewer taxes collected by the local government and, thus, less money available for programs.

Private Litigation

Private parties can recover damages or obtain injunctions for environmental harms under a combination of statutory and common law provisions. The Clean Air Act, the Clean Water Act, and the Noise Control Act, for example, authorized private lawsuits for violations of air, water, and noise pollution standards.

Class-action lawsuits may be filed under these statutes. A **class-action lawsuit** is a suit brought by a limited number of individuals on behalf of a much larger group. These particular lawsuits are brought against companies that pollute the air or water, that make excessive noise, or that have handled or use hazardous substances. The plaintiffs can claim personal injury damages or diminution in property values as a result of exposure to environmental hazards. The remedy in class-action suits is the recovery of money, rather than pollution control.

Some federal statutes give the government the exclusive right to file lawsuits for violations of environmental protection regulations. When the government has the exclusive right to sue, state governments and private parties are limited to assisting the federal authorities in the lawsuit.

Regulation by the Federal Government

Congress has changed its attitude toward the environment over the decades. In the first stage, described in the section titled *Historical Background*, little was done to prevent environmental damage or to control pollution. The second stage began in the 1960s, when Congress enacted statutes aimed at environmental cleanup. In the third stage, Congress continued its interest in cleaning up the environment while expanding its focus toward the goal of preventing pollution in the first place. Keep in mind that all the federal statutes described in the following sections represent a financial or health cost to someone: the government, the business community, or the individual.

During the 1960s and 1970s, neither federal nor state governments brought many environmental criminal prosecutions. In the 1980s, this attitude changed and the change continues today. During the early 1980s, the Environmental Protection Agency, the U.S. Department of Justice (DOJ), and the offices of state attorneys general together established special units designed exclusively for the investigation and prosecution of environmental crimes.

Since 1982, the DOJ has brought more than 1,100 indictments for environmental crimes. Of this total, 825 plea bargains were entered into or a trial was held and convictions were obtained. A plea bargain is a process in criminal court in which the defendant bargains with the prosecutor to plead guilty, usually on a reduced charge compared to the original charge, such as pleading guilty to manslaughter when the original charge was murder. More than 430 years of prison time were imposed, of which 227 years were actually served. More than $254 million was paid in criminal fines. For example, Rockwell International was fined $18.5 million for hazardous waste and water quality criminal violations at the Rocky Flats nuclear weapons plant near Denver, Colorado. Exxon was fined $125 million for the Valdez, Alaska, oil spill. This spill was discussed in detail in Chapter 2.

National Environmental Policy Act

The **National Environmental Policy Act (NEPA)** of 1969 created the Environmental **Protection Agency (EPA)**.[1] The EPA makes the regulatory rules for the various federal environmental acts.

NEPA also mandated the **environmental impact statement (EIS)**. The EIS is undertaken by the particular federal agency that proposes to build or fund a project. For example, the Federal Bureau of Investigation (FBI) needs to construct a new building to house its fingerprinting center. The FBI must file an EIS that analyzes the impact on the environment of the proposed building. Every proposed major federal project or federally funded project must have an EIS. The EIS has become an instrument for private citizens, businesses, and federal agencies to help shape the final outcome of federal projects.

The EIS must contain (1) the environmental impact of the proposed action; (2) any adverse effects to the environment, along with alternative actions that might be taken; and (3) the irreversible effects that the action might create.

---

[1]The Web site for the Environmental Protection Agency is http://www.epa.gov.

Air Pollution

Federal involvement with air pollution goes back to the 1950s, when Congress authorized funds for air pollution research. In 1963, Congress passed the **Clean Air Act**,[2] which focused on multistate air pollution and provided assistance to states for the implementation of antipollution measures. Various amendments over the years have strengthened the government's authority to regulate air quality. In 1990, Congress passed a sweeping overhaul of the Clean Air Act. The reform measures provided stronger cleanup provisions and formulated prevention measures.

Air pollution silently damages human and animal health, vegetation, lakes, and forests. The original act distinguished between two types of air pollutants. The first type causes death or serious illness at low levels and is discussed in a later subsection titled *Air Toxics*. The second type are criteria pollutants, so named because the EPA must issue criteria documents identifying the effects of each pollutant. These pollutants are discussed in a later subsection titled *National Ambient Air Quality Standards*.

Although both types of pollutants were included in the original Clean Air Act, the 1990 amendments gave the EPA more authority. In 1989, Congress determined that more than 150 million people were still living in areas that failed to meet the air quality standards. The reasons for the failure to achieve healthy air are diverse.

State Implementation Plans. Although the 1990 Clean Air Act is a federal law affecting the entire country, the states do much of the work to carry out the act. The EPA sets limits on the amounts of different pollutants that can be in the air anywhere in the United States. These limitations ensure that all Americans have the same basic environmental protections. The law allows individual states to set stronger pollution controls, but states are prohibited from adopting weaker pollution controls than those set by the EPA.

Each state must take a complete emissions inventory of all polluters, designating them as stationary or mobile. The law recognizes that states should take the lead in carrying out the Clean Air Act because pollution control problems often require special understanding of local industries, geography, housing patterns, traffic patterns, and climate conditions.

---

[2]A copy of the Clean Air Act can be obtained at http://www.law.cornell.edu/uscode/42/7403.shtml.

Although taking an emissions inventory sounds like a relatively easy task, sometimes the source of an emission is elusive, such as dust sources, particularly in arid areas of the western United States. Air pollution often travels from its source in one state to another state. In many metropolitan areas, people live in one state and work or shop in another. Air pollution generated from cars and trucks as people and goods move about daily spreads throughout the interstate area. The Clean Air Act encourages the creation of interstate commissions to develop regional strategies for cleaning up air pollution.

Air pollution also moves across national borders. The law covers pollution that originates in Mexico and Canada and drifts into the United States and vice versa. Under the Clean Air Act, each state was required to develop its own **state implementation plan** (SIP). A SIP is a collection of state regulations for cleaning up polluted areas. The state must involve the public, through hearings and opportunities to comment, in the development of its SIP.

The EPA approves each SIP, and if a SIP is unacceptable, the EPA can take over enforcement of the Clean Air Act in that state. The EPA assists the states by providing scientific research, expert studies, engineering designs, and money to support clean air programs.

National Ambient Air Quality Standards. The EPA uses six criteria pollutants as indicators of air quality.[3] The EPA has set a maximum concentration above which adverse effects on human health may occur. These threshold concentrations are called the **National Ambient Air Quality Standards (NAAQS)**. These standards set uniform, nationwide ambient air quality standards.

Primary ambient standards are adopted to protect public health. These standards set the lowest level of pollution at which an effect on health is observed and

[3]More information about ozone and particulate matter and related programs can be found on the EPA's Office of Air Quality Planning and Standards Web page: http://www.epa.gov/oar/oaqps.

LEGAL HIGHLIGHT

Benefits and Costs of the Clean Air Act

Recently, the EPA conducted a study to estimate and report the benefits and costs of historical air pollution control programs under the Clean Air Act by comparing the differences between two scenarios: (1) an actual scenario reflecting historical economic and environmental conditions observed with the Clean Air Act in place and (2) a hypothetical scenario projecting the economic and environmental conditions that would have prevailed without the federal, state, and local programs developed pursuant to the goals of the 1970 and 1977 Clean Air Acts.

Using a sophisticated array of computer models, the EPA found that by 1990 the differences between the scenarios were so great that, under the so-called "no-control" case, an additional 205,000 Americans would have died prematurely and millions more would have suffered illnesses ranging from mild respiratory symptoms to heart disease, chronic bronchitis, asthma

attacks, and other severe respiratory problems. In addition, the lack of Clean Air Act controls on leaded gasoline use would have resulted in IQ (Intelligence Quotient) loss in children and major increases in hypertension, heart disease, and stroke in adults. Other quantified benefits expressed in dollar terms included visibility improvements, improvements in some agricultural crop yields, improved worker attendance and productivity, and reduced household soiling damage.

When the human health, human welfare, and environmental effects were added up for the entire twenty-year period, the total benefits of Clean Air Act programs were estimated to be about $6 trillion to about $50 trillion, with a mean estimate of about $22 trillion. These benefits represented the value Americans place on avoiding the dire air quality conditions and dramatic increases in illness and premature death that would have prevailed without the 1970 and 1977 Clean Air Acts and their associated state and local programs. By comparison, the actual costs of achieving the pollution reductions observed over the twenty-year period were $523 billion, a small price for the benefits received.

LEGAL HIGHLIGHT

Outer Continental Shelf Activities

Air pollution comes from unlikely sources, such as the outer continental shelf (OCS) activities. Translated, this term refers to offshore drilling and to ships causing emissions in excess of 500 tons of oxides of nitrogen (NOx) annually. The emissions from constructing one drilling platform are 350 tons of NOx.

Drilling a single exploration well can exceed 100 tons of NOx. A major offshore oil project easily exceeds the air pollution caused by 100,000 automobiles that meet 1988 California emission standards, each traveling 10,000 miles. The 1990 Clean Air Act marked the beginning of regulation of OCS activities. The standards for controlling this source of pollution are the same as those for similar onshore areas.

include a safety margin. Primary standards are based on the impact of air quality on human health without consideration of the costs in attaining the standards.

Secondary ambient standards protect public welfare. These standards protect against adverse impacts on human welfare, such as visibility, vegetation, animals, wildlife, crops, buildings, transportation, and property. Secondary ambient standards must be attained within a reasonable time period.

The six criteria pollutants for which ambient standards have been set are ozone, lead, sulfur dioxide, particulates, nitrogen dioxide, and carbon monoxide. Three potentially critical pollutants are ozone, carbon monoxide, and particulates.

Ozone is fatal at high concentrations. Of the ozone people inhale, 90 percent is never exhaled. It reacts rapidly with cells and irritates and inflames the lungs. Nearly 58 million people in the United States live in areas with high ozone concentrations.

Carbon monoxide absorbs more readily into blood than does oxygen. Carbon monoxide displaces oxygen and threatens bodily functions. High concentrations are fatal. Because it poses particular harm to fetal development, pregnant women are especially at risk. Nearly 1.4 million pregnant women live in areas with high concentrations of carbon monoxide. Motor vehicles are the single largest source of ozone and carbon monoxide pollution. As a result, an annual $2 fee is assessed on motor vehicle registration in areas where the air quality fails to meet the standards.

Particulate matter measuring less than ten microns in diameter (PM-10) can produce a range of effects from temporary lung dysfunction to death. A *micron* is

a unit of length equal to one-millionth of a meter. Particulates come from wood stoves, power station emissions, exhausts from diesel vehicles, and common dust.

Particulates impair visibility so much that the National Park Service reports that scenic views are visually impaired 90 percent of the time. People in the United States spend $40 billion per year in health-care costs because of particulate matter. Legislators anticipate that if the new air quality standards are met, the amount saved in health costs will offset the plan's estimated $2.79 billion in pollution control costs.

Attainment and Nonattainment Areas. A geographic area that meets or does better than the National Ambient Air Quality Standards is called an **attainment area**. The Clean Air Act defines a **nonattainment area** as a locality where air pollution levels persistently exceed National Ambient Air Quality Standards.[4]

Designating an area nonattainment is a formal rule-making process and EPA normally takes this action only after the area exceeds air quality standards for several consecutive years. Nonattainment areas fall into one of five classifications based on the air pollution's severity: (1) marginal area, (2) moderate area, (3) serious area, (4) severe area, or (5) extreme area.

Market Approaches. The 1990 Clean Air Act includes many features designed to clean up air pollution

---

[4]Designating an area nonattainment requires a formal rule-making process (see Chapter 6). The EPA normally takes this action only after air quality standards have been exceeded for several consecutive years. The EPA lists all the nonattainment sites at http://www.epa.gov/airs/nonattn.html.

LEGAL HIGHLIGHT

Even Lawn Mowers Pollute

Gasoline-powered lawn mowers, edgers, trimmers, and leaf blowers pollute the atmosphere. One gasoline-powered lawn mower used for one hour releases into the air as much pollution as thirty automobiles will release during the same time period. And if you live in Southern California, this makes for a lot of smog.

First seen in 1903, Los Angeles suffered a severe smog attack in 1947.[a] Deciding that it was time for action, Los Angeles created the Los Angeles County Air Pollution Control District. By 1953, a task force recommended the following steps be taken within Los Angeles County:

- Reduce hydrocarbon emissions by cutting vapor leaks from refineries and fueling operations.

- Establish automobile exhaust standards.

- Burn propane instead of diesel in trucks and buses.

- Slow the growth of heavily polluting industries.

- Ban open trash burning.

- Develop a rapid transit system.

The Air Pollution Control District evolved into the South Coast Air Quality Management District (AQMD).[b] It serves as the smog control agency for all or portions of Los Angeles, Orange, Riverside, and San Bernardino Counties, California, where 14 million people breathe the dirtiest air in the United States. What actions does the AQMD recommend today for you to do?

- Purchase an electric or battery-powered lawn mower.

- Use water-based paints labeled "zero-VOC" (volatile organic compound) when painting homes. The lower the VOC content, the better.

- When reroofing a home, use a lighter shade of roofing material to reduce the need for air conditioning and cut electricity bills in the summer. Plant trees for shade.

- Fire up the barbecue briquettes with an electric probe instead of starter fluid, or use a barbecue fueled by natural gas or propane.

- Purchase high-fuel efficiency and low-emissions automobiles, or even an electric vehicle.

- When filling the car's gas tank, latch the nozzle on to avoid breathing toxic gasoline fumes. Avoid topping off the gas tank to prevent spilling fuel, a significant source of air pollution.

- Keep the car tuned.

- Car pool and consolidate errands whenever possible to reduce driving.

- Report smoking vehicles, faulty gasoline nozzles, and industrial or commercial polluters suspected of violating air quality regulations to the proper authorities.

Although the Los Angeles area still suffers from smog, the air is cleaner than it has been for decades.

[a] In London, in December 1952, a killer smog so thick that residents could see no more than three feet claimed 4,000 lives.
[b] The Southern California AQMD Web site is http://www.aqmd.gov.

---

as efficiently and inexpensively as possible. The act encourages businesses to choose the best ways to reach pollution cleanup goals. These new flexible programs are called market-based approaches. For instance, the acid rain cleanup program offers businesses choices of methods for reaching their pollution reduction goals and includes pollution allowances that can be traded, bought, and sold. Gasoline refiners receive credits for producing cleaner gasoline than required, which they can then use on those occasions when their gasoline fails to meet cleanup requirements.

The federal government allows companies that pollute, such as utilities, a limited ability to pollute. Otherwise, the electrical utilities in some major metropolitan areas would have to cease operations. But sometimes these limited allowances are insufficient to cover actual pollution so a utility is allowed a number of credits to trade for a limited ability to continue to pollute.

Comparison of two companies, Clean Utility and Dirty Utility, illustrates the trading market operation. Clean Utility has installed emission control and therefore releases only small amounts of pollution. Dirty Utility has not yet been able to afford the costly pollution controls. Under the regulations, both utilities can pollute up to 100 tons of sulfur dioxide a year. Clean Utility releases only 10 tons per year, while Dirty Utility releases 150 tons. Dirty Utility can release 100 tons legally, and can purchase credits for the other 50 tons. Clean Utility can sell credits for the 90 tons that it does not release because of the pollution controls it installed.

These credits are traded on the Chicago Board of Trade. Recently, the credits rose from $68.14 to $110.36 for each ton that is discharged into the atmosphere. Trading of these credits gives a business an additional reason to install antipollution equipment.

Air Toxics. Hazardous air pollutants are toxic and generally cancer causing. Toxic releases from major manufacturing facilities amount to approximately 2.7 billion pounds a year. Cancer incidences may be as high as 500,000 fatal cases for Americans alive in 1992.

In 1985, in Institute, West Virginia, the Union Carbide plant had an accidental toxic release. An Occupational Safety and Health Administration (OSHA) investigation discovered 221 safety and health violations at Union Carbide's Institute plant. OSHA imposed a fine of $1.38 million for willful disregard of health and safety.

Accidental releases of extremely hazardous substances during a recent four-year period caused 309 deaths, 11,341 injuries, and the evacuation of 464,677 people from homes and jobs. Seventy percent of the events occurred at stationary facilities, and 30 percent were related to transportation.

As a result of the harm caused by air toxics, the EPA established a list of hazardous air pollutants, and the list can be amended as needed. A national air toxics clearinghouse was established to coordinate and disseminate information.

Acid Rain. Acid rain is extremely corrosive and can damage humans and materials. It can dissolve heavy metals and destroy materials such as stone, rubber, zinc, steel, leather, and paint. Congress convened a task force to investigate acid rain and to study the impact of acid rain on bodies of water, forests, and crops.

Ozone Layer and Climate Protection. The earth's main shield against the sun's harmful ultraviolet radiation is the ozone layer. Scientific evidence now shows that this layer is being destroyed. At the same time, global warming, commonly called the *greenhouse effect*, has been detected. The national goal is to correct these two problems.

First, the government has programs in place to eliminate the emissions that destroy the ozone layer (for example, chlorofluorocarbon-based automobile refrigerants will no longer be manufactured). Second, the emissions that have led to, and that perpetuate, the warming of the climate are being reduced.

The EPA has issued standards to protect the ozone. The most recent standards are based on averaging air quality over an eight-hour block of time instead of the one hour used previously. This new standard helps protect people who spend significant time outdoors. The air quality standard is an average concentration of pollutants over an eight-hour period during a week, month, or year.

Enforcement. The EPA can issue administrative citations for which the penalties can go up to $200,000 in any given case. Criminal liability can be imposed for unlawful releases of toxic pollutants, including negligent releases.[5] The Office of Enforcement and Compliance Assurance (OECA) works in partnership with EPA regional offices, state governments, tribal governments, and other federal agencies to ensure compliance with the nation's environmental laws. Employing an integrated approach of compliance assistance, compliance incentives, and innovative civil and criminal enforcement, OECA and its partners seek to maximize compliance and reduce threats to public health and the environment.

Water Pollution

Federal regulations governing water pollution can be traced back over a century to the **Rivers and Harbors Act** of 1886, amended in 1890 and in 1899. These regulations required a permit for discharging or depositing refuse in navigable waterways. The courts

---

[5]The Office of Regulatory Enforcement (ORE) is located within the EPA. The ORE's Web site is located at http://www.epa.gov/compliance. Some penalties that have been imposed are available for review at http://www.epa.gov/ozone/enforce.

Enforcement by EPA

The Environmental Protection Agency regulates approximately 8 million government and business sources of potential pollution. The EPA has a number of devices to ensure compliance that are backed by a program of compliance monitoring and civil and criminal penalties. In a partnership with the state governments, the EPA has delegated enforcement to state and local government. On average, the states conduct 80 percent of the inspections and are responsible for 84 percent of the formal enforcement actions.

In 1999, the EPA conducted 21,410 inspections and started 3,935 civil judicial and administrative enforcement actions. As a result of its enforcement program, 6.8 billion pounds of pollutants were not placed in the environment. Polluters spent more than $3.6 billion to correct violations and to take the steps necessary to prevent further pollution.

Some examples are the following:

- The EPA and the Department of Justice announced a settlement with seven manufacturers of diesel engines. Although the engines were set to meet the EPA requirements and were tested at that setting, the manufacturers advised purchasers (trucking companies, bus companies, and other users) on how to readjust the engine settings. At the new settings, the engines polluted the air. The settlement will prevent 75 million tons of harmful pollutants from entering the atmosphere between the years 1999 and 2025. The manufacturers paid a $83.4 million penalty, the largest civil penalty ever for violations of environmental laws.

- The EPA and the state of Georgia reached a settlement with the city of Atlanta. The city paid a civil penalty of $700,000 and agreed to bring its sewer system into compliance with the Clean Water Act and the Georgia Water Quality Control Act.

Atlanta is implementing a $27.5 million program to create a greenway corridor and to clean up various streams. Lastly, Atlanta paid a $2.5 million penalty, the largest Clean Water Act penalty ever assessed against a municipality.

- Royal Caribbean Cruises, Ltd., pled guilty to twenty-one violations and paid an $18 million for violating the Clean Water Act and the Oil Pollution Act. Video-toting passengers captured a number of violations on videotape, including the dumping of waste oil and hazardous chemicals into the ocean. Royal Caribbean also made false statements to the Coast Guard. The cruise line agreed to institute a five-year environmental compliance plan.

- The EPA has an audit policy. If a company conducts an audit and discovers violations, it can self-report those problems and can apply for penalty relief. The EPA granted relief to GTE after more than 600 Emergency Planning and Community Right-to-Know Act and Spill Prevention Control and Countermeasures violations at 314 GTE facilities in twenty-one states were reported. It was the largest EPA settlement reached through the EPA's self-disclosure policy. Seventeen telecommunications companies found, disclosed, and corrected more than 2,000 environmental violations at more than 600 facilities nationwide.

The EPA operates nine Compliance Assistance Centers designed to help small businesses and small governmental entities, such as towns and counties, to comply with their obligations under the environmental laws. The centers offer plain English summaries of the regulations and provides a number technical resources. A survey of those covered reflected positive results. More than 50 percent reported a cost savings and more than 75 percent indicated environmental improvements. More than 80 percent found the centers to be useful in understanding environmental regulations.

---

determined that even hot water can be considered refuse because it affects fish and aquatic plant life.

Clean Water Regulation. The most important and comprehensive legislation plan to eliminate pollution

in our waters took place in 1972. The 1972 **Clean Water Act** established these goals: (1) to make waters safe for swimming, (2) to protect fish and wildlife, and (3) to eliminate the discharge of pollutants into the water. Regulations for the most part specify that businesses and governments install the best available technology.

The act requires both municipal and industrial dischargers to apply for permits before they discharge wastes into the nation's navigable waters. The act also confers legal standing on citizens (or organizations) when their interests are affected by parties that violate EPA or state standards. Both injunctive relief and damages can be sought through claims under the act. Like the Clean Air Act, anyone bringing legal action under this act may not obtain damages personally. All damages that are recovered are required to be turned over to the federal government. The following case involves private parties filing an action against a polluter of water.

CASE 24.2

Supreme Court of the United States, 2000
528 U.S. 120, 120 S. Ct. 693, 145 L. Ed. 2d 610
http://supct.law.cornell.edu/supct/html/98-822.ZS.html

FRIENDS OF THE EARTH, INC. v. LAIDLAW ENVIRONMENTAL SERVICES, INC.

BACKGROUND AND FACTS The defendant, Laidlaw Environmental Services, Inc., purchased a hazardous waste incinerator facility in South Carolina, which included a wastewater treatment plant. Shortly after Laidlaw acquired the facility, the South Carolina Department of Health and Environmental Control (DHEC) granted Laidlaw a permit authorizing the company to discharge treated water into the North Tyger River.

The permit placed limits on Laidlaw's discharge of pollutants into the river, including mercury, an extremely toxic pollutant. Once the permit was received, Laidlaw began to discharge pollutants into the waterway; repeatedly, Laidlaw's discharges exceeded the limits set by the permit.

Friends of the Earth, Inc. (FOE), took the preliminary step necessary to filing suit. A letter was sent to Laidlaw notifying the company of FOE's intention to file a citizen suit against it under the act after the expiration of the requisite sixty-day notice period. Shortly thereafter, Laidlaw's lawyer contacted DHEC to ask whether DHEC would consider filing a lawsuit against Laidlaw.

Laidlaw's reason for requesting that DHEC file a lawsuit against it was to bar FOE's proposed citizen suit. DHEC agreed to file a lawsuit against Laidlaw; the company's lawyer drafted the complaint for DHEC and paid the filing fee. On the last day before FOE's sixty-day notice period expired, DHEC and Laidlaw reached a settlement requiring Laidlaw to pay $100,000 in civil penalties and to make "every effort" to comply with its permit obligations.

FOE filed a citizen suit against Laidlaw alleging noncompliance with the National Pollutant Discharge Elimination System (NPDES) permit and seeking an award of civil penalties. Laidlaw moved to dismiss the action on the ground that the citizen suit was barred by DHEC's prior action against the company. The district court held that DHEC's action against Laidlaw had not been "diligently prosecuted"; consequently, the court allowed FOE's citizen suit to proceed. The district court found that Laidlaw had violated the mercury limits on 489 occasions between 1987 and 1995 and further found that after FOE initiated the suit, but before the court rendered its judgment, Laidlaw violated the mercury discharge limitation in its permit 13 more times.

The district court found that Laidlaw had gained a total economic benefit of $1,092,581 as a result of its extended period of noncompliance with the mercury discharge limit in its permit. The court imposed a civil penalty of $405,800. The district court stated that the penalty was appropriate, taking into account the judgment's "total deterrent effect." In reaching this determination, the court "considered that Laidlaw will be required to reimburse plaintiffs for a significant amount of legal fees."

FOE appealed the civil penalty judgment, arguing that the penalty was inadequate. Laidlaw cross-appealed, arguing that FOE lacked standing to bring the suit and that DHEC's action qualified as a diligent prosecution precluding FOE's litigation.

The Court of Appeals for the Fourth Circuit . . . held that the case had become moot. The appellate court held that the elements of standing—injury, causation, and redressability—must persist at every stage of review or else the action becomes moot. The court of appeals reasoned that the case had become moot because the only remedy available was civil penalties payable to the government and that payment would not redress any injury FOE suffered.

After the court of appeals issued its decision but before the Supreme Court granted *certiorari,* the entire incinerator facility in Roebuck was permanently closed, dismantled, and put up for sale, and all discharges from the facility permanently ceased. Laidlaw, however, did not surrender its permit.

The U.S. Supreme Court granted *certiorari.* The Court discussed whether the case was moot and whether FOE had standing to sue.

Justice GINSBURG delivered the opinion of the Court.

. . . .

This case presents an important question concerning the operation of the citizen-suit provisions of the Clean Water Act. . . . In the Clean Water Act citizen suit now before us, the District Court . . . assess[ed] a civil penalty of $405,800. The "total deterrent effect" of the penalty would be adequate to forestall future violations, the court reasoned, taking into account that the defendant "will be required to reimburse plaintiffs for a significant amount of legal fees and has, itself, incurred significant legal expenses."

. . . .

We reverse the judgment of the Court of Appeals. The appellate court erred in concluding that a citizen suitor's claim for civil penalties must be dismissed as moot when the defendant, albeit after commencement of the litigation, has come into compliance. . . . A defendant's voluntary cessation of allegedly unlawful conduct ordinarily does not suffice to moot a case. . . .

. . . .

In *Lujan v. Defenders of Wildlife,* we held that, to satisfy Article III's standing requirements, a plaintiff must show (1) it has suffered an "injury in fact" that is (a) concrete and particularized and (b) actual or imminent, not conjectural or hypothetical; (2) the injury is fairly traceable to the challenged action of the defendant; and (3) it is likely, as opposed to merely speculative, that the injury will be redressed by a favorable decision. An association has standing to bring suit on behalf of its members when its members would otherwise have standing to sue in their own right, the interests at stake are germane to the organization's purpose, and neither the claim asserted nor the relief requested requires the participation of individual members in the lawsuit.

Laidlaw contends first that FOE lacked standing from the outset . . . because the plaintiff organizations failed to show that any of their members had sustained or faced the threat of any "injury in fact" from Laidlaw's activities. In support of this contention Laidlaw points to the District Court's finding, made in the course of setting the penalty amount, that there had been "no demonstrated proof of harm to the environment" from Laidlaw's mercury discharge violations. . . .

The relevant showing for purposes of Article III standing, however, is not injury to the environment but injury to the plaintiff. To insist upon the former rather than the latter as part of the standing inquiry is to raise the standing hurdle higher than the necessary showing for success on the merits in an action alleging noncompliance with an NPDES permit. Focusing properly on injury to the plaintiff, the District Court found that FOE had demonstrated sufficient injury to establish standing. For example, FOE member Kenneth Lee Curtis averred in affidavits that he lived a half-mile from Laidlaw's facility; that he occasionally drove over the North Tyger River, and that it looked and smelled polluted; and that he would like to fish, camp, swim, and picnic in and near the river between 3 and 15 miles downstream from the facility, as he did when he was a teenager, but would not do so because he was concerned that the water was polluted by Laidlaw's discharges. . . .

Other members presented evidence to similar effect. . . .

. . . .

. . . Here, the civil penalties sought by FOE carried with them a deterrent effect that made it likely, as opposed to merely speculative, that the penalties would redress FOE's injuries by abating current violations and preventing future ones—as the District Court reasonably found when it assessed a penalty of $405,800.

. . . .

Satisfied that FOE had standing under Article III to bring this action, we turn to the question of mootness.

The only conceivable basis for a finding of mootness in this case is Laidlaw's voluntary conduct—either its achievement by August 1992 of substantial compliance with its NPDES permit or its more recent shutdown of the Roebuck facility. It is well settled that a defendant's voluntary cessation of a challenged practice does not deprive a federal court of its power to determine the legality of the practice. "[I]f it did, the courts would be compelled to leave '[t]he defendant . . . free to return to his old ways.'" In accordance with this principle, the standard we have announced for determining whether a case has been mooted by the defendant's voluntary conduct is stringent: "A case might become moot if subsequent events made it absolutely clear that the allegedly wrongful behavior could not reasonably be expected to recur." The "heavy burden of persua[ding]" the court that the challenged conduct cannot reasonably be expected to start up again lies with the party asserting mootness.

The Court of Appeals justified its mootness disposition by reference to *Steel Co.*, which held that citizen plaintiffs lack standing to seek civil penalties for wholly past violations. In relying on *Steel Co.*, the Court of Appeals confused mootness with standing. The confusion is understandable, given this Court's repeated statements that the doctrine of mootness can be described as "the doctrine of standing set in a time frame: The requisite personal interest that must exist at the commencement of the litigation (standing) must continue throughout its existence (mootness)."

. . . .

Standing doctrine functions to ensure, among other things, that the scarce resources of the federal courts are devoted to those disputes in which the parties have a concrete stake. In contrast, by the time mootness is an issue, the case has been brought and litigated, often (as here) for years. To abandon the case at an advanced stage may prove more wasteful than frugal. This argument from sunk costs does not license courts to retain jurisdiction over cases in which one or both of the parties plainly lacks a continuing interest, as when the parties have settled or a plaintiff pursuing a nonsurviving claim has died. . . .

. . . .

Laidlaw also asserts, in a supplemental suggestion of mootness, that the closure of its Roebuck facility, which took place after the Court of Appeals issued its decision, mooted the case. The facility closure, like Laidlaw's earlier achievement of substantial compliance with its permit requirements, might moot the case, but—we once more reiterate—only if one or the other of these events made it absolutely clear that Laidlaw's permit violations could not reasonably be expected to recur. The effect of both Laidlaw's compliance and the facility closure on the prospect of future violations is a disputed factual matter. FOE points out, for example—and Laidlaw does not appear to contest—that Laidlaw retains its NPDES permit. These issues have not been aired in the lower courts; they remain open for consideration on remand.

DECISION AND REMEDY The Court found that even with Laidlaw closing the plant, the case was not moot. The Court found that the FOE satisfied the requirements to bring an action under the Clean Water Act and left it to the trial court to determine the civil penalties.

CRITICAL THINKING: POLITICAL QUESTION Why do you think that the government has not banned all pollution? After all, this would save our planet. Explain your answer.

INFOTRAC RESEARCH ACTIVITY

InfoTrac has articles that are directed toward farming operations. Individuals may not realize how much pollution is created by livestock or poultry. Search InfoTrac and type in either "sewage" or "sewage disposal in rivers." Review four recent articles about this problem and compare these articles.

Oil Pollution. In 1990, the **Oil Pollution Act** was signed into law. The act is a result of the *Exxon Valdez* oil spill off the Alaskan shore and other spills that occurred during the same period. Spills containing a variety of polluting elements happened to the Delaware River, the Arthur Kill, Montana's Whitefish Lake, the southern California coast, and Galveston Bay. Both the EPA and the U.S. Coast Guard have responsibilities under this act.

The strict liability limit increased eightfold. For a spill equivalent to that of the *Exxon Valdez*, the liability cap has been increased from $14.3 million to $114 million under the act. This liability is in addition to damages that may be awarded under other theories. Liability now covers cleanup costs, natural resource damages, losses to subsistence resources, and costs to local government.

The $1 billion Oil Spill Liability Trust Fund (OSLTF), established under the act, is financed by oil companies. The OSLTF is used for costs not directly paid by a responsible party and for "mystery spills" when the responsible party cannot be identified. In the future, new oil tankers must be double hulled, and single-hulled tankers are scheduled to be phased out by 2015. The statute also established the Oil Spill Recovery Institute, a research center.

Quality Standards. Every day millions of gallons of wastewater flow into effluent treatment plants, are cleaned, and are returned to navigable streams. Today, the quality standard for the water leaving the treatment plants is higher than that applied to drinking water supplied to homes. A higher cleaning standard also has been imposed for water containing toxic wastes than for water with normal pollutants.

Wetlands. Land that lies between solid land and open bodies of water, such as lakes, large rivers, or the ocean, is designated as wetlands. Often under water, wetlands are home to wildlife and birds.

In the past, wetlands were filled in by developers, and homes and businesses were built on the filled wetlands. Today, a permit issued by the Army Corps of Engineers is necessary to fill in wetlands. The following case involves an agency representing municipalities that wanted to fill in wetlands with nonhazardous solid wastes.

CASE 24.3

Supreme Court of the United States, 2001 531 U.S. 159, 121 S. Ct. 675, 148 L. Ed. 2d 576

SOLID WASTE AGENCY OF NORTHERN COOK COUNTY v. U.S. ARMY CORPS OF ENGINEERS

BACKGROUND AND FACTS Petitioner, the Solid Waste Agency of Northern Cook County (SWANCC), was a consortium of twenty-three suburban Chicago cities and villages that united in an effort to locate and develop a disposal site for nonhazardous solid waste. SWANCC found a 533-acre parcel, which had been the site of a sand and gravel pit mining operation for three decades until 1960. Long since abandoned, a forest grew over the old mining site and its excavation trenches evolved into scattered permanent and seasonal ponds of varying size.

The municipalities decided to purchase the site for disposal of their nonhazardous solid waste. By law, SWANCC was required to file for various permits from Cook County and the state of Illinois before it could begin operation. In addition, because the operation called for the filling of some of the permanent and seasonal ponds, SWANCC contacted the U.S. Army Corps of Engineers (Corps) to determine if a federal landfill permit was required under Section 404(a) of the Clean Water Act (CWA).

Section 404(a) grants the Corps authority to issue permits "for the discharge of dredged or fill material into the navigable waters at specified disposal sites." The term *navigable waters* is defined under the act as "the waters of the United States, including the territorial seas." The Corps issued regulations defining the phrase *waters of the United States* to include

> *waters such as intrastate lakes, rivers, streams (including intermittent streams), mudflats, sandflats, wetlands, sloughs, prairie potholes, wet meadows, playa lakes, or natural ponds, the use, degradation or destruction of which could affect interstate or foreign commerce. . . . 33 CFR § 328.3(a)(3) (1999).*

In an attempt to "clarify" the reach of its jurisdiction, the Corps stated in its Migratory Bird Rule that Section 404(a) extends to intrastate waters:

a. Which are or would be used as habitat by birds protected by Migratory Bird Treaties; or

b. which are or would be used as habitat by other migratory birds which cross state lines; or

c. Which are or would be used as habitat for endangered species; or

d. Used to irrigate crops sold in interstate commerce.

The Corps initially concluded that it had no jurisdiction over the site because it contained no "wetlands." After the Illinois Nature Preserves Commission informed the Corps that a number of migratory bird species had been observed at the site, the Corps reconsidered and ultimately asserted jurisdiction over the site pursuant to subpart (b) of the Migratory Bird Rule. The Corps found that approximately 121 bird species had been observed at the site, including several known to depend on aquatic environments for a significant portion of their life requirements. Thus, on November 16, 1987, the Corps formally "determined that the seasonally ponded, abandoned gravel mining depressions located on the project site, while not wetlands, did qualify as 'waters of the United States' . . . based upon the following criteria: (1) the proposed site had been abandoned as a gravel mining operation; (2) the water areas and spoil piles had developed a natural character; and (3) the water areas are used as habitat by migratory bird [sic] which cross state lines."

SWANCC filed suit in federal district court challenging the Corps' jurisdiction over the site. The district court granted summary judgment to respondents on the jurisdictional issue. On appeal to the Court of Appeals for the Seventh Circuit, SWANCC renewed its attack on respondents' use of the Migratory Bird Rule to assert jurisdiction over the site. SWANCC argued that respondents had exceeded their statutory authority in interpreting the Clean Water Act (CWA) to cover nonnavigable, isolated, intrastate waters based on the presence of migratory birds and, in the alternative, that Congress lacked the power under the commerce clause to grant such regulatory jurisdiction.

The Court of Appeals held that under the constitution the Congress has the authority to regulate such waters based on "the cumulative impact doctrine, under which a single activity that itself has no discernible effect on interstate commerce may still be regulated if the aggregate effect of that class of activity has a substantial impact on interstate commerce." The aggregate effect of the "destruction of the natural habitat of migratory birds" on interstate commerce, the court held, was substantial because each year millions of Americans cross state lines and spend more than a billion dollars to hunt and observe migratory birds. The court of appeals then turned to the regulatory question. The court held that the CWA reaches as many waters as the commerce clause allows and, given its earlier commerce clause ruling, it therefore followed that respondents' Migratory Bird Rule was a reasonable interpretation of the act. SWANCC filed with the U.S. Supreme Court, which granted *certiorari*.

Chief Justice REHNQUIST delivered the opinion of the Court.

. . . .

Where an administrative interpretation of a statute invokes the outer limits of Congress' power, we expect a clear indication that Congress intended that result. This requirement stems from our prudential desire not to needlessly reach constitutional issues and our assumption that Congress does not casually authorize administrative agencies to interpret a statute to push the limit of congressional authority. This concern is heightened where the administrative interpretation alters the federal–state framework by permitting federal encroachment upon a traditional state power. ("[U]nless Congress conveys its purpose clearly, it will not be deemed to have significantly changed the federal–state balance"). Thus, "where an otherwise acceptable construction of a statute would raise serious constitutional problems, the Court will construe the statute to avoid such problems unless such construction is plainly contrary to the intent of Congress."

Twice in the past six years we have reaffirmed the proposition that the grant of authority to Congress under the Commerce Clause, though broad, is not unlimited. Respondents argue that the "Migratory Bird Rule" falls within Congress' power to regulate intrastate activities that "substantially affect" interstate commerce. They note that the protection of migratory birds is a "national interest of very nearly the first magnitude," and that, as the Court of Appeals found, millions of people spend over a billion dollars annually on recreational pursuits relating to migratory birds. These arguments raise significant constitutional questions. For example, we would have to evaluate the precise object or activity that, in the aggregate, substantially affects interstate commerce. This is not clear, for although the Corps has claimed jurisdiction over petitioner's land because it contains water areas used as habitat by migratory birds, respondents now, post litem motam, focus upon the fact that the regulated activity is petitioner's municipal landfill, which is "plainly of a commercial nature." But this is a far cry, indeed, from the "navigable waters" and "waters of the United States" to which the statute by its terms extends.

These are significant constitutional questions raised by respondents' application of their regulations, and yet we find nothing approaching a clear statement from Congress that it intended § 404(a) to reach an abandoned sand and gravel pit such as we have here. Permitting respondents to claim federal jurisdiction over ponds and mudflats falling within the "Migratory Bird Rule" would result in a significant impingement of the

States' traditional and primary power over land and water use. Rather than expressing a desire to readjust the federal–state balance in this manner, Congress chose to "recognize, preserve, and protect the primary responsibilities and rights of States . . . to plan the development and use . . . of land and water resources . . . ." We thus read the statute as written to avoid the significant constitutional and federalism questions raised by respondents' interpretation, and therefore reject the request for administrative deference.

. . . .

DECISION AND REMEDY The Court held that the Migratory Bird Rule exceeded the authority granted to the U.S. Army Corps of Engineers. The water involved here was not a navigable waterway in that this was solely an intrastate waterway with no ability to navigate it.

CRITICAL THINKING: POLITICAL ISSUE In the past, when deciding issues involving interstate commerce, the U.S. Supreme Court has upheld federal statutes and administrative rules by looking at the governed area in the aggregate. In this case, the U.S. Supreme Court did not follow this approach. Do you think the Court adequately explained why it did not follow this concept?

Other Regulations. In 1972, Congress passed the **Marine Protection, Research, and Sanctuaries Act**. This act established a system of permits that regulates the discharge and introduction of materials into coastal waters and continuous marine areas.

The **Safe Drinking Water Act** of 1974 authorized the EPA to establish standards for safe drinking water purity. All owners or operators of public water systems must comply with health-related standards. The law focuses on all waters actually or potentially designated for use for drinking water, whether located aboveground or underground. The rules, which are similar to those of the Clean Water Act, provide that states assume the primary responsibility for complying with national standards. The federal government assumes responsibility if states fail to institute or enforce drinking water standards. In most cases, explicit penalties are imposed on parties that pollute the water. The polluting party also can be required to clean up the pollution or to pay the cost of doing so.

Nuclear Wastes

Millions of pounds of nuclear waste, in both liquid and solid form, are generated each year. Most of this waste is radioactive and will remain dangerous for thousands of years. In 1982, Congress passed the **Nuclear Waste Policy Act (NWPA)**. This act required the building of a permanent repository for the disposal of spent nuclear fuel and high-level wastes. In the meantime, Congress provided that a monitored retrievable storage (MRS) facility could be built as a temporary measure until the permanent site was developed.

Shore Protection

In the 1980s, medical wastes, such as needles and bandages, washed ashore on New Jersey beaches crowded with bathers. Soon other reports of such garbage washing ashore caused the local governments to react quickly by closing the beaches. Federal statutes now forbid the indiscriminate disposal into the oceans of potentially infectious medical waste. Regulations provide for proper disposal.

Similarly, Congress passed a statute, entitled the **Shore Protection Act**[6] of 1988, that controls the disposal of solid wastes in oceans and lakes. The act created a permit system to track and control the solid waste as it is transported to its final place of disposal. The law also provides for study and recommendations as this problem grows.[7]

---

[6]A copy of this act can be obtained at http://www.law.cornell.edu/uscode/33/2601.shtml.

[7]The Office of Ocean and Coastal Resource Management's mission is to effectively manage multiple uses of the nation's coastal and ocean resources. Its Web address is http://www.ocrm.nos.noaa.gov/welcome.html.

Noise Pollution

In 1972, Congress prescribed standards and regulations for the control of aircraft noise, including sonic booms, and the control of sound emissions of railroad and motor vehicles involved in interstate commerce. The **Noise Control Act** of 1972 established the goal of creating an environment free from noise that injures public health and welfare. The courts ruled that local noise control is preempted when state regulations conflict with those established by federal statutes.

The Federal Aviation Administration, the Environmental Protection Agency, and the Department of Transportation administer regulations under the Noise Control Act. The EPA, for example, can establish noise emission levels for equipment, motors, and engines. It also reviews production processes, verifies reports for compliance with the law, conducts audit tests, and inspects manufacturers' records.

Toxic Substances

The **Toxic Substances Control Act**[8] was passed in 1976. This law requires the EPA to track more than 75,000 industrial chemicals produced or imported into the United States. The EPA can investigate harmful effects from new chemical compounds. Manufacturers, processors, and other organizations planning to use chemicals are required to first determine their effect on human health and the environment. The EPA regulates those toxic substances that potentially create a hazard or an unreasonable risk of injury. This act supplements the Clean Air Act.

Pesticide and Herbicide Control

The use of chemical pesticides to kill insects and herbicides to kill weeds has significantly increased agricultural productivity. A growing body of evidence, however, shows that the environment has failed to absorb residuals from these chemicals. In some cases, buildups of residuals have killed animals. Some potential long-term effects detrimental to the public also have been identified.

The original regulations governing pesticides were established by the **Federal Insecticide, Fungicide, and Rodenticide Act** of 1947, as amended in 1972 by the **Federal Environmental Pesticide Control**

Act. The Environmental Protection Agency requires that pesticides cannot cause unreasonable harm to the environment.

Pesticides must be (1) registered before they can be sold; (2) certified, labeled, and used only for approved applications; and (3) used in amounts that meet established limits when they are applied to crops that provide food for animals or people. The EPA also inspects manufacturing establishments. In some situations, it controls the supply of pesticides to keep hazardous chemicals off the market. Substances that are identified as harmful are subject to suspension and cancellation of registration. The applicators of pesticides must take an examination before being certified to use and apply these chemicals.

Waste Disposal

Waste disposal can occur on the land, in the water, or in the air. Thus, regulations protecting these resources from pollution also apply to waste disposal. In 1965, Congress passed the **Solid Waste Disposal Act**, an act designed to reduce solid waste disposal by encouraging the recycling of waste and the reuse of materials by society. The act encourages the development and use of technology that converts garbage into useful products.

The **Resource Conservation and Recovery Act (RCRA)** of 1976, as amended in 1984, governs EPA studies and recommendations on solid waste disposal, ranging from glass and plastic waste to landfill used at airports. The RCRA provides a cradle-to-grave (from creation to disposal) tracking system of hazardous waste. Both the federal and state governments regulate companies that generate, store, transport, dispose of, or handle hazardous waste at any time. The EPA issues permits for, and conducts on-site inspections of, hazardous waste facilities.

The RCRA was amended by the **Hazardous and Solid Waste Amendments (HSWA)** in 1984. HSWA required the phasing out of the land disposal of hazardous waste. The act provides for stringent hazardous waste management standards and a comprehensive underground storage tank program.

In 1980, Congress passed the **Comprehensive Environmental Response, Compensation, and Liability Act (CERCLA)**,[9] commonly known as the

---

[8]The full act is available at http://www.law.cornell.edu/uscode/15/2601.shtml.

[9]A copy of this act can be obtained at http://www.law.cornell.edu/uscode/42/9601.shtml.

Superfund. When hazardous waste finds its way into the soil, the polluter must pay for cleanup to the land until it meets drinking water standards. In other words, after the cleanup, a person should be able to drink the water that comes from the ground. If the polluter cannot be found, the Superfund monies are used to clean up the site. The trust fund is mandated to be at $8.5 billion. Residential property is exempt from this act.

In 1986, the Superfund law was amended by the **Emergency Planning and Community Right-to-Know Act (EPCRA)** to increase the information about the presence of hazardous chemicals in communities and their release into the environment. Each state appoints a State Emergency Response Commission (SERC) to plan a response to such a hazardous release.

The polluter comes from one of these categories: (1) the generator of the wastes disposed of at the site; (2) the transporter of the wastes to the site; (3) the owner or the tenant who operated the site at the time of the waste disposal; (4) the current owner and operator of the site; or (5) a lending institution, if it managed the property. Companies are liable for their past actions in waste disposal.

In the past, the Superfund mandated a strict and harsh liability standard. Multiple defendants had *joint and several liability,* which meant that one or more of the responsible parties could be sued. If the court rendered a money judgment on the plaintiff's behalf, the money could be collected from one or all of the wrongdoers. Usually, the defendants jointly paid their respective share of the judgment. At other times, a company that was responsible for only a fraction of the share of the judgment could be held liable to pay all of the judgment. This happened when the other co-defendants were unable to pay their share.

As a result of the harshness of strict liability, a number of reforms were adopted. Today, a polluter pays a proportional cost of the cleanup in a ratio to its degree of fault. The government rarely pursues a small-volume polluter. Any monies collected by the government from companies as fines for polluting a particular site is spent on cleaning up that site.

Heavy pesticide use, leaking underground storage tanks (LUST), and general waste disposal have made real property subject to cleanup. The practical effect of this law is seen in the purchase of real property. Under the act, the land's owner is liable and must clean it up. Cleanup costs may range from a few hundred dollars to millions. Today, a lending institution requires verification that the soil is free from contamination before it lends money for a buyer to purchase the property. Additionally, before the lender repossesses any property, it must verify that no environmental problems exist.

Three defenses exist: (1) act of God, (2) act of war, and (3) act of a third party (an innocent purchaser can use this defense). A property owner will not be liable if someone dumps hazardous waste on the property without permission. The innocent purchaser defense occurs when a person purchases property without knowledge of, or without reason to know of, the hazardous waste already on the property.

In the following case, a current land owner sought damages from the prior owner under the Superfund provisions. The property was purchased in 1977 and the CERCLA statute was passed in 1980. Even though no law existed when the property was sold, the CERCLA statute applied retroactively to the land's seller.

CASE 24.4

United States Court of Appeals, Fifth Circuit, 1989
889 F.2d 664

AMOCO OIL CO. v. BORDEN, INC.

BACKGROUND AND FACTS In 1977, Amoco Oil Company wanted to purchase certain property from Borden, Inc. The parties discussed two prices: $1.8 million for the site "as is" or $2.2 million if Borden removed the phosphogypsum, a combination of phosphorus and gypsum, a by-product of the fertilizer manufacturing process. Amoco accepted the "as is" option.

The Texas Department of Water Resources informed Amoco that phosphogypsum is radioactive. Amoco hired several consultants to measure the radioactivity. The consultants' reports revealed various elevated radiation levels throughout the site. The site was secured with fences and guards to prevent access. Amoco claimed that cleanup costs would be between $11 million and $17 million.

Amoco sued Borden on a number of counts, including sharing liability under the Superfund (CERCLA). Borden's primary defenses against liability were (1) that the levels of radiation emanating from the site were not high enough to be considered a release of a hazardous substance within the meaning of CERCLA and (2) that the property was sold "as is" and that this fact and the doctrine of caveat emptor precluded a finding of liability.

Circuit Judges BROWN, REAVLEY, and HIGGINBOTHAM

. . . .

The term "release" is defined to mean: any spilling, leaking, pumping, pouring, emitting, emptying, discharging, injecting, escaping, leaching, dumping, or disposing into the environment (including the abandonment or discarding of barrels, containers, and other closed receptacles containing any hazardous substance or pollutant or contaminant).

. . . .

Borden's actions met the release requirement in two ways. First, it did so by disposing of the phosphogypsum and highly radioactive wastes on the property. . . . Second, the gas emanating from the radionuclides constitutes a release within the meaning of the statute. . . .

. . . .

It is undisputed that Amoco's property falls within the statutory definition of a "facility"; that Borden is a responsible party within the meaning of CERCLA, and that the statutory defenses to liability are inapplicable. . . .

. . . .

The hazard on the property constitutes an indivisible harm. As an owner of a facility that continues to release a hazardous substance, Amoco shares joint and several liability for remedial actions with Borden. When one liable party sues another to recover its equitable share of the response costs, the action is one for contribution, which is specifically recognized under CERCLA.

Under that provision, a court has considerable latitude in determining each party's equitable share. After deciding the appropriate remedial action, the court will have to determine each party's share of the costs. Possible relevant factors include: the amount of hazardous substances involved; the degree of toxicity or hazard of the materials involved; the degree of involvement by parties in the generation, transportation, treatment, storage, or disposal of the substances; the degree of care exercised by the parties with respect to the substances involved; and the degree of cooperation of the parties with government officials to prevent any harm to public health or the environment. Additionally, the circumstances and conditions involved in the property's conveyance, including the price paid and discounts granted, should be weighed in allocating response costs.

Borden . . . claim[s] that the equities in this case require Amoco to bear the full cost of cleanup. However, because both parties are liable under CERCLA, this is a question more properly decided by the district court, after it has determined the proper scope of the cleanup efforts.

DECISION AND REMEDY The case was sent back to the trial court to decide the equitable share that each party must pay. CERCLA imposes responsibility on every owner of real property that contains hazardous materials and creates joint and several liability in these situations.

CRITICAL THINKING: POLITICAL CONSIDERATION In the past, when a person purchased a property under the term "as is," that was interpreted as taking the property with all faults. This meant that a purchaser could not bring legal action against the seller for problems with the property. This decision changed this rule. Should this rule have been changed for a Superfund property?

Occasionally, the acts of a business or individual will violate both the RCRA and CERCLA because these statutes overlap. The next case shows companies and individuals to be in violation of the RCRA when the hazardous waste was transported, as well as in violation of CERCLA for failing to report the dumping of this same waste.

CASE 24.5

United States Court of Appeals, First Circuit, 1991

933 F.2d 35

UNITED STATES v. MACDONALD & WATSON WASTE OIL CO.

BACKGROUND AND FACTS Master Chemical Company, located in Boston, Massachusetts, manufactured chemicals primarily for use in the shoe industry. Among the chemicals Master Chemical used was toluene, which it stored in a 2,000-gallon underground storage tank. When Master Chemical personnel discovered in the late fall of 1982 that water was entering the tank and contaminating the toluene, the tank was emptied and its use discontinued. Some toluene had leaked out and contaminated the soil.

Master Chemical retained an environmental consulting firm to prepare a study. The environmental consulting firm solicited a bid from MacDonald & Watson Waste Oil Company for the excavation, transportation, and disposal of the toluene-contaminated soil. Although MacDonald & Watson was in the business of transporting and disposing of *hazardous* waste oils and *nonhazardous* contaminated soil, it lacked a permit to dispose of *solid hazardous wastes*, such as *hazardous* contaminated soil, at all of its disposal sites. The disposal facility in Rhode Island was leased from Narragansett Improvement Company (NIC). MacDonald & Watson operated the disposal facility under NIC's Resource Conservation and Recovery Act (RCRA) permit that authorized the disposal of *liquid hazardous* wastes and soils contaminated with *nonhazardous* wastes, such as petroleum products. Neither MacDonald & Watson nor NIC had a permit authorizing the disposal of *solid hazardous* wastes, such as toluene-contaminated soil, at this disposal facility.

Master Chemical accepted the bid from MacDonald & Watson to remove the waste and clean up the site. The defendant Slade, an employee of MacDonald & Watson, signed the contract on behalf of MacDonald & Watson. A MacDonald & Watson employee stamped the transportation manifests "Non-hazardous in Rhode Island, Accepted for Processing."

The Environmental Protection Agency discovered that the toluene-contaminated soil was disposed of at a facility that only had a permit for soil that was not contaminated with a hazardous waste. The EPA referred the matter to the Department of Justice for criminal prosecution.

In a complicated trial, the court convicted several employees of MacDonald & Watson, several employees of NIC, and both businesses, MacDonald & Watson and NIC, on various criminal charges. One employee, Ritarossi, supervised the soil's transportation. He was convicted of knowingly transporting and causing the transportation of hazardous waste, namely, toluene and soil contaminated with toluene, to a facility that lacked a permit, in violation of the RCRA. Following is a small portion of the judge's decision that discusses Ritarossi's conviction.

Circuit Judge LEVIN H. CAMPBELL

. . . .

Ritarossi contends that the evidence was insufficient to prove that he either knew that the material shipped to NIC was subject to RCRA regulation as toluene-contaminated soil or to prove he knew the substance and limitations of NIC's permit. However, Ritarossi could be found to have signed several of the "Authorization to Accept Shipment" forms which describes [sic] the "spilled material" as toluene and provides [sic] "toluene and gravel" as the "Description of petroleum product spilled and material spilled into." [A witness from Master Chemical] testified that he discussed the circumstances surrounding the leaking toluene tank with Ritarossi during excavation of the tank. Moreover, [the] environmental consultant testified that he asked Ritarossi to include options in MacDonald & Watson's bid both for disposal at MacDonald & Watson's facility and for disposal at an out-of-state RCRA secure landfill because the consultant did not know whether MacDonald & Watson had the proper permits to dispose of the material at their facility. We find sufficient evidence from which the jury could determine that Ritarossi knew the material was toluene-contaminated soil and also to infer that he either knew that NIC's permit did not permit acceptance of such material or, at very least, willfully failed to determine the material's status under NIC's permit.

. . . .

We conclude that the reportable quantity for the toluene-contaminated soil was 1,000 pounds. . . . It was never a subject of dispute that the toluene-contaminated soil was delivered to the [disposal facility] in other than nine 25-yard dump trucks and one 20-yard dump truck. We see no basis on which it could be rationally concluded by any juror that less than 1,000 pounds of contaminated soil was released.

DECISION AND REMEDY The RCRA was violated when Ritarossi authorized the transportation of the contaminated soil knowing (or willfully failing to find out) that it would be dumped in an unauthorized disposal facility without the proper permits. Failure to report the solid hazardous waste's dumping was a criminal violation of CERCLA.

CRITICAL THINKING: MANAGEMENT CONSIDERATION If you were employed in a business that might have problems with hazardous materials through accidental discharge, how would you protect yourself from criminal and civil liability?

The **Pollution Prevention Act (PPA)** was passed in 1990. It focuses on reducing the amount of pollution through cost-effective changes in production, operation, and use of raw materials. The reduction of pollution is more desirable and fundamentally different than managing waste or controlling pollution. This act focuses on increasing the efficiency in the use of energy, water, or other natural resources through conservation. Some conservation practices are recycling, reduction of pollution at its source, and the use of renewable energies, such as solar energy.

CYBERLAW

Record Research on the Web

The *Practical Tips* section, later in this chapter, discusses the three phases of an environment audit required by the Environmental Protection Agency. Within phase I (surface analysis), one step is to review the public records of ownership for at least the last fifty years. These records reflect the business activities conducted on the land, such as gasoline station, photography shop, dry cleaning business, restaurant business, or farming.

All of these businesses just mentioned use hazardous materials that today are required by regulation to be disposed of in a specific manner. Realizing that these types of businesses have been previous owners of the real estate should send out a red flag that environmental problems might exist. For example, the gasoline station handles oil, gas, and underground storage tanks; in the past, the process of developing film included silver and lead; dry cleaners handle solvent chemicals; restaurants use cooking oils and cleaning supplies; and farming involves pesticides and herbicides. In addition to ownership, public records show past and existing environmental cleanup liens.

A search of the public records for the first phase currently can be achieved through the use of the World Wide Web (WWW) in a only few counties.[10] These counties have placed their public records of property ownership on the Web. The placement of the recorded documents on a Web site allows any person to access this information from a home or office. No longer is it necessary to travel to the local recording office to research the names of those who have owned the property. Although today not many states and counties have placed the documents recorded in the county on the Web, as money becomes available, more government recording offices will place these records on the Web as a routine matter.

Endangered Species Act

Congress adopted the **Endangered Species Act (ESA)** in 1973 both to conserve the species themselves and to protect the ecosystems of the endangered species. Endangered species, unlike timber, are nonrenewable resources. In a congressional hearing, the assistant secretary of the interior testified that "half of the recorded extinctions of mammals over the past 2,000 years have occurred in the most recent 50-year period."

Federal agencies are mandated to conserve endangered species. The secretary of the interior enforces the ESA. In 1993, Congress created the National Biological Survey to catalog all species within the United States. Species include mammals, birds, reptiles, fish, crustaceans, trees, flowers, and grasses. A total of 853 species were placed on the endangered species list during the 1980s and 1990s. Today, the Department of Interior lists 632 endangered species (326 are plants) and 190 threatened species (78 are plants).

In the past, the government focused on one endangered species at a time. Today, the approach is broader because it considers ecosystems. An ecosystem is a community of animals, birds, insects, trees, bushes, plants, flowers, grasses, bacteria, fungi, and soil types, just to mention a few items. If a large enough portion of land that comprises an ecosystem is preserved, such as the Florida Everglades, everything within the land is protected. It is believed that this holistic approach will prevent any one species from becoming extinct

because the community is interrelated and interdependent. For example, a species of birds may depend on one type of tree, but the tree is dependent on a particular type of soil or flooding condition. To protect only the bird may be useless if its habitat is destroyed.

Private individuals can challenge a federal agency's decision involving endangered species. In the case of *Bennett v. Spear*[11] the United States Supreme Court allowed private persons to challenge actions of the Department of Interior involving the maintenance of minimum water levels on several lakes to protect two endangered species of fish. The private persons who would have been affected by this federal action because they depended on water for irrigation challenged the acts of the government. The Court stated that they had standing to litigate this issue.

Exhibit 24–1 shows the expensive costs of protecting a few endangered species. When a species is placed on the endangered list, the Department of Interior can restrict the free use of private property and can slow or stop economic development on it.

Exhibit 24-1 **Costs of Protecting Some Endangered Species**

Species	Cost
Atlantic green turtle	$88,236,000
Loggerhead turtle	$85,947,000
Blunt-nosed leopard lizard	$70,252,000
Kemp's Ridley sea turtle	$63,600,000
Colorado squawfish	$57,770,000
Black-capped vireo	$53,538,000
Swamp pink	$29,026,000

Source: National Wilderness Institute.

Judicial Limits

In the first half of the 1970s, federal and state legislators enacted many statutes that regulate environmental quality. Judicial interpretations of these statutes gener-

---

[10]An example of a progressive county is Maricopa County, Arizona, where public records are accessible through the Web. See http://recorder.maricopa.gov/recdocdata/GetRecDataSelect.asp?mcrs=1.

[11]520 U.S.154, 117 S. Ct. 1154, 137 L. Ed. 2d 281 (1997); located on the Web at http://supct.law.cornell.edu/supct/html/95-813.ZS.html.

ally have given broad discretionary powers to the administrative agencies that carry out these statutes' directives.

Beginning in the mid-1970s, however, the courts began to place stricter limits on administrative discretion. Court decisions imposed a **cost–benefit standard** on administrative decisions.[12] Under the cost-benefit standard, courts will consider the cost of an action and compare it with the benefit that may result from the action. For example, in *Union Electric Co. v. Environmental Protection Agency,*[13] the utility claimed that it would cost $500 million to comply with the Clean Air Act and that this sum could not be obtained through financial markets. The United States Supreme Court turned down this argument and held

that the clean air regulations "are expressly designed to force regulated sources to develop pollution control devices that might at the time appear to be economically or technologically infeasible."

Environmental Side Agreement to NAFTA

The United States, Mexico, and Canada, in addition to signing the North American Free Trade Agreement (NAFTA) and the North American Agreement on Labor Cooperation (NAALC was discussed along with NAFTA in Chapter 22), signed the North American Agreement on Environmental Cooperation. This side agreement establishes, maintains, and enforces each country's domestic environmental law.

The agreement encourages public participation in the lawmaking and enforcement process. Provisions include

---

[12]See the Environmental Protection Agency's Web site on cost–benefit analysis at http://yosemite.epa.gov/ee/epa/eed.nsf/webpages/Guidelines.html.

[13]427 U.S. 246, 96 S. Ct. 2518, 49 L. Ed. 2d 474 (1976).

LEGAL HIGHLIGHT

Economic and Environmental Concerns

Everyone is in favor of protecting the environment. Everyone is in favor of earning an honest living. But what happens when these two values conflict? This conflict is played out when environmentalists clash with the logging industry. In the Pacific Northwest, for example, the loggers are pitted against those who want to protect old-growth forests and spotted owls.

The logging industry either owns the land it logs or leases the land from the federal or state government and then operates under permits to log the forest. This work creates employment and thus a tax base. The monies earned by employees support other private industries, such as grocery and furniture stores, and also generate taxes paid to the local and federal governments. Since the 1920s, many logging companies have cooperated with the Save-the-Redwoods League and the Sierra Club.

If the spotted owl, along with the Harris's hawk, Henslow's sparrow, loggerhead shrike, seaside

sparrow, snowy plover, and vermilion flycatcher, is placed on the endangered species list, this effectively would stop all logging. The designation would protect 1.5 million acres of old-growth forest from future logging. Keep in mind that since the pilgrims arrived in the early 1600s, more than 90 percent of the original woodland in the United States has been destroyed.

Is it ethical to protect birds and forests over the jobs of people who are generally second- and third-generation loggers—especially since these people contribute to the community's economic basis?

Most old-growth wood is shipped overseas for use in other countries. Should this be allowed? Would the decision differ if the old-growth wood were used in the United States?

Destruction of habitat poses the greatest threat to the survival of wild species. Birds, animals, and plants have evolved over centuries to survive in specific environments. Destruction of the old-growth forests would mean the destruction of some species. Each species plays a part in the ecosystem's delicate balance. Is it ethical to allow these wild species to perish?

government-to-government dispute settlement procedures for patterns of failure to enforce domestic environmental statutes effectively. The side agreement also creates mechanisms for collaboration among the parties.

The environmental side agreement establishes the Commission for Environmental Cooperation (CEC), which is a council composed of each country's top environmental officials. The CEC also includes an independent secretariat under the direction of an executive director and a joint advisory committee composed of nongovernmental organizations from the three countries to advise the council.

Under the agreement, any individual or organization residing in any of the three countries may file a complaint with the secretariat alleging that a country failed to enforce its environmental laws. The secretariat determines whether the complaint warrants a response. After the offending country responds, on a two-thirds vote, the record is made public. If evidence exists that a continuing pattern has developed that violates environmental law, an action plan will be established to correct the situation. If this plan of action fails, monetary assessments can be imposed. If an assessment is not paid, trade sanctions may be imposed on the United States and Mexico. Monetary sanctions enforceable by a court order can be imposed on Canada.

International Consideration

Global Antipollution Actions

Pollution knows no international boundaries. The radioactive pollution from Chernobyl was detected over a weekend by Sweden and Norway before it was reported by the former Union of Soviet Socialist Republics. The radioactivity eventually encircled the earth and led to a ban of agricultural products from some countries because some products, such as milk, plants, and grain crops, contained radioactive elements.

The more developed nations have passed legislation similar to that of the United States. The European Union (EU), then called the European Community, passed the Single Europe Act, which requires it to issue a comprehensive regulatory scheme to protect the environment. Adopted in 1987, this program contains laws similar to those of the United States.

The less developed countries have fewer resources for protecting the environment. In 1992, a number of nations signed the Climate Change Treaty,[14] which is sponsored by the United Nations. This treaty set out a number of meetings that would establish goals and timetables. In 1997, a conference was held in Kyoto, Japan, to set legal global limits on the emissions of carbon dioxide and other "greenhouse" gases—mostly by-products of fossil fuel burning—that trap the heat that Earth emits.[15]

The conference wrapped up two years of negotiations to determine a compromise formula assigning various levels of gas reductions to the thirty-four industrialized countries. Two main proposals emerged. The European Union wanted industrialized nations to reduce greenhouse gas emissions to 15 percent below 1990 levels by 2010. The United States, on the other hand, suggested lowering emissions only to 1990 levels.

Although most parties agree that global warming is taking place, the question of how to handle the problem remains.[16] On one side, the automobile manufacturers, coal companies, and oil producers argued that no timetables should be imposed to meet goals for the reduction of carbon dioxide and other gases. On the other side, companies selling fuel-efficient technologies, environmentalists, and insurance companies that pay damages caused by global warming, such as for flood or hurricane damage claims, supported specific reductions.

Less developed nations want and need industrial development and are willing to accept pollution to obtain that goal. Slowly, however, these countries are making ecological progress. For example, the **Association of Southeast Asian Nations (ASEAN)** is an intergovernmental agency of Indonesia, Malaysia, the Philippines, Singapore, and Thailand that was founded in 1967. This organization seeks economic and cultural cooperation among its members. In 1985, ASEAN's members entered into the Agreement on

[14]See Kyoto Protocol to the United Nations Framework Convention on Climate Change Treaty at http://unfccc.int/resource/convkp.html.

[15]The Kyoto Conference has a Web site at http://www.globalissues.org/EnvIssues/GlobalWarming/Kyoto.asp.

[16]For more information about research on the topic of climate warming, see the Hadley Center for Climate Prediction and Research located at http://www.meto.gov.uk/sec5/CR_div/Brochure. The Hadley Center provides data based on temperature records dating back to the mid-nineteenth century. The data are considered among the most reliable in climate science.

the Conservation of Nature and Natural Resources. In this agreement, each county recognized its responsibility for controlling pollution and preventing it from migrating to other countries.

Global international treaties making up the Ozone Treaties are the **Montreal Protocol on Substances that Deplete the Ozone Layer**, which has been modified five times: London (1990), Copenhagen (1992), Vienna (1995), Montreal (1997), and Beijing (1999). The protocol aims to reduce and eventually eliminate the emissions of man-made ozone-depleting substances.

The Montreal Protocol was signed by twenty-four nations in 1987. This treaty is unique in that its goal is to prevent pollution rather than simply to provide cleanup measures. The treaty requires all nations to reduce both production and consumption of chemicals that deplete the ozone layer. Production of the most damaging ozone-depleting substances was eliminated, except for a few critical uses, by 1996 in developed countries and will be eliminated by 2010 in developing countries.[17]

Under the auspices of the United Nations Environment Programme, various nations sponsored the **Vienna Convention on the Protection of the Ozone Layer** in 1985. Through this convention, governments committed themselves to protect the ozone layer and to cooperate with each other in scientific research to improve understanding of the atmospheric processes.

The **United Nations Convention on the Law of the Sea**[18] imposes on signatory members the duty to avoid polluting the oceans from land or from vessels, including legislation against dumping raw wastes from ships. Many video-toting vacationers on cruise ships have taped a number of incidents of cruise ships violating the law.

The **Convention on the Law of the Non-Navigational Uses of International Watercourses**[19] of 1997 provides for the exchange of information among countries if water-related hazards occur. Another article requires nations to take all measures to prevent harmful conditions, such as toxic chemical spills.

The United Nations Educational, Scientific, and Cultural Organization (UNESCO) also supports pollution control.[20] It has been particularly successful in compiling data and arranging for regional agreements to stop pollution. In addition, the World Bank requires pollution controls as part of each applicant's business plan before it loans for industrial purposes.

[18]The United Nations' Oceans and Law of the Sea Home Page is located at http://www.un.org/Depts/los/index.htm.
[19]The United Nations' International Law Commission's Web site for this convention is at http://www.un.org/law/ilc/texts/nnavfra.htm.
[20]The UNESCO home page is at http://www.unesco.org.

[17]See the United Nations Environment Programme Web page entitled The Ozone Secretariat at http://www.unep.org/ozone.

PRACTICAL TIPS

Considerations When Purchasing Real Property

A person must be very careful when purchasing real property. In the past, one had to consider zoning laws, financing, and engineering studies of the land and any projected buildings. Today, a purchaser must take into consideration the various federal statutes concerning the environment. If an environmental hazard exists on the property, the property owner must correct it. In reality, only one defense is available: that of the innocent purchaser. Auditing can help a purchaser establish this defense.

The Environmental Protection Agency issued a policy statement on auditing. An environmental audit has three parts that may be implemented: (1) a surface analysis (phase I) and (2) a technical subsurface study (phase II). If necessary, a cleanup becomes phase III. A phase II study is very expensive and normally is unnecessary if phase I does not reveal an environmental problem. Legally, neither audit is required. Without an audit, however, the EPA takes a hard stand against a purchaser claiming no knowledge. Generally, an audit is required to meet the innocent purchaser defense.

A professional known as an environmental consultant should perform a phase I analysis. The public records of ownership for at least the last fifty years must be reviewed. The names in the public record may reveal the types of business activities in which previous owners, such as an oil company, engaged. The public record also shows existing environmental cleanup liens.

The consultant reviews aerial photographs that might show prior use of the property. He or she examines federal, state, and local records to identify building permits and reports or environmental records of previous land use. A visual inspection of the property and adjacent property also is necessary, because hazardous materials may have migrated from an adjoining property onto the property for sale.

The phase II audit includes physical sampling and testing. The soil and groundwater are sampled to identify and isolate the type and extent of the contamination. A phase II audit is accomplished only when a phase I audit indicates environmental problems. Phase III occurs when the property is cleaned up. Potential purchasers and their lending institutions always should perform a phase I audit before purchasing raw land. Otherwise, they may be held liable.

Prior to purchasing real estate, the purchaser should investigate the property. Here are suggested actions.

Checklist

✔ *Public Records* Review the public records to investigate information about the prior use of the property over the prior years. Prior usage as a gasoline station or a dry cleaners should be a red flag that chemicals may exist.

✔ *Photographs* Review photographs of the area that were taken over past decades to see if any past property use might have caused environment problems. Photographs sometimes can be obtained from public utilities, private companies, or government offices. Compare the photographs with the public records.

✔ *Confirmation* Check for building permits. If the building has been modified, does it meet current standards?

✔ *Inspection* Make a visual inspection of the property and adjacent land. A condition on a neighboring property may contaminate this property.

Following these suggested actions will help to prevent problems. Be sure to read other material to be able to take more preventive actions.

Chapter Summary

Private persons and state and local governments have sued polluters to protect the environment. The lawsuits focus on the tort theories of nuisance, trespass, negligence, and strict liability. Most private suits faced legal defenses that prevented a party from successfully restricting activity that has harmed or might harm the environment. Local government tried to protect the environment by regulating building design and noise and by controlling the use of property through zoning laws.

Congress in 1969 passed the Environmental Protection Act and created the Environmental Protection Agency. The law requires an environmental impact statement (EIS) for projects using federal funds or built by federal agencies. The EIS is prepared to determine the effect of the federal project on the environment.

The federal government has passed a number of statutes, including the Clean Air Act, that was last amended in 1990. The 1990 act requires states to create state implementation plans, which are intended to inventory air polluters. The Clean Water Act was passed to make the waters safe for swimming, to protect fish and wildlife, and to eliminate the discharge of pollutants into the waters. The Oil Pollution Act placed strict liability limits on oil polluters, created the Oil Spill Liability Trust Fund, and established the Oil Spill Recovery Institute.

The Nuclear Waste Policy Act governs the disposal of spent nuclear fuel and high-level wastes. The Shore Protection Act controls the disposal of solid wastes in oceans and lakes. The Noise Control Act protects the public's health and welfare from excessive noise.

The Resource Conservation and Recovery Act provides a cradle-to-grave tracking system of hazardous waste. The Comprehensive Environmental Response, Compensation, and Liability Act requires polluters and land owners to clean up the hazardous waste sites.

In 1973, Congress passed the Endangered Species Act, administered by the Department of Interior. The act protects those species that are endangered or threatened on private or public land.

The courts attempt to balance the adverse effect of activities that affect the environment with the cost of protecting the environment. The courts use the cost–benefit standard on administrative decisions. The courts consider the cost of the EPA's action with the benefit that may result from the action.

Using the World Wide Web

EPA's Office of Air and Radiation (OAR) deals with issues that affect the quality of our air and protection from exposure to harmful radiation. OAR develops national programs, technical policies, and regulations for controlling air pollution and radiation exposure. Areas of concern to OAR include indoor and outdoor air quality, stationary and mobile sources of air pollution, radon, acid rain, stratospheric ozone depletion, radiation protection, and pollution prevention.

For *Web Activities*, links to Web sites mentioned in the chapter, and additional Web sites that relate to the chapter topics, go to **http://bohlman.westbuslaw. com**, click on "Internet Applications," and select Chapter 24 .

Web Activities

Go to **http://bohlman.westbuslaw.com**, click on "Internet Applications," and select Chapter 24.
24–1 Air Pollution
24–2 EPA

Key Terms

Association of Southeast Asian Nations (ASEAN)
attainment area
class-action lawsuit
Clean Air Act 1963
Clean Water Act 1972
Comprehensive Environmental Response, Compensation, and Liability Act (CERCLA) 1980
Convention on the Law of the Non-Navigational Uses of International Watercourses
cost-benefit standard
Emergency Planning and

Community Right-to-Know Act (EPCRA)
Endangered Species Act (ESA)
environmental impact statement (EIS)
Environmental Protection Agency (EPA)
Federal Environmental Pesticide Control Act 1972
Federal Insecticide, Fungicide, and Rodenticide Act 1947/1972 Amend
Hazardous and Solid Waste Amendments (HSWA)
Marine Protection,

Research, and Sanctuaries Act
Montreal Protocol on Substances that Deplete the Ozone Layer
National Ambient Air Quality Standards (NAAQS)
National Environmental Policy Act (NEPA) 1969
Noise Control Act 1972
nonattainment area
Nuclear Waste Policy Act (NWPA)
Oil Pollution Act
Pollution Prevention Act (PPA)

Resource Conservation and Recovery Act (RCRA)
Rivers and Harbors Act
Safe Drinking Water Act 1974
Shore Protection Act
Solid Waste Disposal Act
state implementation plan (SIP) 1965
Toxic Substances Control Act 1976
United Nations Convention on the Law of the Sea
Vienna Convention on the Protection of the Ozone Layer

Questions and Case Problems

24–1 Nuisance Oakhill is a development-home building corporation that primarily develops retirement communities. Washington Feeds owns several feed lots in Buckeye. Oakhill purchased 20,000 acres of farmland in the same area and began building and selling homes on this acreage. In the meantime, Washington Feeds continued to expand its feedlot business. Eventually only 500 feet separated the two operations. Because of the odor and flies from the feedlots, Oakhill found it difficult to sell the homes in its development. Oakhill wants to enjoin Washington Feeds from operating its feedlots

in the vicinity of the retirement home development. Under what theory would Oakhill file this action? Explain.

24–2 Noise Control Act Flylight, Inc., manufactures a 250-seat passenger airplane that is fuel efficient and that travels at a cruising speed of 900 miles per hour. The plane is only cost effective for flights of 1,000 miles or more. Traveling at 900 miles per hour creates a sonic boom lasting for no more than five seconds. The sound measured during the five-second period exceeds aircraft noise levels established by the Environmental Protection Agency. Should Flylight, Inc., aircraft be banned from flying over the United States? Explain.

24–3 Clean Water Act Atlantic Richfield Co. (ARCO) had an accidental oil spill, which it reported to the Coast Guard in accordance with the law. ARCO cleaned up the oil spill to the Coast Guard's satisfaction. The Coast Guard assessed a civil penalty for this accidental discharge. ARCO refused to pay, claiming that it cleaned up the spill and that the spill was accidental. ARCO also argued that such penalties are criminal. The federal government sued to collect the penalty. What was the result? Explain. [*United States v. Atlantic Richfield Co.*, 429 F. Supp. 830 (E. D. Pa. 1977)]

24–4 National Environmental Policy Act The Government Services Administration (GSA) entered into an agreement with a private individual to construct a building to the GSA's specifications and to lease it to the GSA. Under the contemplated lease provision, the GSA would use the entire building for a five-year (renewable) period. As many as 2,300 government employees would be assigned to the building, and most would commute by automobile. The cost of the lease was approximately $11 million. The GSA proceeded with its plans for the building without preparing an environmental impact statement. Was a statement necessary? Explain. [*S. W. Neighborhood Assembly v. Eckard*, 445 F. Supp. 1195 (D.D.C. 1978)]

24–5 Standing to Sue Citizens Against Toxic Sprays, Inc., was an organization established to challenge the use of toxic sprays in places where they could be harmful to humans, animals, or vegetation. The group sought to enjoin the U.S. Forest Service from using the herbicide TCDD, because of its hazardous effect on people who breathed it. TCDD was used only in national forests, not in any residential areas. Citizens Against Toxic Sprays alleged that some of its members were affected by the use of TCDD in two of the national forests because they lived near them, worked in them, or used them for recreational activities. Does Citizens Against Toxic Sprays, Inc., have the standing to sue the U.S. Forest Service? Explain. [*Citizens Against Toxic Sprays, Inc., v. Bergland*, 428 F. Supp. 908 (1977)]

24–6 Wetlands A dispute arose over 153 acres of undeveloped land owned by Leslie Salt Company. The land abuts the San Francisco National Wildlife Refuge and lies approximately one-quarter mile from the Newark Slough, a tidal arm of the San Francisco Bay. The condition of the property in 1985 resulted from artificial changes during the last 100 years. Starting out as pastureland, it was excavated for salt until 1959. The salt pits remained and temporarily filled with water during the winter rainy season. Fish lived in the ponds and migratory birds used the pits as habitat during the winter and spring. An endangered species, the salt marsh harvest mouse, also inhabited the property.

The California Department of Transportation (Caltrans) constructed culverts adjacent to Leslie's land. Caltrans breached the levee on the wildlife refuge adjacent to Leslie's property, which allowed water to flow through the culverts onto Leslie's land. Caltrans failed to place effective floodgates on the culverts, creating wetlands conditions over time. In 1985, Leslie started to dig a ditch to drain and fill in the land. The Army Corps of Engineers (Corps) became aware of this activity and issued a cease-and-desist order pursuant to its authority under the Clean Water Act. The Corps claimed jurisdiction over the majority of the property, which Leslie then challenged. What result and why? [*Leslie Salt Co. v. United States*, 896 F.2d 354 (9th Cir. 1989)]

24–7 Nuisance Judy Godwin began construction of her home. At about the same time, Exxon began the construction of a "separation" plant 700 feet north of the home site. The residence and plant were completed at about the same time. The plant emitted noise, vibration, and sulfurous odors around the clock. These gave Godwin headaches and the odor prevented her from inviting friends to her residence. What legal theories could she use against Exxon? What result would be obtained under them? Explain. [*Exxon Corp., U.S.A. v. Dunn*, 474 So. 2d 1269 (Fla. Dist. Ct. App. 1985)]

24–8 Clean Water Act Interpretation of the language in environmental statutes is very important. The Clean Water Act authorizes private citizens to commence a civil action for an injunction and/or the imposition of civil penalties in federal district court against any person "alleged to be in violation" of the conditions of a National Pollutant Discharge Elimination System (NPDES) permit. The NPDES is a federal statute that authorizes permits to be granted to businesses that apply for permission to discharge effluent into a river or lake. The permit limits the amount and type of effluent authorized to be discharged. Between 1981 and 1984, Gwaltney of Smithfield repeatedly violated the conditions of its NPDES permit by exceeding authorized effluent limitations. Because of the installation of new equipment, Smithfield's last reported violation occurred in May 1984. Nevertheless, in June 1984, having given notice of its intent to sue to the Environmental Protection Agency and to sue state authorities, as required by the act, the Chesapeake Bay Foundation filed a suit alleging that Smithfield "has violated . . . [and] will continue to violate its NPDES permit." Smithfield filed a motion to dismiss, alleging that the federal statute required that it be in violation of the act at the time the action was filed. What was the result? Explain. [*Gwaltney of Smithfeld v. Chesapeake Bay Foundation*, 484 U.S. 49, 108 S. Ct. 376, 98 L. Ed. 2d 306 (1987)]

24–9 Endangered Species Act The secretary of the interior declared a small fish known as the snail darter to be endangered under the Endangered Species Act of 1973. The snail darter lived in a portion of the Little Tennessee River in which more than $100 million dol-lars had been spent on the Tellico Dam's construction. The secretary ordered all federal agencies to take action to ensure that the critical habitat of the snail darter was maintained. A group of concerned citizens brought legal action to stop any further construction of the dam on the basis that if the dam were completed, all the snail darters would be killed. Should the court grant an injunction to stop the construction? Explain. [*Tennessee Valley Authority v. Hill*, 437 U.S. 153, 98 S. Ct. 2279, 57 L. Ed. 2d 117 (1978)]

24–10 Internet The EPA Web site lists all the ozone nonattainment areas by state, area, and county. Is your area listed as a nonattainment area? Go to **http://www.epa.gov/ttncaaa1/title1/bgilbert/greenbk/oncs.htm** to find out.

The Constitution of the United States of America

Note: THE FOLLOWING TEXT IS A TRANSCRIPTION OF THE CONSTITUTION. TO ASSIST THE READER, TEXT IN ITALICS REPRESENTS SECTIONS THAT HAVE BEEN AMENDED OR SUPERSEDED. TEXT IN SMALL CAPS REPRESENTS INFORMATIONAL MATERIAL.

Preamble

WE THE PEOPLE of the United States, in Order to form a more perfect Union, establish Justice, insure domestic Tranquility, provide for the common defence, promote the general Welfare, and secure the Blessings of Liberty to ourselves and our Posterity, do ordain and establish this Constitution for the United States of America.

Article I

Section 1. All legislative Powers herein granted shall be vested in a Congress of the United States, which shall consist of a Senate and House of Representatives.

Section 2. The House of Representatives shall be composed of Members chosen every second Year by the People of the several States, and the Electors in each State shall have the Qualifications requisite for Electors of the most numerous Branch of the State Legislature.

No Person shall be a Representative who shall not have attained to the Age of twenty five Years, and been seven Years a Citizen of the United States, and who shall not, when elected, be an Inhabitant of that State in which he shall be chosen.

Representatives and direct Taxes shall be apportioned among the several States which may be included within this Union, according to their respective Numbers, which shall be determined by adding to the whole Number of free Persons, including those bound to Service for a Term of Years, and excluding Indians not taxed, three fifths of all other Persons.[1] The actual Enumeration shall be made within three Years after the first Meeting of the Congress of the United States, and within every subsequent Term of ten Years, in such Manner as they shall by Law direct. The Number of Representatives shall not exceed one for every thirty Thousand, but each State shall have at Least one Representative; and until such enumeration shall be made, the State of New Hampshire shall be entitled to chuse three, Massachusetts eight, Rhode Island and Providence Plantations one, Connecticut five, New York six, New Jersey four, Pennsylvania eight, Delaware one, Maryland six, Virginia ten, North Carolina five, South Carolina five, and Georgia three.

When vacancies happen in the Representation from any State, the Executive Authority thereof shall issue Writs of Election to fill such Vacancies.

The House of Representatives shall chuse their Speaker and other Officers; and shall have the sole Power of Impeachment.

Section 3. The Senate of the United States shall be composed of two Senators from each State, *chosen by the Legislature thereof*[2] for six Years; and each Senator shall have one Vote.

Immediately after they shall be assembled in Consequence of the first Election, they shall be divided as equally as may be into three Classes. The Seats of the

---

[1] Changed by the XIV amendment.
[2] Changed by the XVII amendment.

Senators of the first Class shall be vacated at the Expiration of the second Year, of the second Class at the Expiration of the fourth Year, and of the third Class at the Expiration of the sixth Year, so that one third may be chosen every second Year; *and if Vacancies happen by Resignation, or otherwise, during the Recess of the Legislature of any State, the Executive thereof may make temporary Appointments until the next Meeting of the Legislature, which shall then fill such Vacancies.*[3]

No Person shall be a Senator who shall not have attained to the Age of thirty Years, and been nine Years a Citizen of the United States, and who shall not, when elected, be an Inhabitant of that State for which he shall be chosen.

The Vice President of the United States shall be President of the Senate, but shall have no Vote, unless they be equally divided.

The Senate shall chuse their other Officers, and also a President pro tempore, in the Absence of the Vice President, or when he shall exercise the Office of President of the United States.

The Senate shall have the sole Power to try all Impeachments. When sitting for that Purpose, they shall be on Oath or Affirmation. When the President of the United States is tried, the Chief Justice shall preside: And no Person shall be convicted without the Concurrence of two thirds of the Members present.

Judgment in Cases of Impeachment shall not extend further than to removal from Office, and disqualification to hold and enjoy any Office of honor, Trust, or Profit under the United States: but the Party convicted shall nevertheless be liable and subject to Indictment, Trial, Judgment, and Punishment, according to Law.

Section 4. The Times, Places and Manner of holding Elections for Senators and Representatives, shall be prescribed in each State by the Legislature thereof; but the Congress may at any time by Law make or alter such Regulations, except as to the Places of chusing Senators.

The Congress shall assemble at least once in every Year, and such Meeting shall *be on the first Monday in December,*[4] unless they shall by Law appoint a different Day.

Section 5. Each House shall be the Judge of the Elections, Returns, and Qualifications of its own Members, and a Majority of each shall constitute a Quorum to do

Business; but a smaller Number may adjourn from day to day, and may be authorized to compel the Attendance of absent Members, in such Manner, and under such Penalties as each House may provide.

Each House may determine the Rules of its Proceedings, punish its Members for disorderly Behavior, and, with the Concurrence of two thirds, expel a Member.

Each House shall keep a Journal of its Proceedings, and from time to time publish the same, excepting such Parts as may in their Judgment require Secrecy; and the Yeas and Nays of the Members of either House on any question shall, at the Desire of one fifth of those Present, be entered on the Journal.

Neither House, during the Session of Congress, shall, without the Consent of the other, adjourn for more than three days, nor to any other Place than that in which the two Houses shall be sitting.

Section 6. The Senators and Representatives shall receive a Compensation for their Services, to be ascertained by Law, and paid out of the Treasury of the United States. They shall in all Cases, except Treason, Felony and Breach of the Peace, be privileged from Arrest during their Attendance at the Session of their respective Houses, and in going to and returning from the same; and for any Speech or Debate in either House, they shall not be questioned in any other Place.

No Senator or Representative shall, during the Time for which he was elected, be appointed to any civil Office under the Authority of the United States, which shall have been created, or the Emoluments whereof shall have been increased during such time; and no Person holding any Office under the United States, shall be a Member of either House during his Continuance in Office.

Section 7. All Bills for raising Revenue shall originate in the House of Representatives; but the Senate may propose or concur with Amendments as on other Bills.

Every Bill which shall have passed the House of Representatives and the Senate, shall, before it become a Law, be presented to the President of the United States; If he approve he shall sign it, but if not he shall return it, with his Objections to the House in which it shall have originated, who shall enter the Objections at large on their Journal, and proceed to reconsider it. If after such Reconsideration two thirds of that House shall agree to pass the Bill, it shall be sent together with the Objections, to the other House, by which it shall likewise be reconsidered, and if approved by two thirds of that

---

[3] Changed by the XVII amendment.
[4] Changed by the XX amendment.

House, it shall become a Law. But in all such Cases the Votes of both Houses shall be determined by Yeas and Nays, and the Names of the Persons voting for and against the Bill shall be entered on the Journal of each House respectively. If any Bill shall not be returned by the President within ten Days (Sundays excepted) after it shall have been presented to him, the Same shall be a Law, in like Manner as if he had signed it, unless the Congress by their Adjournment prevent its Return in which Case it shall not be a Law.

Every Order, Resolution, or Vote, to which the Concurrence of the Senate and House of Representatives may be necessary (except on a question of Adjournment) shall be presented to the President of the United States; and before the Same shall take Effect, shall be approved by him, or being disapproved by him, shall be repassed by two thirds of the Senate and House of Representatives, according to the Rules and Limitations prescribed in the Case of a Bill.

Section 8. The Congress shall have Power To lay and collect Taxes, Duties, Imposts and Excises, to pay the Debts and provide for the common Defence and general Welfare of the United States; but all Duties, Imposts and Excises shall be uniform throughout the United States;

To borrow Money on the credit of the United States;

To regulate Commerce with foreign Nations, and among the several States, and with the Indian Tribes;

To establish an uniform Rule of Naturalization, and uniform Laws on the subject of Bankruptcies throughout the United States;

To coin Money, regulate the Value thereof, and of foreign Coin, and fix the Standard of Weights and Measures;

To provide for the Punishment of counterfeiting the Securities and current Coin of the United States;

To establish Post Offices and post Roads;

To promote the Progress of Science and useful Arts, by securing for limited Times to Authors and Inventors the exclusive Right to their respective Writings and Discoveries;

To constitute Tribunals inferior to the supreme Court;

To define and punish Piracies and Felonies committed on the high Seas, and Offenses against the Law of Nations;

To declare War, grant Letters of Marque and Reprisal, and make Rules concerning Captures on Land and Water;

To raise and support Armies, but no Appropriation of Money to that Use shall be for a longer Term than two Years;

To provide and maintain a Navy;

To make Rules for the Government and Regulation of the land and naval Forces;

To provide for calling forth the Militia to execute the Laws of the Union, suppress Insurrections and repel Invasions;

To provide for organizing, arming, and disciplining the Militia, and for governing such Part of them as may be employed in the Service of the United States, reserving to the States respectively, the Appointment of the Officers, and the Authority of training the Militia according to the discipline prescribed by Congress;

To exercise exclusive Legislation in all Cases whatsoever, over such District (not exceeding ten Miles square) as may, by Cession of particular States, and the Acceptance of Congress, become the Seat of the Government of the United States, and to exercise like Authority over all Places purchased by the Consent of the Legislature of the State in which the Same shall be, for the Erection of Forts, Magazines, Arsenals, dock-Yards, and other needful Buildings;—And

To make all Laws which shall be necessary and proper for carrying into Execution the foregoing Powers, and all other Powers vested by this Constitution in the Government of the United States, or in any Department or Officer thereof.

Section 9. The Migration or Importation of such Persons as any of the States now existing shall think proper to admit, shall not be prohibited by the Congress prior to the Year one thousand eight hundred and eight, but a Tax or duty may be imposed on such Importation, not exceeding ten dollars for each Person.

The privilege of the Writ of Habeas Corpus shall not be suspended, unless when in Cases of Rebellion or Invasion the public Safety may require it.

No Bill of Attainder or ex post facto Law shall be passed.

No Capitation, or other direct, Tax shall be laid, *unless in Proportion to the Census or Enumeration herein before directed to be taken.*[5]

No Tax or Duty shall be laid on Articles exported from any State.

No Preference shall be given by any Regulation of Commerce or Revenue to the Ports of one State over

---

[5] Changed by the XVI amendment.

those of another: nor shall Vessels bound to, or from, one State be obliged to enter, clear, or pay Duties in another.

No Money shall be drawn from the Treasury, but in Consequence of Appropriations made by Law; and a regular Statement and Account of the Receipts and Expenditures of all public Money shall be published from time to time.

No Title of Nobility shall be granted by the United States: And no Person holding any Office of Profit or Trust under them, shall, without the Consent of the Congress, accept of any present, Emolument, Office, or Title, of any kind whatever, from any King, Prince, or foreign State.

Section 10. No State shall enter into any Treaty, Alliance, or Confederation; grant Letters of Marque and Reprisal; coin Money; emit Bills of Credit; make any Thing but gold and silver Coin a Tender in Payment of Debts; pass any Bill of Attainder, ex post facto Law, or Law impairing the Obligation of Contracts, or grant any Title of Nobility.

No State shall, without the Consent of the Congress, lay any Imposts or Duties on Imports or Exports, except what may be absolutely necessary for executing its inspection Laws: and the net Produce of all Duties and Imposts, laid by any State on Imports or Exports, shall be for the Use of the Treasury of the United States; and all such Laws shall be subject to the Revision and Controul of the Congress.

No State shall, without the Consent of Congress, lay any Duty of Tonnage, keep Troops, or Ships of War in time of Peace, enter into any Agreement or Compact with another State, or with a foreign Power, or engage in War, unless actually invaded, or in such imminent Danger as will not admit of delay.

Article II

Section 1. The executive Power shall be vested in a President of the United States of America. He shall hold his Office during the Term of four Years, and, together with the Vice President, chosen for the same Term, be elected, as follows:

Each State shall appoint, in such Manner as the Legislature thereof may direct, a Number of Electors, equal to the whole Number of Senators and Representatives to which the State may be entitled in the Congress; but no Senator or Representative, or Person holding an Office of Trust or Profit under the United States, shall be appointed an Elector.

The Electors shall meet in their respective States, and vote by Ballot for two Persons, of whom one at least shall not be an Inhabitant of the same State with themselves. And they shall make a List of all the Persons voted for, and of the Number of Votes for each; which List they shall sign and certify, and transmit sealed to the Seat of the Government of the United States, directed to the President of the Senate. The President of the Senate shall, in the Presence of the Senate and House of Representatives, open all the Certificates, and the Votes shall then be counted. The Person having the greatest Number of Votes shall be the President, if such Number be a Majority of the whole Number of Electors appointed; and if there be more than one who have such Majority, and have an equal Number of Votes, then the House of Representatives shall immediately chuse by Ballot one of them for President; and if no Person have a Majority, then from the five highest on the List the said House shall in like Manner chuse the President. But in chusing the President, the Votes shall be taken by States, the Representation from each State having one Vote; A quorum for this Purpose shall consist of a Member or Members from two thirds of the States, and a Majority of all the States shall be necessary to a Choice. In every Case, after the Choice of the President, the Person having the greater Number of Votes of the Electors shall be the Vice President. But if there should remain two or more who have equal Votes, the Senate shall chuse from them by Ballot the Vice President.[6]

The Congress may determine the Time of chusing the Electors, and the Day on which they shall give their Votes; which Day shall be the same throughout the United States.

No person except a natural born Citizen, or a Citizen of the United States, at the time of the Adoption of this Constitution, shall be eligible to the Office of President; neither shall any Person be eligible to that Office who shall not have attained to the Age of thirty five Years, and been fourteen Years a Resident within the United States.

In Case of the Removal of the President from Office, or of his Death, Resignation or Inability to discharge the Powers and Duties of the said Office, the same shall devolve on the Vice President, and the Congress may by Law provide for the Case of Removal, Death, Resignation or Inability, both of the President and Vice President, declaring what Officer shall then act as President, and such Officer shall act accordingly, until the Disability be removed, or a President shall be elected.[7]

The President shall, at stated Times, receive for his Services, a Compensation, which shall neither be

---

[6] Changed by the XII amendment.
[7] Changed by the XXV amendment.

increased nor diminished during the Period for which he shall have been elected, and he shall not receive within that Period any other Emolument from the United States, or any of them.

Before he enter on the Execution of his Office, he shall take the following Oath or Affirmation: "I do solemnly swear (or affirm) that I will faithfully execute the Office of President of the United States, and will to the best of my Ability, preserve, protect and defend the Constitution of the United States."

Section 2. The President shall be Commander in Chief of the Army and Navy of the United States, and of the Militia of the several States, when called into the actual Service of the United States; he may require the Opinion, in writing, of the principal Officer in each of the executive Departments, upon any Subject relating to the Duties of their respective Offices, and he shall have Power to grant Reprieves and Pardons for Offenses against the United States, except in Cases of Impeachment.

He shall have Power, by and with the Advice and Consent of the Senate to make Treaties, provided two thirds of the Senators present concur; and he shall nominate, and by and with the Advice and Consent of the Senate, shall appoint Ambassadors, other public Ministers and Consuls, Judges of the supreme Court, and all other Officers of the United States, whose Appointments are not herein otherwise provided for, and which shall be established by Law; but the Congress may by Law vest the Appointment of such inferior Officers, as they think proper, in the President alone, in the Courts of Law, or in the Heads of Departments.

The President shall have Power to fill up all Vacancies that may happen during the Recess of the Senate, by granting Commissions which shall expire at the End of their next Session.

Section 3. He shall from time to time give to the Congress Information of the State of the Union, and recommend to their Consideration such Measures as he shall judge necessary and expedient; he may, on extraordinary Occasions, convene both Houses, or either of them, and in Case of Disagreement between them, with Respect to the Time of Adjournment, he may adjourn them to such Time as he shall think proper; he shall receive Ambassadors and other public Ministers; he shall take Care that the Laws be faithfully executed, and shall Commission all the Officers of the United States.

Section 4. The President, Vice President and all civil Officers of the United States, shall be removed from Office on Impeachment for, and Conviction of, Treason, Bribery, or other high Crimes and Misdemeanors.

Article III

Section 1. The judicial Power of the United States, shall be vested in one supreme Court, and in such inferior Courts as the Congress may from time to time ordain and establish. The Judges, both of the supreme and inferior Courts, shall hold their Offices during good Behaviour, and shall, at stated Times, receive for their Services a Compensation, which shall not be diminished during their Continuance in Office.

Section 2. The judicial Power shall extend to all Cases, in Law and Equity, arising under this Constitution, the Laws of the United States, and Treaties made, or which shall be made, under their Authority;—to all Cases affecting Ambassadors, other public Ministers and Consuls;—to all Cases of admiralty and maritime Jurisdiction;—to Controversies to which the United States shall be a Party;—to Controversies between two or more States;—*between a State and Citizens of another State;*[8]—between Citizens of different States;— between Citizens of the same State claiming Lands under Grants of different States, and between a State, or the Citizens thereof, and foreign States, Citizens or Subjects.

In all Cases affecting Ambassadors, other public Ministers and Consuls, and those in which a State shall be a Party, the supreme Court shall have original Jurisdiction. In all the other Cases before mentioned, the supreme Court shall have appellate Jurisdiction, both as to Law and Fact, with such Exceptions, and under such Regulations as the Congress shall make.

The Trial of all Crimes, except in Cases of Impeachment, shall be by Jury; and such Trial shall be held in the State where the said Crimes shall have been committed; but when not committed within any State, the Trial shall be at such Place or Places as the Congress may by Law have directed.

Section 3. Treason against the United States, shall consist only in levying War against them, or, in adhering to their Enemies, giving them Aid and Comfort. No

[8] Changed by the XI amendment.

Person shall be convicted of Treason unless on the Testimony of two Witnesses to the same overt Act, or on Confession in open Court.

The Congress shall have Power to declare the Punishment of Treason, but no Attainder of Treason shall work Corruption of Blood, or Forfeiture except during the Life of the Person attainted.

Article IV

Section 1. Full Faith and Credit shall be given in each State to the public Acts, Records, and judicial Proceedings of every other State. And the Congress may by general Laws prescribe the Manner in which such Acts, Records and Proceedings shall be proved, and the Effect thereof.

Section 2. The Citizens of each State shall be entitled to all Privileges and Immunities of Citizens in the several States.

A Person charged in any State with Treason, Felony, or other Crime, who shall flee from Justice, and be found in another State, shall on Demand of the executive Authority of the State from which he fled, be delivered up, to be removed to the State having Jurisdiction of the Crime.

No Person held to Service or Labour in one State, under the Laws thereof, escaping into another, shall, in Consequence of any Law or Regulation therein, be discharged from such Service or Labour, but shall be delivered up on Claim of the Party to whom such Service or Labour may be due.[9]

Section 3. New States may be admitted by the Congress into this Union; but no new State shall be formed or erected within the Jurisdiction of any other State; nor any State be formed by the Junction of two or more States, or Parts of States, without the Consent of the Legislatures of the States concerned as well as of the Congress.

The Congress shall have Power to dispose of and make all needful Rules and Regulations respecting the Territory or other Property belonging to the United States; and nothing in this Constitution shall be so construed as to Prejudice any Claims of the United States, or of any particular State.

Section 4. The United States shall guarantee to every State in this Union a Republican Form of Government,

and shall protect each of them against Invasion; and on Application of the Legislature, or of the Executive (when the Legislature cannot be convened) against domestic Violence.

Article V

The Congress, whenever two thirds of both Houses shall deem it necessary, shall propose Amendments to this Constitution, or, on the Application of the Legislatures of two thirds of the several States, shall call a Convention for proposing Amendments, which, in either Case, shall be valid to all Intents and Purposes, as part of this Constitution, when ratified by the Legislatures of three fourths of the several States, or by Conventions in three fourths thereof, as the one or the other Mode of Ratification may be proposed by the Congress; Provided that no Amendment which may be made prior to the Year One thousand eight hundred and eight shall in any Manner affect the first and fourth Clauses in the Ninth Section of the first Article; and that no State, without its Consent, shall be deprived of its equal Suffrage in the Senate.

Article VI

All Debts contracted and Engagements entered into, before the Adoption of this Constitution shall be as valid against the United States under this Constitution, as under the Confederation.

This Constitution, and the Laws of the United States which shall be made in Pursuance thereof; and all Treaties made, or which shall be made, under the Authority of the United States, shall be the supreme Law of the Land; and the Judges in every State shall be bound thereby, any Thing in the Constitution or Laws of any State to the Contrary notwithstanding.

The Senators and Representatives before mentioned, and the Members of the several State Legislatures, and all executive and judicial Officers, both of the United States and of the several States, shall be bound by Oath or Affirmation, to support this Constitution; but no religious Test shall ever be required as a Qualification to any Office or public Trust under the United States.

Article VII

The Ratification of the Conventions of nine States shall be sufficient for the Establishment of this Constitution between the States so ratifying the Same.

Attest: William Jackson, Secretary

---

[9] Repealed by the XIII amendment.

Done in Convention by the unanimous Consent of the Senate present the Seventeenth Day of September in the Year of our Lord one thousand seven hundred and Eighty seven and of the Independence of the United States of America the Twelfth. In witness whereof, We have hereunto subscribed our Names,

G⁰. Washington
    Presidt and deputy from Virginia

Delaware
    Geo: Read
    Gunning Bedford jun
    John Dickinson
    Richard Bassett
    Jaco: Broom

Maryland
    James McHenry
    Dan of St Thos. Jenifer
    Danl. Carroll

Virginia
    John Blair
    James Madison Jr.

North Carolina
    Wm. Blount
    Richd. Dobbs Spaight
    Hu Williamson

South Carolina
    J. Rutledge
    Charles Cotesworth Pinckney
    Charles Pinckney
    Pierce Butler

Georgia
    William Few
    Abr Baldwin

New Hampshire
    John Langdon
    Nicholas Gilman

Massachusetts
    Nathaniel Gorham
    Rufus King

Connecticut
    Wm. Saml. Johnson
    Roger Sherman

New York
    Alexander Hamilton

New Jersey
    Wil: Livingston
    David Brearley
    Wm. Paterson
    Jona: Dayton

Pennsylvania
    B. Franklin
    Thomas Mifflin
    Robt. Morris
    Geo. Clymer
    Thos. FitzSimmons
    Jared Ingersoll
    James Wilson
    Gouv Morris

The First 10 Amendments to the Constitution as Ratified by the States

Note: THE FOLLOWING TEXT IS OF THE FIRST 10 AMENDMENTS TO THE CONSTITUTION. THESE AMENDMENTS WERE RATIFIED DECEMBER 15, 1791, AND FORM WHAT IS KNOWN AS THE "BILL OF RIGHTS."

THE PREAMBLE TO THE BILL OF RIGHTS

CONGRESS OF THE UNITED STATES
BEGUN AND HELD AT THE CITY OF NEW-YORK, ON
WEDNESDAY THE FOURTH OF MARCH, ONE THOUSAND
SEVEN HUNDRED AND EIGHTY NINE.

THE CONVENTIONS OF A NUMBER OF THE STATES, HAVING AT THE TIME OF THEIR ADOPTING THE CONSTITUTION, EXPRESSED A DESIRE, IN ORDER TO PREVENT MISCONSTRUCTION OR ABUSE OF ITS POWERS, THAT FURTHER DECLARATORY AND RESTRICTIVE CLAUSES SHOULD BE ADDED: AND AS EXTENDING THE GROUND OF PUBLIC CONFIDENCE IN THE GOVERNMENT, WILL BEST ENSURE THE BENEFICENT ENDS OF ITS INSTITUTION.

RESOLVED BY THE SENATE AND HOUSE OF REPRESENTATIVES OF THE UNITED STATES OF AMERICA, IN CONGRESS ASSEMBLED, TWO THIRDS OF BOTH HOUSES CONCURRING, THAT THE FOLLOWING ARTICLES BE PROPOSED TO THE LEGISLATURES OF THE SEVERAL STATES AS AMENDMENTS TO THE CONSTITUTION OF THE UNITED STATES, ALL, OR ANY OF WHICH ARTICLES, WHEN RATIFIED BY THREE FOURTHS OF THE SAID LEGISLATURES, TO BE

VALID TO ALL INTENTS AND PURPOSES, AS PART OF THE SAID CONSTITUTION; VIZ.

ARTICLES IN ADDITION TO, AND AMENDMENT OF THE CONSTITUTION OF THE UNITED STATES OF AMERICA, PROPOSED BY CONGRESS AND RATIFIED BY THE LEGISLATURES OF THE SEVERAL STATES, PURSUANT TO THE FIFTH ARTICLE OF THE ORIGINAL CONSTITUTION.

Amendment I [1791]

Congress shall make no law respecting an establishment of religion, or prohibiting the free exercise thereof; or abridging the freedom of speech, or of the press; or the right of the people peaceably to assembly, and to petition the Government for a redress of grievances.

Amendment II [1791]

A well regulated Militia, being necessary to the security of a free State, the right of the people to keep and bear Arms, shall not be infringed.

Amendment III [1791]

No Soldier shall, in time of peace be quartered in any house, without the consent of the Owner, nor in time of war, but in a manner to be prescribed by law.

Amendment IV [1791]

The right of the people to be secure in their persons, houses, papers, and effects, against unreasonable searches and seizures, shall not be violated, and no Warrants shall issue, but upon probable cause, supported by Oath or affirmation, and particularly describing the place to be searched, and the persons or things to be seized.

Amendment V [1791]

No person shall be held to answer for a capital, or otherwise infamous crime, unless on a presentment or indictment of a Grand Jury, except in cases arising in the land or naval forces, or in the Militia, when in actual service in time of War or public danger; nor shall any person be subject for the same offence to be twice put in jeopardy of life or limb; nor shall be compelled in any criminal case to be a witness against himself, nor be deprived of life, liberty, or property, without due process of law; nor shall private property be taken for public use, without just compensation.

Amendment VI [1791]

In all criminal prosecutions, the accused shall enjoy the right to a speedy and public trial, by an impartial jury of the State and district wherein the crime shall have been committed, which district shall have been previously ascertained by law, and to be informed of the nature and cause of the accusation; to be confronted with the witnesses against him; to have compulsory process for obtaining witnesses in his favor, and to have the Assistance of Counsel for his defence.

Amendment VII [1791]

In Suits at common law, where the value in controversy shall exceed twenty dollars, the right of trial by jury shall be preserved, and no fact tried by jury, shall be otherwise re-examined in any Court of the United States, than according to the rules of the common law.

Amendment VIII [1791]

Excessive bail shall not be required, nor excessive fines imposed, nor cruel and unusual punishments inflicted.

Amendment IX [1791]

The enumeration in the Constitution, of certain rights, shall not be construed to deny or disparage others retained by the people.

Amendment X [1791]

The powers not delegated to the United States by the Constitution, nor prohibited by it to the States, are reserved to the States respectively, or to the people.

Amendments 11–27 to the Constitution of the United States

Amendment XI [1798]

PASSED BY CONGRESS MARCH 4, 1794. RATIFIED FEBRUARY 7, 1795.
Note: ARTICLE III, SECTION 2, OF THE CONSTITUTION WAS MODIFIED BY AMENDMENT XI.

The Judicial power of the United States shall not be construed to extend to any suit in law or equity, commenced or prosecuted against one of the United States by Citizens of another State, or by Citizens or Subjects of any Foreign State.

Amendment XII [1804]

PASSED BY CONGRESS DECEMBER 9, 1803. RATIFIED JUNE 15, 1804.

The Electors shall meet in their respective states, and vote by ballot for President and Vice-President, one of whom, at least, shall not be an inhabitant of the same state with themselves; they shall name in their ballots the person voted for as President, and in distinct ballots the person voted for as Vice-President, and they shall make distinct lists of all persons voted for as President, and of all persons voted for as Vice-President, and of the number of votes for each, which lists they shall sign and certify, and transmit sealed to the seat of the government of the United States, directed to the President of the Senate;—The President of the Senate shall, in the presence of the Senate and House of Representatives, open all the certificates and the votes shall then be counted;—The person having the greatest number of votes for President, shall be the President, if such number be a majority of the whole number of Electors appointed; and if no person have such majority, then from the persons having the highest numbers not exceeding three on the list of those voted for as President, the House of Representatives shall choose immediately, by ballot, the President. But in choosing the President, the votes shall be taken by states, the representation from each state having one vote; a quorum for this purpose shall consist of a member or members from two-thirds of the states, and a majority of all states shall be necessary to a choice. *And if the House of Representatives shall not choose a President whenever the right of choice shall devolve upon them, before the fourth day of March next following, then the Vice-President shall act as President, as in the case of the death or other constitutional disability of the President.*[10] The person having the greatest number of votes as Vice-President, shall be the Vice-President, if such number be a majority of the whole number of Electors appointed, and if no person have a majority, then from the two highest numbers on the list, the Senate shall choose the Vice-President; a quorum for the purpose shall consist of two-thirds of the whole number of Senators, and a majority of the whole number shall be necessary to a choice. But no person constitutionally ineligible to the office of President shall be eligible to that of Vice-President of the United States.

Amendment XIII [1865]

PASSED BY CONGRESS JANUARY 31, 1865. RATIFIED DECEMBER 6, 1865.

Section 1. Neither slavery nor involuntary servi- tude, except as a punishment for crime whereof the party shall have been duly convicted, shall exist within the United States, or any place subject to their jurisdiction.

Section 2. Congress shall have power to enforce this article by appropriate legislation.

Amendment XIV [1868]

PASSED BY CONGRESS JUNE 13, 1866. RATIFIED JULY 9, 1868.

Section 1. All persons born or naturalized in the United States, and subject to the jurisdiction thereof, are citizens of the United States and of the State wherein they reside. No State shall make or enforce any law which shall abridge the privileges or immunities of citizens of the United States; nor shall any State deprive any person of life, liberty, or property, without due process of law; nor deny to any person within its jurisdiction the equal protection of the laws.

Section 2. Representatives shall be apportioned among the several States according to their respective numbers, counting the whole number of persons in each State, excluding Indians not taxed. But when the right to vote at any election for the choice of electors for President and Vice President of the United States, Representatives in Congress, the Executive and Judicial officers of a State, or the members of the Legislature thereof, is denied to any of the male inhabitants of such State, *being twenty-one years of age,*[11] and citizens of the United States, or in any way abridged, except for participation in rebellion, or other crime, the basis of representation therein shall be reduced in the proportion which the number of such male citizens shall bear to the whole number of male citizens twenty-one years of age in such State.

Section 3. No person shall be a Senator or Representative in Congress, or elector of President and Vice President, or hold any office, civil or military, under the United States, or under any State, who having previously taken an oath, as a member of Congress, or as an officer of the United States, or as a member of any State legislature, or as an executive or judicial officer of any State, to support the Constitution of the United States, shall have engaged in insurrection or rebellion against

[10] Superceded by Section 3 of the XX amendment.

[11] Changed by Section 1 of the XXVI amendment.

the same, or given aid or comfort to the enemies thereof. But Congress may by a vote of two-thirds of each House, remove such disability.

Section 4. The validity of the public debt of the United States, authorized by law, including debts incurred for payment of pensions and bounties for services in suppressing insurrection or rebellion, shall not be questioned. But neither the United States nor any State shall assume or pay any debt or obligation incurred in aid of insurrection or rebellion against the United States, or any claim for the loss or emancipation of any slave; but all such debts, obligations and claims shall be held illegal and void.

Section 5. The Congress shall have power to enforce, by appropriate legislation, the provisions of this article.

Amendment XV [1870]

PASSED BY CONGRESS FEBRUARY 26, 1869. RATIFIED FEBRUARY 3, 1870.

Section 1. The right of citizens of the United States to vote shall not be denied or abridged by the United States or by any State on account of race, color, or previous condition of servitude.

Section 2. The Congress shall have power to enforce this article by appropriate legislation.

Amendment XVI [1913]

PASSED BY CONGRESS JULY 2, 1909. RATIFIED FEBRUARY 3, 1913.

The Congress shall have power to lay and collect taxes on incomes, from whatever source derived, without apportionment among the several States, and without regard to any census or enumeration.

Amendment XVII [1913]

PASSED BY CONGRESS MAY 13, 1912. RATIFIED APRIL 8, 1913.

The Senate of the United States shall be composed of two Senators from each State, elected by the people thereof, for six years; and each Senator shall have one vote. The electors in each State shall have the qualifications requisite for electors of the most numerous branch of the State legislatures.

When vacancies happen in the representation of any State in the Senate, the executive authority of such State shall issue writs of election to fill such vacancies: Provided, That the legislature of any State may empower the executive thereof to make temporary appointments until the people fill the vacancies by election as the legislature may direct.

This amendment shall not be so construed as to affect the election or term of any Senator chosen before it becomes valid as part of the Constitution.

Amendment XVIII [1919] [Repealed]

PASSED BY CONGRESS DECEMBER 18, 1917. RATIFIED JANUARY 16, 1919. REPEALED BY XXI AMENDMENT.

Section 1. After one year from the ratification of this article the manufacture, sale, or transportation of intoxicating liquors within, the importation thereof into, or the exportation thereof from the United States and all territory subject to the jurisdiction thereof for beverage purposes is hereby prohibited.

Section 2. The Congress and the several States shall have concurrent power to enforce this article by appropriate legislation.

Section 3. This article shall be inoperative unless it shall have been ratified as an amendment to the Constitution by the legislatures of the several States, as provided in the Constitution, within seven years from the date of the submission hereof to the States by the Congress.

Amendment XIX [1920]

PASSED BY CONGRESS JUNE 4, 1919. RATIFIED AUGUST 18, 1920.

The right of citizens of the United States to vote shall not be denied or abridged by the United States or by any State on account of sex.

Congress shall have power to enforce this article by appropriate legislation.

Amendment XX [1933]

PASSED BY CONGRESS MARCH 2, 1932. RATIFIED JANUARY 23, 1933.

Section 1. The terms of the President and Vice President shall end at noon on the 20th day of January, and the terms of Senators and Representatives at noon on the 3d day of January, of the years in which such terms would have ended if this article had not been ratified; and the terms of their successors shall then begin.

Section 2. The Congress shall assemble at least once in every year, and such meeting shall begin at noon on the 3d day of January, unless they shall by law appoint a different day.

Section 3. If, at the time fixed for the beginning of the term of the President, the President elect shall have died, the Vice President elect shall become President. If the President shall not have been chosen before the time fixed for the beginning of his term, or if the President elect shall have failed to qualify, then the Vice President elect shall act as President until a President shall have qualified; and the Congress may by law provide for the case wherein neither a President elect nor a Vice President elect shall have qualified, declaring who shall then act as President, or the manner in which one who is to act shall be selected, and such person shall act accordingly until a President or Vice President shall have qualified.

Section 4. The Congress may by law provide for the case of the death of any of the persons from whom the House of Representatives may choose a President whenever the right of choice shall have devolved upon them, and for the case of the death of any of the persons from whom the Senate may choose a Vice President whenever the right of choice shall have devolved upon them.

Section 5. Sections 1 and 2 shall take effect on the 15th day of October following the ratification of this article.

Section 6. This article shall be inoperative unless it shall have been ratified as an amendment to the Constitution by the legislatures of three-fourths of the several States within seven years from the date of its submission.

Amendment XXI [1933]

PASSED BY CONGRESS FEBRUARY 20, 1933. RATIFIED DECEMBER 5, 1933.

Section 1. The eighteenth article of amendment to the Constitution of the United States is hereby repealed.

Section 2. The transportation or importation into any State, Territory, or possession of the United States for delivery or use therein of intoxicating liquors, in violation of the laws thereof, is hereby prohibited.

Section 3. This article shall be inoperative unless it shall have been ratified as an amendment to the Constitution by conventions in the several States, as provided in the Constitution, within seven years from the date of the submission hereof to the States by the Congress.

Amendment XXII [1951]

PASSED BY CONGRESS MARCH 21, 1947. RATIFIED FEBRUARY 27, 1951.

Section 1. No person shall be elected to the office of the President more than twice, and no person who has held the office of President, or acted as President, for more than two years of a term to which some other person was elected President shall be elected to the office of President more than once. But this Article shall not apply to any person holding the office of President when this Article was proposed by the Congress, and shall not prevent any person who may be holding the office of President, or acting as President, during the term within which this Article becomes operative from holding the office of President or acting as President during the remainder of such term.

Section 2. This article shall be inoperative unless it shall have been ratified as an amendment to the Constitution by the legislatures of three-fourths of the several States within seven years from the date of its submission to the States by the Congress.

Amendment XXIII [1961]

PASSED BY CONGRESS JUNE 16, 1960. RATIFIED MARCH 29, 1961.

Section 1. The District constituting the seat of Government of the United States shall appoint in such manner as the Congress may direct:

A number of electors of President and Vice President equal to the whole number of Senators and Representatives in Congress to which the District would be entitled if it were a State, but in no event more than the least populous state; they shall be in addition to those appointed by the states, but they shall be considered, for the purposes of the election of President and Vice President, to be electors appointed by a state; and they shall meet in the District and perform such duties as provided by the twelfth article of amendment.

Section 2. The Congress shall have power to enforce this article by appropriate legislation.

Amendment XXIV [1964]

PASSED BY CONGRESS AUGUST 27, 1962. RATIFIED JANUARY 23, 1964.

Section 1. The right of citizens of the United States to vote in any primary or other election for President or Vice President, for electors for President or Vice President, or for Senator or Representative in Congress, shall not be denied or abridged by the United States, or any State by reason of failure to pay any poll tax or other tax.

Section 2. The Congress shall have power to enforce this article by appropriate legislation.

Amendment XXV [1967]

PASSED BY CONGRESS JULY 6, 1965. RATIFIED FEBRUARY 10, 1967.

Section 1. In case of the removal of the President from office or of his death or resignation, the Vice President shall become President.

Section 2. Whenever there is a vacancy in the office of the Vice President, the President shall nominate a Vice President who shall take office upon confirmation by a majority vote of both Houses of Congress.

Section 3. Whenever the President transmits to the President pro tempore of the Senate and the Speaker of the House of Representatives his written declaration that he is unable to discharge the powers and duties of his office, and until he transmits to them a written declaration to the contrary, such powers and duties shall be discharged by the Vice President as Acting President.

Section 4. Whenever the Vice President and a majority of either the principal officers of the executive departments or of such other body as Congress may by

law provide, transmit to the President pro tempore of the Senate and the Speaker of the House of Representatives their written declaration that the President is unable to discharge the powers and duties of his office, the Vice President shall immediately assume the powers and duties of the office as Acting President.

Thereafter, when the President transmits to the President pro tempore of the Senate and the Speaker of the House of Representatives his written declaration that no inability exists, he shall resume the powers and duties of his office unless the Vice President and a majority of either the principal officers of the executive department or of such other body as Congress may by law provide, transmit within four days to the President pro tempore of the Senate and the Speaker of the House of Representatives their written declaration that the President is unable to discharge the powers and duties of his office. Thereupon Congress shall decide the issue, assembling within forty-eight hours for that purpose if not in session. If the Congress, within twenty-one days after receipt of the latter written declaration, or, if Congress is not in session, within twenty-one days after Congress is required to assemble, determines by two-thirds vote of both Houses that the President is unable to discharge the powers and duties of his office, the Vice President shall continue to discharge the same as Acting President; otherwise, the President shall resume the powers and duties of his office.

Amendment XXVI [1971]

PASSED BY CONGRESS MARCH 23, 1971. RATIFIED JULY 1, 1971.

Section 1. The right of citizens of the United States, who are eighteen years of age or older, to vote shall not be denied or abridged by the United States or by any State on account of age.

Section 2. The Congress shall have power to enforce this article by appropriate legislation.

Amendment XXVII [1992]

ORIGINALLY PROPOSED SEPTEMBER 25, 1789. RATIFIED MAY 7, 1992.

No law, varying the compensation for the services of the Senators and Representatives, shall take effect, until an election of Representatives shall have intervened.

Appendix B

Web References for Selected Materials

Introduction

Please go to **http://bohlman.westbuslaw.com** to find a rich source of materials and statutes. Materials that are found on the Web site are *Spanish Equivalents for Important Legal Terms in English, Selected World Wide Web Addresses, Critical Thinking,* and *International Top-Level Domains.* Selected statutes that are linked include the *Uniform Commercial Code, Sherman Act, Clayton Act, Federal Trade Commission Act, National Labor Relations Act,* and various *Federal Civil Rights Acts.*

Guide to Appendices C–G

Appendix C Spanish Equivalents for Important Legal Terms in English

Please go to **http://bohlman.westbuslaw.com** for a link to Spanish equivalents. This appendix includes an abundance of terms that related English legal words to Spanish.

Appendix D Selected World Wide Web Addresses

Please go to **http://bohlman.westbuslaw.com** for a link to a number of World Wide Web addresses. Once on the West Business Law site, links are available to these Web sites so the reader does not need to retype lengthy Web addresses.

Appendix E Critical Thinking

Please go to **http://bohlman.westbuslaw.com** to link to the *Critical Thinking* site. The *Critical Thinking* appendix is a reference source that provides basic methods to use when faced with different legal, ethical, and business problems. Included are methods of evaluating evidence, using a reasoning process that includes explanations of inductive reasoning and deductive reasoning, evaluating fallacies in reasoning, and providing rules to remember.

Appendix F International Top-Level Domains (ITLDs)

Please go to **http://bohlman.westbuslaw.com** to link to the top-level domains for each country in the world. This chart is a handy reference when surfing the Web to determine the country that is the top-level domain in the Web address. The reader can click directly to this Web site at: **http://www.iana.org/cctld/cctld-whois.htm**.

Appendix G Selected Statutes

Please go to **http://bohlman.westbuslaw.com** to link directly to the various statutes that are referenced in the following section. Alternative Web sites are also provided.

Uniform Commercial Code. Please go to **http://bohlman.westbuslaw.com** to link directly to Cornell University Law School Web site. Alternatively, the reader can go directly to Cornell at the following Web address: **http://www.law.cornell.edu**. Once on the Web site, on the left side, hold the mouse over the second bar that reads "Constitutions and codes". A frame will appear that near the bottom reads "Uniform Commercial Code". Click on the "Uniform Commercial Code". The user may be asked to fill out a short questionnaire. The reader can fill out the form and submit it or use the following Web address to go directly to the Uniform Commercial Code: **http://www.law.cornell.edu/ucc/ucc.table.html**.

Other Uniform Codes, such as the Uniform Partnership Act, are available at the Cornell Web site. Once on the Web site, on the left side, hold the mouse over the second bar that reads "Constitutions and codes". A frame will appear that near the bottom reads "Other uniform laws". Click on the "Other uniform laws". Once on the next page, on the right side, under "Uniform law locators" click on "Business and Finance Laws". The reader can access the information directly at the following Web address: **http://www.law.cornell.edu/uniform/vol7.html**.

Selected Federal Statutes. Please go to **http://bohlman.westbuslaw.com** to link directly to the *Sherman Act, Clayton Act, Federal Trade Commission Act, National Labor Relations Act,* and various *Federal Civil Rights Acts.* Alternatively, the reader may directly link to U.S. House of Representatives' Web site at **http://uscode.house.gov/usc.htm**. Once on the U.S. House of Representatives' Web site, in the "Title" box, type in title number provided and in the "Section" box, type in the section number provided. A list of documents will appear. Search the database of documents carefully to find the exact match. In some cases, the exact match will appear twice, where one match may be an update. The reader needs to click on both entries to see which one contains the statute. Click on the citation to access the text of the statute. Materials following the text will include the source of the material; any amending legislation, including the dates of the amendments and the amending text; effective dates; and short title. Located on the top left of the Web page are two arrows. Clicking on the right arrow takes the reader through the statutory scheme, while clicking on the left arrow, takes the reader back to the previous section. The Office of the Law Revision Council of the U.S. House of Representatives maintains this Web site.

Sherman Act, 15 U.S.C. § 1. In the "Title" box, type "15", and in the "Section" box, type "1". Click on "Search", and in the list of "documents found", click on the citation to access the text of the statute.

Sherman Act, 15 U.S.C. § 2. No direct link exists at the time of this writing. Follow the previous directions to link to Sherman Act, 15 U.S.C. § 1. Located on the top left of the Web page are two arrows. Clicking on the right arrow allows the reader to access the remaining sections of the Sherman Act, which consists of sections 1–7.

Clayton Act, 15 U.S.C. § 12. In the "Title" box, type "15", and in the "Section" box, type "12". Click on "Search", and in the list of "documents found", click on the citation to access the text of the statute. Located on the top left of the Web page are two arrows. Clicking on the right arrow allows the reader to access the remaining sections of the original and amended sections of the Clayton Act, sections 12–19.

Clayton Act, 15 U.S.C. § 13 (Robinson-Patman Act). In the "Title" box, type "15", and in the "Section" box, type "13". Click on "Search", and in the list of "documents found", click on the citation to access the text of the statute. Located on the top left of the Web page are two arrows. Clicking on the right arrow allows the reader to access the remaining sections §§ 13(a), 13(b), and 13(c) of the Robinson–Patman Act, which amends Section 2 of the Clayton Act.

Clayton Act, 15 U.S.C. § 18 (Celler-Kefauver Act amended by the Hart-Scott-Rodino Antitrust Improvement Act). In the "Title" box, type "15", and in the "Section" box, type "18". Click on "Search", and in the list of "documents found", click on the citation to access the text of the statute. Located on the top left of the Web page are two arrows. Clicking on the right arrow allows the reader to access the remaining sections of the Clayton Act.

Clayton Act, 15 U.S.C. § 19 (Interlocking directorates and officers). In the "Title" box, type "15", and in the "Section" box, type "19". Click on "Search", and in the list of "documents found", click on the citation to access the text of the statute. Located on the top left of the Web page are two arrows. Click on the left arrow takes the reader back through the Clayton Act.

Federal Trade Commission Act, 15 U.S.C. § 41. In the "Title" box, type "15", and in the "Section" box, type "41". Click on "Search", and in the list of "documents found", click on the citation to access the text of the statute. Located on the top left of the Web page are two arrows. Clicking on the right arrow allows the reader to access the remaining sections of the Federal Trade Commission Act, sections 41–77.

National Labor Relations Act, 29 U.S.C. § 151. In the "Title" box, type "29", and in the "Section" box, type "151". Click on "Search", and in the list of "documents found", click on the citation to access the text of the statute. Located on the top left of the Web page are two arrows. Clicking on the right arrow allows the reader to access the remaining sections of the National Labor Relations Act, sections 151–169.

Federal Civil Rights Laws, 42 U.S.C. § 1981 (Equal Rights Under the Law). In the "Title" box, type "42", and in the "Section" box, type "1981". Click on "Search", and in the list of "documents found", click on the citation to access the text of the statute. Clicking on the arrows allows the reader to access various sections of the Civil Rights Acts.

Federal Civil Rights Laws, 42 U.S.C. § 1981a (1964 Civil Rights Act). In the "Title" box, type "42", and in the "Section" box, type "1981a". Click on "Search", and in the list of "documents found", click on the citation to access the text of the statute. Located on the top left of the Web page are two arrows. Clicking on the arrows allows the reader to access various sections of the Civil Rights Acts.

Federal Civil Rights Laws, 42 U.S.C. § 2000a (Public Accomodations). In the "Title" box, type "42", and in the "Section" box, type "2000a". Click on "Search", and in the list of "documents found", click on the citation to access the text of the statute. Located on the top left of the Web page are two arrows. Clicking on the arrows allows the reader to access various sections of the Civil Rights Acts.

Federal Civil Rights Laws, 42 U.S.C. § 2000e-2 (Equal Employment Opportunities). In the "Title" box, type "42", and in the "Section" box, type "2000e-2". Click on "Search", and in the list of "documents found", click on the citation to access the text of the statute. Located on the top left of the Web page are two arrows. Clicking on the arrows allows the reader to access various sections of the Civil Rights Acts.

Federal Civil Rights Laws, 42 U.S.C. § 3604 (Fair Housing). In the "Title" box, type "42", and in the "Section" box, type "3604". Click on "Search", and in the list of "documents found", click on the citation to access the text of the statute. Located on the top left of the Web page are two arrows. Clicking on the arrows allows the reader to access various sections of the Civil Rights Acts.

Federal Civil Rights Laws, 42 U.S.C. § 12101 (Equal Opportunity for Individuals with Disabilities). In the "Title" box, type "42", and in the "Section" box, type "12101". Click on "Search", and in the list of "documents found", click on the citation to access the text of the statute. Located on the top left of the Web page are two arrows. Clicking on the arrows allows the reader to access various sections of the Civil Rights Acts.

Glossary

A

abandoned property Property discarded by the true owner who has no intention of reclaiming it.

absolute privilege Applies to judicial and legislative proceedings where defamatory statements are made, but the maker cannot be held liable under conditions protected by law.

acceptance Voluntary act by word or by conduct of the offeree that shows assent or agreement to the terms of the offer.

acceptor Drawee who, by signature, agrees to pay a drawer's instrument.

accession Something added on, as in value added to a piece of personal property by labor or materials.

accord and satisfaction An agreement to settle a disputed debt. The accord is the offer and the satisfaction is normally the payment of the amount.

accounting A remedy in equity whereby the court requires a finding as to the amount of money due and owing.

accredited investor Investor who is not likely to need government protection when making investment decisions; includes institutional investors, seller's directors and officers, individual investors with large annual incomes or net worths, and any corporation or charitable organization with total assets of more than $5 million.

act of state doctrine Doctrine created by the judiciary that provides that the judicial branch of one country will not examine the validity of public acts committed by a recognized foreign government within its own territory.

actual authority Authority held by an agent of a principal; consists of expressed and applied authority.

actual knowledge Knowledge in fact.

actual malice Refers to a statement made with the knowledge that it is false or with reckless disregard of whether or not it is false.

actus reus Criminal conduct.

ad valorem tariff Tax based on a percentage of the value of the imported goods.

administrative agency Agency of the federal government created by the executive or legislative branch for a specific purpose; endowed with legislative, executive, and judicial powers, agency interprets and enforces congressional statutes and rules.

administrative law Body of law that governs the powers, procedures, and practices of administrative agencies.

Administrative Procedure Act of 1946 (APA) Federal statute that acts as a constitution for administrative agencies; provides standardized administrative agency practices and governs how an administrative agency conducts its business.

administrative regulations and rules Rules adopted by administrative agencies to implement and administer statutes. They have the force of law, absent successful challenge in the courts.

adversary system System in which the judge or jury acts as the decision maker between two opposing sides, the plaintiff and defendant, at trial.

adverse possession Means of obtaining title to land without a deed being delivered. To establish title, the adverse possessor must prove nonpermissive use that is actual, open, notorious, exclusive, and adverse for the period prescribed by statute.

affidavit Short written statement of facts given under oath and sometimes used as evidence in court.

affirm Act of appellate court when deciding to uphold a lower court's decision.

affirmative action Based on an executive order issued by the U.S. president requiring the federal government and businesses that contract with the federal government to affirmatively seek out people in protected classes based on race, religion, national origin, or sex, in order for the workforce to reflect the makeup of the community.

affirmative defense A defense raised in answer to an attempt to defeat the allegations in a complaint.

affirmative disclosure order An order from a FTC administrative law judge requiring a seller to place affirmative disclaimers in its advertising disclosing that the product will not benefit all members of the public and specifying which members will not be aided; a remedy for past deceptive advertisements.

Age Discrimination in Employment Act (ADEA) A federal statute that protects older workers from discrimination in matters of hiring, promotions, and layoffs.

age of majority Age when a person is no longer a minor, which is set by state statute.

agency by estoppel Occurs when a principal leads a third person to believe that another person is the principal's agent.

agency law Defines the relationship between an agent, who agrees to represent or act on behalf of a principal, who has the right to control the agent's conduct in matters entrusted to the agent.

agency shop Under federal law, states may pass a statute whereby workers cannot be required to be members of a union, but it might require workers to pay an amount equal to initiation fees and union dues under the theory that these workers enjoy the benefits of the union.

agent Person or business who agrees to represent another person or business.

agreement The act of two or more persons who express a mutual and common purpose.

alien corporation Corporation that originated outside the United States, but does business within the United States.

alternative dispute resolution (ADR) Speedy and just means of resolving a dispute at a reasonable cost to both the parties and to the taxpayers; for example, arbitration, conciliation.

Alternative Disputes Resolutions Act In 1998, Congress adopted this act. Mandates all federal courts, including bankruptcy courts, to send litigants to ADR before proceeding with litigation.

American Arbitration Association (AAA) Private nonprofit organization established in 1926, whose purpose is to foster study of arbitration, to perfect the techniques of arbitration law, and to advance the science of arbitration for the prompt and economic settlement of disputes.

Americans with Disabilities Act (ADA) A federal statute amending the Civil Rights Act prohibiting discrimination against people with disabilities.

analytical school of law Approach to the study of law that uses logical analysis to extract the principles underlying a legal code.

annual percentage rate (APR) True rate of interest being charged on a yearly basis.

answer Document filed by defendant that answers a complaint and admits or denies the allegations stated in the complaint.

Anticybersquatting Consumer Protection Act Law imposes a penalty if a person deliberately registers a domain name that reflected the name of an existing business or uses a domain name that is identical or confusingly similar to a trademark.

antitrust laws Laws that regulate economic competition in order to prevent monopolists from controlling the economy.

apparent authority See *agency by estoppel*.

appellant The party appealing a case to a higher court.

appellate courts Courts of appeal or courts of review; courts whose subject-matter jurisdiction is limited to hearing appeals.

appellate jurisdiction Power of appeals courts to hear appeals only on issues of law, not on issues of fact.

appellee The party defending an appeal of a case to a higher court.

arbitration Procedure in which the parties to a dispute submit their case to an impartial third person (arbitrator).

arbitrator Person selected by the parties to a dispute to make a decision based on evidence submitted by both parties.

arson Intentional, willful, and malicious burning of another's or one's own property.

articles of dissolution Resolution adopted by a corporation's board of directors and majority shareholders

when the decision has been made to cease operation of the corporation.

articles of incorporation Initial incorporation process that provides basic information about the corporation and is the primary source of authority for future operation of the business.

articles of organization These articles are prepared for a limited liability company. They normally have a brief statement of who are the owners and/or managers of the business. This document is normally filed in a public office.

assault Intentional act (not excused or allowed on grounds of self-defense or defense of others) that creates in another person a reasonable, imminent apprehension of fear of harm.

assignee Third party to whom rights of a party to a contract have been transferred.

assignment A transfer of all or part of one's property, interest, or rights.

assignor Original party to a contract who assigns rights to a third party.

Association of Southeast Asian Nations (ASEAN) Organization among some southeast Asian nations that seeks economic and cultural cooperation among its member nations: Indonesia, Malaysia, the Philippines, Singapore, and Thailand.

assumption of risk Doctrine that says a plaintiff is barred from legal recovery if plaintiff entered into a known and appreciated danger that caused the plaintiff injury or damage.

attainment area Geographic area defined by the Clean Air Act where air pollution levels meet or exceed the minimum requirements mandated by the National Ambient Air Quality Standards.

attempt Intent along with some overt action to commit a criminal act that falls short of committing the act itself.

automatic stay In bankruptcy law, an order that stops or suspends all civil litigation against a debtor.

avoidance In bankruptcy law, power invested in a trustee to rescind a debtor's obligations.

award Arbitrator's decision.

B

backward vertical integration When a business goes back up the supply chain and merges with a supplier; for instance, when an automobile manufacturer purchases an automobile parts manufacturing company.

bailee Person who is entrusted with personal property and who holds the property for a limited time.

bailment Usually formed by agreement, it is the delivery of personal property, without transfer of title, by a bailor to a bailee for a particular purpose, such as storage. On completion of the purpose, the bailee must return the bailed property to the bailor.

bailor Person who owns personal property and who entrusts that property to another for a limited time period.

bankruptcy A federal right guaranteed under Article I, Section 8, of the U.S. Constitution allowing the bankrupt to reorganize or discharge debts.

bankruptcy fraud Dishonesty with the bankruptcy court on the part of the person who has declared bankruptcy.

Bankruptcy Reform Acts of 1978, 1994, and 2001 Federal statutes that govern bankruptcy law.

bargain and sale deed Deed that conveys title to real property to a purchaser, but it does not warrant or guarantee title.

battery An intentional act that results in harm to another person as a result of physical contact.

bearer Person who has physical possession of a negotiable instrument.

bearer paper Instrument that is payable to any person holding the paper. May start as order paper that is converted to bearer paper through use of a blank indorsement. Contrast with *order paper.*

beneficiary Person who benefits from the income of property placed in a trust.

Berne Convention for the Protection of Literary and Artistic Works Agreement signed in 1988 that provides citizens of other countries that are signatories with the same copyright protections that it provides its own citizens.

beyond a reasonable doubt A high level of proof that requires a jury to be convinced the defendant committed the crime.

bilateral contract Contract in which one person makes an offer and receives an acceptance from the offeree; most contracts are of this nature.

bill of exchange Draft drawn upon the buyer of the goods; used as one type of method of making payments when dealing internationally.

bill of information Varies from state to state. Normally, the prosecutor submits an affidavit to a judge who then issues the bill of information charging a person with a crime. Used instead of a grand jury indictment.

bill of lading Document used in the transportation industry that indicates who holds title to goods or who has a right to possession of the goods.

Bill of Rights First 10 amendments to the U.S. Constitution adopted in 1791.

bill of sale A sworn document use to transfer ownership of personal property.

binding arbitration Arbitration that is binding once parties have agreed in writing to submit a controversy to arbitration. A legal action cannot be brought if the parties have agreed to submit a controversy to arbitration.

blank indorsement A signature on reverse side of a negotiable instrument which does indicate who will take it next or include any restrictions.

blue sky laws Statutes that regulate the sales of securities within a state.

board of directors Board consisting of directors elected by shareholders to set and oversee a corporation's overall policies and management. The board hires officers to implement policy set by the board and to oversee the daily operations of the corporation.

bona fide occupational qualification (BFOQ) Job requirement that is unique and specific to a job but that could be discriminatory; for example, the requirement that a wet nurse be female is a BFOQ, and this fact would be a possible defense to an employment discrimination charge.

bona fide seniority or merit system A system allowing differences in the terms, conditions, or privileges of employment based on a seniority or merit system, but the differences cannot result from an intent to discriminate. Commonly, a system that is the result of a union contract.

bond Method of financing (as for a business) that is a long-term commitment in which the loan earns interest at a fixed rate, and repayment to the creditor is commonly secured by property.

breach of contract Failure to perform what a party is under an absolute duty to perform based on an express or an implied-in-fact contract.

bribery Crime of offering, giving, receiving, or soliciting something of value for the purpose of influencing an official in the discharge of his or her public or legal duties. In some states, covers private persons, such as business executives.

browser Computer software program that provides a graphical user interface with the World Wide Web.

burglary Act of entering into the building of another with the intent to commit a felony.

business format franchise Franchise for which the franchisor provides the franchisee with the right to use a franchisor's trademark. The franchisee is responsible for the manufacture and sale of the end product.

business judgment rule Law stating that directors and officers will not be held liable for honest errors in business decisions if they made the decisions as reasonable and prudent businesspersons and in good faith.

bylaws Statutes of a corporation setting forth the internal rules of management for the corporation.

C

cartel A combination of producers that join to control the production, sale, and price of goods or services and potentially to obtain a monopoly or near monopoly over a particular industry or product.

cartelization A banding together of competing firms.

case law See *common law.*

cashier's check Draft in which the bank is both the drawer and drawee.

causation Action that causes something to be produced or to happen. One of the elements necessary to prove negligence.

cease-and-desist order This order is an administrative remedy that directs a person to refrain from engaging in further violative conduct. Several major federal agencies have the authority to issue these orders. If they are violated the business can be fined damages and eventually be held in contempt of court.

Celler-Kefauver Act Section 7 of the Clayton Act, established in 1950; controls corporate mergers.

Center for Medicare & Medicaid Services (CMS) Administers Medicare for the federal government.

certificate of deposit (CD) Acknowledgment by a bank of the receipt of money; carries an agreement to repay the money with interest.

certified check Check that is recognized and accepted by a bank office as a valid appropriation of the specified amount drawn against the funds held by the bank.

challenge for cause During *voir dire*, an attorney's request to dismiss a prospective juror because of apparent bias.

chancellor In early England, the principal minister who handled petitions for redress. In American law, this is the name given in some states to the judge of a court of chancery.

changing-market-conditions defense In an antitrust price discrimination case, this defense is used by a business to show that a business is selling a product at a lower price because it was discontinuing a product or product line or was offering the items at fire or bankruptcy sale prices.

chattel real Chattel that concerns real property, such as a lease.

check Paper drawn on a bank, ordering it to pay a sum of money on demand.

checks and balances Scheme of the government that balances the power of one branch with the other two branches, so no one branch can usurp power.

Children's Online Privacy Act (COPA) Prohibits Internet operators from collecting information about children while they are on the Internet.

choice-of-forum clause A clause used in international contracts that designates the forum, or location, in which the case will be heard in the event of any dispute.

choice-of-law clause Clause in an international business contract that designates the forum in which adjudication will take place and the substantive law that will be applied in the event of any dispute.

civil law The legal rights and duties that exist among persons or between citizens and their government. Not criminal law.

civil law system Based on the continental European legal system, which deals strictly with statutory provisions and does not take into consideration decisions by courts.

class-action lawsuit Suit brought by a limited number of individuals on behalf of a much larger group.

Clayton Act Federal statute enacted in 1941 to strengthen federal antitrust laws; aimed at restraining specific monopolistic practices.

Clean Air Act A federal statute that mandates antipollution controls by air polluters, such as utilities; provides assistance to states for the implementation of antipollution measures.

Clean Water Act A federal statute that established the goals of (1) making water safe for swimming, (2) protecting fish and wildlife, and (3) controlling or eliminating the discharge of pollutants into the water.

clear and convincing evidence The level of proof that requires a plaintiff to present evidence that goes beyond a well-founded doubt. This level of proof falls between that of a preponderance of the evidence and the level of proof needed in a criminal case, which is evidence beyond a reasonable doubt.

close corporation Corporation with a small number of shareholders, often family members. Its stock is not traded publicly.

closed shop Firm that recognizes union membership by its workers as a condition for employment.

code A statute or ordinance.

codified law A series of statutes or ordinances.

Colgate doctrine Rule that resulted from United States v. Colgate decision in which the U.S. Supreme Court allowed Colgate to refuse unilaterally to deal with retailers who did not follow suggested retail prices; that is, Colgate can deal with whomever it desires.

collateral contract Express written contract made by a third person who guarantees to pay a debt or perform a duty to one party (the creditor) of an original contract if the original debtor is unable to do so.

collateral installment note Negotiable instrument that is payable in installments, during which time the owner of the negotiable instrument has a lien against the maker's personal property.

collateral note Written promise to pay secured by the payee-creditor in which the maker-debtor creates a lien against his or her personal property.

collect on delivery (C.O.D.) Delivery method in which the delivery company collects from the buyer the money owed for goods when it delivers them.

comity Deference that one nation gives to the laws and judicial decrees of another nation, based on respect.

commerce clause Clause in the U.S. Constitution that gives Congress the power "to regulate commerce with foreign nations, and among the several states, and with the individual tribes."

common law Body of judge-made law comprised of principles and the rules of how these principles relate to the government and to the security of persons and property.

common stock Method of financing a business in which stock is held by a shareholder and carries voting rights and the right to a share of the profits of the business if a dividend is declared; has indefinite duration unless redeemed by the corporation.

community property Property of married couples in which each spouse owns an undivided half interest in any property acquired during the marriage.

compact See *treaty.*

comparative negligence Doctrine that enables computation of both the plaintiff's and the defendant's negligent acts when determining recovery amounts.

compensatory damages Award to the injured party as a result of a lawsuit to make up for the monetary loss suffered because the other party breached the contract.

complaint Type of pleading issued by the plaintiff to the defendant that states the purpose of the lawsuit.

Comprehensive Environmental Response, Compensation, and Liability Act (CERCLA) A federal statute requiring polluting hazardous waste to be cleaned up by the polluter; if the polluter cannot be found, monies appropriated to the act are used. Commonly known as Superfund.

computer crime Crime committed by use of a computer; for example, electronic thefts of money through issuing an extra paycheck, shaving funds, or depositing funds in personal accounts.

Computer Software Rental Amendments Act A federal statute that allows a computer program's copyright holder to control the rental, leasing, or lending of the computer program after the first sale.

conciliation Third party successfully gets conflicting parties to accept an agreement, but does not participate in the negotiations.

concurrent jurisdiction Power to hear a case held by both federal and state courts.

concurrent powers Power of either Congress or state legislatures to make laws on the same subject matter.

confiscation Taking property without proper public purpose or just compensation being awarded.

confusion Mixing one person's personal property that is fungible with another's fungible goods, such as grains. Once mixed, no way exists to reseparate the goods.

conglomerate merger Consolidation of two or more firms dealing in unrelated products and operating in markets not horizontally or vertically linked.

consent decree Agreement signed by an administrative law judge after the government and business have reached a voluntary agreement. This type of decree can be enforced in court.

consequential damages Foreseeable damages that result when a party breaches a contract.

consideration Something of legal value given in exchange for a promise; essential element of a contract.

consignment Situation in which an owner of goods turns the goods over to a person who sells this type of goods and who agrees to sell them in the ordinary course of business.

Consolidated Omnibus Budget Reconciliation Act (COBRA) A federal statute providing that when an employee leaves an employer, the employee may buy group health coverage for themselves and their families for a limited time period, usually no longer than eighteen months.

conspiracy Occurs when two or more persons plan, along with some overt action, to commit a criminal act.

constitutional law Public law that involves questions of whether the government has the power to act.

constructive knowledge Knowledge that is imputed, such as what the agent knows, the principal knows; or, for example, what is publicly recorded is presumed to be known by all persons.

constructive notice All documents that are recorded in a public office, such as a county recorder's office. A public recording provides every person the ability to find the recorded document.

This public recording means that every person either has actual notice or has imputed knowledge of the information actually recorded. If the information is imputed to a person, it is said that he or she has constructive notice of the publicly recorded document.

Consumer Credit Cost Disclosure Act See *Truth-in-Lending Act*.

Consumer Credit Protection Act (CCPA) Federal statute that is the primary source of federal law covering credit transactions; enforced by several federal agencies.

consumer credit transaction Transaction that occurs when a consumer enters into a contract to purchase an item and at the same time receives credit from the seller or a financial institution to purchase the item specified in the contract.

Consumer Leasing Act A federal statute act requiring full disclosure of all financial terms in consumer leasing contracts.

Consumer Product Safety Act A federal statute that created the Consumer Product Safety Commission, which is designed to protect consumers from unreasonable risk of injury from hazardous consumer products.

Consumer Reporting Reform Act A federal statute requiring all credit bureaus to provide toll-free numbers and to make an employee, not a recording, available when a consumer calls a credit bureau. Amended the Consumer Reporting Act.

contract Promise or set of promises for the breach of which the law gives a remedy, and the performance of which the law in some way recognizes as a duty.

contract for future goods Contract for the sale of goods that do not yet exist.

contractual agreement to arbitrate Arbitration established by contractual agreement entered into either before or after a dispute occurs.

contributory negligence Negligence on the part of both parties; each party contributes to the negligence.

convention Law adopted by an international organization that was created by a treaty.

Convention on Contracts for the International Sale of Goods (CISG) International agreement on rules providing guidance for international contracts.

Convention on the Law of the Non-Navigational Uses of International Watercourses Convention providing for the exchange of information among countries if water-related hazards occur; includes an article requiring nations to take all measures to prevent harmful conditions, such as toxic chemical spills.

Convention on the Limitation Period in the International Sale of Goods Convention that established unified rules for determining the statute of limitations in a lawsuit.

conversion Taking personal property from its rightful owner or possessor and placing it in the service of another; civil law side of stealing.

copyright Right granted by statute to the author or originator of certain literary or artistic productions.

corporation A legal entity created by the state or federal government and owned by shareholders.

corrective advertising order An order from a FTC administrative law judge requiring a seller to alert consumers to false statements in past advertising.

cost and freight (C.&F.) Delivery term that indicates that the purchase price of goods includes freight charges of those goods during transportation.

cost, insurance, and freight (C.I.F.) Delivery term that indicates that the purchase price of goods includes insurance and freight charges of those goods during transportation.

cost–benefit standard Standard created by statute and applied by courts; involves considering the cost of an action and comparing it with the benefit that may result from the action.

cost-justification defense In an antitrust price discrimination case, this defense is used by a business to show that the cost was lower per unit to manufacture or transport; therefore, the sale of the unit at lower cost is justified.

counterclaim Claim in which the defendant sets forth allegations against the claims made by the plaintiff in a lawsuit.

Counterfeit Access Device and Computer Fraud and Abuse Act Act that makes it a federal crime to knowingly access a computer to obtain restricted federal government information, to obtain financial records from financial institutions, or to obtain con-

sumer reports from consumer reporting agencies. It also made it a crime to counterfeit or use unauthorized access devices to obtain items of value or to traffic in such devices.

counteroffer Rejection of original offer and the simultaneous making of a new offer.

countervailing duty Import tax equal to the grant extended to an exporter by its home country to encourage exportation or to assist the exporters in meeting competition.

course of dealing Principle encouraged by the Uniform Commercial Code that defers to previous conduct between parties of a contract to establish a basis for understanding and interpreting their expressions in a current contract.

court of equity Court that grants a legal means to enforce personal rights or to correct a wrong.

Court of International Trade (CIT) Court that has the power of a federal district court involving trade matters, such as dumping and countervailing duty.

court of law Court that grants a monetary damage award.

court's opinion Decision by the court.

courts of appeal Courts of review.

covenant not to compete This clause can be included in one of two types of agreements, either the purchase of a business or an employment contract. The seller of the business or the employee agrees not to compete against the other party to the contract. These clauses are valid if they are reasonable both as to time and area.

covenant not to sue Contract between two parties in which one party waives the right to sue the other party, usually in return for a settlement.

cover Ability to obtain goods similar to those required by the contract, after it has been breached, from other available sources.

creditor beneficiary Person who purchases the right to receive proceeds owed under a contract. Has the right to institute legal action to enforce rights under the original contract.

criminal law Body of law that deals with violations of wrongs committed against society as a whole.

cross-claim Claim brought by a defendant against a codefendant.

cumulative preferred stock Stock in a corporation that carries the right to accumulate unpaid dividends and has preference at dissolution of the corporation.

Currency Transaction Report (CTR) Report required by federal law that must be submitted by financial institutions (1) if they suspect criminal activity by a customer who is involved in a financial transaction of $1,000 or more or (2) when a single transaction of a series of related transactions of currency amounts to more than $10,000.

customs brokers Licensed people who conduct customs business on behalf of others.

D

damages for pain and suffering Damages awarded to compensate the plaintiff who has endured pain and suffering as a result of the defendant's actions.

debenture Form of bond that is unsecured.

debt securities Bonds of debentures that represent a loan to the corporation.

deceit See *fraud*.

decree Decision that determines a party's equitable rights in a case before a court.

deed Writing signed by an owner of property by which title to the property is transferred to another.

defamation Act of making any untrue statement or statements that harm the reputation of another person or corporation.

defamation by computer Production by a computer of erroneous information about a person's credit standing or business reputation that may impair the person's ability to obtain further credit.

default judgment Court order awarding one party everything it requested because opposing party failed to respond in time.

defendant Person being sued and accused of causing harm by a plaintiff.

deficiency judgment Award that represents the deficient amount (difference between the mortgage debt and the amount received from the proceeds of the foreclosure sale).

delegation Transfer of a contract's duties to another person.

demand draft See *sight draft*.

demurrer Defendant's motion to dis-

miss the complaint, stating that, even if the facts are true, their legal consequences are such that there is no reason to go further with the lawsuit and no need for the defendant to present an answer.

deontology Philosophical practice of defining and adhering to an absolute set of standards by which ethical behavior can be measured.

deposition Sworn oral testimony by opposing party or by witness(es) taken by interrogatories, not in open court.

derivative authority Authority accorded the agent by the principal to carry out the principal's business.

Digital Millennium Copyright Act (DMCA) A federal statute that limits the liability of online service providers for copyright infringement and covers other issues, such as distance education, libraries, and webcasting of sound recordings.

director (of a corporation) Person elected by shareholders to oversee the corporation's overall policies and management. The board of directors hires officers to implement the policy and to oversee the daily operations of the corporation.

disaffirm Person who has a legal right to rescind a contract and therefore does not have a duty to perform.

discharge To perform a contract fully.

disclosed principal Principal whose identity is known by the third party at the time the contract is made by the agent.

discovery Process of obtaining information from opposing party or from witnesses in a lawsuit.

disgorgement This order is issued by the SEC to require a wrongdoer to return any profits that have been made in violation of the security laws.

dishonest employee rule A theft using checks by an employee who endorses legitimate checks made out to the employer and cashes the check or deposits these checks into a banking account not controlled by the employer.

disparagement of goods False statement made about a person's product.

disparate impact Employment discrimination practice that appears neutral on the surface but that actually affects a protected class adversely.

disparate treatment Employment discrimination practice in which treat-

ment of a certain class differs from the treatment of other employees or applicants.

dissociation The end of a relationship with a partnership.

dissolution Through court action, an order terminating a business entity so that it no longer exists.

dissolve The act of a corporation liquidating itself in preparation for going out of business.

distributorship franchise Type of franchise where a manufacturing concern (franchisor) licenses a dealer (franchisee) to sell its products; for example, an automobile dealership.

diversity of citizenship cases Cases involving: (1) citizens of different states, (2) a foreign country as plaintiff and citizens of a state or different states, or (3) citizens of a state and citizens or subjects of a foreign country where the amount in controversy is greater than $50,000 and does not involve a federal question.

divestiture Through court action, an order taking away from a defendant something of value, such as illegally gained profits or property used in the commission of a crime.

doctrine of exhaustion of remedies A business or person must use all procedures for appeal of an administrative agency before filing an action in court.

doctrine of laches Rule that states that individuals who fail to look out for their rights until after a reasonable time has passed will not be helped.

doctrine of *respondeat superior* Rule that makes the principal liable for the agent's torts if the torts are committed within the scope of the agency or the scope of employment.

doctrine of selective incorporation Under the Fourteenth Amendment, the U.S. Supreme Court has applied many, but not all, clauses of the first ten amendments to the states.

document of title Paper representing ownership of goods.

domestic corporation Corporation doing business in the state in which it was incorporated.

donee beneficiary Person who receives the proceeds of a contract as a gift even though not a party to the contract. Often has the right to institute legal action to enforce rights under the original contract.

double jeopardy Protection provided in the Fifth Amendment that says a person cannot be tried by the same level of government more than once for the same crime.

draft Unconditional written order; debt owed by the drawee to the drawer.

drawee Debtor of the drawer.

drawer One who creates or executes the order-to-pay instrument.

due diligence defense Under the Securities Act of 1933, a defense available to a defendant who signed a false statement about a security, but did so after a good faith attempt to verify the truth of the statement

due process clause Part of the Fifth and Fourteenth Amendments.

dumping Practice of selling goods in the buyer's country below the price costs to manufacture in, and transport from, the seller's country.

duress Compulsion by threat; forcing someone to do something out of fear.

E

easement Right of a person to make limited use of another person's property without taking anything from the property.

easement by prescription A right to a nonpossessory interest in real property by establishing the right contrary to, and without the permission of, the owner.

economic regulation One aspect of the powers of administrative agencies authorizing an agency to regulate and monitor a type of business, such as the banking industry.

economic school of law Approach to the study of law that holds that most laws may be evaluated in accordance with economic theory; developed by Richard A. Posner in the 1970s.

economic strike Strike in which employees seek economic benefits, such as higher wages and benefits; management may permanently replace the striking employees, although these employees have priority when management rehires after the strike.

Electronic Communications Privacy Act (ECPA) A federal crime to intercept an electronic communication at the point of or during transmission, when transmitted through a router or server, or after receipt by the intended recipient; includes any electronic transfer of signals.

Electronic Data Gathering, Analysis, and Retrieval (EDGAR) System that performs automated collection, validation, indexing, acceptance, and forwarding of submissions by companies that are required by law to file forms with the SEC.

Electronic Freedom of Information Act A federal statute that makes it possible for the public to have free electronic access to government documents on the Internet without having to make a formal request under the Freedom of Information Act.

electronic funds transfer (EFT) Automatic payment or direct deposit using teller machines, point-of-sale systems, and automated clearinghouses.

Electronic Payment Association (NACHA) A not-for-profit trade association, which develops operating rules and business practices for electronic payments and deposits.

Electronic Signatures in Global and National Commerce Act Law to eliminate legal barriers to using electronic technology to engage in contracting. Provides that contracts cannot be denied legal effect solely because they are in electronic form.

embezzlement Fraudulent conversion of another's property or money by a person in lawful possession of that property.

Emergency Planning and Community Right-to-Know Act (EPCRA) A federal statute requiring the release of information to affected communities about the presence of hazardous chemicals and their release into the environment.

eminent domain Power of government to condemn land in order to take it for public use.

Employee Polygraph Protection Act A federal statute making polygraph use unlawful except under restricted conditions, including (1) national defense; (2) ongoing investigations; (3) drug security, drug theft, or drug diversion investigations; and (4) armored car and security personnel.

Employee Retirement Income Security Act (ERISA) Federal statute that established a supplement to social security to be set up by employers for their employees.

employment at will This form of employment exists when there is no contractual arrangement for the employee to work for a given time period such as one year. The employer may terminate the employee with or without cause.

employment law State and federal statutes that define the relationship between an employer and its employees.

enabling act Congressional legislation that creates an administrative agency, determines its structure, and defines its powers.

Endangered Species Act (ESA) A federal statute designed to conserve endangered species and protect their ecosystems.

entitlement program Government program that administers benefits to those who qualify for them. Economic regulation to control the public welfare.

enumerated (delegated) powers Provisions in the U.S. Constitution that delegate certain powers to the three branches of the federal government.

environmental impact statement (EIS) Any federal agency that will build or fund the building of a project must conduct an EIS under the National Environmental Policy Act. The EIS must contain information on the (1) environmental impact of project, (2) any adverse effects that might result, and (3) the irreversible effects that the action might create.

Environmental Protection Agency (EPA) Federal agency created in 1970 that assembles various organizations responsible for environmental protection.

Equal Access to Justice Act A federal statute that allows an individual or small business to recover legal fees, expert witness fees, and other expenses involving an action by the U.S. government, if the government action was not substantially justified.

Equal Credit Opportunity Act Federal statute that forbids discrimination based on race, sex, religion, national origin, marital status, age, or person's income from public assistance in determinations of creditworthiness.

Equal Employment Opportunity Commission (EEOC) Five-member commission created in 1964 to administer Title VII; members are appointed by the president of the United States with consent of the Senate; issues interpretive guidelines and regulations but does not have force of law; investigates, holds hearings, keeps statistics.

Equal Pay Act Amendment to the

Fair Labor Standards Act of 1938, administered by the EEOC; prohibits discrimination based on sex in wages paid for equal work on jobs which performance requires equal skills, effort, and responsibility and that are performed under similar conditions (job content rather than job description).

equal protection clause Legal right in the Fourteenth Amendment that holds that government must treat similarly situated individuals in a similar manner.

equitable remedy Remedy granted by court; an appropriate remedy, based on fairness, justice, and honesty is awarded to the harmed party in order to correct the situation.

equity securities Shares of stock representing an ownership interest in a corporation.

estoppel To bar, to impede, to stop.

ethics Principles used to differentiate right from wrong and govern a person's conduct.

exclusive dealing agreement Legal vertical restraint of trade in which the manufacturer or distributor may require the retailer not to sell products of competing firms, provided there is no boycott but each decision is made on an individual basis.

exclusive jurisdiction Power to hear a case held by only a federal court (as in federal crimes, bankruptcy, patents, copyrights, and suits against the United States) or by only a state court (as in divorce, probate, and adoption cases).

exclusive power Power exclusively delegated to the federal or state government.

exculpatory clause Contract clause that limits liability for negligent acts.

executed contract Contract that is fully performed.

executive agency See *line agency.*

executive agreement Agreement made by the president of the United States without need for the consent of the Senate; used in making agreements with foreign countries.

executive branch Branch of the U.S. government that includes the president and is charged with enforcing the law; the powers of the president, as established in Article II of the Constitution.

executive order Issued by an executive, such as the president, and broad in nature. May be issued to give guidance on policy, to coordinate activities

among agencies, or to create an administrative agency.

executory contract Contract that has not been performed.

exempt property Debtor's property protected by state or federal statute from seizure by a creditor of a debtor or trustee in bankruptcy; such property cannot be sold. Contrast with *nonexempt property.*

exempt security Security issued by governments, nonprofit organizations, and certain businesses that is exempt from registration under the Securities Act of 1933.

exempt transaction Transaction that is exempt from the registration requirements of the Securities Act of 1933. See *small offering exemption, private offering exemption,* and *intrastate offering exemption.*

Exon-Florio provision Allows the U.S. president to prevent the purchase by a foreign business of any U.S. firms, such as airline companies or defense companies, if such purchase would threaten national security.

Export Administration Act A federal statute that governs the export of goods and restricts the export of goods and technology in the military field when release of these would be detrimental to the United States.

Export-Import Bank (Eximbank) Created by Congress, a bank that provides financial assistance, primarily in the form of credit guarantees, to exporting and importing firms.

Export Trading Company Act A federal statute designed to increase U.S. exports of goods and services; allows competing producers to apply for an exemption from antitrust laws for business conducted overseas if the U.S. government grants the export trade certificate of review.

exporting Selling of goods manufactured in, and sent from, the domestic country to a foreign country.

express authority Authority that provides an agent with specific instructions on behalf of the principal.

express contract Contract in which the terms are stated exactly whether written or spoken.

express warranty Explicit statements made by the seller to the buyer regarding the condition or quality of the goods purchased.

expropriation Government seizure of a privately owned business or goods for

a proper public purpose and with just compensation.

extortion The obtaining of property from another, with his or her consent, but the consent is induced by wrongful use of actual or threatened force, violence, fear, or under color of official right.

extradition Process to deliver an accused or convicted person to the country in which the crime allegedly occurred.

F

fact finding Investigative process by which a third party will investigate the issues and make findings of fact to present to the court or other body charged with ruling on the issues.

factor A factor is one who provides short-term financing, from 30 to 180 days, to businesses exporting to developed countries. The exporter sells the export receivable to the factor who in turn is paid by the importer or its import factor. The factor works in developed countries in order to use the banking, legal, and accounting systems when necessary. The difference between a factor and using a letter of credit is that a factor provides nonbank financing while a letter of credit is issued by a bank.

failing-company defense Defense used by a business to justify a merger with a company confronting with complete failure and no known prospective purchasers. In such a case, the courts may allow a merger that could create a monopoly.

Fair Credit Billing Act Amendment to Truth-in-Lending Act (TILA) that requires creditors to correct errors promptly and without damage to a person's credit rating.

Fair Credit Reporting Act Title VI of the Consumer Credit Protection Act, which requires that consumers be informed of the nature and scope of a credit investigation, the kind of information that is being compiled, and the names of persons who will be receiving the report.

Fair Debt Collection Practices Act Part of the Consumer Credit Protection Act; adopted in 1977, it prohibits certain practices in the collection of consumer debt by debt collection agencies.

Fair Labor Standards Act (FLSA) Federal statute that established minimum wage, overtime standards, record-keeping, and child labor prohibitions; provides for administrative procedures for the enforcement of and compliance with these standards as they apply to employees engaged in commerce, production of goods to be placed in commerce, or employees of an enterprise engaged in commerce.

Fair Packaging and Labeling Act (FPLA) A federal statute that requires certain disclosures by any firm that packages or labels consumer products.

False Claims Act A federal statute authorizing government to sue any party filing a fraudulent payment claim for products or services.

false imprisonment Intentional confinement or restraint of another person without justification.

False Statement Act A federal statute that makes criminal making a false statement to the U.S. government to obtain a monetary return. The making of a false statement is a crime.

Family and Medical Leave Act A federal statute providing that employees can take up to twelve weeks of unpaid leave for the birth or adoption of a child, for the care of an immediate family member, or for a serious health condition.

Federal Anti-Injunction Act A federal statute restricting the federal courts' power to issue injunctions against unions engaged in peaceful strikes. Also known as the Norris-LaGuardia Act.

Federal Arbitration Act Federal statute favoring arbitration that withdraws from the states the power to require a judicial forum for the resolution of disagreements if the parties by contract have agreed to solve the problem by arbitration.

Federal Environmental Pesticide Control Act A federal statute that amends the Federal Insecticide, Fungicide, and Rodenticide Act.

Federal Insecticide, Fungicide, and Rodenticide Act A federal statute that requires licensing of those handling and applying insecticides, fungicides, and rodenticides; requires EPA to inspect manufacturing sites; EPA controls supply of pesticides to keep hazardous chemicals off the market. Pesticides must be (1) registered before they can be sold; (2) certified, labeled, and used only for approved applications; and (3) used in amounts that meet

established limits when they are applied to crops that provide food for animals or people.

Federal Insurance Contributions Act Federal statute that provides funding for the social security program.

federal question case Case with a legal question that involves the federal Constitution, treaty, or statute. Federal courts have jurisdiction over federal question cases.

Federal Trade Commission Act of 1914 Federal statute that created the Federal Trade Commission.

Federal Trademark Dilution Act Amends the Lanham Act. Sets out guidelines for determining which marks are truly distinctive.

Federal Unemployment Tax Act (FUTA) Federal statute that established a state system of providing unemployment compensation to eligible individuals.

federalism System of government organization in which state governments and the federal government share powers.

fee simple absolute Estate in property in which the owner has the greatest aggregation of rights, privileges, and power possible; is indefinite in duration.

fee simple defeasible Type of estate of real property for which the title can be taken away automatically from the current owner under certain conditions created by the original seller.

fee simple subject to a condition subsequent Type of estate of real property for which the title can be taken away from the current owner if a specified event occurs as set out by the original seller.

felony Crime punishable by imprisonment in a federal or state penitentiary for more than one year, by fine, or by death.

feminist school of law School that believes that the feminine viewpoint is not represented in the law.

fictitious name filing Filing with a public office and prepared by the owner of a business to alert the public to the fact that he or she is doing business under a fictitious name.

fictitious payee rule A theft using checks by an employee who writes checks drawn on the employer's bank that are payable to a fictitious payee.

fiduciary duty Duty of an agent to

act on behalf of the principal with the utmost good faith.

finance charge Total amount of interest paid on a loan.

financing statement Document required by the UCC and signed by a debtor that describes the goods used as collateral in a security agreement and must be filed in a public office in order to be effective against all persons.

firm offer Under the UCC, Section 2-205, a firm offer is created when a merchant makes a written, signed offer to buy or sell goods and indicates in the offer that the offer is irrevocable. The purchaser does not need to pay the merchant to hold the offer open if the time period is less than three months.

fixture Object affixed to realty by roots, embedded in it, or permanently attached by cement, nails, bolts, plaster, or screws.

flat-rate tariff Tax based on a unit, such as a barrel, or on weight.

Food, Drug, and Cosmetic Act A federal statute that created the Food and Drug Administration and also prohibits adulteration or misbranding of food, drugs, and cosmetics.

foreclosure A judicial document filed by a mortgagee-creditor against a mortgagor-debtor that exercises the mortgagee's lien right under the mortgage to have the real property sold for nonpayment of a note for real property. With a deed of trust, a foreclosure can be a nonjudicial action by a trustee.

foreign corporation Corporation doing business in a state other than the one in which it was incorporated.

Foreign Corrupt Practices Act of 1977 (FCPA) Federal statute that prohibits bribes given to foreign government officials by representatives of American companies and their directors, officers, shareholders, employees, or agents for the purpose of obtaining or retaining business for the American company.

foreseeability Test for proximate cause that asks whether the defendant's unreasonable conduct could have been foreseen to cause the plaintiff's injury or damage.

forfaiter A forfaiter is one who provides medium- to long-term financing from 180 days to ten years to businesses exporting or working in developing countries. A forfaiter will purchase an export receivable from the exporter.

The export receivable is guaranteed by the country's bank or the country itself where the work or item was delivered.

forgery Crime of obtaining goods by false pretenses.

formal contract Written contract between parties.

formal rule making Rule making that requires an agency to conduct a hearing before it can adopt a rule. Contrast with *informal rule making*.

forward-looking statement A statement issued by a business that projects earnings and losses.

forward vertical integration When a business goes forward in the supply chain and merges with a purchaser; for instance, when an automobile manufacturer purchases a car rental company.

franchise Arrangement in which the owner of a trademark, a trade name, or copyright licenses another person under specified conditions or limitations to use the trademark, trade name, or copyright in marketing goods or services.

franchisee The holder of a franchise.

franchisor A franchisor licenses a franchisee to use the franchisor's trademark, trade name, or copyright in the marketing of specific goods and services.

fraud Involving (1) a misrepresentation of material facts, (2) the intent to deceive or the reckless disregard of the facts' truthfulness, (3) the knowledge that the facts are false, (4) the victim's justifiable reliance on these facts, and (5) damages.

free on board, destination (F.O.B. destination) Transportation term denoting that risk and title of goods transfer to the buyer on notification that goods have arrived at the destination.

free on board, point of shipment (F.O.B.) Transportation term denoting that risk and title of goods transfer to the buyer on delivery of the goods to the transportation company.

Freedom of Information Act of 1966 (FOIA) Amendment to the Administrative Procedure Act that makes all nonexempt information held by federal agencies available to the public.

freehold estate Estate in real property of uncertain duration.

freight forwarders Licensed businesses that arrange the transportation of goods.

full faith and credit clause Clause in the U.S. Constitution that mandates the enforcement of a state's valid judgment, decree, or order in other states.

full warranty A promise that ensures some type of buyer satisfaction in case a product is defective; provides for free repair or replacement of any defective part.

fungible goods Identical goods by nature or usage of trade, such as grains.

G

garnishment Statutory procedure in which a person's property in possession of another is applied to payment of that person's debts.

General Agreement on Tariffs and Trade (GATT) The GATT was created in 1948 as only an agreement. Since then it has grown to be both an agreement and an organization. Several rounds of GATT have been negotiated over the decades in order to continually update the tariff and trade rules. The GATT organization was replaced by the World Trade Organization (WTO) in 1995.

General Agreement on Trade in Services (GATS) Agreement adopted by the World Trade Organization to govern trade in the services industry, such as securities, banking, and insurance services.

general jurisdiction Power to hear almost any subject matter in a lawsuit; authority of the court of original jurisdiction.

general license General authority to ship and export goods; not a license in the usual sense.

general partner In a business, a partner who has unlimited liability.

general policy statement Statement that sets out in broad terms the particular philosophy, mission, and objectives of a government agency.

general warranty deed Deed that provides the buyer protection against defects in the title to land.

gift Voluntary transfer of ownership of property.

goods All things that are movable and tangible.

government agency Administrative agency created by Congress to administer a quasi-business venture generating its own revenue; for example, U.S. Postal Service.

Gramm-Leach-Bliley Act (GLBA) Federal act providing consumers with privacy rights in the financial area. Businesses must inform customers that it may share nonpublic information with others and the consumers can choose whether to participate.

gratuitous agency Occurs when an agent performs services without compensation.

gray-market goods Foreign-manufactured goods for which a valid U.S. trademark has been registered; also known as a *parallel import*.

group boycott Per se violation of the Sherman Act in which a group refuses to deal with some third party or parties.

H

hardware Computer equipment itself.

Hart-Scott-Rodino Antitrust Improvements Act A federal statute requiring businesses that intend to merge to provide the Federal Trade Commission and the Department of Justice with a premerger notification.

Hazardous and Solid Waste Amendments (HSWA) A federal statute requiring the phasing out of land disposal of hazardous waste; provides for stringent hazardous waste management standards and a comprehensive underground storage tank program.

Health Insurance Portability and Accountability Act (HIPAA) A federal statute mandating that when a person moves from one employer with group health insurance to another employer with group health insurance, the new group health insurance company must accept that person and charge the same premium and may not exclude or charge a higher premium for a preexisting medical condition.

hearsay evidence Out-of-court information given by someone other than a witness to prove the truth of a contested fact. Not allowed at trial.

Herfindahl-Hirschman Index Statistical formula used by the Department of Justice to determine nonmarket considerations of a proposed merger, such as the ease of entry into the business and the resulting competitive strength of the merged firms.

historical school of law Approach to the study of law based on the origin and history of the legal system; looks to the past to discover what the principles of contemporary law should be.

holder Person who possesses negotiable instruments drawn, issued, or indorsed to his or her order or to the bearer or in blank.

holder in due course (HDC) Special-status transferee of a negotiable instrument.

homestead exemption Exemption of certain types of real and personal property from levy of execution or attachment in the event of mortgage default and deficiency judgment.

horizontal market division Per se violation of the Sherman Act that involves dividing a market for the sale of a specific product among competitors.

horizontal merger Merger of comparable companies.

horizontal price fixing Occurs when two or more potential competitors on the same level set a fixed price for their goods or services.

I

identified goods Existing goods that have been identified to a particular contract.

Identity Theft and Assumption Deterrence Act Law making it a federal crime to steal a person's identity.

illusory promise A statement that appears to be a promise but in reality does not create any contractual obligation.

Immigration Act A federal statute that overhauled previous immigration acts, changing the emphasis from immigration based on family ties with U.S. citizens or nationals to immigration based on the potential ability of the immigrant to contribute to the economy.

Immigration Reform and Control Act A federal statute providing for civil and criminal sanctions for employers if they fail to verify their workers' employment eligibility and knowingly hire any individual unauthorized to work. Also, employers cannot discriminate against workers based on their national origin or lack of citizenship.

implied authority Authority that is ordinary in that type of business.

implied-in-fact contract Contract formed in whole or in part from the conduct of the parties.

implied-in-law contract This contract exists when one person is unjustly enriched at the expense of another. No actual contract actually exists, but the law implies a promise to pay by the person who has been enriched.

implied warranty of authority When a person acts for another, he or she guarantees that he or she has the right to so act.

implied warranty of fitness for a particular purpose Warranty that arises when any seller knows the particular purpose for which a buyer will use the goods and knows the buyer is relying on the seller's skill and judgment to select suitable goods.

implied warranty of merchantability Warranty that goods are reasonably fit for the purpose for which they are sold, are properly packaged and labeled, and are of proper quality; arises in the sale of goods by a merchant who deals in goods of that kind.

importing Buying of goods manufactured in a foreign country that are brought into the domestic country.

impostor rule A theft using a check by a person posing as the person entitled to the check.

inadequate-resources defense Defense used by a company to justify a merger with a business that has inadequate financial resources to compete. In such a case, the courts may allow a merger that could create a monopoly.

incidental beneficiary Person who receives a benefit from a contract in an indirect way, even though the person is not a party to the contract and has no right to enforce the contract.

incorporator Person who starts a corporation.

independent agency Administrative agency that is not under the control of the president or Congress but is free-standing; has a commission created by Congress and is headed by a commissioner.

independent contractor Person who contracts with another to do something for him or her but who is not controlled by the other or subject to the other's right to control with respect to his or her physical conduct in the performance of the undertaking.

indictment Formal charge of wrongdoing issued by a grand jury prior to trial.

indorsee Person who receives a signed negotiable instrument from an indorser.

indorsement Signature of the person known as the indorser written on the back of the instrument itself.

indorser Anyone, other than the maker or acceptor, who signs a negotiable instrument.

infliction of mental distress Intentional act that involves extreme and outrageous conduct and that results in severe emotional distress to another.

informal contract Written or oral contract.

informal rule making Rule making that consists of notice and comment; most commonly used by administrative agencies to promulgate rules.

injunction Equitable remedy in which an order is issued to a person or a business to refrain from doing wrongful act(s).

Information Infrastructure Protection Act Law making it a federal crime to intentionally transmit a computer virus or to trespass into an Internet-connected computer.

insider trading Under Section 16, the act by any director, officer, or shareholder holding 10 percent or more of any one class of stock who buys and sells or sells and buys within six months. Under Section 10(b), the act by any director, officer, majority shareholder, or anyone having access to or receiving information of a nonpublic nature from an insider who uses the nonpublic information to trade.

Insider Trading and Securities Fraud Enforcement Act A federal statute that amended the Insider Trading Sanctions Act by enlarging the types of people subject to civil liability and provided the SEC with the power to reward informants, required securities firms to prevent insider trading, and increased criminal penalties.

Insider Trading Sanctions Act (ITSA) A federal statute that gave the SEC additional powers to institute legal action against any person who trades on nonpublic information through a national securities exchange or a registered broker-dealer.

in personam **(personal) jurisdiction** Jurisdiction over the person.

in rem jurisdiction Jurisdiction over property.

installment note Negotiable instrument that is payable in installments.

intangible property Property that possesses an invisible value, such as an annuity, checks, or bonds, and is reported by a piece of paper with rights recognized by law.

intended beneficiary Person who intended to benefit from the contract as either a creditor beneficiary or a donee beneficiary.

intentional interference with a contractual or business relationship Tort in which the plaintiff must prove the defendant intentionally induced the breach of a valid contractual or business relationship.

intentional tort Intentional acts that cause injuries either against the person or against property.

InterAmerican Convention on International Commercial Arbitration (Panama Convention) Convention that created the agreement among the United States, Mexico, and Latin American countries to submit disputes surrounding commercial transactions to arbitration.

intermediate scrutiny test Discrimination test for which two requirements must be met: (1) an important governmental objective and (2) a substantial relationship between the means and the end.

international agent A specialized type of agent that can help a business find buyers in another country.

International Antitrust Enforcement Assistance Act (IAEAA) A federal statute providing antitrust guidance to businesses engaged in international operations, concerning the enforcement policies of the Department of Justice and the Federal Trade Commission.

International Court of Justice (ICJ) Principal judicial organ of the United Nations.

international custom General practice among nations that is accepted as law.

international law Law considered legally binding among otherwise independent nations.

International Organization of Securities Commission Organization created by the International Securities Enforcement Cooperation Act to cooperate with other countries in regulating the securities markets and transactions.

International Securities Enforcement Cooperation Act Act that allows the SEC to cooperate with other countries to regulate security markets and transactions.

International Trade Administration (ITA) Promotes world trade and strengthens the international trade and investment position of the United States; part of the Department of Commerce.

International Trade Commission (ITC) Independent agency that imposes tariff adjustments and import quotas for goods.

interpretive rule Statement by an administrative agency as to how it interprets the statute it is charged with administering; published in the Federal Register.

interrogatories Written questions sent to the opposing party that must be answered under oath.

Interstate Land Sales Full Disclosure Act A federal statute designed to decrease the opportunities for fraud and deception when consumers purchase property they have not seen. Developers are required to (1) make full disclose their financial position; (2) register with the Office of Interstate Land Sales Registration within the Department of Housing and Urban Development before commencing sales; and (3) provide purchasers with a copy of a property report before a contract is signed.

intrastate offering exemption Offerings made within the boundaries of one state by a seller who resides in that state. Federal regulations do not apply to these types of offerings.

invasion of privacy An intentional act that invades a person's intangible right to be left alone.

issue To sign and deliver a negotiable instrument for the first time.

issuer Party, such as a corporation or limited partnership, that issues securities.

J

joint tenancy with right of survivorship Situation in which two or more persons own an undivided interest in either personal or real property, and, on the death of one of the joint tenants, his or her interest transfers to the remaining joint tenant, not to his or her heirs.

judgment Verdict that has been signed by a judge and that states who won the case and the conditions of the award.

judgment rate Interest rate set by statute and used when the parties to a negotiable instrument or other contracts have failed to specify an interest rate.

judicial arbitration Compulsory, court-mandated arbitration.

judicial branch Branch of the U.S. government that consists of the federal judicial system and its powers as established by Article III of the U.S. Constitution.

judicial deference Term meaning that a court does not reverse an agency action unless the court finds that agency in violation of a condition set out by the Administrative Procedure Act.

judicial review Process for deciding whether a law is in conflict with the mandates of the Constitution.

judicial sale Sale conducted by a sheriff, as directed by a court order, to sell off property seized from a nonpaying debtor.

jurisdiction Power of a court to hear a particular dispute, civil or criminal, and to make a binding decision.

jurisprudence Science or philosophy of law.

K

know-how license License granted to a foreign licensee by a U.S. business to use a trade secret or the know-how to use certain technology.

L

Labor Management Relations Act Also known as the Taft-Hartley Act; amendment to the Wagner Act that provides protection for employers as well as employees in labor-related issues.

Labor Management Reporting and Disclosure Act Also known as the Landrum-Griffith Act; statute that established an employee bill of rights and reporting requirements for union activities; regulates internal union business.

landlord Owner of a piece of property that is rented to a tenant.

Lanham Act A federal statute prohibiting false descriptions about products or services in advertisements; forbids deceptive advertising that is likely to mislead.

larceny Wrongful or fraudulent taking and carrying away by any person of the personal property of another.

law System that gives order to society; a system of moral conduct by which society achieves justice; a body of rules.

law merchant Rules resulting from the resolution of disputes and from transactions of merchants and other commercial traders; consists primarily of general customs of the trades that remain law unless displaced by specific statutes.

lease Transfer of real or personal property by landlord or lessor to the tenant or lessee for a period of time in exchange for a consideration (usually payment of rent); on termination, the property reverts to the lessor.

legal benefit Occurs when a person obtains something that he had no prior legal right to obtain.

legal capacity An element of a contract. It denotes the competence (or legal ability) of a party to a contract, which includes the issues of age, mental capacity, or intoxication. Generally considered to be the fourth requirement for a valid contract.

legal detriment Occurs when a person does, or promises to do, something that he had no prior legal duty to perform or when the person gives up the legal right.

legal entity Individuals and various forms of business that can sue and be sued in a court, pay taxes, and hold title to property.

legal ethics Moral and professional duties that lawyers owe other lawyers, their clients, the courts, and the public.

legal fiction A construction by the law to reach a just result.

legal remedy Remedy awarded by the court; the harmed party could be awarded land, money, items of value, or a combination of all three.

legality An element of a contract. The subject matter and performance by the parties must be legal. An agreement is illegal if either its formation or its performance is criminal, tortious, or otherwise opposed to public policy. Generally considered to be the fifth requirement for a valid contract.

legislative branch Branch of the U.S. government that consists of Congress and its powers as established by Article I of the U.S. Constitution.

letter of credit Contract used in international business that assures the seller of payment while assuring the buyer that payment will not be made until all terms and conditions of the instrument are complied with.

letter ruling Document stating the official position of a federal administrative agency with respect to a particular issue.

libel Act of false and malicious statements in writing to others about another person or business.

lien Another name for a secured transaction to ensure repayment of the loan by taking an interest against the property that is securing the loan. Repayment in full discharges the lien.

life estate Type of ownership of real property for the life of an individual.

limited jurisdiction Jurisdiction limited to certain subject matters.

limited liability company (LLC) This is a new form of organization that allows the owners to have limited liability like a corporation, but treats the organization as a partnership (which does not pay taxes) for tax purposes. The owners may lose their investment in the business if it fails, but otherwise are not liable for other debts of the business.

limited liability partnership This form of organization is of recent origin. It allows partners to have limited liability from the debts of the business. All of the rules of a general partnership apply to this business organization except for limited liability. In a regular general partnership all of the partners are liable for the debts of the business.

limited partner In a limited partnership, a partner who has limited liability up to the amount of his or her contribution to capital.

limited partnership A business that is created by statute where there must be at least one general partner and one limited partner.

limited warranty A promise that is limited in its scope of coverage. Less than a full warranty.

line agency Administrative agency under the direct control of the president of the United States; for example, the Department of Labor.

liquidated damages Amount stipulated in a contract to serve as the measure of damages in case of a breach.

liquidated debt A debt that is not disputed between the contracting parties.

liquidation The selling of assets so they can be converted into cash.

long-arm statute A state statute that allows a court to obtain jurisdiction over a defendant who lives outside that state.

lost property Property that is not voluntarily left and forgotten.

M

Maastricht Agreement Officially, the Treaty on European Unity, signed in Maastricht, the Netherlands. Amends the Treaty of Rome by replacing the EEC with the European Union and by providing the basis for a political, monetary, and economic union. Created a single market

Magnuson-Moss Federal Trade Improvement Act A federal statute that broadened the scope of the Wheeler-Lea Act; eliminated holder-in-due course rights when consumer goods are financed; provided FTC with more enforcement powers.

Magnuson-Moss Warranty Act Federal statute designed to prevent deception in warranties by making them easier to understand; enforced by the Federal Trade Commission.

mailbox rule Under common law, an acceptance is effective when dispatched when it uses the same means of communication as the offer.

maker Person who signs and issues a promissory note agreeing to pay a certain sum of money.

manager The person(s) who manage(s) a limited liability company, as determined by the operating agreement for the company.

manufacturing or processing plant franchise Type of franchise in which the franchisor transfers to the franchisee essential ingredients or the formula to make a particular product.

Marine Protection, Research, and Sanctuaries Act A federal statute that established a system of permits that regulates the discharge and introduction of materials into coastal waters and continuous marine areas.

market power The business becomes so dominate in the marketplace that it no long competes but instead can force its decisions on other competitors.

Market Reform Act A federal statute that addresses the stability of U.S. securities markets when extraordinarily volatile situations occur.

maskwork A series of related images, fixed or encoded, in a three-dimensional pattern on a silicon chip. The pattern is layered in a series, so that each image has a pattern. Similar to a film negative that is black on clear plastic. As it is processed into a picture, various layers of plastic with images are placed on top of one another. Eventually the final product, a colored photograph, is produced. May be copyrighted.

McCarran-Ferguson Act A federal statute exempting all activities that involve insurance businesses from the antitrust laws.

med/arb Hybrid system that first uses mediation and then arbitration to reach a resolution.

mediation Process of promoting voluntary compromise or resolution of a dispute usually initiated before arbitration.

Medicare Health insurance program administered by the Social Security Administration to people sixty-five years of age and older and for those under sixty-five years of age who are disabled.

meeting the competition defense In an antitrust price discrimination case, this defense is used by a business to justify its selling of a product at a lower price to some customers to meet a competitor's price.

member As used in this textbook, the owner(s) of a limited liability company.

mens rea Criminal intent.

merchant Under the UCC, a person who regularly deals in a particular type of goods.

merchant protection legislation A state statute that allows a merchant to detain a suspected shoplifter, provided that reasonable cause for suspicion exists and that the detention is executed in a reasonable way.

merger Combination of two or more firms into one firm.

merit registration State security registration that is reviewed for its merits rather than just for its disclosures.

military orders As commander-in-chief, the president, or those authorized in the military, can issue orders.

minitrial A form of alternative dispute resolution in which the parties present their arguments or part of a case to a judge or advisory jury that renders a decision in order to encourage settlement.

minor Person under the statutory age limit, which is normally 18 years of age.

mirror-image rule A common law rule that requires an offeree's acceptance to match the offeror's offer exactly.

misapplication of trust funds A special form of embezzlement in which funds entrusted to a person or business are not used for their original intention.

misdemeanor Crime punishable by a fine or by confinement for up to a year; for example, trespass or disorderly conduct.

mislaid property Property that has been placed somewhere by the owner voluntarily and then inadvertently forgotten.

misrepresentation A factually incorrect statement or conduct made during contract negotiations on which the other party relies.

Model Business Corporation Act (MBCA) A model statute that has had its major provisions adopted by most states.

Money Laundering Control Act A federal statute that requires the tracking of large sums of currency to prevent the free flow of currency gained from criminal acts.

monopoly Situation in which a business has exclusive control or nearly total control of the market share of a particular business or even of a whole industry.

Montreal Protocol on Substances that Deplete the Ozone Layer Protocol aimed at reducing and eventually eliminating the emissions of man-made ozone-depleting substances.

mortgage Special type of lien against real property to secure repayment of a debt.

mortgage note Type of collateral note used to buy a house.

mortgagee Creditor or lender; the beneficiary of the mortgage.

mortgagor Debtor or borrower who creates a mortgage on real estate.

motion Application made to a judge by a party to a lawsuit seeking relief for a wrong committed or asserting a procedural right.

motion to dismiss See *demurrer*.

multiple product order An order from an FTC administrative law judge requiring a seller's future advertisements for specific products to be accurate. Order covers more products than the product involved in a past false advertisement.

mutual assent Meeting of the minds of the offeror and the offeree; offer must be made by one person and accepted by another for the same item or service.

mutual (bilateral) mistake Mistake made by both of the contracting parties as to either the identity or existence of the subject matter of the contract.

N

National Ambient Air Quality Standards (NAAQS) Standards set by the Environmental Protection Agency that regulate uniform nationwide ambient air quality standards.

National Environmental Policy Act (NEPA) Federal statute established in 1970 that created the Council of Environmental Quality and mandated that an environmental impact statement be prepared for every recommendation or report on legislation or major federal action significantly affecting the quality of the environment.

National Export Strategy Expanded and streamlined program to promote U.S. exports by the federal government.

National Labor Relations Act Also known as the Wagner Act; federal statute enacted in 1935 that established rights of employees to engage in collective bargaining and to strike.

National Labor Relations Board (NLRB) Agency created by the Wagner Act to oversee union elections and to prevent employers from engaging in unfair and illegal union-labor activities and practices.

national law Body of law that pertains to a particular nation.

National Securities Markets Improvement Act A federal statute that ended dual regulation (by the state and federal governments) of investment advisers by providing the SEC authority over any adviser who manages $25 million or more of assets.

national treatment Required under World Trade Organization (WTO) rules, a nondiscrimination principle that calls for an importing country to treat goods from other WTO member countries as if they were domestic goods.

natural law school Approach to the study of law that holds ethics to be the source of legal authority; ethical values are used to make legal decisions.

negative option rule Federal Trade Commission rule that requires book, video, and other similar clubs to provide members enough time to respond if they choose to decline a monthly selection.

negligence Conduct that falls below the duty of care and that results in another's personal injury or property damage.

negotiable To make an instrument negotiable, it must be in writing and signed, be an unconditional promise or order to pay a fixed amount of money, payable to bearer or order, and payable on demand or at a definite time.

negotiable instrument A specialized written document signed by the debtor acknowledging a debt to be paid on demand or at a specified time in the future. The document is an unconditional promise or order to pay a fixed sum of money.

negotiation Process in which two or more people meet to discuss their differences and attempt to arrive at a settlement that is acceptable to both.

Noerr-Pennington Doctrine Derives from two U.S. Supreme Court cases that allows businesses to work together to lobby Congress to pass appropriate favorable laws.

Noise Control Act A federal statute establishing the goal of creating an environment free from noise that injures public health and welfare.

nolo contendere Plea by the defendant that does not admit guilt but that allows the court to impose the same penalty as for a guilty plea.

nonattainment area Geographic area defined by the Clean Air Act where air pollution levels persistently exceed national ambient air quality standards.

nonexempt property Debtor's property that is not protected by state or federal statute from seizure and sale by a creditor or trustee in bankruptcy with proceeds from sale used to pay off the outstanding debts. Contrast with *exempt property*.

nonfreehold estate Chattel real; estate consisting of possession of land without possessing a freehold estate in it.

normal trade relations Required under the World Trade Organization (WTO) rules, a nondiscrimination principle that calls for equal treatment of goods exported and imported among countries that are members of WTO. Formerly called most-favored-nation principle.

Norris-LaGuardia Act Federal statute established in 1932 that permits employees to organize and restricts federal courts from issuing injunctions against unions engaged in peaceful strikes.

novation Written agreement entered into by all the parties in which one party is substituted for another party; that is, one party is completely dismissed, and another party is substituted.

Nuclear Waste Policy Act (NWPA) A federal statute requiring the building of a permanent repository for the disposal of spent nuclear fuel and high-level wastes.

nuisance Improper activity that interferes with another's enjoyment or use of his or her property.

O

objective standard of care All persons must act as a reasonable and prudent person would act under the same facts or circumstances. One of the elements necessary to prove negligence.

obtaining goods or money by false pretenses Crime of obtaining title to another's property using an intentionally false statement of a past or existing fact with the intent to defraud another.

Occupational Safety and Health Act Federal statute that requires health and safety protections for employees at their place of employment.

Occupational Safety and Health Administration (OSHA) Organization that promulgates and enforces workers' safety and health standards, conducts inspections and investigations, keeps records, and performs research.

offer In contract law, conduct or statement by a person with the objective intent to be bound that proposes definite terms and is communicated to the other party, permitting that person receiving the offer to accept or reject it.

offeree Person receiving the offer.

offeror Person making the offer.

officer (of a corporation) Person hired by a corporation's board of directors to implement policy set by the board and to oversee the daily operations of the corporation.

Oil Pollution Act A federal statute that increased the strict liability limit eightfold for spills containing polluting elements. Liability fines cover cleanup costs, natural resource damages, losses to subsistence resources, and costs to local government.

Old Age, Survivors, and Disability Insurance (OASDI) Another name for Social Security, which provides retirement and disability payments and acts as a life insurance annuity by providing funds to minor children whose parent(s) is(are) deceased.

Older Workers Benefit Protection Act (OWBPA) A federal statute prohibiting employers from discrimination in benefits packages for older workers.

Omnibus Trade and Competitive-

ness Act (OTCA) A federal statute having four purposes: (1) to authorize the negotiation of reciprocal trade agreements; (2) to strengthen U.S. trade laws; (3) to improve the development and management of U.S. trade strategy; and (4) through these actions, to improve living standards in the world.

operating agreement Agreement in a limited liability company that determines who will have the responsibility of management, control, and division of profits.

operation of law Broad concept used by a court or statute to impose rights or liabilities on a party without any action taken by the party.

opt-in provision Clause in contract that the customer must take affirmative action and request to have information made available to a data bank.

option contract Contract separate from the main contract that removes the offeror's right to revoke an offer for the time period specified in the option; money for time.

opt-out provision Cause in contract that the customer must take affirmative action to have name excluded from data banks. No action means that the customer allows name to be included in the data bank to be shared (usually sold) to others.

order Decision of the administrative law judge; final disposition of a case between the government and a party in a lawsuit.

order paper Instrument that is payable to a specific person. May start as bearer paper that is converted to order paper by designating the next holder. Contrast with *bearer paper*.

ordinance Law enacted by a city or county legislative body.

original jurisdiction Jurisdiction held by the original court, the trial court.

overt act An act committed in anticipation of committing a criminal act.

P

parallel import See *gray-market imports*.

Paris Convention for the Protection of Industrial Property Convention that attempts to achieve uniformity in the patent area by having countries adopt a universal system of granting and recognizing patents.

parol evidence rule Rule that allows

courts to prevent being placed into evidence any oral statements made prior to or at the time of a written contract's signing; also known as the *best evidence rule.*

partially disclosed principal Principal whose identity is not known by the third party but the third party knows that the agent is acting for a principal at the time the contract is made.

partially protected speech Speech that cannot be regulated by the government, but can be restricted as to time and place, but must be fully truthful.

partnering This term is used in large construction contracts to assist in building a framework to handle any disputes that may arise among the contractors. Normally a neutral facilitator arranges a procedure to handle these disputes in an expeditious manner. The purpose is to take care of small disputes when they arise in order to prevent larger disputes.

partnership A business that is run for profit in which two or more people have an undivided, and sometimes unequal, ownership interest.

partnership by estoppel When a person allows his name to be used in a partnership and does not deny it when others imply that he is a partner. The person becomes liable as if he really were a partner.

pass-through tax treatment The passing of profits and losses through a partnership, limited liability company, or S corporation to the individual owners for federal taxation purposes.

patent Grant from the government that conveys and secures to an inventor the exclusive right to make, use, and sell an invention for a period of seventeen years.

patent license License granted to a foreign licensee by a U.S. business that allows access to and use of a patent.

payee Bearer of an instrument.

payment order Under the UCC, Article 4A, order for an electronic transfer of funds that deletes money from the originator's account and places it in the payee's account.

per se **rule** Illegality that requires for proof only the fact that an agreement existed; for example, horizontal price fixing.

peremptory challenge During *voir dire*, an attorney's request that a prospective juror be dismissed for an unstated reason.

perfection A series of steps a secured party must take to protect its rights in the collateral against all persons.

Personal Data Protection Directive European Union directive that requires contracts to have an opt-in provisions in contracts between consumers and businesses.

personal defense A defense against paying a negotiable instrument to an ordinary holder; it is not a defense against a holder in due course.

personal jurisdiction See *in personam jurisdiction.*

personal property All property that is basically movable and is not real property.

petition Written request made to a court.

petty offense Civil offense not classified as a crime, which is punishable by a fine, imprisonment, or both; for example, a traffic violation.

pierce the corporate veil Action taken by a court to ignore the corporate structure and look to the shareholders' personal assets to satisfy corporate obligations.

plaintiff Person filing a lawsuit to seek relief from harm.

Plant Closing Act See *Worker Adjustment and Retraining Notification Act.*

plead To present a case before a court.

pleading Document written by one of the parties to a lawsuit and sent to the other parties and to the court to be included in the judge's case file; provides information to the other parties.

police power Authority possessed by states to regulate private activities in order to protect or promote the health, safety, morals, or general welfare of their citizens.

Pollution Prevention Act (PPA) A federal statute that focuses on the reduction of the amount of pollution through cost-effective changes in production, operation, and use of raw materials.

power of attorney Notarized written document that grants a person the authority to perform acts on another person's behalf, such as signing papers, opening accounts, or making purchases.

precedent Decision made in a previous, similar case that is used to decide the outcome of a current case.

preemption doctrine Doctrine that allows Congress to act exclusively in areas that affect primarily national, as opposed to local, matters. If Congress chooses to preempt a particular area, the states no longer have any authority to enact legislation in that area.

preferential lien As defined by federal statute, a lien voluntarily made by a debtor, prior to a bankruptcy, to enable a favored creditor to receive payments prior to payments owed to other creditors.

preferential payment As defined by federal statute, payments made within a specific time period by a debtor to favored creditors, but not to all creditors, prior to the filing of a bankruptcy.

preferred stock Equity security in a corporation that carries certain preferences, such as dividends at a fixed rate; may or may not carry voting rights and is entitled to preference over common stock in payment of assets in the event the corporation is liquidated.

Pregnancy Discrimination Act A federal statute that redefined gender discrimination to include discrimination based on pregnancy, childbirth, or related medical conditions.

preponderance of the evidence To prevail in a lawsuit, the level or proof that requires a plaintiff to present evidence that is just slightly more persuasive than the defendant's evidence.

pretrial hearing Hearing that serves to identify and narrow the subject matter that is in dispute and to plan the course of the trial.

price discrimination Occurs when the same goods or services are sold to competing purchasers at different prices.

prima facie **case** Evidence presented by the plaintiff that will prove the case unless contradicted and overcome by other evidence presented by the defendant.

principal Person or business who hires an agent to represent them.

Privacy Act 1974 amendment to the Administrative Procedures Act that protects individuals who are citizens or legal aliens from uncontrolled transfer of certain personal information to federal agencies for nonroutine uses.

private judge A judge, usually retired, who is hired by parties to resolve a dispute because of his or her subject matter expertise in the area of the dispute. Also called a *referee.*

private law Subdivision of substantive law; addresses direct dealings between persons.

private nuisance Tort that interferes with the property interest of a limited number of individuals.

private offering exemption Securities offered to only a few people and exempt from registration with the SEC.

Private Securities Litigation Reform Act A federal statute that curtails lawsuits against businesses based on securities law violations.

privileges and immunities clause Clause that prevents one state from discriminating against the citizens of another state based solely on their residency.

privilege of immunity Person cannot be held liable for defamatory statements when made under conditions that are protected by law.

privileged information Information obtained through a confidential communication in a protected relationship, such as an attorney–client, husband–wife (in some states), or priest–penitent relationship. Not allowed at trial.

privity of contract Requirement that an injured party suing for product liability must have been a party to the original contract.

probable cause Reasonable ground for supposing that an individual has committed a crime.

probate Legal process of settling a person's estate by collecting property owned by the deceased, paying his debts, and transferring ownership of the deceased's property to his heirs.

procedural due process Guarantee granted to individuals that requires any government decision to take a person's life, liberty, or property to be made fairly.

procedural law Established methods or processes of enforcing the rights created by substantive law.

procedural rule Type of administrative agency rule that governs the internal practices of an agency.

process Document that is an order coming from the court, signed by the judge or representative; three stages of process exist: issued, served, filed.

product liability Potential responsibility that a manufacturer or seller has for injuries or damages caused by defective goods.

production Means of acquiring ownership of personal property by creating that property.

professional agent One who handles contracts in a particular field; for example, real estate broker.

professional association Organized group of professionals with common interests; subject to antitrust laws.

professionally developed ability test Tests that can be given by employers to potential employees to measure specific abilities related to job performance. An ability test, its administration, and the actions based on the results must not be intended to discriminate illegally.

promisee Person receiving the promise.

promisor Person making the promise.

promissory estoppel Doctrine that prevents the promisor from revoking the offer.

promissory note Written promise to pay made between two parties; payable at a definite time or on demand.

promoter Person who takes the preliminary steps to organize a corporation.

prospectus Document the supplies information to prospective buyers of a security.

protected speech Speech that cannot be restricted or regulated in any manner by the government, thus allowing a full exchange of ideas to take place.

Protection of Semiconductor Chip Products Act A federal statute that allows the maskwork of a semiconductor chip to be copyrighted.

protocol Official agreement between different countries' diplomats that does not have the force of a treaty.

proximate cause Reasonable, causal relationship between a defendant's unreasonable conduct and the plaintiff's injury or damage. Limits the defendant's liability as a result of the misconduct. One of the elements necessary to prove negligence.

proxy Written authorization empowering another person to act for the signer at, for instance, a shareholders' meeting.

public law Subdivision of substantive law; addresses the relationship between individuals and their government.

public nuisance Crime that disturbs or interferes with the public.

public welfare Government protection and entitlement programs that benefit the public at large.

punitive (exemplary) damages Damages awarded to punish a party for intentional and willful conduct that he or she knew at the time would harm someone.

purchase Acquiring property or services by the payment of money or services.

purchase money security loan Security interest created as part of a purchase agreement.

Q

qualified indorsement Instrument of indorsement used by the indorser to disclaim or limit liability on the instrument.

qualified privilege The law gives a limited right of protection to a person who makes defamatory statements, as long as they are made under conditions protected by law.

quasi in rem jurisdiction Jurisdiction over the interests of particular persons in particular property.

quasi-contract Implied-in-law contract in which the parties did not make any promise by word or conduct but the law imposed a promise on the party who benefited.

quasi-executive function Administrative agency power to ensure compliance with the rules and to conduct investigations.

quasi-judicial function Administrative agency power to prosecute cases, render judgments, and impose penalties if violations occur.

quasi-legislative function Administrative agency power to promulgate rules that have the effect of law.

quasi-official agency Created by Congress, but the agency does not have the same authority as line, independent, or government agencies.

quiet title action Action filed in court whereby the court determines who has title to real property.

quitclaim deed Deed conveying to the buyer whatever interest the grantor had in the property, if any.

quota Limit, as on the number of goods that can be imported to a country.

R

Racketeer Influenced and Corrupt Organizations Act of 1970 (RICO) Amendment to the Organized Crime Control Act of 1970; designed to control the investment by organized crime into legitimate businesses and to force forfeiture of any profits made as a result of such criminal activity.

ratification Occurs when a principal approves a contract, by word or by action, that has been negotiated by a purported agent. Ratification binds the principal to the agent's acts and treats the acts or contracts as if the principal had authorized them.

rational basis test Discrimination test that does not involve a protected class. Two requirements must be met: (1) a legitimate governmental interest and (2) a rational relationship between the governmental interest and the means used to accomplish that interest.

reaffirm As defined by federal statute, an agreement by a debtor with a creditor to repay debts that could have been forgiven by bankruptcy court.

real defense A complete defense against paying a negotiable instrument to any owner.

Real Estate Settlement Procedures Act (RESPA) Federal statute that governs the purchase of a house and the borrowing of money to pay for it.

real property Land and the objects permanently attached to it.

receiving stolen goods Crime in which the recipient of the stolen goods knows or should have known that the goods were stolen.

recording statute State statute that allows certain documents, such as deeds and liens, to be recorded in a specified public office so prospective buyers or lenders are provided with a way to check a property's history and to determine any outstanding claims against the property's title.

red herring prospectus Preliminary prospectus; so named because the legend printed across it is in red ink and states that the SEC registration has been filed but is not yet effective.

reformation of the contract Rewriting of the contract because of errors in the written document.

registration statement Document filed with the SEC by a business that desires to issue a security; provides information about the business, such as the names of directors and officers and financial and economic infor- mation.

regular trustee Court-appointed trustee who is elected or appointed to represent the creditors in a specific

bankruptcy case. Contrast *U.S. trustee.*

Regulation A An SEC rule that provides a simplified registration statement for issues of $1.5 million or less in one year.

Regulation D An SEC rule that has three provisions that exempt different situations from registration.

Regulation C, Rule 415 An SEC rule, known as shelf registration, that allows an issuer to register stock without needing to sell it. The stock is placed on a shelf to be sold at a later time.

Regulatory Flexibility Act 1980 amendment to the Administrative Procedures Act that requires an agency to publish in the Federal Register twice each year a special regulatory flexibility agenda.

rejection In contract law, act of refusing to accept an offer.

relevant geographic market Part of the structural analysis used by the courts to determine whether a monopoly exists; considers the area where the product is sold, transportation costs, and how far consumers must travel to purchase the product.

relevant product market Part of the structural analysis used by the courts to determine whether a monopoly exists; considers the characteristics of the product, its substitutes.

remand Act of sending a case back to a lower court to carry out the appellate court's decision.

remedy Relief provided for an innocent party when the other party has breached a contract. A remedy enforces a right.

remedy at law Legal remedy awarded by the court; the harmed party could be awarded land, money, or items of value, or a combination of all three.

reorganization Also known as Chapter 11 in a business bankruptcy filing; situation in which the creditors and debtors formulate a plan under which the debtor pays a portion of the debts and is discharged of the remainder, and the debtor is allowed to continue in business.

reply Pleading filed by a plaintiff in response to a defendant's counterclaim.

repossession Situation in which the secured party takes possession of the collateral covered by the security agreement in the event of default.

request for physical or mental examination Court order requiring a

party to a lawsuit to submit to an examination by a doctor.

request to produce Court order requiring a party to a lawsuit to make available physical evidence it has in its possession.

res ipsa loquitur Latin for "the thing speaks for itself." Doctrine that says the event causing the damage must not occur in the absence of negligence, the conduct of the plaintiff or any other third party could have caused the event, and the defendant owes the plaintiff a duty of reasonable care.

res judicata Rule that states once a case has been fully litigated, neither party can institute another action based on the same facts or circumstances.

resale price maintenance agreement Vertical restraint of trade agreement in which the buyer and the seller agree to the price at which the buyer will resell the product.

rescission Remedy that cancels the agreement and returns the parties to the contract to the status quo; may be by mutual consent, by conduct, or by decree of a court of equity.

Resource Conservation and Recovery Act (RCRA) A federal statute governing Environmental Protection Agency studies and recommendations on solid waste disposal; provides a creation-to-disposal tracking system for hazardous waste.

response See *answer.*

Restatement, Second Body of law created by the judiciary and revised in 1979; covers the areas of law regarding contracts, property, trusts, and torts.

restitution Equitable remedy in which a person is restored to his or her original position prior to loss or injury, or is placed in the same position as if a breach had not occurred.

restraint of trade Agreement among competitors that has a wrongful intent to increase prices on products or services by minimizing competition.

restricted securities Securities acquired in unregistered, private sales from an issuer.

restrictive indorsement Indorsement on an instrument that requires the indorser to comply with certain instructions regarding the funds involved.

retention Under the merit system, judges who were originally appointed must stand for election to retain their judicial office.

reverse Act of appellate court when deciding to disagree with a lower court's decision.

Revised Model Business Corporation Act (RMBCA) A model statute that revised the then-existing law by simplifying its procedures.

Revised Uniform Arbitration Act (RUAA) In 2000, the National Conference of Commissioners on Uniform State laws promulgated the act. Under consideration by state governments.

Revised Uniform Limited Partnership Act (RULPA) A uniform statute that has been adopted by several states that revised the then-existing limited partnership rules.

Revised Uniform Partnership Act (RUPA) A uniform statute that has been adopted by many states that revised the then-existing partnership laws. Under this act, a partnership is treated as an entity rather than as a collection of individuals

revocation Withdrawing of the offer by the offeror.

Right to Financial Privacy Act Passed in 1978, act restricts power of federal government to obtain a person's financial records. Customer the right to know who has accessed the financial records. Amended by the USA Patriot Act in 2001.

right-to-work laws Statutes making it illegal for union membership to be required for employment.

Rivers and Harbors Act A federal statute regulating the discharge into or depositing of refuse in navigable waterways.

robbery Wrongful or fraudulent taking and carrying away by any person of the personal property of another, involving the use of fear or force.

Robinson-Patman Act Section 2 of the Clayton Act; promotes economic equality in the purchasing and selling of goods; prohibits price discrimination.

Rule 10b-5 Rule issued by the SEC implementing Section 10(b) of the Securities Exchange Act of 1934 that makes it unlawful for any person, directly or indirectly, to defraud or mislead anyone in the purchase or sale of a security.

Rule 144 An SEC rule that allows an owner of a securities to sell them if they have been held for more than one year and adequate public information is available.

Rule 144A An SEC rule that allows a safe harbor for the owner when reselling securities to qualified institutional buyers or registered broker-dealers.

Rule 415 An SEC rule, known as shelf registration, that allows an issuer to register stock without needing to sell it. The stock is placed on a shelf to be sold at a later time.

Rule 504 An SEC rule stating that a noninvestment company can sell up to $1 million in securities that it issues in any one year without registration if the company does not advertise or make any general solicitations.

Rule 505 An SEC rule stating that a private, noninvestment company may sell up to $5 million in securities in any one year to any number of accredited investors and no more than 35 unaccredited investors if the company does not advertise or make any general solicitations.

Rule 506 An SEC rule stating that a private, noninvestment company may offer an unlimited number of securities if they generally do not solicit or advertise them.

rule of reason Doctrine by which the court reviews all the circumstances of a case to decide whether the defendant's practice was an unreasonable restraint on trade.

S

S corporation A corporation that is treated as a partnership for federal tax purposes.

Safe Drinking Water Act A federal statute authorizing the Environmental Protection Agency to establish standards for safe drinking water purity.

safe harbor exemption An SEC rule that exempts parties from having to register certain securities.

Safe Harbor Privacy Principles U.S. Department of Commerce issued this document setting out principles for businesses to adopt. EU agreed to allow U.S. companies to conduct business within the EU if they have adopted these principles.

sale on approval Contract clause that states that no sale occurs until the ultimate consumer is satisfied.

sale or return Contract clause that states that the business purchaser can return the goods if not sold. Buyer has risk of loss and title unless the goods are returned.

Sarbanes-Oxley Act Amends the securities law by increasing regulation of stock markets, reforming the deterrence of business fraud, and increasing corporate accountability. Created the Public Company Accounting Oversight Board to oversee the activities of the auditing profession.

scam bankruptcy A plan to swindle creditors by purchasing goods in advance, while at the same time planning a bankruptcy proceeding.

school of legal realism School that stresses the pragmatic and empirical sides of law; looking at how well the law meets the needs of society.

scienter Guilty knowledge that is greater than simple negligence.

scope of employment Within the time and space of a work assignment.

Section 10(b) Section of the Securities Exchange Act of 1934 that makes it unlawful to use or employ, in connection with the purchase or sale of a security, any deceptive device.

Section 16 Section of the Securities Exchange Act of 1934 that requires directors, officers, and owners of more than 10 percent of the shares of any one class of stock of a company registered with the SEC to file reports of their holdings and transactions with the SEC; such persons are known as "insiders."

Section 18 Section of the Securities Exchange Act of 1934 that requires publicly held corporations registered with the SEC to file periodic and intermittent reports that include audited financial statements, current financial status, and securities holdings.

secured transaction Type of transaction secured by collateral.

Securities Act of 1933 First securities regulation statute enacted by Congress; often referred to as the "truth in securities" law because it requires full and truthful disclosure by companies issuing securities.

Securities and Exchange Commission (SEC) Federal body that regulates securities, financial markets, business practices, and specific industries, such as stockbrokers.

Securities Enforcement Remedies and Penny Stock Reform Act A federal statute that strengthens the enforcement powers of the SEC and regulates the penny stock market.

Securities Exchange Act of 1934 A federal statute that (1) ensures the integrity of stock and securities sold through national stock exchanges and over-the-counter markets; (2) informs the investing public of the financial condition of a business; (3) protects the public from fraudulent activity; and (4) created the Securities and Exchange Commission.

Securities Investor Protection Corporation (SIPC) A corporation created by Congress that manages a fund that protects investors from the financial harm caused when stockbrokerage houses fail.

security An investment of money or other consideration in a common enterprise, with the investor expecting a profit and with the profit derived primarily through the efforts of a promoter or a third party other than the investor.

self-defense Doctrine that gives a person the right to defend his or her person.

self-incrimination Protection provided in the Fifth and Fourteenth Amendments that says a person cannot be forced to testify against himself or herself.

server Computer software program that allows mainframe and personal computers to host World Wide Web sites.

service mark Mark used to distinguish the services of one person from those of another; the title, character names, or other distinctive features of radio and television programs may be registered as service marks.

shelf registration See *Rule 415*.

Sherman Act A federal statute that attempts to end monopolies and restraints of trade.

Shore Protection Act A federal statute controlling the disposal of solid wastes in oceans and lakes.

short trial One day trial conducted with a minimum of four jurors.

sight (demand) draft Instrument payable on sight when the holder presents it for payment.

slander Act of verbally making false and malicious statements to others about another person or business.

slander of title Defaming the title a person has to his or her property and possibly preventing the sale of the property.

small offering exemption Offerings from an issuer that are not large enough

for the federal government to regulate; includes certain types of bank loans, privately negotiated sales of securities to large institutional investors, and business-venture promotions by a few closely related persons.

Social Security Act Federal statute that established a federal insurance program covering the financial impact of retirement, death, disability, hospitalization, and unemployment of a worker through contributions by a worker and his or her employer.

software Programming involved with a computer system.

sole proprietorship A business owned by one person.

Solid Waste Disposal Act A federal statute designed to reduce solid waste disposal by encouraging the recycling of waste and the reuse of materials by society.

sovereign immunity Doctrine that states a person cannot sue the government without its permission.

special indorsement Indorsement on an instrument that indicates a specific person to whom the indorser intends to make the instrument payable.

special warranty deed Deed in which the seller warrants that he or she has not previously done anything to lessen the value of the real estate for sale.

specific performance Equitable remedy in which the defendant is ordered to perform the act(s) promised in the contract.

spending power Authority possessed by the federal and state governments to spend public monies.

spot rate Market rate for goods or exchange rate for currencies.

stakeholder Persons or entities affected by the activities of a business, such as shareholders, employees, customers, suppliers, government, and the community or public at large.

standing to sue Doctrine that requires a litigant to demonstrate a direct harm as a result of the other party's action.

stare decisis "Let the decision stand"; the practice of deciding a case with reference to former decisions.

state implementation plan (SIP) Plan required by the 1991 Clean Air Amendments that requires states to collect information about mobile and stationary sources of pollution and to issue

regulations for cleaning up polluted areas.

status quo Maintaining the same position.

statute Law passed by Congress or a state legislature.

statute of frauds Statute providing that certain contracts are not enforceable in court unless they are in writing and signed by the party to be charged.

statute of limitations Statutes that set limitations on the amount of time that can elapse during which a lawsuit must be filed.

statutory duty Obligation imposed by a legislative act.

statutory law Body of law enacted by state and federal legislatures.

statutory liens Liens granted by statute, such as a landlord's lien against the tenant's property for nonpayment of rent.

stay Court order to stop a proceedings.

stop-payment order Request made by a customer that his or her bank stop payment on an issued check.

straight bankruptcy Bankruptcy in which the debtor lists debts and turns his or her assets over to a trustee for settlement of the bankruptcy action.

strict scrutiny test Discrimination test for which two requirements must be met: (1) a compelling government interest and (2) use of the least restrictive means available to satisfy that interest.

strict liability Situation in which no defenses exist; applies to dangerous activities where all risk and responsibility for injury is assumed by the party involved or doing the hazardous activity.

subject matter jurisdiction Jurisdiction that limits the type of cases a court can hear as a result of the subject of the case or the amount of money disputed.

subpoena Process document that secures the attendance of a witness at a trial.

subpoena *duces tecum* Process document that requires evidence to be brought to court.

substantial evidence Evidence that a reasonable person might accept as adequate to support a conclusion.

substantive due process Doctrine that holds that the content or substance of a piece of legislation must be in compliance with the Constitution.

substantive law Law that defines, describes, regulates, and creates legal rights and obligations of individuals with respect to each other.

substantive rule Administrative agency rule that is not procedural or interpretive in nature.

summary judgment Written request by either party to a lawsuit to the court to grant judgment on grounds that there is no genuine issue of material fact and the requesting party is entitled to judgment as a matter of law.

summons Process document that requires the defendant to defend against the claim of the plaintiff in a lawsuit.

sunset law Law that establishes the automatic expiration date for an administrative agency.

Sunshine Act Amendment to the Administrative Procedures Act that prohibits administrative agencies from holding secret meetings.

superseding (intervening) force In a negligent tort case, it may break the causal connection between a wrongful act and injury to another. If so, no liability results.

supremacy clause Clause in Article VI of the Constitution that governs the relationship between the states and the federal government; the federal Constitution, statutes, and treaties take priority over state laws if a conflict arises between the two.

T

tangible property Visible property that has physical existence; for example, land, cattle, buildings, computers.

tariff Tax placed on imported goods based on either an ad valorem or a flat-rate basis.

tenancy by the entirety Ownership where the husband and wife own property without separate transfer rights.

taxing power Authority possessed by the federal government and state governments to levy and collect taxes.

temporary restraining order (TRO) A person is ordered for a temporary time to refrain from an activity.

tenancy at will Rental agreement in which either the tenant or the landlord can terminate the tenancy without notice.

tenancy by sufferance Possession of land without right; not a true tenancy.

tenancy by the entirety Only a husband and wife can hold property in ten-ancy by the entirety, which is created when they purchase the property. Neither spouse can transfer his or her interest.

tenancy for years Nonfreehold estate created by express contract by leasing property for a specific period of time.

tenancy from period to period Nonfreehold estate created by a lease that does not specify length of time but states that rent is to be paid at certain intervals.

tenancy in common Co-ownership in which two or more persons can own an undivided fractional interest in the property, but, on one tenant's death, that interest passes to his or her heirs.

tenant Person who rents a piece of property from the landlord (owner).

tender Offer of money or goods.

termination The final act of a partnership when it goes out of business.

termination statement Statement showing that a debt has been paid.

territorial and customer division Where competitors engage in an agreement to divide sales among certain customers or territory and agree not to compete for those customers or territory.

theft of trade secrets Tort of stealing confidential information.

third-party complaint Complaint filed against a party who was not an original party to the lawsuit.

thrust-upon defense Defense used by a business to justify its monopoly that it is selling a superior product or follows better business practices and, hence, the monopoly was created through no wrongful act or intent on the business's part.

time draft Draft that is payable at a definite future time.

tippee People to whom material information about a security is given that could be used for insider trading.

tipper People who give out material information about a security that could be used for insider trading.

Title VII of the Civil Rights Act of 1964 Federal statute that prohibits discrimination in all areas of employment on the basis of race, color, religion, national origin, sex, including pregnancy, childbirth, and abortion, by state, local, and federal agencies and employers of at least fifteen employees and involved in or a part of interstate commerce; administered by the Equal Employment Opportunity Commission.

tombstone advertisement Written advertising for a security that simply tells the investor where and how to obtain a particular security's prospectus; so named because it is outlined in black and resembles a tombstone.

tort French word meaning "wrong"; wrongdoing for which a civil action in court is possible.

Toxic Substances Control Act A federal statute requiring the Environmental Protection Agency to track more than 75,000 industrial chemicals produced or imported into the United States in order to regulate those toxic substances that potentially create a hazard or an unreasonable risk of injury to people. This act supplements the Clean Air Act.

trade acceptance Draft frequently used with the sale of goods in which the purchaser becomes liable to pay the draft. Equivalent to note receivable of the seller and note payable of the buyer, a trade acceptance permits the seller to raise money on it before it is due.

Trade Act A federal statute that governs trade; first time Congress granted the U.S. president fact-track authority, now called trade promotion authority.

Trade Agreement Act A federal statute that regulates the practice of dumping in the United States.

trade association Group of organized competitors pursuing a common interest, such as dissemination of information, advertising campaigns, codes of conduct; subject to antitrust laws.

trade promotion authority Procedure passed by Congress requiring it, once the U.S. president has signed a trade agreement with another country or countries, either to approve or disapprove of the agreement as signed; amendments are not allowed. Formerly called fast-track authority.

trade regulation rule Administrative rule issued by the FTC that applies to an industry's policies and practices; this rule has the force of law.

Trade-Related Aspects of Intellectual Property Rights (TRIPS) Agreement adopted by the World Trade Organization for the protection of intellectual property rights, such as copyrights and patents.

trademark Distinctive mark, motto, device, or implement that a manufacturer stamps, prints, or otherwise affixes to the goods it produces.

Trademark Counterfeiting Act A federal statute that makes dealing in goods or services under a counterfeit trademark a federal crime.

traveler's check Draft from a financial institution.

treaty Agreement or contract between two or more nations that must be authorized and ratified by the supreme power of each nation.

tribunal administrator Person who manages the administrative matters and all communication between the parties and the arbitrator in an arbitration.

trust Legal entity in which a trustee holds title to property for the benefit of another.

trustee Person who holds title to the property placed in a trust and manages the property for the benefit of the beneficiaries.

trustor Person who creates a trust and names the trustee and beneficiary.

Truth-in-Lending Act (TILA) Title I of the Consumer Credit Protection Act; deals with deceptive credit practices and requires notice and disclosure to prevent sellers and creditors from taking unfair advantage of consumers.

tying arrangement Arrangement in which the buyer must purchase one item in order to purchase the tied product.

U

unaccredited investor An investor who is likely to need protection when making investments. Compare with *accredited investor.*

unconscionable contract or clause Clause in a contract, or the entire contract, that is so one-sided as to be unjust after considering the needs of the particular case.

undercapitalization Situation of a corporation when it has insufficient capital (money and property).

unconscionability In the sale of goods, the UCC provides that when a clause in the contract is so one-sided as to be harsh and shocking to the conscience of the court under the circumstances, the court may refuse to enforce a contract or a clause, if it is found to be unconscionable.

undisclosed principal Principal whose identity is totally unknown by the third party and the third party has

no knowledge that the agent is acting in an agency capacity at the time the contract is made.

undue influence Arises from special relationships that allow one party to greatly influence another, thus overcoming the weaker party's free will.

unenforceable contract Contract that began as a valid contract, but for some legal reason cannot now be enforced against the other party.

unfair labor practices strike Strike whereby workers strike because management is alleged to be in violation of the law. If workers are correct, management must rehire these workers.

unfair or deceptive acts or practices Language contained in the Wheeler-Lee Act to enable the FTC to provide consumers with protections from these types of acts or practices. Not defined by statue, but interpreted by the courts on a case-by-case basis.

Uniform Arbitration Act Act designed to make legislation on arbitration more uniform throughout the country; has been adopted by 34 states and the District of Columbia.

Uniform Commercial Code (UCC) Uniform act consisting of eleven articles that applies to both interstate and intrastate business transactions governing the conduct of business among individuals and businesses.

Uniform Consumer Credit Code (UCCC) Comprehensive body of rules governing the most important aspects of consumer credit; has been adopted by only a few states.

Uniform Customs and Practices for Documentary Credits (UCP) The International Chamber of Commerce created this document covers particularly letters of credit.

Uniform Limited Partnership Act (ULPA) A uniform statute that has been adopted by many states that established the rules for limited partnerships.

Uniform Partnership Act (UPA) A uniform statute adopted by most states that establishes the law on general partnerships.

unilateral contract Contract in which a person makes a promise that requires in return an act (not a promise) by the other party; for example, a reward situation.

unilateral mistake Mistake made by one of the contracting parties.

union shop Business that does not

require union membership of applicants in order to be hired but can and usually does require workers to join the union after a specific period of time on the job.

United Nations Commission on International Trade Law (UNCITRAL) Commission that develops model laws that cover international commercial transactions.

United Nations Convention on International Bills of Exchange and Promissory Notes Agreement among nations concerning the rules governing documents that are orders to pay (bills of exchange) and promises to pay (promissory notes).

United Nations Convention on the Law of the Sea Convention imposing on signatory members the duty to avoid polluting the oceans from land or from vessels; includes legislation against dumping raw wastes from ships.

United Nations Convention on the Recognition and Enforcement of Foreign Arbitral Awards (New York Convention) Convention that created the agreement that allows the enforcement of arbitrated awards in any of the signature.

Universal Copyright Convention Agreement signed in 1952 that grants an author copyright protection in other countries that are signatories when the work is first published and notification given to the other country's copyright office.

unliquidated debt A disputed debt is called an unliquidated debt. This dispute occurs when one person claims more is owed than what the other party believes is owed.

unprotected speech Any speech not protected by the First Amendment. Includes dangerous speech, fighting words, speech that incites violence or revolution, defamatory speech, obscenity, and child pornography.

USA Patriot Act Passed in 2001 in reaction to the terrorist attacks on September 11, 2001, the act grants the executive branch of the federal government additional powers to investigate and detain suspected terrorists.

U.S. Customs and Border Protection Service housed within the Department of Homeland Security that assesses and collects customs duties, excise taxes, fees, and penalties owed on imported merchandise.

U.S. trade representative Chief representative of the United States in the formulation of trade policy and in activities involving bilateral and multilateral trade negotiations; cabinet-level official with the rank of ambassador.

U.S. trustee Government employee in an administrative position within the bankruptcy court who monitors the administration of bankruptcy cases. Contrast *regular trustee*.

usage of trade Principle encouraged by the Uniform Commercial Code that calls for the application of the rules of a particular trade to fill in missing terms in a contract or to guide a court when interpreting a contract clause.

use of the mails to defraud Crime of (1) mailing a writing for the purpose of executing a scheme to defraud or (2) an organized scheme to defraud by false pretenses.

use permit Permit issued by a governmental body that grants permission to operate a given type of business in a certain area.

usury Rate of interest that is above the amount allowed by statute; applies to cash loans only.

utilitarianism Approach to establishing ethical standards based on the consequences of an action.

V

valid contract Contract that meets all requirements of a contract to be enforced in a court.

validated license Limited authority to ship and export certain types of high-technology goods; limits or prohibits certain types of high-technology goods from being shipped to countries of concern that may pose a military threat to the United States.

variance Exception to a zoning ordinance.

venue Particular geographic area within a judicial district where a suit should be brought.

verdict Decision of the jury.

vertical merger Merger of a company at one stage of production with another company at a higher or lower stage of production.

vertical restraint Trade practice that involves firms at different levels of the production and distribution process and that violates antitrust laws.

Vienna Convention on the Law of Treaties Convention that codified the entire body of law on treaties; covers issues such as the legal difference between treaties and other types agreements, constitutional limitations on treaty-making powers, terminology, legal designation of parties, and general rules that apply to interpreting treaties.

Vienna Convention on the Protection of the Ozone Layer Convention through which governments committed themselves to protecting the ozone layer and to cooperating with each other in scientific research to improve understanding of the atmospheric processes.

void agreement Agreement in which the purpose is illegal and hence cannot be enforced by law.

voidable contract Situation in which one party to a contract is bound but the other party may disaffirm it; for example, a contract by a minor.

voir dire The process of selecting a jury, during which attorneys can question prospective jurors to determine bias.

W

warehouse receipt Document that indicates who holds title to goods or who has a right to possession of the goods stored by a distributor.

warrant To promise a fact or facts shall be as represented in a contract or negotiable instrument.

warranty of title Guarantee to the buyer that the goods are not stolen, have no lien against them, and do not infringe a patent or copyright.

Webb-Pomerene Act A federal statute exempting acts or agreements made in the course of export trade by associations of competing producers formed solely for the purpose of engaging in export trade.

Wheeler-Lea Act A federal statute strengthening the power of the Federal Trade Commission to regulate anticompetitive business behavior and to provide consumer protection.

whistleblower Person who discloses wrongful behavior on the part of a company or person.

white-collar crime Monetary offense usually against a business; nonviolent crimes committed by corporations or by individuals against corporations.

winding up The process whereby the assets of a partnership are sold and proceeds distributed.

Worker Adjustment and Retraining Notification Act (WARN) A federal statute requiring businesses to notify employees sixty days in advance if a plant will close. Businesses must also give workers advance notice if more then one-third of a company's employees will be laid off. Also known as the Plant Closing Act.

workers' compensation laws Laws that provide economic protection for workers who are injured or killed on the job.

World Trade Organization (WTO) Created by the Uruguay Round of GATT in 1994, the WTO has two purposes: to administer the GATT and the dispute-resolution system. The WTO replaced the 47-year-old GATT organization on January 1, 1995, although the GATT organization and the WTO will both be in place while the administrative duties are transferred.

writ of attachment Process document issued after judgment has been made by the court; may take the form of an order to take or seize property or persons to bring them under control of the court.

writ of *certiorari* Formal notice from the U.S. Supreme Court or other appellate courts that it will accept a case for review.

writ of execution Process document issued after judgment has been made by the court; puts in force the court's decree or judgment.

writ of garnishment Process document issued after judgment has been made by the court; garnishes the wages or property of the party at fault.

Table of Cases

Index

Selected World Wide Web Addresses

United States Government General Information

FirstGov, your first click to the U.S. government; a complete Web site to all government Web sites
   http://www.firstgov.gov
Consumer Information Center
   http://www.pueblo.gsa.gov
Declaration of Independence
   http://lcweb2.loc.gov/const/declar.html
or
   http://www.nara.gov/exhall/charters/charters.html
Federal Business Opportunities
   http://www.fedbizopps.gov/
Federal Consumer Information
   http://www.pueblo.gsa.gov/money.htm
Federal Consumer Information Center, National Contact Center (operates like a federal Yellow Book)
   http://www.info.gov
Federal statistics
   http://www.fedstats.gov/
Federalist Papers
   http://lcweb2.loc.gov/const/fedquery.html
Government Information Locator Service
   http://www.access.gpo.gov/su_docs/gils/index.html
Government Printing Office Online databases
   http://www.gpoaccess.gov/databases.html
National Archives and Records Administration (NARA)
   http://www.nara.gov/
NARA, Exhibit Hall
   http://www.nara.gov/exhall/exhibits.html
NARA, Office of the Federal Register
   http://www.gpoaccess.gov/nara/index.html
U.S. Constitution
   http://lcweb2.loc.gov/const/constquery.html
or
   http://www.nara.gov/exhall/charters/charters.html
U. S. Government Manual
   http://www.gpoaccess.gov/gmanual/index.html
U.S. Government Printing Office
   http://www.gpoaccess.gov/index.html
World Wide Web Virtual Library
   http://www.law.indiana.edu/v-lib

United States Government Libraries

Library of Congress (LOC)
   http://www.lcweb.loc.gov
LOC, online exhibitions
   http://www.loc.gov/exhibits/
LOC, searchable electronic global library
   http://lcweb.loc.gov/homepage/lchp.html
LOC, U.S. Copyright Office
   http://www.loc.gov/copyright/
Department of Energy, digital archive
   http://www.doedigitalarchive.doe.gov/

National Agricultural Library
   http://www.nalusda.gov
National Library of Education
   http://www.ed.gov/NLE
National Library for the Environmental Protection Agency
   http://www.epa.gov/natlibra/
National Library of Medicine
   http://www.nlm.nih.gov
National Library Service for the Blind and Physically Handicapped
   http://www.loc.gov/nls/
National Resources Library, Department of Interior
   http://www.doi.gov/nrl/
National Transportation Library
   http://www.bts.gov/NTL/
Newspaper and Current Periodical Reading Room
   http://lcweb.loc.gov/global/ncp/ncp.html

Article I, Legislative Branch

General Accounting Office (GAO)
   http://www.gao.gov
Library of Congress, THOMAS site; legislative information on current and past bills
   http://thomas.loc.gov
United States Capitol
   http://www.aoc.gov
U.S. Code of Federal Regulations
   http://www.gpoaccess.gov/cfr/index.html
U.S. Code
   http://www.gpoaccess.gov/uscode/index.html
or
   http://www.law.cornell.edu/uscode/
U.S. Code, Table of Popular Names
   http://www4.law.cornell.edu/uscode/topn/
U.S. Electoral College
   http://www.archives.gov/federal_register/electoral_college/electoral_college.html
U.S. House of Representatives
   http://www.house.gov
U.S. House of Representatives, Office of the Clerk
   http://clerk.house.gov/index.php
U.S. Senate
   http://www.senate.gov
U.S. Senators
   http://www.senate.gov/senators/index.cfm

Article II, Executive Branch and Executive Departments

Office of the President
   http://www.whitehouse.gov/
Executive Office of the President
   http://www.firstgov.gov/Agencies/Federal/Executive/EOP.shtml
Department of Agriculture